W9-BSZ-463

CRYPTOGRAPHY: A NEW DIMENSION IN COMPUTER DATA SECURITY

CRYPTOGRAPHY: A NEW DIMENSION IN COMPUTER DATA SECURITY

A Guide for the Design and Implementation of Secure Systems

CARL H. MEYER
STEPHEN M. MATYAS

Cryptography Competency Center
IBM Corporation, Kingston, New York

A Wiley-Interscience Publication

JOHN WILEY & SONS

New York • Chichester • Brisbane • Toronto • Singapore

Library of Congress Cataloging in Publication Data:

Meyer, Carl, Ph.D.
Cryptography: A New Dimension in Computer Data Security—A Guide for the Design and Implementation of Secure Systems

Bibliography: p.
Includes index.
1. Cryptography–Handbooks, manuals, etc.
I. Matyas, Stephen. II. Title.

Z103.M55 001.54′36 82-2831
ISBN 0-471-04892-5 AACR2

Printed in the United States of America

10 9 8 7 6 5 4 3

Preface

This book deals with today's cryptography. Unlike past classical schemes used for the concealment of diplomatic and military secrets of monarchs and government officials at all levels, today's cryptography must provide cost-effective, secure approaches for protecting the vast amounts of digital data gathered and communicated with electronic data processing (EDP) systems. Consequently, the material in this book is intended for the increasing number of both technical and nontechnical people concerned with computer data security and privacy.

Advances in cryptography appeared with unprecedented frequency in the 1970s as strong encryption-based protocols and new cryptographic applications emerged. On January 15, 1977, the National Bureau of Standards adopted an encryption algorithm as a Federal standard—The Data Encryption Standard (DES)—marking a milestone in cryptographic research and development. Subsequently, in December 1980, the American National Standards Institute adopted the same algorithm for commercial use in the United States. Another milestone was set by the proposal of a new concept called Public Key Cryptography, an approach still being developed and no standard algorithm yet agreed upon.

Many readers may find themselves unacquainted with cryptography, but confronted with problems of cryptographic design or the implementation of cryptographic protection at some level within a communications network or EDP system. To meet the approaching challenges to the technical world, full coverage of these aspects of cryptography is provided.

It is noteworthy that cryptography is the only known practical means for protecting information transmitted through a large communications network, be it telephone line, microwave, or satellite. A detailed discussion of how cryptography can be used to achieve communications security (COMSEC) is provided. Moreover, various attack scenarios are discussed so that the engineer and systems designer can understand and appreciate the problems and difficulties involved in providing a cryptographically secure COMSEC solution.

Cryptography can be used to achieve file security. A protocol is developed for the encryption of data stored on removable media. Enhanced authentication protocols, including personal verification, message authentication, and digital signatures, can also be achieved through cryptographic techniques. These subjects are of particular interest to those concerned with electronic funds transfer and credit card applications within the banking and finance industry, or any other area where the originator, timeliness, contents, and intended receiver of a message must be verified.

The banking and finance industry has been the leader in promoting the use of cryptography for protecting assets transferred via messages sent through large networks of computers and terminals. To address this subject properly, we have reprinted a significant portion of the *PIN Manual,* prepared by the staff of MasterCard International, Inc., and previously available only through MasterCard's Security Department. This material is augmented by our detailed analysis of EFT systems security. A set of EFT security requirements is presented. It should be evaluated by those designing or planning EFT applications. Various implementations are discussed, including design trade-offs and techniques for achieving superior security in future systems.

Any key-controlled cryptographic algorithm, such as the DES, requires a protocol for the management of its cryptographic keys. The details of a key management scheme providing support for the protection of communications between individual end users (end-to-end) and for the protection of data stored or transported on removable media are given. Procedures for the safe and secure generation, distribution, and installation of cryptographic keys are also discussed.

Shannon's treatment of cryptography (in his landmark paper on Secrecy Systems) has been used as a starting point for the coverage of the subjects of unicity distance and work factor. Both statistical and information theory approaches are given, providing the reader with a more thorough understanding of the approaches for achieving cryptographic strength.

This book is intended for those people interested in understanding the role of cryptography in achieving high levels of computer data security. Perhaps of even greater importance is the fact that cryptography is identified as a complete solution to some data security problems. For others, it provides only a partial solution, but this is equally important to an understanding of what problems can and cannot be solved using cryptography. Engineers, designers, planners, managers, academicians, and students can benefit from one or more of the practical and theoretical subjects treated in the text.

The state-of-the-art material for this book was derived from our involvement in research and development efforts in the field of cryptography, and more generally from our work in the field of data security.

The views expressed in this book are those of the authors and not necessarily those of the IBM Corporation.

Starting with the third printing, the function for generating redundant information for a message integrity check has been changed from modulo two addition, which was found to have certain undesirable properties, to modulo 2^{64} addition. The change affects pages 69, 79, 82-83, 101-105, 257-259, 361, 385, 399, 400-401, 411-415.

Carl H. Meyer
Stephen M. Matyas

Kingston, New York
July, 1982

Acknowledgments

We are indebted to David B. Mayer, whose early review of Chapters 1 through 3 was instrumental in setting the presentation format to enable this work to appeal to a broader audience.

David Kahn reviewed Chapter 1 and provided many valuable criticisms that redirected the chapter's content and approach.

Stephen M. Lipton supplied the section Technical Implications of Privacy Legislation in Chapter 1. He also assisted and shared his technical expertise in the preparation of portions of Chapter 9 dealing with the legal significance of digital signatures.

Miles Smid reviewed the material dealing with message authentication and digital signatures. Several weaknesses and one subtle attack against one of the authentication procedures uncovered by Smid are documented in Chapter 9. Both Miles Smid and Carl Campbell reviewed and criticized early versions of Chapter 11, which led to a more precise discussion of alternative cryptographic methods in electronic funds transfer systems.

Jonathan Oseas reviewed the entire manuscript and provided valuable comments, especially for Chapter 11. As our manager, he also made resources available that accelerated the book's completion.

Donald W. Davies and Dr. Wyn L. Price critically reviewed major portions of the manuscript and were responsible for pointing out the existence of semiweak keys.

We are indebted to Stanley A. Kurzban, who reviewed the entire manuscript. His many excellent comments and suggestions improved the manuscript both from a technical and editorial standpoint.

We are indebted also to Ronald K. Freeman for his careful editing skills and his continued support and assistance in the preparation of this manuscript.

We especially wish to thank Richard E. Lennon for his collaboration and suggestions with the material in Chapters 4 and 11. His tireless efforts with the composition and editing of the manuscript are deeply appreciated. Without his help, this book would have been delayed at least one year.

Many of our colleagues generously provided detailed criticism of different portions of the manuscript: Dr. Willis H. Ware reviewed a large part of the work; Robert H. Courtney reviewed Chapter 1; Professors Ronald L. Rivest and Martin E. Hellman reviewed the section on public-key algorithms; Dr. Don Coppersmith collaborated with us in developing a computer procedure to solve simple substitution ciphers and reviewed Chapter 12 and associated appendices; Charles C. Wood reviewed Chapters 1 and 4 and provided many excellent comments; Dr. Glen G. Langdon, Jr. reviewed Chapter 12; Frank S. Piedad, James B. Warner, Marvin Sendrow, and Jerry Svigals reviewed Chapter 11 and associated appendices.

Salim Akl, Stanley Benton, Professor G. R. Blakley, Frank Davis, Whitfield Diffie, William H. Ehrsam, Robert C. Elander, Ronald C. Gault, Horst Feistel, John B. Gillett, Robert R. Jueneman, Dr. Stephen T. Kent, Edwin Lester, Michael J. Martino, Dr. Christian Mueller-Schloer, Louise D. Nielsen, Paul N. Prentice, Mok-Kong Shen, Robert E. Shuck, Albert A. Smith, Jr., Dolfis G. Smith, and Howard Zeidler all offered constructive criticism and ideas that significantly improved this book.

Gracious assistance in the preparation of the manuscript was provided by many of our colleagues. O. Tom Thomas supplied the material from which Appendices C and E were derived. Laura A. Wheatherly assisted by obtaining permission from MasterCard International Inc. to reprint sections 1 through 4 of the PIN Manual. Thomas E. Deuser and John T. Minick helped in the composition of the book. Fern Franke, Frank Marquette, Sherry Collins, Jim Economos, and Susan Swiderski of AGS Typography prepared the manuscript's many excellent figures and tables.

We also owe a debt to Horst Feistel, who started the cryptographic effort at IBM with his LUCIFER algorithm and thus laid the foundation for the DES.

Finally, we wish to thank Dr. Walter L. Tuchman, under whose direction the DES algorithm was developed, and the IBM Corporation for making it possible for us to write this book.

C. M.
S. M.

Contents

Abbreviations

Cipher Modes and Associated Parameters:

CBC	cipher block chaining
CE	compressed encoding
CFB	cipher feedback
ECB	electronic codebook (see block cipher)
ICV	initial chaining value
OCV	output chaining value
OFB	output feedback (see key auto-key cipher
X	plaintext
Y	ciphertext
Z	initializing vector (synonymous with ICV)
DEA	Data Encryption Algorithm (ANSI; synonymous with DES)
DES	Data Encryption Standard (NBS)
PKC	Public Key Cryptosystem
RSA	Rivest, Shamir, Adelman (public key) algorithm

Cryptographic Keys:

K	primary data-encrypting key
KA	authentication key
KC	primary communications key (synonymous with session key)
KF	primary file key
KI	interchange key
KMT	terminal master key
KN	secondary key
KNC	secondary (node) communication key
KNF	secondary node file key
KP	personal key
KPG	personal key-generating key used to generate KP from ID
KPN	PIN generating key used to generate PIN from ID
KS	session key
KSTR	transaction session key
KT	resident terminal key
KTR	transaction key

PK	public key in a public-key cryptosystem	
PKb	public bank key in a PKC	
PKc	public customer key in a PKC	
PKu	public universal key in a PKC	
SK	secret key in a PKC	
SKb	secret bank key in a PKC	
SKc	secret customer key in a PKC	
SKu	secret universal key in a PKC	

Cryptographic Operations:

AF	authenticate forward	(host)
AR	authenticate reverse	(host)
ECPH	encipher data	(host)
EMK	encipher under master key	(host)
ENC	encipher	(terminal)
ENCO	encipher only	(host)
DCPH	decipher data	(host)
DEC	decipher	(terminal)
DECK	decipher key	(terminal)
DECO	decipher only	(host)
GKEY	generate key	(host)
GSK1	generate session key 1	(host)
GSK2	generate session key 2	(host)
LKD	load key direct	(terminal)
MGK	merge key	(host)
RFMK	reencipher from master key	(host)
RTMK	reencipher to master key	(host)
SMK	set master key	(host)
WMK	write master key	(terminal)

Cryptographic Macros:

CIPHER
GENKEY
RETKEY

System Terminology:

ATM	automated teller machine
BSC	binary synchronous communication
CC	communications controller
HPC	host processing center
KDC	key distribution center

LU logical unit
PLU primary logical unit
PU physical unit
RH request/response header
RU request/response unit
SDLC synchronous data link control
SLU secondary logical unit
SNA system network architecture
SSCP systems services control point

Organizations:

ANSI American National Standards Institute
CCITT Consultative Committee on International Telephone and Telegraph
ISO International Standards Organization
NBS National Bureau of Standards
NSA National Security Administration

Parameters Associated with Verification and Authentication

AP authentication parameter
BID bank identifier
CRV cryptographic verification
DGS digital signature
ID user identifier
MAC message authentication code
PAC personal authentication code
PAN primary account number
PIN personal identification number
RN random number
Tcard time-variant information generated by bank card
TID terminal identifier
TOD time-of-day
TR transaction request
Tterm time-variant information generated by terminal
Rf reference
Z initializing vector

CRYPTOGRAPHY: A NEW DIMENSION IN COMPUTER DATA SECURITY

CHAPTER ONE

The Role of Cryptography in Electronic Data Processing

CRYPTOGRAPHY, PRIVACY, AND DATA SECURITY

Organizations in both the public and private sectors have become increasingly dependent on electronic data processing. Vast amounts of digital data are now gathered and stored in large computer data bases and transmitted between computers and terminal devices linked together in complex communications networks. Without appropriate safeguards, these data are susceptible to interception (e.g., via wiretaps) during transmission, or they may be physically removed or copied while in storage. This could result in unwanted exposures of data and potential invasions of privacy. Data are also susceptible to unauthorized deletion, modification, or addition during transmission or storage. This can result in illicit access to computing resources and services, falsification of personal data or business records, or the conduct of fraudulent transactions, including increases in credit authorizations, modification of funds transfers, and the issuance of unauthorized payments.

Legislators, recognizing that the confidentiality and integrity of certain data must be protected, have passed laws to help prevent these problems. But laws alone cannot prevent attacks or eliminate threats to data processing systems. Additional steps must be taken to preserve the secrecy and integrity of computer data. Among the security measures that should be considered is *cryptography,* which embraces methods for rendering data unintelligible to unauthorized parties.

Cryptography is the only known practical method for protecting information transmitted through communications networks that use land lines, communications satellites, and microwave facilities. In some instances it can be the most economical way to protect stored data. Cryptographic procedures can also be used for message authentication, digital signatures, and personal identification for authorizing electronic funds transfer and credit card transactions.

Attack Scenarios

The possibility exists that unauthorized individuals can intercept data by eavesdropping. In fact, there are several methods of eavesdropping.

Wiretapping. Interception of individual transmissions over communication lines by using hardwire connections.

Electromagnetic Eavesdropping. Interception of wireless transmissions, for example, radio and microwave transmissions, or information-bearing electromagnetic energy emanating from electronic devices.

Acoustic Eavesdropping. Interception of sound waves created by the human voice or by printing, punching, or transmitting equipment. (This method of eavesdropping is listed for reference only. In almost all cases, physical security measures rather than cryptography are effective against this threat.)

Eavesdropping is completely passive: the opponent only listens to or records information being transmitted.[1] An attack involving only eavesdropping is called a *passive attack*. If, in addition, the opponent modifies transmitted information or injects information into the communication path, the attack is called an *active attack*.

In a passive attack, a tape recording of digitial data intercepted from a communication path is made. The data can be reconstructed by analyzing the recording tape or playing it back into suitable receiving equipment (e.g., a modem[2] and terminal). In an active attack, a terminal and modem compatible with the transmission line are necessary, and, in some cases, a minicomputer that can quickly modify intercepted information may be required.

Cables running between building offices and telephone company junction boxes located inside the user's premises are particularly vulnerable to wiretapping. The many lines of a telephone cable are separated at the boxes and usually are labeled. A wiretap can be performed by almost anyone; no special technical skills are required and the necessary equipment is relatively inexpensive. However, once the lines are outside the building, and until they reach telephone company switching facilities, access to selected lines becomes more difficult.[3] Effective attacks are nevertheless still possible.

Interception of radio and microwave transmissions poses a particularly subtle threat because a physical connection (tap) to the transmission link is not required. However, because microwave links, including those used in satellite communications, can contain several thousand channels, sophisticated and expensive equipment [1] may be required to intercept and separate channel signals. Despite this cost, the reward for a successful attack can be extremely great.

[1] It is common practice to use the term wiretapping to refer to the interception of all forms of voice and data communications, regardless of whether that information is transmitted via communication lines, radio, or microwave.

[2] A *modem* is a device used to link a terminal (or other transmitting device) and the communication channel. It modulates and demodulates, i.e., converts digital signals to analog, and vice versa.

[3] Within telephone company switching facilities, interception may require collusion with telephone company personnel.

According to a July 1977 article in *The New York Times* [2]:

> the Russians, using advanced scientific equipment, have been "plucking" from the air many long-distance [telephone] calls transmitted by microwaves, or ultrahigh-frequency radio signals. They then used massive high-speed computers to locate sensitive information in the transmissions.[4]

The Russian Embassy in Washington, D.C. and at least five other locations were purportedly used as listening posts to monitor many private and government telephone calls.

Every operating electronic device emits electromagnetic energy. For those devices handling data, it is important to know whether the energy level of any information-bearing emanations is high enough (and distinct enough) for an opponent to detect and interpret the data contained therein. Usually the answer is no. When the equipment in question has integral shielding that can reduce the information-bearing emissions to below threshold levels for all but the most sophisticated detection equipment, such eavesdropping is difficult and expensive [1]. However, for unshielded digital electronic devices employing slow-speed serial data streams, the complexity and costs of eavesdropping diminish.

In the absence of strong cryptographic protection, an eavesdropping opponent may learn enough about the operational procedures of the system, including passwords, to defeat any security mechanisms.

In applications involving automated teller machines (ATMs) that have the capacity to dispense cash, a passive wiretap may permit an opponent to obtain information (personal identifier, password) needed to impersonate legitimate ATM users. With an active wiretap, an opponent could inject unauthorized messages to obtain funds illegally. In other applications involving electronic funds transfer (EFT), the opponent, by masquerading as one bank, could send a message to another bank specifying that money be credited to an account previously established. The opponent could then withdraw from the account before the deception could be detected through normal auditing procedures.

Although there is little evidence publicly available to indicate how much eavesdropping has actually taken place, the potential for such activity has raised concerns about the confidentiality of personal affairs and business transactions. It is reasonable to anticipate problems when eavesdropping is the most practical means to achieve the desired result, especially when the payoff is great enough and the nature of the punishment, if discovered, is small enough to justify the crime!

EFT systems, which move many billions of dollars between financial institutions linked together in a communications network, represent a tempting target. Recognizing the threat, the Federal Reserve System has begun to install cryptographic devices on some of its communication lines [3].

Cryptography is the only practical means for protecting the confidentiality

[4] Computers can locate certain words or sets of words, certain voice prints, and certain dialed numbers for selection of which calls to monitor.

of information transmitted through potentially hostile environments, where it is either impossible or impractical to protect the information by conventional physical means. A cryptographic system properly implemented can prevent much eavesdropping damage. Also, damage resulting from message alteration, message insertion, and message deletion can be avoided. And in some cases a cryptographic system can reduce the severity of problems caused by the accidental exposure of misrouted information.

Administrative and physical security procedures often can provide adequate protection for off-line data transport and storage. However, where file security methods are either nonexistent or weak, encryption may provide the most effective and economical protection.

A more complete treatment of eavesdropping techniques can be found in James Martin's *Security, Accuracy and Privacy in Computer Systems* [1].

Technical Implications of Privacy Legislation

Privacy, as it involves collections of personal data, relates to the right of individuals to control or influence what information about them may be collected and stored, and by whom, for what specific reasons, and to whom that information may then be disclosed. Privacy also relates to the right of individuals to know that information about them has been compiled and that it is correct and complete enough for the intended uses. Furthermore, individuals should be able to expect that information relating to them will not be made available to others they have not authorized, and they should have the right to challenge the accuracy of such information. (See Westin's *Privacy and Freedom* [4]).

From a technical viewpoint, the requirements of privacy legislation, both enacted and pending, generally apply to the categories of data collection (record keeping, information manipulation, communication and storage) and information controls (system accountability and integrity, and information dissemination and presentation). Although privacy is a legal, social, and moral concern, privacy legislation has specific technical implications.

To understand the technical implications of privacy statutes, one must review such legislation and look to concepts borrowed from existing law in an attempt to foresee how courts may interpret and apply new legislation. To date, the Privacy Act of 1974 [5] has been the most significant piece of legislation enacted in the United States concerning computers and data security. The act is prefaced by several congressional findings, such as:

> The increasing use of computers and sophisticated information technology, while essential to the efficient operation of the government, has greatly magnified the harm to individual privacy that can occur from any collection, maintenance, use, or dissemination of personal information.

In view of these findings, the act provides for certain safeguards concerning information systems. Although it is limited to federal agencies and certain government contractors, several provisions are pertinent to a discussion of data security in all computer applications. Each federal agency must accurately record disclosures of certain types of information under that agency's control. The act also requires each agency to establish "rules of conduct" for persons involved in the design, development, operation, or maintenance of any system of records involving personal data.

The act further requires that each agency take certain steps to maintain the confidentiality of records held by that agency. Each agency must

> establish appropriate administrative, technical, and physical safeguards to ensure the security and confidentiality of records and to protect against any anticipated threats or hazards to their security or integrity which could result in substantial harm, embarrassment, inconvenience, or unfairness to any individual on whom information is maintained. [6]

In July 1977, the Privacy Protection Study Commission established under the act urged, in its final report to the President and to Congress, that certain corrections be made to the act so that obligations imposed by the law would be more realistic. For example, the commission recommended that federal agencies should be required to

> establish reasonable administrative, technical, and physical safeguards to assure the integrity, confidentiality and security of its individually identifiable records so as to minimize the risk of substantial harm, embarrassment, inconvenience, or unfairness to the individual to whom the information pertains. [8]

The question of what are reasonable safeguards depends on two factors: standard of care and state of the art. The standard of care as applied by the courts would be the so-called standard of reasonable care—the care that reasonable persons, similarly situated, would take under similar circumstances. In the case of *The T. J. Hooper* [9], a federal court declared

> In most cases, reasonable prudence is in fact common prudence; but strictly it is never its measure; a whole calling may have unduly lagged in the adoption of new and available devices. It never may set its own test, however persuasive be its usages. Courts must in the end say what is required; there are precautions so imperative that even their universal disregard will not excuse their omission.

How then will the courts decide what is required? Reasonable care depends on the probability and gravity of the harm balanced against the burden and cost of taking sufficient precautions to prevent the harm. A common sense cost/benefit analysis is thus one method of determining what is reasonable.

State of the art concerns itself with whether a certain technological device or process is technically feasible and commercially available. While to a scientist the question of technology may be a relatively objective one, to a court it may necessarily involve policy considerations. A court might well consider the question of technological feasibility along with economic and public interest considerations. What, then, can be said with regard to cryptography?

Although its cost may still be significant, cryptography currently is the only known practical method to achieve communication security. It represents the only mechanism that can meet the state of the art requirement in providing such protection. Moreover, for some federal agencies and private organizations, cryptography may be the only practical way to satisfy the requirements of existing or proposed privacy legislation. With a strong encryption procedure available to the general public, and with cryptographic systems also publicly available, cryptographic protection of data has become both technically feasible and commercially achievable.

Further incentive for the implementation of cryptography as a means of protecting assets or data that represent assets may also come from the Foreign Corrupt Practices Act of 1977 [10]. This amendment to the Securities and Exchange Act of 1934 requires every issuer of stock listed on a national exchange to make and keep books, records, and accounts which, in reasonable detail, accurately and fairly reflect the transaction and disposition of corporate assets. The act obliges the corporation and its management to devise and maintain a system of internal accounting controls to provide reasonable assurance that "access to assets is permitted only in accordance with management's . . . authorization" [11].

These provisions apply to all corporate transactions, whether or not they are "foreign" or "corrupt." In addition to corporate fines, criminal penalties of fines and/or imprisonment may be imposed on officers and directors for violations. Assuring that access to assets or data that represent assets is permitted only with management's authorization may require, in certain applications, the use of protective measures that cryptography can offer.

Since laws and regulations are constantly updated, specific applications and security measures should be reviewed with one's own legal counsel. For additional reading material and references dealing with privacy legislation, see Lance J. Hoffman's *Modern Methods for Computer Security and Privacy* [12].

THE DATA ENCRYPTION STANDARD

Martin [1] has stated, "If cryptography is worth using at all, it should be used well." In other words, high-quality cryptography must be the objective of the algorithm designer. Less secure approaches, although attractive for economic or performance reasons, can lead to a false sense of security. And cryptography that is scarcely more than a nuisance to the opponent is therefore worse than no cryptography at all. Thus high-quality cryptography is the best way to ensure effective cryptographic protection of data, even though skilled and determined opponents will always present a threat.

Recognizing the need to adopt a standard algorithm[5] for the encryption of computer data, the National Bureau of Standards (NBS) published a notice in the Federal Register on May 15, 1973, in which it solicited proposals for

[5] An *algorithm* is a procedure for calculating the value of some quantity or for finding the solution to some mathematical problem that frequently involves repetition. (See also Cryptographic Algorithms, Chapter 2.) Note that references outside a chapter are designated by the heading and chapter number, whereas references within a chapter are designated only by the heading.

"cryptographic algorithms for [the] protection of computer data during transmission and dormant storage" [13]. In part, the notice read:

> Over the last decade, there has been an accelerating increase in the accumulations and communication of digital data by government, industry and by other organizations in the private sector. The contents of these communicated and stored data often have very significant value and/or sensitivity. It is now common to find data transmissions which constitute funds transfers of several million dollars, purchase or sale of securities, warrants for arrests or arrest and conviction records being communicated between law enforcement agencies, airline reservations and ticketing representing investment and value both to the airline and passengers, and health and patient care records transmitted among physicians and treatment centers.
>
> The increasing volume, value and confidentiality of these records regularly transmitted and stored by commercial and government agencies has led to heightened recognition and concern over their exposure to unauthorized access and use. This misuse can be in the form of theft or defalcations of data records representing money, malicious modification of business inventories or the interception and misuse of confidential information about people. The need for protection is then apparent and urgent.
>
> It is recognized that encryption (otherwise known as scrambling, enciphering or privacy transformation) represents the only means of protecting such data during transmission and a useful means of protecting the content of data stored on various media, providing encryption of adequate strength can be devised and validated and is inherently integrable into system architecture. The National Bureau of Standards solicits proposed techniques and algorithms for computer data encryption. The Bureau also solicits recommended techniques for implementing the cryptographic function; for generating, evaluating, and protecting cryptographic keys; for maintaining files encoded under expiring keys; for making partial updates to encrypted files; and mixed clear and encrypted data to permit labeling, polling, routing, etc. The Bureau in its role for establishing standards and aiding government and industry in assessing technology, will arrange for the evaluation of protection methods in order to prepare guidelines.

In a second notice on August 27, 1974, the NBS again solicited cryptographic algorithms. Basically, the two notices stated that the NBS recognized the "apparent and urgent" need for data protection within government and the private sector, and that encryption is the "only means" for protecting communicated data, and a "useful means" for protecting stored data. The NBS therefore solicited "proposals for algorithms for the encryption of computer data" and agreed to "arrange for the evaluation" of these algorithms in order to "select those algorithms suitable for commercial and non-defense goverment use."

The requirements that NBS imposed for acceptable encryption algorithms included the following.

1. They must be completely specified and unambiguous.
2. They must provide a known level of protection, normally expressed in length of time or number of operations required to recover the key in terms of the perceived threat.

3. They must have methods of protection based only on the secrecy of the keys.
4. They must not discriminate against any user or supplier.

On August 6, 1974, International Business Machines Corporation (IBM) submitted a candidate algorithm that had been jointly developed by personnel at the company's research laboratory in Yorktown Heights, New York and at its Kingston, New York development laboratory.

According to the NBS, only one algorithm (the one submitted by IBM) was found acceptable. (Because cryptographic expertise within the government is almost totally resident within the National Security Agency (NSA), and NSA is the national communications security authority, NBS requested and obtained assistance from NSA in assessing the strength of candidate algorithms [14]). This algorithm formed the basis for the proposed Data Encryption Standard (DES). On March 17, 1975, the NBS published the algorithm stating its intent to have it considered as a Federal Information Processing Standard and requesting comments on the algorithm and its submission as a standard. On July 15, 1977, the proposed DES became a federal standard.

DES applies only to federal departments and agencies for the cryptographic protection of computer data not classified according to the National Security Act of 1974, as amended, or the Atomic Energy Act of 1954, as amended [15].[6] However, since the standard may be adopted and used by organizations outside the federal government, the NBS has provided the private sector with a cryptographic algorithm that has been found, after intensive analysis,[7] to be free from any known shortcut solution. DES has also been adopted by the American National Standards Institute (ANSI), on the recommendation of the Committee on Computers and Information Processing (X3), as the standard industry algorithm ("Data Encryption Algorithm," X3.92).

Incorporation of DES in computers and related peripheral devices can eliminate cryptographic algorithm incompatability between different manufacturers' equipment. Moreover, costs associated with the development and validation of comparable cryptographic algorithms can be avoided.

For a more detailed history of DES, see Ruth M. Davis' "The Data Encryption Standard in Perspective" [16].

DEMONSTRATING EFFECTIVE CRYPTOGRAPHIC SECURITY

Developing a strong cryptographic algorithm involves two endeavors: design and validation. Algorithm design consists of specifying criteria and inventing

[6] Supplemental interpretation of the standard has allowed its use in selected classified areas [17].

[7] Seventeen man-years of effort were expended by IBM personnel to design and validate DES. Several consultants were employed by IBM to provide additional assistance and analysis. Subsequently, an independent validation of the algorithm was initiated by the NBS and performed by the NSA.

a candidate algorithm that satisfies those criteria. Algorithm validation consists of subjecting the candidate algorithm to a thorough, intensive, and rigorous analysis (cryptanalysis).

Algorithm validation is performed by an "attack" team playing the role of opponent or antagonist. Attempts are made to uncover weaknesses that might lead to an attack against the algorithm, and to break the algorithm by using all known methods of attack for that type of algorithm. In the absolute sense, *a cryptographic algorithm is attack-proof (perfectly strong) only if there is no procedure or method that can be successfully used to attack (break) it.* Thus, to certify that an algorithm is attack-proof requires the proof of a negative hypothesis: the nonexistence of a procedure for breaking the algorithm. In general, such proofs are impossible.[8]

Since it is impossible to prove that an algorithm is attack-proof, a compromise is necessary. The dilemma must be resolved (to an acceptable point) by performing algorithm validation on a best-effort basis. An algorithm is considered strong (resistant to certain types of attack) if no exploitable weakness can be uncovered during the validation effort. Thus the basis for developing or creating a strong cryptographic algorithm requires an extensive knowledge of how to break cryptographic algorithms. The proper application of this knowledge helps to build a strong algorithm. In turn, the quality of this measure of strength depends on the knowledge and expertise of the attack team, and the scope, intensity, and duration of the investigation. Ideally, the two tasks—design and validation—are performed by two independent, and possibly competitive, groups. In practice, however, the design and validation groups may interact. Such interaction is intended to provide the means to uncover flaws and defects, thereby permitting the algorithm's designers to incorporate any necessary improvements.

A properly validated cryptographic algorithm of demonstrated strength is the foundation upon which more sophisticated encryption-based protection schemes (communication and file security, message authentication, and so forth) can be implemented. With any nonsecret, key-controlled cryptographic algorithm, such as DES, the protection achieved through encryption ultimately depends on how well the secrecy of the cryptographic keys can be maintained. An opponent who obtains the key(s), as well as the encrypted data, does not need to perform a cryptanalysis; since the algorithm is publicly available, the key will directly "unlock" the data. Thus a strong cryptographic algorithm alone does not automatically guarantee protection. Effective security requires both a strong algorithm and secure procedures for generating, distributing, installing, and managing keys.

It is not surprising that the problems encountered in cryptographic algorithm design are also encountered in the design of encryption-based protection schemes. These schemes are designed and validated in the same manner as cryptographic algorithms. A favorable validation leads to a conclu-

[8] Such a proof is possible for the so-called *one-time tape* system (see Designing an Algorithm, Chapter 2). A certifiably unbreakable cipher is obtained if a plaintext is combined bit-by-bit or character-by-character with a truly random sequence of bits or characters using a single, elementary, reversible operation (e.g., modulo 2 addition).

sion that penetration of the system, although not certifiably impossible, is at least demonstrably difficult or unlikely.

THE OUTLOOK FOR CRYPTOGRAPHY

In the late 1960s and early 1970s, data security began to be recognized as a major design concern for data processing (DP) systems. During this period, systems were designed to operate reliably only in environments subjected to "random noise"—power line disturbances, spurious electromagnetic radiation, equipment malfunction, programming errors, and the like. Few, if any, precautions were taken to protect the secrecy of computer data, or to defend it against "intelligent noise"—the deliberate actions of people intent on subversion. As a result, many systems were vulnerable to attack. Transmitted data could be intercepted and data could be modified, deleted, or added to a system. But today data processing system designers are more aware of these threats, and cryptography is recognized as an important factor in the design of secure systems.

Within the computer industry there is a movement toward more secure systems. Cryptography is being used in selected high-risk applications. For example, significant numbers of cash-issuing terminals employ DES to verify the identity of customers. At IBM's Thomas J. Watson Research Center at Yorktown Heights, New York, a DES-based cryptographic system, known as the Information Protection System (IPS), is used to protect stored computer data [18]. International Flavors and Fragrances, Inc., uses DES to protect valuable formulas transmitted via voice-grade public telephone lines [19]. Other designs for new and better cryptographic applications are being developed. Therefore, those responsible for the security of computer operations and data should be prepared to include cryptographic measures in their security system. Although many companies might not feel the need to encrypt their data, and even if they do, they might not use DES, according to a statement in the December 1979 issue of *EDP Analyzer,* "there is a fairly good chance they would be making a mistake on both counts—and particularly the second" [20].

However, to derive the maximum benefits from cryptography, significant planning is required to integrate it into system architectures properly, and standards are necessary to assure cryptographic compatibility within applications and among devices implementing DES. In addition to establishing the standard for computer data encryption [15], the NBS has published a standard on modes of DES operation [21] and is investigating file encryption in order to issue yet another standard for this cryptographic application.

Efforts by the Technical Committee on Encryption (X3.T1) on behalf of the American National Standards Institute (ANSI) have resulted in the adoption of DES as an ANSI standard [22]. In addition, the committee is developing standards for DES modes of operation and DES devices operating at the communications link level. Work is in progress to develop additional cryptographic standards for higher levels of communication protection as well as for removable file media.

ANSI technical committees involved with the finance industry are developing application standards to address the broad subject of electronic funds transfer systems, including methods using DES for consumer-initiated electronic financial transactions as well as transaction data authentication.

Other government agencies besides the NBS have drafted additional application standards involving DES and DES equipment. Proposed Federal Standard 1026 [23] specifies the interoperability and security requirements for use of DES. Proposed Federal Standard 1027 [24] specifies the minimum physical and electrical security features of devices implementing DES.

The development of cryptographic standards is a lengthy process. Proposed Federal Standard 1026, for example, represents more than three years of work. ANSI adopted DES more than three years after its adoption by the U.S. Federal Government. The time necessary to draft and adopt cryptographic standards is relative to the time necessary to design, test, manufacture, and install cryptographic computer equipment. Thus to meet the challenges and demands in the emerging field of system security, data processing people should begin their cryptographic education, research, and planning now.

REFERENCES

1. Martin, J. T., *Security, Accuracy and Privacy in Computer Systems,* Prentice-Hall, Englewood Cliffs, NJ, 1973.
2. Burnham, D., and Horrock, N. M., "Administration Maps Secret Plan to Fight Telephone Intrusion," *The New York Times,* pp. 1, 34 (July 10, 1977).
3. O'Toole, T., "Fed Is Testing 'Unbreakable' Code System," *Washington Post,* p. A10 (August 13, 1978).
4. Westin, A. F., *Privacy and Freedom,* Atheneum, New York, 1968.
5. Privacy Act of 1974, Public Law 93-579, 5 U.S.C. 552a(e) (10).
6. 5 U.S.C. 552(a), Sec. 3(E) (10).
7. 5 U.S.C. 552(a), Sec. 5(B) (1), (2).
8. *Personal Privacy in an Information Society—The Report of the Privacy Protection Study Commission,* p. 527 (July 1977).
9. *The T. J. Hooper,* 60F. 2d 737 N2d Cir. (1932), cert. den 287 U.S. 662 (1933).
10. Public Law 95-213, Title I S102, 91 Stat. 1494.
11. 15 U.S.C. 78m(b)(2).
12. Hoffman, L. J., *Modern Methods for Computer Security and Privacy,* Prentice-Hall, Englewood Cliffs, NJ, 1977.
13. "Cryptographic Algorithms for Protection of Computer Data During Transmission and Dormant Storage," *Federal Register* **38**, No. 93 (May 15, 1973).
14. *Report of the Workshop on Cryptography in Support of Computer Security,* NBSIR 77-1291, Held at the National Bureau of Standards, September 21–22, 1976, National Bureau of Standards, U.S. Department of Commerce, Washington, D.C. (September 1977).
15. *Data Encryption Standard,* Federal Information Processing Standard (FIPS) Publication 46, National Bureau of Standards, U.S. Department of Commerce, Washington, D.C. (January 1977).
16. Davis, R. M., "The Data Encryption Standard in Perspective," *IEEE Communications Society Magazine* **16**, No. 6, 5–9 (1978).

17. Inman, B. R., "The NSA perspective on Telecommunications Protection in the Non-Governmental Sector," *Signal* **33**, No. 6, 7–13 (1979).
18. Konheim, A. G., Mack, M. H., McNeill, R. K., Tuckerman, B., and Waldbaum, G., "The IPS Cryptographic Programs," *IBM Systems Journal* **19**, No. 2, 253–283 (1980).
19. "With Data Encryption, Scents Are Safe at IFF," DP Dialogue, Data Processing Division, IBM Corporation, printed in *Computerworld* **14**, No. 21, 95 (1980).
20. "Data Encryption: Is It for You?," *EDP Analyzer* **16**, No. 12, 1–13 (1978).
21. *DES Modes of Operation,* Federal Information Processing Standards (FIPS) Publication 81, National Bureau of Standards, U.S. Department of Commerce, Washington, D.C. (1981).
22. ANSI X3.92-1981, *Data Encryption Algorithm,* American National Standards Institute, New York (December 31, 1980).
23. Proposed Federal Standard 1026, *Telecommunications: Interoperability and Security Requirements for Use of the Data Encryption Standard in the Physical and Data Link Layers of Data Communications,* General Services Administration, Washington, D.C., Draft (January 21, 1982).
24. Federal Standard 1027, *Telecommunications: General Security Requirements for Equipment Using the Data Encryption Standard,* General Services Administration, Washington, D.C. (April 14, 1982).

Other Publications of Interest

25. Parker, D. B., *Crime by Computer,* Scribner, New York, 1976.
26. Kahn, D., "Cryptology Goes Public," *Foreign Affairs* **58**, No. 1, 141–159 (1979).

CHAPTER TWO

Block Ciphers and Stream Ciphers

A basic problem in cryptography is devising procedures to transform messages (*plaintext*) into cryptograms (*ciphertext*) that can withstand intense cryptanalysis—the techniques used by opponents to penetrate encrypted communications and recover the original information.

The procedures used to accomplish such transformations involve either a *code system* or a *cipher system*. Code systems require a code book or dictionary that translates words, phrases, and sentences of plaintext vocabulary into their equivalent ciphertext code groups. However, the number of plaintext groups that can be converted depends on the size of the code book. Therefore, not every message can be encoded, and the versatility of these code systems is limited.

On the other hand, cipher systems are versatile. They require two basic elements: a *cryptographic algorithm* (a procedure, or a set of rules or steps that are constant in nature); and a set of variable *cryptographic keys*. A key is a relatively short, secret sequence of numbers or characters selected by the user.

After introducing several concepts relevant to ciphers, this chapter discusses two particularly useful ciphers: block ciphers and stream ciphers. Both conventional algorithms (e.g., DES) and public-key algorithms (e.g., the RSA algorithm and the trapdoor knapsack algorithm) are covered under the subject of block ciphers.

Both block and stream ciphers can be used in communications and data processing systems. With a block cipher, data are encrypted and decrypted in blocks, whose length are predetermined by the algorithm's designer. With a stream cipher, the algorithm's user determines the length of data to be encrypted and decrypted. This flexibility requires that stream ciphers, in addition to the algorithm and key, employ another parameter defined as an initializing vector.

Different modes of encryption can be obtained with block and stream ciphers by employing feedback methods (*chaining*), which establish dependencies to past information. Chaining not only strengthens a cipher, but can also be used to authenticate data even when privacy is not required. At the end of the chapter, a comparison is made between block and stream ciphers. Their relative strengths and ease of implementation are discussed.

CRYPTOGRAPHIC ALGORITHMS

The cryptographic algorithm can be thought of as an extremely large number of transformations, the particular transformation in effect depending on the cryptographic key being used. Each transformation changes sequences of intelligible data (plaintext) into sequences of apparently random data (ciphertext). The transformation from plaintext to ciphertext is known as *encipherment* or *encryption.* Each transformation must have a unique inverse operation, also identified by a cryptographic key. The inverse transformation from ciphertext to plaintext is called *decipherment* or *decryption.* (The term that encompasses both enciphering and deciphering operations is *ciphering.*)

There are two types of cryptographic algorithms, *conventional* and *public-key.* With a conventional cryptographic algorithm, the enciphering and deciphering keys are either identical, or, if different, are such that each key can be easily computed from the other. Thus knowledge of the enciphering key is equivalent to knowledge of the deciphering key—when you have one, you also have the other.[1]

A public-key algorithm, on the other hand, permits many users or nodes within a communications system to encipher data using the same public key, but only the specific user or node possessing the secret deciphering key can "unlock" or recover the data. In contrast, a conventional cryptographic algorithm provides effective data security between two users or nodes within a communications system only if these users or nodes have knowledge of the same secret key.[2]

A parameter of a cryptographic algorithm that provides security because of its secrecy is defined as a *cryptographic variable.* The cryptographic key used in a conventional cryptographic algorithm and the private key used in a public-key algorithm are examples of cryptographic variables. They are analogous to the secret combination for a safe.

Enciphering And Deciphering

Consider a representation for the process of enciphering and deciphering with a cryptographic algorithm. (Boldface capital letters are used to define sets, whereas set members are identified by either the corresponding lowercase letters or in some cases the same capital letter not in boldface.) Let **P** represent the collection of all possible plaintext combinations, and **C** the col-

[1] In a conventional cryptographic algorithm it is common to treat the enciphering key and corresponding deciphering key as identical quantities, even though they may differ.

[2] The assumption is made here that the algorithm is known to the opponent and therefore that the strength of the system depends on the key. Moreover, to be useful, the approaches described above must be based on a cryptographic algorithm of validated strength (e.g., DES). The public-key concept is relatively new, and even though several public-key algorithms have recently evolved, their strength has yet to be validated. Therefore, emphasis is given here to encryption schemes based on conventional algorithms such as DES.

lection of all possible ciphertext combinations. The sets **P** and **C** are described by displaying their members inside braces.

$$\mathbf{P} = \{p_1, p_2, \ldots, p_n\}$$
$$\mathbf{C} = \{c_1, c_2, \ldots, c_m\}$$

The notation $|\mathbf{P}|$ represents the number of elements contained in the set **P**. Hence $|\mathbf{P}| = n$ and $|\mathbf{C}| = m$.

The enciphering process (Figure 2-1) can be described by a rule (E for encipher) that associates with each element p in **P** a single element, $c = E(p)$, in **C**. Each plaintext combination is assigned to a single ciphertext combination. The deciphering process is described by another rule (D for decipher) that relates each ciphertext element E(p) in **C** with its original plaintext, thus assuring that the plaintext is correctly recovered from the ciphertext. It is assumed here that the number of ciphertext combinations (six in Figure 2-1, i.e., c_1 through c_6) is larger than the number of plaintext combinations

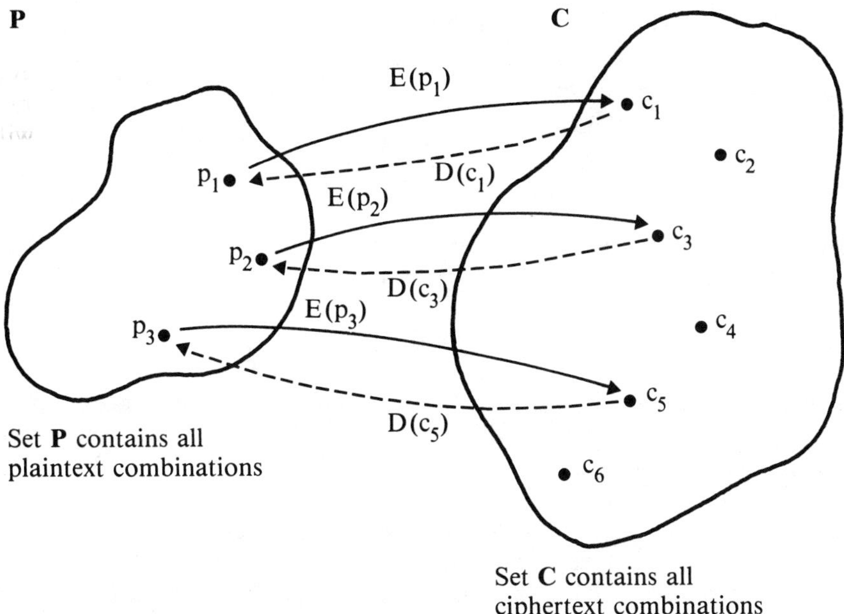

Rule E (encryption process, solid lines) assigns to each element in **P** one element in **C**.

Rule D (decryption process, broken lines) assigns to each of the elements in **C** previously selected by Rule E, one element in **P**, such that the correct plaintext combination is recovered.

Figure 2-1. The Ciphering Process

(three in Figure 2-1, i.e., p_1 through p_3). This situation can be illustrated with a trivial example where plaintext consists of 26 alphabetic characters and ciphertext consists of 26 alphabetic and 10 numeric characters. Thus any one of the 36 ciphertext symbols can be used as a substitute for any one of the 26 plaintext symbols.

The ideas discussed so far can be expressed in mathematical terms by using the concept of a function. A function may also be called a transformation, an operator, or a mapping. This concept can be explained in terms of the ciphering operation illustrated in Figure 2-1. The *function* is defined by the following:

1. A set **P** called the *domain* of the function.
2. A set **C** called the *co-domain* of the function.
3. A *rule* E which associates with each element p of **P** a single element c of **C**.

The function that describes the encipher operation is defined by two sets (**P** and **C**) and a rule which assigns to each element in **P** one element in **C**. Hence the encipher operation can be described by the notation (**P**, **C**, E). It is customary to use the same symbol for the function and its rule. Hence, if (**P**, **C**, E) is a function, then it is said that E is a function from **P** to **C**. This statement can be written as

$$E : \mathbf{P} \rightarrow \mathbf{C}$$

If p is an element in **P** and c the element in **C** that correponds to it under the transformation (function) E, then one writes

$$E(p) = c$$

The set of all E(p) in **P**, also expressed as E(**P**), is defined as the *range* (or *image*) of E. Hence the range E(**P**) is a subset of **C**. In Figure 2-1, the domain of E is **P**, whereas the range of E is the set of elements $\{c_1, c_3, c_5\}$.

There are two properties of functions that need to be distinguished at this point. A function $f : \mathbf{P} \rightarrow \mathbf{C}$ is called *one-to-one* whenever no two different elements in **P** are represented by the same element in **C**; that is, whenever $p_i \neq p_j$ for p_i and p_j in **P** implies that $f(p_i) \neq f(p_j)$. An equivalent statement is that if $f(p_i) = f(p_j)$, then $p_i = p_j$ if f is a one-to-one function. Since plaintext can be recovered correctly only if each ciphertext element represents one and only one plaintext element, all functions representing a cryptographic algorithm must be one-to-one. Otherwise, upon decipherment there would be more than one possible recovered plaintext, thus introducing ambiguity into the decipherment process.

The number of possible one-to-one functions from the set of plaintext elements (**P**) to the set of ciphertext elements (**C**) is determined as follows. The first plaintext element may be transformed to any of $|\mathbf{C}|$ elements, the second plaintext element to $|\mathbf{C}| - 1$ elements, whereas the last plaintext element may be mapped to any of $(|\mathbf{C}| - |\mathbf{P}|) + 1$ elements. Therefore, the total number of one-to-one functions is equal to the product of the number of elements in **C** available to each plaintext element, namely

$$|\mathbf{C}| \cdot (|\mathbf{C}| - 1) \cdot \ldots \cdot (|\mathbf{C}| - |\mathbf{P}| + 1) = \frac{|\mathbf{C}|!}{(|\mathbf{C}| - |\mathbf{P}|)!}$$

where

$$n! = 1 \cdot 2 \cdot 3 \cdot \ldots \cdot n \qquad \text{(called n factorial)}$$

(Note that $0! = 1$.) In the example shown in Figure 2-1, where $|\mathbf{P}| = 3$ and $|\mathbf{C}| = 6$, there are 120 possible one-to-one functions $(6 \cdot 5 \cdot 4 = 120)$, of which only one is shown.

If **S** denotes the set of possible one-to-one functions from **P** to **C**, then there are $|\mathbf{S}|$ such functions, any one of which is a candidate to be used for ciphering. Specifying a cipher key is the same as selecting one of these functions. (How this is achieved in an actual design is explained in Chapter 3). Since the cryptographic key is a cryptographic variable, the symbol v is used to denote a key and the symbol **V** to denote a set of keys. (The symbols **V** and v are used here to avoid conflicts with the symbols K and k, which are used below to denote specific keys.) Since the total number of possible keys is equal to $r = |\mathbf{V}|$, the set **V** can be expressed as

$$\mathbf{V} = \{v_1, v_2, \ldots, v_r\}$$

Let

$$\mathbf{E} = \{E_{v_1}, E_{v_2}, \ldots, E_{v_r}\}$$

specify the corresponding set of functions defining the encipherment procedure, and let

$$\mathbf{D} = \{D_{v_1}, D_{v_2}, \ldots, D_{v_r}\}$$

specify the corresponding set of functions defining the decipherment procedure. Thus the algorithm consists of enciphering (E) and deciphering (D) procedures, where **E** represents the set of all possible enciphering functions (or transformations) and **D** represents the set of all possible deciphering functions.

If the number of keys which can be independently specified exceeds the number of one-to-one functions (i.e., $|\mathbf{V}| > |\mathbf{S}|$) there must be cases where all plaintext-to-ciphertext correspondences are identical even though different keys are used (i.e., $E_{v_i} = E_{v_j}$, even though $v_i \neq v_j$). Such keys are called *equivalent keys*. Even if the number of keys is less than the number of one-to-one functions, $|\mathbf{V}| < |\mathbf{S}|$, equivalent keys may exist. In fact, for highly complex algorithms, it may be too difficult to prove or disprove the existence of equivalent keys.

Nevertheless, a good design principle that reduces the likelihood of equivalent keys is to ensure that the number of possible keys is much less than the number of possible one-to-one functions, (i.e., the condition $|\mathbf{V}| \ll |\mathbf{S}|$ is satisfied). For DES, the following conditions hold.

$|\mathbf{P}| = |\mathbf{C}| = 2^{64}$ (64 binary digits of data are enciphered at a time)

$|\mathbf{V}| = 2^{56}$ (56 binary digits uniquely identify a key)

$|\mathbf{S}| = (2^{64})!$

Since $2^{(64-56)} = 256$, it follows that

$$|\mathbf{S}| = 256 \cdot |\mathbf{V}| \cdot (2^{64} - 1)!$$

and therefore it can be seen that $|\mathbf{V}| \ll |\mathbf{S}|$ for DES.

A function f : $\mathbf{P} \rightarrow \mathbf{C}$ is called *onto* if the range of f is all of **C** (i.e., for any given c in **C** there exists at least one p in **P** such that f(p) = c). The function shown in Figure 2-1 is not onto, since some ciphertext combinations (c_2, c_4, and c_6) will not be generated as a result of enciphering all possible plaintext combinations.

It has been established that all functions associated with a cryptographic algorithm must be one-to-one. If they are also onto, then the number of elements in the sets **P** and **C** will be equal (i.e., the number of plaintext combinations is equal to the number of ciphertext combinations). Figure 2-2 shows two such cases, where there are $3 \cdot 2 \cdot 1 = 3!$ functions that are one-to-one and onto. In general, there are $|\mathbf{P}|!$ such functions if $|\mathbf{P}| = |\mathbf{C}|$. In mathematical terms, this implies that each function f_v has an *inverse function,* f_v^{-1}:

$$c = f_v(p)$$

and

$$p = f_v^{-1}(c)$$

Work Factor

To implement a cryptographic algorithm conveniently, the key must be fixed in length, relatively short, and capable of being used repeatedly without weakening security. However, an algorithm that uses a finite key can, theoretically, always be broken (if by no other means than trial and error using every possible key). The only question concerns how much work and resources the opponent must expend. Fortunately, it is not necessary to implement unbreakable algorithms provided that the work (or work factor) required to break the algorithm is sufficiently great to discourage an opponent from attacking it.

Work factor measures what is needed to carry out a specific analysis or attack against a cryptographic algorithm. The attack is conducted under a given set of assumptions which includes the information available to achieve

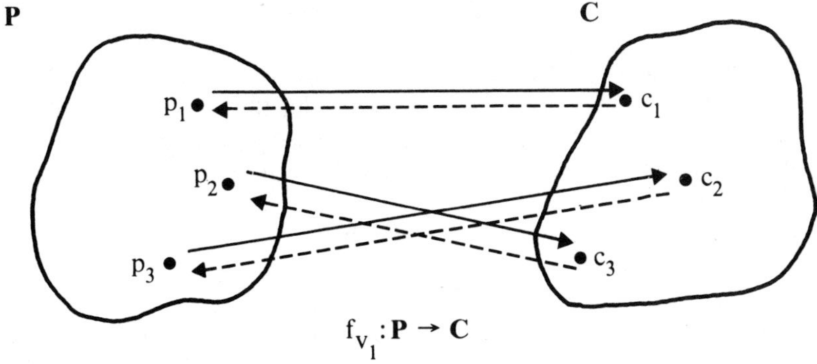

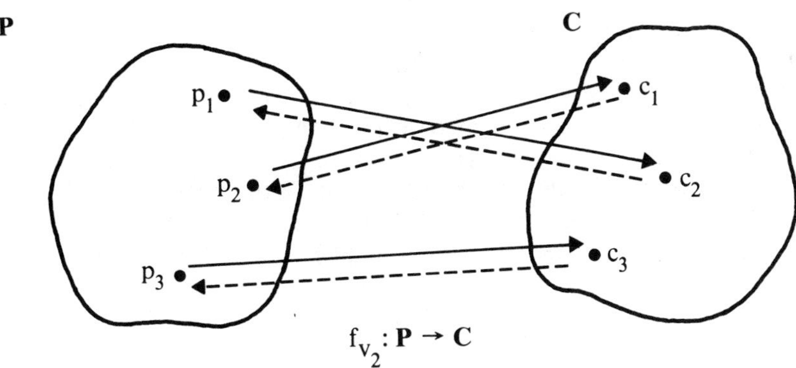

Encipherment: denoted by a solid line

Decipherment: denoted by a broken line

Figure 2-2. Examples of Functions that are One-To-One and Onto

a predetermined goal such as the recovery of the plaintext or key.[3] A good cryptographic algorithm design maximizes the amount of work that an opponent must expend to break it. Thus, for a given algorithm and set of assumptions, the work factor is an expression of the minimum amount of work necessary for a successful attack.

In practice, there is no universally accepted, fixed set of parameters used to express the work factor. However, it is frequently measured in one or more of the following: cryptanalyst hours, number of mathematical or logical operations, computing resources (such as data storage and processing requirements), special hardware, and calendar time. To be useful, the work factor should be expressed using parameters which can be translated for the purpose of comparison into a common base, such as cost in dollars.

[3]With some cryptographic attacks, there may only be a probability of success associated with the recovery of the plaintext or key.

Types of Attacks

In an *exhaustive attack,* an attempt is made to recover the plaintext or key by using direct search methods. For example, in key exhaustion, a known plaintext is enciphered with a trial key and the result is compared for equality with the known corresponding ciphertext.[4] If only ciphertext is available, it can be decrypted with the trial key and the resulting plaintext can be inspected to see if it makes any sense. In this way, it can be determined if the trial key is a candidate for the unknown key or not.

Exhaustive attacks can be thwarted by making the number of required trials very large. However, the work factor of an exhaustive attack, which is directly proportional to the number of trials, is easily determined even when the number of trials is so large that the attack is not feasible. This is not the case with some other attacks.

In an *analytical attack,* a set of mathematical equations (obtained from a definition of the cryptographic algorithm)[5] is solved for the variable or variables representing the unknown message or key. One way to thwart this purely mathematical attack is to construct the algorithm so that each plaintext bit is a sufficiently complex mathematical function of the ciphertext and key, and each key bit is a sufficiently complex mathematical function of the ciphertext and plaintext. If the mathematical equations describing the algorithm's operation are so complex that an analytical attack cannot be successful, then a work factor for this method cannot be calculated. In that case, one usually says that the work factor is very large, implying that the algorithm cannot be broken in the practical sense.

Designing an Algorithm

It is possible to design *unbreakable ciphers* [1]. To do so, the key must be randomly selected (i.e., each key must have the same chance of being chosen) and used only once. Furthermore, the length of the key must be equal to or greater than the length of the plaintext to be enciphered.[6] Unfortunately, long keys of this type, known as *one-time tapes,* are impractical for most applications where there is considerable message traffic, since a large number of keys must be transported and stored before communications can be established.

There are two ways to design a strong cryptographic algorithm [2]. First, one can study the possible methods of solution available to the cryptanalyst —describing them in the most general terms possible—and then define a set of design rules to thwart any one of these methods. An algorithm is then constructed which can resist these general methods of solution. Second, one can construct an algorithm in such a way that breaking it requires the

[4] This attack method assumes that the opponent knows the cryptographic algorithm and possesses a fragment of plaintext and corresponding ciphertext.

[5] The attack assumes that the opponent has knowledge of the cryptographic algorithm.

[6] The cipher is unbreakable because *every* message of the same length is equally likely to have yielded the given ciphertext.

solution of some known problem, but one that is difficult to solve. The DES algorithm was designed using the first approach (Chapter 3), whereas some public-key algorithms have been designed using the second approach (Chapter 2).

Any procedure for attacking a cryptographic algorithm requires that certain cryptographic information (such as ciphertext, plaintext and corresponding ciphertext) be available to carry out the attack. Therefore, the set of procedures that can be used to attack an algorithm depends on the information available to an opponent. Knowing the cryptographic information an opponent might reasonably be able to obtain is thus the basis for determining the class of attacks that the algorithm must be designed to resist.

The cryptographic algorithm, as well as the key, could be kept secret—an approach employed by the military where tight security measures can be enforced. (However, even here, it is ordinarily assumed during threat analyses that attackers have everything except keys and, where applicable, sequencing variables.) In nonmilitary sectors, however, where comparable security measures are impractical or unenforceable, it is unlikely that the secrecy of an algorithm installed at many locations with differing levels of physical security can be maintained for an extended period of time. Moreover, where there are many competing organizations and businesses, a policy of keeping the algorithm secret would promote the widespread use of differing and therefore incompatible algorithms with varying levels of cryptographic strength. An approach that overcomes these difficulties is to adopt a single standard algorithm whose strength has been carefully validated. Such an algorithm would be in the public domain, and its security would depend only on the secrecy of the cryptographic key. This strategy was used by the NBS in adopting the DES algorithm.

Data useful in attacking cryptographic algorithms can be categorized as follows.

1. Ciphertext only.
2. Unselected plaintext and corresponding ciphertext.
3. Selected plaintext and corresponding ciphertext.
4. Selected ciphertext and corresponding plaintext.

Encrypted messages (ciphertext) can be intercepted by wiretapping during transmission; encrypted data files can be copied or stolen from their storage locations (see Attack Scenarios, Chapter 1).

A fragment of plaintext can usually be deduced from some intercepted ciphertext because of the highly formatted text present in most messages and data files. On the other hand, an opponent who could obtain the use of a cryptographic device containing a secret key might (depending on the particular implementation) be able to encipher selected plaintext or decipher selected ciphertext. However, proper physical security and access control procedures are an effective means to prevent unauthorized use of cryptographic devices.

While an opponent's access to certain information (such as ciphertext) cannot be denied, other information may become known as a result of one or more of the following:

1. A deliberate act that depends on the opponent's skill, daring, and persistence.
2. An unintentional act involving carelessness or ignorance on the part of a cryptographic system's user.
3. An unknown and hence unanticipated event for which no present defense exists.

Except in rare cases, it is impossible to state absolutely that certain information will never become available to an opponent under all operating conditions and environments in which the algorithm may be implemented. Therefore, a conservative approach must be used in algorithm design. It is assumed that the opponent has a wide range of information that might be useful in attacking the algorithm. The algorithm is then designed to resist all known attacks made possible by this information.

Also, it is impossible to state absolutely that an algorithm is free from all possible attacks. Therefore, a conservative approach must likewise be used in the design of a system, such as a communication or file security system, which implements a cryptographic algorithm. It is assumed that the opponent has knowledge of a wide range of attacks that might be capable of breaking the algorithm. The system is then designed to deny the opponent the information needed to carry out the attacks.

In summary, the design of a *strong* cryptographic algorithm must satisfy the following conditions:

1. The mathematical equations describing the algorithm's operation are so complex that, for all practical purposes, it is not possible to solve them using analytical methods.
2. The cost or time required to recover the message or key is too great when using methods that are mathematically less complicated, because either too many computational steps are required (as in the case of message or key exhaustion), or too much data storage is required (as in the case of attacks requiring large accumulations of information such as frequency tables and dictionaries).

Furthermore, it is assumed that the above conditions are satisfied even when the opponent has the following advantages:

1. Relatively large amounts of plaintext (specified by the opponent, if he so desires) and corresponding ciphertext are available.
2. Relatively large amounts of ciphertext (specified by the opponent) and corresponding plaintext are available.
3. All details of the algorithm are available. (It is not assumed that

cryptographic strength depends on maintaining the secrecy of the algorithm.)

4. A number of large high-speed computers (determined by the resources available to the opponent) can be used for cryptanalysis.

The distinction between strong and unbreakable should be apparent. While in theory a strong algorithm can always be broken, in the practical sense it cannot. Unbreakable is an absolute attribute and means that even with an unlimited amount of computational power, data storage, and calendar time, there is no way to obtain the message or key through cryptanalysis. So to speak, strong is a variable, and unbreakable is its maximum value.

Block ciphers and stream ciphers are two fundamentally different approaches which can be used to achieve strong encryption-based protection schemes. The study of these two approaches is thus basic to an understanding, and even a full appreciation, of the direction in which cryptography is currently moving.

Since the main thrust here is to show how cryptography can be used in computer systems, all cryptographic discussion will assume that information is expressed in binary form. The treatment is still general, since any characters can be encoded into binary equivalents.

BLOCK CIPHERS

A *block cipher* (Figure 2-3) transforms a string of input bits of fixed length (an input block) into a string of output bits of fixed length (an output block). The enciphering and deciphering functions are such that every bit in the output block depends jointly on every bit in the input block and on every bit in the key.

A cipher's *blocksize* (the number of bits in a block) is determined by considerations of cryptographic strength, and it must be large enough to

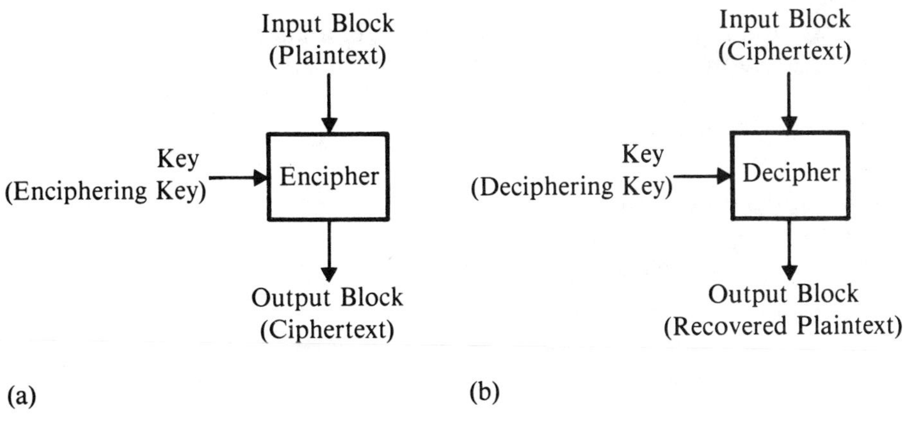

Figure 2-3. Block Cipher

foil simple *message exhaustion* attacks. For example, by enciphering all possible plaintext combinations with a given key, an opponent could build a dictionary of ciphertext (sorted into sequence) and corresponding plaintext. A message could then be recovered by searching the dictionary and relating each intercepted ciphertext block to its corresponding plaintext block. However, if the blocksize is large enough, the dictionary will be too large to construct or store.

In the method of message exhaustion described above, the opponent must be able to encipher data with a key being used by the cryptographic system. In a public-key cryptographic system, the public enciphering-key (or enciphering-transformation) is available to anyone. In a conventional cryptographic system, a conservative assumption is made that the opponent has access to a cryptographic device containing a secret key, even though proper physical security and access control are effective measures against such unauthorized access.[7] (While the opponent can encipher data using the cryptographic device, the key remains unknown.)

Other attacks must also be considered before arriving at an acceptable blocksize. For example, advantage could be taken of the fact that some data blocks are more likely to occur than others. Therefore, the frequency of occurrence should be taken into account. This type of attack is called *block frequency analysis* and uses statistical methods. It is similar to an analysis which could be performed on a simple substitution cipher by taking into account letter frequencies.

By expressing cipher operations in purely mathematical form as a set of equations, it may be possible to solve for the unknown variables directly using analytical methods. This approach is called a *deterministic attack*. To foil deterministic attacks, every bit in the output block must be a sufficiently complex mathematical function of every bit in the input block and key. This property is defined as *strong intersymbol dependence*. From the discussion of work factor, it thus follows that a complex mathematical function must be one for which it is computationally infeasible to solve for the key, even if plaintext and corresponding ciphertext are known (i.e., the work factor is too high).

As part of a mathematical structure for further analysis, several terms useful in a discussion of block ciphers and stream ciphers are defined below.

X: Input (plaintext)
Y: Output (ciphertext)
K: Cryptographic (or cipher) key
Z: Initializing vector (seed value)
U: Intermediate initializing vector
R: Cryptographic bit-stream

[7] Another form of message exhaustion does not require access to the cryptographic device. Instead, each possible plaintext combination is enciphered with each possible key. The opponent then builds a dictionary of plaintext and corresponding ciphertext for each possible key. Later, interception of plaintext and corresponding ciphertext allows the unknown key to be determined.

Since computer data are in binary format, vector notation is used to express such quantities. An input block (X) of b bits is thus denoted by

$$X = (x_1, x_2, \ldots, x_b)$$

where x_i is a 0 or 1 for each i = 1, 2, . . . , b. Using, as before, the notation |*| to represent the number of elements in *, the number of elements in the vector X is denoted |X|. Note that in the example above, the length of X is b, (i.e., |X| = b). In some situations, it is helpful to speak of a sequence or time-sequence of vectors. Here, a sequence of n input blocks is denoted by

$$(X(1), X(2), \ldots, X(n))$$

and specifies the time sequence or relative order of encipherment of each block. If each input block contains b bits, then the vector of input bits at time i is denoted by

$$X(i) = (x_1(i), x_2(i), \ldots, x_b(i))$$

and |X(i)| = b.

In describing a block cipher, it is not necessary to distinguish between the encipherment of block X at time i and the encipherment of the same block X at time j. Simply, encipherment of block X at any time will result in the same block Y. Of course, it is assumed that the same cryptographic key is used. This independence with regard to the order of encipherment does not hold when block chaining is used (a concept discussed later).

Before further details are introduced, a frequently used operation, *modulo 2 addition* or *Exclusive OR* (symbol ⊕), is defined (Table 2-1).

A	B	A ⊕ B
0	0	0
0	1	1
1	0	1
1	1	0

Table 2-1. Modulo 2 Addition

From the rules for modulo 2 addition, it follows that

$$A \oplus A = 0$$

$$A \oplus 0 = A$$

$$A \oplus 1 = \overline{A}$$

where $\overline{A}$ is the complement of A. $\overline{A}$ is obtained by inverting the bits in A, that is, 0 becomes 1 and 1 becomes 0. It follows that if

$$A \oplus B = C$$

then

$$A = C \oplus B$$

$$B = C \oplus A$$

(Note that $A \oplus B \oplus B = A \oplus 0 = A = C \oplus B$.)

Let K be a key in the set {K1, K2, . . . , Kn} of possible keys and let f_K be a function in the set $\{f_{K1}, f_{K2}, \ldots, f_{Kn}\}$ of one-to-one functions corresponding to these keys that transforms an input block (X) of b bits into an output block (Y) of b bits, (i.e., $|Y| = |X| = b$). Hence there are 2^b possible plaintext combinations and 2^b possible ciphertext combinations within the domain and co-domain of each function f_K, respectively. In general, only the condition $|Y| \geqslant |X|$ need be satisfied to yield an unambiguous system (a system where no two plaintext combinations map to the same ciphertext combination). For engineering reasons, however, the choice $|Y| = |X|$ is usually made. In that case, the function f_K is one-to-one as well as onto, and hence the inverse function (f_K^{-1}) also exists (Figure 2-2).

Conventional Algorithms

A block-cipher design similar to that used in DES algorithm is now considered. The operations of encipherment and decipherment are described as follows (Figure 2-4).

$$f_K(X) = Y$$

for encipherment, and

$$f_K^{-1}(Y) = X$$

for decipherment. Subscript K designates which particular key (and hence function, f_K) is selected out of the set of all possible keys (and hence functions).

Although f_K must be one-to-one for decipherment to be possible, it is interesting that a one-to-one function f_K can in the most simple case be constructed from a *many-to-one* function (a function that produces the same output for several different inputs). Let such a many-to-one function be defined as g_K. The idea here is to *exercise* g *in the encipherment as well as in the decipherment process.*

To achieve this, the input block (X) consisting of b bits is split into two blocks, L(0) (left) and R(0) (right), each consisting of b/2 bits. Hence X can be expressed as a concatenation of L(0) and R(0):

$$X = L(0),R(0)$$

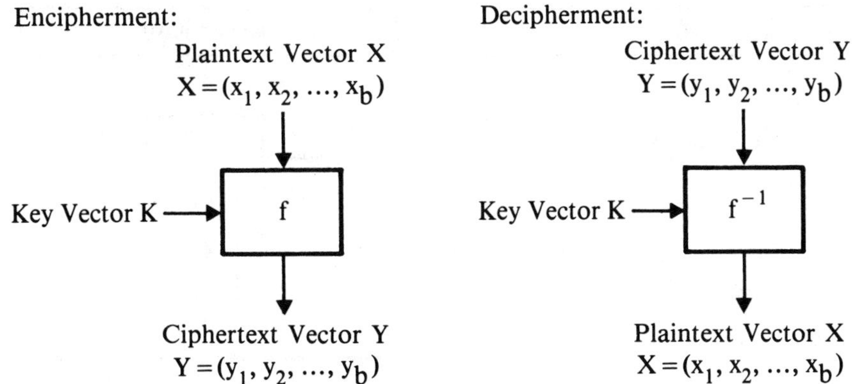

Figure 2-4. Block Cipher (Conventional Cryptographic Algorithm)

g transforms R(0) into g_K(R(0)) under control of cipher key K; as indicated in Figure 2-5. L(0) is brought into play by adding it modulo 2 to g_K(R(0)) to obtain R(1):

$$R(1) = L(0) \oplus g_K(R(0))$$

The operation is completed by setting L(1) equal to R(0).

If L(1),R(1) represents the ciphertext or scrambled version of L(0),R(0), then the question arises how this ciphertext could be unscrambled without introducing an inverse operation for function g_K. With this goal in mind, the reader should observe that since the ciphertext contains L(1) and since L(1)

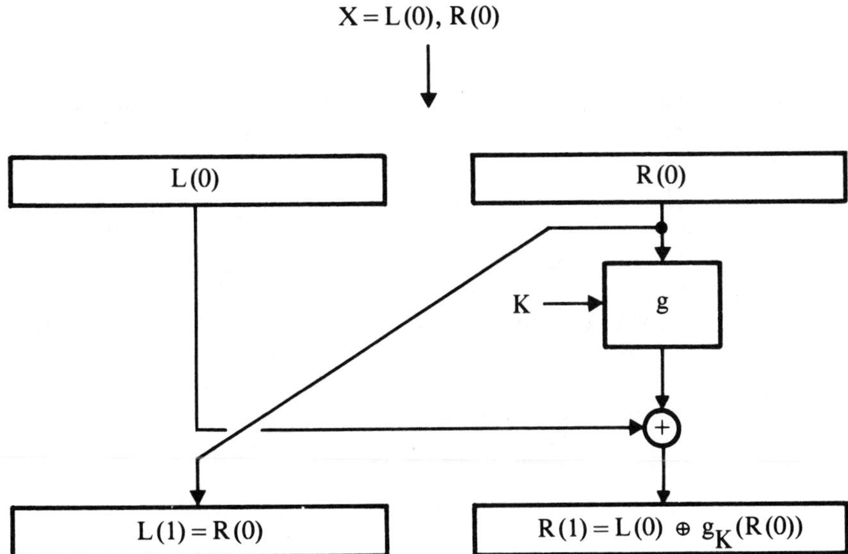

Figure 2-5. Transformation of Input Block (L(0), R(0))

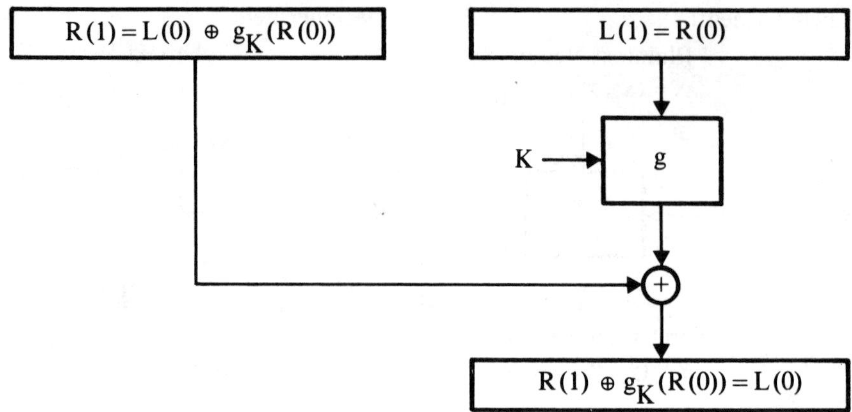

Figure 2-6. Recovery of L(0)

equals R(0), half of the original plaintext is immediately recovered. The remaining half, L(0), can also be recovered, as indicated in Figure 2-6, by recreating $g_K(R(0))$ from R(0) and adding $g_K(R(0))$ modulo 2 to R(1):

$$\begin{aligned} R(1) \oplus g_K(R(0)) &= L(0) \oplus g_K(R(0)) \oplus g_K(R(0)) \\ &= L(0) \end{aligned}$$

However, to use the procedure in Figure 2-5 for encipherment as well as decipherment, the left and right halves of the output are interchanged. That is, the ciphertext (Y) is defined as

$$Y = [L(0) \oplus g_K(R(0))],\ R(0)$$

This scheme is, of course, extremely weak, since half of the input block, namely R(0), remains unenciphered in the output block. However, cryptographic strength can be obtained by repeating the process (exercising g) n times, where n is called the *number of rounds*, and by using a different key for each round. The basic idea for a two-round system is illustrated in Figure 2-7. The reader should understand that deciphering in such a system is possible only if the internal keys, K(1) and K(2) in Figure 2-7, are exercised in the order K(1), K(2) for encipherment and K(2), K(1) for decipherment. In general, the plaintext can be recovered in an n-round system by exercising the internal keys in the order K(1), K(2), . . . , K(n − 1), K(n) for encipherment and K(n), K(n − 1), . . . , K(2), K(1) for decipherment.

So far it has been assumed that the same key had to be used for encipherment and decipherment, that is,

$$f_K(X) = Y \quad \text{(for encipherment)}$$
$$f_K^{-1}(Y) = X \quad \text{(for decipherment)}$$

where the internal keys are derived from the external key K (the key supplied by the user). However, in the n-round system, the following relations also hold:

$$f_K(X) = Y$$
$$f_{K'}(Y) = X$$

The external keys, K and K′, are defined to have the following schedule of internal keys:

round:	1,	2,	..., n − 1,	n	
K:	K(1),	K(2),	..., K(n − 1),	K(n)	(2-1)
K′:	K(n),	K(n − 1),	..., K(2),	K(1)	(2-2)

Hence, it follows that f_K^{-1} is equivalent to $f_{K'}$.

As discussed earlier, the ciphering process can in general be described by a set of functions, namely

$$\mathbf{E} = \{E_{v_1}, E_{v_2}, \ldots, E_{v_r}\}$$

for encipherment, and

$$\mathbf{D} = \{D_{v_1}, D_{v_2}, \ldots, D_{v_r}\}$$

for decipherment. Selecting a common key (K) for encipherment and decipherment thus determines the enciphering transformation (E_K) as well as the deciphering transformation (D_K). A cryptographic system using the approach shown in Figure 2-7 could, however, be described by defining only one set of functions, that is, by defining only **E**. The set of functions for the deciphering process does not have to be separately specified, since for each key K that is used for enciphering with function (E_K) there is a key K′ that can be used for deciphering with function ($E_{K'}$). In the former case, a common key is used together with the sets of enciphering and deciphering functions (**E** and **D**, respectively) and in the latter case two different keys are used for enciphering and deciphering together with one set of enciphering functions, **E**. It follows, therefore, that

$$E_{K'}(E_K(X)) = E_K(E_{K'}(X)) = X$$

for all possible plaintext (X). And, if K and K′ were to have a much more complex relationship than the one indicated by Equations 2-1 and 2-2, the cryptographic scheme shown in Figure 2-7 could be used as a public-key cryptographic algorithm.

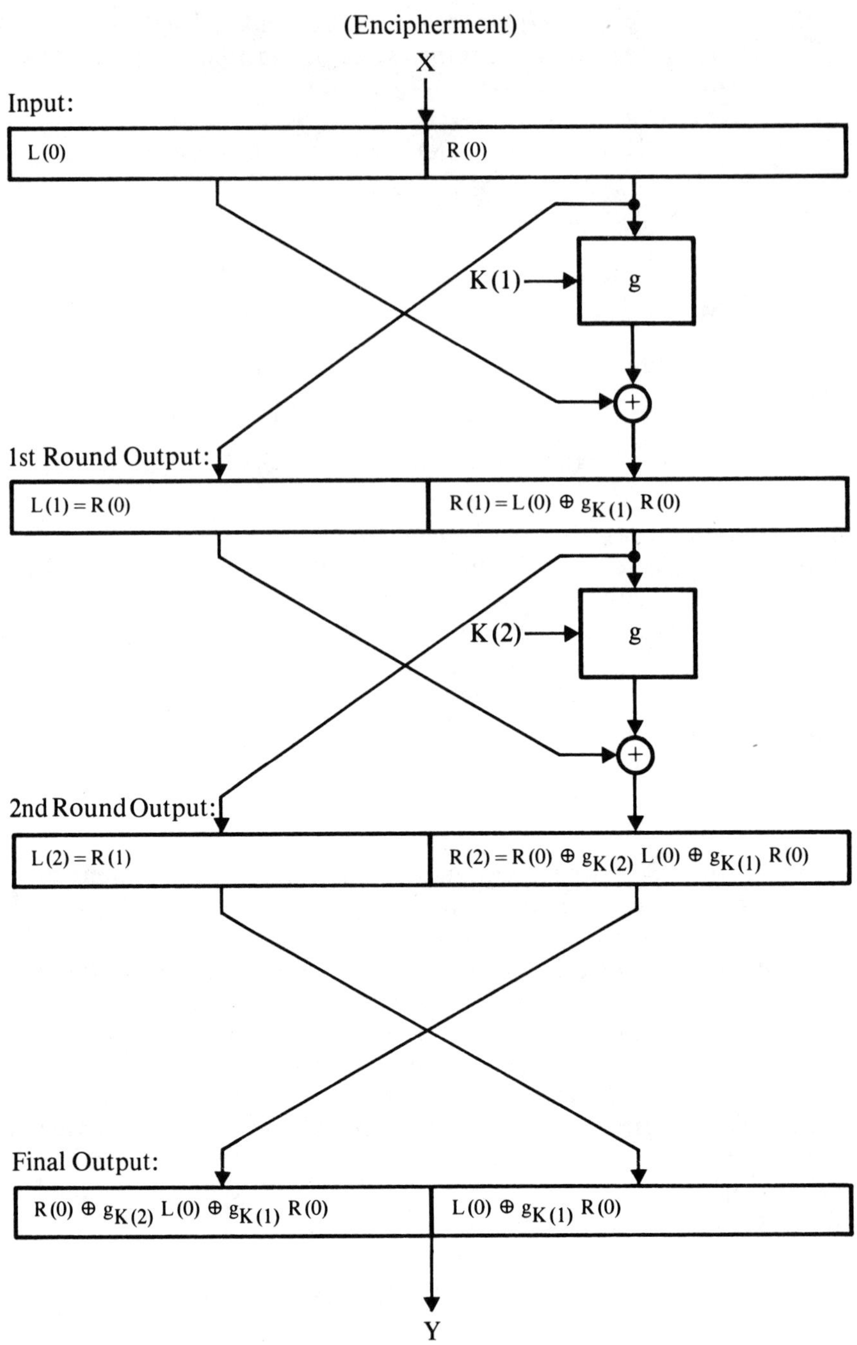

Figure 2-7. A Two-Round Block Cipher

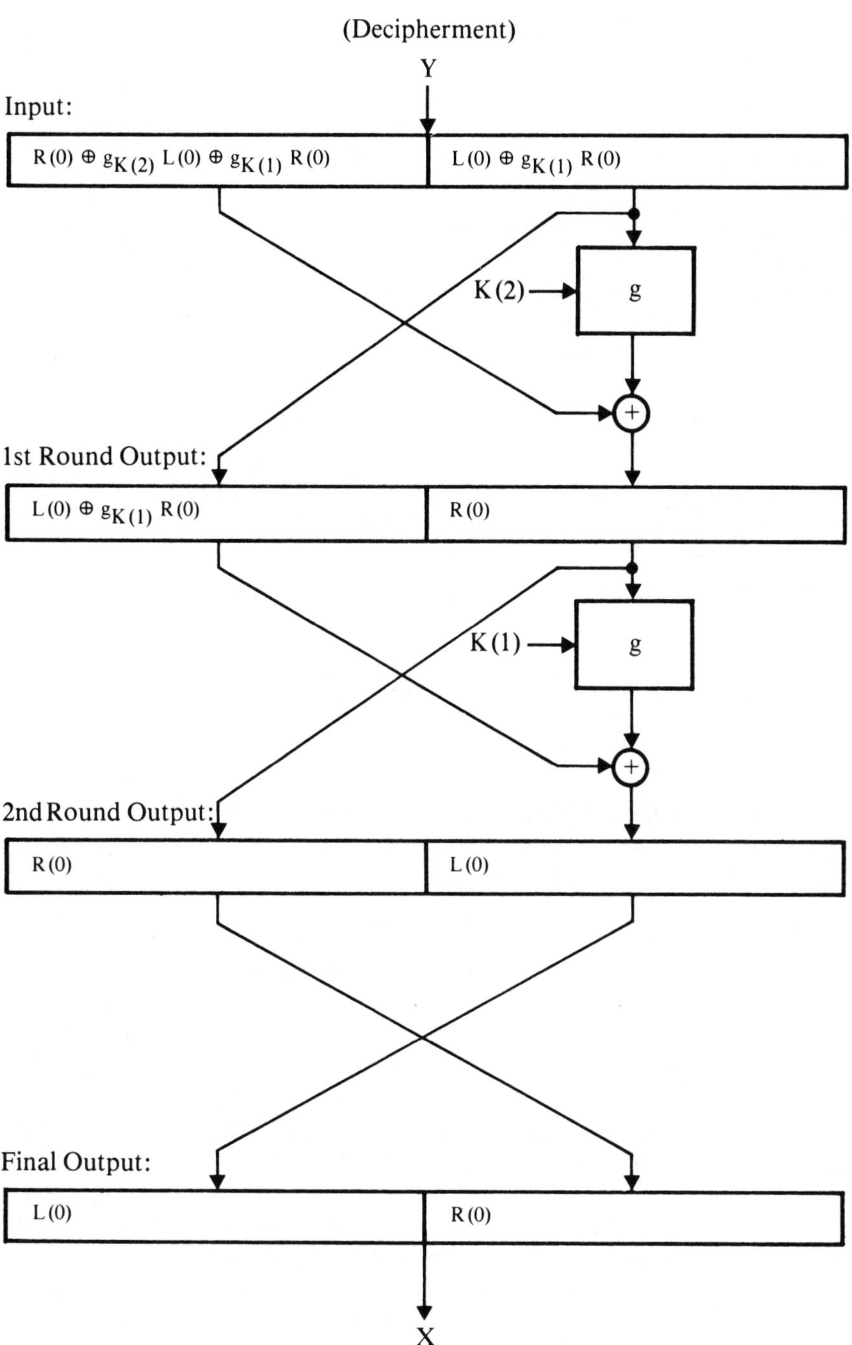

Figure 2-7 (cont'd). A Two-Round Block Cipher

Public-Key Algorithms

Public-key cryptography [3] uses an enciphering key (PK) which is in the public domain and a deciphering key (SK) which is kept secret. Anyone can encipher data using the public key of another user, but only those users with knowledge of the secret key can decipher enciphered data. The enciphering algorithm (E) and the deciphering algorithm (D) might be different, though it is possible for E and D to be identical. (In the discussion that follows, it is assumed that E and D are made public.)

To be used privately, or for private data communications, a public-key algorithm must have the following properties:

1. Users must be able to compute a pair of public and private keys, PK and SK, efficiently.
2. Knowledge of PK must not permit SK to be computed efficiently. (Note: There is no requirement that knowledge of SK prevent PK from being computed efficiently.)
3. Encipherment followed by decipherment causes the original message (X) to be recovered, that is,

$$D_{SK}(E_{PK}(X)) = X$$

for all X in the domain of E_{PK}.

If, in addition to meeting conditions (1) and (2), the public-key algorithm is such that decipherment followed by encipherment causes the original message (X) to be recovered, that is,

$$E_{PK}(D_{SK}(X)) = X$$

for all X in the domain of D_{SK}, then the algorithm can be used to generate a digital signature[8] that authenticates the message's sender (see Chapter 9).

Greater design restrictions are placed on a public-key algorithm than on a conventional algorithm because the public key represents additional information which the opponent can use to attack the algorithm. A public-key algorithm must be designed to withstand attacks made possible by this additional information. (See Cryptographic Strength Considerations.)

In a conventional algorithm, such as DES, the designer has complete freedom to choose the substitutions, permutation, number of rounds, and key schedule (i.e., key bits used in each round) without considering whether the enciphering process reveals the deciphering process. In DES, the deciphering process can be automatically determined if the enciphering key is known, since all steps taken in the enciphering process can easily be retraced to obtain the deciphering process.

On the other hand, in a public-key algorithm it must not be possible to

[8] Merkle and Hellman [4] have shown that digital signatures can be obtained if $E_{PK}(D_{SK}(X)) = X$ holds for only a fraction of the set of possible Xs.

retrace the steps in the enciphering process to determine the deciphering process. Enciphering follows one path and deciphering follows a different path, and knowledge of the former must not reveal the latter.

There are other notable differences between conventional and public-key algorithms. The public-key algorithms invented thus far [4–6] are easily described in mathematical terms, and rely for their strength on the underlying assumption that a particular, known mathematical problem is difficult to solve. On the other hand, a conventional algorithm like DES is designed so that the mathematical equations describing its operation are so complex that for all practical purposes it is not possible to solve them using analytical methods.

Another difference relates to the disciplines needed to attack an algorithm. With a public-key algorithm, these disciplines appear to be few in number and fixed by the algorithm's mathematical description. With a conventional algorithm, on the other hand, the designer has the freedom to ensure that many (possibly chosen) disciplines are required.

Also, the manner in which keys are generated is different for conventional and public-key algorithms. In a conventional algorithm, the key can be randomly selected in a straightforward way, since knowledge of the enciphering key is equivalent to knowledge of the deciphering key, and vice versa. However, in a public-key algorithm, the relationship between the public and private keys is purposely made obscure (i.e., knowledge of the public key does not reveal the private key). Thus, a special procedure is needed to compute the public and private keys, and this procedure must also be computationally efficient.

RSA Algorithm

The RSA algorithm [5] (named for the algorithm's inventors: Rivest, Shamir, and Adleman) is based on the fact that in the current computing art factorization of composite numbers with large prime factors involves overwhelming computations. Indeed, cumulative experience has shown this problem to be intractable [7]. (For more details, see Cryptographic Strength Considerations.)

A number p (p = 1, 2, 3, . . .) is called *prime* if its only divisors are the trivial ones, ±1 and ±p, otherwise it is called *composite*. The primes below 100 are

2	13	31	53	73
3	17	37	59	79
5	19	41	61	83
7	23	43	67	89
11	29	47	71	97

All primes are odd except for the number 2. Every composite number can be factored uniquely into prime factors. For example, 6 is a composite number whose factors are 2 and 3 (i.e., $6 = 2 \cdot 3$). The composite number 999,999 on the other hand is factored by the prime numbers 3, 7, 11, 13, and 37 (i.e., $999{,}999 = 3^3 \cdot 7 \cdot 11 \cdot 13 \cdot 37$).

To describe the RSA algorithm, the following quantities are defined.

1. p and q are primes (secret)
2. $r = p \cdot q$ (nonsecret)
3. $\phi(r) = (p-1)(q-1)$ (secret)
4. SK is the private key (secret)
5. PK is the public key (nonsecret)
6. X is the message (plaintext) (secret)
7. Y is the ciphertext (nonsecret)

Because the suggested approach involves modulo arithmetic, congruences are defined in the way they were first introduced by Gauss. Two integers a and b are *congruent* for the modulus m if their difference $a - b$ is divisible by the integer m.[9] This is expressed in the symbolic statement

$$a \equiv b \pmod{m}$$

When a and b are not congruent, they are called *incongruent* for the modulus m, and this is written

$$a \not\equiv b \pmod{m}$$

For any pair of integers a and b, one or the other alternative holds (i.e., a and b are either congruent or incongruent). For example,

$$16 \equiv 1 \pmod{5}$$

$$-7 \equiv 15 \pmod{11}$$

$$-7 \not\equiv 15 \pmod{3}$$

One can state the congruence $a \equiv b \pmod{m}$ slightly differently by saying that b is congruent to a when it differs from a by some multiple (c) of m.

$$b = a + cm$$

The RSA algorithm is based on an extension of Euler's theorem [7], which states that

$$a^{\phi(r)} \equiv 1 \pmod{r}$$

[9] Congruent means agreeing with or corresponding to while modulus (shortened to mod) signifies "little measure."

where

1. a must be relatively prime to r. (Integers a and b are *relatively prime* if their greatest common divisor, gcd, is one.)
2. $\phi(r) = r(1 - 1/p_1)(1 - 1/p_2) \ldots (1 - 1/p_n)$, where $p_1, p_2, \ldots, p_n$ are the prime factors of r.

$\phi(r)$ is Euler's ϕ-function of r (also called indicator or totient) which determines how many of the numbers 1, 2, . . . , r are relatively prime to r.

For example, the composite number $20 = 2^2 \cdot 5$ has two prime factors, 2 and 5. Thus there are $\phi(20) = 20(1 - \frac{1}{2})(1 - \frac{1}{5}) = 8$ integers which are relatively prime to 20 (i.e., which have neither 2 or 5 as a factor):

$$1, 3, 7, 9, 11, 13, 17, 19$$

In the discussion that follows, the reader is expected to be familiar with elementary number theory [7].

To obtain the mathematical relationship between the public and private keys, PK and SK, Euler's result is extended as follows. First, it is shown that $a \equiv b \pmod{r}$ implies that $a^m \equiv b^m \pmod{r}$ for any exponent m [7]. Thus Euler's formula $a^{\phi(r)} \equiv 1 \pmod{r}$ can be rewirtten as

$$a^{m\,\phi(r)} \equiv 1 \pmod{r} \tag{2-3}$$

where, as before, a is relatively prime to r. From the fact that $a \equiv b \pmod{r}$ implies that $ac \equiv bc \pmod{r}$ for any integer c, and from Equation 2-3, it follows that

$$X^{m\,\phi(r) + 1} \equiv X \pmod{r} \tag{2-4}$$

where plaintext X is relatively prime to r (a restriction that is removed below). Let the public key (PK) and the secret key (SK) be chosen so that

$$SK \cdot PK = m\phi(r) + 1 \tag{2-5}$$

or, equivalently,

$$SK \cdot PK \equiv 1 \pmod{\phi(r)} \tag{2-6}$$

(A method for finding SK and PK satisfying this equation is discussed below.) Equation 2-4 can therefore be rewritten as

$$X^{SK \cdot PK} \equiv X \pmod{r}$$

which holds true for any plaintext (X) that is relatively prime to the modulus (r). (Actually, as shown below, the relation holds for any plaintext (X), and thus the restriction can be removed.)

Encipherment and decipherment can now be interpreted as follows:

$$E_{PK}(X) = Y \equiv X^{PK} \pmod{r} \tag{2-7}$$

$$D_{SK}(Y) \equiv Y^{SK} \pmod{r} \equiv X^{PK \cdot SK} \pmod{r} \equiv X \pmod{r} \tag{2-8}$$

Moreover, because multiplication is a commutative operation (i.e., SK·PK = PK·SK), it follows that encipherment followed by decipherment is equivalent to decipherment followed by encipherment:

$$D_{SK}(E_{PK}(X)) = E_{PK}(D_{SK}(X)) \equiv X \pmod{r} \tag{2-9}$$

As mentioned above, this property is useful for generating digital signatures (see Digital Signatures, Chapter 10).

Because $X^{PK} \pmod{r} \equiv (X + mr)^{PK} \pmod{r}$ for any integer m, each plaintext X, X+r, X+2r, . . . , results in the same ciphertext. Thus the transformation from plaintext to ciphertext is many-to-one. But restricting X to the set $\{0, 1, \ldots, r - 1\}$ makes the transformation one-to-one, and thus encipherment and decipherment can be achieved as described in Equations 2-7 and 2-8.

Consider the example in which r equals $2 \cdot 3 = 6$ and $\phi(r)$ therefore equals $1 \cdot 2 = 2$. As predicted by Euler's theorem, $X^{\phi(r)} \equiv 1 \pmod{r}$ for values of X in the set $\{0, 1, \ldots, 5\}$ which are relatively prime to $r = 6$. However, one observes that $X^{\phi(r)+1} \equiv X \pmod{r}$ for all values of X in the set $\{0, 1, \ldots, 5\}$, as shown in Table 2-2. A proof is now given that the relationship $X^{m\,\phi(r)+1} \equiv X$

X	$X^{\phi(r)} \pmod{r}$	$X^{\phi(r)+1} \pmod{r}$
0	0	0
1	1	1
2	4	2
3	3	3
4	4	4
5	1	5

Legend:
$p=2,\ q=3,\ r=6,\ \phi(r)=2$
Set of Xs relatively prime to r: {1, 5}
Set of Xs relatively prime to p: {1, 3, 5}
Set of Xs relatively prime to q: {1, 2, 4, 5}

Table 2-2. Evaluation of $X^{\phi(r)+1} \pmod{r}$

(mod r) holds for any plaintext, X, where r = pq is the product of two prime factors and X is restricted to the set {0, 1, . . . , r − 1}—a condition which is necessary for encipherment and decipherment.

The theorem holds trivially for X = 0, and so only the case X > 0 must be considered. If X is not relatively prime to r = pq, then X must contain either p or q as a factor. Suppose p is a factor of X, so that the relation X = cp holds for some positive integer c. Since X is restricted to the set {0, 1, . . . , r − 1}, and r equals pq, it follows that X must be relatively prime to q. Otherwise, X would also contain q as a factor, in which case it would exceed r − 1. Using Euler's theorem, we have

$$x^{\phi(q)} \equiv 1 \pmod{q}$$

where $\phi(q) = q - 1$. But

$$X^{m(p-1)\phi(q)} \equiv 1^{m(p-1)} \equiv 1 \pmod{q}$$

for any integer m, and $(p-1)\phi(q) = (p-1)(q-1) = \phi(r)$, so that

$$X^{m\phi(r)} \equiv 1 \pmod{q}$$

or, for some integer n

$$1 = X^{m\phi(r)} + nq$$

Multiplying each side by X = cp results in

$$\begin{aligned} X &= X^{m\phi(r)+1} + (nq)(cp) \\ &= X^{m\phi(r)+1} + ncr \end{aligned}$$

or,

$$X^{m\phi(r)+1} \equiv X \pmod{r}$$

The case in which q is a factor of X can be handled in the same manner, thus completing the proof.

Procedures are now discussed for using the proposed algorithm. In particular it is shown how a user can create a pair of keys: public key (PK) and secret key (SK).

The user selects two prime numbers, p and q, where p ≠ q. The product r = pq is made public, but p and q are kept secret. Note, for example, that the choice p = q is unacceptable, since p could then be obtained by taking the square root of the publicly known modulus (r). Even if the difference d = (p − q) is nonzero, d must still be unpredictable, since otherwise p and q could be determined from r. Note that (p + q) is the square root of $(p-q)^2 + 4r$, and q is half the difference of (p + q) and (p − q).

The public and secret keys must now be selected such that they satisfy Equation 2-6, that is,

$$PK \cdot SK \equiv 1 \ (\text{mod } \phi(r))$$

In addition, it must be easy to compute PK and SK. The question thus arises as to how PK and SK can be chosen to satisfy these requirements. The following theorem [7] provides the answer.

Let the notation d = (a, n) be used to indicate that d is the greatest common divisor (gcd) of a and n. Then the congruence $aX \equiv b \ (\text{mod } n)$ is solvable (i.e., an integer X can be found that satisfies the congruence) only if the gcd of a and n divides b, and when this is the case there are d solutions [7].

If a and n are respectively defined as SK and $\phi(r)$, then gcd (SK, $\phi(r)$) divides 1 if and only if gcd (SK, $\phi(r)$) = 1, that is, if and only if SK is relatively prime to $\phi(r)$. And so, the congruence $SK \cdot X \equiv 1 \ (\text{mod } \phi(r))$, where X is defined as PK, has a solution only if SK is relatively prime to $\phi(r)$. (Note that if a = PK, the solution X would be SK.) Moreover, because Euclid's algorithm (discussed below) provides an efficient method both to test whether a randomly chosen SK is relatively prime to $\phi(r)$ and to find the solution (X) of the congruence $SK \cdot X \equiv 1 \ (\text{mod } \phi(r))$, the theorem above provides an efficient means of finding PK and SK.

For example, let p = 47 and q = 61. (Methods for generating prime numbers are treated separately. See Testing for Primality.) Thus r = pq = 2867 and $\phi(r) = (p - 1)(q - 1) = 2760$.

The method for determining the gcd of two integers, and therefore, a test as to whether two integers are relatively prime, is based on the *Euclidean algorithm* (from Euclid's *Elementa*, seventh book, circa 300 B.C.); namely, if a = bn + c, then the gcd of a and b equals the gcd of b and c. Thus, one can solve for gcd (a, b) by progressively reducing the size of the numbers whose gcd we are trying to find. For purposes of illustration, let a = 38 = 2 · 19 and b = 26 = 2 · 13. Observe that 19 and 13 are primes, and therefore that 2 is the greatest common divisor of a and b. The same result is obtained with Euclid's algorithm.

1. $38 = 26 \cdot 1 + 12$ — 26 divides 38 one time with a remainder of 12
2. $26 = 12 \cdot 2 + 2$ — 12 divides 26 two times with a remainder of 2
3. $12 = 2 \cdot 6$

The last nonvanishing remainder (the value of 2 in the above example) is the gcd of a = 38 and b = 26. Even for very large integers, the Euclidean algorithm requires only a small number of steps to find the gcd.

With the aid of Euclid's algorithm, it can now be shown (for the example p = 47, q = 61, and $\phi(r) = 2760$) that SK = 167 is a candidate for the secret key.

$$2760 = 167 \cdot 16 + 88 \qquad (2\text{-}10a)$$

$$167 = 88 \cdot 1 + 79 \qquad (2\text{-}10b)$$

$$88 = 79 \cdot 1 + 9 \tag{2-10c}$$

$$79 = 9 \cdot 8 + 7 \tag{2-10d}$$

$$9 = 7 \cdot 1 + 2 \tag{2-10e}$$

$$7 = 2 \cdot 3 + 1 \quad \text{(1 is the last nonvanishing remainder)} \tag{2-10f}$$

$$2 = 1 \cdot 2 \tag{2-10g}$$

The value of PK can be found by using a variation of Euclid's algorithm, which has already been used in computing the gcd of SK and $\phi(r)$. The goal is to rewrite Equations 2-10a through 2-10g in such a way that the final result is in the form

$$(\text{factor}_1 \cdot \text{SK}) + (\text{factor}_2 \cdot \phi(r)) = 1$$

in which case, factor_1 is interpreted as PK. (Note that this expression is equivalent to $\text{PK} \cdot \text{SK} \equiv 1 \pmod{\phi(r)}$.)

Let SK = 167 and $\phi(r) = 2760$, where p = 47 and q = 61. The public key can be computed using Equation 2-10f.

$$1 = 7 - 2 \cdot 3 \tag{2-11a}$$

Substituting $2 = 9 - 7 \cdot 1$ (Equation 2-10e) into Equation 2-11a results in

$$1 = 7 - 9 \cdot 3 + 7 \cdot 3 = 7 \cdot 4 - 9 \cdot 3 \tag{2-11b}$$

Substituting $7 = 79 - 9 \cdot 8$ (Equation 2-10d) into Equation 2-11b results in

$$1 = 79 \cdot 4 - 9 \cdot 32 - 9 \cdot 3 = 79 \cdot 4 - 9 \cdot 35 \tag{2-11c}$$

Substituting $9 = 88 - 79 \cdot 1$ (Equation 2-10c) into Equation 2-11c results in

$$1 = 79 \cdot 4 - 88 \cdot 35 + 79 \cdot 35 = 79 \cdot 39 - 88 \cdot 35 \tag{2-11d}$$

Substituting $79 = 167 - 88 \cdot 1$ (Equation 2-10b) into Equation 2-11d results in

$$1 = 167 \cdot 39 - 88 \cdot 39 - 88 \cdot 35 = 167 \cdot 39 - 88 \cdot 74 \tag{2-11e}$$

Finally, substituting $88 = 2760 - 167 \cdot 16$ (Equation 2-10a) into Equation 2-11e results in

$$1 = 167 \cdot 1223 - 2760 \cdot 74 \tag{2-11f}$$

From Equation 2-11f, it can be seen that 1223 is the multiplicative inverse of 167 modulo 2760, and therefore that PK = 1223 is the public key corresponding to SK = 167.

In summary, the following numerical values were obtained in the example.

$$p = 47 \qquad \text{(chosen)}$$
$$q = 61 \qquad \text{(chosen)}$$
$$r = pq = 47 \cdot 61 = 2867 \qquad \text{(derived)}$$
$$\phi(r) = (p-1)(q-1) = 46 \cdot 60 = 2760 \qquad \text{(derived)}$$
$$SK = 167 \qquad \text{(chosen)}$$
$$PK = 1223 \qquad \text{(derived)}$$

A message to be enciphered is first divided into a series of blocks such that the value of each block does not exceed $r - 1$. (Otherwise, a unique plaintext representation is not possible.) This could be achieved by substituting a two-digit number for each letter of the message). For example, blank = 00, A = 01, B = 02, . . . , Z = 26. Thus, the message "RSA ALGORITHM" would be written in blocks as

1819 0100 0112 0715 1809 2008 1300

The first plaintext block, 1819, is enciphered by raising it to the power PK = 1223, dividing by r = 2867, and taking the remainder, 2756, as the ciphertext. Likewise, 2756 is deciphered by raising it to the power SK = 167, dividing by r = 2867, and taking the remainder, 1819, as the recovered plaintext. The total ciphertext of the example is as follows:

2756 2001 0542 0669 2347 0408 1815

Since PK = 10011000111 in binary (or $2^{10} + 2^7 + 2^6 + 2^2 + 2^1 + 2^0$ or $1024 + 128 + 64 + 4 + 2 + 1$), the first plaintext block, 1819, is enciphered as:

$$\begin{aligned} 1819^{1223} &\equiv 1819^{1024} \cdot 1819^{128} \cdot 1819^{64} \cdot 1819^{4} \cdot 1819^{2} \cdot 1819^{1} \\ &\equiv 2756 \pmod{2867} \end{aligned}$$

Since PK contains 11 bits, there are 10 repeated squaring operations needed to compute the intermediate quantities: $1819^2, 1819^4, 1819^8, \ldots, 1819^{1024}$. The cumulative total is then multiplied by each intermediate result if there is a corresponding 1 bit in the key.[10] Except for the value of the exponent, the operations of encipherment and decipherment are the same.

The following summary describes the procedure for selecting keys and performing the steps of encipherment and decipherment:

1. Two secret prime numbers, p and q, are selected randomly.

[10]The computation is easier than it may seem, since the mod r can be applied to each intermediate result with the same end result.

2. The public modulus, $r = pq$, is calculated.
3. The secret Euler totient function, $\phi(r) = (p - 1)(q - 1)$, is calculated.
4. A quantity, K, is selected, which is relatively prime to $\phi(r)$. K is defined as either the secret key, SK, or the public key, PK.
5. The multiplicative inverse of K modulo $\phi(r)$ is calculated using Euclid's algorithm, and this quantity is defined to be either the public key, PK, or the secret key, SK, depending on the choice made in (4).
6. Encipherment is performed by raising the plaintext, X (whose value is in the range 0 to $r - 1$), to the power of PK modulo r, thus producing the ciphertext, Y (whose value is also in the range 0 to $r - 1$).
7. Decipherment is performed by raising the ciphertext, Y, to the power of SK modulo r.

The Distribution of Primes

To thwart an opponent using exhaustive methods to obtain the secret primes, one must choose p and q from a sufficiently large set. But at the same time the method used to find p and q must be computationally efficient.

The largest tables of prime numbers ordinarily contain only a few thousand entries and are too small to be of use. On the other hand, computing and storing a table of prime numbers large enough to provide adequate security is clearly out of the question.

At the present, the most practical method of selecting primes suitable for use in the RSA algorithm is to test randomly selected integers until the required number of primes have been found. The approach works only because the proportion of primes to nonprimes is high enough.

By actual count, one finds that each group of 100 numbers from 1 to 1000 (1 to 100, 101 to 200, etc.) contains respectively, the following number of primes:

25, 21, 16, 16, 17, 14, 16, 14, 15, 14

In each group of 100 numbers from 1,000,001 to 1,001,000, the corresponding frequency of primes is

6, 10, 8, 8, 7, 7, 10, 5, 6, 8

and from 10,000,001 to 10,001,000 the corresponding frequency is

2, 6, 6, 6, 5, 4, 7, 10, 9, 6

A computation by M. Kraitchik [7] shows that for each group of 100 numbers in the interval from $10^{12} + 1$ to $10^{12} + 1000$ the corresponding frequency of primes is

4, 6, 2, 4, 2, 4, 3, 5, 1, 6

Even though the prime numbers gradually become more scarce as the numbers within the groups become larger, there are still infinitely many primes.

According to the prime number theorem, the ratio of $\pi(x)$, the number of primes in the interval from 2 to x, and $x/\ln(x)$ approaches 1 as x becomes very large, that is,

$$\lim_{x \to \infty} \frac{\pi(x)}{x/\ln(x)} = 1$$

where ln(x) is the (natural) logarithm of x to the base $e = 2.71828\ldots$ For different intervals, a comparison of the actual number of primes [7] to the estimated number of primes (given by x/ln(x)) is shown in Table 2-3.[11]

x	a π (x)	b x/ln(x)	a/b
1,000	168	145	1.159
10,000	1,229	1,086	1.132
100,000	9,592	8,686	1.104
1,000,000	78,498	72,382	1.084
10,000,000	664,579	620,421	1.071
100,000,000	5,761,455	5,428,681	1.061
1,000,000,000	50,847,478	48,254,942	1.054

Table 2-3. Number of Primes in Interval 2 to x

The probability that a randomly selected value in the interval from 2 to x is prime is approximately equal to $\pi(x)/(x-1)$, that is, the ratio of the number of primes ($\pi(x)$) to the total number of integers $(x-1)$. It can be shown that on the average about $(x-1)/\pi(x) \simeq \ln(x)$ values must be tested before a prime is found.[12] For example, if the magnitude of p and q were on the order of 2^{200}, then about $\ln(2^{200}) = 140$ trials (or 70 trials using odd numbers) would be needed to find a prime. (See Cyptographic Strength Considerations for a discussion of the magnitude of r.)

Testing for Primality

Several methods can be used to test a randomly selected number for primality. However, the most straightforward approaches are not computationally

[11] A better approximation of $\pi(x)$ can be obtained by evaluating the integral $\int_2^x dt/\ln(t)$.

[12] If the probability of finding a prime number is equal to p at each trial, then it takes on the average 1/p trials to find a prime number, assuming that the trials are statistically independent.

feasible. For example, a test could be based on Wilson's theorem [7], which states that

$$(p - 1)! \equiv -1 \pmod{p} \qquad \text{if } p \text{ is prime}$$

where

$$(p - 1)! = 2 \cdot 3 \cdot \ldots \cdot (p - 1)$$

In all other cases (except n = 4), it can be shown that

$$(n - 1)! \equiv 0 \pmod{n} \qquad \text{if } n \text{ is not prime}$$

Several examples are shown below.

$$\begin{array}{ll} (2-1)! \equiv -1 \pmod{2} & (7-1)! \equiv -1 \pmod{7} \\ (3-1)! \equiv -1 \pmod{3} & (8-1)! \equiv 0 \pmod{8} \\ (4-1)! \equiv 2 \pmod{4} & (9-1)! \equiv 0 \pmod{9} \\ (5-1)! \equiv -1 \pmod{5} & (10-1)! \equiv 0 \pmod{10} \\ (6-1)! \equiv 0 \pmod{6} & (11-1)! \equiv -1 \pmod{11} \end{array}$$

It should be obvious, however, that a test based on Wilson's theorem is useless for large values of p, since too many multiplications would be required to compute $(p - 1)!$.

A different test could be based on the simple fact that if a number n is not prime, then n must contain a factor less than or equal to the square root of n. But even here the test is useless for large primes p, since to show that p is not divisible by any number between 2 and $\sqrt{p}$, and thus prove that p is prime, would still require too many computations.

The methods described thus far will determine with absolute certainty whether a number is prime or composite. However, adopting a procedure that is less reliable permits a favorable trade-off between computation time and the risk of accepting a number as prime when it is really composite. (Efficient procedures for testing a large number for primality are given in references 8 through 11.) To test a large number n for primality, one could use the elegant "probabilistic" algorithm of Solovay and Strassen [8]. It picks a random number a from a uniform distribution $(1, 2, \ldots, n - 1)$ and tests whether

$$\gcd(a, n) = 1 \qquad \text{and} \qquad J(a, n) \equiv a^{(n-1)/2} \pmod{n} \qquad (2\text{-}12)$$

where J(a, n) is the *Jacobi symbol* [12]. If n is prime, then Equation 2-12 always holds. If n is composite, the Equation 2-12 will be false with probability of at least 1/2.

The number n can now be tested for primality by using a set of integers, $\mathbf{A} = \{a_1, a_2, \ldots, a_m\}$, where each a in **A** is less than n. The test requires that, for each value of a in **A**, Equation 2-12 holds. Thus n is found to be composite if there is an a in **A** for which Equation 2-12 does not hold; otherwise n is accepted as prime.

The procedure does not guarantee that a selected number is prime, but only that it has not failed the test of primality. The greater the number of integers in **A**, the greater the probability that a selected number is prime. This can be argued as follows. If **A** contains m randomly selected integers from 1 to $n - 1$, then the probability that Equation 2-12 holds when n is composite is less than 0.5 for each value of a in **A**. So for a composite number, the probability that Equation 2-12 holds for all m values in **A** is less than 0.5^m. In other words, the probability that a composite number will pass the primality test is less than 0.5^m. If m is large, then the chance for error is small. For example, 0.5^m is 0.00098 and 0.00000095 for $m = 10$ and $m = 20$, respectively.

When n is odd, $a \leqslant n$, and $\gcd(a, n) = 1$, the Jacobi symbol, $J(a, n)$, has a value in $\{-1, 1\}$ and can be efficiently computed by the following recursive procedure [5]:

$$\begin{aligned} J(a, n) = {} & \text{if } a = 1 \text{ then } 1 \text{ else} \\ & \text{if } a \text{ is even then } J(a/2, n)(-1)^{(n^2 - 1)/8} \\ & \text{else } J(n \ (\text{mod } a), a)(-1)^{(a-1)(n-1)/4} \end{aligned}$$

A simple numerical example of testing a number for primality illustrates a different approach, one based on Euler's theorem. (The method is not recommended, but is given here because it is easy to understand.) Recall that Euler's theorem states that if p is prime, then

$$a^{p-1} \equiv 1 \pmod{p}$$

where a and p are relatively prime.

The number p is tested for primality by using a set of integers $\mathbf{A} = \{a_1, a_2, \ldots, a_m\}$ where each a in **A** is less than p. The test consists of ensuring that for each value of a in **A**, 1 is the remainder obtained when a^{p-1} is divided by p. (The procedure for evaluating a^{p-1} (mod p) is the same as that described earlier for enciphering and deciphering data with the RSA algorithm.) Thus p is found to be composite if there is an a in **A** for which 1 is not the remainder obtained when a^{p-1} is divided by p; otherwise p is accepted as prime.

A further example illustrates the procedure's result when a prime number ($p = 1151$) and a composite number ($n = 1147$) are tested for primality using the set of integers $\mathbf{A} = \{106, 750, 479, 808, 1111, 223, 55, 848, 378, 729\}$ (Table 2-4). If the test for primality was based on the set $\mathbf{A} = \{750, 1111, 223\}$, then an incorrect conclusion would have been reached for the value $n = 1147$ (i.e., one would have said that the composite number 1147 is prime).

a	a^{p-1} (mod p)	a^{n-1} (mod n)
106	1	915
750	1	1
479	1	566
808	1	591
1111	1	1
223	1	1
55	1	841
848	1	1120
378	1	776
729	1	667

Table 2-4. Test of a Prime Number (p = 1151) and a Composite Number (n = 1147) for Primality

Cryptographic Strength Considerations

One approach that enables an opponent to break the RSA algorithm is to factor r. Once p and q are known, (p − 1) and (q − 1) can be used to compute $\phi(r) = (p-1)(q-1)$, and then SK could be calculated from $\phi(r)$ and PK by using Euclid's algorithm.

However, in the proposed scheme, each user chooses a pair of secret primes (p and q) which are large enough so that factorization of the nonsecret modulus (r = pq) is not feasible, even with the help of high-speed computers, and given the fastest known method of factoring. It is therefore absolutely essential that r is large enough to make the work needed to factor r sufficiently great.

The fastest known factoring algorithm is that of Richard Schroeppel [5]. It can factor r in approximately $\ln(r)^{\mathrm{sqrt}(\ln(r)/\ln(\ln(r)))}$ steps. (ln denotes the natural logarithm function.) As a first order approximation, assume that the computation time needed to perform one step in the Schroeppel algorithm is the same as that to search one key in a hypothetical exhaustive attack against DES. In this case a blocksize of 388 bits would mean that the work needed to factor r is equivalent to the work needed to exhaust 2^{56} DES keys. Instead, if the computation time required to perform a step in the Schroeppel algorithm were 1000 (1 million) times greater than that required to search a single key in DES, then a blocksize of 280 (186) bits would be required to maintain equivalency.

According to the algorithm's inventors [5], additional protection against sophisticated factoring algorithms can be achieved by ensuring that the following conditions are met:

1. p and q differ in length by only a few bits.

2. Each number $(p - 1)$ and $(q - 1)$ contains a large prime factor, p' and q', respectively.
3. The gcd of $(p - 1)$ and $(q - 1)$ is small.

Moreover, it has also been pointed out that further protection is possible by ensuring that $(p' - 1)$ and $(q' - 1)$ have large prime factors, p'' and q'', respectively [13,14].

To find a suitable p, first find a large prime p'' and let p' be the first prime in the sequence $i \cdot p'' + 1$, for $i = 2, 4, 6, \ldots$, etc. Repeating the process, let p be the first prime in the sequence $i \cdot p' + 1$, for $i = 2, 4, 6, \ldots$, and so on. (A value for q can be found in a similar fashion.)

Without regard for the usual methods of factoring composite numbers, it is noteworthy that r could easily be factored if either $\phi(r)$ or SK were available. The significance of this fact is that it is just as hard to determine $\phi(r)$ or SK as it is to factor r. By way of an illustration, if $\phi(r)$ were available, then r could be obtained by the following steps:

1. Obtain $(p + q)$ from r and $\phi(r) = r - (p + q) + 1$.
2. Obtain $(p - q)$ from the equation $(p + q)^2 = p^2 + 2r + q^2 = (p - q)^2 + 4r$ by taking the square root of $(p + q)^2 - 4r$.
3. Obtain q as half the difference of $(p + q)$ and $(p - q)$.

On the other hand, having SK would permit $SK \cdot PK - 1$ to be computed, which is a multiple of $\phi(r)$. But an efficient method of factoring r is available if a multiple of $\phi(r)$ is known [9].

It should be obvious that finding a number (X) not relatively prime to r would be equivalent to breaking the algorithm. This is because the gcd of X and r would be equal to either p or q, and its value could be easily computed using Euclid's algorithm. However, in the practical sense, there is no need to be concerned that the algorithm will be broken by finding such a number (X), provided that r is sufficiently large. In the interval from 1 to r there are

$$\phi(r) = (p - 1)(q - 1) = pq - (p + q) + 1$$

numbers relatively prime to r, and

$$r - \phi(r) = (p + q) - 1$$

numbers not relatively prime to r. The probability of accidentally discovering a number having p or q as a factor is therefore equal to

$$\frac{r - \phi(r)}{r} = 1 - \frac{\phi(r)}{r} = \frac{p + q - 1}{pq} \simeq \frac{1}{q} + \frac{1}{p}$$

which is extremely small for large values of p and q.

Factoring large numbers is a well-known problem that has engaged mathematicians for many hundreds of years. Experience has shown it to be an intractable problem. Yet this evidence does not prove that the cryptographic approach is strong. In fact, until the advent of high-speed computers, mathematicians weren't looking for methods that might require very complicated tests. Furthermore, the general problem of factoring and the special case of factoring associated with the RSA algorithm are different. The classical problem of factoring, not yet solved despite a considerable effort, can be stated as follows:

Factor a composite number r, where r may be any product of two or more prime factors.

The cryptographic problem, which must take into account attacks using selected ciphertext and is not yet sufficiently investigated, can be stated as follows:

Factor a composite number r, where r is the product of two prime factors[13] *($r = pq$) and where there exists a public key PK and a secret key SK that satisfies the relation*

$$PK \cdot SK = 1 \ (\mathrm{mod}\ (p-1)(q-1))$$

such that the opponent has knowledge of chosen ciphertext, Y_1, Y_2, . . . , and corresponding recovered plaintext, X_1, X_2, . . . (without having knowledge of SK) which satisfy the relation

$$Y_i^{SK} \equiv X_i \ (\mathrm{mod}\ r)$$

In the cryptographic problem, knowledge of PK (i.e., a value relatively prime to (p − 1)(q − 1)) does not provide an opponent with much information beyond that present in the classical problem. This is because in the classical problem it would be a simple matter to select a large prime (i.e., a value relatively prime to (p − 1)(q − 1)) that could be used as a public key to carry out a chosen plaintext attack. However, in the cryptographic problem, the public key can be used in conjunction with a chosen ciphertext attack to produce quantities that are functions of both PK and SK. In this sense, the public key is potentially of greater value in the cryptographic problem than it is in the classical problem.

As yet there is no evidence to support a claim that the additional information available to the opponent in the cryptographic problem will allow the modulus to be factored. However, one cannot conclude that the problem of factoring in the cryptographic problem is hard merely on the basis that the classical problem of factoring is known to be hard. And while factoring the modulus in the RSA algorithm leads to breaking the algorithm, there is no proof that breaking the algorithm is the same as solving the classical problem of factoring.

It is entirely possible that the proposed RSA algorithm is cryptographically strong. However, this conclusion cannot be reached from previous work done to solve the theoretic problems of factoring composite numbers. It can only be reached by taking into account the requirements that must be satis-

[13] In a more general approach, the RSA algorithm could specify that r is the product of more than two prime factors.

fied for strong algorithms and by performing a thorough validation. Since the algorithm is in the public domain and has become a topic of great interest among academicians and cryptologists [15-21], it is only fair to say that a validation effort of sorts has already begun. Nevertheless, in addition to such an effort, a well-organized approach by a group of dedicated people whose only task is to uncover weaknesses in the algorithm is needed. Finally, it would be highly desirable for the National Security Agency, where significant cryptographic expertise resides, to certify the algorithm's strength. This certification would be based on a similar government-organized validation effort.

Trapdoor Knapsack Algorithm[14]

A public-key algorithm can also be based on the classical problem in number theory known as the knapsack problem [4]. The following is an introduction to this approach. Let A be a nonsecret (published) vector of n integers ($a_1, a_2, \ldots, a_n$) and let X be a secret vector of n binary digits (0s and 1s) whose components are designated ($x_1, x_2, \ldots, x_n$), that is,

$$A = (a_1, a_2, \ldots, a_n)$$

$$X = (x_1, x_2, \ldots, x_n)$$

Defining Y to be the *dot product* of A and X results, by definition, in

$$Y = A \cdot X = a_1x_1 + a_2x_2 + \ldots + a_nx_n = \sum_{i=1}^{n} a_ix_i$$

Calculation of Y is simple, involving only a sum of at most n integers. However, finding X from Y and A is generally difficult when n is large and A is properly chosen. This is called the *knapsack problem.*

Let the knapsack problem be illustrated by the following simple example: If

$$X = (\quad 1, \quad 0, \quad 1, \quad 1, \quad 0, \quad 0, \quad 0, \quad 1)$$

$$A = (2453, 6394, 941, 1076, 4791, 4404, 9549, 6639)$$

then

$$Y = A \cdot X = 2453 + 941 + 1076 + 6639 = 11109$$

In the knapsack problem, one is asked to find X such that $A \cdot X = Y$, where A and Y are given. In the most general case, one would like to have a function g to calculate X from A and Y such that g satisfies the relation $X = g(A, Y)$.

One way to find X is by the method of direct search. (In the above example, there are $2^8 = 256$ values for X.) This consists of computing $A \cdot X$

[14] At the time of publication of this book, the trapdoor knapsack algorithm reportedly has been broken [22].

for each enumerated value of X, and comparing the result with Y for equality. Function g, in this case, is a procedure to test all possibilities for X, and select the first which works. However, if the number of elements in A (and thus in X) is large, and A is properly chosen, then such an exhaustive approach is not practical. A different method of solution would be required.

In the described public-key algorithm, A represents the public key. Anyone can produce ciphertext Y from plaintext X by the equation $Y = A \cdot X$. But for this approach to be cryptographically strong, it must not be computationally feasible to obtain X from information assumed to be known to the cryptanalyst, thus preventing the process from being inverted by discovery of function g.

An example of a cryptographically weak approach (since it allows the process to be easily inverted) is a public key A whose elements satisfy the following conditions:

$$a_{i+1} > a_1 + a_2 + \ldots + a_i = \sum_{j=1}^{i} a_j; \qquad i = 1, 2, \ldots, n-1$$

Using the notation

$$\begin{aligned} Y_1 &= x_1 a_1 \\ Y_2 &= x_1 a_1 + x_2 a_2 \\ &\vdots \\ Y_n &= x_1 a_1 + x_2 a_2 + \ldots + x_n a_n \end{aligned}$$

where $Y = Y_n$ is the ciphertext, one can recover X from Y_n and A as follows. If Y_n is less than a_n, then x_n is set equal to 0 and Y_{n-1} is set equal to Y_n. Otherwise, x_n is set equal to 1 and Y_{n-1} is set equal to $Y_n - a_n$. Now, using the computed value of Y_{n-1}, one can compute the values of x_{n-1} and Y_{n-2} in a similar manner. The procedure continues until $X = (x_1, x_2, \ldots, x_n)$ has been recovered.

The recovery of X can be illustrated by the following example:

$$A = (15, 92, 108, 279, 563, 1172, 2243, 4468) \qquad (2\text{-}13)$$

$$Y = A \cdot X = 4870$$

Thus

$$\begin{aligned} x_8 &= 1, &&\text{since } Y_8(= 4870) > a_8(= 4468) \\ x_7 &= 0, &&\text{since } Y_7(= 402) < a_7(= 2243) \\ x_6 &= 0, &&\text{since } Y_6(= 402) < a_6(= 1172) \\ x_5 &= 0, &&\text{since } Y_5(= 402) < a_5(= 563) \\ x_4 &= 1, &&\text{since } Y_4(= 402) > a_4(= 279) \end{aligned}$$

$$x_3 = 1, \quad \text{since } Y_3(= 123) > a_3(= 108)$$
$$x_2 = 0, \quad \text{since } Y_2(= 15) < a_2(= 92)$$
$$x_1 = 1, \quad \text{since } Y_1(= 15) = a_1(= 15)$$

and the value of X is (1, 0, 1, 1, 0, 0, 0, 1).

A trapdoor knapsack [4] is one in which the careful choice of vector A allows the designer to recover X from Y easily using the secret trapdoor (identified by the secret key), but which makes it difficult for anyone else to find the solution. The introduction of a secret quantity makes it possible to find a transformation such that $X = g'$ (A, Y, secret quantity), where the function g' is easily calculated. The way the problem is solved here is to transform Y to Y' by the following method:

1. Choose secret integers, r and t, which are relatively prime.
2. Calculate another quantity, s (also kept secret) from r and t, which is the multiplicative inverse of t modulo r.

In that case, the relations

$$Y' = Y s \pmod{r}$$
$$Y' = A'X$$

exist which allow easy recovery of X, since A' falls into the class of knapsack problems which have easy solutions. In other words, a trapdoor is introduced (identified by the secret parameters r and t) that transforms a hard knapsack problem (vector A) into a trivial knapsack problem (vector A').

To construct a trapdoor knapsack, let $A' = (a'_1, a'_2, \ldots, a'_n)$ be a secret vector of n integers such that $a'_i > a'_1 + a'_2 + \ldots + a'_{i-1}$ for all i. The vector

$$A' = (15, 92, 108, 279, 563, 1172, 2243, 4468)$$

used in the last example (Equation 2-13) satisfies this condition. Now choose secret integers r and t such that these three conditions hold:

1. $r > a'_1 + a'_2 + \ldots + a'_n$
2. $r > t$
3. r and t are relatively prime (i.e., gcd (r, t) = 1)

The choice r = 9291 and t = 2393 satisfies the necessary conditions. That they are relatively prime can be shown as follows, using Euclid's algorithm:

$$9291 = 2393 \cdot 3 + 2112$$
$$2393 = 2112 \cdot 1 + 281$$
$$2112 = 281 \cdot 7 + 145$$

$$281 = 145 \cdot 1 + 136$$
$$145 = 136 \cdot 1 + 9$$
$$136 = 9 \cdot 15 + 1$$
$$9 = 1 \cdot 9$$

The last nonvanishing remainder (the value 1 in the above computation) is the gcd of 9291 and 2393.

The easily solved knapsack vector A′ is now transformed into a trapdoor knapsack vector A via the relation

$$a_i \equiv a_i' t \pmod{r}$$

Since

$$Y = A \cdot X = \sum_{i=1}^{n} a_i x_i$$

it follows that

$$Y \equiv \sum_{i=1}^{n} [a_i' t \pmod{r}]\, x_i$$
$$\equiv \sum_{i=1}^{n} a_i' x_i t \pmod{r}$$

Defining

$$Y' = \sum_{i=1}^{n} a_i' x_i = A' \cdot X$$

to be the transformed ciphertext from which X can be easily recovered, since A′ is chosen that way, one obtains

$$Y \equiv Y' t \pmod{r} \tag{2-14}$$

The idea here is to use the secret quantities t and r to transform Y to Y′ and thus transform the hard knapsack problem into an easy one. To achieve this let a quantity s be defined such that

$$st \equiv 1 \pmod{r}$$

Hence s is the multiplicative inverse of t modulo r. If one defines t and r to be relatively prime (as stated in condition 3), there is a unique solution for s.

(This was discussed before in conjunction with the RSA algorithm. See Equations 2-10a through 2-10g.) Furthermore, to assure a unique relation between plaintext and ciphertext, choose a value of r that exceeds the maximum value of Y, that is,

$$r > \sum_{i=1}^{n} a_i$$

which satisfies condition 1.

Multiplying Y by s (see Equation 2-14) results in

$$Ys \equiv Y'st \pmod{r} \equiv Y' \pmod{r}$$

or equivalently

$$Y' \equiv Ys \pmod{r}$$

which is the desired result.

In the current example, $a_1 = 8022 \equiv 15 \cdot 2393 \pmod{9291}$, $a_2 = 6463 \equiv 92 \cdot 2393 \pmod{9291}$, and so on, and therefore vector A can be computed to be

$$A = (8022, 6463, 7587, 7986, 64, 8005, 6592, 7274)$$

Vector A (the public key) is published by the user. Anyone desiring to communicate a message (X) to the user enciphers the message using vector A. The ciphertext (Y) is obtained via the relation $Y = A \cdot X = \sum_{i=1}^{n} a_i x_i$. To recover the original message (X) from the ciphertext (Y), Y is transformed into Y′ using s, namely

$$Y' = Y \cdot s \bmod r$$

and the solution is obtained using the knapsack vector A′.

In the present example, the value of s is computed by rewriting the equations previously obtained with Euclid's algorithm:

$$1 = 136 - 9 \cdot 15$$

$$1 = 16 \cdot 136 - 16 \cdot 145$$

$$1 = 16 \cdot 281 - 31 \cdot 145$$

$$1 = 233 \cdot 281 - 31 \cdot 2112$$

$$1 = 233 \cdot 2393 - 264 \cdot 2112$$

$$1 = 1025 \cdot 2393 - 264 \cdot 9291$$

Thus s = 1025 is the multiplicative inverse of t = 2393 modulo r = 9291.

The trapdoor knapsack public-key algorithm is illustrated by the following example:

$A' = (15, 92, 108, 279, 563, 1172, 2243, 4468)$	(secret, chosen)
$r = 9291$	(secret, chosen)
$t = 2393$	(secret, chosen)
$s = 1025$	(secret, derived)
$A = (8022, 6463, 7587, 7986, 65, 8005, 6592, 7274)$	(nonsecret, derived)

A message

$$X = (1, 0, 1, 1, 0, 0, 0, 1)$$

is enciphered using vector A, as follows.

$$Y = A \cdot X = (8022 + 7587 + 7986 + 7274) = 30869$$

Multiplying Y by the secret value of s results in

$$Y' = Y \cdot s \pmod{r} = 30869 \cdot 1025 \pmod{9291} = 4870$$

Subsequently, $X = (1, 0, 1, 1, 0, 0, 0, 1)$ is recovered from $Y' = 4870$ and vector A', as previously shown in Equation 2-13.

STREAM CIPHERS

A *stream cipher* (Figure 2-8) employs a bit-stream generator to produce a stream of binary digits called a *cryptographic bit-stream,*[15] which is then combined either with plaintext (via the $\boxplus$ operator) to produce ciphertext, or with ciphertext (via the $\boxplus^{-1}$ operator) to recover plaintext.

Vernam [23] was the first to recognize the merit of a cipher in which ciphertext (Y) is produced from plaintext (X) by combining it with a secret bit-stream (R) via a simple and efficient operation. In his cipher, Vernam used an Exclusive-OR operation, or modulo 2 addition (Table 2-1), to combine the bit-streams. Thus encipherment and decipherment are defined by $X \oplus R = Y$ and $Y \oplus R = X$, respectively, and the condition $\boxplus = \boxplus^{-1} = \oplus$ is satisfied. Since in most stream cipher designs modulo 2 addition is used as the combining operation, it will be used in the remainder of the discussion on stream ciphers.

[15] Traditionally, the term key-stream has been used to denote the output of the bit-stream generator. Instead, the term cryptographic bit-stream is used here to avoid possible confusion with a fixed-length cryptographic key in cases where a cryptographic algorithm is used as the bit-stream generator.

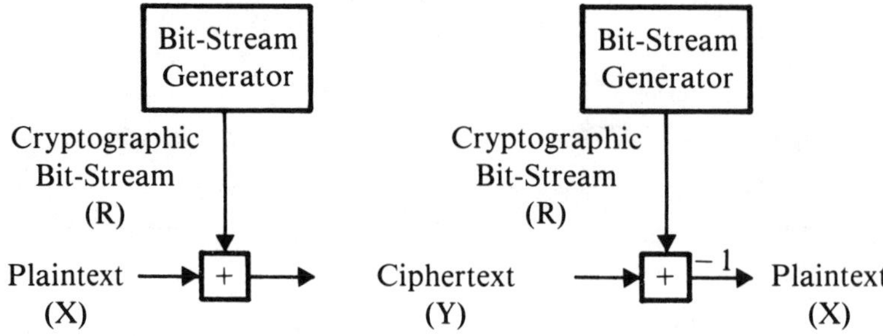

Figure 2-8. Stream Cipher Concept

If the bit-stream generator were truly random, an unbreakable cipher could be obtained by Exclusive-ORing the plaintext and cryptographic bit-stream. (See the discussion of one-time tape systems, Cryptographic Algorithms.) In that case, the cryptographic bit-stream is used directly as the key and is equal in length to the message. But because the cryptographic bit-stream is random, it must be provided to the users in advance via some independent and secure channel. This, of course, introduces insurmountable logistical problems if the intended data traffic is very large. Hence, for practical reasons, the bit-stream generator must be implemented as an algorithmic procedure, so that the cryptographic bit-stream can be produced by both users. In such an approach (Figure 2-9), the bit-stream generator is a key-controlled algorithm and must produce a cryptographic bit-stream which is cryptographically strong.

When modulo 2 addition is used as the combining operation, each bit in the output ciphertext (recovered plaintext), is dependent upon the corresponding bit in the input plaintext (ciphertext), but not upon any other bits in the input plaintext (ciphertext). This is in marked contrast to the block cipher which exhibits a much more complex relationship between bits in the plaintext (ciphertext) and bits in the ciphertext (recovered plaintext). Both approaches, however, have comparable strength.

In a stream cipher, the ciphering algorithm (G) uses a cipher key (v) to

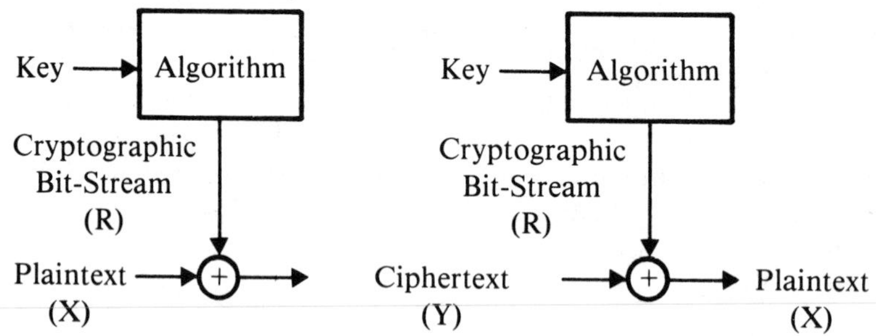

Figure 2-9. Stream Cipher Using an Algorithmic Bit-Stream Generator and Modulo 2 Addition

generate a cryptographic bit-stream (R). If the set of keys is represented, as before, by

$$V = \{v_1, v_2, \ldots, v_r\}$$

it follows that the set of enciphering and deciphering functions (G) can be expressed as follows.

$$G = \{g_{v_1}, g_{v_2}, \ldots, g_{v_r}\}$$

where g_v represents a key-selected transformation which generates a particular bit-stream. Function g should not be confused with the function introduced earlier for the block cipher design (Figure 2-7).

In a stream cipher, the algorithm may generate its bit-stream on a bit-by-bit basis, or in blocks of bits. This is of no real consequence. All such systems are stream ciphers, or variations thereof. Some variations, however, have important characteristics. Moreover, since bit streams can be generated in blocks, it is always possible for a block cipher to be used to obtain a stream cipher. However, in a communications system, because both the sender and receiver must produce cryptographic bit-streams that are equal and secret, their keys must also be equal and secret. In effect, this means that a public-key algorithm can be used to obtain a stream cipher only if it is used as a conventional algorithm. That is, both sender and receiver use the same algorithm (E or D) and the same key. But the key must be kept secret.

Consider the general case where an input block (X) of b bits is enciphered by generating a cryptographic bit-stream (R) of b bits and Exclusive-ORing R with X to produce b bits of ciphertext (Y).

$$Y = X \oplus R$$

From the rules of modulo 2 addition (Table 2-1), it follows that X can be recovered by adding the same cryptographic bit-stream (R) to the ciphertext (Y).

$$X = Y \oplus R$$

The ciphering procedure using modulo 2 addition is thus extremely simple and easy to implement. However, care must be taken to achieve a cryptographically strong design. If, for example, the opponent knows that modulo 2 addition has been performed, and plaintext (X) and corresponding ciphertext (Y) become available, he then could add both quantities together (modulo 2) and recover the cryptographic bit-stream.

$$X \oplus Y = X \oplus (X \oplus R) = R$$

Since the cryptographic key (K) is a constant quantity, it follows that the cryptographic bit-stream (R), or block of bits produced at each iteration of the ciphering algorithm, will not change if it depends only on K. In this case, once the opponent has obtained R, he can decipher any intercepted ciphertext without ever knowing the key (K). This, of course, is unacceptable.

The stream cipher must not start from the same initial conditions in a predictable way, and thereby regenerate the same cryptographic bit-stream at each iteration of the algorithm. In other words, the stream cipher must not *reoriginate.*[16]

Since the key, even though it is secret, does not ensure an unpredictable cryptographic bit-stream, another quantity, defined as the *initializing vector* (Z), must be introduced into the ciphering process. (Other terms used are *seed* and *fill.*) In effect, different initializing vectors cause different cryptographic bit-streams to be generated. And the cryptographic bit-stream is unpredictable as long as the initializing vector satisfies one of the following conditions.

1. *Random.* Z is produced by some natural phenomenon whose statistics have been demonstrated to be random, and Z has enough combinations so that the probability of repeating is extremely small.
2. *Pseudo-random.* Z is produced by a deterministic process whose period (the interval between equal recurring values) is extremely large compared to the length of Z, and whose values have the statistical properties of randomness.
3. *Nonrepeating.* Under certain conditions, Z can be produced by a process that may be predictable, but whose period before repeating is so large that for practical purposes it is of no concern. A 64-bit nonresettable counter would satisfy this condition. Even if the opponent obtains the cryptographic bit-stream associated with one counter setting, he cannot determine what the bit-stream will be for a different counter setting.

In contrast to the cipher key, which must be kept secret, the initializing vector may be a nonsecret quantity. This is because the initializing vector either does not repeat, or else repeats with only a small probability (determined by the length of the initializing vector).

The cryptographic bit-stream R generated by the function g can now be expressed by

$$R = g_K(Z)$$

The encipher and decipher operations are thus defined by

$$Y = X \oplus R = X \oplus g_K(Z)$$
$$X = Y \oplus R = Y \oplus g_K(Z)$$

[16]This is not a requirement for the block cipher, since knowledge of plaintext and corresponding ciphertext does not permit an opponent to decipher without knowledge of the key.

It follows that the set of functions **G**, which determines the cryptographic bit stream, does not have to be a collection of one-to-one functions since an inverse operation is never needed. On the other hand, a set of functions $\mathbf{F} = \{f_{K,Z}\}$ does exist which relates plaintext and ciphertext using the keys and initializing vector as parameters

$$Y = f_{K,Z}(X)$$
$$X = f_{K,Z}^{-1}(Y)$$

where $f_{K,Z}$ is, of course, a one-to-one function. Since the length of the ciphertext is equal to the length of the plaintext, the number of plaintext combinations is equal to the number of ciphertext combinations. Hence $f_{K,Z}$ is also an onto function. (Note that the domain of $f_{K,Z}$ is the set of all plaintext combinations, the co-domain is the set of all ciphertext combinations.) The basic idea of a stream cipher is shown in Figure 2-10.

In a stream cipher, Z is used not only for providing cryptographic strength but also for establishing synchronization between communicating cryptographic devices. It assures that the same cryptographic bit-streams are

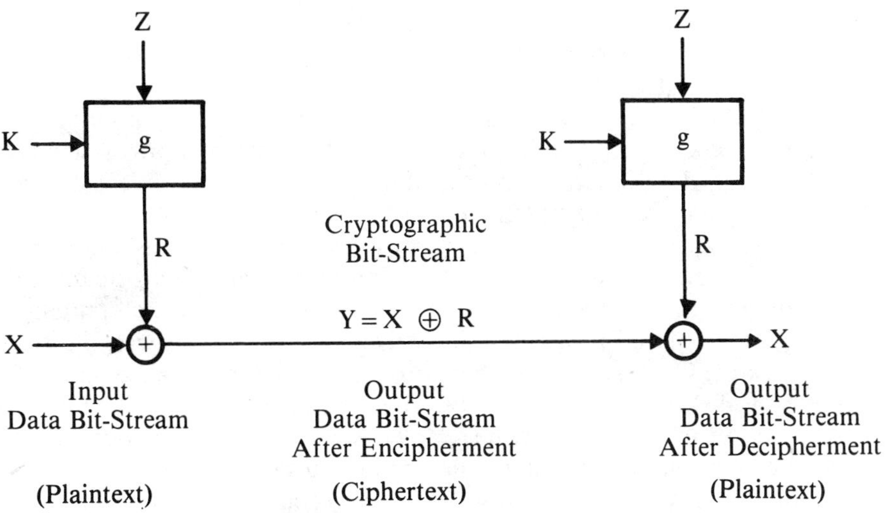

Legend: example of encipherment and decipherment

⊕	Plaintext	0 1 0 1
	Cryptographic Bit-Stream	0 0 1 1
	Ciphertext	0 1 1 0
⊕	Ciphertext	0 1 1 0
	Cryptographic Bit-Stream	0 0 1 1
	Recovered Plaintext	0 1 0 1

Figure 2-10. Stream Cipher

generated for the sender and the receiver. This may be accomplished by generating Z at the sending device and transmitting it in clear form to the receiver. An alternative method is for the receiver to determine Z by transmitting it to the sender. But this requires an additional initialization message, and hence is less efficient. However, it does provide a way to introduce a time-dependent parameter controlled by the receiver.

Recall that for a strong cryptographic algorithm it is assumed that the opponent has the advantage of relatively large amounts of selected plaintext and corresponding ciphertext. However, when the algorithm is a stream cipher this means that the opponent also has knowledge of large portions of the cryptographic bit-stream, since the cryptographic bit-stream can be reconstructed by modulo 2 addition of known plaintext and corresponding ciphertext. (Note that if $Y = X \oplus R$, then $Y \oplus X = R$.) It is important, therefore, that knowledge of part of the cryptographic bit-stream does not allow portions of the remaining cryptographic bit-stream to be determined. Hence, a necessary, although insufficient condition to achieve cryptographic strength with the stream cipher is for the bit-stream produced by the algorithm to be pseudo-random.

A bit-stream is considered to be pseudo-random if on statistical grounds one cannot reject the hypothesis that it is random (i.e., it passes all conceivable tests of randomness). Pseudo-randomness assures that it will be difficult for an opponent to use statistical attacks successfully against the cryptographic algorithm.

In addition to the opponent knowing relatively large amounts of selected plaintext and corresponding ciphertext, it is assumed for a strong stream cipher that the opponent knows the initializing vectors corresponding to the given plaintext and ciphertext.

Cryptographic systems usually treat initializing vectors as nonsecret quantities. Thus in a communications system, initializing vectors are no more difficult to intercept than ciphertext. Since the algorithm and cryptographic key are fixed, a variable cryptographic bit-stream is obtained by varying the initializing vector. One way to do this is to use a new initializing vector for each iteration of the ciphering algorithm (i.e., for each new block of bits produced in the cryptographic bit-stream). However, in a communications system, this has the disadvantage of increasing the amount of transmitted data, since the initializing vector bits are now added to each block of ciphertext bits. A more efficient approach is to use a single initializing vector for each message. (In general, a message consists of several blocks.) At the first iteration of the ciphering algorithm, the initializing vector is used (as before) to produce a block of bits in the cryptographic bit-stream, and these bits are then used to encipher the first block of plaintext. At all subsequent iterations of the ciphering algorithm, the initializing vector is altered by or determined from information obtained using *feedback* techniques. In this case, the bit-streams available at time i are used to produce an *intermediate initializing vector*, U, which is then used in the ciphering process at time $i + 1$.

A feedback can be obtained from several places: the cryptographic bit-stream, the plaintext, the ciphertext, or some combination thereof. Each of these approaches can give rise to a cryptographic system with differing char-

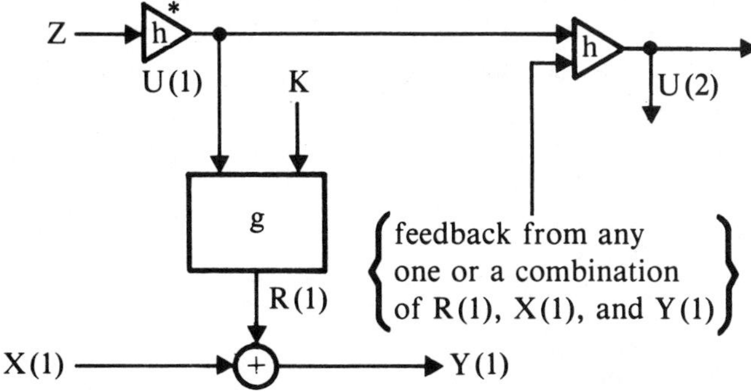

Note: The cryptographic bit-stream used to encipher the first block of plaintext bits depends only on the secret key and the non-secret initializing vector.

Figure 2-11. Encipherment of First Block of Plaintext Using a Stream Cipher

acteristics with respect to recovery from ciphertext errors. But regardless of what feedback technique is used, the first block of plaintext, X(1), is enciphered by a cryptographic bit-stream, R(1), which depends only on an initializing vector, Z, and a cipher key, K (Figure 2-11).

In the most general case, the length of the intermediate initializing vector (U) may not equal the length of the initializing vector (Z). For example, U(1) might be obtained by concatenating zero bits to Z. To accommodate such situations, a function h* is introduced to define how U(1) is obtained from Z:

$$U(1) = h^*(Z)$$

where encipherment of the first block of plaintext is given by

$$Y(1) = X(1) \oplus g_K(U(1))$$

A method for generating the initial condition U(2) is considered next. Let the intermediate initializing vector at time i, U(i), be a function h of the previous initializing vector, U(i − 1), as well as an additional feedback quantity:

$$U(i) = h[U(i - 1), \text{feedback quantity}]$$

However, since U(1) equals h*(Z), it follows that U(2) is given by

$$U(2) = h[h^*(Z), \text{feedback quantity}]$$

as shown in Figure 2-11. It should be understood that the intermediate

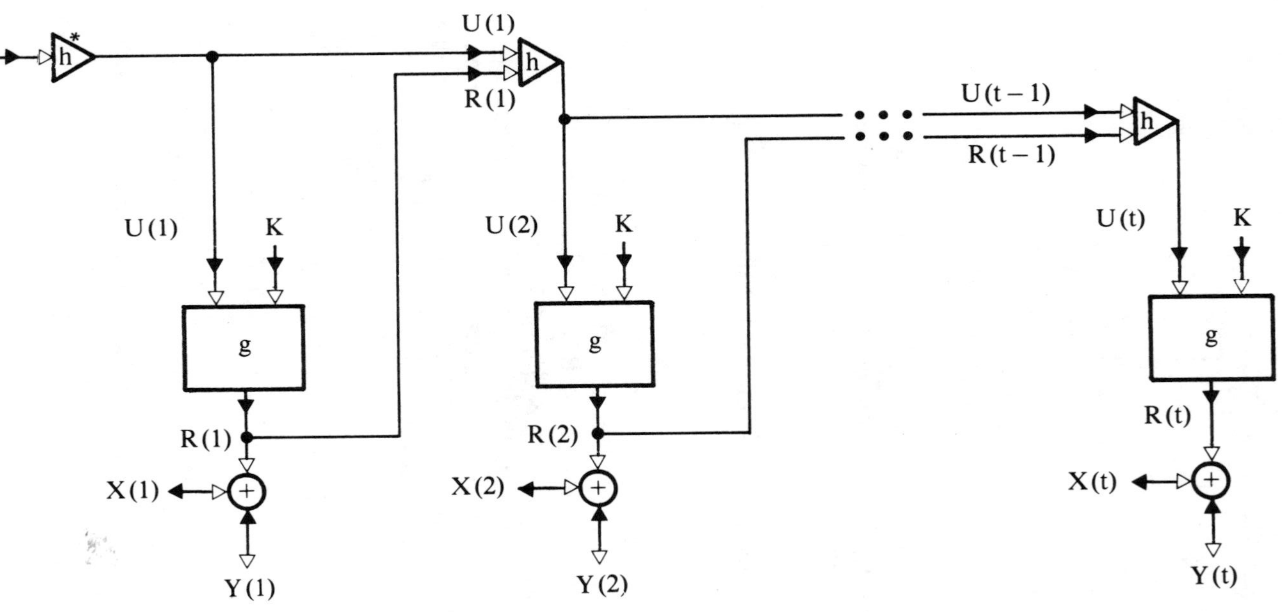

Legend: encipherment mode: ——▷ , decipherment mode: ——▶

Note: Function h* determines the number of bits in each intermediate value U(i). The message is X = X(1), X(2), ..., X(t), where t can be as large as the user desires.

Figure 2-12. Key Auto-Key Cipher

initializing vectors must satisfy the same conditions as the initializing vector Z. The function h must therefore not introduce a bias into the ciphering process that could make the U values predictable.

The special case where the feedback is obtained from the cryptographic bit-stream is shown in Figure 2-12 and is defined as the *key auto-key cipher*. One property of this cipher is that an error in the ciphertext produces an error only in the corresponding bit positions of the recovered plaintext (i.e., there is no error expansion due to the ciphering process).

There are many ways to design a key auto-key cipher. The component common to all of these designs is that the feedback must be obtained from the cryptographic bit-stream. In general, the following relationships hold for a key auto-key cipher:

$$Y(i) = X(i) \oplus R(i)$$

$$X(i) = Y(i) \oplus R(i)$$

where

$$R(i) = g_K(U(i)); \qquad 1 \leqslant i \leqslant t$$

$$U(i) = \begin{cases} h^*(Z); & i = 1 \\ h[U(i-1), R(i-1); & i > 1 \end{cases}$$

where U(1) = h*(Z) is the initial seed value, U(i) is the new seed at iteration $i > 1$, and h is a simple function of two arguments.

Some of the differences between block and stream ciphers can now be stated.

1. The block cipher enciphers a single block of data at one time. It requires a minimum blocksize determined by considerations of cryptographic strength. The stream cipher requires no minimum blocksize; it can be used to encipher, in the extreme case, on a bit-by-bit basis.
2. In the block cipher, every ciphertext bit is a complex function of every plaintext bit in the corresponding input block. In the stream cipher, every ciphertext bit y(i) is related to its corresponding plaintext bit x(i) by the relationship $y(i) = x(i) \oplus r(i)$.
3. The block cipher may or may not require an initializing vector (Z); it is allowed to reoriginate. This is because knowledge of plaintext and corresponding ciphertext does not reveal information in the same way that it would in the case of the stream cipher.[17] A cryptographically strong stream cipher must not reoriginate, and thus requires an initializing vector (Z).

[17] Although an initializing vector is not always a requirement for a block cipher, it is nevertheless used in block chaining. But even there the block cipher may reoriginate, since the initializing vector could be reused for a limited period of time.

BLOCK CIPHERS WITH CHAINING

The overall strength of a cryptographic system can be enhanced by using a technique known as chaining. *Chaining* is a procedure used during the ciphering process which makes an output block dependent not only on the current input block and key, but also on earlier input and/or output.

In certain applications, data to be enciphered may contain patterns that are longer than the cipher's blocksize. Such patterns in the plaintext may result in similar patterns in the ciphertext which could be exploited by an opponent. Chaining significantly reduces the presence of repetitive patterns in the ciphertext, because with chaining two identical blocks of plaintext will, upon encipherment, result in different ciphertext blocks.

Patterns Within Data

Patterns within data may occur because of a definite arrangement or interrelation between the characters or strings of characters that span a data record, that is, because of the data's *structure*. Patterns may also occur within data because only relatively few of the possible characters or strings of characters tend to repeat, that is, because of the data's *redundancy*.

The structural relationship that may exist within data is illustrated by an example of several assembler language statements punched onto 80-column cards (Figure 2-13). When this plaintext is enciphered using DES (no chaining), patterns within the ciphertext are still discernible (Figure 2-14).

Similarly, data intended for visual display may also contain patterns because of a rigidly defined format. For example, a format for medical records might well include such displayed keywords as *name, age, height, weight*, and the like. These constant portions of the displayed data could allow its overall structure to be determined, even though enciphered. Once this underlying structure is known, variable portions of the data may be further exposed to analysis.

If data are highly redundant, then encryption with a block cipher may not prevent cryptanalysis using block frequency analysis. Block frequency analysis determines the frequency of each ciphertext block from a large sample of intercepted ciphertext. By relating the observed frequencies of the ciphertext blocks to the expected frequencies of the plaintext blocks, an opponent may be able to draw certain inferences concerning the nature of the plaintext corresponding to a given ciphertext.

Data redundancy can be exploited to attack a cryptographic system by the method illustrated in the following example. Assume that a cryptographic system uses a block cipher (no chaining) to protect messages transmitted among the nodes of a communication network. Assume further that each pair of nodes shares a different cipher key for messages transmitted between them.

At each node, the cipher keys are managed by the system and the user is not aware of the ciphering operations. Most importantly, the cipher keys are kept secret from users, even though users may request that messages be enciphered and deciphered using cipher keys.

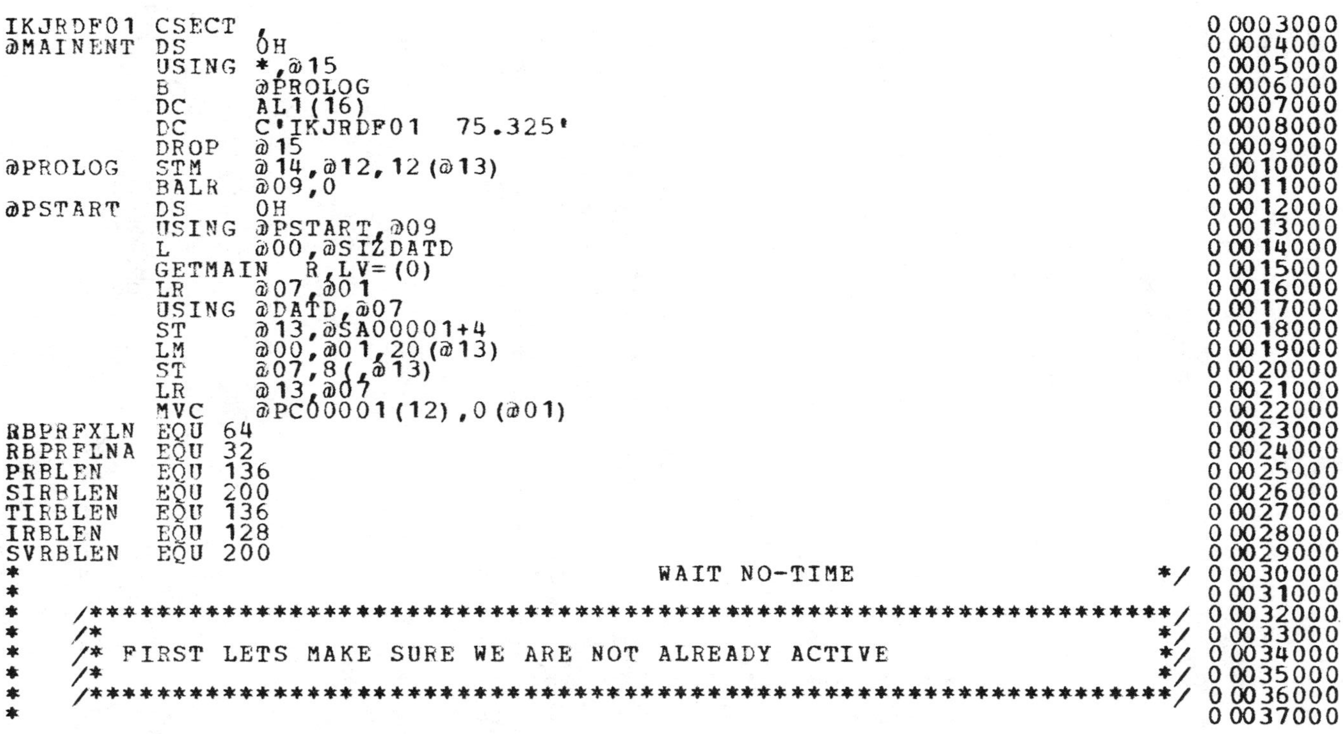

```
IKJRDF01 CSECT ,                                                        00003000
@MAINENT DS    0H                                                       00004000
         USING *,@15                                                    00005000
         B     @PROLOG                                                  00006000
         DC    AL1(16)                                                  00007000
         DC    C'IKJRDF01  75.325'                                      00008000
         DROP  @15                                                      00009000
@PROLOG  STM   @14,@12,12(@13)                                          00010000
         BALR  @09,0                                                    00011000
@PSTART  DS    0H                                                       00012000
         USING @PSTART,@09                                              00013000
         L     @00,@SIZDATD                                             00014000
         GETMAIN  R,LV=(0)                                              00015000
         LR    @07,@01                                                  00016000
         USING @DATD,@07                                                00017000
         ST    @13,@SA00001+4                                           00018000
         LM    @00,@01,20(@13)                                          00019000
         ST    @07,8(,@13)                                              00020000
         LR    @13,@07                                                  00021000
         MVC   @PC00001(12),0(@01)                                      00022000
RBPRFXLN EQU 64                                                         00023000
RBPRFLNA EQU 32                                                         00024000
PRBLEN   EQU 136                                                        00025000
SIRBLEN  EQU 200                                                        00026000
TIRBLEN  EQU 136                                                        00027000
IRBLEN   EQU 128                                                        00028000
SVRBLEN  EQU 200                                                        00029000
*                                   WAIT NO-TIME                     */ 00030000
*                                                                       00031000
*    /****************************************************************/ 00032000
*    /*                                                              */ 00033000
*    /* FIRST LETS MAKE SURE WE ARE NOT ALREADY ACTIVE               */ 00034000
*    /*                                                              */ 00035000
*    /****************************************************************/ 00036000
*                                                                       00037000
```

Figure 2-13. Example of Highly Structured Plaintext

```
   N {   3q1 #   qWa-    n!Wa-    n!Wa-    n!Wa-    n!Wa-    n!Wa-    n!Wa-    n!w s  d
  ! ,#     ?p ±|      ┘   3 Wa-    n!Wa-    n!Wa-    n!Wa-    n!Wa-    n!Wa-    n!     5P
Wa-    n!3  ±@ε  v6r        Wa-    n!Wa-    n!Wa-    n!Wa-    n!Wa-    n!Wa-    n!o yS o
Wa-    n!4┐+3 +   ±  % uAjWa-    n!Wa-    n!Wa-    n!Wa-    n!Wa-    n!Wa-    n!ε  +     E
Wa-    n!; ←    z     e o  Wa-    n!Wa-    n!Wa-    n!Wa-    n!Wa-    n!Wa-    n!  %    C¬≤
Wa-    n!  '— ┘e7o       ┐         )%|  ]y  N  Wa-    n!Wa-    n!Wa-    n!Wa-    n!u     X%F
Wa-    n!  Op+s !%s    4   k]Wa-    n!Wa-    n!Wa-    n!Wa-    n!Wa-    n!Wa-    n!  i v  3 f
Y   5         )       kf   q    F9       Wa-    n!Wa-    n!Wa-    n!Wa-    n!Wa-    n!   Qg   ?
Wa-    n!   Nj               M  Wa-    n!Wa-    n!Wa-    n!Wa-    n!Wa-    n!Wa-    n!B 7 E  ← V
. t  B   2   ?p ±|       ┘   3  Wa-    n!Wa-    n!Wa-    n!Wa-    n!Wa-    n!Wa-    n!   z  } a
Wa-    n!m  B  O(oVt5  $  b    ]*d□   ≠  Wa-    n!Wa-    n!Wa-    n!Wa-    n!Wa-    n!,  - 6b5
Wa-    n!5  5  {32    ]≥  .  ε└ p  $    Wa-    n!Wa-    n!Wa-    n!Wa-    n!Wa-    n!  zN    9
Wa-    n!A4  co     K  q    5¬z  ┌    Wa-    n!Wa-    n!Wa-    n!Wa-    n!Wa-    n!≠  !X  Bo!
Wa-    n!≥-←,3=s  a    q  ■   Wa-    n!Wa-    n!Wa-    n!Wa-    n!Wa-    n!Wa-    n!q    p+
Wa-    n!m  B  O(oV  (  P29 ≠Wa-    n!Wa-    n!Wa-    n!Wa-    n!Wa-    n!Wa-    n!! po  X!
Wa-    n!  CQ       qO ┌e4r  I{□+ =4  -Wa-    n!Wa-    n!Wa-    n!Wa-    n!Wa-    n!;     ¬  └U
Wa-    n!  ¬ L?      D   N9q/  εC    }  Wa-    n!Wa-    n!Wa-    n!Wa-    n!Wa-    n!w '7  V
Wa-    n!  CQ       q    E    :U   Tq       Wa-    n!Wa-    n!Wa-    n!Wa-    n!Wa-    n!  m   q   N
Wa-    n!≥-←,3=s  [Q  LP  e┘Wa-    n!Wa-    n!Wa-    n!Wa-    n!Wa-    n!Wa-    n!  ok9h     Z
Wa-    n!  F  6.      e@    2┘  $  +  E  tC   ┘    b  Q  Wa-    n!Wa-    n!Wa-    n!Wa-    n!     ┘       )S
   x      %  :   N      Wa-    n!Wa-    n!Wa-    n!Wa-    n!Wa-    n!Wa-    n!Wa-    n!              /D
 p         '   !q]%     Wa-    n!Wa-    n!Wa-    n!Wa-    n!Wa-    n!Wa-    n!Wa-    n!┐      └*  n
1bS  6pg          1  %  Wa-    n!Wa-    n!Wa-    n!Wa-    n!Wa-    n!Wa-    n!Wa-    n!              h
7%  e   a{q      f<    AWa-    n!Wa-    n!Wa-    n!Wa-    n!Wa-    n!Wa-    n!Wa-    n!N            4|
3qo └Y   (        1  %  Wa-    n!Wa-    n!Wa-    n!Wa-    n!Wa-    n!Wa-    n!Wa-    n!T $  8   O
 8h  n  u      ≤        FWa-    n!Wa-    n!Wa-    n!Wa-    n!Wa-    n!Wa-    n!Wa-    n!O  4'       ■
 T  ?}      q    f<    AWa-    n!Wa-    n!Wa-    n!Wa-    n!Wa-    n!Wa-    n!Wa-    n!G
 G8  <    hWa-    n!Wa-    n!Wa-    n!    p  □m  ¬≤  5?   ]Wb  S     rWa-    n!   H   z         @ ≠
 G8  <    hWa-    n!Wa-    n!Wa-    n!Wa-    n!Wa-    n!Wa-    n!Wa-    n!Wa-    n!≤+ 9c'
N    └≥≤  L        C        C        C        C        C        C        C M    vb      :2a+  !-
?   e       Wa-    n!Wa-    n!Wa-    n!Wa-    n!Wa-    n!Wa-    n!Wa-    n!   H   z     —  -4p Q
  y6      SP qj'    ┘     +5  )O3   f     K.+     s>2   j  ≠q/{  F   I  8B  Wa-    n!   H   z     f)P   @4
?   e       Wa-    n!Wa-    n!Wa-    n!Wa-    n!Wa-    n!Wa-    n!Wa-    n!   H   z        A   o,
N    └≥≤  L        C        C        C        C        C        C        C M    vb        O Gq
 G8  <    hWa-    n!Wa-    n!Wa-    n!Wa-    n!Wa-    n!Wa-    n!Wa-    n!Wa-    n!O  3ho{ε!
```

Spaces represent nonprintable characters

K = Hex '85CDCB1C9BD0851A ' is the parity-adjusted key used for encipherment. Hexadecimal, or "Hex" for short, is a base-sixteen system for representing numbers. The numbers 0 through 15 are represented by digits 0 through 9, and letters A through F, respectively.

Figure 2-14. Ciphertext Obtained when Plaintext in Figure 2-13 is Encrypted Using the DES (No Chaining)

Although the cryptographic system described above protects users from outsiders, it does not necessarily protect one user from another. For example, a large amount of known plaintext could be transmitted between any two selected nodes by one of the system's users. This user could then recover his own ciphertext, if necessary, by performing a wiretap. A dictionary of equivalent plaintext and ciphertext blocks could then be constructed. This dictionary would permit the user to recover portions of intercepted ciphertext transmitted by another system's user between the same pair of communication nodes.

If the data normally transmitted in the communications network have enough redundancy, then the number of possible meaningful plaintext blocks will be small enough to permit a dictionary to be constructed. For example, 1 million different eight-character groups can be transmitted over a 4800 bit-per-second (baud) line in about four hours. And a dictionary of 1 million plaintext and ciphertext equivalents could easily be stored within most computer systems. Even with a dictionary of 1 million entries, it is likely that some blocks of intercepted ciphertext could be recovered directly from the dictionary. Once a few plaintext blocks have been correctly recovered, new suppositions concerning the content of adjacent blocks can be made. These hypotheses could be tested by transmitting additional blocks of plaintext and intercepting the corresponding ciphertext to determine if the suppositions were correct. Therefore, through a process of trial and error, it may be possible for additional portions of an intercepted message to be recovered.

One way to eliminate the undesirable effects of redundancy and structure within data is by Exclusive-ORing a different random or pseudo-random bit pattern Z with each block of plaintext prior to its encryption. In effect, the previously existing patterns within the data (should they occur) are canceled as a result of the noise vector Z.

However, if the values of Z (chaining values) are selected using a process that cannot be duplicated at the time decipherment takes place, then each chaining value must also be transmitted or stored with each block of ciphertext so that recovery of the plaintext is possible. This requirement is most disadvantageous since it causes the amount of information that must be transmitted or stored to be doubled.

Chaining eliminates the problem of transmitting or storing a separate Z-value for each block of ciphertext, since at each step in the ciphering process an equivalent chaining value is computed from information used within the ciphering process (such as prior plaintext, ciphertext, or key). The chaining value used at the first step in the ciphering process is called the *initial chaining value* or initializing vector (Z), and if it is to be used it must be supplied as input to the ciphering process.

In effect, the chaining value permits noise to be introduced into the ciphering process. The way in which this chaining value is derived and applied determines the type of chaining used. Several different block chaining techniques are discussed below.

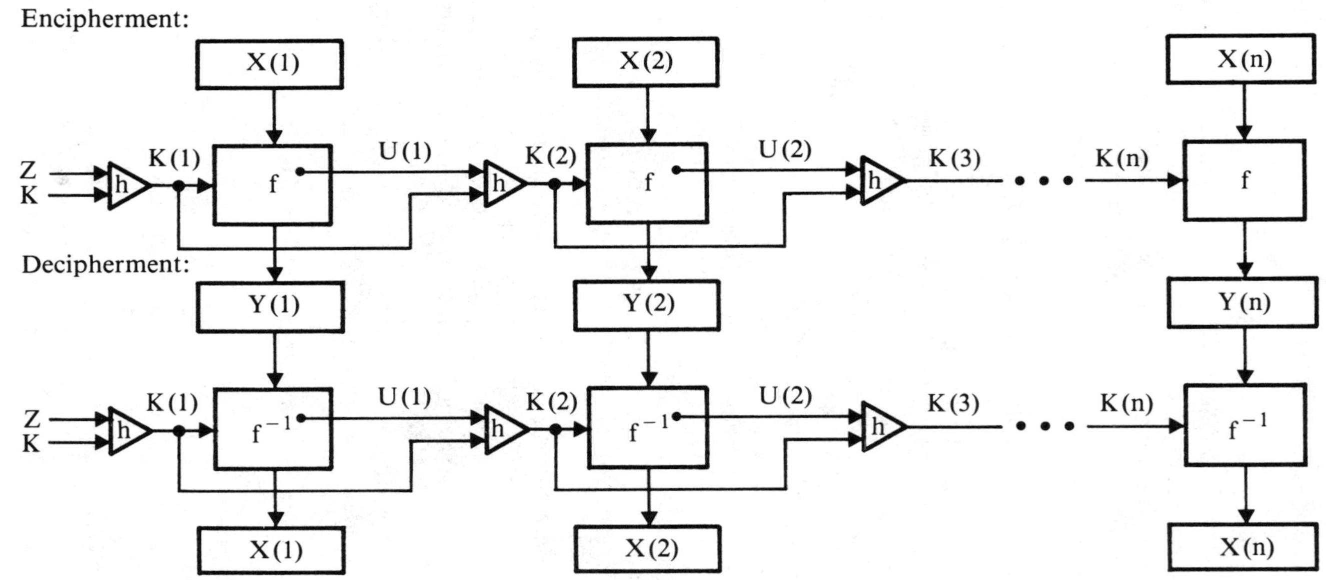

U(1), U(2), ..., U(n) represent intermediate results that are identical for encipherment and decipherment.

Figure 2-15. Block Cipher with Block Chaining (Block Chaining Using Variable Key)

Block Chaining Using a Variable Key

One way to obtain block chaining is to change cipher keys internally at each step in the ciphering process. This could be accomplished by using a feedback from some intermediate value derived within the ciphering function (Figure 2-15).

It must be possible to derive the same intermediate value used for feedback during both encipherment and decipherment. For example, if DES were used, then such an intermediate value could be obtained after the eighth round of encipherment/decipherment. (See Chapter 3 for a discussion of the DES algorithm.)

The cryptographic function f defines the relationship between plaintext and ciphertext. Since the length of plaintext X equals the length of ciphertext Y, function f is one-to-one as well as onto. Function h defines how the cipher keys are changed or altered through the introduction of the initializing vector Z or the feedback vectors U(1), U(2), . . . , U(n − 1). Note that function h may be a many-to-one function since identical inputs to this function will be available during both encipherment and decipherment.

From Figure 2-15, it follows that

$$K(i) = h(K(i-1), U(i-1)); \qquad i \geqslant 1 \tag{2-15}$$

where

$$U(i) = \begin{cases} \text{an intermediate result of the ciphering} \\ \text{operation that is identical during both} \\ \text{enciphering and deciphering operations;} \end{cases} \qquad i > 0$$

$$U(0) \equiv Z$$

$$K(0) \equiv K$$

and ≡ denotes "identically equal to." Hence, encipherment and decipherment are expressed as

$$Y(i) = f_{K(i)}(X(i)); \qquad i \geqslant 1 \tag{2-16a}$$

and

$$X(i) = f^{-1}_{K(i)}(Y(i)); \qquad i \geqslant 1 \tag{2-16b}$$

respectively. Even if the initializing vector (Z) is held constant, patterns in the input data will be eliminated. This is because cipher key K(i) is different from cipher key K(j) so that ciphertext Y(i) is different from ciphertext Y(j), even if plaintext X(i) equals plaintext X(j). In contrast, *stereotyped messages* (such as may occur in a terminal-to-computer inquiry system where frequent yes and no responses are transmitted) are not masked when Z is constant, since identical messages will always result in identical cryptograms.

To eliminate the problem of stereotyped data records, a variable initializing vector (Z) must be used.

Since U(i) is an intermediate result of the encipherment of block X(i), it can be expressed as a function h_1 of K(i) and X(i):

$$U(i) = h_1(K(i), X(i)); \quad i \geqslant 1 \tag{2-17a}$$

Similarly, U(i) is an intermediate result of the decipherment of block Y(i), and so it can also be expressed as a function h_2 of K(i) and Y(i):

$$U(i) = h_2(K(i), Y(i)); \quad i \geqslant 1 \tag{2-17b}$$

But, by the recursive nature of Equations 2-15 and 2-17a, it follows that there exist functions $\phi_1, \phi_2, \ldots, \phi_i$ such that

$$K(i) = \phi_i(K, X(0), X(1), \ldots, X(i-1)); \quad i \geqslant 1 \tag{2-18a}$$

where X(0) ≡ Z. Likewise from Equations 2-15 and 2-17b, it follows that there exist functions $\psi_1, \psi_2, \ldots, \psi_i$ such that

$$K(i) = \psi_i(K, Y(0), Y(1), \ldots, Y(i-1)); \quad i \geqslant 1 \tag{2-18b}$$

where Y(0) ≡ Z.

But from Equations 2-16a and 2-18a, it follows that there exist functions $H_1, H_2, \ldots, H_i$ such that the generated ciphertext, Y(i), is given by

$$Y(i) = H_i(K, X(0), X(1), \ldots, X(i)); \quad i \geqslant 1 \tag{2-19a}$$

and from Equations 2-16b and 2-17b, it follows that there exist functions $G_1, G_2, \ldots, G_i$ such that the recovered plaintext, X(i), is given by

$$X(i) = G_i(K, Y(0), Y(1), \ldots, Y(i)); \quad i \geqslant 1 \tag{2-19b}$$

where X(0) ≡ Y(0) ≡ Z.

Equation 2-19a enables us to determine the most general block cipher. Since the ciphering process is entirely deterministic, an output ciphertext block at time i, Y(i), can depend only on the inputs to the ciphering process from time 1 through time i, namely the cipher key (K), the initializing vector (Z), and all plaintext blocks X(1) through X(i). It follows, therefore, that Equation 2-19a represents the most general relation that could be established for a block cipher. Moreover, since ciphertext block Y(i) depends on the initial conditions established at the beginning of the ciphering process, namely at time 1, it is said that Y(i) is *origin-dependent*.

For similar reasons, it follows that a recovered plaintext block at time i, X(i), can depend only on the cipher key (K), the initializing vector (Z), and all ciphertext blocks Y(1) through Y(i). Equation 2-19b, therefore, represents the most general relation that could be established for a block cipher. In like manner, X(i) is also origin-dependent.

A block cipher which satisfies the general relations expressed in Equations 2-19a and 2-19b is defined as a *general block cipher.* A block cipher for which every bit in the recovered plaintext block X(i) is a function of every bit in ciphertext blocks Y(1) through Y(i) is said to have the property of *error propagation.* Since the corruption of only a single bit of ciphertext may cause each subsequent bit of recovered plaintext to be in error, error propagation can be used as a means for detecting the occurrence of such errors (see Cryptographic Message Authentication Using Chaining Techniques).

Since strong intersymbol dependence is one property of a block cipher, it follows that error propagation is automatically achieved in a general block cipher. However, since a bit in output block (i) does not depend on bits within input blocks (i + 1), (i + 2), . . . , the dependence is not defined as strong intersymbol dependence but rather as *intersymbol dependence.*

Block Chaining Using Plaintext and Ciphertext Feedback

Another way to obtain block chaining is to hold the cipher key constant and modify the input plaintext by making it a function of both the previous block of plaintext and the previous block of ciphertext (Figure 2-16). In this case, encipherment and decipherment are given by

$$Y(i) = f_K(X(i) \oplus U(i)); \quad 1 \geqslant 1 \qquad (2\text{-}20a)$$

and

$$X(i) = f_K^{-1}(Y(i)) \oplus U(i); \quad i \geqslant 1 \qquad (2\text{-}20b)$$

respectively, where

$$U(i) = \begin{cases} Z; & i = 1 \\ h(X(i-1), Y(i-1)); & i > 1 \end{cases} \qquad (2\text{-}21)$$

Suppose that h is simple addition modulo 2^{64}.

$$U(i) = X(i-1) + Y(i-1) \bmod 2^{64}; \quad i > 1$$

Then, from Equation 2-20a, it follows that

$$Y(i) = f_K(X(i) \oplus (X(i-1) + Y(i-1) \bmod 2^{64})); \quad i > 1$$

and so, there exist functions $H_1, H_2, \ldots, H_i$ such that

$$Y(i) = H_i(K, X(0), X(1), \ldots, X(i)); \quad i \geqslant 1 \qquad (2\text{-}22a)$$

where $X(0) \equiv Z$. Similarly, from Equation 2-20b, it follows that

$$X(i) = \begin{cases} f_K^{-1}(Y(i)) \oplus Z; & i = 1 \\ f_K^{-1}(Y(i)) \oplus (Y(i-1) + X(i-1) \bmod 2^{64}) & i > 1 \end{cases}$$

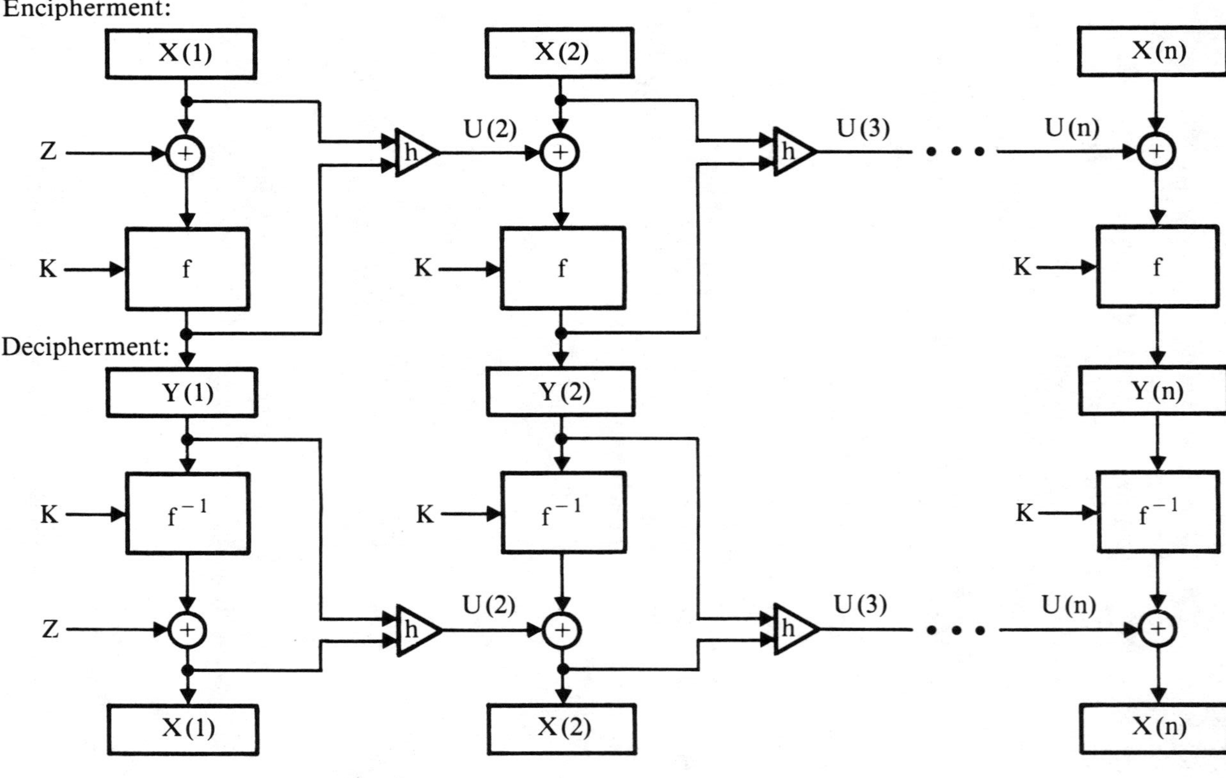

Figure 2-16. Block Cipher with Block Chaining (Block Chaining Using Plaintext-Ciphertext Feedback)

and so, there exist functions $G_1, G_2, \ldots, G_i$ such that

$$X(i) = G_i(K, Y(0), Y(1), \ldots, Y(i)); \quad i \geqslant 1 \tag{2-22b}$$

where $Y(0) \equiv Z$. From Equations 2-22a and 2-22b, it can be seen that origin-dependence has been achieved for X(i) and Y(i), and that Equations 2-19a and 2-19b have been satisfied for the general block cipher.

A Self-Synchronizing Scheme Using Ciphertext Feedback

A cryptographic procedure or device is said to be *self-synchronizing* if after an error has occurred the ciphering operation automatically corrects itself (i.e., all plaintext can be recovered correctly except the portion affected by the error). Consider the case of two cryptographic devices that produce identical outputs for identical inputs. Suppose that an error is now introduced into the ciphering process of one device, so that the outputs of the two devices are different. If after some period of time the outputs again become equal, then the devices are said to be self-synchronizing.

A self-synchronizing block chaining scheme can be obtained by omitting the plaintext feedback in Figure 2-16 (referred to as Cipher Block Chaining, CBC [26]). Mathematically, this can be expressed by defining function h in Equation 2-21 as follows.

$$h(X(i-1), Y(i-1)) = Y(i-1); \quad i \geqslant 1$$

Hence, encipherment and decipherment can be expressed by

$$Y(i) = f_K(X(i) \oplus Y(i-1)); \quad i \geqslant 1$$

and

$$X(i) = f_K^{-1}(Y(i)) \oplus Y(i-1); \quad i \geqslant 1$$

where $X(0) \equiv Y(0) \equiv Z$ (see Figure 2-17).

Again, it follows that there exist functions $H_1, H_2, \ldots, H_i$ and $G_1, G_2, \ldots, G_i$ such that

$$Y(i) = H_i(K, X(0), X(1), \ldots, X(i)); \quad i \geqslant 1 \tag{2-22c}$$

and

$$X(i) = G_i(K, Y(i-1), Y(i)); \quad i \geqslant 1 \tag{2-22d}$$

From Equations 2-22c and 2-22d, it follows that patterns within the input data are masked since ciphertext block Y(i) depends on plaintext blocks X(1), X(2), . . . , X(i). However, since the recovered plaintext block X(i) does not depend on all ciphertext blocks Y(1), Y(2), . . . , Y(i), the scheme is not a general block cipher.

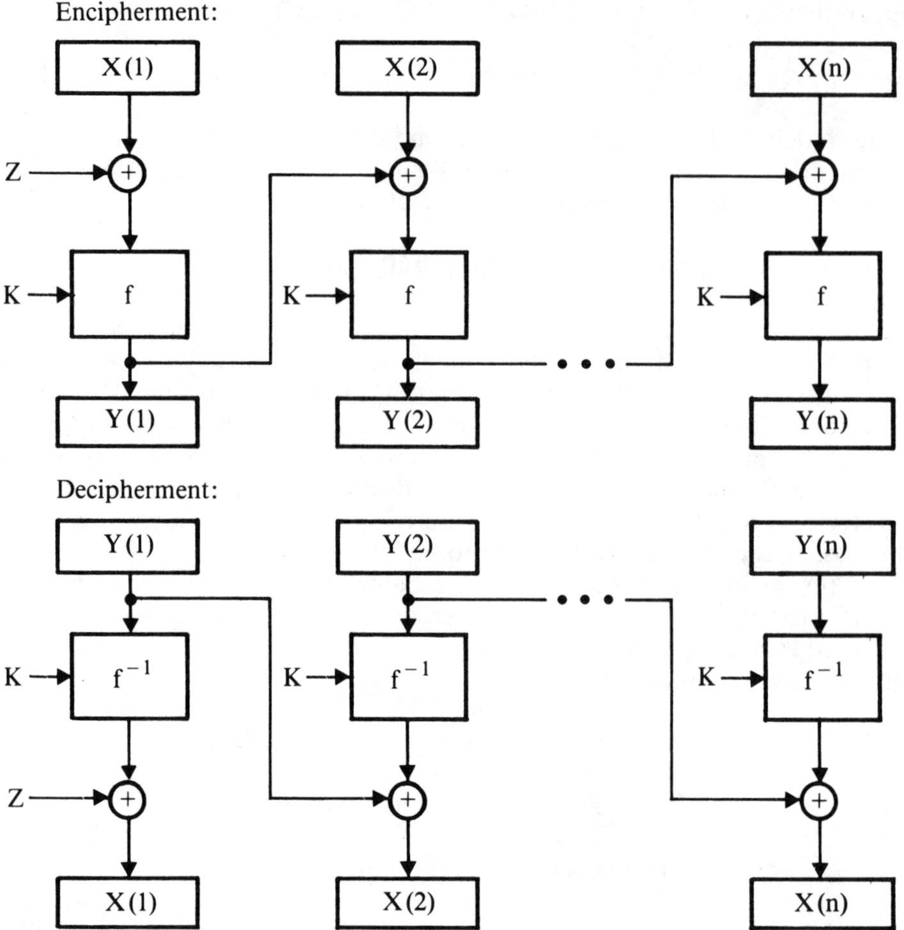

Figure 2-17. Block Cipher with Block Chaining (Block Chaining Using Ciphertext Feedback)

An error occurring in ciphertext block Y(i − 1) can affect every bit in the recovered plaintext block X(i − 1), but it will affect only the corresponding bit positions in the recovered plaintext block X(i). In other words, if the seventh and thirteenth bits in Y(i − 1) are in error, then the seventh and thirteenth bits in X(i) are in error. None of the bits in the recovered plaintext blocks X(i + 1), X(i + 2), and so forth, will be affected by an error occurring in ciphertext block Y(i − 1). Since most of the plaintext can be recovered, even when an error occurs in the ciphertext, the scheme is said to be self-synchronizing.

However, since an error in ciphertext does not propagate, the scheme cannot be directly used for message authentication (see Cryptographic Message Authentication Using Chaining Techniques). Hence the choice of a block chaining method must involve the weighing of the benefit of direct cryptographic authentication against that of self-synchronization.

A practical application for the self-synchronizing approach is the protection of stored data. When cryptography is used for communication security, one can recover from an error in transmission simply by retransmitting the original message. When a file is encrypted, recovery from an error must be effected with ciphertext alone. If a ciphering procedure with error propagation is used for file security, subsequent inability to read a portion of the ciphertext, because of damage either to the physical medium or to the recorded bits, may prevent all following ciphertext from being deciphered. In certain applications for cryptography, therefore, a self-synchronizing approach may be the most desirable.

Examples of Block Chaining

To illustrate how block chaining can be used to eliminate patterns within data, the plaintext in Figure 2-13 was enciphered using block chaining with ciphertext feedback (Figure 2-17). Figure 2-18 illustrates the situation where each 80-character line or 80-column card is enciphered as a separate data record so that only the blocks within each line or card are chained together. Figure 2-19 illustrates the case where the entire text is enciphered as a single data record so that all blocks are chained together.

Short Block Encryption

Since a block cipher enciphers and deciphers only blocks of bits at a time, it is important to know how a block cipher can cope with data whose length is not an integral multiple of the cipher's blocksize. A block whose length is less than the cipher's blocksize is called a *short block*, whereas a block whose length is equal to the blocksize is called a *block* or *standard block*.

A short block will always occur as the last block of data when the data's length is not an integral multiple of the cipher's blocksize. A short block will also occur as the first (and only) block of data when the data's length is less than the cipher's blocksize.

If a short block is first padded with enough additional bits to produce a standard block, it is always possible to encipher a short block in a secure way using a block cipher (see Effects of Padding and Initializing Vectors). *Padding* is the operation of appending additional data bits (or bytes) to plaintext so that its length becomes a multiple of the cipher's blocksize. For security purposes, it is best if pad characters are produced by a random process, although in most cases a pseudo-random process is sufficient. If pad characters could be predicted by an opponent, then, in terms of the work factor, the blocksize would be effectively reduced. The technique of short block encryption using padding is illustrated below (Figure 2-20).

Generally, when cryptography is used for communication security, padding is an acceptable solution for handling messages that may be variable in length. This, however, is not always the case when cryptography is used for file security, because padding bits may cause overflow of secondary storage.

When ciphering operations are not length-preserving, it may no longer be convenient, practical, or even possible to substitute ciphertext freely for

```
     @  q    d.E P J1   P    x u□G   t    Z          6 ( (J[u J   y   ≥i   ≠#+5X   a? 8[   6S T
G  X "  .b$ A  89(2C    Dsx 5 Ze)          ? V@o  V       Y   K 8    ]L =┘     - D    p t*xv)  |
   0     u o   5            -  391  V  .C   < n L F≤q≥5 6 2z./r +)r  y      Q I >    E*>
   0     j+   S    t    ←■ P-] 3#   ■ }5- ≥¬/Z   &t          6 a≤ 6     -    < P      9
   0    w%    i ┘    5[ d     t   kS   dr z &  @      N     'f B   ●  r3C   Y LZ¬   'G    4S
   0    Smf      })I    9 6 I   ,  /1     4   Rtd     UX 05i● O    @   . D Y8   nS   Y 2b  qE!
   0     K    N KVtd   bVJ    v   ObXkW   =@ 4Xi ■S8≥>&   28   t □    w%   /    8 % @ K I  ●
        L   ┘X jK;k  N +    [[  1     X ←X o5   XRPcXo Xw  4  W c   4 y8 j—       o =    i
   0    ? ←gu         u4     1L OCh≠ 7V   i &$ (   +r[ 6 h      %e    5  kCI    =   5        ■
)!    9[  U;    >5S   V       L )-5 1 *H   ┘   W&d      kp ≥K Sx-M      N  $ U          S 1     :S
   0      -Kf 8b J    .  <"Ng, <    9  M   9   3   :      +S 4 ■ c       R    <  x        ●C(Z Y
   0      2        o!k S/0       QV          ?|}>-6ey.Q] ,( (   7□   8 4   0[  LWH5    r LDq{W[  a
   0               r 5  Y □? ±!         P U    ±C   .(Tt jx   +   ]≥   H,Y  8M  ]    s    }≠c       &
   0     / aD d' 43    R         1L        :hJb$     y J   z 4    yx   m   S   LoU >b     b  B2<I
   0       -Kf 8b    t5 ¬  &¬15 3┘  ,1       .&    0+7     2%6   yo  81           4 ! k    c9[-PC
   0       o (    @       B<   t   1] ±       9    ;zY    ● )    1  | W        jA)   9I    *  uv    +  @
   0     x ZQa   4B      &  ' :   )  -=      +          ( V            zb -,         <1        2"   F m
   0       o (    @      ylT  +#i           !      )1 &7 C'o [S  r-           ←, - HYb D@+ □ ←   hUH   <
   0     / aD d'         4      =    q mqf[        i &t   S       +             ┘ & (1 J3● v ]  o -
   0       L  #G □?    8w   (L({¬7≠ :         3 @  8Z@       b¬     rC9          +  "  4 0  um9       g (
   ≥    m<  /LKqK    q DV  Pp   S   ?   ≤F      N6      g         +  ←  &1G7    ft !1     R ?6E>       < 7
R=  (1t     ¬     U|    .*)         -8  + q    L6I6  6  2rM    -     9    -k6       ●JD      ]≠       ;X )    I
□¬   E'(Y    p    [      V    f    )b:   G8  pCE up 8    T ≠S          [F± P )< V/ B     5  Y      Y      "
k≥ )  Y d      m  GZ b7r  5       ] U≥      $ X(    @         /X4uq□    ?   R      7K BIp v      -Z"     >mD>     8
6         i      C≠"     ●   {{5       d      4±4C←X  :   No  ¬      ●61  5  #  U≠± c  :] 6 +      & K  + y; 0  2G5
¬ X  1k        ≠r  b¬     15(L      o  B    $$ @ NO        n       Q      V¬E. &E 6  +<, i        ±  j".     G}   (
F≥ +        h        [  Q±9●    han≥      o2 )■     m     Y       #  ' □  4!4         z   g●  ≥&fA     7   m    M?
 :    Vw□    sg    HLG $  /    v□ %  k  ≤          iN     ±w1G "@     tq          #r□w +@□9   ?   q d9     3 W    #
 :    Vw□    sg    HLG $  /    v□ %  k  ≤    ≥    +   , aG ze          ]           0    a   LK] 7 1≥              )     v[
4 ≥      n  (.    k      B     +  T≥6Z  Sr8      Ck ┘       ■    SO       R ?w    k  6h  t←   d GZrVt E.
)+8-      G  (bh  ?y  s  6     u8  6  Dk  )    (□ %       2  X5[ {N+(2      jw    3-Zf  y    Y T  b   |r     tC 1L J
< u      N ow       )   15    k   {rw2Js          )● H.    Os  9&K u?Qu       [N2/   % g( 9.A|        p -q          3
)+8-      G  (bh  ?y  s  6     u8  6  Dk  )    (□ %       2  X5[ {N+(2      jw    3  Zf  y    Y T  b   |r  o      n
4 ≥      n  (.    k      B     +  T≥6Z  Sr8      Ck ┘       ■    SO       R ?w    k  6h  t←   d GZrVt     V      ┘
 :    Vw□    sq    HLG $  /    v□ %  k  ≤    ≥    +   , aG ze          ]           0-   a   LK} 7 1≥                  pM    9
```

Spaces represent nonprintable characters.

Z = Hex '5555555555555555' is the constant initializing vector, which is the same for each line of plaintext to be encrypted.

K = Hex '85CDCB1C9BD0851A' is the parity-adjusted key used for encipherment.

Figure 2-18. Ciphertext Obtained when the Plaintext in Figure 2-13 is Encrypted Line-By-Line Using the DES Block Cipher with Ciphertext Feedback

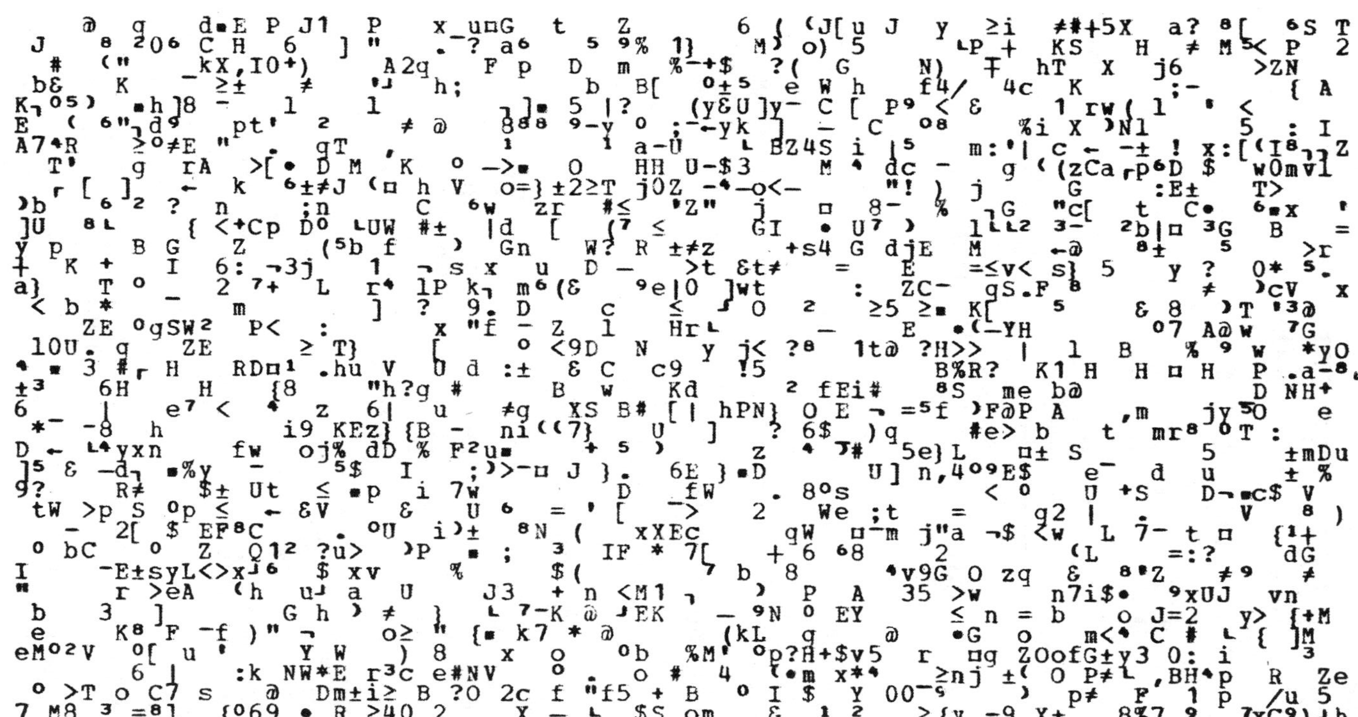

Spaces represent nonprintable characters.

Z = Hex ' 5555555555555555 ' is the initializing vector.

K = Hex ' 85CDCB1C9BD0851A ' is the parity-adjusted key used for encipherment.

Figure 2-19. Ciphertext Obtained when the Plaintext in Figure 2-13 is Encrypted as a Single Aggregate Message Using the DES Block Cipher with Ciphertext Feedback

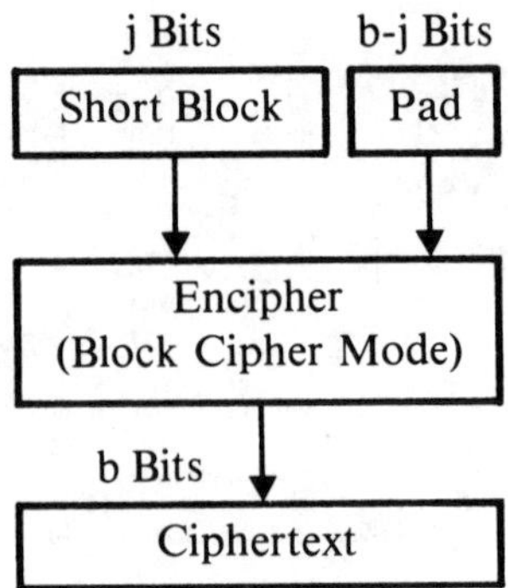

Figure 2-20. Encipherment of a Short Data Block Using Block Cipher Mode

plaintext within a computer data base. Expanded ciphertext may cause a file to overflow the physical boundaries of the recording medium. Encipherment of selected fields within records, or of selected records within files may require that record formats be redefined and may in turn require existing files to be restructured. Such dependencies between the encryption algorithm and stored data are undesirable.

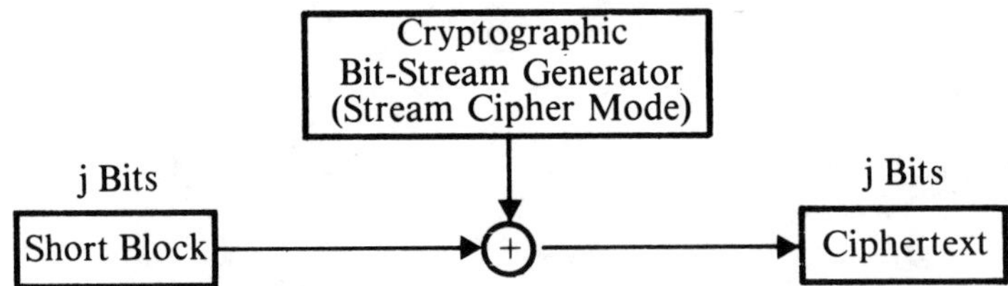

Figure 2-21. Encipherment of a Short Data Block Using Stream Cipher Mode

One way to avoid data expansion would be to use the stream cipher mode of operation to handle the special situations of short blocks (Figure 2-21). In this mixed mode of operation, the block cipher mode is used for ciphering standard blocks and the stream cipher mode is used for ciphering short blocks. One way to implement the stream cipher mode is to generate the cryptographic bit-stream by reenciphering the previous block of ciphertext or, in the case of the first block, by enciphering the initializing vector. This scheme is shown in Figure 2-22.

Consider the following plaintext whose length is greater than, but not an integral multiple of, the cipher's blocksize.

b Bits		b Bits	j Bits	
X(1)	• • •	X(n − 1)	X(n)	

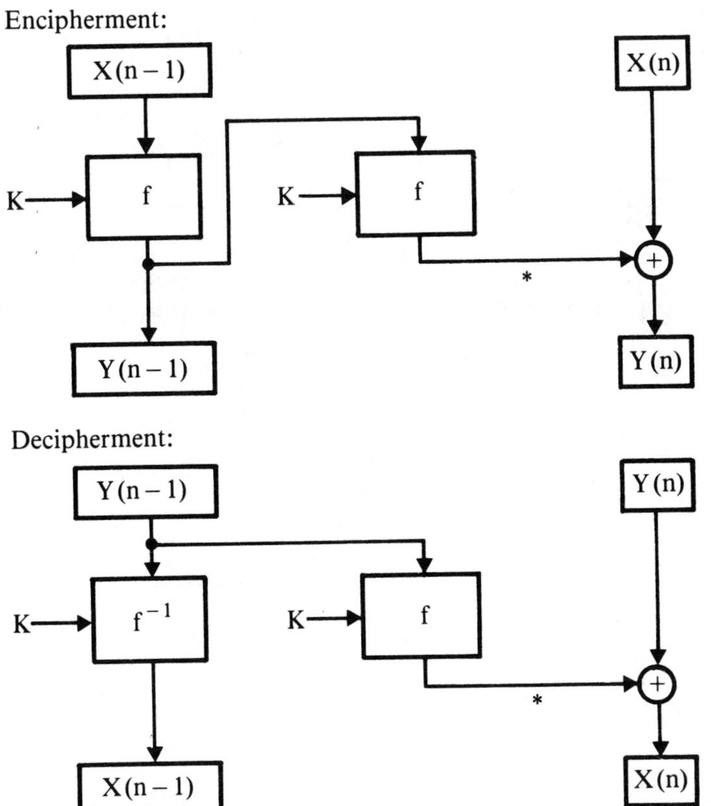

* | X(n) | bits are used to encipher X(n), where | X(n) | is the length of X(n) in bits. If n = 1, then the initializing vector (Z) is enciphered under K to produce the cryptographic bit-stream.

Figure 2-22. Stream Cipher Mode for Encipherment of Short Blocks

where

$$b = \text{blocksize}$$

$$1 \leqslant j < b$$

Instead of using a mixed mode of operation (i.e., a block cipher for standard blocks and a stream cipher for short blocks) one can use a block cipher to encipher short blocks provided that the data's length is greater than the cipher's blocksize.

Another approach for enciphering a short block, X(n), is to make use of a technique called *ciphertext-stealing mode* (Figure 2-23). In this mode, the short block, X(n), is first padded by stealing (removing) just enough bits from the ciphertext Y(n − 1) to make the length of X(n) equal to the cipher's blocksize. This results in Y(n − 1) becoming a short block and Y(n)

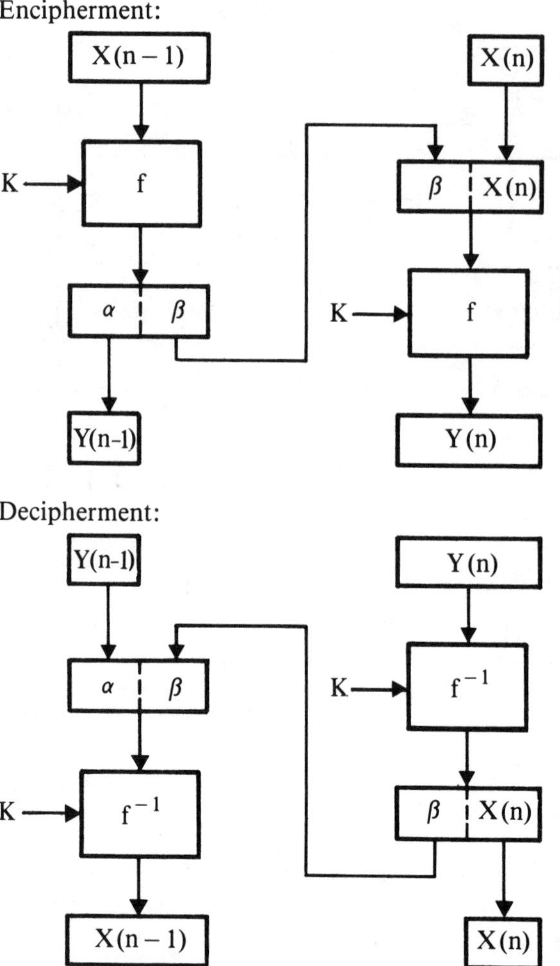

Figure 2-23. Ciphertext-Stealing Mode for Encipherment of Short Blocks

becoming a standard block. Since the number of bits removed from Y(n — 1) equals the number of bits added to X(n), no expansion occurs. The enciphering process is reversed by deciphering Y(n) prior to Y(n — 1) and recovering the original stolen bits from Y(n — 1). The reconstructed value of Y(n — 1) is then deciphered.

Both the stream cipher mode and the ciphertext-stealing mode display a certain awkwardness in the manner in which short blocks are handled. With the stream cipher mode, the cryptographic bit-stream is generated by encipherment of Y(n — 1) regardless of whether encipherment or decipherment is taking place. Complete symmetry between encipherment and decipherment is therefore lost. With the ciphertext-stealing mode, the serial fashion in which blocks are normally enciphered or deciphered is not preserved. Here, the two trailing ciphertext blocks are deciphered in reverse order. Again, complete symmetry between encipherment and decipherment is lost.

The encryption of short blocks also affects error propagation. In the stream cipher mode (Figure 2-22), a bit change in Y(n − 1) will affect all bits in the recovered plaintext, (X(n − 1), X(n)), whereas a bit change in Y(n) will cause only a corresponding bit change in the recovered plaintext, X(n). Hence the error propagation property discussed earlier for the general block cipher is lost as far as the last short block of ciphertext is concerned. (There is no strong intersymbol dependence between plaintext and ciphertext in the last block.) In the ciphertext-stealing mode (Figure 2-23), any bit change in the short ciphertext block Y(n − 1) will affect only the recovery of plaintext block X(n − 1), but will not affect the recovery of plaintext short block X(n). Hence, any error in ciphertext block Y(n − 1) will not propagate, and again the error propagation property is affected.

When implemented properly, the stream cipher and ciphertext-stealing modes provide equivalent cryptographic strength, although a somewhat unlikely set of circumstances can be found in which these two techniques are not equivalent. Suppose that these two techniques are implemented in a cryptographic system which uses a block cipher with no chaining. Assume further that it is possible for an opponent to request enciphering operations but not deciphering operations, and that the cipher keys are managed by the system (i.e., unknown to the system's users). If the stream cipher mode is used, the short block X(n) can be recovered by intercepting Y(n − 1) and Y(n) via a wiretap, retransmitting Y(n − 1) as text in a second message, intercepting the ciphered version of Y(n − 1) via a second wiretap, and finally, Exclusive-ORing Y(n) with the ciphered version of Y(n − 1). This attack could be prevented either by using X(n − 1) + Y(n − 1) mod 2^{64} instead of Y(n − 1) as the value to be ciphered, or by using chaining.

Figures 2-24 through 2-27 illustrate how the stream cipher and ciphertext-stealing modes can be used in conjunction with the block chaining schemes previously discussed. Without loss of generality, only two full blocks are shown, X(1) and X(2), respectively. Block X(3) is a short block. Generally speaking, all of these schemes are equivalent in cryptographic strength provided that the basic cryptographic algorithm is strong (i.e., an algorithm comparable in strength to DES is used).

In each case (Figure 2-24 and 2-26), the stream cipher mode is implemented in such a way that it is not possible for an opponent to recover X(3) by intercepting Y(2) and Y(3) via a wiretap, retransmitting Y(2) as data, intercepting the encipherment of Y(2) via a second wiretap, and finally Exclusive-ORing the enciphered version of Y(2) with Y(3). In Figure 2-24, the attack is not possible because Y(2) is enciphered with a variable key that is chained back to the origin. In Figure 2-26, the attack is not possible because the cryptographic bit-stream used to encipher X(3) via the Exclusive-OR operation is a function of both plaintext and ciphertext.

For all practical purposes, the ciphertext-stealing mode is implemented in such a way that a frequency analysis on the short block is not possible. In Figure 2-25, observe that the variable key K(2) used to encipher X(2) is the same key used to encipher the quantity β concatenated with X(3), and that

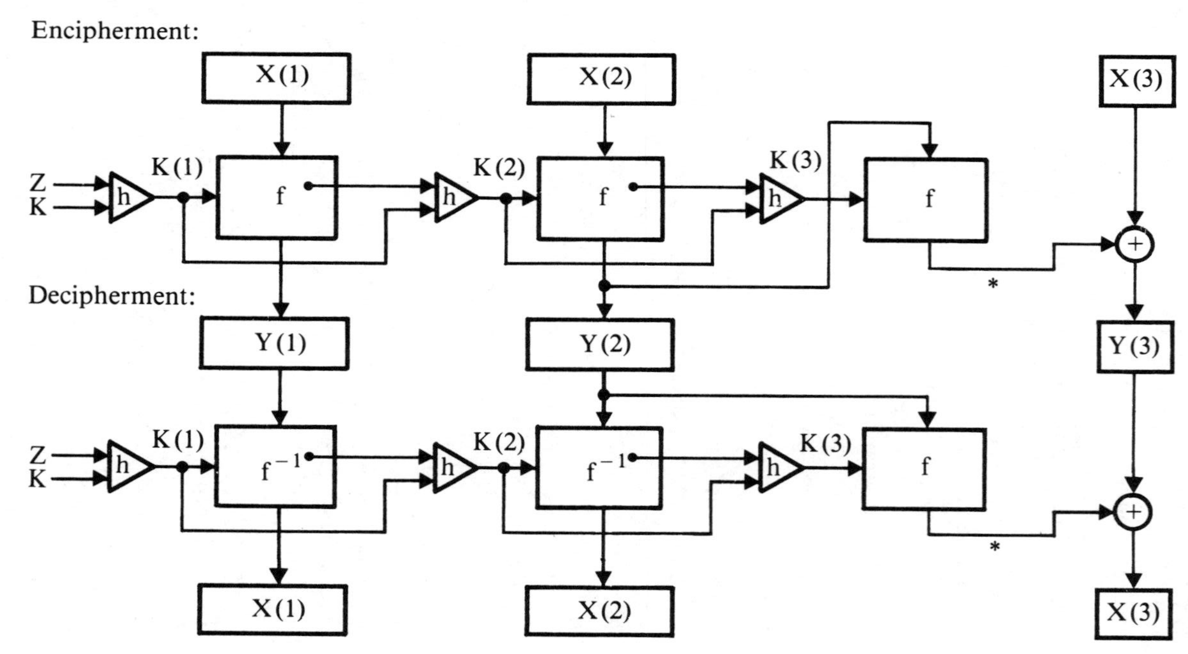

* Number of bits used equals | X(3) |

Note: Function h could be an Exclusive-OR operation in an actual implementation. A bit change in Y(3) results only in a corresponding bit change in X(3) and hence is predictable by an opponent. A change of any other ciphertext bit is propagated, and the effect on the recovered plaintext is unpredictable.

Figure 2-24. Block Cipher with Block Chaining
(Block Chaining Using Variable Key, and Stream Cipher Mode for Short Blocks)

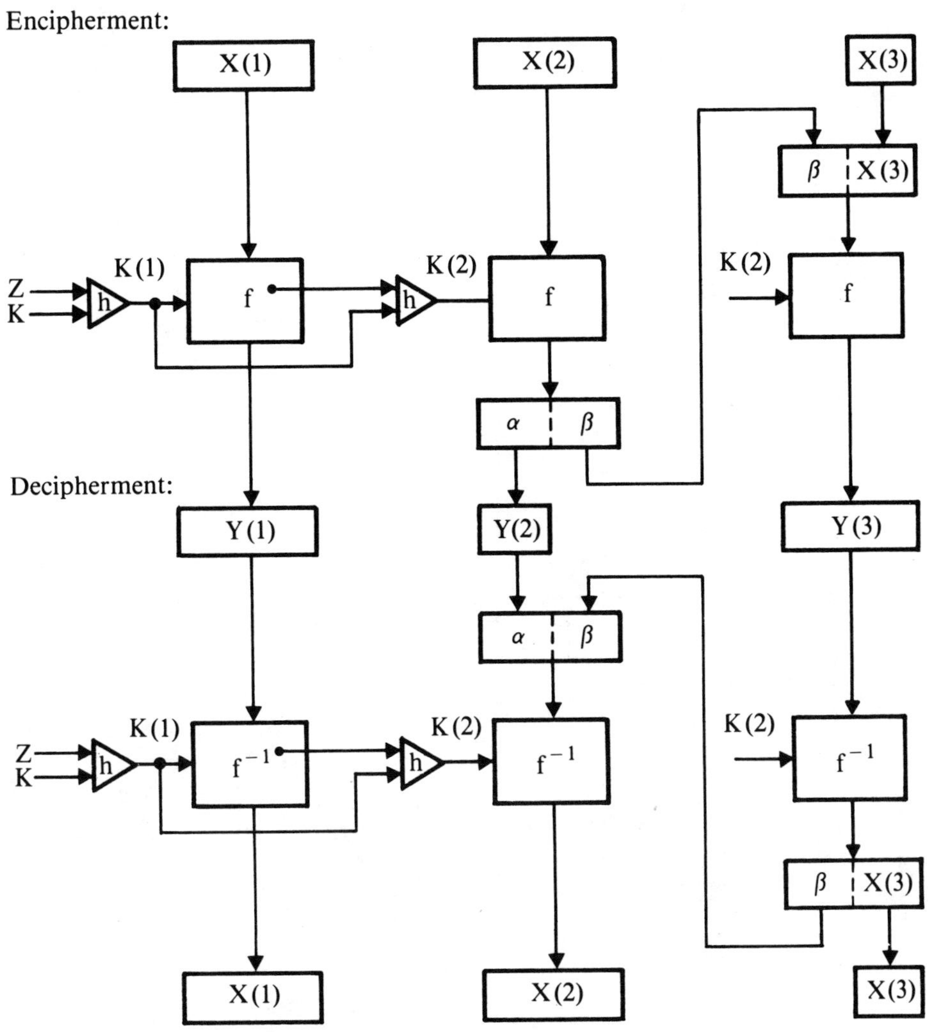

Note: Function h could be an Exclusive-OR operation in an actual implementation. A change in Y(2) affects only the recovery of X(2), and hence the error does not propagate in that case. A change of any other ciphertext bit is propagated, and the effect on the recovered plaintext is unpredictable.

Figure 2-25. Block Cipher with Block Chaining (Block Chaining Using Variable Key, and Ciphertext-Stealing Mode for Short Blocks)

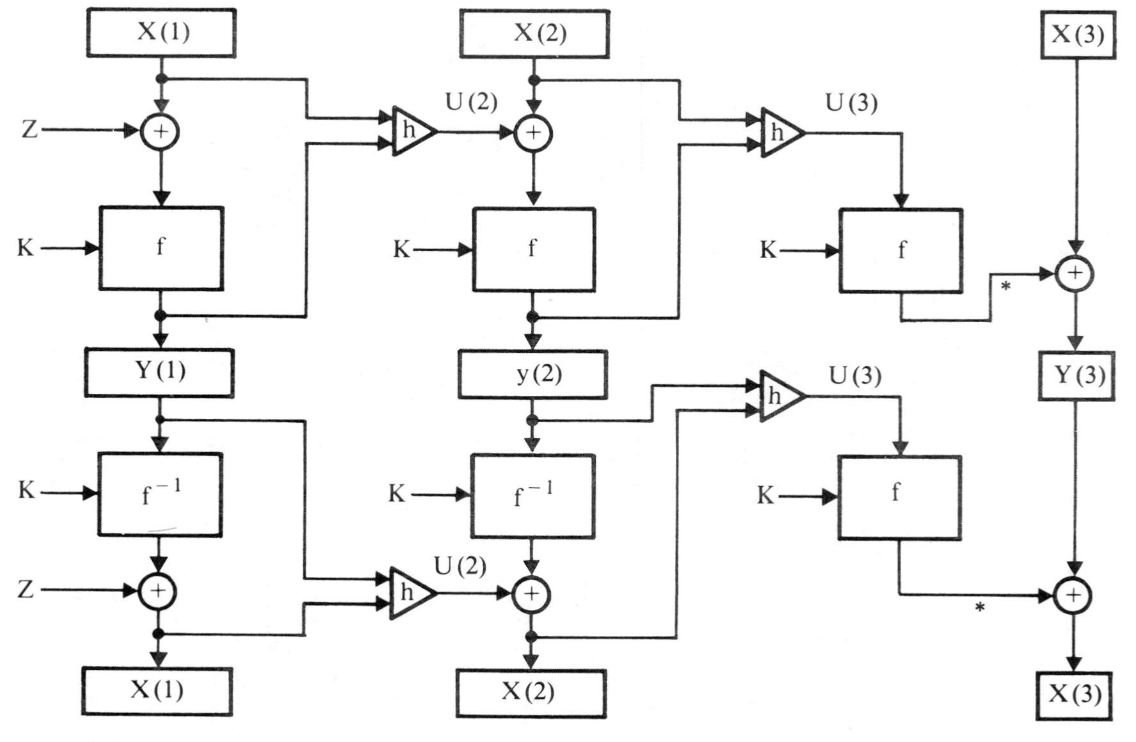

* Number of bits used equals | X(3) |

Note: Function h could be addition modulo 2^{64} in an actual implementation. A bit change in Y(3) results only in a corresponding bit change in X(3) and hence is predictable by an opponent. A change of any other ciphertext bit is propagated, and the effect on the recovered plaintext is unpredictable.

Figure 2-26. Block Cipher with Block Chaining (Block Chaining Using Plaintext-Ciphertext Feedback, and Stream Cipher Mode for Short Blocks)

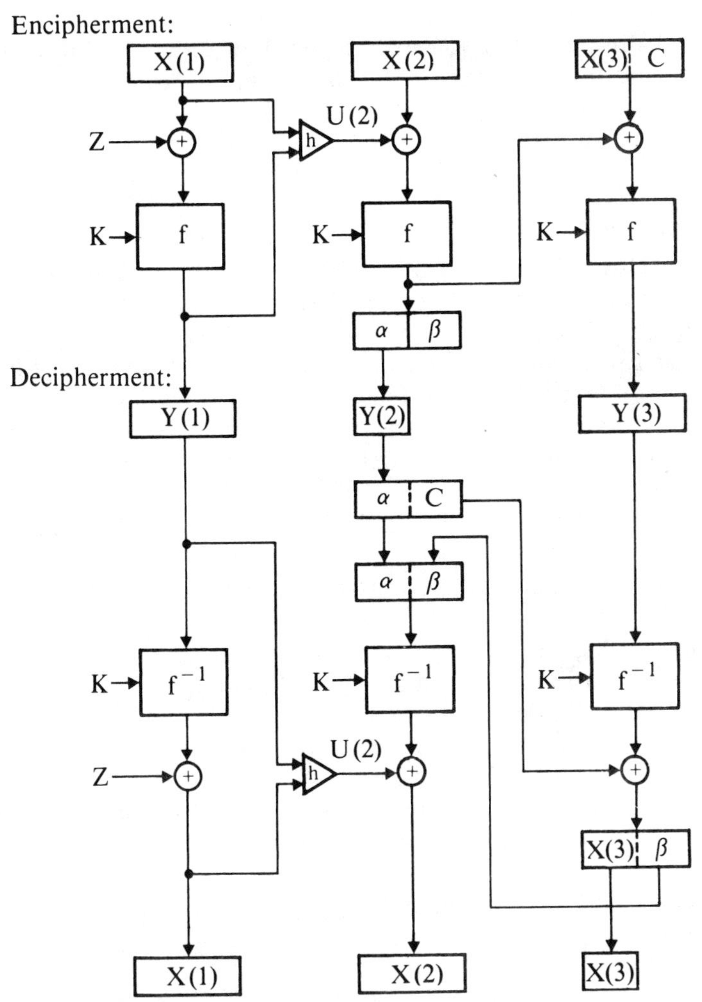

Note: (1) C is a constant, say all zero bits.

(2) Function h could be addition modulo 2^{64} in an actual implementation; or a self-synchronizing system could be obtained by making h depend only on the ciphertext feedback.

A change in Y(2) affects only the recovery of X(2), and hence the error does not propagate in that case. A change of any other ciphertext bit is propagated, and the effect on the recovered plaintext is unpredictable.

Figure 2-27. Block Cipher with Block Chaining (Block Chaining Using Plaintext-Ciphertext Feedback and Ciphertext-Stealing Mode for Short Blocks)

K(2) is chained to the origin. Since X(2) is enciphered prior to X(3) and Y(3) is deciphered prior to Y(2), the same cipher key, K(2), is used for both the encipherment and decipherment of the second and third blocks of plaintext and ciphertext, respectively. In Figure 2-27, observe that the short block is chained using only a ciphertext feedback. Since the last two blocks must be treated in reverse order, using a feedback from the plaintext would prevent recovery.

Observe that the method for implementing the ciphertext-stealing mode in Figure 2-27 is slightly different from that shown in Figure 2-23. In addition to stealing ciphertext and concatenating it with short block X(3), ciphertext is also stolen and Exclusive-ORed with X(3). This extra step is important because for all practical purposes it prevents a successful block frequency analysis on Y(3). With the technique shown in Figure 2-23, this is not necessarily true when the number of bits concatenated to X(n) is small, (e.g., if β were only one bit and the number of plaintext combinations for X(n) were small).

As pointed out in Figure 2-22, the encipherment of data consisting of a single short block of $j < b$ bits can be accomplished by Exclusive-ORing the first j bits of the encipherment of the initializing vector Z. However, such a procedure would be weak if the same Z were used repeatedly to encipher a sequence of short blocks, e.g., a file of records in which each record consists of a single short block. In effect, each short block would be protected using the same cryptographic bit-stream, which would thus allow the plaintext associated with these short blocks to be recovered via a simple cryptanalysis.

In the case of file security, a strong procedure for the encipherment of data records consisting of repeated short blocks is to use a method of *record chaining* [24,25]. Here, the value of Z is a variable that changes for each record to be enciphered. In the recommended approach, Z_i (the initializing vector for the ith record) is specified as the rightmost 64 bits ("right64") of the concatenation (||) of Z_{i-1} and the just-constructed ciphertext (the ciphertext of record $i - 1$), i.e.,

$$Z_i = \text{right64}[Z_{i-1} \; || \; \text{ciphertext of record } i - 1]$$

Thus, the first record is enciphered using the initial value of Z (defined as Z_1). All subsequent records are enciphered using a computed value of Z, as described above.

With record chaining, the chaining process continues across record boundaries. To correctly decipher a record (given the key), only that record and the preceding 64 bits of ciphertext (and possibly the initial value of Z if less than 64 bits of ciphertext are present) are required. Record chaining is ideally suited for sequentially organized files. For nonsequential files, block chaining is best suited. But for block chaining to be strong, each record must have its own (unique or randomly selected) 64-bit initializing vector, Z.

The inherent cryptographic weaknesses associated with the encryption of groups of short data blocks in a sequentially organized file can also be avoided via the implementation. For example, data blocks (of any length) can be temporarily joined (concatenated) into an "artificial" data unit (or *cipher unit*) which is then enciphered as if it were one, large record or collection of data.

In the case of communication security, padding is the preferred technique for short block encryption. Here, the physical boundary limitations that can lead to data overflow, which apply to file security, do not exist.

STREAM CIPHERS WITH CHAINING

In a block cipher, chaining can be used to acquire two important properties. First, it can mask repetitive patterns within data by making each block of ciphertext, Y(i), dependent upon all prior blocks of plaintext, X(1), X(2), . . . , X(i − 1), as well as on the present plaintext block X(i). In a sense, this chaining technique extends the effective blocksize of the cipher. Second, it can extend error propagation across block boundaries by making each block of recovered plaintext, X(i), dependent upon all prior blocks of ciphertext, Y(1), Y(2), . . . , Y(i − 1), as well as on the present ciphertext block, Y(i).

In a stream cipher, patterns occurring within the input plaintext are automatically eliminated as a consequence of Exclusive-ORing the plaintext with the cryptographic bit-stream (Figure 2-10). The cryptographic bit-stream introduces pseudo-random noise into the ciphering process and hence eliminates exploitable statistics associated with the plaintext. The changing initializing vector Z assures that stereotyped messages (if they occur) will result in different ciphertext. Thus chaining is not needed in a stream cipher to mask patterns within the data or to mask stereotyped messages. It can, however, be useful in a stream cipher to achieve either the property of error propagation, if one desires secrecy and authentication in one operation, or self-synchronization, in which case the system does not have to be reinitialized after an error condition occurs.

In the stream cipher, it can be assumed that the cryptographic bit-stream is produced as a series of blocks:

$$R(1), R(2), \ldots, R(t)$$

where

$$R(i) = (r_1(i), r_2(i), \ldots, r_b(i))$$

is a block of b bits generated at iteration i, and b is the blocksize. Encipherment and decipherment are defined as

$$Y(i) = X(i) \oplus R(i); \quad i \geqslant 1 \tag{2-23a}$$

and

$$X(i) = Y(i) \oplus R(i); \quad i \geqslant 1 \tag{2-23b}$$

A Chaining Method with the Property of Error Propagation

Error propagation is present in a block cipher whenever each bit in the recovered plaintext block X(i) is a function of every bit in ciphertext blocks Y(1) through Y(i). In a stream cipher, however, because of the modulo 2 addition shown in Equation 2-23b, the jth bit in the recovered plaintext block X(i) depends on the jth bit in the ciphertext block Y(i), but not on any other bits in ciphertext block Y(i). At best, a scheme could be devised where the jth bit in X(i) is a function of every bit in Y(1) through Y(i − 1). If this were the case, then an error occurring in any of the ciphertext blocks Y(1) through Y(i − 1) could propagate to the recovered plaintext block X(i).

To achieve this dependence, a feedback could be provided from either the plaintext X, the initializing vector Z, or a combination of both, in addition to the feedback from the ciphertext. A stream cipher with the property of error propagation is shown in Figure 2-28.

Note, however, that error propagation due to corruption of the ciphertext could be obtained by providing a feedback only from the plaintext. That is, encipherment is expressed by

$$\begin{aligned} Y(1) &= X(1) \oplus g_K(Z); \qquad i = 1 \\ Y(i) &= X(i) \oplus g_K(X(i-1)); \qquad i > 1 \end{aligned}$$

and decipherment is expressed by

$$\begin{aligned} X(1) &= Y(1) \oplus g_K(Z); \qquad 1 = 1 \\ X(i) &= Y(i) \oplus g_K(X(i-1)); \qquad i > 1 \end{aligned} \tag{2-24}$$

It follows that each bit in the recovered plaintext block X(i) depends on each bit in the initializing vector (Z) and on each bit in the ciphertext blocks Y(1) through Y(i − 1), by the recursive relation shown in Equation 2-24.

If a feedback from plaintext were used, patterns in the plaintext would result in patterns in the ciphertext. This is because Y(i) is not origin-dependent. Recall that patterns were destroyed in the key auto-key cipher (Figure 2-12) because the feedback was taken from the cryptographic bit-stream.

From Figure 2-28 it follows that encipherment and decipherment can be expressed as

$$Y(i) = X(i) \oplus g_K(U(i)); \qquad i \geqslant 1 \tag{2-25a}$$

and

$$X(i) = Y(i) \oplus g_K(U(i)); \qquad 1 \geqslant 1 \tag{2-25b}$$

respectively, where

$$U(i) = \begin{cases} h^*(Z); & i = 1 \\ h(U(i-1), Y(i-1)); & i > 1 \end{cases} \tag{2-26}$$

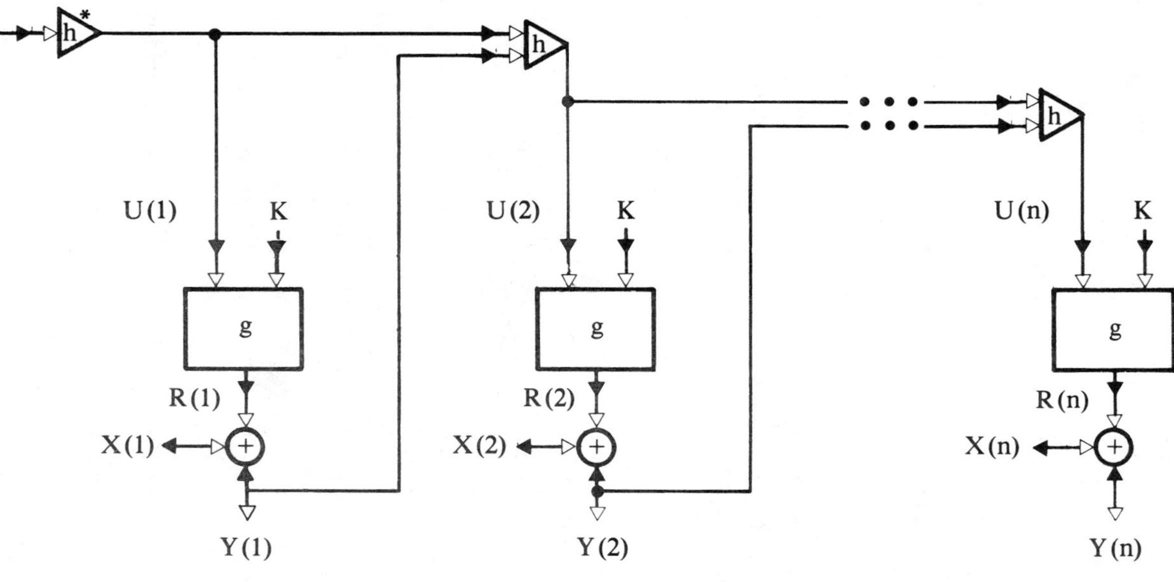

Legend: encipherment mode: —▷ , decipherment mode: —▶

Note: Z, U, R, X and Y are blocks of n bits; h could be an Exclusive-OR function

Figure 2-28. Stream Cipher with Error Propagation

Function h* is again introduced to allow Z to be different in length from U.

From the recursive nature of Equation 2-26, it follows that there exist functions $G_1, G_2, \ldots, G_i$ and $H_1, H_2, \ldots, H_i$ such that

$$Y(i) = X(i) \oplus H_i(K, X(0), X(1), \ldots, X(i-1)); \quad i \geqslant 1 \qquad (2\text{-}27a)$$

and

$$X(i) = Y(i) \oplus G_i(K, Y(0), Y(1), \ldots, Y(i-1)); \quad i \geqslant 1 \qquad (2\text{-}27b)$$

where $X(0) \equiv Y(0) \equiv Z$.

Using the same arguments that led to the definition of a general block cipher (see Block Chaining Using a Variable Key), the reader can see that Equations 2-27a and 2-27b represent the most general relation that can be established for a stream cipher. Whenever such relations hold for a stream cipher, it is called a *general stream cipher.*

It follows (Equation 2-27a) that the jth bit in ciphertext block Y(i) is affected by only the jth bit in plaintext block X(i), whereas it is potentially affected by every bit in plaintext blocks X(1) through X(i − 1). In like manner, it follows (Equation 2-27b) that the jth bit in the recovered plaintext block X(i) is affected by only the jth bit in ciphertext block Y(i), whereas it is potentially affected by every bit in ciphertext blocks Y(1) through Y(i − 1).

Since the recovered plaintext block X(i) is potentially affected by every bit in ciphertext blocks Y(1) through Y(i − 1), error propagation is achieved. However, because the jth bit in the recovered plaintext block X(i) depends only on the jth bit in ciphertext block Y(i), the following statements may be made. *For the general stream cipher, intersymbol dependence can be achieved for all but the final block. For the general block cipher, there is intersymbol dependence throughout all blocks.* This is an important difference between block ciphers and stream ciphers.

A Chaining Method with the Property of Self-Synchronization

A self-synchronizing stream cipher can be obtained from Figure 2-28 by defining function h as

$$h(U(i-1), Y(i-1)) = Y(i-1); \quad i > 1$$

that is, by feeding back the ciphertext as input to the algorithm. By defining $Y(0) \equiv Z$, it follows that

$$g_K(U(i)) = g_K(Y(i-1)); \quad i \geqslant 1$$

and so, from Equations 2-25a and 2-25b, encipherment and decipherment can be expressed as

$$Y(i) = X(i) \oplus g_K(Y(i-1)); \quad i \geqslant 1 \qquad (2\text{-}28a)$$

and

$$X(i) = Y(i) \oplus g_K(Y(i-1)); \quad i \geqslant 1 \qquad (2\text{-}28b)$$

respectively.

It follows (Equation 2-28b) that an error in ciphertext block Y(i − 1) can potentially affect every bit in the computed quantity $g_K(Y(i-1))$, and hence can cause every bit in the recovered plaintext block X(i) to be in error. Moreover, it follows (Equation 2-28b) that an error in ciphertext block Y(i − 1) will cause the corresponding bit positions in the recovered plaintext block X(i − 1) to be in error. That is, if the third, fifth, and eleventh ciphertext bits in Y(i − 1) are in error, then the third, fifth, and eleventh recovered plaintext bits in X(i − 1) will be in error. Finally, it follows (Equation 2-28b) that an error in ciphertext block Y(i − 1) will at most affect only the recovery of plaintext blocks X(i − 1) and X(i), but it will not affect the recovery of subsequent plaintext blocks X(i + 1), X(i + 2), and so forth. Hence the scheme is self-synchronizing.

A specific example of a self-synchronizing stream cipher, the ciphertext auto-key cipher, is shown in Figure 2-29. The cryptographic bit-stream is produced in blocks of 64 bits by enciphering the contents of a 64-bit input register, denoted by Y for the sender and Y′ for the receiver, and storing the result in a 64-bit output register, denoted by R for the sender and R′ for the

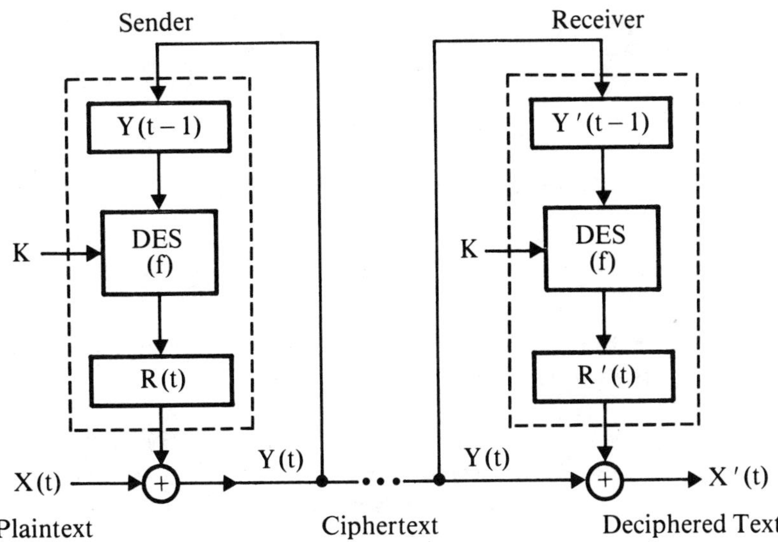

At t = 1: X(t) ≡ Z; Y(t − 1) ≠ Y′(t − 1)

At t > 1: Y(t − 1) = Y′(t − 1) implies in synchronization
Y(t − 1) ≠ Y′(t − 1) implies out of synchronization

Figure 2-29. Ciphertext Auto-Key Cipher

receiver. The contents of registers Y, Y′, R, and R′ at time t are denoted by Y(t), Y′(t), R(t), and R′(t), respectively.

Before communication within the system is possible, the sender and receiver must be synchronized. This is necessary since registers Y and Y′ are assumed to be volatile (i.e., stored information is lost when power to the cryptographic device is turned off). Therefore, it is assumed that at time t = 0

$$Y(0) \neq Y'(0)$$

At time t = 1, synchronization is accomplished by transmitting a 64-bit initializing vector Z, instead of the usual block of plaintext. This causes the same block of ciphertext to be gated into registers Y and Y′ so that Y(1) equals Y′(1), and hence synchronization is achieved. However, unlike subsequent blocks of transmitted plaintext, the first block (the initializing vector) is not presented to the user at the receiving end.

At time t > 0, the input Y(t − 1) is enciphered using key K to obtain

$$R(t) = f_K(Y(t-1))$$

R(t) is Exclusive-ORed with the data block X(t) to obtain

$$Y(t) = R(t) \oplus X(t)$$

Y(t) is then transmitted to the receiving end where the input Y′(t − 1) is enciphered using key K to obtain

$$R'(t) = f_K(Y'(t-1))$$

R′(t) is Exclusive-ORed with the ciphertext block Y(t) to obtain the recovered plaintext, X′(t).

$$X'(t) = Y(t) \oplus f_K(Y'(t-1))$$

If the first data block X(1) is defined as the initializing vector (Z) (i.e., $X(1) \equiv Z$) then the following may be said:

1. At t = 1, $Y(0) \neq Y'(0)$ implies that $X(1) \neq X'(1)$ even though X′(1) is not presented to the user. However, if Y(1) is received without error, then the sender and receiver are in synchronization.
2. At t > 1, $Y(t-1) \neq Y'(t-1)$ implies that $X(t) \neq X'(t)$, (i.e., the receiver obtains incorrect plaintext). However, if Y(t) is received without error, then the sender and receiver are in synchronization. $Y(t-1) = Y'(t-1)$ implies that $X(t) = X'(t)$ (i.e., the receiver obtains correct plaintext).

If errors on the transmission line (bit changes, but not bit additions or deletions) cause sender and receiver to get out of synchronization ($Y(t) \neq$

Y′(t)), then error-free transmission of another block of ciphertext will cause sender and receiver to come back into synchronization (Y(t + 1) = Y′(t + 1)). Generally, the ciphertext blocksize can be less than 64 bits in length if desired. In this case, only the necessary bits from R are Exclusive-ORed with plaintext, and the feedback will affect fewer bits in Y.

For all practical purposes, a 48-bit initializing vector is enough to provide adequate cryptographic strength. If the sender and receiver are able to sense when they are resynchronizing, a protocol can be established whereby only a 48-bit block of ciphertext is sent for this purpose. Both sender and receiver pad this 48-bit block of ciphertext with a designated constant (all zeros), so that the values placed into registers Y and Y′ are the same. Furthermore, attacks on initializing vectors should be prevented by generation of these quantities within the secure area of the cryptographic device.

Cipher Feedback Stream Cipher

By definition, a ciphertext auto-key cipher produces its cryptographic bit-stream using feedback from ciphertext. The various algorithms differ in the way this ciphertext is manipulated before being used. One such algorithm, mentioned in the proposed U.S. Federal Standard 1026 [26], is called *cipher feedback* (Figure 2-30). In this approach, the leftmost n bits of the DES output are Exclusive-ORed with n bits of plaintext to produce n bits of ciphertext, where n is the number of bits enciphered at one time ($1 \leqslant n \leqslant 64$). These n bits of ciphertext are fed back into the algorithm by shifting the current DES input n bits to the left, and then appending the n bits of ciphertext to the right side of the shifted input to produce a new DES input used for the next interaction of the algorithm.

A seed value, which must be the same for both sender and receiver, is used as an initial input to DES in order to generate the cryptographic bit-stream. Standard 1026 allows seed length to vary from 8 to 64 bits, but to ensure compatability among users it requires that all cipher feedback implementations must be capable of using a 48-bit seed. Both the sender and receiver are synchronized by right justification of the seed in the input to DES and setting the remaining bits equal to 0.

An Example of Seed Generation

One method of producing seed values is to use the DES algorithm as a generator of pseudo-random numbers. (See Stream Ciphers for a discussion of requirements for initializing vectors, or seed values.) The seed values are unpredictable because the key used by DES to produce the cryptographic bit-stream is also used to produce the seed values.

During an initialization phase, a nonsecret quantity, such as the ID of the device in which the algorithm is installed, is placed in a nonvolatile storage that can be accessed (read) only by the cryptographic algorithm. A seed is produced by enciphering this initial quantity with the installed cryptographic key and using the leftmost m bits ($m \leqslant 64$) from the DES output. The entire 64-bit DES output, however, is used to replace the initial quantity in nonvolatile storage. The content of this nonvolatile

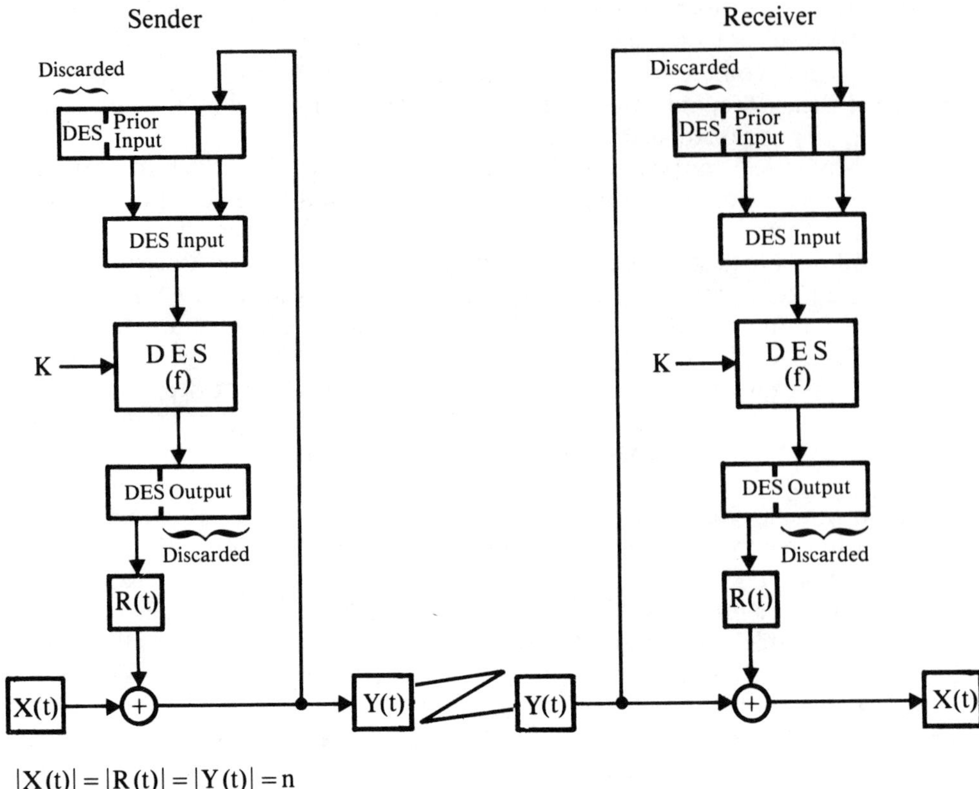

Figure 2-30. Cipher Feedback

storage continually changes and, in addition, cannot be manipulated by external means.

Let IC_0 be the starting value supplied by the user and placed in non-volatile storage, where IC stands for *initial condition*. During the first seed generation, IC_1 is produced by encrypting IC_0

$$f_K(IC_0) = IC_1$$

and IC_1 replaces IC_0. During the second seed generation, IC_2 is produced by encrypting IC_1 and IC_2 replaces IC_1. The process continues in this manner. The method of generating and using a seed in cipher feedback is illustrated in Figure 2-31.

The Cipher Feedback approach is self-synchronizing, since any bit change occurring in the ciphertext during transmission gets shifted out of the DES input after 64 additional ciphertext bits are sent and received. If, for example, 8 bits are enciphered at one time, as shown in Figure 2-30, and a bit is altered in $Y(t_1)$, changing it to $Y^*(t_1)$, then the DES inputs at sender and receiver are as shown in Figure 2-32, where the 5-byte seed is defined as S1, S2, . . . , S5. In this case, the blocks of ciphertext, given by $Y^*(t_1)$, $Y(t_2)$, . . . , $Y(t_8)$,

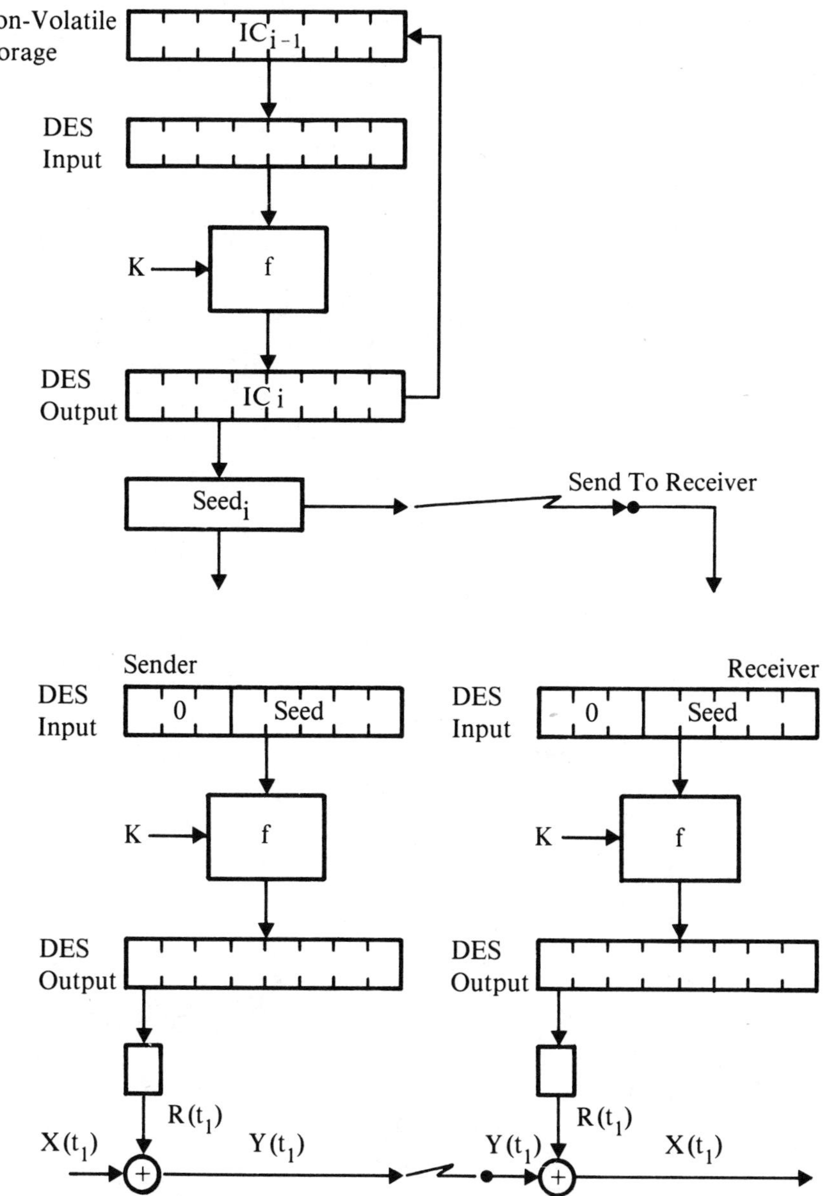

Figure 2-31. Cipher Feedback with a 40-bit Seed and 8-bit Plaintext

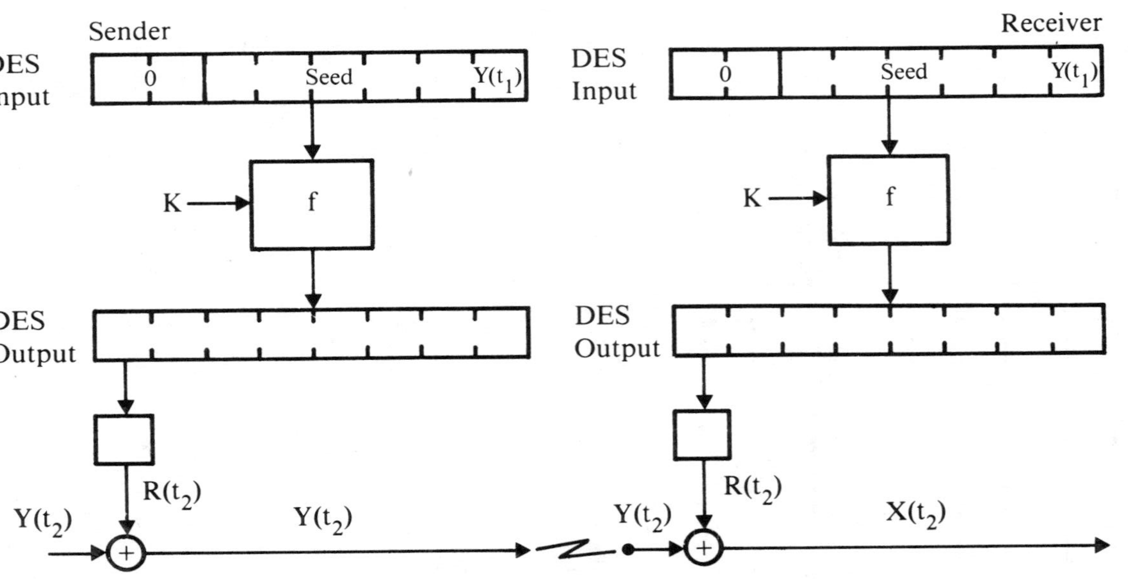

Figure 2-31 (cont'd). Cipher Feedback with a 40-bit Seed and 8-bit Plaintext

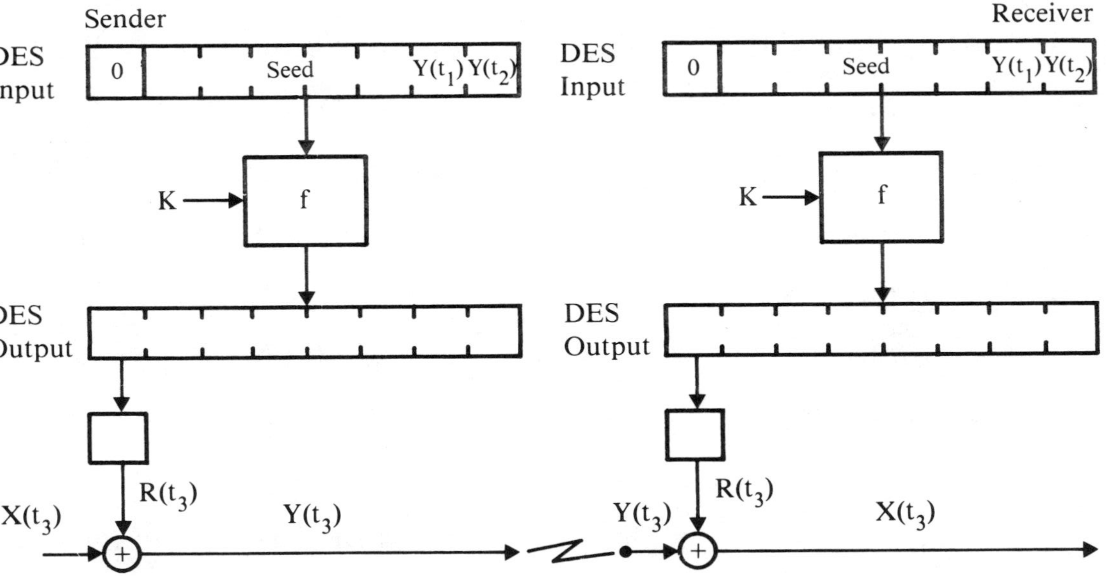

Figure 2-31 (cont'd). Cipher Feedback with a 40-bit Seed and 8-bit Plaintext

Iteration	DES Input At Sender								DES Input At Receiver							
0	0	0	0	S1	S2	S3	S4	S5	0	0	0	S1	S2	S3	S4	S5
1	0	0	S1	S2	S3	S4	S5	$Y(t_1)$	0	0	S1	S2	S3	S4	S5	$Y^*(t_1)$
2	0	S1	S2	S3	S4	S5	$Y(t_1)$	$Y(t_2)$	0	S1	S2	S3	S4	S5	$Y^*(t_1)$	$Y(t_2)$
3	S1	S2	S3	S4	S5	$Y(t_1)$	$Y(t_2)$	$Y(t_3)$	S1	S2	S3	S4	S5	$Y^*(t_1)$	$Y(t_2)$	$Y(t_3)$
4	S2	S3	S4	S5	$Y(t_1)$	$Y(t_2)$	$Y(t_3)$	$Y(t_4)$	S2	S3	S4	S5	$Y^*(t_1)$	$Y(t_2)$	$Y(t_3)$	$Y(t_4)$
5	S3	S4	S5	$Y(t_1)$	$Y(t_2)$	$Y(t_3)$	$Y(t_4)$	$Y(t_5)$	S3	S4	S5	$Y^*(t_1)$	$Y(t_2)$	$Y(t_3)$	$Y(t_4)$	$Y(t_5)$
6	S4	S5	$Y(t_1)$	$Y(t_2)$	$Y(t_3)$	$Y(t_4)$	$Y(t_5)$	$Y(t_6)$	S4	S5	$Y^*(t_1)$	$Y(t_2)$	$Y(t_3)$	$Y(t_4)$	$Y(t_5)$	$Y(t_6)$
7	S5	$Y(t_1)$	$Y(t_2)$	$Y(t_3)$	$Y(t_4)$	$Y(t_5)$	$Y(t_6)$	$Y(t_7)$	S5	$Y^*(t_1)$	$Y(t_2)$	$Y(t_3)$	$Y(t_4)$	$Y(t_5)$	$Y(t_6)$	$Y(t_7)$
8	$Y(t_1)$	$Y(t_2)$	$Y(t_3)$	$Y(t_4)$	$Y(t_5)$	$Y(t_6)$	$Y(t_7)$	$Y(t_8)$	$Y^*(t_1)$	$Y(t_2)$	$Y(t_3)$	$Y(t_4)$	$Y(t_5)$	$Y(t_6)$	$Y(t_7)$	$Y(t_8)$
9	$Y(t_2)$	$Y(t_3)$	$Y(t_4)$	$Y(t_5)$	$Y(t_6)$	$Y(t_7)$	$Y(t_8)$	$Y(t_9)$	$Y(t_2)$	$Y(t_3)$	$Y(t_4)$	$Y(t_5)$	$Y(t_6)$	$Y(t_7)$	$Y(t_8)$	$Y(t_9)$

Figure 2-32. Self-Synchronizing Feature in Cipher Feedback

will be correctly deciphered at the receiver only by chance, since the DES input in each case is incorrect. After eight blocks of uncorrupted ciphertext have been received, given by $Y(t_2)$, . . . , $Y(t_9)$, both the sender's and receiver's cryptographic devices will have equal DES inputs again.

In general, any bit change in an n-bit block of ciphertext can cause a change in any of the corresponding n bits of recovered plaintext and in any of the 64 bits of recovered plaintext immediately following. However, one should realize that a permanent out-of-synch condition will result if a ciphertext bit is added or dropped, since the integrity of the block boundary is lost. To recover from such an error, the sender and receiver would have to have a way to establish the beginning and end of blocks of bits that are enciphered at one time (n = 8 bits in the given example). On the other hand, if enciphering takes place on a bit-by-bit basis (n = 1), then the property of self-synchronization is maintained even when bits are lost or added. This is because blocks are bits, and therefore the block boundary cannot be disturbed. (Note that in the example where n = 8, self-synchronization would be maintained if bits were dropped or added in blocks of 8 bits.)

Examples of Cipher Feedback

Figures 2-33 and 2-34 illustrate two examples of cipher feedback using 8-bit blocks and the described method of seed generation.

Key (external) = 1 3 3 4 5 7 7 9 9 B B C D F F 1

Key (internal) = F 0 C C A A F 5 5 6 6 7 8 F

IC_{i-1} = 5 4 5 4 5 4 5 4 5 4 5 4 5 4 5 4

IC_i = 9 9 A D F 9 4 D 9 C E 6 3 0 C 7

Plaintext = 0 1 2 3 4 5 6 7 8 9 A B C D E F

Seed Length	Seed (underlined) Followed by Ciphertext
16 bits	<u>99AD</u>190E35C419F818AA
24 bits	<u>99ADF9</u>38B80C2CF1E1F7CC
32 bits	<u>99ADF94D</u>B347FC9D5F21D142
40 bits	<u>99ADF94D9C</u>8C266744C539AA59
48 bits	<u>99ADF94D9CE6</u>E88A57084C7A0E57

Figure 2-33. Cipher Feedback—Example 1

Key (external) = 4 9 B C 2 6 4 6 9 E B A 7 3 0 4

Key (internal) = 3 2 4 9 6 6 7 7 C 9 E 3 3 2

IC_{i-1} = 2 8 5 B C 7 4 6 8 4 B C D 7 3 4

IC_i = 7 3 B 3 5 D 2 0 E E 0 3 4 A 7 3

Plaintext = F E D C B A 9 8 7 6 5 4 3 2 1 0

Seed Length	Seed (underlined) Followed by Ciphertext
16 bits	73B3554CE44CA6A60601
24 bits	73B35DDE02A95F890D110E
32 bits	73B35D202B4EC26CCD9A882B
40 bits	73B35D20EE56852B80C35CB1AF
48 bits	73B35D20EE032E69D50427AB6B27

Figure 2-34. Cipher Feedback—Example 2

EFFECTS OF PADDING AND INITIALIZING VECTORS

When the block cipher is used for communication security, padding is generally the easiest and most straightforward way to handle short blocks. The small amount of message expansion which results from padding can normally be tolerated within the communication network.

When padding is used, an additional character called the *pad count* must be included as part of the pad characters. The pad count specifies the number of pad characters, including itself, which have been appended to the block. This procedure works well for short blocks, but it creates a problem for standard blocks. Strictly speaking, an extra block of pad characters must be appended to a message whenever its length is a multiple of the blocksize. This allows the procedure to be applied uniformly to all transmissions.

The problem of performance degradation, which may result from adding an extra block of pad characters when the block is already a multiple of the cipher's blocksize, can be greatly reduced by using a *pad indicator bit.* (For example, a 0 indicates no padding and a 1 indicates padding.) The pad indicator bit is transmitted with each message as part of the message's header.

As a measure of the amount of message expansion caused by padding, the *cryptographic throughput factor* (ξ) is defined as

$$\xi = \frac{N_x}{N_y}$$

where

N_x = the length in bits of message X

N_y = the length in bits of cryptogram Y
(Y is enciphered from X)

If $N_y = nb$, where n represents the number of blocks in Y and b the block-size in bits, and n_p represents the number of required bits of padding, then

$$\xi = \frac{(nb - n_p)}{nb} = 1 - \frac{n_p}{nb}$$

Figure 2-35 shows a plot of ξ versus message length (in characters), when the DES block cipher is used.

When the stream cipher is used for communication security, practically no throughput degradation results from transmission of the initializing vector Z, provided that this is done only at sign-on or power-up time. In most situations, however, this assumption is not justified. In practice, each communication node is required to multiplex its transmissions among several different nodes which are all competing for the right to transmit data. This requires that the last initial state be stored and saved for each temporarily inactive session. Generally speaking, this procedure is less desirable than transmitting a new initializing vector each time communication is reactivated. In addition to multiplexing problems, line errors may create an out-of-synch condition between a pair of communicating nodes. This problem appears to

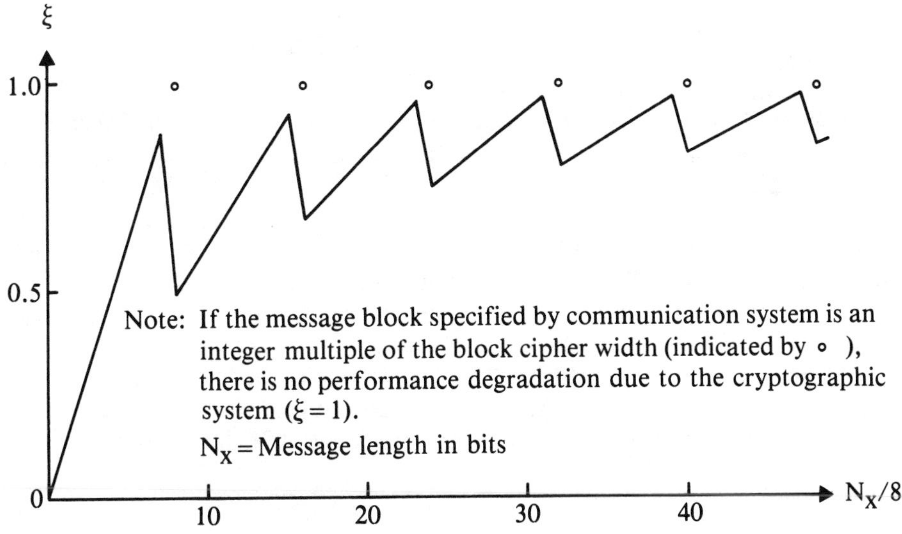

Figure 2-35. Degradation of Throughput in Block Ciphers due to Padding

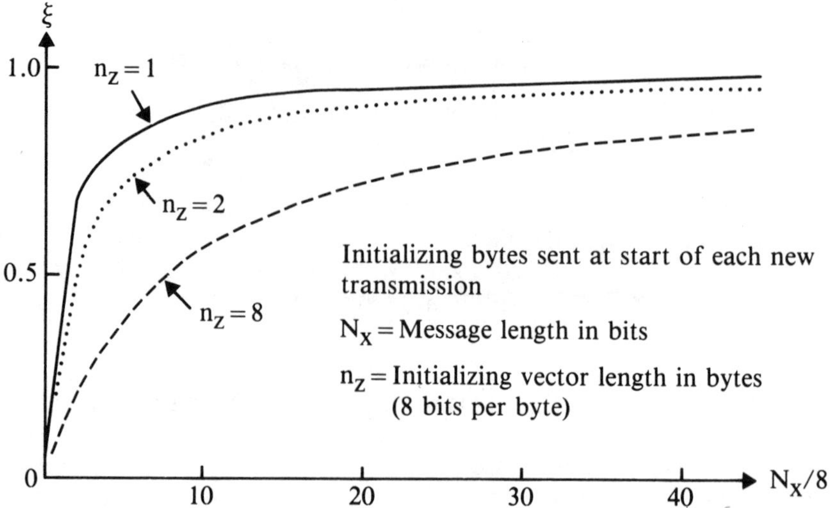

Figure 2-36. Degradation of Throughput in Stream Ciphers due to Initializing Vector

be best resolved by sending another initializing vector. Let n_z represent the number of bytes in Z. Figure 2-36 shows several plots ($n_z = 1, 2, \ldots, 6$) of ξ versus message length (in characters) when the stream cipher is used.

CRYPTOGRAPHIC MESSAGE AUTHENTICATION USING CHAINING TECHNIQUES

The authentication technique described below permits one to determine with a high level of confidence whether a string of text (plaintext or ciphertext) has been altered (accidentally or intentionally). When enciphered data are transmitted or stored within a computing system, either the ciphertext or the recovered plaintext may be authenticated, depending on which is more convenient for the particular application. For example, in the case of enciphered keys used by a cryptographic system's key manager, it may be impractical to decipher these keys to authenticate them. In contrast, authenticating plaintext may be useful in situations where the data are not confidential (i.e., where data are transmitted or stored within the computing system in unenciphered form).

Authentication is accomplished by verifying a bit pattern, called the *authentication code* (AC), that has been computed and appended to the text (plaintext or ciphertext) at a prior time when the data was assumed or known to be correct (see Figure 2-37).

The AC must be a function (ϕ) of the text (TXT), and should have the following properties.

1. It should be computationally infeasible for an opponent to compute $\phi(\text{TXT}')$ for a different text, $\text{TXT}' \neq \text{TXT}$. Otherwise, an opponent could replace TXT and $\phi(\text{TXT})$ with TXT′ and $\phi(\text{TXT}')$, respectively.

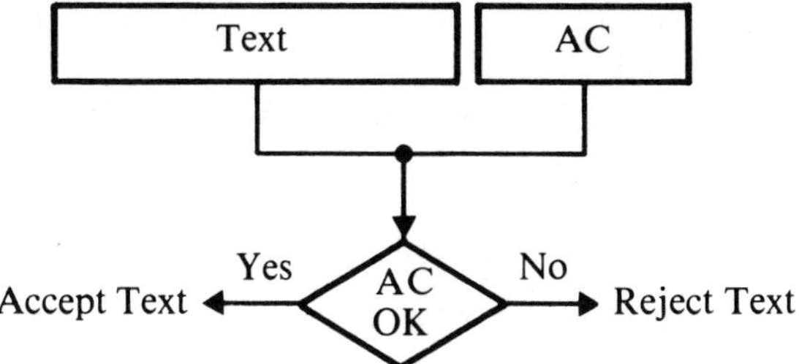

Figure 2-37. Text Checking Procedure Using an Authentication Code

2. It should be computationally infeasible for an opponent to find a different text, TXT′, such that ϕ(TXT′) equals ϕ(TXT). Otherwise, an opponent could replace TXT with TXT′, while leaving ϕ(TXT) unchanged.
3. ϕ(TXT) should be uniformly distributed in the sense that for TXT′ $\neq$ TXT, the probability that $\phi(\text{TXT}') = \phi(\text{TXT})$ is $1/2^c$, where c is the number of bits in AC. In that case, there is only a small chance ($1/2^c$) that a different text (changed either deliberately or accidentally) will be accepted as genuine when C is chosen large enough.

One way to implement an authentication scheme is to exploit the error propagation property obtained with certain chaining techniques. This idea can be explained by reference to the block chaining method that incorporates a plaintext and ciphertext feedback (Figure 2-16). It has the advantage that secrecy and authentication can be achieved in one operation.

For purposes of discussion, function h is assumed to be addition modulo 2^{64}, and the length of the initializing vector Z is equal to the cipher's blocksize. (Using an Exclusive-OR for function h has been shown to be weak, see Authentication by an Encryption Method Without the Property of Error Propagation, Chapter 8.) Let X(1), X(2), . . . , X(n) denote plaintext blocks to be enciphered with key K and initializing vector Z, and let Y(1), Y(2), . . . , Y(n) denote the resulting ciphertext.

$$Y(1) = f_K(X(1) \oplus Z)$$

$$Y(2) = f_K(X(2) \oplus (Y(1) + X(1) \bmod 2^{64}))$$

$$\vdots$$

$$Y(n) = f_K(X(n) \oplus (Y(n-1) + X(n-1) \bmod 2^{64}))$$

The AC could then be defined as follows.

$$AC = f_K(Z \oplus (Y(n) + X(n) \bmod 2^{64}))$$

Note that an additional plaintext block, X(n + 1), is appended to the end of the text to permit the computation of Y(n + 1) = AC. In the example, the additional block is defined to be equal to the initializing vector Z. In another approach it could be a designated constant, say all zero bits, or it could be a repetition of the first block, X(1).

Assume that the length of the AC equals the cipher's blocksize. Upon decipherment, the recovered plaintext is given by

$$X(1) = f_K{}^{-1}(Y(1)) \oplus Z$$

$$X(2) = f_K{}^{-1}(Y(2)) \oplus (Y(1) + X(1) \bmod 2^{64})$$

$$\vdots$$

$$X(n) = f_K{}^{-1}(Y(n)) \oplus (Y(n-1) + X(n-1) \bmod 2^{64})$$

$$X(n+1) = f_K{}^{-1}(Y(n+1)) \oplus (Y(n) + X(n) \bmod 2^{64})$$

where X(n + 1) was originally defined to be equal to the initializing vector Z.

By comparing X(n + 1) and Z for equality, a decision can be made to accept or reject the message (Figure 2-38). The receiver accepts the message if X(n + 1) equals Z, since only the sender who knows the secret key K could have properly created Y(n + 1) in the first place. Otherwise, the message is rejected.

It is also possible to authenticate a message by reconstructing the AC (Figure 2-39) instead of deciphering Y(n + 1) and recovering Z. In that case, Y(1) through Y(n) are deciphered as before, but then Z, X(n), and Y(n) are combined to form Z $(X(n) + Y(n) \bmod 2^{64})$ and this quantity is enciphered with the secret key K to produce AC. The receiver accepts the message if Y(n + 1) equals AC, otherwise, the message is rejected.

The latter method has the advantage that the AC does not have to be a full block (i.e., one could use c bits for AC, where $c < b$ and b is the number of bits in a block). The probability of accepting a message as genuine when it is not is in that case $1/2^c$ (provided that no error cancellation occurs). Thus, the value of c depends on the risk one is willing to take in accepting a forged or corrupted message as genuine.

To analyze the effects of error propagation, let ciphertext block Y(i) be the last corrupted block. The decipherment of ciphertext block Y(i) is shown in Figure 2-40. If Y(i) is the only ciphertext block in error, then the following is true. The only case in which the error is not propagated all the way through to the recovered plaintext block X(n + 1) occurs when the corrupted ciphertext block Y(i)′ and the deciphered value of Y(i)′ under key K are such that

$$Y(i)' + (f_K{}^{-1}(Y(i)') \oplus Q) = Y(i) + (f_K{}^{-1}(Y(i)) \oplus Q)$$

where Q is the value produced at point 2 (i.e., the feedback value at point 1 in Figure 2-40 is unchanged). (Note that the input at point 2 in Figure 2-40 is unchanged and hence cancelled out.) Assuming that an error in Y(i) causes each bit in $f_K{}^{-1}(Y(i)')$ to differ from its corresponding bit in $f_K{}^{-1}(Y(i))$ with a probability approximately equal to 0.5, it follows that the probability of the event that error cancellation occurs is approximately equal to $1/2^b$.

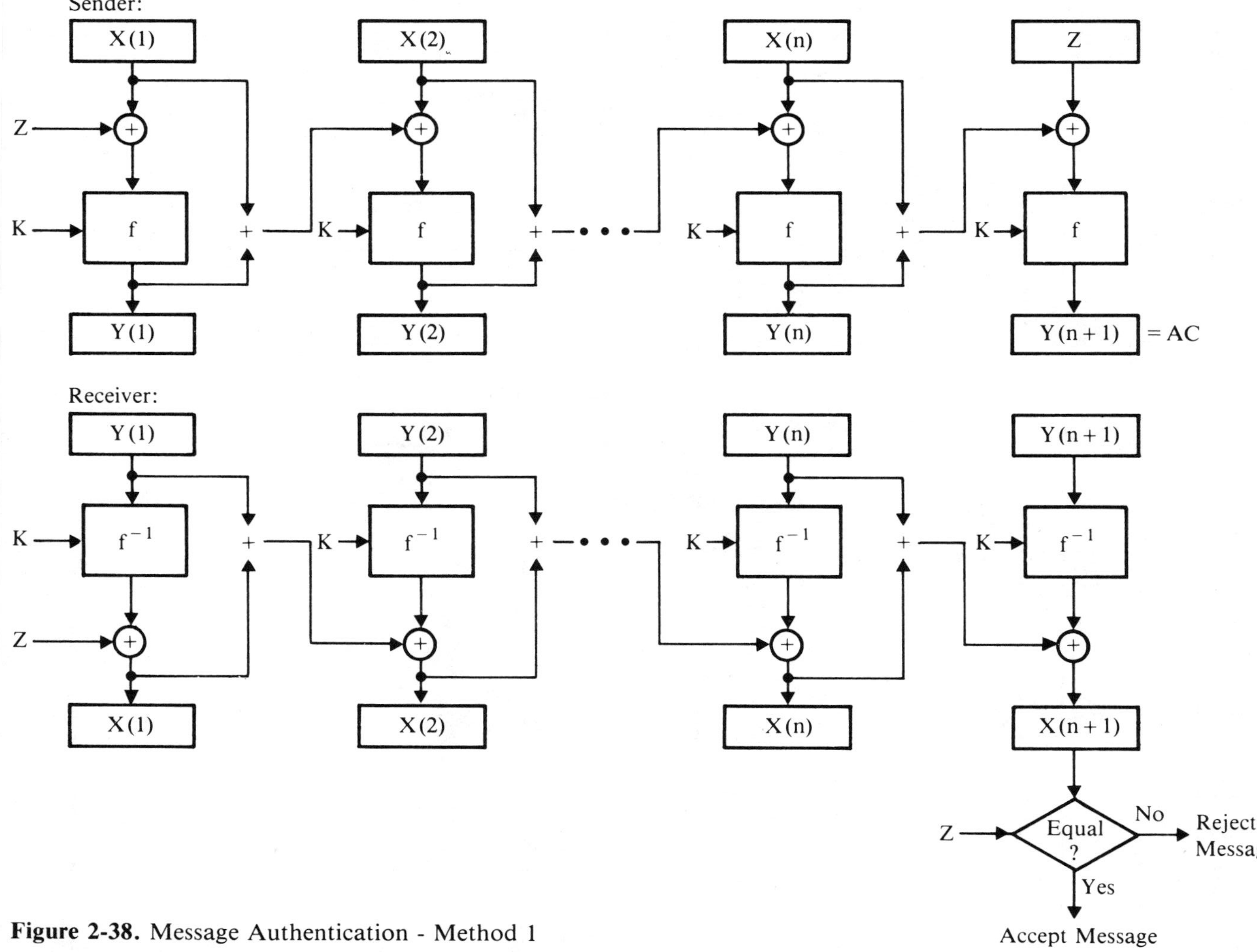

Figure 2-38. Message Authentication - Method 1

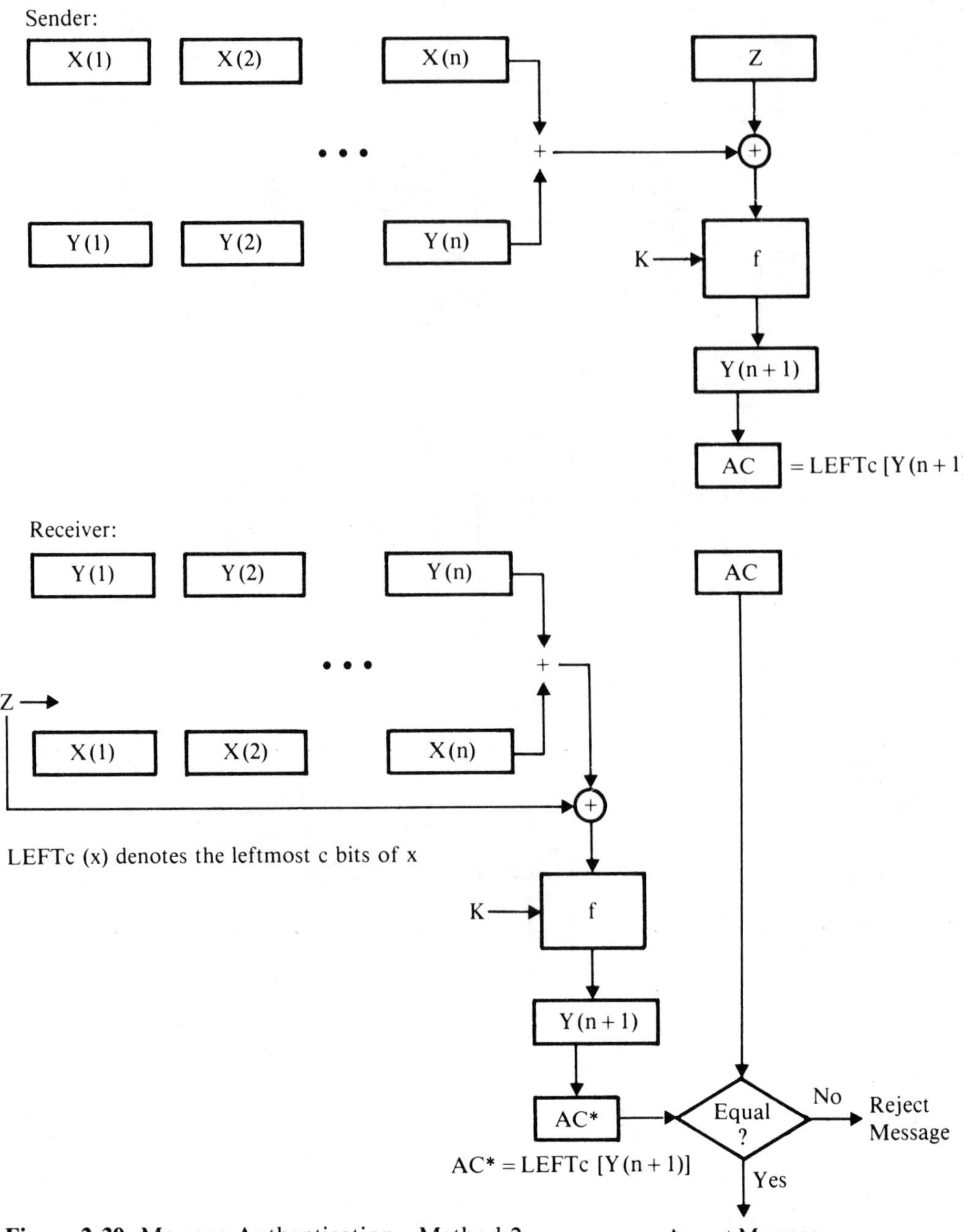

Figure 2-39. Message Authentication - Method 2

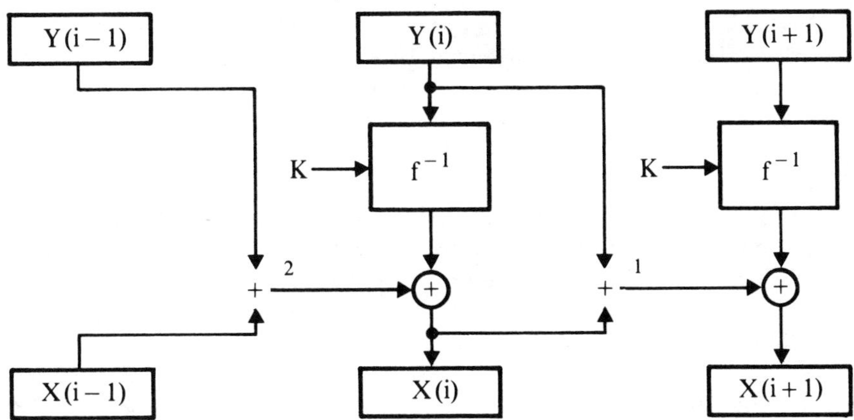

Figure 2-40. Decipherment of Ciphertext Block Y(i)

If, in addition, there are also errors in blocks of ciphertext preceding ciphertext block Y(i), then the following is true. The only case in which the error is not propagated all the way through to the recovered plaintext block X(n + 1) occurs when the corrupted ciphertext block Y(i)′ is such that the deciphered value of Y(i)′ under key K cancels the errors both in Y(i)′ and in the feedback value at point 2 in Figure 2-40 (i.e., the feedback value at point 1 is unchanged).

$$Y(i)' + X(i)' = Y(i) + X(i) \text{ Mod } 2^{64}$$

Again, for all practical purposes, the probability that Y(i)′ will give rise to a $f_K^{-1}(Y(i)')$ that in turn produces an X(i)′ that is self-canceling is approximately equal to $1/2^b$.

Properties one and two for authentication, given above, are satisfied because, under normal conditions an opponent will not know the secret cipher key K, and without knowledge of this key it is computationally infeasible to compute the authentication code or to make systematic changes to the ciphertext that would escape detection. Property three is satisfied if the length c of the AC is large enough.

So far, examples have been given to authenticate messages enciphered with a block cipher. Similar techniques exist for stream ciphers but are not shown here.

COMPARISON OF BLOCK CIPHERS AND STREAM CIPHERS

In the discussion on block ciphers, it was shown that a block cipher need not use an initializing vector (the block cipher could reoriginate). It was also shown that cryptographic strength depends on a minimum required blocksize (the blocksize for DES is 64 bits).

The discussion on stream ciphers showed that a stream cipher must always use an initializing vector (the stream cipher must not reoriginate). A minimum blocksize is not required for the stream cipher, although it was shown that (if desired) the cryptographic bit-stream could be generated in blocks of bits (up to 64 bits per block for DES), and that encipherment could be performed on a block-by-block basis.

In certain applications where highly redundant or structured data are enciphered using a block cipher, patterns in the input stream can be masked or hidden through the use of chaining techniques (block chaining). Stereotyped messages are also masked if an initializing vector is used in conjunction with block chaining. Again, by way of contrast, chaining is not needed in a stream cipher to mask patterns in the input stream, since this is automatically accomplished by the cryptographic bit-stream. Stereotyped messages are also masked, since initializing vectors are always required in a stream cipher.

In certain applications involving authentication, it is desirable for the ciphering technique to have the property of error propagation, that is, an error in the ciphertext causes the recovered plaintext (measured from the point of the error to the end of the recovered plaintext) to be in error. Error propagation can be achieved within block ciphers and stream ciphers through the use of chaining techniques.

A block cipher for which there exist functions $G_1, G_2, \ldots, G_i$ and $H_1, H_2, \ldots, H_i$ such that

$$Y(i) = H_i(K, X(0), X(1), \ldots, X(i)); \quad i \geqslant 1$$

and

$$X(i) = G_i(K, Y(0), Y(1), \ldots, Y(i)); \quad i \geqslant 1$$

where

$$X(0) \equiv Y(0) \equiv Z$$

was defined to be a general block cipher. Two examples of general block ciphers are the block cipher using a variable key (Figure 2-15), and the block cipher using plaintext-ciphertext feedback (Figure 2-16). The self-synchronizing scheme using ciphertext feedback (Figure 2-17) is not a general block cipher. This is because the general relation for X(i) is given by $X(i) = G_i(K, Y(i-1), Y(i))$ (see equation 2-22d) rather than $X(i) = G_i(K, Y(0), Y(1), \ldots, Y(i))$, as shown above.

A stream cipher for which there exist functions $G_1, G_2, \ldots, G_i$ and $H_1, H_2, \ldots, H_i$ such that

$$Y(i) = X(i) \oplus H_1(K, X(0), X(1), \ldots, X(i-1)); \quad i \geqslant 1$$

and

$$X(i) = Y(i) \oplus G_i(K, Y(0), Y(1), \ldots, Y(i-1)); \quad i \geqslant 1$$

where

$$X(0) \equiv Y(0) \equiv Z$$

was defined to be a general stream cipher. An example of the general stream cipher is shown in Figure 2-28. The self-synchronizing scheme using ciphertext feedback (Figure 2-29) is not a general stream cipher. This is because the general relation for X(i) as derived from Equation 2-25b is given by $X(i) = Y(i) \oplus G_i(K, Y(i-1))$ rather than $X(i) = Y(i) \oplus G_i(K, Y(0), Y(1), \ldots, Y(i-1))$, as shown above.

There are two important differences between the general block cipher and the general stream cipher.

1. In the general block cipher, an intersymbol dependence can exist for all blocks. In the general stream cipher, an intersymbol dependence can only exist for all but the last block.
2. The initializing vectors used with the general block cipher need not be frequently changed. They could, for example, be held constant for the duration of a terminal-to-computer communication session lasting the entire day. Hence, the block cipher reoriginates during that session. Since stream ciphers must not reoriginate,the initializing vectors used with the general stream cipher can only be used once.

Instead of frequent generation and transmission of initializing vectors within a communication system, the initializing vectors, or their equivalent condition, could be stored within each system node. Recall that in the key autokey cipher (Figure 2-12), the vectors U(1), U(2), . . . , U(t) represent states that could be used for the purpose of initialization. This is true of stream ciphers in general. The initializing vector Z determines the initial state of the system ($Z \equiv U(1)$). Once the initial state of the system has been set, only the current state of the system need be remembered to maintain synchronization. For example, suppose at the beginning of a session, node A sends vector Z to node B. Transmission of message X from node A to node B leaves both node A and node B in the same state, say U(i). Hence at this point either node A or node B can continue to transmit using U(i) as the initialization vector. A new Z is not required. Although this method works very well in a system with two communication nodes, it becomes extremely complex when several nodes are involved. In practice, this is avoided by generating a new initializing vector each time a cryptographic device changes from a decryption mode into an encryption mode.

A block cipher has the problem of coping with a short block. A record whose length is less than the cipher's blocksize can be enciphered only after it has been padded with enough bits to make it a standard blocksize. However, the last short block within a record whose length is greater than the cipher's blocksize can be enciphered with no data expansion using a technique known as ciphertext-stealing mode.

With a stream cipher, there is no problem enciphering a short block since only as many bits from the cryptographic bit-stream are used as are

	General Block Cipher	General Stream Cipher
Encipherment	$Y(i) = H_i(K, X(0), \ldots, X(i))$	$Y(i) = X(i) \oplus H_i(K, X(0), \ldots, X(i-1))$
Decipherment	$X(i) = G_i(K, Y(0), \ldots, Y(i))$	$X(i) = Y(i) \oplus G_i(K, Y(0), \ldots, Y(i-1))$
	The jth bit of Y(i) depends	
Intersymbol Dependence Within Ciphertext	on every bit in X(1), X(2), ..., X(i)	only on the jth bit in X(i), but, on every bit in X(1), X(2), ..., X(i − 1)
	The jth bit of X(i) depends	
Intersymbol Dependence Within Recovered Plaintext	on every bit in Y(1), Y(2), ..., Y(i)	only on the jth bit in Y(i), but, on every bit in Y(1), Y(2), ..., Y(i − 1)

Table 2-5. Comparison between a General Block Cipher and a General Stream Cipher

	General Block Cipher	General Stream Cipher
Initializing Vector Z	Not mandatory, but highly desirable. If used, Z can be constant over a session. Z should be 64 bits for DES.	Required for all applications. In the practical case, Z must be frequently changed. To achieve maximum security, Z should contain 48 bits for the DES.
Number of bits which may be enciphered at a single time	Equal to the blocksize of the block cipher (64 bits for the DES). It is not possible to encipher short blocks in a secure way. A short block preceded by a complete block can be enciphered securely, but this will affect error propagation.	Any number from 1 to the maximum determined by design (64 if the DES is used).
Implementation Considerations	Straightforward when Z is not used. Slightly more complicated if Z is infrequently generated.	More complicated because of the frequent generation of Z.

Table 2-5 (cont'd). Comparison between a General Block Cipher and a General Stream Cipher

needed to encipher the plaintext. Hence as an alternative to enciphering short blocks using block cipher mode, these special cases could be handled using stream cipher mode.

When the length of a data record is less than the cipher's blocksize, enciphering the record causes data expansion—regardless of whether block cipher mode or stream cipher mode is used. In a block cipher, these extra bits are used for padding, while in a stream cipher they manifest themselves in the form of a required initializing vector.

With a stream cipher, an initializing vector of 48 bits is sufficient for most applications whenever DES is used. If a weaker system can be tolerated, a 40-bit initializing vector may be sufficient. With fewer than 40 bits, however, the system may be considerably weakened as far as the protection of the first part of the enciphered message is concerned, and an analysis should be performed to determine if this situation can be tolerated. (In applications where data travel over low-speed communication lines, it could very well happen that 16 bits are sufficient.)

Table 2-5 summarizes the similarities and differences between block ciphers and stream ciphers. Figure 2-41 illustrates the effect that a single bit change in ciphertext can have on recovered plaintext, when several different ciphering protocols are considered. Figure 2-42 illustrates the effect that a single bit change in the plaintext can have on the resulting ciphertext (during encipherment).

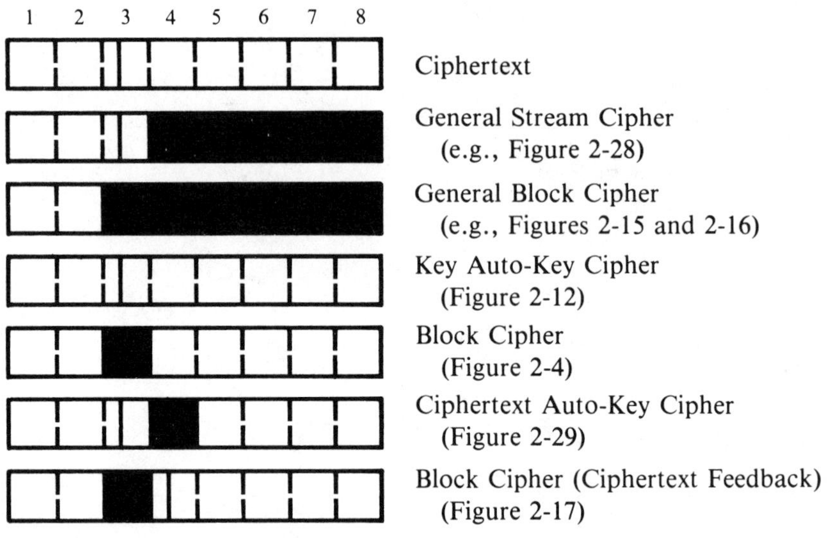

Figure 2-41. Effect on Recovered Plaintext for a One-Bit Ciphertext Change

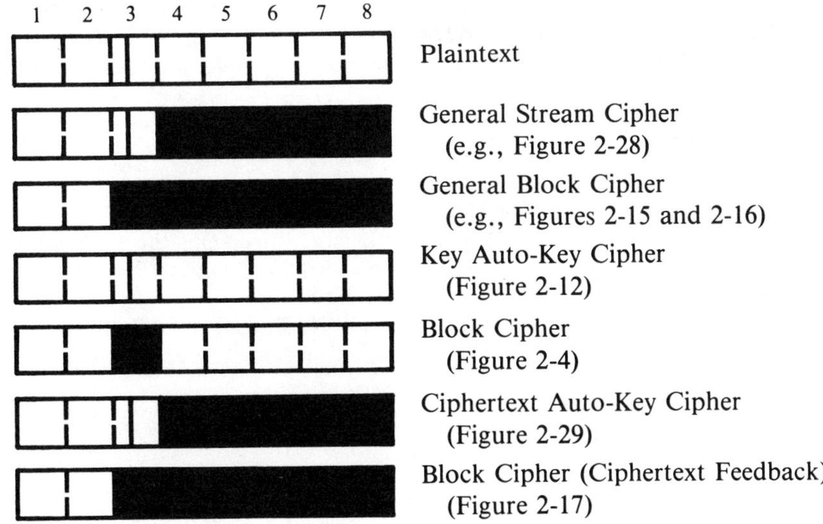

Figure 2-42. Effect on Produced Ciphertext for a One-Bit Plaintext Change

REFERENCES

1. Kahn, D., *The Codebreakers,* Macmillan, New York, 1972.
2. Shannon, C. E., "Communication Theory of Secrecy Systems," *Bell System Technical Journal,* **28**, 656–715 (1949).
3. Diffie, W., and Hellman, M., "New directions in cryptography," *IEEE Transactions on Information Theory,* **22**, 644–645 (November 1976).
4. Merkle, R., and Hellman, M., "Hiding Information and Receipts in Trap Door Knapsacks," *IEEE Transactions on Information Theory,* **24**, 525–530 (September 1978).
5. Rivest, R. L., Shamir, A., and Adleman, L., "A Method for Obtaining Digital Signatures and Public-Key Cryptosystems," *Communications of the ACM,* **21**, No. 2, 120–126 (1978).
6. McEliece, R. J., "A Public-Key Cryptosystem Based on Algebraic Coding Theory," Jet Propulsion Laboratory, California Institute of Technology, Pasadena, CA, *DSN Progress Report, 42–44,* 114–116 (January-February 1978).
7. Ore, O., *Number Theory and its History*, McGraw-Hill, New York, 1948.
8. Solovay, R., and Strassen, V., "A Fast Monte-Carlo test for primality, *SIAM Journal on Computing,* **6**, 84–85 (March 1977).
9. Miller, G. L., "Reimann's hypothesis and tests for primality," *Proceedings Seventh Annual ACM Symposium on the Theory of Computing,* Albuquerque, New Mexico, 234–239, May 1975. Extended version available as Research Report CS-75-27, Department of Computer Science, University of Waterloo, Waterloo, Ontario, Canada (October 1975).
10. Rabin, M. O., "Probabilistic algorithms," In J. F. Traub, Ed., *Algorithms and Complexity,* Academic Press, New York, 21–40 (1976).

11. Pollard, J. M., "Theorems on factorization and primality testing," *Cambridge Philosophical Society Proceedings,* **76**, 521–528 (1974).
12. Niven, I., and Zuckerman, H. S., *An Introduction to the Theory of Numbers,* Wiley, New York, 1972.
13. Simmons, G. J., and Norris, J. N., "Preliminary comments on the M.I.T. public-key cryptosystem," *Cryptologia,* **1**, No. 4, 406–414 (1977).
14. Rivest, R. L., "Remarks on a proposed cryptanalytic attack on the M.I.T. Public-Key Cryptosystem," *Cryptologia,* **2**, No. 1, 62–65 (1978).
15. Williams, H. C., and Schmid, B., "Some Remarks Concerning the M.I.T. Public-Key Cryptosystem," *Science Report No. 91,* Department of Computer Science, University of Manitoba, Winnipeg, Manitoba, Canada (1979).
16. Davies, D. W., Price, W. L., and Parkin, G. I., "An Evaluation of Public-Key Cryptosystems," *NPL Report CTU 1,* National Physical Laboratory, Teddington, Middlesex TW11 OLW, UK (1979).
17. Herlestam, T., "Critical Remarks on Some Public-Key Cryptosystems," *BIT,* **18**, 493–496 (1978).
18. Rivest, R. L., "Critical Remarks on 'Some Critical Remarks on Public-Key Cryptosystems' by Tore Herlestam," *BIT,* **19**, 1–3 (1978).
19. Blakley, B., and Blakley, G. R., "Security of Number Theoretic Public Key Cryptosystems Against Random Attack, I," *Cryptologia,* **2**, No. 4, 305–321 (1978).
20. Blakely, B., and Blakley, G. R., "Security of Number Theoretic Public Key Cryptosystems Against Random Attack, II," *Cryptologia,* **3**, No. 1, 29–42 (1979).
21. Blakley, B., and Blakley, G. R., "Security of Number Theoretic Public Key Cryptosystems Against Random Attack, III," *Cryptologia,* **3**, No. 2, 105–118 (1979).
22. Shamir, A., "A Polynomial Time Algorithm for Breaking Merkle-Hellman Cryptosystems," (extended abstract) Applied Mathematics, The Weizmann Institute, Rehovot, Israel (April 1982).
23. Vernam, G. S., "Cipher Printing Telegraphy Systems for Secret Wire and Radio Telegraphic Communications," *Journal of the AIEE,* **45**, 109–115 (February 1926).
24. Matyas, S. M., Meyer, C. H., and Tuckerman, L. B., "Method and Apparatus for Enciphering Blocks Which Succeed Short Blocks in a Key-Controlled Block-Cipher Cryptographic System," U.S. Patent No. 4,229,818 (October 21, 1980).
25. Konheim, A. G., Mack, M. H., McNeill, R. K., Tuckerman, B., and Waldbaum, G., "The IPS Cryptographic Programs," *IBM Systems Journal,* **19**, No. 2, 253–283 (1980).
26. Proposed Federal Standard 1026, *Telecommunications: Interoperability and Security Requirements for Use of the Data Encryption Standard in the Physical and Data Link Layers of Data Communications,* General Services Administration, Washington, D.C., Draft (January 21, 1982).

Other Publications of Interest

27. Ryska, N. and Herda, S., *Kryptographische Verfahren in der Datenverarbeitung,* Springer Verlag, Berlin, also New York, 1980.
28. Denning, D. E., *Cryptography and Data Security,* Addison-Wesley, Reading, 1982.

CHAPTER THREE

The Data Encryption Standard

Generally, all ciphers are substitution ciphers since in a cipher a set of plaintext messages is always uniquely transformed into a set of ciphertext messages for a given key, and in effect this constitutes substitution of ciphertext for plaintext. However, three classes of ciphers are ordinarily distinguished: *transposition ciphers, substitution ciphers,* and a combination of both called *product ciphers.*

The chapter begins with a short discussion of these three classes of ciphers. Next, ciphers using a linear feedback approach are shown to be breakable by expressing the relationship between keys, ciphertext, and plaintext as a set of mathematical equations, and then using analytical techniques to solve them. Although the attacks are elementary in nature, they do provide good background information to discuss broad principles followed in cipher design.

A detailed discussion of the Data Encryption Standard (DES) is presented in the second half of the chapter, including the generation procedures for DES's internal keys. Also, there is a simple numerical example that allows the DES's operation to be followed using only paper and pencil. Finally, there is a demonstration, both mathematically and pictorially, of how complexity in the ciphering process builds up with the number of iterations—a process involving substitution and permutation.

CLASSES OF CIPHERS

Transposition ciphers, consisting of rearrangements of plaintext letters, were used by the Greeks as early as 400 B.C. They represent the oldest known method of encryption. To encipher messages, the ancient Greeks used a device called a scytale (Figure 3-1). It consisted of a long narrow strip of papyrus wrapped around a cylinder (the diameter determined the key), with the plaintext written horizontally (row-by-row). When the strip was unwound, the letters were rearranged to conceal the message. To read the message, the recipient merely rewrapped the strip around a cylinder whose diameter was the same as the original.

A substitution cipher replaces plaintext letters, without changing their sequence, with one or more letters, figures, or symbols. An example of an early substitution cipher is the Julius Caesar cipher illustrated in Figure 3-2.

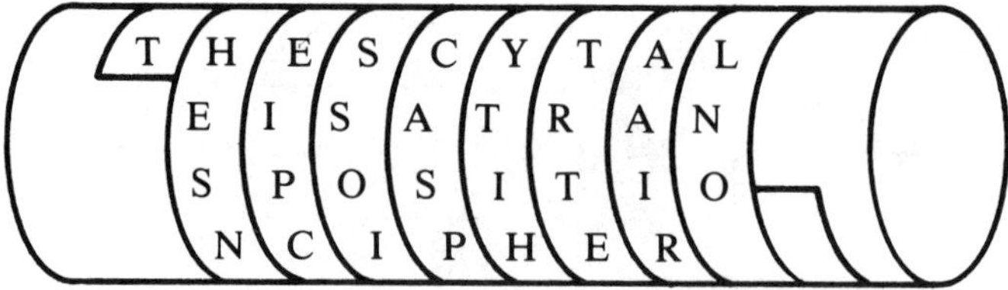

Plaintext: The Scytale is a transposition cipher.

Figure 3-1. The Scytale

For encipherment, each plaintext letter was replaced by the letter obtained when the alphabet was shifted three positions to the left (i.e., A would be replaced by D, B by E, and so forth). In decipherment, the process was simply reversed (i.e., D would be replaced by A, E by B, and so forth).

A product cipher involves the steps of both substitution and transposition. The ADFGVX product cipher illustrated in Figure 3-3 was used by the German Army during World War I. It employed a table having six rows and six columns labeled with the letters A, D, F, G, V, X. The table contained 26 letters (A, B, . . . , Z) and 10 digits (0, 1, . . . , 9) inserted in a random order. Encipherment was accomplished by replacing each plaintext letter with the pair of letters that described its position (row and column) within the ADFGVX table. This intermediate text was then written (row-by-row) into a transposition rectangle, and the columns read according to a numerical key. For example, the sorted alphabetical order for the key DEUTSCH became CDEHSTU, since letter C is ranked lowest or first in alphabetical sequence, letter D is ranked next, and so forth. Thus, to obtain the ciphertext, the column under C is read first, the column under D is read second, and so forth.

Decipherment is accomplished by writing the ciphertext back into the transposition rectangle (column-by-column) according to the same numerical key, reading the transposition rectangle (row-by-row) to obtain the intermediate text, and then finding each plaintext letter by using each pair of letters in the intermediate text as coordinates in the ADFGVX table.

Key:

Plaintext Letter:	ABCDEFGHIKLMNOPQRSTVXYZ
Ciphertext Letter:	DEFGHIKLMNOPQRSTVXYZABC

(In Latin the letters J, U, and W were not used.)

Message:	E	P	L	V	R	I	B	V	S	V	N	V	M
Cryptogram:	H	S	O	Z	V	M	E	Z	X	Z	Q	Z	P

Figure 3-2. Substitution Cipher Used by Julius Caesar

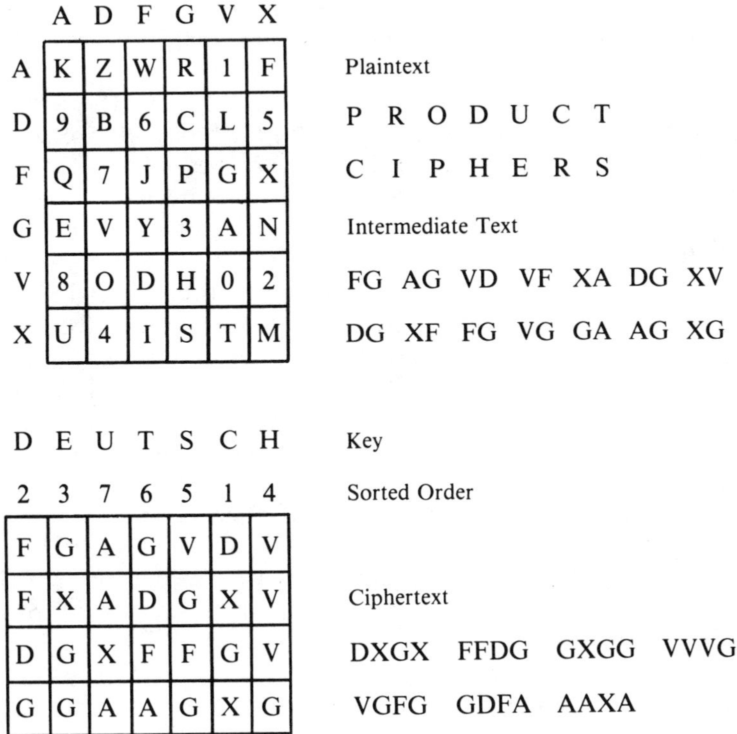

A D F G V X
A K Z W R 1 F
D 9 B 6 C L 5
F Q 7 J P G X
G E V Y 3 A N
V 8 O D H 0 2
X U 4 I S T M
Plaintext
P R O D U C T
C I P H E R S
Intermediate Text
FG AG VD VF XA DG XV
DG XF FG VG GA AG XG
D E U T S C H
Key
2 3 7 6 5 1 4
Sorted Order
F G A G V D V
F X A D G X V
D G X F F G V
G G A A G X G
Ciphertext
DXGX FFDG GXGG VVVG
VGFG GDFA AAXA

Figure 3-3. The ADFGVX Cipher—an Example of a Product Cipher

Cryptographic research conducted during World War II showed that strong encryption algorithms could be obtained using alternate steps of substitution and transposition, resulting in a product cipher. In his classic paper on secrecy systems, Shannon [1] pointed out that mixing functions–functions obtained as the product of two simple noncommutative operations–could be used to achieve cryptographic strength. Although based on the principle of mixing functions, the ADFGVX cipher is actually a weak algorithm, since substitution and transposition are used only once and the substitution is not under control of a key.

By the late 1960s, threats to computer data began to be viewed as real problems. The need for a strong method of encryption in the private sector was at last apparent. At the same time, large scale integration (LSI) technology permitted a highly complex cryptographic algorithm to be implemented on a single chip, thus achieving the high-speed encryption essential to data processing.

Research into the development of strong product ciphers was undertaken by private industry between 1968 and 1975. A block product cipher designed by Feistel [2] was implemented in a cryptographic system known as LUCIFER [3]. A new cryptographic algorithm based on the LUCIFER design was developed shortly thereafter at IBM under the leadership of Dr. W. L. Tuchman [4]. The new algorithm consisted of 16 alternate steps (or rounds) of key-controlled substitution and fixed permutation. This algorithm, approved by the NBS, was embodied in a federal standard that became effective on July 15, 1977.

Known as the Data Encryption Standard (DES) [5] the algorithm enciphers a 64-bit block of plaintext into a 64-bit block of ciphertext under the control of a 56-bit cryptographic key. The process of encryption consists of 16 separate rounds of encipherment, each round using a product cipher approach, or *cipher function*. The interaction of data, cryptographic key K, and cipher function g is illustrated in Figure 3-4. The externally supplied key K consists of 64-bits: 56 bits are used by the algorithm and eight bits may be used for parity checking. A different subset of 48 key bits from the 56-bit key is used in each round. The subsets of key bits used for encipherment are denoted K(1), K(2), . . . , K(16). During decipherment, the keys are used in reverse order (K(16) in round one, K(15) in round two, and so forth). The initial and inverse initial permutations allow the algorithm to be implemented more easily on a single chip, provided that the data and key are serially loaded.

DES can be thought of as a huge key-controlled substitution box (S-box) with a 64-bit input and output. With such an S-box, a total of $(2^{64})!$ different transformations or functions from plaintext to ciphertext are possible. The 56-bit key used with DES thus selects only a small subset (2^{56}) of the total set's possible functions.

A single huge S-box is impossible to construct. Therefore, DES is implemented by using several smaller S-boxes (6-bit input and 4-bit output) and permuting their concatenated outputs. By repeating the substitution and permutation process several times, cryptographic strength increases.

When referring to the cryptographic transformations of encipherment and decipherment, E denotes encipherment and D denotes decipherment. The notation used to express these operations is

$$E_K(X) = Y$$

which means that ciphertext Y is produced by the encipherment of plaintext X under key K, and

$$D_K(Y) = X$$

which means that plaintext X is produced by the decipherment of ciphertext Y under key K.

In DES, a cryptographic relationship exists among the plaintext, ciphertext, and cryptographic keys on the one hand and the complements of those quantities on the other hand. That relationship, called the *complementary property* of DES, can be expressed as

$$E_K(X) = \overline{E_{\overline{K}}(\overline{X})}$$

where the bars represent complementation, or bit inversion. (This property can be used advantageously for testing purposes, as demonstrated in Chapter 6.)

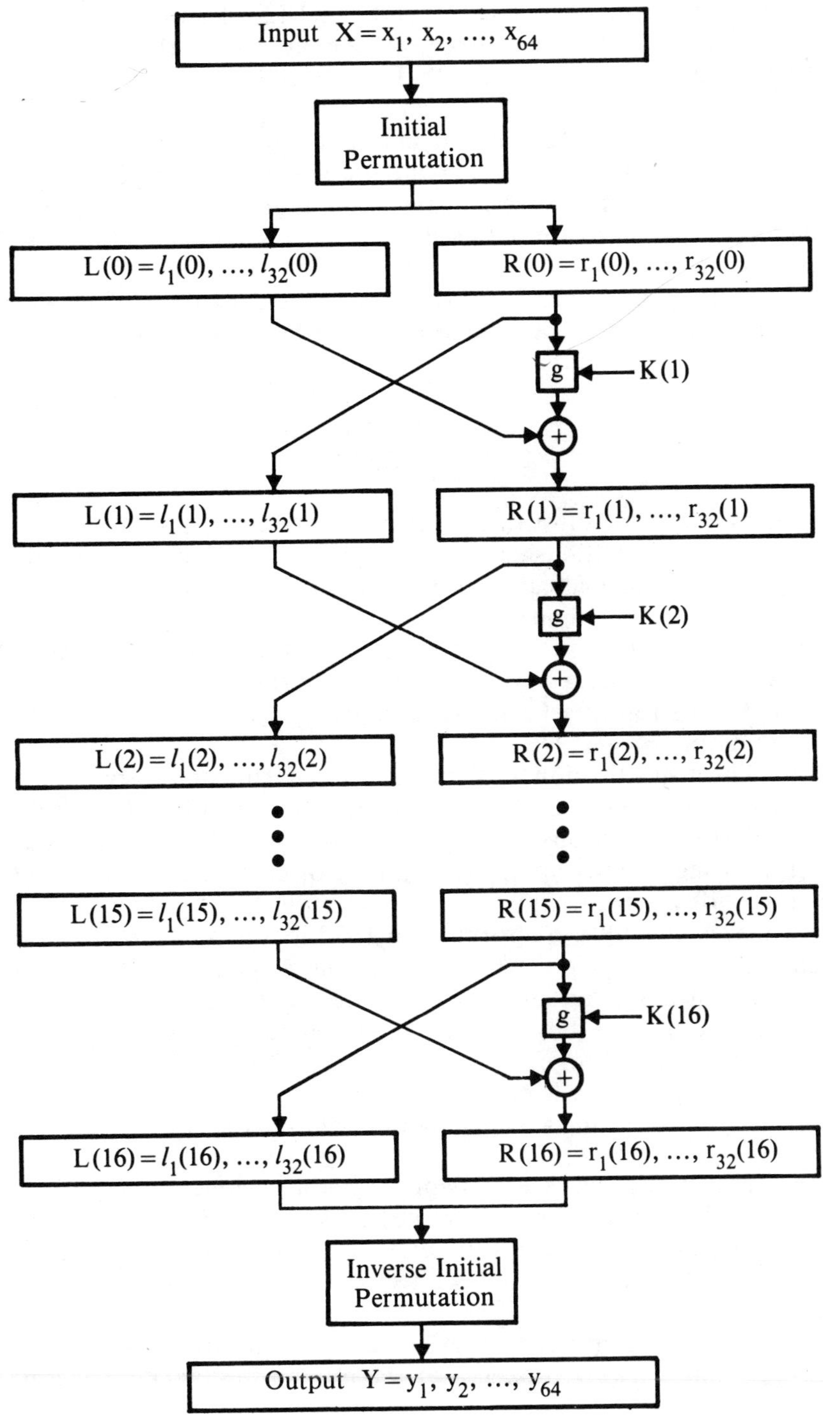

Figure 3-4. Enciphering Computation

Because of the complementary property of DES, if an analyst could obtain $E_K(X)$ and $E_K(\overline{X})$ for an arbitrary X, he could reduce the size of the key space he must search from 2^{56} to 2^{55}. Therefore, the key space could be exhausted in 2^{55} trials instead of 2^{56} trials. However, depending on the implementation, it may not be possible for an opponent to obtain plaintext X and its complement $\overline{X}$ enciphered under the unknown cipher key. Moreover, it has been suggested that in special cases, when more security is desired, multiple encryption methods can be used as a means of increasing the work factor associated with breaking the system (see also Appendix D). At this writing, the authors are unaware of any demonstrated method of using DES-ciphered data to solve for a single key bit, other than by key exhaustion (trying each possible key).

DESIGN CRITERIA

Generally, the steps of substitution and permutation in the DES algorithm have the following relationship to the algorithm's strength. Deterministic attacks (purely mathematical and nonstatistical in nature) are deterred mainly by the use of nonlinear functions in the substitution process. Statistical attacks are deterred mainly by the permutation of bits after each step of substitution (smoothing out the statistics). In the strict sense, both deterministic and statistical attacks are deterred by a combination of substitution and permutation.

Why nonlinear substitution functions are essential to strong product ciphers is illustrated by a cryptanalysis of three different encryption algorithms that make use of linear functions. Such an analysis is useful in arriving at design criteria for strong cryptographic algorithms. For example, a common pitfall in the design of a stream cipher is the assumption that a strong algorithm can be achieved merely by ensuring that the bit stream, which is added to the plaintext using modulo 2 addition, is a long sequence of pseudo-random bits (perhaps on the order of billions of bits). Even so, if there is a linear relationship among the bits in the pseudo-random bit stream, then the algorithm can easily be broken.

Breaking a System with Two Key-Tapes

In 1926, Vernam [6] suggested an approach for enciphering large amounts of plaintext using two relatively short key-tapes. His idea was to use the two original key-tapes to produce a very long bit stream. This key, or bit stream, could then be added to the plaintext, using modulo 2 addition, to produce the ciphertext.

However, Vernam's method of producing the bit stream from two key-tapes is weak and is easily broken. Let the bits on the two key-tapes be denoted by

$$U = u_1, u_2, \ldots, u_{p_1}, u_1, u_2, \ldots, u_{p_1}, \ldots$$

$$V = v_1, v_2, \ldots, v_{p_2}, v_1, v_2, \ldots, v_{p_2}, \ldots$$

The periods (intervals between equal recurring values) of U and V are p_1 and p_2, respectively. If p_1 and p_2 are chosen to be relatively prime, the bit stream resulting from the modulo 2 addition of U and V will have a period $p = p_1 p_2$. Let

$$R = r_1, r_2, \ldots, r_p, r_1, r_2, \ldots$$

denote the resulting bit stream. Assume that the number of enciphered plaintext bits is less than or equal to p, thus avoiding repetition of bits in the cryptographic bit-stream R. The operations of encipherment and decipherment are represented, as in the case of the key auto-key cipher (Chapter 2), by the following.

$$Y(i) = X(i) \oplus R(i)$$
$$X(i) = Y(i) \oplus R(i) \qquad (3\text{-}1)$$

where $\oplus$ represents modulo 2 addition, and

$X(i) = x_1(i), x_2(i), \ldots, x_n(i)$	denotes an n-bit plaintext
$Y(i) = y_1(i), y_2(i), \ldots, y_n(i)$	denotes the resulting n-bit ciphertext
$R(i) = r_1(i), r_2(i), \ldots, r_n(i)$	denotes the ith subset of bits from R that is used to encipher the ith block of plaintext.

At first glance, this scheme may appear to employ a one-time tape, thus satisfying the conditions for an unbreakable cipher. In an unbreakable cipher (see Chapter 2), the key (or the bit stream R in the present case) must be randomly selected and used only once. But the bits denoted by R in the present example are not random—at best, they are only pseudo-random. And because the bits in R can be represented by a set of linear equations, the scheme can be broken by solving for the unknown key tapes U and V. While p equations can be written to describe the bits in R, the analyst must cope with no more than $p_1 + p_2 - 1$ equations to break the system, as shown below.

Let the period of the first tape be 3 and the period of the second tape be 2, and let one bit be enciphered at a time. In that case, $R(i) = r(i)$, and hence

$$r(1) = u_1 \oplus v_1 \qquad (3\text{-}2a)$$
$$r(2) = u_2 \oplus v_2 \qquad (3\text{-}2b)$$
$$r(3) = u_3 \oplus v_1 \qquad (3\text{-}2c)$$
$$r(4) = u_1 \oplus v_2 \qquad (3\text{-}2d)$$
$$r(5) = u_2 \oplus v_1 \qquad (3\text{-}2e)$$
$$r(6) = u_3 \oplus v_2 \qquad (3\text{-}2f)$$

where it is assumed, without loss of generality, that r(1) coincides with the start of the tape. The period of R is $2 \cdot 3 = 6$.

If the opponent has a fragment of plaintext and corresponding ciphertext available for analysis (see Chapter 2), he can recover a fragment of the bit stream R by adding the plaintext to the ciphertext using modulo 2 addition. The problem then is to calculate the $p_1 + p_2$ bits comprising tapes U and V by knowing only a portion of the p_1p_2 bits from R.

Since $u_i \oplus v_j = \bar{u}_i \oplus \bar{v}_j$, it follows that the unknown key tapes U and V always have two solutions:

$$u_1, u_2, \ldots, u_{p_1}; v_1, v_2, \ldots, v_{p_2}$$

and

$$\bar{u}_1, \bar{u}_2, \ldots, \bar{u}_{p_1}; \bar{v}_1, \bar{v}_2, \ldots, \bar{v}_{p_2}$$

Thus a single bit in one of the two key-tapes can be assigned an arbitrary value (either 0 or 1). The remaining unknown bits in U and V are expressed in terms of a subset of the bits in R and the arbitrarily assigned bit in U or V. Let u_1 be the choice for the independent bit.

In the example ($p_1 = 3$, $p_2 = 2$), the dependent variables v_1, v_2, u_2, and u_3 can be represented as follows.

$$v_1 = r(1) \oplus u_1 \qquad \text{from 3-2a}$$

$$v_2 = r(4) \oplus u_1 \qquad \text{from 3-2d}$$

$$u_2 = r(2) \oplus v_2 = r(2) \oplus r(4) \oplus u_1 \qquad \text{from 3-2b}$$

$$u_3 = r(3) \oplus v_1 = r(3) \oplus r(1) \oplus u_1 \qquad \text{from 3-2c}$$

This shows that the arbitrary assignment of $u_1 = 0$ or $u_1 = 1$ and knowledge of four bits in R, namely r(1), r(2), r(3), and r(4), are enough to permit the unknown bits in U and V to be calculated. Thus to solve a pair of key-tapes, U and V, the analyst must have knowledge of as many bits in R as there are unknown bits in U and V. And the number of unknown bits in U and V is $p_1 + p_2 - 1$, since one bit can be arbitrarily assigned to either 0 or 1. U and V can then be used to calculate the remaining unknown bits in R.

With matrix notation, the set of linear equations (3-2a through 3-2f) is expressed as follows.

$$\begin{bmatrix} 1 & 0 & 0 & 1 & 0 \\ 0 & 1 & 0 & 0 & 1 \\ 0 & 0 & 1 & 1 & 0 \\ 1 & 0 & 0 & 0 & 1 \\ 0 & 1 & 0 & 1 & 0 \\ 0 & 0 & 1 & 0 & 1 \end{bmatrix} \begin{bmatrix} u_1 \\ u_2 \\ u_3 \\ v_1 \\ v_2 \end{bmatrix} = \begin{bmatrix} r(1) \\ r(2) \\ r(3) \\ r(4) \\ r(5) \\ r(6) \end{bmatrix} \qquad (3\text{-}3)$$

In the present example, the *rank* [7] of the (0, 1) matrix, as well as the augmented matrix [7], is four. Therefore, there are only four independent variables and only four bits in R are needed to solve for the unknown bits in U and V. In general, it can be shown that the rank of these matrices is equal to $p_1 + p_2 - 1$, which means that $p_1 + p_2 - 1$ bits in R are needed to solve for U and V.

Breaking a Key Auto-Key Cipher Using Linear Shift Registers

A linear shift register is a hardware circuit that can produce a stream of pseudo-random bits. It consists of a sequence of flip-flops[1] (Figure 3-5), denoted by $FF_1, FF_2, \ldots, FF_n$, and n initial switch settings which are the secret key, denoted by $k_1, k_2, \ldots, k_n$, where

$$k_j = 0 \quad \text{if the jth switch is open}$$

$$k_j = 1 \quad \text{if the jth switch is closed}$$

At each clock pulse of the circuit, a single bit in the pseudo-random bit stream is generated, so that r(1), r(2), . . . , r(t) denotes the bits produced by the linear shift register at clock times 1, 2, . . . , t. The mathematical equations defining the operation of a 3-stage shift register and used for calculating r(1) through r(t) are given below.

The operations of encipherment and decipherment are represented, as in the case of the key auto-key cipher (Chapter 2), by the following.

$$y(i) = x(i) \oplus r(i) \quad \text{encipherment}$$

$$x(i) = y(i) \oplus r(i) \quad \text{decipherment}$$

where x(i) and y(i) denote the ith plaintext and ciphertext bits, respectively. The output from the jth shift register stage (FF_j) at time t is denoted by $s_j(t)$. The initial conditions at clock time t = 1 are given by $z_j = s_j(1)$, for j from 1 to n.

It might seem that linear shift registers would give rise to strong cryptographic algorithms. A 61-stage linear shift register, for example, produces $2^{61} - 1$ different bit streams, whose period is $2^{61} - 1$ bits.[2] A communication terminal operating at a rate of 2400 bits per second would take over 30 million years to use up the entire bit system.

While the period is very long, the linear relationship among the generated bits represents a fundamental weakness. In an n-stage shift register, the bit stream is uniquely determined by the n initial conditions and n switch positions (see Figure 3-5). Thus to break the cipher, all that an opponent has to do is solve 2n independent equations involving the initial conditions and the

[1] A flip-flop is an electronic circuit having two stable states, 0 and 1, and the ability to change from one state to the other on application of a signal in a specified manner.

[2] The period of every bit stream is $2^{61} - 1$, because 61 is a Mersenne prime [8,9]. The maximum period of the bit stream is $2^n - 1$ when n is not a Mersenne prime.

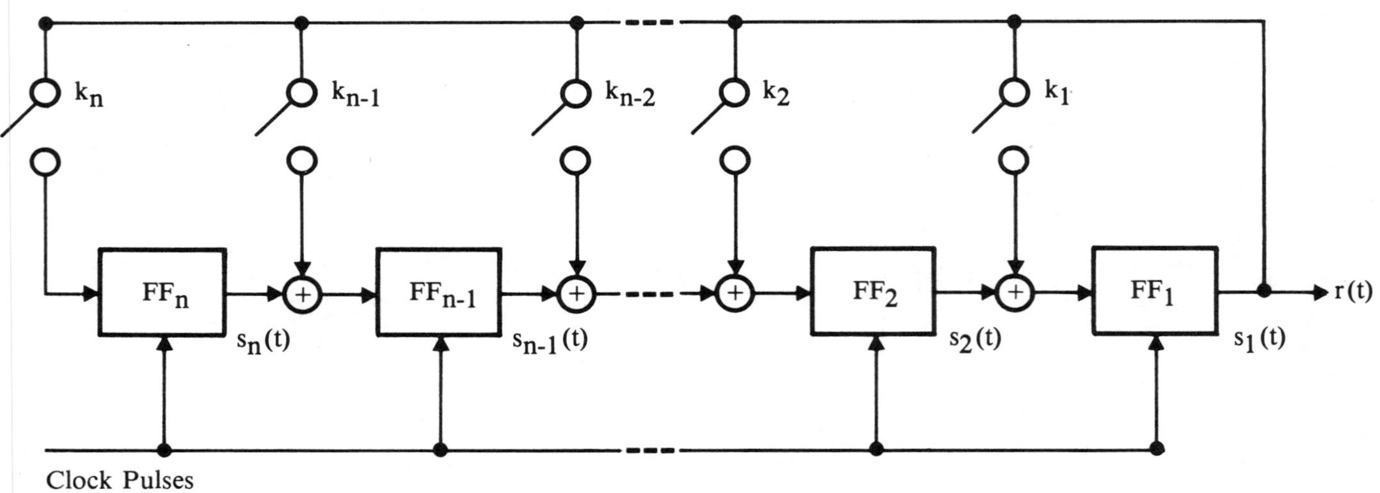

The initial conditions at clock time $t=1$ are represented by $z_j = s_j(1)$ for $j = 1, 2, \ldots, n$.

n = number of stages (flip-flops); $k_1, k_2, \ldots, k_n$ are switches where $k=0$ if the jth switch is open and $k=1$ if the jth switch is closed; $s_j(t)$ is the output from the jth flip-flop at time t.

Figure 3-5. Key Auto-Key Cipher Design Using an n-Stage Linear Shift Register

positions of the feedback switches. For all practical purposes, this could be accomplished here if 122 bits of plaintext and corresponding ciphertext were available for analysis.

To appreciate how the cipher under discussion is implemented, consider a 3-stage shift register (Figure 3-6). An analysis of the operation of the shift register at clock times t = 1, 2, . . . , 6 is given in Table 3-1. Since $s_1(t) = r(t)$, it follows that

$$\begin{aligned}
r(1) &= z_1\\
r(2) &= z_2 \oplus k_1 r(1)\\
r(3) &= z_3 \oplus k_2 r(1) \oplus k_1 r(2)\\
r(4) &= k_3 r(1) \oplus k_2 r(2) \oplus k_1 r(3)\\
r(5) &= k_3 r(2) \oplus k_2 r(3) \oplus k_1 r(4)\\
r(6) &= k_3 r(3) \oplus k_2 r(4) \oplus k_1 r(5)
\end{aligned}$$

This can be expressed in matrix notation as

$$\begin{bmatrix} r(1)\\ r(2)\\ r(3)\\ r(4)\\ r(5)\\ r(6) \end{bmatrix} = \begin{bmatrix} 0 & 0 & 0 & 1 & 0 & 0\\ r(1) & 0 & 0 & 0 & 1 & 0\\ r(2) & r(1) & 0 & 0 & 0 & 1\\ r(3) & r(2) & r(1) & 0 & 0 & 0\\ r(4) & r(3) & r(2) & 0 & 0 & 0\\ r(5) & r(4) & r(3) & 0 & 0 & 0 \end{bmatrix} \begin{bmatrix} k_1\\ k_2\\ k_3\\ z_1\\ z_2\\ z_3 \end{bmatrix} \qquad (3\text{-}4)$$

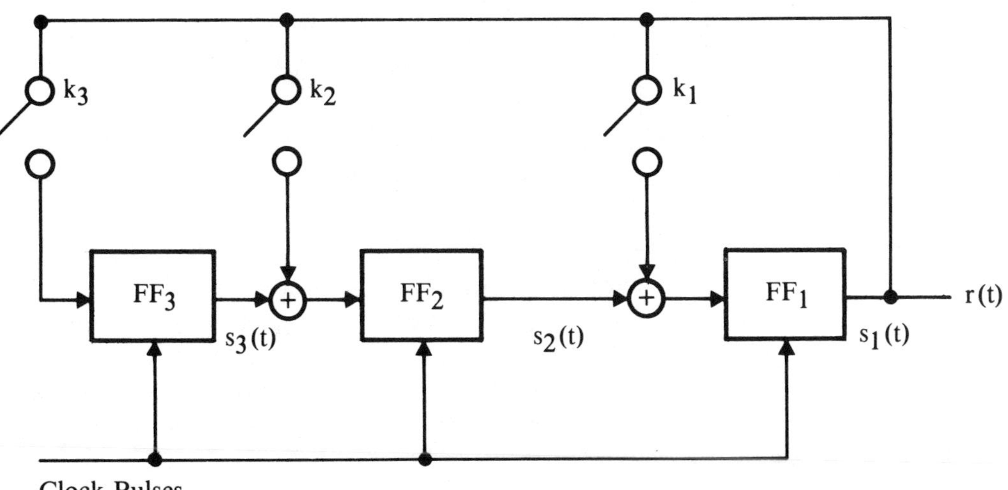

For t = 1, the initial conditions hold: $z_1 = s_1(1)$, $z_2 = s_2(1)$, $z_3 = s_3(1)$

Figure 3-6. Key Auto-Key Cipher Design Using a 3-Stage Linear Shift Register

t	$s_3(t)$	$s_3(t) \oplus k_2 r(t)$	$s_2(t)$
1	z_3	$z_3 \oplus k_2 r(1)$	z_2
2	$k_3 r(1)$	$k_3 r(1) \oplus k_2 r(2)$	$z_3 \oplus k_2 r(1)$
3	$k_3 r(2)$	$k_3 r(2) \oplus k_2 r(3)$	$k_3 r(1) \oplus k_2 r(2)$
4	$k_3 r(3)$	$k_3 r(3) \oplus k_2 r(4)$	$k_3 r(2) \oplus k_2 r(3)$
5	$k_3 r(4)$	$k_3 r(4) \oplus k_2 r(5)$	$k_3 r(3) \oplus k_2 r(4)$
6	$k_3 r(5)$	$k_3 r(5) \oplus k_2 r(6)$	$k_3 r(4) \oplus k_2 r(5)$

t	$s_2(t) \oplus k_1 r(t)$	$s_1(t)$
1	$z_2 \oplus k_1 r(1)$	z_1
2	$z_3 \oplus k_2 r(1) \oplus k_1 r(2)$	$z_2 \oplus k_1 r(1)$
3	$k_3 r(1) \oplus k_2 r(2) \oplus k_1 r(3)$	$z_3 \oplus k_2 r(1) \oplus k_1 r(2)$
4	$k_3 r(2) \oplus k_2 r(3) \oplus k_1 r(4)$	$k_3 r(1) \oplus k_2 r(2) \oplus k_1 r(3)$
5	$k_3 r(3) \oplus k_2 r(4) \oplus k_1 r(5)$	$k_3 r(2) \oplus k_2 r(3) \oplus k_1 r(4)$
6	$k_3 r(4) \oplus k_2 r(5) \oplus k_1 r(6)$	$k_3 r(3) \oplus k_2 r(4) \oplus k_1 r(5)$

Initial conditions: $z_1 = s_1(1)$, $z_2 = s_2(1)$, $z_3 = s_3(1)$

Table 3-1. Analysis of a Key Auto-Key Cipher that Uses a 3-Stage Linear Shift Register

While it is possible to solve the k_1, k_2, k_3, z_1, z_2, and z_3 in terms of bits r(1) through r(6) by using the matrices above, generally, one is not interested in the initial conditions z_1, z_2, and z_3. Thus, the key can be found using the reduced form:

$$\begin{bmatrix} r(4) \\ r(5) \\ r(6) \end{bmatrix} = \begin{bmatrix} r(3) & r(2) & r(1) \\ r(4) & r(3) & r(2) \\ r(5) & r(4) & r(3) \end{bmatrix} \begin{bmatrix} k_1 \\ k_2 \\ k_3 \end{bmatrix} \tag{3-5}$$

Although the approach seems straightforward, it should be noted that a solution may not exist for certain values of r(1) through r(6). Before elaborating on this idea, assume (without loss of generality) that $k_3 = 1$.

When $k_3 = 1$, only r(1) through r(5) must be known before one can solve for k_1 and k_2 (i.e., only five independent equations are needed). Hence Equation 3-5 can be reduced to the following:

$$\begin{bmatrix} r(4) \oplus r(1) \\ r(5) \oplus r(2) \end{bmatrix} = \begin{bmatrix} r(3) & r(2) \\ r(4) & r(3) \end{bmatrix} \begin{bmatrix} k_1 \\ k_2 \end{bmatrix} \tag{3-6}$$

Solving for k_1 and k_2 using Cramer's Rule, one obtains

$$k_1 = \frac{\begin{vmatrix} r(4) \oplus r(1) & r(2) \\ r(5) \oplus r(2) & r(3) \end{vmatrix}}{\begin{vmatrix} r(3) & r(2) \\ r(4) & r(3) \end{vmatrix}} = \frac{r(2)[r(5) \oplus r(2)] \oplus r(3)[r(4) \oplus r(1)]}{r(2)r(4) \oplus r(3)}$$

$$k_2 = \frac{\begin{vmatrix} r(3) & r(4) \oplus r(1) \\ r(4) & r(5) \oplus r(2) \end{vmatrix}}{\begin{vmatrix} r(3) & r(2) \\ r(4) & r(3) \end{vmatrix}} = \frac{r(3)[r(5) \oplus r(2)] \oplus r(4)[r(4) \oplus r(1)]}{r(2)r(4) \oplus r(3)}$$

provided that $r(2)r(4) \oplus r(3) \neq 0$. The denominator of the two expressions above is zero if either

1. $r(3) = 0$ and $r(2)r(4) = 00, 01$, or 10
2. $r(3) = 1$ and $r(2)r(4) = 11$

However, even in the situation where $r(2)r(3)r(4) = 001$ or 100, a solution can still be found. When $r(2)r(3)r(4) = 001$, Equation 3-6 is written as

$$\begin{bmatrix} 1 \oplus r(1) \\ r(5) \end{bmatrix} = \begin{bmatrix} 0 & 0 \\ 1 & 0 \end{bmatrix} \begin{bmatrix} k_1 \\ k_2 \end{bmatrix}$$

which results in

$k_1 = r(5)$ and $k_2 =$ any value (i.e., k_2 has no unique solution, denoted no solution)

When $r(2)r(3)r(4) = 100$, Equation 3-6 is written as

$$\begin{bmatrix} r(1) \\ 1 \oplus r(5) \end{bmatrix} = \begin{bmatrix} 0 & 1 \\ 0 & 0 \end{bmatrix} \begin{bmatrix} k_1 \\ k_2 \end{bmatrix}$$

which results in

$k_1 =$ any value and $k_2 = r(1)$

A summary of these results is given in Table 3-2.

Table 3-3 shows the bit streams produced by the 3-stage linear shift register (calculated in terms of the initial conditions, z_1, z_2, and z_3, by using Equation 3-4), where $k_3 = 1$ and k_1 and k_2 are variables. The maximum period of $2^3 - 1 = 7$ is obtained for keys (switch positions) 101 and 110, while keys 111 and 100 result in bit streams with periods of 4 and 3, respectively.

	r(2) r(3) r(4)	r(2) r(3) r(4)
	010 011 101 110	000 001 100 111
	$D = r(2)r(4) \oplus r(3) \neq 0$	$D = r(2)r(4) \oplus r(3) = 0$
Expression For k_1	$(1/D)[r(2)[r(5) \oplus r(2)] \oplus r(3)[r(4) \oplus r(1)]]$	* r(5) * *
Expression For k_2	$(1/D)[r(3)[r(5) \oplus r(2)] \oplus r(4)[r(4) \oplus r(1)]]$	* * r(1) *

Note: It was assumed that $k_3 = 1$; * denotes no solution

Table 3-2. Solutions for the Key in a Key Auto-Key Cipher Using a 3-Stage Linear Shift Register

Numerical values for the output bits r(1) through r(5) in Table 3-3 can be calculated by assigning z_1, z_2, and z_3 each of their possible values of 0 and 1. The results of such a calculation, where the five output bits are expressed in decimal notation for ease of presentation, are shown in Table 3-4. Out of the 32 possible values for bits r(1) through r(5), the values 1, 2, 3, 8, 15, 16, 17, 24, and 30 do not occur. The values 0, 9, 14, 18, 25, and 31 occur respectively, 4, 2, 2, 2, 2, and 2 times. As the number of stages is increased, the frequency of each value, r(1) through r(5), will be about the same, and hence the distribution will become more uniform.

r(t)	Switch Position Combinations: k_3, k_2, k_1			
	100	101	110	111
r(1)	z_1	z_1	z_1	z_1
r(2)	z_2	$z_1 \oplus z_2$	z_2	$z_1 \oplus z_2$
r(3)	z_3	$z_1 \oplus z_2 \oplus z_3$	$z_1 \oplus z_3$	$z_2 \oplus z_3$
r(4)		$z_2 \oplus z_3$	$z_1 \oplus z_2$	z_3
r(5)		$z_1 \oplus z_3$	$z_1 \oplus z_2 \oplus z_3$	
r(6)		z_2	$z_2 \oplus z_3$	
r(7)		z_3	z_3	

It is assumed that $k_3 = 1$; the periods for the bit streams produced by the keys 100, 101, 110, and 111 are 3, 7, 7, and 4, respectively.

Table 3-3. Pseudo-Random Bit Streams Produced by a 3-Stage Linear Shift Register for Different Switch Positions (Keys)

Initial Conditions	Feedback Switch Position (k_1, k_2)			
	00	01	10	11
z_1 z_2 z_3	Output r(1) through r(5) for given values of k's and z's			
0 0 0	0	0	0	0
0 0 1	4	5	7	6
0 1 0	9	11	14	12
0 1 1	13	14	9	10
1 0 0	18	23	29	25
1 0 1	22	18	26	31
1 1 0	27	28	19	21
1 1 1	31	25	20	19

Note: the value of r(1), r(2), ..., r(5) for $z_1z_2z_3 = 100$ and $k_1k_2 = 01$ is 010111 in base 2 and 23 in base 10

Table 3-4. Output from the First Stage of a 3-Stage Linear Shift Register

The mathematical equations for k_1 and k_2 given in Table 3-2 are next evaluated for each of the output values, r(1) through r(5), given in Table 3-4. From this, one gets a rough idea of the number of times that these equations either have a solution (identified by 0 or 1), or have no solution (identified by an *), as shown in Table 3-5. Since the row and column headings in Table 3-5 were chosen to match those in Table 3-4, one can estimate the probability of successfully solving for the key.

Consider the output value (r(1)r(2) · · · r(5) = 00100 (equivalent to decimal 4), which is produced by feedback switch positions k_1k_2 = 00 and initial conditions $z_1z_2z_3$ = 001 (see Table 3-4). Using only the output value 00100 and the equations in Table 3-2, it follows that

$$D = (0 \cdot 0) \oplus 1 = 1$$

and therefore that a unique solution for k_1 and k_2 can be obtained as

$$k_1 = (1/1)[0(0 \oplus 0) \oplus 1(0 \oplus 0)] = 0$$

$$k_2 = (1/1)[1(0 \oplus 0) \oplus 0(0 \oplus 0)] = 0$$

Hence the entry in Table 3-5 corresponding to column 00 (k_1k_2 = 00) and row 001 ($z_1z_2z_3$ = 001) is 00. Now consider the output value r(1)r(2) · · · r(5) = 10011 (equivalent to decimal 19), which is produced by feedback switch positions k_1k_2 = 10 and initial conditions $z_1z_2z_3$ = 110, or by k_1k_2 = 11 and $z_1z_2z_3$ = 111 (see Table 3-4). The output value 10011 and the equations in Table 3-2 lead to

$$D = (0 \cdot 1) \oplus 0 = 0$$

and therefore the equations for k_1 and k_2, as given by

$$k_1 = (1/0)[0(1 \oplus 0) \oplus 0(1 \oplus 1)] = 0/0$$

$$k_2 = (1/0)[0(1 \oplus 0) \oplus 1(1 \oplus 1)] = 0/0$$

are indeterminate forms. This condition can be resolved for k_1, since r(2)r(3) r(4) = 001 and thus k_1 = r(5) = 1 (see Table 3-2). However, there is no solution for k_2. Hence, the entries in Table 3-5 corresponding to column 10 and row 110, and column 11 and row 111, are labeled 1*.

By repetition of this approach for each entry in Table 3-4, a solution for k_1 is obtained in 22 out of 32 cases, for k_2 in 17 cases, and for both k_1 and k_2 in 14 cases (see Table 3-5). The probability of obtaining a solution is therefore about 0.5. The values of k_1k_2 that cause the output bits r(1)r(2) · · · r(5) to be equal to 00000 or 11111 (decimal 0 or 31) should not be used, since the plaintext and ciphertext are forced to be either identical or complements of each other. If those instances are excluded from Table 3-4, a solution for k_1 is obtained in 21 out of 26 cases, k_2 in 17 cases, and both k_1 and k_2 in 14 cases.

Initial Conditions for which r(1) through r(5) are Evaluated	Feedback Switch Positions (k_1, k_2) for which r(1) through r(5) are Evaluated							
	00		01		10		11	
	Evaluated Values of (k_1, k_2) Based on Knowledge of r(1) through r(5)							
z_1 z_2 z_3	k_1	k_2	k_1	k_2	k_1	k_2	k_1	k_2
0 0 0	*	*	*	*	*	*	*	*
0 0 1	0	0	0	1	1	0	1	1
0 1 0	*	0	0	1	*	*	1	1
0 1 1	0	0	*	*	*	0	1	1
1 0 0	0	*	0	1	1	0	1	1
1 0 1	0	*	0	*	1	0	1	*
1 1 0	0	*	0	*	1	*	1	1
1 1 1	*	*	*	1	1	0	1	*

P[solution for k_1] = 22/32; (21/26) (see footnote 3)
P[solution for k_2] = 17/32; (17/26) (see footnote 3)
P[solution for k_1 and k_2] = 14/32; (14/26) (see footnote 3)

* denotes no solution

Table 3-5. Solution of Feedback Switch Positions for a 3-Stage Linear Shift Register

[3] Instances where r(1) · · · r(5) = 00000 or 11111 are excluded from the calculation.

The calculation of keys—based on knowledge of $r(1)r(2) \cdots r(2n)$, where n is the number of stages—is successful in about 50 percent of the cases. The likelihood that a key can be solved for is increased if the number of bits available for analysis is greater than 2n. For example, if 2n + 9 bits are available, and consecutive bit streams of 2n bits are used, then 10 sets of 2n output bits would be available for analysis. Now, for each set of 2n output bits, assume that the probability of obtaining no solution for the key is 0.5—an assumption that is reasonable for the previous example. Thus the probability that no solution is obtained for all 10 sets of 2n output bits is $0.5^{10} = 1/1024$, and so the probability of a successful attack is 1023/1024.

When two or more linear shift registers are used one after another, the resulting algorithm still employs linear functions, and an identical method of analysis can be applied.

Breaking a Plaintext Auto-Key Cipher Using Linear Shift Registers[4]

The key auto-key cipher analyzed in the previous section does not employ feedback from either plaintext or ciphertext, but rather uses only internal feedback. To show that a similar analysis also applies to a cipher (based on linear shift registers) that uses an external feedback, a plaintext auto-key cipher is analyzed.

To reduce the number of required calculations, but still provide enough insight into the problem, the analysis is limited to a 5-stage linear shift register (n = 5), whose key is $k_1k_2 \cdots k_5 = 00101$. Enciphering and deciphering with the shift register is shown in Figures 3-7 and 3-8, respectively.

The shift-register circuits in Figures 3-7 and 3-8 can be represented analytically by the delay operator (D). If τ represents the delay of one shift register, then the transfer function of n shift register stages can be represented by $D^n\tau$. The input and output sequences are represented by $x(t - n\tau)$ and $y(t - n\tau)$, respectively.

All additions are done with Exclusive-ORs and therefore obey modulo 2 rules. All operations are linear. From Figure 3-7, it follows that

$$\begin{aligned} y(t) &= x(t)[(D^{2\tau} \oplus 1)D^{3\tau} \oplus 1] \\ &= x(t)(D^5 \oplus D^3 \oplus 1) \end{aligned} \qquad (3\text{-}7)$$

where the τ notation is dropped for purposes of convenience. Similarly, analysis of the circuit in Figure 3-8 shows that

$$\begin{aligned} w(t) &= [w(t)[(D^2 \oplus 1)D^2] \oplus y(t)]D \\ &= w(t)(D^5 \oplus D^3) \oplus y(t)D \end{aligned}$$

and so

$$y(t)D = w(t)(D^5 \oplus D^3 \oplus 1) \qquad (3\text{-}8)$$

[4]© 1972 Hayden Publishing Co. The text describing the method to be used is reprinted from *Electronic Design,* November 9, 1972 [10].

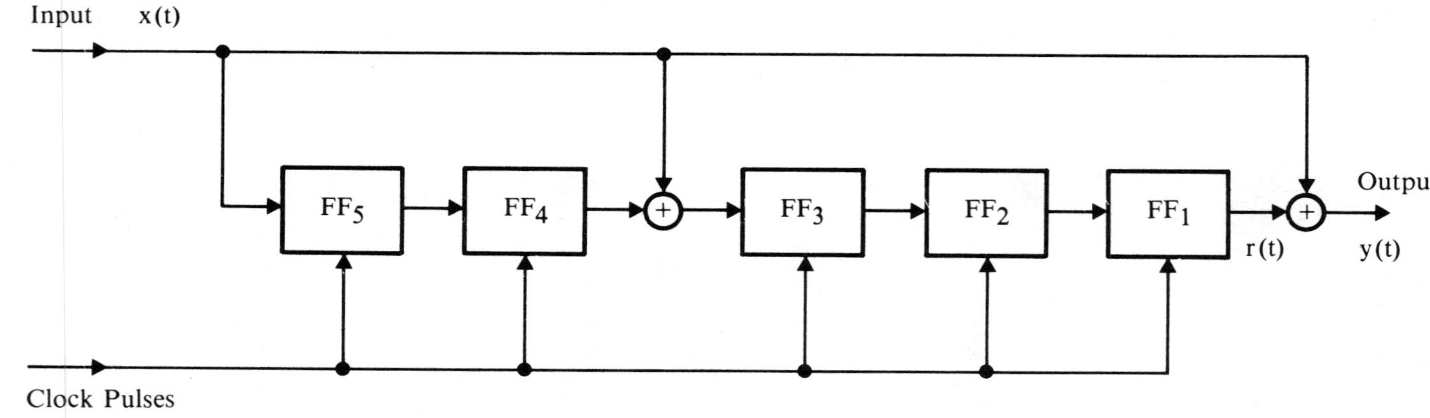

Figure 3-7. Plaintext Auto-Key Cipher Operating in Encipher Mode

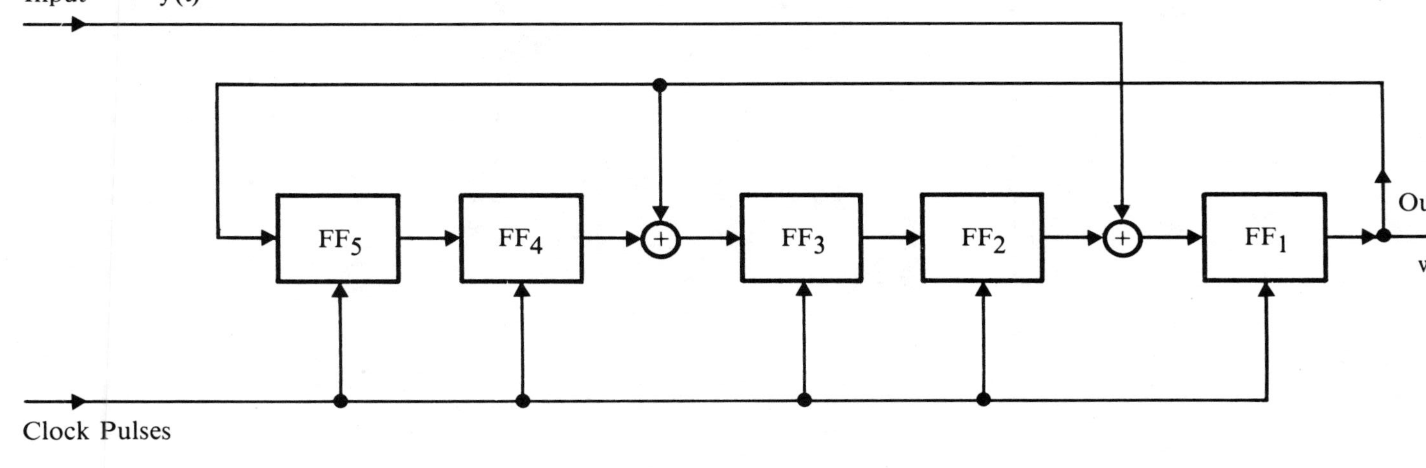

Figure 3-8. Plaintext Auto-Key Cipher Operating in Decipher Mode

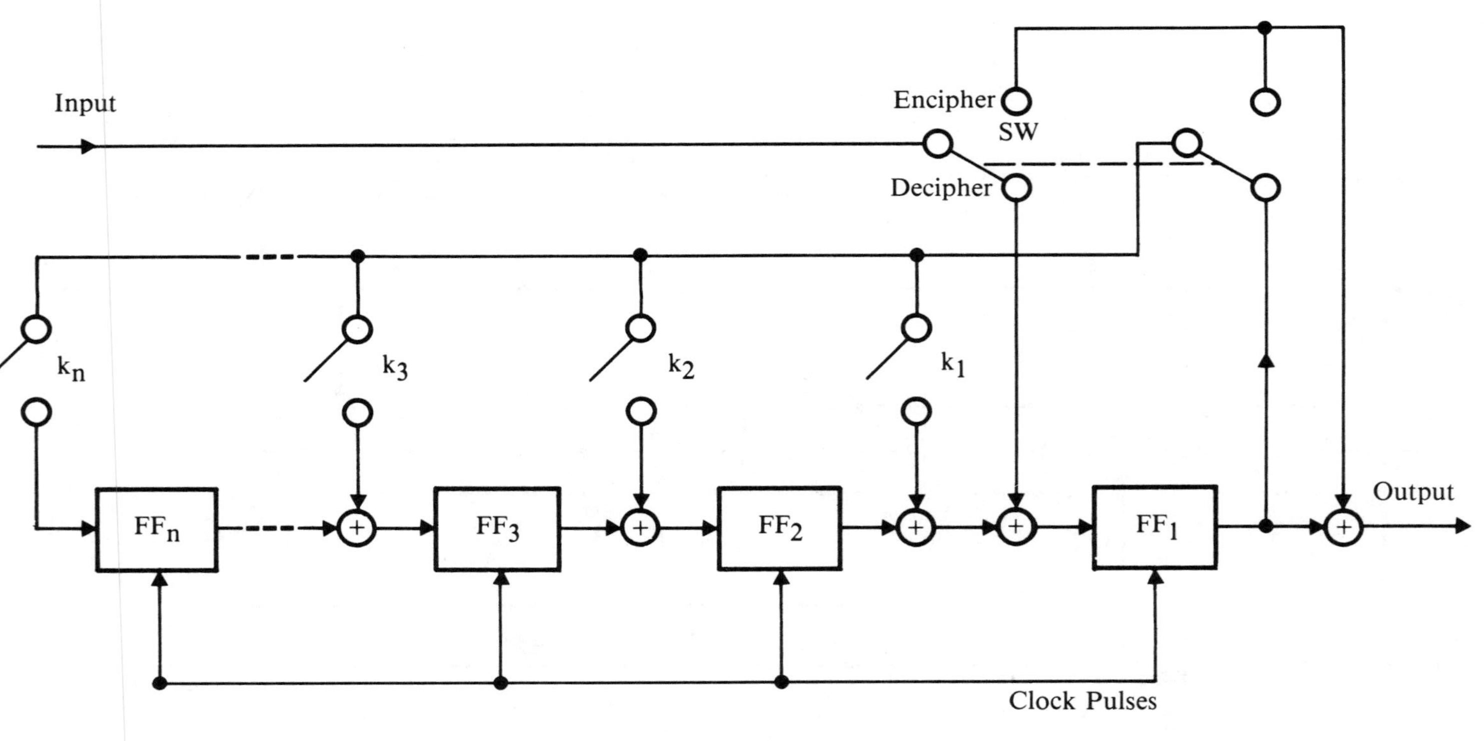

Switch SW is shown set in decipher mode.

Figure 3-9. Plaintext Auto-Key Cipher Using Linear Shift Registers

Multiplying Equation 3-7 by D results in

$$y(t)D = x(t)D(D^5 \oplus D^3 \oplus 1)$$

and so, from Equation 3-8 it follows that

$$w(t) = x(t)D$$

Thus the final output of the pair of cascaded circuits shown in Figures 3-7 and 3-8 equals the input delayed by 1 bit. The original input text x(t) is correctly recovered as w(t) delayed by 1 bit.

A generalized combined encipher/decipher circuit is shown in Figure 3-9. In general, the scheme with arbitrary feedback—with switches k_1 to k_n arbitrarily set (see Figure 3-9)—can be broken with any 2n bits of clear and corresponding ciphertext. Breaking the cipher involves determining the switch settings and the initial states of the flip-flop stages. Once these conditions are known, the complete text can be deciphered.

Consider the n-stage circuit in Figure 3-9. Assume that the plaintext data consisting of bits x(1), x(2), . . . , x(2n) and the corresponding ciphertext data y(1), y(2), . . . , y(2n) are known. The most important information—the cryptographic key—is represented by the states (open and closed) of the various switches $k_1, k_2, \ldots, k_n$.

An open switch at point i is specified by $k_i = 0$, whereas a closed switch at point i is specified by $k_i = 1$. The initial states of the shift register stages are designated by $z_1, z_2, \ldots, z_n$, where each z_i can assume the values of 1 or 0.

An analysis of the 5-stage linear shift register scheme indicates that the cipher can be represented by

$$x(1) \oplus y(1) = z_1$$

$$x(2) \oplus y(2) = k_1x(1) \oplus z_2$$

$$\vdots$$

$$x(6) \oplus y(6) = k_1x(5) \oplus k_2x(4) \oplus k_3x(3) \oplus \cdots \oplus k_5x(1)$$

$$\vdots$$

$$x(10) \oplus y(10) = k_1x(9) \oplus k_2x(8) \oplus k_3x(7) \oplus \cdots \oplus k_5x(5)$$

and is also represented in matrix form in Figure 3-10. All additions and multiplications are performed modulo 2.

Let the switch settings of $k_1, k_2, \ldots, k_5$ correspond to the configuration of Figure 3-7. Therefore, the ratio of y(t) to x(t) within the circuit, as previously derived in Equation 3-7, is

$$k_5 \oplus k_3 \oplus 1 = D^5 \oplus D^3 \oplus 1$$

For example, the input signal

$$x(1), x(2), \ldots, x(10) = 1011100001$$

is represented by delay operators as

$$(1 \oplus D^2 \oplus D^3 \oplus D^4 \oplus D^9)$$

Multiplying

$$(D^5 \oplus D^3 \oplus 1)(1 \oplus D^2 \oplus D^3 \oplus D^4 \oplus D^9)$$

and noting that in modulo 2 addition $D^n \oplus D^n = 0$ and ignoring values where $n > 10$ results in

$$\begin{aligned} y(1), y(2), \ldots, y(10) &= 1 \oplus D^2 \oplus D^4 \oplus D^6 \oplus D^8 \\ &= 1010101010 \end{aligned}$$

and

$$r(1), r(2), \ldots, r(10) = 0001001011$$

Although the 10 unknowns, k_1 through k_5 and z_1 through z_5, can be derived from the 10 equations represented by the matrix shown in Figure 3-10, to simplify the computation it is assumed that all register stages are initially reset ($z_1 = z_2 = \ldots = z_5 = 0$). In this case, only the entries in the lower left quarter of the matrix equation must be derived. This results in

$$\begin{bmatrix} x(6) \oplus y(6) \\ x(7) \oplus y(7) \\ x(8) \oplus y(8) \\ x(9) \oplus y(9) \\ x(10) \oplus y(10) \end{bmatrix} = \begin{bmatrix} x(5) & x(4) & x(3) & x(2) & x(1) \\ x(6) & x(5) & x(4) & x(3) & x(2) \\ x(7) & x(6) & x(5) & x(4) & x(3) \\ x(8) & x(7) & x(6) & x(5) & x(4) \\ x(9) & x(8) & x(7) & x(6) & x(5) \end{bmatrix} \begin{bmatrix} k_1 \\ k_2 \\ k_3 \\ k_4 \\ k_5 \end{bmatrix}$$

Substituting values for x and y, one obtains

$$\begin{bmatrix} 0 \\ 1 \\ 0 \\ 1 \\ 1 \end{bmatrix} = \begin{bmatrix} 1 & 1 & 1 & 0 & 1 \\ 0 & 1 & 1 & 1 & 0 \\ 0 & 0 & 1 & 1 & 1 \\ 0 & 0 & 0 & 1 & 1 \\ 0 & 0 & 0 & 0 & 1 \end{bmatrix} \begin{bmatrix} k_1 \\ k_2 \\ k_3 \\ k_4 \\ k_5 \end{bmatrix}$$

which results in

$$\begin{aligned} k_1 \oplus k_2 \oplus k_3 \oplus k_5 &= 0 \\ k_2 \oplus k_3 \oplus k_4 &= 1 \\ k_3 \oplus k_4 \oplus k_5 &= 0 \\ k_4 \oplus k_5 &= 1 \\ k_5 &= 1 \end{aligned}$$

$$
\begin{bmatrix} x(1)\oplus y(1) \\ x(2)\oplus y(2) \\ x(3)\oplus y(3) \\ x(4)\oplus y(4) \\ x(5)\oplus y(5) \\ \hline x(6)\oplus y(6) \\ x(7)\oplus y(7) \\ x(8)\oplus y(8) \\ x(9)\oplus y(9) \\ x(10)\oplus y(10) \end{bmatrix}
=
\left[\begin{array}{ccccc|ccccc}
0 & 0 & 0 & 0 & 0 & 1 & 0 & 0 & 0 & 0 \\
x(1) & 0 & 0 & 0 & 0 & 0 & 1 & 0 & 0 & 0 \\
x(2) & x(1) & 0 & 0 & 0 & 0 & 0 & 1 & 0 & 0 \\
x(3) & x(2) & x(1) & 0 & 0 & 0 & 0 & 0 & 1 & 0 \\
x(4) & x(3) & x(2) & x(1) & 0 & 0 & 0 & 0 & 0 & 1 \\
\hline
x(5) & x(4) & x(3) & x(2) & x(1) & 0 & 0 & 0 & 0 & 0 \\
x(6) & x(5) & x(4) & x(3) & x(2) & 0 & 0 & 0 & 0 & 0 \\
x(7) & x(6) & x(5) & x(4) & x(3) & 0 & 0 & 0 & 0 & 0 \\
x(8) & x(7) & x(6) & x(5) & x(4) & 0 & 0 & 0 & 0 & 0 \\
x(9) & x(8) & x(7) & x(6) & x(5) & 0 & 0 & 0 & 0 & 0
\end{array}\right]
\begin{bmatrix} k_1 \\ k_2 \\ k_3 \\ k_4 \\ k_5 \\ z_1 \\ z_2 \\ z_3 \\ z_4 \\ z_5 \end{bmatrix}
$$

By arranging the enciphering circuit's variables and constants in a matrix, the established rules of matrix maniputation can be used to crack the cipher with only (2n) bits of plaintext and corresponding ciphertext (n = flip-flop stages).

Figure 3-10. Matrix Representation of the Variables and Constants for a 5-Stage Linear Shift Register Enciphering Circuit Using Plaintext Feedback

Solving these five simultaneous equations yields

$$k_1 = 0$$
$$k_2 = 0$$
$$k_3 = 1$$
$$k_4 = 0$$
$$k_5 = 1$$

Instead of this procedure, a more elegant approach is to calculate the inverse of the 5 X 5 matrix:

$$\begin{bmatrix} k_1 \\ k_2 \\ k_3 \\ k_4 \\ k_5 \end{bmatrix} = \begin{bmatrix} 1 & 1 & 0 & 1 & 0 \\ 0 & 1 & 1 & 0 & 1 \\ 0 & 0 & 1 & 1 & 0 \\ 0 & 0 & 0 & 1 & 1 \\ 0 & 0 & 0 & 0 & 1 \end{bmatrix} \begin{bmatrix} 0 \\ 1 \\ 0 \\ 1 \\ 1 \end{bmatrix} = \begin{bmatrix} 0 \\ 0 \\ 1 \\ 0 \\ 1 \end{bmatrix}$$

In the previous section, it was noted that some randomly chosen sets of 2n bits of plaintext and corresponding ciphertext will not provide the information needed to solve the 2n unknowns. These same considerations apply to the present situation. Hence to increase the likelihood of a solution more than 2n bits are required (an additional 9 bits will suffice in most situations).

For those applications where an accomplice can be used to send a predetermined message, a shortcut for obtaining the key can be employed. First, enough zero bits are sent to reset all the shift register stages to zero. (This has been achieved when the ciphertext consists of all zeros.) Next, any convenient message (at least n + 1 bits long) starting with a 1 bit is sent. The key can then be determined by a simple tabular approach.

Since all initial conditions are represented by zeros, the following general relationship holds:

$$x(t) \oplus y(t) = \sum_{i=1}^{n} k_i x(t - i\tau)$$

Initially, it is assumed that all possible feedback paths are used. The input message X = 1011100001 is used as before and delayed step by step, one unit at a time, up to 5 units (see Table 3-6). (Note that Y = 1010101010.) Because all shift register stages are reset to 0, zeros can be inserted to fill out the locations in front of the delayed input message. Asterisks indicate the zeros that are appended to the front of the message (see Table 3-6).

Bits in position 2 show that there are zeros in the plaintext and ciphertext. Because $x(t - \tau)$ shows a 1 in bit position 2, it can be concluded that $x(t - \tau)$ cannot contribute to the output. Hence it follows that $k_1 = 0$.

Bit Position	1	2	3	4	5	6	7	8	9	10	Conclusion
Input X(t)	1	0	1	1	1	0	0	0	0	1	
$X(t-\tau)$	*	1	0	1	1	1	0	0	0	0	$k_1 = 0$
$X(t-2\tau)$	*	*	1	0	1	1	1	0	0	0	$k_2 = 0$
$X(t-3\tau)$	*	*	*	1	0	1	1	1	0	0	$k_3 = 1$
$X(t-4\tau)$	*	*	*	*	1	0	1	1	1	0	$k_4 = 0$
$X(t-5\tau)$	*	*	*	*	*	1	0	1	1	1	$k_5 = 1$
Output Y(t)	1	0	1	0	1	0	1	0	1	0	

Table 3-6. Chosen Plaintext Attack Against a Plaintext Auto-Key Cipher

In a similar manner, $x(t - 2\tau)$ and $x(t - 4\tau)$ cannot contribute. Therefore, $k_2 = k_4 = 0$. Finally, it can be concluded that $k_3 = k_5 = 1$, a result that agrees (again) with the actual switch positions. It should be observed that only $n + 1$ bits of plaintext and corresponding ciphertext were needed in this case to determine the key.

Designing a Cipher[5]

The methods for attacking a cryptographic algorithm fall into two categories: cryptanalysis and "brute force," or exhaustive, methods. Exhaustive methods can be further divided into two subcategories: key exhaustion and message exhaustion.

Exhaustive attacks are easily thwarted either by adjusting certain parameters in the algorithm, such as blocksize (if a block cipher is used) and key length, and/or by restricting the way a cryptographic procedure or system uses the algorithm, such as requiring the use of initializing vectors and chaining. The major challenge in algorithm design is to devise a procedure that can withstand determined efforts at cryptanalysis.

A successful method of cryptanalysis is often called a shortcut solution. A shortcut solution is defined here as a cryptanalytic break to distinguish it from an exhaustive break. In the former case the algorithm must be redesigned, whereas in the latter case the problem may be remedied by the way the algorithm is implemented (e.g., by using block chaining, multiple encryption, and the like).

[5]© 1978 IEEE. Reprinted from *Proceedings COMPCON 78* [11].

Shortcut Methods

Cryptanalytic or shortcut methods can be divided into two subcategories: deterministic or analytical methods, and statistical methods. In a deterministic approach, the cryptanalyst first attempts to express a desired unknown quantity (such as the key or message) in terms of some other known quantity or quantities (such as given ciphertext, or given plaintext and corresponding ciphertext) whose relationship to the unknown quantity depends on the nature of the algorithm. Then the cryptanalyst solves for the unknown quantity.

Let Y denote the ciphertext produced by enciphering plaintext X with cryptographic key K, and let f_K represent the function that relates X and Y:

$$Y = f_K(X)$$

In a deterministic attack against the key, the opponent tries to find a function F, where

$$K = F(X, Y)$$

such that F can be represented by an easily computed procedure.

In a poorly designed algorithm, it may be possible to solve for the key by decoupling F into a set of equations

$$\begin{aligned} k_1 &= F_1(Y, X) \\ k_2 &= F_2(Y, X, k_1) \\ &\vdots \\ k_n &= F_n(Y, X, k_1, \ldots, k_{n-1}) \end{aligned}$$

and then to solve for the key bits $k_1, k_2, \ldots, k_n$, one at a time. While analytical methods will generally succeed in breaking an algorithm that uses linear functions, this method of attack can be effectively thwarted if the algorithm makes use of nonlinear functions of sufficient complexity.

In a statistical approach, the cryptanalyst attempts to exploit statistical relationships between plaintext, ciphertext, and key. Consider a simple substitution cipher on English text. It can be shown (Chapter 12) that about 100,000 characters of ciphertext are required to deduce the key when only letter frequency statistics are used in the analysis. However, only about 300 characters of ciphertext are required to recover the key when digram statistics are used [12]. It can be shown that the theoretical limit is about 25 characters (Chapter 12).

To thwart statistical attacks, the algorithm's output (ciphertext) should be pseudo-random. In other words, for a large set of plaintext and key inputs, one must not be able, on the basis of statistical analysis, to reject the hypothesis that the output bit stream is random.

During the validation of DES, no shortcut solution could be found by its investigators, including the NSA [13]. This same conclusion was reaffirmed in September 1977 at a workshop conducted by the National Bureau of Standards, Institute for Computer Sciences and Technology (ICST), to investigate the complexity of the DES algorithm [14]. Though additional attempts to break DES have been made, the authors are unaware of any shortcut method that can solve for even a single bit in the key.

Brute Force Methods

In a brute force approach, one attempts to find a desired unknown quantity (such as the message or key) by using a method of direct search, trial and error, or exhaustion. In key exhaustion, a known plaintext is enciphered with a trial key and the output is compared for equality with a given ciphertext. (The attack assumes that the cryptographic algorithm is known to the opponent, and that plaintext and corresponding ciphertext are available for analysis.) If the comparison is favorable, then the trial key is a candidate for the unknown key. While in theory the correct key can always be found by repeated trials, in practice the attack is thwarted if the computational and data storage requirements are too great, or if the cost of the attack is too great.

In August 1976, ICST sponsored a workshop to determine the feasibility of building a machine that could recover a 56-bit DES key from a given fragment of plaintext and corresponding ciphertext [15]. The workshop participants were asked to design a hypothetical key-exhaustion machine using their own specialized knowledge and taking full advantage of anticipated technical advances. Factors to be considered were the architecture of such machines, types of circuitry, speed of operation, reliability and maintainability, size, power, and cooling requirements.

The members of the workshop, which included 20 representatives from industry, research organizations, universities, and government agencies, together with a number of ICST staff members, reached the following conclusion:

> A machine which finds, on the average, one key per day could probably not be built until 1990 and the probability factor of it being available even then is estimated to be between .1 and .2. In addition, the cost of such a machine would be several tens of millions of dollars.

While it is important to determine the work factor for key exhaustion, and therefore to establish how vulnerable the algorithm is to this method of attack, it is far more important to establish that the algorithm has no shortcut solution. When the algorithm has no shortcut solution, its *effective key length*, and hence the work factor to perform key exhaustion, is determined by the way the algorithm is implemented in a particular cryptographic procedure or system.

By using multiple encryption methods, DES's effective key length can be increased to any desired value [16]. And there are efficient ways to expand the key in a migratable way. This, in effect, allows strong DES-based cryptographic procedures and systems to be used for an indefinite period (as long as no shortcut solution is found).

Under the assumption that an opponent can exercise the cryptographic device containing an unknown key, it is possible in theory to build a dictionary of plaintext and corresponding ciphertext—by enciphering all possible plaintext combinations—that would then allow the opponent to recover messages without ever solving for or knowing the key. But in practice this form of message exhaustion is thwarted if the computational and data storage requirements to build and store the dictionary are too great.

To improve efficiency, exhaustive methods may use a combination of precomputed tables together with a method of direct search, although the construction of such tables may also take days, months, or even years.

Effective countermeasures to thwart exhaustive methods are obtained by

1. Making both the effective key length and blocksize (if a block cipher is used) large enough, and/or
2. "Whitening" the plaintext and/or ciphertext by adding pseudo-random "noise" to the message. In a block cipher, this can be achieved by the use of initializing vectors combined with block chaining techniques, whereas in a stream cipher, it is automatically achieved as a result of the required initializing vector (see Chapter 2).

For some applications, whitening may be necessary even if the algorithm's key length and blocksize are large. For example, if "buy" and "sell" are the only possible messages ever sent by the application, then a dictionary with only two entries would be enough to defeat the intended security, and therefore some type of whitening would be mandatory.

In summary, a well-designed cryptographic algorithm is one that will withstand all known shortcut and brute force methods of solution. But it should also be realized that if an algorithm has no shortcut solution, then it can always be implemented in such a way that the minimum work factor of all brute force attacks is larger than any desired value.

Classified Design Principles

History has shown that many supposedly strong ciphers were broken using cryptanalysis (e.g., the Japanese PURPLE cipher and the German Enigma cipher used during World War II). These ciphers were cracked despite the fact that the design principles and the methods of analysis to validate the algorithm's strength were not available to the cryptanalyst. In fact, it can be argued that a cryptanalyst would be better off unprejudiced by knowledge of the design principles and methods of analysis used to validate the algorithm's strength.

Some of the methods of analysis used by IBM to validate the DES, and all such methods used by NSA, have been classified by the U.S. government. Therefore, some critics of DES have inferred that one cannot be sure that statements by IBM and NSA about DES are as claimed. To answer this criticism, the Senate Committee on Intelligence conducted an investigation into the matter. The following summarizes the conclusions that were reached [13].

1. DES is more than adequate for its intended applications.
2. IBM invented and designed DES.
3. NSA did not tamper with the design.
4. NSA certified that the DES was free of any known statistical/mathematical weakness.
5. NSA recommended that the Federal Reserve Board use DES for electronic funds transfer applications.

DESCRIPTION OF THE DATA ENCRYPTION STANDARD

Although a complete description of the DES algorithm has been published [5], the reader may find that treatment difficult to follow. For this reason, a more detailed description of the algorithm is given here, providing the reader with a greater insight and understanding of DES's operation. A numerical example of a one-round encryption is also given. (Frequent references are made to the description of the DES, which is reprinted in its entirety, including original page numbers, in Appendix A.)

A block cipher design consisting of n rounds of encipherment/decipherment is described in Chapter 2. The steps performed at each round are summarized below.

1. The input block is split into two parts, a left half and a right half.
2. The right half (step 1) is then operated on using a cipher function g (see Figures 2-5 and 2-6).
3. This output (step 2) is combined (via an Exclusive-OR operation) with the left half (step 1).

The particular design has the property that the ciphering process can be reversed regardless of the nature of function g. This is accomplished merely by reversing the order in which the keys are exercised at each round in the ciphering process. For example, if during encipherment the keys are exercised in the order K(1) through K(n), then during decipherment they must be exercised in the order K(n) through K(1).

The block cipher design described above is also used in DES, where $n = 16$ and K(1) through K(16) are 48-bit keys. For reasons of security, all of these keys should be different. This is achieved by selecting, at each round, a different subset of 48 bits from the 56-bit key supplied to the algorithm. This procedure (key schedule calculation) is based on a simple shifting and bit-selection algorithm. Figure 3-11 illustrates the key schedule calculation used for encipherment. For decipherment, left shifts become right shifts, except for the shift performed between (C_0, D_0) and (C_1, D_1), which is not required. (See the discussion below.)

The key schedule calculation begins with an initial permutation defined by permuted choice 1, PC-1 (see page 16 of [5]). PC-1, which is the same for encipherment and decipherment, selects 56 of the 64 external key bits (in

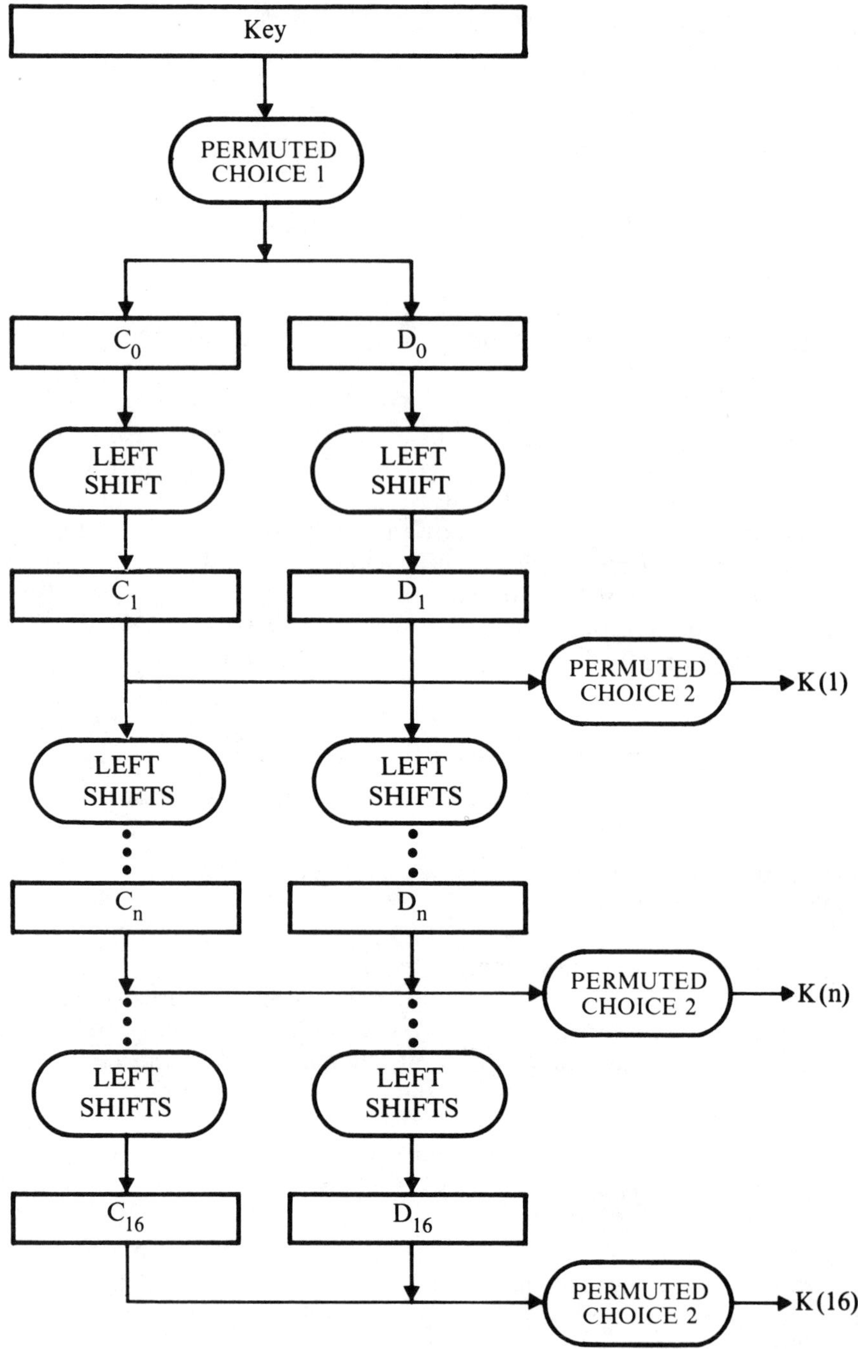

Figure 3-11. Key Schedule Calculation for Encipherment

Iteration Number i	Number of Left Shifts
1	1
2	1
3	2
4	2
5	2
6	2
7	2
8	2
9	1
10	2
11	2
12	2
13	2
14	2
15	2
16	1

Table 3-7. Shift Schedule for Encipherment

effect stripping off the parity bits) and loads them into two 28-bit shift registers (C and D). Thus parity checking of the external key must be performed prior to PC-1.

During an enciphering operation, the contents of registers C_{i-1} and D_{i-1} are shifted one or two positions to the left, according to the schedule of left shift operations (page 18 of [5]), as shown in Table 3-7. K(i) is then derived from (C_i, D_i) via a second permutation defined by permuted choice 2, PC-2 (page 18 of [5]). Moreover, the shift schedule is such that $C_{16} = C_0$ and $D_{16} = D_0$.

During a decipher operation, K(16) must be used in round one, K(15) in round two, and so forth. But the contents of registers C_0 and D_0 are the same for enciphering and deciphering, since the external key is loaded in both cases via PC-1. This means that K(16) can be created at round one merely by omitting the first shift operation, K(15) can be created at round two by shifting C_0 (C_{16}) and $D_0(D_{16})$ one bit to the right, and the remainder of the internal keys can be created in the same manner using the shift schedule in Table 3-7, except that left shifts are changed to right shifts.

Generation of Key Vectors Used for Each Round of DES

Let the externally entered key K (including parity bits stripped off before the key is used by DES) be defined as

$$K = k_1, k_2, \ldots, k_{64}$$

The permuted choice PC-1 (page 16 of [5]) determines how 56 of these initial 64 bits are loaded into two 28-bit registers, C_0 and D_0:

$$
\begin{aligned}
C_0 = {} & k_{57}, k_{49}, k_{41}, k_{33}, k_{25}, k_{17}, k_9, \\
& k_1, k_{58}, k_{50}, k_{42}, k_{34}, k_{26}, k_{18}, \\
& k_{10}, k_2, k_{59}, k_{51}, k_{43}, k_{35}, k_{27}, \\
& k_{19}, k_{11}, k_3, k_{60}, k_{52}, k_{44}, k_{36}, \\
D_0 = {} & k_{63}, k_{55}, k_{47}, k_{39}, k_{31}, k_{23}, k_{15}, \\
& k_7, k_{62}, k_{54}, k_{46}, k_{38}, k_{30}, k_{22}, \\
& k_{14}, k_6, k_{61}, k_{53}, k_{45}, k_{37}, k_{29}, \\
& k_{21}, k_{13}, k_5, k_{28}, k_{20}, k_{12}, k_4
\end{aligned}
$$

It can be seen that bits 57, 49, and 41 of K are the first, second, and third bits of register C_0, respectively, while bits 63, 55, and 47 of K are the first, second, and third bits of register D_0, respectively. It can also be observed that the 64 input bits have been reduced to 56 bits, because the parity bits k_8, k_{16}, k_{24}, k_{32}, k_{40}, k_{48}, k_{56}, and k_{64} have been systematically removed as part of the initial loading process.

The key vectors K(1), K(2), . . . , k(16), which consist of 48 key bits each, cannot be created until the vectors C_1 through C_{16} and D_1 through D_{16} (Figure 3-11), which consist of 28 key bits, have been formed. These vectors are derived by using the schedule given on page 18 of [5] and Table 3-7.

Let (C_i, D_i) denote the concatenation of registers C_i and D_i. In general, (C_{i+1}, D_{i+1}) is produced from (C_i, D_i) by shifting the bits in C_i and D_i, respectively, one or two positions to the left. The shifting employs wraparound (i.e., bits shifted off the left side of the register are reinserted at the right side of the register). The results are shown in Tables 3-8 and 3-9. As an example, it can be seen that $C_1, D_1)$ is derived from (C_0, D_0) by shifting the bits in C_0 and D_0 one position to the left.

Permuted choice 2 (PC-2) is the rule (page 18 of [5]) that defines how the 48-bit key vectors K(1), K(2), . . . , K(16) are derived from the vectors (C_1, D_1), (C_2, D_2), . . . , (C_{16}, D_{16}), respectively. The bit patterns stored in registers C_i and D_i are referred to here also as vectors C_i and D_i, respectively. Specifically, K(i) is derived from (C_i, D_i) by taking the key bits located in positions

$$
\begin{matrix}
14, 17, 11, 24, 1, 5, 3, 28, 15, 6, 21, 10 \\
23, 19, 12, 4, 26, 8, 16, 7, 27, 20, 13, 2
\end{matrix}
\qquad (3\text{-}9a)
$$

from vector C_i and concatenating them with the key bits located in positions

$$
\begin{matrix}
41, 52, 31, 37, 47, 55, 30, 40, 51, 45, 33, 48 \\
44, 49, 39, 56, 34, 53, 46, 42, 50, 36, 29, 32
\end{matrix}
\qquad (3\text{-}9b)
$$

from vector D_i.

Round (i)	Index of Elements in Vector C_i																												Round (1)
	1	2	3	4	5	6	7	8	9	10	11	12	13	14	15	16	17	18	19	20	21	22	23	24	25	26	27	28	
1	49	41	33	25	17	9	1	58	50	42	34	26	18	10	2	59	51	43	35	27	19	11	3	60	52	44	36	57	1
2	41	33	25	17	9	1	58	50	42	34	26	18	10	2	59	51	43	35	27	19	11	3	60	52	44	36	57	49	2
3	25	17	9	1	58	50	42	34	26	18	10	2	59	51	43	35	27	19	11	3	60	52	44	36	57	49	41	33	3
4	9	1	58	50	42	34	26	18	10	2	59	51	43	35	27	19	11	3	60	52	44	36	57	49	41	33	25	17	4
5	58	50	42	34	26	18	10	2	59	51	43	35	27	19	11	3	60	52	44	36	57	49	41	33	25	17	9	1	5
6	42	34	26	18	10	2	59	51	43	35	27	19	11	3	60	52	44	36	57	49	41	33	25	17	9	1	58	50	6
7	26	18	10	2	59	51	43	35	27	19	11	3	60	52	44	36	57	49	41	33	25	17	9	1	58	50	42	34	7
8	10	2	59	51	43	35	27	19	11	3	60	52	44	36	57	49	41	33	25	17	9	1	58	50	42	34	26	18	8
9	2	59	51	43	35	27	19	11	3	60	52	44	36	57	49	41	33	25	17	9	1	58	50	42	34	26	18	10	9
10	51	43	35	27	19	11	3	60	52	44	36	57	49	41	33	25	17	9	1	58	50	42	34	26	18	10	2	59	10
11	35	27	19	11	3	60	52	44	36	57	49	41	33	25	17	9	1	58	50	42	34	26	18	10	2	59	51	43	11
12	19	11	3	60	52	44	36	57	49	41	33	25	17	9	1	58	50	42	34	26	18	10	2	59	51	43	35	27	12
13	3	60	52	44	36	57	49	41	33	25	17	9	1	58	50	42	34	26	18	10	2	59	51	43	35	27	19	11	13
14	52	44	36	57	49	41	33	25	17	9	1	58	50	42	34	26	18	10	2	59	51	43	35	27	19	11	3	60	14
15	36	57	49	41	33	25	17	9	1	58	50	42	34	26	18	10	2	59	51	43	35	27	19	11	3	60	52	44	15
16	57	49	41	33	25	17	9	1	58	50	42	34	26	18	10	2	59	51	43	35	27	19	11	3	60	52	44	36	16

k_{49}, k_{41}, k_{33}, ..., etc. are the 1st, 2nd, 3rd, ..., etc. key bits in C_1, i.e., in register C during the 1st round.

Table 3-8. Key Bits Stored in Register (C) for Each Individual Round

Round	Index of Elements in Vector D_i																												Round
(i)	29	30	31	32	33	34	35	36	37	38	39	40	41	42	43	44	45	46	47	48	49	50	51	52	53	54	55	56	(i)
1	55	47	39	31	23	15	7	62	54	46	38	30	22	14	6	61	53	45	37	29	21	13	5	28	20	12	4	63	1
2	47	39	31	23	15	7	62	54	46	38	30	22	14	6	61	53	45	37	29	21	13	5	28	20	12	4	63	55	2
3	31	23	15	7	62	54	46	38	30	22	14	6	61	53	45	37	29	21	13	5	28	20	12	4	63	55	47	39	3
4	15	7	62	54	46	38	30	22	14	6	61	53	45	37	29	21	13	5	28	20	12	4	63	55	47	39	31	23	4
5	62	54	46	38	30	22	14	6	61	53	45	37	29	21	13	5	28	20	12	4	63	55	47	39	31	23	15	7	5
6	46	38	30	22	14	6	61	53	45	37	29	21	13	5	28	20	12	4	63	55	47	39	31	23	15	7	62	54	6
7	30	22	14	6	61	53	45	37	29	21	13	5	28	20	12	4	63	55	47	39	31	23	15	7	62	54	46	38	7
8	14	6	61	53	45	37	29	21	13	5	28	20	12	4	63	55	47	39	31	23	15	7	62	54	46	38	30	22	8
9	6	61	53	45	37	29	21	13	5	28	20	12	4	63	55	47	39	31	23	15	7	62	54	46	38	30	22	14	9
10	53	45	37	29	21	13	5	28	20	12	4	63	55	47	39	31	23	15	7	62	54	46	38	30	22	14	6	61	10
11	37	29	21	13	5	28	20	12	4	63	55	47	39	31	23	15	7	62	54	46	38	30	22	14	6	61	53	45	11
12	21	13	5	28	20	12	4	63	55	47	39	31	23	15	7	62	54	46	38	30	22	14	6	61	53	45	37	29	12
13	5	28	20	12	4	63	55	47	39	31	23	15	7	62	54	46	38	30	22	14	6	61	53	45	37	29	21	13	13
14	20	12	4	63	55	47	39	31	23	15	7	62	54	46	38	30	22	14	6	61	53	45	37	29	21	13	5	28	14
15	4	63	55	47	39	31	23	15	7	62	54	46	38	30	22	14	6	61	53	45	37	29	21	13	5	28	20	12	15
16	63	55	47	39	31	23	15	7	62	54	46	38	30	22	14	6	61	53	45	37	29	21	13	5	28	20	12	4	16

Table 3-9. Key Bits Stored in Register (D) for Each Individual Round

This rule used in conjunction with the C_i and D_i vectors given in Tables 3-8 and 3-9 allows the evaluation of key vector K(i). The first 24 bits of K(i) which are derived from C_i are shown in Table 3-10. The second 24 bits of K(i) which are derived from D_i are shown in Table 3-11. The total key vector K(i) associated with the ith round is thus obtained by concatenating row i from Table 3-10 with row i from Table 3-11. The entries in Tables 3-10 and 3-11 correspond to the indices of the associated key bits within the key $k_1, k_2, \ldots, k_{64}$ which are to be used. For example, from Tables 3-10 and 3-11, it can be seen that

$$K(1) = k_{10}, k_{51}, \ldots, k_{41}, k_{22}, k_{28}, \ldots, k_{31}$$

$$K(2) = k_2, \; k_{43}, \ldots, k_{33}, k_{14}, k_{20}, \ldots, k_{23}$$

$$\vdots \qquad\qquad \vdots$$

$$K(16) = k_{18}, k_{59}, \ldots, k_{49}, k_{30}, k_5, \; \ldots, k_{39}$$

Observe that $C_{16} = C_0$ and $D_{16} = D_0$. This results in the following difference between encipherment and decipherment. Since the externally supplied key is the same for encipherment and decipherment, the bit patterns in registers C_0 and D_0 are independent of the chosen operation. During encipherment, the process starts with K(1). This requires that (C_1, D_1) be created from (C_0, D_0) by one left shift, and K(1) be created from (C_1, D_1). During decipherment, the process starts with K(16). However, since (C_{16}, D_{16}) equals (C_0, D_0), it follows that K(16) can be created from (C_0, D_0) directly (i.e., an initial left shift is not required). The shift schedule is, of course, traced then in reverse order, left shifts becoming right shifts.

Weak and Semiweak Keys

It must be realized that the mathematical complexity of the DES algorithm, and hence its cryptographic strength, would be reduced if the internal keys at each round were the same. For this reason, the condition $K(1) = K(2) = \ldots = K(16)$ should be avoided.

There is, however, a set of *weak* keys within DES which satisfy the above condition. This occurs whenever the bits in register C are all ones or zeros, and the bits in register D are all ones or zeros. In this case, C_1 and D_1 are, respectively (see Tables 3-8 and 3-9),

$$k_{49} = k_{41} = \ldots = k_{57} = 0 \text{ or } 1$$

and

$$k_{55} = k_{47} = \ldots = k_{63} = 0 \text{ or } 1$$

Round (i)	Index of Elements in Vector K(i)																								Round (i)
	1	2	3	4	5	6	7	8	9	10	11	12	13	14	15	16	17	18	19	20	21	22	23	24	
	Index of Selected Element in Vector C_i (Obtained from PC-2)																								
	14	17	11	24	1	5	3	28	15	6	21	10	23	19	12	4	26	8	16	7	27	20	13	2	
1	10	51	34	60	49	17	33	57	2	9	19	42	3	35	26	25	44	58	59	1	36	27	18	41	1
2	2	43	26	52	41	9	25	49	59	1	11	34	60	27	18	17	36	50	51	58	57	19	10	33	2
3	51	27	10	36	25	58	9	33	43	50	60	18	44	11	2	1	49	34	35	42	41	3	59	17	3
4	35	11	59	49	9	42	58	17	27	34	44	2	57	60	51	50	33	18	19	26	25	52	43	1	4
5	19	60	43	33	58	26	42	1	11	18	57	51	41	44	35	34	17	2	3	10	9	36	27	50	5
6	3	44	27	17	42	10	26	50	60	2	41	35	25	57	19	18	1	51	52	59	58	49	11	34	6
7	52	57	11	1	26	59	10	34	44	51	25	19	9	41	3	2	50	35	36	43	42	33	60	18	7
8	36	41	60	50	10	43	59	18	57	35	9	3	58	25	52	51	34	19	49	27	26	17	44	2	8
9	57	33	52	42	2	35	51	10	49	27	1	60	50	17	44	43	26	11	41	19	18	9	36	59	9
10	41	17	36	26	51	19	35	59	33	11	50	44	34	1	57	27	10	60	25	3	2	58	49	43	10
11	25	1	49	10	35	3	19	43	17	60	34	57	18	50	41	11	59	44	9	52	51	42	33	27	11
12	9	50	33	59	19	52	3	27	1	44	18	41	2	34	25	60	43	57	58	36	35	26	17	11	12
13	58	34	17	43	3	36	52	11	50	57	2	25	51	18	9	44	27	41	42	49	19	10	1	60	13
14	42	18	1	27	52	49	36	60	34	41	51	9	35	2	58	57	11	25	26	33	3	59	50	44	14
15	26	2	50	11	36	33	49	44	18	25	35	58	19	51	42	41	60	9	10	17	52	43	34	57	15
16	18	59	42	3	57	25	41	36	10	17	27	50	11	43	34	33	52	1	2	9	44	35	26	49	16

Table 3-10. First Set of 24 Key Bits in K(i), the Key Used at Round (i)

Round (i)	25	26	27	28	29	30	31	32	33	34	35	36	37	38	39	40	41	42	43	44	45	46	47	48	Round (i)
	Index of Selected Element in Vector D_i (Obtained from PC-2)																								
	41	52	31	37	47	55	30	40	51	45	33	48	44	49	39	56	34	53	46	42	50	36	29	32	
1	22	28	39	54	37	4	47	30	5	53	23	29	61	21	38	63	15	20	45	14	13	62	55	31	1
2	14	20	31	46	29	63	39	22	28	45	15	21	53	13	30	55	7	12	37	6	5	54	47	23	2
3	61	4	15	30	13	47	23	6	12	29	62	5	37	28	14	39	54	63	21	53	20	38	31	7	3
4	45	55	62	14	28	31	7	53	63	13	46	20	21	12	61	23	38	47	5	37	4	22	15	54	4
5	29	39	46	61	12	15	54	37	47	28	30	4	5	63	45	7	22	31	20	21	55	6	62	38	5
6	13	23	30	45	63	62	38	21	31	12	14	55	20	47	29	54	6	15	4	5	39	53	46	22	6
7	28	7	14	29	47	46	22	5	15	63	61	39	4	31	13	38	53	62	55	20	23	37	30	6	7
8	12	54	61	13	31	30	6	20	62	47	45	23	55	15	28	22	37	46	39	4	7	21	14	53	8
9	4	46	53	5	23	22	61	12	54	39	37	15	47	7	20	14	29	38	31	63	62	13	6	45	9
10	55	30	37	20	7	6	45	63	38	23	21	62	31	54	4	61	13	22	15	47	46	28	53	29	10
11	39	14	21	4	54	53	29	47	22	7	5	46	15	38	55	45	28	6	62	31	30	12	37	13	11
12	23	61	5	55	38	37	13	31	6	54	20	30	62	22	39	29	12	53	46	15	14	63	21	28	12
13	7	45	20	39	22	21	28	15	53	38	4	14	46	6	23	13	63	37	30	62	61	47	5	12	13
14	54	29	4	23	6	5	12	62	37	22	55	61	30	53	7	28	47	21	14	46	45	31	20	63	14
15	38	13	55	7	53	20	63	46	21	6	39	45	14	37	54	12	31	5	61	30	29	15	4	47	15
16	30	5	47	62	45	12	55	38	13	61	31	37	6	29	46	4	23	28	53	22	21	7	63	39	16

Table 3-11. Second Set of 24 Key Bits in K(i), the Key Used at Round (i)

Thus there are four weak keys altogether and they are represented by the following (parity-adjusted) external keys:

01	01	01	01	01	01	01	01
1F	1F	1F	1F	0E	0E	0E	0E
E0	E0	E0	E0	F1	F1	F1	F1
FE	FE	FE	FE	FE	FE	FE	FE

Weak keys also have the property that there is no difference between the operations of encipherment and decipherment. Whereas, in general, the relations $D_K E_K(X) = X$ and $E_K D_K(X) = X$ hold for any key K and plaintext X, the special relation $E_K E_K(X) = X$ also holds for weak keys. Moreover, since $D_K D_K E_K E_K(X) = X$, the relation $D_K D_K(X) = X$ also holds.

There is another set of keys defined as *semiweak*. These have the property that only two different internal keys are produced, each occurring eight times. A semiweak key occurs whenever

1. Register C or D contains bit pattern 0101 . . . 0101 or 1010 . . . 1010.
2. The other register (D or C) contains bit pattern 0000 . . . 0000, 1111 . . . 1111, 0101 . . . 0101, or 1010 . . . 1010.

An alternating sequence of 0 and 1 bits has the interesting property that no matter how the sequence is shifted only two bit patterns are produced in registers C and D, namely, 0101 . . . 0101 and 1010 . . . 1010.

By way of illustration, let register C_0 contain 1010 . . . 1010 and register D_0 contain 0101 . . . 0101. The bit patterns shown in Table 3-12, from which the internal keys are derived, are produced in registers C_i and D_i.

In the above example, C_1 and D_1 (see Tables 3-8 and 3-9) are, respectively,

$$k_{49}, k_{41}, \ldots, k_{36}, k_{57} = 01 \ldots 01$$

and

$$k_{55}, k_{47}, \ldots, k_4, k_{63} = 10 \ldots 10$$

which results in (parity-adjusted) external key

$$K_{01,10} = \text{1F E0 1F E0 0E F1 0E F1}$$

where the subscripts (01 and 10) indicate the repeating bit patterns in C_1 and D_1.

Let K denote $K_{01,10}$. Note that one can recover plaintext also by applying the encipher operation, since there is a K′ (where $K' \neq K$) whose internal keys satisfy the relation

$$K'(i) = K(17 - i) \qquad \text{for } i = 1, 2, \ldots, 16$$

Index i	Number of Left Shifts	Content of Register C_i (28 bits)	Content of Register D_i (28 bits)
0		1010...1010	0101...0101
1	1	0101...0101	1010...1010
2	1	1010...1010	0101...0101
3	2	1010...1010	0101...0101
4	2	1010...1010	0101...0101
5	2	1010...1010	0101...0101
6	2	1010...1010	0101...0101
7	2	1010...1010	0101...0101
8	2	1010...1010	0101...0101
9	1	0101...0101	1010...1010
10	2	0101...0101	1010...1010
11	2	0101...0101	1010...1010
12	2	0101...0101	1010...1010
13	2	0101...0101	1010...1010
14	2	0101...0101	1010...1010
15	2	0101...0101	1010...1010
16	1	1010...1010	0101...0101

Table 3-12. Example of an Enciphering Key Which Produces Only Two Different Internal Keys

(a fact pointed out by D. W. Davies and W. L. Price of the National Physical Laboratory, Teddington, Middlesex, England). In the example, $(C_1, D_1) = (C_{16}, D_{16}) = (1010 \ldots 1010, 0101 \ldots 0101)$, and therefore C_1 and D_1 (see Tables 3-8 and 3-9) are, respectively,

$$k_{49}, k_{41}, \ldots, k_{36}, k_{57} = 10 \ldots 10$$

and

$$k_{55}, k_{47}, \ldots, k_4, k_{63} = 01 \ldots 01$$

which results in (parity-adjusted) external key

$$K_{10,01} = \text{E0 1F E0 1F F1 0E F1 0E}$$

Note that $K_{10,01}$ is also a semiweak key, and $K_{01,10}$ can be used in an encipher operation to recover plaintext enciphered with $K_{10,01}$. In general, it can be shown that for any semiweak key (K) there is another semiweak key ($K' \neq K$) such that

$$E_K E_{K'}(X) = X \text{ and } E_{K'} E_K(X) = X \tag{3-10}$$

for any X. Altogether there are 12 semiweak keys. They are represented by the (parity-adjusted) external keys shown in Table 3-13. The six pairs of semiweak keys shown in Table 3-14 satisfy Equation 3-10.

There are other keys which exhibit the property of having some identical internal keys. For example, this occurs when

1. Register C or D contains bit pattern 0011 . . . 0011, 0110 . . . 0110, 1001 . . . 1001, or 1100 . . . 1100.
2. The other register (D or C) contains bit pattern 0000 . . . 0000, 0011 . . . 0011, 0101 . . . 0101, 0110 . . . 0110, 1001 . . . 1001, 1010 . . . 1010, 1100 . . . 1100, or 1111 . . . 1111.

Again, by way of illustration, let register C_0 contain 1100 . . . 1100 and register D_0 contain 0011 . . . 0011. The bit patterns produced in registers C_i

$K_{00,01}$	=	E0	FE	E0	FE	F1	FE	F1	FE
$K_{00,10}$	=	FE	E0	FE	E0	FE	F1	FE	F1
$K_{01,00}$	=	1F	FE	1F	FE	0E	FE	0E	FE
$K_{01,01}$	=	01	FE	01	FE	01	FE	01	FE
$K_{01,10}$	=	1F	E0	1F	E0	0E	F1	0E	F1
$K_{01,11}$	=	01	E0	01	E0	01	F1	01	F1
$K_{10,00}$	=	FE	1F	FE	1F	FE	0E	FE	0E
$K_{10,01}$	=	E0	1F	E0	1F	F1	0E	F1	0E
$K_{10,10}$	=	FE	01	FE	01	FE	01	FE	01
$K_{10,11}$	=	E0	01	E0	01	F1	01	F1	01
$K_{11,01}$	=	01	1F	01	1F	01	0E	01	0E
$K_{11,10}$	=	1F	01	1F	01	0E	01	0E	01

Table 3-13. List of Semiweak Keys Represented as (Parity-Adjusted) External Keys

$(K_{00,01}, K_{00,10})$
$(K_{01,00}, K_{10,00})$
$(K_{01,01}, K_{10,10})$
$(K_{01,10}, K_{10,01})$
$(K_{01,11}, K_{10,11})$
$(K_{11,01}, K_{11,10})$

Table 3-14. Pairs of Semiweak Keys (K, K′) that Satisfy the Relation $E_K E_{K'}(X) = E_{K'} E_K(X) = X$ for all X

Index i	Number of Left Shifts	Content of Register C_i (28 bits)	Content of Register D_i (28 bits)
0		1100...1100	0011...0011
1	1	1001...1001	0110...0110
2	1	0011...0011	1100...1100
3	2	1100...1100	0011...0011
4	2	0011...0011	1100...1100
5	2	1100...1100	0011...0011
6	2	0011...0011	1100...1100
7	2	1100...1100	0011...0011
8	2	0011...0011	1100...1100
9	1	0110...0110	1001...1001
10	2	1001...1001	0110...0110
11	2	0110...0110	1001...1001
12	2	1001...1001	0110...0110
13	2	0110...0110	1001...1001
14	2	1001...1001	0110...0110
15	2	0110...0110	1001...1001
16	1	1100...1100	0011...0011

Table 3-15. Example of an Enciphering Key which Produces Only Four Different Internal Keys

and D_i, from which the internal keys are derived, are shown in Table 3-15. Each of the bit patterns–(1100, 0011), (1001, 0110), (0011, 1100), and (0110, 1001)–occurs four times in the registers (C_i, D_i), i = 1, 2, . . . , 16. Moreover, the pattern of recurrence is such that the same internal key never occurs twice in succession, although it will occur alternately. 48 (parity-adjusted) external keys whose internal keys recur in the manner described are listed in Table 3-16.

Finally, the reader should realize that the described set of keys (weak, semiweak, etc.) pose no threat to the algorithm's security. This is because the number of such keys is small in comparison to the total set of 72,057,594,037,927,936 possible different keys. And, provided that keys are randomly selected, the likelihood of selecting such a key in the first place is therefore very small. However, these keys could easily be avoided during key generation (e.g., if they were intended to be installed in a system for relatively long periods of time).

Details of the DES Algorithm

The basic scheme for encipherment used by DES is shown in Figure 3-4. The initial permutation (IP) and the enciphering function (g) are discussed in more detail at this point.

Indices (i,j)		External Key $K_{i,j}$ (Parity-Adjusted)
0000	0011	1F 1F 01 01 0E 0E 01 01
	0110	01 1F 1F 01 01 0E 0E 01
	1001	1F 01 01 1F 0E 01 01 0E
	1100	01 01 1F 1F 01 01 0E 0E
0011	0000	E0 E0 01 01 F1 F1 01 01
	0011	FE FE 01 01 FE FE 01 01
	0101	FE E0 1F 01 FE F1 0E 01
	0110	E0 FE 1F 01 F1 FE 0E 01
	1001	FE E0 01 1F FE F1 01 0E
	1010	E0 FE 01 1F F1 FE 01 0E
	1100	E0 E0 1F 1F F1 F1 0E 0E
	1111	FE FE 1F 1F FE FE 0E 0E
0101	0011	FE 1F E0 01 FE 0E F1 01
	0110	E0 1F FE 01 F1 0E FE 01
	1001	FE 01 E0 1F FE 01 F1 0E
	1100	E0 01 FE 1F F1 01 FE 0E
0110	0000	01 E0 E0 01 01 F1 F1 01
	0011	1F FE E0 01 0E FE F1 01
	0101	1F E0 FE 01 0E F1 FE 01
	0110	01 FE FE 01 01 FE FE 01
	1001	1F E0 E0 1F 0E F1 F1 0E
	1010	01 FE E0 1F 01 FE F1 0E
	1100	01 E0 FE 1F 01 F1 FE 0E
	1111	1F FE FE 1F 0E FE FE 0E

Indices (i,j)		External Key $K_{i,j}$ (Parity-Adjusted)
1001	0000	E0 01 01 E0 F1 01 01 F1
	0011	FE 1F 01 E0 FE 0E 01 F1
	0101	FE 01 1F E0 FE 01 0E F1
	0110	E0 1F 1F E0 F1 0E 0E F1
	1001	FE 01 01 FE FE 01 01 FE
	1010	E0 1F 01 FE F1 0E 01 FE
	1100	E0 01 1F FE F1 01 0E FE
	1111	FE 1F 1F FE FE 0E 0E FE
1010	0011	1F FE 01 E0 0E FE 01 F1
	0110	01 FE 1F E0 01 FE 0E F1
	1001	1F E0 01 FE 0E F1 01 FE
	1100	01 E0 1F FE 01 F1 0E FE
1100	0000	01 01 E0 E0 01 01 F1 F1
	0011	1F 1F E0 E0 0E 0E F1 F1
	0101	1F 01 FE E0 0E 01 FE F1
	0110	01 1F FE E0 01 0E FE F1
	1001	1F 01 E0 FE 0E 01 F1 FE
	1010	01 1F E0 FE 01 0E F1 FE
	1100	01 01 FE FE 01 01 FE FE
	1111	1F 1F FE FE 0E 0E FE FE
1111	0011	FE FE E0 E0 FE FE F1 F1
	0110	E0 FE FE E0 F1 FE FE F1
	1001	FE E0 E0 FE FE F1 F1 FE
	1100	E0 E0 FE FE F1 F1 FE FE

Table 3-16. Partial List of (Parity-Adjusted) External Keys that Produces Four Equally Recurring Internal Keys

The 64-bit input block of data to be enciphered,

$$X = x_1, x_2, \ldots, x_{64}$$

is first subjected to an initial permutation IP. This results in

$$\begin{aligned} L(0) = {} & x_{58}, x_{50}, x_{42}, x_{34}, x_{26}, x_{18}, x_{10}, x_2, \\ & x_{60}, x_{52}, x_{44}, x_{36}, x_{28}, x_{20}, x_{12}, x_4, \\ & x_{62}, x_{54}, x_{46}, x_{38}, x_{30}, x_{22}, x_{14}, x_6, \\ & x_{64}, x_{56}, x_{48}, x_{40}, x_{32}, x_{24}, x_{16}, x_8 \end{aligned} \tag{3-11a}$$

$$\begin{aligned} R(0) = {} & x_{57}, x_{49}, x_{41}, x_{33}, x_{25}, x_{17}, x_9, x_1, \\ & x_{59}, x_{51}, x_{43}, x_{35}, x_{27}, x_{19}, x_{11}, x_3, \\ & x_{61}, x_{53}, x_{45}, x_{37}, x_{29}, x_{21}, x_{13}, x_5, \\ & x_{63}, x_{55}, x_{47}, x_{39}, x_{31}, x_{23}, x_{15}, x_7 \end{aligned} \tag{3-11b}$$

L(0) and R(0) can be used in conjunction with the derived key vectors K(1) through K(16) to produce L(16) and R(16), as shown in Figure 3-4. This 64-bit block of pre-output data

$$\begin{aligned} L(16), R(16) = {} & l_1(16), l_2(16), \ldots, l_{32}(16), \\ & r_1(16), r_2(16), \ldots, r_{32}(16) \end{aligned} \tag{3-12}$$

is then subjected to an inverse initial permutation (IP^{-1}), which reverses the effect of the initial permutation, as follows:

$$\begin{aligned} Y = {} & y_1, y_2, \ldots, y_{64} \\ = {} & l_8, r_8, l_{16}, r_{16}, l_{24}, r_{24}, l_{32}, r_{32}, \\ & l_7, r_7, l_{15}, r_{15}, l_{23}, r_{23}, l_{31}, r_{31}, \\ & l_6, r_6, l_{14}, r_{14}, l_{22}, r_{22}, l_{30}, r_{30}, \\ & l_5, r_5, l_{13}, r_{13}, l_{21}, r_{21}, l_{29}, r_{29}, \\ & l_4, r_4, l_{12}, r_{12}, l_{20}, r_{20}, l_{28}, r_{28}, \\ & l_3, r_3, l_{11}, r_{11}, l_{19}, r_{19}, l_{27}, r_{27}, \\ & l_2, r_2, l_{10}, r_{10}, l_{18}, r_{18}, l_{26}, r_{26}, \\ & l_1, r_1, l_9, r_9, l_{17}, r_{17}, l_{25}, r_{25} \end{aligned} \tag{3-13}$$

where the indices, which refer to a particular round, have been dropped for convenience of representation. The reader should observe that the inverse initial permutation described above is different from that described on page 9 of [5]. This is because the pre-output in Figure 3-4 is defined as L(16), R(16) whereas the pre-output on page 8 of [5] is defined as R(16), L(16).

It remains now only to discuss the enciphering function (g). The kernel of this operation (i.e., a one-round operation) is shown in Figure 3-12. First, the right half of the input to round i, denoted by

$$R(i-1) = r_1(i-1), r_2(i-1), \ldots, r_{32}(i-1)$$

is expanded from 32 bits to 48 bits, denoted by $E(R(i-1))$, using the E Bit-Selection Table (page 11 of [5]). The result is

$$\begin{array}{ll} E(R(i-1)) & r_{32}, r_1, r_2, r_3, r_4, r_5, \\ & r_4, r_5, r_6, r_7, r_8, r_9, \\ & r_8, r_9, r_{10}, r_{11}, r_{12}, r_{13}, \\ & r_{12}, r_{13}, r_{14}, r_{15}, r_{16}, r_{17}, \\ & r_{16}, r_{17}, r_{18}, r_{19}, r_{20}, r_{21}, \\ & r_{20}, r_{21}, r_{22}, r_{23}, r_{24}, r_{25}, \\ & r_{24}, r_{25}, r_{26}, r_{27}, r_{28}, r_{29}, \\ & r_{28}, r_{29}, r_{30}, r_{31}, r_{32}, r_1 \end{array} \qquad (3\text{-}14)$$

where the indices again have been dropped for convenience of representation. The expansion scheme is shown in Figure 3-13. The purpose of using the E expansion is to achieve a dependence of each bit of ciphertext on all plaintext and key bits in as few rounds as possible.

Once $E(R(i-1))$ is generated, it is added modulo 2 to K(i). This results in a 48-bit vector A.

$$\begin{aligned} A &= E(R(i-1)) \oplus K(i) \\ &= a_1, a_2, \ldots, a_{48} \end{aligned} \qquad (3\text{-}15)$$

(Although A is different for each round, and hence should be indexed by i, to avoid confusion this is not done here. In Figure 3-12, the elements of vector A are used as arguments in the substitution operations (S-boxes) S_1 through S_8 (pages 15 and 16 of [5]). Each S-box is described as a matrix of four rows (labeled 00, 01, 10, 11) and 16 columns (labeled 0000, 0001, . . . , 1111).

Each S-box can now be represented by four substitution functions, S_i^{00}, S_i^{01}, S_i^{10}, S_i^{11} for S-box S_i, where the superscript identifies the row of the matrix, each mapping four input bits (which determine the column of the matrix) to four output bits given by the element of the matrix. The first and last of the six entries to DES substitution box S_i in Figure 3-12 determine which of the four substitution functions in S_i are selected. Because these bits are derived from input bits as well as key bits, the selection of substitution functions depends not only on the key but also on the input data. Thus the E expansion, in effect, introduces an *autoclave* or self-keying feature. Because i ranges from 1 to 8, 32 functions are obtained with the eight S-boxes.

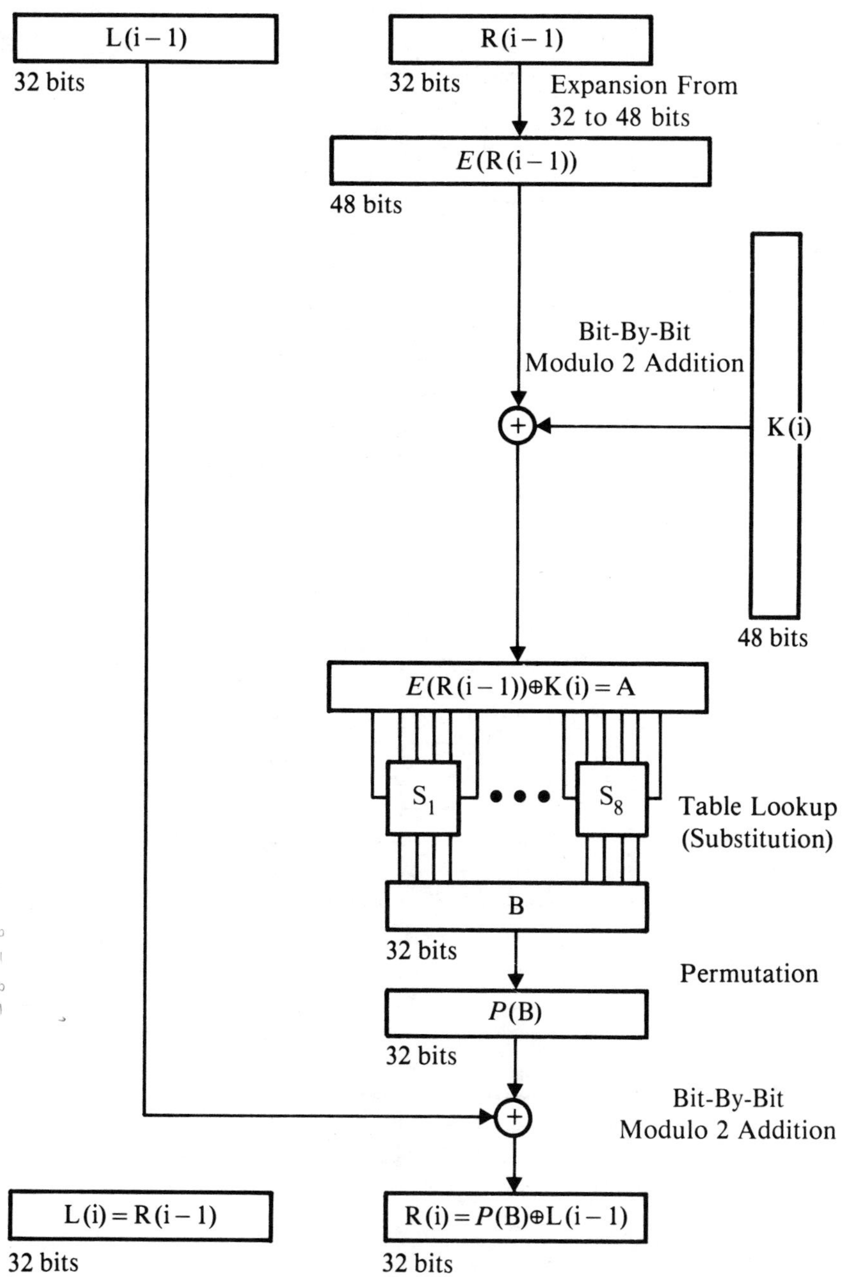

Figure 3-12. Details of Enciphering Function (g)

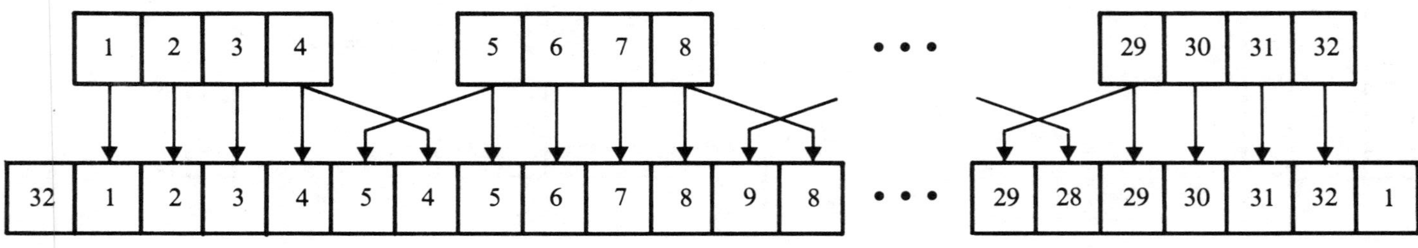

Figure 3-13. Expansion *(E)* of Right Half of Input to Each Round

With a_1 through a_6 being the inputs to the first S-box,

$$S_1^{a_1, a_6}(a_2, a_3, a_4, a_5)$$

represents the first four bits of B (i.e., bits b_1 through b_4). The last four bits, from S_8, (i.e., b_{29} through b_{32}) are given by

$$S_8^{a_{43}, a_{48}}(a_{44}, a_{45}, a_{46}, a_{47})$$

Knowledge of the 48 bits represented by vector A therefore allows one to determine the 32 bits represented by vector B. By permuting the elements of B (page 12 of [5]), one obtains P(B), where P stands for permutation.

$$\begin{aligned} P(B) = {} & b_{16}, b_7, b_{20}, b_{21}, b_{29}, b_{12}, b_{28}, b_{17}, \\ & b_1, b_{15}, b_{23}, b_{26}, b_5, b_{18}, b_{31}, b_{10}, \\ & b_2, b_8, b_{24}, b_{14}, b_{32}, b_{27}, b_3, b_9, \\ & b_{19}, b_{23}, b_{30}, b_6, b_{22}, b_{11}, b_4, b_{25} \end{aligned} \tag{3-16}$$

The output of round i thus becomes

$$L(i), R(i) = R(i-1), P(B) \oplus L(i-1)$$

By recognizing that P(B) is a function g of K(i) and R(i − 1), the following relationship can be established:

$$L(i) = R(i-1) \tag{3-17}$$

$$R(i) = L(i-1) \oplus g[K(i), R(i-1)] \tag{3-18}$$

Summary of the DES Procedure

Initialization:

1. Specify the 64-bit, externally supplied, cryptographic key, k_1, k_2, . . . , k_{64} (composed of 56 key bits and 8 nonkey bits).
2. From k_1, k_2, . . . , k_{64}, construct 16 key vectors, K(1) through K(16), of 48 bits each, which are used in rounds 1 through 16, respectively. (K(1) through K(16) are expressed in terms of the external key bits via Tables 3-10 and 3-11.)
3. Specify the 64-bit, externally supplied, input (plaintext), x_1, x_2, . . . , x_{64}.
4. From x_1, x_2, . . . , x_{64}, construct the 32-bit vectors L(0) and R(0), as shown in Equations 3-11a and 3-11b.
5. Set iteration counter to i = 1.

Iteration i:

6. Derive $E(\mathrm{R}(\mathrm{i}-1))$ from $\mathrm{R}(\mathrm{i}-1)$ using the expansion function E given by Equation 3-14.
7. Use K(i) if encipherment is being performed, otherwise use K(17 − i) for decipherment.
8. Add (modulo 2) the results of steps 6 and 7, and define the result to be the 48-bit vector $A = a_1, a_2, \ldots, a_{48}$.
9. Form $S_1^{a_1, a_6}(a_2, a_3, a_4, a_5)$ and define the 4-bit result as b_1, b_2, b_3, b_4. Repeat this process for

$$S_2^{a_7, a_{12}}(a_8, a_9, a_{10}, a_{11}) \text{ through } S_8^{a_{43}, a_{48}}(a_{44}, a_{45}, a_{46}, a_{47})$$

   defining the result as $b_5, b_6, \ldots, b_{32}$. The result of this step is the 32-bit vector B.
10. Derive P(B) by permuting B according to the permutation function (P) given by Equation 3-16.
11. Add (modulo 2) P(B) to L(i − 1) and define the result to be R(i).
12. Define L(i) = R(i − 1).
13. Increment the iteration counter i by 1.
14. If iteration counter is 16 or less, then repeat steps 6 through 14, otherwise derive the output from L(16), R(16), as shown in Equations 3-12 and 3-13.

Numerical Example

In the numerical example presented here, the value L(1), R(1) is derived for a one-round encipherment. It is assumed that

$$X = K = 0\ 1\ 2\ 3\ 4\ 5\ 6\ 7\ 8\ 9\ A\ B\ C\ D\ E\ F$$

in hexadecimal notation, or

$$\begin{aligned} X = K = &\ 0000\ 0001\ 0010\ 0011\ 0100\ 0101\ 0110\ 0111 \\ &\ 1000\ 1001\ 1010\ 1011\ 1100\ 1101\ 1110\ 1111 \end{aligned}$$

in binary notation. From Tables 3-10 and 3-11, it follows that

$$\begin{aligned} K(1) = &\ 0000\ 1011\ 0000\ 0010\ 0110\ 0111 \\ &\ 1001\ 1011\ 0100\ 1001\ 1010\ 0101 \quad \text{(binary)} \\ = &\ 0\ B\ 0\ 2\ 6\ 7\ 9\ B\ 4\ 9\ A\ 5 \quad \text{(hexadecimal)} \end{aligned}$$

From Equations 3-11a and 3-11b, it follows that

$$\begin{aligned} L(0) &= 1100\ 1100\ 0000\ 0000\ 1100\ 1100\ 1111\ 1111 \\ &= C\quad C\quad 0\quad 0\quad C\quad C\quad F\quad F \end{aligned}$$

and

$$\begin{aligned} R(0) &= 1111\ 0000\ 1010\ 1010\ 1111\ 0000\ 1010\ 1010 \\ &= F\quad 0\quad A\quad A\quad F\quad 0\quad A\quad A \end{aligned}$$

Expanding R(0) with the aid of Equation 3-14 yields

$$\begin{aligned} E(R(0)) = {} & 011110\ 100001\ 010101\ 010101 \\ & 011110\ 100001\ 010101\ 010101 \end{aligned}$$

Modulo 2 addition of this with K(1) yields

$$\begin{aligned} A &= E(R(0)) \oplus K(1) \\ &= 011100\ 010001\ 011100\ 110010 \\ &\quad\ 111000\ 010101\ 110011\ 110000 \end{aligned}$$

Grouping these 48 bits into sets of 6 bits allows the convenient evaluation of the substitution operation (page 15 of [5]).

$$\begin{aligned} S_1^{00}(1110) &= S_1^0(14) = 0 \quad \text{(base 10)} \quad = 0000 \quad \text{(base 2)} \\ S_2^{01}(1000) &= S_2^1(8) \ \ = 12 \qquad = 1100 \\ S_3^{00}(1110) &= S_3^0(14) = 2 \qquad = 0010 \\ S_4^{10}(1001) &= S_4^2(9) \ \ = 1 \qquad = 0001 \\ S_5^{10}(1100) &= S_5^2(12) = 6 \qquad = 0110 \\ S_6^{01}(1010) &= S_6^1(10) = 13 \qquad = 1101 \\ S_7^{11}(1001) &= S_7^3(9) \ \ = 5 \qquad = 0101 \\ S_8^{10}(1000) &= S_8^2(8) \ \ = 0 \qquad = 0000 \end{aligned}$$

Concatenating all of these results yields

$$\begin{aligned} B &= 0000\ 1100\ 0010\ 0001\ 0110\ 1101\ 0101\ 0000 \\ &= 0\quad C\quad 2\quad 1\quad 6\quad D\quad 5\quad 0 \end{aligned}$$

Applying the permutation P according to Equation 3-16, the result

$$\begin{aligned} P(B) &= 1001\quad 0010\quad 0001\quad 1100\quad 0010\quad 0000\quad 1001\quad 1100 \\ &= 9\quad 2\quad 1\quad C\quad 2\quad 0\quad 9\quad C \end{aligned}$$

is obtained. Modulo 2 addition of P(B) with L(0) yields

$$\begin{aligned} \text{R}(1) &= 0101\ 1110\ 0001\ 1100\ 1110\ 1100\ 0110\ 0011 \\ &= \ \ 5 \quad\ \text{E} \quad\ 1 \quad\ \text{C} \quad\ \text{E} \quad\ \text{C} \quad\ 6 \quad\ 3 \end{aligned}$$

and hence the right half output after round one is obtained. Furthermore,

$$\text{L}(1) = \text{R}(0) = \text{F}\ 0\ \text{A}\ \text{A}\ \text{F}\ 0\ \text{A}\ \text{A}$$

which completes the one-round sample computation.

Some Remarks about the DES Design

Methods of analysis (attacks), including heuristic approaches, were gathered during an initial study phase. These techniques were then used to obtain a set of design principles, or criteria, that govern the design of the algorithm. By requiring that the candidate algorithm meet all design criteria, the previously defined methods of attack were rendered ineffective.

The initial study phase for DES extended over a 5-year period. The resultant design criteria were then used to design DES's permutation (P-box), substitutions (S-boxes), and key schedules (see Description of the Data Encryption Standard). For example, one design criterion for DES was that the permutation schedule must ensure that each output (ciphertext) bit is a function of all input (plaintext and key) bits after a minimum number of rounds. (See also Analysis of Intersymbol Dependencies for the Data Encryption Standard.)

Since it is common for statisticians to employ randomization techniques in the design of experiments (procedures for collecting, analyzing, and interpreting data), mathematicians, or people with strong mathematical backgrounds, frequently suggest that parameters such as permutation, substitution, and key schedule should be randomly chosen. This indeed was the first thought of the designers of DES. However, realization early in the development process that random parameter selection introduced weaknesses into the algorithm led to abandonment of these random approaches.

In the actual design process, parameters were randomly generated and then tested against the design criteria. A significant portion of the random designs were rejected in this process. For example, S-box functions were selected on the basis of strength and ease of implementation (see Implementation Considerations for the S-Box Design). Thus it should not be surprising that the final solutions contain some structural properties different from those expected to result from use of purely random selection. However, let it again be stated that the results of the DES design effort showed that carefully selected S-box functions will produce a much stronger algorithm than one based on random designs.

The question of S-box structure is an issue that was raised as part of an independent analysis of DES [17], and was also dealt with as part of the second ICST workshop to investigate the complexity of DES [14]. The members of the ICST workshop concluded that these structures offer no known shortcut solutions.

Implementation Considerations for the S-Box Design

An interesting result, which appears to relate cryptographic strength to the number of logic circuits describing an S-box, was encountered in the design of DES's S-box functions. The minimum number of logic circuits needed to implement the final (nonrandom) S-box design was significantly greater than that required for a preliminary (nearly random) design. This result suggests that the number of logic circuits can be used as an indicator or heuristic to reject weak S-box functions. For example, if an S-box function is selected using a different set of design criteria and the minimum number of logic circuits falls below an established threshold, then the cryptographic strength of the S-box functions is highly suspect.

The measurements upon which this heuristic is based are given below. However, before discussing the measurements, a few preliminaries are necessary. An S-box is a function that maps 6 input bits ($x_1, x_2, \ldots, x_6$) into 4 output bits ($y_1, y_2, \ldots, y_4$). Moreover, each output bit (y_i) can be represented as a boolean expression of the 6 input bits, that is, y_i can be represented as one or more *minterms* that are combined using a logical OR operation [18]. In the example, each of the 6 input bits is either 0 or 1, and so there are $2^6 = 64$ minterms, as shown:

1. $x_1 \cdot x_2 \cdot \ldots \cdot x_6$
2. $\overline{x}_1 \cdot x_2 \cdot \ldots \cdot x_6$
3. $x_1 \cdot \overline{x}_2 \cdot \ldots \cdot x_6$
4. $\overline{x}_1 \cdot \overline{x}_2 \cdot \ldots \cdot x_6$

$\vdots$

64. $\overline{x}_1 \cdot \overline{x}_2 \cdot \ldots \cdot \overline{x}_6$

where "•" denotes here the logical AND operation and $\overline{x}$ denotes the complement of x.

To see how to determine the boolean expression for a given S-box function, consider the following example (toy system) in which an S-box has three inputs (x_1, x_2, and x_3) and two outputs (y_1 and y_2), where

	(x_2, x_1) 0	1	2	3
(x_3) 0	1	3	2	0
1	2	1	0	3

"Toy" S-box Function

The outputs (y_2, y_1) can be expressed in terms of the inputs (x_3, x_2, x_1) as follows:

x_3 x_2 x_1	y_2 y_1
0 0 0	0 1
0 0 1	1 1
0 1 0	1 0
0 1 1	0 0
1 0 0	1 0
1 0 1	0 1
1 1 0	0 0
1 1 1	1 1

For example, the boolean expression for y_1 is

$$y_1 = \bar{x}_3 \cdot \bar{x}_2 \cdot \bar{x}_1 + \bar{x}_3 \cdot \bar{x}_2 \cdot x_1 + x_3 \cdot \bar{x}_2 \cdot x_1 + x_3 \cdot x_2 \cdot x_1$$

where "+" denotes here the logical OR operation. A minterm is included in the boolean expression if the corresponding output bit (y_1) is equal to 1. For example, note that $y_1 = 1$ when $x_1 = 0$, $x_2 = 0$, and $x_3 = 0$.

A derived boolean expression would normally be reduced to find an equivalent expression that would be better with respect to some measure. In the case of the DES algorithm, a single chip design was desired, and therefore it was important at that time (about 1974) to reduce the number of logic circuits needed to implement the S-box functions. The S-boxes were designed using a multidimensional approach in which the boolean expressions for each output bit were reduced jointly [19].

For an early design of the S-box, with only a few design criteria, the distribution of minterms after reduction (based on a sample of 18 S-boxes) was found to be as shown in Table 3-17. However, as more and more design criteria were added, making the design less and less random, a corresponding increase in the number of required minterms was observed. For example, in the final

No. of Minterms per S-box	No. of S-boxes
40	1
41	1
44	3
45	3
46	4
47	2
48	4

Table 3-17. Distribution of Minterms for a Preliminary Design of the S-box

No. of Minterms per S-box	No. of S-boxes
52	3
53	7
54	9
55	22
56	16
57	20
58	4
59	2

Table 3-18. Distribution of Minterms for Final Design of S-box

S-box design, the distribution of minterms after reduction (based on a sample of 83 S-boxes) was found to be as shown in Table 3-18. Therefore, introducing more stringent design criteria caused the required number of minterms to shift significantly, from about 45 to 55, toward the maximum number of 64.

To make it as easy as possible for an LSI logic designer to implement the design on a single chip, the left tail of the distribution was chosen (52 and 53). (Many cryptographic applications that have been proposed require a single chip design for economic and performance reasons.)

ANALYSIS OF INTERSYMBOL DEPENDENCIES FOR THE DATA ENCRYPTION STANDARD[6]

One property of DES is that each bit of ciphertext is a complex function of all plaintext bits and all key bits. A method is developed later which evaluates how fast this dependence (defined as intersymbol dependence) builds up as a function of repeated mathematical operations called rounds. With the DES algorithm, the minimum number of rounds needed to achieve intersymbol dependence for plaintext as well as key is five.

To analyze the intersymbol dependence, consider the basic design approach shown in Figure 3-14. It is not necessary to take into account the initial permutation IP and final permutation IP^{-1} (Figure 3-4). Some of the relations already developed are repeated in this section to make the analysis easier to understand and independent of other sections.

For strength, DES relies on the complexity of the function g, which incorporates substitution as well as transposition (or permutation), and exercising the function g a number of times (defined as rounds).

After 16 rounds have been employed by DES, the 64 bits of plaintext

[6]© 1978 AFIPS press. The material describing the analysis is reprinted in part from *AFIPS Conference Proceedings,* 1978 National Computer Conference [20].

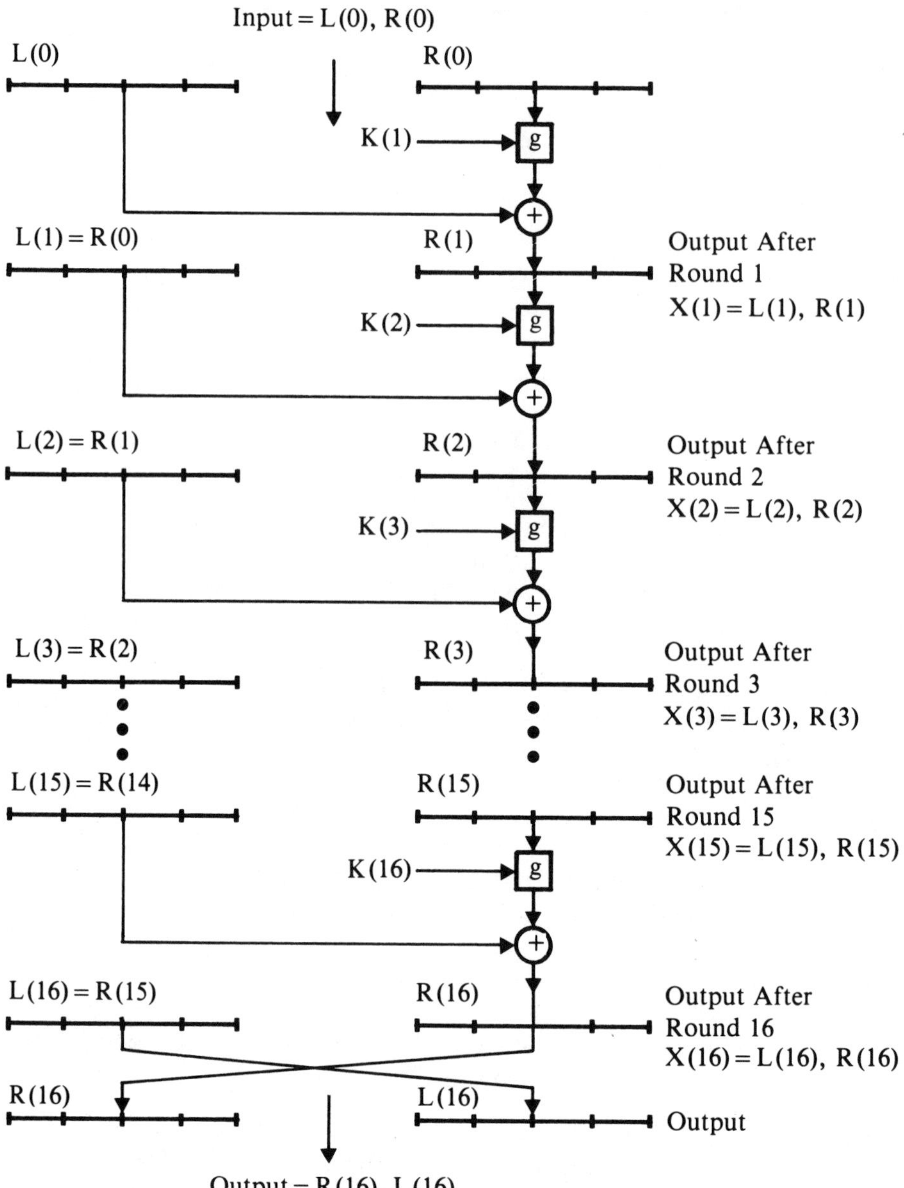

Figure 3-14. Basic Block Cipher Design Used by the Data Encryption Standard

are transformed into 64 bits of ciphertext under the control of a 56-bit key. During each round a subset of the key (defined as K(i) for round i; i = 1, 2, . . . , 16) is used. The input to round i, X(i − 1), is expressed as the concatenation of two 32-bit quantities. L(i − 1) represents the 32 input bits of the left half of the one-round cipher operation (Figure 3-13), and R(i − 1) represets the 32 input bits of the right half:

$$L(i-1) = l_1(i-1), l_2(i-1), \ldots, l_{32}(i-1)$$

$$R(i-1) = r_1(i-1), r_2(i-1), \ldots, r_{32}(i-1)$$

Hence the input to round i is defined as

$$X(i-1) = L(i-1), R(i-1)$$

whereas the output from round i is defined as

$$X(i) = L(i), R(i)$$

Thus each bit of the ciphertext produced by DES is a complex function of all 64 plaintext bits and all 56 key bits.

The following example illustrates the marked change produced in a recovered plaintext when only one bit is changed in the ciphertext or key. Hexadecimal notation is used. If the plaintext 1000000000000001 is enciphered with a (56-bit) key 30000000000000, then the ciphertext 958E6E627A05557B is produced. The original plaintext is recovered if 958E6E627A05557B is deciphered with 30000000000000. However, if the first 9 in the ciphertext is changed to 8 (a 1-bit change) and the ciphertext 858E6E627A05557B is now deciphered with key 30000000000000, the recovered plaintext is 8D4893C2966CC211, not 1000000000000001. On the other hand, if the first 3 in the key is changed to 1 (another 1-bit change) and the ciphertext 958E6E627A05557B is now deciphered with key 10000000000000, the recovered plaintext is 6D4B945376725395. (The same effect is also observed during encipherment.)

The dependence of each ciphertext bit on all bits of the plaintext and key is defined as intersymbol dependence. Many applications can take advantage of this. Two applications, discussed in Chapter 2 and again here, effectively expand the block size of DES by using chaining methods. When block encryption is used, each 64-bit block of data is enciphered separately. In chained block encryption, on the other hand, the encipherment of each block is made dependent on prior information (plaintext, ciphertext, or the like) available when the block is enciphered. Two techniques for block chaining, ciphertext feedback and plaintext-ciphertext feedback, are defined below.

Let $X_1, X_2, \ldots, X_n$ denote blocks of plaintext to be chained using key K, let Y_0 be a nonsecret quantity defined as the initializing vector, and let $Y_1, Y_2, \ldots, Y_n$ denote the blocks of ciphertext produced. When ciphertext feedback is used, the following relationship holds:

$$Y_1 = E_K(X_i \oplus Y_{i-1}) \qquad \text{for } i \geqslant 1$$

where $\oplus$ represents modulo 2 addition. When plaintext-ciphertext feedback is used, the following relationships hold:

$$Y_1 = E_K(X_1 \oplus Y_0)$$

and

$$Y_i = E_K(X_i \oplus Y_{i-1} \oplus X_{i-1}) \qquad \text{for } i \geqslant 2.$$

With block chaining, a ciphertext bit in block i depends not only on all plaintext bits in block i, but also on the plaintext bits of block 1 through (i − 1). Thus chained block encryption (or block chaining) can be used to extend the intersymbol dependence between ciphertext and plaintext.

Plaintext-ciphertext feedback has the additional property of error propagation. Corruption of a single bit of ciphertext will cause each subsequent bit of recovered plaintext to be in error with a probability approximately equal to 0.5. Appending a known pattern of bits to the end of the plaintext prior to encryption, and comparing that value to the value recovered, allows the error propagation feature to be used for checking the true content of a message. Chaining techniques are useful for encrypting data, and the block cipher (with no chaining) is useful for key transformation (see Chapters 4 and 5).

In the analysis below, a method is developed which shows how fast the intersymbol dependence builds up as a function of the number of rounds. A basic assumption is made that the substitution functions are *nonaffine*,[7] such that cancellation of dependencies does not occur. Since, in the design of DES, great care was taken to select S-boxes with the nonaffine property, it is assumed in the analysis that the assumption stated above holds for DES.

At each step, the analysis considers whether or not an output bit depends upon an input bit. Although the degree of complexity is not measured, a distinction is made among three kinds of functional relationships. Details of g (the kernel of the DES cryptographic approach), as illustrated in Figure 3-12, must be considered in a discussion of these relationships.

For DES, the right half of the input is expanded from 32 bits to 48 bits (see Figures 3-12 and 3-13, and Equation 3-14), an S-box has six input bits and four output bits. The first and last input of the six entries to the DES substitution box S_i in Figure 3-12 determine which of the four substitution functions in S_i is selected. Because these bits are derived from the 32 input bits (i.e., message bits if the input is interpreted as a message) as well as key bits due to the modulo 2 addition of K(i) and E(R(i − 1)), the selection of substitution functions not only depends on the key but also on the input data. This, in effect, introduces a self-keying feature, or *autoclave*.

In the following two analyses, the dependencies of output X(i) on plaintext X(0) and on the key are treated separately.

Interdependence between Ciphertext and Plaintext

To investigate the functional relationship between the input to round i + 1 (which is equal to the output of round i, i = 1, 2, 3, . . . , 16) and the input to the first round, a matrix is defined. It consists of 64 rows and 64 columns and is referred to as $G_{i,j}$. Its element $a_{l,m}$ in row l and column m shows the

[7]A function is nonaffine if, for an operator □, the condition f(x □ y) ≠ f(x) □ f(y) □ c holds, where c is not dependent on x and y.

type of relationship which exists between the lth bit of X(i) and the mth bit of X(j). In particular, $a_{l,m}$ is blank if a dependency does not exist between $x_l(i)$ and $x_m(j)$. If there is a dependency via message bits only, $a_{l,m}$ is set to x. If the dependency is via autoclave, $a_{l,m}$ is set to –. If message bits as well as autoclave bits influence the output, $a_{l,m}$ is set to *.

In a well designed system, an output bit depends on more and more input bits as the number of rounds increases. These input bits come into play via message dependence (x), autoclave dependence (–), or both (*). The design goal is to have each output bit depend on each input bit after only a few rounds, with autoclave as well as message dependence being achieved.

It is advantageous to partition matrix $G_{i,j}$ into four submatrices of 32 rows and 32 columns each:

$$G_{i,j} = \begin{bmatrix} G_{i,j}^{(L,L)} & G_{i,j}^{(L,R)} \\ G_{i,j}^{(R,L)} & G_{i,j}^{(R,R)} \end{bmatrix}$$

Using the definition of $G_{i,j}$, one can see that the elements of the submatrices express the relationships shown in Table 3-19. Let the relationships between the output and the input of one round ($G_{i,i-1}$) be evaluated first. The dependence of the output bits from the substitution operation (vector B in Figure 3-12) on the input bits R(i – 1) is shown in Figure 3-15. (Note that the dependence of B on R(i – 1) is identical to the dependence of R(i) on R(i – 1) if the permutation is not present.)

The selection of the substitution function (S-function) in the first S-box, S_1, depends on bits 32 and 5 of R(i – 1). This follows from the fact that the first and sixth input bits to S_1 select the S-function, and the first and sixth bits of the expanded version of R(i – 1), which are determined by $E(R(i-1))$, are equal to $r_{32}(i-1)$ and $r_5(i-1)$, respectively, according to Equation 3-14 and Figure 3-13. Therefore, all output bits from S_1 (b_1 through b_4) depend on $r_{32}(i-1)$ and $r_5(i-1)$ via autoclave. However, they depend on $r_1(i-1)$ through $r_4(i-1)$ via message. R(i – 1) is considered to be the second 32 bits of input message in this case. Hence the entries in rows 1

Submatrix	Relationship Expressed in Submatrix
$G_{i,j}^{(L,L)}$	L(i) vs. L(j)
$G_{i,j}^{(L,R)}$	L(i) vs. R(j)
$G_{i,j}^{(R,L)}$	R(i) vs. L(j)
$G_{i,j}^{(R,R)}$	R(i) vs. R(j)

Table 3-19. Functional Relationships

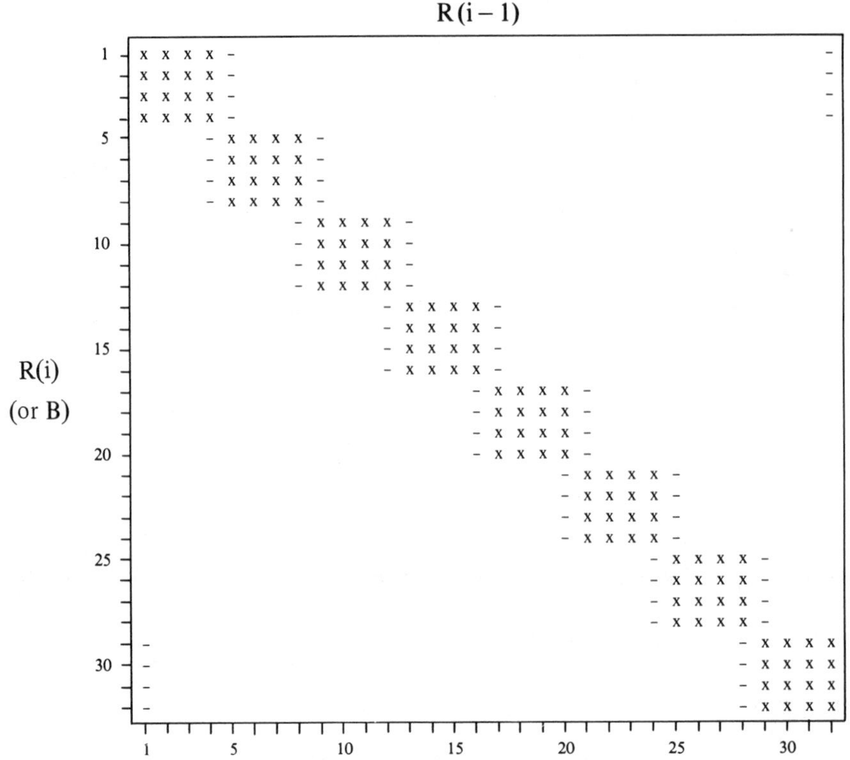

Figure 3-15. Functional Dependence of R(i) on R(i – 1) without Permutation

through 4, columns 32 and 5 in Figure 3-15, are equal to –. The corresponding entries in columns 1 through 4 are equal to x. All other entries of rows 1 through 4 are blank since b_1 through b_4 only depend on six input bits. Repeating this analysis for S_2 through S_8 results in the matrix of Figure 3-15.

Taking permutation into account, the matrix rows have to be rearranged according to the permutation schedule given by *P*(B) in Equation 3-16. The result is shown in Figure 3-16 and represents the type of relationship that exists between R(i) and R(i – 1); thus, $G_{i,i-1}^{(R,R)}$ is obtained (see Table 3-19).

Since L(i) = R(i – 1) (Equation 3-17), one can see that L(i) does not depend on L(i – 1) but has a linear dependence on R(i – 1). Hence the elements of $G_{i,i-1}^{(L,L)}$ are blank since they express the relationship between L(i) and L(i – 1).

The relationship between L(i) and R(i – 1) is expressed by the elements of $G_{i,i-1}^{(L,R)}$. Due to the linear relationship between L(i) and R(i – 1), the elements located on the diagonal are set to x as shown in Figure 3-17. Equation 3-18 shows the relationship among R(i), L(i – 1), K(i), and R(i – 1). Since the dependence on K(i) is not of interest here, the expression

$$R(i) = L(i-1) \oplus h[R(i-1)] \tag{3-19}$$

is used henceforth. The relationship between R(i) and L(i – 1) is also linear.

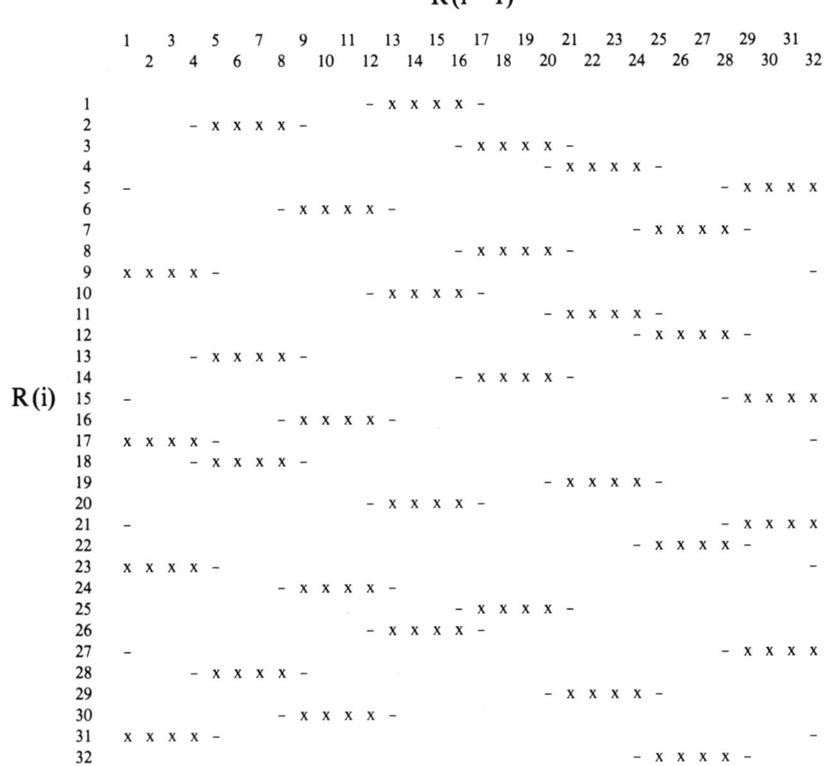

Figure 3-16. Functional Dependence of R(i) on R(i – 1), Matrix $G^{(R,\,R)}_{i,i-1}$

Hence the diagonal elements of $G^{(R,L)}_{i,i-1}$, which relate R(i) and L(i − 1), are set to x, whereas the remaining elements are blank (Figure 3-17). Since $G^{(L,L)}_{i,i-1}$ through $G^{(R,R)}_{i,i-1}$ have now been evaluated, the matrix $G_{i,i-1}$ is completely defined. It is shown in Figure 3-17.

Let $G_{i+1,i-1}$ be expressed next in terms of $G_{i,i-1}$. From Equation 3-17, the relation L(i + 1) = R(i) can be established. Thus the functional dependence of L(i + 1) on X(i − 1) is identical to the functional dependence of R(i) on X(i − 1). Since the dependence of L(i + 1) on X(i − 1) = [L(i − 1), R(i − 1)] is given by $G^{(L,L)}_{i+1,i-1}$, $G^{(L,R)}_{i+1,i-1}$, and the dependence of R(i) on X(i − 1) is given by $G^{(R,L)}_{i,i-1}$, $G^{(R,R)}_{i,i-1}$, according to Table 3-19, it follows that

$$G^{(L,L)}_{i+1,i-1} = G^{(R,L)}_{i,i-1} \tag{3-20}$$

and

$$G^{(L,R)}_{i+1,i-1} = G^{(R,R)}_{i,i-1} \tag{3-21}$$

Before the derivation of $G^{(R,L)}_{i+1,i-1}$ and $G^{(R,R)}_{i+1,i-1}$, a more general case is considered, the evaluation of $G^{(R,L)}_{j+1,i-1}$ and $G^{(R,R)}_{j+1,i-1}$ from $G_{j,i-1}$ $(j \geqslant i)$. (Note that for j = i the special case described above is obtained.)

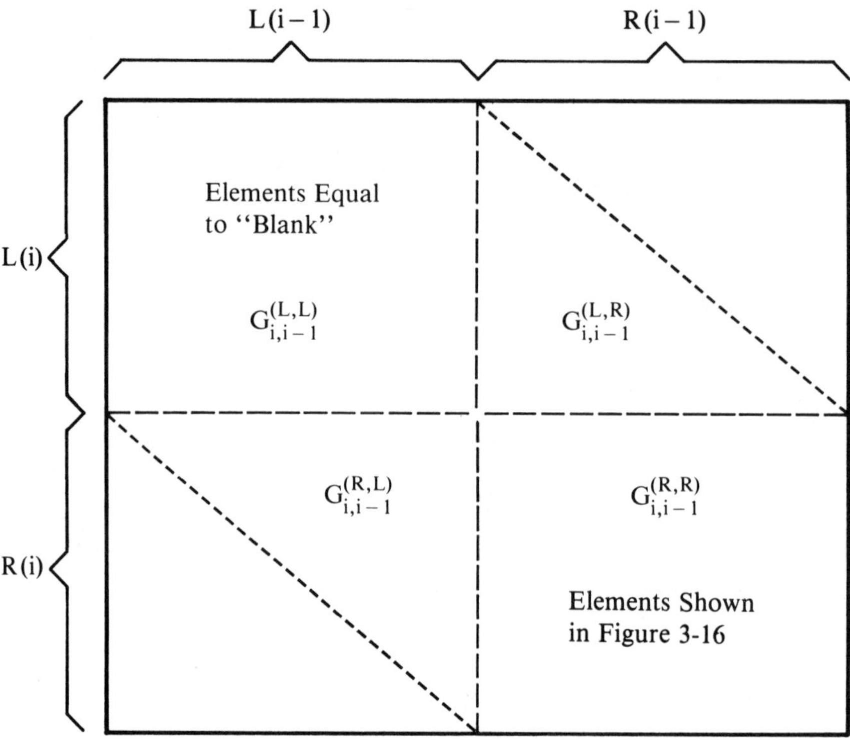

Elements of $G^{(L,R)}_{i,i-1}$ and $G^{(R,L)}_{i,i-1}$ located on the indicated diagonal are equal to "x" whereas the remaining elements are equal to blank.

Figure 3-17. Functional Relationship between $X(i) = L(i), R(i)$ and $X(i-1) = L(i-1), R(i-1)$, Matrix $G_{i,i-1}$

The elements of row s of $G^{(R,L)}_{j+1,i-1}$ give the relationship between bit s of R(j + 1) (i.e., $r_s(j+1)$) and L(i − 1), whereas the elements of row s of $G^{(R,R)}_{j+1,i-1}$ give the relationship between bit s of R(j + 1) and R(i − 1). To evaluate these elements, one must first obtain the relationship between $r_s(j+1)$ and X(j) = [L(j), R(j)] by using Figures 3-16 and 3-17. Bit s of R(j + 1) linearly depends on L(j), as shown in Figure 3-17 (i.e., on bit s of L(j) via message dependence (x)). From Figure 3-16, it follows that bit s of R(j + 1) depends on R(j) via —xxxx— (i.e., bit s depends on two bits of R(j) via autoclave and on four bits of R(j) via a message relationship). Let the columns of these entries in $G^{(R,R)}_{i,i-1}$ (equal to $G^{(R,R)}_{j+1,j}$ if i = j + 1) be designated as $m_1(s)$ through $m_6(s)$. For example (Figure 3-16), the following is obtained for s = 4: $m_1(s) = 20$, $m_2(s) = 21$, $m_3(s) = 22$, $m_4(s) = 23$, $m_5(s) = 24$, and $m_6(s) = 25$. Since the dependence of X(j) on X(i − 1) is given by $G_{j,i-1}$ and the dependence of bit s of R(j + 1) on X(j) is known, the relationship between R(j + 1) and X(i − 1), given by rows 33 to 64 of matrix $G_{j+1,i-1}$ can be determined by properly combining elements of row s, $m_1(s) + 32$, . . . , $m_6(s) + 32$ of $G_{j,i-1}$. This method is indicated in Figure 3-18.

The rule that should be used to combine the rows of matrix $G_{j,i-1}$ so that the dependence of $x_{s+32}(j+1)$ on $X(i-1)$ can be evaluated still must be decided. Since the main objective of this analysis is to determine how fast the functional dependence between output and input builds up, it would be sufficient simply to indicate if a functional relationship between an output bit and an input bit exists. However, to provide more insight on the influence of autoclave, a rule is derived which highlights autoclave influence. Thus all elements of $G_{j,i-1}$ for rows $m_1(s)+32$ and $m_6(s)+32$ are set to –, indicating an autoclave relationship. Note that the elements of row $s+32$ of $G_{j+1,i-1}$ describe the dependence of $x_{s+32}(j+1)$ on $X(i-1)$. Since $x_{s+32}(j+1)$ depends on $x_{m_1(s)+32}(j)$ and $x_{m_6(s)+32}(j)$ via autoclave, the dependence of $x_{m_1(s)+32}(j)$ and $x_{m_6(s)+32}(j)$ on $X(i-1)$ is changed from –, x, or * to an autoclave dependence –. Adoption of this rule permits the

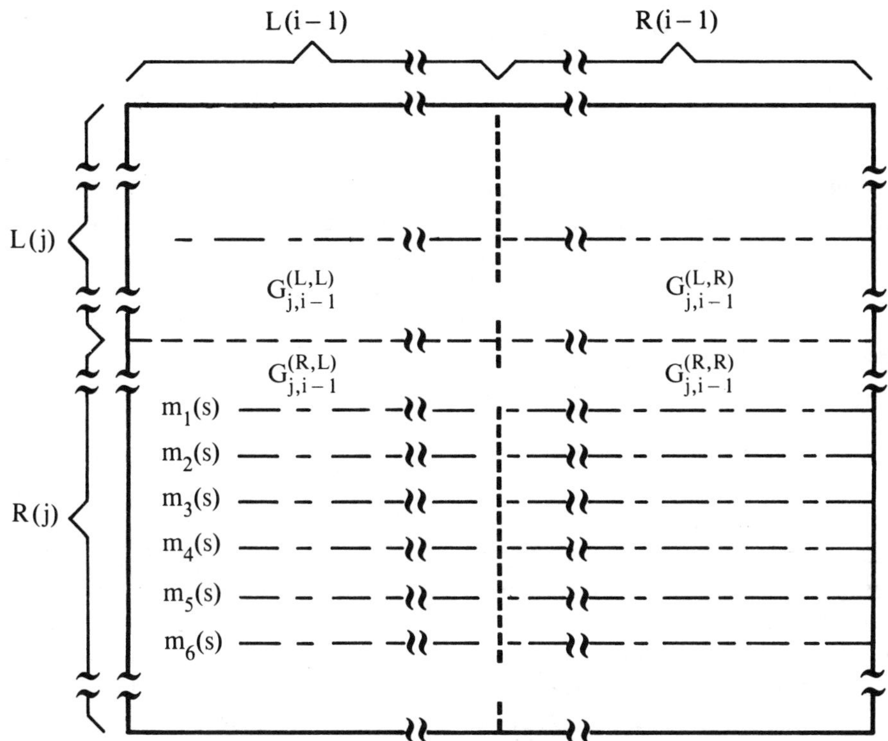

Note: $X(j+1) = [L(j+1), R(j+1)]$ vs. $X(i-1)$ is obtained by combining the elements of row s, $m_1(s)$ through $m_6(s)$, where $m_1(s)$ through $m_6(s)$ are the columns in which the elements in row s of $G^{(R,R)}_{i,i-1}$ occur. $(1 \leqslant s \leqslant 32.)$ $G^{(R,R)}_{i,i-1}$ is defined in Figure 3-16.

Figure 3-18. Evaluation of Functional Dependence of $X(j+1)$ vs. $X(i-1)$ from $X(j)$ vs. $X(i-1)$.

elimination of previous history as far as the autoclave entry to an S-box is concerned, thereby increasing the emphasis on the last autoclave dependence.

In order to take into account previous history for the entries to an S-box not associated with autoclave, the elements of $G_{j,i-1}$ are left unchanged for rows s, $m_2(s) + 32$, $m_3(s) + 32$, $m_4(s) + 32$, and $m_5(s) + 32$.

When the proper rows of $G_{j,i-1}$ are combined, one or more entries can occur in the same column. Only if entries are either all x or all – will the final dependence be correspondingly set. If mixed entries (x and –) occur, the final dependence is set to *. If the entry * occurs at least once, then the final dependence is set to *, regardless of the other entries.

Summary of the Procedure

The elements of row s + 32 of matrix $G_{j+1,i-1}$, for $1 \leq s \leq 32$, can be generated from matrix $G_{j,i-1}$ by determining $m_1(s)$ through $m_6(s)$ from the given matrix $G^{(R,R)}_{i,i-1}$. They are the columns in which the nonblank elements in row s of $G^{(R,R)}_{i,i-1}$ are located. (Figure 3-16 shows these entries.) Take matrix $G_{j,i-1}$ and select row s, $m_1(s) + 32$ through $m_6(s) + 32$. The entries in row s + 32 of matrix $G_{j+1,i-1}$ are now obtained by combining the elements in the indicated rows using the established rules.

As a corollary, the following can be stated. Elements in row s of $G^{(R,L)}_{j+1,i-1}$ are obtained by combining row s of $G^{(L,L)}_{j,i-1}$ with rows $m_1(s)$ through $m_6(s)$ of $G^{(R,L)}_{j,i-1}$. Elements in row s of $G^{(R,R)}_{j+1,i-1}$ are obtained by combining row s of $G^{(L,R)}_{j,i-1}$ with rows $m_1(s)$ through $m_6(s)$ of $G^{(R,R)}_{j,i-1}$.

Consider now the special case j = i (i.e., let $G_{i+1,i-1}$ be evaluated from $G_{i,i-1}$). The submatrix $G^{(R,R)}_{i+1,i-1}$ can be derived by using the stated rules. The result is shown in Figure 3-19.

For ease of understanding, the detailed steps for obtaining the elements of row s (for s = 4) of $G^{(R,R)}_{i+1,i-1}$ from $G_{i,i-1}$ are shown in Figure 3-20. Note that for s = 4, one obtains (from Figure 3-16) $m_1(s), \ldots, m_6(s)$ equal to 20, 21, 22, 23, 24, 25, as stated above.

$G^{(R,L)}_{i+1,i-1}$ can now be computed. According to the established rule, elements of row s of $G^{(L,L)}_{i,i-1}$ and of rows $m_1(s)$ through $m_6(s)$ of $G^{(R,L)}_{i,i-1}$ must be combined. But the elements of $G^{(L,L)}_{i,i-1}$ are all blank, so that it does not come into play. Elements of row $m_1(s)$ through $m_6(s)$ at $G^{(R,L)}_{i,i-1}$ are equal to x at columns $m_1(s)$ through $m_6(s)$. (See Figure 3-17.) According to the established rule, the entries at columns $m_1(s)$ and $m_6(s)$ are changed to – before all entries are combined to obtain the elements of row s in $G^{(R,L)}_{i+1,i-1}$. These entries are then equal to –xxxx– at columns $m_1(s)$ through $m_6(s)$, that is, identical to the ones in $G^{(R,R)}_{i,i-1}$.

Therefore, it can be concluded that

$$G^{(R,L)}_{i+1,i-1} = G^{(R,R)}_{i,i-1}$$

Combining this result with Equation 3-21 yields the following relationship:

$$G^{(R,L)}_{i+1,i-1} = G^{(L,R)}_{i+1,i-1} = G^{(R,R)}_{i,i-1} \tag{3-22}$$

Equation 3-20 permits the evaluation of $G_{i+1,i-1}$ in terms of $G_{i,i-1}$.

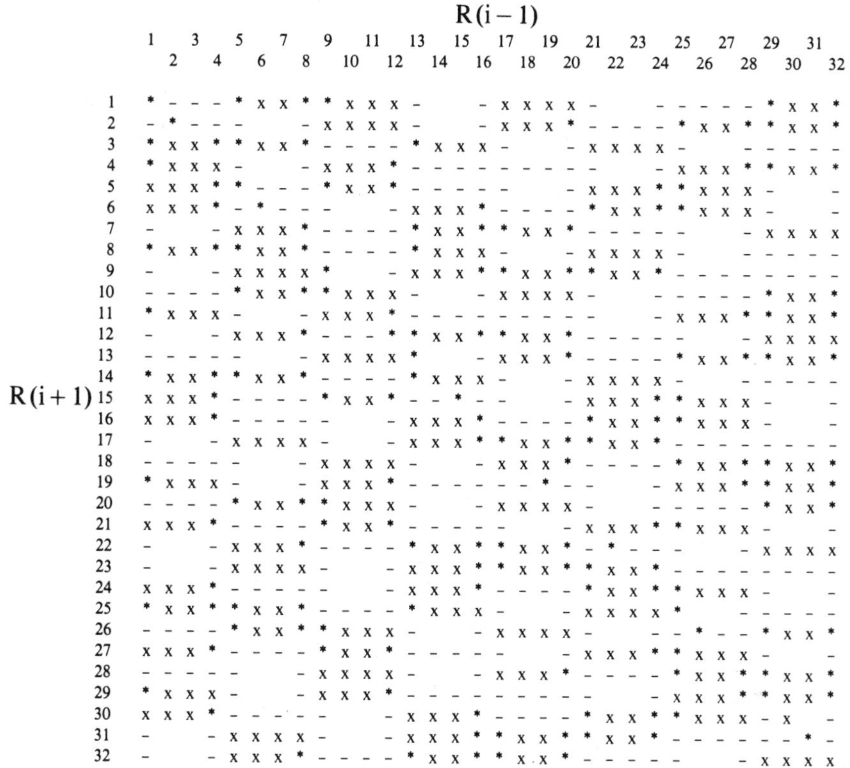

Figure 3-19. Functional Dependence of R(i + 1) on R(i − 1), Matrix $G^{(R,R)}_{i+1,i-1}$

The proof by induction is used next to show that the following general rule (for $j \geqslant i$) holds:

$$G^{(L,L)}_{j+1,i-1} = G^{(R,L)}_{j,i-1} \tag{3-23}$$

$$G^{(L,R)}_{j+1,i-1} = G^{(R,R)}_{j,i-1} \tag{3-24}$$

$$G^{(R,L)}_{j+1,i-1} = G^{(L,R)}_{j+1,i-1} = G^{(R,R)}_{j,i-1} \tag{3-25}$$

The first stage of the proof–the demonstration that these statements are correct for the smallest value of j, j = i–is given above. (See Equations 3-20, 3-21, and 3-22.)

From the relationship (Equation 3-17)

$$L(j+1) = R(j)$$

it can be determined that L(j + 1) depends on X(i − 1) in the same way R(j) depends on X(i − 1). Thus

$$G^{(L,L)}_{j+1,i-1} = G^{(R,L)}_{j,i-1}$$
$$G^{(L,R)}_{j+1,i-1} = G^{(R,R)}_{j,i-1}$$

which proves Equations 3-23 and 3-24.

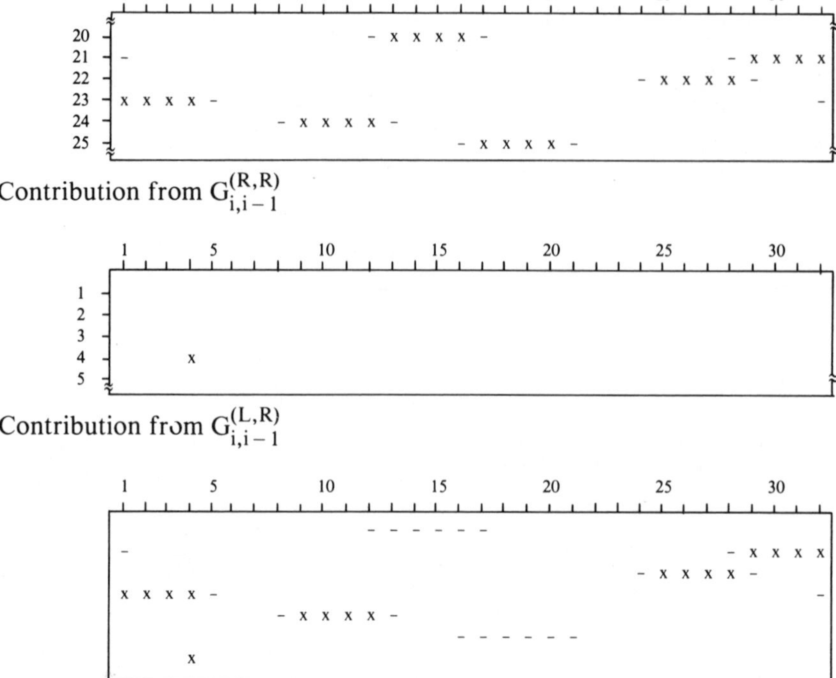

Contribution from $G^{(R,R)}_{i,i-1}$

Contribution from $G^{(L,R)}_{i,i-1}$

Entries to be combined

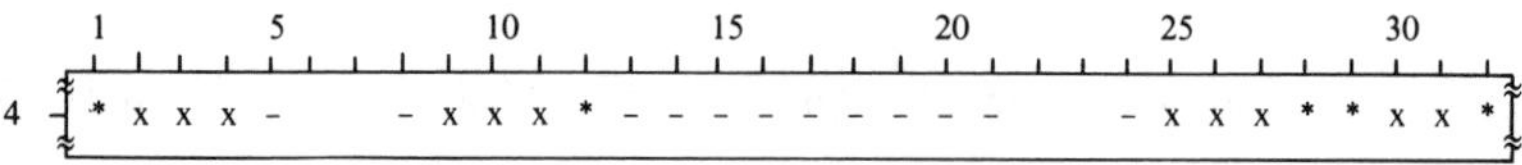

Combined entries resulting in row four of $G^{(R,R)}_{i+1,i-1}$

Figure 3-20. Functional Dependence of 4th Bit of $R(i+1)$ on $R(i-1)$

The results stated in the corollary are used to prove Equation 3-25 as follows. $G^{(R,L)}_{j+1,i-1}$ is obtained by combining the elements of $G^{(L,L)}_{j,i-1}$ (row s) and $G^{(R,L)}_{j,i-1}$ (rows $m_1(s)$ through $m_6(s)$). But $G^{(L,L)}_{j,i-1} = G^{(R,L)}_{j-1,i-1}$, $G^{(R,L)}_{j,i-1} = G^{(R,R)}_{j-1,i-1}$, if the stated rule holds. $G^{(L,R)}_{j+1,i-1} = G^{(R,R)}_{j,i-1}$ is obtained by combining the elements of $G^{(L,R)}_{j-1,i-1}$ (row s) and $G^{(R,R)}_{j-1,i-1}$ (rows $m_1(s)$ through $m_6(s)$). But $G^{(L,R)}_{j-1,i-1} = G^{(R,L)}_{j-1,i-1}$ if the stated rule holds. Hence, $G^{(R,L)}_{j+1,i-1}$ is obtained just as $G^{(R,R)}_{j,i-1}$ was and, likewise, $G^{(L,R)}_{j+1,i-1}$ is obtained. Therefore, $G^{(R,L)}_{j+1,i-1} = G^{(L,R)}_{j+1,i-1}$. That completes the proof. (See Figure 3-21.)

Minimum Number of Rounds Required to Achieve Ciphertext/Plaintext Intersymbol Dependence

For each output bit to depend on all plaintext bits after round j, no element of $G_{j,0}$ can be blank. When this condition is satisfied, it follows from the relationships developed between $G_{j,0}$ and $G_{j-1,0}$ and $G_{j-2,0}$ that no ele-

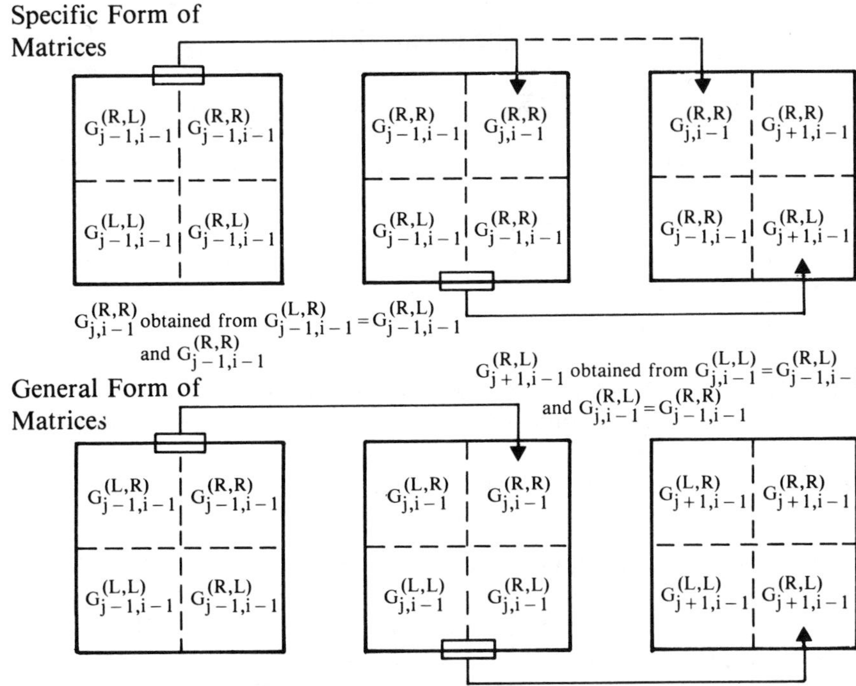

Figure 3-21. Graphical Presentation of Proof that $G^{(R,L)}_{j+1,i-1}=G^{(L,R)}_{j+1,i-1}$

ment of $G^{(L,R)}_{j-1,0} = G^{(R,L)}_{j-1,0}$ can be blank and no element of $G^{(R,R)}_{j-2,0}$ can be blank.

If all row entries of the matrices were independent, an approximate result for the minimum number of rounds could be obtained as shown below. (In actuality, the elements of eight sets of four rows each of $G^{(R,R)}_{i,i-1}$ are highly correlated. Therefore, the increase of intersymbol dependence will be slower than predicted by the approximation.) Since $G^{(R,R)}_{1,0}$ has six entries in each row (Figure 3-16) and $G^{(L,R)}_{1,0}$ has one entry in each row (Figure 3-17), then $G^{(R,R)}_{2,0}$ can have at most $1 + 6 \cdot 6$ or 37 entries. (Note that $G^{(R,R)}_{2,0}$ is obtained from $G^{(L,R)}_{1,0}$ and $G^{(R,R)}_{1,0}$.) There are, however, only 32 columns in $G^{(R,R)}_{2,0}$. Therefore, it is possible that none of the elements of $G^{(R,R)}_{2,0}$ are blank. Thus it is possible to fill all 32^2 entries of $G^{(R,R)}_{2,0}$, $G^{(L,R)}_{3,0} = G^{(R,L)}_{3,0}$, $G^{(R,R)}_{4,0}$ after rounds 2, 3, and 4, respectively. Hence all 64^2 entries of $G_{4,0}$ could be filled after four rounds.

The approximate analysis shows that four is the minimum number of rounds needed to achieve intersymbol dependence between ciphertext and plaintext. The accurate analysis below shows that after four rounds complete interdependence has not been achieved and for the specific design of DES five rounds are required.

From the evaluation of $G^{(R,R)}_{i+1,i-1}$ (Figure 3-19) one can see that there are 28 nonblank elements in each row, except for row 30 which contains 29 elements. It can also be shown that all entries of $G^{(R,R)}_{i+2,i-1}$ are equal to *.

Round	Output/Input Relation				
j	L(j)vs.L(0)	L(j)vs.R(0)	R(j)vs.L(0)	R(j)vs.R(0)	X(j)vs.X(0)
1	0.00	3.13	3.13	18.75	6.25
2	3.13	18.75	18.75	87.60	32.06
3	18.75	87.60	87.60	100.00	73.49
4	87.60	100.00	100.00	100.00	96.90
5	100.00	100.00	100.00	100.00	100.00

Note: Table entries express the degree of intersymbol dependence, i.e., the percentage of nonblank elements in the appropriate relation.

Table 3-20. Ciphertext/Plaintext Intersymbol Dependence

Thus after round 4 each output bit of L(4), except bit 30, depends on 28 bits of L(0) and all 32 bits of R(0). Bit 30 of L(4) depends on 29 bits of L(0) and all 32 bits of R(0). Each bit of R(4), on the other hand, individually depends on the 32 plaintext bits of L(0) and R(0).

Let the degree of intersymbol dependence be measured by a factor ξ, which is obtained by evaluating the percentage of nonblank elements. Respectively, for $G_{1,0}^{(L,L)}$ through $G_{1,0}^{(R,R)}$ (Figures 3-16 and 3-17), ξ is 0%; $100 \cdot 32/32^2 = 3.125\%$; 3.125%; and $100 \cdot 32 \cdot 6/32^2 = 18.75\%$. With the total $G_{1,0}$, ξ is equal to $(0 + 3.125 + 3.125 + 18.75)/4$ or 6.25%. Using either the results above or Figure 3-19, $\xi = 100[32^2 - ((31 \cdot 4) + 3)]/32^2 = 87.60\%$ for $G_{2,0}^{(R,R)}$. Hence according to the rules for obtaining $G_{3,0}$ from $G_{1,0}$, the values of ξ associated with $G_{2,0}^{(L,L)}$ through $G_{2,0}^{(R,R)}$ are 3.13, 18.75, 18.75, and 87.60%, respectively, whereas ξ for $G_{2,0}$ is equal to $\frac{1}{4}$ (3.125 + 18.75 + 18.75 + 87.60) or 32.06%. Because none of the elements of $G_{3,0}^{(R,R)}$ are blank (they are actually all *), ξ, as associated with $G_{3,0}^{(R,R)}$, is equal to 100%. The results are summarized in Table 3-20.

Interdependence Between Ciphertext and Key

For the investigation of the functional relationship between the input to the (i + 1)th round (equal to the output of the (i)th round, i = 1, 2, . . . 16) and the key, a matrix F_i of 64 rows and 56 columns is defined. The elements of the matrix, $a_{l,m}$, for row l and column m show the type of relationship which exists between the lth bit of X(i) and the mth bit of U where

$$U = u_1, u_2, \ldots, u_{56}$$

is a vector whose elements are related to the externally entered key

$$K = k_1, k_2, \ldots, k_{64}$$

as follows:

$$\begin{aligned} U = {} & k_{49}, k_{41}, k_{33}, k_{25}, k_{17}, k_9, k_1, \\ & k_{58}, k_{50}, k_{42}, k_{34}, k_{26}, k_{18}, k_{10}, \\ & k_2, k_{59}, k_{51}, k_{43}, k_{35}, k_{27}, k_{19}, \\ & k_{11}, k_3, k_{60}, k_{52}, k_{44}, k_{36}, k_{57}, \\ & k_{55}, k_{47}, k_{39}, k_{31}, k_{23}, k_{15}, k_7, \\ & k_{62}, k_{54}, k_{46}, k_{38}, k_{30}, k_{22}, k_{14}, \\ & k_6, k_{61}, k_{53}, k_{45}, k_{37}, k_{29}, k_{21}, \\ & k_{13}, k_5, k_{28}, k_{20}, k_{12}, k_4, k_{63} \end{aligned} \tag{3-26}$$

The vector U represents the key obtained by loading the external key of 64 bits into two 28-bit shift registers after the parity bits k_8, k_{16}, k_{24}, k_{32}, k_{40}, k_{48}, k_{56}, and k_{64} have been systematically removed as part of the loading procedure (Tables 3-8 and 3-9). Of the 56 register positions, 48 are connected to the Exclusive-OR circuits which perform the modulo 2 addition between $R(i-1)$ and $K(i)$ (Figure 3-12). If the register positions are labeled 1 through 56, it follows that $K(i)$ is obtained by taking the key bits located in positions

14, 17, 11, 24, 1, 5, 3, 28, 15, 6, 21, 10,
23, 19, 12, 4, 26, 8, 16, 7, 27, 20, 13, 2

of the first register, and positions

41, 52, 31, 37, 47, 55, 30, 40, 51, 45, 33, 48,
44, 49, 39, 56, 34, 53, 46, 42, 50, 36, 29, 32

of the second register. (See Equations 3-9a and 3-9b.)

Since U represents the key stored in the register at the start of the enciphering process, K(1) is related to U as follows:

$$\begin{aligned} K(1) = {} & u_{14}, u_{17}, u_{11}, u_{24}, u_1, u_5, u_3, u_{28}, u_{15}, u_6, u_{21}, u_{10}, \\ & u_{23}, u_{19}, u_{12}, u_4, u_{26}, u_8, u_{16}, u_7, u_{27}, u_{20}, u_{13}, u_{29}, \\ & u_{41}, u_{52}, u_{31}, u_{37}, u_{47}, u_{55}, u_{30}, u_{40}, u_{51}, u_{45}, u_{33}, u_{48}, \\ & u_{44}, u_{49}, u_{39}, u_{56}, u_{34}, u_{53}, u_{46}, u_{42}, u_{50}, u_{36}, u_{29}, u_{32} \end{aligned} \tag{3-27}$$

After each round, the key bits located in the shift register are shifted to the left by either one or two positions. The shifting employs wraparound (i.e., bits shifted off the left side of the registers are reinserted at the right side of the registers).

K(2) is obtained by shifting the contents of each register 1 bit to the left, whereas K(3) is obtained by a 2-bit shift to the left. (See Reference 5 or Tables 3-8 and 3-9.) Hence with K(1) specified, the relationship of the other keys, K(2) and K(3), to U can be expressed as follows:

$$\begin{aligned} K(2) = {} & u_{15}, u_{18}, u_{12}, u_{25}, u_{2}, u_{6}, u_{4}, u_{1}, \\ & u_{16}, u_{7}, u_{22}, u_{11}, u_{24}, u_{20}, u_{13}, u_{5}, \\ & u_{27}, u_{9}, u_{17}, u_{8}, u_{28}, u_{21}, u_{14}, u_{3}, \\ & u_{42}, u_{53}, u_{32}, u_{38}, u_{48}, u_{56}, u_{31}, u_{41}, \\ & u_{52}, u_{46}, u_{34}, u_{49}, u_{45}, u_{50}, u_{40}, u_{29}, \\ & u_{35}, u_{54}, u_{47}, u_{43}, u_{51}, u_{37}, u_{30}, u_{33} \end{aligned} \tag{3-28}$$

$$\begin{aligned} K(3) = {} & u_{17}, u_{20}, u_{14}, u_{27}, u_{4}, u_{8}, u_{6}, u_{3}, \\ & u_{18}, u_{9}, u_{24}, u_{13}, u_{26}, u_{22}, u_{15}, u_{7}, \\ & u_{1}, u_{11}, u_{19}, u_{10}, u_{2}, u_{23}, u_{16}, u_{5}, \\ & u_{44}, u_{55}, u_{34}, u_{40}, u_{50}, u_{30}, u_{33}, u_{43}, \\ & u_{54}, u_{48}, u_{36}, u_{51}, u_{47}, u_{52}, u_{42}, u_{31}, \\ & u_{37}, u_{56}, u_{49}, u_{45}, u_{53}, u_{39}, u_{32}, u_{35} \end{aligned} \tag{3-29}$$

The functional relations can be seen if F_i is partitioned into two matrices of 32 rows and 56 columns:

$$F_i = \begin{bmatrix} F_i^{(L)} \\ F_i^{(R)} \end{bmatrix}$$

where the elements in the submatrices express the relations shown in Table 3-21.

Evaluate F_1 first. From Equation 3-17, it follows that

$$L(1) = R(0)$$

hence L(1) does not depend on any key bits. Define the elements of the matrix F_i to be blank, as before, if no dependence on U exists. The elements of $F_1^{(L)}$ are thus blank.

Similarly, from Equation 3-18,

$$R(1) = L(0) \oplus g[K(1), R(0)]$$

hence R(1) depends on U via K(1) since L(0) and R(0) do not depend on U. As a first step in obtaining $F_1^{(R)}$, the dependence of the output bits from the substitution operation, vector B in Figure 3-12, on the key bits K(i) is evaluated in Figure 3-22. (Note that the dependence of B on K(i) is identical to

Submatrix	Relationship Expressed in Submatrix
$F_i^{(L)}$	L(i) vs. U
$F_i^{(R)}$	R(i) vs. U

Table 3-21. Functional Relationships

the dependence of R(i) on K(i) if the permutation is not present.) The selection of the substitution function in the first S-box, S_1, depends on the first and sixth bits of K(i) because the values of these bits are Exclusive-ORed with the first and sixth input bits to the S-box. The result of this operation in turn determines which of the four S-functions in S_1 is selected. Key bits 1 and 6 of K(i) therefore affect the output bits from $S_1(b_1$ through $b_4)$ by influencing the selection of an S-function. This functional relationship is indicated by —. The other four key bits (bits 2, 3, 4, and 5 of K(i)) affect b_1 through b_4 by influencing the arguments of the S-function. This kind of dependence is indicated by the symbol x. If a bit from the key affects the

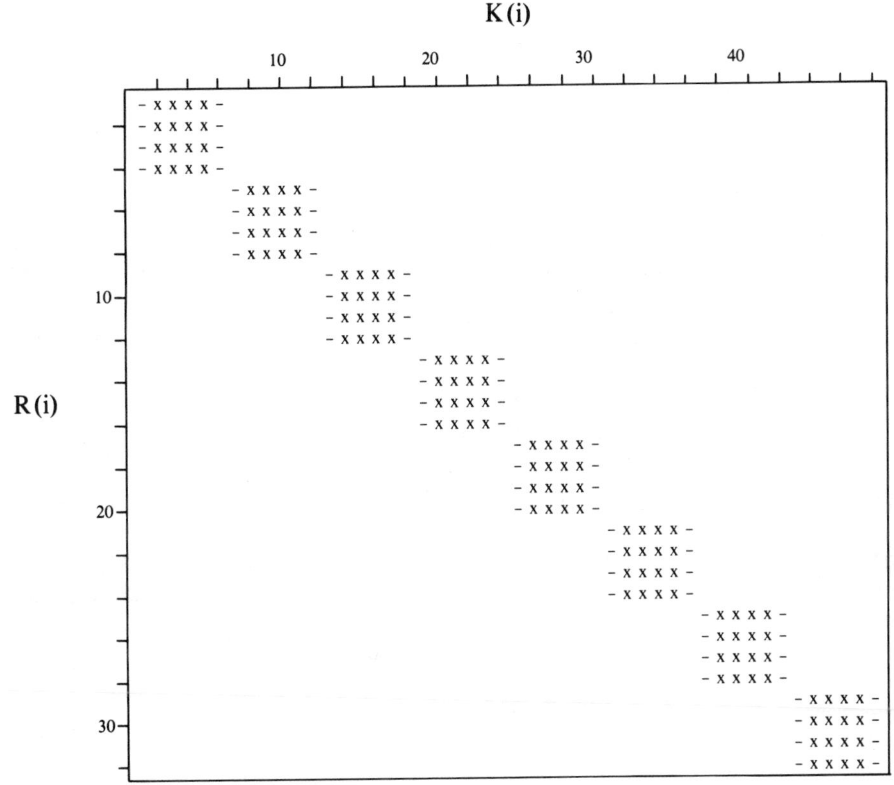

Figure 3-22. Functional Dependence of R(i) on K(i) without Permutation

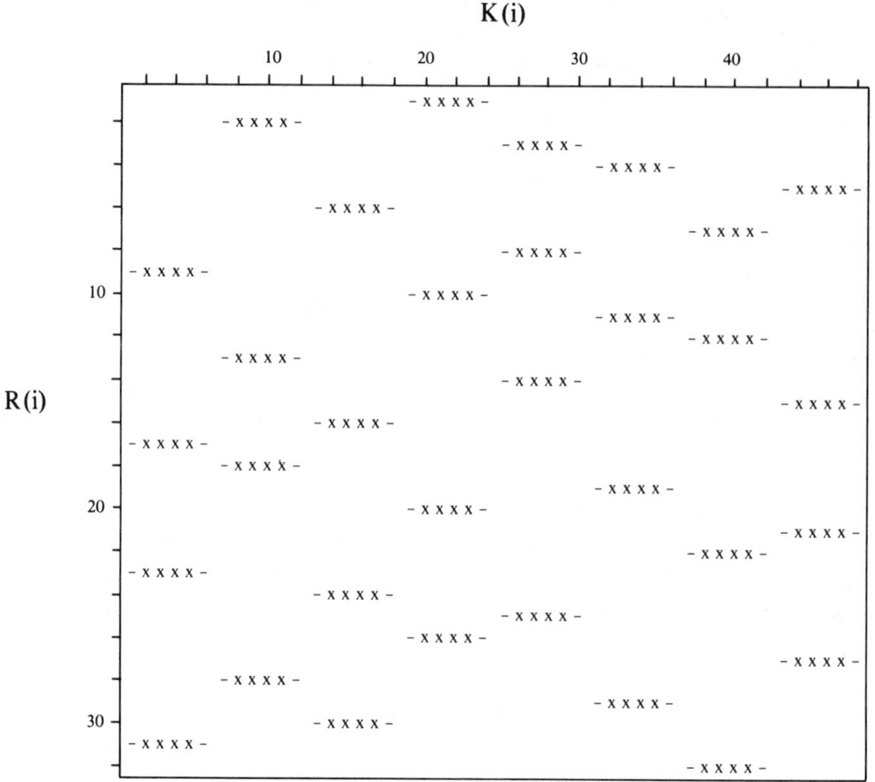

Figure 3-23. Functional Dependence of R(i) on K(i)

output by selecting an S-function as well as by selecting an argument, the symbol * is used. If the output does not depend on the key, a blank is used. This approach, used for all other bits of K(i), leads to Figure 3-22.

Because of this permutation, the rows of Figure 3-22 must be rearranged according to the relation given by *P*(B) in Equation 3-16. The result is shown in Figure 3-23 and represents the type of relationship that exists between R(i) and K(i). The dependence of R(1) on U can be determined, in order to construct $F_1^{(R)}$, by using Equation 3-27, which relates each bit of K(1) to each bit of U. Figure 3-24 is constructed by replacing each bit of K(1) with the appropriate bit of U, and thus $F_1^{(R)}$ is obtained.

Evaluate F_2 next. From Equation 3-17, it follows that L(2) = R(1) and hence L(2) depends on U in the same way R(1) does. Since the dependence of L(2) on U is shown by $F_2^{(L)}$, and the dependence of R(1) on U is shown by $F_1^{(R)}$, according to Table 3-21 it follows that

$$F_2^{(L)} = F_1^{(R)} \tag{3-30}$$

From Equation 3-18, one obtains

$$R(2) = L(1) \oplus g\,[K(2), R(1)]$$

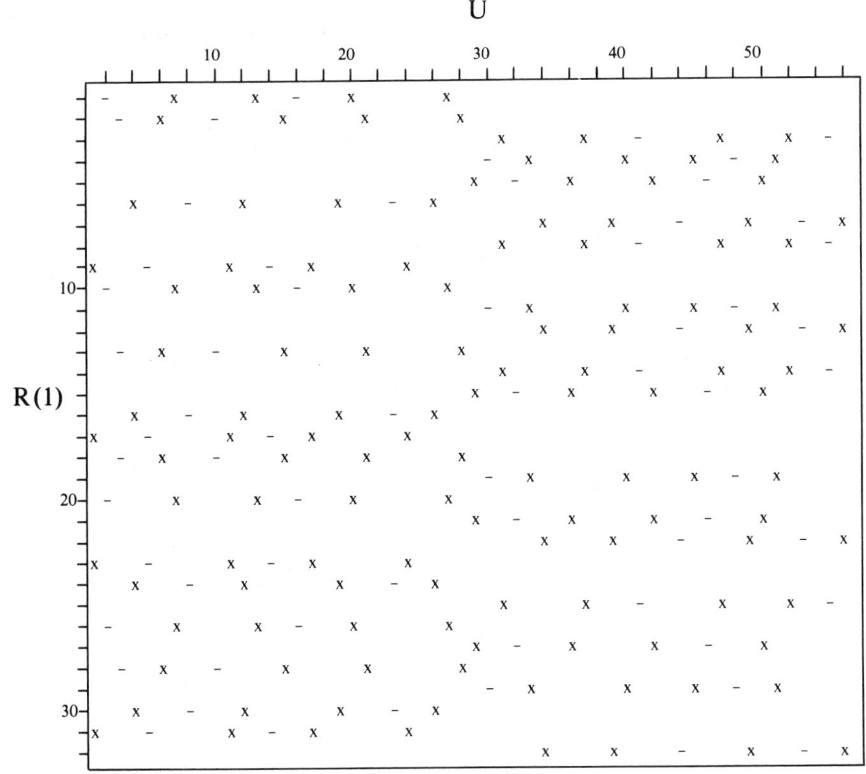

Figure 3-24. Functional Dependence of R(1) on U, Matrix $F_1^{(R)}$

The relationship between R(2) and R(1) was already established with the evaluation of $G_{i,i-1}^{(R,R)}$ (see Figures 3-16 and 3-17 for i = 2), whereas the relationship between R(1) and U is given by $F_1^{(R)}$ (see Figure 3-24). The relationship between R(2) and L(1) was also established before with the evaluation of $G_{i,i-1}^{(R,L)}$ (see Figure 3-17 for i = 2). But since L(1) does not depend on U, it can be ignored here. By the reasoning which led to Figure 3-18, it can be concluded that row s of $F_2^{(R)}$ can be constructed from F_1 by:

1. Combining rows $m_1(s)$ through $m_6(s)$ of $F_1^{(R)}$ with row s of $F_1^{(L)}$ (the elements of which are blank),
2. Taking into account the influence of K(2).

The impact of K(2) can be evaluated by using the entries of row s of Figure 3-23 and translating the elements of K(2) into the appropriate U-values via Equation 3-28. The method illustrated is by the construction of the fourth row of $F_2^{(R)}$. From Figure 3-23, it follows that the dependence of R(2) on K(2) is indicated by —xxxx— for bits 31 through 36 of K(2). The bits correspond to u_{31}, u_{41}, u_{52}, u_{46}, u_{34}, and u_{49}, respectively, according to Equation 3-28. The appropriate entries are shown in Figure 3-25. From Figure 3-16, one observes that for s = 4, m_1 (s) through m_6 (s) are equal to 20 through 25,

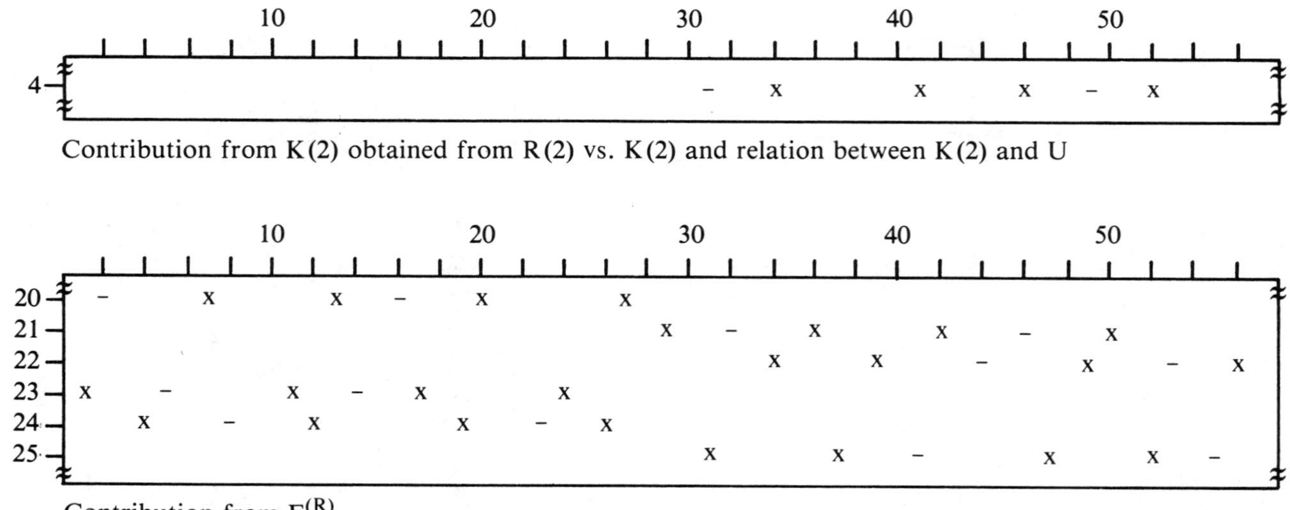

Figure 3-25. Detailed Steps to obtain Functional Dependence of 4th Bit of R(2) on U

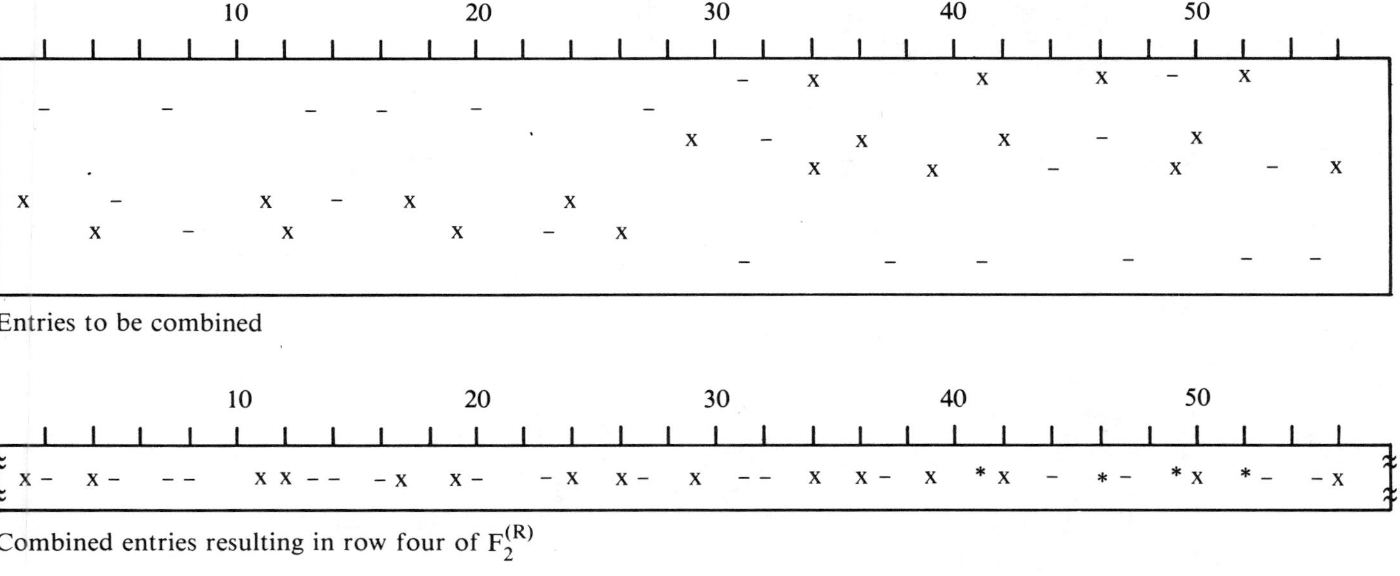

Figure 3-26. Functional Dependence of 4th Bit of R(2) on U

respectively. Hence rows 20 through 25 of Figure 3-24 must be used to obtain the contribution of R(1) to U. Details are shown in Figure 3-25. Due to rules similar to the ones established above for the ciphertext/plaintext dependence, the entries in the rows $m_1(s)$ and $m_6(s)$ of $F_1^{(R)}$ are changed to –, yielding the entries shown in Figure 3-26. The selection of an S-function is similar to autoclave-dependence, whereas the selection of an argument was treated like message-dependence above. By the same rules for combining several elements that were used above, the final result of the functional dependence of the fourth bit of R(2) on U is obtained as shown in Figure 3-26. Repetition of this procedure for $1 \leqslant s \leqslant 32$ yields Figure 3-27 and hence $F_2^{(R)}$ is obtained. Since $F_2^{(L)} = F_1^{(R)}$, as shown before, the matrix F_2 is thus obtained by combining Figure 3-24 and Figure 3-27. Let F_3 be evaluated next. The steps followed to obtain the functional dependence of the fourth bit of R(3) on U are shown in Figure 3-28. The final result (also shown in Figure 3-28) is obtained by following the same rules that led to the combination of Figure 3-25 and Figure 3-26. Repeating this procedure, all rows of $F_3^{(R)}$ shown in Figure 3-29 can be obtained. By using the relation $F_3^{(L)} = F_2^{(R)}$ the matrix F_3 is then obtained by combining Figure 3-27 and Figure 3-29.

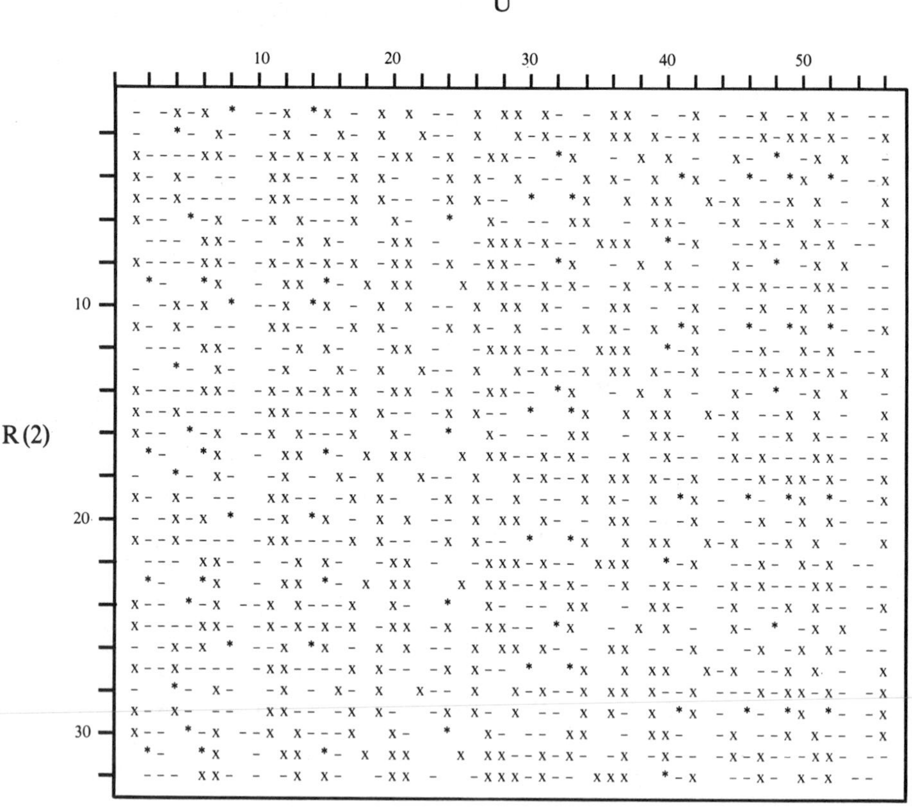

Figure 3-27. Funtional Dependence of R(2) on U, Matrix $F_2^{(R)}$

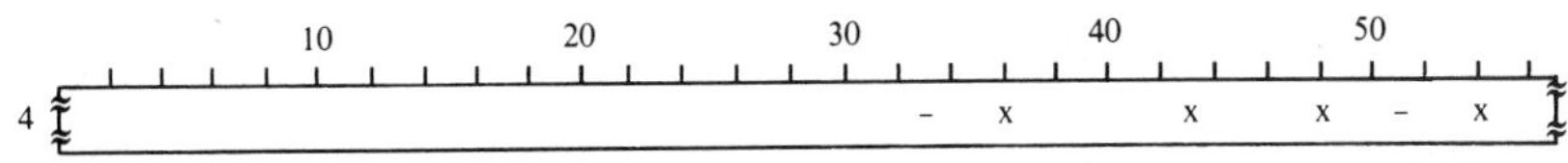

Contribution from K(3) obtained from R(3) vs. K(3), Figure 3-23, and relation between K(3) and U, Equation 3-29.

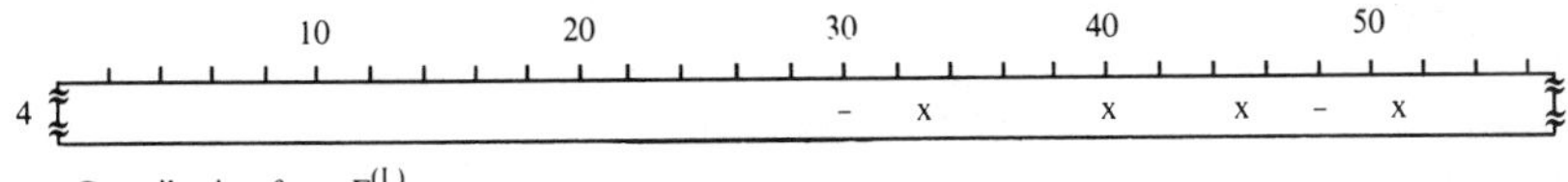

Contribution from $F_2^{(L)}$

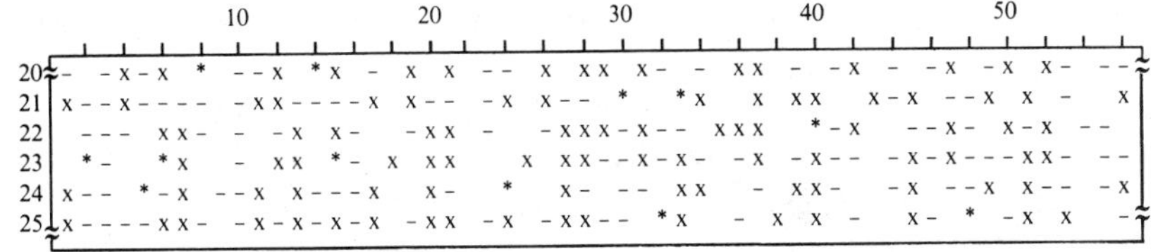

Contribution from $F_2^{(R)}$. (Entries in row 20 and 25 must be set equal to – before combining.)

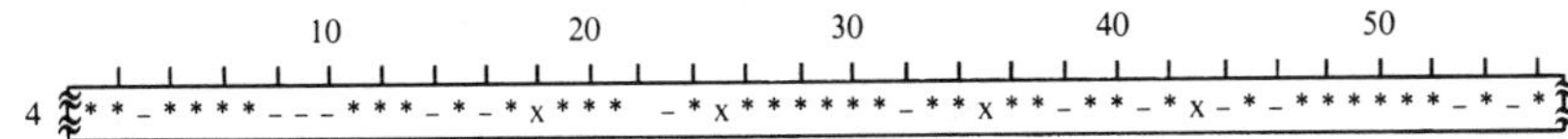

Combined entries resulting in row four of $F_3^{(R)}$

Figure 3-28. Functional Dependence of 4th Bit of R(3) on U

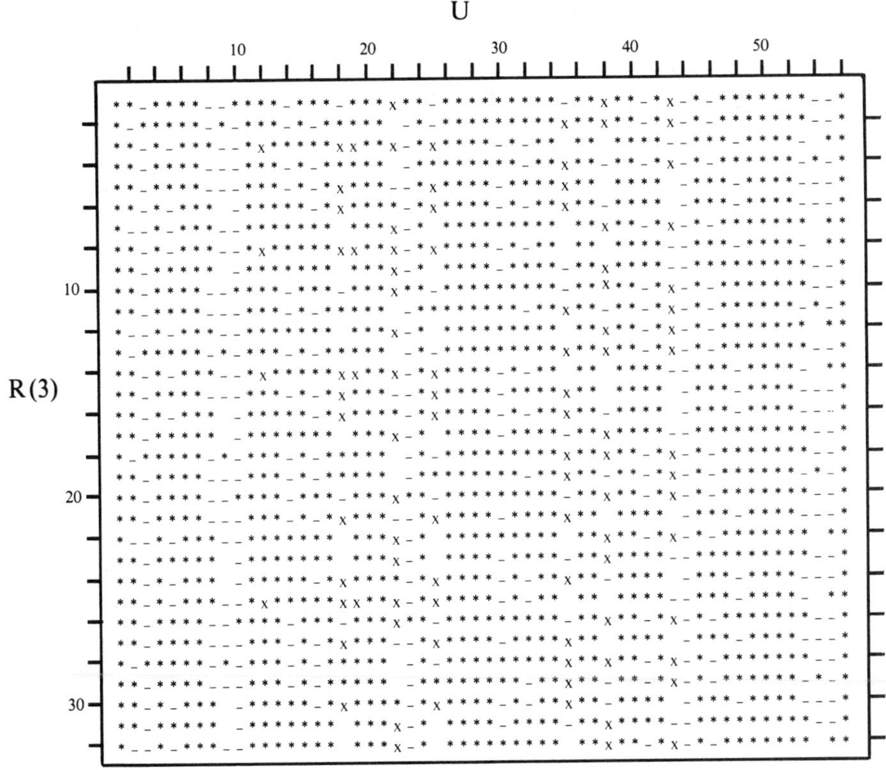

Figure 3-29. Functional Dependence of R(3) on U, Matrix $F_3^{(R)}$

Minimum Number of Rounds Required to Achieve Ciphertext/Key Intersymbol Dependence

For each output bit to depend on all bits of the key after round j, no element of F_j must be blank. If this condition is satisfied, then it follows from Equation 3-30 that no element of $F_{j-1}^{(R)}$ is blank.

An approximate calculation of the minimum number of rounds can be performed as follows. Figure 3-23 shows that K(j) always affects six columns in each row of $F_j^{(R)}$. Since L(0) and R(0) do not depend on the key, there are six nonblank entries in each row of $F_1^{(R)}$ (see also Figure 3-24), whereas all entries of $F_1^{(L)}$ are blank as shown before. Six rows of $F_1^{(R)}$ of six nonblank entries each and one row of $F_1^{(R)}$ (entries all blank) are combined to obtain $F_2^{(R)}$ to take into account the relationship between R(2) and X(1), whereas K(2) is taken into account in deriving six entries in each row (see also Figure 3-25). The maximum possible number of nonblank entries in each row of $F_2^{(R)}$ is thus $(6 \cdot 6) + 6 = 42$. (In the accurate analysis for DES shown in Figure 3-26, only 36 entries of the fourth row of matrix $F_2^{(R)}$ are nonblank since there is an overlap between elements of the rows to be combined.) Six rows of $F_2^{(R)}$ of at most 42 nonblank entries each, one row of $F_1^{(R)}$ of six nonblank entries each and six entries determined by the relationship between R(3) and K(3) are combined to obtain $F_3^{(R)}$. Since the total, $(6 \cdot 42) + 6 + 6$, exceeds the maximum number of possible entries (56) it is concluded that all rows of $F_3^{(R)}$ could be nonblank, which implies that at most all elements of $F_4^{(L)}$ could be nonblank. (In the accurate analysis for DES shown in Figure 3-28, there is still one nonblank entry, in row four of matrix $F_3^{(R)}$, again due to overlap between entries to be combined.) The conclusion of this approximate analysis is therefore that all $64 \cdot 56$ entries of F_4 could be nonblank after four rounds.

If an accurate analysis to calculate the percentage of nonblank elements, ξ, is performed, it is seen from Figures 3-24, 3-27, and 3-29 that $F_1^{(2)}$, $F_2^{(2)}$,

Round	Output/Input Relation		
j	L(j) vs. U	R(j) vs. U	X(j) vs. U
1	0.00	10.71	5.36
2	10.71	79.02	44.87
3	79.02	96.43	87.72
4	96.43	100.00	98.21
5	100.00	100.00	100.00

Note: Table entries express the degree of intersymbol dependence, i.e., the percentage of nonblank elements in the appropriate relations.

Table 3-22. Ciphertext/Key Intersymbol Dependence

$F_3^{(2)}$ have 1600, 376, and 64 blank entries, respectively. With this information and the fact that $F_j^{(2)} = F_{j-1}^{(1)}$ the values of ξ shown in Table 3-22 can be obtained. Since U is directly related to the supplied key (ignoring parity bits) according to Equation 3-26, the table entries do not change when U is replaced by K. Hence the relationships shown in Table 3-22 also indicate how the intersymbol dependence between ciphertext and key build up.

Summary and Conclusions

One property of DES is that each bit of ciphertext is a function of all plaintext bits and all cipher key bits. This property, defined as intersymbol dependence, has been analyzed above by evaluating how fast intersymbol dependence was achieved as a function of repeated mathematical operations defined as rounds. Each of these operations consists basically of substitution and transposition.

Three different forms of dependencies were considered:

1. If an input bit affects the selection of a substitution function in one round, the corresponding output was said to have an autoclave dependence on the input.
2. If an input bit affects the argument of a substitution function in one round, the corresponding output was said to have a message dependence on the input.
3. Finally, since the basic operation involving substitution and transposition is repeated several times, the functional relation between a ciphertext bit and a plaintext bit can be a combination of both of the relations defined above.

It has been shown that after five rounds each ciphertext bit depends on all plaintext bits via message- as well as autoclave-dependence. In addition, a similar analysis has revealed that each ciphertext bit depends on all key bits after five rounds.

The method applied to DES is, in general, applicable to ciphers which split up the input into two parts, operate on one part first, and combine the results of that operation with the other part using modulo 2 addition. In addition, the assumption is made that the S-box functions are nonaffine such that cancellation of dependencies does not occur.

REFERENCES

1. Shannon, C. E., "Communication Theory of Secrecy Systems," *Bell System Technical Journal,* **28**, 656–715 (1949).
2. Feistel, H., "Block Cipher Cryptographic System," U.S. Patent No. 3,798,359 (March 19, 1974).
3. *IBM Research Reports,* **7**, No. 4, IBM Research, Yorktown Heights, NY (1971).

4. Ehrsam, W. F., Meyer, C. H., Powers, R. L., Smith, J. L., and Tuchman, W. L. "Product Block Cipher System for Data Security," U.S. Patent No. 3,962,539 (June 8, 1976).
5. *Data Encryption Standard,* Federal Information Processing Standard (FIPS) Publication 46, National Bureau of Standards, U.S. Department of Commerce, Washington, DC (January 1977).
6. Vernam, G. S., "Cipher Printing Telegraph Systems for Secret Wire and Radio Telegraphic Communications," *Journal of the AIEE,* **45**, 109-115 (February 1926).
7. Kolman, B., *Elementary Linear Algebra,* Macmillan, London, 1971.
8. Golomb, S. W., *Shift Register Sequences,* Holden-Day, San Francisco, 1967.
9. Oystein, O., *Number Theory and Its History,* McGraw-Hill, New York, 1948.
10. Meyer, C. H. and Tuchman, W. L., "Pseudorandom Codes can be Cracked," *Electronic Design,* **23**, 74–76 (November 9, 1972).
11. Tuchman, W. L. and Meyer, C. H., "Efficacy of the Data Encryption Standard in Data Processing," *Proceedings COMPCON,* **78**, 340–347 (September 1978).
12. Bahl, L., "An Algorithm for Solving Simple Substitution Cryptograms," *International Symposium on Information Theory,* Ithaca, NY (October 1977).
13. Unclassified Summary, Involvement of NSA in the Development of the Data Encryption Standard, United States Senate Select Committee on Intelligence, Washington, DC (April 1978).
14. Branstad, D., Gait, J., and Katzke, S., *Report of the Workshop on Cryptography in Support of Computer Security,* Held at the National Bureau of Standards, NBSIR 77-1291, Systems and Software Division Institute for Computer Sciences and Technology, National Bureau of Standards, Washington, DC 29234 (September 1977).
15. Meissner, P., *Report of the 1976 Workshop on Estimation of Significant Advances in Computer Technology,* Held at the National Bureau of Standards, August 30-31, 1976 NBSIR 76-1199, Computer Systems Engineering Division, Institute for Computer Sciences and Technology, National Bureau of Standards, Washington, DC 29234 (December 1976).
16. Hoffman, L. J., *Modern Methods for Computer Security and Privacy,* Prentice-Hall, Englewood Cliffs, NJ, 1977.
17. Hellman, M., Merkle, R., Schroeppel, R., Washington, L., Diffie, W., Pohlig, S., and Schweitzer, P., *Results of an Initial Attempt to Cryptanalyze the NBS Data Encryption Standard,* Information Systems Laboratory Report, Stanford University (September 9, 1976) (Revised November 10, 1976.)
18. Harrison, M. A., *Introduction to Switching and Automata Theory,* McGraw-Hill, New York, 1965.
19. Hong, S. J., Cain, R. G., and Ostapko, D. L., "MINI: A Heuristic Approach for Logic Minimization," *IBM Journal of Research and Development,* **18**, No. 5, 445–458 (September 1974).
20. Meyer, C. H., "Ciphertext/Plaintext and Ciphertext/Key Dependence vs. Number of Rounds for the Data Encryption Standard," *AFIPS Conference Proceedings,* **47**, 1119–1126 (June 1978).

Other Publications that Treat Cryptanalysis

21. Coppersmith, D., and Grossman, E., "Generators for Certain Alternating Groups with Applications to Cryptography," *SIAM Journal on Applied Mathematics,* **29**, 624–627 (December 1975).
22. Grossman, E., "Group Theoretic Remarks on Cryptographic Systems Based on Two Types of Addition," IBM T. J. Watson Research Center, Yorktown Heights, NY, RC 4742 (February 1974).

23. Tuckerman, B., "A Study of the Vigenere-Vernam Single and Multiple Loop Enciphering Systems," IBM T. J. Watson Research Center, Yorktown Heights, NY, RC 2879 (May 1970).

24. Tuckerman, B., "Solution of a Substitution Fractionation Transposition Cipher," IBM T. J. Watson Research Center, Yorktown Heights, NY, RC 4537 (September 1973).

25. Konheim, A. G., *Cryptography: A Primer*, John Wiley, New York, 1981.

CHAPTER FOUR

Communication Security and File Security Using Cryptography[1]

Previous chapters have introduced the reader to the fundamentals of cryptography from a conceptual and, at times, abstract viewpoint. The discussion has centered around the types of cryptographic algorithms in use today, their salient properties, and some principles used in designing strong algorithms.

Beginning with this chapter and continuing throughout most of the book, cryptographic applications are described that provide data privacy, data integrity, or both. Communication security (**COMSEC**), file security (**FILESEC**), personal verification, message authentication, and digital signatures are discussed. This chapter deals mainly with methods for incorporating a conventional cryptographic algorithm, such as DES, in a data processing network to provide communication security. Also described are methods of using DES to secure data stored on removable media, such as tapes and disks. Methods for implementing public-key algorithms are not described, although some of the material may be applied to the design of public-key cryptographic systems.

For COMSEC, end-to-end encryption—the encipherment of data at their point of origin and decipherment only at their final destination—is emphasized because it provides the most security. When properly implemented, a host processor's encryption capability can be used for communication security, file security, and other applications involving cryptography. Before a step-by-step discussion of how end-to-end encryption can be implemented in a data processing network, an overview of network configurations and the various ways that cryptography can be implemented is appropriate.

NETWORKS

Soon after the first computers were developed for scientific data processing applications, people realized that they might be applied to accounting tasks. System designers and manufacturers then tried to extend the benefits of the

[1] The material contained in this chapter elaborates and extends the ideas contained in References 1 and 2.

computer to more people and businesses. The application of computers to communications was inevitable.[2]

At first, typewriter-like devices were designed and attached to the computer in the same way that punched card readers, magnetic tape devices, and line printers were. Through the keyboard the user could request programming services without punching cards. Similarly, program execution was performed immediately, or in real time, as opposed to the delay normally experienced between submission of a job for batch processing and receiving the output, or results. Systems programs called operating systems made program execution in real time possible. Useful results and reports of errors were returned to the user with almost no noticeable delay.

While such devices were satisfactory for users near the computer, they did not serve remote users. This problem was solved when it became possible to send computer data over voice-grade analog telephone lines.

The development of the transmission control unit, a device capable of controlling the telephone line and attached devices, contributed to this breakthrough. System programming at the computer formatted data and managed the control unit and device through standardized protocols: the agreements reached between two parties on the format and meaning of control messages and the sequence of control messages to be exchanged between the two parties. Unfortunately, application development was inhibited by the need for device-dependent support in each application program for each type of device. Architectures were subsequently developed to unify network operations (see Incorporation of Cryptography into a Communications Architecture, Chapter 7).

At the same time, advances in technology, specifically the development of microprocessors, led to the introduction of programmable communications control units and programmable device control units. These units assumed line and device control functions previously performed by application programs. As a result, a major portion of the network management responsibility was relocated to various network devices thus allowing the host processor to perform other functions. Gradually, data communications between hosts as well as between a host and its attached devices (terminals, printers, facsimile machines, etc.), over switched (public) or nonswitched (dedicated) lines, became generalized such that any node (terminal, communications controller, or host processor) could communicate with any other node.

The microprocessor revolution also had an effect on the computational capability of terminals and control units. In addition to the fixed functions of line and device control, particular applications could be performed by specialized devices because sufficient computing power was available for additional functions. As the capacity of microprocessors increased, additional functions were off-loaded from host processors and performed by various microprocessor-driven devices. Systems evolved wherein data processing functions were performed by devices situated in different places and connected by transmission facilities. Thus data could be partially or wholly processed

[2] A short history of this development can be found in Reference 3.

at any number of network nodes—a concept that became known as *distributed data processing*. The common element in this development was the network architecture which established the basis for device attachment and specified the protocols necessary for device interaction.

A *data processing network* (Figure 4-1) is a configuration of data processing devices, such as processors, control units, and terminals, which normally are connected by data links for the purpose of data processing and information exchange. The links may be processor channels, satellite and microwave links, or switched and nonswitched communications lines. A network may be de-

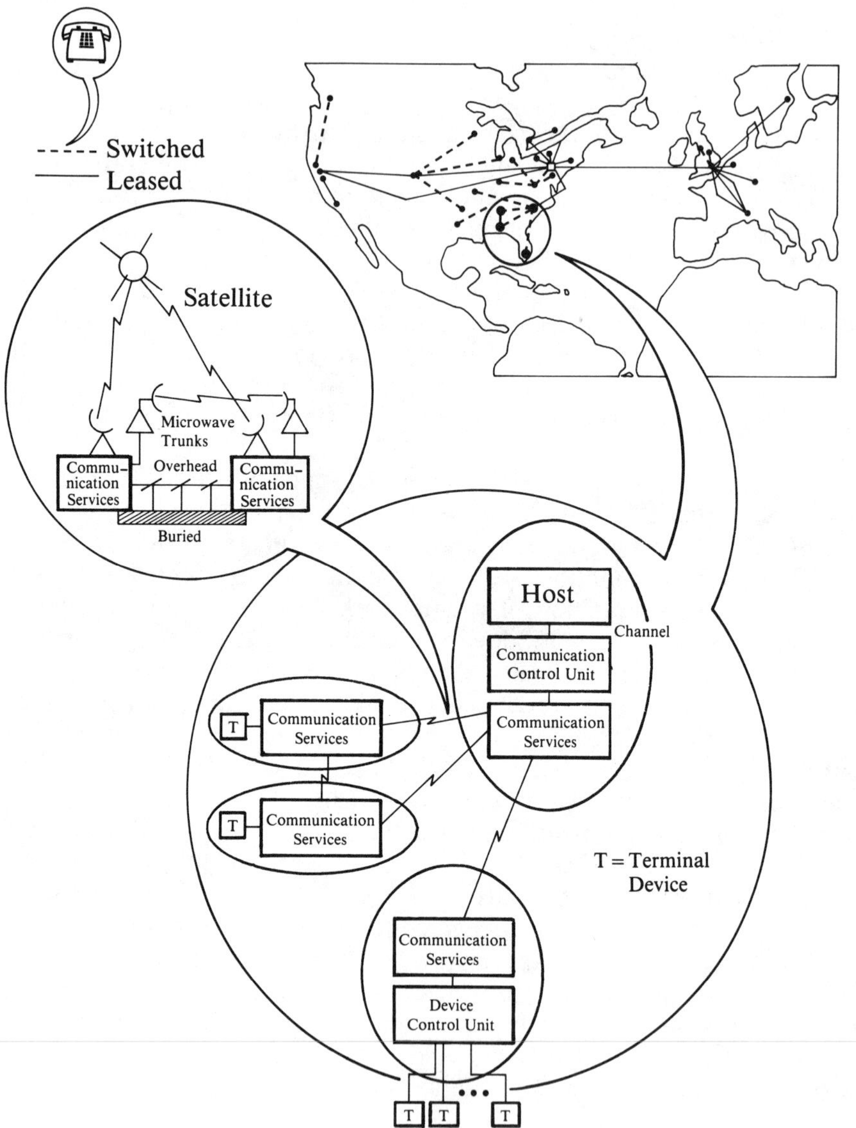

Figure 4-1. Data Processing Network

scribed, in terms of the patterns formed by its links, as a star, loop, tree, or mesh. In any case, the network's basic function is to provide *access paths* by which a *user* (person or program) at one location can communicate with another user at some other location [4].

As more network facilities are used to process and transmit data, there is an increased dependency on communication facilities provided by a communication common carrier for hire by the general public. Likewise, the opportunity and ease with which data can be intercepted increase. An architecture for networks must therefore provide a capability to implement appropriate security measures should they be required.

NETWORK ENCRYPTION MODES

There are three ways to incorporate cryptography into a communications system: *link*, *node*, and *end-to-end* encryption.

Link encryption (Figure 4-2) protects data between adjacent network nodes. The algorithm is implemented in cryptographic devices that bracket (i.e., are situated at opposite ends of) a communication line between two network nodes. The two devices are positioned between their respective nodes and associated modems (modulators/demodulators) and are equipped with identical keys.

Node encryption (Figure 4-3) is similar to link encryption in that each pair of nodes shares a key to protect data communicated between them. However, data passing through an intermediate node are not in the clear, as would be the case with link encryption. Rather, at an intermediate node, the enciphered data are transformed from encipherment under one key to encipherment under another key (deciphered and reenciphered) within a security module or protected peripheral device attached to the node. (Node encryption is defined solely for completeness and discussed only in this section.)

End-to-end encryption (Figure 4-4) continuously protects data during transmission between users. Unlike link and node encryption, end-to-end encryption permits each user to have several keys, one key for each user who uses encryption. Data are deciphered only at their final destination—they never appear in clear form at intermediate nodes or their associated security modules.

With link and node encryption, the user is normally not aware that messages are receiving cryptographic protection (i.e., the cryptographic function is provided by the network, and is transparent to the user). A user-transparent form of end-to-end encryption occurs if the cryptographic function is provided automatically through system services. If the user makes specific requests for cryptography, its use is not transparent. This latter case is referred to as *private* cryptography.[3]

One system service required to support transparent end-to-end encryption involves the selection or assignment of a cryptographic key for enciphering

[3] Private cryptography is not the opposite of, nor should it be confused with, cryptography using a public-key algorithm. For a description of public-key algorithms, see Cryptographic Algorithms and Public-Key Algorithms, Chapter 2.

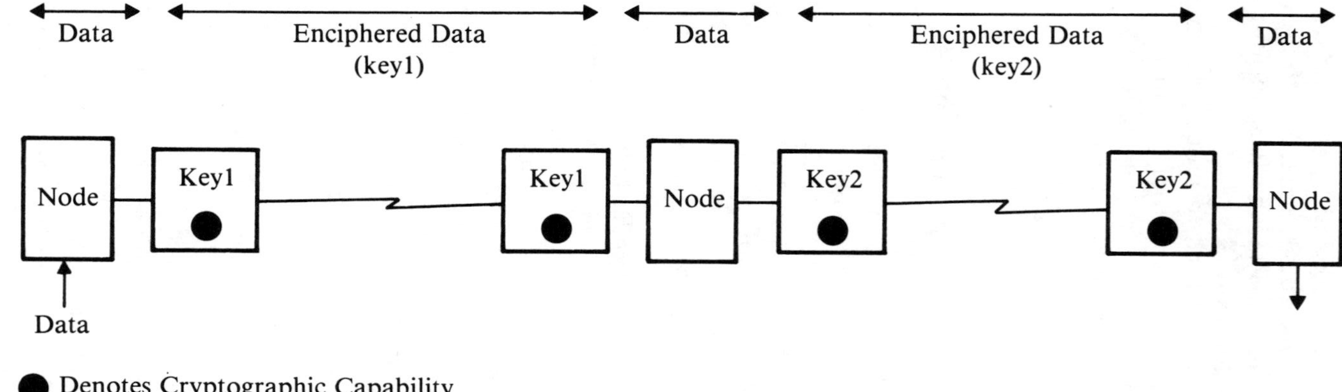

Figure 4-2. Link Encryption

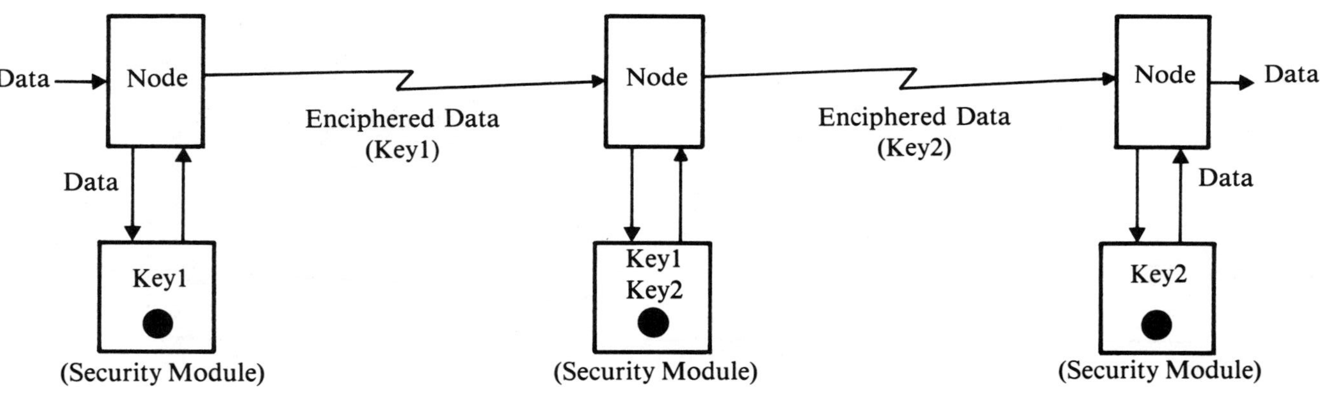

Figure 4-3. Node Encryption

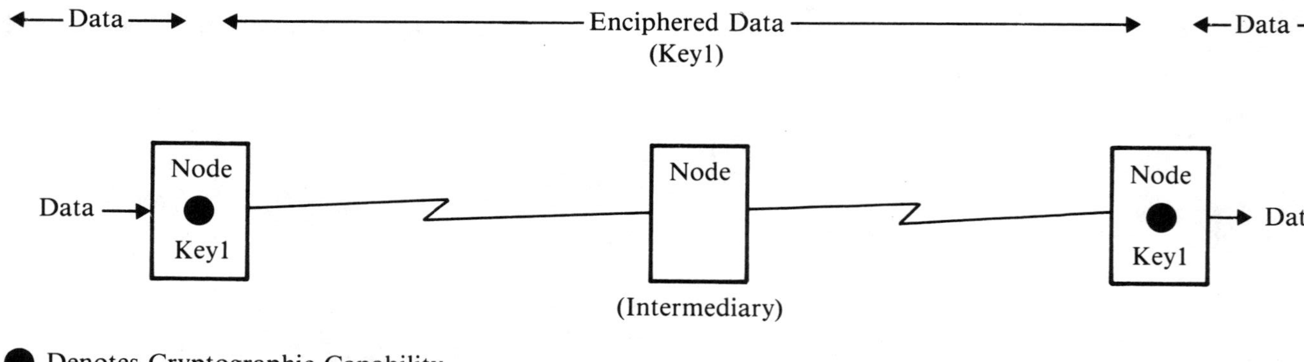

Figure 4-4. End-to-End Encryption

and deciphering data between communicating users (or the network nodes at which the users are located). If one or more nodes in the system cannot use encryption, or if encryption of only selected messages is desired, an additional system mechanism is required to enable and disable the encryption function. In either case, if cryptography is to be used by a network node, then the encryption capability must be integrated (logically or physically) into the node. In effect, this means that key management for end-to-end encryption is not affected by the way a node is attached to the communication channel.

A host processor's encryption capability can be integrated into the central processing unit (CPU), into a front-end processor, or into a separate unit attached to a CPU's channel—a device that connects the CPU and main storage with input/output control units. There are many trade-offs between cost and performance that must be considered in selecting an approach. However, the latter approach, being compatible with many CPU designs, has the advantage that only a single device need be designed.

With link encryption, every node in the selected path over which encrypted data pass must have a standalone cryptographic device connected to its input and output ports. With node encryption, every node in the selected path over which encrypted data pass must have its own security module (integrated or attached). With end-to-end encryption, only those nodes that originate or receive encrypted messages require an encryption capability; this can significantly reduce the places where cryptography, or cryptographic devices, must be used in the network.

In general, the information communicated between network nodes consists of a message, or the data to be exchanged between users, and a message header. Generally, a header contains routing information; for example, the intended destination, the message's sequence number, the identity of the message's source, indicators denoting the start and end of text, the classification of the message (i.e., whether it contains control commands, data, or both), and possibly its format.

With link encryption, both a message and its header could be encrypted (Figure 4-5). With either end-to-end or node encryption, only the message, but not the routing information, can be encrypted. This is because each intermediate node in the communications path must examine the routing information in order to direct the message to its intended destination. Of course, if link encryption and either end-to-end or node encryption were implemented in the same network, messages would be doubly encrypted and headers would therefore be encrypted on a link basis.

If clear and encrypted messages are intermixed, a mechanism must exist to separate them. In one approach, a bit in the message's header is used to indicate whether the message is encrypted. In another approach, consistent with some line protocols, special control messages specify when to start and stop encryption. Finally, a high security mode of operation is possible if the mechanism for turning encryption on and off is ignored and all message traffic is encrypted.

Since with end-to-end and node encryption, and in some cases with link encryption, the header is in clear form, data communications are susceptible to a form of *traffic analysis* wherein an opponent obtains statistics related to

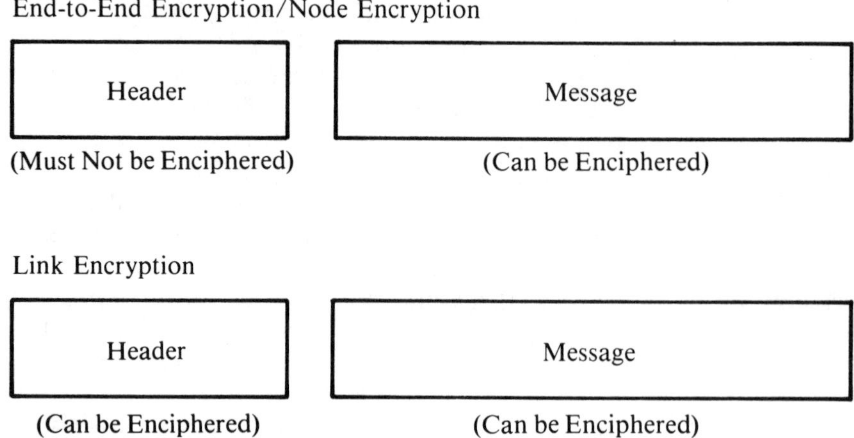

Figure 4-5. Message and Header Encryption

the number of messages transmitted to or from a given node. Other forms of traffic analysis are possible when headers are encrypted. Used by the military, traffic analysis has often given advance warning of enemy activity in a particular sector or combat zone. Traffic analysis can be prevented easily (at the expense of efficiency) by deliberately keeping a line active with bogus message traffic, thus masking the occasions when an unusual amount of meaningful traffic is transmitted. However, since traffic analysis is less of a threat in commercial applications, it is not discussed.[4]

In terms of cost, flexibility, and security, end-to-end encryption appears most attractive for systems requiring many protected links. Thus a cryptographic architecture—the definition and allocation of keys, cryptographic operations, macro instructions, and the like—for end-to-end encryption in a communications network is the subject of most of the remainder of this chapter. Based on this architecture, methods are also developed for the encryption of data files. (The communication architecture to support such a system is discussed in Chapter 7.)

However, link encryption may be more attractive than end-to-end encryption for certain networks and teleprocessing configurations. For example, where the number of links requiring protection is small, only a few link encryption devices are necessary, and therefore the cost of protection is low. Link encryption devices operate transparent to existing programs, and they require no operator action. Moreover, most link encryption devices operate at line speed, thus causing no noticeable degradation in transmission performance. Finally, some teleprocessing devices, because of their design or the way they are managed by programming, will not support end-to-end encryption. For these reasons, link encryption is discussed in greater detail before developing the subject of end-to-end encryption.

[4] The interested reader may wish to consult Baran [5] and Chaum [6], who address the traffic analysis problem.

FUNDAMENTALS OF LINK ENCRYPTION

Whereas the objective of end-to-end encryption is to protect data over the entire path it must traverse from a source node to a destination node, the objective of link encryption is to protect only the portion of the total path, or link(s), where the opportunity for interception exists or is the greatest.[5] The definition of link includes terrestrial (telephone wires, microwave, optical fiber, cable television, etc.) and satellite communication services which (1) accept a signal from a portion of a data processing system (or business machine), (2) transport that signal to a distant point, and (3) deliver the signal with exactly the same bit sequence it had when it was received. Such services are provided by communication common carriers (Western Union Telegraph Co., American Telephone and Telegraph Co., General Telephone and Electronics Co., and numerous independent telephone companies), specialized carriers, satellite carriers in the United States, and the Postal Telephone and Telegraph Administrations (PTTs) in many other countries. Excluded from the definition are the CPU's channel and the input/output (I/O) bus used to attach I/O control units (i.e., devices not connected to a communication channel).

From a practical point of view, an encryption device operating independently of the communication channel is independent of, and does not require redesign of, existing data processing and communications equipment (Figure 4-2). However, the placement of the encryption device need not be external to a terminal or its modem. Encryption apparatus could, in fact, be included "under the covers," along with a modem (should the design of either piece of equipment so specify). The ultimate decision rests with the manufacturer of the equipment and is based on the requirements of the market.

Regardless of implementation, however, the data encryption equipment (DEE) must conform to the established interface between system components, generally called data terminal equipment (DTE) and data circuit-terminating equipment (DCE).[6] (This terminology has been accepted by the International Consultative Committee for Telegraph and Telephone (CCITT), the International Organization for Standardization (ISO), the American National Standards Institute (ANSI), and the Electronic Industries Association (EIA).) Included are the electrical signal characteristics, interface mechanical characteristics, and the functional description of interchange circuits needed to establish, maintain, and disconnect the physical connection between a DTE and DCE or between two DTEs.

In some cases, improved link efficiency can be realized if the DEE is designed to a specific data link control protocol. These rules regulate the initiation, checking, and retransmission (if any) of each data unit presented to the link for transmission, and are independent of the media used. This improves the DEE's ability to determine when to start and stop encrypting/decrypting.

[5] Much of the information in this section regarding link protocols was taken from Chapter 11 in Reference 7. Interested readers are referred to this text for supplemental reading.

[6] A DTE corresponds to a data terminal or communications controller. A DCE corresponds to a modem or its functional equivalent in a public data network.

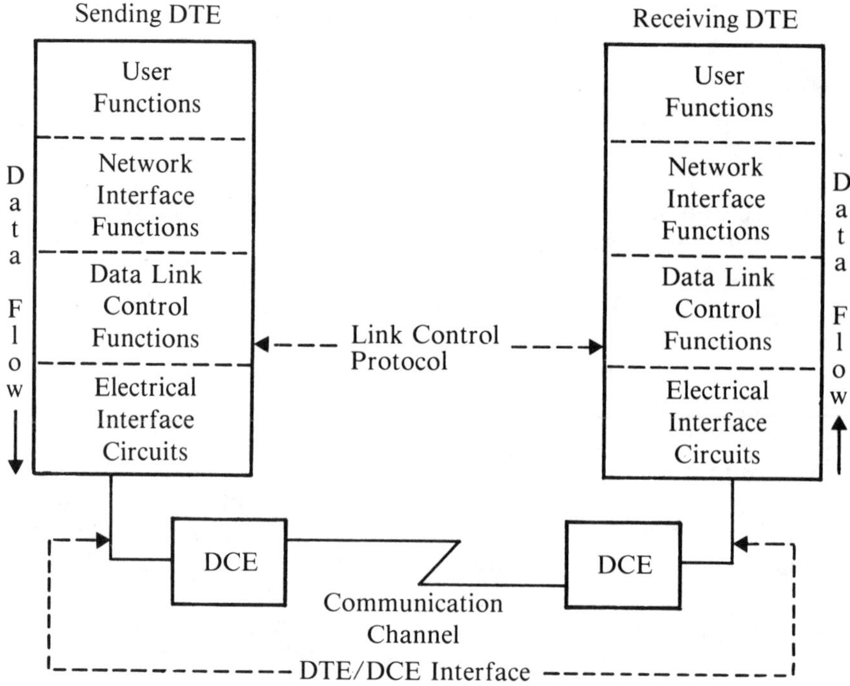

Figure 4-6a. DTE/DCE and Link Control Interface

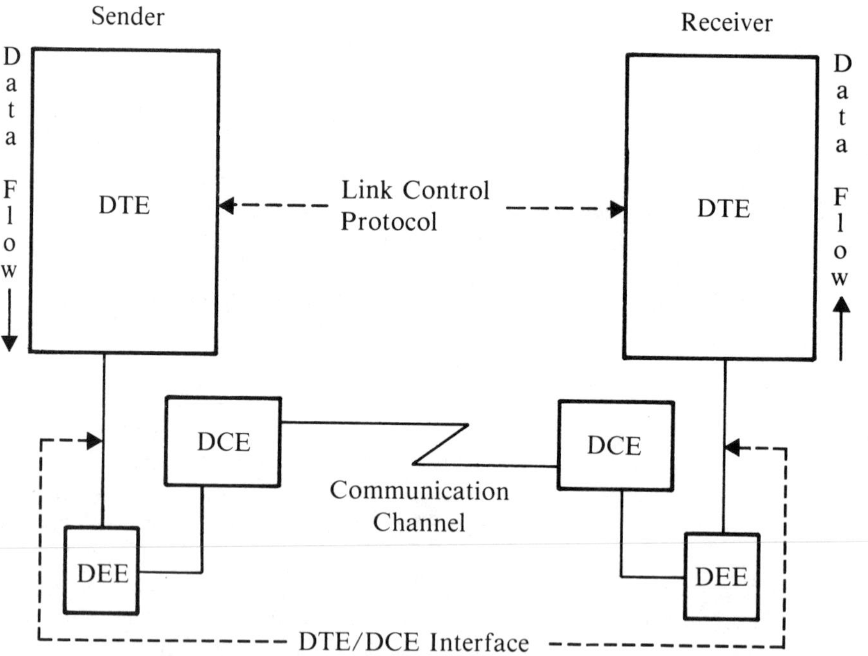

Figure 4-6b. DEE Placement—Link Encryption

Implementations which are not link protocol-dependent also exist. In these cases *every* bit is cryptographically processed without consideration by the DEE as to the format of the data unit being transmitted. Figure 4-6a illustrates the DTE/DCE interface and the arrangement of functions within DTEs.

DTE/DCE interfaces between data processing equipment and communication equipment are standardized in the United States through the efforts of the EIA, and worldwide through CCITT. Almost all manufacturers adhere to the EIA and CCITT standards so that products of different manufacturers can communicate with one another.

For the same reason, link protocols are standardized in the United States by ANSI, and worldwide through ISO. Practically then, link encryption devices must be implemented in conformance with these standards. Thus the presence of the DEE, residing on the DTE/DCE interface (Figure 4-6b), is transparent to both DTE and DCE.

Link protocols applicable to character-coded information generally fall into two broad classes: *asynchronous* and *synchronous*. The difference is related to the mechanism used to provide (bit) synchronization of the transmitted data character(s).

With an asynchronous protocol, the bits within each character, or block of characters, are sent at distinct time intervals as determined by clock pulses generated by the DTE. The receiving DTE receives the transmitted bits at the same rate, having the ability to produce clock pulses identical to those of the sender. But the first bit of each character, or block of characters, can be sent at any time. By contrast, the time of occurrence of each bit or byte transmitted synchronously, including the start bit or start character, is related to clock pulses synchronized between the sending and receiving DTEs. The protocols commonly used for asynchronous and synchronous transmissions are discussed below. A method for incorporating cryptography in each is suggested.

Asynchronous

With this protocol, each data character is preceded by a *start* bit and followed by at least one *stop* bit (popularly referred to as start/stop protocol). The start and stop bits delimit each character being sent. Depending on the character code/set in use, a character could be represented by 5, 6, 7, or 8 bits.

The start bit must always be sent in the clear. Encryption can, and usually does, begin with the first data bit and normally ends with the last data bit. The stop bit may or may not be enciphered, although in most present designs it is sent in the clear. A DEE supporting this protocol could be designed to operate with a specific character code, for example, 7-bit ASCII (American National Standard Code for Information Interchange), or with multiple codes. In this latter case, the device must be initialized via some external input to operate with one code during one period and then be reinitialized to operate with another code during a different period. Implementation options, such as these, may vary from one manufacturer to another.

Byte-Synchronous

This protocol is suitable for 7- and 8-bit ASCII and 8-bit EBCDIC (Extended Binary-Coded Decimal Interchange Code). Characters entered at a keyboard are first collected in a buffer. The entire message is then transmitted at intervals determined by the clocking mechanism supported by the two DTEs. Rather than rely on start and stop bits for character synchronization, the DTE uses a different source of timing. For example, some DCE's maintain a master clock signal (referred to as modem clocking). However, it is still desirable (as in the start/stop protocol) to derive the bit-synchronizing signal from the 0-to-1 and 1-to-0 transitions in the bit-stream itself. This is accomplished in the DTE with a bit-clock, the primary component of a business machine clock, since this avoids the consequences of any tendency of the DCE's clock to drift. In binary synchronous communication (BSC), for example, sufficiently frequent 0-to-1 bit transitions are provided through the use of the special PAD and SYN characters.

The PAD character (a set of alternating 1s and 0s) helps establish bit synchronization between the DTE and DCE. The SYN character, which may repeatedly appear in the data, helps the receiving DTE maintain character (byte) synchronization with the sending DTE. For example, initial synchronization, following a line turnaround, is assisted by the control-character sequence of PAD SYN SYN. Additional synchronizing (SYN) characters in the data stream not only ensure that the receiving DTE stays in bit synchronization but also establish which bits are the first and last in each character (i.e., they provide character synchronization as well). The content of the message is delineated by the following additional control characters:

SOH (start of header)
STX (start of text)
ETX (end of text)

With this very brief explanation, the use of cryptography to protect a message can now be understood. In one approach, intended to protect only the text portion of the message, the DEE scans the data stream for an STX character, used to signal the beginning of encryption/decryption. Encryption/decryption terminates when a corresponding ETX character is encountered. (ETX may or may not be encrypted.) Alternatively, the SOH character could signal the DEE to begin encrypting/decrypting, if it was desired to protect header information. But note that in this case the entire message is encrypted/decrypted. Therefore, throughput is adversely affected since encryption is always applied, even for messages containing no text. (In BSC, control messages are used to convey link commands.)

Ordinarily, a group of bits (called the block check character) is added to the message after the ETX. These bits, which are a function of all the bits in the message (including the header), are used to detect errors that can occur during transmission. When encryption is employed, the block check character can and may be encrypted, in which case its recomputation by the receiver is performed after decryption.

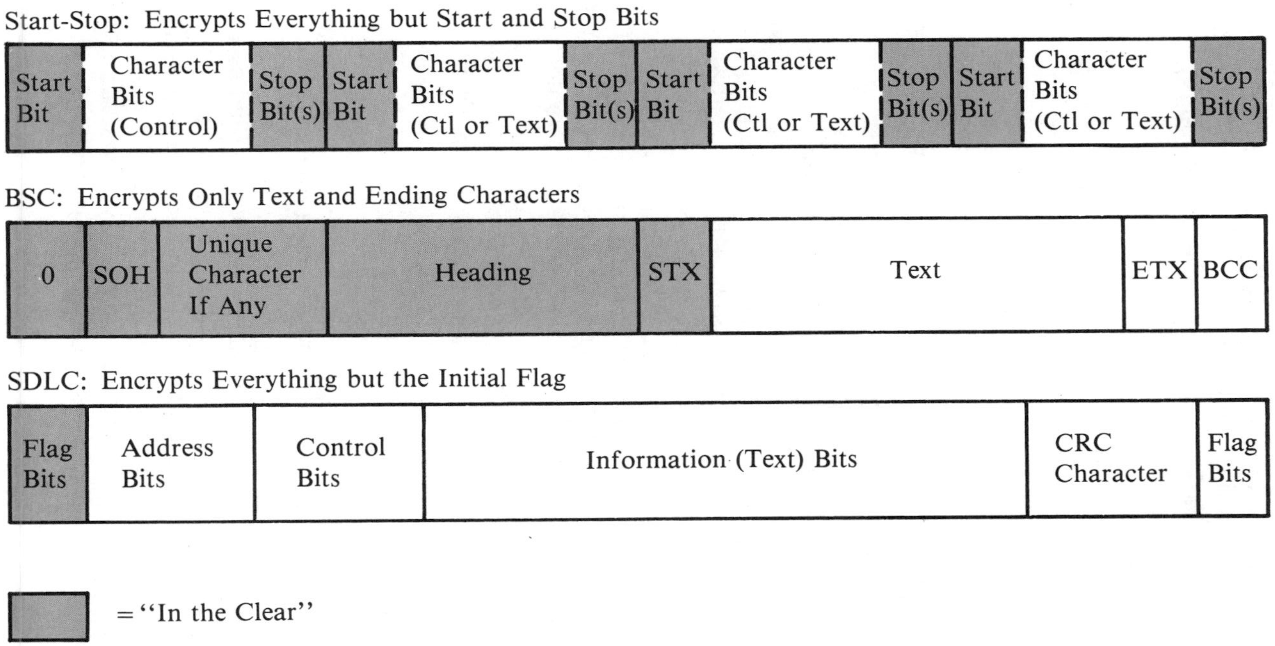

Start-Stop: Encrypts Everything but Start and Stop Bits

Start Bit	Character Bits (Control)	Stop Bit(s)	Start Bit	Character Bits (Ctl or Text)	Stop Bit(s)	Start Bit	Character Bits (Ctl or Text)	Stop Bit(s)	Start Bit	Character Bits (Ctl or Text)	Stop Bit(s)

BSC: Encrypts Only Text and Ending Characters

0	SOH	Unique Character If Any	Heading	STX	Text	ETX	BCC

SDLC: Encrypts Everything but the Initial Flag

Flag Bits	Address Bits	Control Bits	Information (Text) Bits	CRC Character	Flag Bits

= "In the Clear"

Figure 4-7. Example of Extent of Encryption, by Protocol

Reprinted by permission from IBM 3845 Data Encryption Device IBM 3846 Data Encryption Device General Information. © 1977 by International Business Machines Corporation.

Bit-Synchronous

Some link protocols are bit-oriented, rather than character-oriented.[7] Therefore, the bit pattern of a particular character is ignored by the DTE and the protocol is said to be character-code independent. Each transmission is synchronized by a unique delimiter called a *flag* (F). Transmitted data are identified by leading and trailing flags, and a unit of transmission is referred to as a *frame*. The generalized format of a frame is:

[Link Header] [Information] [Link Trailer]

or

[F] [Information] [F]

When a series of frames is sent as a group, the trailing flag of one frame is also the leading flag of the next frame (i.e., the frames are separated by a single flag). By convention, sequences of eight or more consecutive 1-bits are never transmitted except to indicate an idle line condition.

Even though the discussion above is brief, a generalized approach to encryption can be inferred therefrom by means of an example using IBM's Synchronous Data Link Control (SDLC). Because link encryption is effected between two adjacent nodes, in which case routing information must be unencrypted at the nodes but not on the link, SDLC encryption can commence with the detection of a leading F (where F is the bit string 01111110) and terminate after the trailing F (F followed by eight or more 1-bits). Decryption follows the same rule. Of course, the trailing flag would have to be identified after decryption to delimit the frame. Calculation and comparison of the block check character, which is included in the information segment of the frame, likewise is performed after decryption. Figure 4-7 illustrates one of many possible encryption implementations to achieve link data protection and serves to summarize this subject.

AN OVERVIEW OF END-TO-END ENCRYPTION

In a data communications network, assume that a person (end user) at a terminal is communicating with an application program (also an end user) through a processor of some type. These communicating end users share a common key, which may be a personal (private) key provided by and agreed upon by the users in advance or, for *transparent* cryptographic data protection, a key dynamically generated and assigned to these users by the system. This latter *data-encrypting* (or *data-decrypting*)[8] *key* is active only for the

[7] Several bit-synchronous protocols have evolved from ANSI's Advanced Data Communications Control Procedure (ADCCP), and the ISO equivalent, High Level Data Link Control (HDLC).

[8] Recall that a conventional algorithm is assumed.

duration of a single communications session, and therefore is called a *session key*.

For file security, applications programs are the participants (end users that encipher or decipher files). The data-encrypting key used to protect a file is called a *file key*. And a different file key, which is provided by either the end user or the system, may be assigned to each file. Subsequently, an encrypted file may be decrypted (recovered) at any host with an encryption capability, including the one at which it was created, provided that the file key is made available to that host.

For communication security, session keys are generated at a host and then transmitted to a receiving node (terminal or host) via a communications network (assumed nonsecure). The session key is kept secret by enciphering it under another key, defined a *key-encrypting* (or *key-decrypting*) *key,* which has been installed in advance at the receiving node. This approach allows each receiving node to have a unique key-encrypting key. Therefore, if a key-encrypting key at a terminal is compromised, the security exposure is localized to that specific terminal and does not jeopardize the security of the entire network—a highly desirable feature.

In the particular system under consideration, one set of key-encrypting keys is used to encipher session keys transmitted from host to host, and another set of key-encrypting keys is used to encipher session keys transmitted from host to terminal. Each host must therefore store the key-encrypting keys of each host and terminal that it communicates with. Potentially, many key-encrypting keys may be required. A terminal, on the other hand, is required to store only one key-encrypting key, called a *terminal master key*. Session keys are sent from a host to a terminal enciphered under the terminal's master key.

The terminal master key's secrecy is achieved by storing it in a protected area called the *cryptographic facility*. The cryptographic facility is a secure implementation containing the cryptographic algorithm (DES is assumed), and a nonvolatile memory where the master key is stored. It can be accessed only through inviolate interfaces (secure against intrusion, circumvention, and deception), which allow processing requests, key, and data parameters to be presented, and transformed output to be received. A similar cryptographic facility is available at the host.

Key-encrypting keys stored at a host processor are kept secret by enciphering them under a *host master key*. This method of protecting keys is referred to as the *master key concept*. The host master key, like the terminal master key, is kept secret by storing it in the host's cryptographic facility.

Because of the large number of cipher keys used at a host processor, automated procedures are required to generate and manage these keys. The key generator and the key manager are two host programs provided for this purpose. The key generator generates the key-encrypting keys that are required by the host. However, key-encrypting keys can also be specified by installation personnel (e.g., personal keys that have been created by individual users, or keys that have been generated at some other location by another key generator). In any case, the key-encrypting keys used by a host are stored in a key table. A second copy of each key-encrypting key is transmitted securely (by courier or some other means) and installed in the respective terminal or host.

Due to the large number of keys required at a host, it is customary to store the key table on a disk or drum (i.e., in secondary storage rather than in the computers main memory). In this discussion the key table is called the *Cryptographic Key Data Set* (**CKDS**). It resides on secondary storage and is assumed to be accessible during normal system operation. The key generator has exclusive write privilege to this data set to add, change, and delete keys. The key manager and key generator have exclusive read privilege to the data set to accomplish the tasks of translating keys. Access to the CKDS is denied to all other programs.

The translation function of the key manager involves reenciphering a key from encipherment under one key to encipherment under another key. Requests for key translation are made via **GENKEY** (Generate Key) and **RETKEY** (Retrieve Key), two *programming calls* used to invoke the key manager function.

Another programming call, denoted **CIPHER**, invokes the encipher and decipher data function. It also provides a way for the calling program to specify extended options, such as block chaining (see Block Ciphers with Chaining, Chapter 2).

Six basic cryptographic operations are defined to the host's cryptographic facility. These operations, either alone or in combination, provide the cryptographic services requested by the GENKEY, RETKEY, and CIPHER calls, and all other key management functions required by the system. The implementation of the basic operations is such that a clear key cannot be recovered outside the cryptographic facility, regardless of the order in which the basic operations are exercised. Since this property is a requirement for the cryptographic system to be secure, let it be restated in a stronger form:

It must not be possible to recover keys in the clear outside a designated physically secure area, such as a cryptographic facility, regardless of the inherent security of the supporting host operating system.

CIPHER KEY ALLOCATION

The formal treatment of end-to-end encryption begins with a discussion of cipher key allocation. To provide good overall security, different cryptographic applications require different types of cipher keys. (This will be demonstrated later when analyzing a particular implementation.) Thus an important step in the design of any cryptographic system is the initial specification of its cipher keys. This includes a statement or declaration of the intended purpose and use of each class or type of key and the procedures for their protection.

Technically, cryptographic keys are data. However, it is useful in a discussion involving cryptography to distinguish between keys (key data) and data that are not keys (nonkey data, or simply data).

Specification of Cipher Keys

The designer of a cryptographic system must answer the following questions:

1. What nodes in the system require cipher keys and how are these keys initialized or set into the nodes?
2. How often are cipher keys changed, that is, what is the expected life of a key?
3. Where in the system, and under what conditions, are cipher keys created?
4. How are data and cipher keys protected?

In the system to be described, both terminals and host processors can have encryption capabilities. The encryption capability (a *facility* capable of performing encryption and decryption) is invoked by a user located at the terminal or host processor.

For terminals capable of input and output operations, the end user is a human being (Figure 4-8). It is assumed that only one end user can be active at any given time. Terminal control units (also called cluster control units) that can support several terminals and their respective end users concurrently are, for simplicity, not specifically identified in this discussion. However, the developed key management scheme would support these devices, provided that the control unit's cryptographic operations were designed differently to accommodate several enciphered session keys.

At the host processor, end users are application programs. Because of multiprogramming (concurrent execution of two or more programs by a host processor), many application programs can contend for the use of the host's cryptographic service at the same time (Figure 4-9).

For the encryption capability in a node to function, it must have a copy of the cryptographic algorithm (DES is assumed) and the specific cryptographic key to be used for ciphering data. The key that is in use at any given time is defined as the *working key*. To prevent the working key and intermediate rounds of encipherment from being probed by an opponent (since knowledge of intermediate rounds reduces the work factor associated with the algorithm), the cryptographic algorithm and working key are maintained or stored in a

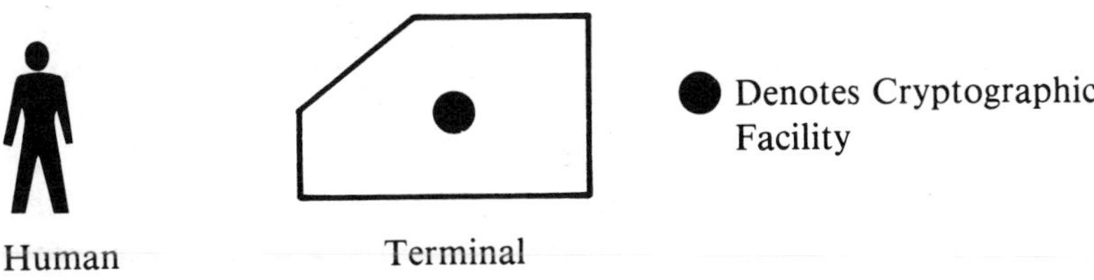

Figure 4-8. Terminal End User

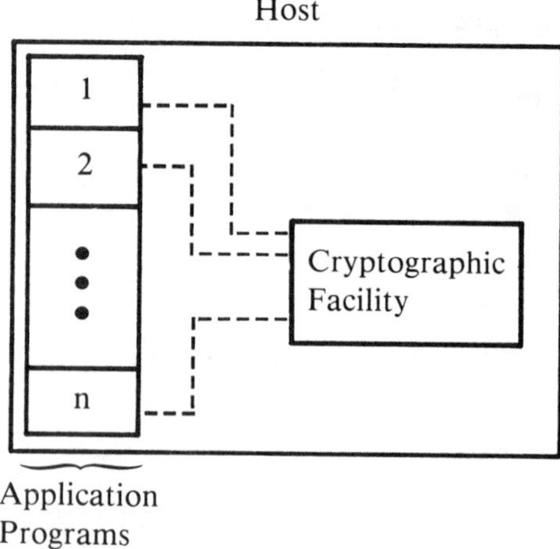

Figure 4-9. Host End Users

protected area defined as the *cryptographic facility* (Figure 4-10; see also The Cryptographic Facility).

It may be helpful for the reader to think of the cryptographic facility as a physical object, for example, a standalone hardware device or security module with its own protective covers [8]. Or one can think of the cryptographic facility as a special component integrated into another device, such as a terminal or computer. In either case, the security of the cryptographic facility is a function of the protection features associated with or provided by its physical embodiment and/or the device within which it is integrated; for example, probe resistant packaging, automatic tamper-proof detection features, covers, and the like, and the access control measures (administrative controls, locks and keys, badges, guards, fences, and so forth) that are present to limit access to the cryptographic facility or its embodying cryptographic device. The cryptographic facilities shown in Figures 4-8 and 4-9 are integrated into their respective devices.

When implemented in software, the boundaries of the cryptographic facility are not well-defined. In such cases, the physical protection achieved in hardware must now be achieved logically through programming. Ultimately, the degree of protection will depend on a processor's hardware protection features as utilized by the resident operating system (e.g., store and fetch protection, privileged operations, program execution modes, and the like). Thus the security of software implementations is no better than that of the underlying operating system.

To be initialized, at least one cipher key must be inserted into the cryptographic facility in clear form. This initial key must be transmitted to the facility in a secure manner, without compromising its secrecy. Subsequently, other keys can be introduced into the cryptographic facility by the system automatically. A key can be transmitted to a cryptographic facility over a nonsecure path as long as it is first enciphered under a key already present in the receiving cryptographic facility.

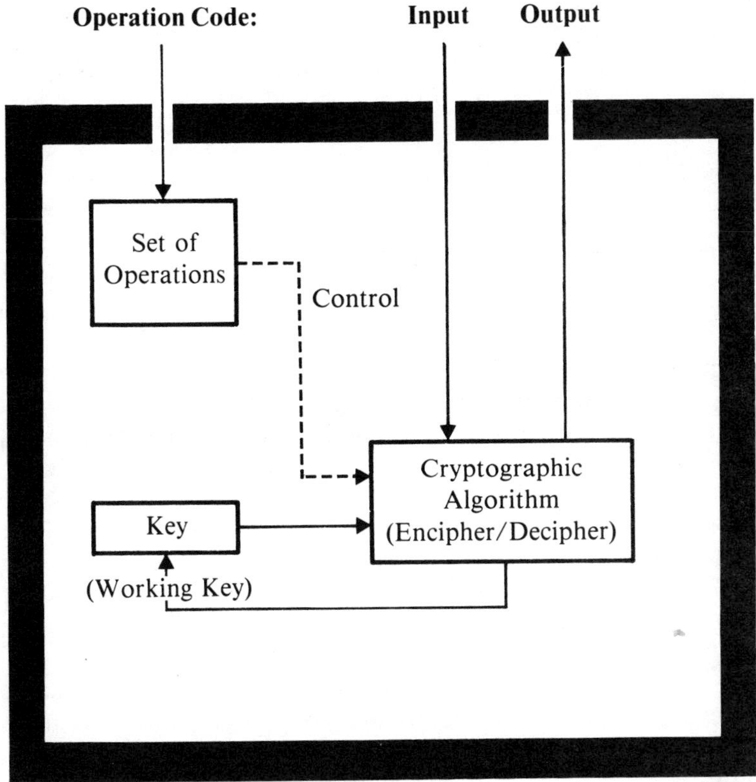

Figure 4-10. Cryptographic Facility—General Concept

The cryptographic facility provides the means for inserting data or keys to be ciphered. A control line is provided to activate the desired operation. The results of the operation are provided as output, except when an enciphered key is deciphered to produce a working key. In this case, the result is retained within the cryptographic facility.

The initial key may be a personal key associated with a particular user, or a system-supplied key associated with a particular node. In either case, the key is manually entered into the node's cryptographic facility. A personal key is normally entered by the user at the time ciphering is required. Conversely, a key supplied by the system is entered by installation personnel at the time the system is first initialized.

The described method of key management allows keys to be managed entirely by the system and its operating personnel, thus achieving cryptographic transparency. As indicated earlier, transparency is a highly desirable feature. However, the design does allow for user-supplied keys, and users have the option to manage keys and invoke the system's cryptographic operations themselves.

Nodes at which data encryption is desired must be equipped with identical encryption algorithms, and each node must have a copy of the same cipher

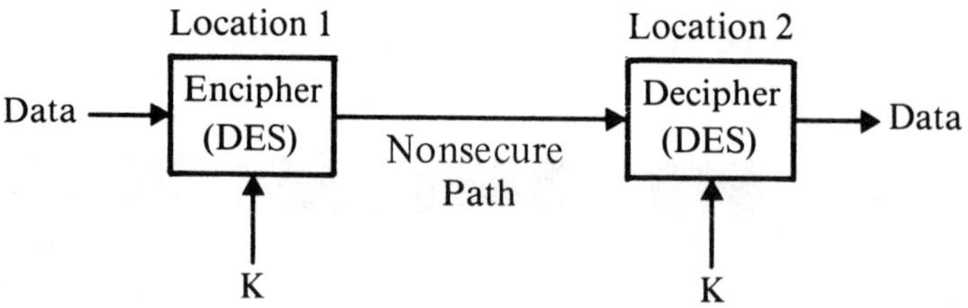

Figure 4-11. Transmission of Enciphered Data from Location 1 to Location 2

key K (Figure 4-11). Though two nodes must always share a common data-encrypting (or data-decrypting)[9] key to permit enciphered communications, greater security is achieved if different data-encrypting keys are used by each pair of communicating nodes. Such a design minimizes the resulting damage if a key should become compromised.

Using different data-encrypting keys for enciphered communications between each pair of communicating nodes has other advantages. Information intended for one node cannot be surreptitiously decrypted at another node, and misdirected messages cannot be accidentally deciphered by unintended recipients.[10]

The cryptographic system being described uses a different key for enciphering the data transmitted or transferred between each pair of end users. These data may be transmitted electronically or they may be magnetically encoded on a removable storage medium and transported from one location to another. Subsequent diagrams will use the following notation to differentiate between nodes and end users:

Circle: Denotes a network node (terminal or host)
Square: Denotes an end user (human being or application program)

In this discussion, a key used to protect (encipher and decipher) data is called a *primary key* (**K**). A primary key is also called a *data-encrypting* (or *data-decrypting*) *key*. When a primary key is used directly to provide communication security, it is called a primary communication key (**KC**), or simply, a communication key. The primary communication key used to protect data during a communications session is called a *session key* (**KS**). When a primary key is used directly to provide file security, it is called a primary file key (**KF**), or simply, a *file key*. A primary key (K) that protects data between end users 1 and 2 can be represented by the following diagram (Figure 4-12).

Primary keys are automatically generated by the system at the request of an end user, although primary keys can be supplied by end users as well. During periods of storage outside the cryptographic facility, these primary

[9] A conventional algorithm is assumed so that the enciphering and deciphering keys are equal.

[10] This is also true for a public-key algorithm.

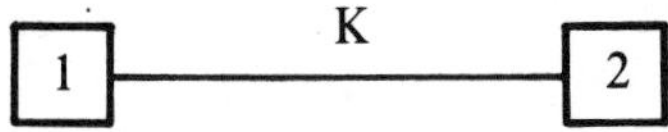

Figure 4-12. Shorthand Notation Representing Data Protection Between Users 1 and 2 Using Primary Key K

keys are protected by encipherment under another key, a *key-encrypting* (or *key-decrypting*) *key*. Keys must be kept secret for the period of their existence or until the data they protect are deemed no longer of value.

A *secondary key* (**KN**), where N stands for node, is one type of key-encrypting key used to protect primary keys (Figure 4-13). A second type of key-encrypting key, defined *master key*, is described below. When a secondary key is used to provide key protection in a communications environment, it is called a *secondary communication key* (**KNC**). When a secondary key is used to provide key protection in a data base environment, it is called a *secondary file key* (**KNF**).

Secondary keys are ordinarily introduced into the system at the request of installation personnel via the key generator, although secondary keys can be specified by installation personnel as well. Secondary keys, as a rule, remain unchanged for relatively long periods of time—months or perhaps years. With the benefit of physical protection, the risk of compromise is reduced.

Once the secondary keys have been manually set in their respective network nodes, data-encrypting keys can be sent from one node to another by encipherment under the secondary key of the receiving node. Similarly, data communicated between end users can be protected by encipherment under an established data-encrypting key.

Both COMSEC and FILESEC subscribe to the same concept of data protection: cryptography is used to protect data in an uncontrolled and presumably hostile environment by encipherment under a data-encrypting key. There are, however, differences in the expected life of the keys.

In a communications environment, a primary key exists only for the time required for two end users to exchange data. Ordinarily, the key would exist for a matter of minutes, perhaps an hour, but rarely for more than a day. In cases where encrypted files are transported between data processing locations, the key would exist for a matter of days or weeks. In contrast, a primary key used to protect archival data could exist for a period of years, or as long as the file is retained.

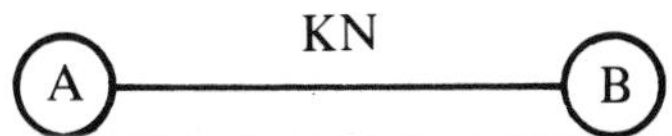

Figure 4-13. Shorthand Notation Representing Key Protection Between Nodes A and B Using Secondary Key KN

During the initiation of a communications session, a session key (either dynamically generated by the cryptographic system or supplied by the end user) is assigned to the session. At the completion of the session, the session key is erased or overwritten. Thus each session carries on cryptographic communications with a different key, thereby reducing the amount of data encrypted under a single key.

When used in a data base environment, the cryptographic system dynamically provides, or accepts from the end user, a key analogous to the session key (a file key) which it then assigns to a file. The file keys are protected via a secondary file key, which is analogous to the secondary communication key mentioned above. The net result is that different files are encrypted with different file keys, just as the data for different sessions are encrypted with different session keys. When a personal key is used as a file key, access to encrypted data also depends upon the user's ability to supply the correct key.

The sequence of events involved in gaining cryptographic protection for data communications between two end users can now be summarized. In order for the two nodes to establish a common primary key (data-encrypting key) on behalf of their respective end users, they must share, or have access to, a common secondary key. For good security, a different secondary key should be used between each pair of nodes. During the initiation phase (Figure 4-14), a dynamically generated primary key (K) is sent from node A to node B enciphered under a secondary key (KN) previously installed at each node. During the communication phase (Figure 4-15), end users 1 and 2 located at nodes A and B, respectively, communicate using primary key K.

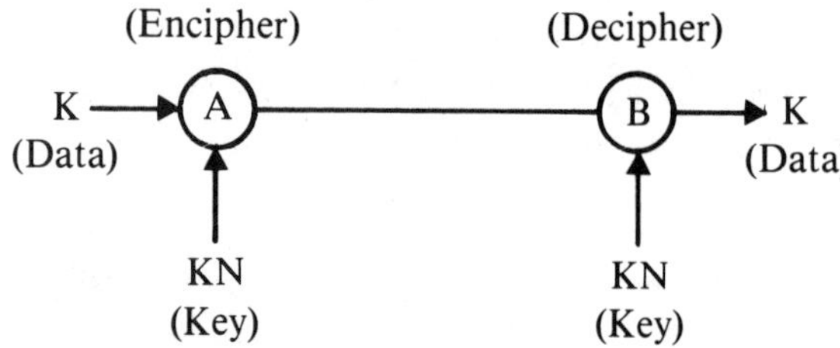

Figure 4-14. Initiation Phase

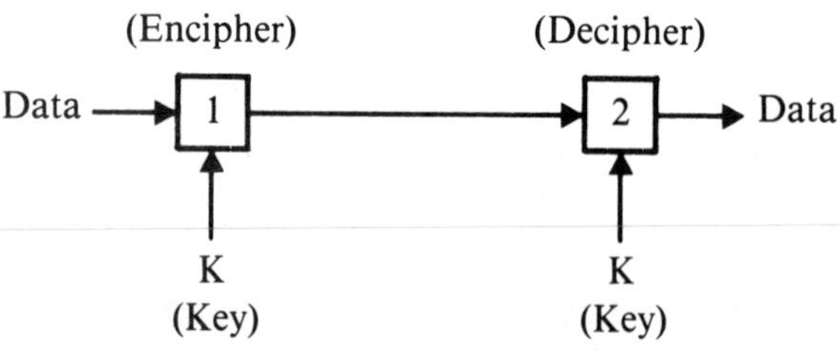

Figure 4-15. Communication Phase

In a communications environment, key distribution occurs at the time a session is established. Where nodes A and B are hosts and the data being transmitted are in the form of an encrypted file, key distribution can precede, be part of, or follow the transmission of data.

Let us now expand on this concept. It is evident that in a system with n network nodes, all of which require and support cryptography, there are

$$\binom{n}{2} = \frac{n(n-1)}{2}$$

ways in which nodes may be selected two at a time (i.e., in pairs). A total of n(n − 1)/2 different secondary keys is needed within the system, where each node is required to store n − 1 different secondary keys, one for each of the other nodes in the system. This is illustrated by a simple four node system (Figure 4-16).

In a system with a realistic number of nodes, say 100, each node would have to store 99 different secondary keys. A total of 4950 different secondary keys would have to be stored in the system. Clearly, the task of installing and managing such a large number of cipher keys would be difficult. However, recognizing that data processing systems have different processing and storage capabilities, one can reduce the number of secondary keys to a more manageable number by concentrating keys at host nodes and installing only one key in each terminal node.

Each terminal, as a rule, is, or can be, associated with a single managing host. In effect, a terminal has a logical owner (the host). Therefore, the collection of terminals and other nodes managed by a single host is defined here as a *domain* or *single domain*. When two or more hosts are logically connected, the resultant network is said to have *multiple domains*. This concept of ownership allows keys to be assigned more simply.

The path between each terminal and its owning host (a single domain) is protected with a unique secondary communication key, installed in the terminal and stored in the host's key table. The path between each pair of hosts

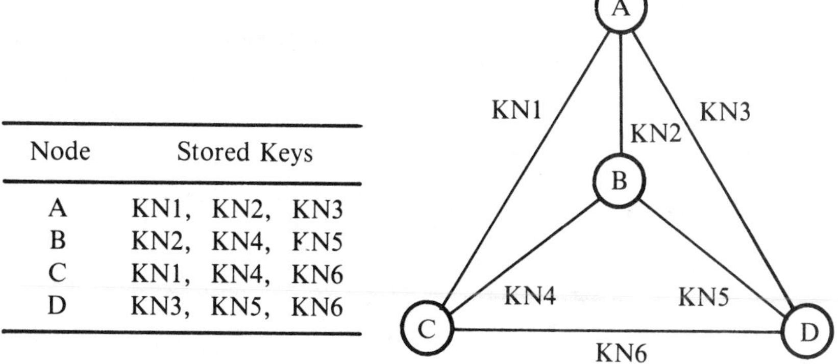

Node	Stored Keys
A	KN1, KN2, KN3
B	KN2, KN4, KN5
C	KN1, KN4, KN6
D	KN3, KN5, KN6

Figure 4-16. Allocation of Secondary Keys in a Four Node System

is protected with a pair of unique secondary communication keys, stored in the key table at each host. These key-encrypting keys are *unidirectional*: they are used for data movement in only one direction. The property of unidirectionality is actually enforced via the system's cryptographic operations, which must be appropriately designed (see Chapter 5). In effect, the cryptographic operations permit decryption of encrypted information only at the intended destination node.

Assume that a session key is generated at a host (for matters of economy and practicality). It is enciphered under the secondary communication key (obtained from the host's key table) assigned to each of the receiving nodes. In this form, the session key can be safely transmitted to each receiving node, while enjoying the protection provided by the secondary communication key. The operations defined to the host's cryptographic facility are such that the session key, once enciphered, cannot be recovered at the generating host (under the assumption that the generating host is not a receiving node), preserving the unidirectional property of the secondary communication key.

In an environment with multiple domains, each host must be able to send as well as receive session keys enciphered under a unidirectional secondary communication key. The two different cases (single and multiple domains) are shown below (Figure 4-17), where the unidirectional nature of the secondary communication key is illustrated through the use of a right or left-directed arrow.

In summary, each host shares two different secondary communication keys with each of the other hosts in the network, and a single secondary communication key with each of the terminals within its own domain. Thus in a network with 3 hosts and 2 terminals per host (Figure 4-18), each host must store 4 different secondary keys, each terminal must store 1 secondary key, and a total of 12 different secondary keys are required in the system. The

Single Domain COMSEC:

Multiple Domain COMSEC:

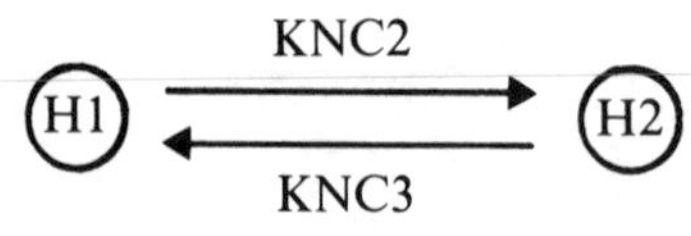

Figure 4-17. Allocation of Secondary Communication Keys

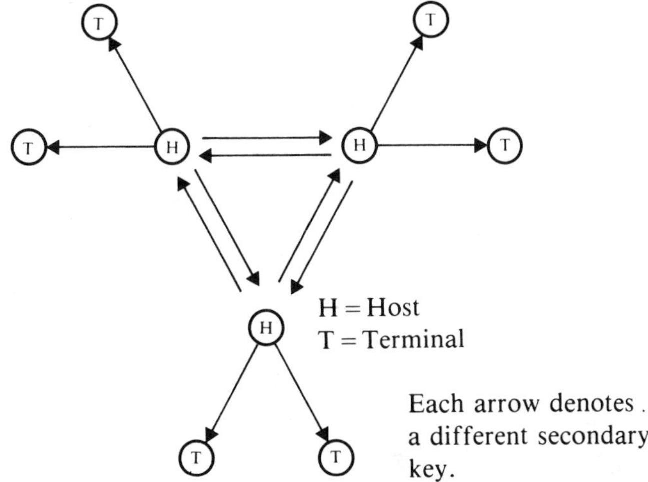

Figure 4-18. Allocation of Secondary Communication Keys in a Communications Network with 3 Hosts and 2 Terminals per Host

allocation of these secondary communication keys can be illustrated by a directed graph, where each arrow denotes a different secondary communication key, KNC (Figure 4-18).

A system with 4 hosts and 24 terminals per host yields a network with 100 nodes. Each host would have to store 30 different secondary communication keys, each terminal would be required to store 1 secondary communication key, and a total of 108 secondary communication keys would be needed by the system. This compares favorably with the prior system of 100 nodes, where the path connecting each pair of nodes was protected with a different secondary communication key. Recall that in such an approach 99 different secondary communication keys were stored at each host and each terminal, resulting in a total of 4950 different keys in the system.

The allocation of secondary keys for FILESEC (Figure 4-19) is similar to that described for COMSEC. However, encrypted files can be created and recovered (decrypted) only at host nodes.[11] Therefore, secondary file keys are needed to protect only the paths connecting two hosts, but not the paths leading to or from terminals. Encrypted files can also be created and recovered at the same host, and so a secondary file key is used to protect the path leading from a host back to itself.[12]

In a network with three hosts (Figure 4-20), each host must store five different secondary file keys, and a total of nine different file keys are required within the network.

[11] This is a convention, not a requirement. The developed key management scheme could be extended to handle file encryption and decryption at terminals, but is not shown.

[12] The corresponding case in COMSEC would involve data communications among application programs within a single host. Data protection for such an environment is a function of hardware protection features and access control procedures, *not cryptography*.

Multiple Domain FILESEC:

Single Domain FILESEC:

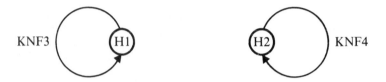

Figure 4-19. Allocation of Secondary File Keys

A procedure in which files are encrypted at one host and decrypted at another is analogous to a communication session in which data are transmitted only in one direction. As one might expect, the similarity between COMSEC and FILESEC is reflected in their respective key management schemes. Thus in FILESEC, the secondary key plays the same role that it does in COMSEC; namely, it protects the primary key until it is loaded into the cryptographic facility and used to decipher enciphered data.

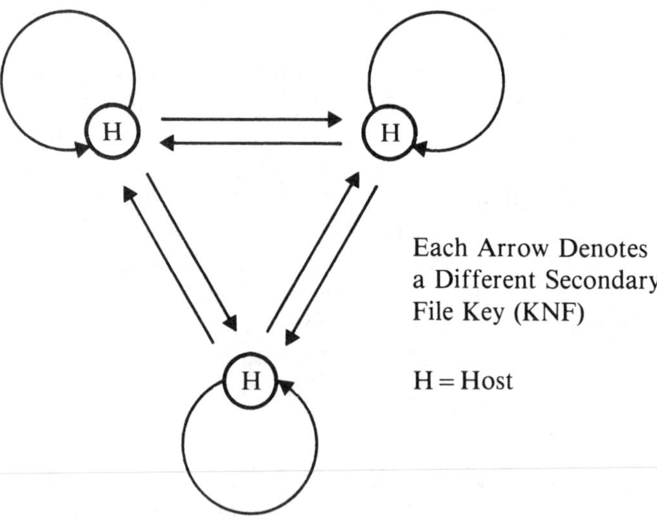

Figure 4-20. Allocation of Secondary File Keys in a Network with 3 Hosts

Let domain i and domain j be two domains within a multiple domain network. The following instances of data encryption are treated within the protocols for COMSEC and FILESEC:

Single Domain COMSEC
Terminal user (domain i) ⟷ terminal user (domain i)
Terminal user (domain i) ⟷ application program (domain i)
Multiple Domain COMSEC
Terminal user (domain i) ⟷ terminal user (domain j)
Terminal user (domain i) ⟷ application program (domain j)
Application program (domain i) ⟷ application program (domain j)
Single Domain FILESEC
Application program (domain i) ⟷ application program (domain j)
Multiple Domain FILESEC
Application program (domain i) ⟷ application program (domain j)

An Example of the Encryption of Transmitted Data

An example is now given, using the concept of multiple domains, to show how a user located at a terminal in one domain can initiate a communications session with a user located at a terminal in a different domain. Cryptography is transparent in this example. In the following diagrams, for simplicity, only the relevant key transformation functions are depicted. Although the complexities of an actual network implementation are purposely omitted, bear in mind that the described operations require a host system which has a full complement of programming support, including an operating system to control the execution of application programs and telecommunication access methods to manage data transmission between the host and other network nodes.

Suppose that user 1 is located at terminal 1 in domain i and that user 2 is located at terminal 2 in domain j. The network configuration and allocation of secondary keys are shown in Figure 4-21.

Each host generates the secondary communication keys for its respective domain, and these keys are securely distributed and inserted into designated nodes by authorized personnel. The means for protecting the keys while they are stored at each node, and the means for using the keys to perform the required key transformation functions, are topics to be covered in the remainder of this chapter.

User 1 initiates the session by invoking the appropriate *logon* procedure, specifying a designated application program in host i. The logon message would, in this case, identify the sending terminal (T1) and the requested destination terminal (T2). As a result, at host i, a pseudo-random number (session key) is generated, which then is enciphered under both KNC1, for secure transmission to T1, and KNC2, for secure transmission to host j (Figure 4-22).

The copy of the session key enciphered under KNC1 is transmitted to

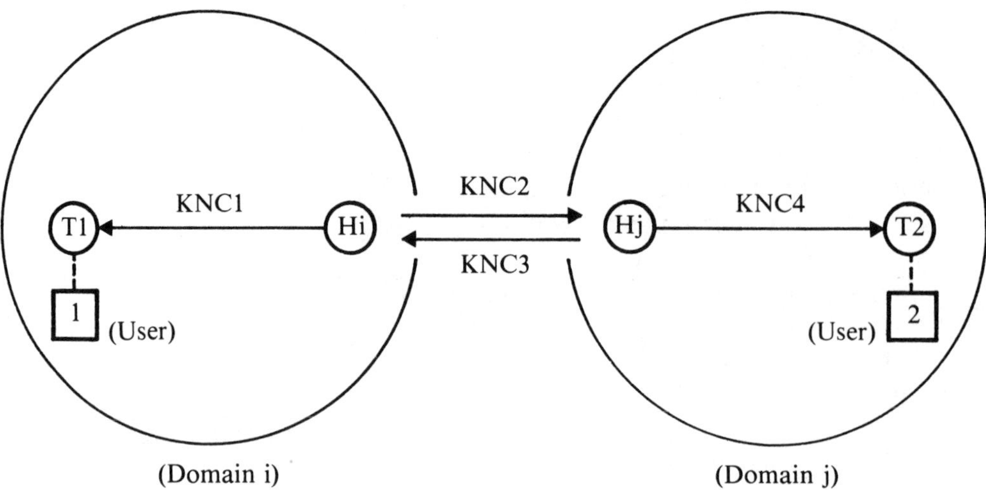

Note: It is assumed in this and subsequent Figures that KNC1 ≠ KNC2 ≠ KNC3 ≠ KNC4.

Figure 4-21. Initial Configuration

terminal 1 and the copy enciphered under KNC2 is transmitted to host j. At host j, a transformation is performed to reencipher the session key from encipherment under KNC2 to encipherment under KNC4 (Figure 4-23). The copy of the session key reenciphered from KNC2 to KNC4, is now transmitted to terminal 2.

Terminals 1 and 2 each recover the session key by deciphering the enciphered value of KS using the stored values of KNC1 and KNC4, respectively,

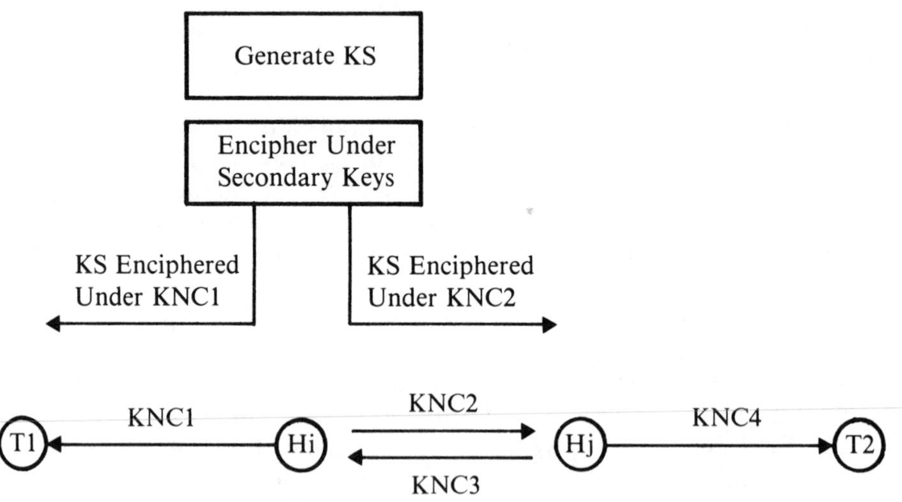

Figure 4-22. Session Key Generation/Encryption—Host i

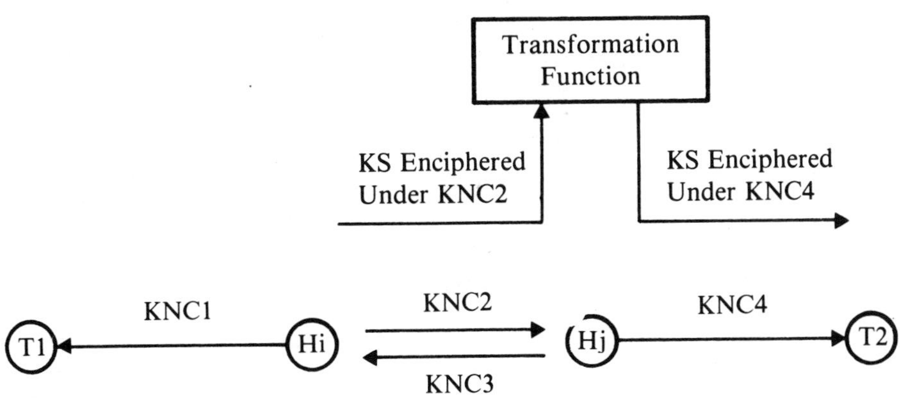

Figure 4-23. Session Key Transformation—Host j

and the recovered session key is then stored in a secure area in the respective cryptographic facilities (Figure 4-24).

At the end of the session initialization process, the communicants, 1 and 2, have a common session key (KS). Encrypted data can now be sent and received, thus completing the communication protocol.

Using a similar approach, an application program executing in one host can encipher data that are to be written to a portable storage medium, such as a reel of tape. The same data, after having been transported to another host, can be read and deciphered by a second application program.

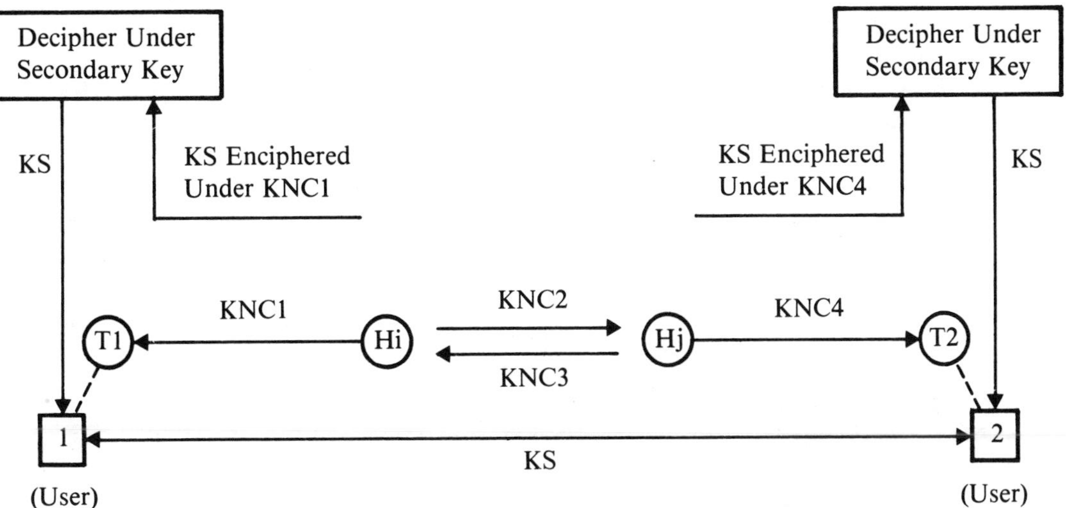

Figure 4-24. Session Key Recovery at Terminal 1 and Terminal 2

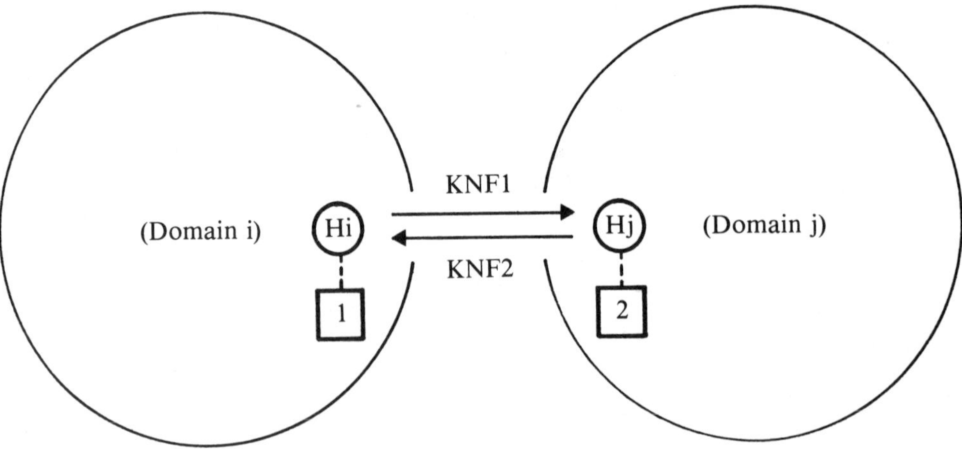

Note: It is assumed in this and subsequent Figures that KNF1 ≠ KNF2.

Figure 4-25. Initial Configuration

An Example of the Encryption of a Data File

Suppose that application program 1, executing in host i, creates an enciphered file for transmission to host j, and that at host j, the file is deciphered by application program 2. The network configuration and allocation of secondary keys are as shown in Figure 4-25.

Application 1 initiates the procedure by requesting a file key from host i. In response, host i generates a random file key, KF, and provides this value in a form that can be used by host i's cryptographic facility. In addition, a second copy of the file key is enciphered under a secondary file key, KNF1, and this value is written to the file's header record. This latter step allows the enciphered file to be recovered at its intended destination. Once the file has been enciphered, it is transported to host j. The entire process is illustrated in Figure 4-26.

At host j, the enciphered file key is read from the file header, and KF is recovered by deciphering under KNF1. The resulting value of KF is stored in a secure area of host j's cryptographic facility, where it is then used to decipher the enciphered file, as illustrated in Figure 4-27.

THE CRYPTOGRAPHIC FACILITY

The basic cryptographic operations of key transformation and data ciphering are performed by a cryptographic facility (Figure 4-28). The cryptographic facility is a secure implementation containing a conventional cryptographic algorithm (DES is assumed) and storage for a small number of key and data parameters. It can be accessed only through inviolate interfaces (secure

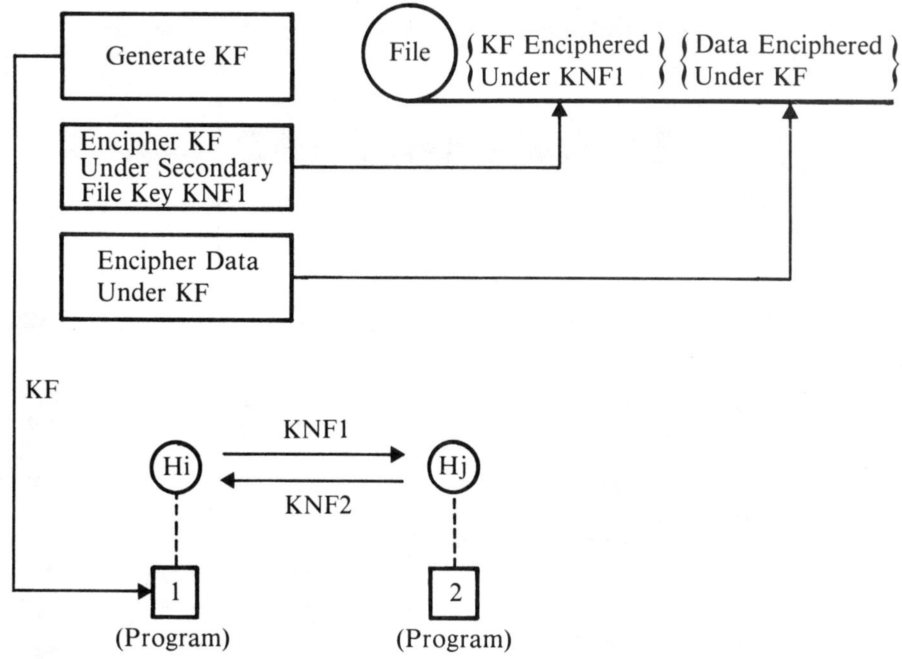

Figure 4-26. File Key Generation and Encipher Data Operations—Host i

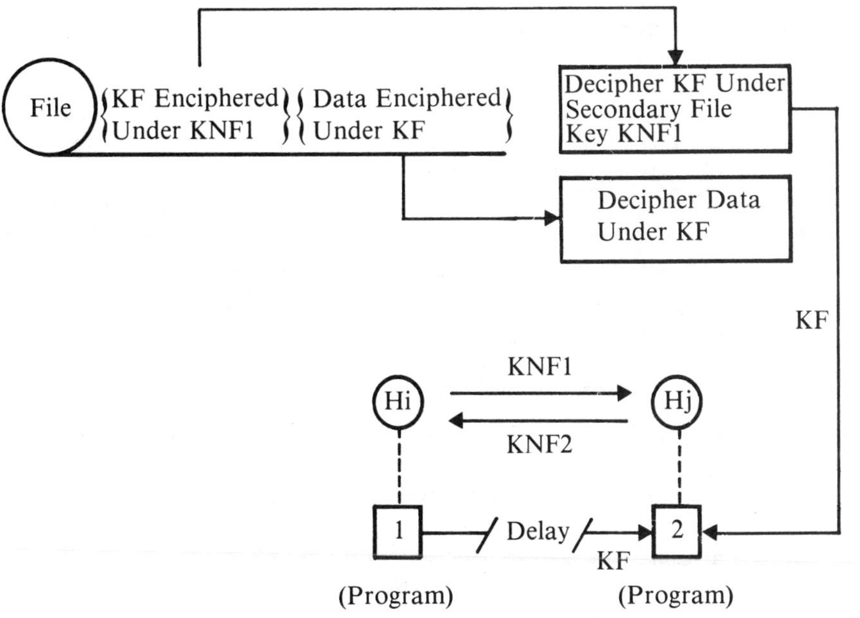

Figure 4-27. File Key Recovery and Decipher Data Operations—Host j

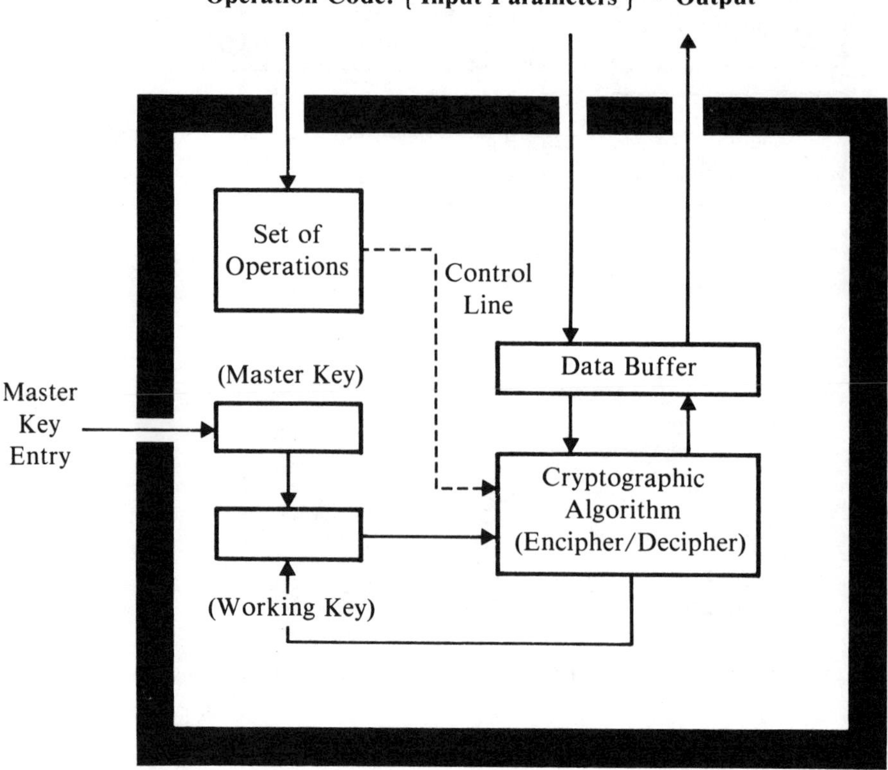

Figure 4-28. Cryptographic Facility

against intrusion, circumvention, and deception) which allow processing requests (via the indicated control line), key, and data parameters to be presented, and transformed output to be received. This strategy ensures that *clear keys and results of intermediate rounds of encipherment and decipherment are kept secret*. Access to the cryptographic facility can be controlled by a combination of physical and logical means that vary depending on whether the cryptographic facility is implemented in hardware or software.[13] Cryptographic operations are described using the following notation:

Operation Code: {**Input Parameters**} ⟶ **Output**

A cryptographic facility is assumed present at every host and terminal using cryptography. (It is assumed that useful processing of encrypted data is not possible.) However, since a terminal receives, but never produces enciphered keys, the cryptographic operations required at a terminal are different from those required at a host (see Basic Cryptographic Operations).

The cryptographic facility contains storage for both a master key and a working key. The working key, which is the key actively used by the cryp-

[13] Hardware is emphasized because it is more secure than software and it is required, per FIPS Publication 46 [10] for equipment procured for U.S. Government use.

tographic algorithm at any given time, normally changes from operation to operation. The master key, on the other hand, is a permanently stored quantity, and is maintained in a nonvolatile memory (i.e., a memory under battery power to prevent its loss when power to the device is shut off). A volatile memory (erased when power to the device is interrupted) or data buffer is also provided for the storage of input key and data parameters, intermediate results, and transformed output.

For simplicity, certain nonessential or unimportant elements (e.g., set of operations, control line, key and data storage elements) are omitted in subsequent figures depicting the cryptographic facility. Rather, emphasis is placed on the sequence of encipher and decipher operations required to perform a cryptographic operation and the key and data parameters used therein.

The cryptographic facility performs only two primitive operations: encipherment and decipherment. That is, the contents of the data buffer are either enciphered or deciphered under the cryptographic key contained in the working key storage, as illustrated in Figure 4-29.

Encipherment is denoted by the letter **E** and decipherment by the letter **D**. Each operation has two inputs (the data to be enciphered or deciphered and the working key) and a single output (the transformed data). The cryptographic algorithm is represented by a box, and by convention, the key enters from the left, data enter at the top, and output exits at the bottom. The notation used to express these operations is

$$\mathbf{E}_{\mathrm{K}}(\mathbf{X}) = \mathbf{Y}$$

which means that ciphertext Y is produced by the encipherment of plaintext X under key K, and

$$\mathbf{D}_{\mathrm{K}}(\mathbf{Y}) = \mathbf{X}$$

which means that plaintext X is produced by the decipherment of ciphertext Y under key K.

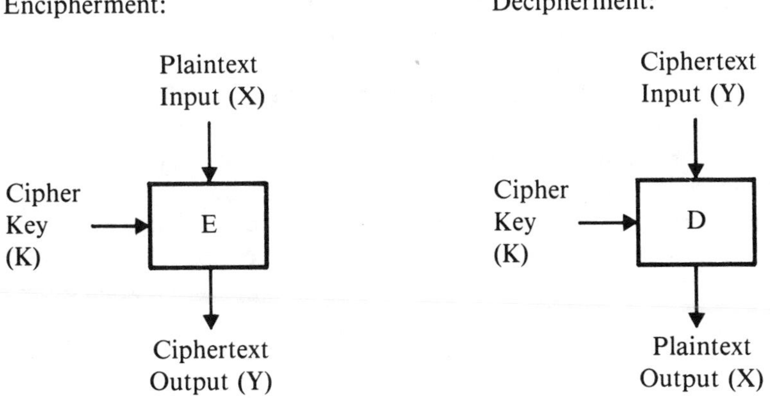

Figure 4-29. "Primitive" Operations of Encipherment and Decipherment

The basic cryptographic operations invoked through the programmed interface are performed by repeated executions of the primitive operations of encipherment and/or decipherment. During this process, the master key may be used as the working key if it is first transferred to the working key storage. In the same manner, an output from one operation may be used as an input (data or working key) to the next operation (described in more detail in the next section, Cipher Key Protection). Accordingly, when a series of encipher/decipher executions is required to satisfy a request, the contents of the working key storage will typically change as each encipher and decipher operation is performed.

Insertion of the master key into the cryptographic facility may be accomplished by a direct manual process, in which case a key is entered from mechanical switches, dials, or from a hand-held device, and is read directly into the master key storage. Alternatively, insertion of the master key may be accomplished by an indirect entry process, in which case a key entered from a nonvolatile medium, such as a card with a magnetic stripe, or entered through a keyboard-entry device, is first read into main memory and is then transferred to the master key storage. In this case, the residual copy of the master key in main memory must be erased (overwritten) after transfer to the master key storage is complete.

The master key is only used by the cryptographic facility to encipher and decipher other keys, and therefore is classified as a key-encrypting key. Being stored in nonvolatile memory, it can remain in use for long periods of time without having to be reentered.

CIPHER KEY PROTECTION

Because the cryptographic algorithm is assumed to be nonsecret, the degree of protection provided by the cryptographic system depends on how well the secrecy of the cryptographic keys is maintained. Therefore, the objective of sound key management is to ensure that *cryptographic keys never occur in clear form outside the cryptographic facility*, except under secure conditions during the period when keys are first generated, distributed, and installed, or when they are stored for backup or recovery in a safe or vault.

Protection of Terminal Keys

Since only one secondary communication key needs to be stored at a terminal (the one shared with its owning host), this key can be stored directly in the master key storage of the cryptographic facility. (Accordingly, the secondary communication key (KNC) used by a terminal is referred to as the *terminal master key*, **KMT**.) In effect this means that the terminal's cryptographic operations are less complicated than those required by the host, since the terminal must manage only a single secondary communication key. On the other hand, the host must manage the activities of the entire cryptographic system and therefore must cope with greater numbers of secondary and primary keys. In such a system, the terminal plays a passive role by responding to requests made by the host, while the host plays a more active role by managing and initiating requests.

As previously stated, a terminal master key provides a means for the host to transmit securely to a terminal a primary communication key (KC), referred to as a session key (KS). The process of recovering a session key at a terminal is illustrated in Figure 4-30.

First the terminal master key is copied from master key storage to working key storage, and the enciphered session key is accepted as input to the cryptographic algorithm (step 1). The cryptographic algorithm deciphers the input

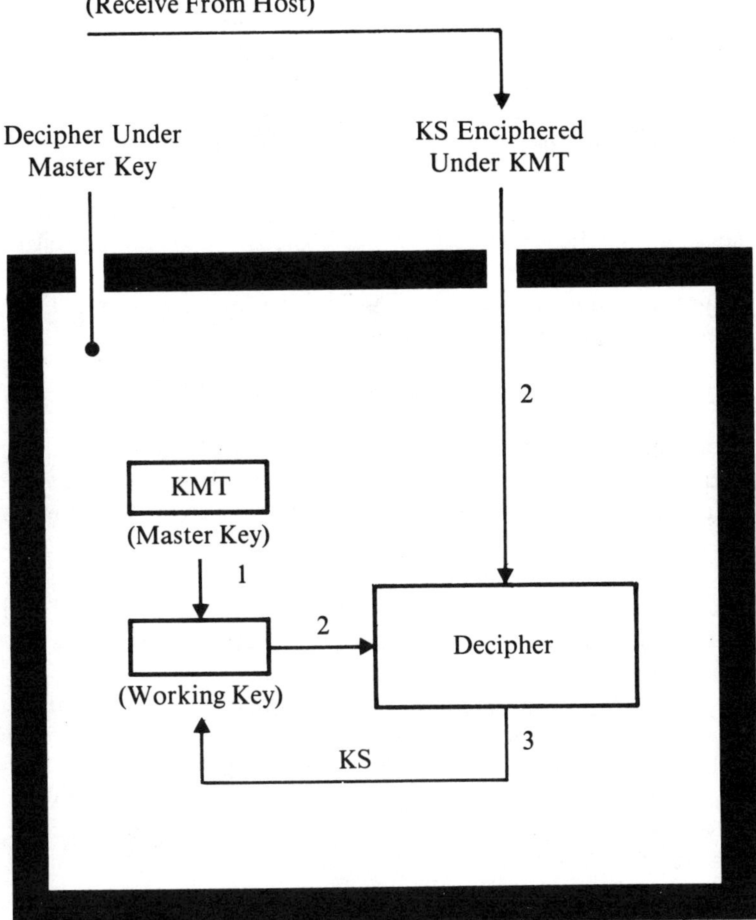

KMT = Secondary Communication Key (Terminal Master Key)
KS = Primary Communication Key (Session Key)

Note: To improve readability, some nonessential elements of the cryptographic facility are omitted in this and subsequent figures.

Figure 4-30. Session Key Recovery at the Terminal's Cryptographic Facility

data, under control of the terminal master key located in the working key storage, to obtain the clear session key (step 2). The session key is then transferred to the working key storage, replacing the terminal master key (step 3). The terminal can now initiate requests for data to be ciphered using the session key.

Protection of Host Keys

Because the host system has a greater role than a terminal in managing and controlling the operation of the cryptographic system, proportionately more demands are placed upon it to store and protect many different cipher keys (see Cipher Key Allocation).[14] Likewise, it becomes a more desirable target to an opponent.

Since several primary keys may be in use at any given time (typically, one per application program using cryptography), the host's cryptographic facility must be shared among the various applications. And when the working key storage will accommodate only one key, it is impractical to retain a primary key until its associated application program terminates. Instead, governed by the priority scheduling rules imposed by the host, the working key storage is regularly reinitialized with the primary key corresponding to the active application program. Thus primary keys must be protected when they are not being used by the cryptographic facility.

The Master Key Concept

One way to keep primary keys secret is to store them (in clear form) in a memory that can be read only by the cryptographic facility (i.e., a protected memory). However, an equally acceptable alternative is to encrypt keys and control their use via the host system. In the approach suggested here, all primary keys stored outside the cryptographic facility are enciphered under a single *host master key* (**KM0**) stored within the cryptographic facility. Therefore, before it can be used, an enciphered primary key, $E_{KM0}(K)$, must first be deciphered under KM0.

The concept of using one key to protect many other keys is defined as the *master key concept*. Basically, the problem of providing secrecy for a large number of cipher keys is reduced to that of providing secrecy for only a single key. More generally, cryptography reduces the problem of protecting large amounts of information (the plaintext) to that of a small amount of information (the cryptographic keys).

Encrypted vs. Unencrypted Primary Keys

When encrypted primary keys are used, an opponent must either compromise the security of the cryptographic facility containing KM0 or gain access to the system and invoke the decipher data operation, specifying $E_{KM0}(K)$ and data enciphered under K as input parameters. (It is assumed that a cryp-

[14]©1979 IEEE. Reprinted from NTC 79 Conference Record, November 27–29, 1979, Washington D.C. [9]

tographic operation designed to produce a clear key does not exist.[15]) Unencrypted primary keys, on the other hand, offer no protection if they become known.

In a network with multiple hosts, good security (i.e., independence among hosts) dictates that the master key at each host (KM0) should be different from that at any other host, or equal only by pure chance. Thus the points at which an encrypted primary key can be attacked are further reduced.

Not only must the secrecy of keys be protected, either by storing them in a protected memory or by enciphering them, but key usage must also be controlled, that is users must be able to access and use only those keys for which they are authorized.[16] Cryptography alone does not provide a solution to this problem, even though it provides effective measures to augment system services (see Authentication Techniques Using Cryptography, Chapter 8). Instead, security features provided by the host processor hardware and the host operating system must be used in conjunction with cryptography to ensure the security of data when resident in the host's main memory. Examples of hardware security features include store and fetch protection and special operations that may be used only by a supervisory program (or when the host processor is operating in the supervisory state).

Multiple Master Keys

Secondary keys stored at the host system can also be protected through encryption. These enciphered keys are stored in a data set accessible only to the cryptographic system (see The Host Cryptographic System). However, enciphering the keys using the host master key is not sufficient for protection since it allows primary keys to be recovered in clear form via selected cryptographic operations (see The Host System Cryptographic Operations, Chapter 5). To prevent this, a second host master key, KM1, is used. A third host master key, KM2, is defined to guarantee the unidirectional property of secondary communication keys (used to encipher primary keys while they are routed through a communications network). Thus three master keys are required: KM0, KM1, and KM2.

Note that multiple master keys are broadly applicable to cryptography since they allow the cryptographic operations for one application or purpose to be separated from those used for another (see Partitioning of Cipher Keys). The discussion of multiple master keys presented in this section has been kept brief deliberately and is intended only to give the reader enough information to allow the hierarchical structure of keys and the system's cryptographic operations to be discussed. The full justification for having three separate master keys is presented in Chapter 5.

Within the cryptographic facility, storage could be provided for three

[15] To create such an operation, an opponent would have to modify or replace the cryptographic facility. It is assumed that adequate physical security measures are present to deny an opponent such an opportunity.

[16] In a cryptographic system which operates transparent to the user, the system provides the keys, not the user. In contrast, if private or personal keys are allowed, the user provides the key, not the system.

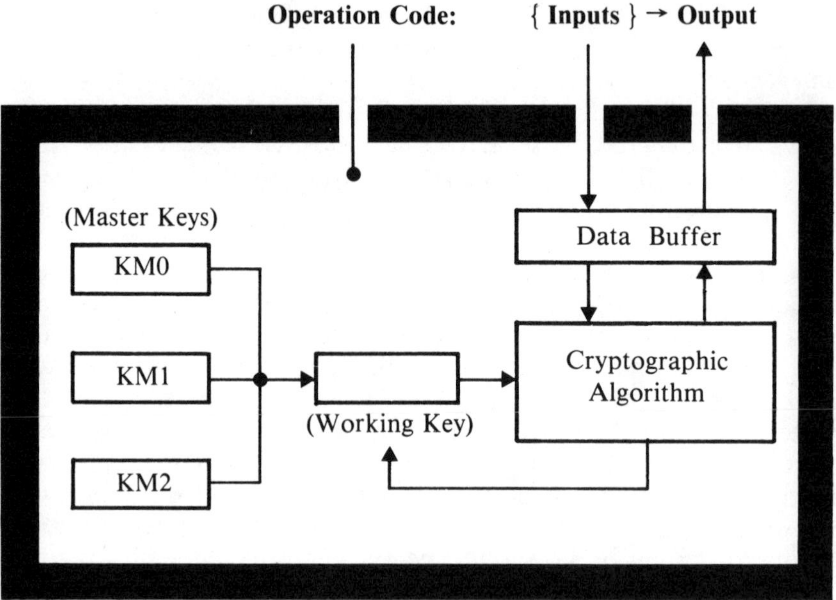

Figure 4-31. An Implementation Using Three Independent Host Master Keys

independent master keys (Figure 4-31). One or more of these keys (KM0, KM1, and KM2) would be selected as the working key and used to perform a sequence of encipher and decipher operations, depending upon the particular operation code presented to the cryptographic facility.

In a different approach, the three master keys could be derived from a seed key, KM, stored in the cryptographic facility. This requires an additional computation, but less storage. The keys could be obtained, for example, by defining KM0 as the encipherment of 0 under the key KM, KM1 as the encipherment of 1 under key KM, and KM2 as the encipherment of 2 under key KM (Figure 4-32).

When a master key is needed, KM is copied to the working key storage, a value is then selected for j (0, 1, or 2 depending upon the particular operation specified), and j is placed in the data buffer (step 1). The contents (j) of the data buffer are enciphered under the key (KM) located in the working key storage to produce the desired master key, KMj (step 2). The computed master key is then returned to the working key storage, overwriting the value of KM (step 3).

Master Key Variants

Another procedure for implementing multiple master keys is to store KM0 in the cryptographic facility and then derive KM1 and KM2 from KM0, as needed, by simply inverting selected bits in KM0. In such an approach, KM1 and KM2 are called *variants* of the host master key.

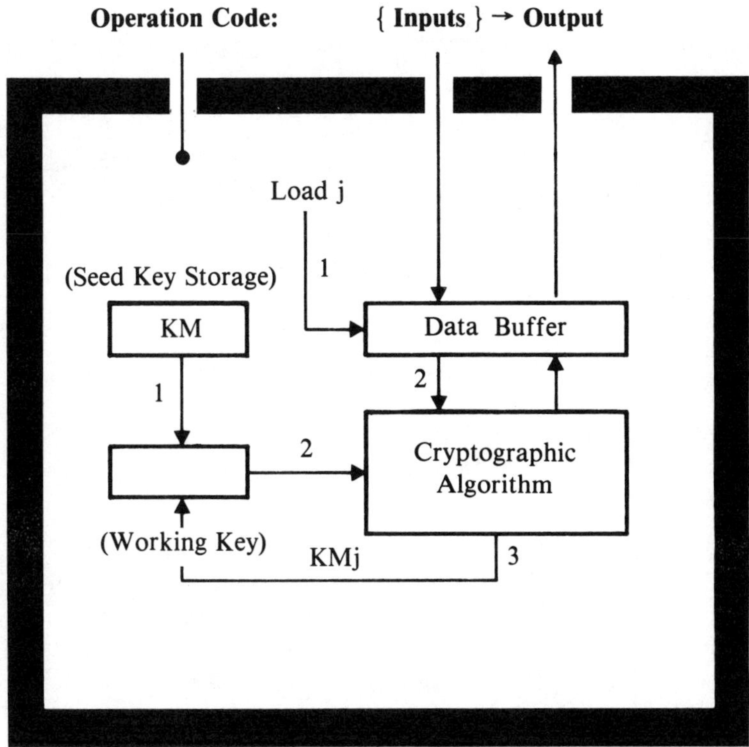

j = 0, 1 or 2

Figure 4-32. Implementation in which Multiple Master Keys are Derived from a Seed Key

KM0: Host master key

KM1: First variant of KM0

KM2: Second variant of KM0

Different variants are derived by inverting different bits. Such an operation can be easily performed within a cryptographic facility at the time KM0 is transferred from master key storage to the working key storage (Figure 4-33). (Note that the particular bits inverted to produce KM1 and KM2 are not important to this discussion.)

Obviously, a knowledge of any one of the keys (KM0, KM1, or KM2) is equivalent to a knowledge of all the keys, and therefore, using variants of KM0 must, by definition, provide less overall security than using either three independent master keys or three dependent master keys derived from one seed key using an irreversible operation. However, the trade-off between key storage, key computation time, and key independence is a good one. The resulting key management scheme is strong in any case.

Note that using three closely related keys is worthwhile only if a high correlation between keys does not result in exploitable correlations in the

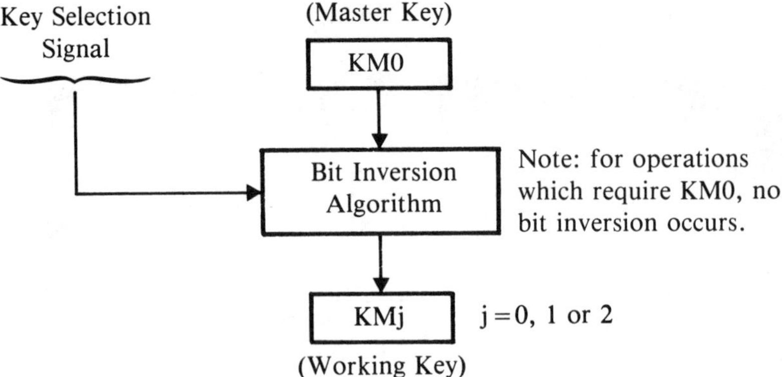

Figure 4-33. Derivation of Variants within the Cryptographic Facility Using Selected Bit Inversion

ciphertext which is produced by enciphering the same plaintext. Since, for DES, a single bit change in the key has a drastic effect on the ciphertext (see Analysis of Intersymbol Dependencies for the Data Encryption Standard, Chapter 3), there is no computationally feasible way to deduce one enciphered value from another. For example, given $E_{KMx}(K)$, for x = 1, 2, or 3, where KMx and K are unknowns, it is not presently possible to compute, deduce, or otherwise infer $E_{KMy}(K)$, for y = 1, 2, or 3 and $y \neq x$.

Summary

Figure 4-34 illustrates the overall scheme for protecting cipher keys at the host system.

Hierarchy of Cipher Keys

The discussion of cipher key allocation and protection implicitly defined a hierarchy of cipher keys and of key protection. This hierarchy is illustrated in Figure 4-35.

Large amounts of data are protected through the use of a smaller number of dynamically generated data-encrypting keys (primary keys), and the data-encrypting keys are protected through a still smaller number of relatively constant key-encrypting keys (secondary keys) or with the host master key (KM0). The key-encrypting keys are, in turn, protected with the variants of the host master key (KM1 and KM2). As a consequence, only a small number of keys need to be stored in clear form within the cryptographic facility, whereas the remainder of the keys can be stored outside the cryptographic facility in enciphered form. The various cipher keys defined to the cryptographic system are summarized in Figure 4-36, by name, category, use, and item protected (key or data).

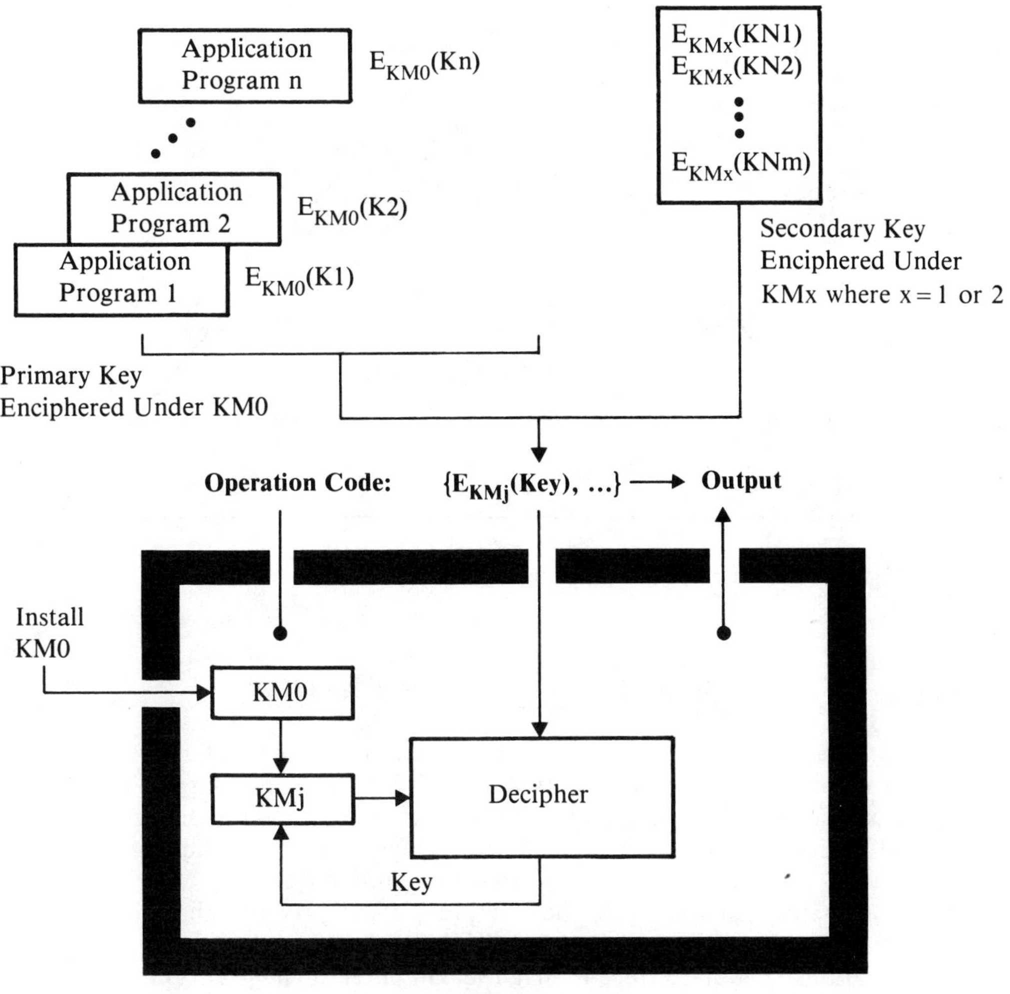

KM0 = Host Master Key
KM1 = First Variant of the Host Master Key
KM2 = Second Variant of the Host Master Key
j = 0, 1, or 2 Depending on the Requested Operation Code

Figure 4-34. Host Cipher Key Protection—Summary

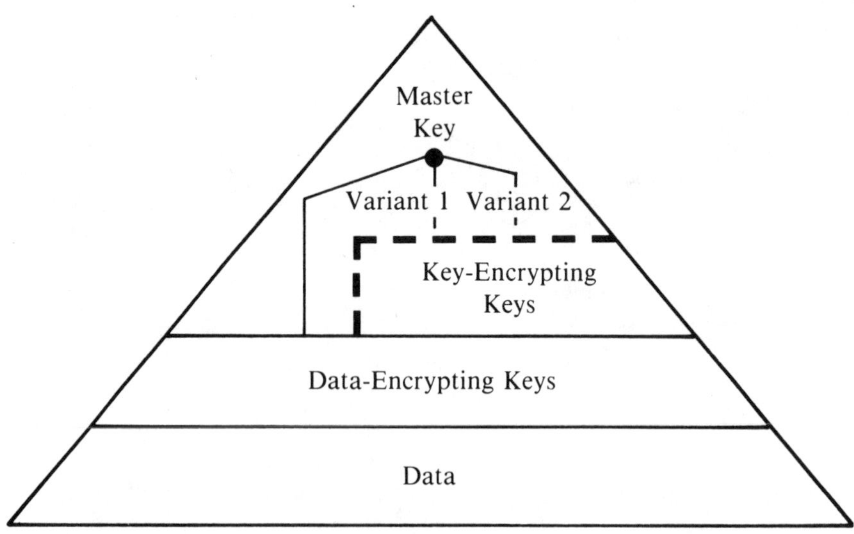

Figure 4-35. Hierarchy of Key Protection

THE HOST CRYPTOGRAPHIC SYSTEM[17]

Even for a modest-sized cryptographic system, the number of data-encrypting keys required over a period of time may indeed be quite large. Therefore, manual techniques for key generation and key management would soon prove to be inadequate. Automated procedures which are fast and eliminate security exposures resulting from human errors are required.

Fortunately, in this case, the computer itself provides the answer. Key generation and key management can both be effectively handled as computer applications. The net effect is that the computer augments cryptography by generating and managing the system's cipher keys, and in turn, cryptography protects the computer's data.

The host cryptographic system is comprised of three basic elements:

1. **Cryptographic Facility** The cryptographic facility, as previously described (Figure 4-28), is a secure implementation (hardware and/or software) containing the cryptographic algorithm (DES is assumed) and storage for a small number of key and data parameters. It can be accessed only through inviolate interfaces which allow processing requests (basic cryptographic operations), key, and data parameters to be presented, and transformed output to be received.
2. **Key Generator** The key generator is a computer program that

[17]The material in this and subsequent sections represents the details of one particular implementation [2]. This implementation illustrates the operation and interrelationships between the various components of an actual cryptographic system. Other designs are possible.

Category	Key Name	Use	Item Protected
Key-Encrypting Keys	Host Master Key (KM0)	Encipher Keys Actively Used or Stored at Host	Primary Key
	First Variant of Host Master Key (KM1)	"	Secondary Key
	Second Variant of Host Master Key (KM2)	"	Secondary Key
	Secondary Communication Key	Encipher Keys External to Host	Primary Communication Key
	Secondary File Key	"	Primary File Key
Data-Encrypting Keys	Primary Communication Key	Encipher or Decipher Data	Data in Motion
	Primary File Key	"	Data in Storage

KMT = Terminal Master Key (Secondary Communication Key Stored at Terminal)

KS = Session Key (Primary Communication Key that is Unique for Each Session)

Figure 4-36. Summary of Cipher Keys

creates the key-encrypting keys required by a host. Key-encrypting keys can also be specified by installation personnel. These keys are enciphered under a variant of the host master key, either KM1 or KM2, and then written in a file called the Cryptographic Key Data Set (CKDS). The CKDS resides on secondary storage (either disk or drum) and is assumed to be accessible by the cryptographic system during normal operations. A discussion of which secondary keys are enciphered under KM1 and which are enciphered under KM2 is given in the section called Key Management Macro Instructions. A label, or symbolic name, is associated with each enciphered key stored in the CKDS. The key manager accesses a key in the CKDS by using the label of the key (i.e., the key's name). The label could, for example, be the name of a resource protected by the referenced key. The generated keys (in clear form) and their respective identifying labels are recorded on a second output medium, such as a printer listing or punched cards. This allows the keys to be distributed to other locations and installed within their nodes. It also permits a backup record of the keys to be kept in a secure repository (safe, vault, or the like). Whenever the existing host master key is changed, the key generator is also used to decipher the secondary keys on the CKDS and reencipher them under the appropriate variant of the new host master key.

3. **Key Manager** The key manager is a program that creates primary keys, accesses the CKDS using a key's name supplied as input, and exercises the cryptographic facility in response to requests for key translation operations. In short, the key manager is the resource manager for the host's cryptographic keys. It has programming interfaces through which processing requests, keys, and data are presented, and generated or transformed outputs are received.

Figure 4-37 provides an overview of the basic elements needed at a host to implement a cryptographic system; namely, cryptographic facility, key generator program, and key manager program. GENKEY and RETKEY, which denote programming interfaces to the key manager, are used by programs to request key translation functions. CIPHER, another programming interface to the cryptographic facility, is used by programs for ciphering data. GENKEY, RETKEY, and CIPHER are implemented as programming *macro instructions*.

A macro instruction is commonly used with programs written in the basic assembly language of a particular computer. It approximates a higher level language in that with one uniquely named statement a programmer can incorporate a predefined sequence of instructions needed to satisfy a particular (and normally repetitive) function. The substitution of assembler language instructions for the macro instruction is performed during the compilation of the source program. For additional flexibility, macro instructions can be customized through the use of input parameters to vary the sequence of, and values associated with, the substituted assembler language instructions.

The macro instructions GENKEY, RETKEY, and CIPHER, when placed on the system macro library, can be used by system programs (where transparent cryptography is desired) or by user application programs (where private cryptography is desired).[18]

In the particular implementation discussed here, GENKEY, RETKEY, and CIPHER are implemented through the use of four basic cryptographic operations defined to the host's cryptographic facility; namely, encipher data (ECPH), decipher data (DCPH), reencipher from master key (RFMK), and reencipher to master key (RTMK). Two additional operations, set master

[18] Restricted access to a macro is achieved by placing it on a private library, addressable only by authorized users.

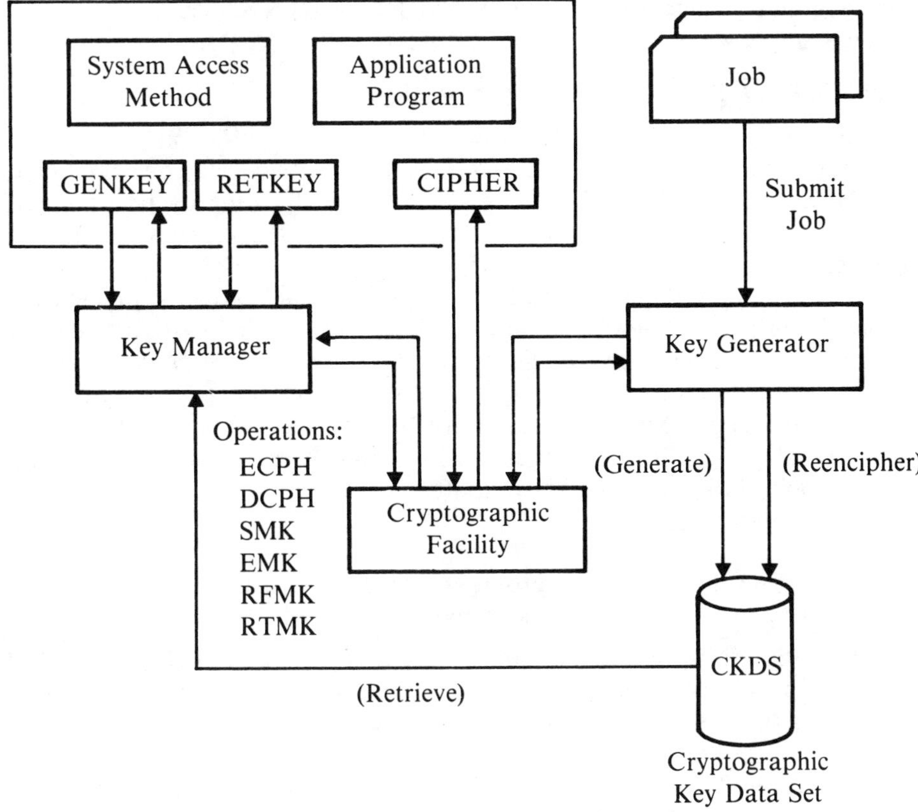

Figure 4-37. Host Cryptographic System

key (SMK) and encipher under master key (EMK), permit, respectively, installation of the host master key and encipherment of user-supplied data-encrypting keys (private or personal keys) under the host master key. (See The Host System Cryptographic Operations, Chapter 5.)

BASIC CRYPTOGRAPHIC OPERATIONS

There are two categories of cryptographic operations within the cryptographic system: those that transform data (data-ciphering operations), and those that initialize and transform cipher keys (key-ciphering operations). Since the host has an active role in managing the system's cipher keys (as compared to the terminal's less active role), the key-ciphering operations at the host system are more complex than those at the terminal.

In any case the cryptographic operations performed by a cryptographic facility are defined as *basic* since they are the most elementary operations that can be requested by the system. Recall that a cryptographic operation is described by its operation code, one or more input parameters (enclosed in braces), and output (pointed to by a right arrow) (see also The Cryptographic Facility):

Operation: {**Input Parameters**} ⟶ **Output**

An input, as well as the operation's output, can be either a key or data parameter. Keys and data parameters may be in either clear or enciphered form. However, operations involving clear keys will ordinarily be exercised only when the system is sterile, that is, no other users or application programs are active.[19]

The basic cryptographic operations provide a means for implementing high level key management functions in the cryptographic system.[20] But, if not properly designed, they could allow an opponent to perform complex cryptographic transformations leading to the recovery of keys and data. Therefore, the cryptographic system must be designed so that if one or more of the operations are used together with any enciphered keys or data parameters that are routinely generated, routed, or stored within the system, it is not possible to recover:

1. Clear keys outside the cryptographic facility, regardless of the inherent security of the supporting host operating system.
2. Plaintext from ciphertext outside the cryptographic facility, except in the specific manner intended (using a decipher data operation), and under the specific conditions anticipated.

The same method used to validate the strength of a cryptographic algorithm (Chapter 1) is used to certify that cryptographic operations are dependable and secure. The process of subjecting cryptographic operations to a series of hypothetical attacks is called *threat analysis*. A favorable result (validation by threat analysis) leads to the conclusion that exposure of keys and data, although not provably impossible, is at least demonstrably difficult or unlikely.

As an aid to the reader in interpreting the meaning of the cryptographic operations described below, a summary of common abbreviations is given.

X: Plaintext block
Y: Ciphertext block
K: Primary key (data-encrypting key)
KN: Secondary key (key-encrypting key)
KM0: Host master key
KM1: First variant of host master key
KM2: Second variant of host master key

[19] For example, clear keys would exist at a host when the key generator program is executed or when a key is installed in the cryptographic facility. The key generator program might even be executed on a separate system, if the host's system programs cannot be trusted.

[20] They represent one way in which the high level key management functions can be achieved, but not the only way.

Recall that the notation $E_K(X)$ denotes the encipherment of plaintext X under key K, and the notation $D_K(Y)$ denotes the decipherment of ciphertext Y under key K.

Cryptographic Operations at a Terminal

The following basic cryptographic operations are used at a terminal:

Load Key Direct (LKD)
Write Master Key (WMK)
Decipher Key (DECK)
Encipher (ENC)
Decipher (DEC)

The LKD, WMK, and DECK operations are used for initializing and transforming keys, while ENC and DEC are used to transform data.

Since a terminal participates in only one communication session at a time, it is possible for the session key to be placed into the working key storage of the terminal's cryptographic facility at the beginning of a session, and remain there unchanged for the session's duration. The terminal's cryptographic operations are designed to avoid the overhead of reinitializing the working key storage whenever possible.[21]

LOAD KEY DIRECT

LKD: {K} ⟶ Load Cipher Key K into Working Key Storage

The LKD operation (Figure 4-38) is used to load a clear key into the working key storage of the terminal's cryptographic facility. No inverse operation is available for reading the working key. The LKD operation allows the terminal user to enter a private key which can be used for ciphering data. (This operation is not needed if only system-initiated session keys are used.)

WRITE MASTER KEY

WMK: {KN} ⟶ Write Cipher Key KN in Master Key Storage

The WMK operation (Figure 4-39) is used to write a key into the master key storage of the terminal's cryptographic facility. No inverse operation is available for reading the master key. The WMK operation may be exercised only in an authorized state. Such a state may be created by a physical key-operated switch which enables or disables the operation. (This is an example of an authorized state that is not automated, that is, the machine is placed in an authorized state manually by a designated user or security administrator. See also the Set Master Key operation.)

[21] The cryptographic operations for a terminal control unit (or cluster controller), which can service several terminals and terminal users concurrently, would need to be designed to accommodate several enciphered session keys, associating each with the corresponding session. The details of such a design are not provided in this discussion.

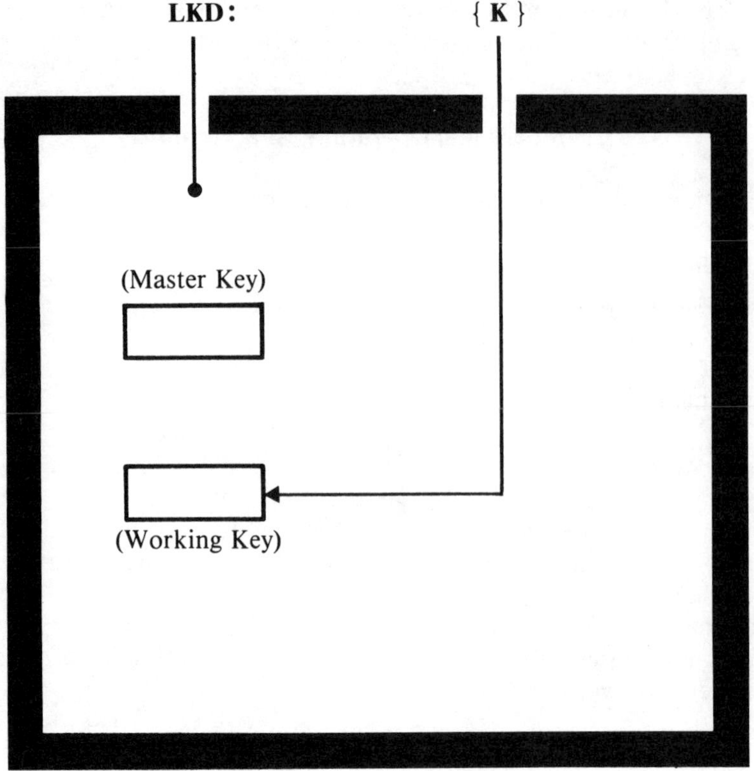

Figure 4-38. Load Key Direct Operation at Terminal

DECIPHER KEY

DECK: $\{E_{KN}(K)\} \longrightarrow$ **Load Cipher Key K into Working Key Storage**

The DECK operation (Figure 4-40) is used to decipher a key under the cipher key stored in the master key storage of the terminal's cryptographic facility, and place the result in working key storage. By definition, the input key parameter is a primary key enciphered under the terminal master key, and hence the value placed in the working key storage (as a result of the DECK operation) will be the intended data-encrypting key.

ENCIPHER

ENC: $\{X\} \longrightarrow E_K(X)$

The ENC operation (Figure 4-41) is used to encipher data. A 64-bit block of plaintext (X) is enciphered under the data-encrypting key (K) stored in the working key storage of the terminal's cryptographic facility. A 64-bit block of ciphertext, denoted by $E_K(X)$, is produced.[22] As long as the cryptographic

[22] The described implementation of DES is called the Electronic Code Book Mode (ECB). As a rule, block encryption (see also the DEC, ECPH, and DCPH operations) is used to protect keys. A different method, called chained block encryption (see CIPHER Macro Instruction), is used to protect data. (See also Block Ciphers with Chaining, Chapter 2.)

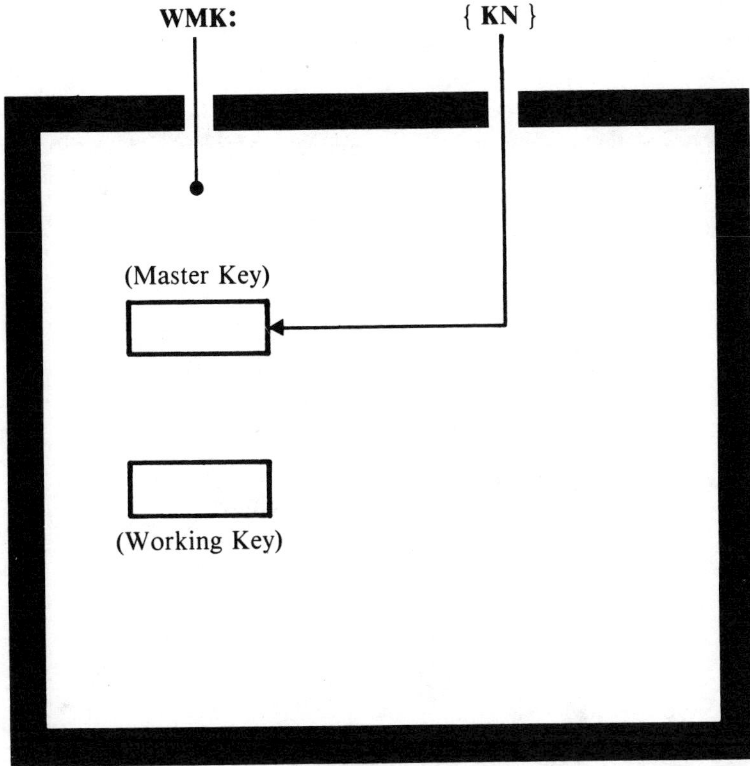

Figure 4-39. Write Master Key Operation at Terminal

facility's controls remain set to the encipher mode of operation, a message of multiple 8-byte blocks of plaintext can be enciphered as a series of steps in which each 8-byte block of plaintext is presented to the cryptographic facility in succession. Thus message encipherment can be expressed by the notation

$$\text{ENC: } \{X(1), X(2), \ldots, X(n)\} \longrightarrow Y(1), Y(2), \ldots, Y(n)$$

where X(1), X(2), . . . , X(n) denotes a message of n 8-byte blocks of plaintext, Y(1), Y(2), . . . , Y(n) denotes the resulting ciphertext, and Y(1) = $E_K(X(1))$, Y(2) = $E_K(X(2))$, and so on.

DECIPHER

$$\text{DEC: } \{E_K(X)\} \longrightarrow X$$

The DEC operation (Figure 4-42) is used to decipher data. A 64-bit block of ciphertext (denoted by $E_K(X)$) is deciphered under the data-encrypting key (K) stored in the working key storage of the terminal's cryptographic facility. A 64-bit block of plaintext (X) is recovered. As long as the cryptographic facility's controls remain set to the decipher mode of operation, a message of multiple 8-byte blocks of ciphertext can be deciphered as a series of steps in which each 8-byte block of ciphertext is presented to the cryptographic

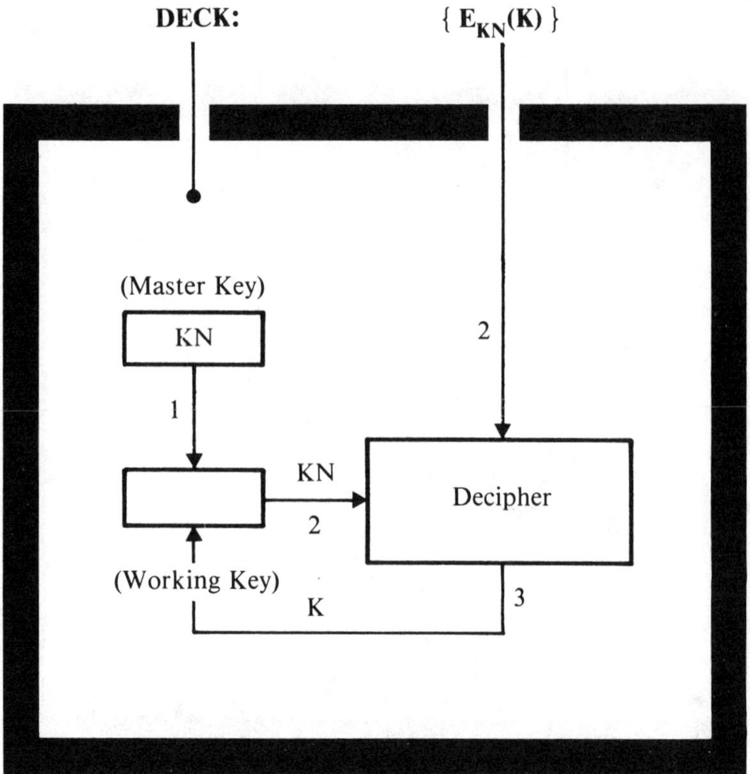

Note: The numbers indicate the order in which the individual steps are performed.

Figure 4-40. Decipher Key Operation at Terminal

facility in succession. Thus message decipherment can be expressed by the notation

$$\textbf{DEC: } \{Y(1), Y(2), \ldots, Y(n)\} \longrightarrow X(1), X(2), \ldots, X(n)$$

where Y(1), Y(2), . . . , Y(n) denotes a message of n 8-byte blocks of ciphertext, X(1), X(2), . . . , X(n) denotes the recovered plaintext, and X(1) = $D_K(Y(1))$, X(2) = $D_K(Y(2))$, and so on.

Once the session key has been placed into the working key storage using the DECK operation, there is no need to repeat the step of loading and deciphering the working key as a precondition of requesting subsequent encipher (ENC) and decipher (DEC) operations, since the session key is still present in working key storage. Hence all data ciphering operations can be performed using an implicit cipher key (the cipher key present in the working key storage), rather than an explicit cipher key (a cipher key supplied as an input parameter to the requested cryptographic operation).

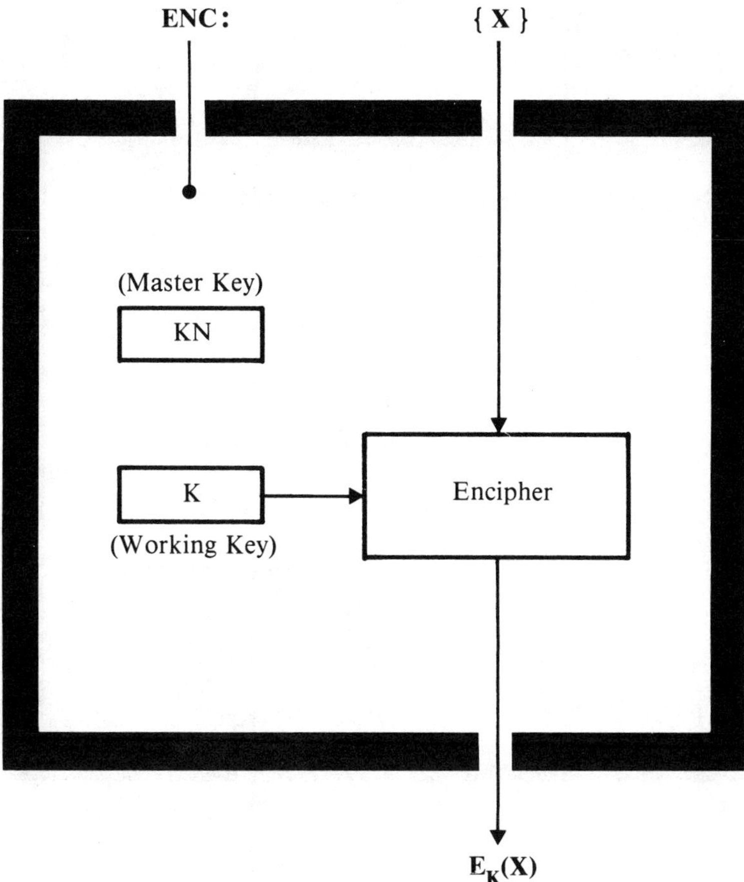

Figure 4-41. Encipher Operation at Terminal

Cryptographic Operations at a Host

There are two categories of basic cryptographic operations defined to the host's cryptographic facility, those that transform data:

Encipher Data (ECPH)
Decipher Data (DCPH)

and those that are used to initialize and transform keys:[23]

Set Master Key (SMK)
Encipher Under Master Key (EMK)

[23] In an actual implementation, the steps describing each cryptographic operation vary depending upon the number of storage elements within the cryptographic facility available for storing intermediate results produced by the operation.

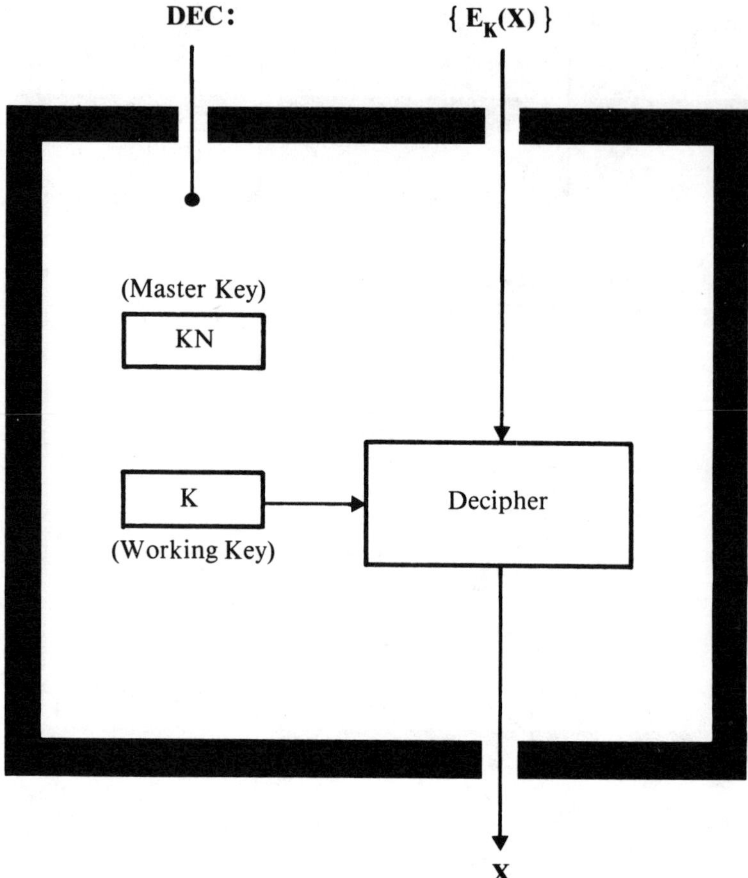

Figure 4-42. Decipher Operation at Terminal

Reencipher from Master Key (RFMK)
Reencipher to Master Key (RTMK)[24]

Data Ciphering Operations

Since several application programs may be involved in communication sessions at one time, the cryptographic facility must be shared among these several different users. In the approach described here, the primary key is provided as an input parameter to all requests for enciphering and deciphering data.

ENCIPHER DATA

$$\text{ECPH: } \{E_{KM0}(K), X\} \longrightarrow E_K(X)$$

The ECPH operation (Figure 4-43) is used to encipher data. A 64-bit block of plaintext (X) is enciphered under the data-encrypting key (K) to produce

[24] In an actual implementation, effective security could require that the RTMK operation be restricted to privileged programs (see Key Management Macro Instructions).

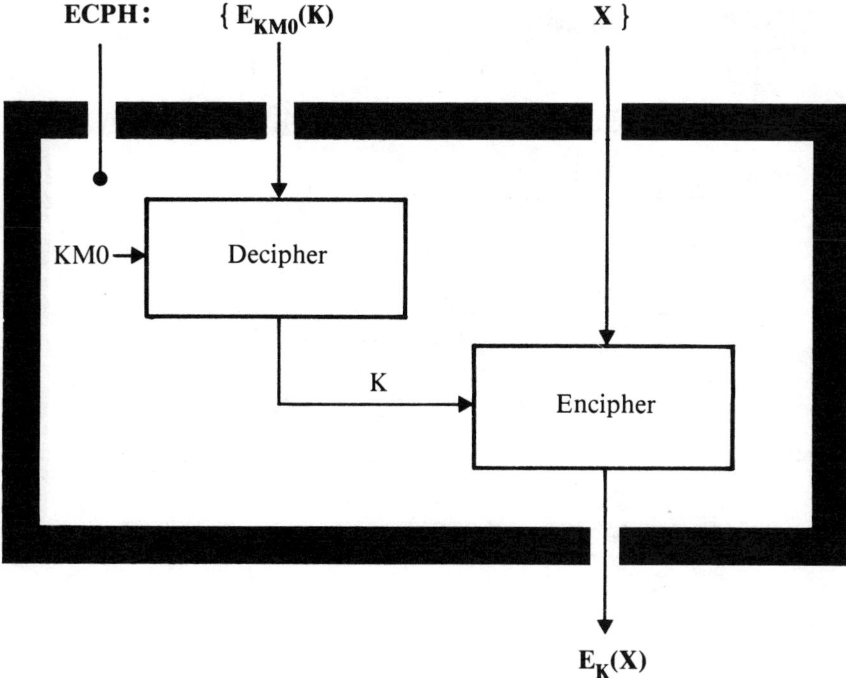

Figure 4-43. Encipher Data Operation at Host System

a 64-bit block of ciphertext, denoted by $E_K(X)$. As long as the cryptographic facility's controls remain set to the encipher data mode of operation, a message of multiple 8-byte blocks of plaintext can be enciphered as a series of steps in which each 8-byte block of plaintext is presented to the cryptographic facility in succession. Message encipherment can be expressed by the notation

$$\text{ECPH: } \{E_{KM0}(K), X(1), X(2), \ldots, X(n)\} \longrightarrow Y(1), Y(2), \ldots, Y(n)$$

where X(1), X(2), . . . , X(n) denotes a message of n 8-byte blocks of plaintext, Y(1), Y(2), . . . , Y(n) denotes the resulting ciphertext, and $Y(1) = E_K(X(1))$, $Y(2) = E_K(X(2))$, and so on.

DECIPHER DATA

$$\text{DCPH: } \{E_{KM0}(K), E_K(X)\} \longrightarrow X$$

The DCPH operation (Figure 4-44) is used to decipher data. A 64-bit block of ciphertext, denoted by $E_K(X)$, is deciphered under the data-encrypting key (K) to recover a 64-bit block of plaintext (X). As long as the cryptographic facility's controls remain set to the decipher data mode of operation, a message of multiple 8-byte blocks of ciphertext can be deciphered as a series of steps in which each 8-byte block of ciphertext is presented to the cryptographic facility in succession. Message decipherment can be expressed by the notation

$$\text{DCPH: } \{E_{KM0}(K), Y(1), Y(2), \ldots, Y(n)\} \longrightarrow X(1), X(2), \ldots, X(n)$$

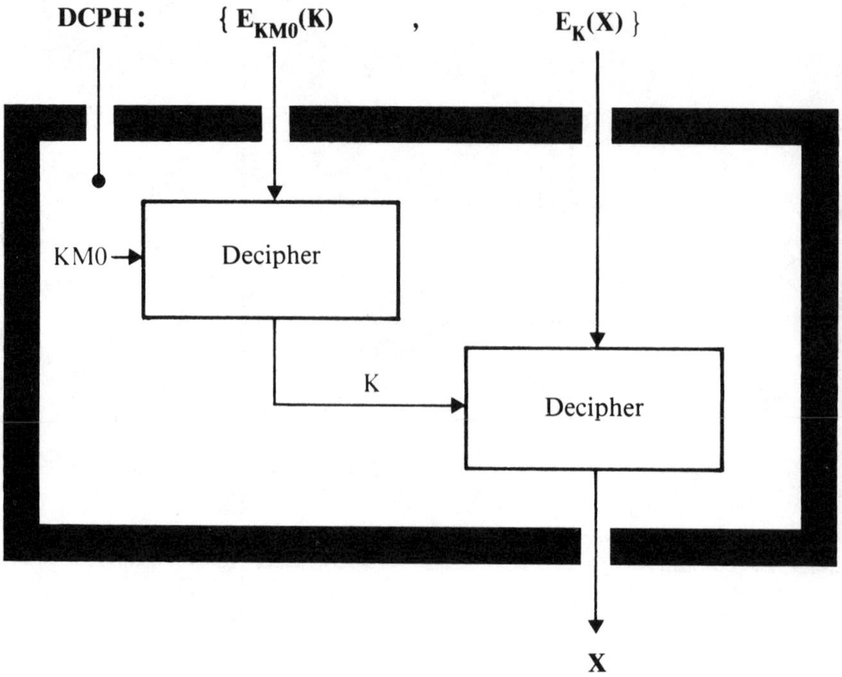

Figure 4-44. Decipher Data Operation at Host System

where Y(1), Y(2), . . . , Y(n) denotes a message of n 8-byte blocks of ciphertext, X(1), X(2), . . . , X(n) denotes the recovered plaintext, and X(1) = $D_K(Y(1))$, X(2) = $D_K(Y(2))$, and so on.

Key Management Operations

SET MASTER KEY

SMK: {KM0} ⟶ Write Cipher Key KM0 in Master Key Storage

The SMK operation (Figure 4-45) is used to write a key into the master key storage of the host's cryptographic facility. No inverse operation is available for reading the master key. The SMK operation can be invoked only in an authorized state. Such a state may be controlled by a physical key-operated switch which enables or disables the operation.

ENCIPHER UNDER MASTER KEY

EMK: {K} ⟶ $E_{KM0}(K)$

The EMK operation (Figure 4-46) is used to encipher a data-encrypting key under the host's master key (KM0). No inverse operation is available which allows decipherment under KM0. (A description of how keys can be enciphered under the variants of the host master key is given in Chapter 6.)

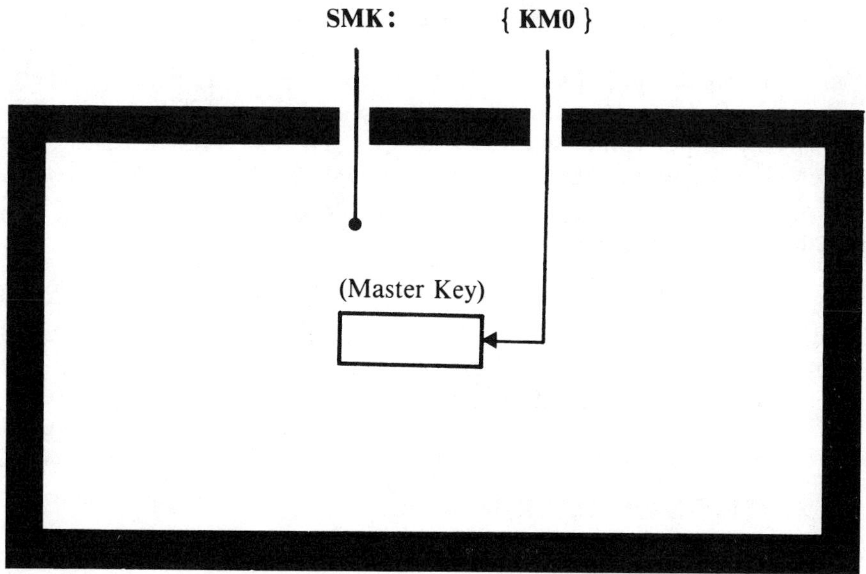

Figure 4-45. Set Master Key Operation at Host System

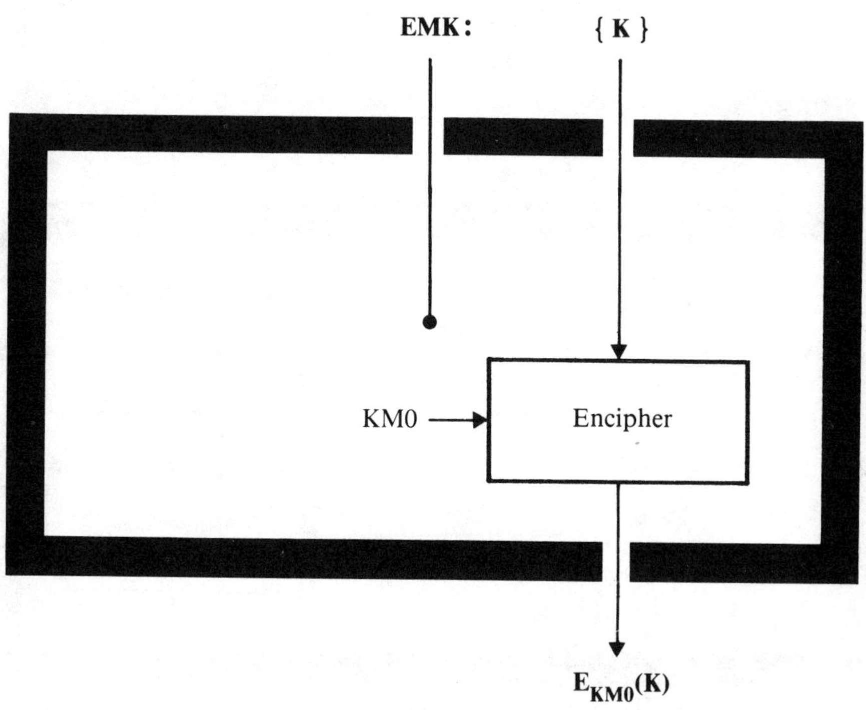

Figure 4-46. Encipher Under Master Key Operation at Host System

An EMK operation is provided at the host to support the use of personal (user-supplied) keys. Without EMK it would be impossible to encipher a personal key under the host master key so that it could be used to encipher and decipher data (see CIPHER Macro Instruction).

REENCIPHER FROM MASTER KEY

RFMK: $\{E_{KM1}(KN), E_{KM0}(K)\} \longrightarrow E_{KN}(K)$

The RFMK operation (Figure 4-47) is used by the key manager to transform a primary key (K) from encipherment under the host master key (KM0) to encipherment under a secondary key (KN).

REENCIPHER TO MASTER KEY

RTMK: $\{E_{KM2}(KN), E_{KN}(K)\} \longrightarrow E_{KM0}(K)$

The RTMK operation (Figure 4-48) is used by the key manager to transform a primary key (K) from encipherment under a secondary key (KN) to encipherment under the host master key (KM0).

Although it may appear that the RFMK and RTMK operations are the inverse of each other, this is true only if the same secondary key is enciphered under both KM1 and KM2. Two variants are introduced specifically so that the operations are not reversible (see Chapter 5). Translation of a key from

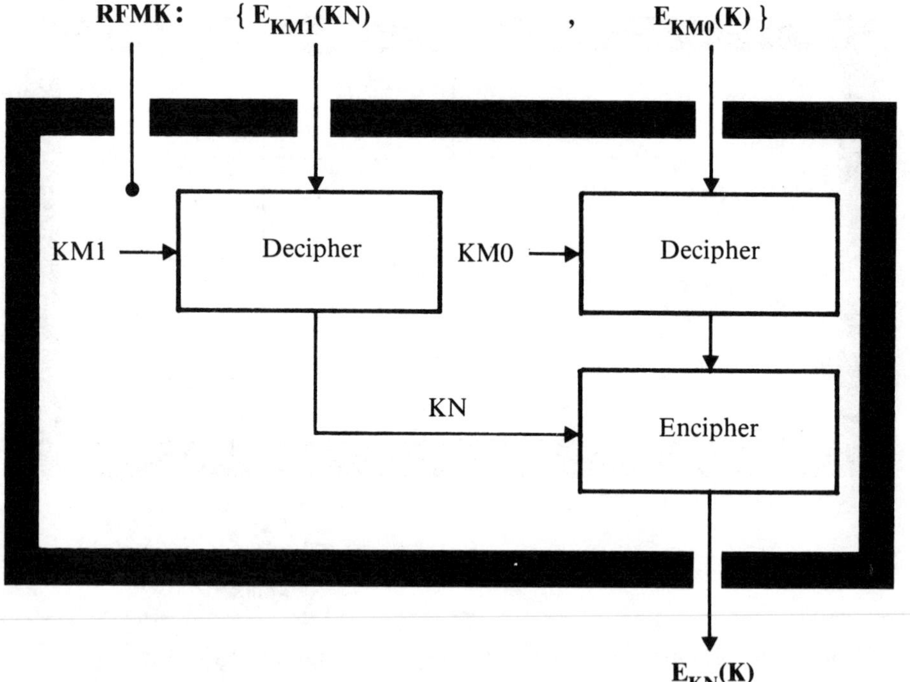

Figure 4-47. Reencipher From Master Key Operation at Host System

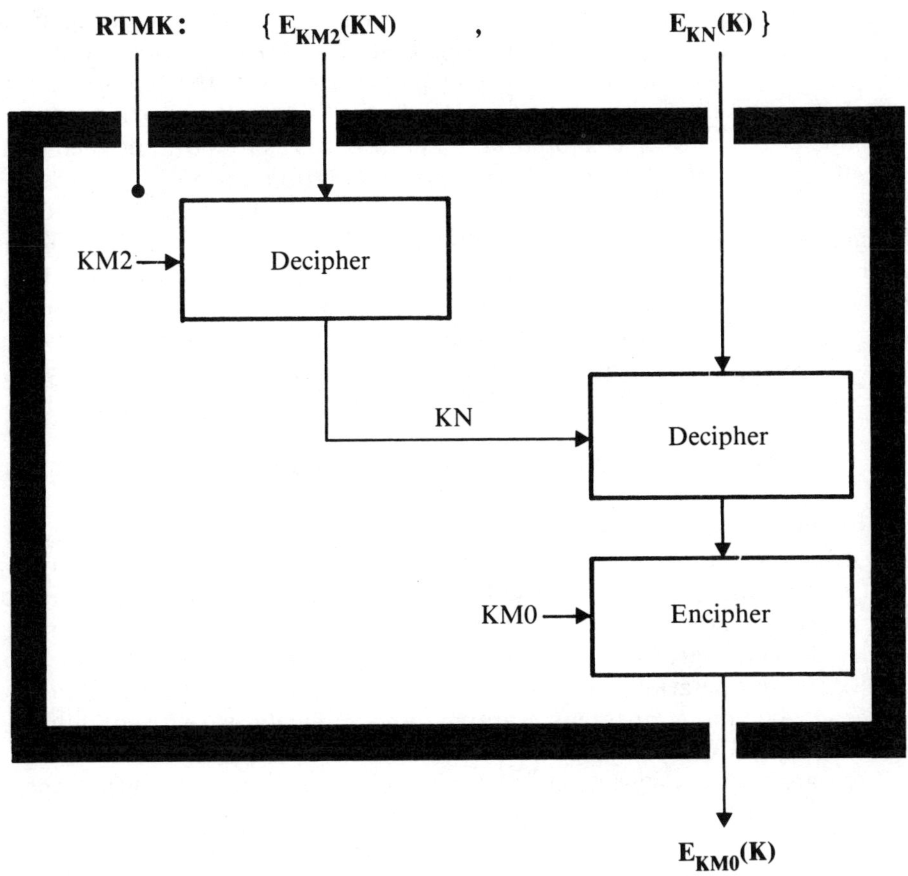

Figure 4-48. Reencipher To Master Key Operation at Host System

encipherment under one secondary key to encipherment under another secondary key would be accomplished using a combination of RTMK and RFMK.

Key Parity

A DES key consists of 64 bits of which 56 bits are used directly by the algorithm and 8 bits (the last bit of each 8-bit byte) can be used for error detection [9]. (See also The Data Encryption Standard, Chapter 3.) For example, the bits can be used to assure that each byte in the key has *odd parity* (i.e., that the number of 1 bits in each byte is odd). If used, keys are parity adjusted when they are created.

Since some of the concepts pertinent to key parity are applicable to this section, the topic is presented here. The topic of key generation is discussed in detail in Chapter 6.

Key-encrypting keys are generated in clear form. Prior to encipherment—in this case, with a variant of the host master key—each byte in the key can easily be adjusted to have odd parity. When retrieved within the cryptographic facility, during execution of the various basic cryptographic operations, the clear key may be examined for correct parity. However, there is no firm requirement per FIPS Publication 46 [10] to test for parity, nor is there any recommended action that should be taken if parity is found to be incorrect. Therefore, parity checking remains an implementation option.

In the discussed implementation, data-encrypting keys are generated in an enciphered form. Thus, there is no way of knowing, short of deciphering the key and making a test, whether a generated key has correct parity or not. Furthermore, there is only a $1/2^8 = 1/256$ chance that correct parity will occur. Needless to say, ensuring correct parity for data-encrypting keys would be complex and time-consuming. Therefore, data-encrypting keys (as discussed here) are not parity adjusted.

Partitioning of Cipher Keys

The host master key (KM0) and its variants (KM1 and KM2) permit cipher keys to be separated or *partitioned* into functionally different groups.[25] Such partitioning ensures that the keys defined to one cryptographic operation, or set of cryptographic operations, cannot be used, misused, or manipulated meaningfully by another cryptographic operation, or set of cryptographic operations. This in turn is the basis for achieving isolation or independence among different cryptographic applications (e.g., communication security and file security).

Key partitioning may be achieved if the cipher keys used by a first operation are enciphered under the first variant of the host master key (KM1) and the cipher keys used by a second operation are enciphered under the second variant of the host master key (KM2). Assume that encipherment under the variants is restricted to personnel authorized to install keys, and that decipherment under the variants is possible only within the cryptographic facility where the variants are derived from the stored host master key (Figure 4-49).

Once a key has been enciphered under its appropriate variant (either KM1 or KM2) it can be specified as a parameter in a cryptographic operation. An enciphered key can be recovered only in the cryptographic facility. And only a key that has been specifically selected and enciphered in advance under one of the variants of the host master key can be recovered when specified as a parameter in a cryptographic operation. If a key not intended for use with a particular cryptographic operation is specified as a parameter of that operation, it will produce a final output that cannot be interpreted, understood, or used in a meaningful way.

This principle can be explained further through the use of a hypothetical cryptographic operation defined as OP1. OP1 has a single input parameter:

OP1: {Key Parameter} ⟶ Output

[25] ©1979 IEEE. Reprinted from *NTC 79 Conference Record*, November 27–29, 1979, Washington, D.C. [9].

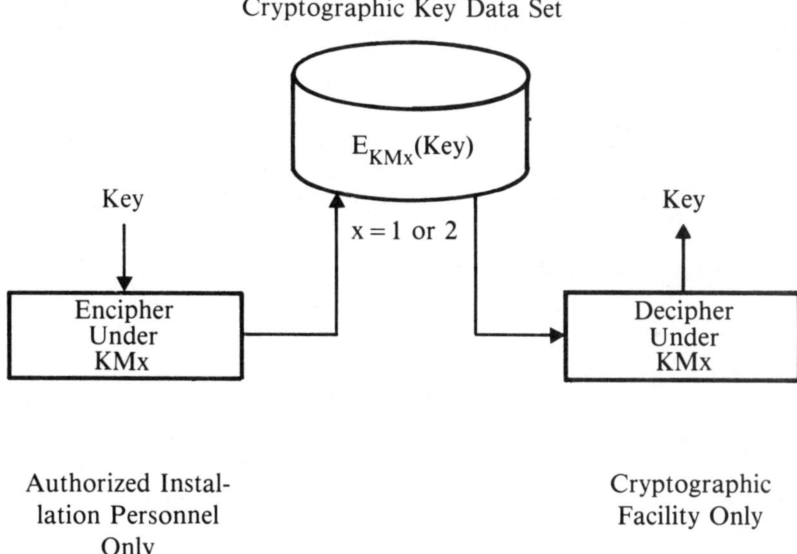

Figure 4-49. Encipherment and Decipherment Under the Variants of the Host Master key

and a set of secondary keys (KN1, KN2, . . . , KNn) that are to be used with it. Selected secondary keys are coupled to OP1 by enciphering them under the first variant of the host master key (KM1):

$$P1 = E_{KM1}(KN1)$$

$$P2 = E_{KM1}(KN2)$$

$$\vdots$$

$$Pn = E_{KM1}(KNn)$$

It is assumed that KM1 is used only with OP1. If $E_{KM1}(KNi)$ is used as a key parameter in OP1, then KNi is recovered within the cryptographic facility. Afterwards, KNi participates in additional ciphering operations to produce a final output. (A precise specification of the additional ciphering operations is not important to the present discussion.)

If the input key parameter (P) is an element in the set $E_{KM1}(KN1)$, $E_{KM1}(KN2)$, . . . , $E_{KM1}(KNn)$, then the recovered value of KN is a valid key known to the system (i.e., the recovered key-encrypting key is in the set KN1, KN2, . . . , KNn). However, if P is any other key parameter (e.g., a key enciphered under KM0 or KM2), or a key not in the set KN1, KN2, . . . , KNn, then the recovered value of KN is a key unknown to the system. The output of the cryptographic operation therefore involves a key whose value is both unpredictable and uncontrollable.

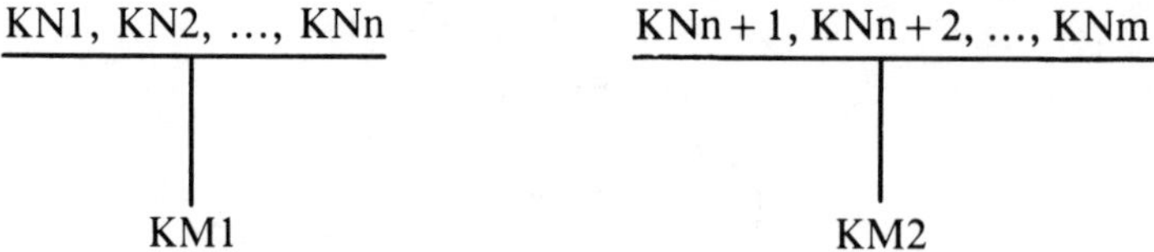

Figure 4-50. Hypothetical Scheme for the Protection of Keys

Suppose that a second hypothetical cryptographic operation is defined as OP2. OP2 also has a single input parameter:

OP2: {**Key Parameter**} ⟶ **Output**

and a set of cipher keys (KNn + 1, KNn + 2, . . . , KNm) that are to be used with it. However, in this case, the cipher keys to be used with OP2 are enciphered under the second variant of the host master key (KM2).

Encrypting KN1 through KNn with KM1, and encrypting KNn + 1 through KNm with KM2, cryptographically separates the secondary keys (Figure 4-50).

Since the results of OP1 or OP2 are meaningful only if the input key parameter is a key-encrypting key enciphered under KM1 or KM2, respectively, it is possible to eliminate shortcut methods of attack which either manipulate the cryptographic operations or use enciphered keys not intended for use with a specific operation. This point is illustrated below by showing the effect of using different key parameters with the example operations (Figure 4-51).

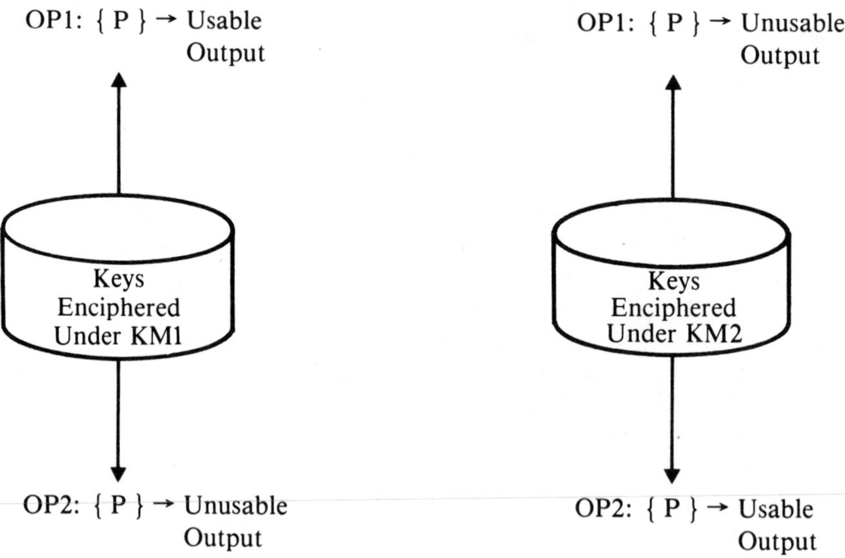

Figure 4-51. Correct and Incorrect Use of OP1 and OP2

An important advantage results from using multiple master keys; the cryptographic operations, higher-level functions, and applications provided by the cryptographic system can be isolated (logically separated) from one another. Cryptographic operations can also be made irreversible, thus limiting the function provided to the system and its users and thereby reducing the ways in which an opponent could attack the system. Whether implemented through variants of a single master key, or several different master keys, the concept of multiple master keys offers the cryptographic system designer flexibility in the development of provably secure cryptographic operations (see Extended Cryptographic Operations, Chapter 5).

CIPHER MACRO INSTRUCTION

The reader is reminded that this and subsequent macro instructions represent only sample specifications for the purpose of illustration. A byte is defined as a sequence of 8 contiguous bits.

The CIPHER macro instruction allows users of the system to encipher and decipher data. The CIPHER macro is defined as follows:

name	**CIPHER**	**PLNTXT**	= **address of plaintext**
		CHRTXT	= **address of ciphertext**
		KEY	= **address of enciphered primary key**
		LENGTH	= **address of length parameter**
		FNC	= **ENCPHR | DECPHR**
		ICV	= **address of initial chaining value**
		CHAIN	= **CHR | BLK | PLNCHR**
		OCV	= **address of output chaining value**
		SHORT	= **PAD | STREAM**

The symbol | denotes "or", whereas the underscore symbol indicates the defaulted parameter.

- PLNTXT = Address of Plaintext

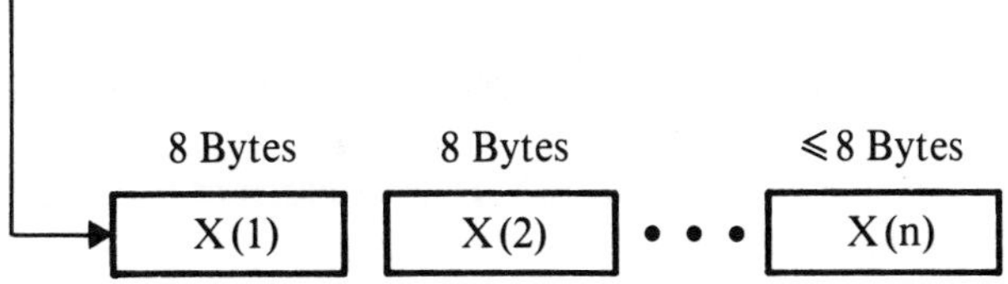

If the function specified is encipher (FNC = ENCPHR), then PLNTXT is the address of the data to be enciphered. If the function specified is decipher (FNC = DECPHR), then PLNTXT is the address of the storage location where the deciphered data are placed.

- CHRTXT = Address of Ciphertext

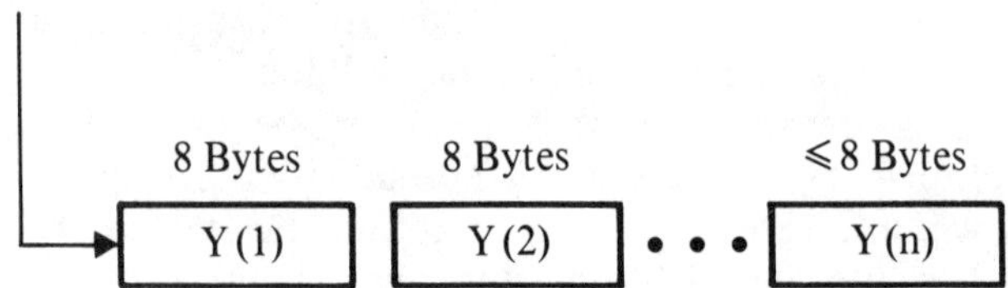

If the function specified is encipher (FNC = ENCPHR), the CHRTXT is the address of the storage location where the enciphered data will be placed. If the function specified is decipher (FNC = DECPHR), then CHRTXT is the address of the data to be deciphered.

- KEY = Address of Key Parameter (Primary Key Enciphered Under Host Master Key, KM0)

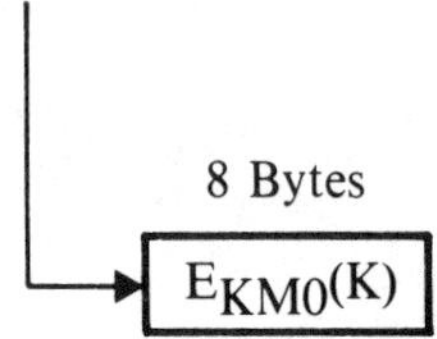

Data ciphering is performed using primary key K, where K is obtained by deciphering the input key parameter with KM0.

- LENGTH = Address of the Location Containing the Length of the Data in Bytes

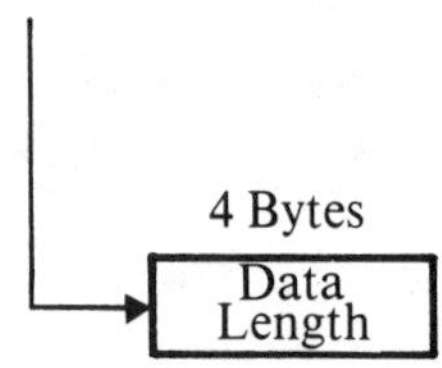

If FNC = ENCPHR, then LENGTH denotes length of plaintext. If FNC = DECPHR, then LENGTH denotes length of ciphertext.

- FNC = <u>ENCPHR</u> | DECPHR

ENCPHR specifies the function of encipherment and DECPHR specifies the function of decipherment.

- ICV = Address of Initial Chaining Value

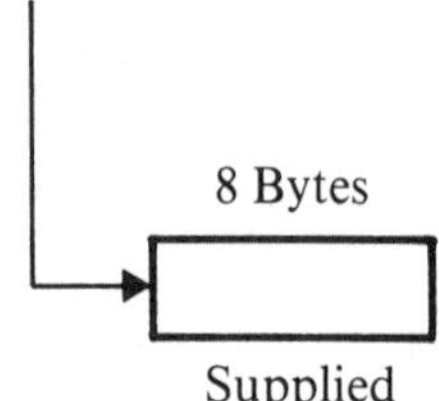

When block chaining is used, a chaining value (CV) is required for each block of data to be ciphered. The CV used to cipher the initial block is called the initial chaining value (ICV). The ICV is a nonsecret, 8-byte, random or pseudo-random value which is supplied as input. It is also called the initialization vector Z (see Block Ciphers and Stream Ciphers, Chapter 2). Except for the ICV, all other chaining values are derived from information supplied or derived when ciphering takes place, and depend on the particular chaining scheme employed.

- CHAIN = CHR | BLK | PLNCHR

The function CHAIN = BLK specifies that ciphering is performed on a block-by-block basis, with no chaining. In this case, the LENGTH parameter must be an exact multiple of 8 bytes. Since the SHORT parameter is used only in situations where LENGTH is not a multiple of 8 bytes, SHORT is invalid when BLK is specified. The method of ciphering data using the BLK function is in Figure 4-52.

The function CHAIN = CHR (CHR being the default parameter for routine encipherment of data) specifies that block chaining with ciphertext feedback is used for data ciphering. The LENGTH parameter, in this case, does not have to be a multiple of 8 bytes. The method of ciphering data using the CHR function is in Figure 4-53.

Encipher		Decipher	
Input Plaintext	Output Ciphertext	Input Ciphertext	Output Plaintext
X(1) X(2) • • • X(n)	$E_K(X(1))$ $E_K(X(2))$ • • • $E_K(X(n))$	Y(1) Y(2) • • • Y(n)	$D_K(Y(1))$ $D_K(Y(2))$ • • • $D_K(Y(n))$

K is a Primary Key.
Input and Output Blocks are 64 Bits in Length

Encipherment:

$$\text{ECPH:}\quad \{E_{KM0}(K), X(1), X(2), \ldots, K(n)\} \rightarrow Y(1), Y(2), \ldots, Y(n)$$

Decipherment:

$$\text{DCPH:}\quad \{E_{KM0}(K), Y(1), Y(2), \ldots, Y(n)\} \rightarrow X(1), X(2), \ldots, X(n)$$

Figure 4-52. Ciphering Operation Using the BLK Function

Chaining Value	Encipher: Input Plaintext	Encipher: Output Ciphertext	Decipher: Input Ciphertext	Decipher: Output Plaintext
$CV(1) = ICV$	$X(1)$	$Y(1) = E_K(X(1) \oplus CV(1))$	$Y(1)$	$X(1) = D_K(Y(1)) \oplus CV(1)$
$CV(2) = Y(1)$	$X(2)$	$Y(2) = E_K(X(2) \oplus CV(2))$	$Y(2)$	$X(1) = D_K(Y(2)) \oplus CV(2)$
• • •	• • •	• • •	• • •	• • •
$CV(n) = Y(n-1)$	$X(n)$	$Y(n) = E_K(X(n) \oplus CV(n))$	$Y(n)$	$X(n) = D_K(Y(n)) \oplus CV(n)$

Where: K is a Primary Key
Input and Output Blocks are 64-bits
$\oplus$ = Modulo 2 Addition (Exclusive-OR (XOR) Operation)

Encipherment:

$$\text{ECPH: } \{ E_{KM0}(K),\ X(1) \oplus ICV,\ X(2) \oplus Y(1),\ \ldots,\ X(n) \oplus Y(n-1) \} \rightarrow Y(1),\ Y(2),\ \ldots,\ Y(n)$$

Decipherment:

$$\text{DCPH: } \{ E_{KM0}(K),\ Y(1),\ Y(2),\ \ldots,\ Y(n) \} \rightarrow D_K(Y(1)),\ D_K(Y(2)),\ \ldots,\ D_K(Y(n))$$

Then XOR the Appropriate Chaining Value to Each Intermediate Block to Recover the Original Plaintext, Namely:

$$D_K(Y(1)) \oplus ICV = X(1)$$
$$D_K(Y(2)) \oplus Y(1) = X(2)$$
$$\vdots$$
$$D_K(Y(n)) \oplus Y(n-1) = X(n)$$

Figure 4-53. Ciphering Operation Using the CHR Function

The function CHAIN = PLNCHR specifies that block chaining with plaintext-ciphertext feedback is used for data ciphering. The method of ciphering data using the PLNCHR function (Figure 4-54) is similar to that described in Figure 4-53, except that the chaining values are defined differently.

In the case of CHAIN = CHR, the chaining values are CV(1) = ICV, CV(2) = Y(1), . . . , CV(n) = Y(n − 1). In the case of CHAIN = PLNCHR, the chaining values are CV(1) = ICV, CV(2) = X(1) + Y(1) mod 2^{64}, . . . , CV(n) = X(n − 1) + Y(n − 1) mod 2^{64}.

- OCV = Address of Output Chaining Value

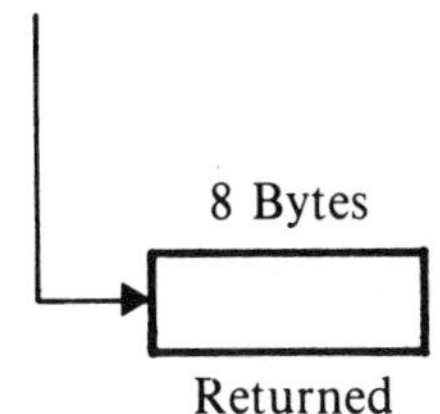

The OCV is a nonsecret, 8-byte, pseudo-random value which is computed from information supplied to or derived by the CIPHER macro at the time ciphering is performed. The method of computation depends upon the particular chaining scheme employed.
The OCV is defined here as the encipherment of the last block of ciphertext (Figure 4-55), although there are other ways in which an OCV could be derived.

- SHORT = <u>PAD</u> | STREAM

The SHORT parameter defines how short blocks (blocks of fewer than 8 bytes) are to be treated during the ciphering process. Basically, short blocks may be handled in two ways: they may be padded and then ciphered, or they may be ciphered directly with a stream cipher. The SHORT parameter is ignored for data that is a multiple of 8 bytes.

If SHORT = PAD is specified, then pad characters are added to a short block prior to its encipherment, and the pad characters are removed from the recovered plaintext block. Up to 7 pad characters can be added to a short block. The last pad character is a binary count of the total number of pad characters; the other pad characters are random or pseudo-random data (Figure 4-56).

If SHORT = STREAM is specified, then blocks 1, 2, . . . , n − 1 are ciphered using block chaining and block n (the short block) is ciphered using a stream cipher. The procedure for ciphering the short block consists of first enciphering the chaining value, CV(n), with the primary key K, and then

$$CV(1) = ICV$$

$$CV(2) = X(1) + Y(1)$$

$$\vdots$$

$$CV(n) = X(n-1) + Y(n-1)$$

Encipherment:

$$\text{ECPH: } \{ E_{KM0}(K),\ X(1) \oplus ICV,\ X(2) \oplus (X(1) + Y(1)),\ \ldots,\ X(n) \oplus (X(n-1) + Y(n-1)) \} \rightarrow Y(1),\ Y(2),\ \ldots,\ Y(n)$$

Decipherment:

$$\text{DCPH: } \{ E_{KM0}(K),\ Y(1),\ Y(2),\ \ldots,\ Y(n) \} \rightarrow D_K(Y(1)),\ D_K(Y(2)),\ \ldots,\ D_K(Y(n))$$

Then XOR the Appropriate Chaining Value to Each Intermediate Block to Recover the Plaintext Values, Namely:

$$D_K(Y(1)) \oplus ICV = X(1)$$
$$D_K(Y(2)) \oplus (X(1) + Y(1)) = X(2)$$
$$\vdots$$
$$D_K(Y(n)) \oplus (X(n-1) + Y(n-1)) = X(n)$$

Note that addition is modulo 2^{64}.

Figure 4-54. Ciphering Operation Using the PLNCHR Function

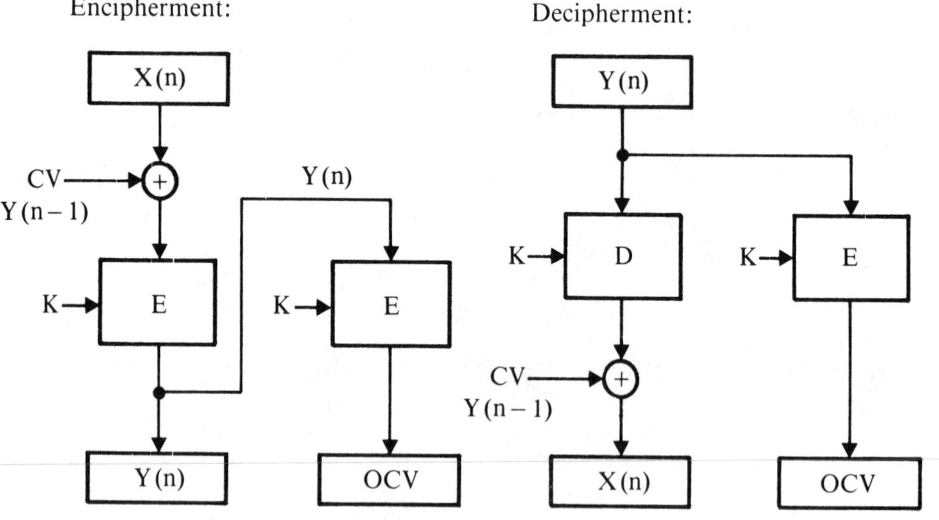

Figure 4-55. Procedure for Computing OCV

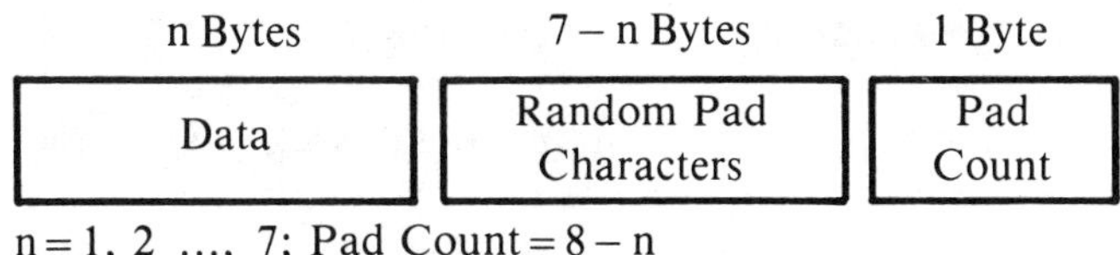

Figure 4-56. Padding of Short Blocks

Exclusive-ORing as many of the produced bits with the short block as necessary. Thus each bit in the short block is Exclusive-ORed with a corresponding bit in the enciphered chain value (Figure 4-57).

In the context of the present discussion, the SHORT parameter is invalid whenever CHAIN = BLK is specified. If CHAIN = CHR and SHORT = STREAM are specified, then the output chaining value is defined as

$$\mathbf{OCV} = \mathbf{E_K(RIGHT64[CV(n) \,||\, Y(n)]\,)}$$

where RIGHT64 denotes a function that extracts the rightmost 64 bits from the bit string variable enclosed in brackets, and || denotes concatenation. By definition, OCV = $E_K(Y(n))$ whenever the length of X(n) is 64 bits. If CHAIN = PLNCHR and SHORT = STREAM are specified, then the output chaining value is defined as

$$\mathbf{OCV} = \mathbf{E_K(RIGHT64[CV(n) \,||\, (Y(n) + X(n) \bmod 2^{64})\,]\,)}$$

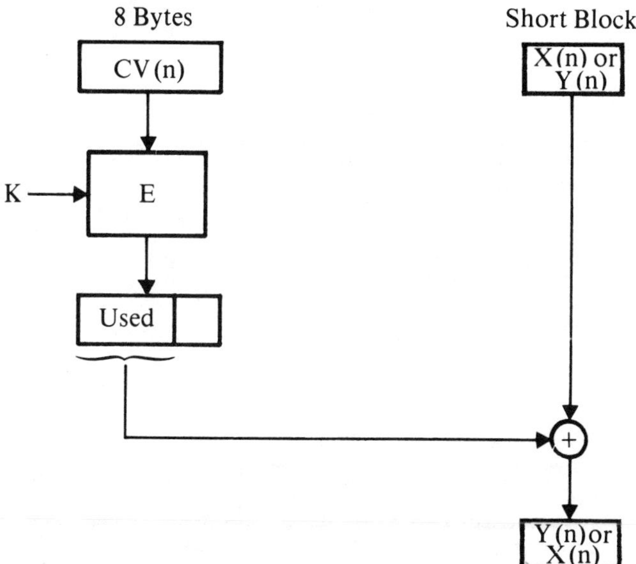

Figure 4-57. Ciphering a Short Block Using the STREAM Parameter

KEY MANAGEMENT MACRO INSTRUCTIONS

The key management macro instructions, GENKEY (generate key) and RETKEY (retrieve key), allow users of the cryptographic system to perform key transformations via the key manager program. In turn, the key manager program effects the desired key transformations by using one or more of the basic cryptographic operations. Used in the process are the key and data parameters specified by the macro, and other parameters stored in a key table that are available to the key manager program. The required transformations are performed by the key manager program using the cryptographic operations RFMK and RTMK, although in a different implementation they might be performed using a different set of cryptographic operations.

GENKEY and RETKEY Macros

Possible specifications for the GENKEY and RETKEY macros are as follows:

GENKEY

name GENKEY TOKEY1 = address, TOKEY2 = address

The TOKEY1 and TOKEY2 parameters each specify the address of a 16-byte area that contains an 8-byte key name (the name of a cryptographic resource) and an 8-byte answer area for the generated key enciphered under the named key-encrypting key.

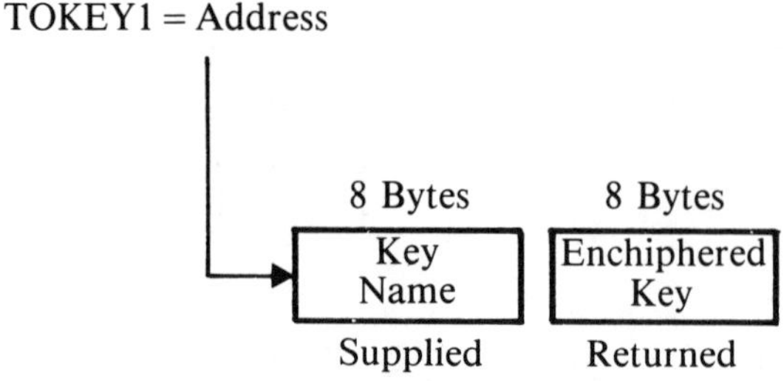

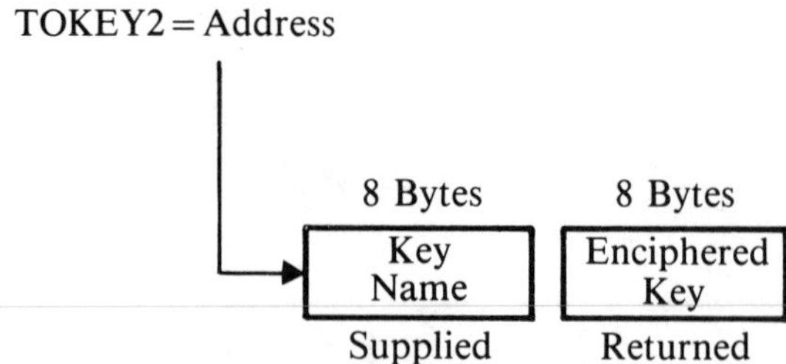

Execution of the GENKEY macro instruction causes the key manager to create a data-encrypting key (K) and to encipher this key under the key-encrypting keys (KN1 and KN2) specified by the key names in the TOKEY1 and TOKEY2 parameters.[26] Each enciphered key is then placed in its respective 8-byte answer area.

RETKEY

name RETKEY FROMKEY = address, TOKEY = address

The FROMKEY parameter specifies the address of a 16-byte area consisting of an 8-byte key name, and an 8-byte data-encrypting key which has been enciphered under the key-encrypting key specified.

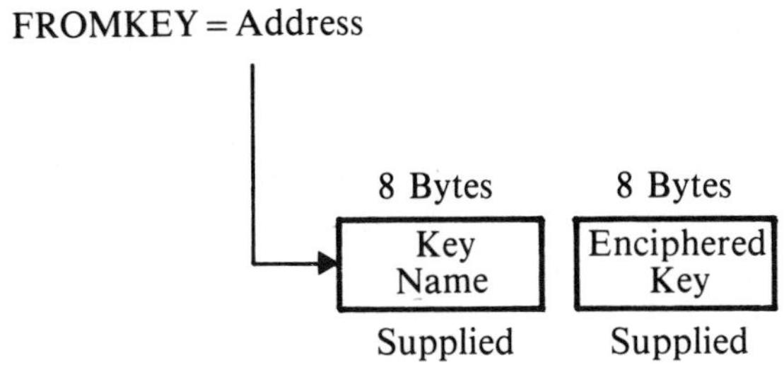

The TOKEY parameter specifies the address of a 16-byte area that contains an 8-byte key name and an 8-byte answer area.

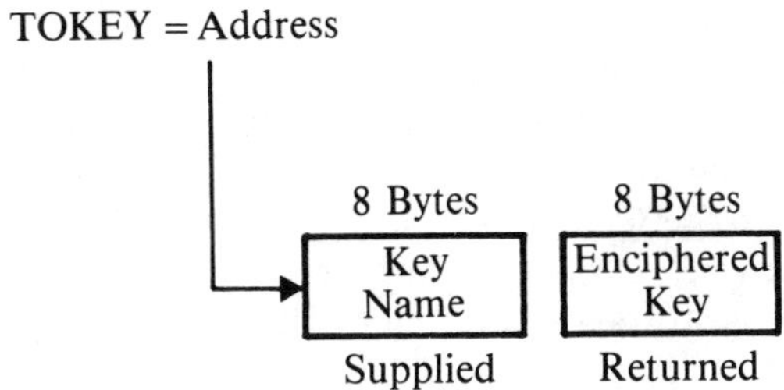

Execution of the RETKEY macro instruction causes the enciphered key supplied in the FROMKEY parameter to be deciphered under the key-encrypting key identified by the supplied key name also in the FROMKEY parameter. The result is then enciphered under the key-encrypting key identified by the supplied key name in the TOKEY parameter.

The qualifiers local and remote are used to distinguish the various cryptographic resources managed by a host processor. For a given host, a *local* resource is one located in the domain of that host; a *remote* resource is one located in or shared with another domain. Each host is a resource itself. There are five types of key-encrypting keys used by the cryptographic system: LOCAL TERMINAL, LOCAL FILE, LOCAL HOST, REMOTE FILE,

[26] Instead of producing K in clear form and then enciphering it under KN1 and KN2, the key manager generates a pseudo-random number, RN, which is defined as $E_{KN1}(K)$. $E_{KN2}(K)$ is then produced by deciphering RN with KN1 and reenciphering the resulting value (K) with KN2.

Local/Remote	Resource	Indicated Key	Key Location
LOCAL	TERMINAL	KMT	CKDS (Host i) & Terminal (Domain i)
	FILE	KNF	CKDS (Host i)
	HOST	KM0i	Cryptographic Facility (Host i)
REMOTE	FILE	KNFij; KNFji	CKDS (Host i & j)
	HOST	KNCij; KNCji	CKDS (Host i & j)

Notes:

LOCAL refers to domain i; REMOTE refers to domain j or something shared with domain j. Lower case letters (i, j) are used to indicate the referenced domain. Letter "i" is sometimes omitted when referring to a LOCAL resource, e.g. KM0 is used in place of KM0i. CKDS denotes the Cryptographic Key Data Set.

Table 4-1. Resources, Keys, and Key Storage Locations

and REMOTE HOST. The relationships among resources, keys, and key storage locations is shown in Table 4-1.

Every key-encrypting key stored at a host is assigned a unique key name. A key name is used by the key manager to locate a key stored in either the cryptographic facility or the CKDS. The key name could, for example, consist of a resource name (either the name of a resource protected by the key, or the location where it is stored) and an identifier:

<key name> = <resource name>, <identifier>

The name of the key installed in the first of a set of terminals might be TERM0001.

The parameters of the GENKEY and RETKEY macros provide a general framework for a user to request key translations. However, it must be realized that only certain combinations of parameter values (as specified by their supplied key names) will be accepted as valid, whereas others will not.[27] The reasons for this are:

1. Certain key translations may be inhibited because they cannot be performed (i.e., the basic cryptographic operations may not permit effective translation).
2. Certain key translations may be inhibited for reasons of security (i.e., the translation, if provided, would lead to an exposure of keys or data).

[27] Error reporting mechanisms are not presented here but can be assumed.

3. Certain key translations may be inhibited simply because the function is not needed by the cryptographic system. The user is only able to do those things that are absolutely required for cryptography.

For example, if the key name of a local terminal and the key name of a local host could be specified for the FROMKEY and TOKEY parameters, respectively, then it would be possible to translate a wiretapped session key (KS) from encipherment under a terminal master key (KMT) to encipherment under a host master key (KM0). Once $E_{KM0}(KS)$ is obtained, anyone with access to the host system could then decipher intercepted ciphertext (enciphered under KS) via the CIPHER macro instruction.

A truth table (matrix of 1s and 0s) could be used by the key manager to determine if certain parameter combinations are valid or invalid. The row and column headings could be identified by LOCAL TERMINAL, LOCAL FILE, LOCAL HOST, REMOTE FILE, and REMOTE HOST (Table 4-2). A

GENKEY

(TOKEY1) \ (TOKEY2)	LOCAL TERMINAL	LOCAL FILE	LOCAL HOST	REMOTE FILE	REMOTE HOST
LOCAL TERMINAL	1	1	1	1	1
LOCAL FILE	1	0	1	1	1
LOCAL HOST	1	1	X	1	1
REMOTE FILE	1	1	1	1	1
REMOTE HOST	1	1	1	1	1

"1" Denotes Requested Translation Allowed
"0" Denotes Requested Translation Denied
"X" Denotes a Null Translation

Note: The cryptographic operations will not permit the encipherment of a common data-encrypting key under two different LOCAL FILE keys.

Table 4-2. Valid and Invalid Parameter Combinations in the GENKEY Macro

similar truth table can be constructed for the parameters of the RETKEY macro (Table 4-3).

In each case, it can be shown that the defined key transformations (Tables 4-2 and 4-3) can be effected by using the RFMK and RTMK operations. For example, a GENKEY request where TOKEY1 designates a local host and TOKEY2 designates a local terminal could be handled as follows. A random number (RN) is produced and defined to be the required data-encrypting key (K) enciphered under the host master key (KM0). RN = $E_{KM0}(K)$ is returned in the 8-byte answer area of the TOKEY1 parameter. An RFMK operation is then used to transform K from encipherment under KM0 to

RETKEY

(FROM-KEY) \ (TOKEY)	LOCAL TERMINAL	LOCAL FILE	LOCAL HOST	REMOTE FILE	REMOTE HOST
LOCAL TERMINAL	□ 0	□ ▽ 0	□ 0	□ 0	□ 0
LOCAL FILE	1	▽ 0	1	1	1
LOCAL HOST	1	▽ 0	X	1	1
REMOTE FILE	1	▽ 0	1	1	1
REMOTE HOST	1	▽ 0	1	1	1

"1" Denotes Requested Translation allowed
"0" Denotes Requested Translation Denied
"X" Denotes a Null Translation

Notes: ▽ No cryptographic operation(s) will permit a data-encrypting key to be transformed to encipherment under a LOCAL FILE key.

□ No cryptographic operation(s) will permit a data-encrypting key enciphered under a LOCAL TERMINAL key to be transformed to encipherment under any other key.

Table 4-3. Valid and Invalid Parameter Combinations in the RETKEY Macro

encipherment under the master key of the specified terminal (KMT). $E_{KMT}(K)$ is returned in the 8-byte answer area of the TOKEY2 parameter. In the described communications environment, the transformations provided by GENKEY would be effected with the RFMK operation. The logical inverse transformation provided by RETKEY is effected with the RTMK operation. As a general rule, key translations related to a file key involve the use of RTMK for both GENKEY and RETKEY. (See also The Host System Cryptographic Operations, Chapter 5.)

The translation functions of RETKEY are necessary to effect proper key management within the cryptographic system but also provide an opponent with a way to subvert the system's security. For example, interdomain communications require that there be a way for one domain to receive an enciphered session key from another domain, and translate that key (via the RETKEY macro instruction) into a form usable for deciphering data. In effect, this means that an opponent who has intercepted an enciphered session key and data enciphered under that key can perform the same translation by invoking the RETKEY macro, provided that access can be gained to the receiving host system.

It is absolutely essential that the cryptographic system have a way of *controlling* the use of the RETKEY macro. Control can be effected, for example, by requiring that the calling program have privilege equal to that of the host's operating system. In addition, the CKDS can be made a protected data set, thus making it the exclusive resource of the key generator and key manager. Recording denied RETKEY requests on a system log is also advisable as an extra precautionary measure.

Using GENKEY and RETKEY

In a previous example (see An Example of the Encryption of Transmitted Data), user 1 located at terminal 1 in domain i established a communications session, using cryptography in a transparent manner, with user 2 located at terminal 2 in domain j. The network configuration and allocation of secondary keys for this example is shown in Figure 4-58.

User 1 initiates the session by logging on via a terminal. This causes a message to be transmitted to host i requesting that a communications session be established between terminal 1 in domain i and terminal 2 in domain j. As a consequence of this action (Figure 4-59), the teleprocessing access method invokes the key manager via the GENKEY macro instruction, passing as parameters the names of KNC1 and KNC2. The key manager generates a session key (KS) and then causes KS to be enciphered under secondary key KNC1 so that it can be transmitted to terminal 1, and under secondary key KNC2 so that it can be transmitted to host j.

The quantity $E_{KNC1}(KS)$ is transmitted to terminal 1, and the quantity $E_{KNC2}(KS)$ is transmitted to host j. At host j, the teleprocessing access method invokes the key manager via the RETKEY macro and passes as parameters the names of KNC2 and KNC4. The key manager then causes the session key (KS) to be transformed from encipherment under KNC2 to encipherment

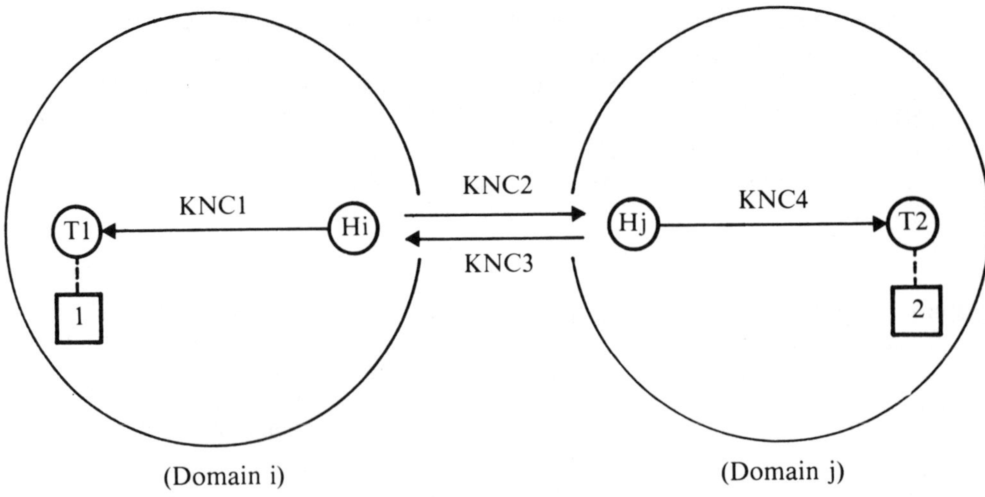

Figure 4-58. Initial Configuration

under KNC4 (Figure 4-60). The quantity $E_{KNC4}(KS)$ is transmitted to terminal 2.

At terminal 1, the session key is recovered by deciphering the quantity $E_{KNC1}(KS)$ with the cipher key KNC1. KNC1 is maintained within the master key storage of terminal 1's cryptographic facility. Similarly, at terminal 2, the session key is recovered by deciphering the quantity $E_{KNC4}(KS)$ with the cipher key KNC4. KNC4 is maintained within the master key storage of terminal 2's cryptographic facility. The cipher keys KNC2 and KNC4 are terminal master keys, although the notation KMT is not used in the present example. As a result of the process of initiating the session, end users 1 and 2 share a common session key (KS) that can be used for ciphering data.

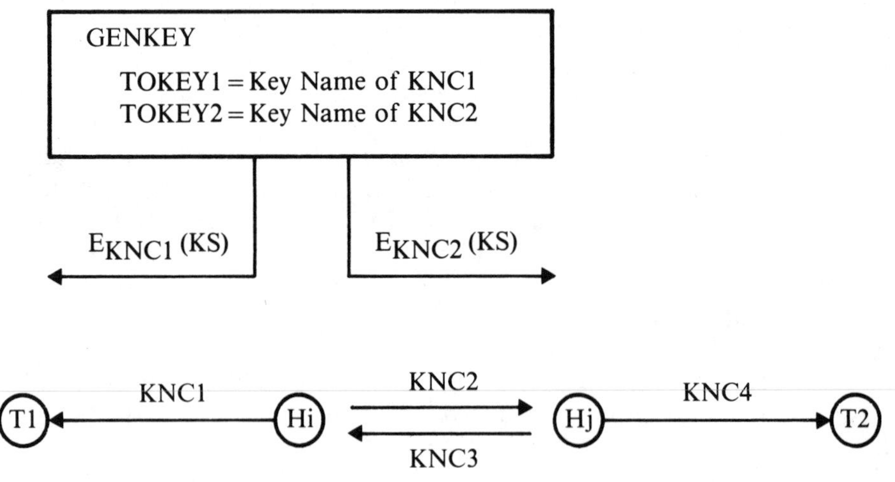

Figure 4-59. Session Key Generation at Host i

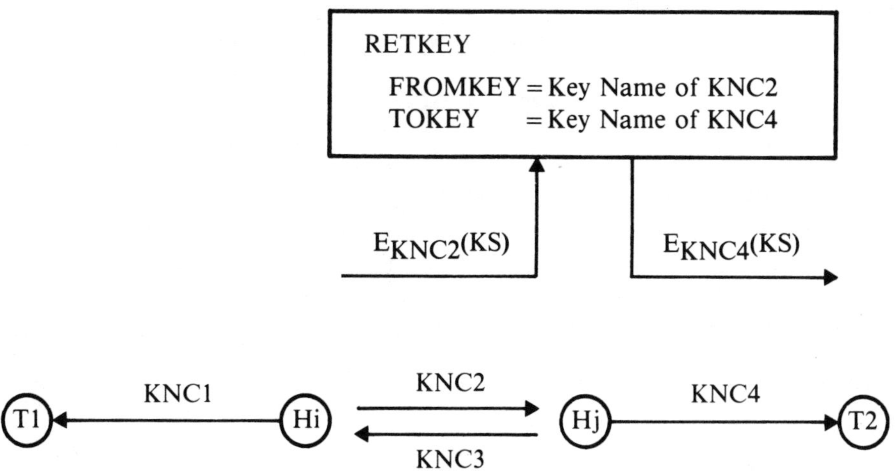

Figure 4-60. Session Key Translation at Host j

THE CRYPTOGRAPHIC KEY DATA SET

The *Cryptographic Key Data Set* (CKDS) is the repository for all secondary keys (other than the host master key) used by the key manager to perform key translation functions. These keys are protected (during their period of storage) by being enciphered under either the first (KM1) or second (KM2) variant of the host master key.

The CKDS is created and maintained by the key generator. A separate input statement is supplied to the key generator for each entry or record in the CKDS that is to be added, updated, or deleted. The input statement has the general format shown in Figure 4-61. The format of each entry (record) in the CKDS is shown in Table 4-4.

The key name is a parameter used to locate an entry in the CKDS. The key type indicates to the key generator whether the stored key is enciphered

Key Type:	Type 1, Type 2, or Type 3 (representing LOCAL TERMINAL, LOCAL FILE, and REMOTE HOST or REMOTE FILE, repectively)
Key Name:	Installation Specified Name
Key1:	Optional 64-Bit Key If a key is required and no key is specified, then a key will be generated automatically.
Key2:	Same as for Key1
Action:	Add, Update, or Delete

Figure 4-61. Input Statement to Add, Update, or Delete a CKDS Record

Field Position (Bytes)	Field Length (Bytes)	Field Description
0	8	Key Name
8	8	Key1 Enciphered Under KM1
16	8	Key2 Enciphered Under KM2
24	1	Resource Type (1, 2, or 3)
25	8	Test Pattern (Optional)

Table 4-4. CKDS Record Format

under KM1 (designated type 1) or KM2 (designated type 2), or whether two different keys are stored under KM1 and KM2 (designated type 3). The resource type indicates to the key manager what cryptographic operations must be performed by the cryptographic facility in order to satisfy requests for translation. The test pattern is an optional parameter that can be used to authenticate stored keys (see Authentication Techniques Using Cryptography, Chapter 8).

Local Terminal:

Terminal Name	E_{KM1}(KMT)	(Unused)	Type 1	Test Pattern (Optional)

Local File:

File Name	(Unused)	E_{KM2} (KNF)	Type 2	Test Pattern (Optional)

Remote Host:

Host j Name	E_{KM1}(KNCij)	E_{KM2}(KNCji)	Type 3	Test Pattern (Optional)

Remote File:

File Name	E_{KM1}(KNFij)	E_{KM2}(KNFji)	Type 3	Test Pattern (Optional)

Legend: Local = Host i
Remote = Host j

Figure 4-62. CKDS Entries

Secondary keys stored in the CKDS are of the types described in Figure 4-62. A secondary communication key associated with a local terminal is of type 1 (i.e., it is stored enciphered under KM1). A secondary file key associated with a local file is of type 2 (i.e., it is stored enciphered under KM2). A pair of secondary communication keys or secondary file keys associated with a remote host or remote file, respectively, are of type 3, (i.e., one of the keys is stored enciphered under KM1 and the other key is stored enciphered under KM2). A secondary key which allows a primary key to be sent to another host is stored enciphered under KM1, whereas a secondary key which allows a primary key to be received from another host is stored enciphered under KM2.

SUMMARY

The main thrust of this chapter has been to show how the DES algorithm can be implemented in a network of connected computers to provide end-to-end encryption for communication security and file security. (Link encryption was treated briefly for the sake of completeness.) Emphasis has been placed on describing a method for allocating keys (including a hierarchical structure of keys for both key and data protection) and defining a set of basic cryptographic operations that use these keys. The cryptographic operations are performed by a cryptographic facility, or secure implementation, that can be invoked through a programming interface (e.g., with program macro instructions). The intent was to provide the reader with an insight into the design of a cryptographic system and to give enough details of the implementation to allow its operation to be understood. A justification for the particular cryptographic operations and keys (including multiple master keys) defined herein is given in Chapter 5.

REFERENCES

1. Ehrsam, W. F., Matyas, S. M., Meyer, C. H., and Tuchman, W. L., "A Cryptographic Key Management Scheme for Implementing the Data Encryption Standard," *IBM Systems Journal*, **17**, No. 2, 106–125 (1978).
2. *IBM Cryptographic Subsystem Concepts and Facilities,* IBM Systems Library Order Number GC22-9063, IBM Corporation, Data Processing Division, White Plains, NY (1977).
3. McFayden, J. H., "Systems Network Architecture: An Overview," *IBM Systems Journal,* **15**, No. 1, 4–23 (1976).
4. Green, P. E., "An Introduction to Network Architectures and Protocols," *IBM Systems Journal,* **18**, No. 2, 202–222 (1979).
5. Baran, P., "On Distributed Communications: IX. Security, Secrecy and Tamper-free Considerations," Memo. RRM-3765-PR, Rand Corporation, Santa Monica, CA (August 1964).
6. Chaum, D. L., "Untraceable Electronic Mail, Return Address, and Digital Pseudonyms," Memo. UCB/ERLM79/9, Electronic Research Laboratory, University of California, Berkeley (February 1979).

7. Cypser, R. J., *Communications Architecture for Distributed Systems,* Addison-Wesley, Reading, MA, 1978.
8. *IBM 3848 Cryptographic Unit Product Description and Operating Procedures,* IBM Systems Library Order Number GA22-7073, IBM Corporation, Data Processing Division, White Plains, NY (1979).
9. Lennon, R. E. and Matyas, S. M., "Unidirectional Cryptographic Functions Using Master Key Variants," *National Telecommunications Conference Record,* **3**, 43.4.1-43.4.5 (1979).
10. *Data Encryption Standard,* Federal Information Processing Standard (FIPS) Publication 46, National Bureau of Standards, U.S. Department of Commerce, Washington, DC (January 1977).

Other Publications that Treat Key Management in Conventional and/or Public-Key Cryptographic Systems

11. Kent, S. T., "Encryption Based Protocols for Interactive User-Computer Communication," *Proceedings Fifth Data Communications Sysmposium,* 5-13 (September 1977). Available from ACM, New York.
12. Everton, J. K., "A Hierarchical Basis for Encryption Key Management in a Computer Communications Network," *Trends and Applications 1978: Distributed Processing,* IEEE Computer Society, Long Beach CA (1978).
13. Merkle, R., "Secure Communications Over Insecure Channels," *Communications of the ACM,* **21**, No. 4, 294-299 (April 1978).
14. Popek, G. J., and Kline, C. S., "Encryption Protocols, Public Key Algorithms, and Digital Signatures in Computer Networks," in *Foundations of Secure Computation,* edited by R. A. DeMillo, D. P. Dobkin, A. K. Jones, and R. J. Lipton, Academic Press, New York, 1978, pp. 133-153.
15. Needham, R. M., and Schroder, M. D., "Using Encryption for Authentication in Large Networks of Computers," *Communications of the ACM,* **21**, No. 12, 993-999 (December 1978).
16. Kohnfelder, L. M., "Towards a Practical Public-Key Cryptosystem," B.S. Thesis, Department of Electrical Engineering, Massachusetts Institute of Technology, Cambridge (May 1978).
17. Smid, M. E., *A Key Notarization System for Computer Networks,* NBS Special Publication 500-54, U.S. Department of Commerce, National Bureau of Standards, Washington, DC (October 1979).
18. Konheim, A. G., Mack, M. H., McNeill, R. K., Tuckerman, B., and Waldbaum, G., "The IPS Cryptographic Programs," *IBM Systems Journal,* **19**, No. 2, 253-283 (1980).
19. Blakley, G. R., "Safeguarding Cryptographic Keys," *AFIPS Conference Proceedings,* **48,** 313-317 (June 1979).
20. Shamir, A., "How to Share a Secret," *Communications of the ACM,* **22,** No. 11, 612-613 (1979).

CHAPTER FIVE

The Host System Cryptographic Operations[1]

Since an opponent masquerading as an authorized user could access the host's cryptographic facility, the cryptographic operations at a host (Chapter 4) must be such that keys are not exposed as a result of exercising these operations in some chosen manner. For this reason, the operations are discussed in depth, providing the reader with additional insight into their design.

The host's basic cryptographic operations are invoked via a programmed interface to the host's cryptographic facility. However, a *set master key* operation, used to store a host master key in the cryptographic facility, is enabled via a physical key lock that operates an associated electromechanical lock. The key lock isolates the set master key operation from the other cryptographic operations, thus affording maximum protection to the master key.

In a data communications network, a host system's domain refers to the set of resources managed by that host system. Data communications involving only a single host system are referred to as *single-domain communications*, whereas those involving more than one host system are referred to as *multiple-domain communications.*

One master key provides adequate security for single-domain communications when pregenerated data-encrypting keys are used. Two master keys are necessary if dynamically generated data-encrypting keys are desired. And if file security (the storage of ciphered data) is also desired, three master keys are required. Also, three master keys are sufficient to provide for single-domain and multiple-domain COMSEC and FILESEC using dynamically generated data-encrypting keys.

SINGLE-DOMAIN COMMUNICATION SECURITY USING PREGENERATED PRIMARY KEYS

Pregenerated primary keys are primary keys generated under secure conditions in a single large group before they are needed, and stored within the

[1] © 1978 IBM Corporation. Reprinted in part from *IBM Systems Journal,* **17**, No. 2 (1978) [1].

system for later use. A cryptographic system with one master key permits single-domain communication security using pregenerated primary keys.

Let KC1, KC2, . . . , KCn denote the pregenerated primary communication keys used for ciphering data. If there is only one master key, KM0, then KM0 is used to protect all primary communication keys stored at the host system for use in subsequent data ciphering operations. Keys are stored in the form

$$E_{KM0}(KC1), E_{KM0}(KC2), \ldots, E_{KM0}(KCn)$$

The host master key KM0 is inserted into the master key storage of the host's cryptographic facility via a *set master key* (SMK) operation, as follows:

$$\text{SMK: } \{KM0\}$$

It is assumed that the primary communication keys are generated ahead of time, and that these keys are enciphered under the host master key KM0 with the *encipher under master key* (EMK) operation, as follows:

$$\text{EMK: } \{KC\} \longrightarrow E_{KM0}(KC)$$

The *encipher data* (ECPH) and *decipher data* (DCPH) operations at the host system are defined as

$$\text{ECPH: } \{E_{KM0}(\text{Key}), \text{Data}\} \longrightarrow E_{KEY}(\text{Data})$$

$$\text{DCPH: } \{E_{KM0}(\text{Key}), E_{\text{Key}}(\text{Data})\} \longrightarrow \text{Data}$$

and hence the enciphered primary communication keys stored at the host system are in a form that can be used directly as inputs to these operations. The ECPH and DCPH operations are defined in such a way that a primary communication key (KC) can be used for ciphering data only after the quantity $E_{KM0}(KC)$ has been deciphered under KM0 and the resulting value of KC transferred to the working key storage of the host's cryptographic facility. This complies with the requirement that KC should not appear in clear form outside the cryptographic facility, except when it is generated and initially enciphered under KM0.

Each terminal in the domain of the host system has its own unique secondary communication key, also called the terminal master key (KMT). The terminal master keys are generated under secure conditions at the host system, and each key is distributed in a secure manner (as by courier) to its respective terminal where it is installed in the master key storage element of the terminal's cryptographic facility.

Once installed, the terminal master key is used to protect the primary communication keys as they are sent from the host system to the terminal. At the terminal, the enciphered primary communication key is first deciphered under the terminal master key, and the resultant value of KC is transferred to the working key storage of the terminal's cryptographic facility (where it can be used for subsequent ciphering operations).

Also, as part of the initialization, the list of primary communication keys is divided into as many separate groups of keys as there are terminals. Each group of keys is then enciphered under a different terminal master key. For example, if there were 5 terminals and 5000 primary communication keys, then the table of enciphered keys would be shown by Table 5-1.

This table of enciphered primary communication keys is stored at the host system, and individual keys are selected from the table and sent to their respective terminals as needed. Alternatively, the keys in each row of the table could be stored at their respective terminals. Individual keys could then be selected, as needed, from this locally stored list.

The table of enciphered primary communication keys is produced by using both the *encipher under master key* (EMK) operation and the *encipher data* (ECPH) operation. A terminal master key (KMT) is first enciphered under the host master key (KM0) using an EMK operation. The quantity $E_{KM0}(KMT)$ is then used in an ECPH operation to encipher a primary communication key (KC) under the terminal master key (KMT):

$$\text{EMK: } \{\text{KMT}\} \longrightarrow E_{KM0}(\text{KMT})$$

$$\text{ECPH: } \{E_{KM0}(\text{KMT}), \text{KC}\} \longrightarrow E_{KMT}(\text{KC})$$

After the table of enciphered primary communication keys has been produced, all quantities used in its generation are erased from the host system's main storage.

To implement the approach described here, four basic cryptographic operations are needed at the host system: *set master key* (SMK), *encipher under master key* (EMK), *encipher data* (ECPH), and *decipher data* (DCPH). (See Cryptographic Operations at a Host, Chapter 4.) The approach requires, in addition, only one master key (KM0).

The disadvantages of this approach are that the number of primary communication keys needed by the cryptographic system must be determined in advance, and the storage space for these keys must be provided by the host system. There is also a danger that one or more of these enciphered keys may become known to an opponent. In that case, the quantity $E_{KM0}(KC)$ could be used by an opponent directly as input to a *decipher data* operation

Terminal 1	$E_{KMT1}(KC1)$,	$E_{KMT1}(KC2)$,	..., $E_{KMT1}(KC1000)$
Terminal 2	$E_{KMT2}(KC1001)$,	$E_{KMT2}(KC1002)$,	..., $E_{KMT2}(KC2000)$
⋮	⋮	⋮	⋮
Terminal 5	$E_{KMT5}(KC4001)$,	$E_{KMT5}(KC4002)$,	..., $E_{KMT5}(KC5000)$

Table 5-1. Table of Primary Communication Keys Enciphered Under Terminal Master Keys

to decipher intercepted ciphertext, provided that access to the host system could be obtained.

SINGLE-DOMAIN COMMUNICATION SECURITY USING DYNAMICALLY GENERATED PRIMARY KEYS

The previous section described a protocol in which one host master key was needed to protect the pregenerated keys used for communication security in a single domain. The question now arises whether one master key is sufficient if dynamically generated session keys are used.

Let KS1, KS2, . . . , KSn denote the dynamically generated primary communication keys used for ciphering data. Each KS is operational only for the duration of a communications session, and hence is called a *session key* (see Cipher Key Allocation, Chapter 4). Since there is only one host master key, KM0, session keys are maintained at the host system in the form

$$E_{KM0}(KS1), E_{KM0}(KS2), \ldots, E_{KM0}(KSn)$$

Session keys required by the cryptographic system are generated at the host processor. This is because a single host facility is more economical than multiple facilities duplicating the same function at several terminals.

To satisfy the condition that no clear key occurs outside the cryptographic facility, and yet avoid a requirement to generate KS directly within the cryptographic facility, an indirect method of generating session keys is adopted. A 64-bit pseudo-random number (RN) is generated (Chapter 6) and defined to be the session key enciphered under the requesting node's host master key (KM0):

$$RN = E_{KM0}(KS)$$

Session keys are therefore produced as a sequence of pseudo-random numbers:

$$RN1, RN2, \ldots, RNn$$

where the ith pseudo-random number (RNi) corresponds to the ith encrypted session key (i.e., RNi = $E_{KM0}(KSi)$).

This method for generating session keys also has the advantage that the quantity RN can be used directly at the host system to encipher and decipher data:

$$\text{ECPH: } \{RN, Data\} \longrightarrow E_{D_{KM0}(RN)}(Data)$$

$$\text{DCPH: } \{RN, E_{D_{KM0}(RN)}(Data)\} \longrightarrow Data$$

where

$$D_{KM0}(RN) = KS$$

Because session keys are generated in enciphered form, it is not possible to encipher them directly under a terminal master key (KMT) by using the EMK and ECPH operations (see Single Domain Communication Security Using Pregenerated Primary Keys). Thus to obtain $E_{KMT}(KS)$, which is required at the terminal, a cryptographic operation is needed to transform KS from encipherment under KM0 to encipherment under KMT. This transformation is accomplished by deciphering $E_{KM0}(KS)$ with the value of KM0 stored in the host's cryptographic facility and reenciphering KS with the terminal master key (KMT). (KMT is stored at the host system and is provided as an input parameter to the host's cryptographic facility as needed.)

A cryptographic system, like the one being discussed, could be constructed with one master key if KMT were stored enciphered under KM0. Such a system, however, would expose session keys, since using $E_{KM0}(KMT)$ and $E_{KMT}(KS)$ as inputs to a *decipher data* operation would yield a clear value of KS:

$$\text{DCPH: } \{E_{KM0}(KMT), E_{KMT}(KS)\} \longrightarrow KS$$

This condition violates the stated requirement that *it must not be possible to recover keys in the clear outside a designated physically secure area, such as a cryptographic facility.*

Two Master Keys

The situation described above can be avoided by defining a second master key, KM1. In this case, session keys are maintained at the host system in the form

$$E_{KM0}(KS1), E_{KM0}(KS2), \ldots, E_{KM0}(KSn)$$

and terminal master keys are maintained at the host system in the form

$$E_{KM1}(KMT1), E_{KM1}(KMT2), \ldots, E_{KM1}(KMTn)$$

The terminal master keys are generated under secure conditions at the host system, and each key is distributed in a secure manner (as by courier) to its respective terminal where it is installed in the master key storage of the terminal's cryptographic facility. This approach, however, requires a translation capability, defined as the *reencipher from master key* operation:

$$\text{RFMK: } \{E_{KM1}(KMT), E_{KM0}(KS)\} \longrightarrow E_{KMT}(KS)$$

Even though the relationship between KM0 and KM1 is publicly known, this information is not enough to permit the algorithm to be broken. For instance, $E_{KM0}(KMT)$ cannot be deduced from $E_{KM1}(KMT)$ for a strong cryptographic algorithm (see Protection of Host Keys, Chapter 4).

The attack described above for recovering session keys is thwarted when KMT is stored enciphered under KM1. Neither is it possible to deduce

$E_{KM0}(KMT)$ from $E_{KM1}(KMT)$, nor is it possible to enter $E_{KM1}(KMT)$ and $E_{KMT}(KS)$ as inputs to a *decipher data* operation and recover a clear session key (KS):

$$\text{DCPH: } \{E_{KM1}(KMT), E_{KMT}(KS)\} \longrightarrow D_K(E_{KMT}(KS)) \neq KS$$

because

$$K = D_{KM0}(E_{KM1}(KMT)) \neq KMT$$

The host master key (KM0) is inserted into the master key storage of the host's cryptographic facility with an SMK operation (as previously discussed). Because session keys are generated in a form enciphered under the host master key (KM0), the EMK operation is not needed to encipher dynamically generated primary keys as it is for pregenerated primary keys.

Encipherment Under KM1

Encipherment of the terminal master keys under KM1 can be accomplished under secure conditions by a combination of cryptographic operations already discussed.[2] The steps involved in this procedure are as follows. The host master key (KM0) is first read into the main storage of the host system, where the variant KM1 is derived by inversion of appropriate bits of KM0. The intermediate quantity $E_{KM1}(KM1)$ is then derived as follows:

$$\text{EMK: } \{KM1\} \longrightarrow E_{KM0}(KM1)$$

$$\text{ECPH: } \{E_{KM0}(KM1), KM1\} \longrightarrow E_{KM1}(KM1)$$

Using the intermediate quantity $E_{KM1}(KM1)$, each terminal master key (KMT) is then enciphered under KM1 as follows:

$$\text{EMK: } \{KMT\} \longrightarrow E_{KM0}(KMT)$$

$$\text{RFMK: } \{E_{KM1}(KM1), E_{KM0}(KMT)\} \longrightarrow E_{KM1}(KMT)$$

Once the list of terminal master keys is enciphered, all intermediate values used in the computation are erased from the host's main storage.

An Example of Communications Encryption

A communication session between a terminal and an application program in a host is initiated as follows. A 64-bit pseudo-random number (RN) is generated at the host system and is defined to be the session key (KS) enciphered under the host's master key (KM0), that is, $RN = E_{KM0}(KS)$. Since the host's master key (KM0) is unavailable at the terminal, $E_{KM0}(KS)$ must be transformed into a form usable at the terminal, that is, into the form $E_{KMT}(KS)$.

[2] Another approach is to use a new cryptographic operation (see Encipherment of Keys Under the Master Key's Variants, Chapter 6).

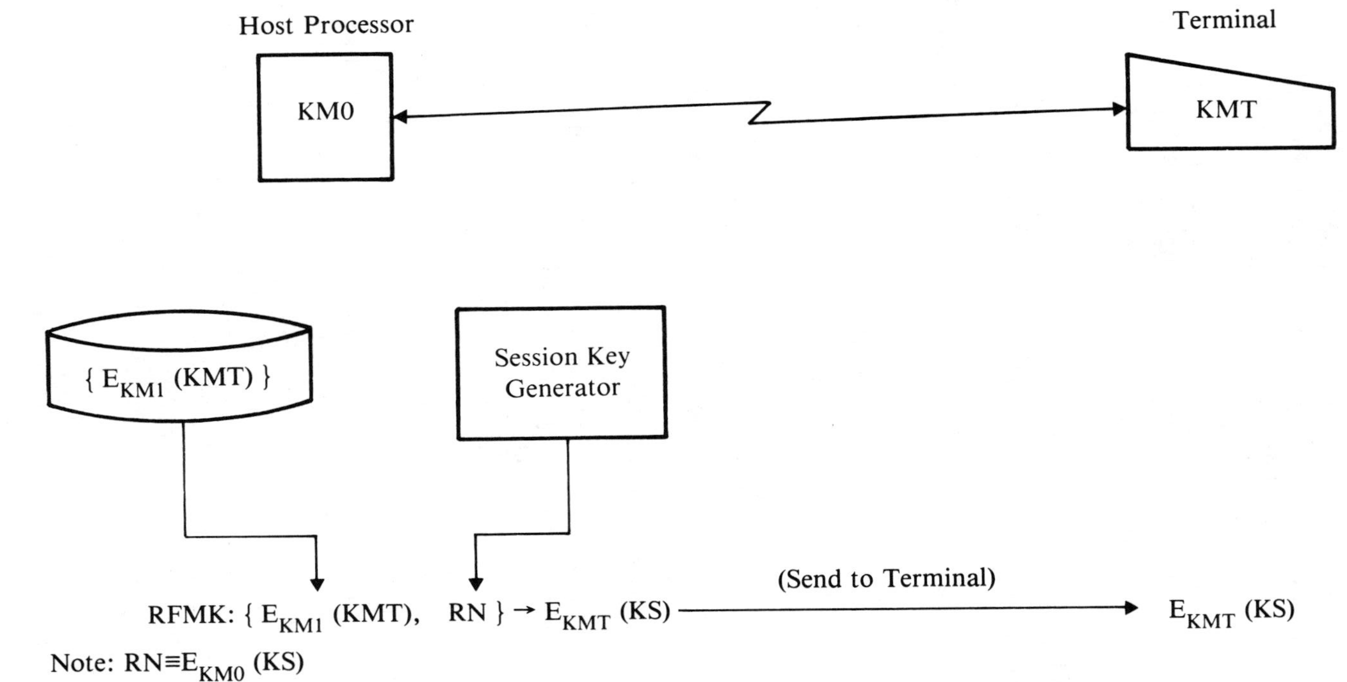

Note: $RN \equiv E_{KM0}$ (KS)

Figure 5-1. Initiation of a Dynamically Generated Session Key (KS) Between a Terminal and Host Application Program in a Single Domain

This is accomplished through the use of the RFMK operation, as described above. $E_{KMT}(KS)$ is then transmitted to the terminal, where KS is recovered and transferred to the working key storage in the terminal's cryptographic facility. $E_{KM0}(KS)$ is given to the application program in the host. At this point, both the terminal and the application program have identical session keys (KS) that can be used for ciphering data (Figure 5-1).

Requirements

In the approach described here, five basic cryptographic operations are needed at the host system: *set master key* (SMK), *encipher under master key* (EMK), *encipher data* (ECPH), *decipher data* (DCPH), and *reencipher from master key* (RFMK). The approach also requires two master keys: KM0 and KM1.

SINGLE-DOMAIN COMMUNICATION SECURITY AND FILE SECURITY USING DYNAMICALLY GENERATED PRIMARY KEYS

A cryptographic system with two master keys permits single-domain communication security using dynamically generated primary keys. If stored data must be protected as well, then a third master key is needed.

Problems Associated with Storing Enciphered Data

The previous section described a protocol for single-domain communication security using dynamic session keys. It therefore seems natural to ask if the same scheme could be adapted for use in file security to protect stored data.

Suppose one wishes to protect stored data in the same way that communicated data are protected, that is, one wishes to use a session key in the form $E_{KM0}(KS)$ as an input parameter to the *encipher data* and *decipher data* operations for the purpose of creating and recovering data files, respectively. However, for this approach to be workable (i.e., to be able to recover data with a DCPH operation), either $E_{KM0}(KS)$ must be saved for later use or else it must be possible to recreate it when it is needed (Figure 5-2).

If $E_{KM0}(KS)$ is stored within the system, especially for long periods, it must be protected by a suitable method of controlled access, since knowledge of $E_{KM0}(KS)$ would allow data to be recovered directly with a *decipher data* operation. This difficulty could be avoided, of course, by using the quantity $E_{KM0}(KS)$ as a personal key and therefore not storing it within the system. However, the advantage of a personal key must be weighed against that of cryptographic transparency (where the user is relieved of any responsibility for handling keys). When stored information is shared among many users, the use of personal keys may be impractical. For example, if there are 10 different users and 10 different data files, such that the first user must have access to all but the first data file, the second user must have access to all but the second file, and so forth, then each file must be enciphered under a different key and each user must be given nine different personal keys to manage.

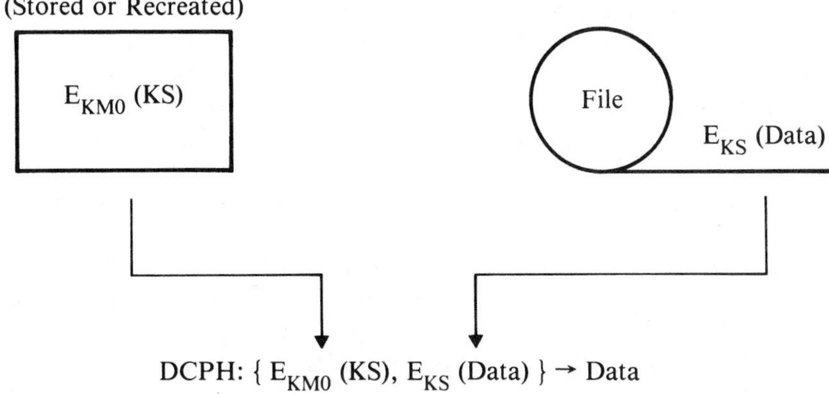

Figure 5-2. Recovery of Data Using the DCPH Operation

Whether $E_{KM0}(KS)$ is stored in the system or used as a personal key, key management must permit the host master key (KM0) to be changed periodically. Either there must be a method for recovering KS in clear form so that it can be reenciphered under the new host master key, or else there must be a method for translating KS directly from encipherment under the old master key to encipherment under the new master key. In either case, the procedure would be cumbersome because of the many different session keys.

Still another disadvantage of basing a file recovery strategy on the stored quantity $E_{KM0}(KS)$ is that recovery at a different host system would not be possible unless KM0 was shared with that other host system. *But no good key management scheme would require a host master key to be shared with another host system.*

Because of these disadvantages, $E_{KM0}(KS)$ should not be the quantity saved for later use in file recovery operations. The disadvantages are overcome, however, if KS is stored enciphered under a *secondary file key* (KNF), rather than under KM0.

In the described approach, quantity $E_{KNF}(KS)$ is saved in a place that will be accessible during later file recovery operations, such as in the file header or in a separate file. At the host system, KNF is stored under the encipherment of some suitable key-encrypting key. (The choice of this key-encrypting key is discussed below.) Recovery of data is accomplished by reading $E_{KNF}(KS)$ from its saved location, obtaining access to the value of KNF stored at the host system, and regenerating the quantity $E_{KM0}(KS)$ using an appropriate translation operation.

The question now arises as to what key KNF can safely be enciphered under during its period of storage. Suppose KNF is stored enciphered under KM0. If it were, then a *decipher data* operation could be used to obtain a clear session key:

$$\text{DCPH: } \{E_{KM0}(KNF), E_{KNF}(KS)\} \longrightarrow KS$$

Again, this would violate the requirement that it must not be possible to recover keys in the clear outside the cryptographic facility.

If, on the other hand, KNF is stored enciphered under KM1, then the cryptographic operation that permits $E_{KM0}(KS)$ to be recovered from $E_{KM1}(KNF)$ and $E_{KNF}(KS)$ would also permit $E_{KM0}(KS)$ to be recovered from $E_{KM1}(KMT)$ and $E_{KMT}(KS)$. The said cryptographic operation would permit an attack against ciphered data by an opponent who could gain access to the system.

The attack is as follows. During a communication session between a user at a terminal and an application program in a host, the opponent obtains the quantities $E_{KMT}(KS)$ and $E_{KS}(Data)$ via a wiretap. By gaining access to the host system, the opponent first recovers $E_{KM0}(KS)$ by entering the quantities $E_{KM1}(KMT)$ and $E_{KMT}(KS)$ as inputs to the said cryptographic operation. Data is then recovered by entering the quantities $E_{KM0}(KS)$ and $E_{KS}(Data)$ as inputs to a DCPH operation.

Incorporation of file security within a cryptographic system, as described here, weakens the protection afforded by communication security. This is because the cryptographic operation that permits $E_{KM0}(KS)$ to be recovered from $E_{KNF}(KS)$ also permits $E_{KM0}(KS)$ to be recovered from $E_{KMT}(KS)$. Such a condition should be avoided; COMSEC and FILESEC applications should be cryptographically separated (see Partitioning of Cipher Keys, Chapter 4).

Three Master Keys

Enciphering the terminal master keys and secondary file keys under different host master keys permits the file security system to be implemented without affecting the integrity of the communication security system. The terminal master keys (which are secondary communication keys) are stored enciphered under a second variant of the host master key (KM1), and the secondary file keys are stored enciphered under a second variant of the host master key (KM2). KM2 is derived from KM0 in a manner similar to that used for deriving KM1: by inverting (different) selected bits in KM0. (A precise specification for KM2 is not important to the present discussion).

In file security, the primary key used for ciphering data is called a *file key* (KF). Let KF1, KF2, . . . , KFn denote the dynamically generated primary file keys used for ciphering stored data. It is assumed that KF is operational for the life of the enciphered file, that is, until the file is no longer maintained enciphered under KF.

The cryptographic operation that allows a file key (KF) to be transformed from encipherment under a secondary file key (KNF) to encipherment under the host master key (KM0), defined as the *reencipher to master key* (RTMK) operation, is given by

$$\text{RTMK: } \{E_{KM2}(KNF), E_{KNF}(KF)\} \longrightarrow E_{KM0}(KF)$$

Even though the relationship between the host master key and its first and second variants is publicly known, this information is not enough to permit the algorithm to be broken. For instance, $E_{KM0}(KNF)$ and $E_{KM1}(KNF)$ cannot be deduced from $E_{KM2}(KNF)$ for a strong cryptographic algorithm (see Protection of Host Keys, Chapter 4).

The attack described above for recovering session keys is thwarted when KNF is stored enciphered under KM2. That is, it is not possible to enter $E_{KM2}(KNF)$ and $E_{KNF}(KF)$ as inputs to a *decipher data* operation and recover a clear file key (KF):

$$\text{DCPH: } \{E_{KM2}(KNF), E_{KNF}(KF)\} \longrightarrow D_K(E_{KNF}(KF)) \neq KF$$

because

$$K = D_{KM0}(E_{KM2}(KNF)) \neq KNF$$

In like manner, it is not possible to enter $E_{KM1}(KMT)$ and $E_{KMT}(KS)$ as inputs to a *reencipher to master key* operation and recover the quantity $E_{KM0}(KS)$:

$$\text{RTMK: } \{E_{KM1}(KMT), E_{KMT}(KS)\} \longrightarrow E_{KM0}(D_K(E_{KMT}(KS))) \neq E_{KM0}(KS)$$

because

$$K = D_{KM2}(E_{KM1}(KMT)) \neq KMT$$

Host Key Protection

Having justified the need for three master keys, the intended use of each of these keys is now summarized. KM0 is used to protect both file keys and session keys. Thus primary keys are maintained at the host system in the form

$$E_{KM0}(KS1), E_{KM0}(KS2), \ldots, E_{KM0}(KSn)$$

$$E_{KM0}(KF1), E_{KM0}(KF2), \ldots, E_{KM0}(KFn)$$

KM1 is used to protect terminal master keys. Terminal master keys are maintained at the host system in the form

$$E_{KM1}(KMT1), E_{KM1}(KMT2), \ldots, E_{KM1}(KMTn)$$

KM2 is used to protect secondary file keys. Secondary file keys are maintained at the host system in the form

$$E_{KM2}(KNF1), E_{KM2}(KNF2), \ldots, E_{KM2}(KNFn)$$

Encipherment under KM1 and KM2

Encipherment of the secondary file keys under KM1 is performed under secure conditions by a combination of the cryptographic operations already described (see Encipherment Under KM1). The host master key (KM0) is first entered into the main storage of the host system, where the variant KM2 is derived by inverting appropriate bits in KM0. (It is assumed that KM0 has already been inserted into the master key storage of the host's cryptographic facility using an SMK operation.) The intermediate quantity $E_{KM1}(KM2)$ is then derived as follows:

$$\text{EMK: } \{KM1\} \longrightarrow E_{KM0}(KM1)$$

$$\text{ECPH: } \{E_{KM0}(KM1), KM2\} \longrightarrow E_{KM1}(KM2)$$

Through the use of the intermediate quantity $E_{KM1}(KM2)$, each secondary file key (KNF) is then enciphered under KM2 as follows:

$$\text{EMK: } \{KNF\} \rightarrow E_{KM0}(KNF)$$

$$\downarrow$$

$$\text{RFMK: } \{E_{KM1}(KM2), E_{KM0}(KNF)\} \rightarrow E_{KM2}(KNF)$$

Once the list of secondary file keys has been enciphered, all intermediate values used in the computation are erased from the host's main memory.

File Key Generation

To satisfy the condition that no clear key occurs outside the cryptographic facility, and yet avoid a requirement to generate KF directly within the cryptographic facility, an indirect method of generating file keys is adopted. A 64-bit pseudo-random number (RN) is generated and defined to be the file key enciphered under the secondary file key associated with the named file:

$$RN = E_{KNF}(KF)$$

The encrypted file keys required by the cryptographic system are therefore produced as a sequence of pseudo-random numbers

$$RN1, RN2, \ldots, RNn$$

where the ith pseudo-random number (RNi) corresponds to the ith encrypted file key (i.e., $RNi = E_{KNF}(KFi)$).

The rationale for defining RN as the file key (KF) enciphered under the secondary file key (KNF), rather than as the file key enciphered under the host master key (KM0), is as follows. If RN were to be defined as the quantity $E_{KM0}(KF)$, then the RFMK operation would have to be used at file creation to derive $E_{KNF}(KF)$ from $E_{KM0}(KF)$. Recall that $E_{KNF}(KF)$ is saved in a location that will be accessible during later file recovery operations, whereas $E_{KM0}(KF)$ is used with an ECPH operation to encipher the file. But at file recovery, the RTMK operation would have to be used to derive $E_{KM0}(KF)$ from $E_{KNF}(KF)$. Thus both the RFMK and RTMK operations would be needed for file security. This in turn would require that KNF be stored enciphered under both KM1 and KM2. An undesirable reversibility would then exist between RFMK and RTMK.

In contrast, if RN is defined as the quantity $E_{KNF}(KF)$, then the RTMK operation can be used to derive $E_{KM0}(KF)$, both when the file is created and when the file is recovered, and KNF need only be stored enciphered under KM2.

An Example of File Encryption

The following example describes how a host application program can encipher a file to be stored on a secondary storage medium, and how this file can later be recovered. Recovery is at the same host where the file was originally enciphered. (Enciphering a file at one host and deciphering it at another host is discussed in Multiple-Domain Encryption.) A 64-bit pseudo-random number (RN) is generated at the host system and defined to be the file key (KF) enciphered under the secondary file key (KNF) of the named file (i.e., RN = $E_{KNF}(KF)$). In this example, RN is written in the file header. The RTMK operation is used by the key manager to transform RN into the quantity $E_{KM0}(KF)$. The quantity $E_{KM0}(KF)$ is then returned by the key manager to the host application program, whereupon the program uses it as an input parameter to the CIPHER (FNC = ENCPHR) macro instruction for the purpose of enciphering the file. During recovery, the quantity RN is read from the file header. The RTMK operation is used by the key manager to transform RN into the quantity $E_{KM0}(KF)$. Again, the quantity $E_{KM0}(KF)$ is returned by the key manager to the application program, whereupon the program uses it as an input parameter to the CIPHER (FNC = DECPHR) macro instruction for the purpose of deciphering the file. Figure 5-3 illustrates the procedures for creating and recovering a file.

Because of the level of indirection provided by the secondary file key (KNF), the quantity $E_{KNF}(KF)$ does not depend on the host master key. Therefore, changing the host master key will not require that $E_{KNF}(KF)$ be reenciphered, as would be the case if $E_{KM0}(KF)$ were written in the file header. The only change that must be made when a new host master key is installed is that the secondary keys stored at the host system are reenciphered under the new variants of the master key, KM1′ and KM2′ (where ′ indicates new). Moreover, since the secondary file key (KNF) can be disclosed to other host systems, recovery is also possible at remote locations.

If cryptographic transparency is desired, the quantity $E_{KNF}(KF)$ can be written in the header of the data file. Access to the data, in this case, can be controlled by controlling the use of the RETKEY macro and thereby controlling access to the quantity $E_{KM2}(KNF)$, which is stored at the host system. In an alternate approach, $E_{KNF}(KF)$ can be treated as a personal key and stored outside the system. In this case, access to the data requires also that the secret quantity $E_{KNF}(KF)$ be provided to the system at the time data are to be deciphered.

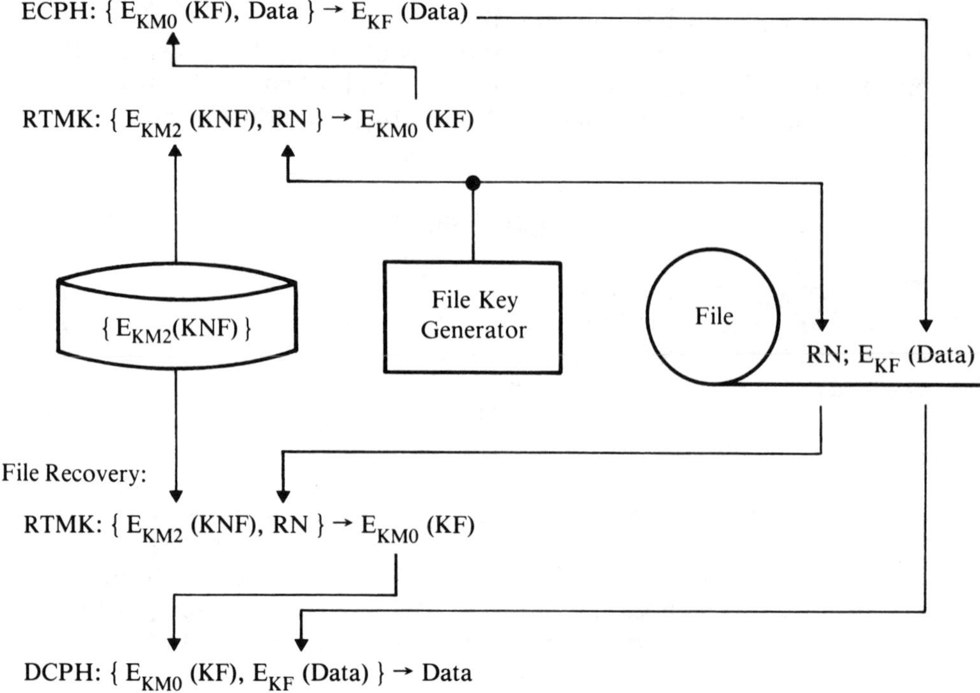

Figure 5-3. Single-Domain File Security Using a Dynamically Generated File Key (KF)

Requirements

In the approach described here, six basic cryptographic operations are needed at the host system: *set master key* (SMK), *encipher under master key* (EMK), *encipher data* (ECPH), *decipher data* (DCPH), *reencipher from master key* (RFMK), and *reencipher to master key* (RTMK). The approach also requires three master keys: KM0, KM1, and KM2.

MULTIPLE-DOMAIN ENCRYPTION

The set of basic cryptographic operations defined in the previous section permits communication security and file security to be achieved within a single-domain network, that is, in a communications network consisting of a single host node and one or more terminal nodes. In this section, it is shown that this same set of cryptographic operations is sufficient to achieve communication security and file security within a multidomain network, that is, in a communications network with many host nodes.

A Protocol For Communication Security

Let i and j denote host nodes whose master keys are KM0i and KM0j, respectively. To permit establishment of a common KS between domains i and j,[3] the two host systems must first share a common key. However, *the common key shared by each pair of host systems should not be the host master key of either system.* Instead, the host systems should share a special key that is used only for sending session keys from one domain to the other. The cryptographic key used for this purpose is called a secondary communication key (KNC).

In the protocol discussed, the following secondary communication keys are defined:

KNCii Known only by host node i; permits a session key generated at host node i to be established between two nodes within domain i. KNCjj is similarly defined at host node j.

KNCij Shared by host nodes i and j; permits a session key generated at host node i to be transmitted to and recovered at host node j. A similar key KNCji is available at host nodes j and i to permit a session key to be transmitted in the reverse direction.

Generally speaking, there should be only one KNCij key and one KNCji key, but possibly many KNCii and KNCjj keys. Within the domain of host node i, the secondary communication keys are used as a means for establishing a common KS between the host and one of its (n) terminals, or between two of its (n) terminals. Hence the set {KNCii} actually represents the set {KMTi1, KMTi2, . . . , KMTin}, where i refers to domain i and the numbers 1 through n denote the specific terminal.

At host node i, KNCij is stored enciphered under KM1i, thus allowing KS to be transmitted to host node j. At host node j, KNCij is stored enciphered under KM2j, thus allowing KS to be reenciphered under KM0j. A symmetrical specification also exists for KNCji. At host node j, KNCji is stored enciphered under KM1j, thus allowing KS to be transmitted to host node i. At host node i, KNCji is stored enciphered under KM2i, thus allowing KS to be reenciphered under KM0i. The form in which KNCij and KNCji are stored at host nodes i and j is shown in Figure 5-4.

The method for establishing a common session key (KS) between two domains, say domain i and domain j, is shown in Figure 5-5.

At host node i, a pseudo-random number (RN) is generated and defined as

$$RN = E_{KM0i}(KS)$$

RN can be used directly in the ECPH and DCPH operations for ciphering data or it can be used in an RFMK operation to transform KS from encipherment

[3]The collection of nodes consisting of host node i and all its logically connected terminal nodes is defined as domain i. A similar domain is defined for host node j.

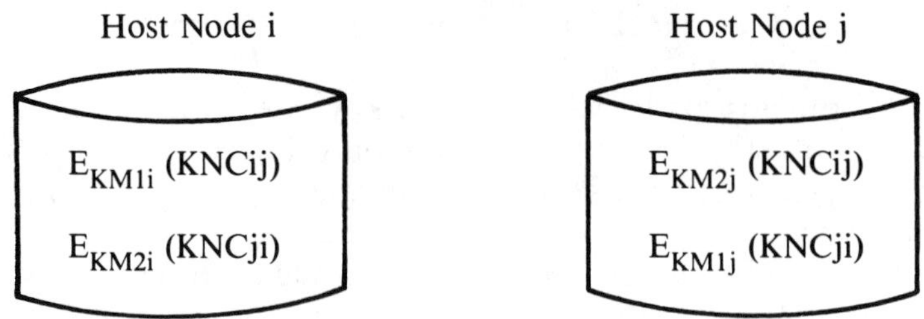

Figure 5-4. Storage of Secondary Communication Keys Shared by Domain i and Domain j

under KM0i to encipherment under a terminal master key (a key in the set {KMTi1, KMTi2, . . . , KMTin}). To send KS to domain j, the RFMK operation is used to transform KS from encipherment under KM0i to encipherment under the appropriate secondary communication key (KNCij):

$$\text{RFMK: } \{E_{KM1i}(\text{KNCij}), E_{KM0i}(\text{KS})\} \longrightarrow E_{KNCij}(\text{KS})$$

The quantity E_{KNCij}(KS) is then transmitted to host node j, where the RTMK operation is used to transform KS from encipherment under KNCij to encipherment under KM0j:

$$\text{RTMK: } \{E_{KM2j}(\text{KNCij}), E_{KNCij}(\text{KS})\} \longrightarrow E_{KM0j}(\text{KS})$$

The quantity E_{KM0j}(KS) can then be used directly in the ECPH and DCPH operations for ciphering data at host node j, or it can be used in an RFMK operation to transform KS from encipherment under KM0j to encipherment under a terminal master key (a key in the set {KMTj1, KMTj2, . . . , KMTjn}).

Because the RFMK and RTMK operations are designed to use, respectively, only the first and second variants of the host master key, a unidirectional process of transformation involving secondary keys (secondary communication keys in the present example) is achieved. A unidirectional transformation process is one that is irreversible at the sender's location, that is, recovery of the primary key (session key in the present example) can only be done at a predefined receiver.

In the example above (of host-to-host communication), unidirectionality from the first host to the second host is achieved because the secondary communication key (KNCij) is known to the first host only in the form E_{KM1i}(KNCij), and the output of the sender's RFMK operation, E_{KNCij}(KS), is usable only by the intended receiver's RTMK operation. In other words, the first host can produce E_{KNCij}(KS) from E_{KM0i}(KS) because E_{KM1i}(KNCij) is available, but it cannot retrieve E_{KM0i}(KS) from E_{KNCij}(KS) because E_{KM2i}(KNCij) is not available. Conversely, the second host can retrieve E_{KM0j}(KS) from E_{KNCij}(KS) because E_{KM2j}(KNCij) is available, but it cannot produce E_{KNCij}(KS) from E_{KM0j}(KS) because E_{KM1j}(KNCij) is not available.

Thus the unidirectionality property ensures that an opponent who recovers

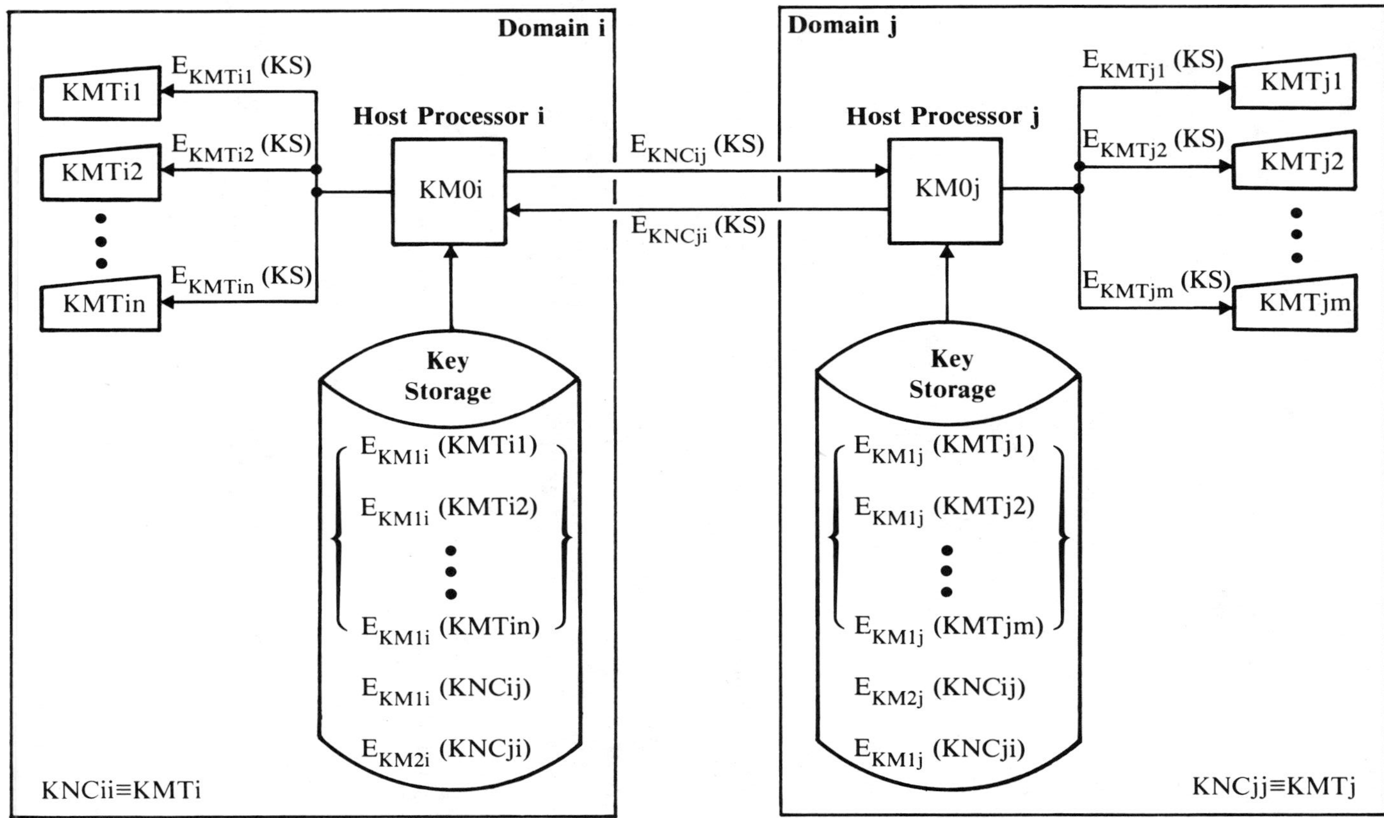

Figure 5-5. Secondary Communication Key Protocol Between Domain i and Domain j

the quantity $E_{KNCij}(KS)$ via a wiretap cannot make use of this quantity at host node i. At host node j, however, the same protocol that permits host node j to recover $E_{KM0j}(KS)$ from $E_{KNCij}(KS)$ can potentially be misused by an opponent. For this reason, the RTMK operation should be privileged, and its use controlled by the key manager.

In summary, then, when a secondary communication key is used to transmit a session key from one domain to another, recovery of that session key at the destination host must be controlled by means other than cryptography.

A Protocol For File Security

To permit establishment of a common KF between domains i and j, the host systems must first share a common key. The cryptographic key used for this purpose is called a secondary file key (KNF).

In the protocol discussed, the following secondary file keys are defined:

KNFii Known only to host node i; permits a file key generated at host node i to be recovered at host node i. KNFjj is similarly defined at host node j.

KNFij Shared by host nodes i and j; permits a file key generated at host node i to be safely stored and later recovered at host node j. A similar key KNFji is available at host nodes j and i to permit a file key to be transmitted in the reverse direction.

At host node i, KNFij is stored enciphered under KM1i, thus allowing KF to be transmitted to host node j. At host node j, KNFij is stored enciphered under KM2j, thus allowing KF to be reenciphered under KM0j. Conversely, at host node j, KNFji is stored enciphered under KM1j, thus allowing KF to be transmitted to host node i. And at host node i, KNFji is stored enciphered under KM2i, thus allowing KF to be reenciphered under KM0i. Note the similarity between KNCij and KNFij, and between KNCji and KNFji. The form in which KNFij and KNFji are stored at host nodes i and j is shown in Figure 5-6.

Transporting a New File

The method for generating a file key (KF) at one domain (say domain i) which can be recovered at another domain (say domain j) is shown in Figure 5-7.

At host node i, a pseudo-random number (RN) is generated and defined as

$$RN = E_{KM0i}(KF)$$

RN can be used directly in the ECPH operation to encipher the file, as follows:

$$\text{ECPH: } \{RN, \text{Data}\} \longrightarrow E_{KF}(\text{Data})$$

To send KF to domain j, the RFMK operation is first used to transform KF

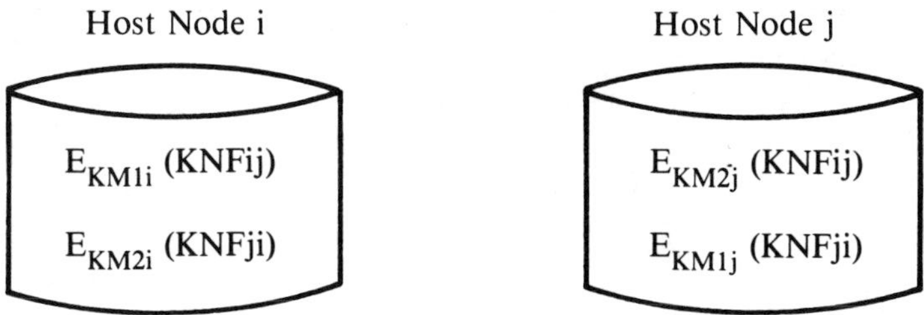

Figure 5-6. Storage of Secondary File Keys Shared by Domain i and Domain j

from encipherment under KM0i to encipherment under the secondary file key (KNFij):

$$\text{RFMK: } \{E_{KM1i}(\text{KNFij}), E_{KM0i}(\text{KF})\} \longrightarrow E_{KNFij}(\text{KF})$$

The quantity $E_{KNFij}(\text{KF})$ is, for this example, recorded in the file header. The enciphered file is then sent to host node j. At host node j, the RTMK operation is used to transform KF from encipherment under KNFij to encipherment under KM0j:

$$\text{RTMK: } \{E_{KM2j}(\text{KNFij}), E_{KNFij}(\text{KF})\} \longrightarrow E_{KM0j}(\text{KF})$$

The quantity $E_{KM0j}(\text{KF})$ can then be used directly in the DCPH operation to recover data:

$$\text{DCPH: } \{E_{KM0j}(\text{KF}), E_{KF}(\text{Data})\} \longrightarrow \text{Data}$$

Transporting an Existing File

The protocol described here has the advantage that a file created and intended to be recovered at host node i can easily be sent to and recovered at host node j *without the data having to be deciphered and reenciphered under a new KF.* This is accomplished by using an RTMK operation to recover $E_{KM0i}(\text{KF})$ from $E_{KNFii}(\text{KF})$, and then using an RFMK operation to produce $E_{KNFij}(\text{KF})$ from $E_{KM0i}(\text{KF})$:

$$\text{RTMK: } \{E_{KM2i}(\text{KNFii}), E_{KNFii}(\text{KF})\} \longrightarrow E_{KM0i}(\text{KF})$$

$$\text{RFMK: } \{E_{KM1i}(\text{KNFij}), E_{KM0i}(\text{KF})\} \longrightarrow E_{KNFij}(\text{KF})$$

Hence the file can be sent to host node j by merely replacing $E_{KNFii}(\text{KF})$ with $E_{KNFij}(\text{KF})$ in the file header. (Note that the procedure may require the file to be copied to another volume.)

Again, because of the property of unidirectionality (see A Protocol for

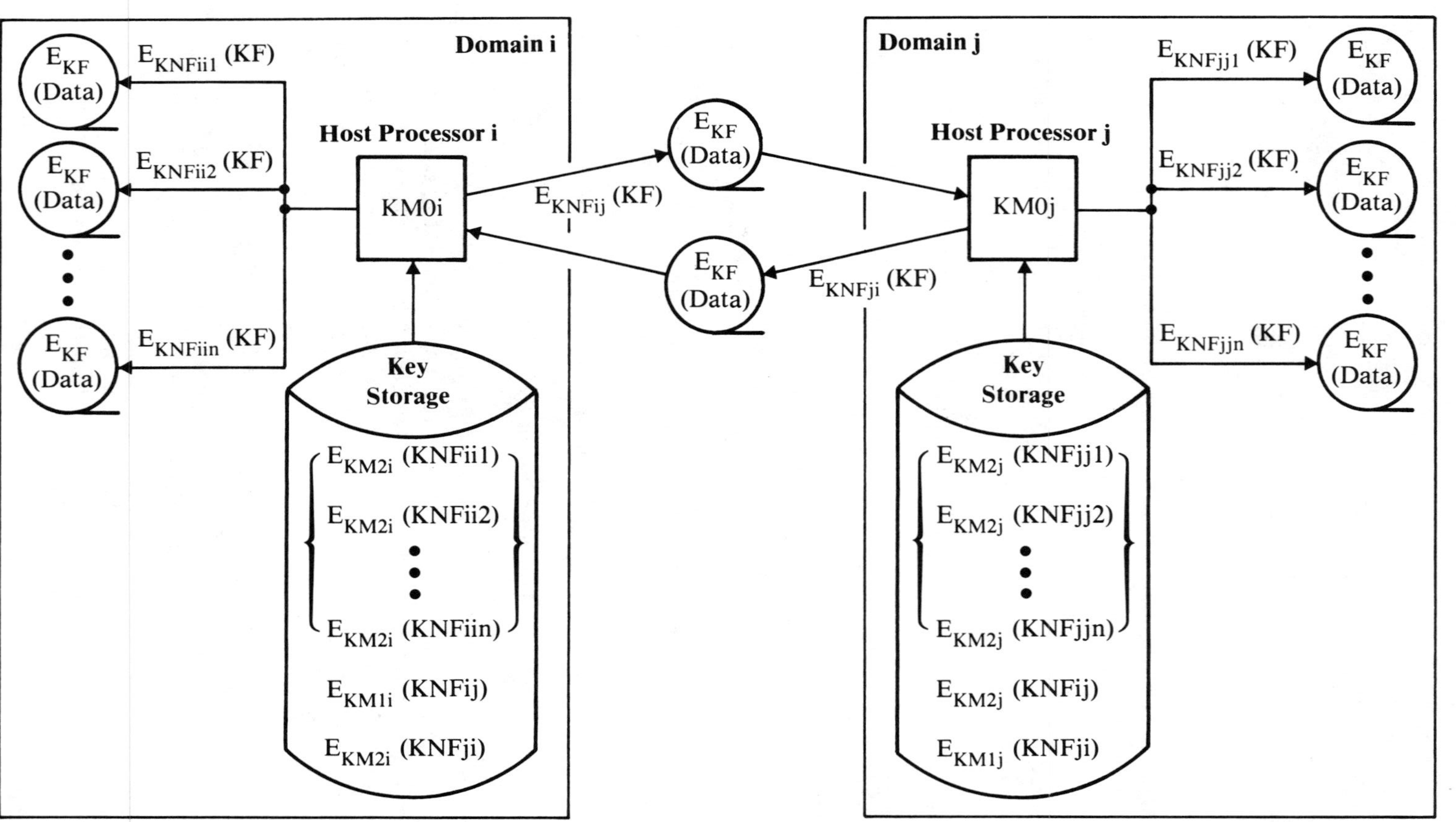

Figure 5-7. Secondary File Key Protocol Between Domain i and Domain j

Communication Security), an opponent who obtains the quantity $E_{KNFij}(KF)$ from the file header can make no use of it at host node i. However, at host node j the RTMK operation could be used to recover $E_{KM0\,j}(KF)$ from $E_{KNFij}(KF)$, provided that access to the system is obtained. Hence the RTMK operation should be privileged, and its use controlled by the key manager.

ADDITIONAL CONSIDERATIONS

It is assumed that only installation-specified cryptographic keys are stored enciphered under KM1 or KM2, and that these keys are secret and known only to authorized installation personnel.

If an opponent could encipher under the host master key variants (KM1 and KM2), then it might be possible to replace existing installation-specified keys with those selected by the opponent. For example, to attack a terminal an opponent could do the following: encipher an alien terminal master key (KMT′) under KM1, replace KMT with KMT′ at the terminal, and replace $E_{KM1}(KMT)$ with $E_{KM1}(KMT')$ in the host's key table. The opponent could then recover session keys sent to the terminal in the form $E_{KMT'}(KS)$, and thus recover data sent to or from the terminal in the form $E_{KS}(Data)$.

Variations of the above attack include the following: requesting or causing installation personnel to encipher, under KM1 or KM2, a value which the opponent knows, or compromising the security of the system by obtaining $E_{KM1}(KMT)$ from the host's key table, and KMT from the terminal.

If an opponent can encipher a known value X under KM1, or can cause installation personnel to encipher a known value X under KM1, or can discover the value of an unknown quantity enciphered under KM1, then an attack can recover primary keys in clear form. Let X, $E_{KM1}(X)$, and $E_{KM0}(K)$ be the values known to an opponent, where K is the unknown primary key to be recovered. The operations involved in the attack are shown below.[4]

$$\text{RFMK: } \{E_{KM1}(X), E_{KM0}(K)\} \longrightarrow E_X(K)$$

$$\text{EMK: } \{X\} \longrightarrow E_{KM0}(X)$$

$$\text{DCPH: } \{E_{KM0}(X), E_X(K)\} \longrightarrow K$$

Elements in the set $\{E_{KMx}(KMy) : x, y = 0, 1, 2; x = y \neq 2\}$ must be kept secret from any potential opponent, since they could be used as parameters with the available cryptographic operations to encipher and/or decipher under one or more of the keys: KM0, KM1, and KM2, as indicated in Table 5-2.

The quantities $E_{KM0}(KM0)$, $E_{KM0}(KM1)$, and $E_{KM0}(KM2)$ could be used with an ECPH operation to encipher under KM0, KM1, and KM2, respectively,

[4] In a sense, the attack is academic because knowledge of $E_{KM0}(K)$ (where K = KS) would allow data enciphered under K to be recovered with the ECPH operation.

Function	Operation	Key Used For Ciphering KM0	KM1	KM2
Encipher	ECPH	$E_{KM0}(KM0)$	$E_{KM0}(KM1)$	$E_{KM0}(KM2)$
Decipher	DCPH	$E_{KM0}(KM0)$	$E_{KM0}(KM1)$	$E_{KM0}(KM2)$
Encipher	RFMK	$E_{KM1}(KM0)$	$E_{KM1}(KM1)$	$E_{KM1}(KM2)$
Decipher	RTMK	——	$E_{KM2}(KM1)$	$E_{KM2}(KM2)$

Table 5-2. Special Quantities that Permit Encipherment and Decipherment Under KM0, KM1, and KM2

or they could be used with a DCPH operation to decipher under KM0, KM1, and KM2, respectively. For example, an arbitrary quantity X could be enciphered and deciphered under KM1 as follows:

$$\text{ECPH: } \{E_{KM0}(KM1), X\} \longrightarrow E_{KM1}(X)$$

$$\text{DCPH: } \{E_{KM0}(KM1), X\} \longrightarrow D_{KM1}(X)$$

The quantities $E_{KM1}(KM0)$, $E_{KM1}(KM1)$, and $E_{KM1}(KM2)$ could be used with an RFMK operation to encipher quantity X under KM0, KM1, and KM2, respectively:

$$\text{EMK: } \{X\} \longrightarrow E_{KM0}(X)$$

$$\text{RFMK: } \{E_{KM1}(KM1), E_{KM0}(X)\} \longrightarrow E_{KM1}(X)$$

Finally, the quantities $E_{KM2}(KM1)$ and $E_{KM2}(KM2)$ could be used with an RTMK operation to decipher quantity X under KM1 and KM2, respectively, provided that decipherment under KM0 is also available:

$$\text{RTMK: } \{E_{KM2}(KM1), X\} \longrightarrow E_{KM0}(D_{KM1}(X))$$

$D_{KM1}(X)$ is recovered by deciphering $E_{KM0}(D_{KM1}(X))$ under KM0.

EXTENDED CRYPTOGRAPHIC OPERATIONS

Additional cryptographic operations can be defined to satisfy specific security requirements. In each case, the primitive operations of encipher and decipher act as building blocks to achieve the desired goal. Similarly, additional variants of the host master key can be defined to isolate further the desired functions served by a particular operation. In this manner, the property of irreversibility is built-in, thus preventing an opponent from manipulating an operation to reverse and defeat its intended purpose.

Although the opportunity for designing special purpose cryptographic operations is virtually infinite, in the interest of economy only one example will be presented here—a method using composite keys to effect session key distribution. Through the use of a unique variant of the host master key, the technique, applicable to COMSEC applications, reduces the system's dependency on the RTMK operation. A second example extends the idea of additional master key variants to produce test patterns used in cryptographic authentication (see Implementing AF and AR, Chapter 8).

Cryptographic Key Distribution Using Composite Keys[5]

The key management scheme discussed thus far (Chapters 4 and 5) distinguishes between primary keys and secondary keys. The latter are used to encipher other keys and are defined as part of the process of initializing the cryptographic system. Primary keys, on the other hand, are dynamically generated each time a communications session is established and are referred to as session keys (KS). Session keys remain in existence only for the duration of the communications session, which is usually a relatively short time.

A simple method of establishing a session key between any two nodes within a communications system is to generate the key at one node and send it to the other. The key can be protected by enciphering it under a special secondary key that is unique to only these two nodes and is installed in advance. A retrieve function (e.g., the RTMK operation) must be used at the receiving node to transform the session key into a form suitable for enciphering and deciphering data. Thus someone who intercepts both an enciphered key and data enciphered under that key, and who also can gain access at any later time to the session key retrieve function, can transform KS into the form suitable for deciphering data.

In network nodes which provide a programmed interface to their respective cryptographic facility, use of the retrieve function (RTMK) can be controlled through physical means (denying access to the system to all but authorized users), and through logical means (making the designated function privileged and/or implementing an access control mechanism).

A *fixed function* node—one that does not provide user access to the cryptographic facility—already provides a level of protection in this regard. However, even here cryptographic authentication (see Handshaking, Chapter 8) could be required if the retrieve function is exposed to a "midnight" attack.

However, a different and more secure approach for protecting the retrieve function is achieved if composite keys are supported by the key distribution process. This is accomplished by defining the session key to be a composite of random data supplied by each node; for example, by combining a first

[5]© 1978 IEEE. Reprinted from *NTC 78 Conference Record,* December 3–6, 1978, Birmingham, Alabama [2].

random number (RN1) generated at the initiating node with a second random number (RN2) generated at the receiving node:

$$KS = RN1 \oplus RN2,$$

where ⊕ represents modulo 2 addition.[6]

The composite key protocol is such that interception of the enciphered values of RN1 and RN2 will not allow KS to be recovered in a form suitable for deciphering data *at either node*. However, the protocol for composite keys is more complex.

A Composite Key Protocol

A composite key protocol can be used to distribute keys between any two nodes in a communications network. However, because it is the intent here only to illustrate the concept of composite keys, the discussion will be limited to an example of host-to-host communications (Figure 5-8). In this example, an application program resident in one host (host i) requests a communications session with an application program resident in another host (host j). The composite key protocol is described as follows. At host i, a *generate session key 1* (GSK1) operation is used to

1. Generate a random number, RN1 (Figure 5-8).

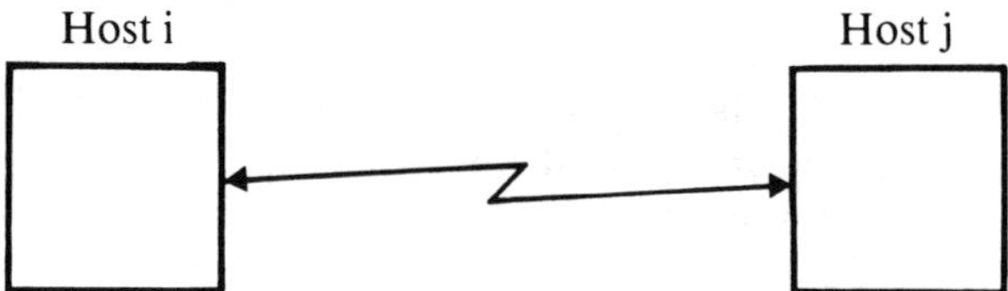

1. Generate RN1.
2. Store RN1 at host i and send RN1 to host j.

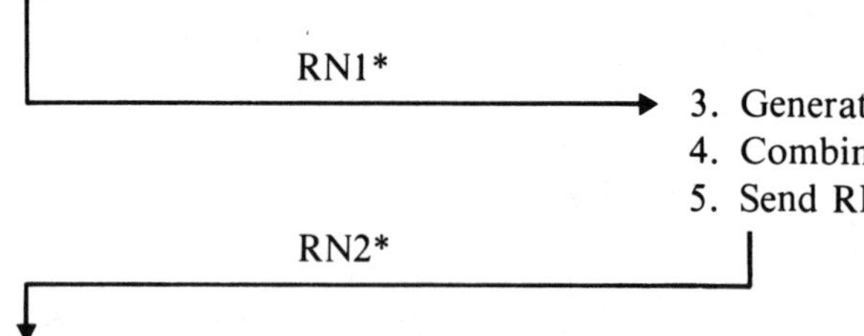

3. Generate RN2.
4. Combine RN2 with RN1 to produce KS
5. Send RN2 to Host i.

6. Retrieve RN1 and combine with RN2 to produce KS.
7. Erase stored copy of RN1.

*Protected by encryption during transmission

Figure 5-8. Overview: Composite Key Protocol

[6] Modulo 2 addition has been chosen for illustrative purposes only. Other suitable techniques for combining RN1 and RN2 exist.

2. Encipher RN1 under KNCij, which permits RN1 to be safely transmitted to host j (Figure 5-8).
3. Encipher RN1 under KM3i, which permits RN1 to be safely stored at host i (Figure 5-9).

A third variant of the host master key (KM3) is used to protect RN1 specifically so that no other parameter (except one enciphered under KM3) can be used in any meaningful way to produce KS. In effect, this isolates and protects the composite key functions from other functions in the cryptographic system. A fourth variant of the host master key (KM4) is defined for the purpose of generating pseudo-random numbers (see An Approach for Generating Keys with the Cryptographic Facility, Chapter 6).

At host j, a *generate session key 2* (GSK2) operation is used to

1. Generate a random number, RN2.
2. Encipher RN2 under KNCji, which permits RN2 to be safely transmitted to host i.
3. Merge RN2 with the value of RN1 received from host i.

Generate Session Key 1 (GSK1):

$$\text{GSK1: } \{ E_{KM1i}(KNCij) \} \rightarrow E_{KNCij}(RN1), E_{KM3i}(RN1)$$

where i designates the originating host of RN1.

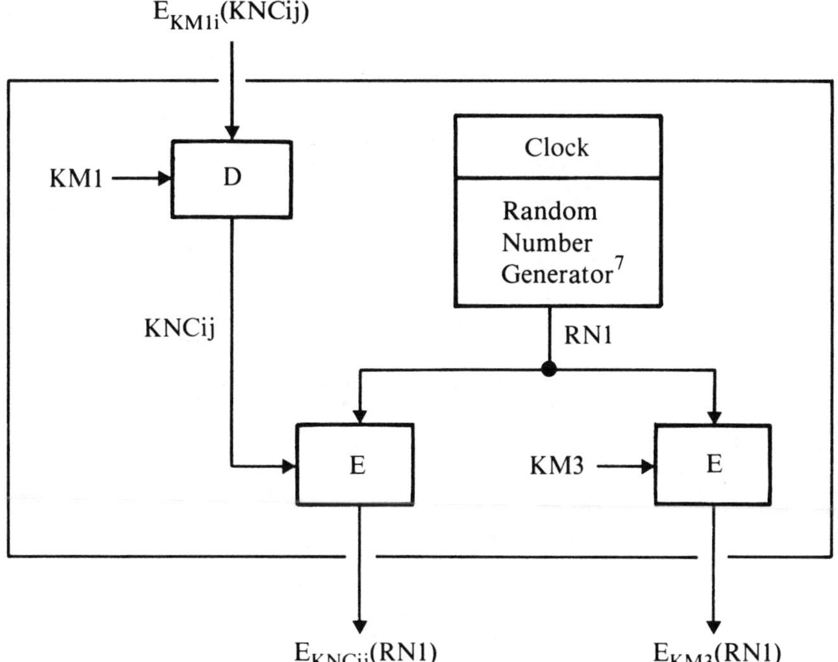

Figure 5-9. Generate Session Key 1

4. Encipher this merged value (KS) under KM0j, which is then in a form usable by an application program at host j for ciphering data.

(See Figure 5-10 and steps 3, 4, and 5 in Figure 5-8). The KS assigned to a particular session cannot be recreated even if someone obtains $E_{KNCij}(RN1)$ and executes GSK2. At each execution of GSK2 a nonresettable clock is read and is used as part of the random number generation process to create RN2.[7] Since KS is a function of RN2, and RN2 changes with each execution of GSK2, the ability to recreate KS is denied.

At host i, a *merge key* (MGK) operation is used to

1. Merge the saved copy of RN1 with the value of RN2 received from host j.
2. Encipher this merged value (KS) under KM0i, which is then in a form usable by an application program at host i for ciphering data.

Generate Session Key 2 (GSK2):

$$GSK2: \{ E_{KM2j}(KNCij), E_{KNCij}(RN1), E_{KM1j}(KNCji) \} \rightarrow E_{KM0j}(KS), E_{KNCji}(RN2)$$

where i designates the originating host of RN1 and j, the originating host of RN2.

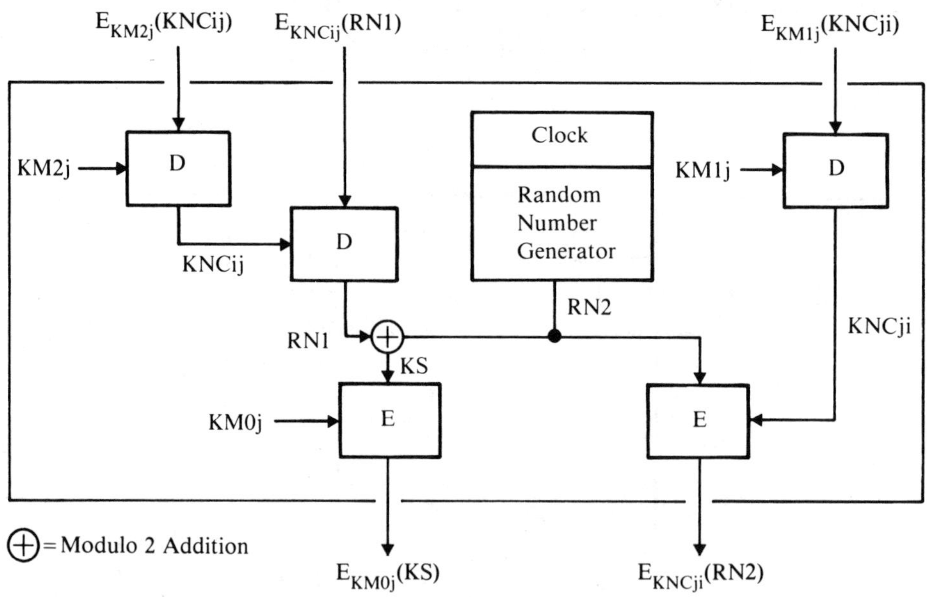

Figure 5-10. Generate Session Key 2

[7] An alternate approach would be to use a nonresettable counter as input to the random number generator and increment it at each GSK2 execution.

Merge Key (MGK):

MGK: { E_{KM2i}(KNCji), E_{KNCji}(RN2), E_{KM3i}(RN1) } → E_{KM0i}(KS)

where i designates the originating host of RN1 and j, the originating host of RN2.

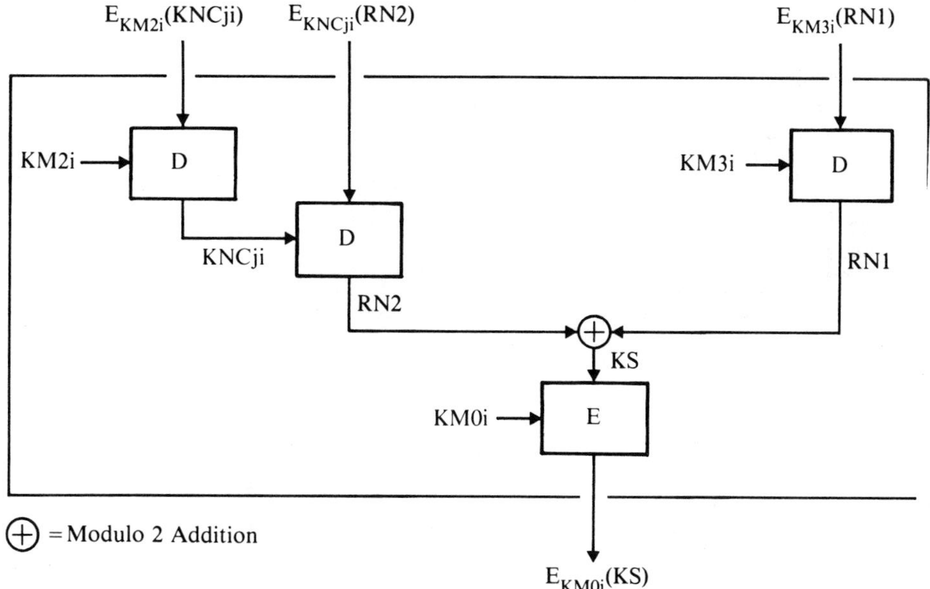

Figure 5-11. Merge Key

(See Figure 5-11 and steps 6 and 7 in Figure 5-8.)

Once the MGK operation is completed, E_{KM0i}(KS) is assigned to the application program, E_{KM3i}(RN1) is erased from host i's main storage, and E_{KM0i}(KS) is returned to the application program. For someone to gain any advantage from the MGK operation, the value E_{KM3i}(RN1) would have to be obtained during its brief period of storage at host i.

Although the present example discusses session initiation between two application programs, it can be coupled with the procedure specified for session key distribution in a single domain network (see Single-Domain Communication Security Using Dynamically Generated Primary Keys) so that a composite key (KS) produced at a host could then be sent to one of its terminals. In this case, E_{KM0i}(KS) is provided as input to an RFMK operation, and KS is transformed from encipherment under the host master key to encipherment under the terminal's master key (KMT):

$$\text{RFMK: } \{E_{KM1i}(\text{KMT}), E_{KM0i}(\text{KS})\} \longrightarrow E_{KMT}(\text{KS})$$

The quantity E_{KMT}(KS) is then sent to the terminal where KS is recovered and used for ciphering data. While this example illustrates a mixture of

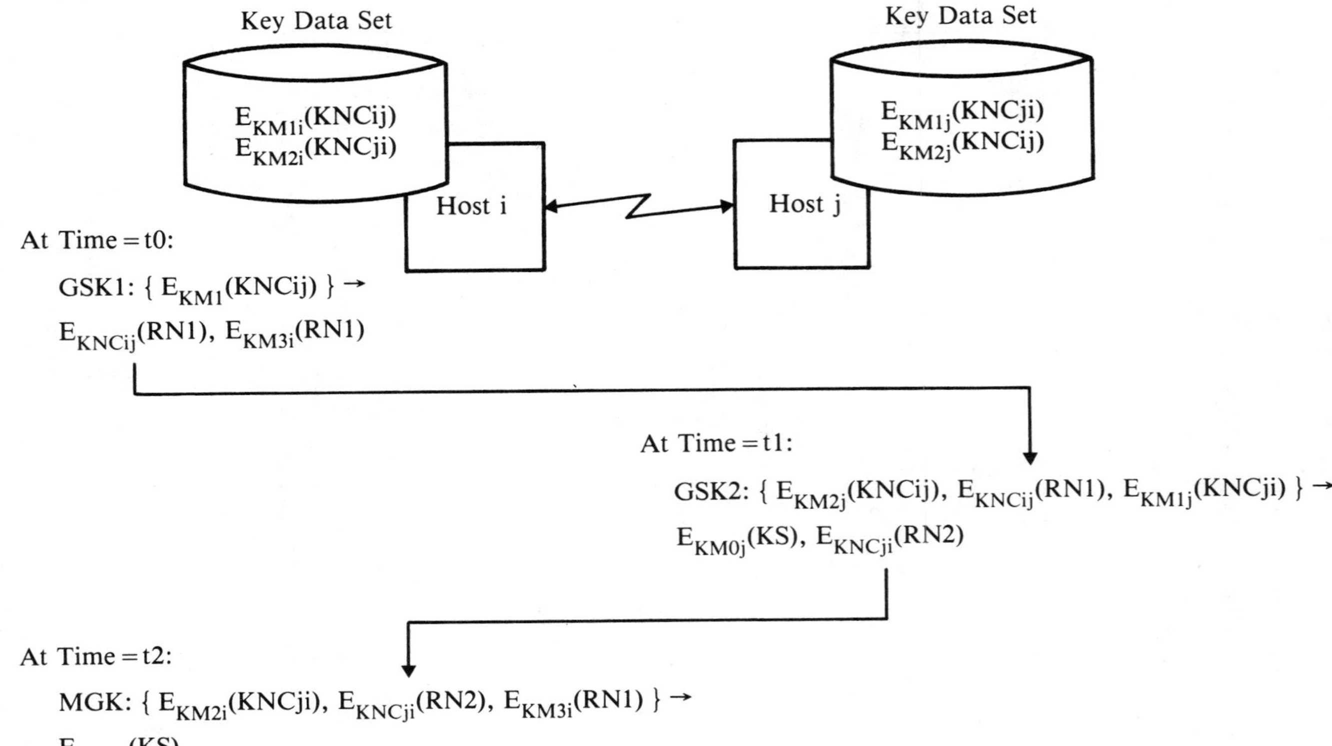

Figure 5-12. Interdomain Exchange of KS

protocols for session initiation, it should be obvious that the composite key protocol could be extended to include terminals.

To implement a composite key protocol, the cryptographic facilities at the affected nodes would have to support the operations GSK1, GSK2, and MGK, and the communications architecture would have to permit the exchange of RN1 and RN2. One such architecture, and the protocol it uses to send session keys between two nodes in a network, is described later (see Incorporation of Cryptography into a Communications Architecture, Chapter 7). Support for composite keys in this architecture could be accomplished by either modifying existing commands or creating new commands. Figure 5-12 illustrates host-to-host key distribution using composite keys.

Without composite keys, a session key could be retrieved and used without authorization provided that the enciphered value of that key and access to the receiving node is obtained. The protocol described here prevents this attack. Thus any attempt to bypass cryptographic protection must be made at the system level during the active session period and involve the retention of the session key in its final enciphered form or be directed at the clear data itself. For all practical purposes, then, no advantage is gained by intercepting RN1 and/or RN2.

SUMMARY

Cryptography reduces the problem of protecting data, in certain clearly defined situations, to that of protecting the secrecy and use of a small set of cryptographic keys. Without cryptography, data is exposed through such external attacks as wiretapping and theft of removable storage. When cryptography is used, the opponent is forced to attack the system from within, requiring a penetration of the operating system.

Control over the execution of the defined cryptographic operations can be exercised by the following means: activating or deactivating certain cryptographic operations with a physical, key-operated switch; maintaining the secrecy of certain special cryptographic quantities used as input to cryptographic operations; and making selected cryptographic operations privileged.

However, it must be emphasized that without system integrity, cryptography will not add significantly to the overall security of a system when the opponent is or can masquerade as an authorized system user. Although cryptography can enhance the integrity of a computer system, it is not a substitute for integrity. When used in conjunction with other security features, cryptography does play an important and valuable role in a total security plan.

REFERENCES

1. Ehrsam, W. F., Matyas, S. M., Meyer, C. H., and Tuchman, W. L., "A Cryptographic Key Management Scheme for Implementing the Data Encryption Standard (DES)," *IBM System Journal,* **17**, No. 2, 106–125 (1978).
2. Lennon, R. E. and Matyas, S. M., "Cryptographic Key Distribution Using Composite Keys," *NTC 78 Conference Record,* 2, 26.1.1–26.1.6 (December 1978).

CHAPTER SIX

Generation, Distribution, and Installation of Cryptographic Keys[1]

Key generation is the process of producing the cryptographic keys required by a cryptographic system. *Key distribution* is the process of transporting or routing cryptographic keys through a cryptographic system for subsequent installation. *Key installation* is the process of entering cryptographic keys into cryptographic devices.

The procedures presented here for the generation, distribution, and installation of cryptographic keys are founded upon the key management scheme developed in Chapters 4 and 5. This scheme for key management distinguishes between key-encrypting keys and data-encrypting keys. The former are used to encipher other keys and are derived as part of the process of initializing the cryptographic system. They remain constant for relatively long periods—changed perhaps once a year. Data-encrypting keys, on the other hand, are generated dynamically during regular system operation. They remain in existence for the life of the data they protect. That period, for communication security, is the length of time the user is signed-on to the system—usually a matter of minutes. For file security, where data are stored in enciphered form, the data-encrypting keys may exist for relatively long periods of time.

One special key-encrypting key, the host master key, should be generated by some random process such as tossing a coin or throwing a die. All other key-encrypting keys are produced by using DES as a generator of pseudorandom numbers. The procedure can be performed under secure conditions on the computer. Data-encrypting keys are generated dynamically at the host processor by exploiting the randomness associated with the many different users and processes that normally are active on a system at any given time.

With DES, each 64-bit cryptographic key consists of 56 independent key bits and 8 bits (the last bit of each 8-bit byte) that may be used for error detection. If used, these bits assure that each byte in the key has odd parity (see Key Parity, Chapter 4).

[1] © 1978 IBM Corporation. Reprinted in part from *IBM Systems Journal* **17**, No. 2, 1978 [1].

Since DES is a publicly known algorithm, cryptographic strength must be based on the secrecy of its cryptographic keys. Even though there are 2^{56} different possible keys, keys should be randomly selected so that an organized search for them would not be likely to meet with early success. If there were a known bias in the selection of keys, an opponent could try the more likely candidates first.

GENERATION OF THE HOST MASTER KEY

Regardless of the procedure used for key generation, organized predictable methods must be avoided. Any procedure based on one's telephone number, name and address, date of birth, or the like, is so frail that no real protection is provided. Also, the programs for generating pseudo-random numbers, which are available on many computer systems, are far too predictable to be used for this purpose and should be avoided.

Since the host master key, either directly or through one of its derived variants, provides protection (through encipherment) for all other keys stored in the system, and since the host master key will in all probability remain unchanged for long periods, great care must be taken to select this key in a random manner. The method recommended here is for the key to be created via a process performed by the user of the system.

Assume that a 64-bit parity-adjusted key is required for the selection process, and that odd parity is used (i.e., every eighth bit is adjusted so that the number of bits in the 8-bit group is odd). Since a change to the key is likely to cause its parity to become incorrect, parity can be used for error detection. For example, parity can be checked to ensure that a master key is properly specified for entry into a cryptographic facility. Or, during regular operation, parity can be checked to ensure that bits in the master key are not inadvertently changed (e.g., because of a malfunction in the cryptographic facility).

Tossing Coins

Let the bit values 0 and 1 in the cryptographic key be determined by the occurrence of heads and tails, respectively. Then toss 56 coins in eight groups of seven coins each, and record the results. Each group is then converted to its corresponding parity-adjusted hexadecimal digits (Table 6-1).

Each group of 7 bits in the 56-bit key is expanded to 8 bits by appending an additional parity bit (odd parity is maintained). This process can be performed with the aid of a table, if desired. In Table 6-2, for example, the first 4 bits index the table row and the last 3 bits the table column. Since every entry in the table has correct parity, a parity-adjusted key will be formed even if there should be an error in indexing. The cryptographic key (the value entered into the system and saved in a secure repository for back up purposes) is defined as that string of hexadecimal digits produced by the table reference process. The values used to index the table are then destroyed.

Trial	Result	Binary	Parity	Hex
(1)	HHHT HTH	0001 010	1	15
(2)	THTH HHT	1010 001	0	A2
(3)	TTHT HHH	1101 000	0	D0
(4)	THHH TTT	1000 111	1	8F
(5)	HHTT TTH	0011 110	1	3D
(6)	TTHH HHH	1100 000	1	C1
(7)	HHHT THT	0001 101	0	1A
(8)	HHTH THH	0010 100	1	29

Parity-Adjusted Key = Hex 15A2D08F3DC11A29

Table 6-1. Results of Coin-Tossing Converted to Binary and Hexadecimal Digits (heads (H) = binary 0, tails (T) = binary 1)

Throwing Dice

The method described above can also be used with dice. Instead of tossing seven coins, the user rolls seven dice. The binary digits can be obtained by an even roll (2, 4, or 6) to represent a 0 bit and an odd roll (1, 3, or 5) to represent a 1 bit.

decimal		0	1	2	3	4	5	6	7
	binary	000	001	010	011	100	101	110	111
0	0000	01	02	04	07	08	0B	0D	0E
1	0001	10	13	15	16	19	1A	1C	1F
2	0010	20	23	25	26	29	2A	2C	2F
3	0011	31	32	34	37	38	3B	3D	3E
4	0100	40	43	45	46	49	4A	4C	4F
5	0101	51	52	54	57	58	5B	5D	5E
6	0110	61	62	64	67	68	6B	6D	6E
7	0111	70	73	75	76	79	7A	7C	7F
8	1000	80	83	85	86	89	8A	8C	8F
9	1001	91	92	94	97	98	9B	9D	9E
10	1010	A1	A2	A4	A7	A8	AB	AD	AE
11	1011	B0	B3	B5	B6	B9	BA	BC	BF
12	1100	C1	C2	C4	C7	C8	CB	CD	CE
13	1101	D0	D3	D5	D6	D9	DA	DC	DF
14	1110	E0	E3	E5	E6	E9	EA	EC	EF
15	1111	F1	F2	F4	F7	F8	FB	FD	FE

Table 6-2. Parity-Adjusted Hexadecimal Digits (Odd Parity)

Random Number Table

A random number table contains a list of numbers that have been generated by a random (or nearly random) process. Once recorded, the numbers are subjected to extensive statistical tests to uncover any nonrandomness. There is one book [2], for example, that lists 1 million random digits arranged in 20,000 rows and 50 columns. The table occupies 400 pages within the text. The basic problem with random number tables is that the opponent may be able to guess which table has been used. For all practical purposes, once this happens a number obtained from the table is no better than the randomly selected starting position.

For example, if a key is selected from the table by using one random starting point, and the table is read from left to right, then there are only 1 million different keys that may possibly be selected. In this instance, the key space is reduced from 72,057,594,037,927,936 (2^{56}) possible different keys to 1,000,000 (approximately 2^{20}) possible different keys. In addition, the tendency of books to open repeatedly to the same page or set of pages, and the tendency to choose numbers near the center of the page, reduce the possible candidates still further.

To overcome these problems, one can choose several random starting points. This would introduce an element of randomness into the routine for generating key bits based on the starting point. But this requires a random process (like coin-tossing) which could instead be used to generate the key directly. Hence the use of random number tables in key generation does not obviate a random process. The use of random number tables complicates, but does not strengthen the key generation process. In fact, the improper use of such tables could actually weaken the procedure. For this reason, random number tables are not recommended for generating keys.

GENERATION OF KEY-ENCRYPTING KEYS

When large numbers of key-encrypting keys are deployed throughout a cryptographic system, there is an increased chance that one or more of these keys will become known to an opponent. Therefore, the procedure for generating keys must be such that if one or more of the keys are discovered, the work factor will remain high enough to protect the remaining keys; that is, a knowledge of part of the keys will not provide a shortcut method to find any of the other keys.

It is recommended that the procedure for generating keys involve the host master key or one of its variants by executing one or more of the cryptographic key management operations. Not only will an opponent be forced to carry out part of his attack on the same host system, but because the operations themselves must be executed as part of the attack, the opponent is constrained by the particular operational characteristics of the host machine itself. For example, since the time it takes to encipher and decipher is known for a specific system, the minimum required computation time can be determined for a given attack.

A Weak Key-Generating Procedure

Suppose that RN is a 64-bit random number supplied as input to the key-generating procedure, and that keys are generated using an *encipher under master key* operation as follows:

Ki = the ith cryptographic key (i = 1, 2, . . . , n) obtained by adjusting each byte in Yi for odd parity

where

$$Y0 = RN$$

$$Yi = E_{KM0}(Yi - 1) \qquad \text{for } i = 1, 2, \ldots, n$$

This procedure is too frail, however, since a compromise of only a single key, say Ki, would with little uncertainty allow an opponent to deduce Yi. By exercising the *encipher under master key* operation, the opponent could then generate the remaining keys, Ki + 1, Ki + 2, . . . , Kn.

A Strong Key-Generating Procedure

The procedure recommended here is to use DES as a generator of pseudo-random numbers and produce the entire set of keys with three 64-bit random values: RN1, RN2, and RN3. Let RN1 and RN2 be generated externally by a human using a random process (such as coin-tossing or rolling dice) similar to that used for generating the host master key, and let RN3 be derived internally within the host system. To defeat the key generating procedure, an opponent must compromise three secret parameters from at least two independent sources. (Three independent sources would be involved if RN1 and RN2 were generated and entered into the system by two different people.)

A straightforward approach for using RN1, RN2, and RN3 in the key-generating procedure is illustrated in Figure 6-1. (Multiple encryption is also discussed in Appendix D.) The procedure is described as follows:

Ki = the ith cryptographic key (i = 1, 2, . . . , n) obtained by adjusting each byte in Yi for odd parity

and

$$Yi = E_{RN3}(E_{RN1}(E_{RN2}(E_{RN1}(i)))) \qquad \text{for } i = 1, 2, \ldots, n \qquad (6\text{-}1)$$

For an opponent to compromise a single key, say Ki, the values of RN1, RN2, and RN3 must be known. Thus even if a set of keys, Ki1, Ki2, . . . , Kij would become known, it would still be impossible to deduce the remaining unknown keys.

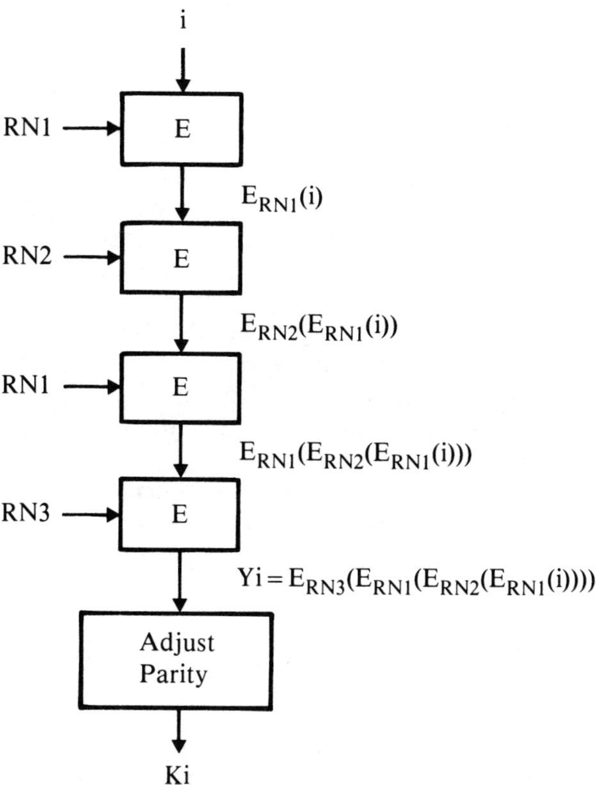

RN1, RN2 = random numbers supplied by the user.
RN3 = a random number generated by the host processor.
i = index number.
E = encipherment.
D = decipherment.

Figure 6-1. Basic Approach for Generating Keys Using the DES

The key-generating procedure illustrated in Figure 6-1 can be implemented within the host cryptographic system by exercising a *reencipher from master key* operation, as shown below:

$$
\begin{aligned}
&\text{RFMK: } \{\text{RN1, i}\} \longrightarrow \text{Ai} \\
&\text{RFMK: } \{\text{RN2, Ai}\} \longrightarrow \text{Bi} \\
&\text{RFMK: } \{\text{RN1, Bi}\} \longrightarrow \text{Ci} \\
&\text{RFMK: } \{\text{RN3, Ci}\} \longrightarrow \text{Yi} \\
&\text{Yi: } \xrightarrow{\text{adjust parity}} \text{Ki}
\end{aligned} \tag{6-2}
$$

where

$$\begin{aligned} i &= \text{index number} \\ R1 &= D_{KM1}(RN1) \\ R2 &= D_{KM1}(RN2) \\ R3 &= D_{KM1}(RN3) \\ Yi &= E_{R3}(D_{KM0}(E_{R1}(D_{KM0}(E_{R2}(D_{KM0}(E_{R1}(D_{KM0}(i)))))))) \end{aligned}$$

and Ai, Bi, and Ci are 64-bit intermediate results.

Assuming that DES does not introduce any bias, then (for i = 1, 2, and 3) Ri is random if RNi is random. Thus the expressions for Yi given in Equations 6-1 and 6-2 are comparable, except for the extra deciphering operations under KM0 in Equation 6-2.

RN3 is generated from several independent readings of a *time-of-day* (TOD) clock. The idea is to issue n different input/output operations of indeterminate length so that the clock values, read at the completion of the operations, denoted

$$\text{TOD1, TOD2, } \ldots \text{, TODn}$$

are unpredictable.

One way to obtain an input/output operation of indeterminate length is to send a message to a terminal's user requesting that one or more terminal keys be struck in response to the issued message. Since the response time is different from user to user, the clock reading obtained at the completion of the event is unpredictable. By repeating the process, the required number of clock readings can be obtained.

If the TOD clock is a 64-bit counter, then a straightforward approach for generating RN3 is to exercise repeatedly the *reencipher from master key* operation:

$$\begin{aligned} &\text{RFMK: } \{\text{TOD1, X0}\} \longrightarrow \text{X1} \\ &\text{RFMK: } \{\text{TOD2, X1}\} \longrightarrow \text{X2} \\ &\qquad\vdots \\ &\text{RFMK: } \{\text{TODn, Xn} - 1\} \longrightarrow \text{RN3} \end{aligned}$$

where:

$$\begin{aligned} X0 &= 0 \\ Xi &= E_{D_{KM1}(TODi)}(D_{KM0}(Xi - 1)) \qquad \text{for } i = 1, 2, \ldots, n \\ RN3 &= E_{D_{KM1}(TODn)}(D_{KM0}(\ldots (E_{D_{KM1}(TOD1)}(D_{KM0}(0))) \ldots)) \end{aligned}$$

The uncertainty in RN3 depends on the uncertainty in each clock value used in its computation. If, for example, each clock value has two possible outcomes of equal likelihood, then there would be 2^n possible combinations for the n-tuple (TOD1, TOD2, . . . , TODn). A value of n equal to 64 would be more than enough to ensure that RN3 is random.

Since, in an actual implementation, the number of unpredictable outcomes for each clock value is much larger than 2, fewer clock readings are needed. For example, if the time a human takes to respond varies as much as one second, and if the responses are spread uniformly over the interval, then a clock with resolution to one microsecond has 2^{20} unpredictable outcomes. Three independent clock values may then be sufficient to generate a random value for RN3.

Where it is undesirable to involve a human in the creation of a random value for RN3, a single clock reading, taken at the time the key-generating procedure is invoked, can be used. However, a single clock value does not have enough different unpredictable combinations to allow RN3 to be used as a cryptographic key, since an opponent may be able to guess the approximate time when the keys were generated. But it does reduce the chance that a duplicate set of keys is accidentally regenerated, should it happen that RN1 and RN2 are inadvertently reentered during a subsequent execution of the key-generating procedure.

An Alternate Approach for Generating Key-Encrypting Keys

An alternate approach also uses DES as a generator of pseudo-random numbers. The basic idea is that a 64-bit random number, RN, can be used in conjunction with the DES algorithm to produce the entire set of key-encrypting keys (except the host master key). RN, in this case, is generated externally by a random process similar to that used in generating the host master key (e.g., coin-tossing or dice-throwing). Yi is the ith pseudo-random number generated in the process, and Ki, which is obtained from Yi by adjusting each byte for odd parity, equals the ith cryptographic key (i = 1, 2, . . . , n).

The approach described here is to use one of the host processor's cryptographic operations so that each value of Yi (i = 1, 2, . . . , n) is a function of the host master key as well as a function of RN. This approach makes use of the *reencipher from master key* (RFMK) operation, as shown below:

$$\text{RFMK: } \{\text{RN, TOD} + \text{i}\} \longrightarrow \text{Ai}$$

$$\text{RFMK: } \{\text{RN, Ai}\} \longrightarrow \text{Yi}$$

$$\text{Yi: } \xrightarrow{\text{adjust parity}} \text{Ki}$$

where

$$R = D_{KM1}(RN)$$

$$Yi = E_R D_{KM0}(E_R(D_{KM0}(TOD + i)))$$

and Ai is a 64-bit intermediate result. Again, assuming that DES does not introduce any bias, the quantity $R = D_{KM1}(RN)$ is random if RN is random.

Therefore, Yi is a function of two secret, independently selected cryptographic keys: one (RN) supplied by the user, the other (KM0) supplied by the system.

Because of the DES algorithm's property of noninvertibility and because of the manner in which the parameters (RN and KM0) are used to compute Yi, a knowledge of several clear keys (Ki1, Ki2, . . . , Kij) or, in fact, even a knowledge of the corresponding Y-values (Yi1, Yi2, . . . , Yij) will not permit RN or KM0 to be deduced. Therefore, a knowledge of one or more of the generated keys will not allow any of the remaining keys to be deduced.

Note that the procedure described above does *not* depend on the randomness provided by the TOD clock. A clock value is introduced in this case to reduce the likelihood that the user will inadvertently regenerate a duplicate list of keys by reentering the same value of RN. A duplicate RN could be reentered, for example, if the medium on which a new value of RN is recorded was accidentally replaced with one containing an old value of RN.

Encipherment of Keys under the Master Key's Variants

Enciphering under the variants of the host master key could be done with operations similar to the *encipher under master key* (EMK) operation. If EMK1 and EMK2 designate encipherment under KM1 and KM2, respectively, then these operations can be described as follows:

$$\textbf{EMK1}: \{X\} \longrightarrow E_{KM1}(X)$$

$$\textbf{EMK2}: \{X\} \longrightarrow E_{KM2}(X)$$

In this approach, use of the EMK1 and EMK2 operations must be carefully controlled (see Additional Considerations, Chapter 5). For example, if an opponent could encipher a known value X under KM1, then knowledge of X and $E_{KM1}(X)$ would permit the opponent to transform $E_{KM0}(Y)$ to $E_X(Y)$ and thus allow the decipherment of any arbitrary quantity (Y) under the host master key (KM0). This would enable recovery of session keys and file keys in clear form. To protect against this threat and thus provide control over enciphering under the host master key's variants, the EMK1 and EMK2 operations could be designed so that they are activated (made operational) only through the use of a physical key-operated switch.

In an alternate approach, encipherment under the variants KM1 and KM2, could be accomplished by using the quantities $E_{KM1}(KM1)$ and $E_{KM1}(KM2)$, respectively. These quantities are called *system activation keys*, and encipherment of an arbitrary value X is accomplished by using a *reencipher from master key* operation, as shown below:

$$\text{EMK}: \{X\} \longrightarrow E_{KM0}(X)$$

$$\text{RFMK}: \{E_{KM1}(KM1), E_{KM0}(X)\} \longrightarrow E_{KM1}(X)$$

$$\text{RFMK}: \{E_{KM1}(KM2), E_{KM0}(X)\} \longrightarrow E_{KM2}(X)$$

How the system activation keys can be created and used for enciphering under the host master key's variants, KM1 and KM2, is further illustrated in the block diagram in Figure 6-2.

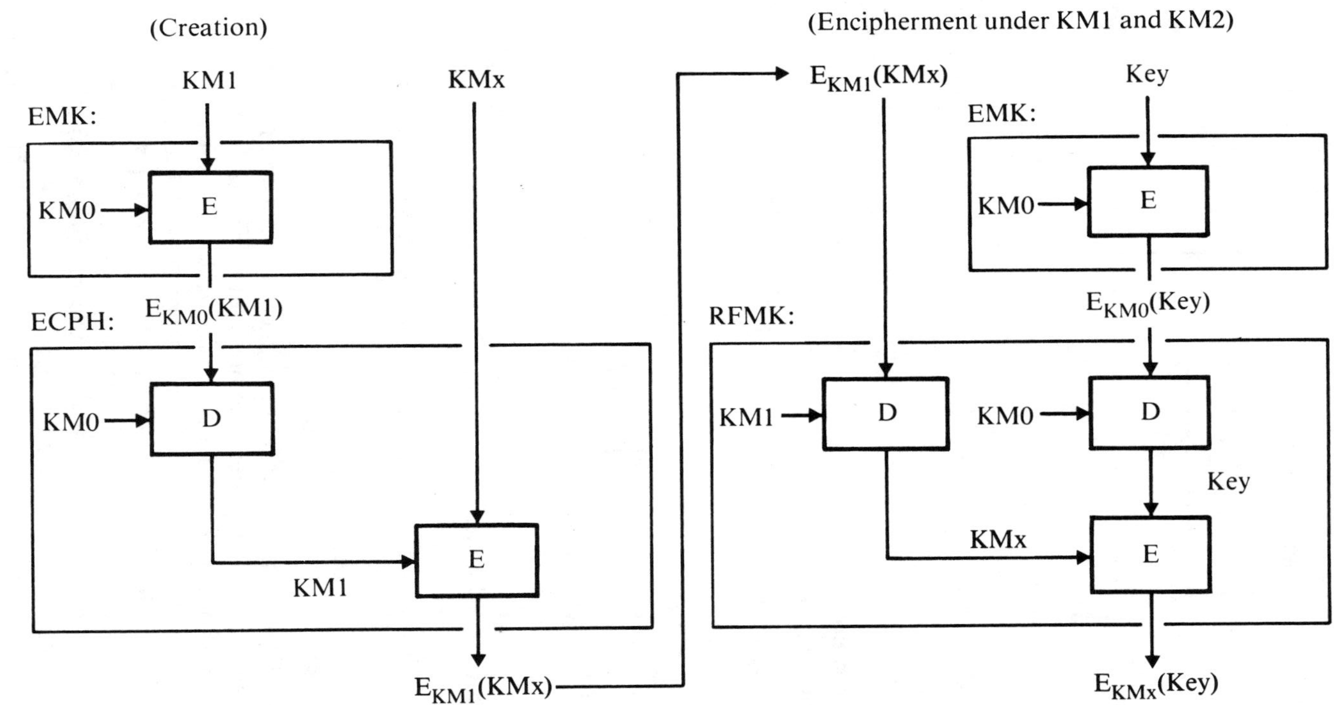

KMx is a variant of the master key (x = 1 or 2).

Figure 6-2. Creation of the System Activation Keys, E_{KM1}(KM1) and E_{KM1}(KM2), and Encipherment Under KM1 and KM2

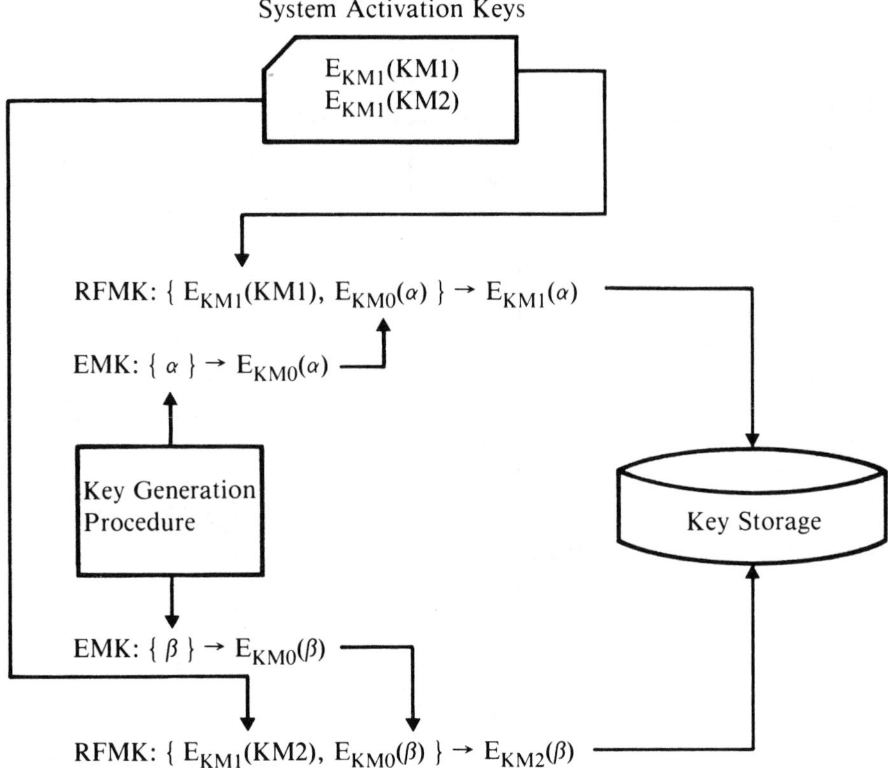

α = key to be enciphered under 1st variant, KM1.
β = key to be enciphered under 2nd variant, KM2.

Figure 6-3. Encipherment of Cryptographic Keys for Local Storage at a Host Processor

Once created, the system activation keys may be saved and later reentered as input parameters to the key-generating procedure (Figure 6-3).

To prevent unauthorized enciphering under KM1 and KM2, the system activation keys are maintained as secret parameters of the cryptographic system. Since deciphering under KM1 and KM2 is not possible with the system activation keys, the design adheres to the strategic principle of providing the cryptographic system with only the minimum functional capability needed to generate and manage its keys.

Alternatively, the quantities $E_{KM0}(KM1)$ and $E_{KM0}(KM2)$ could be used with an ECPH operation to encipher under the respective variants, KM1 and KM2. However, these quantities could also be used with a DCPH operation to decipher under KM1 and KM2. Because of this, it would be less desirable to use $E_{KM0}(KM1)$ and $E_{KM0}(KM2)$—rather than $E_{KM1}(KM1)$ and $E_{KM1}(KM2)$—as system activation keys.

Transforming Cryptographic Keys

It may happen that the host master key is changed within the cryptographic system without the other keys in the system also being changed. Thus a procedure is needed that permits keys stored under the encipherment of variants of the old host master key to be reenciphered under variants of the new host master key.

Let KM0* and KM0 represent the old and new host master keys, respectively. The required function is obtained as follows. KM0* and KM0 are read into the main memory of the host system where the variants KM1*, KM2*, KM1, and KM2 are derived by inverting appropriate bits in KM0* and KM0, respectively. The new host master key, KM0, is then written into the host's cryptographic facility using a set master key operation.

An *encipher under master key* operation is then used to generate the following quantities:

$$\text{EMK: } \{\text{KM1}\} \longrightarrow E_{\text{KM0}}(\text{KM1})$$
$$\text{EMK: } \{\text{KM2}\} \longrightarrow E_{\text{KM0}}(\text{KM2})$$

These quantities are used with an *encipher data* (ECPH) operation to generate the following additional quantities:

$$\text{ECPH: } \{E_{\text{KM0}}(\text{KM1}), \text{KM1}\} \longrightarrow E_{\text{KM1}}(\text{KM1})$$
$$\text{ECPH: } \{E_{\text{KM0}}(\text{KM1}), \text{KM2}\} \longrightarrow E_{\text{KM1}}(\text{KM2})$$
$$\text{ECPH: } \{E_{\text{KM0}}(\text{KM2}), \text{KM1*}\} \longrightarrow E_{\text{KM2}}(\text{KM1*})$$
$$\text{ECPH: } \{E_{\text{KM0}}(\text{KM2}), \text{KM2*}\} \longrightarrow E_{\text{KM2}}(\text{KM2*})$$

If α represents a secondary key stored enciphered under the first variant of the host master key, then reencipherment is accomplished as follows:

$$\text{RTMK: } \{E_{\text{KM2}}(\text{KM1*}), E_{\text{KM1*}}(\alpha)\} \longrightarrow E_{\text{KM0}}(\alpha)$$
$$\text{RFMK: } \{E_{\text{KM1}}(\text{KM1}), E_{\text{KM0}}(\alpha)\} \longrightarrow E_{\text{KM1}}(\alpha)$$

If β represents a secondary key stored enciphered under the second variant of the host master key, then reencipherment is accomplished as follows:

$$\text{RTMK: } \{E_{\text{KM2}}(\text{KM2*}), E_{\text{KM2*}}(\beta)\} \longrightarrow E_{\text{KM0}}(\beta)$$
$$\text{RFMK: } \{E_{\text{KM1}}(\text{KM2}), E_{\text{KM0}}(\beta)\} \longrightarrow E_{\text{KM2}}(\beta)$$

Reencipherment using the RTMK and RFMK operations is further illustrated in the block diagram in Figure 6-4. The general procedure for reencipherment of keys in the cryptographic key data set (CKDS) is illustrated in Figure 6-5.

To ensure that the procedure for transforming cryptographic keys is performed properly, one should verify that the old host master key read into

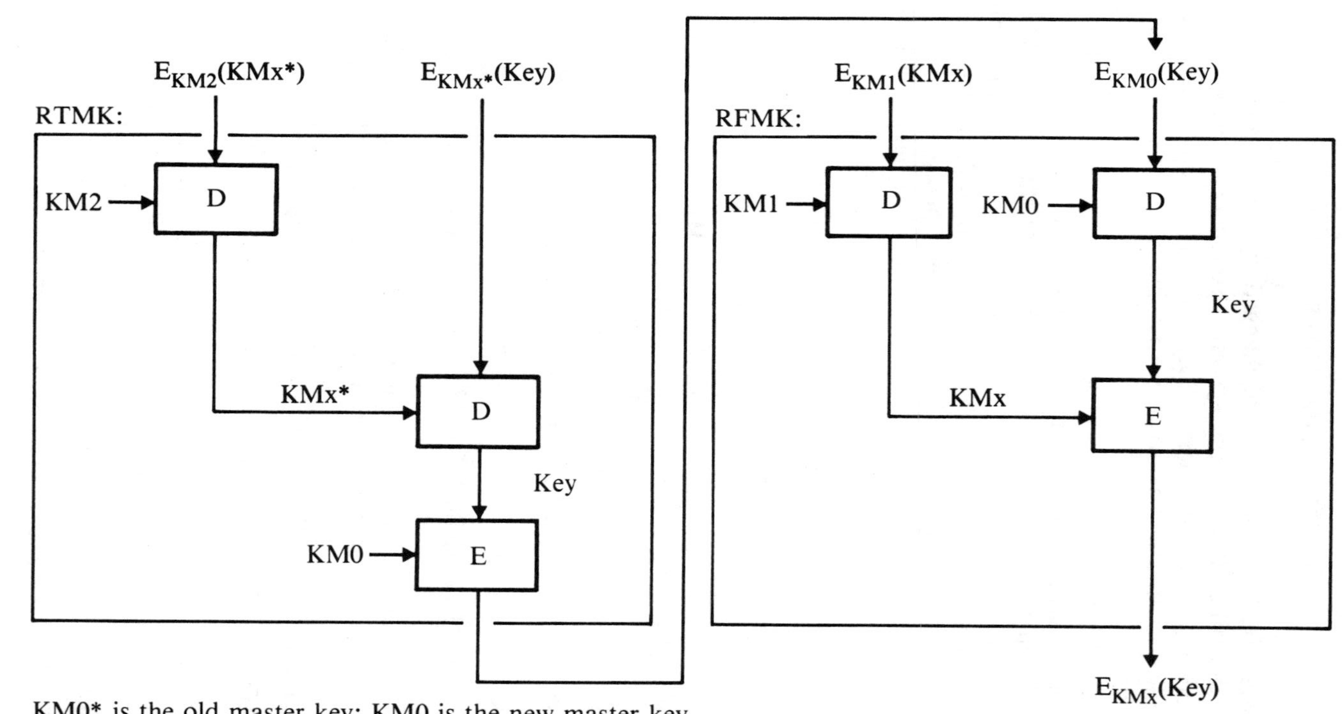

KM0* is the old master key; KM0 is the new master key.
$E_{KM2}(KMx^*)$ and $E_{KM1}(KMx)$ are assumed to be pregenerated.
$x = 1$ or 2.

Figure 6-4. Reencipherment of Cryptographic Keys from an Old to a New Master Key

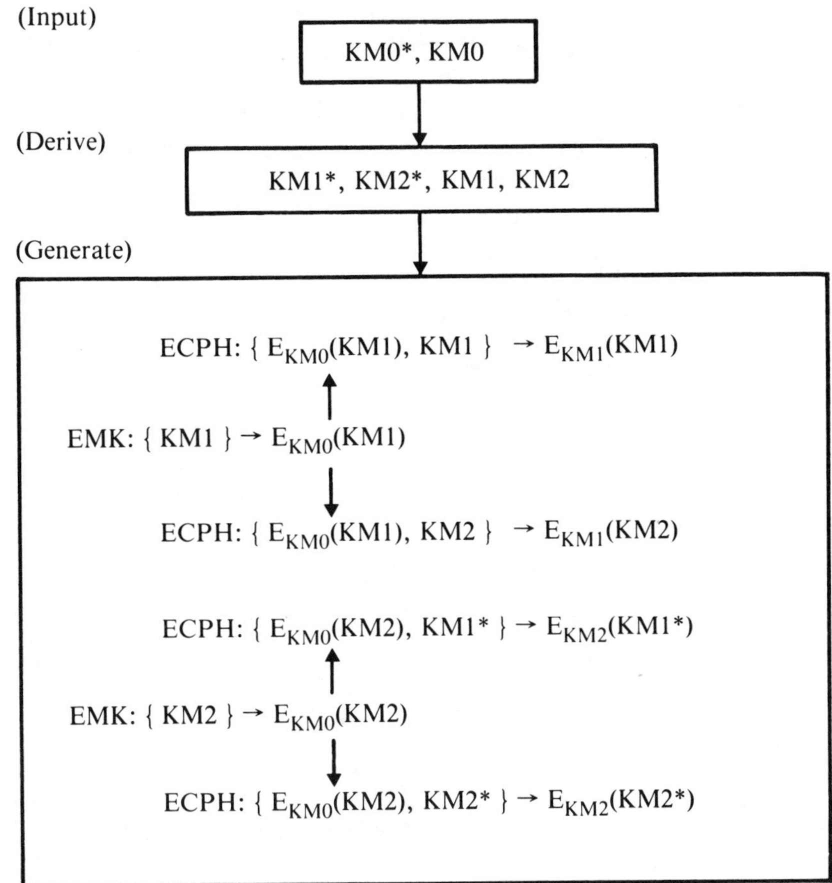

(Input)
KM0*, KM0
(Derive)
KM1*, KM2*, KM1, KM2
(Generate)
ECPH: { E_{KM0}(KM1), KM1 } → E_{KM1}(KM1)
EMK: { KM1 } → E_{KM0}(KM1)
ECPH: { E_{KM0}(KM1), KM2 } → E_{KM1}(KM2)
ECPH: { E_{KM0}(KM2), KM1* } → E_{KM2}(KM1*)
EMK: { KM2 } → E_{KM0}(KM2)
ECPH: { E_{KM0}(KM2), KM2* } → E_{KM2}(KM2*)

KM0*, KM1*, KM2* are old master key and variants.
KM0, KM1, KM2 are new master key and variants.

Figure 6-5. General Procedure for Reencipherment of Keys

the main memory of the host system is equal to the actual host master key stored in the cryptographic facility. This can be accomplished by using the following procedure. Let

KM0* = the old host master key previously written into the host's cryptographic facility

KM0′ = the copy of the old host master key read into main memory of the host system for verification

The following operations are now performed:

$$\text{EMK: } \{\text{KM0}'\} \longrightarrow E_{\text{KM0}*}(\text{KM0}')$$

$$\text{DCPH: } \{E_{\text{KM0}*}(\text{KM0}'), E_{\text{KM0}*}(\text{KM0}')\} \longrightarrow q$$

where

$$q = D_{\text{KM0}'}(E_{\text{KM0}*}(\text{KM0}'))$$

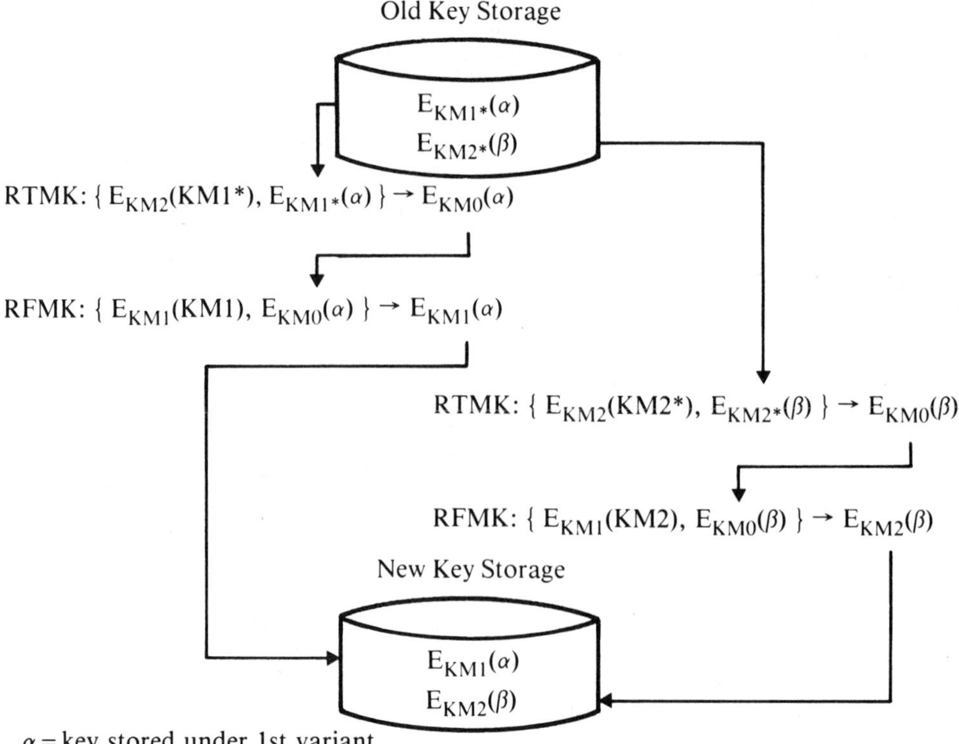

Figure 6-5 (cont'd). General Procedure for Reencipherment of Keys

If KM0′ equals KM0*, then it is always true that q equals KM0′. However, q may equal KM0′ when KM0* is not equal to KM0′, although for DES this is an extremely unlikely event. Assuming that DES is a good pseudo-random number generator, so that each bit in a generated number is equally likely to be a 0 or 1, it follows that the probability of the event that q equals KM0′ and KM0* does not equal KM0′ is about 2^{-64}.

For all practical purposes, if q equals KM0′, then KM0* equals KM0′ (i.e., the entered value of the host master key is equal to the host master key in the cryptographic facility).

GENERATION OF DATA-ENCRYPTING KEYS

A data-encrypting key is produced from a 64-bit random or pseudo-random number (RN) by defining the number to be the desired data-encrypting key already enciphered under a key-encrypting key known to the cryptographic system. For example, in communication security, RN is defined as the session key (KS) enciphered under the host's master key (KM0):

$$RN \equiv E_{KM0}(KS)$$

On the other hand, in file security, RN is defined as the file key (KF) enciphered under a secondary file key (KNF):

$$RN \equiv E_{KNF}(KF)$$

With this strategy, it is not necessary to generate first a data-encrypting key in clear form and then encipher it under the appropriate key-encrypting key. Data-encrypting keys are never exposed in clear form. Rather, they are dynamically produced as needed by the cryptographic system. This is accomplished by using the DES algorithm as a generator of pseudo-random numbers.

An Approach for Generating Keys with the Cryptographic Facility

One way to generate pseudo-random numbers (enciphered data-encrypting keys) is by using a nonresettable counter, or nonvolatile storage, that can be read and incremented only by the cryptographic facility. With this approach, the counter receives the same protection as the master key, working key, or any other intermediate value produced by one of the cryptographic operations.

A pseudo-random number is generated by incrementing the counter and enciphering the resultant value (c + 1) with a special variant of the host master key (KM4), as illustrated in Figure 6-6.

Because the pseudo-random numbers produced from this procedure (RN1, RN2, . . . , RNn) are each based on a different counter value, it follows that RN1 ≠ RN2 ≠ . . . ≠ RNn. The period of the pseudo-random number gen-

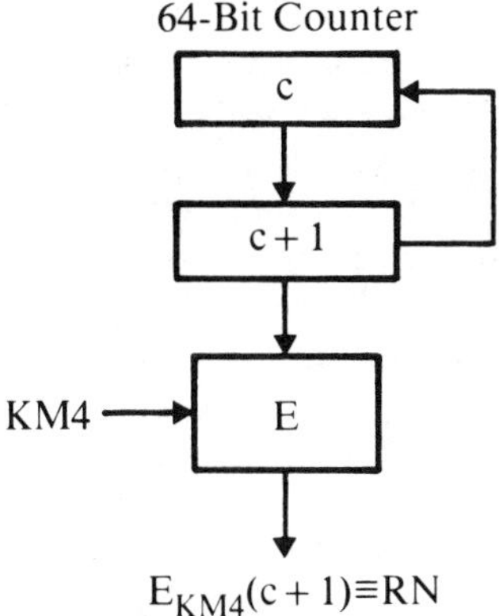

KM4 is a special variant of the host master key used only for the generation of RN. RN is defined as a data-encrypting key enciphered under a key-encrypting key known to the cryptographic system.

Figure 6-6. Procedure for Generating Pseudo-Random Numbers with the Cryptographic Facility

erating process is equal to the period of the counter (n). The procedure is such that it is not computationally feasible to deduce the secret key (KM4) or subsequent unknown values of RN using knowledge of one or more prior values of RN. Furthermore, this process is completely isolated from other cryptographic functions because KM4 is used in the procedure only for generating pseudo-random numbers.

Since the counter can be accessed only by the cryptographic facility, it is not possible for an opponent to reset its value and thereby cause prior data-encrypting keys to be regenerated. Moreover, if the counter is made large enough, say on the order of 64 bits, an opponent cannot cause the counter to recycle by making repeated requests for pseudo-random numbers. Thus previously generated numbers are never recreated. (Note that the counter value need not be kept secret to provide adequate cryptographic strength, but keeping the counter values secret will increase cryptographic strength.)

An Alternate Approach for Generating Data-Encrypting Keys

Basically, a pseudo-random number RN (defined as an enciphered data-encrypting key) is generated within the host processor as a result of the dynamically changing and unpredictable nature of the resource demands placed upon the system by its users.

The alternate approach for generating pseudo-random numbers makes use of the *reencipher to master key* (RTMK) operation in conjunction with two seed values, U and Z. These seed values are derived internally within the processor and are used as input parameters to an RTMK operation. The output of the operation is then used to derive RN. Two independent seed values provide the procedure with added strength, since both values must be compromised before a successful attack is possible. Figure 6-7 illustrates the described procedure for generating pseudo-random numbers.

For example, consecutive seed values Z(1), Z(2), . . . , Z(i) could be generated by combining two or more independent TOD clock values. Independent clock values can be achieved by interleaving an input-output operation of unpredictable duration between successive clock readings. The seed value U(0) could be derived from a combination of user-dependent and process-dependent information stored in the volatile memory of the host processor. Each value U(i), for any value of i greater than zero, is defined as the output of an RTMK operation whose input consists of U(i − 1) and Z(i). Hence it follows that U(i) is a function of U(0) and of Z(1), Z(2), . . . , Z(i).

It should be noted that RN(i) is a function of two independent quantities, U(i − 1) and Z(i), each having enough different values or combinations to prevent discovery by direct search. Each of the U-values, U(1), U(2), . . . , U(i), is generated internally by feeding back the result from the previous RTMK operation. A second RTMK operation is used to produce RN(i) from U(i) and to ensure that it is not possible to deduce U(i) from RN(i). Hence knowledge of one or more of the generated values of RN will not permit an opponent to deduce other (prior or subsequent) values of RN.

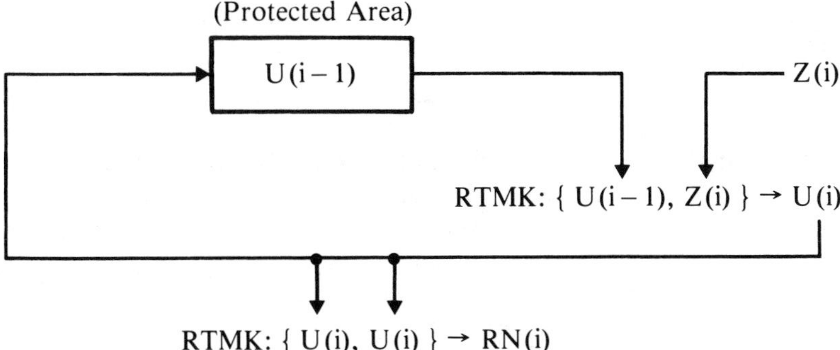

Where:

$U(0)$ = arbitrary value.
$Z(i)$ = function of two or more readings of the time-of-day clock.
$RN(i)$ = generated pseudo-random number.
i = index number.

The specific relations are:

$$U(i) = E_{KM0}(D_{D_{KM2}(U(i-1))}(Z(i)))$$
$$RN(i) = E_{KM0}(D_{D_{KM2}(U(i))}(U(i)))$$

Figure 6-7. DES-Based Pseudo-Random Number Generator for Data-Encrypting Keys

To subvert this process for generating pseudo-random numbers, an opponent must contend with both a changing and unpredictable Z-value and a secret U-value that itself is a function of U(0) and all prior Z-values. Even if one of the seed values should be compromised, the other provides enough cryptographic strength so that an exhaustive attack intended to recover a set of eligible RN(i) would be computationally infeasible.

ENTERING A MASTER KEY AT THE HOST PROCESSOR

For reasons of security, the master key cannot be read once it has been installed in a cryptographic facility. However, the following procedure will allow a security officer to validate, with a high level of confidence, that the master key stored in the cryptographic facility is the one that was intended.

Some function (ϕ) of the master key is computed externally to the system and compared with a similar value computed within the system. For example, KM0 could be used as a key to encipher a 64-bit random number (RN);

$$\phi(KM0) \equiv E_{KM0}(RN)$$

Once the master key has been installed in a cryptographic facility, the *encipher under master key* (EMK) operation could be used to produce the same quantity:

$$\text{EMK: } \{\text{RN}\} \longrightarrow E_{\text{KM0}}(\text{RN})$$

Comparison of these two values could then establish whether the keys used in the two routines were identical. The procedure is not foolproof, however, because the same incorrect key could have been entered in both routines. The objective, therefore, is to reduce the likelihood that an incorrect key is installed in the cryptographic facility in the first place.

Hard-Wired Entry

The reading of temporarily stored keys into the main memory of a system can be avoided by providing a direct wire connection between the point where the key is entered and the nonvolatile key storage area of the cryptographic facility. In this case, the key is entered by means of toggle switches, dials, or the like. The direct wire connection should be so constructed, as by shielding, that probing or tapping of transmitted information is not possible.

Even with hard-wired entry, there is still some chance that the key entered into the cryptographic facility will be different from the key that was intended. The following analysis provides an estimate for **p(UE)**, the probability of undetected error in the entered key (i.e., that an incorrect master key becomes installed in the cryptographic facility).

Of the sources of error affecting the key entry process, human error is the most critical. Mechanical or machine error occurs relatively infrequently, and therefore can be disregarded. At first, it is assumed that only one of the 16 hexadecimal digits entered into the cryptographic facility might be in error. A special case of multiple errors (i.e., double digit transposition of adjacent hexadecimal digits) is considered subsequently.[2]

In the situation described, a mistake in entering the key will not be detected if the parity of the incorrectly entered hexadecimal digit is correct. Since there are 16 possible hexadecimal digits, of which only 8 have odd parity, eliminating the correct digit leaves 7 combinations that have correct parity out of 15 possible combinations. Let

A = the event that the entered value of KM0 has correct parity

B = the event that KM0 is incorrectly entered

Then the probability of an undetected error, P(UE), is given by

$$\begin{aligned} p(\text{UE}) &= p(\text{A and B}) \\ &= p(\text{A}|\text{B})p(\text{B}) \\ &= (7/15)p(\text{B}) \\ &= 0.47p(\text{B}) \end{aligned}$$

[2] It is assumed, as previously stated, that host and terminal master keys are entered in the form of 16 parity-adjusted hexadecimal digits.

where p(A|B) designates the probability of event A given that event B has occurred.

To improve the situation, two quantities, KM0 and a function (ϕ) of KM0, are specified in such a way that errors associated with the entry of KM0 and ϕ(KM0) are statistically independent. The choice of ϕ equal to the identity function would not be practical. This would amount to entering KM0 twice, so that an error in the first entry might well be repeated in the second, implying that the errors in KM0 and ϕ(KM0) could not be considered statistically independent. However, the choice of $\phi(KM0) = \overline{KM0}$ (where overbar indicates the complement) is satisfactory. In this case, the complementary property[3] of the DES algorithm can be advantageously used to validate that the intended KM0 is submitted for entry in the host's cryptographic facility.

The procedure consists of first installing the complement of KM0 ($\overline{KM0}$) in the cryptographic facility and enciphering the arbitrary value U, then installing KM0 in the facility and enciphering the complement of U ($\overline{U}$). The output values are defined as Y1 and Y2, respectively. By the complementary property of the DES, KM0 can be assumed to be installed properly in the cryptographic facility whenever Y1 equals the complement of Y2 ($\overline{Y2}$). Any corruption that may occur in the master key during its transmission between the entry point and the cryptographic facility is also detected with this procedure. Figure 6-8 illustrates this entry procedure.

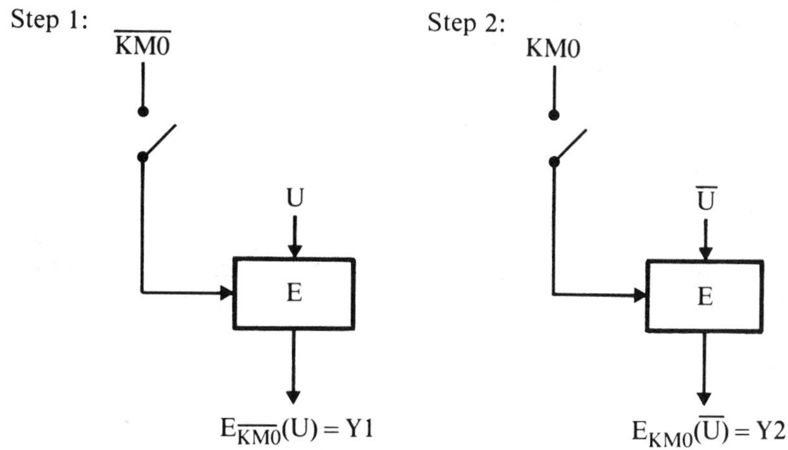

Notes: "——" indicates "the complement of."

Accept KM0 if $Y1 = \overline{Y2}$, otherwise reject KM0.

Figure 6-8. Validation of the Master Key as it is Entered at the Host Processor

[3] The complementary property of the DES algorithm stipulates that EK(X) equals $\overline{E_{\overline{K}}(\overline{X})}$ for every key (K) and plaintext (X). (See also Classes of Ciphers, Chapter 3.)

The following analysis illustrates the superiority of validating the master key using KM0 and $\overline{\text{KM0}}$. Let

E1 = the event that the entered value of $\overline{\text{KM0}}$ is in error, but that the entered value has correct parity

E2 = the event that the entered value of KM0 is in error, but that the entered value has correct parity

E3 = the event that the entered value of $\overline{\text{KM0}}$ and the entered value of KM0 are complements of each other

An undetected error can occur only if all events, E1, E2, and E3, occur simultaneously. The notation (E1, E2, E3) denotes this joint event. The probability of an undetected error is thus given by

$$\begin{aligned} p(UE) &= p(E1, E2, E3) \\ &= p(E3|E1, E2)p(E2|E1)p(E1) \end{aligned}$$

Since it can reasonably be assumed that the events E1 and E2 are statistically independent, it follows that

$$p(E2) = p(E1) = (7/15)p^1$$

and therefore that

$$p(UE) = p(E3|E1, E2)(7/15)^2(p^1)^2 \tag{6-3}$$

where p^1 is the probability that one digit in a key is incorrectly entered (i.e., is in error).

However, given that the events E1 and E2 do occur and that only one hexadecimal digit is in error, it follows that there is a 1/16 probability that the errors in $\overline{\text{KM0}}$ and KM0 occur in the same digital position, a requirement if the errors are to go undetected. Moreover, given that the errors occur in the same digital position, then there is a 1/7 probability that the two incorrect digits will be complements of each other. This is because there are seven incorrect hexadecimal digits with correct parity and only one of these that is the complement of the other incorrectly entered digit. Therefore

$$\begin{aligned} p(UE) &= (1/16)(1/7)(7/15)^2(p^1)^2 \\ &= 0.00194(p^1)^2 \end{aligned}$$

A more general result that takes into account the possibility that multiple errors may occur can be obtained in the following way. Let

E1,i = the event that exactly i digits (i = 1, 2, . . . , 16) in the entered value of $\overline{\text{KM0}}$ are in error, but the entered value has correct parity

E2,i = the event that exactly i digits (i = 1, 2, . . . , 16) in the entered value of KM0 are in error, but the entered value has correct parity

E3,i = the event that the entered value of $\overline{\text{KM0}}$ and the entered value of KM0, as given by E1,i and E2,i, are complements of each other

Then p(UE) can be expressed as

$$p(UE) = \sum_{i=1}^{16} p(E1,i, E2,i, E3,i)$$

$$= \sum_{i=1}^{16} p(E2,e, E3,i \mid E1,i)p(E1,i) \qquad (6\text{-}4)$$

As an example, let double digit transposition of adjacent hexadecimal digits be considered. (This is probably one of the most frequent multiple errors.) Let p2 be the probability of such an event. There are 15 error combinations for this case. Eight of these affect only 1 byte, case (a), with probability (8/15)p2 and 7 of these affect 2 bytes, case (b), with probability (7/15)p2. In the case where transposition takes place within 1 byte, parity is not lost, and thus p(E1,2) = p(E2,2) = (8/15)p2. In the case where transposition affects 2 bytes, the probability of obtaining correct parity is p(E1,2) = p(E2,2) = $(7/15)^2$p2, since there are 7 out of 15 hexadecimal combinations leading to the correct parity.

The conditional probability p(E2,2, E3,2 | E1,2) is equal to (1/15)p2. This is so because the event E3,2, describing the complementary property, occurs only if the same digit pairs are affected in KMO and $\overline{\text{KMO}}$. (Otherwise the transposed digits destroy the complementary property of the entered values.) Thus only one transposition combination out of the 15 satisfies this condition. Given that E1,2 occurs, it also follows that parity is not affected in KMO if the same digit pairs are transposed in both KMO and $\overline{\text{KMO}}$. (Note that if parity is unaffected when a pair of digits in KMO (or $\overline{\text{KMO}}$) are transposed, then parity will also be unaffected when the corresponding pair of digits in KMO (or $\overline{\text{KMO}}$) are transposed.)

Since the events of cases (a) and (b) are mutually exclusive, probabilities can be added, and for i = 2 Equation 6-4 can be rewritten as

$$p(UE) = p2^2(1/15)\,[(8/15) + (7/15)^2] = 0.05p2^2$$

To reduce P(UE) still further, the key entry procedure could cause the key and its complement value to be displayed prior to the key being written in the cryptographic facility. This would allow an additional visual check to be made on the entered values.

Indirect Entry

To enter the master key indirectly, it is read into the main storage of the host processor and a *set master key* (SMK) operation is then used to write the key into the nonvolatile storage area of the cryptographic facility. Once the master key has been transferred, the copy of the master key in main storage is erased.

To reduce the likelihood of human error resulting in an incorrect master key being initialized in the cryptographic facility, it is recommended that the key be entered from a nonvolatile medium such as a punched card or magnetic tape. The card or tape could be stored in a secure location (e.g., a safe or vault) when not being used. As part of the procedure, the master key would be defined as that value which is recorded on the medium—provided, of course, that it has correct parity. Thus any human error committed in recording the key on the medium would be of no real consequence.

Any corruption of the master key between its entry point and the cryptographic facility resulting from either a hardware or software error could be detected by using the previously described procedure in which both the host master key and its complement value are entered (see Hard-Wired Entry).

ATTACK VIA EXTERNAL MANIPULATIONS

While the importance of having a physically protected area for the storage of the master key has been emphasized, the following illustrates that care must also be exercised in choosing a key entry procedure that is safe.

Let K denote an unknown master key and R the contents of the master key storage area in the cryptographic facility. Assume that K and R consist of 16 hexadecimal digits:

$$K = K1, K2, \ldots, K16$$

$$R = R1, R2, \ldots, R16$$

where K1 is stored in R1, K2 in R2, and so forth.

Assume further that the master key is entered into the cryptographic facility in a series of 16 consecutive steps. At each step, a single 4-bit hexadecimal digit of the key is entered into the next available location within R. The procedure is accomplished via manual switches. The storing of digits into R is controlled by an indexing circuit that indicates the next available location. When the switches are deactivated, the index is reset to point R1. However, the procedure has a weakness that can be exploited.

The unknown value of K1 can be attacked by systematically setting R1 to the values 0 through (hexadecimal) F. This can be done by activating the switches for entering the key, entering a trial digit, and deactivating the switches. A list of test messages, previously enciphered under the unknown master key, is now enciphered under each of the 16 different trial master keys. Since R2, R3, . . . , R16 are not changed in the procedure, the value of K1 can be determined by observing which entered digit causes the enciphered test messages to produce the correct ciphertext.

In like manner, K2 can be determined by systematically setting R2 to the values 0 through F. This is done by activating the switches, entering the known value of K1 into R1, entering a trial digit into R2, and deactivating the switches. The list of test messages is again enciphered under each of the 16 different trial master keys. Since R1 is set to K1 and R3, R4, . . . , R16 are not changed in the procedure, the value of K2 can be determined by observing which entered digit causes the enciphered test messages to produce the correct ciphertext.

Repeating the procedure, one can determine the digits K3 through K16. An average of 128 trials, or a maximum of 256 trials, are required. The described attack is thwarted by ensuring that R is automatically overwritten whenever the switches for entering the master key are activated. The process of overwriting the key is called *key zeroization* [3].

MASTER KEY ENTRY AT A TERMINAL

A terminal master key can be set by means of switches, dials, or a hand-held key loading device, or it can be entered at a keyboard. Again, because the terminal master key (KMT) cannot be read once it has been set, one should validate that the key has been properly initialized in the cryptographic facility.

On-Line Checking

One way of determining whether the proper master key has been initialized in a terminal's cryptographic facility is to establish a communications session with the host processor. If the installed terminal master key differs from the copy stored at the host, the session key initiated between the host and terminal will be different, and it will not be possible to send and receive an agreed-upon message.

A simple handshaking protocol could be adopted as part of the process of initiating a session. For example, the terminal could encipher a value N = (N1, N2) with the session key (KS) and send the resulting value to the host processor. Via the established protocol, the host would decipher the received quantity, apply some function to N such as switching the N1 and N2 to produce N′ = (N2, N1), reencipher the value N′ under KS, and send the result to the terminal. At the terminal, a check could then be made to ensure that the first and last halves of the deciphered value of N′ are equal to the last and first halves of N, respectively. If the values agree, the terminal master key would be accepted. Other approaches are possible (see Handshaking, Chapter 8).

Off-Line Checking

It is often desirable to check KMT directly at a terminal without involving the host processor. To do so one can use a validating pattern. This pattern is a nonsecret function of KMT, and is created as part of the process of generating the key.

When a key is generated, the *encipher under master key* (EMK), *encipher data* (ECPH), and *decipher data* (DCPH) operations are used to produce a validating pattern (Vh) at the host system, as follows:

$$\text{EMK: } \{\text{KMT}\} \longrightarrow E_{\text{KM0}}(\text{KMT})$$

$$\text{DCPH: } \{E_{\text{KM0}}(\text{KMT}), \text{TID}\} \longrightarrow D_{\text{KMT}}(\text{TID})$$

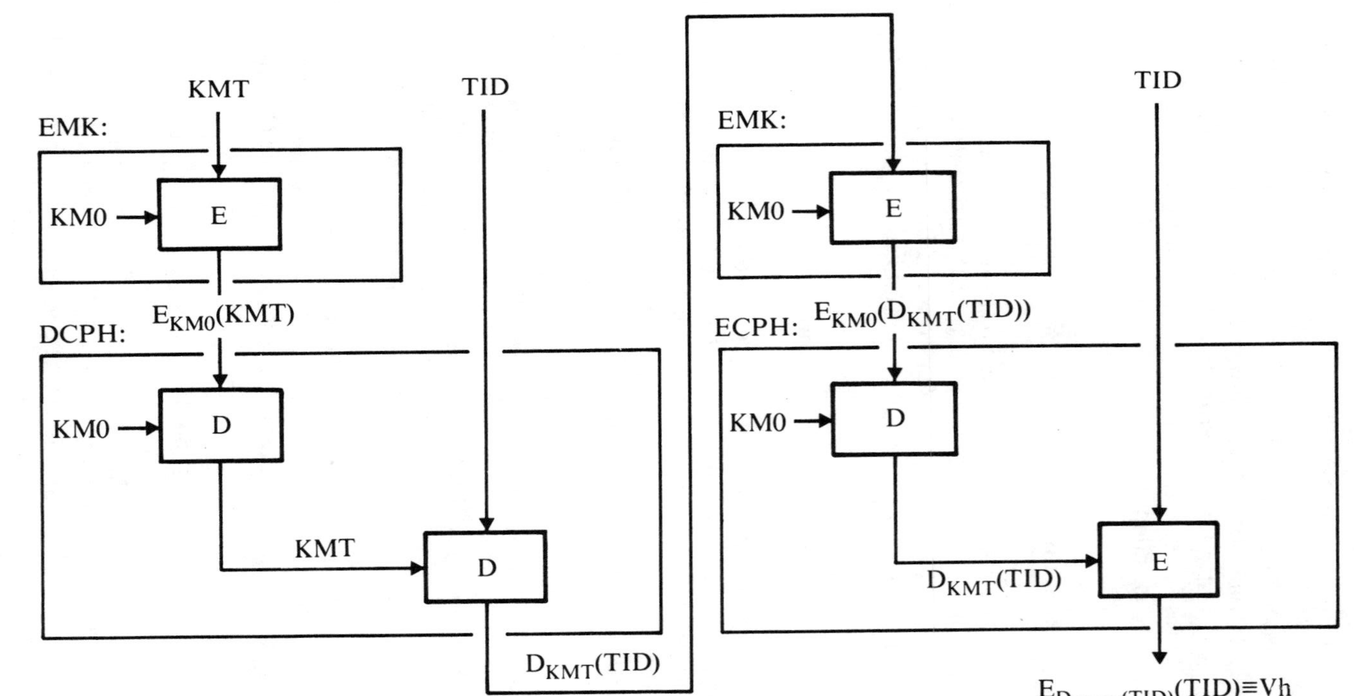

TID = terminal identification number, unique to each terminal in a network.
Vh = validating pattern generated at a host processor.

Figure 6-9. Procedure, at the Host Processor, to Create a Validating Pattern for the Terminal Master Key

$$\text{EMK: } \{D_{KMT}(TID)\} \longrightarrow E_{KM0}(D_{KMT}(TID))$$

$$\text{ECPH: } \{E_{KM0}(D_{KMT}(TID)), TID\} \longrightarrow E_{D_{KMT}(TID)}(TID) = Vh$$

where TID is a terminal identification number unique to each terminal.

The steps to create Vh are shown in block diagram form in Figure 6-9. Later, at the terminal, the *decipher key* (DECK) and *encipher* (ENC) operations are used to produce a similar validating pattern (Vt), as follows:

$$\text{DECK: } \{TID\} \longrightarrow D_{KMT}(TID)$$

$$\text{ENC: } \{TID\} \longrightarrow E_{D_{KMT}(TID)}(TID) = Vt$$

It is assumed here that the terminal can ensure the integrity of TID and that an opponent is not able to cause the terminal to use a value other than TID in the computation of Vt.

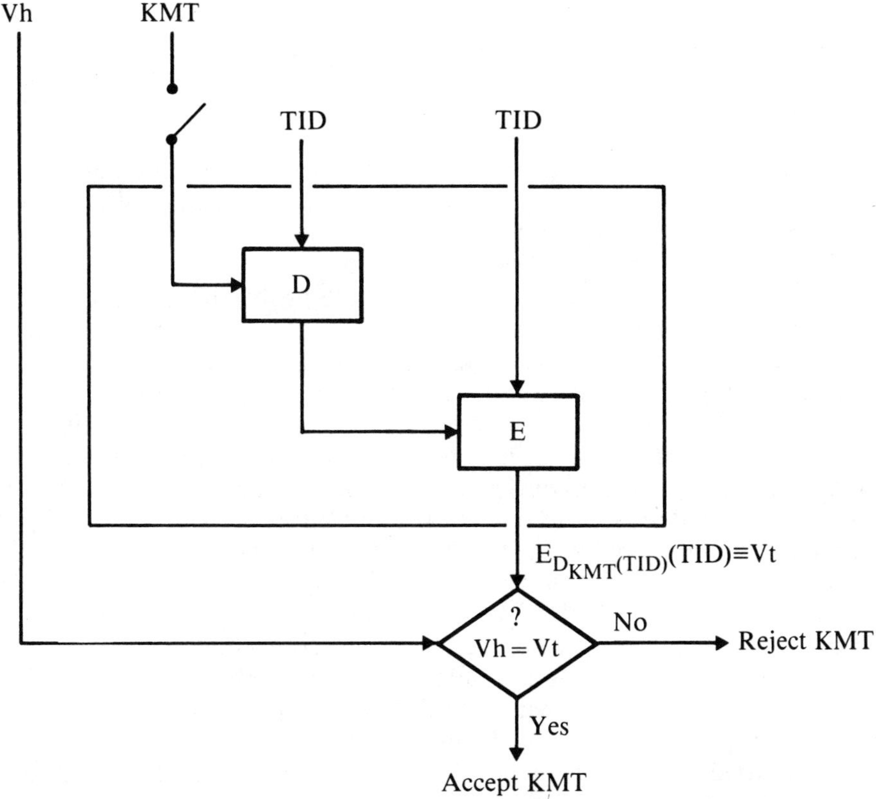

Vh = validating pattern generated at a host processor.
Vt = validating pattern generated at a terminal.
TID = terminal identification number, unique to each terminal in a network.

Figure 6-10. Procedure for Entering and Validating Terminal Master Keys

The person who is authorized to enter KMT at the terminal is given the quantity Vh. As part of the procedure for entering KMT, the terminal will cause the value Vt to be generated and displayed. The operator can determine whether KMT has been entered correctly by comparing Vh with Vt. The steps to create Vt and validate KMT are shown in block diagram form in Figure 6-10.

If Vh is stored in nonvolatile storage at the terminal, frequent checks can be made on the correctness of the terminal master key. Alternatively, Vh could be written down and posted in a conspicuous location at the terminal. A keyboard entry command causing Vt to be generated and displayed would thus allow Vt and Vh to be compared periodically by the terminal operator.

DISTRIBUTION OF CRYPTOGRAPHIC KEYS

Whenever data-encrypting keys (session and file keys) occur outside the cryptographic facility, they are maintained under the encipherment of some key-encrypting key. This allows data-encrypting keys to be routed through the system over paths that are nonsecure. A data-encrypting key can be recovered in a usable form only if the recipient possesses the key-encrypting key under which the data-encrypting key has been encrypted.

Key-encrypting keys are distributed through the system in an altogether different way. One cannot always rely on encryption as a means of protecting the secrecy of these keys, since each node must have at least one key installed initially in clear form. That key must be sent to the node over a path with an acceptable degree of security (i.e., the probability of interception of the key must be very low). One such method is to use a courier, normally the safest and most secure means of transporting keys. Of course, security in this case depends on the reliability of the courier.

Although not necessarily recommended, other means of transmitting keys are by registered mail and by private telephone conversation. These methods are less secure than using a courier because there is a greater chance that an opponent could intercept the key during transmission. The probability of compromise could be reduced, however, by transmitting two or more bit patterns over independent paths and combining them, (e.g., by using an Exclusive-OR operation) at the final destination.

The same approach could be used when entering the key itself. For example, a different bit pattern could be entered into the cryptographic facility by each of several persons. These bits could then be combined within the cryptographic facility to produce the desired key. For the key to be compromised, this protocol would require the collusion of all persons involved in the key entry process.

The procedure for routing keys can be expressed more formally using statistical measures. Let T1, T2, . . . , Tn denote n different bit patterns of 64 bits each, and ϕ a nonsecret function used to produce a cryptographic key (K):

$$K = \phi(T1, T2, \ldots, Tn)$$

For example, ϕ could denote an operation that Exclusive-ORs the bit patterns together, as shown below:

$$K = T1 \oplus T2 \oplus \ldots, \oplus Tn$$

If desired, the technique would permit each of the different bit patterns to be entered into the cryptographic facility by a different person. This, of course, would require that function ϕ be available within the cryptographic facility itself. More likely, the bit patterns would be separately transmitted to a single person, who would in turn combine them using function ϕ and then enter the resulting key into the cryptographic facility.

Let Ai denote the event that bit pattern Ti is transmitted to a designated receiver without being compromised. Note that the complement of Ai ($\overline{Ai}$) denotes the event that Ti is compromised during transmission. Assume, as with the Exclusive-OR operation, that function ϕ is such that T1 through Tn must be compromised in order for the cryptographic key (K) to be compromised. Thus if B represents the event that key K is compromised, then the probability of event B, p(B), can be expressed as follows:

$$p(B) = p(\overline{A1})p(\overline{A1}\,|\,\overline{A2}) \ldots p(\overline{An}\,|\,\overline{A1}, \overline{A2}, \ldots, \overline{An})$$

If the events A1, A2, . . . , An are statistically independent, then p(B) can be expressed as the product of the probabilities;

$$p(B) = p(\overline{A1})p(\overline{A2}) \ldots p(\overline{An})$$

Even though individual values for $p(\overline{A1})$ through $p(\overline{An})$ may not be small enough to justify the transmission of only a single bit pattern, the product of the probabilities may be small enough to be acceptable.

Since assessment of the likelihood that cryptographic keys may become compromised is highly subjective, it is unreasonable to expect that accurate values for the various probabilities in question can ever be obtained. The model is useful mainly to demonstrate the underlying principle involved.

To illustrate this idea, suppose that T1 is sent by registered mail, T2 is sent by telegram, T3 is sent by private conversation, and that K is produced by Exclusive-ORing T1, T2, and T3. Since the bit patterns, T1 through T3, are transmitted via different paths, an assumption of statistical independence ought to hold, in which case, the probability that K is compromised should be the product of the probabilities that T1 is compromised, T2 is compromised, and T3 is compromised. Assuming that the probabilities of the events, p(T1), p(T2), and p(T3), are less than one, it follows that the product of these probabilities is less than any one of the values. Thus, sending the key as T1, T2, and T3 involves less risk than sending the key directly using only one of the paths.

LOST CRYPTOGRAPHIC KEYS

Remember that it is as difficult for the properly authorized user of the system to decrypt data when the key is unknown as it is for the hostile cryptanalyst who never had the key in the first place. Consequently, if for any reason the cryptographic key required to decrypt data should become lost or unknown, the data will not be recoverable. Every effort should be made to adopt a set of administrative procedures and controls that will minimize the probability of losing cryptographic keys.

A copy of all pregenerated key-encrypting keys should be stored in a secure area (e.g., a safe or vault) in the event they are needed for the purpose of backup (see also A Procedure for Authentication of Cryptographic Keys, Chapter 8).

Cryptographic keys may become lost or unknown as a result of hardware malfunction, software error, or human failure. An undetected modification of a cryptographic key stored within the cryptographic system, or failure to use the proper key in the cryptographic facility may cause ciphering operations to proceed using an unknown key. In communication security, two nodes may attempt to communicate using different session keys, or in file security, stored data may be enciphered under a key that is different from that used for recovery.

A simple handshaking procedure at session initiation ensures that both communicants are using the same session key. Message-authentication procedures can also be used to test that plaintext has been recovered with a proper key. Authentication techniques based upon the host master key permit keys to be validated prior to their use. As an extra measure, at the time data are enciphered they could also be deciphered to make sure that recovery is possible. (See Authentication Techniques Using Cryptography, Chapter 8.)

RECOVERY TECHNIQUES

In situations where a cryptographic key will not properly recover plaintext from ciphertext, it may still be possible to decipher the data using techniques for recovery. The underlying principle is that even though the exact key used to encipher the data is not known, one may still be able, using trial and error, to search the key space in a preferred order of likely candidates. If the list of likely candidates is small enough, then such a search may be successful.

Any error by a human, a machine, or software that causes a cryptographic key, K, to be changed to an incorrect key, K′, can be thought of as a function, ϕ, which maps the space of possible keys to itself. Hence recovery can be handled as a two-step procedure: (1) all available information concerning the nature of the error is used to compute a list of functions, $\phi 1$, $\phi 2$, . . . , ϕn, identifying the most probable candidates, $\phi 1(K)$, $\phi 2(K)$, . . . , $\phi n(K)$, for the incorrect key, K′, and (2) the data are then decrypted with each of these candidate keys.

In the present discussion, it is assumed that an incorrect key, K′, is used to encipher data and that the correct key, K, is used to recover the data (Figure 6-11). Alternatively, it may happen that the plaintext is enciphered with the correct key, K, but recovery is later attempted using a corrupted key, K′. In that case, a trial key is in the set of keys to be searched, provided that one of the functions, $\phi 1$, $\phi 2$, . . . , ϕn, maps it to K′.

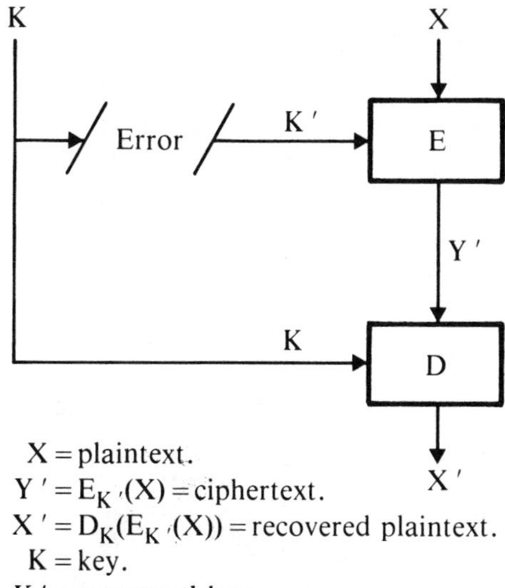

X = plaintext.
$Y' = E_{K'}(X)$ = ciphertext.
$X' = D_K(E_{K'}(X))$ = recovered plaintext.
K = key.
K' = corrupted key.

Figure 6-11. Encipherment Using a Corrupted Key and Decipherment Using the Correct Key

Consider the example of a data file enciphered with a key that in turn is written down on a slip of paper (as 16 hexadecimal digits) and stored in a vault. It is discovered later that the key will not decipher the data. Furthermore, it is suspected that an error occurred in recording the key. Since human error will most likely involve only one, two, or at most, three digits (the occurrence of multiple errors is small) recovery could be attempted by changing each digit, or combination of digits, in the incorrect key to its other possible values and then attempting to decipher and file with each of the keys. If this method does not succeed, it means that more digits were in error. Searching additional keys may be uneconomical, since many trials would be required.

SUMMARY

In connection with the key management scheme discussed in Chapters 4 and 5, two kinds of keys have been described: data-encrypting keys, which protect either data in transit (primary communication keys or session keys) or stored data (primary file keys or file keys); and key-encrypting keys, which encipher other keys—for example, host master keys, secondary communication keys (of which the terminal master key is a special case), and secondary file keys.

Generally speaking, the best method for generating a given class of cryptographic keys depends on the expected number of each type of key that will be needed and the time when the keys will be used. In many cases, the keys can be created dynamically (on demand), but sometimes they are required ahead of time in order to initialize the system.

The host master key is generated by a random process such as tossing coins or throwing dice. Human involvement to that extent is reasonable in the process of generating keys because only one master key is required for each host processor, and the master key is likely to remain unchanged for a relatively long time. Since the master key protects all other keys stored at the host processor, special care should be taken to ensure that it is generated and installed in the cryptographic facility in a secure manner.

It is reasonable to anticipate that the total number of key-encrypting keys (excluding the host master key) may be large enough to warrant mechanical (nonhuman) generation procedures. The desired keys can be produced using the DES algorithm as a generator of pseudo-random numbers. The seed values used in this procedure are generated by the user, employing a random process similar to that used in generating the host master key. Since the key-encrypting keys are used in initializing the cryptographic system, they must be generated ahead of time. This can be accomplished under secure conditions using a computer.

Data-encrypting keys are also required in large numbers (one for each session and file using encryption), but they need not be generated until specifically requested (i.e., until they are needed to protect a communications session or stored data). Hence data-encrypting keys either could be generated ahead of time and stored in table form until needed, or they could be generated dynamically (on demand). Disadvantages in generating them ahead of time are that the keys would be exposed longer to possible compromise by an opponent, and they would require additional storage. One approach for dynamically generating data-encrypting keys is to make use of the randomness associated with the many users and processes normally active on the system at any one time.

Among the more important principles to be followed in key generation is that the compromise of one or more keys should not make it possible for any of the remaining keys to be deduced. With regard to key distribution, it was shown that security can be increased whenever two or more bit patterns of 64 bits are transmitted over different paths and combined at the final destination. To enhance the security of key installation, it is suggested that two different related values, the key and a function of the key, be entered into the cryptographic facility. Any errors that occur in both values will be statistically independent, so the likelihood of an undetected error (i.e., the probability that a wrong key will be installed) will be greatly reduced.

REFERENCES

1. Matyas, S. M. and Meyer, C. H., "Generation, Distribution, and Installation of Cryptographic Keys," *IBM Systems Journal,* **17**, No. 2, 126–137 (1978).
2. The RAND Corporation, *A Million Random Digits With 100,000 Normal Deviates,* Free Press, Glencoe, IL, 1955.
3. Federal Standard 1027, *Telecommunications: General Security Requirements for Equipment Using the Data Encryption Standard,* General Services Administration, Washington, D.C. (April 14, 1982).

CHAPTER SEVEN

Incorporation of Cryptography into a Communications Architecture[1]

Today's versatile, powerful, and complex computer networks have evolved from a modest beginning in the 1950s when users first accessed computer resources from remote terminals. As the evolution proceeded, so did attempts to replace ad hoc network designs with systematic approaches based on defined parameters [2–6].

Fundamental to this approach is a *protocol* (set of agreements) which presents a basis for controlling information transfer within a communications network. Collectively, such protocols, referred to as a *communications architecture*, put the parties served by a network into communication with each other. One architectural approach, IBM's Systems Network Architecture (SNA) [2, 3], is used here to show how cryptography can be incorporated into a communications network. The specifics, discussed here to illustrate how the SNA architecture can be structured to support cryptography, lead to broader concepts which are applicable to other architectures.

In SNA terminology, application programs and terminal devices equate to logical units (LUs). Data transfer between two LUs may occur after a logical connection, or *session*, has been established [4]. Cryptography can be specified as a session parameter at the time a session is established. When this method of protection is in effect, data are enciphered by the originating LU and deciphered only by the destination LU; thus end-to-end protection is achieved (see Chapter 4).

Three architectural levels of cryptography are defined within SNA: session, end user, and private. In *session-level cryptography*, SNA protocols are used by the system to manage cryptography during a session between communicating LUs. In *end-user cryptography*, SNA protocols are used by the system for key distribution, but the end user provides his own rules and protocols regarding the use of cryptography. In *private cryptography*, key selection and distribution, as well as management of the use of cryptography, is performed by the end user according to his own rules and protocols. Because, in this latter case, the use of cryptography is known only to the end user and not to the system, it is transparent to and not in conflict with SNA.

The basic information element that flows between LUs during the LU-LU

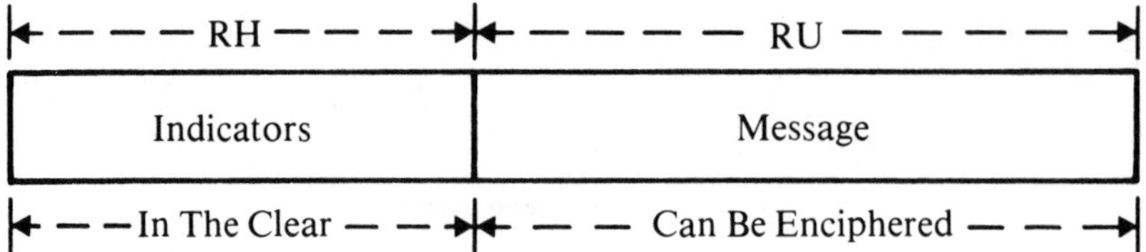

RH - Request/Response Header (contains RU descriptor flags)
RU - Request/Response Unit

Figure 7-1. RH/RU Relationship

session is a request/response unit (RU). It contains either user data or control information (Figure 7-1). The RU is preceded by a request/response header (RH). Only a data request unit is enciphered; the RH remains in the clear. A bit in the RH indicates that the RU contains enciphered data.

The installation, through a definition process, specifies each LU's cryptographic capability, that is whether the LU is equipped with or has access to a cryptographic facility (see The Cryptographic Facility, Chapter 4). Furthermore, particular LUs may be declared secure components, thus making cryptography mandatory for every session in which they participate. The terminal operator may, via the LOGON procedure, select cryptography as a session option. An application program, as part of the OPEN process of a system teleprocessing access method, such as IBM's ACF/VTAM (advanced communication function/virtual telecommunications access method), may request the use of cryptography for the pending session (Figure 7-2). Once cryptography is selected for communicating LUs, it cannot be disabled for the duration of the session.

Three levels of session cryptography are defined: (1) selected cryptography in a transparent mode of operation, (2) selected cryptography in a non-transparent or application-directed mode of operation, and (3) mandatory cryptography.

Transparent cryptography results when the selection of cryptography is unknown to the participating end users. Cryptography may be specified by the installation, perhaps based upon the physical characteristics and not necessarily the logical characteristics of an LU. If selected, cryptographic services are provided by the system, transparent to the end users.

Application-directed cryptography results when the end user makes a specific request for the use of cryptography during a given session. An application program may select which outbound messages are to be enciphered and which are not. Similarly, by using the indicator in the RH, inbound messages can be identified as being enciphered, thus requiring decipherment before being processed.

Mandatory cryptography is a subset of transparent cryptography. As the name implies, this level requires both participating LUs to encipher all outbound messages and to decipher all inbound messages. In this case, the indicator bit in the RH is ignored (as to what or what not to decipher), although it may continue to be set to maintain consistency with other system services.

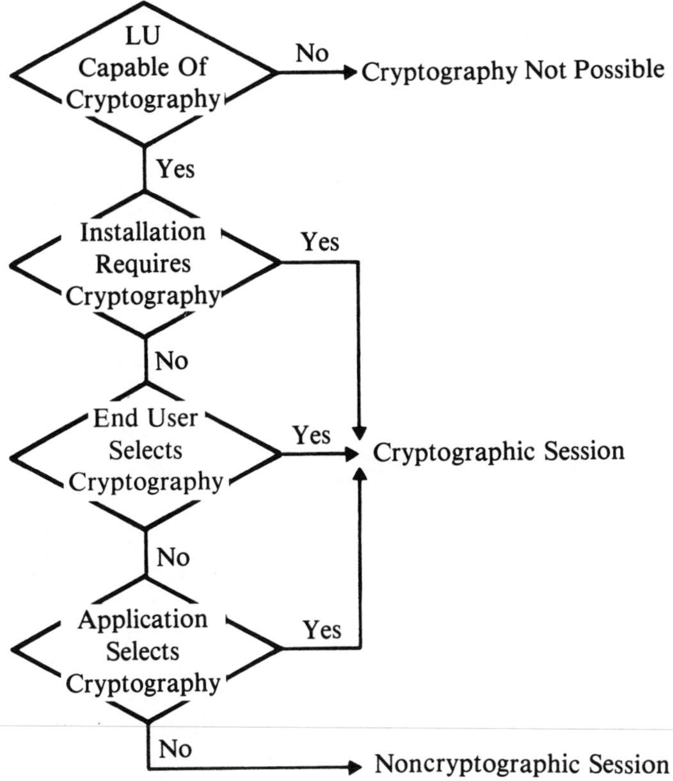

Figure 7-2. Cryptography Selection Process

SESSION-LEVEL CRYPTOGRAPHY IN A SINGLE-DOMAIN NETWORK

Transparent Mode of Operation

SNA provides a set of commands to allow LUs within the communications network to specify and agree on the manner in which the orderly transfer of information from one LU to another will be accomplished. The addition of cryptography, as a means of protecting information from disclosure during its passage through the network, affects the SNA communication network from the standpoint of selection, distribution, and verification of the function. The SNA commands affected by the implementation of communication security will be described.

Figure 7-3 provides a logical view of both commands significant to session initiation, and the network elements between which they flow. The notation **PLU** (primary logical unit) and **SLU** (secondary logical unit) is used because the clarifiers secondary and primary aid in establishing the relationship between the two nodes [3].

Typically, in a terminal-to-application program communications session, the application is the PLU and the terminal (with an installed master key,

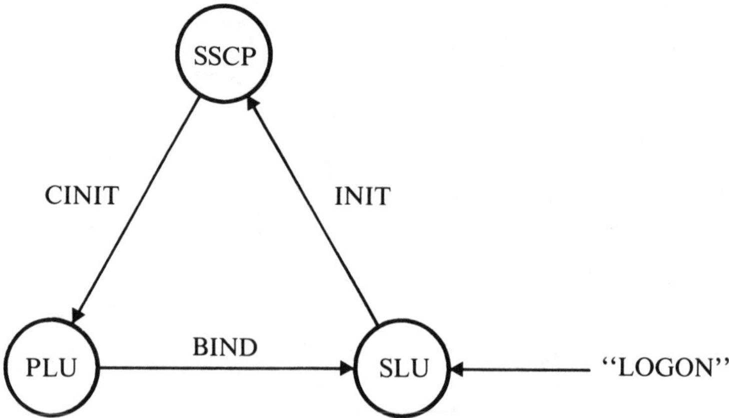

Figure 7-3. SNA Session Initiation Command Flow

KMT) is the SLU. The session initiation process begins with the receipt of an INITIATE (INIT) command at the system services control point **(SSCP)**. The SSCP resides in a host node and is the manager of all sessions between communicating LUs within its *domain* of control. The INIT command is typically generated as the result of a LOGON request (to establish contact with the system) entered at an SLU. An INIT command can also result from actions taken by the host operator or host application programs.

The SSCP resides in a host processor and has available to it tables, built from definition parameters, which completely describe the network or portion of the network that it manages (i.e., the domain of the SSCP). From these tables, the SSCP can determine if cryptography is supported by an LU. Additionally, from the same tables or from LOGON parameters, the SSCP determines if the cryptography function is required or requested for the session corresponding to the INIT. (Refer to Figure 7-2 for clarification of SSCP actions during session initiation.) An error condition occurs if one or both of the candidate LUs cannot support a requested function.

If the use of cryptography is possible, the SSCP obtains a randomly generated number via GENKEY (see Key Management Macro Instructions, Chapter 4), which it defines to be the session key enciphered under the host master key (i.e., in the form $E_{KM0}(KS)$). $E_{KM0}(KS)$ is then inserted in the appropriate field of the CONTROL INITIATE (CINIT) command. If the SLU happens to be a terminal device, then the session key is additionally enciphered under the terminal master key ($E_{KMT}(KS)$) and this quantity is then inserted in the BIND image (which consists of a number of fields in the CINIT command). (The BIND image contains information which specifies the characteristics of the session when established.)

The SSCP forwards the CINIT command to the specified PLU, thus indicating to the PLU that there is a request for a session to be established with an SLU. A PLU, as implemented in SNA, is a host-resident application program. An SLU may be another host-resident application program, or an LU residing in a control unit or terminal.

Upon receipt of CINIT, the PLU can either accept or reject the invitation to go into session with the SLU, regardless of the cryptography level specified. When the PLU accepts, implying also that it acknowledges the use of cryptography, it extracts the session key in the form $E_{KM0}(KS)$ from CINIT and saves it for later use. The PLU uses this quantity for ciphering data which is communicated during the session. The PLU converts the BIND image into a BIND command. The BIND command is then transmitted to the SLU. Upon receipt of BIND, the SLU (if it accepts BIND) extracts from it the quantity $E_{KMT}(KS)$, saving it for later use in the session. The result of this dialogue is that the two participating LUs are each provided with a copy of an identical session key in a form suitable for use with their respective cryptographic facilities.

One additional step is required to complete the process of session initiation (Figure 7-4).[2] It involves an action on the part of the SLU to verify that the PLU has an identical copy of the session key, and that both the PLU and SLU have the ability to encipher and decipher data correctly. If cryptography is specified, a randomly chosen 64-bit number (N) enciphered under the session key (KS) is appended to the positive BIND response. (Note that by SNA protocol, the SLU is required to respond to the BIND command positively if in agreement, negatively if not.) Representing N as the concatenation of two 32-bit quantities, N1 and N2, the resulting quantity, $E_{KS}(N1, N2)$, is thus returned to the PLU in the BIND response.

For those sessions bound using cryptography, the PLU is required to initiate an additional command, the CRYPTO VERIFICATION (CRV) command. The CRV command is used to send the quantity $E_{KS}(\overline{N1}, N2)$ to the SLU, where $\overline{N1}$ denotes the complement of N1. The PLU produces this quantity

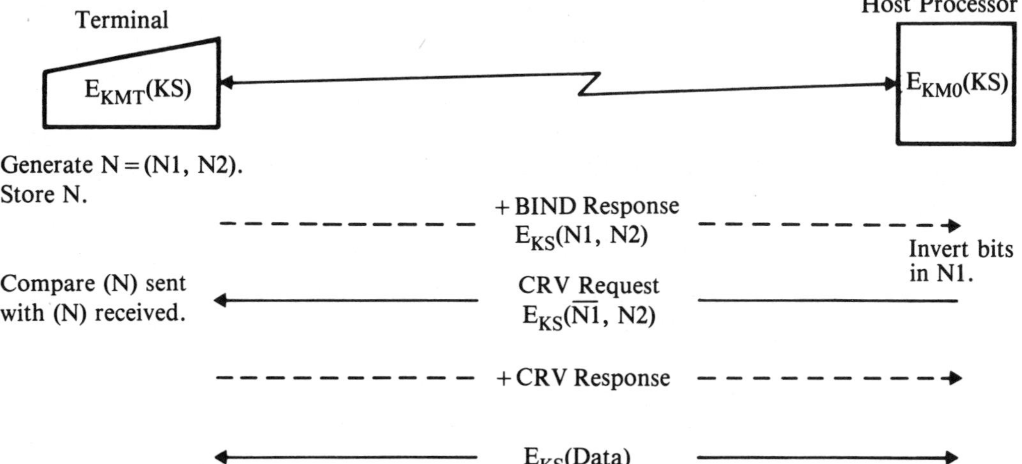

Figure 7-4. Cryptographic Verification Procedure for Session Keys

[2] In this and all subsequent figures, SNA commands are denoted by solid arrows (——→) and responses by broken arrows (- - -→).

by deciphering $E_{KS}(N1, N2)$, which it received from the SLU in the BIND response, inverting N1, and enciphering $(\overline{N1}, N2)$. The quantity $E_{KS}(\overline{N1}, N2)$ is then sent to the SLU (via CRV). Upon receipt of the CRV, the SLU deciphers $E_{KS}(\overline{N1}, N2)$, inverts $\overline{N1}$, and compares the result (N1, N2) with the random number (N) that it originally sent to the PLU in the BIND response. If equal, the SLU responds positively to the CRV (completing the session initiation procedure), and messages may now flow between the two bound LUs, within the constraints of SNA and subject to the agreed upon session cryptographic protocol. If unequal, the SLU overwrites the stored copy of the session key and responds negatively to the CRV. This action then causes the PLU to terminate the session.

Besides verifying that the SLU and PLU have identical session keys and that both LUs can correctly encipher and decipher data, the described handshaking procedure prevents an attack known as the midnight attack, where the data from an entire session is intercepted, recorded, and then later played back into the terminal. (For a more detailed analysis of handshaking, see Authentication Techniques Using Cryptography, Chapter 8.)

Furthermore, random number N is subsequently used by the LUs in session as the initial chaining value (ICV) required with block chaining (see Communication Security and File Security Using Cryptography, Chapter 4). Note that SNA specifies block chaining with ciphertext feedback as the default mode of data encryption.

Figure 7-5 illustrates the session concept in a single domain network where cryptography has not been implemented. Figures 7-6 and 7-7 illustrate session-level cryptography in a single-domain network where the cryptographic system operates in a transparent mode and employs system managed keys (KMTs and KSs).[3]

By employing system keys, the architecture discussed so far allows cryptography to be used in a manner that is transparent to both terminal users and application programs. If personal keys (KPs) are employed, cryptography can still be used in a manner that is transparent to application programs (by treating KP as a master key of a terminal), but requires an action on the part of the user to install the key. For example, KP could be stored on a magnetic stripe card and entered into the terminal during session initiation. A *write master key* operation would then allow KP to be loaded as the terminal's master key.

In this case, KP is used as a key-encrypting key, and session keys are thus sent to the terminal in the form $E_{KP}(KS)$, as shown in Figure 7-8. Except for the fact that KP is identified by the user's ID, whereas KMT was identified by the terminal's ID, the basic protocol has not changed.

[3] The following legend applies to this and all subsequent figures: GENKEY (Generate Key) produces a session key (KS) enciphered under the host master key (KM0) and transforms it to encipherment under the appropriate secondary communication key(s) (KMT, KNC). RETKEY (Retrieve Key) transforms a session key (KS) from encipherment under a secondary communication key (KNC) to encipherment under the host master key (KM0). CIPHER performs data enciphering and data deciphering on behalf of an application program residing in the host. CKDS (Cryptographic Key Data Set) denotes a table of enciphered keys.

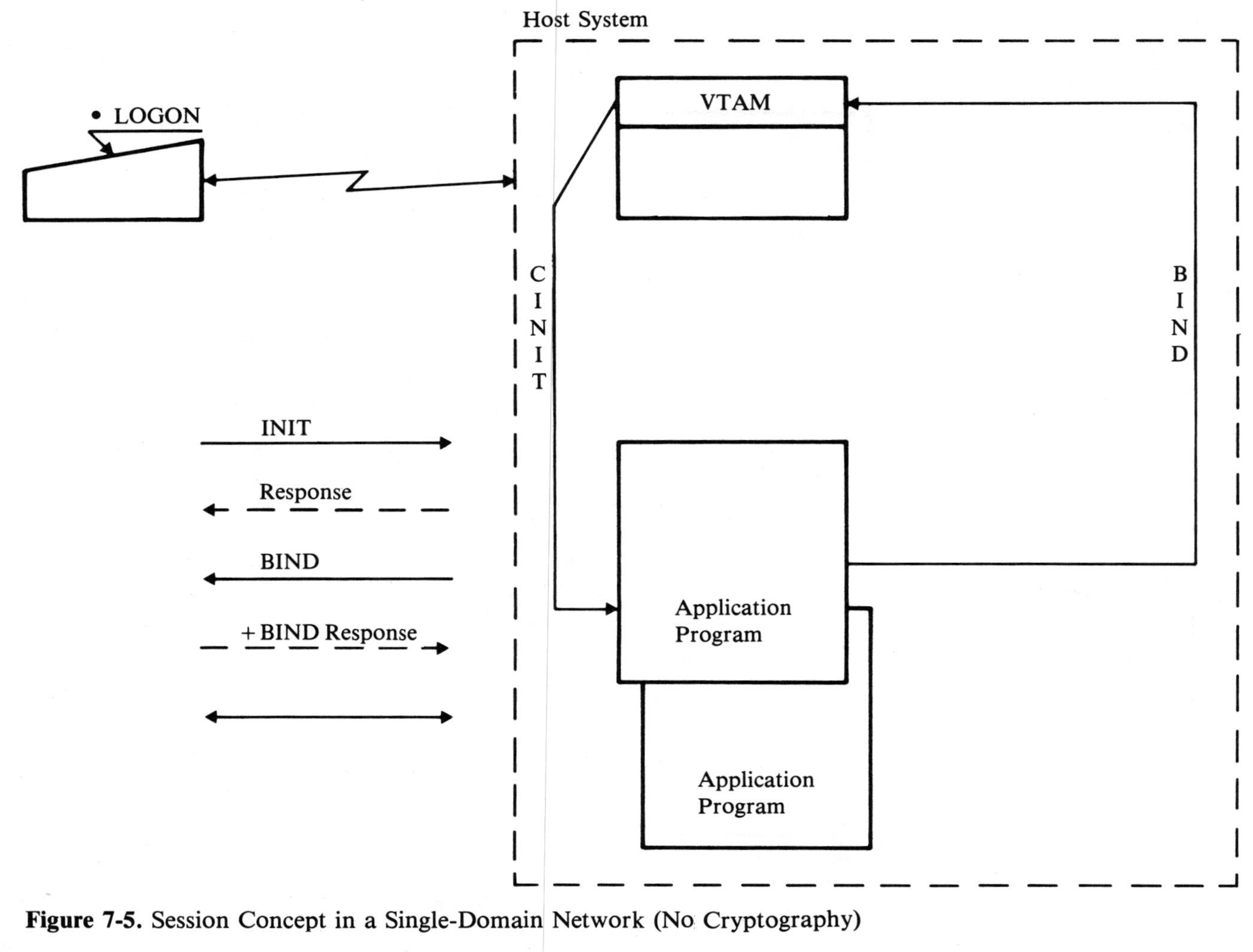

Figure 7-5. Session Concept in a Single-Domain Network (No Cryptography)

Note: ● denotes cryptographic facility in this and subsequent figures.

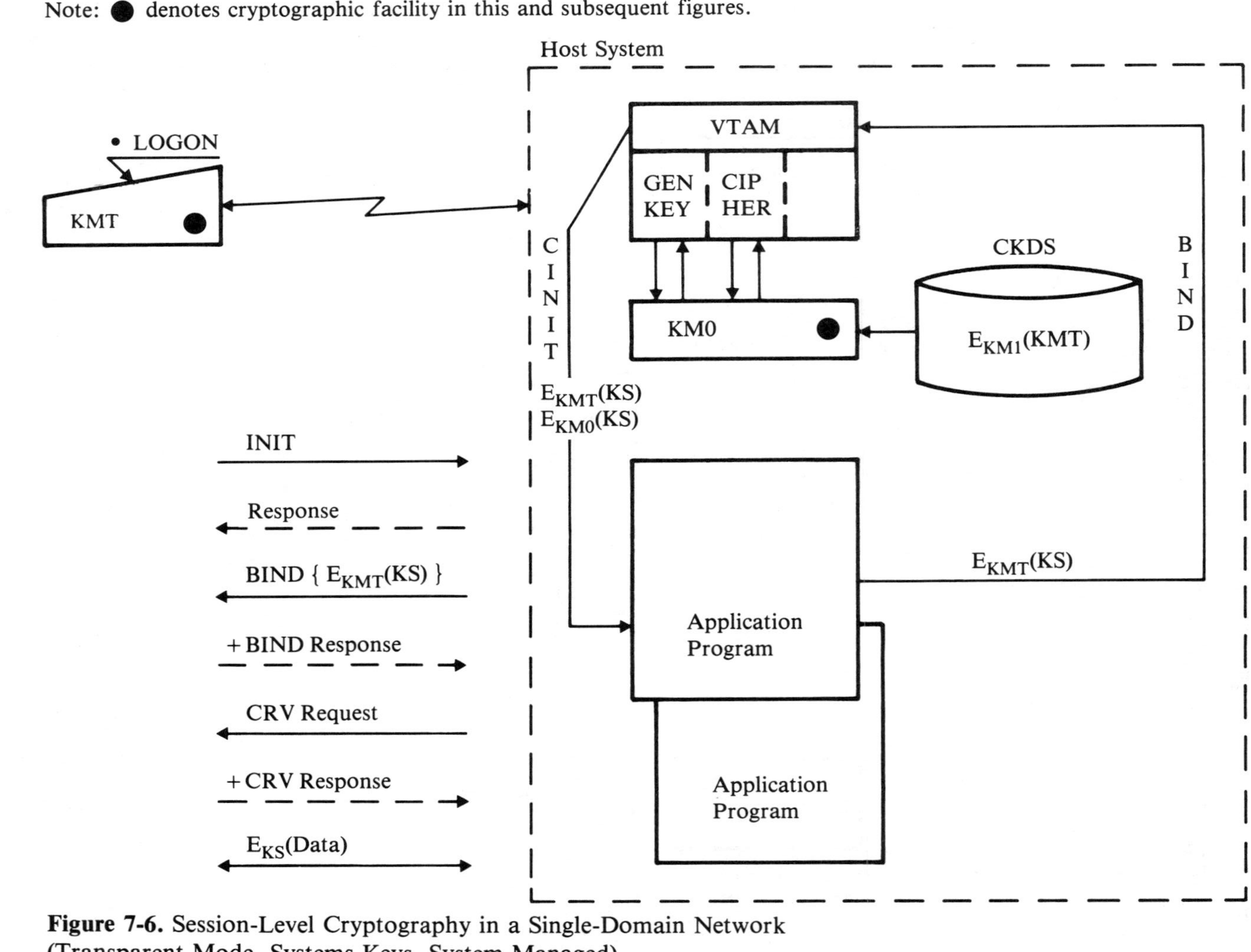

Figure 7-6. Session-Level Cryptography in a Single-Domain Network (Transparent Mode, Systems Keys, System Managed)

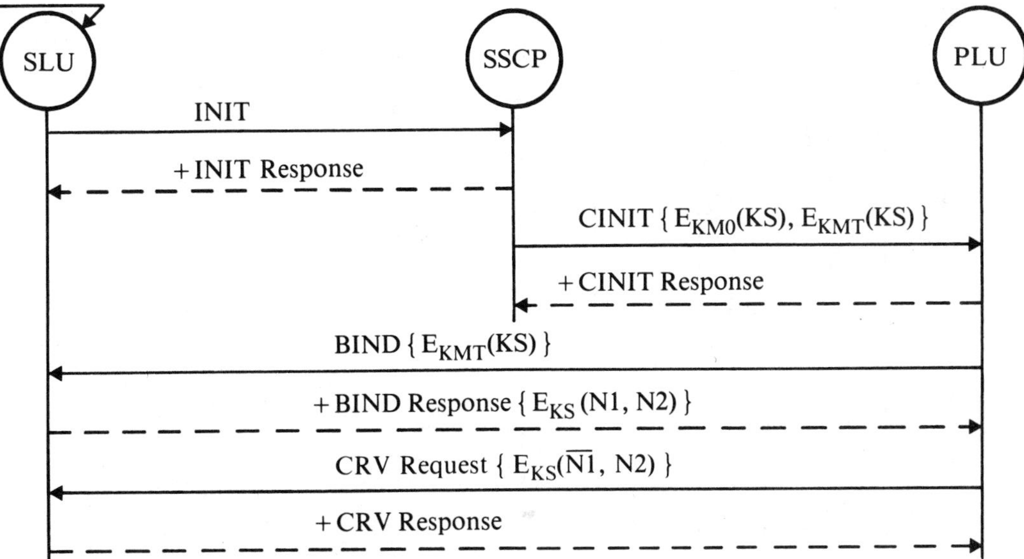

Figure 7-7. Session-Level Cryptography in a Single-Domain Network (SNA Command Flow, Transparent Mode)

Nontransparent Mode of Operation

In this mode, requests for cryptographic services originate with an application program instead of a system routine, and positive action is required on the part of the terminal user to load a personal key in the terminal (Figure 7-9). KP is entered in the terminal at session initiation, and a *write master key* operation is used to load it as the terminal's master key. Session keys are thus sent to the terminal in the form E_{KP}(KS).

A private protocol can be established between the terminal and application program by using the private bit in BIND (provided for this purpose by SNA). But to process the BIND properly, the terminal must be programmable (i.e., the user must be able to program for private cryptography).

In the described protocol, key distribution is accomplished with BIND, but there is no CRV issued. Keys are managed by the application program, not the system, and if handshaking is desired it must be provided by the private protocol.

PRIVATE CRYPTOGRAPHY IN A SINGLE-DOMAIN NETWORK

If a personal key (KP) is used to encipher and decipher data instead of a session key (KS), then *private cryptography* must be used rather than session-level cryptography. Although this mode of operation is not defined by SNA, neither is it precluded. What is needed is a means of synchronization similar to that provided by session-level cryptography (key selection, key generation, cryptography selection mechanism, etc.) that has been agreed to and imple-

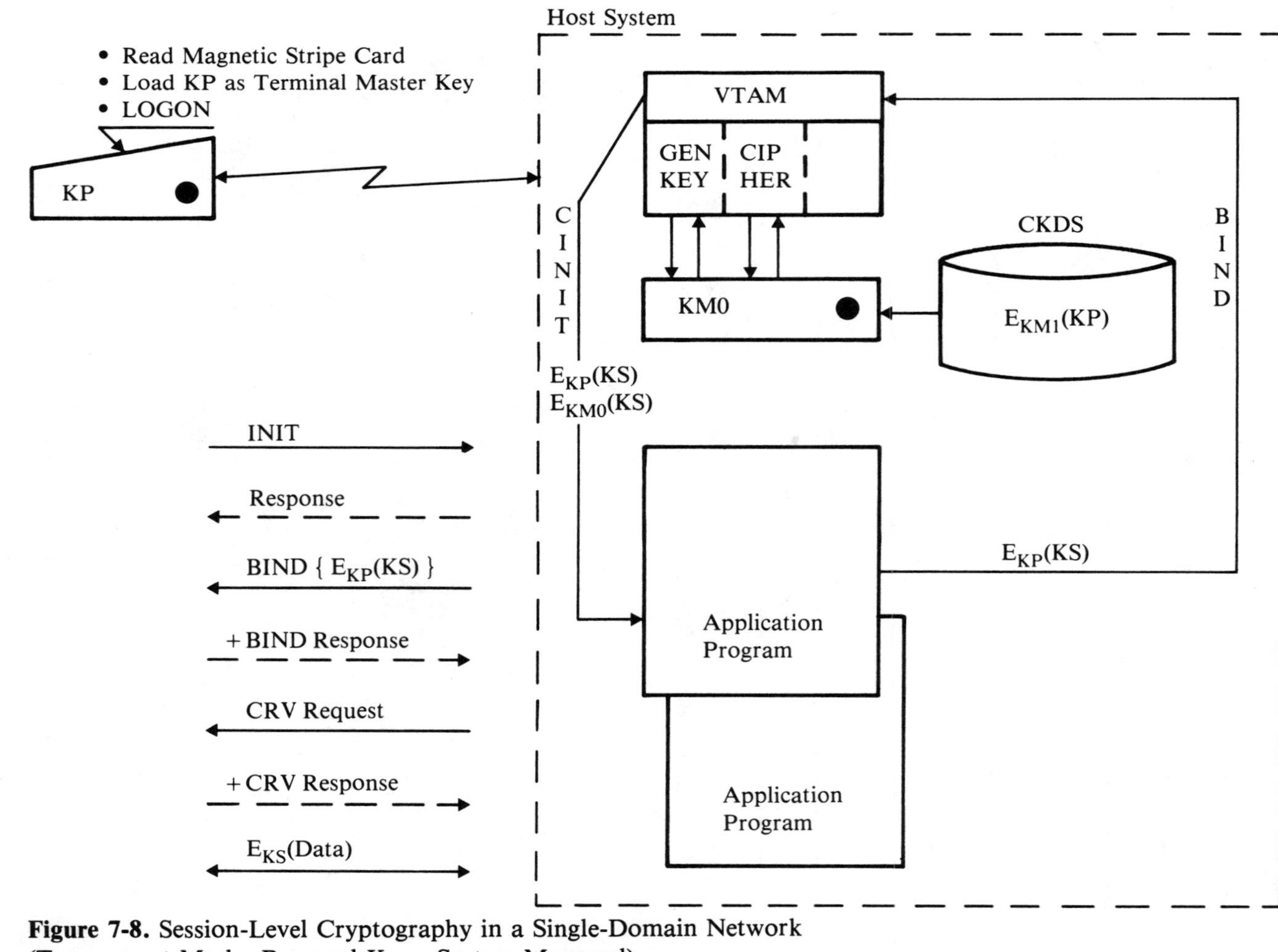

Figure 7-8. Session-Level Cryptography in a Single-Domain Network (Transparent Mode, Personal Keys, System Managed)

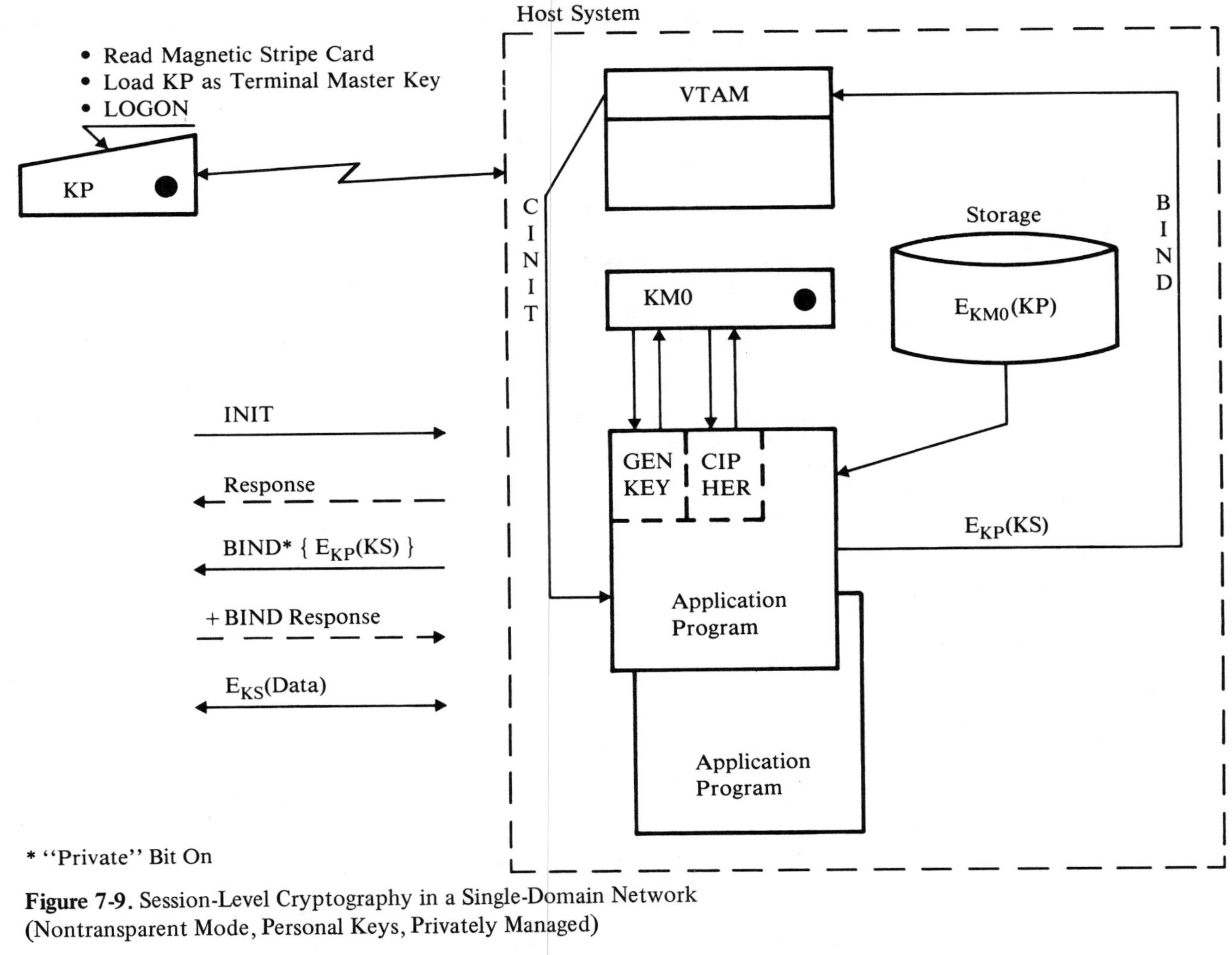

* ''Private'' Bit On

Figure 7-9. Session-Level Cryptography in a Single-Domain Network (Nontransparent Mode, Personal Keys, Privately Managed)

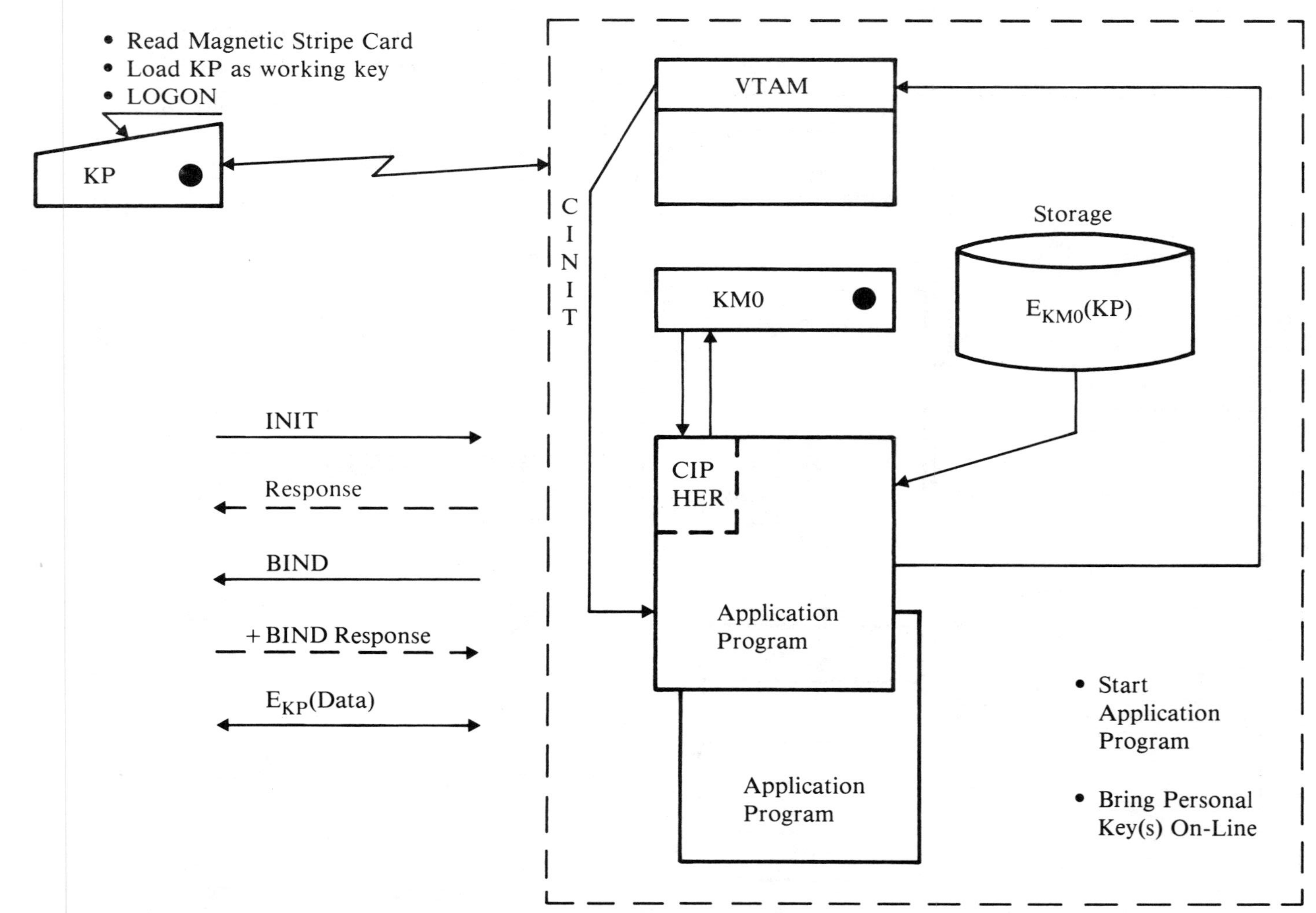

Figure 7-10. Private Cryptography in a Single-Domain Network (Personal Keys, Privately Managed)

mented by the communicants in advance (i.e., the nature of the *private protocol must be defined*).

With private cryptography (Figure 7-10), KP is entered in the terminal at session initiation, and a *load key direct* (LKD) operation is used to transfer it to the terminal's working key storage. KP can then be directly used to encipher and decipher data with the ENC and DEC operations.

At the host, KP is maintained enciphered under the host master key (KM0). In this form, the personal key can be directly used in an *encipher data* (ECPH) or *decipher data* (DCPH) operation. But because the DCPH operation is available to any authorized user of the system, anyone having *access* to KP can decipher data. Thus data security is enhanced if KP is stored off-line and entered as an input parameter only when the using application is executed.

Table 7-1 gives a brief overview of the possible implementations using system managed keys and personal keys.

Approach	Secondary Communication Key	Data-Encrypting Key	Storage of Key at Host
Fig. 7-6	Terminal Master Key (KMT)	Session Key (KS)	E_{KM1}(KMT) Stored On-Line
Fig. 7-8	Personal Key (KP)	Session Key (KS)	E_{KM1}(KP) Stored On-Line
Fig. 7-9	Personal Key (KP)	Session Key (KS)	E_{KM1}(KP) Stored On-Line
Fig. 7-10	None	Personal Key (KP)	E_{KM0}(KP) Typically Stored Off-Line

Table 7-1. Summary of Approaches Using System Managed Keys and Personal Keys

SESSION-LEVEL CRYPTOGRAPHY IN A MULTIDOMAIN NETWORK

The addition of another domain managed by another host requires additional commands to flow in the session initiation process. Figure 7-11 describes the multidomain case. Note that the difference between the multidomain case and the single-domain case is the addition of a cross-domain link. It is over this link that SNA supports a special session known as the *cross-domain session*. The cross-domain session plays an important role in establishing session-level cryptography between two LUs residing in different domains.

As in the single-domain case, the process might begin with the receipt of an INIT command at the SSCP logically owning the SLU. Again, this is typi-

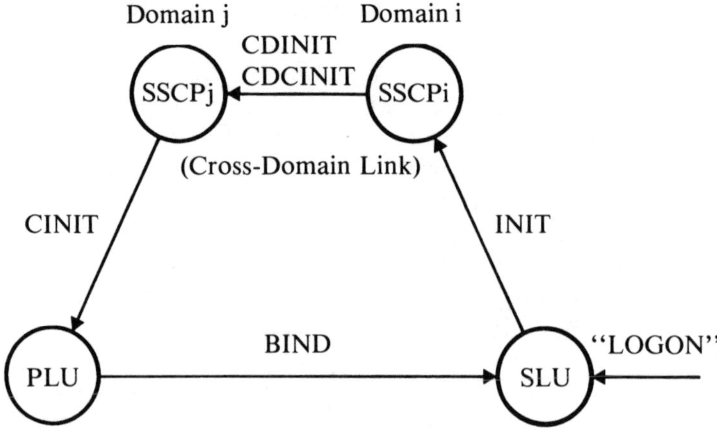

Figure 7-11. SNA Session Initiation Command Flow in a Multi-Domain Network

cally the result of a LOGON sequence entered at a terminal. The PLU (via its SSCP) may also request a session with an SLU. If the SSCP receiving the INIT determines that the requested LU is not in the immediate domain, it initiates cross-domain communication with the appropriate owning SSCP.

The CROSS-DOMAIN INITIATE (CDINIT) command is sent between SSCPs to indicate that an LU in the sender's domain wishes to establish a session with an LU in the receiver's domain. Transmission of CDINIT and its response allows each SSCP to define completely the communicating LUs. The protocol permits session requests to originate in the domain of either LU. No extension to CDINIT is required for cryptography.

A positive acknowledgment to CDINIT results in the creation and transmittal of the CROSS-DOMAIN CONTROL INITIATE (CDCINIT) command. It is through this command that the session key, enciphered under a secondary communication key (KNC), is passed from one domain to another. (SNA defines this key as a *cross-domain key*). In addition to enciphering KS under the cross-domain key, the SSCP must also encipher KS under the SLU's key. This is because the SLU's key is known only to its owning SSCP, and the SSCP therefore is responsible for managing session key initialization. The SLU's key is either a terminal master key (KMT), if the SLU is a terminal, or a special secondary communication key called a *node application key* (KNA), if the SLU is a host application program. (For the distinction between KMT and KNA, see Application Program-to-Application Program Cryptography.) In either case, the session key (KS) is enciphered under the SLU's key and then placed in the BIND image. Both KS (enciphered under the cross-domain key) and the BIND image are included in the CDCINIT command.

The receiving SSCP extracts from CDCINIT the value of KS which was previously enciphered under the cross-domain key. KS is then reenciphered via a RETKEY macro instruction (see Key Management Macro Instructions, Chapter 4) under the host master key of the SSCP, and the result is placed

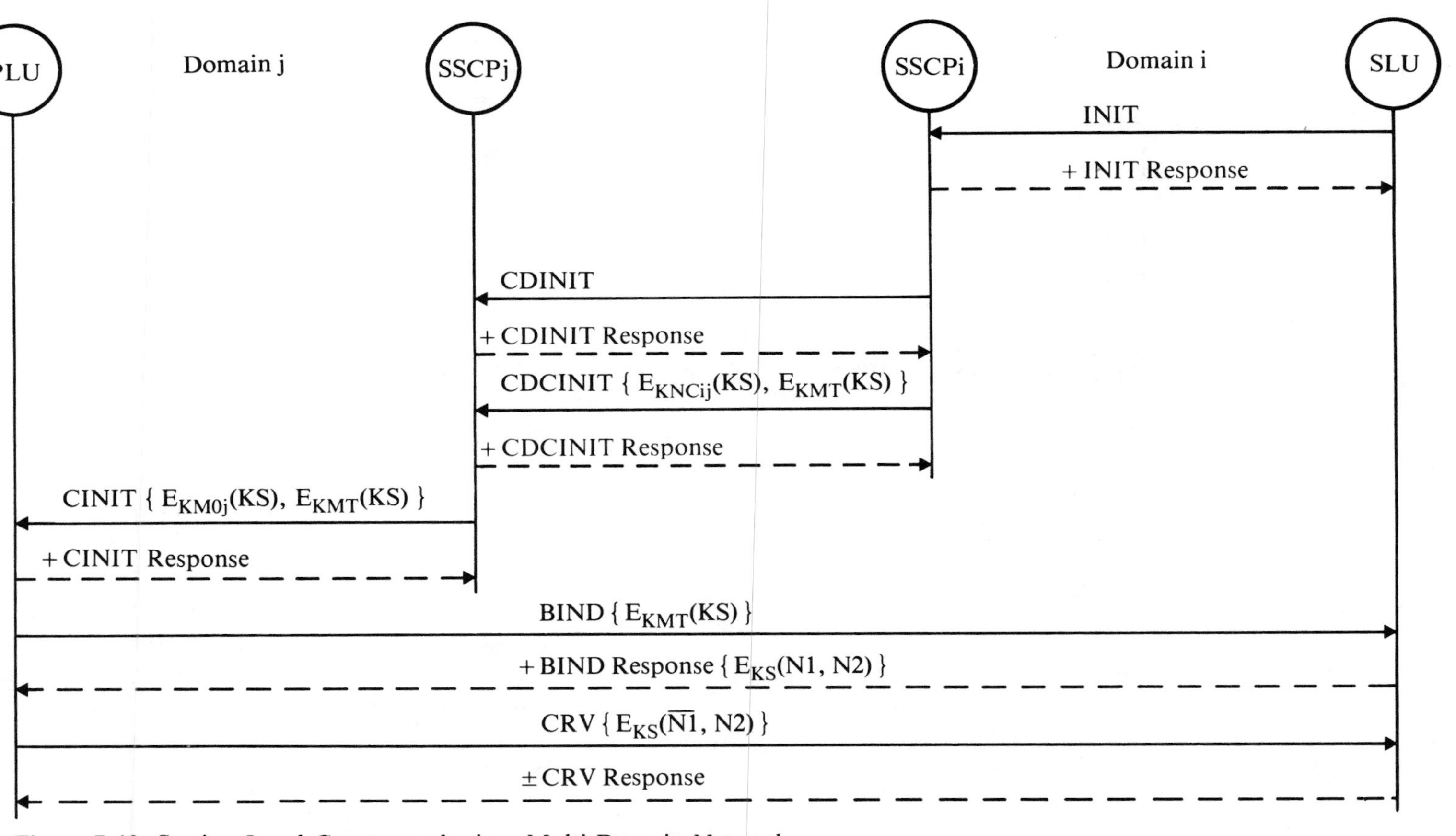

Figure 7-12. Session-Level Cryptography in a Multi-Domain Network (SNA Command Flow, Transparent Mode)

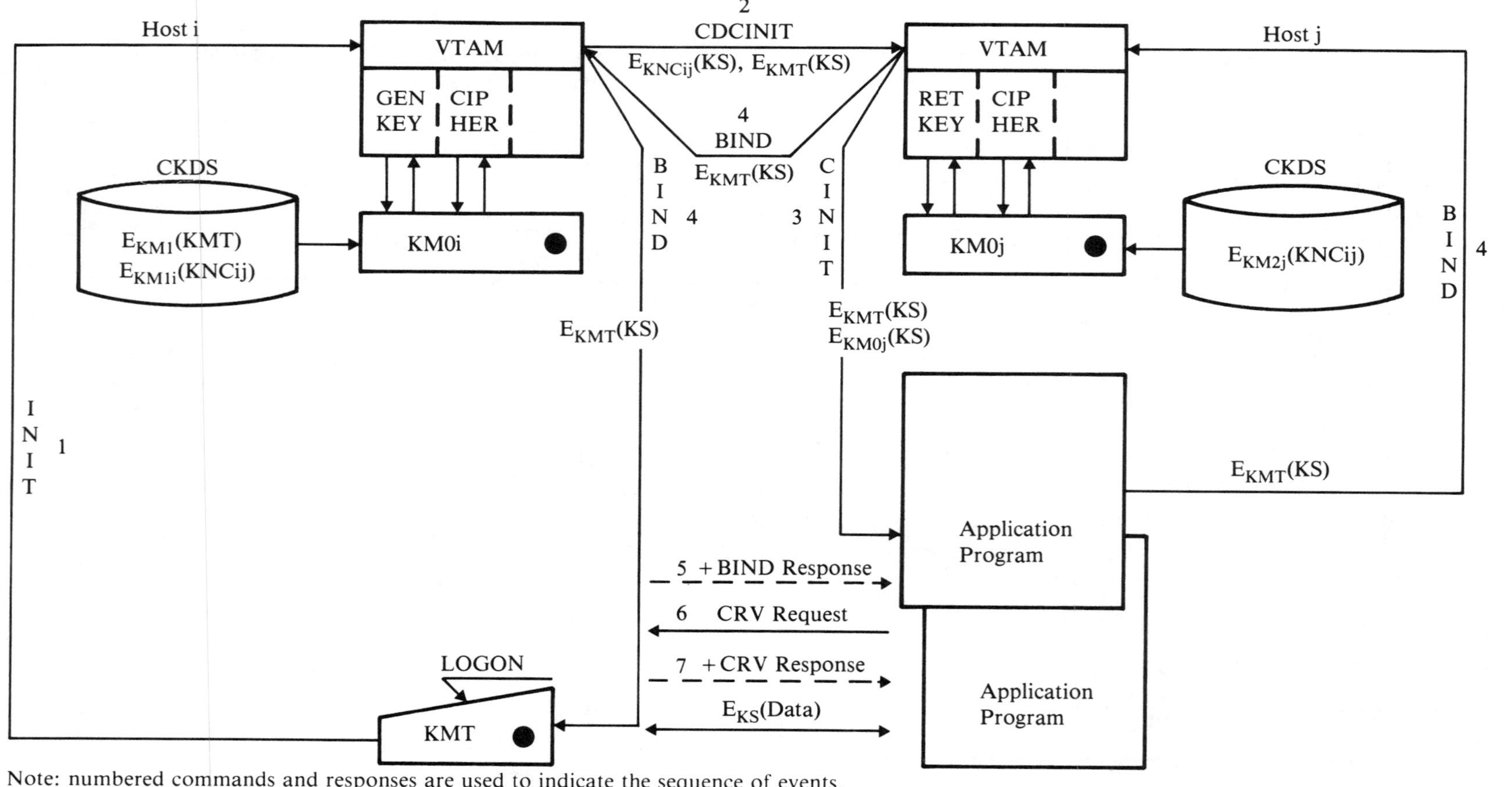

Note: numbered commands and responses are used to indicate the sequence of events. Some responses are not shown to avoid unnecessary complexity.

Figure 7-13. Session-Level Cryptography in a Multi-Domain Network (Transparent Mode, System Keys, System Managed)

in the appropriate field of a CONTROL INITIATE (CINIT) command. The BIND image, which contains KS enciphered under the SLU's key, is also copied to CINIT, and CINIT is then passed to the requested PLU (application program).

From this point, the action taken by the PLU and SLU is the same as discussed earlier (see Session-Level Cryptography in a Single-Domain Network.) To summarize, the receiving PLU extracts from CINIT the value of KS which was previously enciphered under the host's master key, and stores it for later use during the session. It also extracts the BIND image, which contains KS enciphered under the SLU's key, and transmits the enciphered session key to the SLU via BIND. At the end of this exchange, both the PLU and SLU have identical copies of the session key.

Figures 7-12 and 7-13 provide an overview of the command flow and keys contained therein for the establishment of a cryptographic session between two LUs in different domains.

APPLICATION PROGRAM-TO-APPLICATION PROGRAM CRYPTOGRAPHY

Unlike a terminal, an application program has no cryptographic facility of its own; it must use the host's cryptographic facility. Thus to perform encipher and decipher operations, the session key used by an application program must be enciphered under the host master key, that is in the form $E_{KM0}(KS)$. Because of this, the nature of the key transformations that support application-to-application communications vary slightly from those described for application to terminal communications. (In SNA terms, an application program is referred to as an outboard LU.)

Suppose that an SLU residing in host i has requested a session with a PLU in host j. The session key to be used by the SLU thus appears as $E_{KM0i}(KS)$, and is analogous to an outboard SLU's session key which appears in the form $E_{KMT}(KS)$. The SNA protocol for establishing a common session key requires that the key be received by the SLU in BIND. In other words, it must be sent to the SLU by the PLU. In the case of an outboard SLU, the key is directly usable in the form $E_{KMT}(KS)$. However, in the case of an inboard SLU, the equivalent approach of routing $E_{KM0i}(KS)$ to the SLU in domain i via the PLU in domain j is not desirable from a security viewpoint. A session key in the form $E_{KM0i}(KS)$ could be used directly in a *decipher data* operation at host i. Thus if an opponent were able to obtain $E_{KM0i}(KS)$ and data enciphered under KS (via an external wiretap), and obtain subsequent access to host i, then the data could be recovered. The problem is overcome, however, by enciphering the session key under an SLU key (KNA) associated with the specific application program. The quantity $E_{KNA}(KS)$, instead of $E_{KM0i}(KS)$, is sent to the PLU and returned via BIND to the host owning the SLU. After being received, the quantity $E_{KNA}(KS)$ is transformed via a RETKEY macro instruction[4] to the quantity $E_{KM0i}(KS)$, which can then be

[4] To ensure that the transformation cannot be used indiscriminately, the key manager could enforce a requirement that the program invoking RETKEY be privileged (see Protection of Host Keys, Chapter 4).

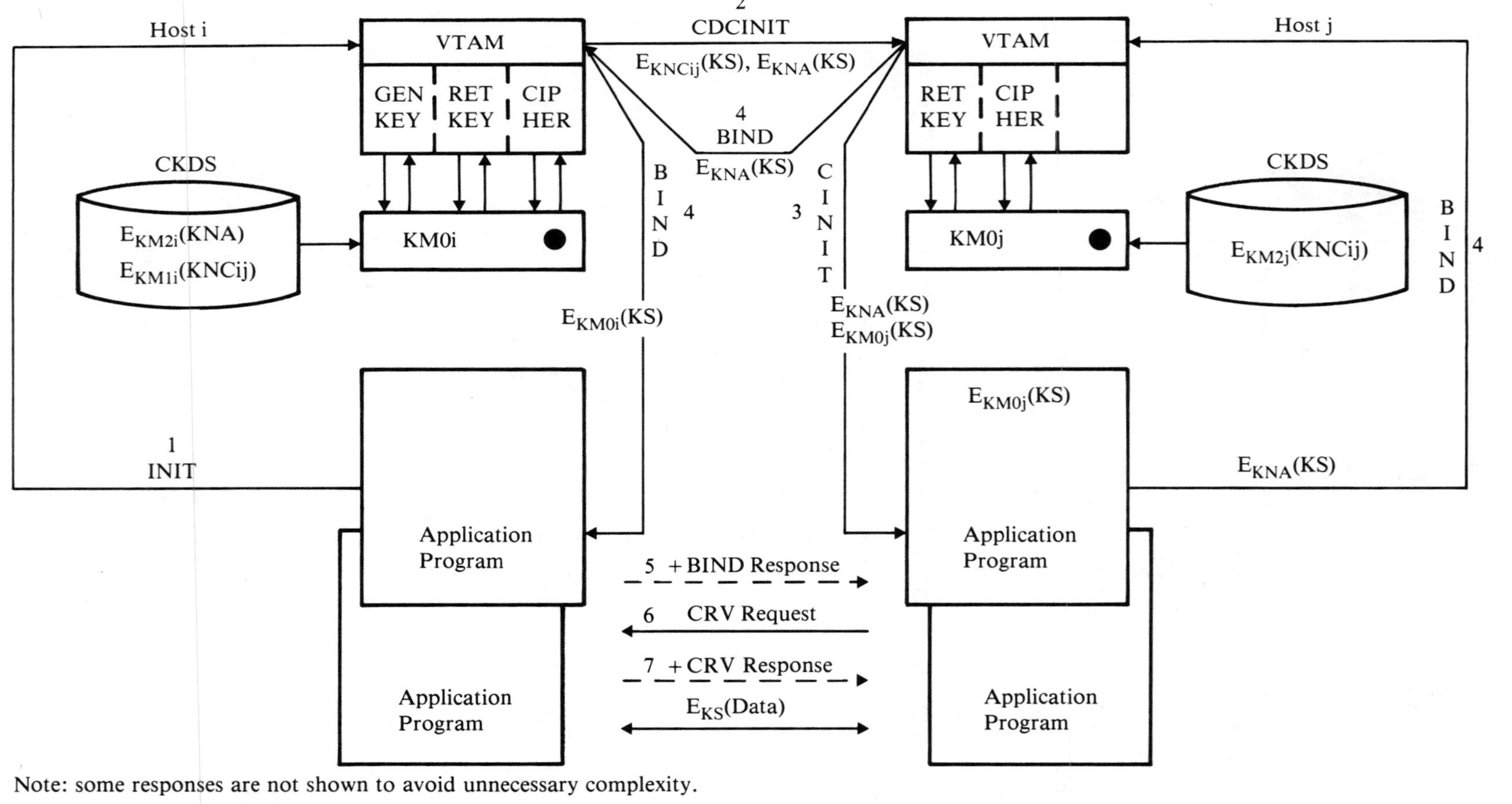

Note: some responses are not shown to avoid unnecessary complexity.

Figure 7-14. Session-Level Cryptography in a Multi-Domain Network (Application Program-to-Application Program Cryptography)

used by the application program at host i to encipher and decipher data. Application-to-application cryptography is illustrated in Figure 7-14.

Personal keys, whether managed privately or by the system, can be implemented in multidomain networks in a manner similar to that described for single-domain networks. The interested reader should have no difficulty in making the necessary extensions.

PADDING CONSIDERATIONS

When the DES algorithm is used in a block cipher mode of operation (e.g., block chaining with ciphertext feedback), a requirement for padding arises because communicated data quite often are not a multiple of 8 bytes (8 bits per byte). (The DES algorithm operates only with blocks of 8 bytes). Therefore, the communications architecture must accommodate a requirement to pad data to 8 bytes.

The cryptographic extensions to SNA provide for message padding. When padding is used, the last message block contains n data bytes ($n = 1, 2, \ldots, 7$), 7-n random pad bytes, and a 1 byte count indicating the number of added (nondata) bytes. A defined bit in the accompanying RH is then set to indicate to the receiver that the message must be stripped of pad characters after decipherment. However, RH is not available to application programs. Thus a private protocol that pads messages must provide a means to identify when padding is used, and identify the number of added pad bytes.

REFERENCES

1. Lennon, R. E., "Cryptography Architecture for Information Security," *IBM Systems Journal,* **17**, No. 2, 138–150 (1978).
2. McFadyen, J. H., "Systems Network Architecture: An Overview," *IBM Systems Journal,* **15**, No. 1, 4–23 (1976).
3. Cypser, R. J., *Communications Architecture for Distributed Systems,* Addison-Wesley, Reading, MA, 1978.
4. Schwartz, M., *Computer-Communication Network Design and Analysis,* Prentice-Hall, Englewood Cliffs, NJ, 1977.
5. Davies, D. W. and Barber, D. L. A., *Communications Networks for Computers,* Wiley, New York, 1973.
6. *Proceedings of the IEEE,* Special Issue on Packet Communication Networks, **66**, No. 11, 1301–1588 (November 1978).
7. Albrecht, H. R. and Ryder, K. D., "The Virtual Telecommunications Access Method: A Systems Network Architecture Perspective," *IBM Systems Journal,* **15,** No. 1, 53-80 (1976).
8. *Advanced Communication Function for VTAM (ACF/VTAM) General Information,* IBM Systems Library, Form No. GC27–0462.

Other Publications of Interest

9. Barber, D. L. A., Davies, D. W., Price, W. L., and Solomonides, C. M., *Computer Networks and Their Protocols,* Wiley, New York, 1979.
10. Kent, S. T., *Protecting Externally Supplied Software in Small Computers,* Doctoral Thesis, Massachusetts Institute of Technology, 1980. Department of Electrical Engineering and Computer Science.

CHAPTER EIGHT

Authentication Techniques Using Cryptography

FUNDAMENTAL CONCEPTS

Authentication is a process which proves that someone or something is valid or genuine. In a computer system or communications network, authentication is an important part of good data security. Cryptography offers a highly secure means to authenticate transmitted messages, stored data, and the identity of people and devices.

Generally, all authentication schemes have a common step in which the validity of one or more parameters must be checked. An authentication scheme is characterized by the nature of the preestablished relationships existing between the checked parameters and the quantities to be authenticated.

For example, authentication of a person's identity requires a special test of legitimacy in which a secret or nonforgeable parameter is supplied by the identified individual together with a claimed identity (ID). By checking the validity of the supplied parameter, the system can decide whether the identified individual is the person he claimed to be. (Personal authentication is discussed in greater detail in Chapters 10 and 11, which treat electronic funds transfer systems.)

Data parameters that remain constant for relatively long periods can be authenticated using bit patterns which are pregenerated under secure conditions. Data parameters which are not constant must be authenticated using bit patterns generated dynamically within the system during normal operations.

The authentication techniques discussed in this chapter are based on a conventional algorithm like DES, and it is assumed that:

1. The cryptographic algorithm is strong, which implies a property of noninvertibility.
2. The cryptographic system can maintain the secrecy and/or integrity of its cryptographic keys.

However, many of the concepts and principles apply to public-key algorithms as well.

As previously defined, encipherment of plaintext X under cipher key K, results in ciphertext $Y = E_K(X)$, and decipherment of ciphertext Y under cipher key K results in plaintext $X = D_K(Y)$.)

A cryptographic algorithm has the *property of noninvertibility* if it is computationally infeasible to determine cipher key K given knowledge of plaintext X and ciphertext $E_K(X)$. Many cryptographic authentication techniques take advantage of this property by treating certain data as cryptographic keys. The idea is similar to that of using one-way functions in the process of personal identification [1-3], in which case the function's input parameter(s) cannot be reconstructed from the function's output parameter.

HANDSHAKING

Handshaking is a procedure to ensure that communication has been established between two genuine nodes (devices) within a communications network. Ordinarily used when communications are initiated, it permits a node to prove that its communicating partner possesses the same data-encrypting key. This is accomplished by testing that enciphered data can be communicated successfully between the two nodes.

In the key management scheme described in Chapter 4, a common session key, KS, is established between a host and terminal by generating KS at the host and transmitting it to the terminal. In this case, KS is protected by enciphering it under the terminal's master key, KMT, which is resident within the terminal's cryptographic facility.

Even though the secrecy of KS is ensured by enciphering it with KMT, without handshaking the procedure is exposed to the so-called midnight attack. In a midnight attack launched against a terminal, the data associated with an entire communication session, including the session key, which is sent to the terminal under KMT encipherment, are wiretapped and recorded (figuratively, by day). Later, (figuratively, by night), the opponent gains unauthorized access to the terminal room and plays back the recording into the terminal. During playback, the terminal is unaware that it is in communication with a fictitious node. The session key is deciphered and initialized in the cryptographic facility. The ciphertext is then deciphered and presented to the opponent who is stationed at the terminal. Handshaking prevents the midnight attack.[1]

Figure 8-1 illustrates a procedure that allows node A (the terminal) to authenticate node B (the host). (By reversing the procedure, node B could also authenticate node A.) Assume that node A generates a pseudo-random number N which it enciphers under the session key KS and transmits to node B. N is padded with null characters if necessary, although it is assumed that N is long enough to ensure that the probability of the same value recurring is very low. N is recovered at node B by deciphering the transmission under

[1] Other cryptographic methods could be used to defend against a midnight attack; for example, a protocol of composite session keys (see Extended Cryptographic Operations, Chapter 5). A midnight attack would also be blocked if (user-supplied) personal keys were used at terminals instead of (system-managed) terminal master keys.

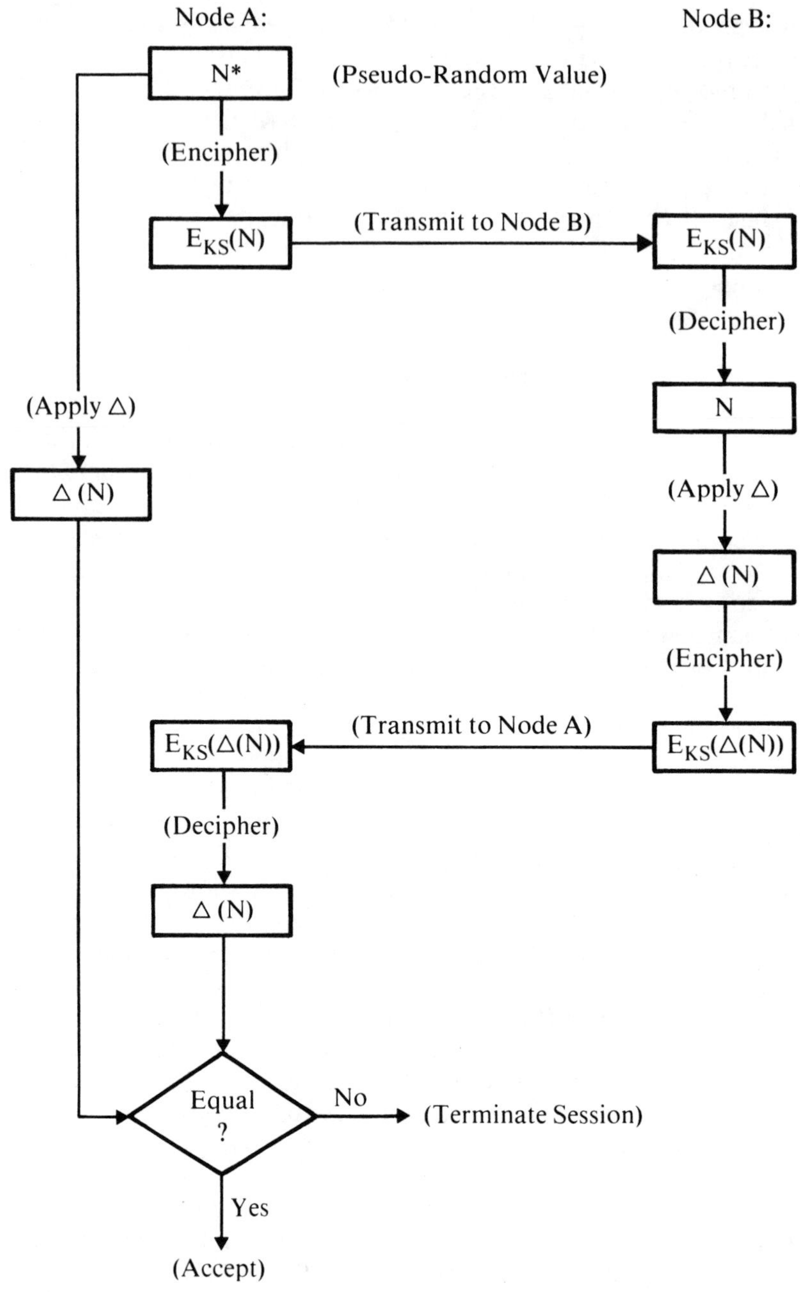

Note: Δ could be a function which inverts certain bits in N.

*Padding with zeros is indicated for the case where N does not have enough bits. N must have enough combinations to prevent a successful attack by trial and error.

Figure 8-1. Authentication of System Nodes via Handshaking

KS. Note that this step is possible only if node B is a genuine node and a copy of the correct KS is available. A nonsecret function Δ is applied to N, and the quantity $\Delta(N)$ is enciphered under KS and sent back to node A. At node A, Δ is similarly applied to the stored or saved value of N so that $\Delta(N)$ can be compared with the corresponding value returned from node B. Node B is accepted as genuine only if the comparison is successful. Otherwise, the session is aborted.

The following example illustrates why an opponent is blocked from carrying out a midnight attack when handshaking is used. Let N1 be a pseudo-random number generated at node A during a session that is wiretapped by an opponent. Assume that node A is a remote terminal. Later, when the recording is played back into the terminal, a value N2 (not equal to N1) is generated within the terminal as part of the handshaking procedure. This means that the prior value $E_{KS}(\Delta(N1))$ returned from node B is no longer correct, and hence the comparison for equality between $\Delta(N1)$ and $\Delta(N2)$ will fail. In an actual implementation, Δ could be a function that inverts certain bits in N.

It is important that N be generated within the terminal and stored in a protected memory. If N is entered by a human operator, or if the stored value of N can be overwritten by a value of the user's choosing, the procedure can be attacked. For example, during an attempted playback, the opponent stationed at the terminal enters $\Delta(N2)$ instead of N2 (Δ is a nonsecret function) and wiretaps the quantity $E_{KS}(\Delta(N2))$, which is sent to node B instead of $E_{KS}(N2)$. The original recording is now modified so that $E_{KS}(\Delta(N1))$ is replaced by $E_{KS}(\Delta(N2))$. A second playback is made. This time the opponent enters N2 into the terminal and the authentication check therefore succeeds.

To block this kind of attack, N can be defined as an operator-entered number RN which is enciphered under the session key KS:

$$N \equiv E_{KS}(RN)$$

Since N is a function of the unknown session key KS, there is no way to subvert the checking procedure unless it is possible to encipher or decipher under the same session key. For example, if an opponent could gain access to an unattended terminal during an actual session, then N2 could be entered as data and the ciphertext $E_{KS}(N2)$ intercepted via a wiretap. Since Δ is a nonsecret function, $\Delta(E_{KS}(N2))$ could be computed from $E_{KS}(N2)$. Then, by entering $\Delta(E_{KS}(N2))$ as data during the same session, the quantity $E_{KS}(\Delta(E_{KS}(N2)))$ could be obtained via a wiretap. Thus to defeat the system, the opponent replaces $E_{KS}(\Delta(E_{KS}(N1)))$ with $E_{KS}(\Delta(E_{KS}(N2)))$ in the original recording, and enters N2 at the terminal.

In an actual implementation, this attack may already be blocked. For example, the attack would not be possible if certain characters in $\Delta(E_{KS}(N2))$ had no corresponding keyboard characters.

Whenever possible, the pseudo-random number N should be generated within a terminal. In theory, this requires a nonvolatile storage in the terminal; otherwise, the terminal will always start from the same initial conditions when power is first supplied to it. However, from a practical viewpoint, a free-running counter starting from the same value (after power-on) may be acceptable provided that the resolution of the counter is such that synchronizing the recorded playback with the power-on sequence is impractical.

MESSAGE AUTHENTICATION

Message authentication is a procedure which, when established between two communicants, allows each communicant to verify that received messages are genuine. Communicants can be people, devices, or processing functions. Typically, a communicant acts as both a sender and receiver of messages, although it is possible for a communicant to participate only as a sender or receiver. Message authentication must allow the receiver of a message to determine that:

1. The message originated with the alleged sender.
2. The contents of the message have not been accidentally or intentionally changed.
3. The message has been received in the same sequence that it was transmitted.
4. The message was delivered to the intended receiver.

In other words, message authentication permits the receiver to validate a message's *origin, contents, timeliness,* and *intended destination.*[2]

Although message authentication permits the receiver to verify that messages are genuine, it does not always permit these properties (origin, contents, timeliness, and intended destination) to be proven to or verified by a third party. (If both the sender and receiver share the same secret information used in the authentication procedure, the sender could later claim that a message was manufactured by the receiver.)

However, an approach using digital signatures does permit the receiver to prove to a third party that messages are genuine (see Digital Signatures, Chapter 9). It provides that the sender cannot later disavow messages as his own, the receiver is unable to forge messages or signatures, and the receiver can prove to an impartial third party (referee) that the content of a message is genuine and that it originated with the sender.

Authentication of a Message's Origin

Two methods for a receiver to verify a message's origin (sender) are discussed. In the first method, the sender's identity is verified through the use of a

[2] Proposed Federal Standard 1026 [4] defines authentication as "the process of assuring that only intended parties or locations exchange and accept a given unit of information as being valid." The standard describes cryptographic methods to achieve the following security objectives: detection of fraudulent insertion of messages; detection of fraudulent deletion of messages; detection of fraudulent modification of messages; and detection of replay of previously valid messages. These security objectives, therefore, represent a subset of those specified herein.

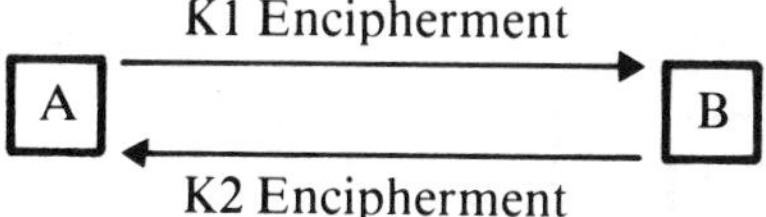

Figure 8-2. Message Encipherment Between A and B

secret data-encrypting key shared by the sender and receiver. The receiver verifies the sender's identity by deciphering the received ciphertext using the agreed upon key (determined by the sender's ID), and checking that the text has been properly recovered. In the second method, the sender's identity is verified through the use of a secret password (known to both the sender and receiver) that is included within the transmitted message.

Suppose that communicants A and B use cryptographic keys K1 and K2, where K1 is used only for transmission from A to B and K2 is used only for transmission from B to A (Figure 8-2). To prove that a message originated with A, B need only demonstrate that the message is properly recovered using K1. Similarly, to prove that a message originated with B, A need only demonstrate that the message is properly recovered using K2.

If the communicants A and B use a common key K there will always be some uncertainty as to which of the two (A or B) was the true originator of a message. For example, it may be possible for a stale message sent from A to B to be injected back into the communication path and redirected to A. Unless steps are taken to prevent such a condition, A could never be certain that a received message originated with B. This problem can be avoided if the sender includes an identifier (ID) in all transmitted messages and the receiver authenticates the contents of the message (Figure 8-3).

When it is either impractical or undesirable to verify a message's sender on the basis of a cryptographic key, a password can be used instead. In that case, A and B must agree ahead of time on the passwords to be used. Let PWa and PWb be the respective passwords assigned to A and B. A includes PWa in all messages sent to B, and B includes PWb in all messages sent to A. To prevent an opponent from finding out the value of one of these passwords, which could then be used to impersonate the respective communicant, passwords are encrypted. But encryption alone is not enough, since an opponent may be able to impersonate a communicant by substituting the communicant's encrypted password in a bogus message. The cryptographic procedure must be such that if an encrypted password is used in a bogus message, it causes either the recovered password to be incorrect or some other part of the message authentication procedure to fail. Various techniques can be used. For example, the password could be encrypted with a dynamically changing data-encrypting key, or block chain encryption could be used with a variable initializing vector (see Block Ciphers with Chaining, Chapter 2). The use of constant passwords is illustrated in Figure 8-4. (The assumption is made here that the number of password combinations is large enough so that it is impractical or impossible for an opponent to cause a correct password to be produced via some process of trial and error.)

In a public-key cryptographic system (see Chapter 2), the sender (A) of an

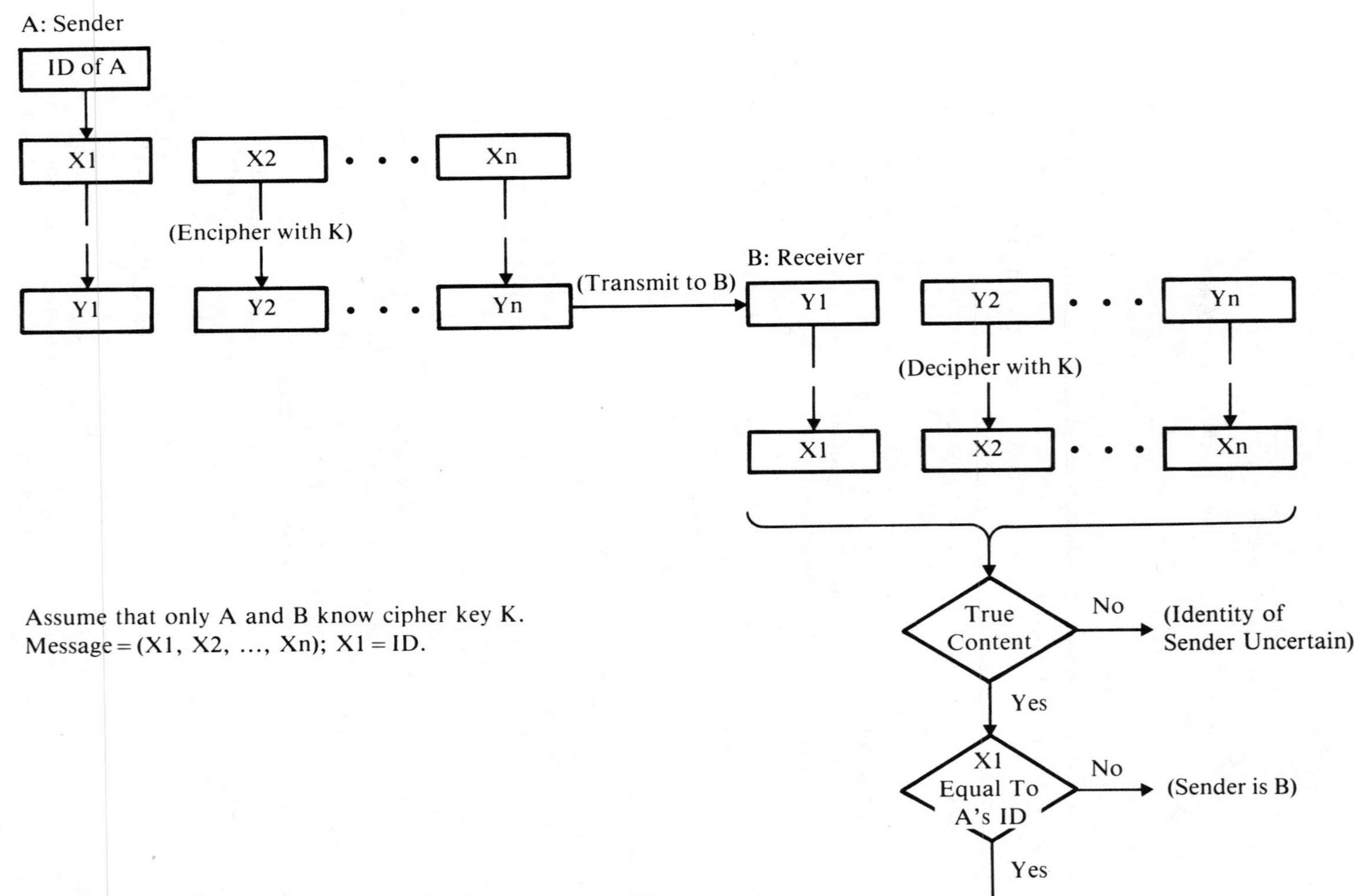

Figure 8-3. Authentication of the Identity of a Message's Sender Using a Common Key, K, and the Sender's ID in the Message

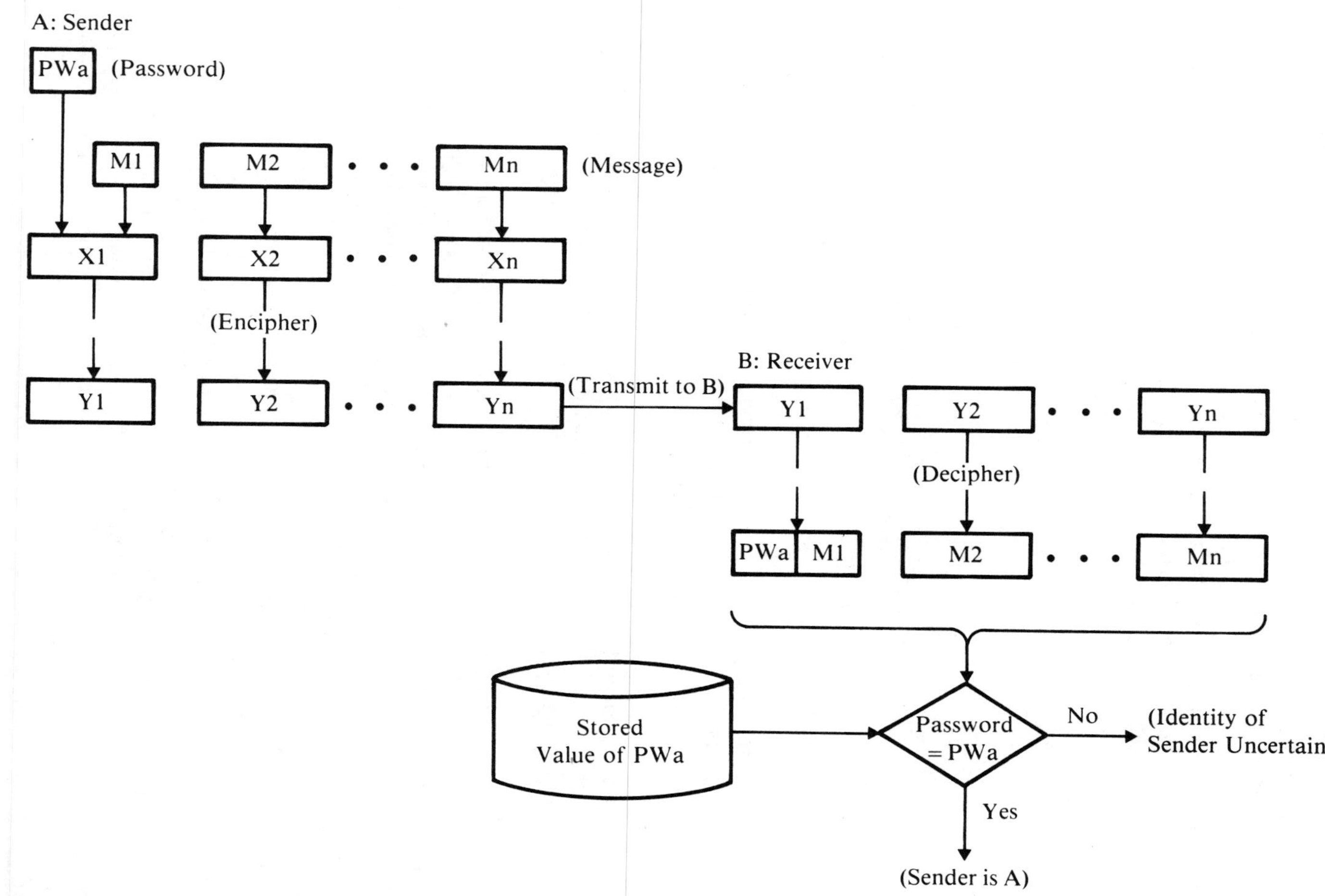

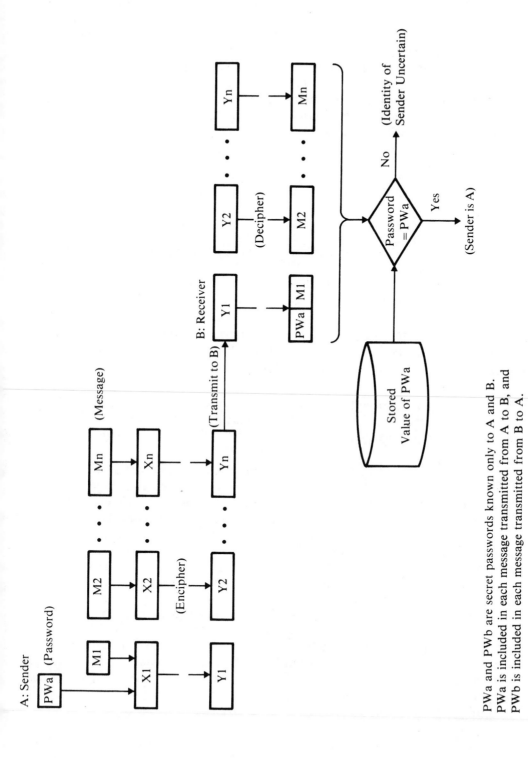

PWa and PWb are secret passwords known only to A and B.
PWa is included in each message transmitted from A to B, and
PWb is included in each message transmitted from B to A.

Figure 8-4. Authentication of the Identity of a Message's Sender Using Constant Passwords

enciphered message cannot be identified with the receiver's (B) secret key (SKb). This is because the receiver's enciphering key (PKb) is not secret (it is in the public domain) and, therefore, anyone can encipher a message with that key. However, the identity of a message's sender can be established if the sender (A) operates on the message with a secret deciphering key (SKa) (e.g., by deciphering the message). In that case, by enciphering the message with the sender's public key (PKa) and checking that it has been properly recovered, anyone can verify that the message originated with A. However, this form of authentication is achieved at the price of having no secrecy. If secrecy is desired (or required), the deciphered message, $D_{SKa}(M)$, must be enciphered with the receiver's public key (PKb). (For more details, see Digital Signatures, Chapter 9.)

Authentication of a Message's Timeliness

A procedure for verifying that messages are received in the same order they were transmitted by the sender is as follows:

1. If a time-variant quantity Z is known in advance to both the sender and receiver, then the order of transmitted messages can be established by requiring that each message be enciphered using Z as an initializing vector.[3]
2. If a time-variant quantity T is known in advance to both the sender and receiver, then the order of transmitted messages can be established by requiring that T be included in the text of each message.

Let Z1, Z2, . . . ,Zn denote time-variant quantities used in transmitting a set of messages, M1, M2, . . . , Mn, respectively. Assume that block chaining with error propagation is used for message encryption (see Figure 2-16). The Z-values establish the sequence of transmitted messages because the ith initializing vector (Zi) allows only the ith enciphered message (Mi) to be recovered. Zi will not permit a different message (Mj) to be recovered. Therefore, to verify that a message is received in its proper sequence, it is necessary only to decipher the message using the appropriate initializing vector, and to verify that it is properly recovered.

Messages can also be sequenced via a time-variant quantity T which is included in the text of each transmitted message. Let T1, T2, . . . , Tn denote the time-variant quantities used in transmitting messages M1, M2, . . . , Mn, respectively. For example, T1, T2, . . . , Tn could be the nonsecret sequence numbers 1, 2, . . . , n. In that case, the recipient could verify that messages are received in their proper sequence if the procedure in Figure 8-3 were changed to include T as well as ID.

[3] There are many ways in which initializing vectors can be established between two communicants. In general, selecting a satisfactory and secure method will depend on the intended application and environment.

Another approach is to use a list of one-time passwords, T1, T2, . . . , Tn, which are agreed upon in advance. These passwords, if used with the procedure in Figure 8-4, allow the receiver to establish the identity of the sender and verify that messages are received in their proper sequence.

The disadvantage of this procedure is that each communicant must keep a record of the next value of T to be used. In addition, the procedure must handle cases where synchronization has been lost. This can be partially overcome if T is a value taken from a TOD clock. In that case, the receiver can authenticate T by using a simple test of reasonableness.

In a different approach, whenever A informs B that it wants to send B a message, B sends A a random number T which A includes in the text of the prepared message. B ensures that the message has been received in its proper sequence by verifying that the correct value of T has been returned in the text of the message. In this procedure, T is a variable that is produced when needed. However, since T is included in the text of the message, the procedure works only if the receiver also verifies the contents of the message.

Authentication of a Message's Contents

The contents of a message are authenticated by verifying the correctness of an *authentication code* (AC), also called a *message authentication code* (MAC), that is computed by the sender and appended to the message (plaintext or ciphertext) before it is sent to the receiver.[4]

Authentication by an Encryption Method with the Property of Error Propagation

Authentication of the contents of a message is easily accomplished if the message is enciphered with an encryption method that has the property of error propagation. A block chaining scheme such as plaintext-ciphertext feedback (see Figure 2-16) could be used. The procedure requires that a quantity known to the receiver (and sender) be appended to the end of the message prior to encipherment (e.g., the initializing vector Z, or the first block of plaintext X(1)). After decipherment, the contents of the message can be authenticated by verifying that the correct quantity appears at the end of the message. If the quantity appended to the end of the message contains c bits, then any change in the ciphertext will be detected with a probability approximately equal to $(2^c - 1)/2^c = 1 - 1/2^c$.

Figure 8-5 illustrates a procedure in which the first c bits of the message are repeated at the end of the message. Upon encryption, these c bits represent the AC. If an error occurs in the ciphertext, the recovered plaintext (after the point of error) will also be in error. In that case, the first c bits of the recovered plaintext will differ from the last c bits with a probability equal to $1 - 1/2^c$.

[4] Procedures to authenticate a message's contents are discussed in Cryptographic Message Authentication Using Chaining Techniques, Chapter 2.

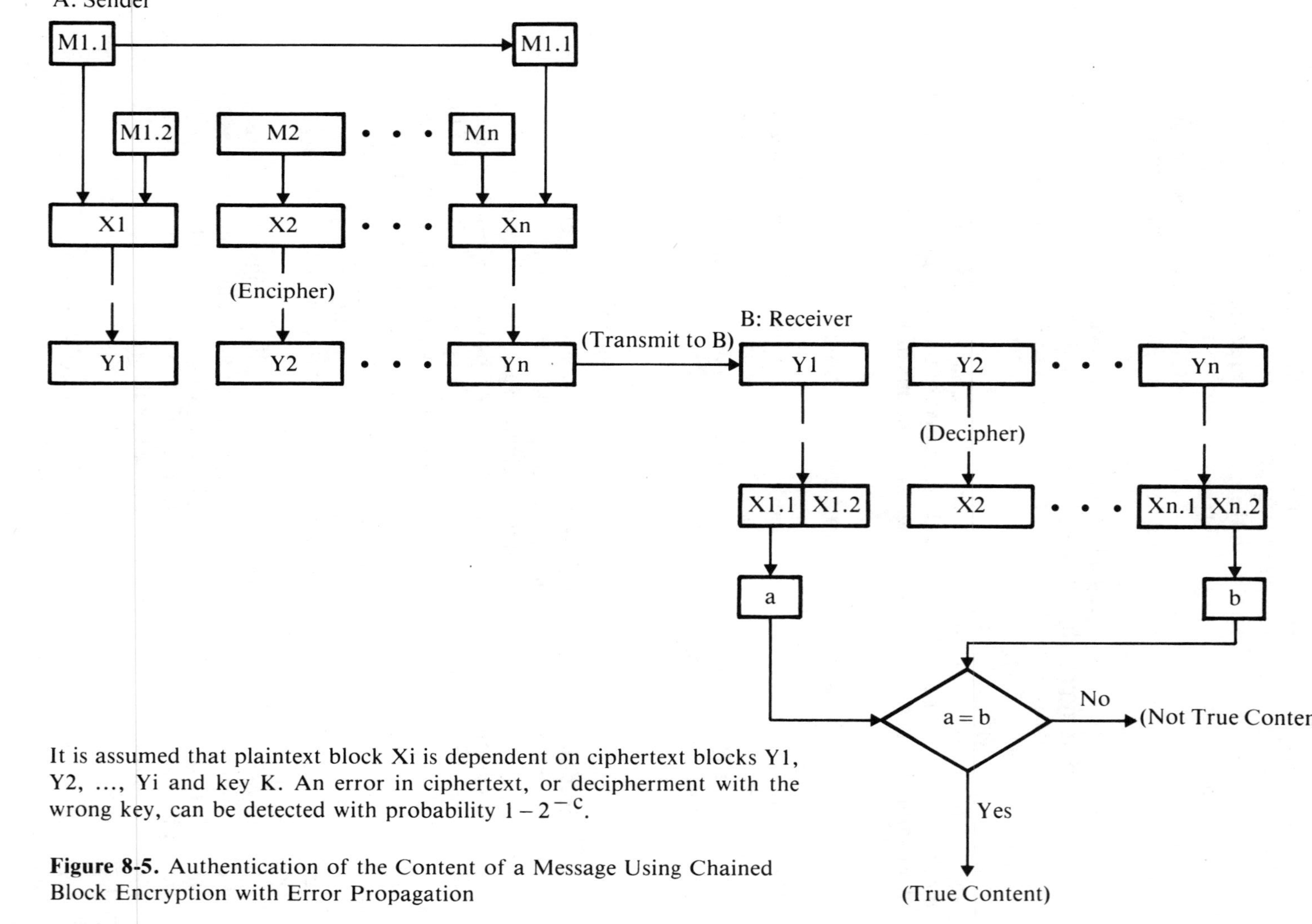

It is assumed that plaintext block Xi is dependent on ciphertext blocks Y1, Y2, ..., Yi and key K. An error in ciphertext, or decipherment with the wrong key, can be detected with probability $1 - 2^{-c}$.

Figure 8-5. Authentication of the Content of a Message Using Chained Block Encryption with Error Propagation

Authentication by an Encryption Method Without the Property of Error Propagation

If the encryption method does not have the property of error propagation (e.g., chained block encryption using ciphertext feedback, Figure 2-17), then a change to the ciphertext may or may not cause the last block of recovered plaintext to be in error. In this case, an approach slightly different from that just discussed can be used to authenticate the contents of a message.

Since an error in the ciphertext is not propagated in the recovered plaintext but instead is localized, the pattern of bits appended to the end of the message must be a function Δ of the entire message (not merely part of the message). The function Δ transforms a message M of arbitrary length into a relatively short, fixed length, pattern of bits Δ(M), such that with high probability Δ(M) will differ from Δ(M′) whenever the recovered message (M′) differs from the original message (M). The enciphered value of Δ(M) represents the AC. (Δ may be a nonsecret function or a secret function known only by the appropriate communicants.) A procedure in which messages are enciphered using block chaining with ciphertext feedback is illustrated in Figure 8-6. (Ciphertext feedback is illustrated in Figure 2-17.)

Even if Δ were such that one could easily find an M and M′ where Δ (M) = Δ(M′), this alone would be insufficient to allow the authentication procedure to be defeated. This is because M and Δ(M) are encrypted. Even if a forged message (M′) could be derived, the opponent could not encrypt it with the proper key. On the other hand, in order to calculate M′ such that Δ(M′) = Δ(M), the value of M or Δ(M) must first be known. But since M and Δ(M) are encrypted, it is assumed that this information is denied to the opponent. Consequently, the opponent can make changes only to the ciphertext, in which case he ordinarily has no control over the recovered plaintext (M′) when the message is deciphered. If the length of Δ(M) is c bits and the bit patterns Δ(M1), Δ(M2), . . . , Δ(Mn), are (nearly) randomly distributed over the set of 2^c possible values for n arbitrarily selected messages, then Δ(M′) will differ from Δ(M) with a probability equal to $1 - 1/2^c$.

Let Δ(M) = X1 ⊞ X2 ⊞ . . . ⊞ Xn, where ⊞ denotes a hashing operator, and let the augmented message M* = X1, X2, . . . , Xn, Δ(M) be encrypted, e.g., using block chaining with ciphertext feedback (Figure 2-17, i.e., CBC mode). The last block of ciphertext is defined as the AC.

Jueneman has shown that defining ⊞ as modulo 2 addition is not secure if encryption of M* is performed using CBC mode [5]. (A permutation of the ciphertext blocks and/or insertion of an even number of spurious ciphertext blocks will produce a recovered message M′ = X1′, X2′, . . . , defining ⊞ as modulo 2 addition is not secure if encryption of M* is performed using cipher feedback (Figure 2-30, i.e., CFB mode) or with a key auto-key cipher (Figure 2-12) [6].

A simple method of computing Δ(M) (still to be more thoroughly analyzed, see Reference 6) is to define ⊞ as modulo 2^{64} addition.

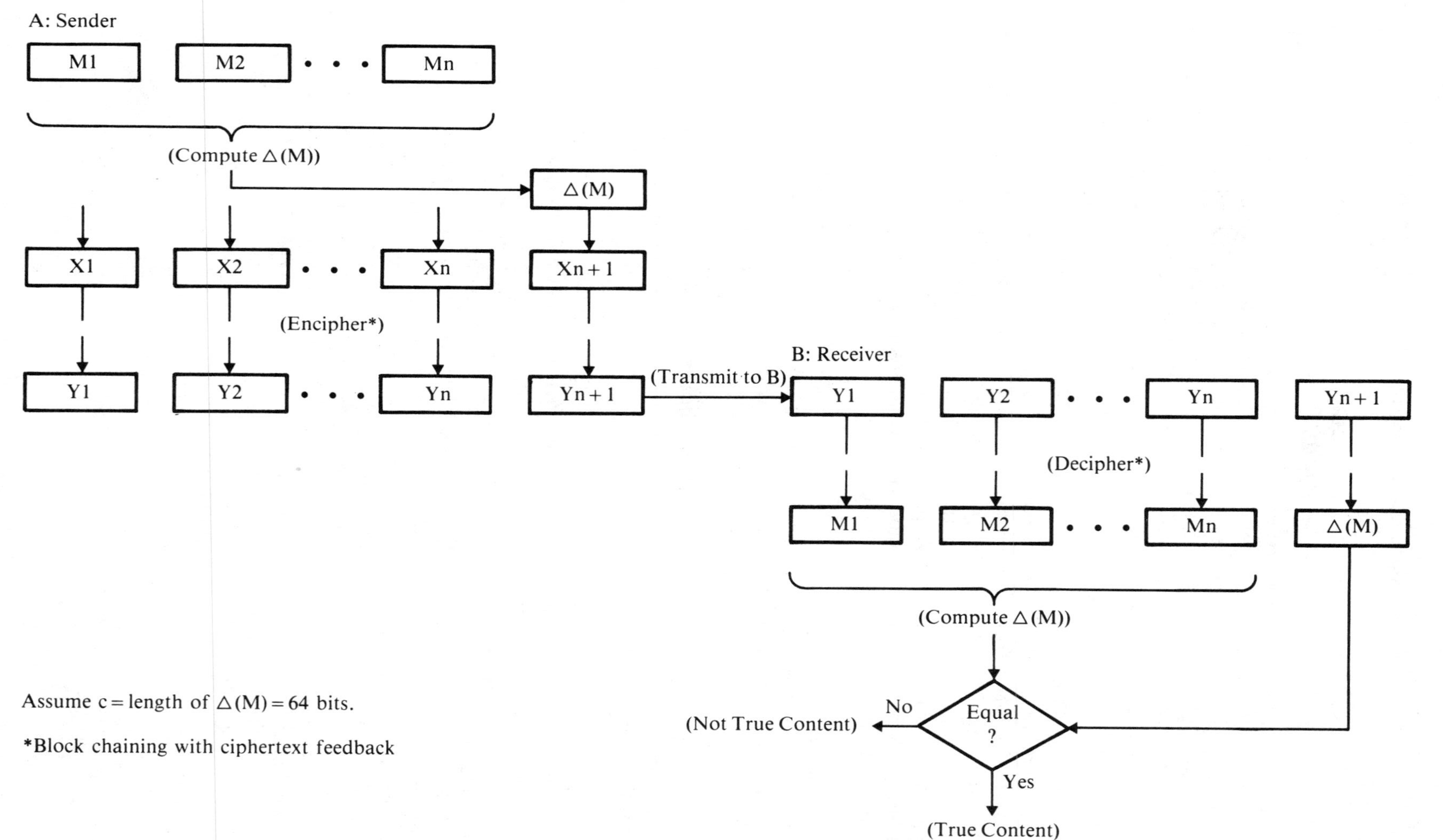

Figure 8-6. Authentication of the Content of a Message where the Authentication Code is $\Delta(M)$ Enciphered Under a Secret Key Known Only to the Sender and Receiver

Another, even more secure, method of computing $\Delta(M)$ would be to encrypt M under a first secret key (using CBC mode) and define $\Delta(M)$ as the last block of ciphertext. The augmented message M* is then encrypted under a second or variant secret key (again using CBC mode).

Authentication Without Message Encryption

It may happen that message authentication is required in cases where messages are sent in unencrypted form, either because there is no need for privacy or because an intermediate network node without an encryption capability must be able to read messages. Thus it is worthwhile to investigate schemes that authenticate unencrypted text (plaintext).

In the discussion that follows, assume that M = (X1, X2, . . . , Xn) is a message to be transmitted in unencrypted form, and that M* = (M, AC) is the augmented message comprised of M and an appended AC. Since M is nonsecret, the authentication procedure must be such that only authorized individuals can compute AC. In effect, this means that the procedure itself, or a parameter used by the procedure, must remain secret. Otherwise, an opponent could compute AC′ for any M′ and substitute (M′, AC′) for (M, AC).

Consider a solution in which the communicants, denoted by the end points in the network, have an encryption capability, whereas the intermediate points in the network have no encryption capability. The cryptographic algorithm and a shared key are used to compute AC. A strong procedure results if the message M is enciphered using block chaining with ciphertext feedback and the AC is defined as the last block of ciphertext (Yn).

However, a weak procedure results if AC is defined as the encipherment of $\Delta(M)$ under K and $\Delta(M)$ is produced by Exclusive-ORing the blocks of plaintext:

$$\Delta(M) = X1 \oplus X2 \oplus \ldots \oplus Xn.$$

Such a scheme is easily defeated by replacing X1 through Xn − 1 with any quantities X′1 through X′n − 1 and replacing Xn with X′n, where X′n is defined as

$$X'n = X'1 \oplus X'2 \oplus \ldots \oplus X'n - 1 \oplus \Delta(M)$$

In this case, knowledge of M provides an opponent with enough extra information to defeat the procedure successfully.

The procedure for authentication without message encryption could also be defeated if $\Delta(M)$ were computed with a polynomial code. Let q be the modulus, and let r be the remainder when M is divided by q. M can be expressed by the equation M = kq + r, where k is an integer that depends on the value of M. However, for a fixed q and r, and any i not equal to k, each message in the set $\{Mi : Mi = iq + r, i \neq k\}$ would be a candidate that could be substituted for M.

If quantity $E_K(\Delta(M))$ is defined as the AC, then it is evident that an opponent cannot merely substitute a bogus message (M′) for M, since without K the new authentication code, $AC' = E_K(\Delta(M'))$, cannot be computed. However, if Δ has the property that an M′ can be easily found such that $\Delta(M') = \Delta(M)$, then the procedure is exposed to an attack wherein M′ is substituted for M.

Authentication of a Message's Receiver

The methods already discussed for authenticating a message's sender are easily adapted so that the message's receiver can authenticate that it is the intended receiver. Let A and B denote the sender and receiver, respectively. The receiver has enough information to verify that the message has been delivered to the correct destination (receiver) whenever any of the following conditions are satisfied:

1. A and B share a pair of secret keys, where one key is used to encipher messages sent from A to B and the other key is used to encipher messages sent from B to A.
2. A and B share one secret key used to encipher messages sent to each other, and the ID of the receiver is included in the text of each message.[5]
3. A and B share a pair of secret passwords, where A's password is included in the text of each message sent to B, and vice versa.
4. A and B share one secret password, but they include ID information in each message, as discussed in condition 2 above.

In a public-key cryptographic system (see Public-Key Algorithms, Chapter 2), the receiver uses its secret deciphering key to verify that it is the message's intended receiver. The receiver knows that a message was directed to it if the correct text is recovered after the message has been deciphered with its secret key.

A Procedure for Message Authentication

Several of the previously discussed ideas are now combined into a single procedure for authenticating messages (Figure 8-7). The procedure has the following characteristics:

1. An encryption method with the property of error propagation is used to authenticate the contents of a message.
2. Passwords are used to authenticate the sender and receiver (i.e., the sender and receiver share secret passwords).

[5] Since there are only two communicants, an acceptable protocol could be established in which only the ID of the sender is included in the text of the message.

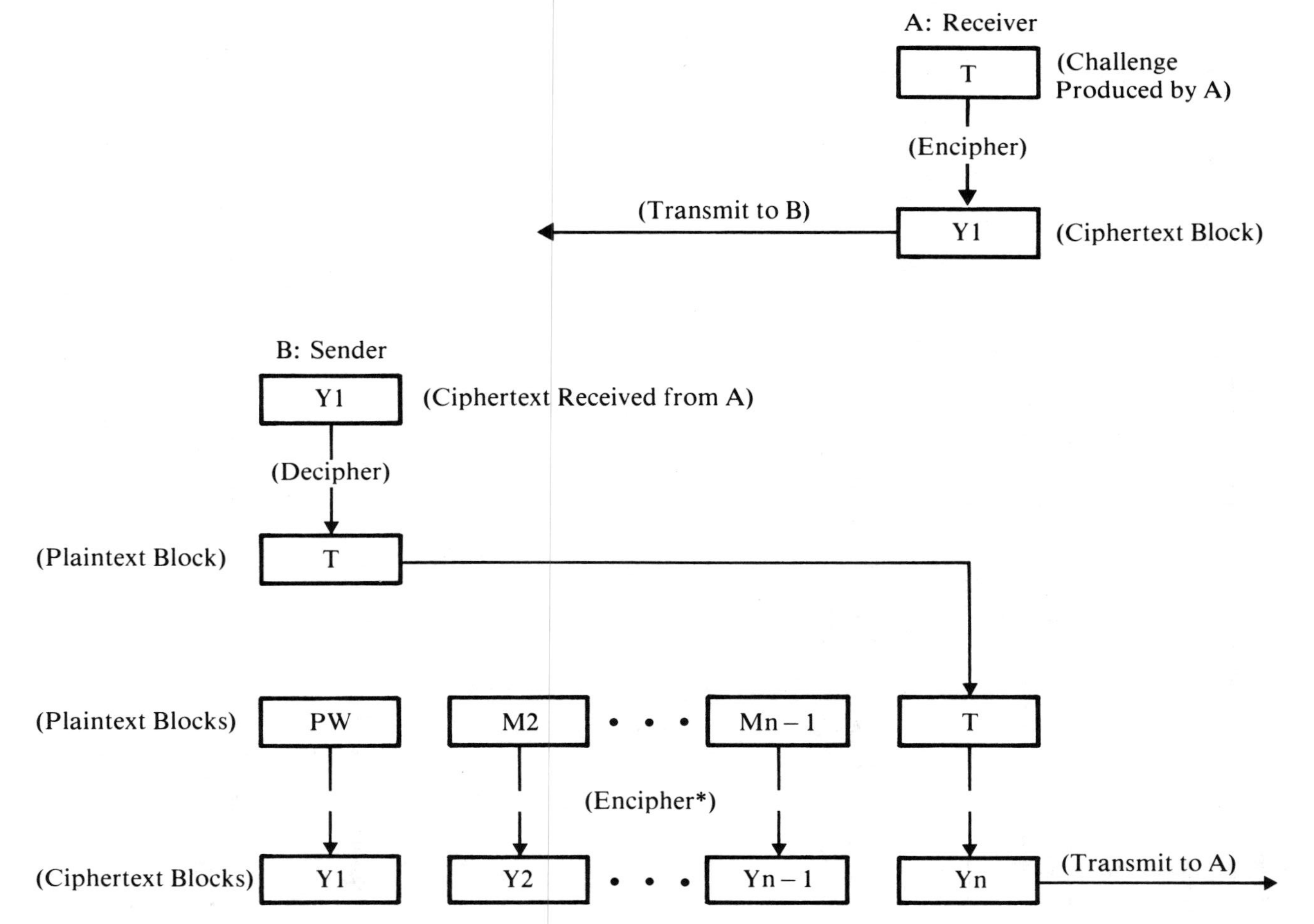

*Block Chaining with Plaintext-Ciphertext Feedback

Figure 8-7. A Procedure for Message Authentication

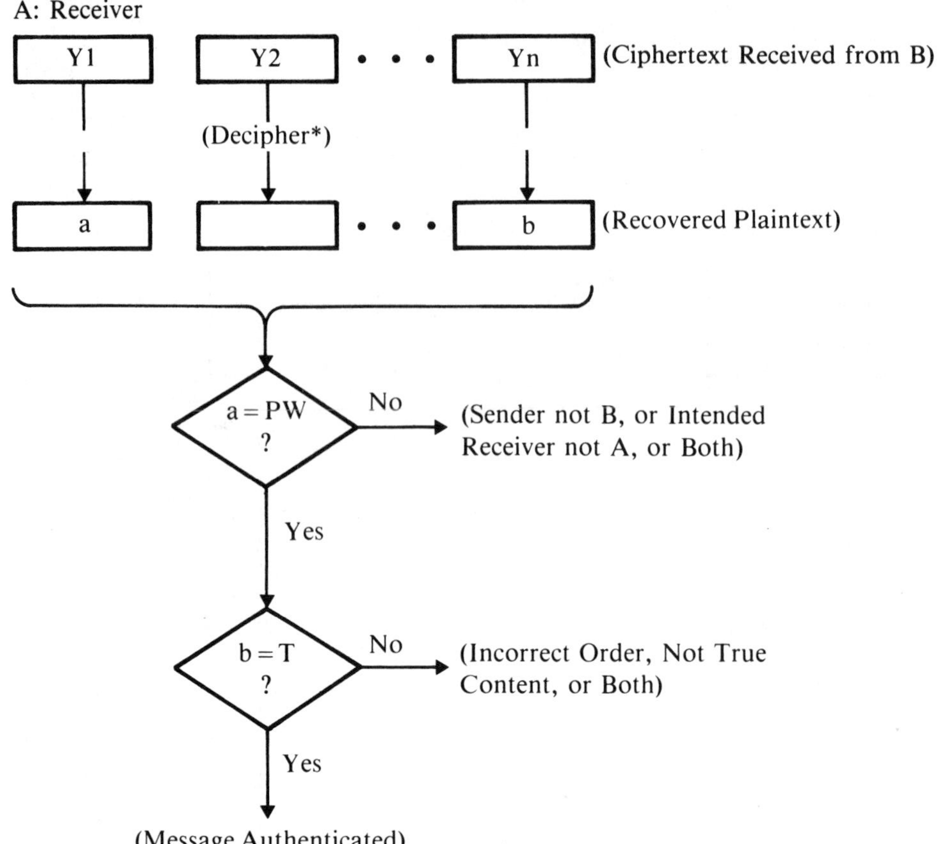

*Block chaining with plaintext-ciphertext feedback

Figure 8-7 (cont'd).

3. A time-variant quantity T is used to verify that messages are received in their proper sequence.

If the cryptographic key used for encipherment is a personal key, KP, then the password, PW, may be omitted from the procedure. On the other hand, if the key used for enciphering is a session key, KS, then the following can be said:

1. The sender need only include PW in the first transmitted message. This is because at session initiation a correspondence between PW and KS is established that lasts for the duration of the session. Once PW has been verified, KS and T can be used to authenticate the message's sender and intended receiver.
2. If T is omitted from the procedure, it is still not possible for messages intercepted during one session to be successfully redirected to one of

the communicants during another session. This is because KS is also a time-variant quantity—a message enciphered with one session key is not properly deciphered with a different session key. In that case, the message's content can be authenticated using the method described in Figure 8-5 (i.e., by appending a known value to the end of the message and enciphering the result with an encryption method that has the property of error propagation).

Generally, the quantity T should contain at least 16 bits (c = 16). If greater integrity is desired, up to 64 bits could be used conveniently with DES.

If passwords are entered into the system through a single standard interface, such as at a remote terminal during sign-on, additional measures can be taken to enhance the security of the personal identification procedure (see Chapters 10 and 11). For example, passwords could be enciphered under a special cryptographic key resident within the terminal, or each password could be treated as a cryptographic key (provided it has enough combinations) and used to encipher a nonsecret value that has been agreed upon in advance. An opponent who intercepts a transformed password cannot enter this value through the standard interface and gain entry to the system.

In the final analysis, there is no set of authentication procedures that can satisfy the processing and security requirements of all conceivable applications implemented under all operating conditions. Thus each method of authentication (origin, contents, timeliness, and intended recipient), or combination thereof, must be evaluated according to the particular application for which it is intended. In so doing, a set of assumptions about the type of information an opponent would have available to defeat the method must also be established. Selection of a method is accomplished by ensuring that it defends against the opponent's anticipated attacks.

AUTHENTICATION OF TIME-INVARIANT DATA

Computer system integrity is the state that exists when there is complete assurance that the system will perform as intended by its designers. Historically, computer system integrity has been based on the concept of accidental error [7]. That is, ways were sought to provide protection only from the accidental loss or destruction of data. No attempt was made to prevent deliberate tampering with the operating system or stored data.

Today it is recognized that data security[6] must include protection from intruders who deliberately attempt to gain unauthorized access to protected resources. Authentication methods that permit only authorized system users to access and manipulate system resources are essential to achieve system integrity. Authentication is the process which proves that someone or something should be accepted as being valid or genuine.

[6] *Data security* is defined as the protection of data from unauthorized disclosure, destruction, and modification, either by accident or intent.

Authentication of Passwords

A common method of authenticating time-invariant data is by comparing the data with a copy of those data which has been stored elsewhere in the system. For example, a user's ID (i.e., the users name or account number) is verified by comparing a supplied password (PW) with a corresponding password stored within the system (Figure 8-8).

This method of checking can be improved whenever passwords are entered into the system from a remote entry device (terminal or hand-held unit attached to a terminal) capable of encryption [2, 3]. A cryptographic operation, Δ, is used to protect the secret PW by transforming it into a nonsecret quantity, Δ(PW). The quantity Δ(PW) is then transmitted to a central facility to verify the user's identity by comparing it with a similarly precomputed value stored in the system.

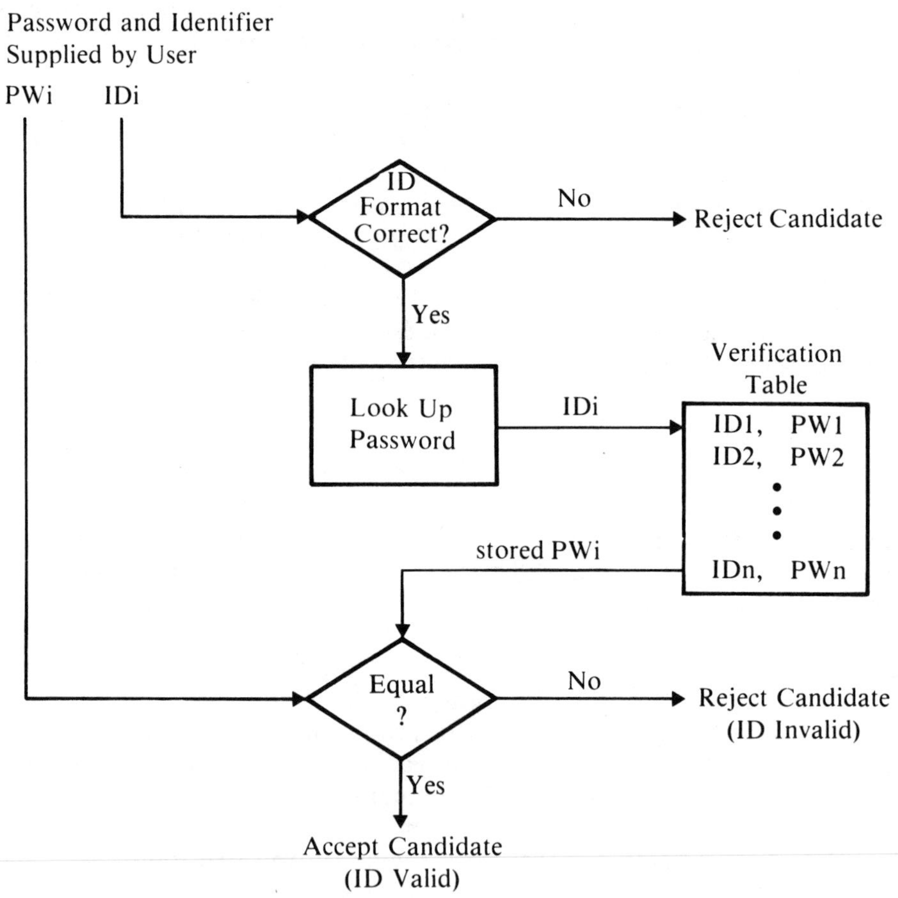

ID is a user identifier (name, account number).

Figure 8-8. Authentication Using a Stored Table of Passwords

When the cryptographic operation (Δ) is based on a strong algorithm such as DES, the value of PW cannot be deduced, even using involved cryptanalysis. In some cases, this degree of protection is absolutely essential (e.g., when PW is the basis for commercial wire transfer of funds as in electronic funds transfer, EFT). In general, the services provided by such a system (debiting and/or crediting customer accounts) are predicated on knowing the customer's identity.

Modern banking methods incorporate self-service terminal devices at which customers conduct their banking business. Such methods do not require customer recognition by an institution employee. Instead, the device and supporting system must be responsible for identifying the customer. Typically, when a transaction is initiated, the customer supplies a secret parameter (a password or more precisely a personal identification number, PIN) together with a claimed ID. The PIN must be managed securely to preserve the integrity of the transaction.

One way to protect PW (or, equivalently, PIN for EFT systems) would be to encipher PW under a secret key available at an entry point to the system (i.e., $\Delta(PW) = E_{Key}(PW)$). Alternatively, when PW has enough combinations, it may be treated as a cryptographic key and used to encrypt (at the entry point) a test phrase such as the user's ID (i.e., $\Delta(PW) = E_{PW}(ID)$). The latter approach has the advantage that only user-supplied quantities are needed to effect the transform Δ, whereas in the former case a system-managed key is required.

However, with most customer-oriented EFT systems, the PIN (PW) is usually comprised of only four to six characters, so that it is easy to remember and convenient to use. The short length also makes the PIN susceptible to exhaustive attacks (methods to determine the PIN using direct searches or trial and error techniques). The PIN's short length thus makes it unsuitable for use as a cryptographic key. However, an approach which overcomes the objection of a short PIN and at the same time enhances key management would be for each customer to supply also a secret *personal key* (KP). With such an approach, exhaustive attacks against PIN and KP could be blocked by defining $\Delta(PIN, KP) = E_{KP \oplus PIN}(ID)$. (See Applying Cryptography to Electronic Funds Transfer Systems–Personal Identification Numbers and Personal Keys, Chapter 11.) In any case, the purpose of Δ is to transform PW into a nonsecret form so that it can be safely transmitted to a central facility (host processor) for authentication.

Upon receipt at the host processor, Δ(PW) is used to verify the user's identity by comparing it with a similarly precomputed value stored in the system (Figure 8-9). Storing Δ(PW) in a verification table at the central facility will protect the secrecy of passwords (Figure 8-9), but it will not protect against an intruder who could alter data stored in the verification table. If an opponent were able to create Δ(X) for an arbitrary value of X, and replace Δ(PWi) with Δ(X) for some user identifier (IDi) in the verification table, then entry to the system could be gained by inputting the known value of X at any entry point. Moreover, a legitimate user of the system with IDj could gain entry under a different identifier, say IDi, by replacing Δ(PWi) with Δ(PWj). In either case, once entry had been achieved, Δ(PWi) could be put back into the verification table to prevent subsequent detection.

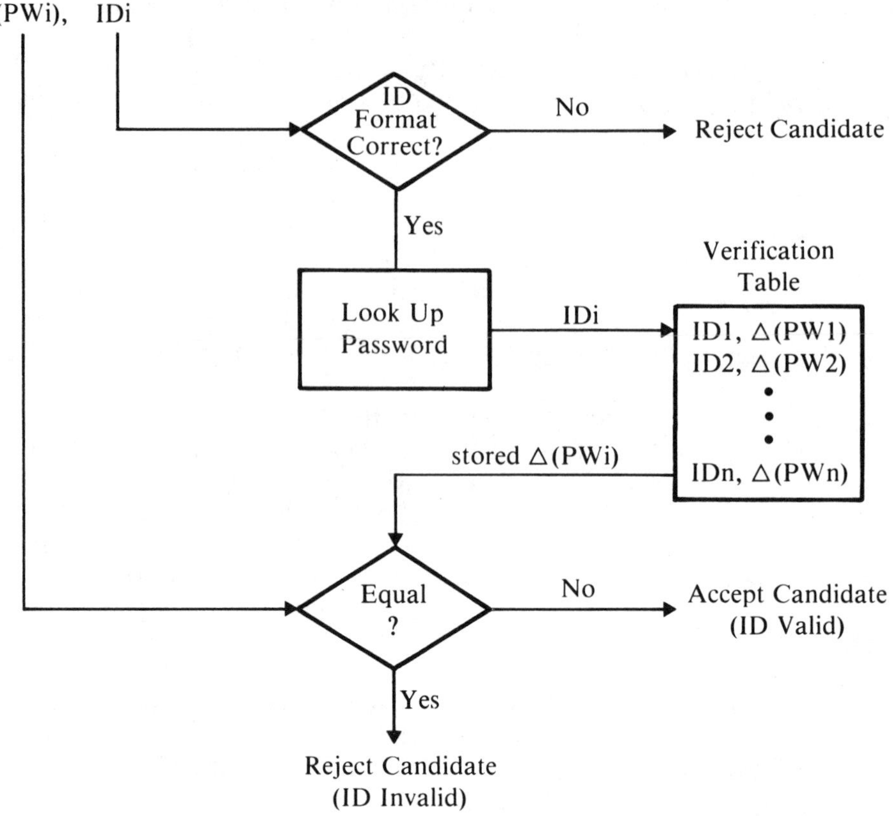

Δ is a cryptographic operation used to transform PW at its entry point into the system. For example, Δ(PW) could be represented by $E_{Key}(PW)$ or $E_{PW}(ID)$, where ID is a user identifier (name, account number).

Figure 8-9. Authentication of Passwords that have been Transformed Under a Cryptographic Operation Δ

An active wiretap threat in which Δ(PWi) and IDi are intercepted and later retransmitted to the host could be blocked by cryptography (e.g., by implementing a protocol for message authentication between the entry point (terminal) and host). However, defenses against the threat of wiretaps in communications networks can be achieved through communication security techniques described in Chapters 4–7 and are not treated in the present discussion.

Gaining unauthorized entry to the system by altering or manipulating the verification table can be prevented by using the technique described for password verification. This technique protects against misuse of information stored in a verification table, even by those who manage and maintain the table and who have legitimate access to it. This authentication technique makes use of a special test pattern (TP) not equal to Δ(PW), which can be used at any later time together with a special cryptographic operation to verify Δ(PW).

In the discussion that follows, ID and Δ(PW) are assumed to be 64-bit quantities. (Parameters less than 64 bits can be padded to 64 bits using some agreed upon protocol; e.g., padding with zero bits.) Moreover, it is assumed that an opponent has read and write access to the verification table.

Authentication Using Test Patterns Generated from the Host Master Key

This procedure, which assumes the DES algorithm, is a general technique to authenticate the contents of a 64-bit block of data (X). For example, password authentication is performed by setting X equal to Δ(PW). However, unlike the method of password authentication described above, this method is not exposed to attacks based on an alteration or manipulation of the verification table.

The basic idea can be implemented within a host processor that has an encryption capability by providing two cryptographic authentication operations: *authentication forward* (AF) and *authentication reverse* (AR). These two operations are defined

$$\mathbf{AF}: \{X, TP\} \longrightarrow VP$$
$$\mathbf{AR}: \{X, VP\} \longrightarrow TP$$

where the contents in the braces indicate the input to the host's cryptographic facility, the arrow points to the result, and

X = the data block to be authenticated
TP = test pattern associated with X
VP = verification pattern assigned to X

TP and VP are nonsecret parameters, each containing 64 bits.

Basically, AR computes the test patterns needed to initialize the system and AF validates data parameters. Hence AR must be restricted to certain special runs with particular users—those responsible for initializing and updating the system. One way to ensure that AR is executed only under secure conditions is to require that it be activated by physically turning a key-operated security lock.[7] AF is available to any program or system user needing to validate data parameters. Therefore, AF must have the property that TP cannot be computed or deduced from X and VP.

For each Xi requiring authentication, there is a corresponding test pattern (TPi) that must be computed in advance. For this reason, the quantity to be authenticated must be known beforehand in clear form. The technique cannot be used when the data to be authenticated are time-variant, such as messages transmitted in a network. Otherwise, this method is completely general; it can be applied to any quantity (Xi).

[7] In general, what is needed to perform the mappings AF and AR is a trapdoor one-way function [8].

Authentication of Xi takes place by exercising the AF operation

$$\text{AF: } \{\text{Xi, TPi}\} \longrightarrow \text{VPi}$$

and comparing the result (VPi) for equality with the corresponding predefined verification pattern to determine whether Xi should be accepted. If the two values are equal, Xi is accepted. Otherwise, Xi is rejected. Only the correct Xi and TPi will produce VPi. A different result ($\neq$ VPi) is produced if one or both of the input parameters are changed.

VPi must be a value related to the identity of Xi. For example, VPi could reflect the name of Xi or the address in main storage where Xi is stored (assuming Xi's storage location does not change). If VP1 = VP2 = . . . = VPn = constant, then by replacing (Xi, TPi) with (Xj, TPj) the system could be deceived into using Xj in place of Xi.

Let the relationship between VPi and IDi (the identifier of Xi) be expressed as

$$\text{VPi} = \nabla(\text{IDi}), \qquad i = 1, 2, \ldots, n$$

where ∇ is a function which prevents ID from being computed from VP. For example, ∇(ID) could be defined as $E_{ID}(C)$, where C is a nonsecret constant value.[8] Figure 8-10 illustrates how the test pattern scheme could be applied to password authentication, where the quantity to be authenticated is Xi = Δ(PWi).

The reason for employing a ∇ function with these properties can be explained by referring to Figure 8-10. Suppose an opponent chooses a password (PW) and obtains Δ(PW) as the result of a sign-on attempt (e.g., via a wiretap). Assume also that VP = ID. The opponent now selects an arbitrary test pattern (TP) and exercises AF using Δ(PW) to obtain VP, which subsequently is specified as ID. By creating an entry in the verification table for the forged values of ID and TP, the opponent could then sign-on the system using the selected password and the corresponding derived identifier.

This attack may already be partially blocked if, for example, the ID consists only of alphameric characters (A, B, . . . Z, 0, 1, . . . , 9) and an initial consistency check is performed to test its validity. This type of consistency check is assumed in Figures 8-8, 8-9, and 8-10 ("ID format correct?" decision block).

VPi does not need to be kept secret because a potential intruder cannot deduce the correct TPi for a given Xi and VPi. (Note that TPi can be created only by using the AR operation and the AR operation is available only to authorized persons.) It should also be realized that VPi must be checked in a dynamic sense (i.e., it must not be compared to a stored system value). Otherwise, an opponent using AF could compute VP for a valid X and an arbitrary TP and replace the correct table value with the value so obtained.

[8] Greater security can be achieved if the method is extended to two test patterns. For example, one could define VPi1 = $E_{ID}(C1)$ and VPi2 = $E_{ID}(C2)$, where C1 and C2 are nonsecret constant values. In that case, Xi and VPi1 would be used to generate TPi1, and Xi and VPi2 would be used to generate TPi2.

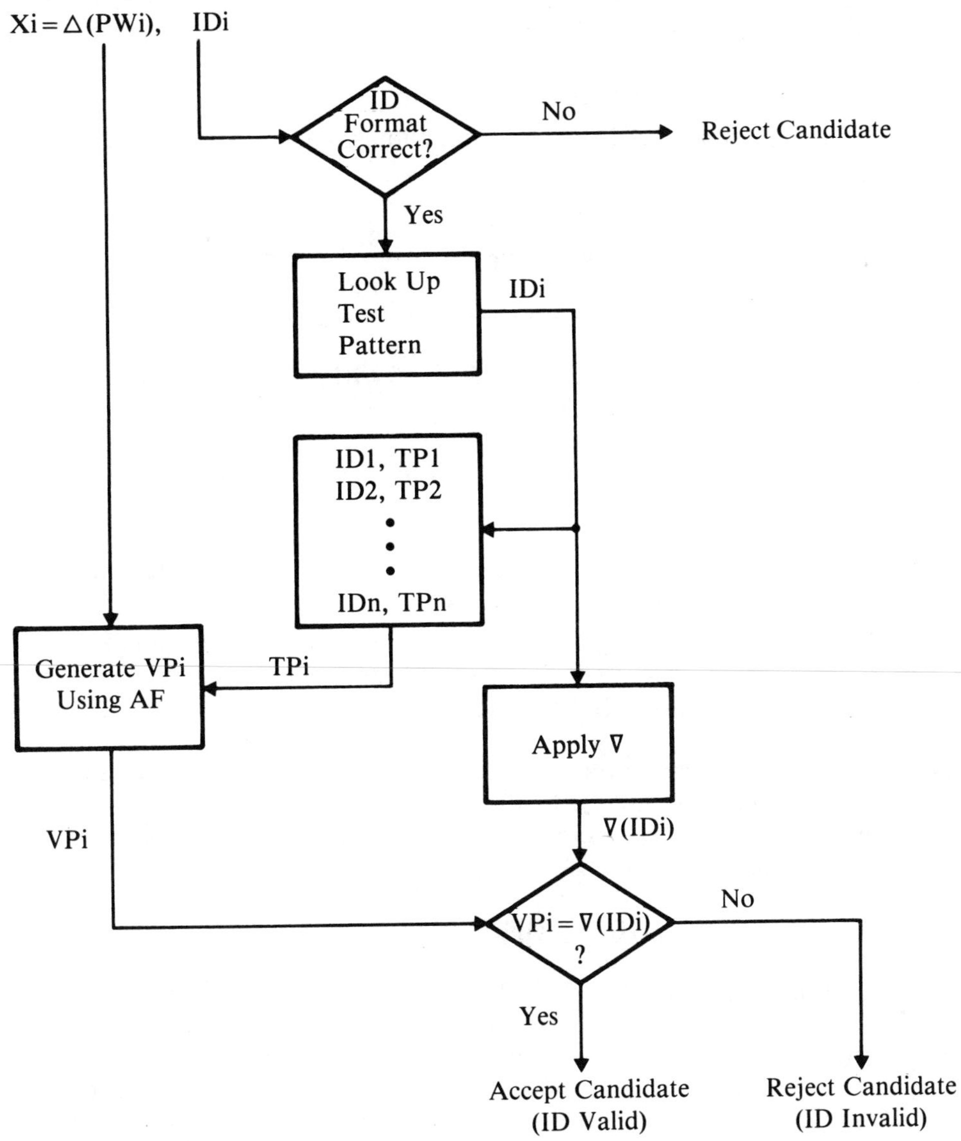

Δ is a cryptographic operation used to transform PW, at its entry point, into a nonsecret quantity. Δ(PW) could be defined as $E_{Key}(PW)$ or $E_{PW}(ID)$, where ID is used as an identifier. ∇ is a cryptographic operation used at the host to transform ID into VP.

Figure 8-10. Authentication Based Upon a Table of Test Patterns

A Short Analysis

It would be unwise to define VP equal to ID. However, to gain further insight into the matter, assume the following for the sake of discussion:

1. The length of ID is less than or equal to 64 bits.
2. VP is defined as the ID padded with enough zero bits to create a 64-bit quantity.

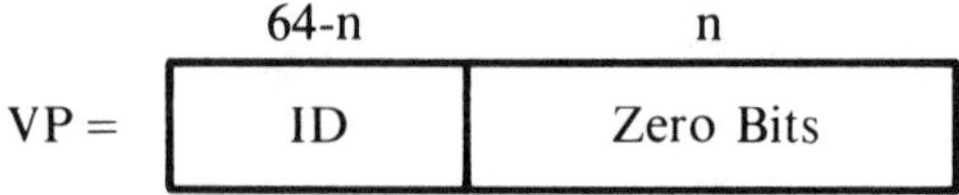

3. Each of the $m = 2^{64-n}$ combinations for ID are valid, and hence there are m possible values for VP.

In theory, the authentication procedure could be attacked in the following way:

1. For each of the m values of ID, the pairs (ID1, ∇(ID1)), (ID2, ∇(ID2)), . . . , (IDm, ∇(IDm)) are computed.
2. For an arbitrary Xi, the AF operation is exercised using different values of TP. This is continued until a VP is found which matches one of the m values in the list: ∇(ID1), ∇(ID2), . . . , ∇(IDm).

Since there are 2^{64} possible verification patterns, the probability that an arbitrary TP will produce a valid verification pattern is $2^{64-n}/2^{64} = 1/2^n$. Therefore, about 2^{n-1} trials (exercising AF) are needed, for a given X, to find a TP that produces a VP in the list:

$$\nabla(\text{ID1}), \nabla(\text{ID2}), \ldots, \nabla(\text{IDm})$$

As a consequence, about $2^{64-n} + 2^{n-1}$ trials are needed to carry out the attack. The ∇ function must be exercised 2^{64-n} times to obtain the relationship between ID and ∇(ID) for each ID, and the AF operation must be exercised 2^{n-1} times to find an appropriate TP. If n is small (the number of IDs is large), then the ∇ function must be exercised more frequently than the AF operation. If n is large (the number of IDs is small), then the AF operation must be exercised more frequently then the ∇ function. The value of n that is selected thus determines the opponent's work factor.

Table 8-1 provides a summary of the effective security achieved with each of the three authentication procedures: unenciphered passwords, transformed passwords, and test patterns.

Implementing AF and AR

One way to implement AF and AR using a conventional cryptographic algorithm like DES would be to define special encipher and decipher opera-

Protection Method	Opponent can read from, but not write into verification table.	Opponent can read from and write into verification table.
Password stored in verification table (Figure 8-8).	Actual Verification information can be obtained. Opponent can LOGON pretending to be someone else.	Actual Verification information can be obtained. New verification information can be created, i.e., a new user can be introduced into the system.
Password stored in verification table (Figure 8-9).	No subversion possible.	Actual verification information cannot be obtained. New verification information can be created, i.e., a new user can be introduced into the system.
Test patterns stored in verification table (Figure 8-10).	No subversion possible.	No subversion possible.

Table 8-1. Comparison of Different Verification Procedures

tions using a new variant[9] of the host master key—a variant defined solely for the purpose of authentication [9]. With a public-key algorithm such as the trapdoor knapsack or the RSA algorithm (see Block Ciphers, Chapter 2), AF and AR would be implemented via the public and private keys, respectively.

Let KM5 represent the fifth variant of the host master key and define

$$\text{AF: } \{\text{Xi, TPi}\} \longrightarrow E_{D_{KM5}(Xi)}(\text{TPi}) = \text{VPi}$$

$$\text{AR: } \{\text{Xi, VPi}\} \longrightarrow D_{D_{KM5}(Xi)}(\text{VPi}) = \text{TPi}$$

Figure 8-11 describes the steps taken by the cryptographic facility to perform the AF and AR operations.

Let KAi be a cryptographic key defined as follows:

$$\text{KAi} = D_{KM5}(\text{Xi}), \qquad i = 1, 2, \ldots, n$$

The integrity of the authentication procedure is assured because of the following:

1. By using a special variant of the host master key (KM5), it is not possible to use other cryptographic operations, singularly or in combina-

[9] A *variant* of the host master key is derived by inverting selected bits in the master key (see Protection of Host Keys, Chapter 4). In effect, a cryptographic system with multiple master keys is achieved when in fact only a single master key is stored in the cryptographic facility. By defining a cryptographic operation to be dependent upon a specific host master key variant, one effectively isolates that operation from all others without loss of cryptographic strength.

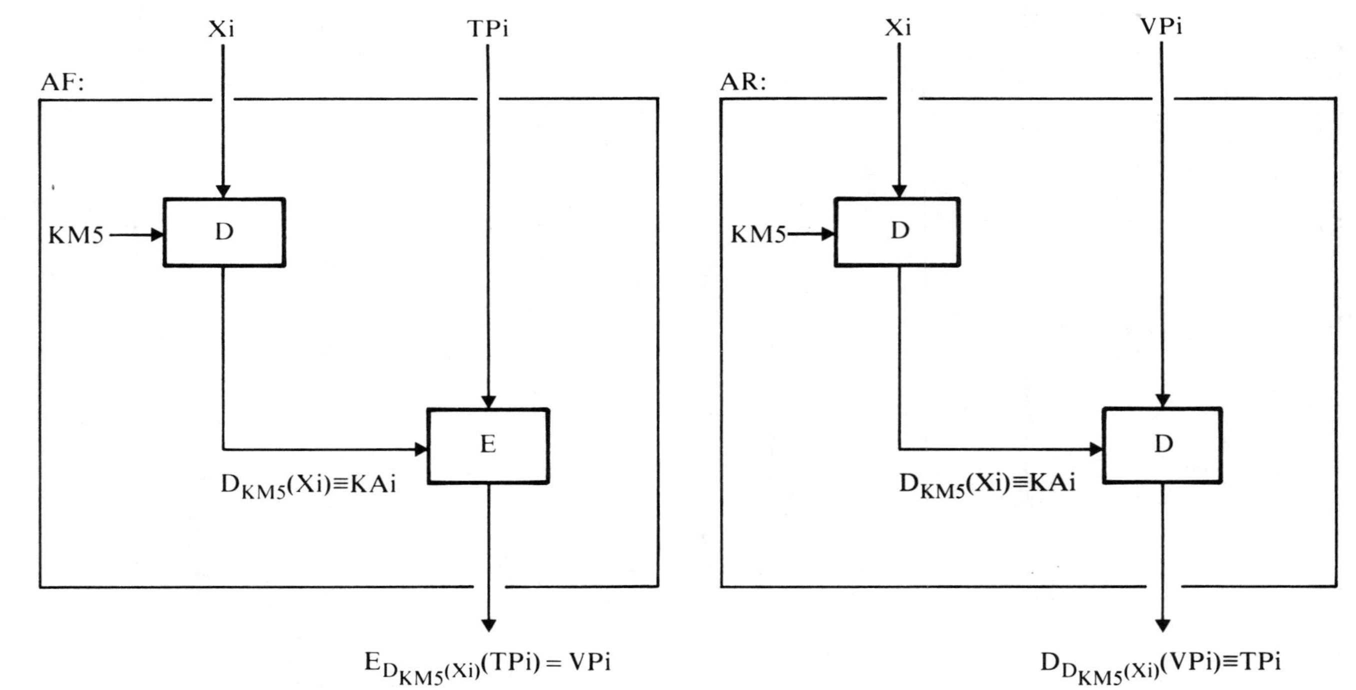

AF is used to authenticate Xi with TPi; AR is used to generate test patterns. Xi is the value to be authenticated; TPi and VPi are the test pattern and verification pattern corresponding to Xi. KM5 is the fifth variant of the host master key.

Figure 8-11. The AF and AR Operations

tion, to subvert or reverse the effect of AF and AR. Likewise, no other operation is provided that will allow encipherment or decipherment under KM5. Furthermore, KAi never appears in the clear outside of the cryptographic facility. Hence for an arbitrary Xi there is no wav to determine the corresponding KAi, and vice versa.

2. AF allows arbitrary encipherment under KAi, but no (inverse) operation is provided to allow decipherment under KAi.

An attack in which the AF operation and the ∇ function are repeatedly exercised in order to find an X, TP, and ID such that

$$\text{AF}: \{X, TP\} \longrightarrow VP = \nabla(ID)$$

can be thwarted by making the number of trials sufficiently large (see also footnote 8).

The method for authentication discussed herein is a general scheme for validating the contents of a time-invariant data variable of arbitrary length. The test of legitimacy is based on a previously computed, nonsecret, nonforgeable test pattern (TP), whose functional relationship to the data is verified (at any later time) using a dynamically generated, nonsecret verification pattern (VP). The method does not rely on either the security or integrity features of a host processor and operating system to protect a verification table.

The cryptographic principles upon which this method is founded include:

1. Ability to create a test pattern using a cryptographically secure operation involving the quantity to be authenticated and a secret key resident in a host.
2. Ability to deny unrestricted usage of AR, the cryptographic operation used to create test patterns. (For all practical purposes, the user sees only a one-way function which allows a verification pattern to be generated from the quantity to be authenticated and the test pattern.)

An Implementation Using the Cryptographic Operations Proposed for Communication and File Security[10]

Except for *set master key*, each of the host's cryptographic operations produce outputs that depend on either the host master key or one of its derived variants (see Chapters 4 and 5). There are many mathematical identities involving the cryptographic operations which might be the basis for an authentication procedure. One such technique is described here.

At the time the host's master key is entered into the cryptographic facility (read into main storage and used as the object of a set master key operation), the following steps are performed:

1. KM1 and KM2 are obtained directly from KM0

[10] Only the cryptographic operations defined in Chapter 4 are used.

2. EMK: $\{KM1\} \longrightarrow E_{KM0}(KM1)$
3. DCPH: $\{E_{KM0}(KM1), C\} \longrightarrow D_{KM1}(C)$
4. EMK: $\{KM2\} \longrightarrow E_{KM0}(KM2)$
5. ECPH: $\{E_{KM0}(KM2), D_{KM1}(C)\} \longrightarrow E_{KM2}(D_{KM1}(C))$

C is an arbitrary nonsecret value which remains constant for all generated test patterns. The quantity

$$KA \equiv E_{KM2}(D_{KM1}(C))$$

is called the *system authentication key*. The system authentication key is a secret parameter used to create test patterns. It is created during a secure computer run, before or during the time when test patterns are created. A copy of KA should be sent to a suitable output device and stored in a secure place for future use. KA and all quantities involved in the computation are erased from main storage when processing is complete.

Test patterns are also created during a secure computer run. KA is made available either by reading it into main storage or by initially creating it. It is assumed that Xi and VPi are available for each required TPi. The procedure is as follows:

1. DCPH: $\{Xi, VPi\} \longrightarrow D_{D_{KM0}(Xi)}(VPi) = Qi$
2. RTMK: $\{KA, Qi\} \longrightarrow E_{KM0}(D_{D_{KM1}(C)}(Qi)) \equiv TPi$

The output of step 2 is defined as the generated test pattern. KA and all quantities involved in the computation are erased from main storage upon completion of this sequence.

Authentication of Xi is performed in the following manner:

1. RFMK: $\{C, TPi\} \longrightarrow D_{D_{KM0}(Xi)}(VPi)$
2. ECPH: $\{Xi, D_{D_{KM0}(Xi)}(VPi)\} \longrightarrow VPi$

The value C used here must be the same as that used to create TPi. If the result at step 2 agrees with the known value of VPi, then Xi is accepted; otherwise, Xi is rejected.

The integrity of the procedure depends on the secrecy of quantity $D_{KM1}(C)$. This quantity appears in clear form only within the cryptographic facility. Moreover, there is no way to use the cryptographic operations to decipher under KM1 (the first variant of the host's master key). Because of this, there is no way for an opponent to derive $D_{KM1}(C)$.

It is important, however, that an opponent not be able to alter or control the value of C. If an opponent could manipulate the value of C and could also obtain X and $E_{KM1}(X)$, for some arbitrary value of X, the procedure would be inadequate for security. For example, if $E_{KM1}(X)$ were substituted for C, this would yield the value X for the intermediate quantity $D_{KM1}(C)$.

Since the opponent knows the value of X, he could now forge test patterns for any desired quantities.

It is conceivable that values of X and $E_{KM1}(X)$ could be acquired, provided that the system's security is violated; for example, if KMT could be illegitimately acquired from a terminal and the corresponding value of E_{KM1} (KMT) could be obtained from the host's key table. On the other hand, if the opponent could manage to capture E_{KM1} (KM1), which is a system activation key (see Generation of Key-Encrypting Keys, Chapter 6), then the EMK and RFMK operations could be used to encipher arbitrary values under KM1.

Figure 8-12 illustrates the procedure for generating KA. Figure 8-13 illustrates the procedure for generating test patterns and for authenticating objects.

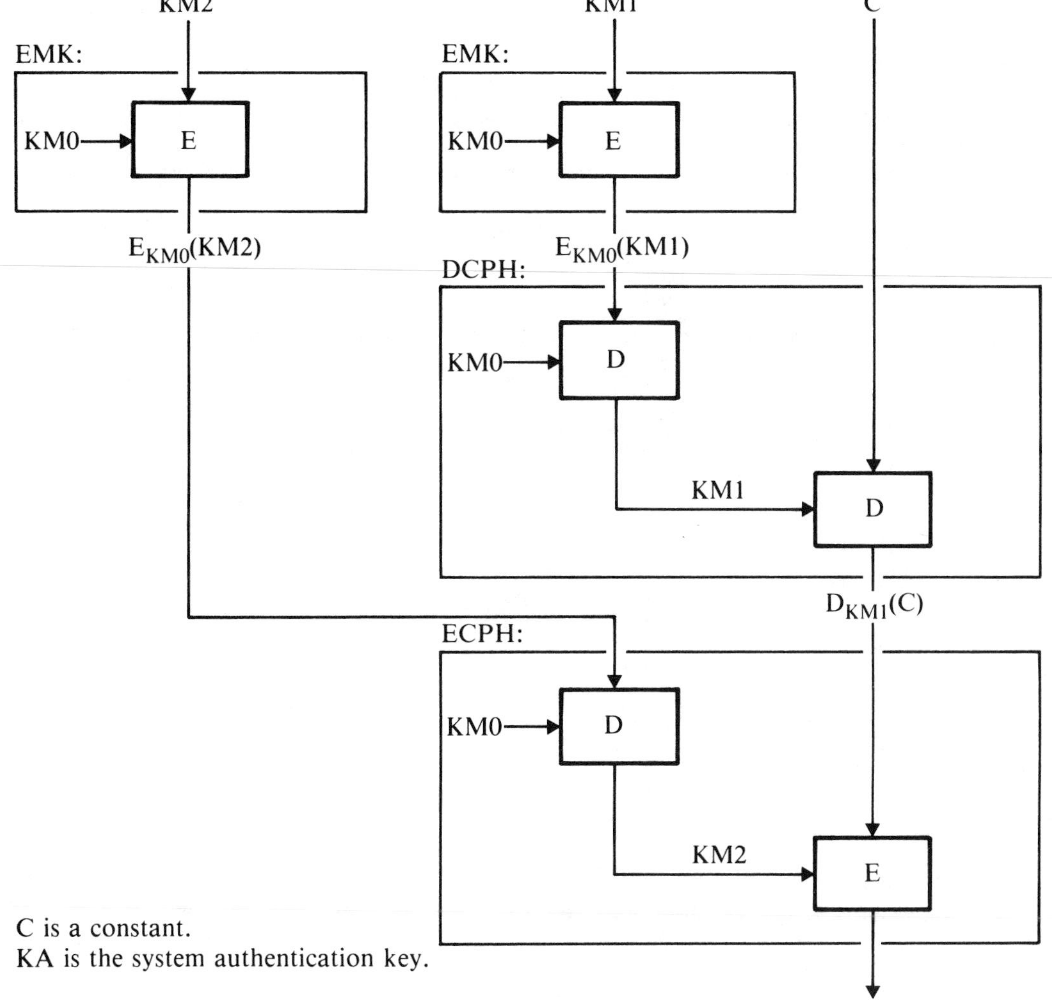

Figure 8-12. Generation of the System Authentication Key

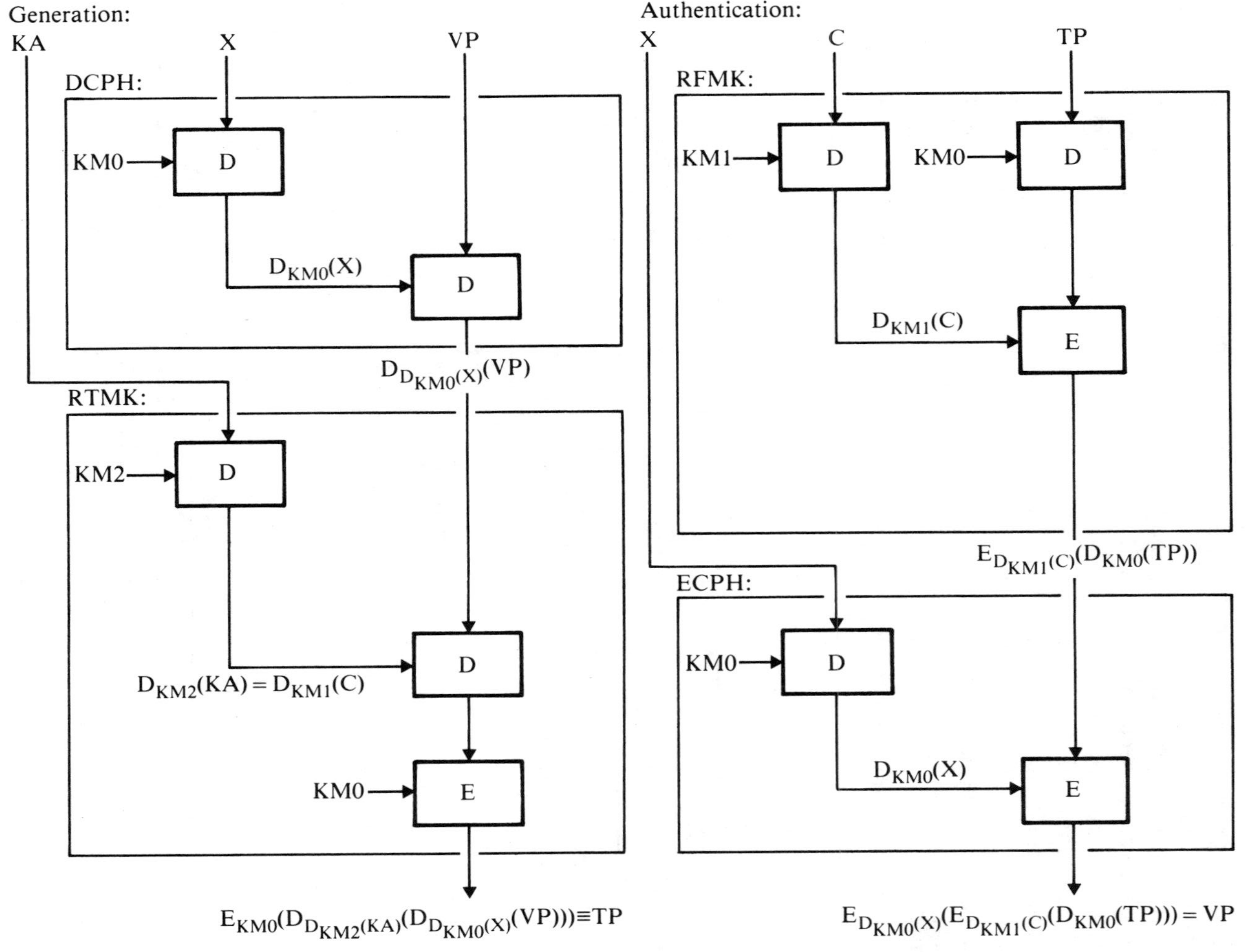

Figure 8-13. Test Pattern Generation and Authentication of Data Parameters

A Procedure for Authentication of Cryptographic Keys

Except for the host master key, which is stored in clear form within the host's cryptographic facility, all keys used by the host system are maintained in enciphered form. Data-encrypting keys, such as session and file keys, are protected by encipherment under the host master key, KM0. Secondary keys, such as terminal master keys, secondary communication keys, and secondary file keys, which are stored in the cryptographic key data set (CKDS), are protected by encipherment under either the first or second variant of the host master key, KM1 or KM2 (see Chapters 4 and 5). Several considerations bear upon any decision to provide authentication for cryptographic keys.

Secondary keys (stored enciphered under KM1 or KM2) could be parity-adjusted at key generation, and the key's parity could be checked at the time it is deciphered in the cryptographic facility. Since each byte in the external key consists of seven key bits and one parity bit, any alteration of the encrypted key due to noise would be detected with a probability of 255/256.

Session keys (KSs) and file keys (KFs) are not parity-adjusted at the time they are created, since they are defined to be enciphered already under KM0 or KNF. A data-encrypting key (KS or KF) is created by generating a random number RN, and defining RN as KS enciphered under KM0, or as KF enciphered under KNF. On the average, about 128 pseudo-random numbers would have to generated before one would be found that provided the recovered KS or KF with correct parity. Such a key generation procedure would be too inefficient for most purposes.

As to communication security, any alteration of stored secondary communication keys or terminal master keys would cause the initiated session keys to be different for each end user. Such a condition would be detected by the handshaking procedure.

As to file security, any alteration of stored secondary file keys would cause the recovered secondary file key to have correct parity with a probability of 1/256. Under such conditions, an incorrect secondary file key would go undetected with probability 1/256, and hence a file (such as one for backup) created using an incorrect secondary file key could not be recovered unless the same altered copy of the secondary file key were used.

If there were no cryptographic authentication, an opponent could transpose keys stored in the CKDS, and indexing errors could cause use of the wrong key without detection of the error. In each case, the parity of the key would still be correct, and this might allow unwanted or unanticipated cryptographic quantities to be derived that could be damaging to the security of the system. If an opponent could encipher under KM1 or KM2, without necessarily knowing the value of either KM1 or KM2, he could systematically replace existing keys with his own keys.

A technique employing test patterns can easily be adapted to validate encrypted keys stored in the CKDS (e.g., prior to their use within the cryptographic facility) (Figure 8-14). However, it should be realized that if the procedure is bypassed due to an unauthorized modification of programming (software), then the intended protection would not be achieved. Therefore, such an authentication procedure reduces the risk associated with

Generation: AR: { Xi, ∇(IDi) } → TPi

Checking:

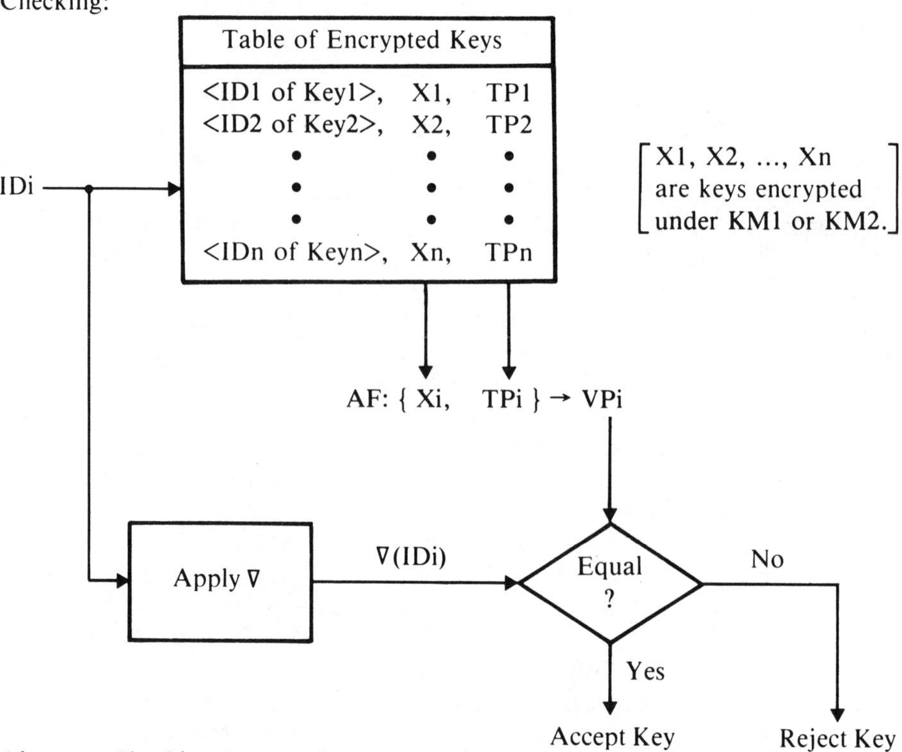

Alternate Checking Approach:

RFMK: { C, TPi } → Ωi
ECPH: { Xi, Ωi } → VPi

Note: C is a dynamically generated constant.

Figure 8-14. Authentication of Cryptographic Keys Using Test Patterns

using an incorrect cryptographic key, but it cannot eliminate the problem altogether.

Another Authentication Method Using Test Patterns Generated from the Host Master Key

Another way to define AF and AR using a conventional cryptographic algorithm like DES is described below:[11]

$$\text{AR: } \{\text{IDi, Xi}\} \longrightarrow \text{TPi}$$

$$\text{AF: } \{\text{IDi, Xi, TPi}\} \longrightarrow \begin{bmatrix} = 1 \text{ if (Xi, IDi, TPi) is a valid triple} \\ \neq 1 \text{ otherwise} \end{bmatrix}$$

[11] The method is based on a similar method suggested by Smid [10]. See also A Key Notarization System for Computer Networks, Chapter 9.

In this case, only test patterns are used. Verification patterns are not required. This is because TPi is tested for validity inside the cryptographic facility, that is, the output of the AF operation indicates only the result of the test (= 1 or ≠ 1).

Let KM5 represent the fifth variant of the host master key and define

$$K0 = E_{KM5}(0)$$
$$K1 = E_{KM5}(1)$$

K0, K1, and KM5 are keys used solely by the AF and AR operations; they effectively isolate AF and AR from the other cryptographic operations defined to the cryptographic facility. AF and AR are defined as follows:

$$\text{AR: } \{IDi, Xi\} \longrightarrow E_{K1 \oplus IDi}(E_{K0}(Xi)) \equiv TPi$$
$$\text{AF: } \{IDi, Xi, TPi\} \longrightarrow D_{K1}(E_{TPi*}(D_{TPi}(E_{K1}(1))))$$

where

$$TPi^* = E_{K1 \oplus IDi}(E_{K0}(Xi))$$

If TPi* = TPi, the output of the AR operation is equal to 1. Otherwise, the output is a complex function of K1, TPi*, and TPi and (in all probability) its value is unequal to 1. Figure 8-15 describes the steps taken by the cryptographic facility to perform the AF and AR operations.

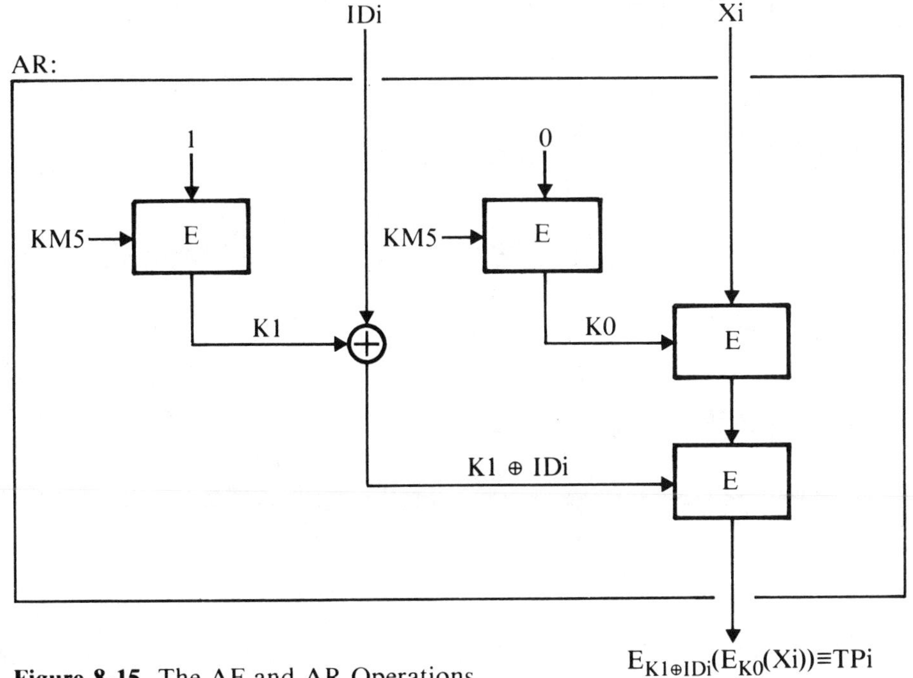

Figure 8-15. The AF and AR Operations

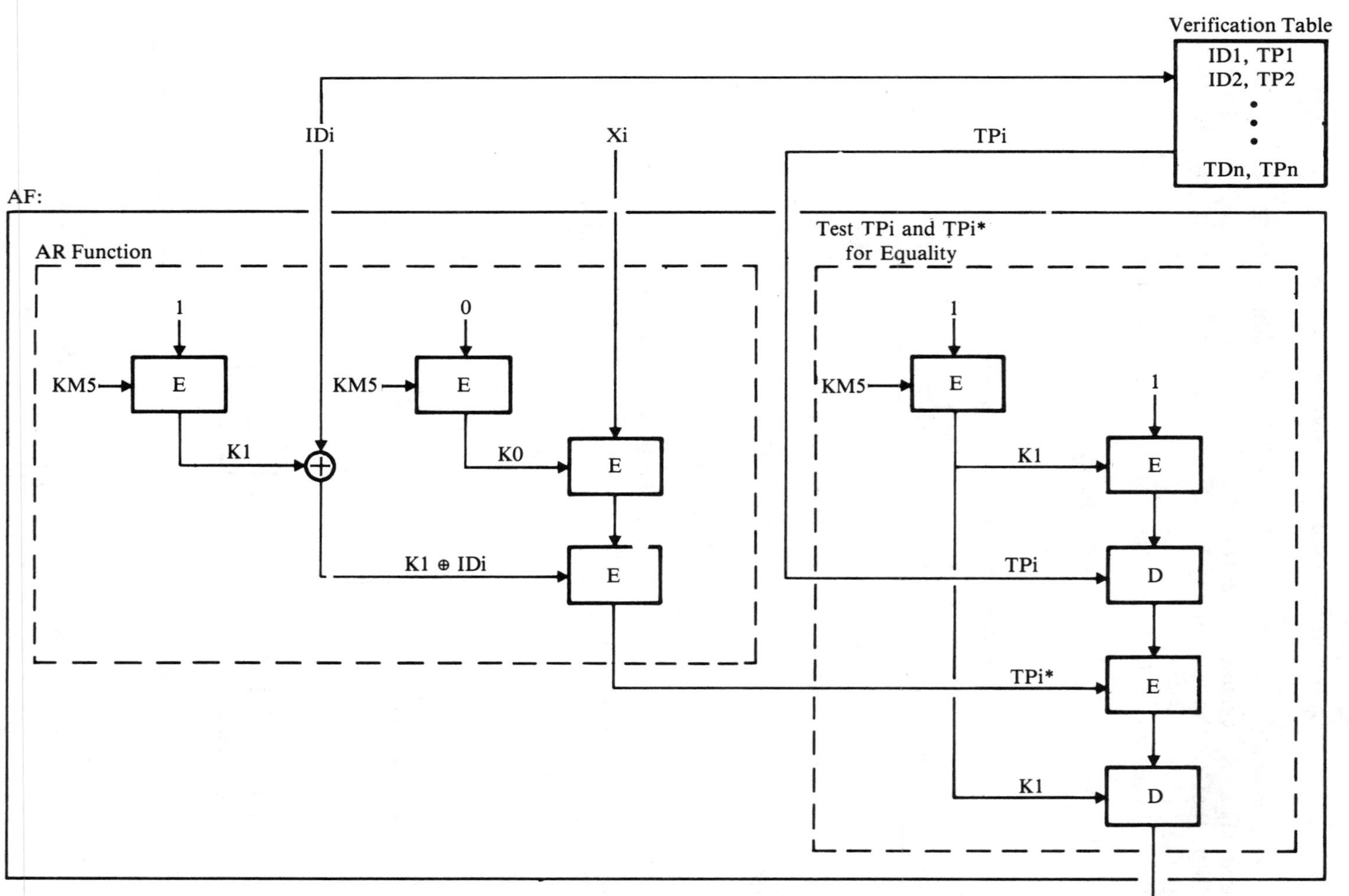

Figure 8-15 (cont'd). The AF and AR Operations

Rather than define K1 as a variant of the host master key, which would allow K1 ⊕ IDi to be manipulated to produce other variants of the host master key, K1 is produced via encipherment using a variant of the host master key. K0 (or the step of encipherment under K0) is introduced to prevent an opponent from directly controlling the input enciphered under K1 ⊕ IDi.

The reader will note that the steps involved in producing the quantity $E_{K1}(D_{TPi}(E_{TPi*}(D_{K1}(1))))$ are an alternate way to compare TPi and TPi* for equality. In effect, the comparison is implemented as a series of encipher and decipher operations.

REFERENCES

1. Wilkes, M. V., *Time-Sharing Computer Systems,* American Elsevier, New York, 1972.
2. Evans, A., Jr., Kantrowitz, W., and Weiss, E., "A User Authentication System Not Requiring Secrecy in the Computer," *Communications of the ACM,* **17**, No. 8, 437–442 (August 1974).
3. Pudy, G. B., "A High Security Log-in Procedure," *Communications of the ACM,* **17**, No. 8, 442–445 (August 1974).
4. Proposed Federal Standard 1026, *Telecommunications: Interoperability and Security Requirements for Use of the Data Encryption Standard in the Physical and Data Link Layers of Data Communications,* General Services Administration, Washington, D.C., Draft (January 21, 1982).
5. Jueneman, R. R., "Analysis of Certain Aspects of Output Feedback Mode," in *Advances in Cryptography: The Proceedings of Crypto 82,* edited by L. M. Adleman, D. L. Chaum, D. E. Denning, W. Diffie, S. T. Kent, R. L. Rivest, A. Shamir, Plenum Publishing Corp., New York (1983).
6. Jueneman, R. R., Matyas, S. M., and Meyer, C. H., "Authentication with Manipulation Detection Code," *Proceedings IEEE '83 Symposium on Security and Privacy,* Oakland, California (April 1983).
7. McPhee, W. S. "Operating System Integrity in OS/VS2," *IBM Systems Journal,* **13**, No. 3, 230–252 (1974).
8. Diffie, W. and Hellman, M., "New Directions in Cryptography," *IEEE Transactions on Information Theory,* IT-22, 644–654 (November 1976).
9. Lennon, R. E., Matyas, S. M., and Meyer, C. H., "Cryptographic Authentication of Time-Invariant Quantities," *IEEE Transactions on Communications, COM-29,* No. 6, 773–777 (June 1981).
10. Smid, M. E., *A Key Notarization System for Computer Networks,* National Bureau of Standards Special Publication 500–54, National Bureau of Standards, U.S. Department of Commerce, Washington, DC (October 1979).

Other Publications of Interest

11. Needham, R. M. and Schroder, M. D., "Using Encryption for Authentication in Large Networks of Computers," *Communications of the ACM,* **21**, No. 12, 993–999 (December 1978).
12. *Guideline on User Authentication Techniques for Computer Network Access Control,* Federal Information Processing Standard (FIPS) Publication 83, National Bureau of Standards, U.S. Department of Commerce, Washington, DC (September 1980).
13. Feistel, H., "Cryptographic Coding for Data-Bank Privacy," IBM T. J. Watson Research Center, Yorktown Heights, NY, RC 2827 (March 1970).

CHAPTER NINE

Digital Signatures[1]

With the quickened pace of business today, and the large distances which are frequently involved, the time required to obtain a signed agreement may undesirably delay a project. The use of an electronic (or digital) signature may remove this inconvenience. If today's paper-based business transactions were to be implemented exclusively via an electronic communications network, the system would have to rely on signed messages or digital signatures.

The signature would have to be such that the receiver could prove to an impartial third party (a court, judge, or referree before whom the parties had agreed to submit for resolution any issue or dispute)[2] that the contents of the message were genuine and that it originated with the sender. The signature would also have to be such that the sender could not later disavow messages, nor could the receiver forge messages or signatures for self-serving purposes.

A signature is a function of (1) the message, transaction, or document to be signed, (2) secret information known to the sender, and possibly, (3) public information known to all parties. The signature may either be a special bit pattern appended to the data, or it may be an integral part of the cryptographically transformed data.

Although digital and written signatures can serve the same purposes, there are obvious physical differences. It should be understood that the several branches of law pertaining to signatures assume a paper-based system as the medium for transacting business. Thus before describing how digital signatures can be obtained, the legal significance of written signatures is discussed.

SIGNIFICANCE OF SIGNATURES[3]

The legal significance of signatures and the use of writings bearing such signatures must be viewed from a perspective which encompasses several branches of the law, including but not limited to the Statute of Frauds, the Law of

[1] This is a technical discussion of an approach to solving a legal problem. The material contained in this chapter does not constitute advice, and those who intend to implement any of the concepts included herein should first consult their legal counsel.

[2] Hereafter, this impartial third party shall be referred to as the referee.

Acknowledgments, the Law of Agency, and the Uniform Commercial Code (UCC). The need for a device or process which may satisfy the requirements of such branches of law in the modern context of electronic (or paperless) signatures can be appreciated by understanding some key areas of the law affecting signatures.

The history of the Statute of Frauds [2] begins in 1677 when "An Act for Prevention of Frauds and Perjuries" was enacted in England. The need for such an act resulted from the peculiar rules of evidence used by English courts during the 17th Century. For example, two parties (A and B) might enter into an oral agreement for the sale of land. It was possible for A to sue B, alleging that B orally agreed to sell the land for a certain amount. In fact, there may never have been any agreement at all, or the price may have been much greater. Under English law, B could not testify in his own behalf. Lawsuits of this kind were frequently tried with professional witnesses, testimony of friends of the parties, and the like. Since perjury was commonplace, the defendant in such cases was at a distinct disadvantage. Suppose that party C testified that he heard B agree to the sale. How could B bring forth a witness who could testify that he did not hear the agreement? The difficulty is that of proving a negative condition.

The difficulty was finally overcome by requiring written evidence that contracts were actually entered into. Specifically, the Statute of Frauds was designed to prevent fraud by excluding from consideration by the courts legal actions on certain contracts, unless there was written evidence of the agreement signed by the party to be charged or his duly authorized agent.

Law of Acknowledgments

Certain documents require acknowledgment or proof of the identity of the person who signs the document, and proof that it was signed on the stated date. This acknowledgment or proof is necessary to prevent the person who signed the document from claiming later that the signature is not genuine. Moreover, certain transactions require that the signature be witnessed by one or more persons. Such transactions may vary according to the law of the jurisdiction in which the document was executed.

Acknowledgment or proof of signature upon a legal document or instrument may normally be made before a judge, an official examiner of title, an official referee, or a notary public. Essentially, the form of an acknowledgment consists of the following:

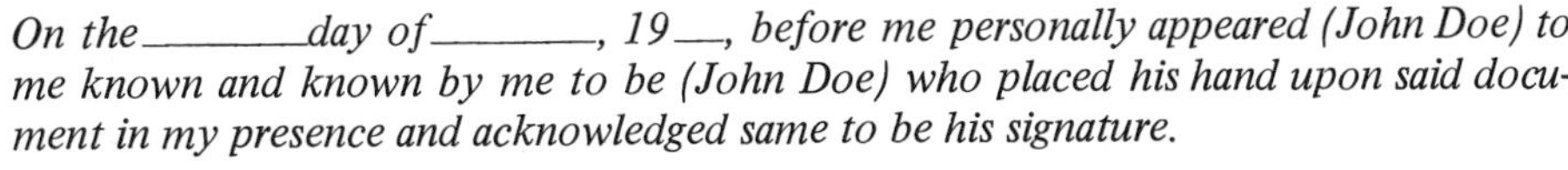

On the _______ day of _______, 19__, before me personally appeared (John Doe) to me known and known by me to be (John Doe) who placed his hand upon said document in my presence and acknowledged same to be his signature.

____

Notary Public

Such acknowledgments together with the signed document are usually recorded in an official registry, like an office of the county clerk or secretary of state.

Law of Agency

The principles of agency law [2] are essential for the conduct of business transactions. A corporation, as a legal entity, can function only through its agents. The law of partnership is to a large degree a special application of agency principles to that particular form of business organization. Agency may be defined as follows:

> Agency is the fiduciary relation (involving a confidence or trust) which results from the manifestation of consent by one person to another that the other shall act on his behalf and subject to his control, and consent by the other so to act. [Restatement of the Law, Agency (2d), p. 7, Sec. 1 (1)]

As a general rule, no particular formalities are required to create an agency relationship. The appointment may be either written or oral, and the relationship may be either expressed or implied. There are two situations in which formalities are required: (1) with a power of attorney, where a formally acknowledged instrument is used for conferring authority upon the agent; and (2) in a few states where it is required that the act which confers authority to perform a certain act must possess the same formalities as the act to be performed. For example, authority to sign a contract which is required to be in writing must itself be granted by a written instrument.

Generally, the law of agency applies to contracts or commercial paper. A principal (the person from whom an agent's authority derives) is bound by the duly authorized acts of his agent. However, if the agent does not possess the requisite authority (express, implied, or apparent), the principal in most instances will not be bound. An agent who fails to bind his principal to an agreement because of the agent's failure to name the principal, or due to lack of the agent's authority, will usually be personally liable to third parties. Thus the correct way for an agent to execute a contract or instrument is to affix the name of his principal followed by his own signature and the capacity in which it is made: "P" Principal, by "A", as Agent.

Uniform Commercial Code

The Uniform Commercial Code (UCC) [3] is a comprehensive modernization and compilation of the various statutes relating to commercial transactions. Its primary objective is to provide uniformity of commercial law throughout American jurisdictions. It has been adopted in all states except Louisiana. The present articles relating to commercial paper, banking transactions, and investment securities are paper-based.

To accommodate electronic funds transfer systems, a special committee was formed to prepare amendments or supplements to these articles. Although the principles governing the transfer of paper-based stocks and bonds (see Article 8 of reference 3, for example) can generally be made applicable to the paperless variety, many technical and mechanical changes are needed to apply those principles to securities without certificates.

According to the current (1972) version of the UCC,

> "Signed" includes any symbol executed or adopted by a party with present intention to authenticate a writing. [UCC: Sec. 1-201 (39)]

and, in case of commercial paper,

> A signature is made by use of any name, including any trade or assumed name, upon an instrument, or by any word or mark used in lieu of a written signature. [UCC: Sec. 3-401 (2)]

The inclusion of the word authenticate in the definition of signed clearly indicates that a complete handwritten signature is not necessary. This authentication may be printed, typed, stamped, or written; it may be initials or thumbprint. It may be on any part of the document, and in certain cases may be found in a billhead or letterhead. No catalog of possible authentications can be complete, and courts must use common sense and commercial experience in passing upon such matters. The question is always whether the symbol was executed or adopted by the party with the intention at that time of authenticating the writing.

A signature may be made by an agent or other representative, and his authority to make such signature may be established according to the Law of Agency. No particular form of appointment is necessary to establish such authority. However, such a signature may be unauthorized if made by an agent who exceeds his actual or apparent authority. An unauthorized signature is one made without actual, implied, or apparent authority, and includes those made by forgers, imposters, and fictitious payees.

The law of commercial paper also recognizes the principle that the drawer—the one who creates a negotiable instrument (a draft, check, note, or certificate of deposit)—has voluntarily entered into relationships beyond his control with subsequent holders of the instrument. The law imposes on the drawer the responsibility to assure that his own negligence does not contribute to the possibility of material alteration of the instrument later in the chain of transfer.

Contributory Negligence

Any person who by his own negligence substantially contributes to a material alteration of the instrument, or to the making of an unauthorized signature, is precluded from asserting the defense of alteration or of lack of authority against anyone who has accepted the instrument in accordance with reasonable commercial standards. An example of such negligence is the situation where space is left in the body of the instrument, such as $ 500, allowing the value to be changed to $2,500, or allowing the words "   five hundred" to be changed to "twenty-five hundred." It also covers the most obvious case where a drawer makes use of a signature stamp or other automatic signing device and is negligent in controlling access to it.

In banking transactions, verification of signatures is a necessary part of the procedure known as the process of posting. Completion of this procedure helps to determine when an item is finally paid in favor of an innocent holder. Posting involves two basic elements: a decision to pay, and some recording of the payment. In certain instances, the recording may actually precede the decision to pay. That is, provisional debits may be entered, and the decision on the authenticity of the signature may be made at a later time.

As incorporated in the UCC, the concept of finality of payment [Sec. 3–418] states that a drawee (the person on whom a bill of exchange is drawn) cannot recover funds paid to a bona fide holder of a draft or check bearing a forged signature of the drawer (one who draws a bill of exchange, or order for payment). This is known as the rule of *Price v. Neal* [3 Burr. 1354 (1762)]. The rule, as enunciated by Lord Mansfield in 1762, imposed upon the drawee the duty to be satisfied that "the bill drawn upon him was in the drawer's hand" [*Price v. Neal*, 3 Burr. 1354, at 1357] before he accepted or paid it, but that it was not the duty of the good-faith holder to inquire into it.

Many banks today rarely review the signature on a small check for its authenticity. Only in cases of stop-payment orders and reports of lost or stolen checks do banks interrupt their otherwise mechanized routines involving such instruments. Generally, losses incurred as a result of forged drawers' signatures are small enough to be absorbed as a cost of operation.

OBTAINING DIGITAL SIGNATURES

For a digital signature procedure to work, there must be enough information available for message and signature validation and yet insufficient information to permit forgery of either message or signature. While a receiver could validate messages and signatures with the same information (algorithm and parameters) used by the sender to create signatures, this could also permit forgery. Therefore, the same information is never sufficient for both signature generation and validation.

Using a data communication system, a sender A may transmit signed messages to a receiver B under a defined procedure which requires that certain information be held by both parties. A must have information that allows it to generate a signature for each message transmitted to B. And B must have information that allows it to validate messages and signatures received from A. The procedure can be extended to permit two-way communication by providing B with signature-generation information similar to that held by A, and by providing A with information that allows it to validate messages and signatures received from B.

If A is concerned that B may later disavow the receipt of messages, A can require that messages be certified. *Message certification* means that the receiver provides some proof to the sender that the message was received. For example, if A sends message M to B, then B could send back to A the signed message "B received M from A," with message M repeated in its entirety.

An initial written and hand-signed agreement is normally required between sender and receiver, regardless of the method used in implementing digital signatures (see Legalizing Digital Signatures). Such an agreement should contain a complete description of the digital signature procedure to be used, including either a list of bit patterns that may be required for validating signatures or the name and location of a registry where the bit patterns are recorded.

There are several cryptographic techniques for generating digital signatures using both conventional and public-key cryptographic algorithms.[4] Digital signatures obtained with a public-key algorithm are referred to here as *universal, general,* or *true* signatures. This is because such signatures can be validated by *anyone* having access to the public-key (or validation parameter) of the sender. To insure that the public-key is genuine and cannot be changed, each sender must publish or record his public-key in a designated registry.

Universal signatures can also be obtained with a conventional algorithm, but the protocols are more involved. As with a public-key algorithm, the sender must share certain nonsecret validation information in advance with the receiver, and this information must also be published or recorded in a designated registry. However, the protocol may also involve certain other secret and/or nonsecret information sent to the receiver at the time the message is validated. However, in no case does the sender share all his secret signature generation information with other communicants or parties.

Arbitrated signatures are another way to obtain digital signatures with a conventional algorithm. An arbitrated signature is validated by a trusted arbiter at the time the message is communicated between parties. To permit validation, each user shares his secret signature-generation information with the arbiter.

Finally, digital signatures can be obtained with a conventional algorithm if the algorithm is first used to obtain the properties of public and private keys. The digital signatures are then created in the same manner as if they were created with a public-key algorithm.

UNIVERSAL SIGNATURES

When universal signatures are involved, the receiver can independently validate each message and signature. A referee is called upon only to settle disputes.

Figure 9-1 illustrates the general approach for obtaining universal signatures. To prevent signatures from being forged, and to associate them uniquely with their senders, each communicant has certain nonshared (secret) information that is used to generate the signature. Usually a signature and message are validated with nonsecret validation information which is included within the initial written agreement or recorded in a designated registry and is available to the parties in advance. But it may also involve certain secret and/or nonsecret information provided to the receiver at the time the message is validated.

[4] A *conventional* cryptographic algorithm is one for which the enciphering and deciphering keys are either identical or are such that each can easily be computed from the other. In contrast, a *public-key* algorithm is one for which there are public and private keys (normally the public key is used for enciphering and the private key for deciphering), and knowledge of the public key does not permit the private key to be computed [4]. See also Cryptographic Algorithms, Chapter 2.

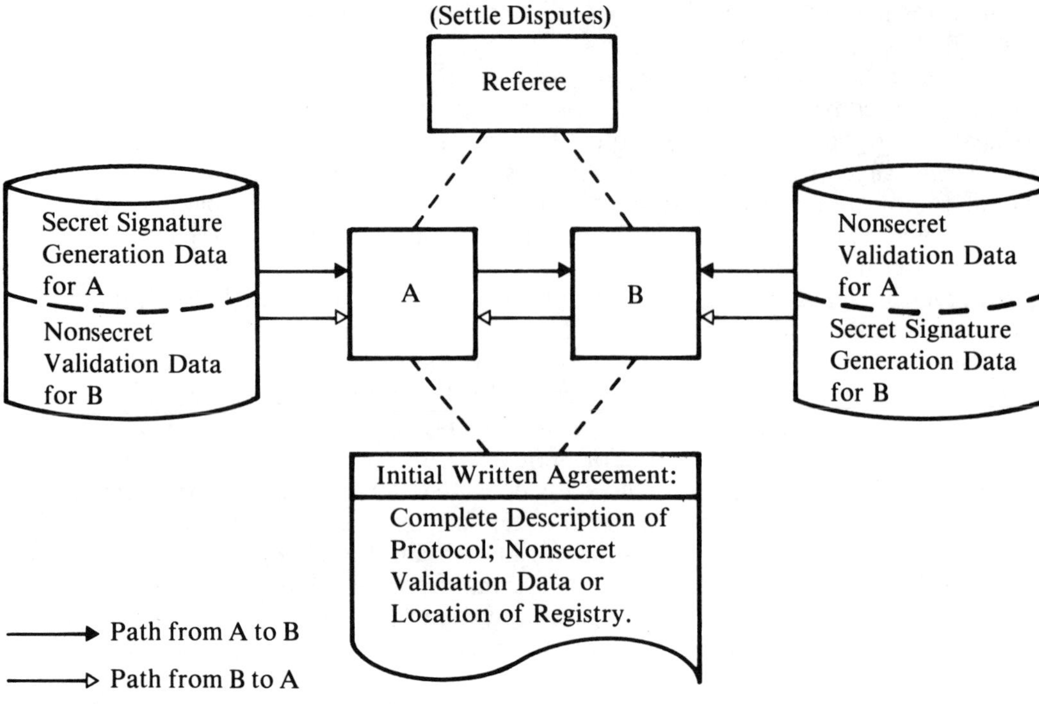

Figure 9-1. A General Approach for Exchanging Universal Signatures

An Approach Using Public-Key Algorithms

Recall that a cryptographic algorithm is composed of enciphering (E) and deciphering (D) procedures which usually are identical or simply consist of the same steps performed in reverse order, but which can be dissimilar.[5] The keys selected by the user consist of sequences of numbers or characters. An enciphering key (Ke) is used to encipher plaintext (X) into ciphertext (Y), as in Equation 9-1, and a deciphering key (Kd) is used to decipher ciphertext (Y) into plaintext (X), as in Equation 9-2.

$$E_{Ke}(X) = Y \tag{9-1}$$

$$D_{Kd}(E_{Ke}(X)) = D_{Kd}(Y) = X \tag{9-2}$$

If E and D are made public, as the present discussion assumes, cryptographic security completely depends on protecting the secret keys.

In a public-key algorithm, the enciphering and deciphering keys, Ke and Kd, are unequal. One key is made public and the other is kept private. However, if the algorithm is to be useful, communicants must be able to compute a public and private pair of keys efficiently, whereas knowledge of the public key alone must not permit the private key to be computed efficiently.

[5] Conventional and public-key algorithms have already been defined and discussed in Chapter 2. However, these subjects are introduced here in a slightly different way.

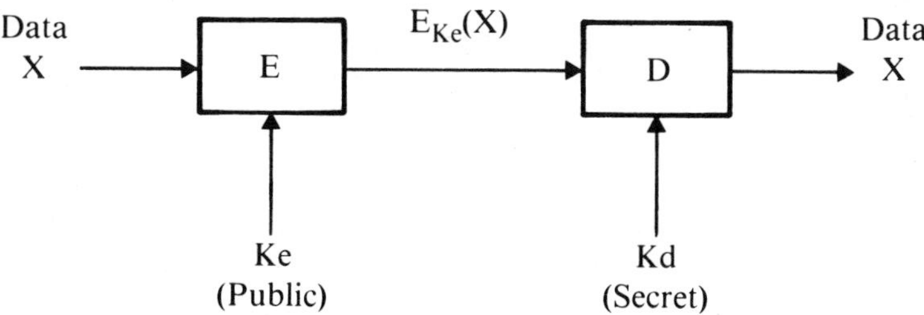

Figure 9-2. Public-Key Cryptographic System Used for Privacy Only

If Ke can be made public without compromising the secrecy of Kd, then the public-key algorithm can be used for private data communications (Figure 9-2). In that case, anyone can encipher data by using the receiver's public enciphering key, but only the authorized receiver can decipher the data through possession of the secret deciphering key.

If Kd can be made public without compromising the secrecy of Ke, then the public-key algorithm can be used to obtain digital signatures, or signed messages (Figure 9-3). In that case, anyone can decipher data using the sender's public deciphering key and thereby prove the origin of the data, but only the authorized sender can encipher the data through possession of the secret enciphering key.

By inserting prearranged information in all messages (such as sender ID, receiver ID, and message sequence number), the messages can be checked to determine if they are genuine. However, because the data are available to anyone having the public deciphering key, privacy is not attained.

If it is also the case that encipherment followed by decipherment, and decipherment followed by encipherment, produce the original plaintext, that is,

$$D_{Kd}(E_{Ke}(X)) = E_{Ke}(D_{Kd}(X)) = X; \quad \text{for all } X \tag{9-3}$$

then the public-key algorithm can be used for both private data communi-

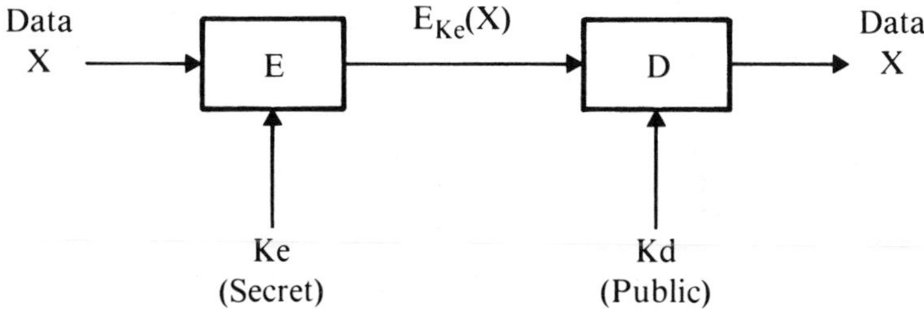

Figure 9-3. Public-Key Cryptographic System Used for Digital Signatures Only

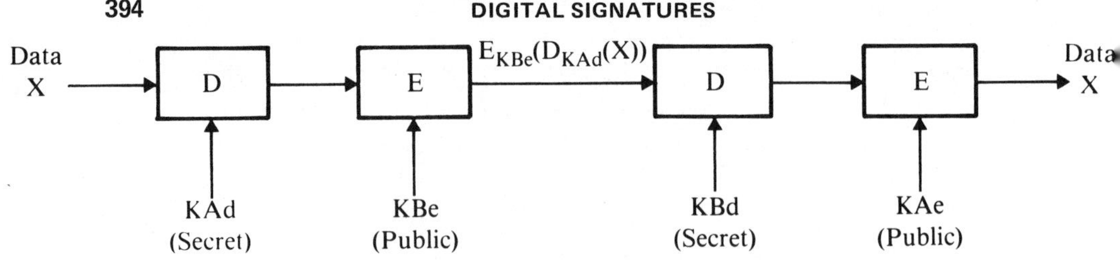

KAe and KAd are enciphering and deciphering keys of the sender (A).
KBe and KBd are enciphering and deciphering keys of the receiver (B).

Figure 9-4. Public-Key Cryptographic System Used for Both Privacy and Digital Signatures

cations and digital signatures (Figure 9-4).[6] A message is signed by deciphering it with the sender's (A's) secret deciphering key (KAd), and privacy is obtained by enciphering the result with the receiver's (B's) public enciphering key (KBe).

However, it must be emphasized that effective data security demands that the correct public key be used; otherwise, the system is exposed to attack. For example, if A can be tricked into using C's instead of B's public key, then C can both decipher the secret communications sent from A to B, and transmit messages to A pretending to be B. Thus key secrecy and key integrity are two distinct, but very important, attributes of cryptographic keys. With a public-key algorithm, the requirement for key secrecy is relaxed for one of the keys, but the requirement for integrity is not.

In order to understand how a public-key algorithm can be used to obtain signed messages, let PA, PB, . . . , PZ denote the public enciphering keys (stored in public files) and SA, SB, . . . , SZ denote the private deciphering keys belonging to the communicants A, B, . . . , Z, as shown in Figure 9-5.

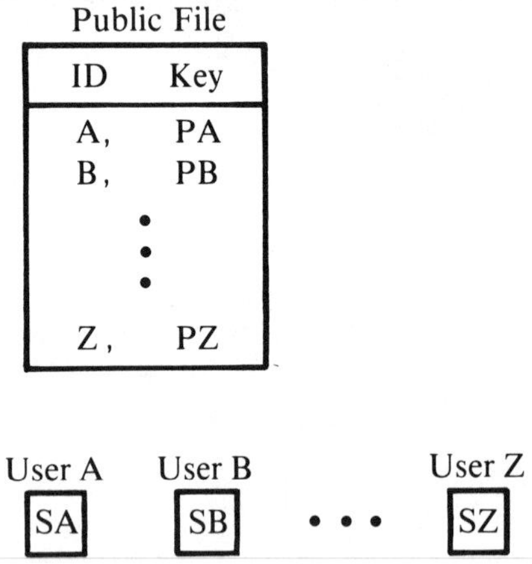

Public File

ID	Key
A,	PA
B,	PB
•	
•	
•	
Z,	PZ

User A: SA   User B: SB   • • •   User Z: SZ

Figure 9-5. NonSecret Enciphering Keys and Secret Deciphering Keys

[6] Merkle and Hellman [5] have shown that a signature capability can be obtained if the relation $E_{Ke}(D_{Kd}(X)) = X$ holds for only a fraction of the set of all messages.

Assume also that the relation in Equation 9-3 is satisfied. Note that for each pair of keys (PA, SA), it follows that $E_{PA}(D_{SA}(M)) = M$ for all M, whereas $E_{PB}(D_{SA}(M)) \neq M$ for almost every M when PB $\neq$ PA.

Assume that all communicated messages contain the sender's ID, the receiver's ID, and a message sequence number in addition to whatever other text is sent in the message; that is, let M denote a message whose format is

M = **<sender ID>**,
<receiver ID>,
<sequence number>, (9-4)
<data>

where the symbols < and > delimit the elements of M. The text of the message is represented by <data>. (A description of the message format would be part of the prior written agreement between the parties.)

In the general case, M will have to be divided into several blocks and enciphered/deciphered separately using methods of chained block encryption (see Block Ciphers and Stream Ciphers, Chapter 2). However, to simplify the discussion, assume that M contains only one block.

Prior to the commencement of the protocol, each communicant reads the public file and obtains the public key of each other communicant. In the present example, A would obtain PB and B would obtain PA from the public file. (Although keys stored in the public file need not be kept secret, they must be protected from accidental or intentional alteration. Methods have been suggested for protecting the integrity of the public-key file [6], but are not discussed here. See also Key Management Considerations–Symmetric Versus Asymmetric Algorithms, Chapter 11).

Let Mi = [A, B, i, T] denote the ith message communicated from A to B. To sign the message using the described protocol, A deciphers Mi with the secret key SA. If private data communications are also required, the result, $D_{SA}(Mi)$, is enciphered with B's public key, PB, and the resulting quantity, $E_{PB}(D_{SA}(Mi))$, is sent to B; otherwise $D_{SA}(Mi)$ is sent to B.

If $E_{PB}(D_{SA}(Mi))$ is received, B recovers $D_{SA}(Mi)$ by deciphering the received quantity with the secret deciphering key, SB.

$$D_{SB}(E_{PB}(D_{SA}(Mi))) = D_{SA}(Mi)$$

Otherwise, $D_{SA}(Mi)$ is received, in which case decipherment with SB is not required. In any event, B then recovers Mi by enciphering $D_{SA}(Mi)$ with A's public key, PA.

$$E_{PA}(D_{SA}(Mi)) = Mi$$

Once the content of Mi has been verified, quantity $D_{SA}(Mi)$ can be used as proof that Mi originated with A. Because SA is available only to A, only A could produce $D_{SA}(Mi)$ in the first place. It is impossible for another communicant to produce $D_{SA}(Mi')$ for a given Mi′ (unless, of course, SA is compromised).

Let Q denote the concatenation of <sender id>, <receiver id>, and <sequence number>, and let c be the length of Q in bits. Assume that the public-key algorithm is a good generator of pseudo-random numbers. Therefore, if $D_{SA}(Mi)$ is enciphered with any key other than PA, or a corrupted value of $D_{SA}(Mi)$ is enciphered with any key including PA, then the probability of producing a correct value Q is approximately equal to $1/2^c$.

Because $1/2^c$ is a very small number (recall that c is the length of Q in bits), the content of Mi can be authenticated by ensuring that the correct value of Q is recovered when $D_{SA}(Mi)$ is enciphered with PA.[7] Therefore, B concludes that M is genuine and that it originated with A if and only if

1. <sender ID> = A (sender's ID),
2. <receiver ID> = B (receiver's ID)
3. <sequence number> = i (next expected value).

In the example, $D_{SA}(Mi)$ is a function of both the message (Mi) and the sender's secret key (SA), and can be computed only by the sender. Moreover, $D_{SA}(Mi)$ satisfies the criteria for a signed message without the need for a digital signature to be appended to the message. This is because the contents of a recovered message can be validated strictly on the basis of known parameters contained in the data, such as <sender id>, <receiver id>, and <sequence number>.

Schemes for obtaining digital signatures with a public-key algorithm have been invented by Rivest, Shamir, and Adleman [7], Merkel and Hellman [5], and Shamir [8].

An Approach Using Conventional Algorithms

Method One

An approach invented by Diffie and Lamport [4], which is based upon a conventional algorithm such as DES, makes use of a digital signature composed of a list of cryptographic keys.

In order that an n-bit message may be signed, the sender randomly generates in advance 2n 56-bit cryptographic keys

$$k1, K1, k2, K2, \dots, kn, Kn \tag{9-5}$$

which are kept secret. The receiver is given in advance two sets of corresponding nonsecret 64-bit validation parameters

$$u1, U1, u2, U2, \dots, un, Un \tag{9-6}$$

[7] If M is divided into blocks and a method of chained block encryption is used, then the last block must contain some data whose value is known to the receiver. This may require that some agreed upon constant, say all zero bits, be included in the last block.

and

$$v1, V1, v2, V2, \ldots, vn, Vn \tag{9-7}$$

where

$$vi = E_{ki}(ui), Vi = E_{Ki}(Ui); \quad i = 1, 2, \ldots, n$$

The validation parameters (Equations 9-6 and 9-7) are also recorded by the sender in an established public registry with recognized and accepted integrity. It is the receiver's responsibility to ensure that the validation parameters received from the sender are genuine (e.g., by comparing them with similar values stored in the public registry).[8]

Later, when message M is sent, the digital signature is generated by selecting k1 or K1 depending on whether the first bit of M is 0 or 1, respectively; selecting k2 or K2 depending on whether the second bit of M is 0 or 1, respectively; and so forth. For example, if M = 0, 1, 1, 0, . . . , the signature would contain the following keys: k1, K2, K3, k4, ...

The receiver validates the digital signature by ensuring that the first 56-bit key in the signature will encipher validation parameter u1 into $E_{k1}(u1)$ if the first bit of M is 0, or that it will encipher U1 into $E_{K1}(U1)$ if the first bit of M is 1; the second 56-bit key in the signature will encipher validation parameter u2 into $E_{k2}(u2)$ if the second bit of M is 0, or it will encipher U2 into $E_{K2}(U2)$ if the second bit of M is 1; and so forth.

For all practical purposes, only the sender, who knows the secret values of ki and Ki (Equation 9-5) and who originally creates vi and Vi from ui and Ui, can disclose a key (to the receiver) that will successfully encipher either ui into vi or Ui into Vi. An opponent would have to discover the value of one of the secret keys (e.g., by using Ui and Vi to solve for Ki), which would not be computationally feasible, or change the value of one of the validation parameters recorded in the registry. For these reasons, and since the procedure is a one-time system (i.e., ki, Ki, vi, and Vi are not reused once ki or Ki has been sent to the receiver), the receiver is unable to forge a single bit in the message.

The above approach demonstrates that digital signatures can be obtained with conventional algorithms and is discussed because it is simple and easy to understand. An obvious disadvantage is that a separate key must be included in the signature for each bit in the message. This could result in very large signatures depending upon the size of the message to be signed. For example, if the DES algorithm were used, the approach would result in a 56-fold data expansion. However, if data compression techniques are used, smaller signatures are possible.

[8] Alternatively, only one validation parameter (a master validation parameter) is stored in the public registry, and this one value is used to validate the entire set of validation parameters received from the sender. The master validation parameter could be published in one or more major newspapers. In such an approach, the master validation parameter would be a complex function of the set of validation parameters (see Compressed Encoding Function). However, such protocols are omitted from the discussion.

Compressed Encoding Function

Let *compressed encoding* (CE) be a function that maps variable length messages of t bits to fixed length bit patterns of m bits, where m and CE are such that it is computationally infeasible to find two different messages, M and M′, for which CE(M) = CE(M′) (Figure 9-6). For a specific M, it ordinarily requires on the order of $2^m/2 = 2^{m-1}$ trials to find an $M' \neq M$ such that CE(M′) = CE(M). However, by trading off time for memory, the number of trials can be reduced with the aid of a precomputed table (see reference 9 and Appendix B). (However, the time to compute such a table may be considerable.) Suppose, for example, the CEs of $2^{m/2}$ messages have been computed and stored in a table. Since the total number of CEs (2^m) is much greater than $2^{m/2}$, the probability that an intercepted CE is included in the table is about $1/2^{m/2}$. In that case, only about $2^{m/2}$ CEs must be intercepted before a match with a table entry occurs. In other words, to find two different messages, M′ and M, such that CE(M′) = CE(M), requires $2^{m/2}$ trials instead of $2^m/2$. If m = 64, the values for 2^{32} and 2^{63} are

$$2^{32} = 4{,}294{,}967{,}296$$

$$2^{63} = 9{,}223{,}372{,}036{,}854{,}775{,}808$$

Thus, the opponent gains an enormous advantage: a computationally infeasible problem is now reduced to a computationally feasible problem.

For example, a digital signature procedure that uses a CE function with 2^m different CE-values could be defeated if it were possible to compute the compressed encoding function of only twice the square root of 2^m messages.[9]

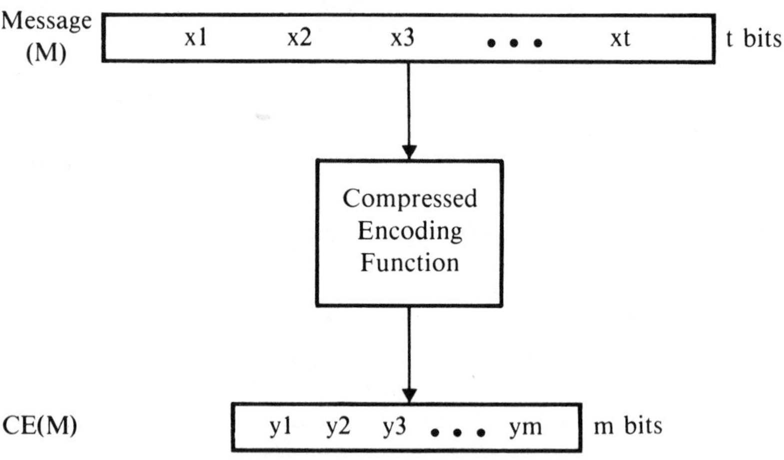

Figure 9-6. The Compressed Encoding Function

[9] If there are 2^m different CE-values, the probability of a match (i.e., any two values being equal) is about 0.5 when only $2^{(m+1)/2}$ CE-values have been precomputed. The attack is described by Yuval [10] in terms of the birthday paradox—a closely related but different problem (see also Appendix B).

Let M1 denote a set of messages that the receiver is willing to accept and let M2 denote a set of messages that the receiver is not willing to accept. The messages in each set could be random perturbations on only two starting messages (i.e., replace words by their synonyms, manipulate the number of blanks between words, and so forth). Generate the compressed encoding for each of these perturbed messages and wait until the same compressed encoding is produced for an acceptable message in M1 and an unacceptable message in M2.

There are many ways in which a suitable CE function could be defined using the DES algorithm. First let M be divided into n 64-bit blocks, X1, X2, . . . , Xn, and define ∇K as a function that transforms n $\times$ 64 bits of data, M = (X1, X2, . . . , Xn), into 64 bits of data (U):

$$\nabla K(M) = U$$

where K is a cryptographic key and U is computed as follows:

$$\begin{aligned} E_K(X1) &= Y1 \\ E_K(X2 \oplus Y1) &= Y2 \\ &\vdots \\ E_K(Xn \oplus Yn-1) &= Yn \\ E_K(X1 \boxplus X2 \boxplus \ldots \boxplus Xn \boxplus Yn) &= U \end{aligned}$$

where $\boxplus$ denotes a hashing operator. For example, $\boxplus$ could be simple modulo 2^k addition, k = 1, 2, . . . , 64, or, in an extreme case, a complex encryption function. Now let K1 and K2 (K1 $\neq$ K2) be two nonsecret keys, and define CE(M) as the 128-bit compressed encoding function

$$CE(M) \doteq (U1, U2) \tag{9-8}$$

where U1 = ∇K1(M) and U2 = ∇K2(M). The CE function described above is shown in Figure 9-7. The number of bits in the compressed encoding function (Equation 9-8) has thus been adjusted to effectively thwart the time-memory attack suggested by Yuval [10].

Method One—Improved

The number of 56-bit keys comprising the signature is reduced by basing the digital signature on the compressed encoding of M, rather than on M itself. Since CE(M) contains m bits, the resulting signature contains 56m bits, rather than 56t bits. If the number of message bits (t) is much larger than the number of bits in the compressed encoding of the message (m), a significant saving is achieved. If the CE function is computed using Equation 9-8, there are 128 keys, or 56·128 = 7168 bits in the signature (Figure 9-8).

The signature is validated against the 128-bit compressed encoding of the received message via the technique described in method one above. However, the size of the signature can be reduced from 128 to 64 keys if the compressed

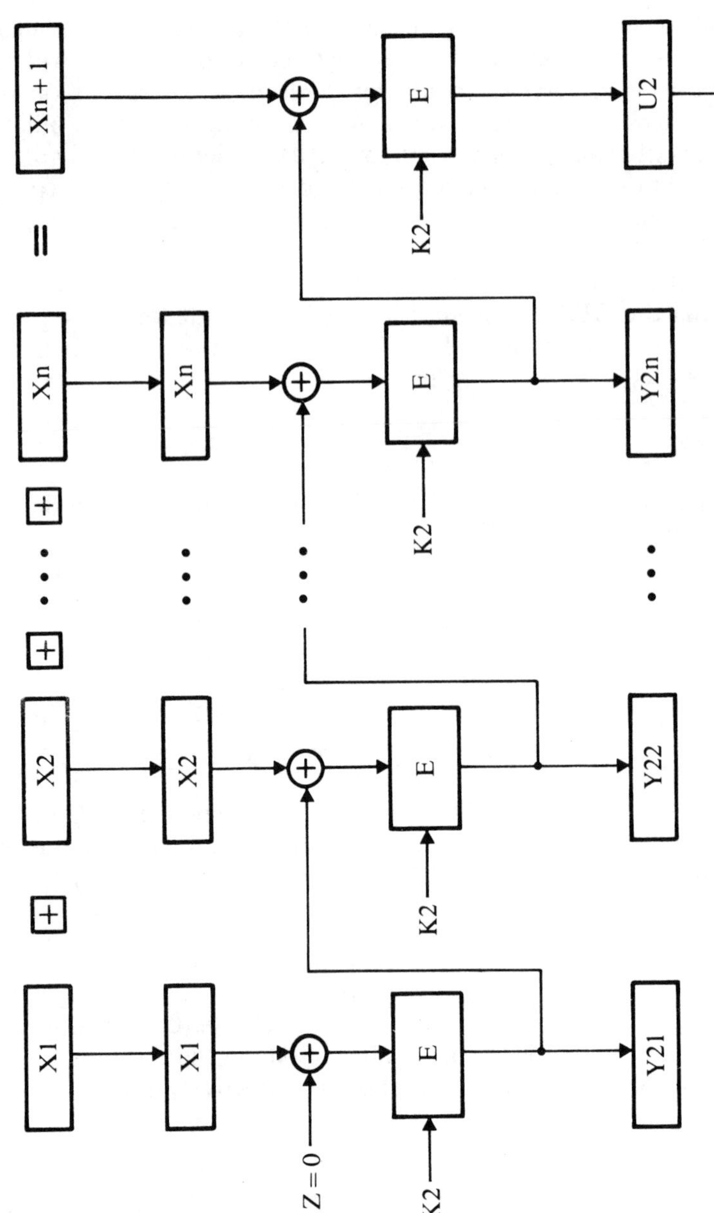

X1
X2
Xn
Xn + 1
X1
X2
Xn
Z = 0
E
E
E
E
K2
K2
K2
K2
Y21
Y22
Y2n
U2

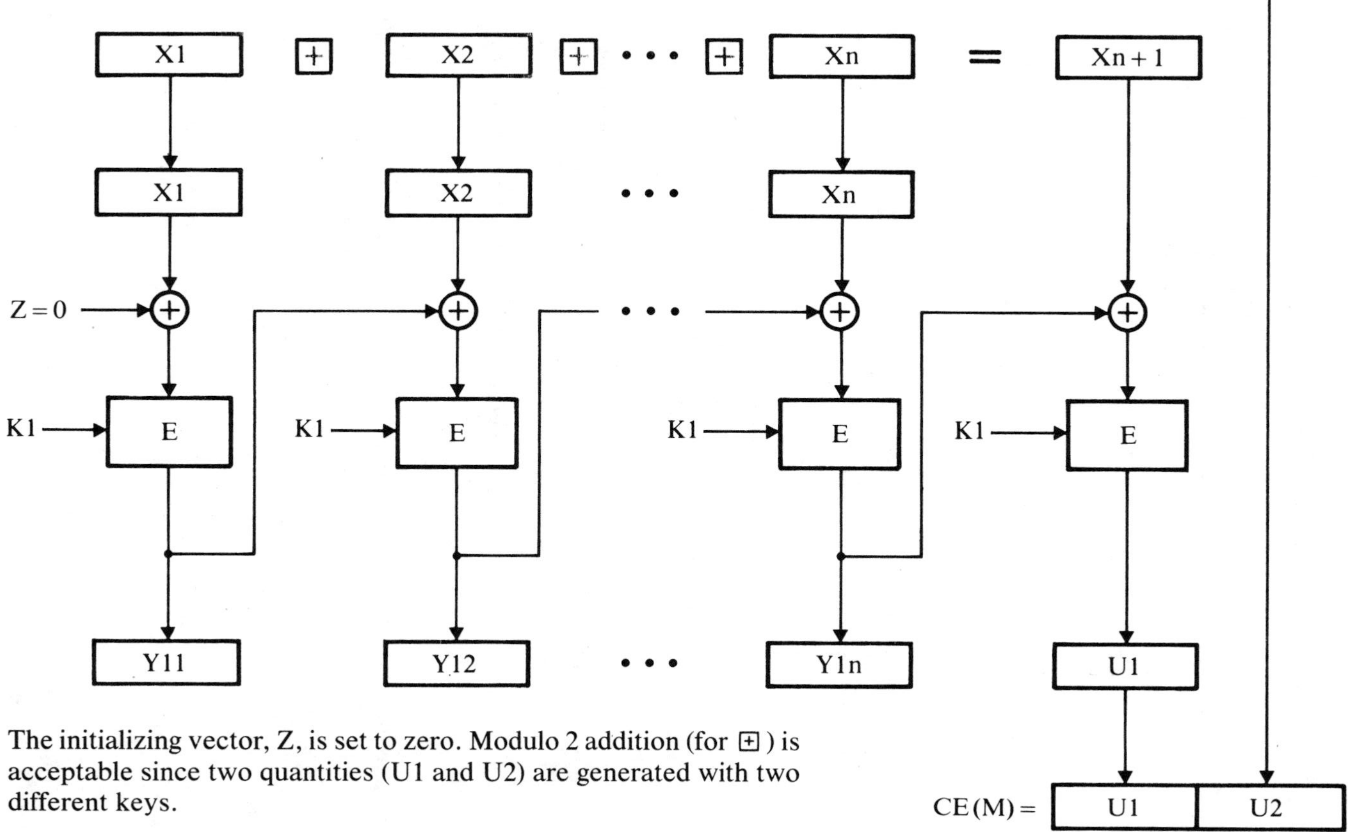

The initializing vector, Z, is set to zero. Modulo 2 addition (for ⊞) is acceptable since two quantities (U1 and U2) are generated with two different keys.

Figure 9-7. Example of a Compressed Encoding Function

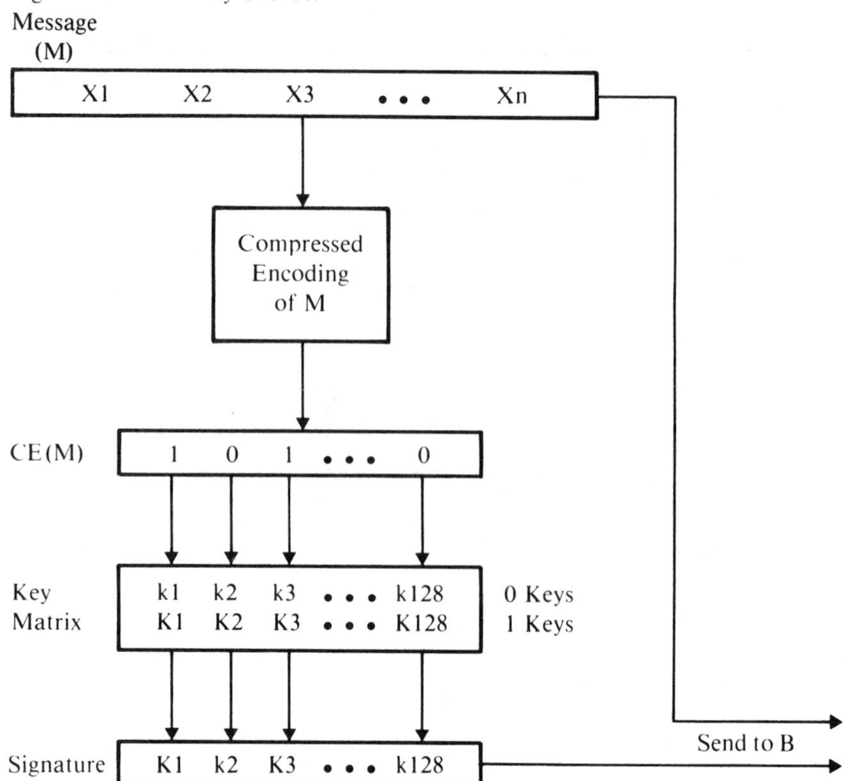

Figure 9-8. A Digital Signature Composed of a List of Cryptographic Keys (Signature Creation)

encoding is divided into 64 2-bit segments instead of 128 1-bit segments, and if the keys k1, k2, . . . , k128, K1, K2, . . . , K128, are arranged in a 4 X 64 table instead of a 2 X 128 table. The rows of the table are denoted 00, 01, 10, and 11, and a key is selected from the appropriate row depending on whether the corresponding bits in CE(M) are 00, 01, 10, or 11.

The same principle could be used to obtain a signature of 32 keys with a 16 X 32 key table, a signature of 16 keys with a 256 X 16 key table, and so on. However, after only a few such reductions, the key table becomes too large to be useful.

Method Two

In a different approach invented by Rabin [11], the digital signature is composed of a list of cryptographic quantities that are formed by enciphering the compressed encoding of a message with a list of randomly selected cryptographic keys. The signature, or list of cryptographic quantities, is validated in a probabilistic fashion by requiring the sender to reveal part of the secret keys that were originally used to produce the cryptographic quantities. Because the particular subset of keys (selected by the receiver) is not known to the sender ahead of time, the properties essential to digital signatures are obtained.

The sender randomly generates 2r cryptographic keys

$$k1, k2, \ldots, k2r - 1, k2r \tag{9-9}$$

which are kept secret. (The value r is determined by security considerations, and is explained later.) The receiver is given, in advance, the corresponding validation parameters

$$u1, u2 \ldots, u2r - 1, u2r$$

and

$$E_{k1}(u1), E_{k2}(u2), \ldots, E_{k2r-1}(u2r - 1), E_{k2r}(u2r)$$

which have also been recorded by the sender in an established registry with recognized and accepted integrity.

The digital signature for message M is formed (Figure 9-9) by enciphering the compressed encoding of M with each cryptographic key in the list denoted by Equation 9-9:

$$E_{k1}(CE(M)), E_{k2}(CE(M)), \ldots, E_{k2r}(CE(M)).$$

(If CE(M) is computed via Equation 9-8, then $E_{Ki}(CE(M)) = [E_{Ki}(u1), E_{Ki}(u2)]$, and each of the entries in the above list is composed of two 64-bit blocks of ciphertext.) The message and signature are then sent to the receiver.

To permit the signature to be validated, the sender discloses to the receiver exactly half (r) of the secret keys (k1, k2, . . . , k2r) used in forming the signature. The remaining r keys are kept secret in order to prevent the receiver from forging signatures. The keys to be disclosed (Figure 9-10) are selected as follows. The receiver randomly generates a vector of numbers, in which there are exactly r ones and r zeros, and sends a copy to the sender. A 1 in position i of the vector signifies that the sender is directed to forward the ith key to the receiver; a 0 signifies that the ith key has not been selected. Once the r keys have been received, the signature is validated by ensuring that ki1 enciphers ui1 into $E_{ki1}(ui1)$, and ki1 enciphers CE(M) into $E_{ki1}(CE(M))$; ki2 enciphers ui2 into $E_{ki2}(ui2)$, and ki2 enciphers CE(M) into $E_{ki2}(CE(M))$; and so forth.

The sender challenges a message M alleged by the receiver to be signed with $E_{k1}(CE(M)), E_{k2}(CE(M)), \ldots, E_{k2r}(CE(M))$ by producing in front of a referee the keys k1, k2, . . . , k2r. These keys and the alleged signature are then validated as before using the corresponding validation parameters obtained from the designated public registry. If r + 1 or more of the elements in the signature are correct, then the receiver is upheld and it is assumed that the sender is attempting to disavow a message he actually sent. On the other hand, if r or fewer of the elements in the signature are correct, then the sender is upheld and it is assumed that the receiver is attempting to forge a message and signature.

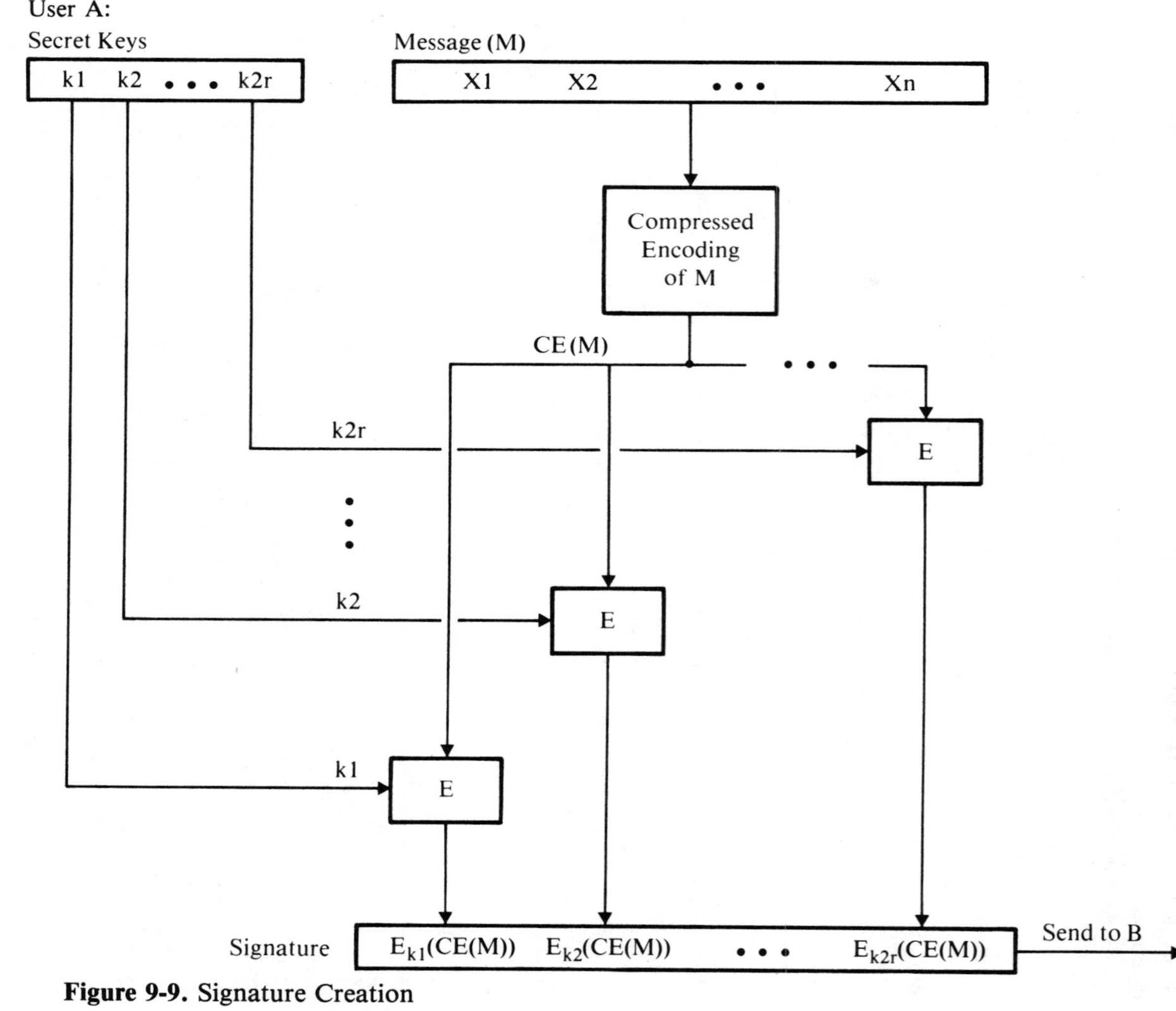

Figure 9-9. Signature Creation

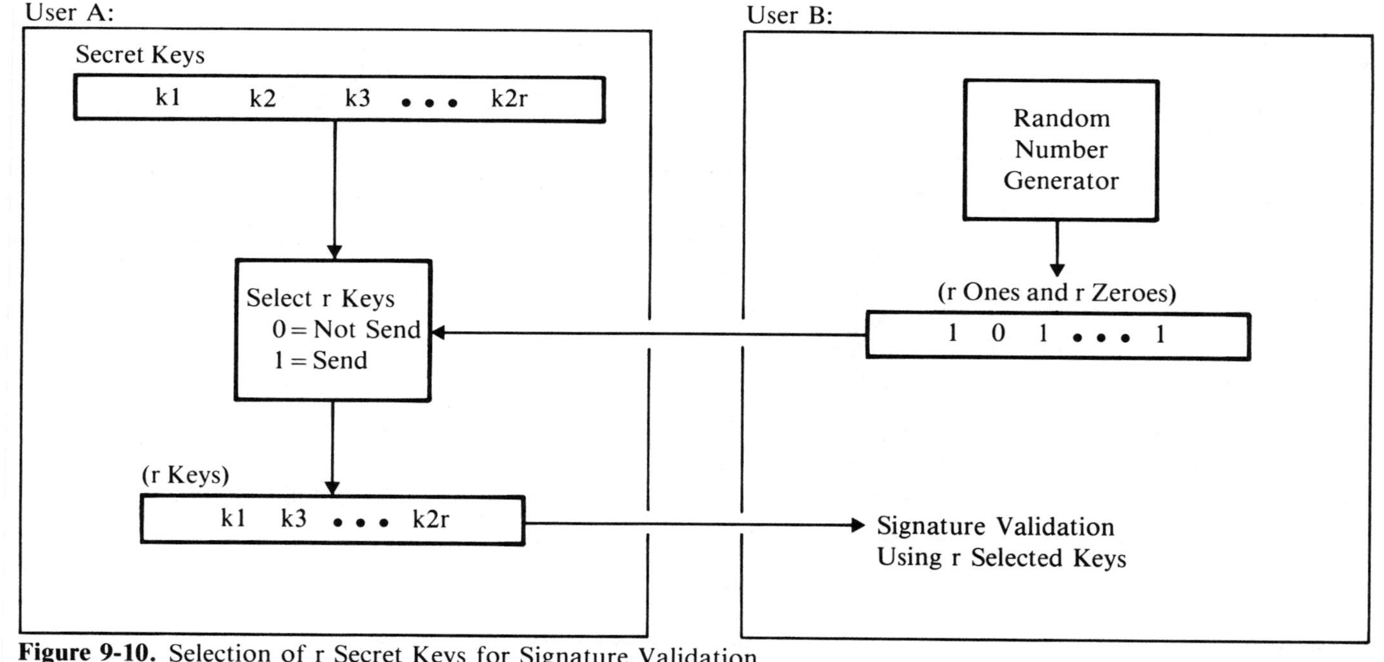

Figure 9-10. Selection of r Secret Keys for Signature Validation

In order for the sender to disavow successfully a message and signature that might also be validated by the receiver, there must be exactly r correct entries in the signature, and the receiver must request and validate the signature using precisely these r entries. But the probability of such an event is given by

$$P = 1/\binom{2r}{r}$$

If 2r = 36, then the probability is about $1/10^{10}$.

Method Three—Matrix Method

In yet another approach invented by the authors [12], the digital signature is a list of 31 cryptographic keys that are selected from a 31 X 31 matrix of secret keys (Figure 9-11) based on the value of the compressed encoding of the message to be signed. A different matrix of keys is required for each signed message.

Initial Keys	k(1,1)	k(1,2)	• • •	k(1,31)
	k(2,1)	k(2,2)	• • •	k(2,31)
	⋮	⋮		⋮
Final Keys	k(31,1)	k(31,2)	• • •	k(31,31)

Figure 9-11. 31 × 31 Matrix of Secret Keys used by the Sender to Form a Signature

Row 1 of the matrix contains 31 *initial keys*, denoted k(1, 1), k(1, 2), . . . , k(1, 31), which are produced via a standard generator of pseudo-random numbers. For example, the initial keys for the nth message could be produced with the DES algorithm using a single secret key-encrypting key K, via the relation

$$E_K(31(n-1)+j) \equiv k(1,j)$$

where

$$j = \text{(matrix) column number}, \ 1 \leqslant j \leqslant 31$$

$$n = \text{message sequence number}$$

In addition to the key matrix, a 30 X 31 matrix of nonsecret *code words* (Figure 9-12) is produced via a generator of pseudo-random numbers. For the purpose of illustration, it is assumed that the code words for the nth message are produced from a single nonsecret seed key U, via the relation

u(1,1)	u(1,2)	• • •	u(1,31)
u(2,1)	u(2,2)	• • •	u(2,31)
⋮	⋮		⋮
u(30,1)	u(30,2)	• • •	u(30,31)

Figure 9-12. 30×31 Matrix of Nonsecret Code Words

$$E_U(31^2(n-1) + 31(i-1) + j) \equiv u(i, j)$$

where

$$i = \text{(matrix) row number}, 1 \leqslant i \leqslant 30$$

$$j = \text{(matrix) column number}, 1 \leqslant j \leqslant 31$$

$$n = \text{message sequence number}$$

(The subscript n, which denotes the message sequence number, is omitted from the discussion.)

This method for generating keys and code words has the advantage that the necessary quantities can be created as needed (i.e., they do not have to be saved).

The keys in rows 2 through 31 of the key matrix are obtained via repeated steps of encipherment using the initial keys and the matrix of code words, as follows:

$$E_{K(i,j)}(u(i, j)) \equiv k(i + 1, j)$$

where

$$1 \leqslant i \leqslant 30$$

$$1 \leqslant j \leqslant 31$$

For example, k(2, j) is produced by enciphering u(1, j) with k(1, j); k(3, j) is produced by enciphering u(2, j) with k(2, j); and so forth. Thus if the receiver is sent key k(i, j), he can compute k(i + 1, j), k(i + 2, j), . . . , k(31, j), but cannot compute k(1, j), k(2, j), . . . , k(i − 1, j).

The keys in row 31 of the key matrix are called the *final keys*. These final keys, which are prepared in advance by the sender and sent to the receiver, represent the validation pattern. (A protocol must be established whereby the receiver can independently validate these final keys; e.g., by requiring the sender to record them in a designated public registry.) In an actual implementation, a large number of these validation patterns would be needed—one for every message to be signed.[10]

[10] To reduce storage further, the receiver could store the compressed encoding of each validation pattern instead of the validation pattern itself. This modified protocol is not discussed.

The first step in forming the signature is to obtain the compressed encoding of the message M that is to be signed. For the purposes of illustration, assume that the compressed encoding of M, or CE(M), is computed via Equation 9-8; that is, CE(M) = (U1, U2) where U1 and U2 are 64-bit quantities. The compressed encoding of M is used together with 31 nonsecret keys, a1, a2, . . . , a31, (also held by the receiver to permit signature validation) to produce 31 unique code words, b1, b2, . . . , b31, as follows:

$$E_{a1}(U1) \oplus E_{a1}(U2) = b1$$
$$E_{a2}(U1) \oplus E_{a2}(U2) = b2$$
$$\vdots$$
$$E_{a31}(U1) \oplus E_{a31}(U2) = b31$$

The keys, a1, a2, . . . , a31, could be established universal constants that are recorded in a public registry.

The 31 b-values are now sorted into numerical sequence. Since each b-value has a position in the sorted and unsorted sequence, it constitutes an index that can be used to select a key from the key matrix. Its position in the sorted sequence specifies the row, and its position in the unsorted sequence specifies the column.

For example, if the sorted and unsorted b-values are given by

Unsorted: b1, b2, b3, . . . , b31

Sorted: b5, b20, b11, . . . , b7

then the keys in the signature are, respectively,

k(5, 1), k(20, 2), k(11, 3), . . . , k(7, 31)

This guarantees that *one and only one key is selected from each row and column.*

As a consequence, one can choose from 31 positions in column 1, 30 positions in column 2, and so on. Altogether, there are 31! or about 2^{112} ways in which the 31 signature keys can be selected from the key matrix. The dimensions of the key matrix have thus been adjusted to eliminate any problem with synonyms (two or more compressed encodings of different messages that result in the same list of signature keys); for example, if the digital signature procedure were attacked using a form of time-memory trade-off [9].

The receiver, except for one additional step, checks the signature by repeating the same steps performed by the sender. First, the compressed encoding of the message is obtained. Then the 31 b-values are computed and sorted into numerical order. This allows the 31 keys in the signature vector to be reinserted into an empty 31 × 31 key matrix. The receiver then uses each signature key to encipher the standard, nonsecret code word to form each lower key in the same column of the matrix, including the final keys that make up the validation pattern. If the final keys (row 31) of the key matrix are equal to the validation pattern previously received from the sender, then the message and signature are accepted as valid; otherwise, the message and signature are rejected.

If the *rank* of a key is defined as the row number of that key in the key matrix, then in order for the receiver to forge a signature, he must know the value of at least one key in one column of the key matrix whose rank is less than the rank of the corresponding key in the signature. But by the non-invertibility property of the DES algorithm, it is computationally infeasible to compute such a key. Only the sender, who possesses the key-generating key, can produce the full set of keys in the key matrix.

The advantage of this method is that it allows a trade-off to be made between computation time (the time to generate and validate signatures) and signature size. The general approach of computing a list of final keys from a list of signature keys leads to a variety of signature methods. For example, an approach in which both the sender and receiver have enough information to disprove a false claim brought by the other, but do not have enough information to prove a self-initiated claim is described in reference 13.

A requirement of all the methods using conventional algorithms is that they are *one-time systems*. This means that *at least one different validation parameter is required for each message and digital signature that is received.* However, with a public-key algorithm, only one validation parameter (the public-key of the sender) is required, regardless of how many signed messages are received.

ARBITRATED SIGNATURES[11]

The requirement of a one-time system of digital signatures based on a conventional algorithm can be overcome if a protocol of arbitrated signatures is adopted. In a communication system with arbitrated signatures, every signed message prepared by the sender is sent to an arbiter. The arbiter authenticates each message and signature, and communicates the result to the intended receiver. Each communicant's signature-generation information must therefore be shared with the arbiter to allow message and signature validation. Message and/or signature forgery is prevented because the signature-generation information is not shared with other communicants.

Figure 9-13 illustrates an approach for generating arbitrated signatures. In an actual implementation, the arbiter might be a combination of software and hardware located at a communications network node. However, because the arbiter has access to every communicants signature-generation information, a high level of physical security and access control is required.

Arbitrated digital signatures seem best suited to users under a common supervising entity (e.g., brokerage house members of a stock exchange, or users whose transactions occur within a single organization's communication network).

Arbitrated signatures are obtained using message authentication tech-

[11]©1979 North-Holland Publishing Co. Reprinted in part from *Computer Networks* **3**, No. 2, April 1979 [14].

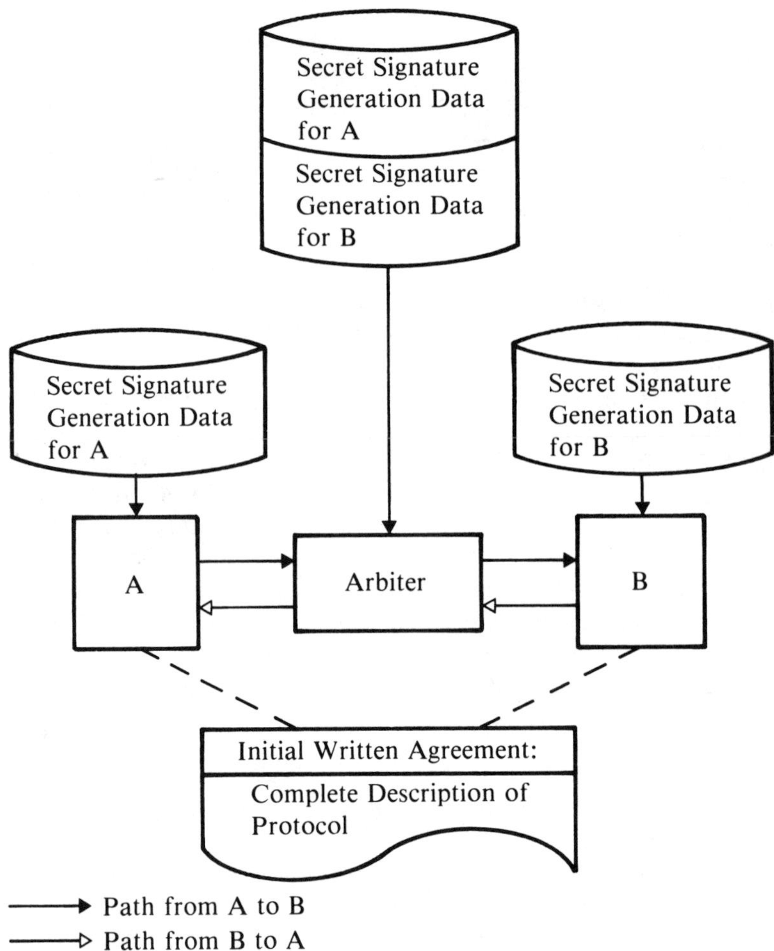

Figure 9-13. Arbitrated Digital Signatures

niques.[12] However, the combination of message authentication and a trusted arbiter (who validates the signature at the time a message is communicated) permits a stronger protocol of digital signatures to be obtained.

Various encryption-based authentication procedures are available that could be used to implement arbitrated signatures. One approach—based on the DES algorithm—is illustrated below.

An Approach Using the DES Algorithm

Suppose each communicant, A, B, . . . , Z, has a secret cryptographic key, KA, KB, . . . , KZ, which is shared with the arbiter (Figure 9-14). With these shared keys it is possible for the arbiter to authenticate messages from each

[12] *Message authentication* is a procedure for authenticating a message's origin, true contents, timeliness, and intended destination. See also Authentication Techniques Using Cryptography, Chapter 8, and Chapters 10 and 11 which treat electronic funds transfer systems.

Arbiter's Key Table

ID	Keys
A,	KA
B,	KB
⋮	
Z,	KZ

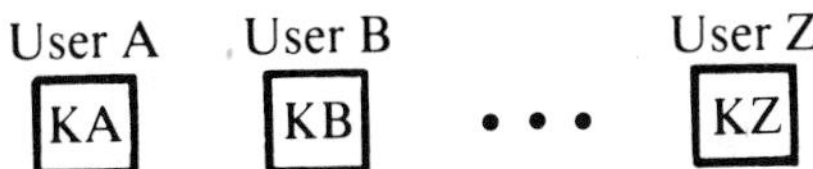

Figure 9-14. Individual Secret Keys Shared With the Arbiter

communicant and for each communicant to authenticate messages from the arbiter. (However, communicants cannot authenticate messages received directly from other communicants.)

In the discussion that follows, let M denote a message whose format is

$$\begin{aligned} M = &\langle \text{sender ID} \rangle, \\ &\langle \text{receiver ID} \rangle, \\ &\langle \text{sequence number} \rangle, \\ &\langle \text{data} \rangle \end{aligned}$$

(see Equation 9-4). Let M be divided into 64-bit blocks of plaintext as follows:

$$M = (X1, X2, \ldots, Xn), \tag{9-10}$$

where Xn could be a short block that is padded to 64 bits. Let X0 be a random 64-bit value that is appended to the front of M and let

$$Xn + 1 = X0 + X1 + \ldots + Xn \pmod{2^{64}}$$

be a block of plaintext appended to the end of M. X0 is used in place of a random initializing vector to mask patterns in the data. X0 can be produced by a generator of pseudo-random numbers. Xn + 1 is a parameter used in the computation of the *authentication code* (AC).

The plaintext X0, X1, . . . , Xn + 1 is enciphered using a form of chained block encryption with ciphertext feedback (Figure 2-17) as follows:

$$\begin{aligned} Y0 &= E_K(X0 \oplus Z) \\ Y1 &= E_K(X1 \oplus Y0) \\ &\vdots \\ Yn + 1 &= E_K(Xn + 1 \oplus Yn) \end{aligned} \tag{9-11}$$

where ⊕ denotes modulo 2 addition, K is the cryptographic key, and Z (the nonsecret initializing vector) is an established constant, say all zero bits.

Once the message has been enciphered, the following information is sent to the receiver:

$$[Y0, Y, AC]$$

where

$$\begin{aligned} Y0 &= \text{the block of ciphertext corresponding to } X0 \\ Y &= \text{the ciphertext } Y1, Y2, \ldots, Yn \\ AC &= \text{the ciphertext } Yn + 1 \end{aligned}$$ [13]

When it is received, the ciphertext (Y0, Y1, . . . , Yn + 1) is deciphered as follows:

$$\begin{aligned} X0 &= D_K(Y0) \oplus Z \\ X1 &= D_K(Y1) \oplus Y0 \\ &\vdots \\ Xn + 1 &= D_K(Yn + 1) \oplus Yn \end{aligned}$$

where X0, X1, . . . , Xn + 1 denotes the recovered plaintext.

Message authentication is made possible because the recovered value Xn + 1 is a complex function of K, and Y0, Y1, . . . , Yn + 1. Therefore, with high probability, decipherment of Y0, Y1, . . . , Yn + 1 with the wrong key, or the corruption of any bits in Y0, Y1, . . . , Yn + 1 will cause the recovered value of Xn + 1 to be incorrect. Thus by comparing the recovered value of Xn + 1 with X0 + X1 + . . . + Xn (mod 2^{64}) for equality, the receiver can determine if the contents of the recovered plaintext (X0, X1, . . . , Xn + 1) are genuine. And, once the contents of the message have been validated, the parameters, <sender id>, <receiver id>, and <sequence number>, can then be checked for correctness.

An Example of Arbitrating a Signature

Let T denote the text of the ith message communicated from A to B, where M is given by

$$M = [A, B, i, T]$$

[13] Greater security can be achieved if AC is defined as the concatenation of Yn + 1 and Y′n + 1, where Yn + 1 and Y′n + 1 are the last blocks of ciphertext that result when X0, X1, . . . , Xn is enciphered with two different keys, K and K′, respectively. This would thwart the described attack in which the opponent generates random perturbations on only two starting messages (see Compressed Encoding Function, and also reference 10).

At A, data (RN, M, ¤) is enciphered using cryptographic key KA and initializing vector Z = 0 to produce ciphertext (Y0, Y, AC), where RN (defined X0 above) is a 64-bit random number, M = X1, X2, . . . , Xn, and ¤ = RN + X1 + X2 + . . . + Xn (mod 2^{64}). Data (A, Y0, Y, AC)—A's unencrypted identifier and the just produced ciphertext–is then sent to the arbiter. Identifier A is included in the transmission so that the arbiter can identify and obtain KA from his key table. (Recall that <sender ID> in M is encrypted.)

At the arbiter, ciphertext (Y0, Y, AC) is deciphered using KA. To prevent messages from being sent under an assumed identity, the arbiter checks that <sender ID> matches the received, unencrypted ID used to retrieve KA (i.e., that <sender ID> = A). If the two identifiers are unequal, an appropriate response is communicated to the sender and the procedure halted. If the two identifiers are equal, the arbiter checks that the last block of recovered plaintext equals RN + X1 + X2 + . . . + Xn (mod 2^{64}), and if so, it is concluded:

1. (Y0, Y, AC) was enciphered using KA and Z = 0, and therefore message M originated with A.
2. M is the true content of the communicated message.

If the last block of recovered plaintext is unequal to RN + X1 + X2 + . . . + Xn (mod 2^{64}), the message is not considered genuine. The arbiter sends the following message to B:

M′ = [A, B, i, T′]

where

T′ = [T, RN, AC, <genuine>] if M is genuine,

or

T′ = [T, RN, AC, <not genuine>] if M is not genuine.

In the example, text T, RN, and AC are repeated in their entirety, whereas <genuine> and <not genuine> denote established code words. A new random number, RN′, is selected and data (RN′, M′, ¤′) are enciphered with key KB and initializing vector Z = 0 to produce ciphertext (Y0′, Y′, AC′). The ID of the receiver, which is included in the received message, is used to locate KB in the arbiter's key table. Data (Y0′, Y′, AC′) are then sent to B.

Having established a communication session with the arbiter, B deciphers (Y0′, Y′, AC′) using Z′ = 0 and KB, and then authenticates M′ in the same way that M was authenticated by the arbiter. B accepts M if and only if

1. M′ is genuine.
2. Code word <genuine> is received in T′.
3. M′ satisfies all other conditions imposed by the digital signature procedure (e.g., parameters <sender ID>, <receiver ID>, and <sequence number> are correct).

RN, M, and AC are retained by B in order to prove later that M was received from A. This can be done by requesting the arbiter to encipher (RN, M, ¤) using Z = 0 and KA (obtained from the arbiter's key table), and then verifying that the last block of produced ciphertext is equal to the value AC (held by B).

In the example, AC is a function of both the message and the sender's secret key. It can be computed by either the arbiter or the sender, but not by the receiver. In that case, AC is the *digital signature* of the message.

A Weak Approach

Consider an approach in which X0 is eliminated and Z is produced via a generator of pseudo-random numbers. The process of encipherment is as follows:

$$Y1 = E_K(X1 \oplus Z)$$

$$Y2 = E_K(X2 \oplus Y1)$$

$$\vdots$$

$$Yn + 1 = E_K(Xn + 1 \oplus Yn)$$

where Xn + 1 = X1 + X2 + . . . + Xn (mod 2^{64}).

At A, data (M,¤), where M = X1, X2, . . . , Xn and ¤ = X1 + X2 + . . . + Xn (mod 2^{64}), are enciphered using cryptographic key KA and initializing vector Z to produce (Y, AC). Data (A, Z, Y, AC) are then sent to the arbiter. In the modified procedure, Z is sent to the arbiter instead of Y0.

The procedure at the arbiter is unchanged, except that Z instead of RN is sent in T′:

T′ = [T, Z, AC, <genuine>] if M is genuine,

or

T′ = [T, Z, AC, <not genuine>] if M is not genuine.

Data (M′, ¤′) are enciphered with key KB and a new initializing vector Z′, which produces ciphertext (Y′, AC′). Data (Z′, Y′, AC′) are then sent to B. The procedure at B is unchanged, except that Z, M, and AC are retained in order to prove later that M was received from A.

This approach allows users to forge messages and signatures.[14] For example, user A could create a forged message and signature, purportedly from user B, as follows. User A sends (A, Z, Y, AC) to the arbiter, where

[14] This weakness was pointed out by Miles Smid, National Bureau of Standards.

(Y, AC) = ciphertext produced from plaintext (M, ¤) using KA

M = [A, B, i, T]

¤ = the 64-bit quantity produced by adding the blocks in M modulo 2^{64}

Except in this case T contains the following:

T = [pad bits, Mf, ¤f]

where

pad bits = enough bits to align Mf on a block boundary

Mf = [B, A, j, Tf] is the forged message

j = sequence number of some message received previously from user B

¤f = the 64-bit quantity produced by adding the blocks in Mf modulo 2^{64}

Thus,

T = [pad bits, B, A, j, Tf, ¤f]

After validating (Y, AC), the arbiter sends (Z′, Y′, AC′) to user B, where

(Y′, AC′) = the ciphertext produced from plaintext (M′, ¤′)

M′ = [A, B, i, T′]

T′ = [T, Z, AC, <genuine>]

Or, upon substituting for T, M′ equals

M′ = [A, B, i, pad bits, B, A, j, Tf, ¤f, Z, AC, <genuine>]

However, user A intercepts (Z′, Y′, AC′) (e.g., by using a wiretap) and jams the transmission to prevent it from reaching user B. The intercepted ciphertext is then used by user A to produce (Zf, Yf, ACf), where

Zf = X(i) ⊕ Y(i); Y(i) is the block of ciphertext produced from X(i) and X(i) is the block of plaintext just prior to the second B in M′

Yf = that portion of the intercepted ciphertext corresponding to Mf

ACf = that portion of the intercepted ciphertext corresponding to ¤f

(Zf, Mf, ACf) can now be given to the arbiter as proof that Mf was received from user B.

The weakness is overcome when Z is held constant and a random X0 is appended to the front of the message as described above.

Additional Weaknesses

There are encryption methods that permit message authentication which would have undesirable properties if used in a procedure for arbitrated signatures. For example, if a form of chained block encryption with plaintext-ciphertext feedback (see Figure 2-16) was used, it would be possible under certain conditions for the sender and receiver to forge messages and signatures.

Consider an implementation in which a message, M = X1, X2, . . . , Xn, is enciphered as:

$$Y1 = E_K(X1 \oplus Z)$$

$$Y2 = E_K(X2 \oplus X1 \oplus Y1)$$

$$\vdots$$

$$Yn + 1 = E_K(Xn + 1 \oplus Xn \oplus Yn)$$

where K is the cryptographic key, Xn + 1 = Z (Z is a random initializing vector), and Yn + 1 is defined as the AC. This encryption method has the peculiar property that for any value D the encipherment of $M' = X1 \oplus D, X2 \oplus D, \ldots, Xn \oplus D$ using cryptographic key K and initializing vector $Z' = Z \oplus D$ is the same as the encipherment of M = X1, X2, . . . , Xn using cryptographic key K and initializing vector Z (i.e., $Y'1 = Y1, Y'2 = Y2, \ldots, Y'n + 1 = Yn + 1$). Consequently, there are numerous easily derived messages that will produce the same AC.

The sender might be able to find values X1, X2, . . . , Xn and D (especially if n is small) such that both M and M′ are valid messages, except that the receiver would be willing to accept M whereas he would be unwilling to accept M′. The sender would send M to the receiver and later claim that M′ was sent.

On the other hand, if a protocol is used in which Xn + 1 is equal to a constant, say all 0 bits, the arbiter could be tricked into accepting an altered message. Let (Z, M, AC) denote a valid triple (initializing vector, message, authentication code) received by the receiver from the arbiter, and let M = X1, X2, . . . , Xn. The receiver can produce a forged triple (Zf, Mf, ACf) provided that he knows the value of some X′1 and Y′1 such that $Y'1 = E_K(X'1)$. X′1 and Y′1 may be determined from previous transmissions. In that case, Z is replaced by $X'1 \oplus X1 \oplus Y'1 \oplus Y1$ and X1 is replaced by $X1 \oplus Y'1 \oplus Y1$:

$$Zf = X'1 \oplus X1 \oplus Y'1 \oplus Y1$$

$$Mf = X1 \oplus Y'1 \oplus Y1, X2, X3, \ldots, Xn$$

and ACf = AC. Observe that the feedback used to encipher block Xi (i =

2, 3, . . . , n + 1) is $Xi - 1 \oplus Yi - 1$ when (X1, X2, . . . , Xn + 1) is enciphered with Z and K, and when ($X1 \oplus Y'1 \oplus Y1$, X2, . . . , Xn + 1) is enciphered with $Zf = X'1 \oplus X1 \oplus Y'1 \oplus Y1$ and K. Thus in either case the second, third, and so on, blocks of ciphertext are the same, and therefore, the same authentication code is produced—proving that (Zf, Mf, ACf) would be accepted by the arbiter.

USING DES TO OBTAIN PUBLIC-KEY PROPERTIES

Even though there are significant differences between public-key and conventional algorithms, a conventional algorithm can provide some of the properties of a public-key algorithm. Thus while the algorithms are markedly different, the cryptographic systems or functions provided the respective systems (i.e., what the user sees or perceives) may be very much alike.

The properties of public and private keys usually associated only with a public-key algorithm can be attained with a conventional algorithm provided that: (1) the public and private (DES) keys are used only at devices and equipment belonging to a specific cryptographic system, and (2) the secrecy and integrity of other system-managed keys stored within these cryptographic devices can be maintained.

Assuming a conventional algorithm, the basic problem involves the design of a trapdoor one-way function that can be used to encrypt/decrypt (transform) time-variant data (e.g., messages transmitted in a communication network). To some degree, the unidirectional cryptographic operations reported in reference 15, and further elaborated on in reference 16, were designed along these lines. Used for key management, one cryptographic operation encrypts keys sent to other devices and a second operation decrypts keys received from other devices. In addition, the two cryptographic authentication operations reported in reference 17, which allow time-variant quantities to be authenticated via a special precomputed test pattern, were also designed around this principle.

A method for implementing unidirectional DES data-encrypting keys was first proposed by Smid [18]. A data key Kij is used to transmit data from user i to user j (i.e., only user i can encrypt with Kij and only user j can decrypt with Kij). A second data key, Kji, is used to transmit data from user j to user i. With this scheme, the key assumes either a transmit (encipher only) or a receive (decipher only) capability. This method permits a protocol for digital signatures to be implemented, similar to that obtained with a public-key algorithm.

A Key Notarization System for Computer Networks[15]

System Design

The key notarization system is designed for computer networks which consist of host computers, user terminals, and key notarization facilities. The

[15] Reprinted in part from NBS Special Publication 500-54, October 1979 [18].

key notarization facility is analogous to the cryptographic facility described in Chapter 4 or to the security module in reference 19.

The host controls the normal operation and communication of the terminals. Terminals have the capability of communicating with the host, with other local terminals through the host, and with terminals of other hosts through communication channels called *interchanges*. Each terminal can use the host key notarization facility by means of user commands. All commands are implemented in the key notarization facility, and every key notarization facility has the capacity to generate keys for distribution to other hosts or facility users.

Two distinct types of keys are used: *interchange keys* (**IK**) and *data keys* (**DK**). Interchange keys and data keys are similar to the secondary and primary keys introduced in Chapter 4. Interchange keys are used for the exchange of data keys between users. One interchange key, called the *facility interchange key*, is used for the encryption of facility user passwords. Other interchange keys may be available for the exchange of data keys between facilities or for subgroups of a facility. Interchange keys are generated outside the network and are entered, unencrypted, directly into the key notarization facility. This permits two facilities to enter the same interchange key. Data keys are used to encrypt data and are generated in the key notarization facility.

The key notarization facility contains the DES algorithm, which employs a secret key to encipher/decipher data or other keys. It has a control microprocessor and memory to implement commands and data transfers. The key notarization facility must also store the unencrypted interchange keys and the states of active users. An *active state* consists of a user identifier, two initializing vectors, and two unencrypted data keys for transmitting and receiving data, respectively. A user is *active* as soon as his identifier is loaded into the key notarization facility. He may then proceed to load the rest of his state.

The key notarization facility contains a key generator which is capable of generating unpredictable keys. Once the 56-bit keys are generated, the proper parity is determined and the entire 64-bit key is encrypted before it is returned to the host. Thus no clear keys are known outside the key notarization facility. The key generator is also used to generate 64-bit initializing vectors which initialize the DES.

Identifiers and Key Notarization

Identifiers are nonsecret binary vectors of up to 28 bits that uniquely identify each user in the network. When a user first attempts to use the key notarization facility, he must submit his identifier along with the correct password to establish an active state in the key notarization facility. Both the host and the key notarization facility employ identifiers to recognize users.

Let i and j be identifiers, and let K be a 64-bit DES key. (i || j) represents the concatenation of i and j. K consists of 8 bytes, each byte containing 7 information bits and a parity bit. K XOR (i || j) is a special function defined as follows. The leftmost 7 information bits of K are Exclusive-ORed with the leftmost 7 bits of i. The eighth bit, a parity bit, is then appended so the modulo two sum of the eight bits is odd. Then the next 7 information bits of K are Exclusive-ORed with the next 7 bits of i and the correct parity bit is appended. This continues until the last 7 information bits of K have been Exclusive-ORed with the last 7 bits of j and the final parity bit has been set. Therefore, K XOR (i || j) is a valid DES key with 56 information bits and 8 parity bits. All passwords and data keys are encrypted under K XOR (i || j) for some K and some i, j pair. In the case of passwords, i = j.

When key notarization is used, keys and passwords are sealed upon encryption by the key notarization facility with the identifiers of the transmitter (or key generator) and the receiver. To generate a notarized key, the transmitter must identify itself to the key notarization facility and provide proof of its identity by supplying the correct password. This is called user authentication. The transmitter must also specify the intended receiver of the key.

A generated key is immediately encrypted under an interchange key Exclusive-ORed with the proper identifier pair, that is IK XOR (i || j). The identifier of the user requesting the key, who is also the transmitter, is always the left identifier (i), and the identifier of the intended receiver is the right identifier (j) in the identifier pair.

Once encrypted, the correct key cannot be decrypted unless the correct identifier pair is again provided. To decrypt the key, the receiver identifies itself and provides password proof of its identity. The receiver must also supply the identifier of the transmitter. If the identification information is not the same as that provided by the transmitter to its key notarization facility, then the decrypted key will not equal the original key and no information can be correctly decrypted. Thus the receiver must know the correct transmitter and be the intended receiver.

User Authentication

Each user has a password used to authenticate and permit him to invoke user commands. The plain password is passed through an encryption function, involving the users identifier, and the result is compared in the key notarization facility with a stored value before the user is activated. No other command will be accepted by the key notarization facility until the user's identity has been authenticated. Each user's password is stored in system memory encrypted under the facility interchange key combined with the users identifier. It is assumed that the host can maintain the correct identity of a user once he has been authenticated. Thus after users are activated, they need not resubmit their passwords each time a new command is issued.

Let $E_K(X)$ indicate the encryption of X under key K using the electronic codebook mode of DES operation [20]. Thus $E_{(IK1\ XOR\ (i\,||\,i))}(PWi)$ denotes the encryption of PWi under IK1 Exclusive-ORed with user i's identifier pair, (i || i). IK1 is used because the passwords are from the system memory of host 1 and IK1 is the facility interchange key of host 1.

To protect against substitution, the password is encrypted under IK1 Exclusive-ORed with the appropriate identifier pair. If identifiers were not used and user j could gain access to the system memory, he might substitute his own encrypted password, $E_{IK1}(PWj)$, for user i's encrypted password $E_{IK1}(PWi)$. User j could then be authenticated as user i by submitting his own password and claiming to be user i. However, if an identifier pair is Exclusive-ORed with the interchange key in the manner described, then $E_{(IK1 \text{ XOR } (i \| i))}(PWj)$ would be calculated upon authentication and it would not compare with $E_{(IK1 \text{ XOR } (j \| j))}(PWj)$ which was submitted as user i's encrypted password.

User i's memory contains personal and shared data keys. *Personal data keys* are encrypted under the facility interchange key Exclusive-ORed with the user's identifier pair. Personal keys may be used to encrypt files and other private data, but they cannot be shared. User i's memory also contains shared data keys. A *shared data key* is encrypted under an interchange key Exclusive-ORed with the concatenation of user i's identifier and another user's identifier, say user j. (i || j) uniquely identifies the communication parties. If (i || j) were not used, another user could substitute his own data key encrypted under the interchange key and could then decrypt any subsequent ciphertext encrypted with that data key. Similarly, when user j receives $E_{(IKp \text{ XOR } (i \| j))}(DKij)$, he must know that he is communicating with user i over interchange p to decipher DKij correctly. Thus the transmitter is prevented from posing as someone else. And since several users may all use the same IKp to communicate, this protection is critical.

Commands

The key notarization facility supports the required commands through a combination of hardware and software. The commands are used for:

1. Data encryption, decryption, and authentication.
2. Password initialization, notarization, change, and reencryption.
3. Reserving and logging out of active user states.
4. Generating notarized data keys and initializing vectors.
5. Loading notarized data keys and initializing vectors.
6. Reencrypting data keys.

A user must authenticate and receive an active state before he can execute any other commands. Password initialization is the only command function which must be privileged to the security officer.

Digital Signatures

Since the key notarization facility combines identifiers with interchange keys for protection against substitution, and employs a separate encryption and decryption key storage, one cannot encrypt data in a key that was generated by another user. Therefore, any encrypted message may be regarded as a signed message (or a signature). It is assumed that messages can be distinguished (e.g., by including redundant data in them). No additional keys or commands are required. All user j needs to do is keep $E_{(IKp \text{ XOR } (i \| j))}(DKij)$, $E_{DKij}(IV)$, and the encrypted message in order to be able to prove that it was received from user i. Of course, user j may send a signed message to user i using data key DKji (≠ DKij).

Suppose user i generates a data key for communication with user j. The encrypted key would be of the form

$$E_{(IKp\ XOR\ (i\,||\,j))}(DKij)$$

where IKp is the interchange key for interchange p and DKij is the data key generated by user i for transmission to user j. Whenever user i generates a key, his identifier is always leftmost in the identifier pair. The only way user j can load DKij is by loading it as a receive key. If user j tries to load DKij as a transmission key (i.e., for the encryption of data going to user i), the key notarization facility will use (j || i) instead of (i || j) when decrypting DKij. If user j tries to load the key as a personal key, then (j || j) will be used. When DKij is loaded as a receive key, only the decryption commands have access to it. Since there is no way for user j to get DKij into the transmit data key active storage, he cannot encrypt a message under DKij or alter a message already encrypted under DKij.

If user j generates a data key for communication with user i, the key will be of the form

$$E_{(IKp\ XOR\ (j\,||\,i))}(DKji)$$

However, user j cannot claim that a message encrypted under DKji came from user i, since he could be challenged to decrypt the encrypted message. To do so, user j would have to load DKji by submitting $E_{(IKp\ XOR\ (j\,||\,i))}(DKji)$ to the key notarization facility and claim to be the receiver. The key notarization facility would not load the correct data key (DKji), since (i || j) instead of (j || i) would be used as the identifier pair when decrypting $E_{(IKp\ XOR\ (j\,||\,i))}(DKji)$. Thus the decrypted message would be garbled.

It is assumed that the key notarization facility of each host is physically secure from all users and that shared interchange keys are securely distributed. One must guard against disclosure and substitution of keys. If one could gain knowledge of the shared key, one could forge all signatures sent between both facilities. Of course, all data keys encrypted under the shared key would also be compromised.

A Method Using Variants of the Host Master Key[16]

A different method for implementing encipher only and decipher only keys with the DES is discussed below. KE (the encipher only key) and KD (the decipher only key) are defined as follows:

$$KE = E_{KMI}(K)$$

$$KD = E_{KMJ}(K)$$

[16]©1980 Horizon House. Reprinted in part from INTELCOM '80 Conference Proceedings [21] with permission of Horizon House Telecommunications, Inc.

where KMI and KMJ are two different variants of the host master key (KM0), unique to the specification of KE and KD respectively, and K is a DES data-encrypting key.

Two new cryptographic operations are also defined to the cryptographic facility: *encipher data only* (**ENCO**) and *decipher data only* (**DECO**), as discussed below:[17]

$$\textbf{ENCO}: \{\textbf{KE}, \textbf{X}\} \longrightarrow E_{D_{KMI}(KE)}(X)$$

$$\textbf{DECO}: \{\textbf{KD}, \textbf{Y}\} \longrightarrow D_{D_{KMJ}(KD)}(Y)$$

where X and Y are the plaintext and ciphertext, respectively. ENCO uses variant KMI and DECO uses variant KMJ.

X is recovered whenever it is enciphered with KE and the result is deciphered with KD:

$$\text{DECO: } \{\text{KD, ENCO: } \{\text{KE, X}\}\} = \text{X}; \quad \text{for all X},$$

and X is recovered whenever it is deciphered with KD and the result is enciphered with KE:

$$\text{ENCO: } \{\text{KE, DECO: } \{\text{KD, X}\}\} = \text{X}; \quad \text{for all X}$$

provided that

$$D_{KMI}(KE) = D_{KMJ}(KD),$$

which is the case whenever KE = $E_{KMI}(K)$ and KD = $E_{KMJ}(K)$.

For an arbitrary value of K, $E_{KMI}(K)$ is generally unequal to $E_{KMJ}(K)$ (i.e., KE $\neq$ KD). This means that when plaintext is enciphered/deciphered with a given key parameter (KE or KD), it cannot be recovered (deciphered/enciphered) with the same key parameter.

Because of the complexity of DES, a knowledge of KE does not reveal KD (and vice versa), even though KMI and KMJ are variants of the same key (KM0). But when used in conjunction with the cryptographic operations ENCO and DECO, KE permits data to be enciphered under a secret DES key (K) and the corresponding KD permits data to be deciphered under the same secret DES key (K). Therefore, as far as the cryptographic system is concerned, enciphering and deciphering are performed with K. But as far as the cryptographic system users are concerned, enciphering is performed with KE and deciphering is performed with KD. That is, the keys and the attributes of those keys are defined respectively different to the user and the cryptographic system.

The properties of a public-key cryptosystem are achieved by making KE (the encipher only key) public and keeping KD (the decipher only key) pri-

[17] ENCO and DECO illustrate the Electronic Codebook (ECB) mode of DES operation [20]. The encipher only and decipher only attributes could also be extended to cover encryption and decryption using block chaining techniques, although such methods are omitted from this discussion.

vate. The approach, however, is not as flexible as a true public-key cryptosystem. KE and KD can be used only at the host system where they were originally created. Moreover, the encipher only and decipher only properties of the keys are guaranteed only as long as the secrecy of KM0 or any of its variants, and the data-encrypting key associated with each KE and KD pair, can be guaranteed.

To allow a user to create a public and private key pair, a key generation function is defined called *generate key* (GKEY):

$$\text{GKEY: } \{\ \} \longrightarrow E_{KMI}(K), E_{KMJ}(K)$$

This operation has no input parameters, and when invoked a random number K is generated within the cryptographic facility and in turn enciphered first under KMI and second under KMJ. The variants KMI and KMJ are derived inside the cryptographic facility by a selected inversion of bits of the host master key KM0.

The principle of encipher only and decipher only keys can also be extended to a network of interconnected terminals and host computers [22]. However, the details are omitted from this discussion.

LEGALIZING DIGITAL SIGNATURES[18]

In the absence of an omnibus statute governing paperless commercial transactions via an electronic communications network, parties are free to enter into their own agreements. However, if disagreements later arise, the party seeking to enforce the contract will prevail only if the agreement complied with certain basic legal requirements. These requirements may include the the provisions of statutes of frauds (as imposed by the UCC and/or local law), acknowledgments, recording, and reasonableness. Modern statutes of frauds require some writing which indicates that a contract for sale has been made between the parties at a defined price, that it reasonably defines the subject matter, and that it is signed by either the party against whom enforcement is sought or by his duly authorized agent. We have seen, however, that the signed requirement may be satisfied by something less than a formal handwritten signature. A mere pattern of bits, whether in clear or encrypted form, would not as a practical matter serve as the required symbol in lieu of a handwritten signature, even though the pattern of bits was transmitted or accepted by a party with the intention at that time of authenticating a writing. This is because a pattern of bits which is used as a signature may be altogether too easily manipulated or forged, and is not part of, or annexed to, a tangible writing. Moreover, unless the pattern of bits were predefined to have a particular meaning to the party receiving it, or unless an established code form were adopted by the parties, it would be utterly without meaning.

Therefore, it seems doubtful that, by itself, a special pattern of bits trans-

[18]©1978 McGraw-Hill, Inc. Reprinted in part from *Data Communications,* February 1978 [1].

mitted together with a message and subsequently recorded on some machine-readable medium would satisfy the necessary legal requirements of signature. On the other hand, when an initial written agreement, signed in the ordinary sense, is entered into by the parties in question, it appears that the legal requirements of signature can be satisfied. The initial written agreement in this case defines the procedures and protocols whereby the parties would conduct a series of future transactions, together with an agreed means and procedure for recording the elements of such transactions.

The UCC specifically authorizes parties to vary the provisions of the code by agreement, except as otherwise stated, and provided that the obligations of good faith, diligence, reasonableness, and care as prescribed by the code may not be disclaimed [Sec. 1-102-(3)]. The UCC further provides for parties involved in banking transactions to stipulate or agree to deviate from its requirements, and to determine for themselves the standards by which their responsibilities are to be measured, provided that a bank may not disclaim responsibility for its own lack of good faith or failure to exercise ordinary care or limit the measure of damages for such lack or failure [Sec. 4-103]. It is under this exception that banks have been able to operate current electronic funds transfer systems, including transactions with their customers and with other banks.

Of course, there are certain classes of transactions for which only accepted paper-based conventions will suffice. For example, to be enforceable, transactions involving real property must (in most states) be in writing, and be acknowledged and recorded in a public registry (the office of the county clerk in which the property is located). Hence to comply with present law, contracts of this nature could not be handled by electronic communications networks with a capability for digital signatures.

Initial Written Agreement

With each of the methods for obtaining digital signatures previously described, each party possesses certain secret and possibly nonsecret, information used in generating his own signature, and other nonsecret information used in checking or validating the signatures of others.

For this protocol to be workable, there must be some mechanism for each party to authenticate independently the nonsecret signature validation information which he holds. This could be done if each party were to record his own signature validation information at some established registry with recognized and accepted integrity, such as an office of the county clerk or the office of a secretary of state. Alternatively, one could include this information within the initial written agreement itself, which was shown to be necessary in order to comply with the underlying legal requirements for conducting signed transactions via an electronic network. Recall that in a public-key cryptographic system, the private deciphering key cannot be efficiently derived from the public enciphering key. Likewise, in a DES-based protocol, the private signature keys cannot be efficiently derived from the corresponding public validation quantities.

As to the question of whether a person who transmits a message signed with an electronic digital signature is in fact authorized, the procedures necessarily imply that only an authorized agent would have access to the secret information needed to generate the signature. Thus, when the secret information used in generating signatures is stored within a computing system, the burden is upon installation management to assure that this information is kept secret, and that an adequate access control mechanism is in place so that signatures can be created only by authorized users (persons, programs, and the like).

Whoever has access to a principal's secret signature generation information will be deemed to be the principal's authorized agent. Therefore, installation management must also implement sufficient security controls in order to be alerted if this secret signature generation information should become exposed, or if the capability to sign messages has been obtained by unauthorized users. Failure of one of the principals to notify other parties that his digital signatures have been compromised may be deemed his own negligence, and might defeat any defenses he may later raise as to the authority of his agents.

Choice of Law

As part of their initial written agreement, the parties must specify a particular jurisdiction under whose laws the agreement is to be governed (such as New York law), and the forum for the litigation of disputes that may arise out of transactions executed via the electronic communications system. Where the parties agree to communicate via a common network and the information needed to validate signatures has been recorded or registered, the jurisdiction wherein such registry is located would be the reasonable and logical choice. Both interstate and international transactions may be accommodated in this manner.

The statute of limitations defines the period of time within which a lawsuit must be commenced from the time a cause of action accrues. In disputes involving contracts, the period in most states is six years. A cause of action upon a contract may accrue at the time the original written agreement was entered into, or at some time thereafter, when a signed message is transmitted. It would appear necessary, therefore, that both parties to a transaction (sender and receiver) retain all data relating to their initial written agreement and to each subsequent signed message for at least the period of the applicable statute of limitations.

Moreover, it would serve the interest of both parties to have a trusted mechanism for the recording of the time and date of the transaction. If the time and date were included as part of the message's content, the receiver would have a means of verifying and proving the time and date of the transaction. This, of course, could be easily accomplished with existing message time-stamping facilities already available in data processing systems.

Regardless of the protocol for implementing electronic digital signatures, the claim is made that if the protocol is implemented as intended, then one can be assured that (1) the sender is not able to later disavow messages as his own, (2) the receiver is not able to forge messages or signatures, and (3) both the sender and receiver are certain that the identity of the sender and the contents of the message can be proved before a referee. As a consequence, the following may be said about the judicial acceptance of the electronic digital signature.

The parties may agree or stipulate as part of their initial written agreement that they will be bound by their digital signatures, that they agree to submit all disputes to a referee, and that they agree the concept of digital signatures is cryptographically sound. However, this agreement will not prevent one of the parties from later raising the claim that the indicated result lacks validity, that he did not understand the underlying scientific principle (not an unreasonable assertion), or that he was forced to sign the stipulation as a condition of his transacting business with the other party. As a practical matter, therefore, it is prudent to assume that such disputes will inevitably arise.

While various techniques exist for proving the validity of written signatures (ranging from expert handwriting analysis to the unique properties of handwritten signature acceleration patterns), the resolution of disputes over digital signatures will be based on validation quantities, the cryptographic strength of the algorithms used in the generation of signatures, and the like. Thus as part of the process of judicial acceptance, the courts must initially pass upon the question of the soundness of the underlying cryptographic technique.

All scientific aids and devices go through experimental and testing phases. During these phases there may be considerable scientific controversy over the validity of the technique, aid, or device. During this period of controversy, there is the danger that a trial of a legal dispute between the parties may result in the trial of the validity of the new scientific technique, rather than a trial of the issues involved in the case. "It is not for the law to experiment but of science to do so" [*State vs. Cary*, 99 N.J. Sup. 323, 239 A.2d 680, aff'd, 56 N.J. 16, 264 A.2nd 209 (1970)].

When scientific aids to the discovery of truth receive general recognition within the relevant scientific community as to their accuracy, courts will not hesitate to take judicial notice of such fact and admit evidence obtained through their use. Judicial notice means that the underlying scientific principle upon which the new device or process is based need not be proved each time the results of the device or process are introduced into evidence.

Judicial Notice Recognized

As an example of judicial notice, each time a police officer testifies that according to the output display of his radar device the defendant was speeding, he need not present expert witnesses to testify to the scientific foundation of radar—that the radar transmitter and receiver can measure the velocity of a moving target based upon the Doppler effect of reflected waves. Radar has now become generally accepted as a means of measuring vehicle speed. All the officer must prove is that, on the particular occasion in question, his particular radar unit was properly set up, calibrated, and operated.[19] Examples

[19] A highly publicized case in Dade County Florida in 1979 regarding the reliability of radar devices and their use by police officers resulted in a ruling "that the reliability of radar speed measuring devices as used in their present modes and particularly in these cases, has not been established beyond and to the exclusion of every reasonable doubt." [23] Subsequent court decisions, however, have generally upheld the accuracy and reliability of police traffic radar.

of other scientific principles that have been reduced to practice and are now judicially noticed include the unique properties of fingerprints and ballistics comparisons [24].

While the digital signature concept could be implemented using any encryption algorithm, its own scientific acceptance would be aided by basing the scheme upon a strong encryption algorithm which itself has already been scientifically recognized and accepted. Of course, if and when additional scientific evidence becomes available to challenge the effectiveness of the algorithm, courts may later reject their reliance upon once accepted principles.

It would be preferable, therefore, for the digital signature to be based on an algorithm whose strength has been certified by the NSA. In all likelihood, this would satisfy the criteria for judicial acceptance of the validity of the underlying scientific principle of digital signatures, and could aid in the eventual acceptance by the courts of the digital signature concept.

REFERENCES

1. Lipton, S. M. and Matyas, S. M., "Making the Digital Signature Legal—and Safeguarded," *Data Communications,* **7**, No. 2, 41–52 (February 1978).
2. Corley, R. N. and Robert, W. J., *Dillavou and Howard's Principles of Business Law,* 9th ed., Prentice-Hall, Englewood Cliffs, NJ, 1971.
3. *Uniform Commercial Code,* 1972 Official Text with Comments, American Law Institute and National Conference of Commission on Uniform State Laws.
4. Diffie, W. and Hellman, M., "New directions in Cryptography," *IEEE Transactions on Information Theory,* **IT-22**, 644–654 (November 1976).
5. Merkle, R. and Hellman, M., "Hiding Information and Receipts in Trapdoor Knapsacks," *IEEE Transactions on Information Theory,* **IT-24**, 525–530 (September 1978).
6. Kohnfelder, L. M., *Towards a Practical Public-Key Cryptosystem,* BS Thesis, Department of Electrical Engineering, Massachusetts Institute of Technology, Cambridge (May 1978).
7. Rivest, R. L., Shamir, A., and Adleman, L., "A Method for Obtaining Digital Signatures and Public-Key Cryptosystems," *Communications of the ACM,* **2**, No. 21, 120–126 (February 1978).
8. Shamir, A., "A Fast Signature Scheme," Massachusetts Institute of Technology, MIT/LCS/TM-107 (July 1978).
9. Branstad, D., Davida, G. I., Hellman, M. E., Tuchman, W. L., and Sugarman, R., "On Foiling Computer Crime," *IEEE Spectrum,* **16**, No. 7, 31–49 (July 1979).
10. Yuval, G., "How to Swindle Rabin," *Cryptologia,* **3**, No. 3, 187–189 (July 1979).
11. Rabin, M. O., "Digitized Signatures," in *Foundations of Secure Computation,* edited by R. A. DeMillo, D. P. Dobkin, A. K. Jones, and R. J. Lipton, Academic Press, New York, 1978, 155–168.
12. Matyas, S. M. and Meyer, C. H., "Electronic Signature for Data Encryption Standard," *IBM Technical Disclosure Bulletin,* **24**, No. 5, 2332–2334 (October 1981).
13. Matyas, S. M. and Meyer, C. H., "Electronic Signature for use with the Data Encryption Standard," *IBM Technical Disclosure Bulletin,* **24**, No. 5, 2335–2336 (October 1981).
14. Matyas, S. M., "Digital Signatures—An Overview," *Computer Networks,* **3**, 87–94 (1979).
15. Ehrsam, W. F., Matyas, S. M., Meyer, C. H., and Tuchman, W. L., "A Cryptographic Key Management Scheme for Implementing the Data Encryption Standard," *IBM Systems Journal,* **17**, No. 2, 106–125 (1978).

16. Lennon, R. E. and Matyas, S. M., "Unidirectional Cryptographic Functions Using Master Key Variants," *1979 National Telecommunications Conference Record,* **3**, 43.4.1–43.4.5 (November 1979).
17. Lennon, R. E., Matyas, S. M., and Meyer, C. H., "Cryptographic Authentication of Time-Invariant Quantities," *IEEE Transactions on Communications,* **COM-29**, No. 6, 773–777 (June 1981).
18. Smid, M. E., *A Key Notarization System for Computer Networks,* NBS Special Publication 500–54, U.S. Department of Commerce, National Bureau of Standards, Washington, DC (October 1979).
19. Campbell, C. M., Jr., "A Microprocessor-Based Module to Provide Security in Electronic Funds Transfer Systems," *Proceedings COMPCON 79,* 148–153 (1979).
20. *DES Modes of Operation,* Federal Information Processing Standard (FIPS) Publication 81, National Bureau of Standards, U.S. Department of Commerce, Washington, DC (1981).
21. Lennon, R. E., Matyas, S. M., and Meyer, C. H., "Cryptographic Authentication Methods for Emerging Data Processing Applications," *Proceedings, INTELCOM '80,* 337–341 (November 1980).
22. Lennon, R. E., Matyas, S. M., and Meyer, C. H., "Public-Key Enciphering/Deciphering Transformations Using a Conventional Algorithm," *IBM Technical Disclosure Bulletin,* **25**, No. 3A, 1241–1249 (August 1982).
23. *Police Traffic Radar,* U.S. Department of Transportation Issue Paper, DOT HS–805 254 (February 1980).
24. Maguire, J. M. and Chadborne, J. H., *Evidence–Cases and Materials,* 6th ed., Foundation Press, Mineola, NY, 1973.

Other Publications of Interest

25. Merkle, R. C., *Secrecy, Authentication, and Public Key Systems,* Technical Report No. 1979–1, Department of Electrical Engineering, Stanford University, Palo Alto, CA (June 1978).
26. Shamir, A., *A Fast Signature Scheme,* MIT Laboratory for Computer Science, Report TM–107 (July 1978).

CHAPTER TEN

Applying Cryptography to Pin-Based Electronic Funds Transfer Systems[1]

Today there are many cryptographic authentication techniques being used and evaluated by major financial institutions for electronic funds transfer systems. Therefore, due to the state-of-the-art, there are divergent opinions as to the order in which problems should be addressed and what methodologies should be used to achieve optimum solutions.

To provide a balanced discussion between the authors' point of view (expressed in Chapter 11) and that of others, permission has been obtained to reprint relevant sections from the *PIN Manual: A Guide to the Use of Personal Identification Numbers for Interchange* [1], which was prepared by the staff of MasterCard International, Inc. (formally Interbank Card Association) in cooperation with MasterCard International's Standing Committees. The material in this chapter, except for two indicated passages, was comprised from the first four sections of the *PIN Manual.* The views expressed and responsibility for the accuracy of the material lies with the originators of that manual.

Helpful footnotes, annotations, and additional material was provided by the authors. (Material added by the authors appears in brackets.) In order to maintain consistency, the original notations for encipherment and decipherment have been changed to conform with the notations used throughout the book.

Pin Manual
A Guide to the Use of
Personal Identification Numbers
in Interchange

INTRODUCTION

In the early 1970's, Interbank Card Association began to investigate the implications of the transition from an off-line paper based funds transfer

[1] By permission of MasterCard International, Inc. (formerly Interbank Card Association). Reprinted in part from *PIN Manual: A Guide to the Use of Personal Identification Numbers in Interchange*, September 1980 [1].

system, exemplified by MasterCard, to an on-line, Electronic Funds Transfer (EFT) system. The investigation soon determined that this transition would present many problems relating to customer acceptance, economic justification, and regulatory policy. However, the only unsolved technological problem was how to insure the system's security.

Interbank soon realized that using secret Personal Identification Numbers, PINs, was the best technique for authenticating customers in EFT. A PIN serves the same role in an electronic system that a written signature serves in a conventional paper based system. While this did not solve the security problem, it did define one major aspect, the need to ensure PIN secrecy everywhere within the EFT environment. Although the assurance of PIN secrecy was the first and foremost EFT security problem, it was not the only one. Insuring the authenticity and integrity of the transaction were also problems.

Since it was apparent that EFT could not progress until these security problems were resolved, Interbank began, in the 1970's, what is believed to be the most extensive study of EFT security ever undertaken. The study, which lasted more than three years, uncovered and assembled a wealth of information regarding virtually every aspect of securing an EFT system. It considered, in detail, the possible fraud threats that could be perpetrated against such a system and developed countermeasures to prevent them. The implementation of each countermeasure was studied in detail to insure that its effectiveness would not detrimentally affect the cost or performance of the EFT system as a whole. The study considered many approaches to the issuance, management, validation, and interchange of PINs, and where choices were available to the financial institution, attempted to determine the pros and cons of the available alternatives. Since the study concluded that most of the required security techniques were cryptographic, considerable thought was given to the practical implementation of cryptography in a retail funds transfer environment. Given special study was the management of the secret keys that are a fundamental ingredient in any secure cryptographic system.

SECTION ONE: BASIC PIN CONCEPTS

Why PINs?

The term PIN refers to personal identification number. It is a secret number assigned to, or selected by, the holder of a debit card or credit card used in an EFT (electronic funds transfer) system and serves to authenticate the cardholder to the EFT system. The PIN is basically the cardholder's electronic signature, and serves the same role in an EFT transaction as a written signature serves in a conventional financial transaction. The PIN is memorized by the cardholder and is not to be recorded by him in a manner that could be ascertained by another person. At the time that the cardholder initiates an EFT transaction, he enters his PIN into the EFT terminal using a keyboard provided for this purpose. Unless the PIN, as entered, is recognized by the EFT system as being correct for this particular account number (read by the EFT terminal from the card's magnetic stripe), the EFT system refuses to accept the transaction. The purpose of all this is so that, should the card be lost or stolen, the finder or thief would be unable to use the card, not knowing the associated PIN. Similarly, it is to prevent someone who would be able to do so from making a usable counterfeit copy of the card. Even if he could make such a counterfeit card he could not use it, not knowing the PIN.

PIN Secrecy

In order for the PIN to serve its required function, it must be known to the cardholder, but to no one else. PIN secrecy is of the utmost importance. If the financial institution wishes the cardholder to be responsible for any compromise of his PIN, and, if a PIN is to be an effective signature substitute, then the institution's own handling of the PIN must be above reproach. It must display to its cardholders extreme care in its PIN management procedures. For example, if a cardholder is given the opportunity of selecting his own PIN and is asked to write the PIN of his choice on the application form containing information identifying him, he will quite likely realize that certain bank employees could ascertain his PIN from this form. This cannot help but influence his own attitude toward the importance of PIN secrecy. On the other hand, if he sees that the institution exercises extreme care to insure that no bank employee can possibly learn his PIN, he will be impressed with the importance of PIN secrecy on his own part.

Some financial institutions tend to view PIN secrecy on a cost-effective basis. That is, they attempt to compare the cost of a certain degree of PIN security with the cost of the fraud losses that might otherwise occur. This is not really a valid comparison, because the impact of fraud due to the compromise of PIN secrecy greatly transcends the actual dollars lost. The most catastrophic type of fraud that can occur because PINs are compromised is the production and use of counterfeit cards, causing the accounts of unsuspecting cardholders to be fraudulently debited. This is not known until the cardholders find their accounts overdrawn or incorrect debits on their monthly statements. Assuming that the fraud losses are not due to negligence on the cardholders' part, the institution must pay not only for the fraud but also for the clerical costs involved in processing cardholder complaints and making restitution. Undoubtedly such fraud would become publicized, and cardholders who had not actually experienced fraud but who could not recall making certain transactions appearing on their statements would suspect that they had been defrauded, and file complaints with the institution. The institution would have no obvious way of distinguishing valid complaints of fraud from invalid ones. As a result, some dishonest cardholders would undoubtedly deny making certain of their transactions, knowing the institution could not prove them wrong. This secondary fraud could be of even greater consequence than the primary fraud. However, the greatest impact of fraud resulting from PIN compromise would probably be on customer relations. A number of honest cardholders would hesitate to trust their funds to such an institution any longer, and would move their accounts elsewhere.

Thus, the net loss to an institution could be many times the loss directly due to PIN compromise.

As electronic banking and other forms of EFT grow as a percentage of total financial transactions, the importance of the PIN, and hence of PIN secrecy, is expected to grow likewise. Only by stringent (though not necessarily costly) security measures can a high degree of PIN secrecy be maintained.

The PIN in its clear (comprehensible) form should never be transmitted over communications lines, because these lines could be tapped. The clear PIN should never reside, even momentarily, in any main frame or any data base, because a clever programmer or computer operator might devise some technique for ascertaining it. It should never be known to, or accessible by, any employee of the institution, not even during the PIN issuing process. (PIN mailers, if used, should be under strict dual control at all times to prevent compromise.)

As stringent as these security measures may be, they can be implemented at modest cost and without noticeable impact upon banking operations. Subsequent sections describe, in detail, security techniques and their implementation.

PIN Length

In order to achieve its intended purpose, the PIN must contain enough digits so that a card finder, thief or counterfeiter would have little probability of hitting the correct PIN by chance, if he simply guessed at values. On the other hand it should not contain very many digits, or it will slow down the EFT transaction time. Therefore it is recommended that the PIN be four, five or six decimal digits in length. A four digit PIN allows ten thousand unique PINs. The criminal has no way of knowing which of these is the correct PIN value for any given stolen or counterfeit card in his possession. Assuming that the number of consecutive incorrect PIN entry attempts per card is limited to a small number (e.g., ten or less), assuming that only one PIN value is usable with any given card, and assuming a best case situation from a card counterfeiter's point of view, namely, an unlimited supply of counterfeit cards (thousands), the unobserved exclusive use of an ATM for hours on end, and no other special system checks to ascertain trial and error PIN determination, he would still require more than forty continuous hours of trial and error (assuming four tries per minute), and nearly one thousand counterfeit cards, before he could determine the PIN for a single card. This is believed to be an unfeasible fraud technique, so a four digit PIN appears adequate. Of course this trial and error procedure would be ten or a hundred times longer for a five or a six digit PIN.

It is assumed that in a properly designed EFT security system, it is impossible for the card counterfeiter to construct an off-line system and use it for trial and error PIN determination. That is, it is assumed that he can attempt this trial and error method only on a terminal connected to the actual EFT network. This assumption is not valid for certain EFT security techniques that have been proposed. Were one of these techniques to be used, a PIN length of six or fewer digits would be extremely non-secure.

Though there is no security disadvantage to having long PINs, there is a practical disadvantage. The longer the PIN, the longer the time the cardholder will require to enter it, and the greater the probability of an entry requiring a repeat. The latter is of special concern in an interchange environment where the PIN must be sent to the card issuer for validation. Several seconds or more could elapse before the cardholder began reentering his PIN. During this time the EFT terminal would be unavailable for other use, and in POS environment, a clerk would also be kept waiting. In addition, there is the delay and inconvenience to the cardholder. Thus long PINs, by increasing the transaction time, are a detriment to the merchant, the cardholder and the financial institution.[2]

Allowable PIN Entry Attempts

It is customary to place a limit on the number of consecutive incorrect PIN entries a cardholder is allowed. This is done to further hinder fraudulent PIN determination by trial and error. Though desirable, this is not as important as it is perhaps believed to be, and would appear unnecessary for all but four digit PINs. Determining a five digit PIN by trial and error would require an average of fifty thousand attempts without such a limit, and this appears unfeasible. If a limit is imposed, it can be either an absolute limit, or a daily limit. An absolute limit gives the cardholder a specified number of attempts to enter his PIN correctly, regardless of the time span. After the allowable attempts have been exhausted, the card is considered invalid. A daily limit restricts the cardholder to a specified number of consecutive incorrect attempts in any one day, but the cardholder starts with a "clean slate" the following day. Only when the number of consecutive incorrect PIN entries in any one day exceeds the limit is the card considered invalid. Of these two approaches, the absolute limit appears preferable, since it more definitively limits criminal attempts at trial and error PIN determination. The benefits of this approach, for a four digit PIN, can be expressed quantitatively. If we let N represent the absolute number of consecutive incorrect PIN entries allowed, where N is small (e.g., ten) relative to ten thousand, then the criminal would have to make an average of about ten thousand tries for each PIN he successfully determined. During this time he would have used up ten thousand divided by N cards. That is, for every card's PIN he successfully determined, he would fail on ten thousand/N cards. Without any type of limit, he would require only a single card, and an average of five thousand tries.

When the PIN is validated using the technique of the American Banking Association PIN Verification Standard, the statistics are somewhat different because this technique uses a "non-reversibly encrypted" PIN, which means that more than one PIN can generally be used with a given card. With this technique and an absolute limit, the criminal requires the average of five thousand trials, and for every counterfeit card on which he succeeds he fails

[2] It is only fair to point out that, at the time of this writing, there are differing opinions as to what constitutes a reasonable and practicable PIN length. Current technology will easily accommodate PINs of up to 16 digits.

on 5,000/N. Without any type of limit he requires a single card and the average of 3,679 tries.

The situation for a daily rather than an absolute limit is essentially the same as in the no limit case, except the criminal is restricted daily to one less than the maximum number of attempts allowed. In this way the card is never declared invalid, and the criminal can make additional attempts the next day. The intent is that long before he has made the five thousand (or 3,679 average) tries required, the legitimate cardholder will have noticed that the card is missing, and report the loss. However, if the criminal is using a counterfeit copy of the card, there is no loss to report.

If some type of limit is imposed on incorrect PIN entries, then the question is whether or not the card should be retained when this limit is reached. In an off-line system, card retention may be necessary to prevent unauthorized card usage. However, as a general rule, it appears better not to retain the card if this can possibly be avoided. In an on-line system, the account can be flagged as invalid in the data base, so there is no practical need to retain the card. If the imposed limit is a daily, card related limit, retaining the card does not significantly affect the criminal who is attempting trial and error PIN determination. He is well aware of the limit, and is careful to stay below it. The only effect of card retention at the limit is to reduce by one the number of tries per card per day that can be made. On the other hand, the cardholder is unaware of the card retention threat, and may keep trying to remember his PIN until he has reached the retention threshold. Thus, retaining the card when this type of limit is used does not appear desirable, unless required by off-line usage of the card.

In summary, some limit on the number of consecutive incorrect PIN entries seems desirable when four digit PINs are used, though unnecessary when the PIN length is longer. This should not be an argument to use a longer PIN, because four digits is, in many ways, the optimum PIN length. With a four digit PIN, the first choice is to use a per card absolute limit, without regard to time. A value in the range of three to ten would seem reasonable. The second choice is to use a per card daily limit, in the range of three to four. The third choice is no limit. This choice introduces some risk, however, this risk is not significant, since it would require the average of fifteen to twenty hours of trial and error at an ATM (assuming the ATM allows four tries per minute) for each four digit PIN thus determined. Finally, retaining the card (should the limit, of whatever type, be reached) appears undesirable, unless there is no other method available for restricting future use of the card.

PIN Issuance

There are two basic PIN issuance techniques. In the first, the financial institution determines what the PIN will be, and conveys it to the cardholder. In the second, the cardholder determines what the PIN will be and conveys it to the institution.

Bank Selected PIN

Again, the card issuing institution has two choices. The PIN can be cryptographically derived from the account number, or it can be a random value.

PIN Cryptographically Derived from the Account Number. In this case, the account number is processed using a cryptographic algorithm so as to produce a decimal value of the appropriate number of digits. With proper generation techniques there is no discernible correlation between the derived PIN and the account number, and the PIN is completely unpredictable to anyone who knows the account number but does not know the secret key (defined in Section Three) used in the cryptographic process.

The advantage of this technique is that it eliminates the necessity for maintaining any record of the PIN. When the PIN of reference is needed to validate the PIN as entered by the (alleged) cardholder, it may be regenerated by simply processing the same account number through the same cryptographic process (utilizing the same secret cryptographic key). The main disadvantage of this technique is that the PIN cannot be changed unless the account number is changed. If a cardholder fears that his PIN may have been compromised and requests a new PIN, the only way to give him a new PIN is to give him a new account number. Another disadvantage is that the cryptographic key cannot be changed without changing every cardholder's PIN.

Random PIN. The use of a random number for the PIN overcomes the disadvantage of having a PIN that is inherently linked to an account number and to a specific cryptographic key. With the random number technique, the card issuing institution generates, in a highly secure manner, a random decimal number that serves as the cardholder's PIN. The disadvantage of this technique is that the institution must maintain a record of the random PIN it issued to serve as the PIN of reference for subsequent validation of the PIN as entered from EFT terminals. As indicated previously, it is unacceptable to store the PIN in its clear form. It must be encrypted, as described in subsequent sections. The encrypted PIN may be (1) stored in the issuer's data base, (2) encoded on the magnetic stripe of the card, or (3) both.

Regardless of which technique is chosen to generate a bank selected PIN, it must be conveyed to the cardholder. This is normally accomplished by means of a PIN mailer, a printed document containing the clear PIN. This document must be printed under conditions of very high security, and dual control throughout must be utilized to insure that no bank employee opens, reads, or even closely examines such a mailer. The most secure PIN mailer is a multi-part sealed form with the PIN printing visible only inside the form. (The form can then, if desired, be placed in a windowed envelope to hide any impression which may have been made upon the top surface of the form.)

The PIN and the associated cards should never be mailed together. Preferably, the PIN is mailed after the cardholder has signed a confirmation receipt for the card.

It is recommended that bank selected PIN should be four digits (not five or six) to simplify its memorization and lessen the probability that it will be carried, in written form, with the card.

Cardholder Selected PIN

Many financial institutions, for reasons to be discussed later, prefer to have the cardholder select his own PIN. In this case, a technique is required where the cardholder can convey his PIN to the institution. There are three such techniques:

1. The PIN may be solicited by mail, with the selected PIN mailed back to the institution.
2. The PIN may be entered by the cardholder via a secure terminal located at one of the institution's offices.
3. The PIN may be selected when the potential cardholder visits the issuer's facility.

Consider each of these techniques:

PIN Solicited by Mail. With this technique the institution prepares a two part form to be mailed to the cardholder. The first part contains the cardholder's name and address, and serves only for mailing purposes. The second part contains a reference number and a place for the cardholder to write the desired PIN. The cardholder is instructed to write only the PIN on the second portion and mail it back to the institution in an opaque envelope provided for the purpose. The first part is to be discarded. The reference number bears no discernible relationship to the cardholder's account number, nor to any other information that would identify the cardholder. Thus, a clerk at the institution may open the returned envelope and manually enter the PIN and the reference number into a special security system. This system can, through a cryptographic process, ascertain the account number from the reference number. Then it passes the PIN, encrypted, and the clear account number to the institution's EDP system. At no point in this process is the clear PIN ever associated with the clear account number, nor with any other information which would serve to identify the cardholder.

PIN Entered via a Secure Terminal. Perhaps the simplest and best way for a cardholder to convey his selected PIN to the financial institution is by entering it via the PIN pad of a secure terminal. A secure terminal is one that encrypts the PIN as soon as it is entered. Such a terminal operating in conjunction with special cryptographic equipment at the institution's EDP facility, provides an environment where the clear PIN is never thereafter available (except within the security system).

With this method of cardholder PIN selection, safeguards must be implemented to protect against someone who steals a card from the mail, impersonates the legitimate cardholder in the PIN selection process, and then draws against the legitimate cardholder's funds. To guard against this, one or more officials at the office where the terminal is located should be responsible for validating the cardholder's identity. Such an official has a special PIN, which he enters into the terminal just before the cardholder begins the PIN selection process, provided the official is satisfied with the cardholder's identity. Only when the cardholder's PIN is preceded by a legitimate official's PIN, is the cardholder's PIN accepted.

Another approach to cardholder PIN selection at a secure terminal is to assign the cardholder an initial PIN with a secure PIN mailer, then allow the cardholder to replace it with a PIN of his own choice. In this case, the cardholder must first correctly enter the assigned PIN, then enter the PIN of his choice. This procedure precludes the necessity of a bank official authenticating the cardholder. The fact that the cardholder knows the assigned PIN is probably sufficient proof of identity.

Regardless of which cardholder authentication method is used, it is suggested that the cardholder be required to enter the PIN identically two consecutive times. This is to prevent accidental errors in entering the selected PIN.

PIN Selected at the Issuer's Facility. Today, a large number of financial institutions utilizing the cardholder selected PIN technique have the cardholder select the PIN at the time he applies for the card. This is logistically simpler than mailing PIN solicitation forms. Furthermore, it allows the card to be prepared immediately thereafter, even if the magnetic stripe is to contain an encrypted version of the PIN. A widely used technique is to have the cardholder write the PIN on the application. This is not a recommended procedure, as certain bank employees would be able to relate the PIN to the name, and then to the account number.

A secure technique for cardholder PIN selection at the issuer's facility uses a prepared form, produced by a special security system. This is a sealed, multi-part form, similar to that suggested previously for PIN mailers. On the top layer the security system prints a clear reference number, and inside the form (where it cannot be seen) it prints this number encrypted. There is no discernible relationship between the clear and the encrypted versions of the reference number, as they are related only via a cryptographic process utilizing a secret key known to no one.

The customer applying for a card is given this sealed form. Privately, he removes the inner portion of the form containing the encrypted reference number, and on this portion writes the PIN of his choice. He writes nothing else, places this portion of the form in an opaque envelope and seals and deposits it in a locked container provided for the purpose. The outer portion of the form containing the clear reference number is submitted along with the application. This clear reference number is entered into the data base of the institution's EDP system as a part of the application and becomes the account number, or is associated with the account number as soon as this number is assigned. At some subsequent time, a bank employee enters the encrypted reference number and the PIN into a special security system which encrypts the PIN, decrypts the reference number, passing the result to the institution's EDP system. This system uses the clear reference number to relate the encrypted PIN to the account number. At no point in this process is the clear PIN associated with any data that identifies the cardholder.

If a secure terminal is available at the office where the customer makes application for the card, another PIN selection procedure is possible. Under this alternate technique, the application is assigned a number. This number is written on the application, and entered into the secure terminal. The customer then enters the PIN of his choice into this terminal, via its PIN pad. The PIN is encrypted at the secure terminal, and remains encrypted thereafter during transmission through, or storage in, communications or EDP equipment. The encrypted PIN will be related to the account number, when the latter is assigned, via the application number.

Another issue concerning a cardholder selected PIN relates to the nature of the PIN itself. Should it be a number or a word? It is often held that a word is preferable, being easier to remember than a number. Since PIN keyboards have (or will have) letters (in the manner of a telephone) associated with each digit, the entry of letters is as convenient as that of numbers. However, the use of a single word for the PIN is not recommended. There are simply not enough different words cardholders would be likely to choose to adequately preclude trial and error PIN determination. For example, one could probably make a list of two hundred words, and have a reasonable probability that any given cardholder would select a PIN from this list.

The recommended technique, where an alphabetic PIN is desired, is to instruct the cardholder to select two unrelated words, using the first two letters of each word to form his four character PIN. If a six character PIN is desired, the first three letters of each word should be used.

When a numeric PIN is used, it is also advisable for cardholders to be given instructions on how to select a PIN. For example, they should be instructed not to select a telephone number that might be readily associated with them (e.g., their own or that of a close relative or business associate). Similarly, they should not select a date that might be readily associated with them (e.g., birthday, anniversary of themselves or a close relative), nor any other number closely associated with them (license number, social security number). These admonitions are designed to guard against the interception of a card in the mail (or the theft or counterfeiting of a card), and determination of the associated PIN by trial and error using readily available information about the cardholder. (While this fraud threat is certainly possible, it is not considered to be a major one.)

Comparison of Bank Selected PIN and Cardholder Selected PIN

There is considerable difference of opinion among financial institutions as to which method of PIN selection is preferable. Operational simplicity favors the institution specifying the PIN. PIN mailers can be printed in an automatic fashion at a very rapid rate. When the PIN is selected by the cardholder, however, each PIN must be individually entered into the system. This is a manual and time consuming procedure with some cost consequences for the financial institution, unless the cardholder can perform the entry without manual assistance.

The advantage of having the cardholders select their PINs is that they will more easily remember such PINs, and be less inclined to write them someplace where they might be associated with their cards. The disadvantage, in addition to the above indicated cost consideration, is that the cardholders may tend to select values which might be surmised, despite admonitions to the contrary. Another factor favoring the cardholder selected PIN is customer relations. It is, presumably, less onerous for customers to memorzie a value they have selected, then one that has been imposed on them.

The recommended approach for PIN selection is one whereby the financial institution issues a PIN to the cardholder with the option of selecting an alternate value. This alternate value is selected, desirably, via a secure terminal with the bank issued value authenticating the cardholder for the PIN change procedure. The bank selected initial value, which most cardholders will probably elect to use as their permanent PIN, should be four digits long, whereas the cardholder might be allowed to select a four, five, or six digit value, depending upon his personal preference.

In many situations it is not feasible to give the cardholder a PIN with the option of changing it. This can be true if the PIN, in an encrypted form, is to be encoded on the card. In such a case the recommended procedure would be for the bank to issue the cardholder a four digit PIN, or else use the previously discussed technique of PIN selection at the time of application. Though the latter may be viewed as somewhat preferable, the former appears acceptable, and is logistically much simpler.

Regardless of the PIN selection technique chosen, the cardholder should be advised of the importance of the PIN and PIN secrecy. The cardholder should be warned against recording the PIN value where it might be located by a finder or thief of the card.

The Forgotten PIN

Regardless of how the PINs are conveyed to the cardholders, it is possible they will forget the PINs. When this happens, there are three possible courses of action for a financial institution.

1. Send the cardholder a PIN mailer advising him of the forgotten PIN.
2. Send the cardholder a completely new PIN.
3. Allow the cardholder to select a new PIN.

From a human factors point of view, the most desirable procedure is probably the first and the least desirable alternative is the second. It is a psychological fact that it is easier to rememorize something than to memorize something completely new. Thus, sending a PIN mailer reminding the cardholder of the original PIN is the preferred technique, even if the cardholder had originally selected the PIN. (Once the cardholder sees the PIN, he will most likely recall why it was selected, and this will reinforce it in the cardholder's mind all the more.) Sending a completely new bank selected PIN is not recommended. If the cardholder could not remember the initial PIN, there is little reason to believe he will remember a different one. Finally, allowing the cardholder to select another PIN is probably acceptable, but less desirable than reminding him of the PIN already selected. Of course, when the PIN in encrypted form has been encoded on the magnetic stripe of the card, the financial institution has no choice but to advise the cardholder of the original PIN, unless the card is to be reissued when the new PIN is chosen.

A PIN mailer, advising the cardholder of a forgotten PIN, must be printed under rigid physical security to prevent bank employees from opening the mailer.

PIN Validation for Local Transactions

Local transaction refers to a transaction in which the institution that issued the card also controls the terminal. By contrast, an interchange transaction is one in which the terminal is controlled by an institution other than the card issuing one. For a local transaction, there are two possible techniques for PIN validation, on-line and off-line.

On-Line PIN Validation

On-line validation refers to PIN validation at the institution's EDP facility, whereas off-line PIN validation refers to PIN validation in the terminal itself. On-line PIN validation is possible only when the terminal in question is on-line to the institution's EDP system (i.e., communicating with an operational EDP system).

In any PIN validation procedure, the PIN as entered by the cardholder is compared against the PIN of reference as recorded by the financial institution. There are three possible techniques for obtaining the PIN of reference. First, it may be stored in encrypted form in the data base of the financial institution. In this case either the encrypted PIN of reference is decrypted and compared with the clear PIN as entered, or else the PIN as entered is encrypted using the same procedure and key as was the PIN of reference, and the two encrypted values are then compared. Second, it may be recorded in encrypted form on the magnetic stripe. Again, either the encrypted PIN of reference is decrypted and compared to the clear cardholder-entered PIN, or else the cardholder-entered PIN is encrypted and compared against the encrypted PIN of reference. Finally, it may be a cryptographic function of the account number, obtained by employing the account number with a cryptographic process.

Encrypted PIN from Data Base. In this approach, the PIN must be encrypted at the terminal, then transmitted to the institution's EDP system along with the other elements of the transaction. Using the account number, the EDP system locates, in its data base, the encrypted PIN for this account. Special security equipment is then (desirably) used to decrypt both the PIN of reference from the data base, and the PIN entered by the cardholder from the terminal. These two decrypted versions of the PIN are compared, and an indication is sent to the EDP system as to whether or not they agree. If the two versions agree, the cardholder entered the correct PIN, and is presumed to be a legitimate user of the card.

Alternately, the PIN as entered by the cardholder is decrypted, then immediately reencrypted using the same key and in the same manner as is the PIN or reference. These two encrypted versions of the PIN are then compared.

Encrypted PIN from the Card. In this approach, the cardholder's PIN is encrypted at the terminal and transmitted, along with the other elements of the transaction, to the EDP system. Included in this transaction data are the contents of the card's magnetic stripe. One of the fields in the stripe contains the encrypted PIN of reference. These two encrypted verions of the PIN, the PIN entered by the cardholder and the PIN of reference from the magnetic stripe, are passed (desirably) from the EDP system to special security equipment which performs appropriate cryptographic operations and then compares both versions as described above. Note, the PIN of reference is encrypted utilizing the account number (which must be passed to the security equipment before it can decrypt this version of the PIN) so that if two cardholders have identical clear PINs, their encrypted PIN will be different.

PIN a Cryptographic Function of the Account Number. As before, the PIN entered by the cardholder is encrypted at the terminal and transmitted to the EDP system, along with the other elements of the transaction. Then the EDP system (desirably) transfers to special security equipment both the encrypted PIN from the terminal and the account number. This security equipment decrypts the encrypted PIN and cryptographically processes the account number to generate the PIN of reference. The two versions of the PIN are then compared, as before.

Off-Line PIN Validation

When the PIN is validated within the terminal (or other remote facility), the terminal (or facility) must have the means to compare the PIN of reference with the PIN entered by the cardholder. Thus the PIN, in an encrypted form, must be encoded on the card's magnetic stripe, or the PIN must be a cryptographic function of the account number. In either case, the terminal must have the cryptographic capability, as well as the necessary encryption keys, to perform the required comparison. The terminal allows the transaction to proceed only if the two versions of the PIN agree.

The use of off-line PIN validation at other than a highly secure terminal like an ATM (automated teller machine) is not recommended. Should a terminal with off-line PIN validation ever be compromised, and the secret encryption keys stored within it ascertained by anyone intent on fraud, they would be able to determine the correct PIN for any lost or stolen card issued by that institution. Furthermore they could, with some additional sophistication, produce usable counterfeit copies of any or all of this institution's cards.

Today off-line PIN validation is widely used in ATMs. This enables the ATM to perform most of its functions (excluding balance inquiry) even when the ATM cannot communicate with the EDP system. This is a useful and valid mode of operation, yet care must be taken, as indicated above, that the secret cryptographic keys are always kept highly secure.

PIN Validation for Interchange Transactions

At some future time it is anticipated that the on-line interchange of EFT transactions will become as common as the present off-line interchange of credit card transactions. It is anticipated that a combination of ATMs, POS (point of sale) terminals, and POB (point of banking) terminals would be included in a nationwide EFT network. Whenever cash is dispensed, the use of a PIN will probably be required. Thus, PIN validation in interchange will become, in the future, a matter of considerable importance.

The use of PINs in interchange poses special security problems. This is due to the fact that the PIN is entered into a terminal under the control of one institution, the acquirer, whereas the card was issued by another institution, the issuer. Should the acquirer's negligence allow the issuer's PINs to be ascertained by someone intent on fraud, the issuer would bear the fraud loss, and there would be no obvious way of determining the identity of the negligent institution because hundreds or thousands participate in a nationwide interchange network.

To provide the highest possible protection for the PIN in an interchange environment, several basic principles appear evident:

1. An acquirer should not be able to validate the PINs of other issuers. Were every institution in an interchange network able to validate the PINs of every other institution, the compromise of a single institution could compromise every PIN of every other institution in the interchange network. This is an unacceptable risk. Therefore, each issuer must validate its own PINs, though an issuer may delegate this responsibility to someone else.
2. Clear PINs should not be allowed over any communications line nor in the EDP system of any acquirer. If clear (intelligible) PINS were transmitted over communications lines, these lines could be tapped and the PINs ascertained. This would not only compromise the PINs of the institution whose lines were tapped, but those of every other institution whose cardholders used terminals of the institution in question. Similarly, clear PINs should not be allowed in any acquirer's or switch's EDP system, because some clever programmer or computer operator might determine a technique for recording the PINs along with the corresponding magnetic stripe information. Even though an issuer might trust its own EDP system to store and/or process its own PINs in a secure manner, such an issuer would quite likely not similarly trust the EDP systems of perhaps thousands of other institutions to be similarly secure. Thus, the PIN should be encrypted at all times as it traverses communications circuits and EDP systems from the terminal where it was entered to the issuer's facility.

Therefore to provide very high security:

1. Every PIN-using terminal in an EFT network should have an integral encryption capability that is physically secure.
2. Every acquirer, as well as certain other nodes that a transaction may traverse, should have a special, physically secure, cryptographic capability to translate the PIN from one cryptographic key to another, in order not to perform any cryptographic operations that might expose clear PINs in a general purpose EDP system.

A "physically secure" cryptographic capability in the above context has a very specific meaning if very high security is desired. The cryptographic capability in question is enclosed, and if the enclosure is penetrated by any means, the cryptographic keys stored within the enclosure are automatically erased. If someone should penetrate the enclosure in an attempt to commit fraud, the cryptographic capability would be rendered inoperative (because it can no longer decrypt PINs) and all the information that could possibly be used to commit the intended fraud would be destroyed.

In order to assure PIN security at all points in the interchange process, it appears that PIN validation in interchange should operate as follows if very high security is desired:

1. PIN is encrypted at the entry terminal, using a secret cryptographic key. The encrypted PIN is then transmitted to the acquirer's EDP system, along with other transaction elements.
2. The acquirer's EDP system routes the encrypted PIN to special security equipment, a security module. Within this physically secure module the PIN is decrypted using the cryptographic key of the terminal, and is immediately reencrypted with a cryptographic key used for interchange. The PIN, thus encrypted, is returned to the acquirer's EDP system. It is then routed to the issuer's EDP system via normal communications channels.
3. The issuer also has a security module, and the PIN from the interchange transaction is routed to this module where it is decrypted, then validated, using any one of the three techniques previously discussed for on-line, local PIN validation.

Although use of the above suggested hardware module provides very high security for PINs in interchange, this degree of security may exceed that which will actually be required by Interbank rules. Main frame software may be acceptable for the decryption and the reencryption of such PINs, especially in the initial steps of nationwide interchange.

The above discussion of interchange applies primarily to the eventual nationwide interchange between hundreds or even thousands of financial institutions. Regional interchange among approximately a dozen institutions is quite likely at an earlier date, and might not operate in conformity to the relatively rigid PIN security principles indicated above. For example, off-line PIN validation within ATMs might be possible in regional interchange, provided all participants clearly understand that the compromise of any one of these shared ATMs could compromise every PIN of every participant. Basically, in regional interchange of this sort, the various institutions trust one another in a way that would not be realistic when interchanging with hundreds or thousands of institutions across the country.

Conclusions

PINs are an essential ingredient of any EFT system, serving as the cardholder's electronic signature to authenticate his right of access to his account. To serve this purpose, the PIN must be kept secret and must be known by no person other than the cardholder. PINs should be from four to six digits in length, long enough to preclude trial and error PIN determination, but not so long as to impede transaction time. When four digit PINs are used, some limit on the number of PIN entry trials is desirable, though it is preferable not to retain the card if this limit is exceeded.

The PIN may either be determined by the institution or selected by the cardholder. There are advantages and disadvantages to each approach, but techniques exist to implement either approach in a secure manner so that no one can determine cardholder PINs. Secure techniques are also available to advise a cardholder of his PIN should he forget it.

A cardholder's PIN is validated by comparing his PIN as entered via an EFT terminal with his PIN of reference. This comparison may be either on-line at the institution's EDP center, or off-line within the EFT terminal itself. On-line PIN validation can be implemented more securely than off-line validation by the use of special security equipment at the institution's EDP center. However, in many cases off-line PIN validation is a necessity, to permit off-line operation of ATMs, for example.

In the forthcoming nationwide interchange of EFT transactions, the PIN cannot be validated off-line in the terminal, but must be transmitted securely to the facility of the issuer (or some institution serving on behalf of the issuer) for validation. Specific security requirements must be placed on acquirers and switches in an interchange environment to insure that an issuer's PINs are not compromised by negligence on the part of another institution.

SECTION TWO: EFT FRAUD THREATS

The preceding section considered general PIN management concepts, and dealt with most of the issues faced by a financial institution that wishes PINs to be used with its debit or credit cards. Insofar as possible, this discussion has been nontechnical, and has avoided the detailed discussion of how security techniques can be implemented.

The remaining sections consider in detail the technical aspects of PIN management, as well as other aspects of EFT security. These sections are intended for those who wish to pursue the subject in greater detail, especially those who are concerned with the design of systems and equipment to be used in an EFT environment, and those who wish to evaluate different equipment designs. This present section serves as an introduction to this detailed technical discussion by considering the general fraud threats against which an EFT system must be protected.

Major EFT fraud is not expected to become a significant risk until a nationwide system for the interchange of EFT transactions is in operation. The relatively small scale of most of today's EFT systems, and the diversity between such systems, tends to discourage fraud. Considerable study and development effort would be required to compromise any one EFT system. Even if such a system were compromised, it would most likely be shut down and/or its security techniques upgraded, long before the criminal had recouped his investment in fraud technology. Though the shutdown of an EFT system would be a mild catastrophe for the institutions involved, it would be preferable to sustaining a substantial fraud loss since EFT is currently more of a convenience (e.g., ATMs as a source of after hours cash) than a necessity. Thus, the potential payoff in compromising an EFT system today would not appear to justify the investment in fraud technology which it would require.

When the nationwide interchange of EFT transactions becomes well established, however, EFT will become a tempting target for a concerted fraud effort. Such a nationwide network will, of necessity, use standardized security techniques throughout. Thus, if organized crime could develop the fraud technology to defeat these techniques, it could be applied against financial institutions all across the country. Furthermore, by this time EFT will be well entrenched, with many thousands of supposedly secure terminals, so the retrofitting of these terminals to counter the exploited vulnerability would be almost prohibitively expensive, and impose nearly insurmountable transition problems. By this time EFT could well have become a major payment system, comparable to checks and credit cards, so shutting down such a system would be virtually unthinkable. Thus, the situation faced by the banking industry would be similar to, though far more serious than, the one faced by the telephone company when Blue Boxes (electronic devices used to make unbillable long distance calls) were first developed. If the banking industry were essentially defenseless against certain fraud threats, these threats would become very attractive to potential perpetrators.

It should also be noted that much of the fraud loss in today's payment system (e.g., bad checks) is borne by merchants. In an EFT system it would be borne primarily by financial institutions.

EFT Fraud Categories

There are three main types of fraud threat to which an EFT system might be susceptible:

1. Fraudulent use of lost or stolen cards.
2. Production and use of counterfeit cards.
3. Manipulation of data.

The use of lost or stolen cards, assuming the PINs for them can be ascertained, is probably the most obvious fraud threat. It requires no technological sophistication (except whatever might be required to determine the associated PIN) and could enable funds to be withdrawn from the corresponding accounts at ATMs or other EFT terminals. However, this exposure to fraud is limited, in an on-line EFT system, to the time between the loss of a card and the reporting of this loss by the cardholder.

The production and use of counterfeit cards is potentially a far more serious fraud threat. In a nationwide EFT system, the flooding of the country with many thousands of counterfeit cards could have a potentially disastrous effect. Unlike the losing or stealing of a card, which is likely to be promptly reported, the use of a counterfeit version of a legitimate card would not be detected until the legitimate cardholder examined his next statement or received notification that his account was overdrawn. Thus, thousands of unsuspecting cardholders would find funds missing from their accounts, an obviously catastrophic occurrence. As indicated in Section One, not only would the banking industry be faced with the resulting direct fraud loss, but, once the fraud had become publicized, inadvertent claims of fraud, or outright fraudulent claims of fraud (cardholders who claim fraud because of transactions they have honestly forgotten, and cardholders who claim fraud knowing that they themselves withdrew the disputed funds) would without doubt occur. This secondary fraud could result in even greater losses than the original direct fraud. Perhaps most serious of all would be the loss of customer good will, and customer confidence in the EFT system. Thus, mass fraud of this type is clearly in a different class from the type which could occur through the fraudulent use of actual issued cards.

The most difficult task in the production and use of counterfeit cards would probably be determination of PINs and corresponding account numbers. The actual encoding of counterfeit cards would not appear to be especially difficult, employing either stolen or handmade card encoders, and using either stolen card stock, plain bank cards, or reencoding expired cards. It should be noted that the same physical card could be reencoded and reused for many different accounts.

The final threat, the manipulation of data, is perhaps the most sophisticated fraud threat of all. In this threat, the EFT system is penetrated and data are inserted or modified in real time. For example, funds may be withdrawn without any account being debited, or with the wrong account being debited. Similarly, credits may be routed into the incorrect account, or credits spuriously originated when no actual deposit or return of merchandise took place. This subject will be considered in greater detail under "Active Fraud Threats."

Fraud techniques can be categorized as either passive or active. Passive techniques are those which simply ascertain information, presumably to enable the subsequent use of lost or stolen cards, or the production and use of counterfeit cards. Active techniques, in contrast, modify or insert data, as indicated above.

Passive Fraud Threats

In order to use lost or stolen cards or to produce and use counterfeit cards at PIN-using EFT terminals, it is necessary to learn PINs and associated account numbers. In the absence of appropriate security safeguards, an identifiable cardholder's PIN might be subject to determination for possible fraudulent use by:

1. The card issuing institution.
2. The PIN delivery system.
3. The cardholder himself.
4. The EFT system.

The following discussion considers each of these, then briefly evaluates the relative risks involved.

The Card Issuing Institution

Improper PIN management and PIN issuing techniques on the part of the card issuing institution can expose the PIN to possible determination. There is a risk of this type of exposure whenever even one member of the institution's staff:

1. Has the opportunity to see or access any cardholder's PIN.
2. Has the ability to change cardholder PINs (enabling him to change PINs to values known by him).
3. Is in a position to authorize others to access or change cardholder PINs.
4. Has the capability to ascertain the cryptographic keys used to protect or derive cardholder PINs, or to enable others to ascertain these keys.

Another area of possible risk within the card issuing institution is the method used to generate cardholder PINs. An improper PIN generation technique might enable information about some or all PINs to be determined from obtainable data.

The Delivery System

The technique used to convey the PIN to the cardholder when the institution selects the PIN, or to the institution when the cardholder makes the selection, is a possible area of PIN compromise. For example, if PINs are sent to cardholders via PIN mailers, there is the possibility that someone might ascertain PINs from these mailers. Risk exists whenever the PIN, together with cardholder identifying information, is conveyed via non-secure channels.

The Cardholder

Careless or improper actions on the part of the cardholder could cause his PIN to be compromised. For example he might:

1. Fail to destroy or secure the PIN mailer. The cardholder might allow his PIN mailer to fall into unauthorized hands.
2. Record the PIN. The cardholder might write the PIN on the card, or in some other place where it could be found and associated with the card.
3. Divulge the PIN. He might tell his PIN to others, who in turn, could allow it to be compromised. Similarly, he might be tricked into giving his PIN to someone purporting to have the authority to receive it.
4. Allow the PIN to be observed. He might allow his PIN to be observed as he enters it into the EFT terminal.

5. Make a poor PIN selection. If the cardholder himself selects his PIN, he might select a value which could be surmised.

The EFT System

The EFT system itself could be vulnerable to PIN compromise if it does not include adequate security techniques.

1. Wire tapping. If PINs are unencrypted or improperly encrypted, they could be ascertained from taps on appropriate communications lines.
2. Computer tapping. If PINs in their unencrypted form exist within a general purpose EDP system even momentarily (perhaps while being decrypted and then reencrypted), the computer software could be surreptitiously modified to cause PINs and corresponding cardholder identifying information to be recorded or otherwise divulged. Similarly, if the cryptographic keys used to encrypt PINs are available within such a system, these keys could be subject to compromise, which would then allow the PINs encrypted under them to be determined. These problems are especially critical in an interchange environment where one institution's PINs pass through EDP systems of switches and other institutions over which it has no control.
3. Terminal tapping. If PIN-using terminals without adequate safeguards are used in a non-secure environment (e.g., point of sale), it would be possible to tap the PIN pad and the magnetic stripe reader, and thus ascertain PINs and corresponding cardholder identifying information.
4. Fake equipment. In a non-secure environment without specialized safeguards, it might be possible to place fake equipment to record PINs. For example, a PIN pad could be installed with a non-PIN using terminal. This PIN pad would go only to a recorder, which would operate in conjunction with a tap in the terminal itself or on the communications line for recording magnetic stripe information.
5. Trial and error PIN determination. If the number of consecutively invalid PIN entry attempts is not appropriately limited, trial and error PIN determination might be possible using the actual EFT system, especially if the finder or counterfeiter of the card had some insight into which PIN values were most likely. Furthermore, PIN determination by exhaustion could be quite feasible if the card finder or counterfeiter could employ some off-line simulation of the EFT system to make and evaluate PIN trials automatically.
6. Compromise of cryptographic keys. If it is possible to ascertain any of the cryptographic keys used to encrypt PINs as they traverse the EFT system; such keys could then be used to decrypt, and thus reveal, the PINs encrypted under them.

Relative Risks

It appears impossible to develop any type of payment system which completely eliminates all fraud risks. In an EFT system, special attention must be paid to those risks which could result in mass fraud, especially the flooding of the country with many thousands of counterfeit cards. Less concern need be focused on those risks which expose only an occasional, specific account.

Though the most difficult risks to counter are those which involve cardholder negligence in the handling of his own PIN, these risks are not of extreme concern. Such risks do not appear to be a source for mass fraud, and furthermore it appears that cardholders can be instructed to treat their PINs with appropriate care.

The greatest fraud risks appear to be in the issuing institution, and in the EFT system itself. Security weaknesses in these areas could result in the compromise of thousands of PINs. For example, security weaknesses which would allow PINs to be determined from an institution's PIN management techniques, or by wiretapping, terminal tapping, or computer tapping the EFT system itself, would appear to pose very great risks. A security weakness cannot be discounted simply because a considerable investment would be required to exploit it. In a nationwide EFT system, the fraudulent payoff from such an investment could be tremendous.

Finally, it should be noted that, once a large-scale nationwide EFT system is in operation, upgrading its security features could be an almost impossibly difficult task because of the standardization and cost inherent in such a system. Thus the system cannot necessarily take advantage of advancing technology. The criminal, however, operates under no such handicap, and can employ the latest technology in his efforts to defraud the system. Therefore an EFT security system must be carefully designed at its inception, with this realization in mind.

Active Fraud Threats

Active fraud threats, the manipulation or insertion of data in real time, require a high degree of technical sophistication. Nevertheless, the continuing advance of computer and electronic technology will make the required technology increasingly available. The two areas in an EFT system where such technology might be applied are the communications lines and the EDP systems.

Communications Lines

There are many ways in which transmitted data could be manipulated to commit fraud in the absence of appropriate security safeguards. The amount field, the transaction type, or the account identifier could be modified in various ways to commit different types of fraud. However, the most likely active fraud threat is probably the simulation of the response message from a host to a terminal, causing every transaction to be approved, but no account to be debited. An ATM would be a likely candidate for this type of fraud. The communications line from the ATM to the host would be found, and a microprocessor system would be placed in series with this line. To the host, this system would look like an idle ATM. To the ATM, this system would look like the host. The criminal would then initiate a transaction from the ATM. The transaction would be intercepted by his microprocessor and would never reach the host. Instead, the microprocessor system would respond to the ATM with "transaction approved" indication, causing the ATM to dispense cash. This procedure would be repeated time after time until the ATM had been depleted of cash.

There are a number of other ways in which such a microprocessor system inserted in a communications line could be used to commit fraud. It could be programmed to pass all transactions unaltered except those for certain specified account numbers. In the case of these accounts, it would modify the message from the terminal to the host then modify the response from host to terminal in the inverse manner. For example, an ATM dispense cash request for $150 might be reduced to $10 by the microprocessor, so the account in question would be debited by only this latter amount. The amount field in the approved response would then be changed from $10 back to $150. Similarly, the amount of a credit transaction could be increased or a debit transaction turned into a credit. Also it might be possible to cause transactions to be misdirected. The account number of a debit transaction might be changed so that the wrong account was debited. Similarly, credit transactions might be misdirected into accounts controlled by the criminal. Finally, it might be possible to introduce spurious credit transactions, or to fraudulently replay previously valid credit transactions.

Another type of active wiretapping would be the substitution of one encrypted PIN for another in an EFT system which encrypted the PIN but did not preclude such substitution. For example, a transaction including an encrypted PIN could be recorded via a passive tap. A counterfeit version of the associated card would be produced and then used at the same terminal with a fictitious PIN. By means of active wiretapping, the encrypted fictitious PIN would then be replaced by the previously recorded encrypted true PIN, causing the transaction to be accepted as valid by the issuer.

EDP Systems

The same types of active fraud which could be perpetrated via communications lines could also be perpetrated within the EDP systems, acquirer's, switch's, and issuer's, which the transaction traverses. This could be accomplished through surreptitious modifications of the CPU software, causing data to be inserted or modified as suggested above. This type of computer fraud would be especially attractive were transactions cryptographically protected only over communications lines and not within EDP systems.

Other opportunities for active fraud exist within the EDP system of the issuer. For example, it might be possible to cause debits against accounts controlled by the criminal to be applied against other accounts instead, with the corresponding journal entries similarly adjusted. In a totally electronic system without backup paper documents, this type of fraud could be quite effective.

Another fraud scenario which might be perpetrated within an issuer's facility is encrypted-PIN substitution. This scenario is possible, for example, when an ATM encrypts the PIN under the PIN KEY (a key shared by all of the institutions' ATMs), then transmits this encrypted PIN to the EDP system for comparison against an identically encrypted PIN of reference in the data base. The criminal would make a counterfeit version of a valid card, then use this card at an ATM with a PIN of his own choosing. The transaction would, of course, be rejected (invalid PIN). However, the criminal would have an accomplice, a skilled programmer at the bank's EDP facility, who would record the criminal's PIN in its encrypted form. At some later time the programmer accomplice would replace the encrypted PIN of reference in the data base with the criminal's encrypted PIN. Thereafter, the criminal could withdraw funds at will from this account, because his PIN would have become the PIN of reference for this account in the data base.

Fraud and Liability

In an interchange environment, the possibility of fraud brings with it the obvious question of which institution is liable in the event that fraud does occur. The concept of liability is that a negligent party must pay any losses which other parties incur because of this negligence. Although liability may be viewed primarily as a legal issue rather than a technological one, liability can be established only if the party responsible for the fraud can be determined. Since technology is generally required to make this determination, the security techniques used in an EFT interchange environment serve not only to counter anticipated fraud threats, but also to provide a basis for establishing liability in the event of fraud.

Considering first the use of lost or stolen cards and the production and use of counterfeit cards, the liability would appear to rest with the card issuer for all transactions in which PINs are used. The main prerequisite for this type of fraud is the ability to ascertain PINs for known accounts. This is most likely to occur in the issuer's PIN management system, PIN distribution system, or as a result of negligence on the part of the cardholders. Since it is impossible for an interchange system to oversee all these aspects of an issuer's internal operations, the interchange system has little choice but to assume that, if PINs are compromised, the issuer is responsible. The result of the above assumption is that the PINs must be extremely well protected in the interchange environment. Were PINs to be compromised in interchange, it would be virtually impossible to establish responsibility. Thus, all aspects of interchange PIN handling must be made especially secure if an ambiguous liability situation is to be avoided.

For example, it may eventually become a fundamental principle of interchange that one institution's clear text (unencrypted) PINs should never exist, even momentarily within the general purpose EDP facility of any other institution. Were this principle to be violated, a devious programmer at an EDP system would be able to ascertain PINs in such large quantities that he could pick and choose among them for fraudulent use so as to give little evidence as to the location of compromise. In such a case many issuers would experience fraud losses, perhaps substantial ones, because of a security compromise over which they had absolutely no control, and for which the guilty party could not be determined.

Another fundamental principle of interchange would appear to be that an institution's PINs are validated only by the issuing institution itself, or by an institution explicitly authorized to do so by the issuing institution. Inherent in the capability to validate PINs is the capability to determine PINs. (There are exceptions to this, but they require the use of very long PINs, eight digits or more.) Thus, in an interchange environment in which every acquirer has the capability to validate the PINs of every issuer, a one-time compromise on the part of a single acquirer could compromise every PIN of every issuer, and leave absolutely no residual evidence as to which acquirer was at fault. Again, many institutions would suffer losses, perhaps very substantial, because of negligence on the part of an institution whose identity could not be determined. Thus the interchange system must be designed to prevent the negligence of one unidentifiable institution from resulting in loss to other institutions.

Fortunately, it is essentially only the passive threats in an EFT interchange environment which can result in losses to some institutions as a result of untraceable negligence on the part of others. In the case of most active threats it is possible to pinpoint the guilty institution and make it financially responsible. Therefore the countering of such active threats in an interchange environment can be left up to the discretion of each participating institution.

In the case of two active threats it is impossible to distinguish negligence on the acquirer's part from negligence on the issuer's part. The first such threat is the substitution of a previously recorded PIN replayed as part of a counterfeit transaction. There is no apparent way to distinguish this fraud threat, due to the acquirer's negligence, from the use of a counterfeit card with a PIN ascertained through negligence on the issuer's part. Probably the simplest resolution to this ambiguity is for the acquirer, who chooses not to use terminals which preclude the active version of this threat, to assume liability unless it can be shown that it was the passive version of the threat which occurred.

The other active threat is the fraudulent replay of a previously valid credit transaction when this replay takes place between an issuer and an acquirer who communicate directly. It would not always be possible to determine whether the replayed message originated from the acquirer's EDP system, the issuer's EDP system, or on the communications link between them. It appears that, in this case, the issuer must assume responsibility for the fraud, since he is better equipped to detect it, as will be shown subsequently.

In other situations it is not possible to distinguish fictitious claims of fraud on the part of dishonest cardholders, the issuer's problem, from certain active fraud threats for which the acquirer should be responsible. For example, the fraudulent misdirecting of credits could, unless precluded by appropriate security measures, occur because of an active wiretap on an acquirer's terminal. On the other hand, a cardholder could claim a credit which he did not receive, and produce a fictitious receipt to prove his claim. Since credits in interchange should be relatively rare (probably limited to the return of merchandise), it is suggested that all terminals with a credit capability protect against this threat. In the absence of such protection, the acquirer should assume liability unless it can be proven otherwise.

Another similarly ambiguous situation might be as follows: A cardholder institutes a debit transaction for what he claims is \$20, and has a receipt to prove it. However, his account is debited for \$200. The possibilities are

(1) that the cardholder himself falsified the receipt and actually received the $200, or (2) that active wiretapping of the acquirer's terminal caused the amount to be increased for transmission to the host, then correspondingly decreased in the response message back to the terminal, with a teller or some other acquirer's employee pocketing the $180 difference.

Fortunately the ambiguous active fraud threats are judged to be relatively improbable. The most probable active threats are unambiguous. For example, the previously suggested "draining" of an ATM (or other EFT terminal) by cutting this terminal off from its host and giving an "approved" response to every request, is clearly the acquirer's liability. The use of active wiretapping to decrease the amount of a debit as reported to the issuer is also clearly the acquirer's liability. Even when a ambiguous situation does exist, it is between two, or at most three potentially responsible parties. In the case of passive fraud threats, it might be impossible to ascertain which one of a thousand or more institutions was responsible for fraud.

Finally, the flooding of the country with tens of thousands of counterfeit cards, the ultimate EFT catastrophe, is possible through passive, not active threats. Thus, it appears acceptable to allow each participating member of an interchange system to decide for itself the degree of protection against active wiretapping which it considers cost effective between its terminals and EDP systems. Whenever an instance of ambiguous fraud occurs (which should be seldom), the associated liability can be stipulated in the Interbank rules.

Another aspect of fraud and liability concerns a cardholder's liability if his PIN is compromised. Consumer protection legislation will make it increasingly difficult for financial institutions to hold the cardholder financially responsible for protection of his own PIN. However, an interchange system which is extremely secure against passive fraud threats, coupled with a highly secure PIN management system on the part of the issuing institution (in which no employee of the institution knows any cardholder's PIN, and all PIN related operations are under strict dual control) can significantly reduce the risk that lost, stolen, or counterfeit cards will be used other than as the result of cardholder negligence. Furthermore, a well publicized, highly secure PIN system should discourage cardholders, who would otherwise fraudulently deny transactions they had in fact actually made (today's main fraud threat), and also convince cardholders to treat their PINs with considerable care. If the precautions taken by the financial institution to prevent any of the institution's employees from learning any cardholder's PINs are highly visible to the cardholder, it cannot help but influence the cardholder's own attitude toward the importance of PIN secrecy, and may, in time, also affect the judicial attitude toward the liability for PIN compromise.

Conclusions

Fraud is not expected to become a major problem for EFT until a nationwide EFT interchange system is in operation. At this point the payoff for fraud technology could be very great, and the result could be mass fraud of perhaps catastrophic proportions. Potentially, the most serious fraud threat is the production and use of counterfeit cards, and the widespread dissemination of large numbers of such cards could be truly disastrous. The use of lost and stolen cards is a potential problem but the use of any sort of PIN system could control this fraud threat. The remaining threat is the modification or insertion of data in real time. Though a serious threat, it would not have nearly as devastating an effect as the massive use of counterfeit cards.

The two main types of fraud threats are passive, the determination of PINs and corresponding account identities to enable the use of lost, stolen, or counterfeit cards, and active, the fraudulent modification or insertion of data in real time. Of these two, the passive is of greater concern in an interchange environment, not only because the passive threats could lead to mass fraud in the form of counterfeit cards, but also because it would be virtually impossible to ascertain the negligent party and thus establish liability for such fraud. Active threats, though potentially serious, are not judged to be catastrophic, and quite often can be traced back to the offending institution.

As a result, it is concluded that an EFT system should protect against passive threats in all aspects of interchange. If very high security is desired, it appears that an issuer's clear PINs should not be allowed, even momentarily, in any general purpose EDP equipment of an acquirer or switch but rather than such clear PINs should be restricted to physically secure cryptographic hardware where they, and the cryptographic keys used to encrypt them, can be physically protected. By imposing stringent security requirements upon all acquirers and switches, it seems more reasonable to then place liability for any use of lost, stolen, or counterfeit cards on the issuer, any compromise of his cardholders' PINs being assumed to result from negligence on the part of the issuer or its cardholders.

A further conclusion is that protection against active fraud threats can be left up to an acquirer's discretion, provided he is willing to assume responsibility for any such fraud against which he does not provide protection. However, it does appear desirable to protect transactions in interchange between institutions against these active threats.

Perhaps the most important conclusion of all is that fraud in a nationwide interchange environment could eventually become a serious problem, if not a major catastrophe. Thus, in planning for interchange, and during the evolution toward it, careful provisions must be made to ensure that adequate security is indeed realized. Security must be an inherent characteristic of EFT from the start. It cannot be added on after the fact.

SECTION THREE: PRINCIPLES OF FRAUD PREVENTION

Cryptography, The Tool for Fraud Prevention

Most of the techniques used to prevent fraud in an EFT system are based upon the use of cryptography. Cryptography involves encryption and decryption. Encryption is the transformation of clear (comprehensible) data by means of an algorithm (i.e., a defined procedure) and a secret number called a key into a form called cipher, which bears no resemblance to the original, clear data. Only someone else possessing the identical secret key is able to decrypt the transformed data and recreate its original clear form.

The Interbank recommended encryption algorithm for use in EFT is the Data Encryption Standard (DES), which is the cryptographic algorithm sponsored by the National Bureau of Standards for data security. It is the only publicly available algorithm which has been certified as highly secure by the United States Government. DES is a block encryption technique. That is, given an input data block of 64 binary bits, a 56 bit secret binary key, and the encrypt command, the algorithm produces 64 cipher bits. These bits bear no obvious relation to the input. In fact, a minor (i.e., one bit) change in the input produces a drastic change in the output. Given these 64 cipher bits, the same 56 bit key, and the decrypt command, the algorithm produces the original clear data.

Though inherently a binary, block encryption technique, DES can be applied in various ways to implement virtually any desired type of encryption.

Preventing Passive Fraud Threats

As described in the preceding section, passive fraud threats are those which enable the PIN for known accounts to be ascertained. As a result, the use of lost, stolen, or counterfeit cards is possible. Given today's technology, the fraud threat can be virtually prevented by:

1. Insuring that the PIN is encrypted at all times except when within a physically secure environment.
2. Insuring that the keys used to encrypt PINs are never available in "clear" form except within physically secure environments.
3. Insuring that physically secure environments, in which clear PINs and clear PIN encrypting keys are found, are in fact secure against physical compromise.

PIN Encryption

To be protected against compromise the PIN should be encrypted using DES and a secret key. Furthermore, the PIN should be encrypted as a function of some quantity which varies from transaction to transaction, or at least from account to account. Were this not done, identical clear PINs encrypted under the same key would produce identical ciphers. This fact could be exploited by a criminal, who would, for example, open ten accounts under fictitious names. He would then know ten PINs and institute transactions from a specific EFT terminal against each of his ten accounts. He would also have tapped the line from his terminal, and would record the encrypted PIN from each of his ten transactions. Next he would use the tap to record transactions from other cardholders. Whenever the encrypted PIN from one of these transactions exactly matched the encrypted PIN from one of his accounts, he would know that the clear PINs were identical. In an environment in which most or all PINs are four digits, he would be able to ascertain the PIN for approximately one account in a thousand which used this particular terminal. For each of these cases, from other information in the recorded transaction, he could determine the contents of the associated card's magnetic stripe, and thus make a counterfeit copy of this card and use it to draw against the cardholder's funds.

One method of encrypting the PIN as a function of a varying quantity (and thus preclude the above indicated fraud threat) is to concatenate the clear PIN with a value six decimal digits or longer, which is:

1. A random or pseudorandom number,
2. A counter, which increments on each transaction, or
3. The least significant digits of the account number.

The result, which must be no more than 64 binary bits in length, is block encrypted using DES and a secret key. The entire 64 bit resulting cipher thus serves as the encrypted PIN for this transaction.

Other equally secure PIN encryption methods exist in which the encrypted PIN is a decimal value of the same number of digits as the clear PIN.

Protection of Cryptographic Keys

PINs should always be encrypted under secret 56 bit DES keys. Maintaining the secrecy of these keys is of the utmost importance, because if any such key becomes compromised the PINs encrypted under it can be similarly compromised. There are two problems associated with key secrecy. The first is the generation and distribution of keys in such a way as to preclude compromise. This is called key management, and will be discussed subsequently. The other, protection of the key while it is within the cryptographic device, will be considered now.

Physical Protection of PINs and Cryptographic Keys

PINs and keys must be physically protected whenever they are in clear (unencrypted) form within cryptographic devices. (For high security, clear PINs and keys should exist nowhere else.) The most effective solution to this problem appears to be the interlocking of the device's enclosure. All of the cryptographic logic is placed within a physically secure enclosure and tamper detection circuitry, built into the enclosure, detects any attempt to gain access to the internal circuitry of the device. The secret keys are interlocked by means of these tamper circuits so that any act of tampering causes the keys to be erased.

The immediate erasure of the keys obviously protects them from compromise. Tapping of the device to ascertain future PINs is prevented also, because opening the device to install the tap erases the secret keys and this renders the device inoperative (i.e., unable to decrypt incoming PINs). As a result, the tap will not successfully capture PINs.

In order to protect the PIN at its point of entry into the system, the PIN keyboard must be a part of this protected enclosure. If it is, and if the enclosure is properly protected via the above suggested interlocks, the terminal tapping threat discussed in the preceding section is precluded.

Preventing Active Fraud Threats

Though passive fraud threats may be countered by simply protecting the PIN from disclosure, countering active threats is more difficult, with different countermeasures needed for different threats.

Data Modification

Many active fraud threats involve the modification of data in real time. These threats can be countered by either of two techniques, message encryption or message authentication. Message encryption, as the name implies, is simply the encryption of all, or at least most, of the message which conveys the transaction. This technique has the advantage of providing privacy as well as security. The disadvantage, however, is that the encrypted message cannot be comprehended or processed by the EDP systems (acquirer's, switch's, issuer's) through which the transaction passes. Thus, the message must be decrypted prior to being processed, but once decrypted, it loses its cryptographic protection, and therefore is susceptible to fraudulent modification within the EDP system.

Message authentication is a technique which produces cryptographic check digits which are appended to the message. These digits are analogous to a parity check or cyclic redundancy check, except that in this case the check digits are cryptographically generated, using DES and a secret key. These digits, called the message authentication code or MAC, are generated by the originator, appended to the transmitted message, and then checked by the recipient, who also holds the same secret key used in the generation process. Should anyone attempt to modify the message between the time the MAC is generated and the time it is checked, he would be detected. Not knowing the secret key, he would be unable to generate the correct MAC for his modified message. Similarly, no one can successfully introduce a spurious message because he could not generate the proper MAC for this message.

The suggested technique for MAC generation is as follows: The first 64 bits of that portion of the transaction to be protected are block encrypted using DES and the secret key. Then the next 64 transaction bits to be thus protected are Exclusive-ORed (modulo 2 added) with the just produced cipher. The result is then block encrypted using the same key, producing a new 64 bits of cipher. This procedure is continued until all critical transaction fields have been included. (The final data block will likely be less than 64 bits, so it is padded with zeros to make a full 64 bits prior to being Exclusive-ORed with the just produced cipher.) Some subset of the final cipher, at least six decimal digits or five hexadecimal digits, serves as the MAC.

As a minimum, the following fields should be included in the MAC generation for a transaction request message:

1. Transaction type (debit, credit, etc.).
2. Cardholder's account number.
3. Amount.

4. Transaction identification information (that information which uniquely identifies a specific transaction from a particular terminal).

In the case of a transaction response message, the equivalent fields plus the response code (approved, disapproved) should be protected. Alternatively, the MAC can be generated only if the transaction is approved, because no known fraud threat could exploit an unprotected disapproved response message.

Though the MAC approach does not provide privacy, its advantage over message encryption is that the protected message is also intelligible, and thus can be processed by EDP systems. With message encryption, the protection is lost when the message is decrypted, so the message is protected against fraudulent modifications only over communications lines but not within EDP systems. Thus message authentication, by protecting the transaction against fraudulent modifications both over communications lines and within EDP systems, is the recommended approach.

As indicated in the preceding section, message authentication can be optional within an acquirer's own network, provided the acquirer is willing to assume any fraud loss which might result from the failure to protect against any "active" fraud threats. However, it is recommended that all transactions in interchange be protected against active fraud by means of message authentication. If subsequent privacy legislation requires encryption, this can be accomplished, for the interchange network, by using link encryption devices, or by encrypting the six or so least significant digits of the account number to conceal the cardholder's identity.

Replay of Debit Authorization

Perhaps the most likely active fraud threat is the isolation of a terminal (especially an ATM) from its host, giving it an "approved" response to every transaction request. Message authentication alone cannot necessarily solve this problem, because it might be possible to record the "approved" response to a valid transaction prior to isolating the unit, then institute identical fraudulent transactions, and replay the previously recorded "approved" response. This fraud threat can be countered only if there is something unique about each transaction (even two transactions for the same amount against the same account), and the transaction-approved response includes this uniqueness, which is checked by the terminal. Furthermore, this unique characteristic must not be something which the criminal can duplicate. For example, the terminal itself can insert a sequence number into the transaction request message. This same number is included in the transaction authorization message back to the terminal protected under the MAC. The terminal checks for agreement between the two values and authorizes the completion of the transaction (e.g., the dispensing of cash) only if the sent and received sequence numbers are identical. Thus, it is impossible to replay the "approved" response to a previous transaction because the sequence number is invalid for any other transaction. Furthermore, the replay version cannot be modified to include the current sequence number, because the MAC would not check.

For this approach to provide the required degree of protection, the sequence number should not repeat within the life of the cryptographic key used in the MAC generation. Alternately, it could be a random, rather than a sequential value, provided it is truly unpredictable, and is at least six decimal digits in length.

Other approaches can provide the same effect. For example, if the terminal key is changed after every transaction, a MAC on the transaction authorization message is unique to a given transaction.

Fraudulent Credits

The four fraud threats associated with credit transactions are:

1. Modified credits (amount field increased, or debit made into a credit).
2. Misdirected credits (account number modified).
3. Spurious credits (totally fictitious credit transaction).
4. Fraudulent replay of previously valid credit transaction.

The first three fraud threats may be countered by the use of message authentication. The use of MAC prevents undetected modifications in any critical transaction field, and also prevents the origination of totally spurious transactions. The fourth fraud threat, however, is somewhat more difficult to counter. Though message sequence numbers are commonly used to detect duplicated messages, these numbers are not considered a part of the security system and thus cannot be relied upon for fraud prevention purposes. That is, they can only be checked in the presumably non-secure main frame, and cannot be checked in special security equipment.

It appears that the responsibility for detecting replayed credits must rest with the issuer. Under this approach, the issuer would be expected to check the previous real time EFT credit transaction for the account in question and verify that it had occurred earlier than the current credit transaction. (This assumes that real time EFT credit transactions are stored in chronological order and that the date/time field in every such credit transaction is protected by the transaction's MAC.) The issuer could then immediately detect a replayed transaction.

It should be noted that real time credits in a retail EFT system should be relatively infrequent. Normal bank deposits are not real time because they are subject to verification and to check clearances. The only expected real time credits would result from the return of merchandise, a relatively uncommon occurrence, so placing the responsibility for detecting the replay of such credits upon the issuer should not be an undue burden.

Encrypted PIN Substitution

Unless appropriately precluded, it would be possible for a criminal to record an encrypted PIN as it leaves a terminal in a valid transaction, then, by active wiretapping at a later time, replay this recorded encrypted PIN as part of a fraudulent transaction. This fraud threat is prevented by techniques which insure that the same PIN when encrypted by the same terminal on two or more different occasions always produces a unique cipher each time. This can be achieved by encrypting the PIN as a function of a variable quantity, such as a terminal generated transaction sequence number (in addition to the secret key). To be fully effective, this terminal should utilize message authentication for the transaction authorization message. This message should include the same variable quantity (e.g., the transaction sequence number) which is used in the encryption of the PIN in the transaction request message. Only if the variable quantity in the authorization message matches the one the terminal used for PIN encryption in the request message, and only if the authorization message is successfully authenticated by the terminal, does the terminal complete the transaction. At the host end, PIN validation and authentication of the authorization message should be performed as a single operation in a physically secure environment, the message authentication code for the authorization message being generated only if the cardholder entered PIN is successfully validated.

If the above indicated procedures are followed, the criminal is prevented from fraudulently replaying a previously recorded encrypted PIN. This PIN would have been encrypted as a function of a previously used variable quantity which could not be successfully reused.

Another technique which can be used to prevent the substitution of the encrypted cardholder entered PIN is key transformation. With this technique, the terminal's key is changed after every transaction. This is accomplished by generating the new key from the old key via a cryptographic procedure. Since the key used to encrypt the PIN changes on each transaction, the criminal is unable to successfully replay the encrypted PIN from a previous transaction. To insure this completely, however, the authorization message to the terminal must be authenticated using the current key.

Other fraud threats are possible if the criminal is able to substitute the encrypted version of a PIN, which the criminal himself knows, for the cardholder's encrypted PIN of reference. Two techniques are required to preclude this threat. First, the cardholder's PIN must be encrypted as a function of his account number. This prevents the criminal from substituting his encrypted PIN of reference for that of the targeted cardholder. Second, the PINs of reference must be encrypted under a cryptographic key never used to encrypt cardholder entered PINs. This prevents the criminal from using an invented PIN with a counterfeit card for the targeted account, then replacing the PIN of reference for this account with the encrypted version of the invented PIN.

It should be noted that the prevention of this fraud threat requires that the PIN of reference and the entered PIN both be decrypted (or that the latter be decrypted, then reencrypted like the former) before a comparison is made since both are encrypted under different keys. This does not permit a commonly used PIN validation technique in which the encrypted cardholder entered PIN is compared in a non-secure environment against a similarly encrypted PIN of reference.

Fraud Prevention in Interchange

The fruad threats associated with interchange are basically no different than those already considered, namely, passive threats to ascertain PINs (for use with lost, stolen or counterfeit cards), and active threats to modify or insert data in real time. Thus, the fraud prevention techniques considered above apply to interchange just as much as to local operations. However, interchange poses a practical problem concerning the implementation of these fraud prevention techniques, the necessity to translate from one cryptographic key to another.

A typical interchange transaction begins when the cardholder enters his PIN at some EFT terminal which also reads his card. At this point the PIN must be encrypted in a key unique to this particular terminal.

Similarly, if message authentication is used, it must be based on a key, the same or different, but still unique to this particular terminal. In an EFT system with thousands or tens of thousands of encrypting EFT terminals, it is not feasible, or even desirable, for every key of every acquirer's terminal to be known at every issuer's facility. Thus, each acquirer must have the capability to translate from the terminal's key to an interchange key known either by the issuer, or by the switch which serves the acquirer (in which case the switch will make a second translation into a key known to the issuer). Furthermore, in the case of the PIN, this translation must take place under conditions of very high security, desirably using special, physically protected, cryptographic hardware. As indicated previously, it may eventually be considered unacceptable for one institution's clear PINs, or the clear keys used to encrypt such PINs, to reside even momentarily in the general purpose EDP equipment of any other institution. Thus, for high security, the acquirer should not perform this translation function of the PIN using CPU software, but rather should use the above indicated physically secure hardware.

In the case of message authentication, however, this does not necessarily apply. Since message authentication is optional on the acquirer's part, he may use CPU software for MAC translation. However, in this case a completely different key must be used for MAC generation than is used for PIN encryption or the clear PIN key would exist in the acquirer's CPU. Since the acquirer may utilize special cryptographic hardware for PIN translation, it is suggested that this same hardware be used for MAC translation as well.

Should an acquirer or a switch find an invalid incoming MAC while performing MAC translation, it is considered acceptable for this institution simply to generate an invalid outgoing MAC. In this way, only the issuer, who performs the final MAC check, need implement the error paths which handle the invalid MAC situation.

Another acceptable technique is to superimpose the MAC on the encrypted PIN and avoid an additional field to the message. This may be accomplished by Exclusive-ORing the MAC and the encrypted PIN. Should the MAC not check, the issuer finds a garbled PIN, and the PIN check fails. While this technique cannot distinguish between an invalid PIN and a modified message, this is of little consequence since the net result in either case is to disallow the transaction.

It is assumed that the EFT system as a whole provides an adequate degree of error control, so that the MAC is relied upon for fraud detection rather than error detection. Since fraud attempts are expected to be virtually non-existent because of the use of message authentication, there is virtually no inefficiency in relaying a message with an invalid MAC all the way to the issuer.

Returning again to a typical interchange transaction, the encrypted PIN is transmitted from the EFT terminal, encrypted in this terminal's secret key. Optionally a MAC, to protect the critical message fields, is also included. The transaction message, including the encrypted PIN, and optionally the MAC, reaches the acquirer's facility. Here the above indicated cryptographic transaction takes place. The PIN is decrypted using the terminal key, and reencrypted using an interchange key. If there is an incoming MAC, this too is translated into the interchange key. If there is no incoming MAC, one is generated.

The interchange key indicated above is either a bilateral key shared by the issuer and the acquirer, or a key shared by the acquirer and his EFT switch. In this latter case, the transaction goes to the switch where a second cryptographic translation occurs, translating the PIN and MAC from the key used between switch and acquirer to that used between switch and issuer. The message with this new encrypted PIN and MAC is then transmitted from switch to issuer, where the MAC is checked and the PIN decrypted and validated. If the transaction is approved by the issuer, a transaction authorization message is sent from issuer to switch. This message is protected by means of a MAC using the key shared by switch and issuer. The switch, upon receiving the transaction authorization message, translates it into the key used between switch and acquirer. The MAC in this key reaches the acquirer. If the MAC is valid, the appropriate authorization response is transmitted to the terminal where the transaction originated. If this terminal expects a MAC with the authorization message, such a MAC is generated, in the terminal key.

Countering the Fake Equipment Threat

Perhaps the most difficult fraud threat to counter is the fake equipment threat, in which a dishonest merchant induces unsuspecting cardholders to use EFT terminals with PIN pads which are fake. Either the entire terminal is fake, or a fake PIN pad is added to a non-PIN-using terminal. In either case the PIN pad output goes to a recorder, as does the output of the magnetic stripe reader. From the information thus collected, the criminal is able to produce usable counterfeit cards. Fortunately, this fraud threat is considered too blatant to be especially probable, but must be considered nevertheless.

This threat can be countered only with the help of the cardholders themselves, some of whom can be induced into cooperating by the offer of substantial rewards (but only after the fraud threat has actually materialized). To enable the cardholders to detect that something is suspicious, a code printed on the EFT receipt must indicate whether or not a PIN was used with the transaction in question. For example, a Transaction Proof Code with a non-zero leading digit printed on the receipt, can indicate that a PIN was used. If the leading digit is zero, a PIN was not used. Thus, an observant cardholder who uses such a terminal with a PIN pad and finds the leading digit of his Transaction Proof Code is zero, would know that he could receive a reward for informing the financial institution of this fact without alerting the merchant.

In a similar manner, an account-related sequence number, maintained by the issuing institution and printed on the EFT receipt, would allow the alert cardholder to immediately detect a totally fake terminal (which did not communicate with his institution) because the sequence number printed on the receipt would not be the number he was expecting.

It is possible that the dishonest merchant could have a non-PIN terminal (with a fake PIN pad) modified so as to change, in real time, the leading Transaction Proof Code digit from zero to some other value. However, the Transaction Proof Code as recorded by the financial institution also prints on the cardholder's monthly statement. Thus, the alert cardholder would also know that he could receive a reward for reporting discrepancies between his EFT receipts and his statement (provided these discrepancies could be confirmed by the institution). The totally fake terminal (which resulted in no statement entry) and the terminal which actively modified the Transaction Proof Code, would be discovered through such cardholder reports. In an interchange environment with on-line EFT, it would be virtually impossible for the dishonest merchant to predict just how soon after using his fake equipment an alert cardholder would receive a statement and report his suspicions. The dishonest merchant would be exposed to an unacceptably high level of detection and therefore would not likely attempt this type of fraud in the first place.

While many cardholders would either not understand, or ignore the above suggested reward offers, a small number of intelligent and alert cardholders should respond. Even these few should be sufficient to pinpoint such dishonest merchants relatively quickly.

Since this fraud threat is considered rather improbable by Interbank, little attention need be paid at this time. Nevertheless, the possibility of the threat, and the techniques for countering it, should be kept in mind.[3]

Conclusions

The two basic techniques used to provide security in an EFT environment are PIN encryption and message authentication. PIN encryption prevents passive fraud threats from ascertaining PINs, and thus precludes the use of lost, stolen, and counterfeit cards. For PIN encryption to be effective, the PIN must be physically protected everywhere that it is not encrypted. Similarly, the cryptographic keys used to encrypt PINs must be protected. Inter-

[3] A fake equipment attack, which cannot be defended against using the above mentioned technique is described in Chapter 11 in the section entitled Threats to the Secrecy of a Key Stored on a Magnetic Stripe Card.

locking these keys with the cryptographic device's enclosure is one obvious technique for providing the required physical protection.

Message authentication insures message integrity, and prevents most active fraud threats. A few active fraud threats, however, require specialized countermeasures, as does the fake equipment.

Interchange does not pose any unique fraud threats, but it does require a special cryptographic capability—translation from one cryptographic key to another under conditions of very high security.

The above discussion has presented only the basic principles of fraud prevention. The following section considers, in some detail, how these principles can be effectively implemented, both in EDP facilities and in EFT terminals. In addition, techniques for secure PIN management and key management will be considered.

SECTION FOUR: IMPLEMENTATION OF FRAUD PREVENTION TECHNIQUES

Section Three considered the general principles which are recommended for preventing fraud in EFT networks. This section will describe in further detail how these principles can be applied, through the use of a "security module." In its preferred implementation, such a module is a physically secure hardware device which serves as a peripheral to an EDP system. Potentially less secure implementations are also possible, in which security module functions are implemented in mainframe software. The implementation used by an issuer for its own PINs is clearly its decision. The implementation used by an acquirer in Interbank interchange may be dictated by future standards, though it is presently premature to indicate what such standards will be.[4]

Suggested Characteristics of Hardware Security Module Implementation

When very high security is desired, hardware implementation of the security module is recommended. The previously mentioned Interbank security study considered in detail how such a hardware device could best be implemented. The hardware implementation as suggested by this study is now considered.

The suggested security module is a self-contained, physically secure, microprocessor controlled cryptographic device programmed to perform the cryptographic functions which the EDP center of a financial institution requires for its EFT operations. A security module interfaces with the institution's EDP system as a peripheral device. Information which requires cryptographic processing is sent from the computer to the module, which almost immediately sends back the results.

Each security module can be programmed to perform virtually any required cryptographic function. These programs are written to insure that the secret ingredients in EFT operations, customer PINs and cryptographic keys, never exist in a clear form outside the physically secure internal circuitry of a security module or of an EFT terminal's cryptographic hardware. In effect,

[4] See Cryptographic PIN Security—Proposed ANSI Method, Appendix E.

the security module takes from a non-secure EDP system all information which must be kept secret to prevent EFT fraud, and concentrates it within a dedicated module where it can be physically protected. Thus, the security module trades computer security, which is now and may always be, elusive, for physical security, which is well understood.

The suggested security module achieves its physical security by means of both locks and interlock circuitry. The module is protected by two different physical locks, requiring two different physical keys. This insures that the module can be legitimately opened only under dual personnel control. Furthermore, whenever the module is opened, whether legitimately using the two keys or by force, interlock circuitry causes all secret data stored within the module (i.e., the cryptographic keys) to be erased. If a criminal breaks into the module, the secret information contained therein will disappear as it is forced open.

The suggested security module system consists of three modules, all electrically and mechanically independent, but sharing a common cabinet. A conventional terminal serves as the keyboard and printer for the system. It is connected to only one of the three modules at any given time, and serves to perform certain subsequently described PIN and key management functions.[5]

Suggested Capabilities[6]

The main functions performed by the security module include PIN management, PIN verification, PIN "translation" in interchange, key management, and message authentication. These functions are based on the National Bureau of Standard's Data Encryption Standard (DES), although proprietary algorithms can be supported as well.

For PIN management, the module can generate a random value for the PIN, then encrypt this value for storage in the mainframe and/or for encoding on the card's magnetic stripe as the "PIN offset" of the "PIN verification field." Alternately, the module can cryptographically derive the PIN from the account number. In either case, the module can print the PIN mailer on a dedicated printer. As a result, the unencrypted PIN is never known to any person and is never present, even momentarily, in the mainframe. If the institution prefers that cardholders select their own PINs, the module implements a system that never allows anyone within or outside the bank, except the actual customer, to associate an unencrypted PIN with the corresponding account number.

For PIN verification, the module decrypts a PIN which has been encrypted by an EFT terminal. It then compares this customer-entered version of the PIN with the "reference" version of the PIN using the technique appropriate to the institution in question, which can be an encrypted PIN from the data

[5] The security module described here was developed and tested in prototype form by Interbank Card Association under the name PINPACK (see also reference 2).

[6] The following six paragraphs are from *Datapro Reports on Banking,* Report No. B61-854-101, "Transaction Security Products Security Module" [3]. Copyright 1980 by Datapro Research Corporation, Delran, New Jersey. All rights reserved. Reprints may be obtained from Datapro Research Corporation.

base, a "PIN offset" or "PIN verification field" from the card's magnetic stripe, or a PIN cryptographically derived from the account number. The module responds with a "valid" or "invalid" indication, but in no case discloses the unencrypted PIN.

For interchange use, the module can "translate" the PIN (and any other data) from the cryptographic key and format used by the EFT terminal to the cryptographic key and format used for interchange. When the module is used for this "translation" function, no unencrypted PINs of any issuer are ever present, even momentarily, within the mainframe of participating institutions, where they might be subject to disclosure.

All functions performed by the DES algorithm are controlled by "keys." A security module is able to generate, control, maintain, and protect all keys associated with the user's network. This includes terminal keys, data storage keys,[7] and interchange keys. Terminal keys are used for encrypting and decrypting PINs and other data transmitted between a terminal and its host. A module can generate terminal keys and can support down-line key loading. Data storage keys protect sensitive data such as PINs stored in a user's data base. Interchange keys are used for transmitting data among various users within a shared system.

The message authentication function performed by a module provides protection against fraudulent modification of messages by cryptographically protecting the text. This is accomplished by processing critical message fields through the DES encryption algorithm, which generates a Message Authentication Code (MAC) appended to the message by the originator and checked by the recipient. Without knowledge of the key used in this process, anyone attempting to modify the message fraudulently would be unable to do so without detection.

PIN management refers to the techniques by which an institution issues, stores, and validates customer PINs. Here the system provides several options.

Bank Selected Random PIN

The security module itself can generate PINs, then print a PIN mailer on its own dedicated terminal printer. This just generated PIN is then encrypted under the PIN Master Key [PMK] and transmitted to the CPU for storage in the EDP system's data base, or, for encoding on the magnetic stripe of the customer's card.

Before the security module will print PIN mailers, it must be put into the "authorized state." To do this, each of two members of the institution's staff must enter a different secret code. Each had previously selected his code, and neither knows the other's code. If both of these codes are entered correctly, the module enters the authorized state, and will print PIN mailers when instructed to do so. If it is not in the authorized state it will respond with an error indication to such an instruction. This would prevent unauthorized personnel from printing PIN mailers at a time when the security module's printer is not properly secured.

[7] Storage keys are equivalent to the master keys discussed below.

PIN Cryptographically Derived from the Account Number

The security module, using DES, can cryptographically derive a PIN from a customer's account number and issue the PIN to this customer on a PIN mailer as discussed above.

Customer-Selected PIN

This may be accomplished by a mailed customer response, by a document given to the customer at the bank's facility, or by having the customer enter his PIN via a secure terminal.

To provide secure management for a customer mailed response, a PIN solicitation document is prepared and mailed to the customer. The portion to be returned, on which the customer writes his PIN, contains no customer identifying information except a reference number. This reference number is really an encrypted account number, intelligible only to the security module. Someone who sees the returned portion of the mailer would be unable to relate the PIN to the account. A bank employee uses this returned portion to enter the selected PIN and the reference number into the security module. The module then decrypts the reference number to determine the account number and encrypts the PIN under the PIN Master Key [PMK]. This resulting information is then transferred to the CPU for storage in the data base. At no point in this process is the clear PIN ever associated with the clear account number.

A similar document can be used by those institutions which have the customer choose his PIN at the time he applies for the account. Another technique which can be used under some conditions is to have the customer convey his PIN selection by entering it into a secure EFT terminal.

PIN Validation

The security module provides a number of different techniques for PIN validation, depending upon the characteristics of the EFT system and how the PIN was issued and stored. In most of today's ATM systems the PIN is validated by the ATM itself. In this case, the only role played by the security module is the preparation, during the PIN issue process, of the encrypted PIN or offset to be encoded on the magnetic stripe of the bank card used to activate the ATM. (Many ATMs use this offset value in the PIN validation process.) In an interchange environment, however, PIN validation must be performed at the EDP system of the card issuing institution, or of some other institution designated by the issuer to perform this function. (As previously indicated, it would be non-secure to have the information needed for the validation of one institution's PINs available to all other institutions.) In this type of environment, the customer's PIN arrives from the EFT terminal or the interchange network, encrypted under a terminal key [TK] or an interchange key [IK] known only to the security module. The module decrypts the customer entered PIN, and then determines the PIN of reference for comparison purposes. In some institutions the security module determines this PIN of reference from the account number, or from data encoded on the bank card (which was previously generated by the module during the PIN issue process). In other institutions there is an encrypted PIN entry in the data base for each account, and this entry is passed to the security module along with the transaction. This entry was generated by the module itself during the PIN issue process, and the security module alone holds the PIN Master Key [PMK] required to decrypt it. After obtaining the PIN of reference and comparing it with the customer entered PIN, the security module informs the EDP system of the comparison result, but does not, under any conditions, output the clear PIN.

Key Management

The preceding discussion has mentioned several types of keys: master keys, terminal keys, and interchange keys. The generation and management of such keys is an important feature of a security module system.

Master keys, of which there are perhaps fifteen in a security module, are common among all the modules which serve a financial institution's EDP facility. However, no two institutions share the same, or even similar, master keys. Master keys are used primarily for encrypting terminal keys [TK1, TK2, ...], interchange keys [IK1, IK2, ...], and PINs. Interbank has developed a special, highly secure Key Management Center for the generation of master keys for use in Interbank interchange. The Interbank personnel who operate this center do not have the capability to ascertain the keys it generates. These keys are conveyed from the center to the institution's security modules via electronic key transfer devices, so no printed record of the keys is ever produced. Though these devices must be transported to the institution under dual controlled conditions of very high security, the use of two independently conveyed devices for each set of keys means that both devices would have to be compromised before any of the conveyed master keys would be revealed.

The keys for an institution's terminals are produced by that institution's security module. The module must first be placed in the authorized state as described previously. Then the module, upon command from the EDP system, generates a random value to use as the terminal key. Ideally, this key is transferred from the security module directly into an electronic key loading device by which it is transported to the terminal in question. Such devices, several versions of which are in use today, prevent the person who loads the key from ascertaining it. As an interim necessity, in the absence of the terminal's ability to interface with such a device, the key may be formed by the addition of two or more sub-keys, each of which is separately printed by the security module's printer, carried to the terminal, manually entered into it, and then the printed record destroyed. Desirably, the key is formed inside the terminal as the sum of two values which are independently conveyed from the security module to the terminal.

After the security module has generated a new terminal key [TK] and transferred it to a key loading device (or to the printer) the module encrypts the just generated key under its Terminal Master Key [TMK], and sends this encrypted value to the EDP system for storage. This eliminates the necessity of internally storing a large number of terminal keys. Every time a transaction comes from a terminal, the EDP system finds the corresponding encrypted key in its data base and passes this to the security module along with the transaction.[8]

Interchange keys are used between the security modules of different institutions to encrypt data in interchange. Such keys for use in Interbank interchange are generated by the Interbank Key Management Center. Usually they are generated on a bilateral basis, two institutions (or an institution and its EFT switch) sharing a common interchange key for transactions between them. The Interbank Key Management Center must first have conveyed to each institution a unique Interchange Master Key [IMK]. The center then generates a random value to serve as this bilateral interchange key [IK], then encrypts this interchange key under the Interchange Master Key of the first institution [IMK1], then under the Interchange Master Key of the second [IMK2]. Thus encrypted [E_{IMK1}(IK) and E_{IMK2}(IK)], the interchange key may be conveyed to each institution via non-secure means.

Note that the security module's PIN management and key management techniques are designed to enforce dual control over all critical manual operations. If the security module is implemented in the suggested physically secure hardware, no cryptographic key can ever be ascertained by anyone, and no PIN can be ascertained except by the customer to whom it is issued, unless there is fraudulent collusion between two explicitly trusted employees of the institution.

MAC Generation[9]

Another security technique provided by the security module is called message authentication. Under this technique, the message is cryptographically processed using a secret key. This process produces a residue, which is then appended to the clear message. This residue, called the message authentication code or MAC, is generated by the originator and checked by the recipient. Should anyone attempt to modify such a message while in transit, he would be unable to do so without detection. Not knowing the secret key used in the authentication process, one would be unable to generate the MAC appropriate to the modified message. This technique is used primarily to prevent messages from being fraudulently modified as they traverse non-secure communications circuits and EDP systems. Since the message is assumed to be in clear (comprehensible) form, it can be comprehended, though not modified, by EDP systems along the way [2].

Utilization

Security module utilization in an operational environment is perhaps best illustrated by means of two examples—its use in a *local* transaction and its

[8] Each ATM which performs PIN validation must internally store the PIN Master Key. To convey this key to an ATM, the security module encrypts it under the terminal key, so that it can be transmitted to the ATM over the nonsecure communications link. Replacement terminal keys can be similarly conveyed from security module to terminal.

[9] The material in this section is taken from reference 2.

use in an *interchange* transaction. A local transaction is one in which the customer uses a terminal controlled by his own institution. An interchange transaction is one in which the customer uses some other institution's terminal.

Figure 10-1 illustrates a local transaction. The cardholder's PIN is entered into the terminal, where it is immediately encrypted under the terminal key [TK]. This encrypted PIN, together with the other elements of the transaction, is then transmitted to the institution's CPU. The CPU examines the just received transaction and determines the identity of the terminal from which it originated, and the identity of the cardholder who initiated it. (The cardholder is identified by his account number, which is read from the card's magnetic stripe by the terminal.) From this information the CPU finds, in its data base, the terminal's key encrypted under the Terminal Master Key, TMK, and the cardholder's PIN of reference encrypted under the PIN Master Key, PMK. (Alternately the encrypted PIN of reference may be encoded on the card's magnetic stripe.) These two encrypted values [E_{TMK}(TK) and E_{PMK}(PIN)] along with pertinent fields from the transaction are conveyed to the security module. The module contains, in its internal storage, the master keys [TMK and PMK]. Using its Terminal Master Key [TMK] it decrypts the terminal key from the data base. This just decrypted value is used to decrypt the cardholder entered PIN as received from the terminal. Then using the PIN Master Key [PMK] it either decrypts the PIN of reference from the data base or encrypts the just decrypted cardholder entered PIN. Either way, the two versions of the PIN are compared. If they disagree, the module sends the CPU a "no" indication. If they agree it sends a "yes" indication.

If the terminal in question uses message authentication, the module will output a valid MAC for the response message only if it finds both the incoming MAC and the PIN to be valid. This prevents a clever CPU programmer from substituting an "approved" response to a terminal for the "disapproved" response which always results from an invalid PIN (or modified message).

An interchange transaction, Figure 10-2, begins just as a local one, with the cardholder's PIN being encrypted under the terminal key [TK] and transmitted as part of the transaction to the acquiring institution. This institution's CPU examines the transaction to learn the identity of the terminal and the cardholder. Again, from the terminal's identity, it locates the terminal's key encrypted under the Terminal Key Master Key in its data base [E_{TMK}(TK)]. It notes, however, that this is an interchange transaction and that this particular cardholder's PIN is not on file here. It thus sends the encrypted terminal key and the transaction to its security module with instructions to perform a PIN translation. The security module decrypts the terminal key, TK, then uses this to decrypt the PIN. It immediately reencrypts the PIN under the appropriate interchange key, IK. In some cases, as illustrated in Figure 10-2, this is a key which the acquirer shares, on a bilateral basis, with the issuer. If it does not share a bilateral key with the issuer in question, the interchange key used is the one the acquirer shares with the interchange switch. The switch will then perform a second key translation, decrypting under the interchange key which it shares with the acquirer [say IK1] and reencrypting with the interchange key it shares with the issuer

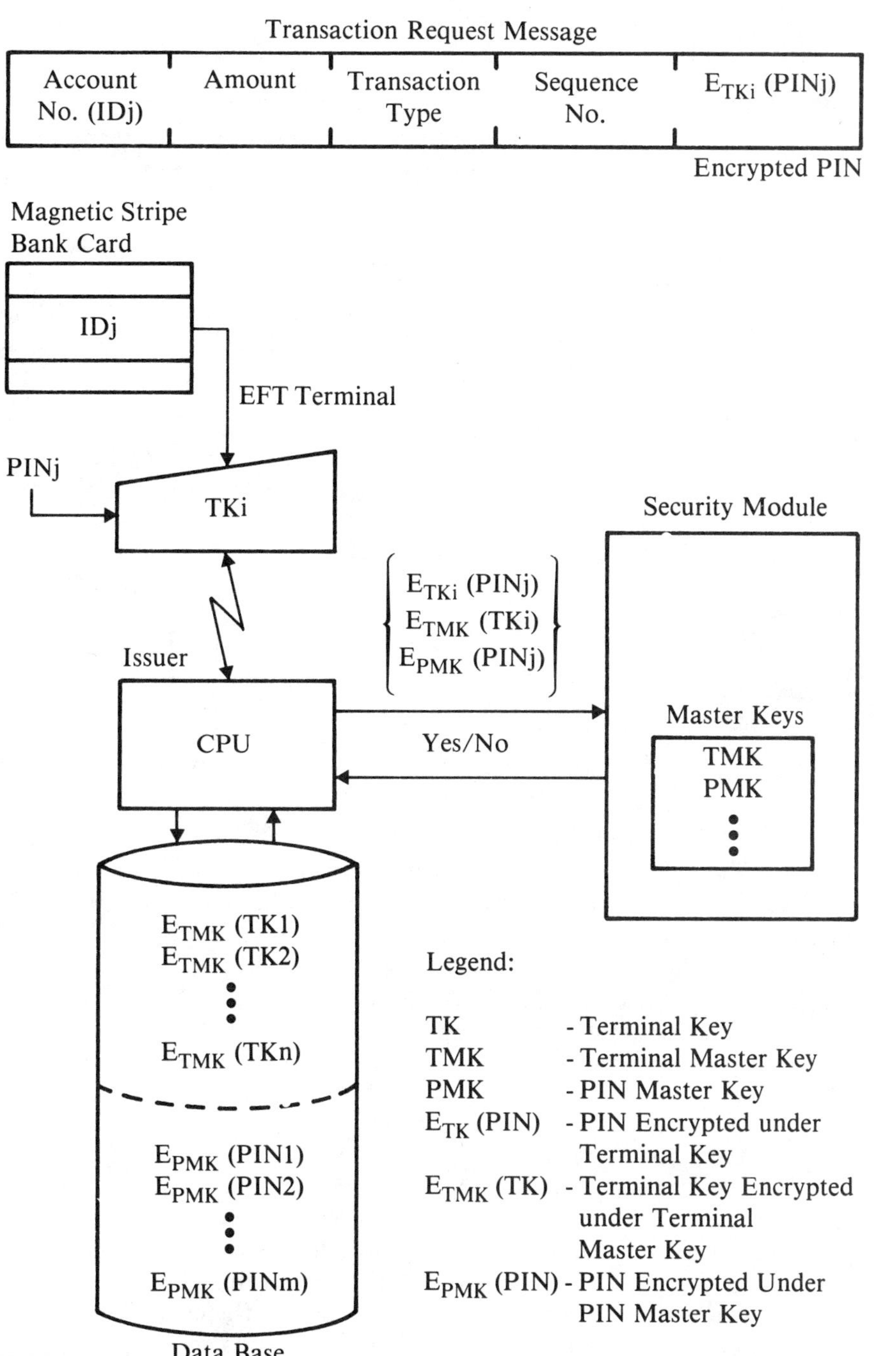

This figure is based on a similar figure in Reference 1.

Figure 10-1. Issuer's PIN Validation - Local Transaction

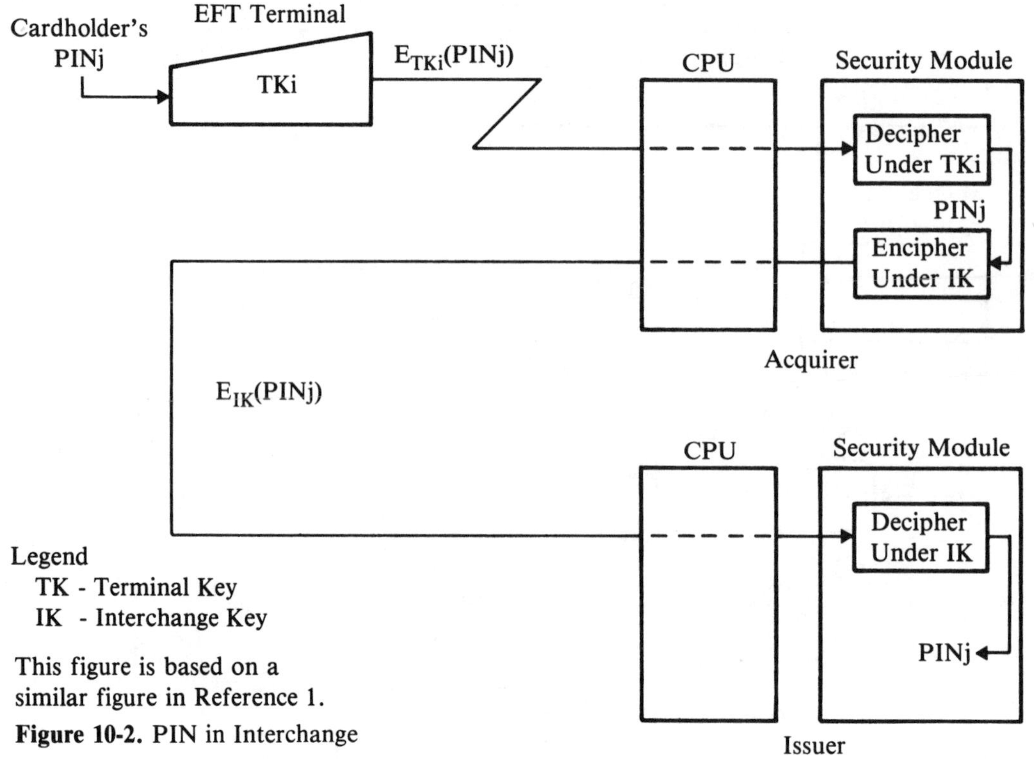

This figure is based on a similar figure in Reference 1.

Figure 10-2. PIN in Interchange

[say IK2]. Either way, the issuer receives the PIN encrypted under an interchange key available to its security module. It then validates the PIN in essentially the same manner described for a local transaction.

Though not shown in Figure 10-2, every interchange transaction is protected by means of a Message Authentication Code, or MAC. This code is generated by the acquirer using the same key used for PIN encryption. The code is validated by the issuer. When the acquirer and issuer do not share a bilateral key, the switch's security module performs a MAC translation as well as the above indicated PIN translation.[10]

Message authentication is also used for the response message from issuer to acquirer, and again a MAC translation, if required, is performed by the interchange switch. If the EFT terminal uses message authentication, the acquirer's security module generates the proper message authentication code for the terminal only if the MAC from the issuer is valid.

Note that throughout this interchange procedure, the clear PIN exists only within the physically secure confines of the originating terminal and the two

[10] For example, the switch decrypts the PIN and checks the MAC using the interchange key shared with the acquirer (IK1). If the incoming MAC is found to be valid, it then reencrypts the PIN and generates an outgoing MAC using the interchange key shared with the issuer (IK2). (It is assumed that each interchange key shared with the switch is stored encrypted under the switch's Interchange Master Key, IMK.)

or three indicated security modules, thus providing the highest possible security for the PIN at all points in the interchange environment.

Conclusions

The above suggested "security module" can be implemented by mainframe software, or by a hardware device. Especially when implemented by a hardware device, the module provides very high security to perform those fraud prevention functions which a financial institution requires in order to participate in a secure EFT interchange network. It provides a means to translate encrypted PINs from one cryptographic key to another without allowing either the clear PINs, or the clear keys used to encrypt them, from existing even momentarily outside of the security module, or of the EFT terminal itself.

Not only does the security module protect PINs in interchange, but it also provides fraud protection for the institution's own PINs as well. It enables a system of PIN issuance, PIN management, and PIN validation by which not even one member of the institution's staff has the capability to ascertain cardholders' PINs. In addition, it performs all other cryptographically related functions (e.g., message authentication) which are required of an institution's EDP facility, and also provides for the required key management capabilities.

REFERENCES

1. *PIN Manual: A Guide to the Use of Personal Identification Numbers in Interchange,* Interbank Card Association (September 1980). Distribution restricted. Contact Security Department, MasterCard International Inc. (formerly Interbank Card Association), 888 7th Avenue, New York, NY 10019.
2. Campbell, C. M., Jr., "A Microprocessor-Based Module to Provide Security in Electronic Funds Transfer Systems," *Proceedings COMPCON 79,* 148–153 (1979).
3. "Transaction Security Products Security Module," Report Number B61-854-101, reprinted from *Datapro Reports on Banking,* Datapro Research Corporation, Delran, NJ (1980).

CHAPTER ELEVEN

Applying Cryptography to Electronic Funds Transfer Systems—Personal Identification Numbers and Personal Keys

One essential requirement of an electronic funds transfer (EFT) system is that institutions must be able to join together in a common EFT network (defined as an *interchange*) such that the EFT security of each institution is independent of the security measures implemented at other institutions. Another requirement is that the process of identification or verification of a user must involve a secret value, commonly called a Personal Identification Number (PIN) which is, on the average, only 4 to 6 digits long.

To discuss EFT security from a more general viewpoint, two terms associated with personal verification are defined: an authentication parameter (AP) and a personal authentication code (PAC). An AP is a function of secret and nonsecret user-supplied information as well as nonsecret system-supplied information. A PAC is a function of the user's identifier (ID), AP, and a secret system-supplied authentication key, KA. A quantity similar to PAC is used in message authentication and is defined as a message authentication code (MAC). Examples of personal verification and message authentication are provided to illustrate the use of AP, PAC, and MAC.

After developing a set of EFT security requirements, implementations based on PIN/system keys and PIN/personal keys are discussed. It is shown that neither implementation satisfies all of the stated requirements, although the PIN/system key approach does provide adequate protection for current EFT systems.

An implementation incorporating PINs, personal and system keys (defined as a *hybrid* key management), and an intelligent secure card is discussed next. This approach, which meets the stated requirements to a higher degree, offers the potential for increased security in future EFT applications.

A glossary of terms and abbreviations is provided at the end of this chapter.

BACKGROUND

Many techniques for cryptographic authentication are used in EFT systems and in those systems being evaluated by major financial institutions and their vendors. The purpose here is to suggest some additional techniques for consideration in the development of these systems.

Every day EFT systems electronically transfer billions of dollars between institutions and individuals. Such transactions (e.g., deposits and withdrawals) cannot be processed safely unless user identities can be validated securely and the correct, unaltered transmission of messages between network nodes (terminals, computers, etc.) can be assured.

The process of validating user identities is called *personal authentication*, *personal verification*, or *personal identification*, whereas the process of validating messages is called *message authentication*. The term personal verification is used throughout this chapter specifically to address validation of secret quantities supplied by a system user. (If a user is verified on the basis of a PIN only, the term PIN validation is commonly used.)

A user is normally provided with an embossed, magnetic stripe identification card (bank card) containing an institution identification number, the card's expiration date, and a *primary account number* (PAN).[1] The institution at which the customer opens his account, and which provides the user with a bank card, is called the *issuer*. At an entry point to the system, information on the user's bank card is read into the system and the user enters a secret quantity called the *personal identification number* (PIN). If the cardholder has supplied the correct PIN and if the balance in the account is sufficient to permit the transaction and if that type of transaction is allowed for that account, the system authorizes the funds transfer.

Consider the network configuration shown in Figure 11-1. The entry point at which transaction requests are initiated, such as a *point of sale* (POS) terminal or an *automated teller machine* (ATM), is defined as an *EFT terminal*. An institution's computer facility, which also happens to manage the connected EFT terminals, is referred to as a *host processing center* (HPC). The three HPCs shown in Figure 11-1 are interconnected via an intelligent *switch*. The switch, which can be another HPC, establishes connections between the HPCs so that information can be routed in the network efficiently. A *communications control unit* (CC), an independent device positioned in the path between an HPC and its associated EFT terminals and between an HPC and adjacent network nodes, is responsible for managing data transmissions over the communications links. Similarly, EFT terminals are assumed to provide complementary support for link management functions. Theoretically, and assumed here, the CC has the capacity to verify system users and data.

The HPC that first acts on information entered at an EFT terminal is the *acquirer* (acquiring HPC).[2] A user who initiates a transaction at an EFT terminal may be a customer of a local institution (HPC X, in which case the acquirer is also the issuer) or a remote (distant) institution (HPC Y or HPC Z). If a user can initiate transactions at an entry point not controlled by the issuer, the supporting network is called an *interchange system*.

[1]The American National Standard Institute's (ANSI) standard magnetic stripe format is given in Appendix C.

[2]The acquirer is normally the HPC associated with the EFT terminal at which PIN and card information are entered.

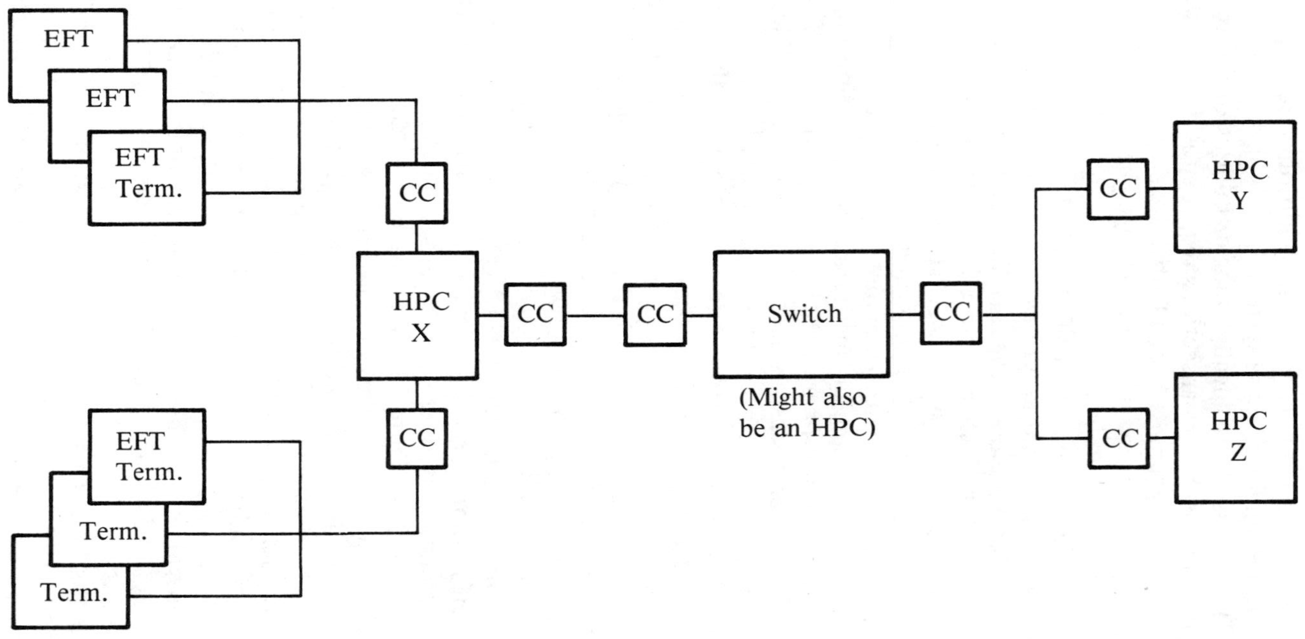

Figure 11-1. Example of an EFT Network Supporting Interchange

For example, consider a simple transaction in which cryptography is not employed. A customer wishes to use a bank card to pay a grocery bill of $35.00 and to receive an additional $50.00 in cash. Assume that the grocer's account is with institution X and the customer's account is with institution Y. The customer's card is inserted into the EFT terminal, either by the customer or by an employee of the retailer attending the EFT terminal, and the customer enters his PIN via a suitable entry device such as a keyboard or a PIN pad, which looks and operates much like a hand-held calculator. Similarly, the grocer enters a transfer request for $85.00 to be transferred from the customer's account to the grocer's account ($35.00 for the groceries plus the $50.00 to be given to the customer).

The information entered at the EFT terminal is assembled into a *debit request* message. This message or *transaction request,* which includes the customer's PIN, his account number (PAN), andsuitable routing information, is then sent via the acquirer (HPC X) and switch to the issuer (HPC Y).

Upon receiving the debit request, HPC Y verifies that the PIN correlates properly with the customer's PAN, and that the customer's account balance is sufficient to cover the $85.00 transfer. If the PIN check fails, the user is normally given at least two more chances to enter the correct PIN. If after the additional trials the PIN is still rejected, HPC Y sends a negative reply to HPC X. If the PIN is correct but the account balance is insufficient to cover the transfer, HPC Y denies the debit request by sending a negative reply or *debit refusal* (insufficient funds) message to HPC X. A message is then sent via the network to the grocer's EFT terminal indicating to the grocer that the funds transfer has been disapproved.

If the debit request is approved, HPC Y records the debit request, reduces the customer's account balance by $85.00, and transmits a positive reply or *debit authorization* message back to HPC X. Upon receiving the debit authorization HPC X takes two actions. A message is sent to the grocer's EFT terminal, indicating to the grocer that the funds transfer has been approved. Then HPC X credits the grocer's account with $85.00. This completes the transaction. (Although other protocols are possible, the one described above will be assumed throughout the present discussion.)

When personal verification is performed by the issuer's HPC (or the HPC of another designated node), the process is said to operate in the *on-line* mode. If personal verification is performed by the terminal, the process is said to operate in the *off-line* mode. If only the terminal and communications controller are involved, the process is said to operate in the *off-host* mode.

In an on-line environment, the highest level of data security can be provided. However, if the system is to be kept available even when the HPCs are not operating (e.g., during weekends, holidays, maintenance, etc.), an off-line or off-host mode of operation must be supported. In general, there is insufficient storage to maintain a verification table at the EFT terminals, and users must be verified without benefit of the HPC's files (of hundreds of millions of characters) which contains the PAN/PIN information of each user. Therefore, off-line and off-host authentication techniques must contend with this limitation, which ultimately results in a decrease in security.

SECURITY EXPOSURES IN EFT SYSTEMS

An EFT system is defined to have the following four components:

1. Communication links
2. Computers
3. Terminals
4. Bank cards

Security considerations for each of these are discussed below (see also reference 1, where part of the material has been taken).

Communication Link Security

Communication links are highly vulnerable to interception of messages by a number of techniques which permit passive (listening), and/or active (data alteration/substitution) attacks. Where there are public telephone line connections between computers and terminals, and that is most common, one normally needs a physical connection to intercept the information. With satellite or microwave transmissions, on the other hand, a physical connection is not required since an appropriate antenna allows the communications channel to be breached between the sending and receiving stations.

If certain data were altered, illegitimate authorization of a transaction could occur. For example, money could be diverted to the wrong institution or account, transaction amounts could be changed, or a debit refusal message could be converted into a debit authorization message. Message authentication techniques eliminate these exposures. They allow the receiver to determine where the message originated, if it is current, what its destination is, and, most importantly, if it has been altered.

Computer Security[3]

Today, time-sharing, real-time interactive terminal communications, and computer-to-computer data links are all common. These technological innovations, coupled with the growth of computer usage, have increased the opportunities for computer abuse. Access to the computer can be gained through a remote terminal or other peripheral device such as a card reader. Thus programs or data stored in or being processed by a computer system could be copied, altered, replaced, or even destroyed. To cope with these problems, a combination of physical security, procedural protection methods, and cryptography can be used.

Cryptography alone does not solve the computer security problem. Other methods are required such as access control, store and fetch protection, and the like. This contrasts with communication security where cryptography may indeed be the only method needed to provide protection.

[3] The security exposures discussed here apply in general to programs or data stored in or processed by a communications control unit or terminal control unit.

Terminal Security

Whenever cipher keys reside in terminals, some physical security is mandatory. Without it, an opponent may be able to probe for a key or change its value. Therefore, both the integrity of nonsecret parameters and the confidentiality of secret parameters must be preserved. In well-designed systems, considerable time would be required to probe for a key successfully.

However, sufficient time to probe for a key would be available if an opponent could steal a terminal. (Note that a resident key is normally stored in volatile storage maintained under battery power so that the key will not be erased if main power is interrupted.) Elaborate interlocks designed to detect penetration and to erase the terminal's key(s) automatically could be defeated with enough time and resources. In that case, previous data encrypted or transformed with the secret terminal-resident key would be exposed. On the other hand, removal of a terminal is likely to be detected and the proper response is to invalidate the terminal and key in the supporting network. This would protect future encrypted data.

Because of the trend toward employment of large numbers of inexpensive terminals (which may be installed in relatively nonsecure locations), the secrecy afforded terminal-resident cryptographic keys may be very little. An inexpensive terminal cannot have elaborate or sophisticated defenses, and penetration of the terminal without its physical removal from the premises becomes increasingly more difficult to defend against.

Even a public-key cryptosystem (PKC) (see Chapters 2 and 9 and references 2 and 3), employing public keys in the EFT terminals, would not provide a secure solution if there were no physical security at the entry points. A PKC would eliminate the need to keep certain (public) keys secret, but it would still be necessary to protect the integrity of these public keys. Otherwise, an attack is possible wherein an opponent replaces the installed public key with a key of his or her own choosing. The opponent, knowing the corresponding secret key, could then produce forged verification information that would be accepted by the terminal. In addition, a public key would only allow the terminal to authenticate transaction response messages received from the issuer. A secret key would still be required for generation of the MACs on transaction request messages sent to the issuer. Hence, even the public-key approach requires a secret key at the entry point.

It may appear that the solution to the exposed terminal problem is to use only externally supplied secret keys (i.e., to use personal keys instead of system keys.) However, it will be shown later that personal keys alone will not lead to a secure implementation.

When transactions are conducted entirely at an EFT terminal (such as a cash-issuing terminal operating in the off-line mode), only personal verification is required—message authentication between the EFT terminal and the issuer is, by definition, not needed. In that case, a public-key cryptosystem with a public key installed in the EFT terminal would suffice to permit personal verification. However, unless the integrity of the public key can be ensured, the system could be attacked.

EFT Terminals in Nonsecure Environments

Ordinarily, information entered into or stored within an EFT terminal would be protected as a consequence of the physical security routinely provided by the owner of an establishment, e.g., the retailer, wherein an EFT terminal is installed. However, if the retailer or an employee of the retailer becomes an opponent, the secrecy and integrity of information at the entry point no longer can be maintained (see the section entitled EFT Security Requirements). Although its physical surroundings (the building, locked doors, employees of the retailer), to some degree, protect an EFT terminal from outsiders who are not authorized to have access, they do not protect an EFT terminal from insiders who are authorized to have access (e.g., the retailer, clerks, cashiers, and sales personnel employed by the retailer).

Those with authorized access to the retailer's premises could subvert security in several ways. For example, by

1. Illicitly reading (skimming) card information.
2. Probing the EFT terminal for secret keys.
3. Replacing keys, algorithms, and hardware devices with parameters, procedures, and devices under the control of the opponent.
4. Tapping (obtaining electronically) information entered at the EFT terminal.
5. Tapping information sent to the issuer.

The insider has an advantage over the outsider simply in terms of the time available to carry out attacks. But the threats are even more insidious because of the insider's ability to coordinate one activity with another (e.g., skimming bank cards and simultaneously tapping the output line).

Fake Equipment Attack

Instead of using indirect methods to obtain the PIN, an opponent can recover PINs directly by subverting the entry process. For example, an opponent could replace the PIN pad[4] and terminal with devices that will display or print the entered values, PIN and personal key (KP), to the opponent stationed out of view. Each PIN and KP so obtained is recorded and reentered into the real terminal which is kept hidden. Upon receiving the transaction response from the issuer, the opponent sends a comparable message to the bogus terminal, leading the user to believe the transaction was completed without interference.

This fake equipment attack points out the vulnerability of entering card and PIN information into devices whose security and integrity cannot be assured. It clearly demonstrates once again that cryptography does not provide the solution to the problem of protecting secret information if that information can be attacked before it is entered into the system. It also

[4] This is a device attached to the terminal, often with an integrated encryption capability, specifically designed to facilitate PIN entry.

argues strongly in favor of a design in which secret user information need not be exposed at the entry point. One approach already suggested involves an intelligent secure card (see the sections entitled Bank Card Security and Personal Key Approach with an Intelligent Secure Card). Since a secret component (KP) is stored on the card, and the card can neither be read nor skimmed by the opponent (the retailer, in this case), its use prevents the exposure at the entry point. The protocol should be such that there is no need to transfer secret card information to another device during normal operation (i.e., transformations involving the secret information are performed directly on the card).

Bank Card Security

The most convenient method of identification or authentication currently in use by financial institutions encompasses something the customer has, a bank card, and something the customer knows, a PIN. The unique correspondence of the account number contained on the card's magnetic stripe and the PIN memorized by the customer serves to identify the customer. Possession of the card without knowledge of the PIN, or knowledge of the PIN without the corresponding card, is insufficient for an imposter to gain access to the system.

Magnetic Stripe Card

Security exposures exist today because it is relatively easy to counterfeit or duplicate magnetic stripe cards. Special knowledge of the card's recorded data is not required to duplicate a card and there are several methods of transferring data from one card to another. Moreover, it does not matter if information on the card is encrypted or in the clear; cryptography does not protect against this exposure.

Two methods of duplicating encoded data previously recorded on the magnetic stripe of a bank card are *skimming* and *buffer recording* [1]. One technique for skimming involves placing a piece of recording tape over the magnetic stripe of a good card and applying heat (e.g., from a common household iron). The recording tape is then placed over the blank stripe of another card and heat is again applied. With this technique, it is possible to produce several duplicate cards without seriously degrading the quality of recorded information on either the original or the duplicate card.

Buffer recording produces a duplicate card of higher quality, but the method is more complex and more expensive than skimming. An electromagnetic reader (a device similar to a tape recorder) and buffer storage are required. Data, read from the card, are stored in the buffer. Later, the data can be read from the buffer and written on a blank card.

Duplication is more readily detectible if cards are constructed with some random property that changes from card to card and which is subsequently verified as part of the users transaction processing [1]. One such technique involves two sets of interleaved magnetic bars printed on the card's inner core. This forms a protective magnetic fingerprint with no two cards being alike. In addition, cards can be constructed of heat- and pressure-sensitive materials that invalidate a card if there are attempts to alter or duplicate it.

But mechanisms that discourage card duplication also increase the cost of both the card and the card reader. If only a few properties are added, the card is less expensive to read but relatively easy to duplicate. As more and more random properties are added, the card becomes more expensive to read and more difficult to duplicate. Furthermore, the special properties must be checked each time the card is read; otherwise a counterfeit card without these properties could be used instead.

Intelligent Secure Card

Recent advances in technology have made it possible to embed a microprocessor on a plastic card permitting identification and authentication computations to be performed directly on the card rather than in the logic of the system entry point device. In addition, small storage arrays permit important customer account information to be stored on the card, thus providing automated record keeping functions equivalent to those provided by a savings passbook. The net effect is to produce a card that is intelligent as well as secure [4, 5]. The intelligent secure card is also referred to as chip card and smart card.

IDENTIFICATION AND AUTHENTICATION OF SYSTEM USERS

A primary objective in the design of a practical authentication method is to find an inexpensive, practicable technique that is difficult to penetrate. The problem is that of properly balancing security against human factors and cost.

User characteristics are grouped into two sets: *transferable*, which means they could be forged, and *nontransferable*, which implies they cannot be forged.

Transferable User Characteristics

Verification can involve something a person has (a magnetic stripe identification card) or knows (a password). Passwords are commonly used, but they are not very secure. They may be compromised without the user, the institution's management, or its auditors knowing.

Nontransferable User Characteristics

Methods of verification involve testing for a unique personal characteristic such as something a person is (voiceprint, fingerprint, hand geometry) or something a person does (handwritten signature). One method, based on a handwritten signature, makes use of a signature pen capable of measuring pen pressure and pen acceleration. Experiments have shown that these two parameters are unique in the process of writing a signature [6].

When a person signs his or her name, the acceleration and pressure motions are not consciously controlled. This can be demonstrated by the close match between a person's signatures written with eyes open and those written with eyes closed. Further development work, however, is needed to bring handwritten electronic signature verification into everyday use.

For the present, a password used in conjunction with a magnetic stripe card and authentication processing performed at an HPC represent the most practical means for achieving personal verification.

REQUIREMENTS FOR PERSONAL VERIFICATION AND MESSAGE AUTHENTICATION

The problems to be solved with cryptography are:

1. Verification of system users, referred to as personal verification.
2. Verification of data (to check for origin, true content, timeliness, and destination), referred to as message authentication.

It must be recognized that

> *applications requiring personal verification very frequently require message authentication, and since both processes are closely related and neither must be allowed to weaken the security of the other, it is prudent to seek a cryptographic solution to both problems simultaneously.*

For example, when the entry node must take some action in response to a transaction request (e.g., to dispense cash or not), the node must receive a message notifying it that the user has or has not been accepted (Figure 11-2). For detection of an attack where a "User Not OK" (or negative) reply is changed to a "User OK" (or positive) reply, message authentication must be used. In this application, the best personal verification scheme could be circumvented were there no message authentication.

The personal verification process starts with the user providing *personal verification information*. This can be categorized in the approaches discussed here as user-remembered information (e.g., a PIN or a *password*) and user-supplied information stored on the bank card (e.g., a primary account number, PAN, or a cryptographic key). If a cryptographic key is stored on the bank card, it is referred to as a *personal key* (KP).

The PAN is also referred to as a *personal identifier*, or *identifier* (ID). Using a unique ID is better than using, for example, the name of a person, since people's names are not always unique. In the discussion that follows, it is assumed that an opponent has knowledge of user IDs. This is a practical assumption, since ordinarily no special precautions are taken to ensure their secrecy (i.e., they are treated as nonsecret quantities). Obtaining them would not be too difficult, since they are frequently used for identification and auditing purposes and are transmitted, stored, and printed on documents in unencrypted form.

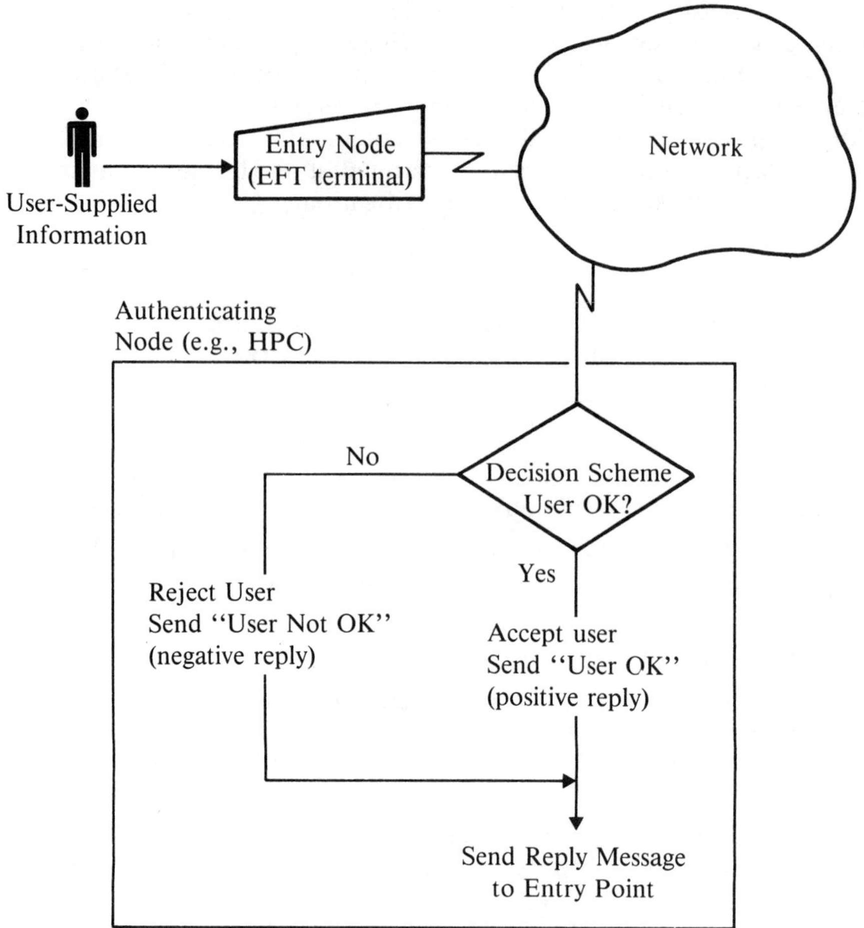

Figure 11-2. The Personal Verification Process

Authentication Parameter

The following discussion of several possible methods for performing personal verification assumes that part or all of the user-supplied verification information is first subjected to a transformation at the entry point. This process creates another quantity defined as a *personal authentication parameter*, or *authentication parameter* (AP) for short (Figure 11-3). An AP is a function satisfying the following conditions:

1. It is always a function of secret user-supplied information, which may or may not be shared with the issuer.
2. It may or may not be a function of other nonsecret user-supplied and/or system-supplied information.
3. It is a function only of the information specified in conditions 1 and 2

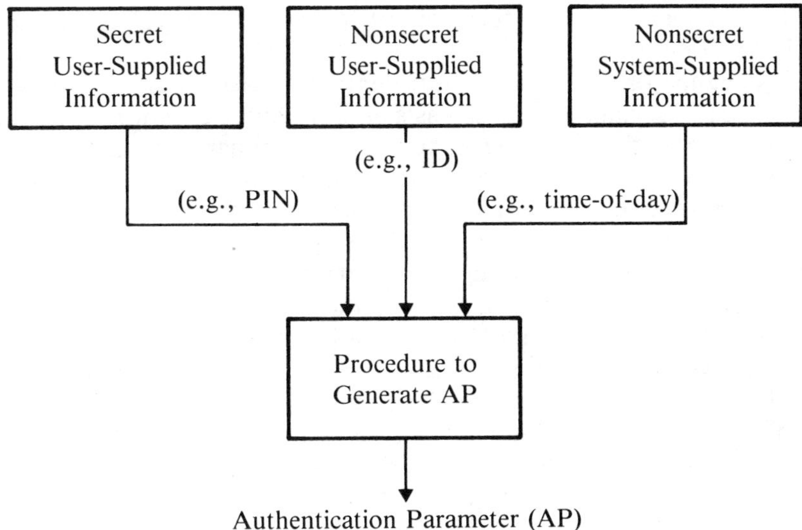

Note: Proper coupling of nonsecret with secret information can lead to a quantity more resistant to analysis.

Figure 11-3. Transformation of User-Supplied Verification Information to a Personal Authentication Parameter at the Entry Point

above (i.e., AP does not depend on secret information known to anyone other than the user or the user and the issuer).[5]

It is fundamental to any cryptographically secure procedure for personal verification that the secret information supplied by the user (which is used by the issuer to authenticate the user) be transformed at the entry point under some cryptographic process to ensure that the secret user-supplied information cannot be ascertained by the unauthorized. It is significant that the secret information used in the computation of AP is known only to the user or to the user and issuer. This is a requirement if personal verification in an interchange environment is to be achieved exclusively between the user and issuer.

For personal verification, AP can be used either alone (by storing an appropriate reference,[6] AP of reference, in a verification table) or in conjunction with other information related to AP via a special cryptographic key defined solely for authentication purposes. The nonsecret information in the computation of AP may be time-invariant (e.g., the primary account number), time-variant (e.g., a time-of-day clock reading), or both. If AP is time-invariant, an AP of reference may be precomputed and stored in a verification

[5] In a discussion of PIN/system key approaches to EFT security, it is likely that the definition of AP would be broadened, allowing AP to depend additionally on secret system-supplied information (e.g., a secret system key).

[6] A reference is a quantity uniquely related to the item to be verified or authenticated. It is a parameter computed or designated, and used, by the authenticator as part of the authentication process.

table at the issuer. If AP is time-variant, then an AP of reference must be dynamically computed.

If AP depends on time-variant information as well as on the transaction request message, it can also be used as a *message authentication code* (MAC). Message authentication (via the MAC) is used primarily to detect stale or bogus messages inserted into the communications path and fraudulently modified messages traversing nonsecure communications systems. However, in such a situation, AP can serve a dual purpose–i.e., it can be used for personal verification as well as message authentication.

The function defining AP may be simple or complex. For example, AP may merely define a process of concatenation of parameters, or it may involve successive encryptions and decryptions, such that it is computationally unfeasible to invert the process (or one-way function) and find secret user-supplied information from AP. The developed set of security requirements places additional constraints on the specification of AP.[7]

Some specifications for AP presently under consideration by the American National Standards Institute (ANSI) technical committees X9 are AP = PIN and AP = PIN||ID, where PIN||ID denotes the concatenation of PIN and ID. If secret information (a 56-bit personal key, KP) is also stored on the bank card, then a better choice for the authentication parameter is AP = $E_{PIN \oplus KP}(ID)$ as discussed later in this chapter. (Note that ⊕ denotes modulo 2 addition and $E_K(X)$ and $D_K(Y)$ define encipherment of X with key K and decipherment of Y with key, K, respectively.)

Personal Authentication Code

In cases where a copy of AP can be safely stored in a verification table at the authenticating node, or where it is possible for the authenticator to compute an AP of reference either by recreating the information that is used to compute each user's AP or by safely storing that information in a table at the authenticating node, personal verification can be based solely on ID and AP. However, if the integrity of the verification table or the secrecy and integrity of stored information used to compute the AP of reference cannot be ensured, or if it is not possible to recreate the information used to compute each user's AP of reference (e.g., if PINs and KPs are selected independently), then personal verification can be based on ID, AP, and a *personal authentication code* (PAC). PAC is a function satisfying the following conditions:

1. It is a function of ID, secret user-supplied information, a secret key known only to the issuer (or authenticator), and possibly other nonsecret information.
2. It does not depend on secret information known to anyone other than the user and the issuer.

[7] For example, AP must be a one-way function of the input parameters which define it, and the secret user-supplied information and AP must each contain on the order of 56 independent bits.

The distinction between AP and PAC is as follows. Either a part of the secret information used in the computation of AP is known only to the user, or, all the secret information used in the computation of AP is shared between the user and issuer. On the other hand, it is always the case that a part of the secret information used in the computation of PAC is known only to the issuer.

There are two approaches for implementing personal authentication codes in an EFT system. In the first approach, PACs are stored directly on the magnetic stripe of the user's bank card thereby eliminating the need for a verification table at the issuer. When needed, the PAC is supplied to the system by the user, and together with AP it is forwarded to the *authenticator* (synonymous with authenticating node). In the second approach, the PACs are stored in a verification table in the issuer's system and only AP is sent to the issuer. In either case, the correct (ID, AP, PAC) relationship is checked via the authentication key, KA.

The authentication parameter and personal authentication code are introduced to broaden and generalize many of the concepts. At the same time, they allow different EFT systems to be discussed using a common, consistent terminology.

Personal Verification Using AP Only

Consider an AP-authenticating procedure that uses a verification table at the issuer, and therefore is an on-line verification method. Assume, for this example, that the quantity to be verified is AP = $E_{KP \oplus PIN}$ (ID), where KP is a 56-bit personal key, and a copy of AP is stored in the verification table of the issuer's HPC during the initialization process. Later, during the verification process, the quantities KP*, PIN*, and ID are entered at an entry point of the system by a user who wishes to be authenticated.[8] At the entry point, AP* = $E_{KP^* \oplus PIN^*}$ (ID) is generated and transmitted (together with ID) to the authenticator. If the stored AP of reference (indexed in the verification table by ID) agrees with the received AP*, the authenticator concludes that KP* ⊕ PIN* = KP ⊕ PIN and the user's identity is ID (as claimed). Otherwise, the user is rejected.

For the approach to be secure, it must not be possible for an opponent to violate the integrity of the verification table (e.g., by overwriting a stored value of AP with another value of AP). If this were possible, the opponent could define his own personal key (KP*) and PIN* for some existing ID, generate AP* = $E_{KP^* \oplus PIN^*}$(ID), and overwrite AP with AP* in the verification table. Subsequently, the opponent could supply KP*, PIN*, and ID at an entry point and be accepted by the system as the user whose identifier is ID.

It is assumed, although not shown at this point, that time-invariant AP values (as described in the example above) are included in the transaction

[8] KP* and PIN* denote the personal key and PIN entered by the user and KP and PIN denote the personal key and PIN (of reference) stored in the system. If the user is legitimate and does not make an error in entering his personal key and PIN, then KP*⊕PIN* equals KP⊕PIN.

request messages sent from the EFT terminal to the issuer, and message authentication is implemented such that the issuer can validate the content, timeliness, sender, and intended receiver of all received messages (see the section entitled Message Authentication Using MAC). Without message authentication, a procedure for personal verification based on time-invariant APs could be attacked in the following manner. A microprocessor is connected to the communications line of the EFT terminal to be attacked. The opponent initiates a transaction at the designated terminal using a bogus PIN and KP and an ID corresponding to a previously intercepted value of AP. The microprocessor is programmed to intercept the transaction request message and replace the bogus value of AP (computed by the terminal from the bogus values of PIN and KP) with the (correct) previously intercepted value of AP. The opponent, masquerading under the assumed ID, is thus validated by the issuer.

Personal Verification Using AP and PAC

An alternative procedure which does not use a verification table is also possible. Consider the on-line case where $AP = E_{KP \oplus PIN}(ID)$, $PAC = K_{KA}(AP)$, and KA is an issuer-controlled, secret authentication key. At the time KP and PIN are created, the issuer (who has KA) computes and stores PAC on the user's bank card (Figure 11-4). Since KA is a secret key, only the issuer can create valid PAC values. During the verification process, both AP and PAC are transmitted to the issuer. This permits the issuer to authenticate AP by enciphering it under KA and testing the result for equality with PAC (Figure 11-4).

To verify the user, the authenticator creates a dynamic *reference* (Rf), or more specifically, a PAC of reference, defined by $Rf = E_{KA}(AP)$. This reference is then compared with the received PAC. If Rf = PAC,[9] the authenticator concludes the following: The received quantities AP and PAC are properly related via the secret authentication key. Since these corresponding quantities could only be generated by someone who knows (or has access to) the secret authentication key, AP is accepted as genuine. Since AP depends on KP, PIN, and ID, authentication of AP also authenticates the triple (KP, PIN, ID) provided that message authentication is also employed to ensure that the transmitted ID is unchanged (i.e., one can conclude that AP was computed from a valid triple).[10] On the other hand, if AP or PAC or both do not have the correct values, then $Rf \neq PAC$ (with high probability) and hence this condition can be detected (with high probability).

[9] It is assumed that AP and PAC are part of the transaction request message whose content, timeliness, sender, and intended receiver are authenticated by the issuer.

[10] PAC is really only coupled to AP. Authentication of AP does not by itself ensure that the claimed ID is the ID in the triple (KP, PIN, ID) that was used to compute AP. Message authentication is also required to ensure that the claimed ID has not been changed. Coupling AP and ID to PAC is discussed in the section Personal Verification with Independent PINs and Personal Keys (Equation 11-4).

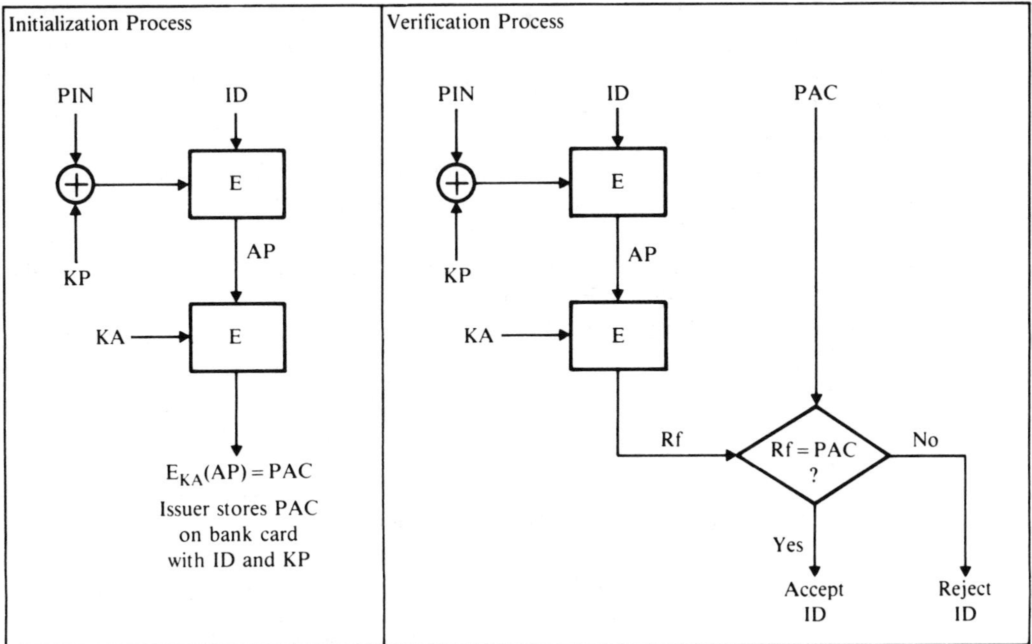

Legend:

AP:	Authentication Parameter	64 Bits
ID:	User Identifier	≤ 64 Bits
KA:	System Authentication Key	56 Bits
KP:	Personal Key	56 Bits
PAC:	Personal Authentication Code	64 Bits (Truncation Possible)
PIN:	Personal Identification Number	≤ 56 Bits
RF:	Reference	64 Bits (Truncation Possible)

Figure 11-4. A Method for Achieving Personal Verification

Message Authentication Using a MAC

To simplify the discussion of message authentication, it is assumed that data secrecy is not required, i.e., a message (M) is sent in the clear and therefore can be read by an opponent.[11] Furthermore, it is assumed that M consists of only one 64-bit data block. The message authentication code (MAC), defined here as quantity $E_K(M \oplus Z)$, is produced by the modulo 2, addition of M with a nonsecret initializing vector (Z) and encipherment of the result with a secret authentication key (K).[12] The initializing vector, Z (used to

[11] If secrecy and authentication are desired at the same time, the data are first encrypted and then one of the authentication methods described below is applied to the resulting ciphertext.

[12] Typically, a message would exceed 64 bits and would contain identification information such as the user's ID, the computed value of AP, a PAC value (if used), as well as other data such as the transaction code and the transaction amount. In that case, a MAC may be generated by using a form of chained block encryption wherein Z is added modulo 2 to the first block of plaintext and each block of ciphertext is added modulo 2 to the next block of plaintext.

introduce time-dependent information into the authentication procedure), may be established between the communicants as part of the session initialization process.[13] By transmitting M and MAC to the receiver, the authenticity of M can be checked by comparing the received MAC for equality with a system-generated MAC of reference (Figure 11-5).

There is a close analogy between personal verification where a PAC is transmitted to the authenticator together with AP (Figure 11-4) and message authentication where a MAC is transmitted to the authenticator together with the corresponding message. (The procedure in Figure 11-4 is actually the same as Figure 11-5 if AP is replaced by $M \oplus Z$, PAC is replaced by MAC, and KA is replaced by K.) The difference is that PAC is precomputed whereas MAC is dynamically computed.

To create a reference (Rf), or more specifically a MAC of reference, the authenticator encrypts $M \oplus Z$ with K using the same procedure as the sender. This reference is then compared with the received MAC. If Rf = MAC, the authenticator concludes the following: The received quantities M and MAC are properly related via the secret authentication key. Since these corresponding quantities could only be generated by someone who knows (or has access to) the secret authentication key, M will be accepted as genuine. On the other hand, if M or MAC or both do not have the correct values, then Rf $\neq$ MAC (with high probability) and hence this condition can be detected (with high probability).

Although prevented from generating a proper MAC for an arbitrary M, an opponent could present a previously intercepted message and MAC. To permit detection of such an event, the MAC must be time-variant—assured here by the quantity Z. It could also be assured by including a unique message sequence number in M, in which case quantity Z (Figure 11-5) would not be needed. In either case, the receiver could then detect stale messages injected into the communication path as well as deleted messages.

In the discussion that follows, personal verification is based on an AP value received in the transaction request message M. Message authentication is based on a MAC attached to the transaction request message. AP is used to validate the originator of the message, whereas MAC is used to validate the content of the message (including the received AP).

EFT Security Requirements[14]

The following EFT security requirements assume that the system must be secure from both insiders (those that have access to privileged system interfaces and internal functions of the system) and outsiders (legitimate users or opponents who have access only to external system interfaces).

[13] It is assumed that the process of establishing Z is such that an outsider cannot alter or predict its value. Otherwise, he may be able to find M^* and Z^* such that $M^* \oplus Z^* = M \oplus Z$. He could then change $[M, E_K(M \oplus Z)]$ to $[M^*, E_K(M \oplus Z)] = [M^*, E_K(M^* \oplus Z^*)]$ which would authenticate when Z^* were used as the initializing vector.

[14] ©1981 IEEE. The section on EFT security requirements is reprinted in part from the authors contribution to the Proceedings of the IEEE 1981 Symposium on Security and Privacy, April 27–29, 1981, Oakland, California [7].

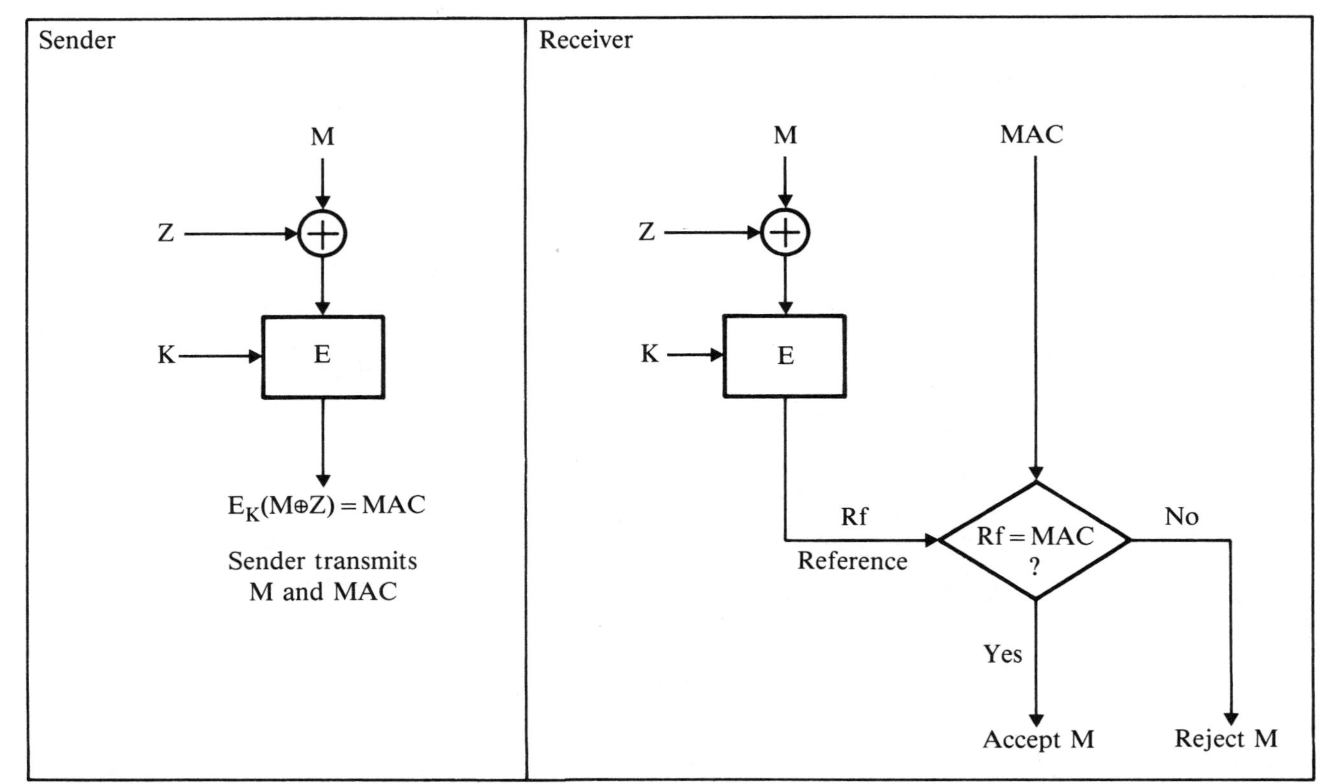

Legend:

K:	Authentication Key	56 Bits
M:	Message	64 Bits
MAC:	Message Authentication Code	64 Bits (Truncation Possible)
Rf:	Reference	64 Bits (Truncation Possible)
Z:	Initializing Vector	64 Bits

Figure 11-5. A Method for Achieving Message Authentication

Although the subject of auditability is not specifically addressed in this chapter, it should be understood that auditability is a prime objective of any well-designed security system. Commonly recognized auditing practices include accountability, cross checks, and sensitivity checks. The EFT security requirements listed below do not obviate the need to implement supportive security practices (e.g., auditing practices, access control, and physical security).

It is not possible to meet every one of the requirements. In some cases, particularly in the case of requirements 1 through 3, they should be considered goals more than requirements. Requirements 4 through 17 assume that cryptography is used (when appropriate) to protect the privacy of data and to authenticate data and users.

Requirement 1. The process of entering information at an EFT terminal must be protected; i.e., the integrity and secrecy of information entered into the EFT terminal must not be compromised as a consequence of the entry process. Furthermore, the information flow within a terminal must be protected.

Requirement 2. Information stored permanently or temporarily within an EFT terminal must be protected; i.e., the integrity of public information and the secrecy as well as integrity of private information must be assured.

Requirement 3. System managers and maintainers of the system (insiders) must be denied the opportunity to misuse the system accidentally or intentionally.

Requirement 4. Messages and system users must be authenticated.

Without personal verification, an opponent who may be a legitimate system user could pose as any system user. Without message authentication, an opponent could alter messages or inject previously communicated messages back into the communications network. This in turn could cause the system to provide some resource to the opponent for which he lacks authorization. Thus, an EFT system (and, for that matter, any communications system) will function securely only if users and messages are genuine.

In implementing authentication methods, the system must provide security measures (other than cryptography) to prevent subversion (e.g., bypassing) of authentication procedures. To the extent that subversion is prevented, the system is said to have the property of integrity.

Requirement 5. The security of the personal verification process implemented at one institution must not depend on security measures implemented at other institutions.

The requirement is based on the principle that a well-designed procedure for personal verification should be such that a user can be authenticated by the issuer without exposing or disclosing (to others) the secret information used in that process and without depending on others, including terminals, terminal control units, communications control units, and Electronic Data Processing (EDP) systems in the network (except the issuer's HPC) to protect the secrecy of that information. The personal verification process must be such that it is unaffected by a breach in security at another node.[15]

The requirement can be satisfied only if the cryptographic parameters, keys, and operations used to authenticate users are controlled and managed by the cardholder and card issuer. In that case, each issuer or institution can specify the security level it desires, independent of other institutions.

Verification could also be performed by some other node, such as a switch designated by the issuer. In this case, the security of the personal verification process would depend on security measures implemented at the designated node. Although employing the services of a designated node should be an option available to the issuer, it should never be a requirement in order to transact business in an interchange.

> *Requirement 6.* Each user must have only one set of user-supplied verification information, and it must be possible to initiate personal verification with this one set of information at any entry point to the system.

Otherwise, institutions could not join together in an interchange unless users were required to know or possess a different set of verification information for each different institution in the system. This would be very impractical.

> *Requirement 7.* The personal verification process must involve user remembered PINs and that process must be secure even if PINs have only four digits.

The PIN is the means by which the EFT system prevents a lost, stolen, or forged bank card from being used at an entry point by someone other than the true cardholder. However, a limitation which any design must cope with is that of human factors. It has been determined that, on the average, people cannot reliably remember a PIN which is longer than six digits. In addition, people prefer PINs as short as possible. In today's EFT systems, the PINs in use are normally between four and six digits long, which is a compromise between usability and security. It is important that this limitation be kept in mind when verification schemes are designed. (Normally, PIN length is a parameter that the issuer can select.) For instance, since verification is based on PIN and card information, it follows that PIN exhaustion (trying one PIN after the other) at the entry point interface is always feasible if card information is available, although six-digit PINs provide greater protection against such attacks than do four-digit PINs. However, exhaustive attacks should not be feasible anywhere else in the system (e.g., within the nodes via a programming interface).

[15] Security at the node designated to perform verification can be obtained through the use of a cryptographic facility (Chapter 4) or security module [8] (see also Implementation of Fraud Prevention Techniques, Chapter 10). With such an approach, important authentication information does not exist in the clear except within the protected confines of hardware. However, additional security measures are needed to prevent unauthorized users from directly exercising the cryptographic facility or security module.

Requirement 8. It must be unfeasible to derive user-remembered information solely from a bank card.

Since bank cards may become lost or stolen, the strength of the personal verification process would be diminished if a PIN could be derived from card information. For the same reason, an opponent who creates a bogus card should not also be able to create a valid corresponding PIN.

Requirement 9. Data can be authenticated only if sufficient nonsubvertible redundant information related to the data to be authenticated is introduced.

Assuming that the sender can generate arbitrary information (e.g., messages, passwords, etc.), the authenticator would have to treat any arbitrary pattern of bits as valid. In simple terms, data cannot always be authenticated by testing only the data. To authenticate random data, the authenticator must be provided with some additional, redundant information that is related to the information to be authenticated and cannot be subverted by an opponent.

The required redundant information may either be an integral part[16] of the data to be authenticated or it may be separate from it (defined here as an authentication code). In a communications system, analogously error-free transmission over a noisy channel requires the introduction of redundancy. Although, in this case, the redundancy is a countermeasure against the introduction of random (unintelligent) noise. In cryptographic applications, one is additionally concerned with the effects of deliberate tampering (intelligent noise) introduced by an intruder.

Requirement 10. Personal verification and message authentication require a reference to be available to the authenticator at the time authentication takes place. This reference, or the process used to generate the reference, must be defined and agreed upon in advance. It must be such that the integrity of the reference (and sometimes its secrecy) or the process that generates the reference or both can be assured by the authenticator.

The authentication process requires a comparison of two quantities (directly or indirectly). If the two quantities are equal, or correlate properly, the quantity to be authenticated is considered genuine; otherwise, it is not. At least one of these two quantities must be determined by the authenticator, and in this discussion, that quantity is called the reference.

Requirement 11. When a personal authentication code is used, it must be a function of user ID, the authentication parameter associated with

[16] For example, consider the (not necessarily practical) case where messages are formed by using only a character set of 36 symbols (A thru Z and 0 thru 9) and each character is represented by 8 bits. In that case, only 36 out of a possible 256 plaintext characters are used. A received message is accepted only if each decrypted character is in the set of 36 valid plaintext characters.

that ID, and a secret authentication key managed, controlled, and known only to the authenticator (issuer, switch, or terminal).

The EFT procedure or protocol must ensure that forged values of PAC will be unacceptable to the authenticator. It must not be possible to subvert the process of personal verification by supplying forged parameters or altering or replacing stored system parameters. This can be accomplished with a secret authentication key that relates PAC to the secret user-supplied information used for authentication. The relationship may actually be one that relates PAC to AP, and hence relates PAC to secret user-supplied information indirectly since AP depends on secret user-supplied information. The key permits valid PACs to be created only by those so authorized.

If a verification table is used by the authenticator and the table is such that stored information cannot be changed, or cannot be changed without detection, then a copy of the user's secret user-supplied information, or AP value, can be stored directly in the table. In that case, a secret authentication key and PAC values are not needed.

Requirement 12. Information included in a transaction request message sent from the entry point to the issuer, which the issuer will use to validate the identity of the user initiating the transaction, must be formed from secret user-supplied information. It may or may not also be formed from nonsecret information, but it must not be formed from secret information known to anyone other than the user or the user and issuer.

This is the only way in which the personal verification process at one institution can be completely isolated from other institutions (see Requirement 5). It also implies that secret cipher keys used in the personal verification process by each institution are not shared with other institutions. Note that an EFT system in which PINs are protected via system keys would not meet this requirement.

Requirement 13. Knowledge of a transaction request message sent from an entry point to the issuer, which includes information that the issuer will use to validate the identity of the user initiating that transaction, must not allow an exposure of secret user-supplied information. And it must not permit equivalent user-supplied information to be derived that would allow an opponent masquerading as a customer of some financial institution to be verified by the system.[17]

Since users may initiate EFT transactions at any entry point in an interchange, information included in the transaction message which the issuer will use to

[17] Requirement 13, however, applies only if user-supplied verification information can be forged or duplicated, e.g., information the user knows (PIN) or has (personal key). On the other hand, if a user is identified by something he does (signature) or is (fingerprint), then duplication of that information may be difficult. Therefore, secrecy in this latter case is not critical. But a solution with PINs, or PINs and personal keys, is pursued here because such an approach is more apt to be used in the foreseeable future.

authenticate that user (e.g., an AP value or a MAC, whose computation involves secret user-supplied information) will often be transmitted through networks under the control of someone other than the issuer. A well-designed procedure for personal verification should not assume that the secrecy or integrity of transaction request messages can be maintained by others except the user and issuer. Therefore, knowledge of data contained in the transaction request message (including the generated MAC) should not expose secret user-supplied information nor should it permit equivalent user-supplied information to be derived that would permit an opponent to be verified by the system.

> *Requirement 14.* Secret user-remembered information (PIN) must be supplemented by additional secret user-supplied information.[18] The information sent from an entry point to the issuer, which the issuer will use to validate the identity of a user, must be a one-way function of the PIN and additional secret user-supplied information.

With short PINs (e.g., 4 to 6 digits), there are insufficient independent secret bits available for computing an authentication parameter (AP) that will prevent recovery of the PIN via exhaustive methods. To overcome this, additional independent secret bits must be made available. However, because of requirement 12, the additional independent secret bits must be user-supplied. At the same time, because of the short PIN, the magnitude and random nature of the additional required secret bits precludes them from being committed to memory. Therefore, since each user has a bank card for initiating transactions at the entry point, it is assumed that the additional secret user-supplied bits (defined to be KP for personal key) are stored on the bank card. Thus, the card must provide storage for an additional quantity to serve as KP (a 56-bit key is assumed). The security issues involved with storing a KP on the bank card (e.g., whether a KP stored on a bank card can be maintained as a secret parameter) are taken up later (see the section entitled Threats to the Secrecy of a Key Stored on a Magnetic Stripe Card).

Since the information used by the issuer to validate the identity of a user must not depend on secret information other than that supplied by the user (requirement 12), and knowledge of that information must not expose secret user-supplied information or allow equivalent user-supplied information to be determined (requirement 13), it follows that this information must be a one-way function of user-supplied information.

> *A function f is a* one-way function *if, for any argument x in the domain of f, it is easy to compute the corresponding value* $y = f(x)$*; yet for almost all y in the range of f, it is computationally infeasible, given a value of y and knowledge of f, to calculate any x whatsoever with the property that* $f(x) = y$*. It is important to note that a function is defined which is not invertible from a computational point of view, but whose*

[18] It is assumed here that verification is based on something the user has (data stored on a magnetic stripe identification card) or knows (a password). Since these data can be forged, they must be kept secret. However, this would not apply if a nonforgeable input parameter were employed (e.g., a fingerprint or the dynamics of a handwritten signature).

noninvertibility is entirely different from that normally encountered in mathematics. A function f is normally called "noninvertible" when the inverse of a point y is not unique; i.e., there exist distinct points x1 and x2 such that f(x1) = y = f(x2). This is not the sort of inversion difficulty that is required here. Rather, it must be overwhelmingly difficult, given a value y and knowledge of f, to calculate any x whatsoever with the property that f(x) = y [2].

The complexity of DES makes it suitable for designing one-way functions. About 56 independent bits of secret input information are needed to obtain a one-way function with DES.[19] The nonsecret output of the one-way function must also be about 56 bits. In subsequent discussions, the one-way function approach will also be defined as the *noninvertible mode;* all other approaches will be referred to as *invertible modes.*[20]

An example of a one-way function of secret user-supplied information is AP = $E_{KP \oplus PIN}$(ID). Advantage is taken here of the fact that, for a strong algorithm, knowledge of plaintext (ID) and corresponding ciphertext (AP) does not permit deduction of the key (KP ⊕ PIN). Thus KP and PIN cannot be obtained from AP and ID. Also a KP* and PIN* cannot be deduced such that AP = $E_{KP^* \oplus PIN^*}$(ID). In that case, AP is a one-way function of KP and PIN.

A more detailed discussion of AP values and one-way functions is given in Appendix D. For the remainder of this chapter, the discussion will be concerned mainly with AP values that are one-way functions of the user's ID and secret user-supplied information, although the computation may also involve nonsecret system-supplied information.

Requirement 15. For message authentication, the authentication code must be a function of the message, a secret authentication key, and time-dependent information. The authentication key must always be known by or accessible to the sender.

Since messages are unpredictable, as far as information content is concerned, message authentication codes (MACs) cannot be precalculated; they must be calculated dynamically. Each MAC is transmitted to the authenticator together with the data that produce it. An opponent is prevented from generating a MAC, since a secret quantity (unknown to the opponent) is used in its generation. Since the procedure or cryptographic algorithm is public, as assumed here, that secret quantity must be a cryptographic key.

Furthermore, the MAC must be time-dependent to permit detection of

[19] As a rule, with approximately 32 independent key bits, the key can be recovered relatively easily using exhaustive methods. As the number of key bits increases, the key may or may not be recoverable depending upon the sophistication and resources of an opponent.

[20] Two other definitions that are closely related but should not be confused with the definitions of invertible and noninvertible functions are those of reversible and irreversible encryption [9]. *Reversible encryption* is defined as a cryptographic transformation of plaintext to ciphertext such that the ciphertext can be converted back to the original plaintext. *Irreversible encryption* is defined as a cryptographic transformation of plaintext to ciphertext such that the ciphertext cannot be converted back to the original plaintext by other than exhaustive methods.

previously transmitted data (stale messages). Requirement 15 differs slightly from requirement 11 because the PAC is time-invariant. Recall that personal verification information (e.g., PINs) remains constant for relatively long periods of time.

Requirement 16. Time dependence in the message authentication code requires that a common time reference be established between the communicants. Furthermore, the receiver must be able to determine the reference's validity independently.

As previously discussed, time dependence allows the receiver to detect whether messages have been deleted or prevented from arriving, and whether stale messages (messages recorded on a prior occasion) have been injected back into the transmission path. But time-dependent quantities per se are not enough to ensure that the receiver rejects stale messages. In addition, the receiver must be able to establish independently the validity of the time reference. A weak procedure would result if the time reference were supplied to the receiver by the sender. In that case an opponent could also do the same and trick the receiver into accepting a previously sent message.

There are two ways in which a time reference could be established between the sender and the receiver: The sender could request a time reference (e.g., a randomly generated quantity) from the receiver, in which case the reference is under exclusive control of the receiver. Or the sender and receiver could maintain a common time reference (e.g., a sequential counter), in which case the reference is under control of both the sender and receiver. For example, a time reference stored on the bank card in a writeable storage element could be automatically updated with each use of the card. The issuer, on the other hand, could track the time reference by storing it in the verification table. The user and issuer could also establish a time reference via some means not under their direct control (e.g., by using a date and time-of-day).

Requirement 17. The security of the message authentication process implemented at one institution must not depend on security measures implemented at other institutions.

The requirement is based on the principle that a well-designed procedure for message authentication should be such that the process of authenticating transaction requests sent from the user to the issuer, and the process of authenticating transaction responses sent from the issuer to the originating terminal, can be effected without exposing the secret information used in these processes and without depending on other institutions and network nodes to protect the secrecy of information used in these processes. This means that message authentication between the user and issuer and between the issuer and originating terminal must be unaffected by the security or lack thereof at any other EDP system or terminal in the interchange.

Comments on the EFT Security Requirements

The reader may note that the six security principles recommended by Kaufman and Auerbach [10] are a subset of the requirements developed here. The basic idea of employing one-way functions for personal verification was discussed in references 11 and 12. The reader may also note that some requirements are derived from preceding requirements. This allows the requirements to be developed in an orderly and progressive manner.

Although there is bound to be some disagreement over what constitutes a true security requirement, the intent here has been to develop a set of requirements that will tend toward maximizing security. In the end, financial institutions and designers and developers of cryptographic systems must weigh their own EFT security requirements against those developed here and decide which are mandatory, which are only desirable, and which are possibly unnecessary. One must always balance the probability and gravity of harm, should it occur, against the cost of implementing sufficient measures to prevent that harm.

PERSONAL VERIFICATION IN THE ON-LINE MODE

There are many ways of using PINs and personal keys to achieve personal verification. Several different designs and design tradeoffs are considered next.

In the design of a procedure for personal verification, the PINs and personal keys may be considered as parameters of the problem, where "secret" and "time-invariant" are attributes of these parameters. The significance of secret versus nonsecret and time-variant versus time-invariant parameters in the design of cryptographic systems has already been discussed. There is, however, another parameter attribute that is important to the design of personal verification procedures, i.e., whether the parameter is *independent* or *dependent*. An independent parameter is one whose value does not depend on any other parameter. It may be arbitrarily selected by the user, systems personnel, or the system. A dependent parameter is one whose value depends on one or more other parameters. Its value is derived from the parameter or parameters upon which it depends.

Independent PINs and personal keys can provide greater security than dependent PINs and personal keys. An independent parameter is not automatically compromised as the result of a compromise of other parameters in a cryptographic system, whereas a dependent parameter is always compromised whenever the secret parameter or parameters and algorithm (if secret) used to compute the parameter are compromised. With an independent parameter, every bit of the parameter must be stored. On the other hand, a dependent parameter can be computed dynamically as needed and thus storage requirements may be substantially reduced. For example, PINs could be derived from the corresponding IDs using a secret system key. This permits the system to regenerate PINs rather than store them in a table. However, such a choice of dependent parameters might be unacceptable because users may want to select their own PINs, and institutions may want to provide this option to their customers.

Note that in the examples below, it is assumed (although not specifically shown) that authentication parameters are sent to the issuer in the transaction request messages and message authentication techniques are used to prevent replay of intercepted AP values.

Personal Verification with Dependent PINs and Dependent Personal Keys

PINs and personal keys can be made dependent variables, for example, by deriving them from users' IDs via a *PIN-generating key* (KPN) and a *personal-key-generating key* (KPG) as indicated by the following relationships:

$$\text{PINi} = E_{\text{KPN}}(\text{IDi}) \quad (11\text{-}1)$$

$$\text{KPi} = D_{\text{KPG}}(\text{IDi}) \quad (11\text{-}2)$$

Encipherment with KPN and decipherment with KPG permit the use of only a single secret key, KPN = KPG.

During the initialization process, the issuer selects KPN and KPG and then produces and issues personal identification numbers, personal keys, and bank cards to each user. ID and KP are stored on the bank card, whereas PIN must be remembered by the user. KPN and KPG are retained by the issuer so that each user's PIN and personal key can be regenerated during the process of personal verification.

A procedure that could be used for verification of a user is as follows (Figure 11-6). User i enters IDi, KPi, and PINi at an entry point (EFT terminal). The EFT terminal computes $\text{APi} = E_{\text{KPi} \oplus \text{PINi}}(\text{IDi})$ and sends IDi and APi to the issuer (via an interchange if necessary). The issuer computes a PINi of reference and a KPi of reference (via Equations 11-1 and 11-2) from the received IDi and the stored values of KPN and KPG. IDi and the derived values of PINi and KPi are then used to compute an APi of reference, or reference Rfi for short. Rfi and the received APi are compared for equality. If Rfi = APi, then IDi is accepted (i.e., the identity of the user is accepted as IDi); otherwise, IDi is rejected.

Deriving PINs and personal keys from seed keys, KPN and KPG, has the disadvantage that it is awkward to reissue new PINs and personal keys.[21] Changing KPN or KPG causes every user's PIN or personal key to change, and thus requires the issuer to reissue a PIN and a bank card to each user and update the associated account file in the issuer's data base. Changing a user's identifier affects only that one user, but requires the issuer to close and open a new account. Compromise of both KPN and KPG allows a global attack against all users whose PINs and KPs were generated with these keys.

[21] To change a user's PIN, one could define the ith updated PIN as the ith encipherment of ID under KPN. However, in that case the system must be able to track the value of i (e.g., by storing it in a verification table).

Initialization Process at Issuer:

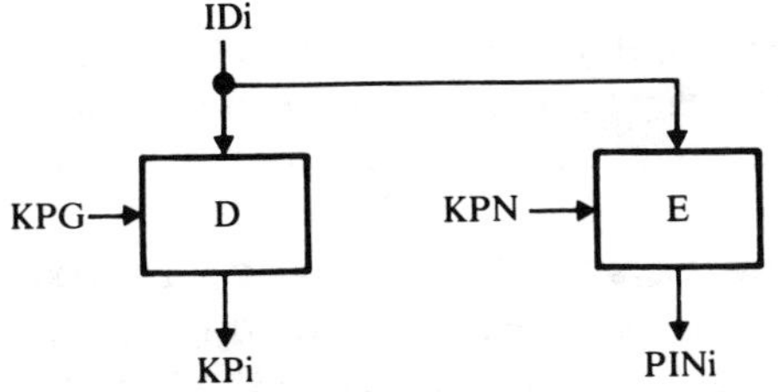

Stored on bank card

Note: Issuer selects KPG and KPN and computes PINi and KPi for each user.

Initiation of Personal Verification at Entry Point:

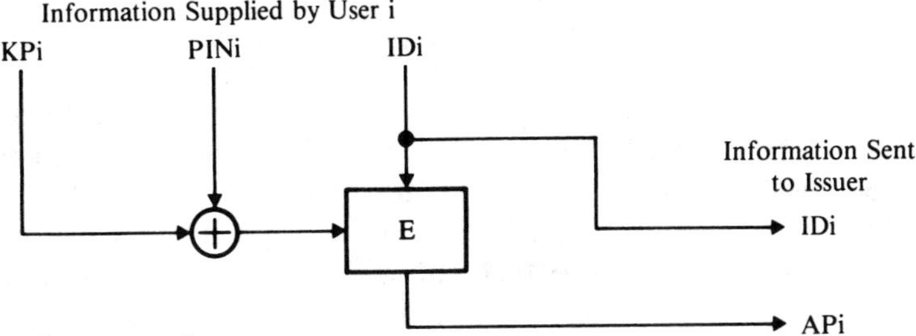

Verification Process at Issuer:

Information Received from Entry Point

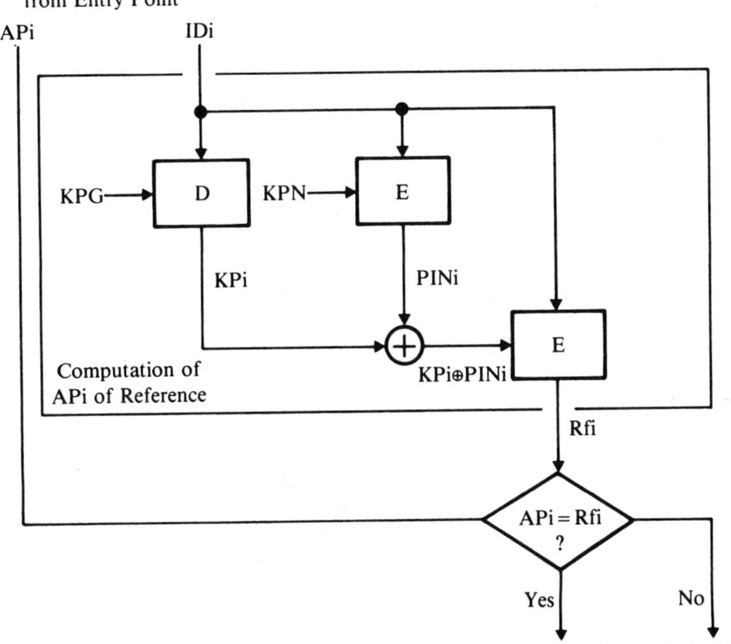

Legend:

KPN:	PIN Generating Key	Independent	Secret
KPG:	Personal-Key Generating Key	Independent	Secret
IDi:	User i's Identifier	Independent	Nonsecret
PINi:	User i's PIN	Dependent	Secret
KPi:	User i's Personal Key	Dependent	Secret
APi:	User i's Authentication Parameter	Dependent	Nonsecret

Figure 11-6. Personal Verification using a PIN Generating KEY (KPN) and a Personal-Key Generating Key (KPG)

The verification procedure does have the advantage that there is no requirement for a personal authentication code (PAC) to be stored on the bank card or in a verification table, i.e., only ID, AP, and the secret system keys are needed.

If banks wish to allow users to choose their own PINs, the scheme could be redefined as follows. From the user's specified PIN, a quantity (defined as the offset) is generated such that the offset equals the modulo 2 addition of PIN and E_{KPN} (ID), where E_{KPN} (ID) is a system-generated personal identification number (defined as pin, Figure 11-7). The offset, which is equal to PIN $\oplus$ pin, is recorded on the user's bank card. When a user is identified to the system, the entered PIN is added modulo 2 to the offset to reproduce the correct dependent value of E_{KPN} (ID) = pin.[22] Thereafter, pin and KP are used together as the basis for user verification.

A disadvantage of this method is that PIN $\oplus$ offset is a constant (C = pin) as long as ID and KPN are not changed. For example, if an opponent ever obtained the PIN and offset, he could calculate C. From then on, the particular ID is compromised even if the user changes his PIN. Note that changing PIN will only change the offset but will not affect pin. Furthermore, since the offset must be stored on the bank card, storage for an additional bit pattern is now required.

Personal Verification with Independent PINs and Independent Personal Keys

When PINs and personal keys are independent variables, they cannot be dynamically regenerated. Therefore, PIN and Personal key generating keys cannot generally be used securely. (The procedure described in Figure 11-7

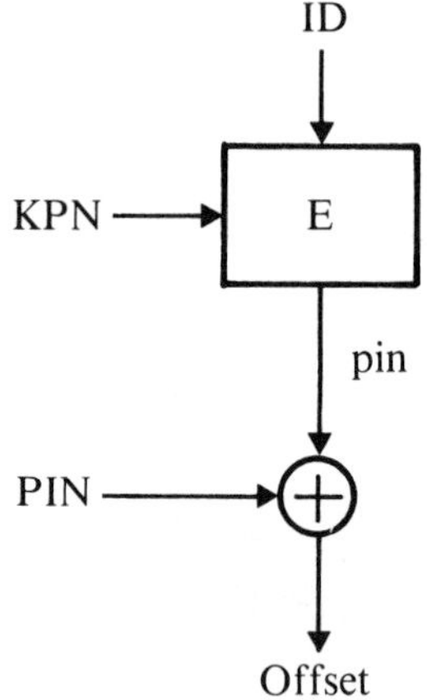

KPN: pin Generating Key

Figure 11-7. Personal Verification Using a PIN Offset

[22] With current magnetic stripe cards, the modulo 2 addition is performed in the EFT terminal. With an intelligent secure card, the operation would be performed on the card.

employed a PIN generating key, and independent PINs were allowed by defining an offset. However, such a scheme has certain security weaknesses, as discussed above.) Hence, a different procedure for personal verification must be used.

One approach is for the issuer to store each user's independently calculated authentication parameter, AP = $E_{KP \oplus PIN}$(ID), in a verification table. Selecting a particular entry in the table is accomplished by using ID as shown in Figure 11-8. Thus, the dynamic computation producing APi of reference, as shown above in Figure 11-6, is replaced by one in which IDi is used to look up the corresponding APi of reference in a table.

Storage of information in a verification table at the issuer can be avoided if an equivalent amount of information is distributed among the users and stored on the bank cards. This additional information, defined here as a personal authentication code (PAC), can be computed using the relationship

$$\text{PACi} = E_{KA}(\text{APi}) = E_{KA}(E_{KPi \oplus PINi}(\text{IDi})) \qquad (11\text{-}3)$$

where KA is a secret *authentication key* known only to the issuer.

A user is now verified when the correct (AP, PAC) pair is supplied. However, the procedure relates PAC to ID only indirectly. Although AP is checked via the procedure, ID itself is not explicitly checked. Thus if the authenticator receives IDj, APi, and PACi instead of IDi, APi, and PACi, there is no way to determine that IDi was changed to IDj—the generated PACi of reference will check only that APi and PACi are a valid pair.

This can be remedied by coupling PAC to AP and ID be defining PAC as follows:

$$\text{PACi} = E_{KA}(E_{KA}(\text{IDi}) \oplus \text{APi}) \qquad (11\text{-}4)$$

If IDi and APi are 8-byte blocks, PACi can be thought of as being produced by encrypting IDi and APi using a form of ciphertext feedback. Thus, PACi validates both APi and the correspondance of APi to IDi. IDi and APi are accepted as valid only if they generate, via KA, a PACi of reference equal to the received PACi.

Since PAC is precomputed, personal verification based solely on the triple (ID, AP, PAC) *without any additional message authentication* is by definition exposed to an active attack wherein previously recorded information is used to modify a transmitted message. For example, an intruder who has previously intercepted the triple (IDi, APi, PACi) can masquerade as user i by entering IDi and any bogus values for KPi, PINi, and PACi at the entry point and then replacing the bogus triple (IDi, AP*, PAC*) transmitted in the transaction request message with the previously recorded triple (IDi, APi, PACi) via an active attack.

Message authentication, which provides a defense against message alteration and the introduction of stale messages, solves the problem. In that case, the relationship between ID and AP is now checked via the MAC and, therefore, personal verification can be based on either Equation 11-3 or 11-4.

During the initialization process (Figure 11-9), PINs are selected by either

Initiation of Personal Verification at Entry Point (Computation on the Intelligent Secure Card):

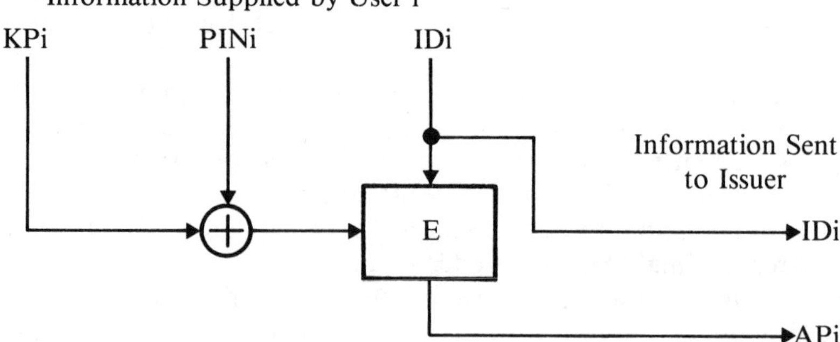

Verification Process at Issuer:

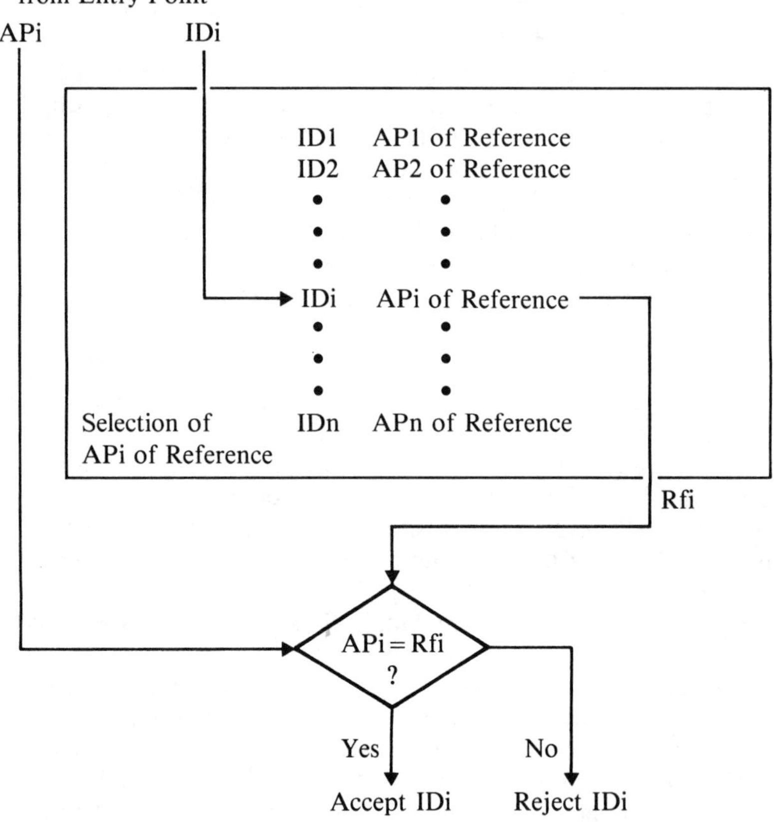

Legend:

IDi:	User i's Identifier	Independent	Nonsecret
PINi:	User i's PIN	Dependent	Secret
KPi:	User i's Personal Key	Dependent	Secret
APi:	User i's Authentication Parameter	Dependent	Nonsecret

Figure 11-8. Personal Verification using Table Lookup

Initialization Process at Issuer:

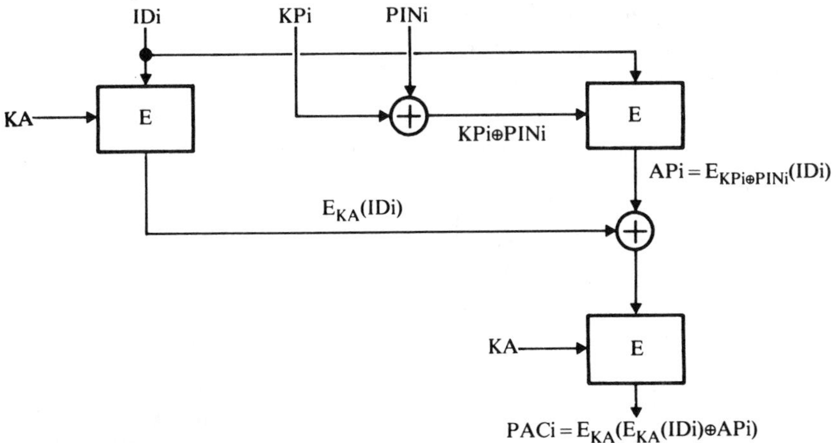

Notes: IDi, KPi, and PACi are recorded on the bank card of the ith user. Issuer or user selects PINi. Issuer selects KPi, records it on the bank card, and computes APi. Issuer also selects KA and computes PACi.

Initiation of Personal Verification at the Entry Point:

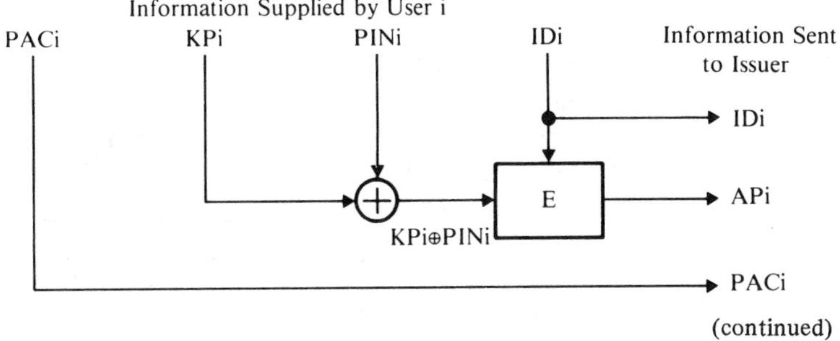

(continued)

Legend:

KA:	Authentication Key	Independent	Secret
IDi:	User i's Identifier	Independent	Nonsecret
PINi:	User i's PIN	Dependent	Secret
KPi:	User i's Personal Key	Dependent	Secret
APi:	User i's Authentication Parameter	Dependent	Nonsecret
PACi:	User i's Personal Authentication Code	Dependent	Nonsecret

Figure 11-9. Personal Verification Using a Secret Authentication Key and Personal Authentication Codes (cont'd next page)

Verification Process at Issuer:

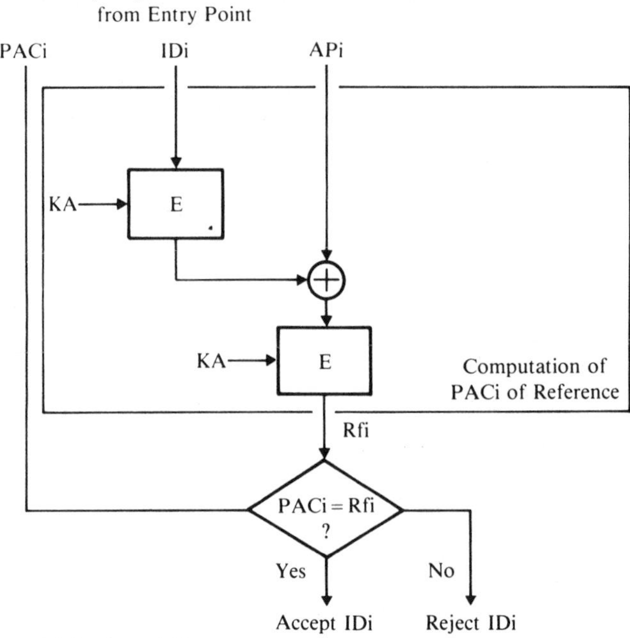

Figure 11-9 (cont'd)

the user or the issuer whereas personal keys are selected by the issuer (to prevent misuse of KPs, see the section entitled Objections to the PIN/ Personal Key Approach). The issuer also selects KA and computes APi = $E_{KPi \oplus PINi}$(IDi)) and PACi = E_{KA} (E_{KA} (IDi) $\oplus$ APi for each user. KA is retained by the issuer so that each user's IDi and APi can be checked against PACi, which is stored on the bank card.

The process of user verification (Figure 11-9) requires user i to enter IDi, KPi, PINi, and PACi at an entry point (EFT terminal). The EFT terminal computes APi = $E_{KPi \oplus PINi}$(IDi)) and sends IDi, APi, and PACi to the issuer–via an interchange if necessary. The issuer computes a PACi of reference, or Rfi for short (via Equation 11-3 or 11-4, as appropriate), from the received values of IDi and APi using the stored value of KA. Next, Rfi and the received PACi are compared for equality. If Rfi = PACi, then (IDi, APi) is accepted as valid and the identity of the user is accepted as IDi. Otherwise, (IDi, APi) is rejected and the user claiming IDi is denied system services.

The approaches in Figures 11-6 and 11-9 are similar in some respects and different in others. Neither requires a verification table, since their references are generated using one or more system keys. In the first case, KPG and KPN are used to generate personal keys and PINs, and in the second case, KA is used to compute PAC. Both approaches provide comparable security because they are equally vulnerable as far as compromise of system keys is concerned. In either implementation, compromise of the system keys KPG and KPN, or KA, will allow global attacks against any user of the system.

The major difference in the two approaches is that an additional quantity,

PAC, must be stored on the bank card when independent KPs and PINs are used. Independence is therefore achieved at the expense of extra storage on the bank card.

Although only three examples of on-line personal verification have been given, variations of these, as well as other designs, are possible. For example, a different KA could be defined for each user, in which case a verification table would be required to store the KAs. Personal authentication codes could also be used to provide cryptographic separation among institutions in an interchange supporting off-line verification. For example, each institution could define two authentication keys for off-line verification. A first key, KAlocal, could be used only to verify an institution's own users (i.e., it would not be shared with other institutions). A second key, KAremote, could be shared and used by all other institutions to verify that institution's users. Such a protocol would require two PACs to be stored on the bank card, one calculated using KAlocal and the other calculated using KAremote. Each entry point would be required to store its KAlocal key and the KA-remote key for each other institution in the interchange.

Minimizing Card Storage Requirements

In any scheme not requiring a verification table, the specification of at least one authentication key is mandatory. If, in addition, the PINs are selected independently, additional storage must be provided on the card for a personal authentication code, as in the method of Figure 11-9. In that method, KP as well as PIN are independent variables and KP and PAC are stored on the bank card. Since security requires that KP be selected by the issuer to eliminate misuse of personal keys (see section Objections to the PIN/Personal Key Approach), it is not really necessary to make KP an independent variable. It is shown next that it is possible, by giving up the freedom to choose KP independently, to reduce storage requirements on the bank card by making KP dependent on PAC and accepting a shorter PAC length (on the order of 16 to 32 bits). Assume that

$$\text{AP} = \text{E}_{\text{KP} \oplus \text{PIN}}(\text{ID}) \tag{11-5}$$

$$\text{PAC} = \text{leftmost m bits of } \text{E}_{\text{KA}}(\text{E}_{\text{KA}}(\text{ID}) \oplus \text{AP})) \tag{11-6}$$

Storage on the bank card can be reduced by generating PAC dynamically from KP.

$$\text{PAC} = \text{leftmost m bits of } \text{E}_{\text{KP}}(\text{ID}) \tag{11-7}$$

The price paid for this advantage is that only certain KPs will satisfy all three equations (11-5, 11-6, and 11-7). Furthermore, due to the complexity of the equations, only trial-and-error methods (i.e., key exhaustion) can be used to generate proper KPs. If the PAC length is m bits, the average number of iterations to find an acceptable KP is 2^{m-1}. To make exhaustion feasible, m should be chosen less than 32.

For analysis of the generation of KPs by the issuer, let

$$\text{APtrial} = E_{\text{KPtrial} \oplus \text{PIN}}(\text{ID}) \tag{11-8}$$

$$\begin{aligned} \text{C1} &= \text{the leftmost m bits of } E_{\text{KA}}(E_{\text{KA}}(\text{ID} \oplus \text{APtrial})) \\ &\quad (= \text{PACtrial}) \end{aligned} \tag{11-9}$$

$$\text{C2} = \text{the leftmost m bits of } E_{\text{KPtrial}}(\text{ID}) \tag{11-10}$$

Due to Equation 11-7, the constraint C1 = C2 is now introduced.

For the generation of KPs that satisfy the condition C1 = C2, trial values of KP (KPtrial) are used for a selected PIN with the corresponding ID to generate a trial AP according to Equation 11-8. A trial PAC (C1 = PACtrial) is then computed from the trial AP using Equation 11-9. A trial value of C2 is also calculated using Equation 11-10. The KPtrial is accepted only if C1 = C2; otherwise, the KPtrial is rejected and the process is repeated (Figure 11-10). Assuming that the probability of a match (C1 = C2) at each trial is 2^{-m}, it takes an average of $2^m/2$ trials to find an acceptable KP.

Once an acceptable KP is found, the initialization process is complete. To initiate the verification process at the entry point requires that AP = $E_{\text{KP} \oplus \text{PIN}}(\text{ID})$ and PAC = the leftmost m bits of $E_{\text{KP}}(\text{ID})$ be generated and transmitted together with the ID to the issuer (Figure 11-11). At the authenticating node (the issuer), the authentication key, KA, is used to generate a PAC of reference, i.e.,

$$\text{PAC of Reference} = \text{leftmost m bits of } E_{\text{KA}}(E_{\text{KA}}(\text{ID}) \oplus \text{AP})$$

Only if this quantity is equal to the received PACi will the user (IDi) be accepted. Otherwise, the user will be rejected (Figure 11-11).

This approach requires, again, proper message authentication. Otherwise, any intercepted triple (ID, AP, PAC) sent to the authenticating node would authenticate the user (Figure 11-11). An opponent could thus masquerade as the user associated with the intercepted triple.

But even if proper message authentication is in place, an opponent could attempt to impersonate another user (say user i) by entering IDi (assumed known) and using a method of trial and error, as follows: an arbitrary personal key and PIN (i.e., KP* and PIN*) are entered so that the entry point calculates AP* = $E_{\text{KP*} \oplus \text{PIN*}}(\text{IDi})$ and PAC* = $E_{\text{KP*}}(\text{IDi})$ (Figure 11-11). At the authenticating node, Rf* = $E_{\text{KA}}(\text{IDi}) \oplus \text{AP*})$ is calculated and checked for equality with the leftmost m bits of PAC*. Since the probability is 2^{-m} that these (fake) quantities are indeed identical, about 2^{m-1} trials are required for the attack to succeed. In the described attack the opponent must manually enter the trial values of KP* and PIN*, which means that the time per trial is measured in seconds. The value of m is selected so that $2^{m-1} \times$ (time per trial) is sufficiently large.

A more serious threat arises if insiders are able to repeatedly exercise the operation that calculates the PAC of reference (Rf in Figure 11-11). In that case, the opponent selects a trial key, KPtrial, and calculates a set of APs by

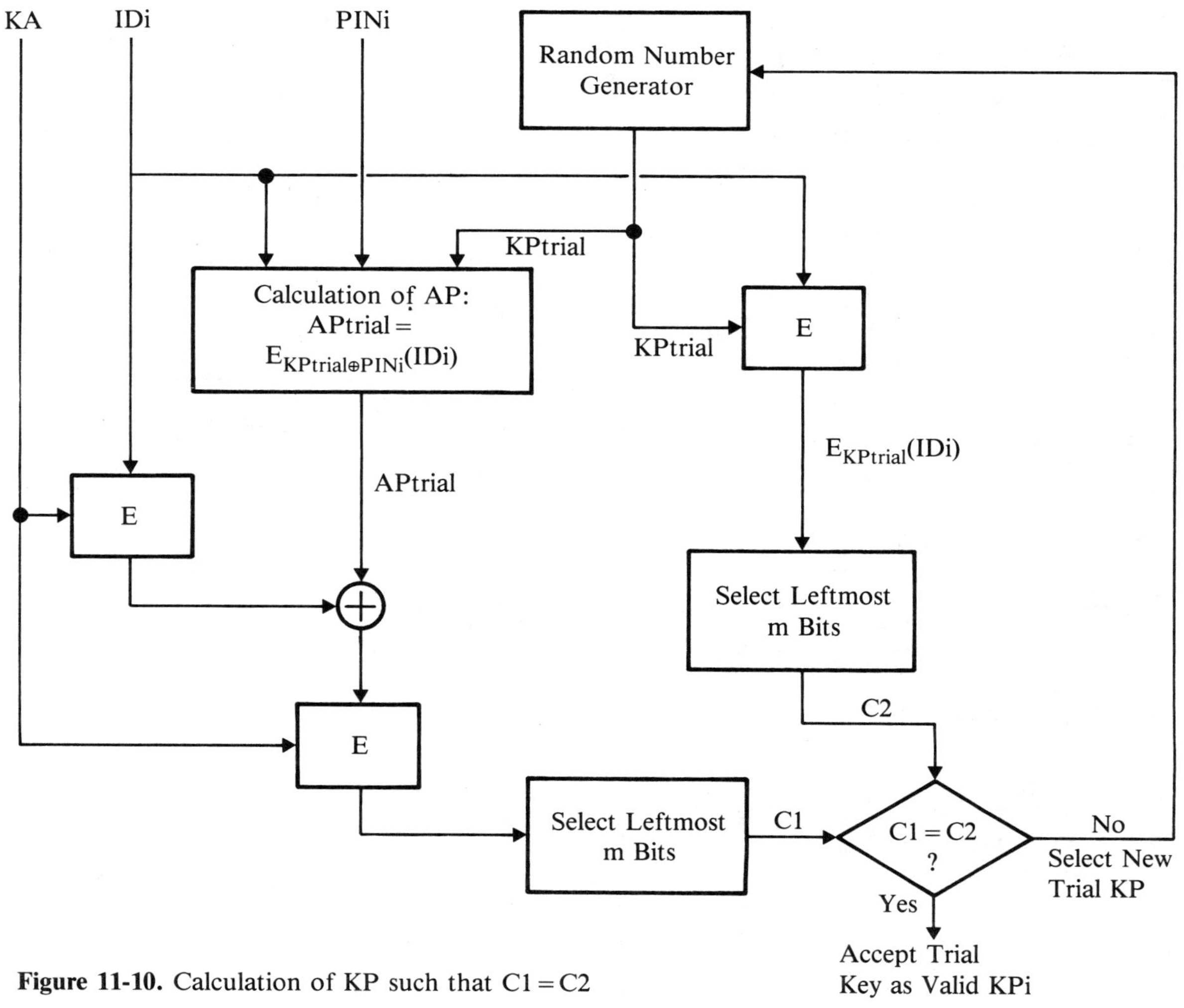

Figure 11-10. Calculation of KP such that C1 = C2

exhausting PIN space (i.e., $\{APj = E_{KPtrial \oplus PINj}(IDi); j = 1,2, \ldots, n\}$ where n is the number of possible PIN combinations). In addition, PACtrial = $E_{KPtrial}(IDi)$ is calculated. The set of APs is then used together with IDi and PACtrial to calculate the set $Q = \{Rfj; j = 1, 2, \ldots, n\}$, where Rfj = $E_{KA}(IDi) \oplus APj$. If Q contains an element Rfj such that Rfj = PACtrial, then the attack succeeds, because in that case an equivalent PIN and KP are found for the IDi. If no match is found, the procedure is repeated using a different KPtrial. This insider attack will succeed only if references can be calculated at will. One way to detect and thwart such an attack is to log all unsuccessful validations. Since most of the time (in an honest environment) the validations will succeed, the statistic of unsuccessful validations is a useful audit tool. The lesson to be learned from this threat analysis is the following: whenever the number of trials required by the issuer to generate certain parameters is small, extreme care must be taken to ensure that an opponent cannot benefit from this efficient computational procedure in the same way. By restricting the opponent to attack the entry point, the described method for reducing card storage can be made sufficiently strong. The value of m is thus chosen so that the issuer can carry out the required

Initialization Process at Issuer:

Notes: Issuer or user selects PINi. Issuer selects KA, generates KPi (as in Figure 11-10), and records KPi on the bank card.

Initiation of Personal Verification at Entry Point:

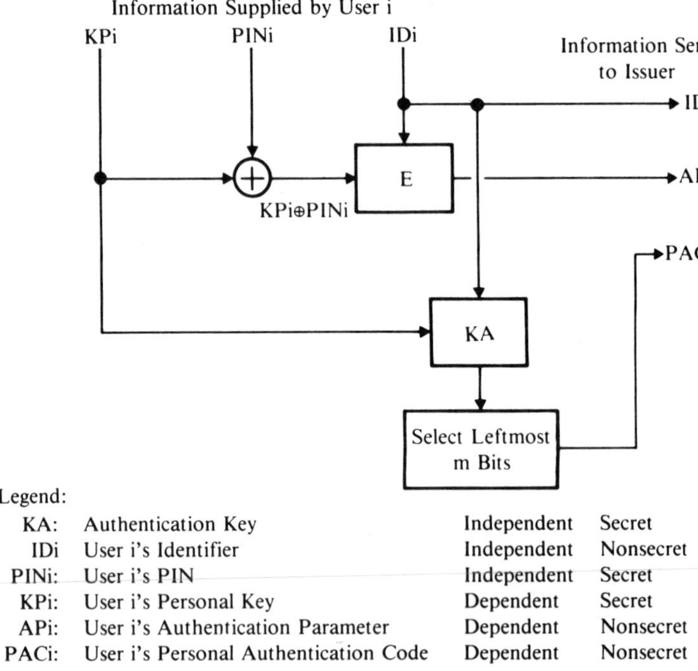

Legend:

KA:	Authentication Key	Independent	Secret
IDi	User i's Identifier	Independent	Nonsecret
PINi:	User i's PIN	Independent	Secret
KPi:	User i's Personal Key	Dependent	Secret
APi:	User i's Authentication Parameter	Dependent	Nonsecret
PACi:	User i's Personal Authentication Code	Dependent	Nonsecret

Figure 11-11. Personal Verification Using a Secret Authentication Key and Personal Authentication Codes

Verification Process at Issuer:

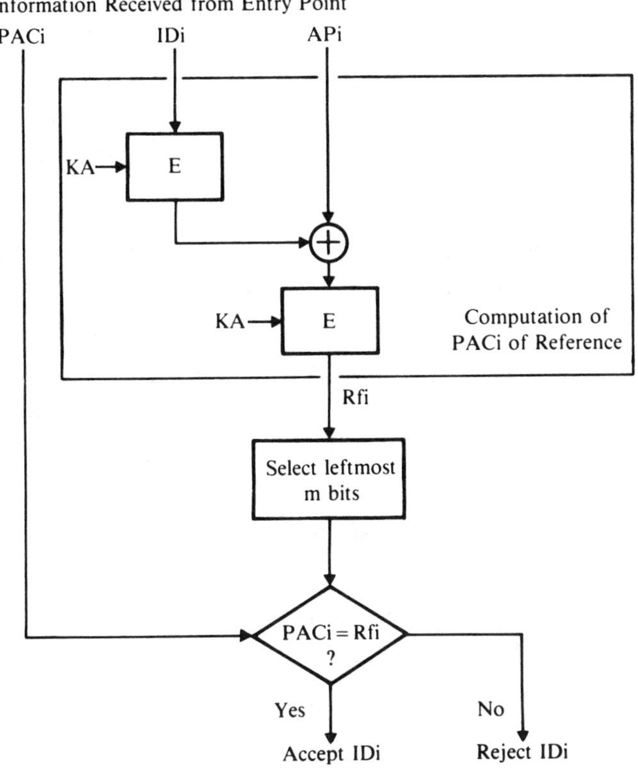

Figure 11-11 (cont'd)

computations efficiently using a high-speed computer whereas an opponent is forced to use a much slower procedure of trial and error involving a manual entry of trial parameters at the entry point.

PERSONAL VERIFICATION IN THE OFF-LINE AND OFF-HOST MODES

When personal verification is performed by a terminal, the process is said to operate in the off-line mode. When a terminal and a communications control unit (Figure 11-1) cooperate to perform personal verification, the process is said to operate in the off-host mode. In the off-line mode, the entry point must additionally assume the role of issuer. It must perform personal verification and manage transaction requests, although it is relieved of other tasks such as opening new accounts and assigning and selecting PINs.

The discussion in this section demonstrates that personal verification using the on-line mode is more secure than either the off-line or off-host modes of operation. The reason for this is that the on-line mode does not involve widely distributed keys as do the other modes. With the off-line and off-host modes, it is not possible to isolate the personal verification process to a single institution. To show why security is reduced in this case, methods are discussed wherein personal verification is performed by a node different from the issuer's node.

Cryptographic system designs for off-line and off-host banking transactions are more straightforward than those for comparable on-line banking transactions. For instance, in an off-line mode, there is no requirement for message authentication, since the entire procedure takes place at the entry point. However, because a terminal and a communications control unit do not, in general, have storage for a verification table, the possible designs are more limited. The following discussion assumes, therefore, that insufficient storage is available for a verification table. Hence, personal verification must be based on testing a preestablished relationship between the ID and secret information supplied by the user.

By definition, when personal verification is performed in the off-line or off-host mode, a widely distributed authentication key must be used to test the relationships among ID, secret user-supplied information, and PAC. If that key is a secret key (using the DES), its compromise globally affects the entire verification procedure. If that key is a public key (using a PKC), compromising its integrity compromises only the verification procedure at that one off-line or off-host location:

An attack against a PKC succeeds if the public key at the entry point is changed by an opponent who then enters a PAC calculated with the corresponding secret key. If the secret key used to compute user PACs is compromised, a global attack against all users is possible (as would be the case with a conventional algorithm). The advantage of the PKC, however, is that the secret key is not stored at the entry point.

Because the authentication key (whether it is a public or a private key) is widely distributed, the soundness of the off-line and off-host modes is questionable. In an interchange environment, for example, the authentication keys may be stored in thousands of terminals. However, the approach may be used safely in networks where the number of institutions and EFT terminals is small and where the EFT terminals are vault-like units. With such an implementation, protecting the secrecy or integrity of a key in the EFT terminal may be less of a problem than providing similar protection to a verification table or authentication key located at a host.

An important requirement of any off-line or off-host personal verification procedure is that a compromise of either of these modes should not compromise or severely weaken security in the on-line mode. (In the discussion it is assumed that both modes are implemented in the network.) In other words, compromising a secret key used in the off-line or off-host mode should not jeopardize secret user-supplied information essential to on-line personal verification.

Personal Verification with System-Selected PINs Employing a PIN Generating Key

The on-line mode can be separated cryptographically from either the off-line or off-host mode if dependent PINs and dependent personal keys are used. For example, assume the on-line scheme illustrated in Figure 11-6, where on-line personal verification is based on PINs and personal keys derived from other keys (KPN and KPG). One way to achieve separation between on-line and off-line personal verification, in this case, would be to base off-line personal verification on PIN only and to base on-line personal verification on PIN as well as KP. This could be achieved by storing only KPN in the terminal (Figure 11-12) and by storing KPN as well as KPG at the issuer's HPC (Figure 11-6). In that case, a compromise of KPN in the off-line mode (resulting in the exposure of PINs) would not compromise the on-line mode since personal keys are still secure.

During the verification process (Figure 11-12), user i enters IDi and PINi at an EFT terminal in which KPN has been installed. The EFT terminal computes $E_{KPN}(IDi)$ = Rfi (i.e., the PIN of reference), and compares Rfi and PINi for equality. If Rfi = PINi, then IDi is accepted; otherwise, if Rfi $\neq$ PINi, IDi is rejected.

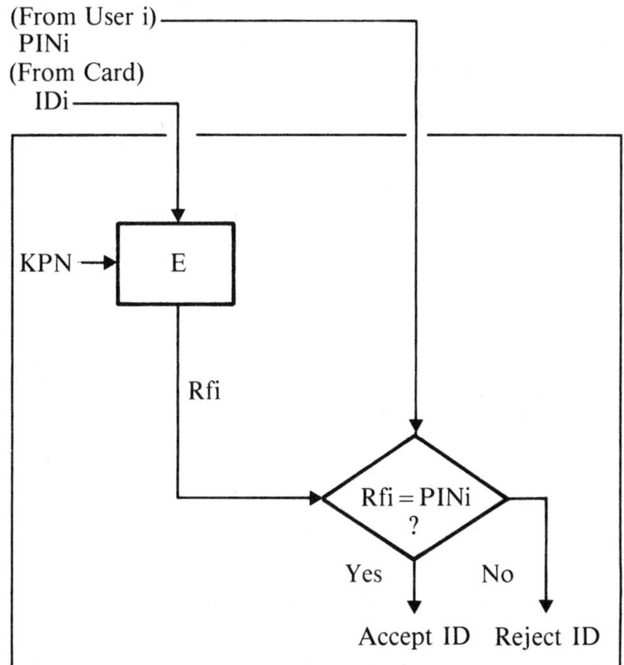

KPN = PIN Generating Key
Rfi = PIN of Reference

Notes: To initialize the system, the issuer selects KPN and computes PINi = $E_{KPN}(IDi)$ for each user (ID1, ID2, ..., IDn). If KPN is compromised a valid PIN can be generated for any given ID.

Figure 11-12. An Example of Off-Line Personal Verification with System Generated PINs

Personal Verification with User-Selected PINs Employing Offsets

Consider a design based on independent PINs which uses an offset field on the card and satisfies the relation

$$E_{KPN}(IDi) = PINi \oplus offseti$$

where KPN is a secret system-managed PIN generating key (see also Figure 11-7).

In this case, KPN, IDi, and PINi are independent variables, whereas E_{KPN} (IDi) and offseti are dependent variables. Verification takes place as illustrated in Figure 11-13. The security weakness here (as discussed before) is that the user-related PIN added to the offset results in a constant, C, as long as ID and KPN remain fixed.

Personal Verification with User-Selected PINs Employing PACs

In a more secure approach, different personal authentication codes (PAC and PACoff) can be used for on-line and off-line (or off-host) transactions, respectively. This is accomplished by using different secret authentication keys (KA and KAoff). For example, one could define

$$PACi = E_{KA}(E_{KA}(IDi) \oplus APi)$$

$$PACoffi = E_{KAoff}(E_{KAoff}(IDi) \oplus APi)$$

where

$$APi = E_{KPi \oplus PINi}(IDi)$$

The on-line verification mode using KA and PACi is shown in Figure 11-9. The off-line and off-host modes use the same procedure as the on-line mode except that KA is replaced by KAoff and PAC is replaced with PACoff (Figure 11-14). KA is stored at the issuer's HPC for on-line verification whereas KAoff is stored in the appropriate terminals and communication controllers to allow off-line and off-host verification.

If KAoff is compromised, a valid PACoff can be generated for any given set of values (ID, KP, PIN) thus compromising the off-line mode. However, the actual KP and PIN cannot be determined, and thus the on-line mode is still secure. Furthermore, since KA is unavailable, PAC cannot be evaluated.

A saving in card space could be achieved by basing on-line personal verification on an authentication parameter stored in a verification table (Figure 11-8). This would eliminate the need to store a personal authentication code associated with on-line verification on the bank card. Storage requirements on the bank card could be reduced further by basing off-line personal verification on a personal authentication code (PACoff) which is related to KP. This idea is discussed above in the section Minimizing Card Storage Requirements.

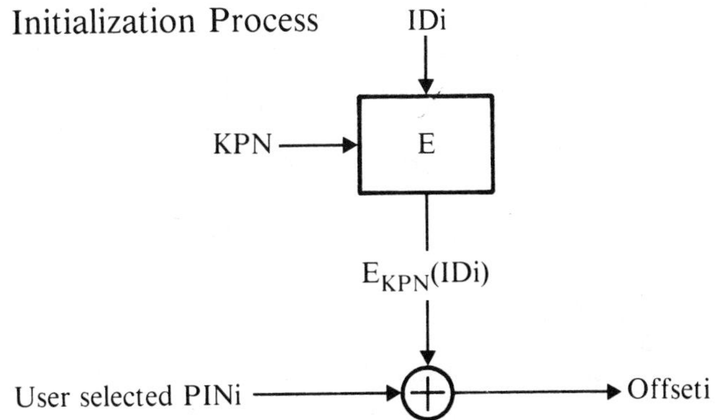

Notes: User selects PIN, whereas issue selects KPN. Issuer computes offset for each user by adding, module 2, the user-selected PIN and the value E_{KPN}(ID).

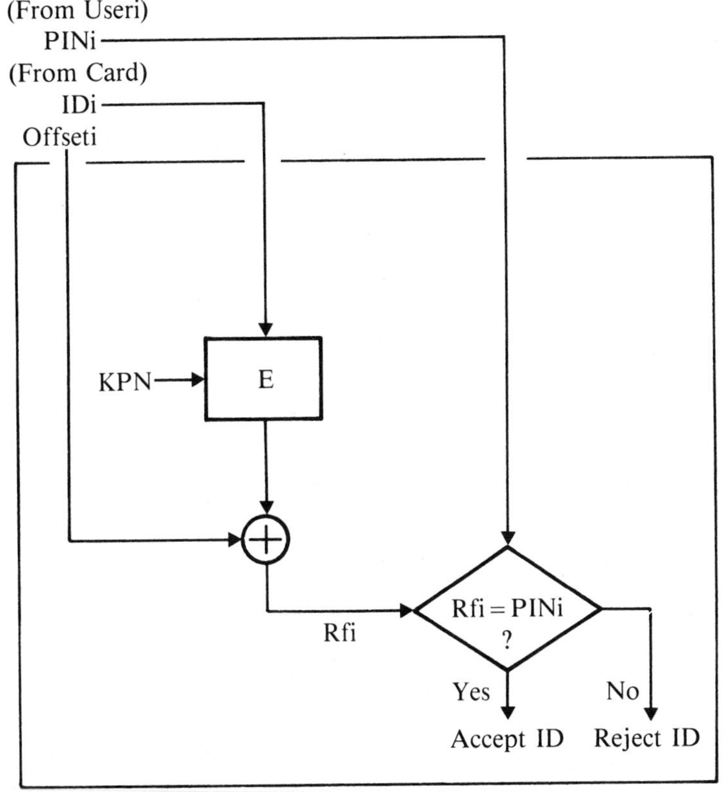

KPN = PIN Generating Key
Rfi = PIN of Reference
Note: If KPN is compromised, actual PINs can be generated.

Figure 11-13. An Example of Off-Line Personal Verification with User-Generated PINs Employing an Offset

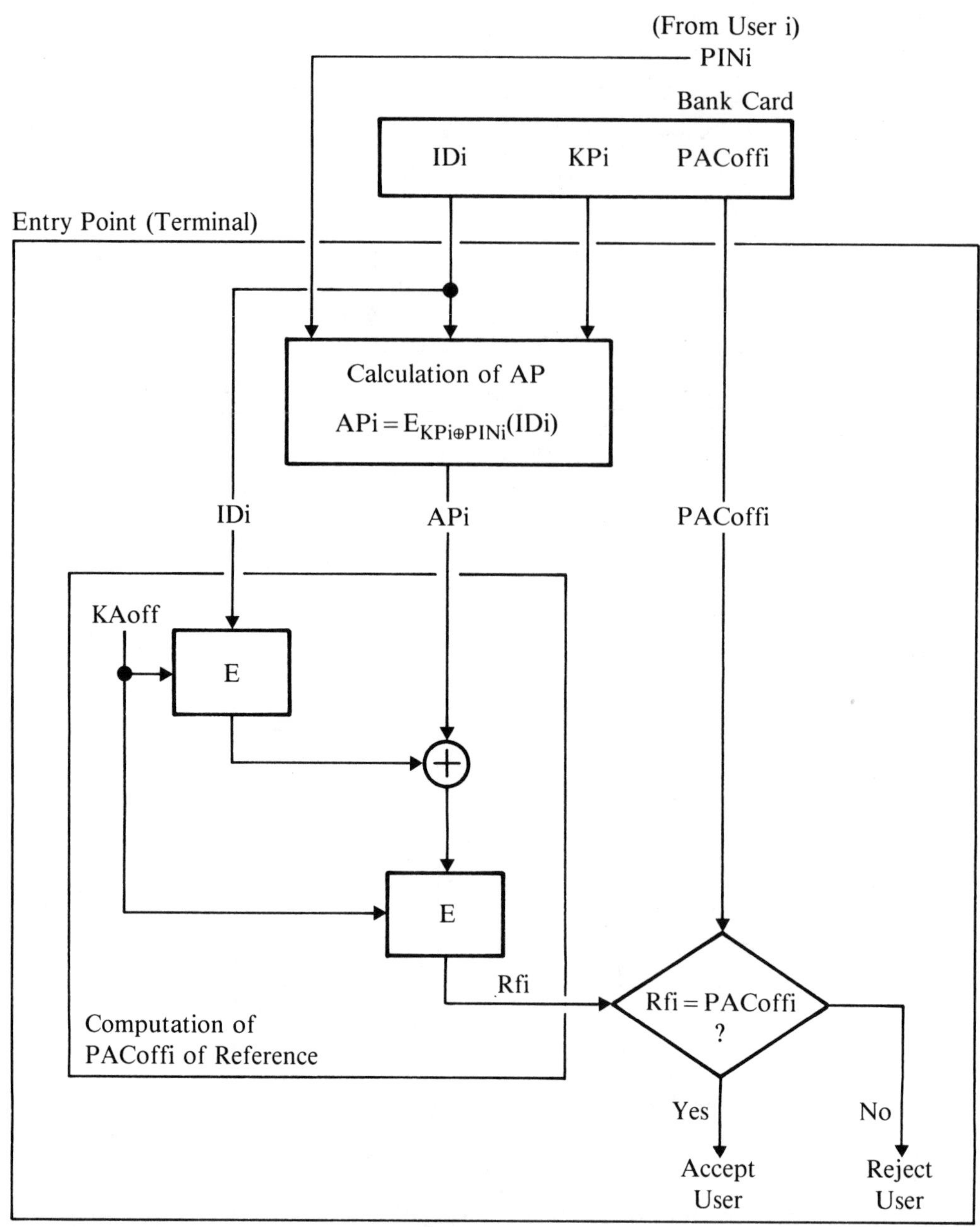

Figure 11-14. Off-Line Personal Verification - PACoffi stored on Bank Card

GUIDELINES FOR CRYPTOGRAPHIC DESIGNS

The EFT security requirements developed above are used in the remainder of the discussion to develop good cryptographic designs. These EFT security requirements may be used effectively to compare and establish trade-offs in different designs (e.g., key management approaches based on system keys only, or personal keys only, or a hybrid approach involving a combination of both).

In the following discussion of methods used to satisfy the various requirements, the focus is on requirements 1, 2, 5, 12, 14, and 17—which are concerned with the integrity of secret information entered into a system, integrity and secrecy of terminal stored information, isolation of the personal verification process, generation of user verification data, one-way functions of secret user-supplied information, and isolation of the message authentication process, respectively. Since requirements 12 and 14 follow from requirement 5, it suffices to compare the different methods with respect to requirements 1, 2, 5, and 17 which are repeated below for the reader's convenience.

> *Requirement 1.* The process of entering information at an EFT terminal must be protected, i.e., the integrity and secrecy of information entered into the EFT terminal must not be compromised as a consequence of the entry process. Furthermore the information flow within a terminal must be protected.
>
> *Requirement 2.* Information stored permanently or temporarily within an EFT terminal must be protected, i.e., the integrity of public information and the secrecy as well as integrity of private information must be assured.
>
> *Requirement 5.* The security of the personal verification process implemented at one institution must not depend on security measures implemented at other institutions.
>
> *Requirement 17.* The security of the message authentication process implemented at one institution must not depend on security measures implemented at other institutions.

To satisfy requirement 1, the following must be true:

1. The entry paths for the PIN and user-supplied key into and within the terminal are not exposed during normal system operation.
2. The entry paths for terminal resident keys into and within the terminal are not exposed during the key loading process.
3. During the entry process, secret card information is not exposed even if bank cards are temporarily in the possession of others.

Requirement 1 is independent of cryptography. It requires that security measures be employed at the entry point to reduce the probability that the PIN and secret card information (e.g., a personnel key, KP) can be ascertained during the entry process. To prevent, or at least make it difficult for card information to be ascertained while the card is in the possession of someone other than the card owner (a bank teller or store clerk), requires a particular approach in the design of the bank card, i.e., the introduction of an intelligent secure card (discussed below) capable of performing computations that involve secret information stored on the card.

To satisfy requirement 2, one must assure that

1. Permanently stored terminal keys are not exposed.
2. Temporarily stored PINs and terminal keys (active for the duration of a transaction) are not exposed.

Keys stored in a terminal can be protected only by physical security measures. Hence, requirement 2 is also independent of cryptography. To avoid the problem of key security at the terminal altogether, one might search for a method which does not require a cryptographic key resident in the terminal. This leads to the idea of using a key supplied by the user, i.e., a personal key. It happens, however, that such an approach is not secure unless a bank card with the following properties could be introduced: counterfeit cards could not be manufactured and information stored on genuine cards could not be read or altered. Such a bank card is defined below as an ideal intelligent secure card. It is concluded, however, that the requirements of the ideal bank card are unattainable at a reasonable cost with current technology.

An intelligent secure card capable of achieving realistic security objectives is defined a practical intelligent secure card (or intelligent secure card for short). It has the property that card information is secure while the card is temporarily in the possession of another person or device for the purpose of transacting business. However, use of an intelligent secure card does not obviate the need to protect the integrity and sometimes the secrecy of information transferred between the card and terminal.

Requirements 1 and 2 can therefore be satisfied partially through the introduction of an intelligent secure card incorporating a personal key. Card information, in this case, is not entered into the EFT terminal. The PIN is not assumed to be entered directly on the card, although, if it were, requirements 1 and 2 could be fully satisfied. Therefore, except for PIN entry, the intelligent secure card is equivalent to a miniature EFT terminal carried by its owner.

Computationally the card would contain the following elements: a one-chip microprocessor, ROS (read only store) containing executable programs, a small RAM (random access memory) for storage of intermediate results (which could be on the microprocessor chip), and a nonvolatile memory for the storage of customer unique information (e.g., account number, secret card key or parameter, and PIN-related information) and dynamic information (e.g., current balance, number of transactions, and a one-up counter or message sequence number). The nonvolatile memory is partitioned and protected so that

1. A portion of the memory can be written to only by the issuing institution during card personalization. Thereafter, secret information stored

in this memory can be read only by the card, whereas nonsecret information stored in this memory can be read by both the card and EFT terminal.

2. A part of the memory can be written to and read only by the card.

Power and timing information would be provided externally by the EFT terminal, although fully self-contained devices are not precluded. Electrical connections for communication between the card and terminal are also provided.

One important design goal is to achieve isolation among institutions with regard to personal verification (requirement 5) and message authentication (requirement 17). A design based solely on PINs and system keys requires a high degree of trust among institutions, since cryptographic transformations are required to translate data from encryption under one key to encryption under another key. This means that PINs or PIN-related information occurs in the clear at nodes not under the control of the issuer. The potential for exposure is minimized if this information occurs in the clear only in secure hardware. But the fact remains that the issuer must trust other institutions to implement secure hardware and maintain its integrity. Hence requirements 5 and 17 cannot be satisfied with a design based solely on PINs and system keys. Details are discussed in the section The PIN/System Key Approach.

Requirement 5 can be satisfied with a design that increases the number of combinations of secret user-supplied information by introducing (in addition to PIN) a personal key (KP) written on an intelligent secure bank card. With PIN and KP, the number of independent bits of secret user-supplied information is sufficient to defend against direct search and dictionary attacks. (Designs based only on PIN are vulnerable to these attacks.) A design based only on KPs and PINs (no system keys) is described in the section The PIN/Personal Key Approach. Specifically, it is shown that KP enhances personal verification and authentication of transaction request messages by satisfying requirement 5. However, the EFT terminal cannot use personal keys to authenticate transaction response messages unless it can be assured that these keys are known only to the issuer (i.e., not even known to the legitimate user). An opponent who enters a fake personal key at an EFT terminal could, for example, inject bogus transaction response messages into the communication line that the EFT terminal would accept as valid. Elimination of these exposures would be possible, and thus requirements 5 and 17 could be satisfied, if a pure personal key approach were used together with an ideal intelligent secure card. But, as a practical matter, the properties of an ideal intelligent secure card are unattainable, and therefore requirement 17 cannot be satisfied with only a personal key approach. *As a consequence, use of a personal key does not eliminate the requirement for a terminal resident key.*

In the section The PIN/Personal Key/System Key (Hybrid Key Management) Approach Using an Intelligent Secure Card, an implementation is discussed that uses a combination of personal and system keys (defined as *hybrid key management*) together with an intelligent secure card capable of achieving realistic security objectives (defined as a practical intelligent secure card in contrast to the ideal intelligent secure card described above). In particular, requirement 5 can be satisfied completely and requirement 17 can be satisfied to a high degree. To satisfy requirement 17 completely requires that electronic digital signatures be implemented (see the section entitled Security Enhancements With Digital Signatures).

The different methods can now be classified as follows:

Method 1. PIN/System Key Approach
Method 2. PIN/Personal Key Approach
Method 3. PIN/Personal Key/System Key Approach

In addition, the following categories can be defined:

Category a. Using a magnetic stripe bank card
Category b. Using a practical intelligent secure card
Category c. Using an ideal intelligent secure card

Hence, altogether there are nine different approaches defined, i.e., 1a, 1b, 1c, 2a, . . . , 3b, 3c. Tables 11-1 and 11-2 indicate the effectiveness of each method with respect to the requirement of separating personal verification and message authentication among institutions (requirements 5 and 17), respectively. Since requirements 1 and 2 require physical security in all approaches, a separate table is not provided for these.

Details of the different designs are discussed in the sections The PIN/System Key Approach, The PIN/Personal Key Approach, and The PIN/Personal Key/System Key (Hybrid Key Management) Approach Using an Intelligent Secure Card. From these discussions it can be concluded that the combination 3b presents a realistic security solution.

Before presenting the details of different designs, some of the fundamental threats to PIN secrecy are highlighted. Furthermore, key management requirements common to all designs are investigated.

Threats to PIN Secrecy

Observation of the PIN

In any nationwide EFT environment, there will be a very large number of PIN-using terminals located in nonsecure locations. The line from the PIN-using terminal could be tapped and one or more cameras or video recorders could be positioned to observe and record customers entering their PINs into the EFT terminal or PIN pad device. This observation is synchronized with reading the corresponding transaction sent over the communication line to establish a relationship between the observed PIN and intercepted account number. After a period of time, a significant number of PINs could be obtained from unsuspecting customers who were not particularly careful during the PIN entry process. A computer could then correlate the recovered PINs with the intercepted transactions to determine the customer's account number and

Method 1			Method 2			Method 3		
a	b	c	a	b	c	a	b	c
Requirement 5: Comparison of Methods Excluding the Entry Point								
not satisfied	not satisfied	not satisfied	satisfied	satisfied	satisfied	satisfied	satisfied	satisfied
Common keys between nodes are necessary.			Secret verification information is processed only at the end points.					
Requirement 5: Comparison of Methods at the Entry Point								
not satisfied	not satisfied	not satisfied	not satisfied	satisfied	satisfied	not satisfied	satisfied	satisfied
Key at entry point is not controlled by the issuer.			Secrecy of input information (PIN and KP) not controlled by the issuer.	Card information (KP) not exposed to others; fake KP and misuse of KP not possible.	Secrecy of card information (KP) guaranteed.	Secrecy of input information (PIN and KP) not controlled by the issuer.	Card information (KP) not exposed to others; fake KP and misuse of KP not possible.	Secrecy of card information (KP) guaranteed.

Table 11-1. Security Properties of Different Cryptographic Methods—Separation of Personal Verification Process.

Method 1			Method 2			Method 3		
a	b	c	a	b	c	a	b	c
Requirement 17: Comparison of Methods Excluding the Entry Point								
not satisfied	not satisfied	not satisfied	satisfied	satisfied	satisfied	satisfied	satisfied	satisfied
Common keys between nodes are necessary.			Secret verification information is processed only at the end points.					
Requirement 17: Comparison of Methods at the Entry Point								
not satisfied	not satisfied	not satisfied	not satisfied	not satisfied	satisfied*	not satisfied	partly satisfied	satisfied*
Key at entry point is not controlled by issuer.			Secrecy of input information not controlled by the issuer. Threat of KP misuse; threat of fake KP.	Threat of KP misuse since user could determine his KP.	Secrecy of card information guaranteed.	Secrecy of input information not controlled by the issuer.**	Threat of KP misuse since user could determine his KP. But attack requires subversion of system keys.	Secrecy of card information guaranteed.

Note: Although the PIN/personal key approach (method 2) provides good separation between institutions, it is not an acceptable solution unless an ideal intelligent secure card is used (method 2c). The security exposure is due to the threat of KP misuse and the use of fake KPs.

*It is assumed that the signal path between the intelligent secure bank card and the terminal is not subverted.

**There is also the threat of KP misuse and the use of fake KPs. But a successful attack is dependent upon subversion of system keys.

Table 11-2. Security Properties of Different Cryptographic Methods—Separation of Message Authentication Process

other information necessary to produce a counterfeit card. This would allow fraud to be perpetrated against each corresponding account.

A suggested defense against this threat is to encrypt the account number and all other information that links the PIN to the cardholder. This prevents the production of a counterfeit card from intercepted information. However, financial institutions may find that encryption of card information conflicts with some other system requirement. For example, it may be necessary for certain intermediate nodes, which do not have an encryption/decryption capability, to read the information contained in the transaction messages.

Bugging of Input Information at EFT Terminals

A bug placed in an EFT terminal allows all PINs entered into that terminal to be intercepted. This, in turn, allows an opponent to successfully masquerade as any one of the users whose PINs are intercepted, thus allowing fraud to be perpetrated against each of the corresponding accounts.

Insertion of Fake Equipment

The most insidious fraud threat is one that uses fake equipment. A dishonest merchant may induce unsuspecting cardholders to use EFT terminals with fake PIN pads. Although there are many variations on this attack (see Countering the Fake Equipment Threat, Chapter 10), some of which can be defended against, there is one that offers no apparent practical defense (no matter what method is employed, personal keys or system keys) if card information and PIN are entered into the retailer's equipment.

In this attack, the merchant replaces the EFT terminal and PIN pad with devices that will display or print the entered PIN at a work station. Every PIN so obtained is automatically recorded. The card information is automatically written on an unused card supplied by the opponent and the PIN and card are entered into the real PIN pad and EFT terminal, which are also hidden. Upon receiving the transaction response from the issuer, the same response is sent to the fake terminal. In this way, the cardholder is made to think that the transaction has completed normally. PINs and counterfeit cards obtained in this manner are then used to commit fraud against the corresponding accounts.

There is no apparent practical defense against the above fake equipment attack. Financial institutions must therefore be willing to accept this threat, realizing that it is impossible to develop protection systems that completely eliminate all risks of fraud.

Key Management Requirements

Fundamental to any key management approach is the requirement (10) that: Personal verification and message authentication require a reference to be available to the authenticator at the time the authentication takes place. This reference, or the process used to generate the reference, must be defined and agreed to in advance. It must be such that the integrity of the reference (and sometimes its secrecy) and/or the process that generates the reference, can be assured by the authenticator.

Thus to check a received MAC at the issuer (associated with the transaction request message) an authentication key must either be stored or dynamically created at the issuer. The same requirement exists at the entry point in order to provide checking procedures for the MAC associated with the transaction response message sent from the issuer to the entry point.

To provide a check for message timeliness, required for detection of the replay of stale messages, the MACs must be time-dependent. Furthermore, for detection of the replay of stale messages and MACs, the time dependence must be controlled by the authenticating node.

This can be accomplished by using a universal time reference, T, e.g., a time-of-day (TOD) clock, which logically ties all nodes together. Here, each node must access T internally since otherwise T is not under the authenticating node's control.

Another way of establishing a common time reference is for the authenticating node to generate a random quantity which is transmitted to the sending node (i.e., the node desiring to send a message to the authenticating node). The sending node places this received random value in the message, generates a MAC on the message, and sends the message and MAC to the authenticating node.

To continue the discussion of authentication concepts: consider two nodes, A and B, which use a common message authentication key, Kauth. This key can be either static (in which case Kauth is stored permanently at both nodes) or dynamic (in which case Kauth may be generated by one or both of the nodes). Figure 11-15 summarizes the concepts discussed thus far.

For the case where Kauth is randomly generated, a key-encrypting key (KNC, or node communication key) must be used to encrypt Kauth so that it may be transmitted safely to the other node where it must be established.

For example, if one node generates Kauth, it can be sent in the form E_{KNC}(Kauth) to the other node. Details of protocols which incorporate the concepts of Figure 11-15 are suggested in Figures 11-16 through 11-19. These figures specifically show that initiation protocols are needed before regular communication can start, unless when a universal time reference is used in conjunction with a static Kauth. If created dynamically, Kauth could be generated either at node A or node B. Another possibility discussed in reference 13 is for Kauth to be formed from random quantities generated at node A and node B.

The notation MAC(argument) is used to show specifically the quantities that MAC depends on. For example, MAC(key, data) is interpreted as the leftmost m bits of the last block of E_{key}(data), where $m \leqslant 64$ is selected by the user and for convenience is omitted from the notation.

Choosing a particular design approach, i.e., system keys, personal keys, or both, affects the way references can be established (discussed below). After one decides how references are established, the major remaining effort must focus on the problem of how best to achieve separation of the personal verification and message authentication processes among different institutions. The details are discussed under the general topic of key management in each of the separate sections covering the PIN/system key approach, the

Authentication Key	Time Reference	
	Universal	System Generated
Kauth	time-of-day clock	Ta generated at node A Tb generated at node B
Static, i.e., Kauth is permanently stored at both nodes	MACa,b and MACb,a are functions of Kauth, TOD, and data sent between node A and node B. No initiation protocol required.	MACa,b is a function of Kauth, Tb, and data sent from node A to node B. MACb,a is a function of Kauth, Ta, and data sent from node B to node A. Initiation protocol required to send Ta from node A to node B and Tb from node B to node A.
Dynamic, i.e., Kauth is randomly generated	MACa,b and MACb,a are functions of Kauth, TOD, and data sent between node A and node B. Initiation protocol required to establish common authentication key (Kauth) between node A and node B.	MACa,b is a function of Kauth, Tb, and data sent from node A to node B. MACb,a is a function of Kauth, Ta, and data sent from node B to node A. Initiation protocol required to send Ta from node A to node B and Tb from node B to node A. In addition, a common authentication key (Kauth) must be established between node A and node B.

Legend:

IDa: Identifier of node A
IDb: Identifier of node B
Kauth: Message authentication key
Ma,b: Message sent from node A to node B
Mb,a: Message sent from node B to node A
MACa,b: Message authentication code for Ma,b
MACb,a: Message authentication code for Mb,a
Ta: System generated time reference at node A
Tb: System generated time reference at node B
TOD: Universal time reference stored at node A and node B

Figure 11-15. Concepts Associated with Authentication

Time Reference: Permanently stored time reference at both nodes, e.g., time-of-day clock (TOD)

Data sent from node A to node B:

TOD, IDa, IDb, Ma,b, MACa,b(Kauth,TOD,IDa,IDb,Ma,b)

Data sent from node B to node A:

TOD, IDb, IDa, Mb,a, MACb,a(Kauth,TOD,IDb,IDa,Mb,a)

Legend:

IDa:	Identifier of node A
IDb:	Identifier of node B
Kauth:	Message authentication key
Ma,b:	Message sent from node A to node B
Mb,a:	Message sent from node B to node A
MACa,b:	Message authentication code for Ma,b
MACb,a:	Message authentication code for Mb,a
TOD:	Universal time reference stored at node A and node B

Figure 11-16. Message Authentication—Universal Time Reference and Static Authentication Key

PIN/personal key approach, and the PIN/system key/personal key (or hybrid key management) approach.

One particular method that assures separation of the personal verification process among institutions uses a secret personal key stored on the card. A system with personal keys faces new threats.

Threats to the Secrecy of a Key Stored on a Magnetic Stripe Card

One major threat to the key-on-the-card (magnetic stripe card) is that cards can be lost and stolen, and information on the card can be copied. Furthermore, information entered into nonsecure terminals can be bugged, and unsuspecting customers can be induced to enter card and PIN information into fake equipment.

However, not all of these exposures present the same threat to EFT security, as will be seen from the discussion below. Note also that many of the exposures could be eliminated with an intelligent secure card (see also the sections entitled Bank Card Security, and Personal Key Approach with an Intelligent Secure Card).

A PIN is analogous to a user-remembered combination to a combination lock; a card with a secret personal key (KP) stored on it is analogous to a physical key to a key lock. It is true that physical keys can be lost, stolen, and duplicated, and therefore, that cards with secret keys written on them would be subject to the same exposures. Yet, keys and locks have been proven to be practical, useful, and worthwhile, even though they do not provide their users with perfect or absolute security. The same would be true of

---

Time Reference: Randomly generated time-variant quantities (Ta at node A and Tb at node B) establish origin of time reference, e.g., Ta and Tb are incremented by one for each message sent

Initiation protocol to exchange Ta and Tb:

From node A to node B: Ta, IDa, IDb
From node B to node A: Tb, IDb, IDa

Data sent from node A to node B:

Tb+i, IDa, IDb, Ma,b, MACa,b(Kauth,Tb+i,IDa,IDb,Ma,b)

Data sent from node B to node A:

Ta+j, IDb, IDa, Mb,a, MACb,a(Kauth,Ta+j,IDb,IDa,Mb,a)

Legend:

IDa: Identifier of node A
IDb: Identifier of node B
Kauth: Message authentication key
Ma,b: Message sent from node A to node B
Mb,a: Message sent from node B to node A
MACa,b: Message authentication code for Ma,b
MACb,a: Message authentication code for Mb,a
Ta: System generated time reference at node A
Tb: System generated time reference at node B
i: Message sequence number for Ma,b
j: Message sequence number for Mb,a

Note: It must not be possible to influence the generation of Ta and Tb externally. Otherwise, stale messages associated with a previously used Ta and Tb can be inserted.

Figure 11-17. Message Authentication–System-Generated Time Reference and Static Authentication Key

bank cards with secret keys stored on them. Information stored on the card would be protected as a consequence of the physical security routinely provided to the card by its holder. Once users were aware of the security implications of exposing card information, it is assumed that they would take the necessary precautions to protect their cards, and by so doing, they would protect the information stored thereon.

Lost Cards

Loss of a card is probably the most common way in which card information becomes exposed, yet this represents the least serious threat to EFT security. An opponent is unlikely to launch an attack by first searching for a lost card, and people who find lost cards are unlikely to be motivated to tap the communications line and recover PINs using cryptographic methods.

Time Reference: Permanently stored time reference at both nodes, e.g., time-of-day clock (TOD)

Initiation protocol to exchange time-variant authentication key (Kauth) generated at node B

From node A to node B: IDa, IDb
From node B to node A: IDb, IDa, E_{KNC}(Kauth)

Data sent from node A to node B:

TOD, IDa, IDb, Ma,b, MACa,b(Kauth,TOD,IDa,IDb,Ma,b)

Data sent from node B to node A:

TOD, IDb, IDa, Mb,a, MACb,a(Kauth,TOD,IDb,IDa,Mb,a)

Legend:

IDa: Identifier of node A
IDb: Identifier of node B
Kauth: Message authentication key
KNC: Node communication key (key-encrypting key)
Ma,b: Message sent from node A to node B
Mb,a: Message sent from node B to node A
MACa,b: Message authentication code for Ma,b
MACb,a: Message authentication code for Mb,a
TOD: Universal time reference stored at node A and node B

Figure 11-18. Message Authentication–Universal Time Reference and Dynamic Authentication Key

It is assumed that the cardholder would notify the issuer upon discovering that he has lost his card. The issuer would then invalidate the account and disallow further transactions until a new card had been issued. Thus the time during which fraud could be committed against an account would be relatively short.

Stolen Cards

Stolen cards are not much of a threat either, although here it must be assumed that the opponent is motivated and capable of attacking the system (which would include the tapping of communication lines, interception of authentication pattern values, and recovery of PINs). However, AP values cannot be intercepted after the cards are stolen, since the cards themselves are needed to initiate transactions. In addition, it is assumed that reissued cards would use different KPs, thus making the APs different.

For stolen cards to be of significant value, they must be stolen from selected individuals whose transaction request messages have been previously

---

Time Reference: Randomly generated time-variant quantities (Ta at node A and Tb at node B) establish origin of time reference, e.g., Ta and Tb are incremented by one for each message sent

Initiation protocol to exchange Ta and Tb as well as Kauth:

From node A to node B: Ta, IDa, IDb
From node B to node A: Tb, IDb, IDa, E_{KNC}(Kauth)

Data sent from node A to node B:

Tb+i, IDa, IDb, Ma,b, MACa,b(Kauth,Tb+i,IDa,IDb,Ma,b)

Data sent from node B to node A:

Ta+j, IDb, IDa, Mb,a, MACb,a(Kauth,Ta+j,IDb,IDa,Mb,a)

Legend:

IDa: Identifier of node A
IDb: Identifier of node B
Kauth: Message authentication key
KNC: Node communication key (key-encrypting key)
Ma,b: Message sent from node A to node B
Mb,a: Message sent from node B to node A
MACa,b: Message authentication code for Ma,b
MACb,a: Message authentication code for Mb,a
Ta: System generated time reference stored at node A
Tb: System generated time reference stored at node B
i: Message sequence number for Ma,b
j: Message sequence number for Mb,a

Note: It must not be possible to influence the generation of Ta and Tb externally. Otherwise, stale messages associated with a previously used Ta and Tb can be inserted. Since Kauth represents time-variant information generated at node B, it is not necessary also to generate Tb at node B. In that case, Ta could be used in place of Tb to generate MACb,a.

Figure 11-19. Message Authentication–System-Generated Time Reference and Dynamic Authentication Key

intercepted. For example, the opponent could tap the communications line from an EFT terminal and accumulate a file of transaction request messages for many different cardholders. (It is assumed that the cryptographically transformed PINs are sent in the transaction request messages.) By stealing the cards of one or more of these people, a computer could then be used to obtain the associated PINs. This would allow fraud to be committed against each account until such time as the card is reported stolen or missing and the issuer updates his data base to reject the invalid card.

Copying Card Information

Copying card information presents a serious threat provided that the card can be read without the cardholder's knowledge. In that case, the issuer has no basis for updating his data base to reject the invalid card. In effect, the opponent has enough time in which to attack the PIN (e.g., by intercepting the user's AP value and recovering the PIN using exhaustive methods, see the section Objections to the PIN/Personal Key Approach Using a Magnetic Stripe Card).

A particular scenario for obtaining card information follows: In any nationwide EFT environment, there is probably a very large number of nonsecure EFT terminals used without PINs for the purchase of merchandise. The same card used in ATMs and other PIN-using terminals could be used in these nonsecure terminals. Thus it is not especially difficult to bug a nonsecure terminal to read and record the key from the card along with the normal magnetic stripe information.

Dishonest retailers or employees who routinely handle customers' cards in the process of transacting business represent another threat. For example, it may be common practice for the cardholder to present his or her card to a clerk, cashier, or salesperson who enters it into the EFT-terminal's card reader. Before returning the card to the cardholder, a skillful opponent could easily skim information from many cards without being observed. The line from the retailer's PIN-using terminal would also be tapped to intercept AP values. After a time, information from a significant number of cards could be skimmed.

Bugging of Input Information at EFT Terminals

Information (PINs and KPs) entered into a terminal could be exposed to a bugging attack. A suggested defense is to interlock the terminal to an alarm so that any penetration of the device causes the alarm to be triggered. However, inexpensive terminals cannot have sophisticated alarm systems. Thus, for inexpensive terminals located in nonsecure retailer environments, there is an increased potential that card information and PINs will be exposed to a bugging attack. For the same reason, terminal-resident keys are also vulnerable in such an environment. Thus, the threat is not restricted to personal keys.

Insertion of Fake Equipment

The fake equipment threat described earlier to obtain PINs (see Threats to PIN Secrecy) is equally effective for obtaining KPs. There is no apparent practical defense to this threat if secret information is entered into a device not under the control of the customer.

THE PIN/SYSTEM KEY APPROACH

In the PIN/system key approach, personal verification is based solely on a secret PIN entered into the EFT terminal by the customer. The PIN is often combined with other nonsecret information such as the cardholder's ID and this combined information is encrypted under a secret system-supplied key.[23] When the ID is coupled to the PIN, attacks against the PIN must take into account the ID. The work factor for certain dictionary attacks against the PIN is increased (see also Appendix D). The ANSI-proposed method for PIN encryption is described in Appendix E.

System keys are used to generate the MACs required for message authentication (Table 11-3). A separate dynamically generated transaction key KTR is used for MAC generation between each logically adjacent pair of nodes (e.g., the terminal and the acquirer, the acquirer and the switch, and the switch and the issuer). The keys KTR1 and KTR2 are used to distinguish further between the MACs generated on transaction request and transaction response messages, respectively. The subscripts x,y denote the sender (x) and the receiver (y). For example, KTR1term,acq represents a transaction key shared by the terminal and the acquirer, and is used by the terminal (the sender) to generate a MAC on a transaction request message sent to the acquirer (the receiver).

It is assumed that the transaction keys are generated at one node (either sender x or receiver y) and transmitted to the other node (receiver y or sender x, as the case may be) encrypted under a permanently installed system key shared by the two nodes (Table 11-3). Transaction keys transmitted between a terminal and the acquirer would be encyrpted under a terminal master key, KMT. Transaction keys transmitted between the acquirer and the switch, and between the switch and the issuer, would be encrypted under an interchange key, KI. The flows of information from an EFT terminal to the issuer and from the issuer back to the EFT terminal (including the keys and MACs used in the message authentication process) are shown in Tables 11-4 and 11-5. The PIN/system key approach is discussed in greater detail in the section Implementation of Fraud Prevention Techniques, in Chapter 10. Some variations on the key management approach shown in Tables 11-4 and 11-5 are listed below.

1. KTR1term,acq = KTR2acq,term
   KTR1acq,sw = KTR2sw,acq
   KTR1sw,iss = KTR2iss,sw
2. KTR1term,acq = KTR1acq,sw = KTR1sw,iss
   KTR2iss,sw = KTR2sw,acq = KTR2acq,term
3. Both 1 and 2 are satisfied (i.e., a single transaction key KTR is used).

In case 1, a different transaction key is established between each logically adjacent pair of nodes, and this key is used to generate the MACs for both Mreq and Mresp. In case 2, a first transaction key (KTR1) is established among the nodes (term, acq, sw, and iss) for the purpose of generating the MAC on Mreq and a second transaction key (KTR2) is established among

[23]If entered into a PIN pad with encryption capability, the PIN may be encrypted under a secret PIN-pad key. However, a terminal key is still required unless the PIN-pad key can also be used to generate the MAC's which are required for message authentication.

		System Nodes			
System User	Bank Card	EFT Terminal	Acquirer's Host	Switch's Host	Issuer's Host
		Permanently Installed Master Keys			
none	none	KMT	KMHacq	KMHsw	KMHiss
		Permanently Installed Interchange Keys			
none	none	none	KIacq,sw	KIacq,sw KIsw,iss	KIsw,iss
		Dynamically Generated Keys Used for MAC Generation on the Transaction Request Message, Mreq			
none	none	KTR1term,acq	KTR1term,acq KTR1acq,sw	KTR1sw,iss KTR1acq,sw	KTR1sw,iss
		Dynamically Generated Keys Used for MAC Generation on the Transaction Response Message, Mresp			
none	none	KTR2acq,term	KTR2acq,term KTR2sw,acq	KTR2iss,sw KTR2sw,acq	KTR2iss,sw

Note: Keys used for personal verification at the issuer and switch are not shown.

Legend:

KMT: Terminal master key
KMH: Host master key
KI: Interchange key
KTR1: Transaction key for MAC generation on transaction request message (Mreq)
KTR2: Transaction key for MAC generation on transaction response message (Mresp)

Table 11-3. Keys Used for Message Authentication—PIN/System Key Approach

System User	Bank Card	System Nodes			
		EFT Terminal	Acquirer's Host	Switch's Host	Issuer's Host
1 Enter PIN into terminal.	2 Enter card into terminal and read card information.	3 Generate AP.	7 Check received MAC1term,acq with KTR1term,acq of reference and TODacq of reference; retain Tterm randomly generated by terminal.	11 Check received MAC1acq,sw with KTR1acq,sw of reference and TODsw of reference.	15 Check received MAC1sw,iss with KTR1sw,iss of reference and TODiss of reference.
		4 Formulate Mreq which includes time dependent information from acquirer (TODacq) and terminal (Tterm).		12 Check for correct destination.	16 Verify user.
		5 Generate MAC1term,acq with KTR1term,acq.	8 Check for correct destination.	13 Generate MAC1sw,iss with KTR1sw,iss.	17 Decide if Mreq is to be honored.
		6 Send Mreq and MAC1term,acq to acquirer.	9 Generate MAC1acq,sw with KTR1acq,sw.	14 Send Mreq and MAC1sw,iss to issuer.	18 Formulate Mresp which includes time information stored at issuer (TODiss) as well as time information generated by the terminal (Tterm).
			10 Send Mreq and MAC1acq,sw to switch.		

Note: It is assumed that the acquirer periodically sends time-of-day information (TODacq) to the terminals in its domain. The terminal, on the other hand, generates random information (Tterm) and sends it to the acquirer. This can be done as part of the initiation protocol (Figure 11-15). The TOD stored at the other network host nodes (TODsw at the switch and TODiss at the issuer) is assumed to be equal to TODacq within an allowable range (ΔTOD).

The integers 1–18 in the table show the sequence of steps in the transaction.

Table 11-4. Information Flow from Terminal to Issuer—PIN/System Key Approach

System User	Bank Card	EFT Terminal	Acquirer's Host	Switch's Host	Issuer's Host
		System Nodes			
	32 Eject card from terminal.	29 Check received MAC2acq,term with KTR2acq,term of reference and Tterm of reference.	25 Check received MAC2sw,acq with KTR2sw,acq of reference and TODacq of reference.	21 Check received MAC2,iss,sw with KTR2iss,sw of reference and TODsw of reference.	18 Formulate Mresp which includes time information stored at issuer (TODiss) as well as time information generated by the terminal (Tterm).
		30 Decide if Mresp is to be accepted or rejected.	26 Check for correct destination.	22 Check for correct destination.	19 Generate MAC2iss,sw with KTR2iss,sw.
		31 If Mresp is accepted, process transaction; otherwise, abort transaction request.	27 Generate MAC2acq,term with KTR2acq,term.	23 Generate MAC2sw,acq with KTR2sw,acq.	20 Send Mresp and MAC2iss,sw to switch.
			28 Send Mresp and MAC2acq,term to terminal.	24 Send Mresp and MAC2sw,acq to acquirer.	

Note: It is assumed that the acquirer periodically sends time-of-day information (TODacq) to the terminals in its domain. The terminal, on the other hand, generates random information (Tterm) and sends it to the acquirer. This can be done as part of the initiation protocol (Figure 11-15). The TOD stored at the other network host nodes (TODsw at the switch and TODiss at the issuer) is assumed to be equal to TODacq within an allowable range (ΔTOD).

The integers 18–32 in the table show the sequence of steps in the transaction.

Table 11-5. Information Flow from Issuer to Terminal—PIN/System Key Approach

the nodes for the purpose of generating a MAC on Mresp. In case 3, a single transaction key KTR is established among the nodes for the purpose of generating the MACs on Mreq and Mresp. In each case, the protocols vary slightly depending on the method used to generate, transmit, and intitialize the various transaction keys.

Key Management Considerations for PIN/System Key Approach

A major objective of the PIN/system key approach is to provide a key management scheme which is transparent to the user (i.e., it does not require keys to be supplied by the user). This means that system keys are used to encrypt PINs and generate message authentication codes. However, the keys at the entry points are not generally known to the issuer (final destination). Thus as messages are routed through the network, encrypted PINs must be decrypted and reencrypted and MACs must be generated.

Sharing of Secret Keys

The PIN/system key approach requires limited sharing of keys so that an institution may recover (decrypt) encrypted PINs and regenerate MACs. Hence financial institutions must be willing to exchange and use interchange keys. On the other hand, key management designs must consider the constraint that financial institutions are unwilling to share, as a condition of joining the interchange, all of their secret keys (e.g., terminal master keys, host master keys) with other institutions.

Cryptographic Translations

In addition to the cryptographic operation or operations required at the EFT terminal to transform PINs and generate MACs, one or more cryptographic operations are required in the security module of the acquiring institution (or designated node) and in the security module of the switch (if used) to allow PINs and MACs traversing the system to be transformed and regenerated, respectively, so that ultimately they are in a form that can be comprehended by the issuing institution.[24]

PIN Translation at the Issuer

If PIN validation is coupled with MAC validation, then PIN translation at the issuer is not required. However, if PIN validation is separate from MAC validation, then a PIN translation is likely to be required at the issuer to transform the PIN of reference, the received PIN, or both, into a form that will allow them to be compared. There are different reasons for this. For example, the issuer may not wish to share the key under which the PIN of reference is encrypted. Or the received PIN may be encrypted under a terminal-generated key, and in turn this key may be transmitted to the issuer

[24]In the PIN/system key approach discussed in Chapter 10, the PIN and MAC must undergo translation at a comparable number of points in the network.

encrypted under the issuer's interchange key. Ultimately, each different key management scheme will have its own different requirement for PIN translation at the issuer.

Protection Against Misrouted Data

Since PINs must be transformed from encryption under one key to encyrption under another key as messages are routed through the system, PIN information may be misrouted accidentally or intentionally. If an opponent were to cause PINs to be translated to encryption under a known key, these PINs would be exposed. Thus the PIN/system key approach must incorporate methods to detect misrouting, thus assuring that PINs are routed only to the proper destinations.

Defending Against the Misrouting Attack

If a PIN/system key approach to EFT security is improperly designed, an intentional misrouting attack may be possible. For example, an opponent might alter the destination bank ID to one of his own choosing. Thus at a selected system node (e.g., the switch) a PIN could be translated from encryption under an interchange key KIi to encryption under an interchange key KIx rather than the intended interchange key KIj. The opponent, who knows KIx, could then recover all misrouted PINs.

A defense against the misrouting attack can be provided by coupling the destination bank ID to the appropriate destination interchange key (see also reference 14). The procedure ensures that the indicated destination bank ID is the one designated at the creation of the transaction request message. At the sender this is made possible by calculating a message authentication code on the information requiring protection (i.e., the transaction request message which contains the bank ID, time-variant information such as a time stamp, and the encrypted PIN).

Before a TRANSLATE operation is attempted, a MAC of reference is generated for the received data = [T, BIDj, E_{KIi}(PIN)],where T denotes the time variant information, BIDj denotes the destination bank ID, and E_{KIi}(PIN) denotes the PIN encrypted under interchange key KIi. The MAC of reference is then compared for equality with the received MAC. If the two MACS are identical, the TRANSLATE operation is enabled. Otherwise an error condition is noted and the TRANSLATE operation is inhibited.

Using the Data Encryption Standard (DES) in the Cipher Block Chaining (CBC) mode (Chapter 2 and Figure 11-20) will suffice to detect as little as a one-bit change in the entire message. Note that MAC does not have to be 64 bits long. A smaller number of bits could be used with a corresponding loss of error detection capability (i.e., the probability of detecting an error is decreased).

The CBC mode can also be used if both secrecy and authentication are required. If two different keys are employed (i.e., one key for encryption and another for MAC generation), a strong procedure is effected. However, this is not the case if only one key is employed. An insecure procedure results if data are first encrypted as shown in Figure 2-17 and a MAC is generated on the encrypted data employing the CBC mode as indicated in principle in Figure 11-20. With known plaintext and matching ciphertext, a string of ciphertext blocks and MAC can be constructed that will pass the authentication check, although the recovered plaintext will be "garbage" (suggested by D. Coppersmith, IBM Thomas J. Watson Research Center, Yorktown Heights, N.Y.). If the MAC is generated first, followed by encryption, a change in ciphertext will not generally be propagated to the MAC field due to the self-synchronizing property of the CBC mode. *Thus, message authentication is not achieved if the same key is used for MAC generation and message encryption.*

Two implementations to detect misrouting are discussed. In the first approach (case 1), interchange keys are stored in the clear in secure hardware and are used directly during execution of the TRANSLATE operation (Figure 11-20).

In the second approach (case 2), the interchange keys are stored in encrypted form outside the secure hardware and are supplied to the TRANSLATE operation as additional parameters. This is a more economical approach, since less storage is required within the secure hardware.

The interchange keys could, for example, be stored encrypted under some unique variant of the master key (KMx) residing in the secure hardware (see Chapters 4 and 5). As a result, there is a table of encrypted keys like this one:

BID1	$E_{KMx}(KI1)$
BID2	$E_{KMx}(KI2)$
⋮	⋮
BIDj	$E_{KMx}(KIj)$
⋮	⋮
BIDn	$E_{KMx}(KIn)$

However, the TRANSLATE operation cannot distinguish between one encrypted key and another, i.e., between $E_{KMx}(KIi)$ and $E_{KMx}(KIj)$, when they are not stored within the confines of the secure hardware. Therefore, a test is needed to ensure that the correct BIDj, $E_{KMx}(KIj)$ pair is used in the TRANSLATE operation.

In devising such a test, advantage can be taken of the fact that the correct bank ID (BIDj) already resides within the secure hardware (Figure 11-20), provided that the MAC check was successfully completed. Using the methods for validating time-invariant data discussed in the section Authentication of Time-Invariant Data, in Chapter 8, a validation pattern (VP) which is a function of this BID, say VP = $E_{BID}(BID)$, is defined. The VP, in turn, is linked to a test pattern (TP) and the quantity to be checked, $E_{KMx}(KIj)$, as shown in Figure 11-21.

The table of encrypted keys is now extended by including the test pattern for each encrypted key, i.e.,

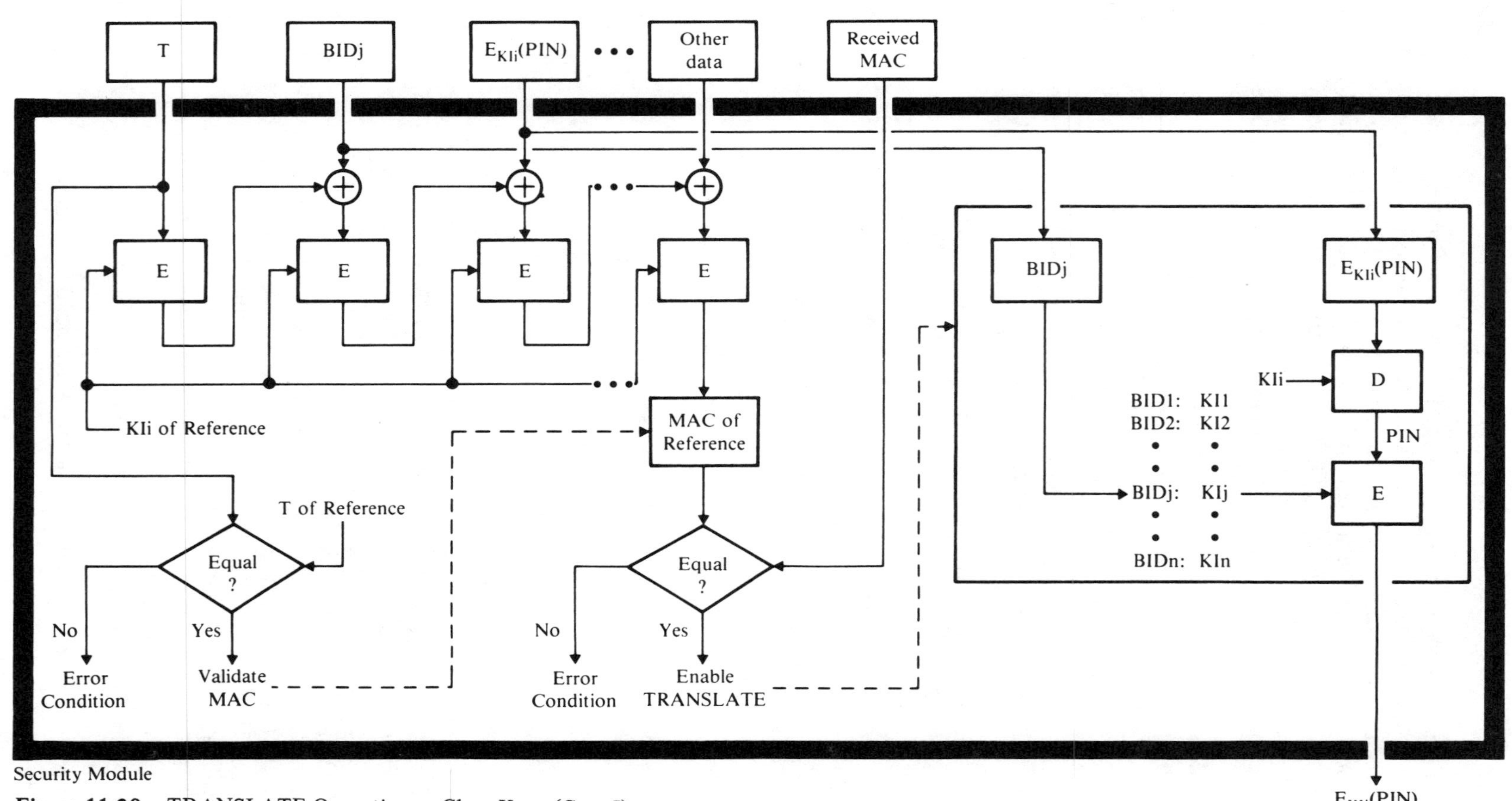

Figure 11-20. TRANSLATE Operation – Clear Keys (Case I)

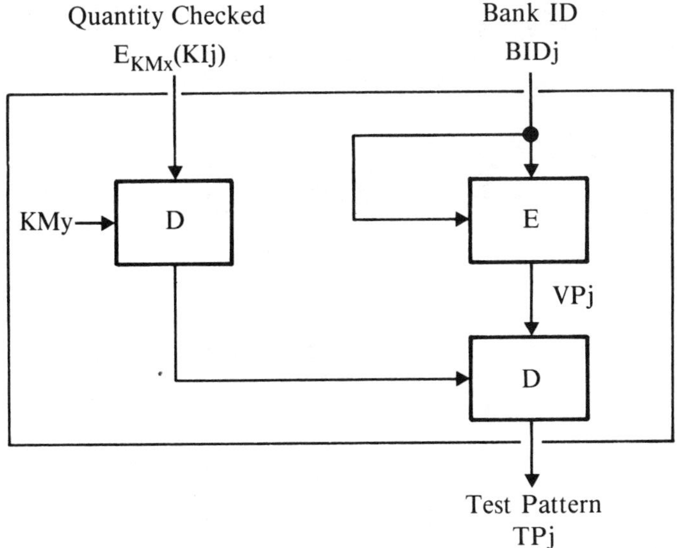

Note: Test pattern is generated under secure conditions and makes use of a special variant of the Master Key (KMy).

Figure 11-21. Generation of Test Pattern

BID1	$E_{KMx}(KI1)$	TP1
BID2	$E_{KMx}(KI2)$	TP2
⋮	⋮	⋮
BIDj	$E_{KMx}(KIj)$	TPj
⋮	⋮	⋮
BIDn	$E_{KMx}(KIn)$	TPn

The encrypted key can now be authenticated using the method indicated in Figure 11-22.

After the checks for content (via MAC), timeliness (via T and MAC), and proper translate key (via TP) have been successfully completed (all in secure hardware), the TRANSLATE operation is enabled and allowed to execute (again in secure hardware, Figure 11-23). If any of the checks fail, the TRANSLATE operation is not enabled.

The approach described here blocks misrouting attacks by enabling the TRANSLATE operation only after the proper bank ID/key relationship has been established. Another defense against the misrouting attack is to transform the personal verification information at the entry point so that the resulting value is a one-way function of the input information. This is achieved by supplementing PINs with personal keys. Misrouting attacks are, in that case, ineffective because the personal key provides end-to-end authentication. An additional advantage is that a simpler key management is achieved [see the section PIN/Personal Key/System Key Approach (Hybrid Key Management) Using an Intelligent Secure Card].

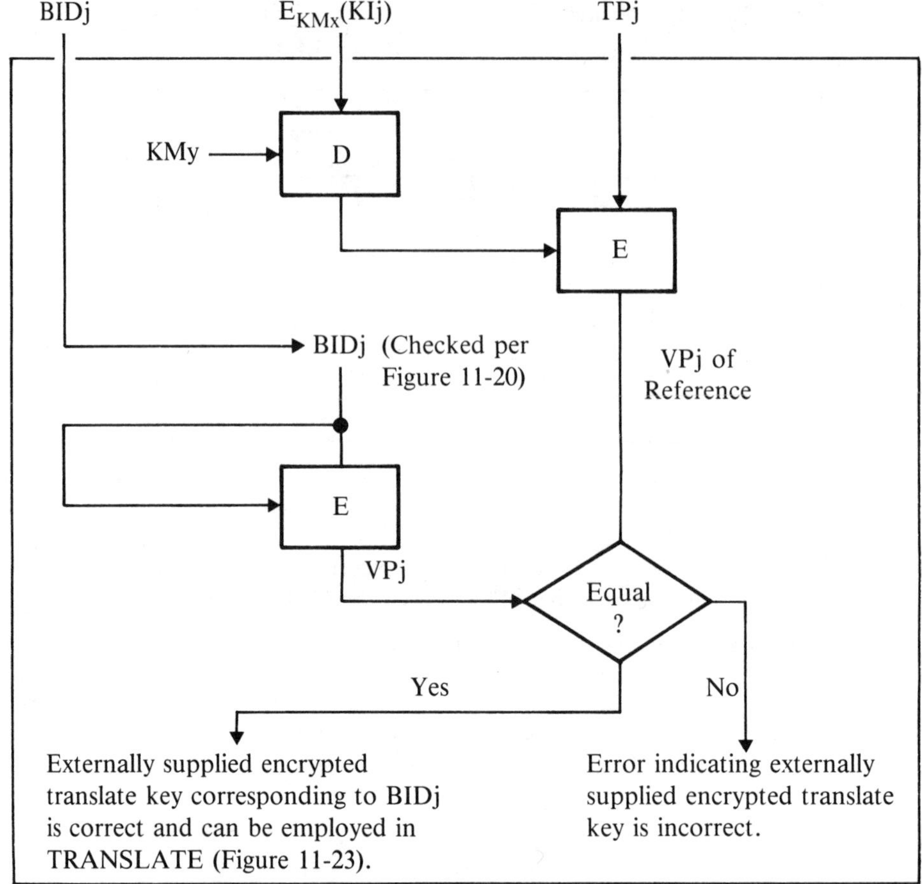

Figure 11-22. Authenticating a Translate Key using a Test Pattern

When personal verification information, i.e., PIN, is protected exclusively via system-controlled keys, key management must be specifically designed to prevent misrouting attacks. The described methods solve the problem by coupling routing information (e.g., bank IDs) with corresponding cryptographic keys via a message authentication code. Only after the proper bank ID/key relationship has been established is the TRANSLATE operation enabled. The TRANSLATE operation works with clear keys stored in secure hardware (case 1) or with encrypted keys stored externally (case 2). But, in the latter case, the encrypted keys must also be coupled to their respective identifiers, which is accomplished here by introducing a checking procedure based on stored test patterns.

Methods to prevent misrouting of PINs could also be extended to include messages. As an illustration of this, consider the case where the MAC on the transaction request message is generated at the EFT terminal using a resident terminal key. At the acquiring institution, the received MAC is replaced with a new MAC generated under KIi. Likewise, at the switch, the MAC generated under KIi is replaced with a MAC generated under KIj. Thus, the generation of a valid MAC on a misrouted message is prevented by enabling the MAC generation operation (as was suggested with the TRANSLATE operation) only if the validated bank identifier BIDj received in the transaction request message agrees with the bank identifier corresponding to the supplied encrypted key $E_{KMx}(KIj)$.

A PIN/System Key Approach for Noninterchange

By definition, a secure PIN/system key approach can be devised for a noninterchange (local) environment, since the acquirer and the issuer are one and the same. Although the processes of personal verification and authentication of transaction request messages involve the user, the EFT terminal, and the HPC, the EFT terminal and the HPC are components of the issuer. Therefore, personal verification and authentication of transaction request messages involve only the user and the issuer.

Authentication of transaction response messages involves only the issuer and EFT terminal. Under the established protocol, the decision to approve or disapprove transactions is made by the issuer; EFT terminals merely respond to the commands received from the issuer's HPC in the transaction response messages. Hence, each institution controls its own EFT security.

A PIN/System Key Approach for Interchange

The EFT security achieved implicitly with a PIN/system key approach in a noninterchange environment is not achieved in an interchange environment. In an interchange environment, the acquirer and issuer may represent different financial institutions, and users may therefore interact with EFT terminals not owned or managed by the issuer. Thus, each institution must trust that:

1. The secret keys it shares with other institutions, or with a switch (if used), will be adequately protected.
2. Each other institution will implement appropriate security measures in its terminals and PIN entry devices to protect PINs.
3. PINs—which may be either included in the message in encrypted form or used in the computation of the MAC—messages and their corresponding MACs will be transmitted via the network to their proper destinations in accordance with an agreed-upon protocol ensuring both PIN secrecy and message integrity.

It follows from these statements that institutions must trust one another and, if used, they must trust the switch. Complete independence, isolation, and separation among the institutions with respect to personal verification and message authentication are thus unattainable with the PIN/system key approach.

Transaction response messages are not merely commands to be acted upon by the originating EFT terminal. Each institution must agree that in its role as an acquiring institution, it will honor transaction requests on the basis

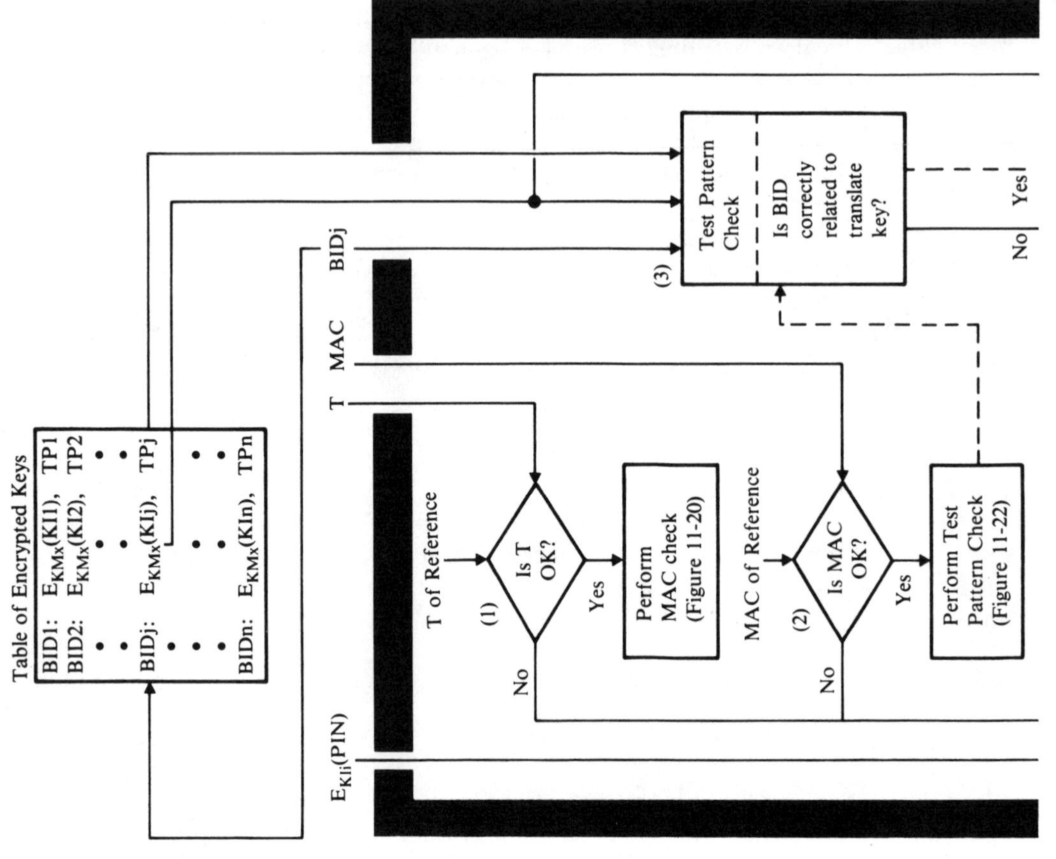

Table of Encrypted Keys
BID1: $E_{KMx}(KI1)$, TP1
BID2: $E_{KMx}(KI2)$, TP2
BIDj: $E_{KMx}(KIj)$, TPj
BIDn: $E_{KMx}(KIn)$, TPn
T
MAC
BIDj
$E_{KIi}(PIN)$
T of Reference
(1)
Is T OK?
Yes
No
Perform MAC check (Figure 11-20)
MAC of Reference
(2)
Is MAC OK?
Yes
No
Perform Test Pattern Check (Figure 11-22)
(3)
Test Pattern Check
Is BID correctly related to translate key?
No
Yes

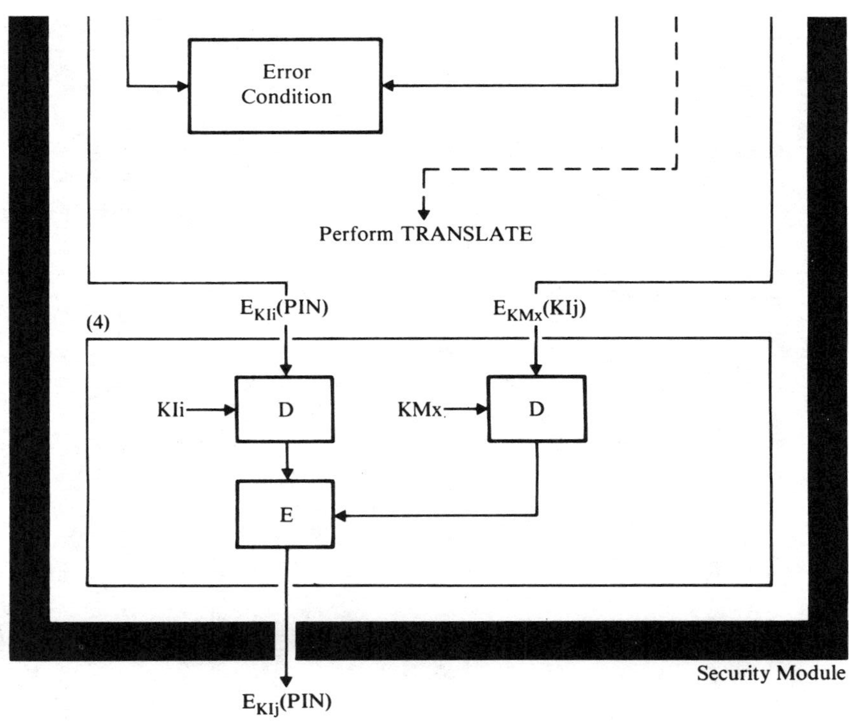

TRANSLATE is enabled only if all the following checks are successful:

1. T for timeliness (Figure 11-20)
2. MAC for content (Figure 11-20)
3. TP for correct translate key (Figure 11-22)

Figure 11-23. TRANSLATE Operation – Encrypted Keys (Case 2)

of receiving a valid transaction response message and MAC from the issuing institution. Message authentication permits the originating EFT terminal to detect bogus response messages that may be injected into the communication line. However, the cryptographic equivalent of a signed message or digital signature (Chapter 9) would be required for the acquirer to have incontrovertible proof that transactions have been authorized by the issuer.

If institutions are willing to join together in an interchange such that each institution trusts all other institutions and the switch, each institution is willing to share secret keys with other institutions or, at least, share one secret key with a switch, and each institution is willing to implement a key management that will allow PINs, messages, and generated MACs to be sent throughout the system in a protected manner in accordance with the established protocol, then an acceptable PIN/system key approach to EFT security is possible.

Disadvantages of the PIN/System Key Approach

Compromise of a System Key Allows Global Attacks Against PINs

The obvious disadvantage of using system keys to protect PINs is that a compromise of any one of these keys will reveal a large number of PINs. (On the other hand, a knowledge of one personal key will reveal at most only the associated PIN for that one account number.) System keys must therefore be provided an especially high degree of security.

For increased security, the PINs could be encrypted with a continually changing key such that the new key is a one-way function of the old key. The purpose of changing the key at time T is to protect traffic encrypted under a previous key, since the new key does not reveal the keys used at times previous to T. As a consequence, PINs cannot be obtained from intercepted encrypted PINs at times previous to T, even if the new key is compromised. One method for achieving this property is to use a decimal counter which holds a cycle count [15]. This counter is incremented whenever a new key is desired, preferably after every transaction. The incremented cycle count, concatenated with the device's identity, is encrypted under the old key, and the resulting cipher is used as a new key. The HPC and security module can track this operation, provided the current cycle count for each transaction is known. This can be accomplished by including the current cycle count in each transaction request sent to the issuer.

Although this method works in principle, a synchronization requirement is introduced, since the communicating nodes must track the keys even in the presence of system errors. This may be unacceptable in some system designs.

Exposure of Keys at the Entry Point

The suggested protection against terminal intrusion, which could lead to an exposure of the secret terminal key, is to interlock the terminal key so that any penetration of the device causes the key to be erased, thus making the device inoperative. However, the manufacture of tamper-proof terminals, although perhaps possible, could lead to unacceptable, increased costs to the respective financial institutions. Even under the assumption that the secret terminal key is interlocked, so that any penetration of the device causes the key to be erased, it must be realized that with enough time and sophisticated equipment the interlock can generally be defeated. Then the terminal key could be recovered.

Key Management is Not Robust

The term robust is used frequently in statistical analyses where the assumption is often made that the underlying probability distributions are Gaussian or normal (i.e., follow a bell-shaped curve). But such an assumption is often incorrect. The question then is: How are the results affected by a deviation from the original assumption of a normal distribution? If deviations do not seriously affect the results, one says the method is robust.

In the PIN/system key approach, key management must defend against dictionary and misrouting attacks. However, weak key management at one network node could expose the PINs of many users, and therefore the security of the entire network could be jeopardized (i.e., a weakness at one point in the system could affect the security of the entire system). Therefore one can say that the PIN/system key approach is not robust.[25]

Advantages of the PIN/System Key Approach

1. Although separation of the authentication process among institutions is not possible with the PIN/system key approach, it nevertheless achieves many of the EFT security requirements stated previously, and provides a strong defense against threats posed by outsiders (those with access only to external system interfaces).
2. The PIN/system key approach can be implemented using existing technology and is in compliance with present bank card format standards and emerging PIN management standards.
3. With secret keys installed in the EFT terminals, there is automatically something with which the terminal can be interlocked (i.e., the secret terminal key) so that any penetration of the device causes the key to be erased and the terminal to become inoperative. Without a secret key, the terminal would have to be interlocked to an alarm or hardware-disabling device.

Conclusion: Although the PIN/system key approach does not satisfy all of the stated EFT security requirements, it does provide a reasonable level of protection, using existing technology and current banking practices and standards, for present EFT systems and those planned for the near future.

[25]A hybrid key management approach is less vulnerable to global exposures as discussed in the section The PIN/Personal Key/System Key (Hybrid Key Management) Approach using an Intelligent Secure Card. Such an approach is thus more robust. In other words, security weaknesses introduced at some nodes in the network do not have a major effect on the overall security of the network.

THE PIN/PERSONAL KEY APPROACH

The personal key approach attempts to improve the process of personal verification by eliminating the need for a secret key in the EFT terminal. Instead a personal key is recorded on each customer's bank card. The key, together with the cryptographic algorithm, is then used to encipher the PIN and generate the MACs needed to authenticate the transaction request and transaction response messages.

The personal key could be stored on either a magnetic stripe card or an intelligent secure card. An intelligent secure card offers greater security, although the magnetic stripe card can provide a migration path to a system incorporating personal keys stored on intelligent secure cards. A PIN/personal key approach using a magnetic stripe card is described first. An approach in which the personal key is stored on an intelligent secure card is described in the section Personal Key Approach with an Intelligent Secure Card.

Description of a PIN/Personal Key Approach Using a Magnetic Stripe Card

Assume that cardholders are authenticated on the basis of an authentication parameter, defined as $AP = E_{KP \oplus PIN}(ID)$, a copy of which is stored in a verification table in the issuer's HPC.[26] Message authentication between the user and issuer, and between the issuer and originating EFT terminal, is based on a MAC produced from the message using a transaction key (KTR) computed dynamically in the EFT terminal from KP, PIN, and ID, as follows: $KTR = D_{KP \oplus PIN}(ID)$.[27] Since $E_{KP \oplus PIN}(ID)$ was already used for an authentication parameter, the decipher operation is used to define KTR. A copy of each user's KTR is also stored in the issuer's verification table.

When a customer initiates a transaction and his card is read, the card information (including KP and ID) is transferred to the terminal and his PIN is entered via a suitable entry device. The PIN and KP are Exclusive-ORed to produce an intermediate key, which is used in turn to produce AP and KTR by enciphering and deciphering the ID, respectively. A transaction request message is then formed, which consists of a time stamp supplied by the acquirer's HPC (TODacq), a message sequence number supplied by the terminal,

[26] The verification table could be eliminated by defining a personal authentication code, $PAC = E_{KA}(AP)$, which is stored on the bank card. In such a case, the issuer would need to store only KA. (See also Figure 11-9.)

[27] A one-way function of KP, PIN, and ID (e.g., $KTR = D_{KP \oplus PIN}(ID)$) has an advantage over a function that is not one-way (e.g., $KTR = KP \oplus PIN$). If KTR were defined as $KP \oplus PIN$, then knowledge of KTR would permit an equivalent KP and PIN (say KP* and PIN*) to be derived such that $KP^* \oplus PIN^* = KP \oplus PIN$. Therefore, unauthorized entry to the system could be gained at any EFT terminal by using KP* and PIN*. On the other hand, if KTR is a one-way function of KP and PIN, there is no practical way to devise KPs and PINs that could be used to gain entry to the system. In that case, an opponent would be forced to conduct an active attack wherein a previously intercepted AP value (corresponding to KTR) is inserted into a bogus message and a MAC is then generated for the message using the compromised KTR.

the user's account number, the user's authentication parameter, the terminal's ID, the transaction type, and the transaction data. The time stamp allows the issuer to check the timeliness of the transaction request message. The message sequence number, which is returned in the transaction response message, allows the EFT terminal to check the timeliness of the response. (See also Figures 11-15 through 11-19 for a discussion of time stamps.) A MAC is then generated for the transaction request message using KTR, and the transaction request message and MAC are sent to the issuer.[28]

The issuer validates the message using the KTR of reference stored in his data base filed under the user's identifier (ID). A MAC of reference is computed from the message and the KTR of reference. The MAC of reference is then checked for equality with the received MAC. The time stamp in the received message is also checked against the time stamp of reference to ensure that the message is current (not a stale message). If both tests succeed, the message is validated. The time stamp of reference is then replaced by the received time stamp.

The received AP value is next compared for equality with the AP of reference also filed under the user's identifier (KD) in the issuer's data base.[29] If the two AP values are equal, the issuer concludes that the secret data supplied by the user (KP and PIN) are properly related to the claimed ID. If the requested transaction can be honored, a positive response is sent to the originating terminal; otherwise, a negative response is sent.

The positive and negative responses could consist of request for transaction granted and request for transaction not granted, respectively (where "transaction" denotes the transaction request message repeated in its entirety). A MAC is also generated for the transaction response message using KTR, and the transaction response message and generated MAC are sent to the EFT terminal.

Upon receipt of the response message, the terminal generates a MAC of reference from the stored KTR of reference and the received message. The received MAC is then compared for equality with the MAC of reference. The message sequence number in the received message is also compared for equality with the message sequence number of reference stored previously in the EFT terminal (at the time it was generated). If both the MACs and message sequence numbers are equal, the response is validated; otherwise, it is not. If a validated positive response is received, the terminal honors the

[28] Since KTR is a function of KP and PIN, MAC is by definition an authentication parameter. Thus, personal verification could be based on the MAC (i.e., an AP value in the message is unnecessary). In the proposed ANSI standard for PIN management and security [11], PIN validation is treated separately from message authentication. For this reason, personal verification and message authentication are treated separately here. An EFT system in which authentication of the transaction request message and personal verification are based solely on the MAC is described in the section The PIN/Personal Key/System Key (Hybrid Key Management) Approach Using an Intelligent Secure Card.

[29] If PAC = E_{KA}(AP) is stored on the bank card, verification takes place as follows. The received value of AP is encrypted with the issuer's KA of reference to generate a PAC of reference. If PAC of reference equals the received PAC, the user is accepted; otherwise, he is rejected.

transaction. If either an invalid or negative response is received, the transaction is denied.

Key Management Considerations for PIN/Personal Key Approach

The major objective of the PIN/Personal Key approach is to devise a key management which minimizes the need for system keys. This means that personal authentication information is a function of KP and PIN only. This also means that message authentication codes associated with transaction request messages are a function of KP (but not a function of system keys). Thus to check a received MAC (associated with the transaction request message) the issuer needs a dynamically computed MAC of reference. This in turn means that KP must be stored or recreated at the issuer dynamically.

The requirement to generate a MAC of reference exists also at the entry point. This allows the MAC associated with the transaction response message sent from the issuer to the entry point to be checked.

A reference must be available at both the issuer and the entry point to permit MACs to be checked. With the PIN/Personal Key approach, that reference would be KP or a secret value related to KP and perhaps PIN. The important thing is that the integrity and secrecy of that reference be assured. It is relatively easy to satisfy this requirement at the issuer where strict security procedures can be enforced. This means that the processes of personal verification and authentication of transaction request messages can be isolated to the respective issuing institutions. However, the situation is different at the entry point. A secret reference cannot be stored in the EFT terminal, since doing so would conflict with the intent of the personal key approach. The personal key approach attempts to eliminate the storage of a secret key (or parameter) in the EFT terminal and thus eliminate the need to manage and maintain the secrecy of terminal resident keys (or parameters). Since storing a reference in the EFT terminal is effectively the same as storing a key, a practical solution is not achieved. The only remaining alternative is to store the reference on the card. However, the price paid for doing this is that the process of authentication of transaction response messages cannot be isolated among the respective institutions.

Advantages of the PIN/Personal Key Approach

Increased Number of Combinations of Secret User-Supplied Information

With an increased number of combinations of secret user-supplied information, discovery of a PIN and personal key via attacks using exhaustive methods are computationally infeasible. Trial and error methods at the entry point interface where the user supplies his information or exhaustive methods performed on the system via a programming interface, are effectively thwarted.

End-To-End Protection Between the User and Issuer

In an interchange environment, a user-supplied key provides true end-to-end cryptographic protection between the user and issuer. Secret interchange keys shared with other institutions or with a switch are unnecessary. Also, cryptographic transformations at the acquirer, the switch, or other intermediate network nodes to decipher data under one key and reencipher them under another key are unnecessary. Thus data are not exposed in the HPC of other institutions, or even in the security modules of those institutions.

In summary, the PIN/personal key approach does not require

1. Sharing of secret keys
2. Cryptographic translation of data
3. Protection against data misrouting
4. PIN translation at the issuer

as would be the case with the PIN/system key approach. This reduces the complexity of key management.

Objections to the PIN/Personal Key Approach Using a Magnetic Stripe Card

Although a magnetic stripe card can be used for storing KP, there are several objections that favor the intelligent secure card as the storage medium for such a KP. For example, a key stored on the magnetic stripe card could be compromised via skimming or bugging. In addition, a key stored on the magnetic stripe card offers no protection against certain active fraud threats as discussed below in the section Exposures Due to Misuse of Personal Keys and Fake Personal Keys.

A Key on the Magnetic Stripe Card Cannot be Protected

One of the major objections raised against storing a key on the magnetic stripe card is that the key cannot be adequately protected, i.e., it cannot be maintained as a secret in a practical EFT system. In a nationwide EFT environment, there is probably a very large number of nonsecure terminals used without PINs and cryptography for the purchase of merchandise. In such an environment a key on the bank card would be exposed. (See also the section above entitled Threats to the Secrecy of a Key Stored on a Magnetic Stripe Card.)

If a cardholder's personal key should become compromised, the associated PIN can also be ascertained with only a small additional effort provided that a transaction request message initiated by the cardholder can be intercepted in the network domain where PINs are used. Consider this case: assume that cardholders are authenticated on the basis of an authentication parameter (AP) included in the transaction request message, where AP is defined as $AP = E_{KP \oplus PIN}(ID)$. With a compromised KP and the corresponding intercepted AP and ID, the PIN can be recovered using a method of direct search. With a four-digit PIN there would be 10,000 combinations, namely, 0000, 0001, . . . , 9999. Starting with the first value, each successive value is tested to see if it is the correct PIN. This is done by Exclusive-ORing the trial PIN with the compromised KP, encrypting ID under this intermediate value, and comparing the result for equality with AP. The trial PIN is therefore the actual PIN in question if the computed value of AP is equal to the intercepted value of AP.

If AP is not sent, the system can still be attacked since the intercepted MAC is a function of KP and PIN. In this case a trial KTR is generated by Exclusive-ORing the trial PIN with the compromised KP and decrypting ID under this intermediate value. The trial KTR is accepted as valid if the MAC generated from the intercepted message (using the trial KTR) equals the corresponding intercepted MAC.

A Key on the Magnetic Stripe Card Must be Shared with the Terminal

By definition, a secret user-supplied key must be used to achieve personal verification and authentication of transaction request messages between the cardholder and issuer such that the cardholder and issuer are completely isolated from all other users, programs, and devices in the EFT system. Although a personal key is required to achieve isolation, it is not by itself sufficient. Isolation is achieved only if the secret personal key is not exposed, disclosed, or shared with others. A key written on a magnetic stripe card must always be read into the EFT terminal, since the terminal contains the cryptographic algorithm. Therefore, in an interchange, the process of personal verification is not isolated to the cardholder and issuer: the secrecy of KP depends additionally on security measures implemented in the acquiring institution's terminals.

Exposure Due to Misuse of Personal Keys and Fake Personal Keys

Although the personal key can be used to generate MACs on EFT transaction request messages and transaction response messages, these MACs are based on a KP and PIN supplied and known to the cardholder. Thus the cardholder himself is able to launch active attacks by generating valid MACs for arbitrary transaction response messages. This action is referred to as a *misuse of personal key attack.* An opponent who supplies a bogus personal key to the EFT terminal can also forge transactions. This action is referred to as a *fake personal key attack.*

Fraud could be perpetrated against the system by initiating a transaction at an EFT terminal using any (bogus or valid) KP and PIN known to the cardholder. A microprocessor previously placed in the communication line between the EFT terminal to its host could be programmed to intercept and prevent all opponent-initiated transactions from reaching the issuer. The microprocessor would then generate a fraudulent response message and valid MAC and send them to the EFT terminal. The EFT terminal would respond as though it were in communication with the issuer, when in fact it would be in communication with the opponent's microprocessor.

The attack illustrates why the process of authenticating transaction response messages must be based on secret information (a secret key) known only to the issuer or to the issuer and originating terminal, but not to the cardholder.

No Interlocking with KP

When a secret terminal key is employed, the suggested protection against bugging and probing is to interlock the terminal key so that any penetration of the device causes the key to be erased and the device to become inoperative. In the personal key approach, there is no secret key to interlock. In that case, a defense against penetration of the terminal must be provided by other methods, e.g., using an integrated alarm system. In addition to increasing cost, alarms may malfunction or become inoperative or be intentionally bypassed during an attack. Moreover, an indication of the alarm's ineffectiveness is not necessarily obvious.

Personal Key Approach with an Intelligent Secure Card

Although several objections have been raised with regard to the personal key, most of these are objections to storing the key on the magnetic stripe card. A valid objection to the personal key, however, is that *authentication of transaction response messages must not be based on a key known to the cardholder (legitimate user or opponent).* Otherwise, the system is exposed to active fraud threats wherein valid MACs would be generated on fraudulent transaction response messages.

An Ideal Intelligent Secure Card

The objection to the "personal key approach," stated above, could be largely overcome by employing an intelligent secure card with the following properties:

1. Secret information stored on the card cannot be probed or read.
2. It is not possible to manufacture counterfeit cards.
3. It is not possible to write a bogus key on a genuine card.

An intelligent secure card with the above properties is defined here as an *ideal intelligent secure card* ("ideal" mainly because the properties of the card are unattainable with present technology).

The intelligent secure card must have some identifying property or feature that could be checked at the time of its use to distinguish it from a bogus card. Otherwise, an opponent may be able to manufacture inexpensive bogus cards which do not have the properties of the intelligent secure cards, but nevertheless satisfy the interface requirements of the entry point.

With an ideal intelligent secure card, all cryptographic operations would be performed on the card using KP. KP would be used to encrypt and protect the PIN and to generate MACs on the transaction request and transaction response messages.

Loss and theft of cards and copying card information present no threat to the secrecy of KP since secret information stored on the card cannot be ascertained due to property 1. The fake personal key attack is blocked since

System User	Ideal Intelligent Secure Bank Card	EFT Terminal	Acquirer's Host (Inst. X)	Switch's Host	Issuer's Host (Inst. Y)
		System Nodes			
		Permanently Installed Keys			
none	KP	none	none	none	KMHiss
		Keys Used for MAC Generation on the Transaction Request Message, Mreq			
none	KTRcard,iss (dynamically generated from KP and PIN)	none	none	none	KTRcard,iss for each member of institution Y (dynamically generated or stored)
		Keys Used for MAC Generation on the Transaction Response Message, Mresp			
none	KTRcard,iss (dynamically generated from KP and PIN)	none	none	none	KTRcard,iss for each member of institution Y (dynamically generated or stored)

Note: Keys associated with personal verification at the issuer (and perhaps the switch) are not shown.

Legend:

KMH: Host master key
KTR: Transaction key (used for message authentication, e.g., KTR1card,iss = $D_{KP \oplus PIN}$(ID))
KP: Personal Key

Table 11-6. Keys Defined for the PIN/Personal Key Approach Using an Intelligent Secure Card

manufacturing or changing a bank card is considered not possible due to properties 2 and 3. Cardholders would not be given their personal keys (only the issuer would know the KPs), thus blocking misuse of personal keys by legitimate users. In effect, the issuer would determine all card information, including the user's personal key. Cardholders would be prevented from obtaining their KPs since they cannot read the information due to property 1.

Furthermore, because all cryptographic operations would be performed on the card, it is unnecessary to transmit KP to the entry point. Thus, KP would not be exposed at the terminal. The ideal intelligent secure card would also eliminate the need for storing a key in the terminal. Hence, an extremely simple key management could be implemented. No additional system keys would be needed with the possible exception of an authentication key at the issuer if personal authentication codes are used.

There is, however, one remaining exposure with this approach. After all checking has been done on the bank card, the terminal must be informed of the outcome (positive or negative). But since there are no keys stored in the terminal, data communications between the card and terminal cannot be authenticated. Therefore the integrity of this communication path must be assured independently. Otherwise, a negative response could be changed to a positive response (again allowing fraud to be committed).

A summary of the keys required with the PIN/personal key approach is provided in Table 11-6. A description of the PIN/personal key approach when used in conjunction with an intelligent secure card is summarized in Tables 11-6 and 11-7. The tables show the flows of information from the card to the issuer (via the EFT terminal) and from the issuer to the EFT terminal (via the card), and include a description of the keys and MACs used in the message authentication process.

Comparing Tables 11-6, 11-7, and 11-8 with those of the PIN/system key approach (Tables 11-3, 11-4, and 11-5), one observes that a simpler key management is achieved with the PIN/personal key approach.

The personal key approach provides adequate EFT security if the requirements of an ideal intelligent secure card are met. However, the approach has one major drawback; it is unlikely that an attractively priced card meeting these requirements can be produced with current technology. Despite this drawback, the intelligent secure card does offer the potential for improved EFT security if used in conjunction with personal and system keys, as discussed in the section The PIN/Personal Key/System Key (Hybrid Key Management) Approach Using an Intelligent Secure Card.

A Practical Intelligent Secure Card

The requirements for an ideal intelligent secure card are unattainable for the following reasons. First, it is unlikely that probing for card information can be prevented. With enough time and resources, information on the card could be recovered. Second, since institutions must be able to arrange for the manufacture of cards, an opponent must be assumed to have the same opportunity.

A more realistic objective would be to make it prohibitively expensive for an opponent to obtain only a few cards, by forcing him to assume the total cost and burden of becoming a manufacturer. Since the opponent would

System User	Ideal Intelligent Secure Bank Card	System Nodes: EFT Terminal	System Nodes: Acquirer's Host	System Nodes: Switch's Host	System Nodes: Issuer's Host
1 Enter PIN and transfer to card via terminal.	2 Generate Tcard and transfer to terminal.	3 Read card information and formulate Mreq which includes TODacq and Tcard.	8 Forward received Mreq and MAC1card,iss to switch.	9 Forward received Mreq and MAC1card,iss to issuer.	10 Check received MAC1card,iss with KTRcard,iss of reference and TODiss of reference.
	5 Compute MAC1card,iss with KTRcard,iss.	4 Send Mreq to intelligent secure card.			11 Verify user.
	6 Send Mreq and MAC1card,iss to terminal.	7 Forward received Mreq and MAC1card,iss to acquirer.			12 Decide if Mreq is to be honored.
					13 Formulate Mresp which includes Tcard.

Note: It is assumed that the acquirer periodically sends time-of-day information (TODacq,term) to the terminals in its domain. The card also generates time-variant information (Tcard) which is transmitted to the issuer. The TOD stored at the other network host nodes (TODsw at the switch and TODiss at the issuer) is assumed to be equal to TODacq within an allowable range (ΔTOD).

The integers 1–13 in the table show the sequence of steps in the transaction.

Table 11-7. Information Flow from Card to Issuer—PIN/Personal Key Approach with Intelligent Secure Card

System User	Ideal Intelligent Secure Bank Card	System Nodes: EFT Terminal	Acquirer's Host	Switch's Host	Issuer's Host
	19 Check received MAC2iss,card with KTR of reference and Tcard of reference.	18 Forward received Mresp and MAC2iss,card to card.	17 Forward received Mresp and MAC2iss,card to terminal.	16 Forward received Mresp and MAC2iss,card to acquirer.	13 Formulate Mresp which includes Tcard.
	20 Decide if Mresp should be accepted or rejected.	22 Initiate action based on decision made by intelligent secure card.			14 Generate MAC2iss,card using KTR.
	21 Notify terminal to process transaction if Mresp is accepted; otherwise notify terminal to abort transaction request*.				15 Send Mresp and MAC2iss,card to intelligent secure card via switch, acquirer, and terminal.

*This response to the terminal cannot be authenticated since there is no terminal resident key.

The integers 13–21 in the table show the sequence of steps in the transaction.

Table 11-8. Information Flow from Issuer to Terminal—PIN/Personal Key Approach with Intelligent Secure Card

normally need only a few cards, the cost per card would be very high. It seems much more reasonable that an intelligent secure card could be manufactured (designed and mass-produced) with the property that secret information stored on the card could not be read, skimmed, or copied during periods when the card is used (and exposed) routinely to transact business. It is assumed that secret information stored on the card would be secure against reading, skimming, or copying even if the card is unwittingly entered into a fake or modified terminal under the control of an opponent, or if, as a part of the procedure for transacting business, the cardholder gives his card to a dishonest merchant (or employee of the merchant) who, in turn, surreptitiously enters the card into a special reading device hidden from view. An intelligent secure card with these properties is defined here as a *practical intelligent secure card,* or *intelligent secure card,* for short.

To summarize, the following properties are assumed for the intelligent secure card.

1. Secret information stored on the card cannot be probed or read by personnel or equipment handling the card during routine business transactions. Sophisticated techniques and expensive equipment would be required to probe or write secret card information, although it is assumed that this could be accomplished in a laboratory environment.
2. It is very expensive to manufacture counterfeit cards on a small scale.
3. It is very expensive to write a bogus key on a genuine card.

The intelligent secure card, as assumed here therefore, only defends against attacks of short duration that do not injure or destroy the card or the secret information stored thereon. It is assumed that a destroyed, injured, or nonfunctional card would be promptly reported to the issuing institution, and that the issuing institution would invalidate the corresponding account and either reissue a new card or reinitialize the existing card with a new key (as appropriate). Likewise, it is assumed that lost and stolen cards would be promptly reported to the issuing institution and that a similar action would be taken by the issuing institution to invalidate the accounts and reissue new cards to the affected cardholders.

However, since one must assume that an opponent could manufacture bogus cards and write bogus keys on them, the PIN/Personal key approach is still exposed to a fake personal key attack. Since one must assume also that a legitimate user can determine his KP if he is willing to overcome the obstacles identified in item 1 above, the exposure to misuse of KPs also exists. For these reasons, the intelligent secure card does not overcome the basic objection to the personal key approach stated previously; namely, authentication of transaction response messages must not be based on a key known to the cardholder (legitimate user or opponent).

This objection (to the personal key approach) can be overcome by basing authentication of transaction response messages on a secret terminal key in addition to a personal key (i.e., the key management employs both personal and system keys). Such hybrid key management used together with an intelligent secure card offers the potential for increased security in future EFT applications.

THE PIN/PERSONAL KEY/SYSTEM KEY (HYBRID KEY MANAGEMENT) APPROACH USING AN INTELLIGENT SECURE CARD

Discussed here is a system which provides a higher level of security than either the PIN/system key or the PIN/personal key approach. From a security point of view, it is thus a preferred solution. The approach combines the features of an intelligent secure card (see the section Personal Key Approach with an Intelligent Secure Card) with that of hybrid key management based on both system keys and personal keys.[30] For reasons of completeness, some of the ideas and terms discussed above are repeated here.

Hybrid key management used together with the intelligent secure card solves the following problems individually associated with the PIN/system key and PIN/personal key approaches, respectively:

1. The PIN/system key approach does not provide isolation of institutions as far as personal verification and message authentication are concerned, although it is an acceptable solution.
2. The PIN/personal key approach in combination with an intelligent secure card, although it provides a higher degree of isolation for personal verification than does the PIN/system key approach, is subject to misuse of KPs and fake KPs. It is, by itself, an unacceptable solution.

With a combination of both approaches (i.e., PIN/system key and PIN/personal key), personal verification can be isolated among institutions and the threats of misused and fake KPs are greatly reduced. As shown below, an attack will succeed only if system keys are subverted and personal keys are manipulated at the same time. In addition, the end-to-end message authentication procedure based on KP and PIN is combined with personal verification eliminating the need for generation of a separate authentication parameter for personal verification.

Although the hybrid approach combines two key management schemes (system and personal key), it is actually less complex than the PIN/system key approach. Rerouting attacks are of no concern because of the personal key, which eliminates some of the functions needed in the PIN/system key approach. It is also more robust since security exposures occurring at intermediate nodes have only a limited effect on overall security.

[30] An increase in security over the PIN/system key approach can be achieved by coupling a hybrid key management with a magnetic stripe card. Storing a personal key on the magnetic stripe card allows a migration path to a hybrid key management approach coupled with an intelligent secure card. The details of such an approach are omitted, although the reader should have no difficulty in adapting the hybrid key management approach described here to work with a magnetic stripe card.

Description of a Hybrid Key Management Approach

The system discussed here is composed of host processing centers (HPCs) and EFT terminals, interconnected in an EFT network supporting interchange.[31] Each network node has a DES cryptographic capability either integrated into the node or contained in a separate dedicated device called a *security module*[32] attached to the node via a secure, local cable. Each security module has a set of cryptographic operations that may be invoked by the supporting device or HPC via a defined interface. The cryptographic operations perform data encryption and decryption and key translations necessary to the management of EFT transactions. No clear cryptographic keys ever exist outside the security module, except during periods when they are initially generated or entered into the system.

Keys stored in a security module are protected by implementing adequate physical security measures and/or providing a set of interlocks that will erase all secret information if penetration of the security module or containing device is detected.

It is assumed (as in the discussion of the PIN/personal key approach, Table 11-6), that a transaction key (a dynamically created key used solely for authentication, denoted by KTR1), is used to generate the MAC on the transaction request message (Mreq). KTR1 is a one-way function of the PIN, the personal key, and the user identifier, so that each user is assigned a different value of KTR1. (Other variations are possible in which different KTR1 keys are generated for the same user on successive transactions, but are omitted from the discussion.) End-to-end authentication is made possible by storing a copy of each user's KTR1 at the issuer. At the entry point, KTR1 is dynamically created from user-supplied information. Since the MAC depends only on secret user-supplied information and other nonsecret information, it is by definition an authentication parameter (AP). Thus authentication of the transaction request message and personal verification are integrated into one procedure.

The response message is authenticated on the basis of a time-variant key KSTR generated randomly at the issuer and transmitted to the terminal in the form $E_{Knode}(E_{KTR2}(KSTR))$ (i.e., doubly encrypted under two keys, KTR2 and Knode). KTR2 is defined by the one-way function KTR2 = $D_{KTR1}(Tcard)$, where KTR1 is the same key used to generate the MAC on the transaction request message and Tcard is a nonsecret time-variant quantity generated by the intelligent secure card. Knode is a time-variant system key shared between two logically adjacent network nodes (e.g., the terminal and acquirer, the acquirer and switch, and the switch and issuer). Thus as KSTR is routed from the issuer to the terminal it is encrypted and reencrypted successively under different Knode keys. For example, Knode

[31] For simplicity, the control units shown in Figure 11-1 are omitted.

[32] The security module provides the same function as a cryptographic facility (see The Cryptographic Facility, Chapter 4). The term "security module" is used here to maintain consistency with the discussion in Chapter 10 of the PIN/System key approach.

would equal the terminal master key KMT on the link between the acquirer and terminal.

At the time Tcard is generated, KTR2 is also generated by the intelligent secure card. KTR2 and Tcard are then sent to the terminal where KTR2 is saved for later use in decrypting KSTR and Tcard is forwarded to the issuer in the transaction request message. The issuer generates KTR2 from Tcard (which it receives in Mreq) and KTR1 (which is stored in the issuer's data base). In a sense, KTR2 is nothing more than a time-variant personal key with the property that knowledge of KTR2 does not reveal KP. Note also that KTR2 is not routed through the system (i.e., the terminal and issuer establish KTR2 without involving other system nodes or depending on these nodes to protect the secrecy of KTR2).

At the terminal, the encrypted KSTR arrives in the form $E_{KMTacq,term}E_{KTR2}(KSTR)$. It is decrypted first with KMT and second with KTR2 to recover KSTR. Mresp is authenticated by generating a MAC of reference from Mresp and KSTR and comparing it for equality with the received MAC.[33]

The Reason for Doubly Encrypting KSTR

The explanation of why KSTR is doubly encrypted under KTR2 and Knode rather than being encrypted only under Knode is now provided. If KSTR is encrypted under both KTR2 and Knode, the message authentication process associated with transaction response messages can be subverted (i.e., bogus messages and MACs acceptable to the terminal could be generated) only if both keys are compromised. An opponent must therefore compromise a Knode key, or some other system key that would allow a Knode key to be determined, and learn the value of KP on some intelligent secure card. With knowledge of KP it would be an easy matter to calculate the value of KTR1 for a bogus PIN and ID entered at the terminal. The value of Tcard could also be intercepted from the transmitted transaction request message, which would allow KTR2 to be calculated. With knowledge of KTR2 and Knode, the opponent (using an active wiretap) could then intercept and block the transaction response message and send a fraudulent transaction response message and MAC to the terminal in its place that would be accepted as valid.

The suggested method of doubly encrypting KSTR under KTR2 and Knode provides additional security (over a method of encrypting KSTR under Knode) only if the cost or work factor to read or write a key on a card or manufacture bogus cards is significant. If the card's defenses can be overcome easily in a laboratory at a low or moderate cost, encryption of KSTR under KTR2 does not add significantly to the security of KSTR. In such a case, the protocol could be modified so that Tcard and KTR2 are not generated by the intelligent secure card and Tcard is eliminated from the transaction request message. At the issuer, KSTR is encrypted only under Knode. Otherwise, the protocol is the same.

[33] There is no need to protect the encrypted value of KSTR with a MAC since, if changed, KSTR will not decrypt correctly and an incorrect MAC of reference will be generated.

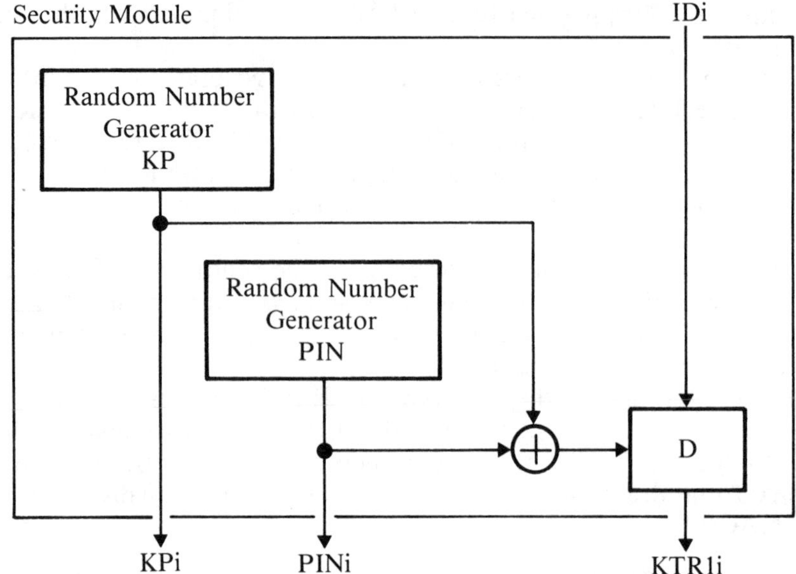

Figure 11-24. Generation of KP, PIN, and KTR1 in Issuer's Security Module - Initialization Process

PIN and KP Selection

While there are several ways in which PINs and personal keys could be selected, it will be assumed that they are produced by the issuer using the security module as a generator of pseudo-random numbers. The generated PIN is printed on a PIN mailer and the corresponding KP is written on the bank card. The PIN mailer and bank card are then forwarded to the designated customer. KP and PIN are also Exclusive-ORed to form the intermediate value KP ⊕ PIN, which is then used as a key to decipher ID and generate a transaction key, KTR1 = $D_{KP \oplus PIN}(ID)$.[34] The generation of KP, PIN, and KTR1 is shown in Figure 11-24. KTR1 is stored in the data base of the issuer's HPC encrypted under a variant of the host master key.

PIN and KP Validation

Each time the customer initiates a transaction at an EFT terminal, the entered PIN is transferred to the bank card where it is Exclusive-ORed with KP to form the intermediate value KP ⊕ PIN (Figure 11-25), which in turn is used with ID to generate KTR1. KTR1 is then used to generate a MAC on the transaction request message. A time-of-day clock value (time stamp) is included in the message to ensure that it is time-variant. (A separate authentication parameter is not transmitted in the message since personal verification is combined with message authentication by basing the MAC on KP and PIN.)

At the issuer, the message is validated using a corresponding KTR1 of

[34] For an explanation of the advantage of making KTR1 a one-way function of KP, PIN, and ID, see footnote 27.

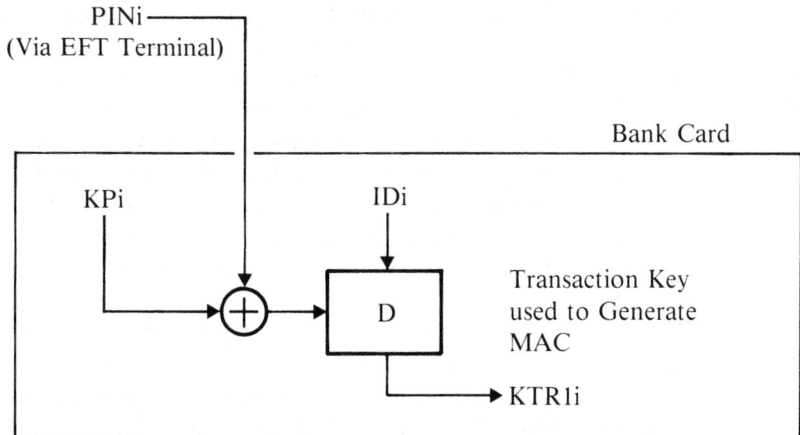

Figure 11-25. Regeneration of the Transaction Key on the Bank Card - Part of the Verification Process

reference which is filed under the user's identifier (ID) in the data base of the issuer's HPC.[35] The KTR1 of reference and the received message are then used to generate a MAC of reference. The MAC of reference and the received MAC are compared for equality. If they are equal, the issuer concludes that the content of the message is correct and that the secret information (KP and PIN) used in the computation of the MAC is properly related to the claimed ID thus verifying the user at the same time. By verifying that the time stamp in the received message correlates properly with the corresponding reference maintained by the issuer, the issuer can determine that the received message is not a stale message. More details are provided below in the sections A Hybrid Key Management Approach for Noninterchange, and A Hybrid Key Management Approach for Interchange.

System Key Generation

The keys for an institution's terminals are produced by that institution's security module, using the module as a generator of pseudo-random numbers. The keys are transferred from the module to a secure device (e.g., a printer) and they are then transported and installed in the appropriate EFT terminals. Each terminal master key is also encrypted under a variant of the host master key (derived in the issuer's security module) and then stored in the data base of the issuer's HPC (filed under the terminal identifier, TID). It is assumed that each terminal in the network has a unique identifier TID, and that the TID is included in each transaction request message.

Key Management Considerations for the Hybrid Approach

The major objective of the PIN/personal key/system key approach is to use externally supplied keys as well as system keys (but only to the extent that

[35] It is assumed that the integrity of the data base can be guaranteed by the issuer's HPC. Various cryptographic techniques can be used to achieve data base integrity (see Authentication of Time-Invariant Data, Chapter 8).

they are of maximum use). Since it is secure to base the required reference at the issuer for MAC checking of the transaction request message entirely on KP and PIN (as discussed above for the PIN/personal key approach), this approach is also used in a hybrid key management scheme. As a consequence, the personal verification process is separated among institutions. On the other hand, since KP alone does not provide a secure method for MAC checking of the transaction response message, the required reference at the entry point is also based, in addition to KP, on a system key. This requires the presence of a terminal resident key (e.g., a terminal master key). In addition, keys used for MAC checking at intermediate nodes must be shared among institutions and thus the message authentication process cannot be isolated to each individual institution. However, greater separation can be achieved by coupling message authentication of transaction response messages to PIN and KP. This is achieved in the implementation discussed here by introducing the end-to-end transaction session key, KSTR, which is routed from the issuer to the terminal encrypted under both KTR2 = D_{KTR1}(Tcard) and Knode. (A still higher degree of separation can be achieved if digital signatures are used as discussed in the section below, Security Enhancements with Digital Signatures.)

In summary, KTR1 is used to generate the MAC on the transaction request message, KSTR is used to generate the MAC on the transaction response message, and KTR2 is one of the keys used to encrypt KSTR for transmission from the issuer to the entry point.

In an interchange environment, the issuer has no knowledge of the acquirer's terminal master keys. In that case, an interchange key (KI), in addition to KTR2, is used to encrypt and forward transaction session keys from one institution to another, e.g., from one institution to a switch, from the switch to an institution, or from one institution to another institution. It is assumed here that interchange keys are generated on a bilateral basis, so that two institutions (or an institution and its EFT switch) can share a common interchange key. An Interchange key is just one special form of node key (Knode). A terminal master key is also a node key.

The MAC generated on the transaction response message using KSTR has the advantage that it can be sent to the originating EFT terminal without undergoing any cryptographic transformation. Only the key (Knode) which protects E_{KTR2}(KSTR) changes as the transaction response message traverses the network.[36]

Hybrid Key Management Approach for Noninterchange

Each time a customer initiates a transaction at an EFT terminal, the customer's card is inserted into the terminal, or suitable read/write device attached to the terminal, and the customer enters his PIN via a suitable entry device (PIN pad or keyboard). The PIN is routed to the card where it is Exclusive-ORed with KP thus generating KTR1 in the manner described

[36] As discussed above, $E_{Knode}E_{KTR2}$(KSTR) is routed back to the terminal which has knowledge of KTR2. Encrypting with Knode, where Knode changes from node to node, assures that attacks which manipulate KP will not succeed.

above (Figure 11-25). The card also generates a random number, Tcard, which is decrypted under KTR1 to produce KTR2. KTR2 and Tcard are then routed to the terminal where KTR2 is stored for later use in authenticating the transaction response message.

Based on the customer's request, the terminal formats a transaction request message, which consists of a time stamp (TOD, time-of-day), time-variant information generated by the terminal (Tterm, a message sequence number), time-variant information generated by the card (Tcard), the user ID, the terminal ID, the transaction type, and the transaction data (Figure 11-26). The time stamp is obtained from the acquirer (which is also the issuer since a local transaction is described),[37] at the request of the EFT terminal. A different request could be made for each customer-initiated transaction. Another possibility is that the acquirer periodically sends time information to the terminal.

The purpose of the time-stamp is to provide the terminal with time-variant data that can be used in the preparation of the transaction request message. This permits the issuer (which, in this case, is the acquirer) to detect stale transaction request messages that may be injected into the communication path. It is assumed that the issuer's HPC maintains a time-of-day clock that can be read to obtain a time stamp.

The purpose of the message sequence number, generated by the EFT terminal, is to provide the issuer with time-variant data that can be used in the preparation of the transaction response message. This permits the EFT terminal to detect stale transaction response messages injected into the communication path. (Without authentication of the transaction response message, a replay attack is possible.) The message sequence number is incremented on each new transaction request message, independent of the customer initiating the transaction.

The purpose of the time-variant information generated by the intelligent secure card is to allow the terminal and issuer to establish a time-variant key, KTR2 = D_{KTR1}(Tcard), without involving other system nodes or relying on these nodes to protect the secrecy of KTR2. In this manner the terminal

Time Stamp (TOD)	Time-Variant Information Controlled By Card (Tcard)	Time-Variant Information Controlled By Terminal (Tterm)	User Identifier (ID)	Terminal Identifier (TID)	Transaction Type	Transaction Data

Figure 11-26. Transaction Request Message Formatted at the EFT Terminal

[37] To eliminate the need for the terminal (acting on behalf of the user) to request a time stamp from the issuer, the issuer could also record a current "time reference" for the user in his HPC's data base. For example, a message sequence number obtained from a one-up counter on the bank card could be used in place of the time stamp.

and issuer share a key that allows end-to-end authentication of Mresp without jeopardizing the security of KTR1, KP, or PIN.

Once the transaction request message has been formatted, it is transferred to the bank card where a MAC is generated using KTR1. The MAC is then returned to the terminal. Generation of a transaction request message and corresponding MAC is shown in Figure 11-27. The message and MAC are then sent to the issuer.

As mentioned earlier, the issuer validates the message using a corresponding KTR1 of reference which is filed under the user's ID in the data base of the issuer's HPC. The KTR1 of reference and the received message are then used to generate a MAC of reference, and the generated MAC of reference is compared for equality with the received MAC. The time stamp is also checked for currency. If both MACs are equal and the time stamp is within the prescribed bounds, the message and user are validated. Message authentication at the issuer's HPC is shown in Figure 11-28.

If the received MAC and time stamp are valid and the transaction request can be honored, the issuer's HPC formats and sends a positive transaction response message to the originating terminal. Otherwise, if any one of the conditions is not met, a negative transaction response message is sent to the originating terminal. Only the positive response is important to the discussion, since a negative response could be defined as any response other than a positive response, e.g., a random bit pattern.

A positive transaction response message consists of a doubly encrypted transaction session key $E_{KMT}E_{KTR2}$(KSTR) and a MAC generated on the transaction request message using KSTR. The procedure for generating a positive transaction response message (Figure 11-29) is as follows: Using the received TID, the HPC identifies the corresponding encrypted terminal master key in its data base and passes this to the security module along with the received transaction request message. The security module first generates a random number, defined as a transaction session key (KSTR), which it then uses to generate a MAC on the transaction request message. Next, KTR1 is recovered from the issuer's data base and used together with the received value of Tcard to generate KTR2 = D_{KTR1}(Tcard). Finally, the encrypted terminal master key is read from the issuer's data base, decrypted, and used with KTR2 to doubly encrypt KSTR. The doubly encrypted transaction session key, $E_{KMT}E_{KTR2}$(KSTR), and MAC are returned to the issuer's HPC whereupon they are sent to the originating terminal.

At the terminal, the procedure for validating the transaction response message (Figure 11-30) is as follows. The doubly encrypted transaction session key, $E_{KMT}E_{KTR2}$(KSTR), is decryted under the terminal master key (KMT) resident in the terminal. Next E_{KTR2}(KSTR) is decrypted under the value of KTR2 forwarded previously from the card to the terminal. KSTR is used to generate a MAC of Reference on the original transaction request message which is assumed to have been saved in the terminal. The MAC of reference is then compared for equality with the received MAC. If the two MACs are equal, the EFT terminal honors the requested transaction; otherwise, the EFT terminal informs the customer that the requested transaction has been

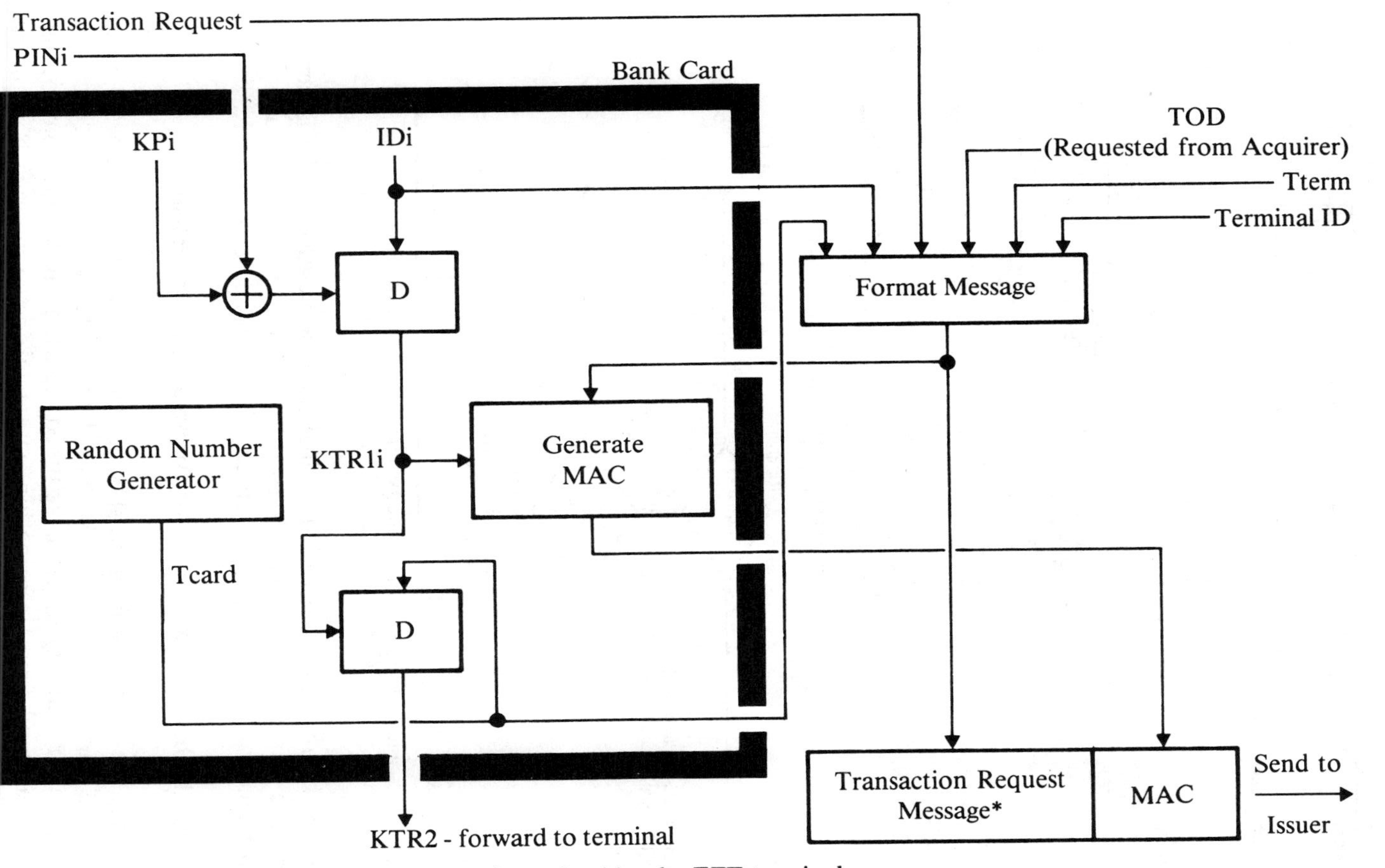

*A copy of the transaction request message is retained by the EFT terminal.

Figure 11-27. Generation of the Transaction Request Message and MAC at the EFT Terminal

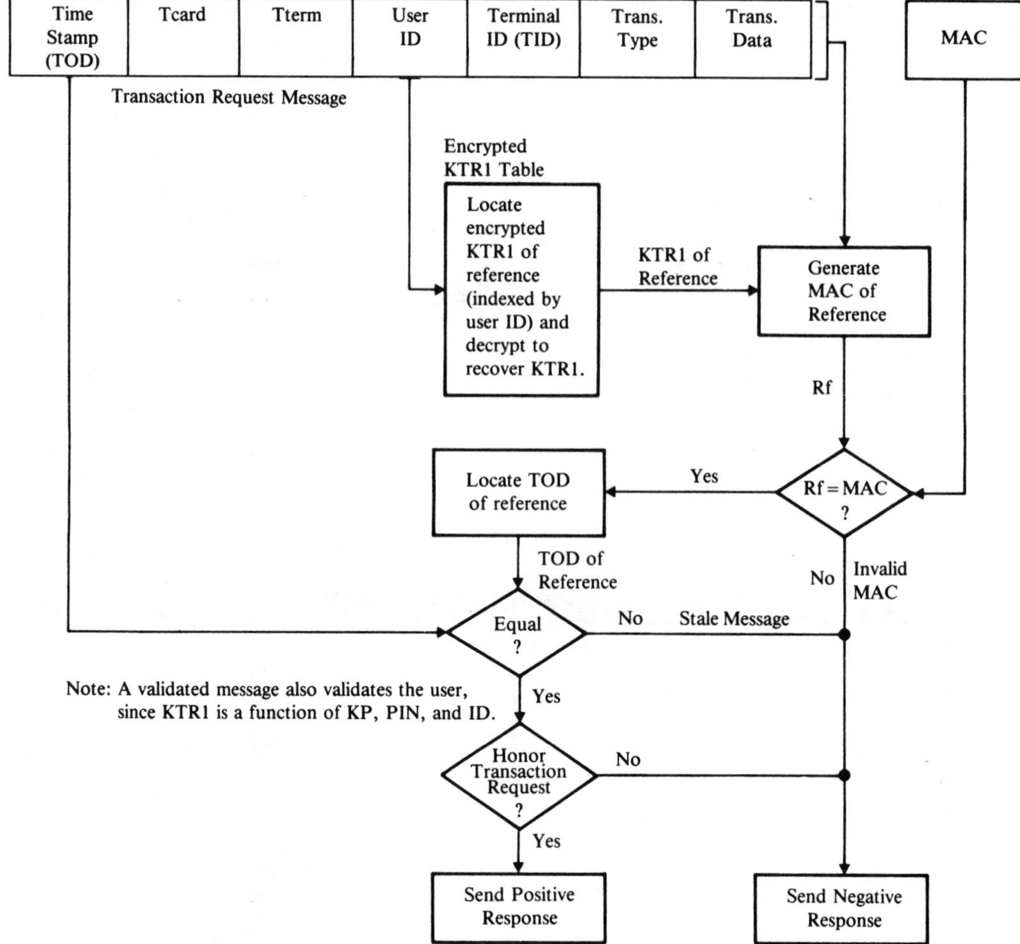

Figure 11-28. Message Authentication at the Issuer's EDP System

disallowed. In any case, the EFT terminal sends a message to the issuer, informing the issuer of the final disposition of the requested transaction. A MAC for this final message can be generated securely based on KSTR.

Hybrid Key Management Approach For Interchange

An interchange transaction originates in the same manner as does a local transaction. The message and MAC based on KTR1 are sent to the issuer via the acquirer and switch. It is assumed that the proper message routing can be determined from information contained in the message.[38] (Current bank card standards call for an institution code to be the first several digits of the personal account number [16].)

[38] Once the destination has been determined, the network routing information will appear in the message's header.

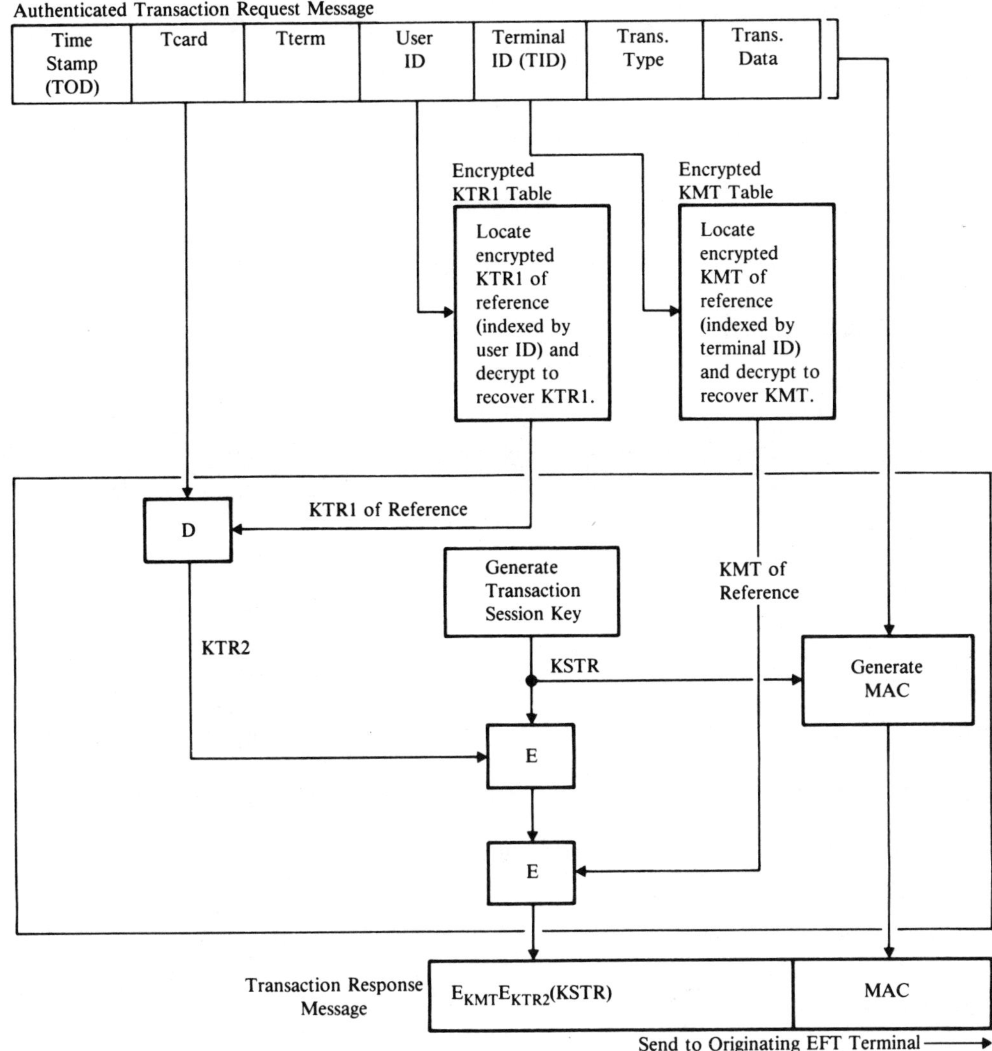

Figure 11-29. Generation of the Positive Transaction Response Message at the Issuer

The issuer validates the message using the KTR1 of reference stored in its data base, as previously described. The time stamp is also checked for currency (i.e., that the clock readings do not vary by more than some fixed limit). In checking for timeliness, it is assumed that the clocks of all institutions are synchronized and do not vary by more than small amounts. Where transactions cross time zones, either automatic adjustments are assumed to be present or a common fixed time is used (e.g., Universal Mean Time).

If the received MAC and time stamp are valid and the transaction request can be honored, the issuer's HPC formats and sends a positive transaction response message to the originating terminal. Otherwise, a negative transaction response message (not discussed here) is sent to the originating terminal.

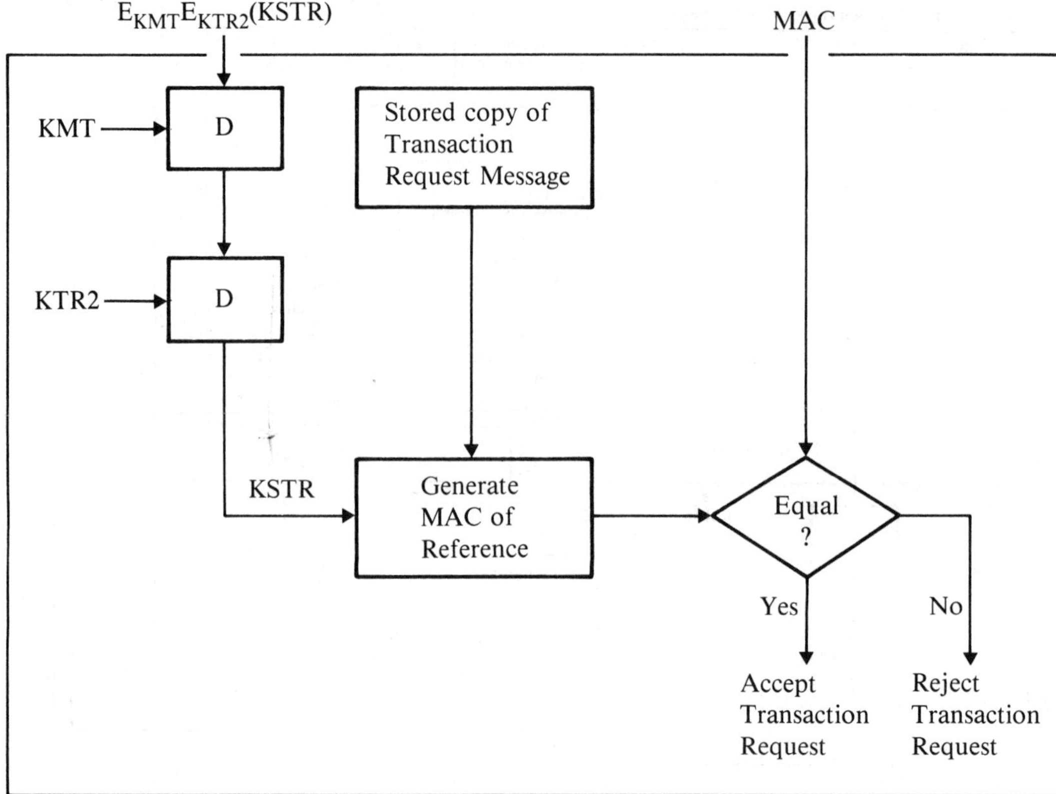

Figure 11-30. Message Authentication at the EFT Terminal

A positive transaction response message consists of a doubly encrypted transaction session key (KSTR) and a MAC generated on the transaction request message using KSTR. The procedure for generating a positive transaction response message is the same as in the case of a local transaction, except that $E_{KTR2}(KSTR)$ is encrypted under a key specified by the appropriate node (an interchange key, KI) rather than a terminal master key. In that case, $E_{KIiss,sw}E_{KTR2}(KSTR)$ and MAC are produced and sent to the switch. At the switch, $E_{KIiss,sw}E_{KTR2}(KSTR)$ is translated from encipherment under KIiss,sw (the issuer's interchange key) to encipherment under KIsw,acq (the acquirer's interchange key). $E_{KIsw,acq}E_{KTR2}(KTSR)$ and MAC are then sent to the acquirer, where $E_{KIsw,acq}E_{KTR2}(KSTR)$ is again translated from encipherment under KIsw,acq (the acquirers interchange key) to encipherment under KMTacq,term (the originating terminal's master key).[39] $E_{KMTacq,term}E_{KTR2}(KSTR)$ and MAC are then sent to the originating terminal. At the terminal, the procedure for validating the transaction response message is the same as in the case of a local transaction.

[39] To thwart message misrouting attacks, the terminal could use KTR2 to generate a MAC on the routing information contained in the message's header.

The general ideas as to the keys to be used as well as how data flows to and from the issuer are shown in Tables 11-9, 11-10, and 11-11.

Cryptographic Considerations for an Intelligent Secure Card

Use of an intelligent secure card does require some additional consideration in the design of secure procedures for personal verification and message authentication. Computation of AP on the bank card poses a problem that is not present when AP is computed inside the EFT terminal.

An authentication parameter computed inside an EFT terminal may or may not involve time-variant information, but an authentication parameter computed on the card *must always involve time-variant information.* The following example explains the reason. A transformation applied to secret user-supplied information inside a terminal (such as a one-way function or encryption under a secret terminal key) prevents an intercepted output from being reentered (in its original form) as input to the terminal. Of course, the issuer must trust that the terminal (acting on its behalf) will perform this transformation with integrity. When an intelligent secure card is used, a similar transformation performed on the card does not achieve the same end. In this case, the issuer cannot trust the cardholder, since the cardholder may be an opponent intent on committing fraud against the system. The issuer also has no way to ensure that the card computes the authentication parameter. A bogus card could store an intercepted value and read it out of storage and pass it to the terminal whenever prompted. To prevent this, the issuer must require the authentication parameter to be a function of time-variant information. This forces the intelligent secure card to compute AP dynamically, and thus prevents the described attack. In the implementation discussed above, this time variance is achieved with time of day (TOD) information.

Security Enhancements with Digital Signatures

If institutions do not wish to share secret keys for purposes of authenticating response messages, digital signatures based on either a conventional or public-key algorithm could be used (see Digital Signatures, Chapter 9). A public-key algorithm, however, is more practical, since there are no restrictions on the number of signed messages that can be sent and received using a single pair of keys. With a conventional algorithm, each digital signature must be validated using a separate validation parameter (or pattern of bits).

Consider a digital signature procedure for authenticating transaction response messages which is based on a public key algorithm. Each institution would have a public and private key, PK and SK, respectively. The public key is shared with each other institution and published in a major newspaper to allow each public key to be independently validated.

In such an approach, the issuer transforms a received transaction request using his secret key and sends the response to the originating acquirer. The acquirer recovers the transaction request using the issuer's public key (which could be stored in the HPC's data base). Since the issuer's secret key is not

System User	Intelligent Secure Bank Card	System Nodes			
		EFT Terminal	Acquirer's Host (Inst. X)	Switch's Host	Issuer's Host (Inst. Y)
Permanently Installed Master Keys					
none	KP	KMT	KMHacq	KMHsw	KMHiss
Permanently Installed Interchange Keys					
none	none	none	KIacq,sw	KIacq,sw KIsw,iss	KIsw,iss
Keys Used for MAC Generation for Transaction Request Message, Mreq					
none	KTR1card,iss (dynamically generated from KP and PIN)	none	none	none	KTR1card,iss for all members of institution Y

Keys Used to Protect the Transaction Session Key Used for MAC Generation of the Transaction Response Message, Mresp					
none	KSTR received from issuer; KTR2card,iss dynamically generated from KTR1card,iss and Tcard, i.e., D_{KTR1}(Tcard)	KMTacq,term	KMTacq,term KIsw,acq	KIiss,sw KIsw,acq	KIiss,sw; KSTR randomly generated by issuer; KTR2card,iss regenerated based on Tcard and KTR1card,iss

Note: Keys associated with personal verification at the issuer (and perhaps the switch) are not shown.

Legend:

KMT: Terminal master key
KMH: Host master key
KTR1: Message Authentication Key for Request Messages (Mreq) (e.g., KTR1 = $D_{KP \oplus PIN}$(ID))
KTR2: Message Authentication Key for Response Messages (Mresp)
KP: Personal Key
KI: Interchange key

Table 11-9. Keys Referenced in the Hybrid Approach

System User	Intelligent Secure Bank Card	System Nodes			
		EFT Terminal	Acquirer's Host	Switch's Host	Issuer's Host
1 Enter PIN and transfer to card via terminal.	2 Generate Tcard and transfer to terminal. 5 Compute MAC1card,iss with KTR1card,iss.	3 Read card information and formulate Mreq which includes Tterm, Tcard, and TODacq,term. 4 Send Mreq to intelligent secure card.	10 Forward received Mreq and MAC1card,iss to switch.	11 Forward received Mreq and MAC1card,iss to issuer.	12 Check received MAC1card,iss with KTR1card,iss of reference and TODiss of reference. 13 Verify user.

6 Generate KTR2 (randomly based on Tcard, i.e., KTR2 = D_{KTR1}(Tcard)).	8 Store Mreq and KTR2 in terminal.	14 Decide if Mreq is to be honored.
	9 Forward received Mreq, MAC1card,iss to acquirer.	
7 Send Mreq, MAC1card,iss and KTR2 to terminal.		

Note: It is assumed that the acquirer periodically sends time-of-day information (TODacq) to the terminals in its domain. The terminal, on the other hand, generates random information (Tterm) and sends it to the issuer. This can be done as part of the initiation protocol (Figure 11-15). The card also generates time-variant information (Tcard) which is transmitted to the issuer. The TOD stored at the other network host nodes (TODsw at the switch and TODiss at the issuer) is assumed to be equal to TODacq within an allowable range (ΔTOD).
The integers 1–14 in the table show the sequence of steps in the transaction.

Table 11-10. Information flow from Terminal to Issuer—Hybrid Approach

System User	Intelligent Secure Bank Card	System Nodes			
		EFT Terminal	Acquirer's Host	Switch's Host	Issuer's Host
		25 Decrypt $E_{KMTacq,term}(Q)$ with KMTacq,term to obtain Q = E_{KTR2}(KSTR).	23 Translate received $E_{KIsw,acq}(Q)$ to $E_{KMTacq,term}(Q)$.	21 Translate received $E_{KIiss,sw}(Q)$ to $E_{KIsw,acq}(Q)$.	14 Decide if Mreq is to be honored. 15 Generate KSTR randomly.
		26 Decrypt Q with KTR2 of reference to obtain KSTR of reference.	24 Send MAC2iss,card and $E_{KMTacq,term}(Q)$ to terminal.	22 Send MAC2iss,acq and $E_{KIsw,acq}(Q)$ to acquirer.	16 Compute MAC2iss,term on received Mreq with KSTR.
		27 Generate MAC2iss,term of reference on stored Mresp with KSTR of reference.			17 Generate KTR2 using KTR1card,iss of reference and received Tcard.

28 Process transaction if MAC2iss,term of reference equals the received MAC2iss,term; otherwise, abort transaction.		18 Encrypt KSTR with KTR2 to obtain Q = E_{KTR2}(KSTR).
		19 Encrypt Q with KIiss.
		20 Send MAC2iss,card and $E_{KIiss,sw}$(Q) to switch.

Note: A check for the correct destination is not necessary since KSTR can only be correctly recovered at the node with the proper KTR1.

The integers 14–28 in the table show the sequence of steps in the transaction.

Table 11-11. Information Flow from Issuer to Terminal—Hybrid Approach

shared with the acquirer, an improvement in security is obtained. Furthermore, the message authentication process is now isolated among institutions. Thus requirement 17 is satisfied.

A MAC based on an acquirer-generated time-variant key (KSTR) is next produced and the MAC and KSTR encrypted under the terminal master key, KMT, is forwarded to the originating terminal. The terminal generates a MAC of reference using the stored KMT, KSTR, and the message of reference, and compares the result for equality with the received MAC. If the two MACs were equal, the terminal honors the request; otherwise not.

In effect, a transaction request transformed under the issuer's secret key provides the acquirer with the equivalent of a signed message authorizing the transaction. The acquirer logs all such signed messages until after they have been cleared via normal accounting methods between respective institutions.

With such an approach, the acquirer has proof of authorization from the issuer, and the issuer need not fear that unwarranted and unprovable claims will be brought against him from other acquirers. The terminal responds only to the orders given it by its owning institution (the acquirer), whereas the acquirer directs the terminal to honor a transaction request only after receiving a signed transaction response message from the issuer.

Advantages

The PIN/personal key/system key approach using an intelligent secure card satisfies the EFT security requirement to a much higher degree than either the PIN/system key or the PIN/personal key approaches. The intelligent secure card

prevents skimming of KP information during routine operations.

It is assumed that cardholders will take appropriate steps to protect their cards during periods of nonuse and that they will promptly report lost or stolen cards. Computations involving KP are performed on the card which means that KP is not read into the EFT terminal. Therefore,

KP is not exposed to a fake equipment attack,
KP is not exposed to probing or bugging of EFT terminals.

Except for the PIN, which is assumed to be entered into the EFT terminal where it exists momentarily before being transferred to the intelligent secure card, secret user-supplied information used in the process of personal verification is known only to the cardholder and issuer. Because KP and PIN together have more than 56 independent secret bits,

exhaustive attacks (trying all PIN and KP combinations) at the point of entry are infeasible,
dictionary and exhaustive attacks (on the system) are infeasible,
a one-way function of PIN and KP is possible,

which implies that it is not possible to deduce PIN and KP or to determine equivalent values of PIN and KP from information transmitted throughout the system, and

> *there is no need to involve or depend on encryption under secret system keys.*

The result is that personal verification and authentication of transaction *request* messages can be isolated to a very high degree, since only the cardholder and issuer are involved. True end-to-end cryptographic protection is thus achieved between the cardholder and issuer, and requirement 5 is satisfied. System keys (in addition to personal keys) are used for the authentication of transaction response messages, which means that

> *EFT terminals are not exposed to a misuse of a personal key attack or a fake personal key attack.*

However, complete isolation with regard to the authentication of transaction *response* messages (requirement 17) is achieved only if a scheme for digital signatures is used by the institutions in the interchange network. With digital signatures,

> *no sharing of secret keys among institutions or with a switch would be required, no cryptographic translations of data as they traverse the network would be required, and the acquirer would have an electronically signed receipt for each transaction request authorized by the issuer.*

KEY MANAGEMENT CONSIDERATIONS—SYMMETRIC VERSUS ASYMMETRIC ALGORITHMS

Frequently, the argument is made that key management is simplified with public-key (asymmetric) algorithms as opposed to conventional (symmetric) algorithms like the DES.[40] To prove or disprove such a general statement, however, is a nontrivial problem.

It must be recognized at the outset that to initialize a system employing symmetric algorithms requires a secure path to distribute the secret keys (e.g., by courier). A system employing asymmetric algorithms also needs a secure path for it's secret keys. But to distribute public keys requires only a channel with integrity (i.e., it must be assured that the correct public keys are distributed). An asymmetric system will obviously not be much simpler than a symmetric system if the number of secret keys to be distributed is comparable. Thus it will depend on the particular application if key management will or will not be simpler with a public-key algorithm.

In the EFT design discussed below (see A Cryptographic System Using an Intelligent Secure Card and A Public-Key Algorithm) an implementation is suggested which uses only public keys at system entry points. Secret keys are required at host nodes and on bank cards in the form of personal keys. Such

[40] The term asymmetric indicates that the encrypting and decrypting keys are different whereas the term symmetric indicates that the encrypting and decrypting keys are (basically) the same.

an implementation offers an advantage over the hybrid key management approach discussed above since it provides a higher degree of isolation among institutions. Before embarking further into EFT system designs, some general ideas are worth examining.

In particular, it is important to distinguish between implementations where (1) cryptographic authentication alone or authentication as well as secrecy is required and (2) where secrecy but not authentication is required. In the former case it is not generally clear if there is a major difference in key management complexity between both approaches. However, in the latter case (secrecy without authentication) the public-key approach definitely results in simpler key management. Comparisons are made here in terms of the number of keys stored in the system. The details of how the system must be initiated are not given. Thus the final verdict of which approach is simpler may very well depend on the protocols which must be used to initialize the system.

Authentication With and Without Secrecy

An implementation that comes to mind first is probably one where n users in the system wish to communicate with each other using personal keys. System involvement is thus minimized in such an approach.

In the asymmetric (e.g., RSA) approach, each user defines his own secret key and corresponding public key. Since the integrity of the public keys must be assured (otherwise authentication is not possible) they will most likely be stored at a system node defined as the key distribution center (KDC).[41] The process of storing public keys requires that users are identified before a public key is accepted by the KDC. (Otherwise an opponent could masquerade as a legitimate system user.) Once this process is completed, the KDC has the added responsibility to route public keys to the appropriate system entry point in such a way that they can be authenticated by the requester. This requires the presence of a secret key belonging to and stored within the KDC. Consequently, a secret key (SKu, or universal secret key) and corresponding public key (PKu) are defined by the KDC.

If user i wants to communicate with user j, he would request user j's public key, PKj, from the KDC. To assure that correct (current, not stale) PKs are received, a handshake protocol between the requesting user and the KDC is defined wherein user i sends a random number, RNi, together with other information, to the KDC in the form IDi, IDj, . . . , $E_{PKu}(D_{SKi}(\text{IDi,RNi}))$. The KDC would then look up user i's public key based on IDi obtained from the request message to recover RNi (using SKu and PKi). The quantity $E_{PKi}(D_{SKu}(\text{IDi, PKj, RNi}))$ is created next and sent to user i who subsequently deciphers with SKi and enciphers with PKu to recover PKj and RN. If the

[41] One might also consider an approach in which the set of public keys are published in a directory, eliminating the need for a KDC. But this requires that users input data (i.e., with the RSA algorithm on the order of 200 decimal digits each, see Chapter 2). In addition, a practical method must be found to periodically update the directory. Furthermore, the integrity of the public keys must be assured. A KDC solves all of these problems very efficiently.

Key Distribution Center		
ID1;	PK1;	D_{SKu}(ID1, PK1)
ID2;	PK2;	D_{SKu}(ID2, PK2)
⋮	⋮	⋮ ⋮
IDn;	PKn;	D_{SKu}(IDn, PKn)

Note: The KDC stores its secret key, SKu, separate from the above table (i.e., in secure hardware). The signatures D_{SKu}(IDi, PKi), i = 1,2, . . . , n, allow the stored public keys to be authenticated.

User Identification Card
IDi · · · user i's identification
PKu · · · public key of KDC
PKi · · · user i's public key
SKi · · · user i's secret key

Figure 11-31. Personal Key Approach with Asymmetric Algorithm (RSA)–Information Stored in the System and on the User Identification Card

recovered RN is identical to the RN originally generated (and presumed saved) by user i, user i concludes that PKj was in fact sent from the KDC and thus is user j's public key. This protocol is repeated by user j who must later obtain user i's public key to participate in a meaningful conversation. The information needed by the KDC and the information supplied by the user (as read from a magnetic stripe on an appropriate identification card, for example), is shown in Figure 11-31. The above suggested handshake protocol is illustrated in Figure 11-32.

A personal key approach using the DES could be implemented by also using a KDC but storing each user's secret personal key KP instead of storing

User i obtains PKj as:

IDi, IDj, $E_{PKu}(D_{SKi}$(IDi, RNi)) ⟶ to KDC
IDi, IDj, $E_{PKi}(D_{SKu}$(IDi, PKj, RNi)) ⟵ from KDC

User i subsequently recovers PKj using SKi and PKu

User j obtains PKi as:

IDj, IDi, $E_{PKu}(D_{SKj}$(IDj, RNj)) ⟶ to KDC
IDj, IDi, $E_{PKj}(D_{SKu}$(IDj, PKi, RNj)) ⟵ from KDC

User j subsequently recovers PKi using SKj and PKu

Figure 11-32. Personal Key Approach with Asymmetric Algorithm (RSA)–Protocol to Establish Authenticated Public Keys

Key Distribution Center	
ID1;	Encrypted KP1
ID2;	Encrypted KP2
⋮	⋮
IDn;	Encrypted KPn

Note: The KDC stores its secret master key used to encrypt personal keys separate from the above table (i.e., in secure hardware)

User Identification Card
IDi · · · user i's identification
KPi · · · user i's secret personal key

Figure 11-33. Personal Key Approach with Symmetric Algorithm (DES)–Information Stored in the System and on the User Identification Card

public keys. The information stored at the KDC and on each user's bank card is shown in Figure 11-33. These secret keys could then be used to securely distribute and authenticate a session key (KS) randomly generated by the KDC (Figure 11-34). To determine that a received session key has indeed originated with the KDC, a random number is generated by the user and sent, encrypted under his personal key, to the KDC. Only if the KDC returns that same random number together with a session key encrypted under the user's personal key, will the session key be accepted as genuine.

The key management requirements of RSA and DES are not much different as far as the user-supplied input information is concerned. The KDC must, in the former case, assure the integrity of n public keys and the integrity and secrecy of its secret key (SKu). In the latter case the integrity

User i obtains KS as:

IDi, IDj, E_{KPi}(IDi, RNi) ⟶ to KDC
IDi, IDj, E_{KPi}(IDi, RNi, KS) ⟵ from KDC

User i recovers KS using KPi

User j obtains KS as:

IDj, IDi, E_{KPj}(IDj, RNj) ⟶ to KDC
IDj, IDi, E_{KPj}(IDj, RNj, KS) ⟵ from KDC

User j recovers KS using KPj

Figure 11-34. Personal Key Approach with Symmetric Algorithm (DES)–Protocol to Establish Authenticated Session Keys

	Asymmetric (RSA) Algorithm	Symmetric (DES) Algorithm
Number of secret keys per user	1	1
Number of public keys per user	1	none
Number of secret keys in KDC	1	n user keys 1 KDC master key
Number of public keys in KDC	n	none

Table 11-12. Required Number of Keys for Asymmetric and Symmetric Algorithms—Personal Key Approach

and secrecy of n user keys and the master key of the KDC must be assured. Either approach requires a secure system node (the KDC). These conclusions are summarized in Table 11-12.

Let it next be assumed that n nodes in a network communicate with each other such that cryptography is transparent to the user (i.e., the user is not required to provide cryptographic parameters). Let it furthermore be assumed that secrecy and authentication are required. This can be achieved (using for example the RSA algorithm) by deciphering with the sender's secret key and enciphering with the receiver's public key as shown in An Approach Using Public Key-Algorithms, Chapter 9.

In a symmetric system, authentication and secrecy are automatically achieved by defining one secret key and performing one operation only (i.e., encryption). Starting with a symmetric system, let KCi,j (where KC denotes a communication key) define the secret key which operates on messages sent from node i to node j. For a three node network, six secret keys (as shown in Figure 11-35) must be defined for complete node to node communication assuming each node manages keys independently of each other node.

For a n node network there are $2(n - 1)$ keys per node required (i.e., $n - 1$ keys to operate on data sent from one node to the $n - 1$ other nodes and $n - 1$ keys to operate on data received by one node from the $n - 1$ other nodes). Hence there are a total of $2n(n - 1)$ keys in the system. Since some identical keys are stored in different nodes (e.g., KCi,j appears in node i and node j), there are only $n(n - 1)$ different keys in the network.

If different keys are not needed to protect data flowing in opposite directions between two nodes, then KCi,j may be identical to KCj,i. This reduces the number of keys required at each node from $2(n - 1)$ to $(n - 1)$. The total number of keys in the network then becomes $n(n - 1)$ and the total number of different keys in the network becomes $n(n - 1)/2$.

Let an asymmetric system (e.g., the RSA algorithm) be discussed next and let SKi define the secret key used at node i to operate on (decipher) data sent to any other node. The corresponding public key, PKi, is made available

Node 1		Node 2		Node 3
KC1,2	⟶	KC1,2		
KC2,1	⟵	KC2,1		
KC1,3	⟶		⟶	KC1,3
KC3,1	⟵		⟵	KC3,1
		KC2,3	⟶	KC2,3
		KC3,2	⟵	KC3,2

The arrow indicates data flow direction and the corresponding entries indicate the keys to be used.

Figure 11-35. Symmetric Algorithm–Keys Required to Achieve Authentication and Secrecy in a Three Node Network

to other system nodes to authenticate messages received from node i. Communications from node i to node j take the form $E_{PKj}D_{SKi}$(Xi,j) where Xi,j are the data sent from node i to node j whose integrity and secrecy must be maintained. For a three node network, three secret and three public keys must be defined as shown in Figure 11-36.

In an n node network, each node stores one secret key and (n − 1) public keys. There are thus a total number of n secret keys in the network and (n − 1)n public keys. The total number of different keys is less because the public key of node i appears in (n − 1) nodes. Hence there are n different secret keys and n different public keys in the network.

If only authentication (not secrecy) is required, the data Xi, j sent from node i to node j are of the form D_{SKi}(Xi, j) instead of E_{PKj}(D_{SKi}(Xi, j)). At the receiver (node j), PKi is used to authenticate Xi, j. Hence the same keys defined above for authentication and secrecy are required for authentication even when secrecy is not required. A summary is given in Table 11-13.

Node 1		Node 2		Node 3
PK2;SK1	⟶	PK1;SK2		
SK1;PK2	⟵	SK2;PK2		
PK3;SK1	⟶		⟶	PK1;SK3
SK1;PK3	⟵		⟵	SK3;PK1
		PK3;SK2	⟶	PK2;SK3
		SK2;PK3	⟵	SK3;PK2

Note: Secrecy as well as integrity of the SKs must be assured whereas for the PKs only integrity must be assured.

The arrow indicates data flow direction and the corresponding entries indicate the keys to be used.

Figure 11-36. Asymmetric Algorithm–Keys Required to Achieve Authentication and Secrecy in a Three-Node Network.

	Asymmetric (RSA) Algorithm	Symmetric (DES) Algorithm
Number of secret keys per node	1	2(n-1) w/ unidirectionality (n-1) w/o unidirectionality
Number of public keys per node	(n-1)	none
Total number of secret keys in network	n	2n(n-1) w/ unidirectionality n(n-1) w/o unidirectionality
Total number of public keys in network	n(n-1)	none
Total number of different secret keys in network	n	n(n-1) w/ unidirectionality n(n-1)/2 w/o unidirectionality
Total number of different public keys in network	n	none

Note: It is assumed that all n nodes of the network communicate with each other without user involvement.

Table 11-13. Required Number of Keys for Asymmetric and Symmetric Algorithms—Transparent Case where Each Node Stores the Required Keys

From Table 11-13 one could easily conclude that key management becomes less complex with asymmetric systems since fewer keys are managed. To make a true comparison, however, system design concepts must also be considered. Most likely an approach where each node stores a set of KCs will not be used. Instead, one would define one secret key per node (KNCi for node i) and store all n of the required keys in a common key distribution center (KDC). Thus the KDC would be the trusted node in the system and would be called upon to generate and distribute session keys to nodes requesting to communicate with one another. For example, a randomly generated session key (KS) would be distributed to nodes i and j in the form $E_{KNCi}(KS)$ and $E_{KNCj}(KS)$, respectively.

The KDC could also be used with an asymmetric algorithm. In that case the KDC would store all n public keys and route them to the system nodes as required. Based on the number of keys stored at the KDC (Table 11-14), one cannot conclude which system (asymmetric or symmetric) is easier to implement. Other investigators analyzing asymmetric and symmetric cryptosystems have concluded that protocols in both systems are strikingly similar [17, 18].

Secrecy Without Authentication

In this section the question to be addressed is: What security penalty (if any) is there if permanently installed keys are not used? The rationale is that each node could generate its public and secret keys dynamically. For ex-

	Asymmetric (RSA) Algorithm	Symmetric (DES) Algorithm
Number of secret keys per system node	1	1
Number of public keys per system node	1	none
Number of secret keys in KDC	1	n user keys 1 KDC master key
Number of public keys in KDC	n	none

Table 11-14. Required Number of Keys for Asymmetric and Symmetric Algorithms—User Transparent Case with Key Distribution Center

ample, the public key generated at node i could be sent over a nonsecure channel to node j. Node j could then encrypt messages for node i with node i's public key (PKi). Only node i, having generated the corresponding secret key SKi can decrypt such a message. Thus, off hand it seems that an acceptable solution has been found for key distribution and key initialization. (For example, the keys required in the three node network shown in Figure 11-36 can easily be generated on demand.)

But there is a major difference between the static situation where keys at each node are defined in an initialization process and the dynamic situation where keys are generated as they are needed. Due to the fact that the keys listed in Figure 11-36 are defined ahead of time as part of system initialization, the corresponding nodes are coupled. After initialization, the sender (node i) has no control over the use of a key by another node (node j). This is in contrast to the case where the keys are generated dynamically. As a consequence there is no way for a node to check the identity of the sender, since the public key sent to the receiving node could have originated with any system node, including a bogus node. The sender, on the other hand, does not really know who is using his personal key to encrypt data addressed to him. To take advantage of these security weaknesses requires, however, an active attack since data on a communications line must be altered enroute. Therefore the described method of dynamically generating keys in lieu of initializing the system with predetermined keys provides data security if the opponent has only the capacity to eavesdrop.

To illustrate the consequences of implementing a cryptographic system without authentication, consider the following case. To send a secret document from A to B, let it be locked in a suitcase. To start with, A seals the suitcase with lock A, which only A can open. After B receives the suitcase, B in turn seals the suitcase with lock B, which only B can open. The doubly locked suitcase is then returned to A. Upon receipt, A removes (his) lock A. The suitcase, still locked with lock B, is returned to B whereupon B removes his lock and retrieves the secret document (Figure 11-37).

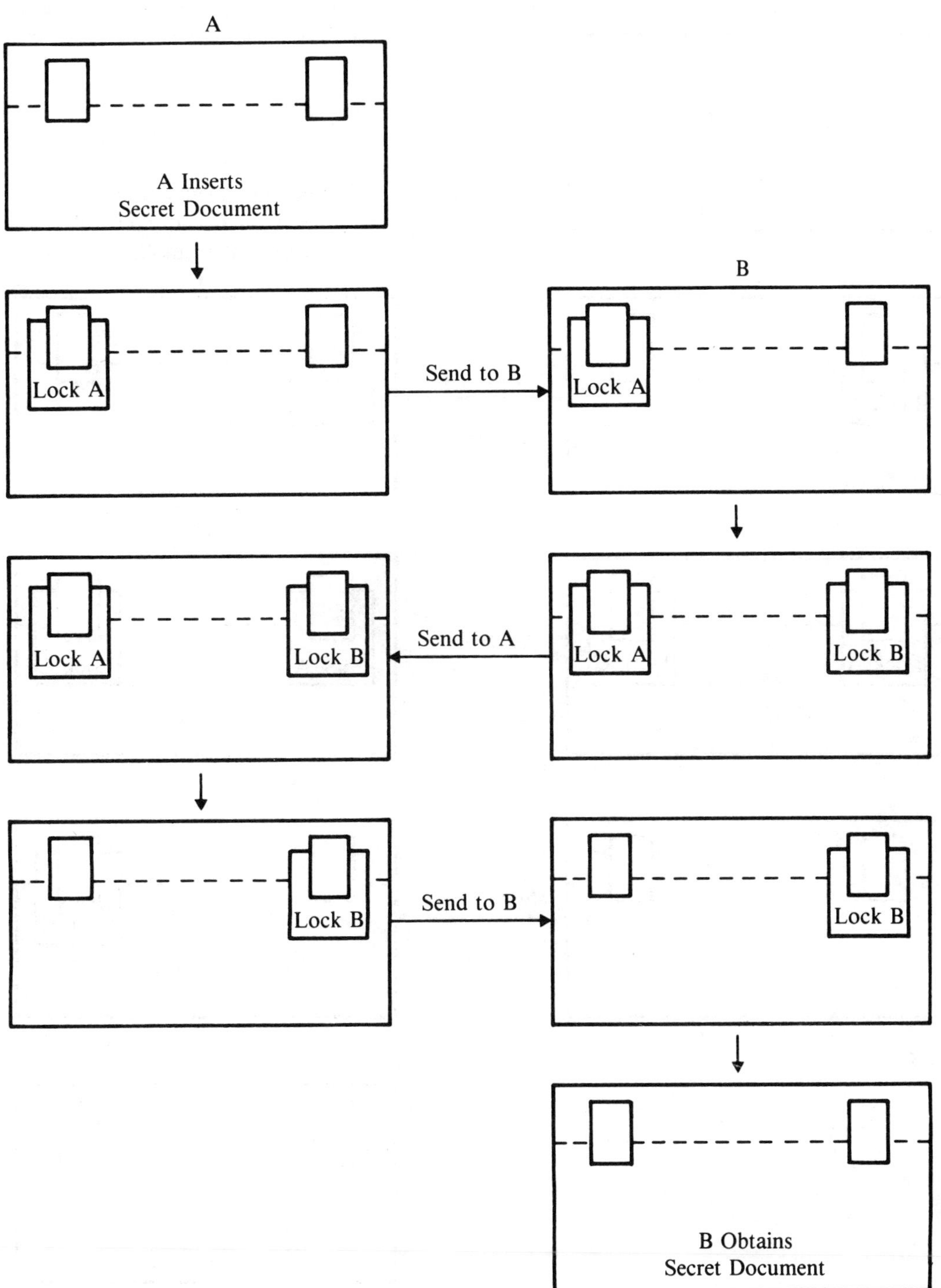

Figure 11-37. Protocol to Send Secret Document from A to B

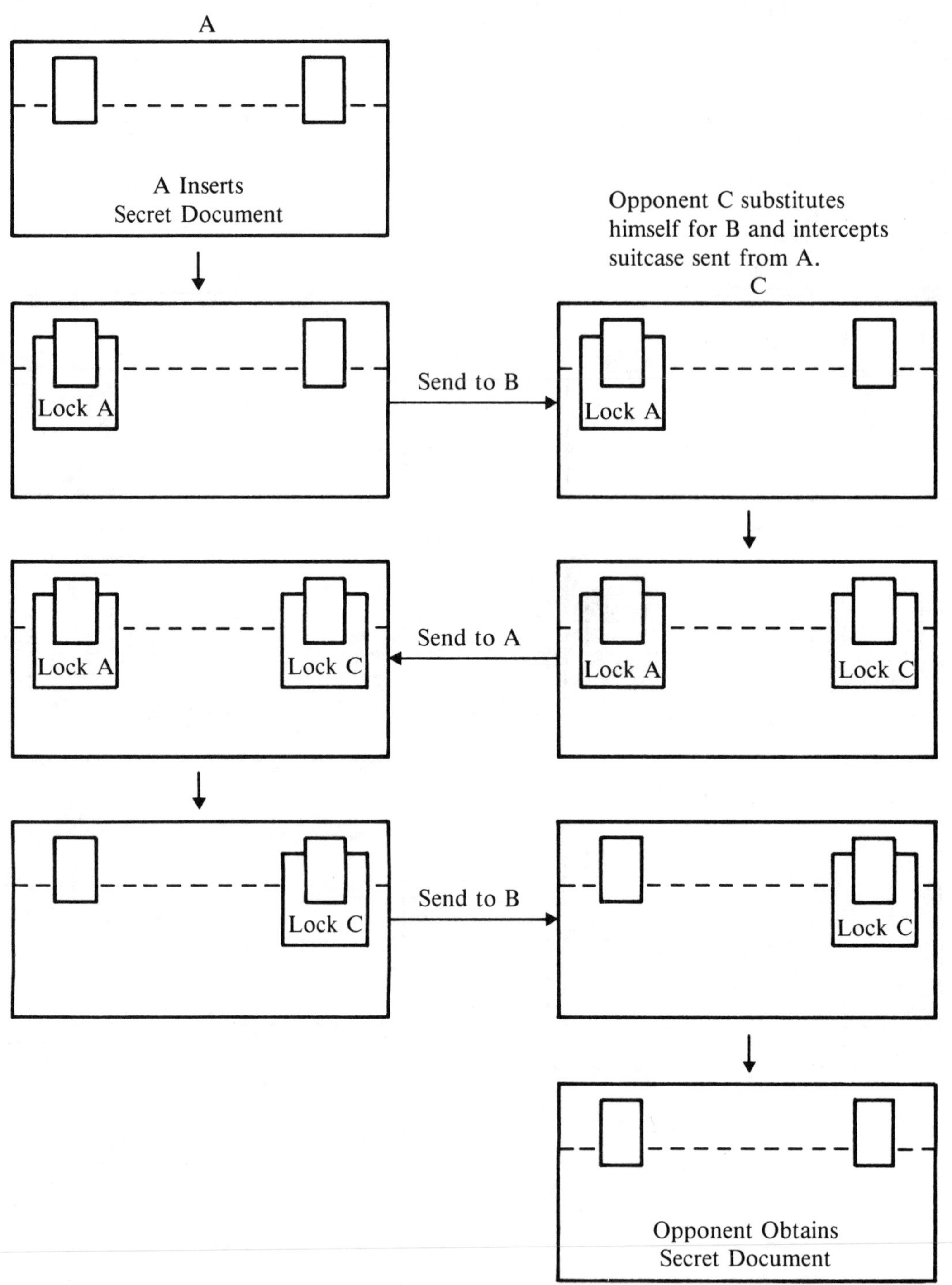

Figure 11-38. Interception of Secret Document by Opponent

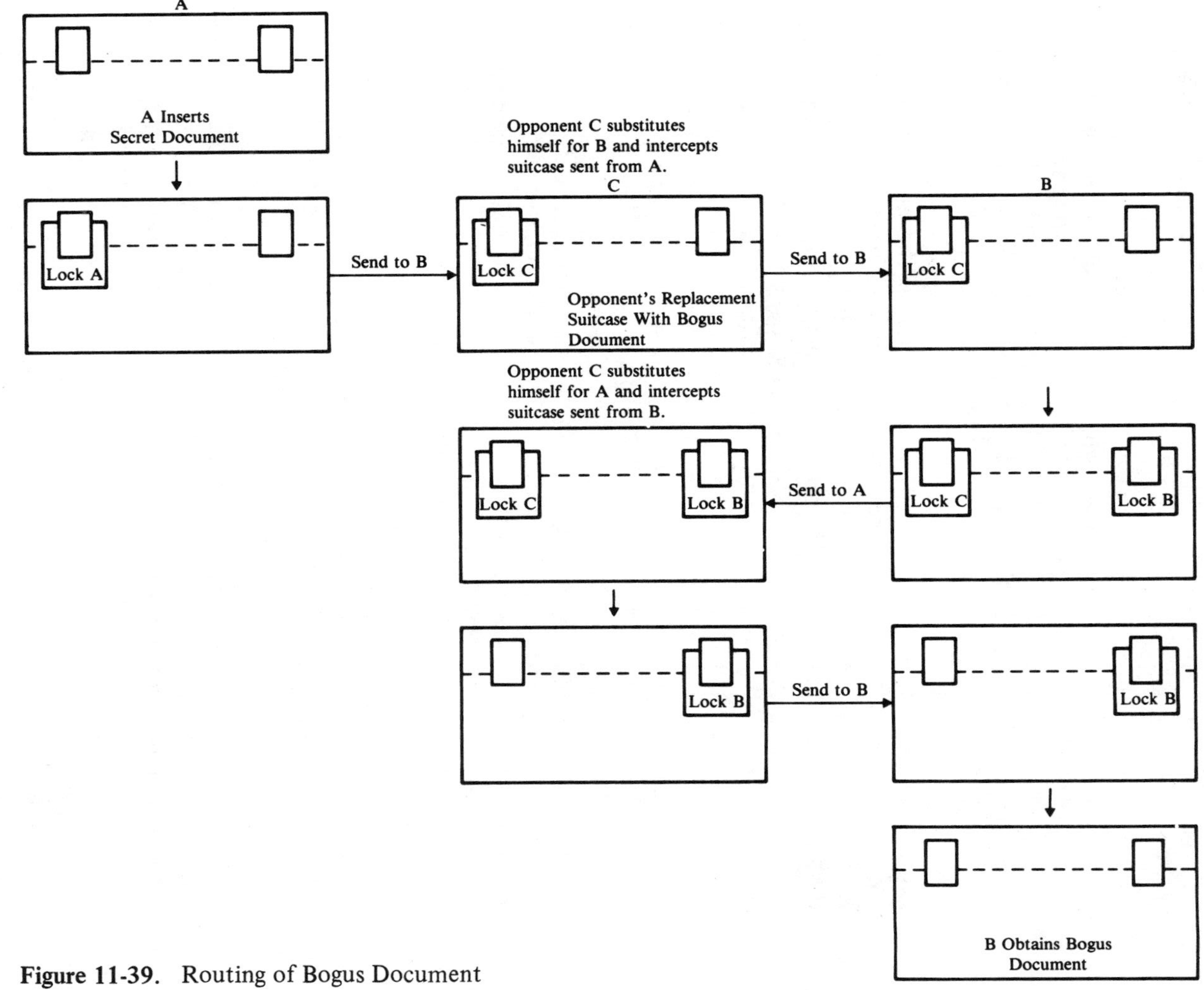

Figure 11-39. Routing of Bogus Document

There are two basic attacks which may be successful in this instance: rerouting and masquerading.

Since A cannot distinguish between B's lock and one supplied by an opponent (due to lack of authentication), it is possible for an opponent to intercept the suitcase and apply his own lock, thus preventing B from applying his lock. As a result the suitcase, sealed with the opponent's lock would be returned to A for removal of A's lock. Once A's lock is removed, the opponent again intercepts the suitcase, removes his lock, and thereby obtains the secret document (Figure 11-38).

In the second attack the opponent again intercepts the suitcase (with A's lock in place) only this time the suitcase and secret document are discarded. The opponent replaces the suitcase with one of his own, complete with a bogus secret document, locks the suitcase with his lock, and forwards the suitcase to B. The protocol requires B to apply his lock and return the suitcase to A, which B does. The opponent again intercepts the suitcase, removes his lock, and returns the case to B. B eventually opens his lock and removes the bogus secret document thinking it originated with A (Figure 11-39). The opponent (posing as B) also sends a bogus suitcase to A to prevent A from detecting the deception.

Figures 11-38 and 11-39 illustrate two attacks against a public-key cryptosystem implementing the particular communication protocol described in Figure 11-37. In general, a public-key cryptosystem's communication protocol is always exposed to active attack if that cryptosystem does not employ preinitialized keys. Although, for applications in which active attacks are considered not a threat, the tradeoff between security and key management complexity may be an attractive one.

A CRYPTOGRAPHIC SYSTEM USING AN INTELLIGENT SECURE CARD AND A PUBLIC-KEY ALGORITHM

The PIN/personal key approach, which was shown to be nonsecure, demonstrates the need for having system keys installed in the EFT terminals. This is true whether a conventional (symmetric) or public-key (asymmetric) algorithm is used. If a conventional algorithm is employed, the terminals must store secret keys. If a public-key algorithm is employed, the terminals may store secret keys, public keys, or both, although, typically, the terminals would store only public keys. (These public keys would be used to authenticate transaction response messages.) When a public-key algorithm is used, one therefore attempts to improve the process of message authentication by eliminating the need for a secret key in the EFT terminal. The requirement for keeping the necessary terminal resident keys secret and assuring their integrity in a conventional approach is thus replaced by the requirement of assuring only the integrity of public terminal resident keys in a public-key approach.

Authentication of transaction request messages, on the other hand, always requires a secret key at the entry point. This key must be supplied by the system user, since otherwise the terminal would have to store a secret key (which is to be avoided).

The main features of the system are thus as follows. Personal verification and authentication of transaction request messages (sent from the terminal to the issuer) are based on a secret user-supplied key derived from the PIN and secret card information and a corresponding public user key stored at the issuer (different for each of the institutions's customers)[42]. Authentication of transaction response messages is based on a secret key available in the security module of the issuer's EDP system and a corresponding public key established at each terminal.

In the described system there is total isolation of the personal verification processes of the various institutions and almost total isolation in the authentication of transaction requests sent from the user to the issuer. These procedures are effected and established solely between the user and the issuer. No secret keys involved in the processes are exposed at the entry point, although the integrity of the public keys must be assured. In an interchange, the acquirer and switch merely act as network routing points to pass nonsecret information to the issuer.

In addition, there is a digital signature capability for transaction responses. The acquirer honors a request from the cardholder only after the issuer has sent a signed message to the acquirer (or to the originating terminal) authorizing the transaction. (Note that this advantage is also obtained with the DES/public-key approach discussed in the section Security Enhancements with Digital Signatures.)

Description of a Public-Key Management Approach

The system discussed here is composed of host processing centers and EFT terminals, interconnected in an EFT network supporting interchange. Each network node has a public-key cryptographic capability that is either integrated into the node or contained in a security module attached to the node via a secure, local cable. Each security module has a set of cryptographic operations that may be invoked by the supporting device or EDP system via a defined interface. No clear cryptographic keys ever exist outside the security module except during periods when they are initially generated or entered into the system.

Each customer is provided with an intelligent secure bank card, which has an installed public-key algorithm and storage for secret and nonsecret information (e.g., keys, encrypted keys, and account-related information). Keys stored in a security module are protected by implementing adequate physical security measures and/or providing a set of interlocks that will erase all secret information if penetration of the security module or containing device is detected.

A secret user key (SKc, where c stands for customer) is used to generate a quantity (DGSreq) which will enable the issuer to authenticate the transaction

[42] PIN secrecy depends entirely on maintaining the secrecy of certain card information (i.e., it is not achieved because of the public-key algorithm). If relevant card information were available to an opponent, the PIN could be derived easily from information in an intercepted transaction request message. The intelligent secure card provides the means to adequately protect card information.

request message, Mreq. In the conventional approach this quantity was called a MAC. Since a public-key approach provides a digital signature capability, the term DGS is used instead of MAC. To demonstrate the parallelism between the public-key and conventional algorithm approaches, assume that (Mreq, DGSreq) is routed to the issuer and define DGSreq as

$$\text{DGSreq} = D_{\text{SKc}}[\text{CE(Mreq)}]$$

where CE(Mreq) represents the compressed encoding of Mreq. As discussed in Chapter 9, CE(M) is a one-way function of M and can be generated with publicly known keys for symmetric as well as asymmetric algorithms. In the implementation discussed here it suffices to specify one public key for generating CE(M) without, at the same time, specifying the corresponding secret key. This is so because the sender and receiver use the same procedure for generating CE(M). To check the signature, the issuer generates the compressed encoding of the received message and compares it with E_{PKc}(DGSreq) (i.e., the received DGSreq encrypted under PKc). If both quantities agree Mreq is accepted; otherwise, not.

This check on DGSreq can be used also to verify the user (e.g., if SKc is defined as SKc = SKc* ⊕ PIN, where SKc* is a secret parameter stored on the card). Since the digital signature (DGS) is now also a function of PIN, personal verification as well as message authentication are combined in one procedure. [The same idea was used in the hybrid key management approach by defining KTR = $D_{\text{KP} \oplus \text{PIN}}$(ID) and is repeated here for the sake of uniformity in the discussion.]

A digital signature on the response message (DGSresp) is generated using a secret key SKb, uniquely defined for each institution (where b stands for bank). Thus,

$$\text{DGSresp} = D_{\text{SKb}}[\text{CE(Mresp)}]$$

To check the received Mresp at the terminal, the public key, PKb, corresponding to SKb, must be available. In the implementation suggested here, PKb and its digital signature D_{SKu}[CE(IDb, PKb)] are stored on the bank card. The key SKu (where u stands for universal) is a key known only to a trusted node or key distribution center. By storing the corresponding public key, PKu, in all terminals, PKb can be authenticated at the terminal before it is used to authenticate Mresp. Authentication of PKb is achieved by enciphering D_{SKu}[CE(IDb, PKb)] with PKu and checking that the result is equal to the compressed encoding of (IDb, PKb), where PKb is the received public key and IDb is the known bank identifier.

To initialize the operation, each institution produces a public and private key-pair (PKb, SKb) for its own use. The private bank key (SKb) is retained in the institution's security module. The public bank key (PKb) is distributed to each other institution in the interchange, and it is also sent (e.g., via a courier) to a key distribution center or designated trusted party. Public keys are distributed securely to assure their integrity (e.g., to avoid masquerading attacks).

Prior to receiving each institution's PKb, the key distribution center produces its own public and private key pair (PKu, SKu) for the purpose of interchange. The secret key, SKu, is employed to generate a digital signature for PKb in the form D_{SKu}[CE(IDb, PKb)]. The user supplies this quantity together with IDb and PKb to the terminal where PKu resides. This enables the terminal to check the DGS and thus authenticate PKb.

The public key of the key distribution center (PKu) and the public bank keys, together with their DGSs, are distributed to each of the respective institutions (banks). SKu is also stored in a safe or vault for recovery purposes. Securely maintaining SKU will also allow other institutions to later join the interchange. The key distribution center can also publish PKu (e.g., in a major newspaper like the New York Times), which will allow each institution to validate the received PKu independently.

Upon receipt of this information from the key distribution center, each issuer validates PKu (by comparing the received PKu with the published PKu) and transfers PKu to its security module where it can be safely stored and used as necessary. The public keys of each bank and their corresponding digital signatures (computed from SKu) are stored in the data base of the institution's EDP system (Figure 11-40).

The issuer also generates a DGS for each users public key, PKc, with the aid of SKb (e.g., D_{SKb}[CE(IDc, PKc)]). The quantities IDc, PKc, and the DGS for PKc, are then stored in the data base of the institution's EDP system (Figure 11-40) and written on the user's bank card (Figure 11-41). A copy of the institution's public bank key PKb and signature D_{SKu}[CE(IDb, PKb)] are also written on the user's bank card. Each institution also installs PKu in each of its terminals (Figure 11-42).

PIN Selection

For this discussion, PINs are assumed to be produced by the issuer using the security module as a generator of pseudorandom numbers. The generated PIN is printed on a PIN mailer and the mailer is sent to the customer. PINs may also be encrypted under a PIN master key and stored off-line for purposes of backup.

Generation of the User's Public and Private Keys

The issuer will produce (in addition to PIN) a public and private key pair (PKc, SKc) for each customer. The user's private key and PIN are Exclusive-ORed to produce a secret card parameter, SKc* (i.e., SKc* = SKc $\oplus$ PIN), which is then written on the user's intelligent secure card.

Validation of the User's PIN and Card Key

Each time the customer initiates a transaction at a terminal, the customer's PIN is entered via a PIN pad or keyboard and transferred to the card. (If the card has its own keyboard, the PIN would not be exposed in the terminal.) On the card, PIN is Exclusive-ORed with the secret card parameter (SKc*) to produce the user's private key, SKc, and SKc is then used to generate a DGS

Secondary Storage

IDc1: PKc1, D_{SKb} [CE (IDc1, PKc1)]
IDc2: PKc2, D_{SKb} [CE (IDc2, PKc2)]
•
•
•
IDcn: PKcn, D_{SKb} [CE (IDcn, PKcn)]

Each customer's identifier, public key, and digital signature (generated with the issuing banks private key) are produced by the issuing bank and stored on the appropriate bank card.

Secondary Storage

IDb1: PKb1, D_{SKu} [CE (IDb1, PKb1)]
IDb2: PKb2, D_{SKu} [CE (IDb2, PKb2)]
•
•
•
IDbn: PKbn, D_{SKu} [CE (IDbn, PKbn)]

Each bank's identifier, public key, and digital signature (generated with the private interchange key) are produced by the key distribution center and sent to each institution. This enables each institution to check digital signatures with PKu.

Security Module

SKb - Private Bank Key
PKb - Public Bank Key
PKu - Public Interchange Key

Public-Key Algorithm

PKb and PKu are stored in the security module to protect their integrity. SKb is stored in the security module to protect its secrecy and integrity.

Figure 11-40. Information Stored in the Data Base of the Issuer's EDP System and in the Issuer's Security Module

on the transaction request message via the public-key algorithm. A time-of-day (TOD) clock obtained from the acquirer via the terminal (as described earlier) is included in the message to ensure that it is time-variant.

At the issuer, the corresponding PKc of reference, which is filed under the user's identifier, is read from the EDP system's data base[43] and used to

[43] See footnote 35.

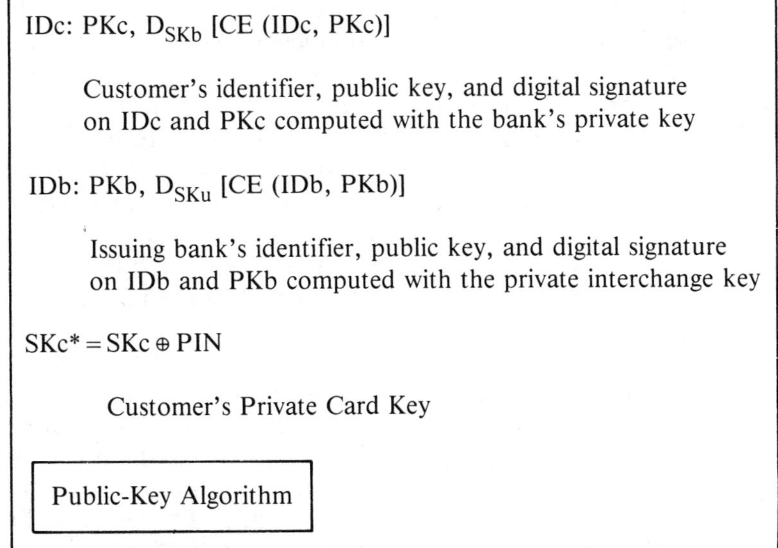

IDc: PKc, D_{SKb} [CE (IDc, PKc)]
Customer's identifier, public key, and digital signature on IDc and PKc computed with the bank's private key
IDb: PKb, D_{SKu} [CE (IDb, PKb)]
Issuing bank's identifier, public key, and digital signature on IDb and PKb computed with the private interchange key
$SKc^* = SKc \oplus PIN$
Customer's Private Card Key
Public-Key Algorithm

Figure 11-41. Information Stored on the Intelligent Secure Card

encrypt the received DGSreq. This result is compared for equality with the compressed encoding calculated on the received message Mreq. Furthermore, the received TOD is checked for currency against a TOD of reference stored in the issuer's EDP system. If both tests succeed, the issuer concludes that the content of the message is correct, the message is not a stale message, and the secret information entered by the customer at the entry point (SKc* and PIN) is properly related to the claimed ID.

Key Management Considerations for Asymmetric Algorithms

To take maximum advantage of the public key idea, secret terminal resident keys should be unnecessary. Only the public keys permanently stored in the terminals are needed to authenticate transaction response messages. To authenticate transaction request messages, however, requires a secret key at the entry point, although a public key can be used at the destination where these messages are checked. Such a secret key must therefore be supplied by the user since, by definition, no secret key should be stored in the terminal permanently. Such a design therefore dictates a personal key ap-

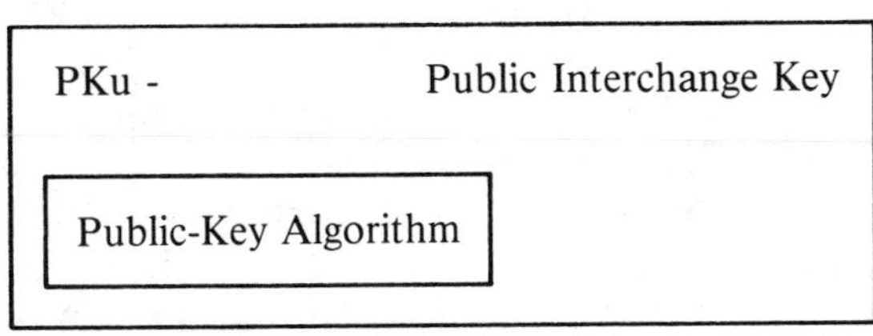

Figure 11-42. Information Stored in the EFT Terminal

proach, where the personal key is equal to the secret key required in the public key approach. The corresponding public key stored at the issuer is used to authenticate request messages.

The most straightforward approach for authenticating transaction response messages would be to store PKu at each EFT terminal and store SKu at each cooperating institution's HPC. A digital signature computed on Mresp at any institution using SKu could be checked at any terminal using PKu. However, this has the disadvantage that institutions share the secret key SKu—an undesirable situation. If SKu should become compromised, an opponent could generate a valid digital signature on any transaction response message.

To avoid sharing secret information and thereby realize separation among the institutions, each subscriber bank can define its own keys (PKb, SKb, where b represents bank). The secret key SKb is used by an individual institution to compute a digital signature on the transaction response message, Mresp. At the EFT terminal, the public key PKb is used to authenticate Mresp and its digital signature. However, such a solution requires that the public key of each institution be available at the entry point. Due to storage limitations (at EFT terminals), such an approach is impractical if there are a large number of subscriber institutions in the interchange network.

The disadvantage of storing a common SKu at each institution in the interchange, or of storing the PKb of each bank in each EFT terminal, can be avoided as follows. A trusted system node or key distribution center is designated to manage the universal secret key, SKu. The individual institutions still define their own (SKb, PKb) key pairs. To establish the correct PKb at an arbitrary entry point, the trusted node generates a digital signature on (IDb, PKb) using SKu. The terminals in which PKu is stored authenticate PKb by encrypting D_{SKu}[CE(IDb, PKb)] with PKu and comparing the result for equality with the compressed encoding of the supplied (IDb, PKb) stored on the bank card. Note that D_{SKu}[CE(IDb, PKb)] is also stored on the bank card. Thus, a hierarchical public-key approach is used in which a universal secret key, SKu, is the dominant system key. This key, known only to the trusted node, provides the means (via the digital signature) for each institution to authenticate the public keys of each other institution (PKb1, PKb2, . . . , etc.). Thus each PKb is checked before being used to authenticate transaction response messages at the entry point. Secret user keys, on the other hand, are used (in conjunction with PINs) to generate digital signatures on the transaction request messages, which in turn allows the issuer (who has the corresponding public keys) to verify users and authenticate transaction request messages.

Off-Line Use

Figure 11-43 illustrates an offline transaction. The customer's card is placed in a card read/write device coupled to or integrated within the terminal. The customer then enters his PIN via a suitable entry device (PIN pad or keyboard). The PIN is transferred to the card where it is Exclusive-ORed with the secret parameter SKc* on the card to form the user's private key, SKc, namely: SKc = SKc* ⊕ PIN. SKc is temporarily stored on the card, i.e., until transaction processing is complete.

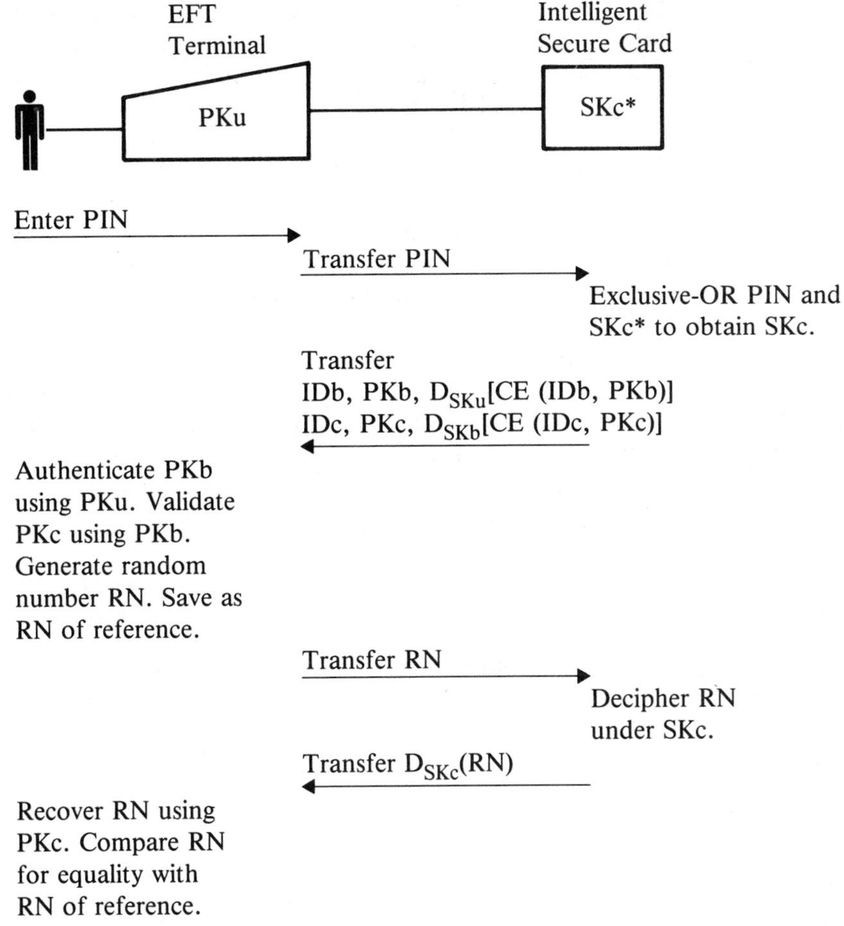

Figure 11-43. Off-Line Use

The two public keys, PKc and PKb, which were originally written on the card by the issuer, are then transferred from the card to the terminal together with their respective digital signatures. This enables the terminal to authenticate PKb and PKc with the aid of PKu (stored in the terminal).

To validate the user, the terminal performs a handshake with the card, as follows: The terminal generates a random number RN, which it transfers to the card and requests that the card decipher the random number under SKc. Upon deciphering the random number under SKc, the card transfers the result to the terminal. The terminal then enciphers the received value under PKc (which it previously authenticated) to recover RN. The recovered value of RN is compared for equality with the RN of reference. If the two quantities are equal, the terminal concludes that (1) the card is capable of cryptographic operations and (2) the card generated the proper SKc. Since SKc is a function of the secret card parameter (SKc*) as well as PIN, personal verification is achieved. The transaction request is then honored according to whatever established limits and prior protocols and arrangements have been implemented.

A variation of the method is for each terminal to also store the public key,

PKb, of the local bank. In that case, if a customer performs an off-line transaction at a terminal belonging to his own bank, the terminal can authenticate PKc directly from D_{SKb}[CE(IDc, PKc)] and avoid the intermediate step of authenticating PKb from D_{SKu}[CE(IDb, PKb)].

On-Line Use in Interchange and Noninterchange

In describing both local and interchange transactions it will be noted that there is no difference in the protocols. Only message routing is different, since different parts of the interchange network are traversed.

The data and computing capability of the customer's card are made available to the terminal (Figure 11-44) when the card is inserted into a suitable read/write device. The customer then enters his PIN via a suitable entry device, the PIN is routed to the card, and the PIN is Exclusive-ORed with the secret card parameter SKc* to form the user's private key, SKc, which is temporarily stored on the card.

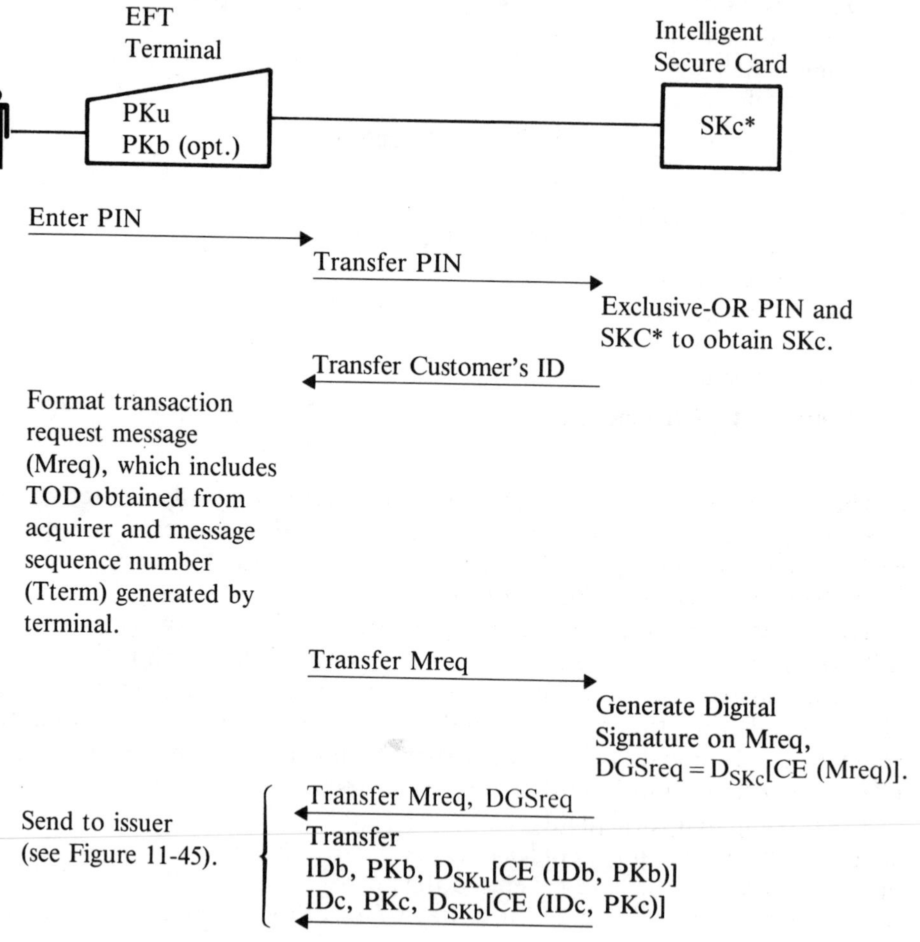

Figure 11-44. On-Line Use—EFT Terminal

To allow the issuer to validate the transaction request message, a DGS is generated using SKc (i.e., D_{SKc} [CE(Mreq)]). This is accomplished by transferring the assembled message to the card where the compressed encoding of Mreq is generated and in turn deciphered under SKc. The message and signature are returned to the terminal for transmittal to the issuer (identical to the acquirer for a local transaction, different from the acquirer for interchange). If it is desired to allow intermediate nodes to authenticate and read the message, the quantities IDb, PKb, D_{SKu}[CE(IDb, PKb)] and IDc, PKc, D_{SKb}[CE(IDc, PKc)] can be read from the card and sent together with the transaction request message.

At the issuer (Figure 11-45), the corresponding PKc of reference is stored in the EDP system's data base, for example, in the form IDc, PKc, D_{SKb}[CE(IDc, PKc)]. Prior to its use, PKc of reference is authenticated using PKb. The received message is then authenticated by generating its compressed encoding and comparing the result for equality with the received DGSreq encrypted under PKb (i.e., with E_{PKb} (DGSreq) = E_{PKb} [D_{SKb} (CE(Mreq))]). If they are identical, and if the TOD checks, then the issuer concludes that the content of the message is correct, the message is not stale, and the secret information supplied by the user, SKc* and PIN, is properly related to the claimed ID. If the requested transaction can be honored, a positive response is sent to the originating terminal. Otherwise, a negative response is sent to the originating terminal.

To send a response, the issuer generates a digital signature on the response message Mresp using SKb (i.e., DGSresp = D_{SKb} [CE(Mresp)]). Mresp and DGSresp are then sent to the EFT terminal. A positive response could consist of sending back the request message (i.e., Mresp = Mreq and DGSresp = D_{SKb} [CE(Mreq)]). This will be assumed here. A negative response can be anything other than a positive response.

To authenticate the response message, the terminal reads IDb, PKb, D_{SKu} [CE(IDb, PKb)] from the card and validates PKb using PKu (stored in the terminal). (If PKb is stored in the terminal, the prior step can be eliminated). The received DGSresp is then enciphered under PKb and the result is compared for equality with the compressed encoding of the Mreq of reference. If the two quantities are equal, the terminal honors the transaction; otherwise, the transaction is denied (Figure 11-46).

A summary of the keys required with the described public key approach is provided in Table 11-15. Tables 11-16 and 11-17 show the flows of information from the card to the issuer (via the EFT terminal) and from the issuer to the EFT terminal. Comparing these tables with those of the hybrid approach (Tables 11-9 through 11-11), one observes that only public quantities are shared among institutions. Thus a higher degree of isolation is achieved with the public key approach. On the other hand, it must be realized that the approach requires a secret universal key. If that key becomes compromised, the security of the entire system is lost. The described public key approach depends, therefore, on one node or key distribution center which is trusted by everyone in the system, and that one party controls and manages the universal secret key.

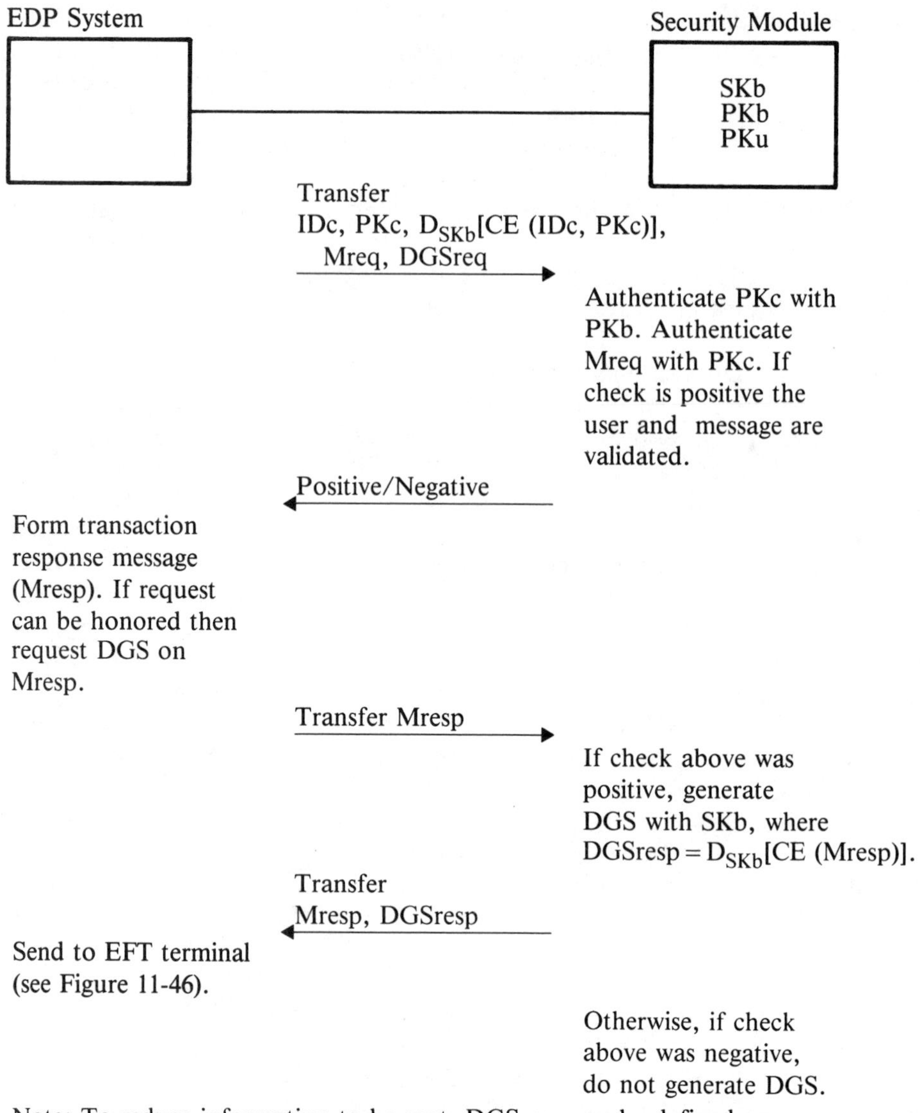

Note: To reduce information to be sent, DGSresp can be defined as DGSresp = D_{SKb} [CE (Mreq)]. In this case the response message is identical to the request message and does not have to be sent. Thus only DGSresp is returned to the terminal as a positive response.

Figure 11-45. On-Line Use—Issuer's EDP System

Additional Comments

In the described approach, PIN secrecy depends on SKc* secrecy. If SKc* were known to an opponent, PIN could be derived easily using only PKc (nonsecret and assumed available). Since PIN has relatively few combinations, and assuming SKc* (Figure 11–43) is available, an opponent could

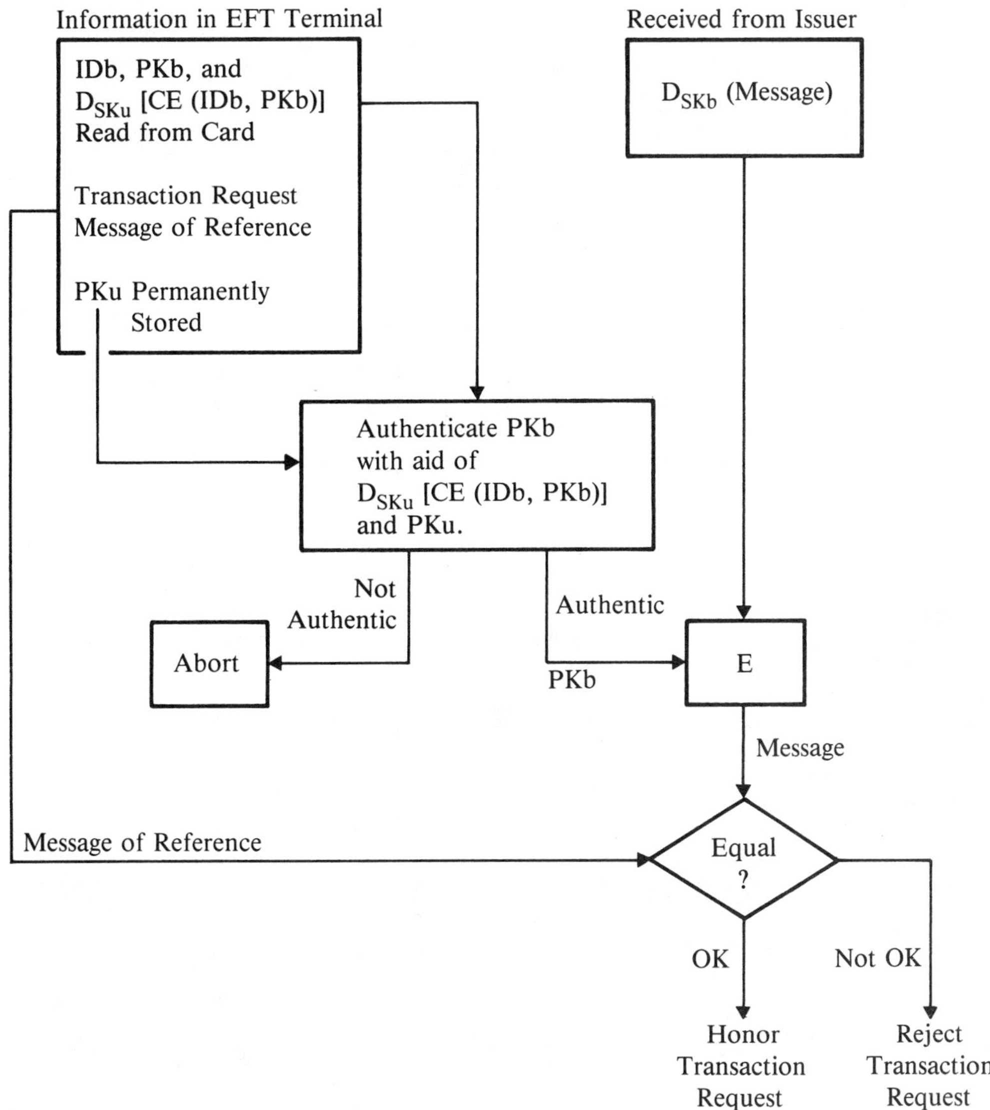

Figure 11-46. On-Line Use—EFT Terminal

enumerate all possible candidates for SKc via the relation SKctrial = SKc* ⊕ PINtrial. SKc is determined by finding the SKctrial satisfying the relation $D_{SKctrial} E_{PKc}(X) = X$.

In an off-line environment, PIN-related information must always be stored on the card, and thus this type of attack will always succeed if card information is available to an opponent. Defense against the attack is therefore based on the high level of data protection afforded by the intelligent secure card. *Hence, strictly speaking requirement 8 (see EFT Security Requirements) cannot be satisfied when a public-key algorithm is used in an off-line environment (i.e., PIN information can always be obtained from card information).*

System User	Intelligent Secure Bank Card	System Nodes: EFT Terminal	System Nodes: Acquirer's Host (Inst. X)	System Nodes: Switch's Host	System Nodes: Issuer's Host (Inst. Y)
Permanently Installed Keys/Parameters					
none	KP SKc* PKc PKb	PKu	none	none	SKMiss PKMiss
Keys Used for Generating and Authenticating Digital Signatures (DSG) on the Transaction Request Messages, Mreqs					
none	SKc (Dynamically Generated from SKc* and PIN, e.g., SKc = SKc* ⊕ PIN)	none	none	none	PKc is stored for all members of institution Y.

Keys Used for Generating and Authenticating Digital Signatures on the Transaction Response Messages, Mresps					
none	PKb (Authenticated Using IDb and D_{SKu}[CE(IDb, PKb)], Also Stored on Bank Card)	PKu (Used to Authenticate PKb)	none	none	SKb is defined by institution Y.

Note: Keys associated with personal verification at the issuer (and, perhaps, the switch) are not shown.

Legend:

SKM: Secret host master key
PKM: Public host master key
SKb: Secret institution (bank) key
PKb: Public institution (bank) key
SKc: Secret user (customer) key
SKc*: Secret card parameter
PKc: Public user (customer) key
SKu: Secret universal key
PKu: Public universal key
IDb: Institution (bank) identifier
IDc: User (customer) Identifier

Table 11-15. Keys Defined for the Public Key Approach Using an Intelligent Secure Card

System User	Intelligent Secure Bank Card	System Nodes: EFT Terminal	Acquirer's Host	Switch's Host	Issuer's Host
1 Enter PIN and transfer to card via terminal.	2 Generate SKc = SKc* ⊕ PIN.	4 Authenticate PKb with PKu and PKc with PKb.	10 Forward received Mreq and DGSreq to switch.	11 Forward received Mreq and DGSreq to issuer.	12 Check received DGSreq with PKc of reference and TODsw of reference.
	3 Read IDb,PKb, D_{SKu}[CE(IDb,PKb)] IDc, PKc and D_{SKu}[CE(IDc,PKc)] from card and transfer to terminal.	5 Read card information and formulate Mreq which includes TODacq and Tterm.			13 Verify user.
		6 Send Mreq to intelligent secure card.			14 Decide if Mreq is to be honored.
	7 Compute DGSreq with SKc (i.e., D_{SKc}[CE(Mreq)]).	9 Forward received Mreq and DGSreq to acquirer.			15 Formulate Mresp which includes Tterm.
	8 Send Mreq and DGSreq to terminal.				

Note: It is assumed that the acquirer periodically sends time-of-day information (TODacq,term) to the terminals in its domain. The TOD stored at the other network host nodes (TODsw at the switch and TODiss at the issuer) is assumed to be equal to TODacq within an allowable range (ΔTOD). The terminal also generates time-variant information (Tterm) which is transmitted to the issuer.

The integers 1–15 in the table show the sequence of steps in the transaction.

Table 11-16. Information Flow from Card to Issuer—Public Key Approach with Intelligent Secure Card

System User	Intelligent Secure Bank Card	System Nodes			
		EFT Terminal	Acquirer's Host	Switch's Host	Issuer's Host
		20 Check received DGSresp with PKb of reference and Tterm of reference.	19 Forward received Mresp, and DGSresp to terminal.	18 Forward received Mresp, and DGSresp to acquirer.	15 Formulate Mresp which includes Tterm.
					16 Generate DGSresp on Mresp using SKb.
		21 Decide if Mresp should be accepted or rejected.			
					17 Send Mresp and DGSresp to intelligent secure card via switch, acquirer, and terminal.
		22 Notify terminal to process transaction if Mresp is accepted; otherwise, abort transaction request.			

The integers 15–22 in the table show the sequence of steps in the transaction.

Table 11-17. Information Flow from Issuer to Terminal–Public Key Approach with Intelligent Secure Card

In an on-line environment, this exposure can be avoided by decoupling SKc and PIN (i.e., by not making SKc a function of PIN). The relation SKc = SKc* ⊕ PIN was used in the present discussion for the sake of uniformity with the approach described in the preceding section, the PIN/Personal Key/System (Hybrid Key Management) Approach Using an Intelligent Secure Card. For example, a better approach would be to define SKc = SKc* and transmit PIN ‖ RN (i.e., PIN concatenated with a random number generated on the card) encrypted under PKb. This approach requires an additional PIN verification step at the issuer, but has the advantage that knowledge of any one of the parameters SKc or PIN does not reveal information about the other.

CONCLUDING REMARKS

The purpose of this chapter has been to suggest various techniques that may be used for cryptographic authentication in future EFT systems. For the present and near term, it appears that PIN/system key-based EFT systems using magnetic stripe cards will predominate. In such systems, a reasonable level of protection can be achieved with existing technology and current banking practices and standards.

In future systems, a nominal increase in security can be achieved if personal keys are combined with the present PIN/system key designs (e.g., using hybrid key management). However, a significant increase in security is achievable if a hybrid key management is implemented in conjunction with intelligent secure cards.

Finally, further enhancements in security are possible by introducing public-key encryption at financial institutions, thereby providing a means for the issuer to give the acquirer an electronically signed receipt for each transaction request authorized by the issuer.

GLOSSARY

For the analysis of the authentication process, the following quantities are defined.

AP = authentication parameter
CC = communications controller
DES = data encrypting standard
DGS = digital signature
HPC = host processing center
ID = user identifier
KA = authentication key
KC = communication key
KDC = key distribution center
KI = interchange key

Knode = node key
KP = personal cryptographic key
KPG = personal key generating key used to generate KP from ID
KPN = PIN generating key used to generate PIN from ID
KMT = terminal master key
KNC = secondary communication key
KSTR = transaction session key
KT = resident terminal key
KTR = transaction key
MAC = message authentication code
PAC = personal authentication code
PAN = primary account number
PIN = personal identification number
PK = public key in a public-key cryptosystem
PKC = public-key cryptosystem
RN = random number
Tcard = time-variant information generated by bank card
TID = terminal identifier
TOD = time of day
Tterm = time-variant information generated by terminal
SK = secret key in a public-key cryptosystem
TR = transaction request
Rf = reference
Z = initializing vector

The notation $E_K(X) = Y$ defines encipherment of the quantity X under the cipher key K, resulting in ciphertext Y. The notation $D_K(Y) = X$ defines decipherment of Y under cipher key K, resulting in plaintext X.

REFERENCES

1. *Introduction to EFT Security,* Division of Management Systems and Economic Analysis, Federal Deposit Insurance Corporation, Washington, DC (August 1976).
2. Diffie, W. and Hellman, M. E., "New Directions in Cryptography," *IEEE Transactions on Information Theory,* **IT-22**, No. 6, 644–654 (1976).
3. Rivest, R. L., Shamir, A. and Adelman, L., "A Method for Obtaining Digital Signatures and Public-Key Cryptosystems," *Communications of the ACM,* **21**, No. 2, 120–126 (1978).
4. Hirsch, P., "French Bring 'Smart' Credit Card to U.S.," *Computerworld,* **16**, No. 43, 1, 8 (October 20, 1980).
5. Orr, W., "The Chip Card is Here, but Where is it Going?," *ABA Banking Journal,* **72**, No. 9, 93–95 (1980).
6. Herbst, N. M. and Liu, C. N., "Automatic Signature Verification Based on Accelerometry," *IBM Journal of Research and Development,* **21**, No. 3, 245–253 (1977).

7. Meyer, C. H., Matyas, S. M., and Lennon, R. E., "Required Cryptographic Authentication Criteria for Electronic Funds Transfer Systems," *Proceedings of the 1981 Symposium on Security and Privacy,* IEEE Computer Society, Oakland, CA, 89–98 (April 1981).
8. Campbell, C. M., Jr., "A Microprocessor-Based Module to Provide Security in Electronic Funds Transfer Systems," *Proceedings COMPCON* **79**, 148–153 (1979).
9. *American National Standard for Personal Identification Number Management and Security, Draft Standard,* American National Standards Institute, Technical Committee X9.A3, Revision 5 (November 5, 1980).
10. Kaufman, D. and Auerbach, K., "A Secure National System for Electronic Funds Transfer," *AFIPS Conference Proceedings 1976 NCC,* **46**, 129–138 (June 1976).
11. Evans, A., Kantrowitz, W., and Weiss, E., "A User Authentication System Not Requiring Secrecy in the Computer," *Communications of the ACM,* **17**, No. 8, 437–442 (1974).
12. Purdy, G. B., "A High Security Log-in Procedure," *Communications of the ACM,* **17**, No. 8, 442–445 (1974).
13. Lennon, R. E. and Matyas, S. M., "Cryptographic Key Distribution Using Composite Keys," *Conference Record, 1978 National Telecommunications Conference,* **2**, 26.1.1–26.1.6 (December 1978).
14. Matyas, S. M. and Meyer, C. H., "Cryptographic Authentication Techniques in Electronic Funds Transfer Systems," *Proceedings of the National Electronics Conference,* **35**, Chicago, 309–314 (October 1981).
15. *PIN Manual: A Guide to the Use of Personal Identification Numbers in Interchange,* MasterCard International, Inc. (formerly Interbank Card Association), New York (1980).
16. Proposed American National Standard X4.16, *Magnetic Stripe Encoding for Financial Transaction Cards,* American National Standards Institute, X4 (Draft, October 1980).
17. Kent, S. T., "Comparison of Some Aspects of Public-Key and Conventional Cryptosystems," *Conference Record of the 1979 International Conference on Communications,* **1**, Boston, 04.3.1–04.3.5 (June 1979).
18. Needham, R. M. and Schroeder, M. D., "Using Encryption for Authentication in Large Networks of Computers," *Communications of the ACM,* **21**, No. 12, 993–999 (1978).

Other Publications of Interest

19. Lennon, R. E. and Matyas, S. M., "Cryptographic PIN Processing in EFT Systems," *Proceedings COMPCON* **79**, 142–147 (September 1979).
20. Meyer, C. H. and Matyas, S. M., "Some Cryptographic Principles of Authentication in Electronic Funds Transfer Systems," *Proceedings of the Seventh Data Security Symposium,* Mexico City, Mexico, 73–88 (October 1981).

CHAPTER TWELVE

Measures of Secrecy for Cryptographic Systems

We agree with the statement that "cryptography is currently an engineering subject in which there are more facts and rules of thumb than theorems or systematic developments" [1]. The science of cryptography has evolved only recently as a result of attempts to explain or define in mathematical terms the facts and rules of thumb that have evolved from the practiced art of cryptography. This chapter reflects this quality and of necessity combines a wide variety of material ranging from the very simple to the very complex.

Cryptographic protection (secrecy) is attainable if plaintext can be recovered from ciphertext only by those authorized. There are in fact two types of secrecy that can be achieved with a cryptographic algorithm: *theoretical secrecy* and *practical secrecy.*

Theoretical secrecy is based on a single axiom: that the information available to or intercepted by an opponent is insufficient for the derivation of a unique cipher solution. In other words, there is always a measure of uncertainty, regardless of what method of analysis is used, as to which candidate among a set of possible values (keys or messages) is correct. For example, cryptographic protection may be based on the assumption that an opponent has only ciphertext available (called a ciphertext-only attack), and that the amount of ciphertext intercepted by an opponent would be insufficient to allow the plaintext or key to be recovered.[1] Today, with the vast amounts of data being transmitted in communication networks, such an assumption cannot be justified. In fact, the designers of a cryptographic system should assume that an opponent can obtain plaintext and matching ciphertext in sufficient quantities to determine the key uniquely (see Cryptographic Algorithms, Chapter 2). Therefore, by and large, theoretical secrecy is unattainable in today's data processing systems and networks.

On the other hand, practical secrecy assumes sufficient information is available to break the cipher, and is measured by the work (work factor)

[1] The following are examples of ciphertext-only attacks in which there are multiple solutions. With transposition on English, cryptogram "nde" would have at least two solutions: "den" and "end." With a simple substitution on English, cryptogram "nde" would have several solutions: "the," "and," "but," and so forth.

required to find the solution to a given cryptanalytical problem (see Cryptographic Algorithms, Chapter 2). This type of secrecy is achieved (e.g., in the DES) by designing the cryptographic algorithm so that it is computationally infeasible to solve for a message or key, even if the analyst has specific knowledge of the cryptographic algorithm and large amounts of chosen ciphertext/plaintext and corresponding plaintext/ciphertext.

Experience has shown that it is difficult to devise a cryptographically strong algorithm. (Note for example the successful cryptanalysis of the German Enigma Cipher and the Japanese PURPLE Cipher used during World War II). To understand why this is so, it is helpful to investigate the mathematical foundations of cryptography. (Theoretical secrecy, which is primarily of value to a general study of cryptography, has been the subject of extensive mathematical analyses. Significant results have been obtained. Practical secrecy, which is significant to the specialized study of cryptographic algorithms, has also been widely investigated; but few substantive results have been obtained.)

Shannon [2,3] invented a particularly useful theoretical model called a *random cipher.* Using information theory, he described the relationship between the amount of intercepted ciphertext and the likelihood of a successful attack. With the model, he was able to determine the *unicity distance* (ud) of a cipher, which he described as follows: with more than ud characters of ciphertext there is only one solution to the cipher, with less than that amount there are several so-called solutions.

More accurate results can be obtained if other probabilistic measures (not based on information theory) are used. The amount of (intercepted) ciphertext defines a specific probability that the ciphertext has a unique solution (only one meaningful decipherment is obtained using the set of all possible keys). By calculating the probability that a correct key or correct plaintext can be obtained for a given amount of ciphertext, more precise statements can be made concerning a cipher's vulnerability.

ELEMENTS OF MATHEMATICAL CRYPTOGRAPHY

The analysis that follows assumes a conventional cryptographic algorithm (an algorithm in which the enciphering and deciphering keys are equal). However, the results can be adapted to public-key algorithms as well. (For a definition of conventional and public-key algorithms, see Cryptographic Algorithms, Chapter 2.)

Information Flow in a Conventional Cryptographic System

Figure 12-1 illustrates the information flow in a conventional cryptographic system. A message (plaintext x) is generated by the sender. An enciphering algorithm E, which depends on a secret key k, is used to encipher x into a cryptogram (ciphertext y):

$$E_k(x) = y$$

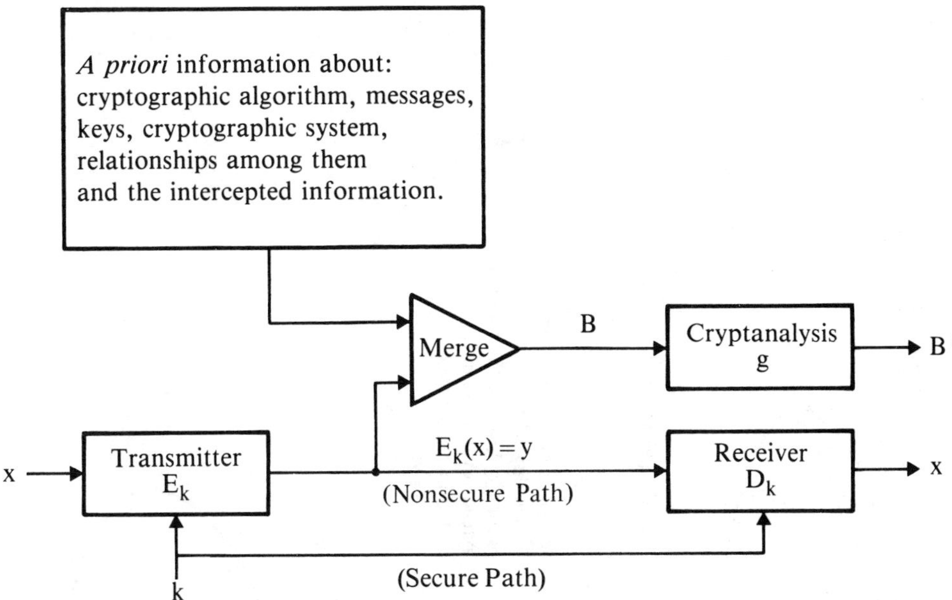

Figure 12-1. Information Flow in a Conventional Cryptographic System

Cryptogram y is then transmitted to the receiver where the deciphering algorithm D, which also depends on secret key k, is used to recover x:

$$D_k(y) = x$$

It is assumed that an opponent does not possess k, and hence cannot recover x from y using D. (Note that algorithms D and E may or may not be kept secret.) In order for k to remain secret, a secure communication path is needed between the sender and receiver.

The opponent's initial information is a variable that can be as little as only ciphertext or as much as complete knowledge of the system (except for the key). If B represents the information available to an opponent and g represents the process of cryptanalysis, then the deduced information, B′, can be expressed as

$$B' = g(B)$$

Practical secrecy assumes that the computational resources and time available for analysis must be within practical bounds. By making these bounds high enough, a sufficiently high work factor is achieved. Theoretical secrecy, on the other hand, assumes that the analyst has unlimited computational resources.

A Cipher with Message and Key Probabilities

A mathematical analysis of ciphers is made possible by assigning probabilities to messages and keys and by making certain simplifying assumptions about

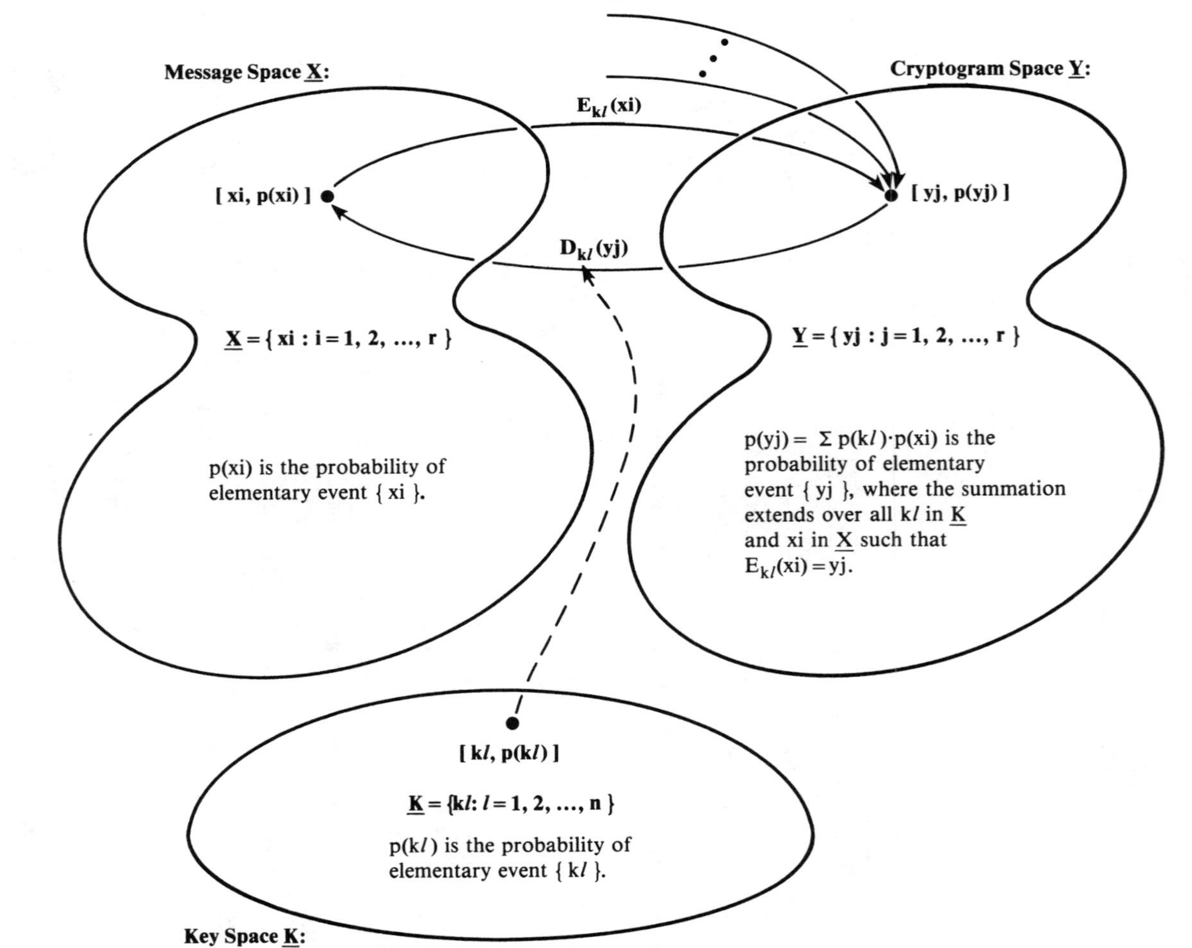

Figure 12-2. A Cipher with Message and Key Probabilities

the enciphering and deciphering transformations, messages, cryptograms, and keys (Figure 12-2). For given enciphering (E) and deciphering (D) algorithms, they are:

1. $\underline{X} = \{xi:i = 1, 2, \ldots, r\}$ is a finite set of r unique messages having associated probabilities of occurrence, p(x1), p(x2), . . . , p(xr).
2. $\underline{K} = \{kl:l = 1, 2, \ldots, n\}$ is a finite set of n unique keys having associated probabilities of occurrence, p(k1), p(k2), . . . , p(kn).
3. $\underline{E} = \{E_k:k = k1, k2, \ldots, kn\}$ is a finite set of one-to-one enciphering functions from the message space ($\underline{X}$) to the cryptogram space ($\underline{Y}$).
4. For every key (k*l* in $\underline{K}$) and message (xi in $\underline{X}$) there is a cryptogram (yj in $\underline{Y}$) such that $E_{kl}(xi) = yj$. The probability of elementary event {yj} is given by

$$p(yj) = \Sigma\ p(kl)p(xi)$$

   where the summation extends over all k*l* in $\underline{K}$ and xi in $\underline{X}$ such that $E_{kl}(xi) = yj$. It is assumed that messages and keys are independently chosen, that is, p(k*l*, xi) = p(k*l*)p(xi).
5. The condition that E_{kl} is a one-to-one function means that the number of elements in $\underline{Y}$, denoted $|\underline{Y}|$, must be equal to or greater than the number of elements in $\underline{X}$. For the special case where $|\underline{X}| = |\underline{Y}|$, each enciphering function in $\underline{E}$ is not only one-to-one but also onto (see Cryptographic Algorithms, Chapter 2), and D_k is the inverse function of E_k. To simplify the analysis, assume that $|\underline{X}| = |\underline{Y}|$. Therefore,

$$\underline{Y} = \{yj:j = 1, 2, \ldots, r\}$$

   is a finite set of r unique cryptograms, and

$$\underline{D} = \{D_k:k = k1, k2, \ldots, kn\}$$

   is a finite set of one-to-one deciphering functions from the cryptogram space ($\underline{Y}$) to the message space ($\underline{X}$).

When no ambiguity exists, the indices (i, j, and *l*) associated with x, y, and k will be omitted from the discussion.

The probabilities assigned to messages and keys represent the analyst's prior knowledge (or assumptions) about the messages and keys selected for encipherment. For example, if there were a known bias in the key selection process, the analyst would assign highest probability to those keys with the greatest chance of being selected. In effect, this would reduce the average number of keys needed to be searched before finding the correct key. However, if keys are randomly selected, or if the selection process is unknown, the analyst would assign equal probability to each key:

$$p(k) = 1/n \qquad \text{for each k in } \underline{K}$$

In the analysis that follows, keys are assumed to be equally probable. Probabilities are assigned to messages using a method suggested by Shannon [2,3]. The message space ($\underline{X}$) is divided into two sets: (1) a set of s meaningfully distinct, or *meaningful messages*, denoted by $\underline{X}'$, and (2) a set of r–s *meaningless messages* denoted by $\underline{X}''$. By assuming that almost all enciphered messages will be meaningful, it follows that the sum of the probabilities of the messages in $\underline{X}'$ is approximately equal to one, and the sum of the probabilities of the messages in $\underline{X}''$ is approximately equal to zero. In the analysis below, assume that the sums of the possibilities of the messages in $\underline{X}'$ and $\underline{X}''$ are one and zero, respectively.[2]

For mathematical simplicity, assume that the analyst has no prior knowledge of the messages' contents and that each message in $\underline{X}'$ is assigned equal probability:

$$p(x) = 1/s \qquad \text{for each x in } \underline{X}'$$

The cryptogram space ($\underline{Y}$) can therefore be divided into a set of *possible cryptograms* (those that can be generated from at least one meaningful message), denoted by $\underline{Y}'$,

$$\underline{Y}' = \{E_k(x):\text{k in } \underline{K} \text{ and x in } \underline{X}'\}$$

and a set of *impossible cryptograms* (those that can be generated only from meaningless messages), denoted by $\underline{Y}''$,

$$\underline{Y}'' = \underline{Y} - \underline{Y}'$$

where $\underline{Y} - \underline{Y}'$ is the *difference* of $\underline{Y}$ and $\underline{Y}'$, defined as the elements in $\underline{Y}$ that are not in $\underline{Y}'$. (The probability, p(y), of each cryptogram (y) in $\underline{Y}'$ is determined by the probabilities of the various messages and keys, as shown above.)

In the definitions given below, y stands for an intercepted cryptogram, that is, y is an element of the set $\underline{Y}'$.

1. M is the random variable defined as the number of keys that will decipher a given intercepted cryptogram (yj) into a meaningful message.
2. M′ is the random variable defined as the number of keys, except for the key originally used to produce the given cryptogram, that will decipher the intercepted cryptogram into a meaningful message ($M' = M - 1$).
3. U is the random variable defined as the number of different meaningful messages that are produced when a given intercepted cryptogram (yj) is deciphered with all possible keys.

[2] Of course, if the sender purposely enciphers random data, then r = s.

4. U′ is the random variable defined as the number of different meaningful messages, except for the message originally used to produce the given cryptogram, that are produced when the intercepted cryptogram is deciphered with all possible keys (U′ = U − 1).

The relationship between M and U is illustrated by the following example in which x1 and k1 are a message and key originally used to produce cryptogram y1; x2 and x3 are incorrect meaningful decipherments; and k2, k3, and k4 are incorrect keys leading to meaningful decipherments (Figure 12-3).

Since 4 keys produce only 3 different meaningful decipherments, it follows that M = 4 and U = 3. It can be seen from the example that the following relations hold in general:

$$u \leqslant m$$

$$m' = m - 1$$

$$u' = u - 1$$

(m and u denote specific values of the random variables M and U, respectively.)

The *probability distribution* of M (the probabilities associated with the occurrence of all possible values of M) is of primary interest to the analyst since the probability of solving successfully for the correct key, denoted by p(SK) (where S stands for success), can be evaluated from M.

Assume that m different keys will decipher an intercepted cryptogram into meaningful messages. Since any of these m keys could be the correct key (the key originally used to produce the given cryptogram), the proba-

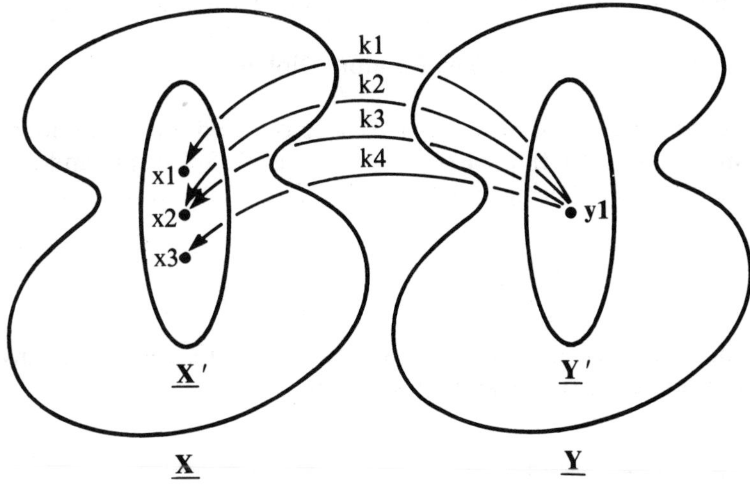

Figure 12-3. Example in which Cryptogram y1 has Four Meaningful Decipherments

bility of guessing or randomly selecting the correct key from among this set is thus

$$p(SK|M = m) = 1/m$$

Since m can range from 1 to n (note that n is the total number of keys, see Figure 12-2), the probability of obtaining the correct key is given by:

$$p(SK) = \sum_{m=1}^{n} (1/m)p(M = m) \qquad (12\text{-}1)$$

where p(M = m) is the probability that M = m. Similarly, the distribution of U allows the probability of successfully solving for the correct message, denoted by p(SM), to be calculated:

$$p(SM) = \sum_{u=1}^{s} (1/u)(p(U = u) \qquad (12\text{-}2)$$

(s is the total number of meaningful messages.) In general, the mathematical relationships that define a cipher—the complex structural relationships dictated by the enciphering and deciphering functions as applied to the set of messages—render it impossible to determine the distributions of M and U. At best, only approximations to these distributions can be found.

Shannon [2] overcame this problem by defining a special theoretical cipher, called a *random cipher*, with the property that the distribution of M is easily determined. He demonstrated that the results obtained with a random cipher are consistent with those obtained with some actual ciphers.

The Random Cipher

Let Q denote the set of all possible one-to-one and onto functions from the set of messages $\underline{X}$ to the set of cryptograms $\underline{Y}$. Select at random, *with replacement,*[3] n enciphering functions, f1, f2, . . . , fn from Q and denote this set by $\underline{E}$:

$$\underline{E} = \{fi: i = 1, 2, \ldots, n\}$$

Corresponding to each enciphering function fi in Q, there is an inverse (deciphering) function, fi^{-1} also in Q, such that

$$fi^{-1}(fi(x)) = x$$

for all x in $\underline{X}$. Let it be assumed that for each enciphering function fi selected

[3] The term "with replacement" means that each selected element is replaced before the next element is selected.

from Q, the corresponding inverse (deciphering) function fi^{-1} is also selected from Q. Thus the set of selected enciphering functions $\underline{E}$ defines a set of associated deciphering functions $\underline{D}$:

$$\underline{D} = \{fi^{-1} : i = 1, 2, \ldots, n\}$$

If f is replaced by E, fi^{-1} is replaced by D, and subscripts are redefined as keys, then $\underline{E}$ and $\underline{D}$ can be rewritten as

$$\underline{E} = \{E_k : k = k1, k2, \ldots, kn\}$$
$$\underline{D} = \{D_k : k = k1, k2, \ldots, kn\}$$

A random cipher can thus be described in terms of the notation used in prior chapters. There is also a natural one-to-one correspondence among ki, E_{ki}, and D_{ki}; selecting any one of the elements is the same as selecting all three elements. The definition of a random cipher given here is different from that given by Shannon [2]. Shannon's random cipher is not a true cipher, since it is possible for the same key to decipher two different cryptograms into the same message. The random cipher defined here eliminates this problem—it is a true cipher.

However, in eliminating one problem, another is created. Because functions are selected from Q with replacement, it may happen that $\underline{E}$ contains two enciphering functions, fi and fj (selected at the ith and jth trials, respectively, such that fi = fj and $i \neq j$ (in other words, $\underline{E}$ may contain an E_{ki} and E_{kj} such that $E_{ki} = E_{kj}$ and $ki \neq kj$). That is, *equivalent* enciphering functions (keys) can occur. But the occurrence of equivalent keys in the definition of a random cipher is not a problem if the total number of such keys remains very small. (Note that in some ciphers it is nearly impossible to prove that equivalent keys do or do not exist.)

Consider a random cipher used to model the DES algorithm. Such a cipher could be constructed by randomly selecting (with replacement) 2^{56} functions (or keys) from Q, where Q contains $(2^{64})!$ different one-to-one and onto functions from the set of all 64-bit messages to the set of all 64-bit cryptograms. Since 2^{56} is very small in comparison to $(2^{64})!$, the probability of selecting the same function (key) twice would be extremely small.

Before proceeding with a mathematical analysis of the random cipher, a computational procedure used to estimate the number of meaningful messages in $\underline{X}$ is discussed. This will allow the results obtained with the random cipher to be applied to several examples of actual ciphers.

Number of Meaningful Messages in a Redundant Language[4]

If an opponent has only ciphertext, but enough is available for analysis, then a necessary and generally sufficient condition for breaking a cipher via

[4] A detailed analysis of the number or meaningful messages is given in Appendix F. Some of the important results derived there are summarized in this section.

the brute-force methods discussed below is that the underlying language from which the messages are selected possess the property known as *redundancy.* A language has redundancy if for any N it can be shown that the possible sequences of N letters are not all equally probable. All natural languages possess redundancy. That English is redundant is demonstrated by a table of the number of times each letter appears in a sample of text. The results of such an experiment using 4 million letters of English text are shown in Table 12-1.

Exactly how redundancy facilitates the process of cryptanalysis can be stated in the following way:

> Redundancy is essentially a series of conditions on the letters of a message, which insure that it be statistically reasonable. These consistency conditions produce corresponding consistency conditions in the cryptogram. The key gives a certain amount of freedom to the cryptogram but, as more and more letters are intercepted, the consistency conditions use up the freedom allowed by the key. Eventually, there is only one [combination of] message and key which satisfies all the conditions and we have a unique solution. [2]

In effect, the reason that a cryptogram eventually has a unique solution, if enough text is available for analysis, is that in a redundant language the messages of N letters can be divided into two sets, those which are intelligible or meaningful and those which are not, and as N is increased the ratio of meaningful to meaningless messages approaches zero. In the English language, for

a	Freq (a)	p(a)	a	Freq (a)	p(a)
A	321712	.0804	N	283561	.0709
B	61472	.0154	O	303844	.0760
C	122403	.0306	P	79845	.0200
D	159726	.0399	Q	4226	.0011
E	500334	.1251	R	244867	.0612
F	92100	.0230	S	261470	.0654
G	78434	.0196	T	370072	.0925
H	219481	.0549	U	108516	.0271
I	290559	.0726	V	39504	.0099
J	6424	.0016	W	76673	.0192
K	26972	.0067	X	7779	.0019
L	165559	.0414	Y	69334	.0173
M	101339	.0253	Z	3794	.0009

p(a) = Freq(a)/4,000,000.
Based on a sample of 8000 excerpts of 500 letters taken from the Brown University Corpus of Present-Day American English. [3]

Table 12-1. Individual Letter Frequencies in 4 Million Characters of English Text

example, the meaningful sequences are just those that are encountered in normal text.

An approximation of s, the number of meaningful messages in $\underline{X}$, can be obtained using a zero-order approximation of message probability (Equation F-2 in Appendix F). When message length N is very large, each message contains about Np1 occurrences of the first letter, Np2 occurrences of the second letter, and so on, where pi is the probability of occurrence of letter i. Hence, for N very large, most messages have a probability p approximately equal to ($\simeq$)

$$p \simeq p1^{Np1} p2^{Np2} \ldots pn^{Npn}$$

where n is the number of different characters in the language. Ignoring statistical variations in p between messages, assume as a first order approximation that all s meaningful sequences have the same probability p. Since the probabilities of all meaningful sequences add up to 1 (as assumed before), it follows that sp $\simeq$ 1 and thus

$$s \simeq 1/p$$

Hence,

$$\log_2 s \simeq -\log_2 p$$

$$\simeq -N \sum_{i=1}^{n} pi \log_2 pi$$

If

$$G_1 = -\sum_{i=1}^{n} pi \log_2 pi$$

is defined as the *entropy per character* (measured in bits per character)[5] for the message source, it follows that

$$s \simeq 2^{NG_1}$$

(See Appendix F.) Using the values for p(a) in Table 12-1, a value of 4.17 bits per character is obtained for G_1. Thus s can be expressed as

$$s \simeq 2^{N4.17}$$

Taking into account probabilities of pairs of letters (digrams), triplets (trigrams), and so on, it is possible to obtain a correspondingly higher-

[5] Since NG_1 denotes the number of bits required to represent s messages and N is the number of characters in each message, G_1 is expressed in bits per character.

order approximation for s (see Appendix F). Groups of n (n = 1, 2, ...) contiguous letters are also referred to as n-grams.

As N approaches infinity (all statistical information about the language is known), one obtains

$$\lim_{N \to \infty} (\log_2 s)/N = R$$

and therefore

$$s = 2^{NR}$$

where R, called the *rate of the language*, is a constant determined by the particular language. For English (26 letters), R is about 1.2 bits per character [4].

PROBABILISTIC MEASURES OF SECRECY USING A RANDOM CIPHER

Probability of Obtaining the Key When Only Ciphertext Is Available for Analysis

Given a random cipher, let y be an intercepted cryptogram which has been enciphered from an unknown meaningful message x. The opponent, who has intercepted y, knows only that x is an element of $\underline{X}'$ and y is an element of $\underline{Y}'$. Assume that kj is the key originally used to encipher x into y. Hence the probability that kj deciphers y into a meaningful message is 1:

$$p[D_{kj}(y) \text{ is meaningful}] = 1$$

In the construction of a random cipher, the enciphering functions in $\underline{E}$ are independently selected from the set Q. Therefore, the process of deciphering y with each of the (n − 1) incorrect keys

$$k1, k2, \ldots, kj - 1, kj + 1, \ldots, kn$$

can be thought of as (n − 1) Bernoulli trials,[6] where s/r represents the probability that a key will successfully decipher y into a meaningful message:

$$p[D_{ki}(y) \text{ is meaningful}] = s/r$$

and 1 − (s/r) is the probability that a key will fail to decipher y into a meaningful message:

$$p[D_{ki}(y) \text{ is meaningless}] = 1 - (s/r)$$

[6] Many problems in probability theory involve independent, repeated trials of an experiment whose outcomes can be classified into two categories called successes and failures. An experiment which has only two possible outcomes is called a *Bernoulli trial* [5].

for all values of i not equal to j. Hence it follows that M′ has a *binomial distribution* [5]:

$$p(M' = m') = \binom{n-1}{m'}(s/r)^{m'}(1-(s/r))^{n-1-m'} \quad \text{for } m' = 0, 1, \ldots, n-1 \tag{12-3a}$$

The expected value (E) and variance (Var) of M′ are, respectively,

$$E(M') = (n-1)(s/r) = \lambda' = \lambda(n-1)/n$$
$$Var(M') = (n-1)(s/r)(1-(s/r)) = \lambda'(1-(s/r))$$

where parameter λ equals ns/r. For s/r much less than 1 (written $s/r \ll 1$), the binomial distribution (Equation 12-3a) can be approximated by the *Poisson distribution* [5], so that

$$p(M' = m') \simeq e^{-\lambda'}(\lambda')^{m'}/m'! \qquad \text{for } s/r \ll 1 \tag{12-3b}$$

Since m′ equals m − 1, it follows that

$$p(M = m) = \binom{n-1}{m-1}(s/r)^{m-1}(1-(s/r))^{n-m} \quad \text{for } m = 1, 2, \ldots, n \tag{12-4a}$$

The expected value and variance of M are, respectively,

$$E(M) = E(M' + 1) = \lambda' + 1 = (\lambda(n-1)/n) + 1 \tag{12-4b}$$

$$Var(M) = Var(M' + 1) = \lambda'(1-(s/r)) \tag{12-4c}$$

The Poisson approximation for p(M = m) is given by

$$p(M = m) \simeq e^{-\lambda'}(\lambda')^{m-1}/(m-1)! \qquad \text{for } s/r \ll 1$$

Using information theory and the above mathematical relationships, Shannon defined the *unicity distance* of a random cipher (the point where there is no uncertainty over which key was used for enciphering) as the value of N(N = cryptogram length in characters) for which λ(λ = ns/r) becomes equal to one [2]. (See also An Expansion of Shannon's Approach Using Information Theory.)

Essentially, when language redundancy is present, the ratio s/r gets smaller as message length (or cryptogram length) gets larger. At some point, s/r is small enough so that ns/r equals 1. However, if data are composed of random, independently-selected characters, in which case there is no language redundancy, s equals r and unicity distance equals infinity.

Unicity distance is often given the following interpretation. *Below the uni-*

city distance ($N < ud$), an attack on the key will not succeed; above the unicity distance ($N \geqslant ud$), an attack on the key will succeed.

However, the interpretation is not strictly correct; there is no abrupt change between the point where the key is ($N \geqslant ud$) and is not ($N < ud$) obtainable. A more precise statement would be that for every cryptogram of N characters, there is an associated probability, p(SK), of obtaining the key used to produce that given (known) cryptogram from the selected (unknown) message.

If information measures are used to determine unicity distance, one concludes that a cipher is vulnerable to attack when λ is close to one. But how vulnerable the cipher is cannot be said. If a probabilistic approach is used instead, more precise statements can be made about the cipher's vulnerability. A value for the probability of successfully obtaining the correct key, p(SK), is derived by combining Equations 12-1 and 12-4a:

$$p(SK) = \sum_{m=1}^{n} (1/m)p(M = m) = (1/\lambda)(1 - (1 - (\lambda/n))^n) \qquad (12\text{-}5)$$

Using the Taylor [6] series expansion for $\ln(1 - (\lambda/n))^n$, it follows that

$$p(SK) \simeq (1/\lambda)(1 - e^{-\lambda}) \qquad \text{for } \lambda/2 \ll 1 \qquad (12\text{-}6)$$

(ln is the natural logarithm to the base e = 2.7182818. . . .) The accurate result for p(SK) (Equation 12-5) depends on n as well as λ, whereas the approximation for p(SK) (Equation 12-6) depends only on λ.

Equations 12-5 and 12-6 show that p(SK) equals one if either the number of keys in $\underline{K}$ is equal to one ($n = 1$), or $\lambda = 0$ (e.g., if the number of characters in the intercepted cryptogram approaches infinity, $N \rightarrow \infty$). Except for the trivial case where $\underline{K}$ contains only one key, the result implies that a random cipher can be broken with certainty only when an infinite amount of ciphertext is available for analysis.

Table 12-2 contains computed values of p(SK) for different values of $\log_2\lambda$ and $\log_2 n$. The values of n for n much greater than 1 ($n \gg 1$) are computed using the approximation for p(SK) (Equation 12-6), while the remainder of the table entries are computed using the accurate expression for p(SK) (Equation 12-5). It can be seen from Table 12-2 that the approximation for p(SK) can be used in all situations where $\log_2 n$ is greater than 10, without much loss of accuracy. Furthermore, it can be seen that the values of interest are all located in a narrow band on either side of the point where $\log_2\lambda$ equals 0.

Shannon [2] defined unicity distance (ud) as the value of N for which λ equals 1. Note that the condition $\{\lambda = 1\}$ is equivalent to the condition $\{\log_2\lambda = 0\}$. Thus when N = ud, it follows from Equation 12-6 that

$$p(SK) = (e - 1)/e = 0.6321 \qquad \text{for } n \gg 1$$

However, if p(SK) is plotted against N, one observes that the transition be-

$\log_2\lambda$ (Bits)	$\log_2 n$ (Bits)				
	0	1	5	10	n>>1
−14	1.0000	0.9999	0.9999	0.9999	0.9999
−12	1.0000	0.9999	0.9999	0.9999	0.9999
−10	1.0000	0.9998	0.9995	0.9995	0.9995
− 9	1.0000	0.9995	0.9990	0.9990	0.9990
− 8	1.0000	0.9990	0.9981	0.9981	0.9980
− 7	1.0000	0.9980	0.9962	0.9961	0.9961
− 6	1.0000	0.9961	0.9925	0.9922	0.9922
− 5	1.0000	0.9922	0.9850	0.9845	0.9845
− 4	1.0000	0.9844	0.9703	0.9694	0.9693
− 3	1.0000	0.9688	0.9418	0.9401	0.9400
− 2	1.0000	0.9375	0.8879	0.8849	0.8848
− 1	1.0000	0.8750	0.7917	0.7871	0.7869
0	1.0000	0.7500	0.6379	0.6323	0.6321
1	0.0	0.5000	0.4366	0.4325	0.4323
2		0.0	0.2465	0.2455	0.2454
3			0.1250	0.1250	0.1250
4			0.0625	0.0625	0.0625
5			0.0313	0.0313	0.0313
6			0.0	0.0156	0.0156
7				0.0078	0.0078
8				0.0039	0.0039
9				0.0020	0.0020
10				0.0010	0.0010
12				0.0	0.0002
14					0.0

Values in the column denoted "n >> 1" were computed using the equation $p(SK) \simeq (1/\lambda)(1 - e^{-\lambda})$, which holds when $\lambda/2n << 1$. Values in all other columns were computed using the equation $p(SK) = (1/\lambda)(1 - (1 - (\lambda/n))^n)$.

Table 12-2. p(SK) Values for a Random Cipher

tween $p(SK) \simeq 0$ and $p(SK) \simeq 1$ is indeed very sharp. This is illustrated below in an example of simple substitution on English. Hence the loose interpretation of unicity distance resulting from information theory is quite good.

An Example of Simple Substitution on English (Ciphertext Only)

An example is given below in which a random cipher is used to model simple substitution on English. It is shown that the unicity distance is about 22 characters, which agrees quite well with reported values for simple substitution ciphers.

In simple substitution on English, there are n = 26! ways in which a 26-letter plain alphabet can be transformed into a 26-letter cipher alphabet (i.e., the maximum number of possible keys is 26!). However, for small and moderate values of N, the number of different letters in the message is usually less than 26. Therefore, the *effective* number of keys is less than 26!.

The average numbers of different letters that occur in messages of N characters, for values of N from 5 to 1500 characters, are shown in Table 12-3. Messages of 25 characters contain about 14 different letters. Therefore, the effective number of keys the analyst must cope with is about

$$\begin{aligned} n &= (26)(25)(24)\ldots(13) \\ &= \frac{26!}{12!} \\ &= 8.4 \times 10^{17} \end{aligned}$$

instead of

$$26! = 4.0 \times 10^{27}$$

Message Length N (Characters)	Average Number of Different Letters per Message
5	4.5
10	7.8
15	10.2
20	12.0
25	13.4
30	14.5
40	16.1
50	17.3
75	19.2
100	20.4
200	22.4
300	23.0
400	23.4
500	23.7
700	24.2
1000	24.6
1500	25.2

The samples were taken from the Brown University Corpus of Present-Day English. [3]
Number of sampled messages = 1000.
On the average, 13.4 different letters occur in a sample of 1000 messages of 25 characters.

Table 12-3. Average Number of Different Letters in N Letters of English Text

Since the unicity distance for simple substitution on English is shown to be about 22 characters, no more than 22-gram statistics should be used to approximate s. In the present analysis, 15-gram statistics are used.

Recall that when J-gram statistics are used ($J \geqslant 1$), the number of meaningful messages ($s_{N, J-1}$) can be approximated by

$$s_{N, J-1} \simeq 2^{NF_J}$$

(See Equation F-14 in Appendix F) where N ($\geqslant$J) is the number of characters in the sample messages, $J - 1$ is the order of the Markov approximation to message probability, and F_J (see Equation F-9 in Appendix F) is a measure of the conditional entropy of the message source.

Using the value $F_{15} = 2.02$ bits per character,[7] $s_{N,14}$ evaluates to

$$s_{N,14} \simeq 2^{N2.02}$$

(To simplify the notation in the discussion below, let s be used in place of $s_{N,14}$.) The total number of messages r is equal to 26^N, which can also be written as

$$r = 2^{(\log_2 26)N} = 2^{4.70N}$$

Therefore, it follows that

$$\begin{aligned} \log_2 \lambda &= \log_2 (ns/r) \\ &= \log_2 n + \log_2 s - \log_2 r \\ &\simeq 59.5 + 2.02N - 4.70N \end{aligned}$$

which can be used to show that $\log_2 \lambda$ is close to 0, or equivalently, that λ is close to 1, when

$$N = 22.2 \text{ characters}$$

This result is interpreted to mean that the unicity distance for simple substitution on English is 22.2 characters when the values of n, s, and r are taken as $26!/12!$, $2^{2.02N}$, and $2^{4.70N}$, respectively. That is, ud = 22.2 characters provided that the message contains about 14 different letters and the cryptanalysis makes use of 15-gram statistics.

Referring now to Table 12-2, one finds that

$$p(SK) = 0.63$$

for a random cipher in which $n = 26!$, $s = 2^{2.02N}$, $r = 2^{4.70N}$, and $N = ud$.

Just how rapidly p(SK) approaches 1 for values of N above 22.2 charac-

[7] F_{15} is computed, using Equation F-18 and values from Table F-3, as follows: $F_{15} = (5.5/4.5)((2.1 - 1.2)/2) = 2.02$.

N (Characters)	18.9	20.0	21.1	22.2	23.3	24.4	25.6
p(SK)	.0020	.0156	.1250	.6321	.9400	.9922	.9990

Values of p(SK) were obtained from Table 12-2 using $\log_2 \lambda$; values of $\log_2 \lambda$ were calculated from the expression $\{\log_2 \lambda = 59.5 + 2.02N - 4.70N\}$ using N.

Table 12-4. Values of p(SK) for N Near ud Given that a Random Cipher is used to Model Simple Substitution

ters, and 0 for values of N below 22.2 characters, can be seen from Table 12-4.

The p(SK) values obtained with a random cipher agree with empirical observations for simple substitution on English. Friedman indicates that

> Practically every example of 25 or more characters representing monoalphabetic encipherment of a 'sensible' message in English can be readily solved [7].

According to Shannon,

> The unicity point . . . can be shown experimentally to lie between the limits 20 and 30. With 30 letters there is nearly always a unique solution to a cryptogram of this type and with 20 it is usually easy to find a number of solutions [2].

Such a close agreement between theoretical and empirical results indicates that the underlying assumptions of a random cipher are good. This same general agreement holds for other ciphers as well (e.g., Caesar, transposition, and Vigenere) [2]. A more detailed treatment of unicity distance computations can be found in Appendix G.

Probability of Obtaining the Key When Plaintext and Corresponding Ciphertext Are Available for Analysis

Consider now a cryptanalysis involving plaintext and corresponding ciphertext. Again, a random cipher is assumed. Let y be the cryptogram produced when a known message x is enciphered with an unknown key kj. In the analysis that follows, x may be a meaningful or meaningless message (i.e., x may be any of the r messages in $\underline{X}$). As before, the probability that kj deciphers y into x is 1:

$$p[D_{kj}(y) \text{ equals } x] = 1$$

Likewise, the process of deciphering y with each of the (n − 1) incorrect keys, k1, k2, . . . , kj − 1, kj + 1, . . . , kn, can be thought of as (n − 1) Bernoulli trials, except now the probability that a key will successfully decipher y into x is 1/r:

$$p[D_{ki}(y) \text{ equals } x] = 1/r$$

and the probability that a key will fail to decipher y into x is $1 - 1/r$:

$$p[D_{ki}(y) \text{ not equal } x] = 1 - 1/r$$

for all values of i not equal to j.

Clearly, cryptanalysis involving plaintext and corresponding ciphertext (where the number of meaningful messages s equals 1) is a special case of the previous analysis. It follows therefore that p(SK) can be calculated from Equations 12-5 and 12-6, except that λ equals n/r instead of ns/r. Since λ is reduced by a factor of s, it is not surprising that the cipher is more vulnerable to attack.

Probability of Obtaining the Plaintext

The emphasis here is on analyzing a random cipher from the viewpoint of obtaining the correct plaintext for a given intercepted cryptogram, without regard to whether one obtains the correct key. Recall that U is defined as the number of meaningful messages that can be recovered from the intercepted cryptogram.

In Appendix H, accurate expressions are derived for the distribution of U (see Equations H-1a and H-3). Using these equations, accurate values were computed for the expected value of U, denoted E(U), and the probability of successfully obtaining the correct plaintext, denoted by p(SM) (see Table 12-5). In particular, values of E(U) and p(SM) are given for the case where the number of keys n equals 32 ($\log_2 n = 5$), and for different values of the number of meaningful messages ($s = 1, 4, 8, 16$, and 32) and λ($\lambda = 2^{-6}, 2^{-3}, 2^{-2}, 2^{-1}, 2^{0}, 2^{1}, 2^{2}$, and 2^{3}). Recall that $\lambda = ns/r$, that is, λ equals the number of keys n multiplied by the number of meaningful messages s divided by the number of cryptograms r.

For purposes of comparison, values for p(SK) from Table 12-2 and values for E(M) computed from Equation 12-4b are also given in Table 12-5. This shows that the difference between p(SM) and p(SK), and the difference between E(U) and E(M), are not too great even for small values of s and n. In an actual cipher, s and n would be much larger than 32; thus no distinction needs to be made between p(SK) and p(SM).

Approximations for $p(U = u)$, E(U), and p(SM) are as follows (see also Equations H-7 thru H-9 in Appendix H):

$$\begin{aligned} p(U = u) \simeq\ & p(M' = u - 1)[1 + \lambda'/s + \\ & (u - 1)(\lambda' - 1)/2s - (u - 1)^2/2s] \\ & \text{for } u \geq 1 \end{aligned}$$

$$E(U) \simeq E(M)[1 - (\lambda'/2s)(\lambda' + (2/\lambda') + 1)]$$

$$p(SM) \simeq p(SK)(1 + \lambda'/2s)$$

where $p(M' = u - 1)$ can be deduced from Equation 12-4a, since $p(M' = u - 1)$ equals $p(M = u)$. The values obtained with these approximations differ by less than 5 percent from the corresponding more accurate values given in Table 12-5.

$\log_2 n = 5$

$\log_2\lambda$ (Bits)	p(SM) $\log_2 s$ (Bits)					p(SK)
	1	2	3	4	5	
−6	0.9962	0.9943	0.9934	0.9929	0.9927	0.9925
−3	0.9706	0.9561	0.9490	0.9454	0.9436	0.9418
−2	0.9430	0.9153	0.9016	0.8949	0.8915	0.8879
−1	0.8925	0.8416	0.8168	0.8047	0.7986	0.7917
0	0.8080	0.7211	0.6800	0.6600	0.6502	0.6379
1	0.6869	0.5533	0.4928	0.4642	0.4503	0.4366
2	0.5676	0.3891	0.3130	0.2785	0.2622	0.2465
3	0.5080	0.2882	0.1974	0.1587	0.1412	0.1250
	E(U)					E(M)
−6	1.008	1.0113	1.0132	1.0142	1.0147	1.0151
−3	1.060	1.0895	1.1052	1.1131	1.1171	1.1211
−2	1.1140	1.1763	1.2087	1.2253	1.2337	1.2422
−1	1.2151	1.3421	1.4113	1.4473	1.4657	1.4844
0	1.3839	1.6453	1.7983	1.8813	1.9244	1.9688
1	1.6263	2.1588	2.5109	2.7139	2.8230	2.9375
2	1.8648	2.8788	3.7040	4.2376	4.5420	4.875
3	1.9841	3.5943	5.3839	6.7940	7.6910	8.75

Note that $0 \leqslant s/r \leqslant 1$, $0 \leqslant \lambda = ns/r \leqslant n$, and $p(SK) = 0$ for $\lambda > n$.

Table 12-5. Values of p(SM) and E(U) where the Number of Keys is Fixed ($n = 32$)

AN EXPANSION OF SHANNON'S APPROACH USING INFORMATION THEORY

In this section, the unicity distance of a cipher with message and key probabilities is discussed in terms of *information theory* [8]. (No assumption is made about the distribution of M, that is, the discussion is not limited to random ciphers but pertains to ciphers in general.)

Consider a message to be a string of symbols, where the symbols belong to a source alphabet. Information theory applies a numerical measure of information to a message, whose value is frequently given in "bits".[8] Based upon this measure is the notion of *entropy*, whose value is frequently given in terms of "bits per symbol". The value of the entropy depends on the statistical or probabilistic properties of the set of messages composed from the source alphabet, rather than the semantics of the particular message. Let $\underline{X}$ = {x1, x2, . . . , xr} denote r different messages with probabilities p1, p2, . . . , pr. The information measure associated with the selection of one member xi from $\underline{X}$, is "$-\log_2$ pi" bits of information. When each message is equally likely, the probability of each message is "1/r" bits, and each message has information value "$\log_2$ r". This is often written as "$-\log_2$ (1/r)"; which is the negative of the $\log_2$ of the probability. For set $\underline{X}$, the average information per message is defined to be the entropy of $\underline{X}$, denoted H($\underline{X}$). Entropy is defined by the expression:

$$H(\underline{X}) = \sum_{i=1}^{r} -(pi)\log_2 (pi)$$

If the messages are equally likely, then H($\underline{X}$) assumes its maximum value of $\log_2$r. In that case, $\log_2$r bits are needed to encode or represent each message and the message bears all the information that is received (i.e., the receiver has no information about which message is selected and sent). For example, if $\underline{X}$ = {x1, x2, x3, x4} and p1 = p2 = p3 = p4 = 1/4, H($\underline{X}$) equals 2. Thus two bits are needed to represent each message.

However, if the messages are unequally likely, one has in advance something that any gambler, speculator, or forecaster would instantly recognize as information. The additional information contributed by the received message is lessened by that amount. For example, if the 4 messages above are assigned probabilities p1 = 1/2, p2 = 1/4, and p3 = p4 = 1/8, then H($\underline{X}$) equals 1.75 bits. On the other hand, if p1 = 1 and p2 = p3 = p4 = 0, then H($\underline{X}$) equals 0. That is, the received message, which is predictable, provides no additional information.

Alternatively, H($\underline{X}$), the entropy function of p1, p2, . . . , pr, can be interpreted as a measure of the *uncertainty* over which message the sender will select and transmit to the receiver. (Recall that H($\underline{X}$) assumes values in the interval 0 to $\log_2$r.) When H($\underline{X}$) = $\log_2$r, there is maximum uncertainty (i.e., the receiver has no information about the message that will be transmitted).

[8] In the pure binary system, a bit is either 0 and 1.

When $H(\underline{X}) = 0$, there is no uncertainty (i.e., the receiver knows in advance which message will be transmitted).

Information theory relies heavily on the mathematical science of probability. For this reason, information theory has been applied to other probabilistic studies in communication theory, cryptanalysis, and the like. In the study of cryptanalysis, $H(\underline{X})$ and $H(\underline{K})$ represent the analyst's prior information over which message and key are selected for encipherment.

Information measures provide an alternative approach for discussing unicity distance. However, because of certain required approximations, the results obtained with this approach are different from those obtained using other probabilistic measures (not based on information theory). In the former case, the relationship between the probability of obtaining the key (or data) and cryptogram length is a step function: the probability is zero when the cryptogram's length is less than the unicity distance, and one when its length is greater than the unicity distance. However, because the transition region—defined by the values of N for which the probability of obtaining the key (or data) is neither close to zero nor close to one—is very small, either approach provides useful results.

Information Measures[9]

The following is a list of common information measures useful to a discussion of theoretical secrecy.

1. Entropy of U:

$$H(U) = -\sum_{u} p(u)\log_2 p(u) \qquad (12\text{-}7a)$$

2. Conditional entropy of U given element v:

$$H(U|v) = -\sum_{u} p(u|v)\log_2 p(u|v) \qquad (12\text{-}7b)$$

3. Equivocation of U given V:

$$H(U|V) = \sum_{v} p(v)H(U|v) \qquad (12\text{-}7c)$$

4. Entropy of U and V:

$$H(U, V) = -\sum_{u,v} p(u, v)\log_2 p(u, v) \qquad (12\text{-}7d)$$

5. Equivocation of U given V and W:

$$H(U|V, W) = -\sum_{u,v,w} p(u, v, w)\log_2 p(u|v, w) \qquad (12\text{-}7e)$$

6. Equivocation of U and V given W:

$$H(U, V|W) = -\sum_{u,v,w} p(u, v, w)\log_2 p(u, v|w) \qquad (12\text{-}7f)$$

[9] Information measures are discussed in greater detail in Appendix F. See also reference 9.

7. Entropy of U, V, and W:

$$H(U, V, W) = -\sum_{u,v,w} p(u, v, w)\log_2 p(u, v, w) \qquad (12\text{-}7g)$$

The following is a list of information identities and relations the proofs of which are left to the reader.

1. $H(U, V) = H(U|V) + H(V)$ (12-7h)
2. $H(U, V, W) = H(U|V, W) + H(V, W)$
   $= H(U, V|W) + H(W)$ (12-7i)
3. $H(U) = H(U|V)$; if U and V are independent, i. e., $p(u, v) = p(u)p(v)$ (12-7j)
4. $H(U) > H(U|V)$; if U and V are dependent, i. e., $p(u, v) \neq p(u)p(v)$ (12-7k)
5. $H(U|V, W) + H(V|W) = H(V|U, W) + H(U|W)$ (12-7l)

In the expressions above, U, V, and W are finite sets whose elements have been assigned probabilities such that

$$\sum_u p(u) = \sum_v p(v) = \sum_w p(w) = 1$$

Unicity Distance for a Cipher When Only Ciphertext Is Available for Analysis

Let it be shown first that $H(\underline{K}, \underline{Y})$ equals $H(\underline{K}, \underline{X})$. From the general relation

$$H(U, V, W) = H(U|V, W) + H(V, W)$$

(see Equation 12-7i) it follows, with an appropriate change of variables, that

$$H(\underline{X}, \underline{K}, \underline{Y}) = H(\underline{X}|\underline{K}, \underline{Y}) + H(\underline{K}, \underline{Y})$$

and

$$H(\underline{Y}, \underline{K}, \underline{X}) = H(\underline{Y}|\underline{K}, \underline{X}) + H(\underline{K}, \underline{X})$$

Hence it follows that

$$H(\underline{K}, \underline{Y}) - H(\underline{K}, \underline{X}) = H(\underline{Y}|\underline{K}, \underline{X}) - H(\underline{X}|\underline{K}, \underline{Y})$$

But since a cipher satisfies $y = E_k(x)$ and $x = D_k(y)$, a knowledge of k and y permits x to be derived, and a knowledge of k and x permits y to be derived.[10]

[10] An exception to this rule is a homophonic substitution cipher (see Appendix G) where $E_k(x)$ defines a set of cryptograms. Encipherment includes the additional step of selecting (usually randomly) one of the cryptograms from this set.

Therefore,

$$H(\underline{X}|\underline{K}, \underline{Y}) = H(\underline{Y}|\underline{K}, \underline{X}) = 0$$

and consequently

$$H(\underline{K}, \underline{Y}) = H(\underline{K}, \underline{X})$$

But, by Equation 12-7h, $H(\underline{K}, \underline{Y})$ can be rewritten as

$$H(\underline{K}, \underline{Y}) = H(\underline{K}|\underline{Y}) + H(\underline{Y})$$

Moreover, since messages and keys are selected independently, that is, $p(x, k) = p(x)p(k)$ for all x in $\underline{X}$ and k in $\underline{K}$, it follows that

$$H(\underline{K}, \underline{X}) = H(\underline{K}) + H(\underline{X})$$

A general equation for $H(\underline{K}|\underline{Y})$ is thus obtained:

$$H(\underline{K}|\underline{Y}) = H(\underline{K}) - H(\underline{Y}) + H(\underline{X})$$

This relationship can now be used to derive the unicity distance of a cipher. Since

$$H(\underline{K}|\underline{Y}) = \sum_{y} p(y)H(\underline{K}|y)$$

$H(\underline{K}|\underline{Y})$ measures the average uncertainty over which key was used to encipher the selected (unknown) message into the given (known) cryptogram. The condition $\{H(\underline{K}|\underline{Y} = 0\}$ implies that there is no uncertainty over which key was used for enciphering (the produced cryptogram is assumed available for analysis). The following definition for unicity distance can now be given.

The *unicity distance* (ud) of a cipher in which only ciphertext is available for analysis is the value of N for which

$$H(\underline{K}) - H(\underline{Y}) + H(\underline{X}) = 0 \qquad (12\text{-}8)$$

provided that such an N exists.

Assume that the analyst has no prior information concerning which message(s) and key(s) are selected for encipherment. In that case, the analyst considers keys to be equally likely, and therefore assigns equal probability to each key in $\underline{K}$. Hence,

$$H(\underline{K}) = \log_2 n$$

(n denotes the number of keys in $\underline{K}$). From the concept of meaningful and meaningless messages, it follows that

$$H(\underline{X}) \simeq \log_2 s$$

(s denotes the number of meaningful messages). Assuming that cryptograms are nearly equally probable, it follows that

$$H(\underline{Y}) \simeq \log_2 r$$

(r denotes the number of cryptograms in $\underline{Y}$). An approximation for $H(\underline{K}|\underline{Y})$ is therefore obtained as follows:

$$\begin{aligned} H(\underline{K}|\underline{Y}) &= H(\underline{K}) - H(\underline{Y}) + H(\underline{X}) \\ &\simeq \log_2 n - \log_2 r + \log_2 s \\ &\simeq \log_2(ns/r) \\ &\simeq \log_2 \lambda \end{aligned} \qquad (12\text{-}9)$$

Equation 12-9 shows that $H(\underline{K}|\underline{Y})$ is near zero when λ equals 1, and therefore that no uncertainty should remain regarding which key was used to encipher the selected (unknown) message into the given (known) cryptogram. However, the results obtained with a random cipher (Table 12-2) are different. When λ equals 1, the probability of obtaining the correct key, p(SK), is 0.6321. The reason for the discrepancy is as follows. In a random cipher, $H(\underline{Y})$ is about equal to $\log_2 r$ only when λ ($\lambda = ns/r$) is much greater than 1. When λ is near 1 the approximation $\{H(\underline{Y}) \simeq \log_2 r\}$ is no longer valid. In that case, the value of $H(\underline{Y})$ is strictly less than $\log_2 r$. This means that the value of N for which the expression $H(\underline{K}|\underline{Y}) - H(\underline{Y}) + H(\underline{X})$ equals zero is greater than the value of N for which λ equals 1. (Since the number of keys n is constant, if an N exists for which $H(\underline{K}|\underline{Y})$ equals zero, then as N becomes very large the ratio s/r will approach 1/n and λ will approach 1.) Equation 12-9 therefore permits only a rough approximation of unicity distance.

Unicity Distance for a Cipher When Plaintext and Corresponding Ciphertext Are Available for Analysis

From the general relationship

$$H(U|V, W) + H(V|W) = H(V|U, W) + H(U|W)$$

(see Equation 12-71) and an appropriate change of variables, it follows that

$$H(\underline{K}|\underline{Y}, \underline{X}) + H(\underline{Y}|\underline{X}) = H(\underline{Y}|\underline{K}, \underline{X}) + H(K|\underline{X})$$

But since a knowledge of k in $\underline{K}$ and x in $\underline{X}$ implies a knowledge of $y = E_k(x)$ in $\underline{Y}$,

$$H(\underline{Y}|\underline{K}, \underline{X}) = 0$$

and keys and messages are selected independently,

$$H(\underline{K}|\underline{X}) = H(\underline{K})$$

it follows that

$$H(\underline{K}|\underline{Y}, \underline{X}) = H(\underline{K}) - H(\underline{Y}|\underline{X})$$

The condition $\{H(\underline{K}|\underline{Y}, \underline{X}) = \text{zero}\}$ means that there is no uncertainty regarding which key was used to encipher the given (known) plaintext into the given (known) ciphertext. Therefore, the *unicity distance* (ud) of a cipher in which plaintext and corresponding ciphertext are available is the value of N for which

$$H(\underline{K}) - H(\underline{Y}|\underline{X}) = 0 \qquad (12\text{-}10)$$

provided that such an N exists. Recall that Shannon defined the ud of a random cipher as the value of N for which ns/r (ns/r = λ) equals one (see Probability of Obtaining the Key When Only Ciphertext is Available for Analysis).

When plaintext and corresponding ciphertext are available for analysis, the set of meaningful messages can be thought of as containing only a single element (the given plaintext):

$$s = 1$$

The remaining $r - 1$ messages are therefore treated as meaningless. Thus the ud of a random cipher in which plaintext and corresponding ciphertext are available for analysis is the value of N for which n/r equals 1. By taking the logarithm (base 2) of each side of the equation and replacing $\log_2 n$ with $H(\underline{K})$, ud becomes the value of N for which

$$H(\underline{K}) - \log_2 r = 0$$

Comparing this with Equation 12-10, one can see that the derived expression provides only a rough approximation to ud. The condition $\{H(\underline{Y}|\underline{X}) \simeq \log_2 r\}$ does not hold when n/r (n/r = λ) is near 1.

Relationships Among $H(\underline{X}|\underline{Y})$, $H(\underline{K}|\underline{Y})$, and $H(\underline{K}|\underline{X}, \underline{Y})$

The information measures $H(\underline{X}|\underline{Y})$, $H(\underline{K}|\underline{Y})$, and $H(\underline{K}|\underline{X}, \underline{Y})$ are of particular interest in cryptanalysis. In each case, the value of N for which the respective measure is equal to zero can be used to define the ud of the cipher. The measure $H(\underline{X}|\underline{Y})$ corresponds to the case where the analyst solves for the plaintext instead of the key, under the assumption that only ciphertext is available for analysis. The measures $H(\underline{K}|\underline{Y})$ and $H(\underline{K}|\underline{X}, \underline{Y})$ have already been discussed.

From Equation 12-71 and an appropriate change of variables, it follows that

$$H(\underline{K}|\underline{X}, \underline{Y}) + H(\underline{X}|\underline{Y}) = H(\underline{X}|\underline{K}, \underline{Y}) + H(\underline{K}|\underline{Y})$$

But a knowledge of k in $\underline{K}$ and y in $\underline{Y}$ implies a knowledge of $x = D_k(y)$ in $\underline{X}$:

$$H(\underline{X}|\underline{K}, \underline{Y}) = 0$$

Therefore, it follows that

$$H(\underline{X}|\underline{Y}) = H(\underline{K}|\underline{Y}) - H(\underline{K}|\underline{X}, \underline{Y}) \tag{12-11}$$

But

$$H(\underline{X}|\underline{Y}) \geqslant 0$$

implies that

$$H(\underline{K}|\underline{Y}) \geqslant H(\underline{K}|\underline{X}, \underline{Y})$$

Thus in a cipher where $H(\underline{X}|\underline{Y})$ and $H(\underline{K}|\underline{Y})$ approach zero as N becomes large and the number of keys in $\underline{K}$ remains constant, it follows that the information measures $H(\underline{X}|\underline{Y})$, $H(\underline{K}|\underline{Y})$, and $H(\underline{K}|\underline{X}, \underline{Y})$ can be plotted as depicted in Figure 12-4. This conclusion can be reached via the following:

1. When N equals zero, it is assumed that $\underline{X}$ and $\underline{Y}$ each contain one element (i.e., $\underline{X}$ contains a null message x_0, and $\underline{Y}$ contains a null cryptogram y_0). Each of the n keys in $\underline{K}$ map x_0 to y_0. Hence $H(\underline{K}|\underline{Y})$ and $H(\underline{K}|\underline{X}, \underline{Y})$ are both equal to $H(\underline{K})$, and $H(\underline{X}|\underline{Y})$ is equal to zero.
2. Generally, when plaintext and corresponding ciphertext are available for analysis, one can solve for the key more easily than when only ciphertext is available for analysis. Thus when N is greater than zero, the value $H(\underline{K}|\underline{X}, \underline{Y})$ is strictly less than the value $H(\underline{K}|\underline{Y})$:

   $$H(\underline{K}|\underline{Y}) > H(\underline{K}|\underline{X}, \underline{Y})$$

   for $N > 0$. This means that $H(\underline{K}|\underline{X}, \underline{Y})$ will approach zero more rapidly than will $H(\underline{K}|\underline{Y})$.
3. When $H(\underline{K}|\underline{X}, \underline{Y})$ is near zero, Equation 12-10 indicates that $H(\underline{X}|\underline{Y})$ is approximately equal to $H(\underline{K}|\underline{Y})$:

   $$H(\underline{X}|\underline{Y}) \simeq H(\underline{K}|\underline{Y})$$

   This in turn says that $H(\underline{X}|\underline{Y})$ and $H(\underline{K}|\underline{Y})$ will nearly coincide and approach zero together. That $H(\underline{X}|\underline{Y})$ is about equal to $H(\underline{K}|\underline{Y})$ at the ud where $H(\underline{K}|\underline{Y})$ equals zero agrees with the previous result for a random cipher (Table 12-5) indicating that p(SK) is about equal to p(SM) at the ud (when λ equals 1).

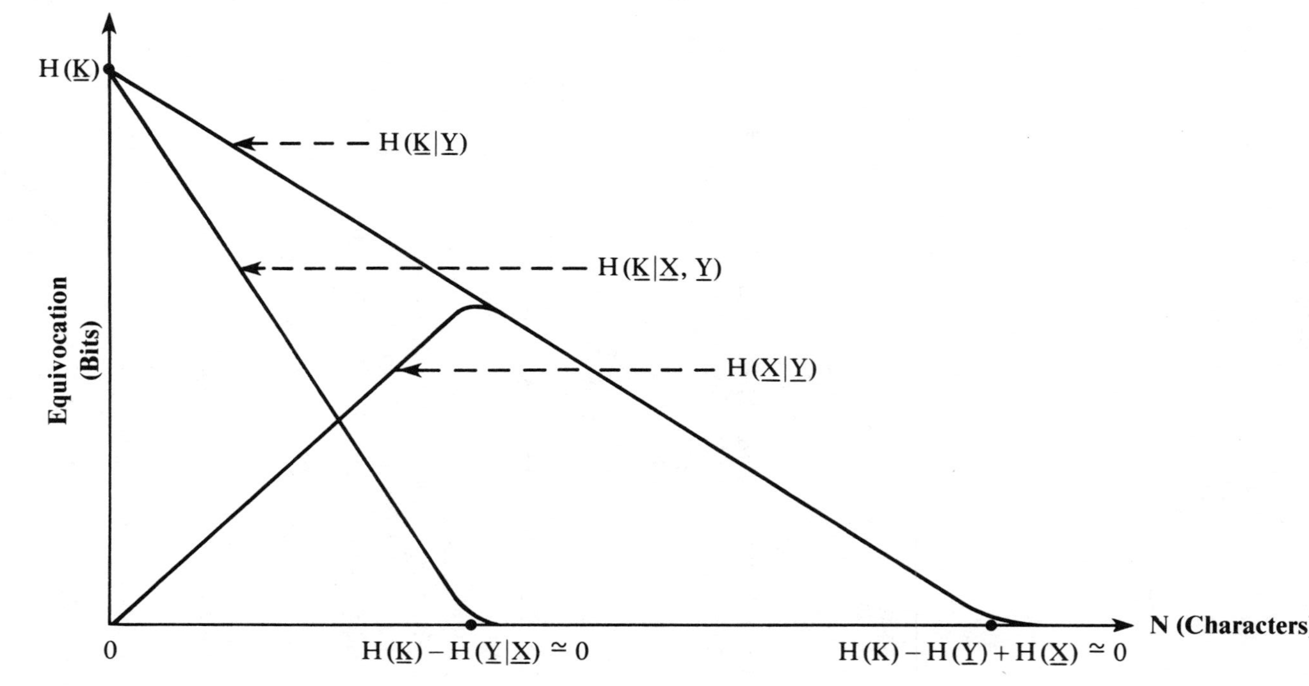

Note: $H(\underline{X}|\underline{Y}) = H(\underline{K}|\underline{Y}) - H(\underline{K}|\underline{X}, \underline{Y})$

Figure 12-4. Plot of $H(\underline{X}|\underline{Y})$, $H(\underline{K}|\underline{Y})$ and $H(\underline{K}|\underline{X}, \underline{Y})$ Against N for a Cipher in which $H(\underline{X}|\underline{Y})$ and $H(\underline{K}|\underline{Y})$ Approach Zero as N Becomes Large

Unicity Distance for the Data Encryption Standard

If plaintext and corresponding ciphertext are available for analysis, the unicity distance of the DES algorithm can be approximated using Equation 12-10. That is, ud is the value of N for which

$$H(\underline{K}) - H(\underline{Y}|\underline{X}) = 0$$

Since there are 2^{56} possible keys in DES, it follows that

$$H(\underline{K}) = 56$$

and therefore, ud is the value of N (in 8-bit characters) for which $H(\underline{Y}|\underline{X}) = 56$. From Equations 12-7b and 12-7c,

$$H(\underline{Y}|\underline{X}) = -\sum_{y,x} p(y, x)\log_2 p(y|x)$$

Thus, $H(\underline{Y}|\underline{X}) = 56$ when $p(y|x) = 1/2^{56}$ for each x and each y produced from x, and $p(y|x) = 0$ for each x and each y not produced form x (i.e., when no two keys map x to the same cryptogram).

If the 2^{56} cryptograms produced by mapping x under each of the 2^{56} keys are considered to be selected at random using replacement from the set of 2^{8N} possible cryptograms, then almost all of the cryptograms will be unique for values of N greater than 8. Thus, a ud of about 8 characters is obtained for DES (i.e., one block of ciphertext is ordinarily enough to determine the key). The precise calculations are omitted.

If only ciphertext is available for analysis, then ud is the value of N for which

$$H(\underline{K}) - H(\underline{Y}) + H(\underline{X}) = 0$$

(see Equation 12-8). If messages in $\underline{X}$ consist of English text (26 letter alphabet with no spaces) and each letter is represented by an 8-bit character, then 26 of the 256 possible 8-bit characters have probabilities corresponding to normal English text, and the other 230 characters have zero probability.

When individual letter probabilities are taken into consideration, the number of meaningful N-character messages, s, can be approximated as follows:

$$s \simeq 2^{4.17N}$$

(See Number of Meaningful Messages in a Redundant Language.) Therefore, it follows that

$$H(\underline{X}) \simeq 4.17N$$

As a first order approximation, assume that each cryptogram in $\underline{Y}$ is equally probable, and hence that

$$\begin{aligned} H(\underline{Y}) &\simeq \log_2 r \\ &\simeq 8N \end{aligned}$$

Substituting the values $H(\underline{K}) = 56$, $H(\underline{Y}) = 8N$, and $H(\underline{X}) = 4.17N$ into equation $\{H(\underline{K}) - H(\underline{Y}) + H(\underline{X}) = 0\}$, one obtains:

$$\begin{aligned} N &= 56/(8 - 4.17) \\ &= 14.6 \text{ characters} \end{aligned}$$

Thus 15 characters or 2 blocks (after rounding up to the nearest block) of ciphertext are enough in theory to solve for the key.

The fact that the ud of DES is only a few characters clearly demonstrates that a cipher which has good practical secrecy does not necessarily have good theoretical secrecy. The strength of DES is based entirely on the prohibitive amount of time and resources required to break it. (See Work Factor as a Measure of Secrecy in this chapter, and Cryptographic Algorithms, Chapter 2.)

Other examples of unicity distance computations can be found in Appendix G.

WORK FACTOR AS A MEASURE OF SECRECY

To show the relationship among the work factor (the time and resources it takes to break a cipher), the sophistication of the attack, and the amount of information available to the cryptanalyst, a simple substitution cipher is analyzed. Although the example is that of a weak cipher, the analysis provides an insight into the approach to be taken with stronger ciphers.

The Cost and Time to Break a Cipher

No matter what method of cryptanalysis is used, the analyst must always expend some amount of time and resources (defined as work factor) to reach his goal. Usually, there is a cost associated with each of the resources used, permitting the overall cost of recovering the key or message to be determined. By increasing available resources, such as computing power, storage, human efforts, and the like, the time required to attack the cipher successfully can often be reduced. Consequently, there is a relationship between cost and time for any given cryptanalytic attack against a cipher.

The information obtained by breaking a cipher also has a value (expressed in financial terms) based on what it is worth to the opponent. Usually, the information decreases in value over its lifetime, which permits a relationship to be established between value and time similar to that between cost and time. The relationships between cost and time and between value and time can then be used in determining the practical secrecy of the cipher.

The cost and time to break a cipher are functions of how it is attacked. Since there may be many different ways to cryptanalyze a cipher, many cost-time relationships are possible. Usually, the cost of breaking a cipher is estimated on the basis of the best known method of attack, even though it may not be the best method altogether.

Cryptanalysis involves high-speed computers and complex, sophisticated computer programs. This includes the following:

1. Computer processors, including special-purpose hardware used to execute the logical and arithmetic operations needed to obtain the solution.
2. Computer storage for the analysis programs and data.
3. Human resources to devise and write analysis programs, gather data, and oversee the analysis.

Simple Substitution on English—Some Preliminaries

An example of simple substitution on English (in which only ciphertext is available for analysis) shows the relationships existing among the cost and time for analysis, the language statistics used for analysis, and the amount of available ciphertext. Results are obtained empirically.

Two different approaches are considered: single-letter frequency analysis, and digram-frequency analysis. To evaluate both approaches, a plaintext is enciphered with a randomly chosen key. The resulting ciphertext is then analyzed to determine how many characters of the key and how many characters of the plaintext are correctly obtained. An important factor is knowing how much better the obtained solution is than a result obtained by pure guessing (random selection).

Let t be the number of characters in the key and p(w) be the probability that w characters of the key are properly obtained by random choice, $0 \leqslant w \leqslant t$. It can be shown [5] that

$$p(w) = (1/w!) \sum_{i=0}^{t-w} (-1)^i (1/i!) \tag{12-12}$$

For a large t, the finite series above can be replaced by an infinite series whose sum is given by 1/e:

$$\lim_{t \to \infty} p(w) = (1/w!)(1/e) = (1/w!)0.368 \tag{12-13}$$

which represents the Poisson distribution with mean equal to 1.

A comparison with the Poisson distribution shows that for $t \geqslant 10$, the values obtained with Equations 12-12 and 12-13 agree to 4 decimal places. Thus when t = 26 (26 letters) or t = 27 (26 letters and space), the Poisson distribution is an excellent approximation to Equation 12-12. Let

$$p(\text{number of correctly guessed key symbols} > c) = a \tag{12-14a}$$

$$p(\text{number of correctly guessed key symbols} \leq c) = 1 - a \qquad (12\text{-}14b)$$

where c can be any value from 0 to t (t = the number of characters in the key). With the aid of a table of Poisson probabilities, the values of a and 1 − a can be evaluated for different values of c (Table 12-6).

If the number of correctly obtained key characters is greater than 5, as one might anticipate when cryptanalysis is performed, then the hypothesis that keys were obtained by random guessing can be rejected at a level of confidence of 99.94% (Table 12-6).

c	6	5	4	3	2	1
a	.0001	.0006	.0037	.0190	.0803	.2692
1 − a	.9999	.9994	.9963	.9810	.9197	.7358

Table 12-6. Values of "a" and "1 − a" for Different Values of c

In one set of tests, using a single-letter frequency analysis on simple substitution on English (26 letters and space), it was determined that about 6 key characters are recovered from a plaintext containing 250 characters. This result is not too useful by itself, since text with only 6 correct (21 incorrect) characters looks more like a cryptogram than an intelligent message. However, a single-letter frequency analysis is helpful if it is used to obtain an initial key for a more powerful digram-frequency analysis. This initial key is usually better than could be obtained using random selection.

In a digram-frequency analysis an initial key (obtained via a single-letter frequency analysis), is used to decipher the cryptogram. The new digram statistics associated with the trial decipherment are then evaluated and used as a basis for adjusting the initial key. This process is repeated several times, so that the final key is likely to contain more correct characters than the starting key. During these iterations, a certain element of randomness is purposely introduced into the algorithm. This has the effect that repeated analysis of the same cryptogram does not (except with low probability) produce the same path to a solution. In that case, repeated analyses with the algorithm can be considered as statistically independent events, and therefore the probability of success (breaking the cipher) can be increased by increasing the number of trials. It is assumed that the probability of success at each trial is the same and that the number of trials are selected in advance. With the assumption of statistical independence, the distribution of the number of successful trials is therefore given by the binomial distribution.

Based on the observation that a text which is 90% recovered can still be read, the analysis is considered a success if at least 90% of the plaintext characters are successfully recovered. A partial printout of a message which is 91.7% correct (21 correct key characters) is shown below.

NATIONAL BUREAU OW STANFARFS CRYPTODRAPHIC ALDORITHMS WOR PROTECTION OW COMPUTER FATA FURIND TRANSMISSION ANF FORMANT

STORADE SOLICITATION OW PROPOSALS THE NATIONAL BUREAU OW STANFARFS UNFER FEPARTMENT OW COMMERCE AUTHORITIES ANF RESPONSIBILITIES WOR WOSTERIND PROMOTIND ANF FEVELOPIND US TRAFE AND COMMERCE ANF BASEF ON THE NATIONAL BUREAU OW STANFARFS RESPONSIBILITY WOR THE CUSTOFY MAINTENANCE ANF FEVELOPMENT OW THE NATIONAL STANFARFS OW MEASUREMENT ANF PROVISION OW MEANS ANF METHOFS WOR MAKIND MEASUREMENTS CONSISTENT GITH THOSE STANFARFS SOLICITS PROPOSALS WOR THE ENCRYPTION OW COMPUTER FATA

Let

p(SM) = the probability that at least 90% of the plaintext is recovered as the result of cryptanalysis (12-15)

Using a method of confidence limits [9], it can be shown that

$$p(\text{pmin} \leqslant p(\text{SM}) \leqslant \text{pmax}) = \gamma \quad (12\text{-}16)$$

where

$$\text{pmin} = x/(x + (n - x + 1)F\gamma)$$

$$\text{pmax} = (x + 1)F\gamma/((n - x) + (x + 1)F\gamma)$$

x = the number of successful attacks in n trials

$F\gamma$ is the *F distribution* with $[2(n - x + 1), 2x]$ degrees of freedom in pmin, and $[2(x + 1), 2(n - x)]$ degrees of freedom in pmax. Thus x/n can be used as an estimate for p(SM).

When a binomial distribution can be approximated by a normal distribution (whenever $\text{Var}(x) > 3$), the following mathematically more convenient approach can be used [10].

$$\text{pmin} = (1/(n + z^2))[x - 0.5 + (z^2/2) - z[(x - 0.5)((n - x + 0.5)/n) + (z^2/4)]^{1/2}] \quad (12\text{-}17a)$$

$$\text{pmax} = (1/(n + z^2))[x + 0.5 + (z^2/2) + z[(x + 0.5)((n - x - 0.5)/n) + (z^2/4)]^{1/2}] \quad (12\text{-}17b)$$

The value of z is determined by the chosen level of confidence γ (Equation 12-16) and the normal distribution function Φ (whose mean is 0 and variance is 1) as follows

$$\Phi(z) - \Phi(-z) = \gamma$$

If $\gamma = 0.95$, then $z = 1.96$. Since the intent here is only to demonstrate the basic approach, the approximations given by Equations 12-17a and 12-17b are used in the computations.

Now, let

$$p(SM, m) = \text{the probability that at least 90\% of the plaintext is recovered in at least one out of m repeated trials of the analysis} \qquad (12\text{-}18)$$

By evaluating p(SM), one is able to approximate p(SM, m). From earlier remarks, it follows that

$$p(SM, 1) = p(SM) \qquad (12\text{-}19a)$$

$$p(SM, m) = 1 - (1 - p(SM, 1))^m \qquad (12\text{-}19b)$$

In practical situations, Equation 12-19b will be useful for moderate values of p(SM). If p(SM) is very small, it means that there is not enough ciphertext available for analysis. Hence allowing large values of m will not result in a significant improvement. Furthermore, as m becomes large, it also becomes impractical for a person to scan all the recovered plaintext solutions. (Remember that the figure of 90% is based on a *person's* ability to enlarge upon a solution known to be incomplete.)

Empirical Results for Simple Substitution on English Using a Digram-Frequency Analysis

The first part of the analysis provides a statistical estimate for p(SM) (defined in Equation 12-15). The following procedure is used. A plaintext and random key are selected and used to produce the ciphertext to be analyzed. Prior to each cryptanalysis of the ciphertext, a starting key is produced using a single-letter frequency analysis. The success of the attack varies according to the search characteristics (determined by a random process). The procedure is executed n times as n independent trials of an experiment. Thus an estimate for p(SM) can be obtained using a sample size of n.

The basic idea (attributed to D. Coppersmith, IBM Thomas J. Watson Research Center, Yorktown Heights, N.Y.) is to make repeated pairwise changes to the starting key, eventually producing a final key close or equal to the actual key. The method used is to interchange the plain characters assigned to two randomly selected cipher characters. If the new digram matrix based on these changes is closer to a standard digram matrix, the key is changed. The measure of closeness is based on whether the dot product of the vectors, defined by the affected rows and columns of the two digram matrices, increases or not.

Analysis is carried out with ciphertext of length N = 250, 275, 300, 350, 400, 500, 600, 700, 800, 900, and 1000 characters, respectively, and a value of n = 120. By rearranging the 120 observed values into 40 groups of 3 each, one obtains an estimate for the probability of success of a multiple digram-frequency analysis with 3 repetitions. If at least 90% of the plaintext is recovered in at least one of the 3 trials, the attack is considered a success.

Plaintext* Length N	Sample Size, n = 120			Sample Size, n = 40		
	p(SM)	Confidence Limits $\gamma = 95\%$		p(SM, 3)	Confidence Limits $\gamma = 95\%$	
250	.008	.000	.052	.025	.001	.147
275	.025	.006	.077	.075	.020	.215
300	.200	.135	.285	.525	.363	.682
350	.433	.344	.527	.850	.695	.938
400	.508	.416	.600	.850	.695	.938
500	.567	.473	.656	.925	.785	.980
600	.817	.733	.879	1.000	.891	1.000
700	.942	.879	.974	1.000	.891	1.000
800	.958	.901	.985	1.000	.891	1.000
900	.967	.912	.989	1.000	.891	1.000
1000	.900	.828	.945	1.000	.891	1.000

*Alphabet consists of 26 letters and space.

Table 12-7. Statistical Estimates for Probability of Successful Message Attack for Simple Substitution on English Using a Digram Frequency Analysis

Thus with 40 groups of 3 trials each, the number of successes can range from 0 to 40. In this way, the value for p(SM, 3) can be estimated for each value of N. The point estimates for p(SM) and p(SM, 3) are given in Table 12-7. The confidence intervals are computed using equations 12-17a and 12-17b, at a 95% level of confidence (z = 1.96).[11]

In addition to p(SM) and p(SM, 3), the mean and standard deviation for the number of correctly recovered plaintext characters, the number of correctly recovered key characters and the computation time to perform the analysis are also evaluated. Assuming a normal distribution for the underlying population, which may not be strictly justified, the confidence limits for each of these parameters are obtained via [9]

$$\bar{x} - (t_\alpha/2)(s/n^{1/2}) < u < \bar{x} + (t_\alpha/2)(s/n^{1/2}) \tag{12-20}$$

where

u = parameter whose confidence limits are determined

$\bar{x}$ = sample mean = $(1/n) \sum_{i=1}^{n} xi$

[11] It was shown before that the distribution of successes, which is a binomial distribution, led to Equation 12-16 and that Equation 12-17 is an approximation of Equation 12-16.

$$s = \text{sample standard deviation} = [(1/(n-1)) \sum_{i=1}^{n} (\bar{x} - xi)^2]^{1/2}$$

n = sample size

{x1, x2, . . . , xn} = the observed values

t is the *student's t distribution* with n degrees of freedom, and $t_\alpha/2$ is related to the level of confidence γ. For $\gamma = 0.95$, which implies $\alpha = 1 - \gamma = 0.05$, one obtains a value of $t_\alpha/2 = 1.98$ when n = 120.

The results are shown in Table 12-8. More elaborate statistical tests could certainly be devised, but the emphasis here is to illustrate only the principles involved.

Empirical Results for Simple Substitution on English Using Single-Letter Frequency Analysis

A single-letter frequency analysis is quite elementary. It is discussed here so that the reader can contrast these results with those obtained for the digram-frequency analysis. The following procedure is used in conjunction with plaintext consisting of 26 letters (no space). First the letters are rearranged according to their relative frequency, from highest to lowest:

E T A O I N S R H L D C U M F P G W Y B V K X J Q Z

For each cryptogram under analysis, this vector is used as the basis for assigning plaintext equivalents to each character of the cryptogram (i.e., the most frequently occurring character in the cryptogram is assigned letter E, the next most frequently occurring character in the cryptogram is assigned letter T, etc.) The recovered plaintext is then compared to the original so that its correctness can be evaluated. The results of this experiment are given in Table 12-9.

Comparison of Results

Figures 12-5 and 12-6 illustrate the superiority of the digram-frequency analysis over the single-letter frequency analysis. They also confirm that the unicity distance is a function of the language statistics used to attack the cipher, and that ud becomes lower as more language statistics are effectively incorporated into the analysis. From Figure 12-6, it can be deduced that analysis with 3-grams, 4-grams, and so on, would give rise to a series of similar curves to the left of that obtained with digrams (the digram curve). In the limit, this series of curves would approach a curve that corresponds to a cryptanalysis performed by a human (90% recovery or more).

Each analysis (1-gram, 2-gram, etc.) has a certain cost associated with it. The single-letter frequency analysis took less than 1.5 CPU seconds on the IBM System 370, Model 168, not counting the input of the ciphertext itself, and required 500 bytes of storage. The digram-frequency analysis, on the

Plaintext* Length N	Sample Mean and Standard Deviation			Confidence Limits for the Mean at Level of Confidence $\gamma = 95\%$		
	Characters of Key Correctly Recovered	% of Plaintext Correctly Recovered	CPU Time (sec)	Characters of Key Correctly Recovered	% of Plaintext Correctly Recovered	CPU Time (sec)
250	10.3 4.8	56.7 23.6	27.6 6.1	9.5 11.2	52.5 61.0	26.5 28.7
275	11.1 4.5	60.2 22.1	28.7 7.4	10.3 12.0	56.2 69.2	27.4 30.0
300	13.8 5.4	69.3 24.4	27.5 8.1	12.9 14.8	64.9 73.7	26.1 29.0
350	20.1 3.8	86.3 14.3	28.8 6.7	19.4 20.8	83.7 88.9	27.6 30.0
400	19.5 4.3	84.6 16.4	30.2 6.7	18.8 20.3	81.7 87.6	29.0 31.4
500	23.2 3.8	90.8 12.8	28.0 6.3	22.5 23.9	88.5 93.1	26.9 29.2
600	24.8 3.3	95.1 11.4	31.0 6.3	24.2 25.4	93.0 97.2	29.9 32.2
700	25.4 2.5	97.6 9.9	31.0 7.2	24.9 25.8	95.8 99.4	29.7 32.3
800	25.9 2.5	97.1 8.2	31.3 6.3	25.4 26.3	95.6 98.6	30.2 32.5
900	25.9 1.8	97.2 6.0	29.6 6.0	25.6 26.2	96.1 98.3	28.5 30.7
1000	25.3 3.2	94.4 12.6	28.9 5.8	24.7 25.8	92.2 96.7	27.8 30.0

Sample Size = 120.
Analysis was performed on an IBM System/370, model 168.
*Alphabet consists of 26 letters and space.

Table 12-8. Statistical Estimates for Key Recovery, Message Recovery, and Processing Time Using a Digram Frequency Analysis

Plaintext Length* N	Sample Size	p(SM)	Confidence Limits $\gamma = 95\%$ (Eqs. 12-17a and 12-17b, $z = 1.96$)	Sample Mean and Standard Deviation: Characters of Key Correctly Recovered	Sample Mean and Standard Deviation: % of Plaintext Correctly Recovered	Confidence Limits for Mean at Level of Confidence $\gamma = 95\%$ (Eq. 12-20): Characters of Key Correctly Recovered	Confidence Limits for Mean at Level of Confidence $\gamma = 95\%$ (Eq. 12-20): % of Plaintext Correctly Recovered
200	120			5.1 2.1	24.5 12.8	4.7 5.5	22.1 26.8
300	120			6.2 2.5	29.3 14.5	5.7 6.7	26.6 31.9
500	120			7.0 2.1	31.7 12.0	6.5 7.3	29.5 33.9
700	120			7.7 2.6	35.1 11.7	7.2 8.2	33.0 37.2
1000	120			7.9 2.9	36.4 12.4	7.3 8.4	34.1 38.6
1500	120			8.2 2.9	38.8 12.4	7.6 8.7	36.6 41.1
2000	120			9.1 2.9	41.6 12.7	8.5 9.6	39.3 43.9
3000	120			10.0 3.0	45.4 13.1	9.4 10.6	43.0 47.8
5000	120			11.4 3.2	50.5 13.7	10.7 12.0	48.0 53.0
7000	120			12.6 3.2	55.0 13.3	11.9 13.1	52.6 57.4
10000	120	.017	.003 .065	12.9 3.7	55.7 14.7	12.2 13.6	53.0 58.4
15000	120	.025	.006 .077	14.1 3.3	60.5 15.3	13.5 14.8	57.7 63.3
30000	120	.025	.006 .077	14.4 3.8	61.6 14.7	13.6 15.1	58.9 64.3
50000	80	.100	.047 .193	14.6 5.3	64.8 18.0	13.4 15.8	60.7 68.8
100000	40	.150	.062 .306	16.4 6.0	70.7 18.8	14.4 18.3	64.6 76.7
500000	8	.375	.102 .741	19.5 6.8	79.2 20.1	13.8 25.2	62.4 96.0

*26 Letters (No Space)

Table 12-9. Statistical Estimates for Probability of Successful Message Attack, Key Recovery, and Message Recovery for Simple Substitution on English Using a Single-Letter Frequency Analysis

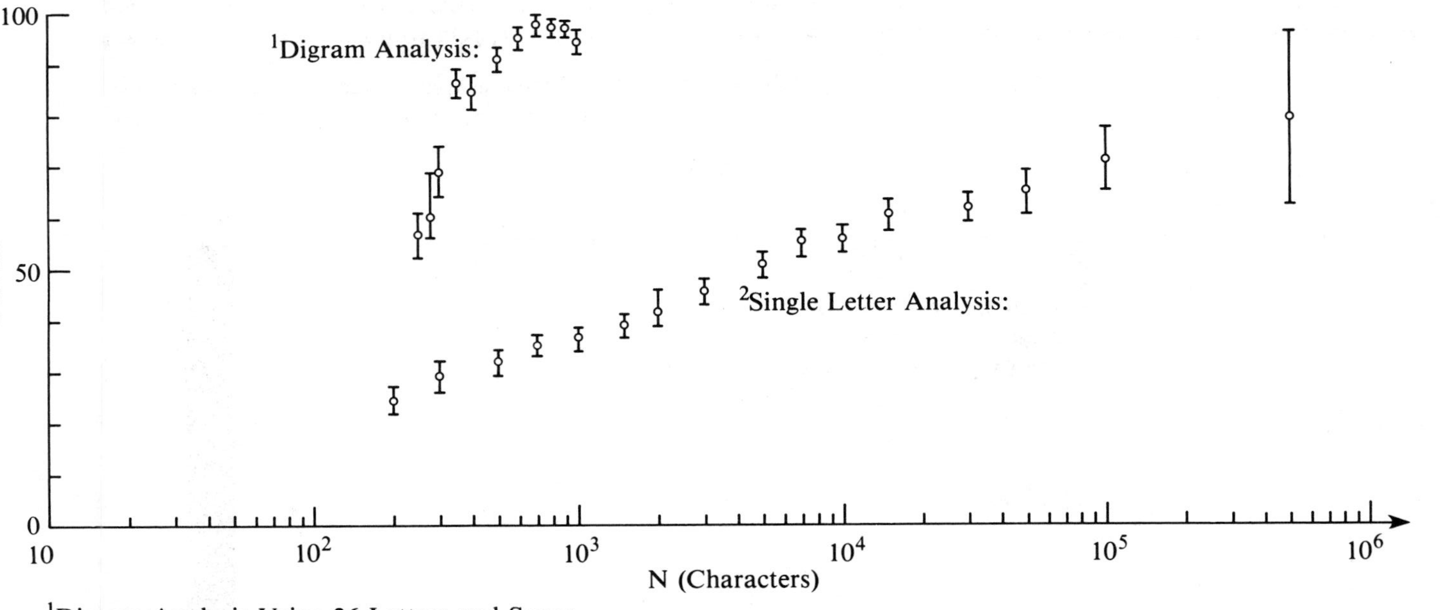

[1]Digram Analysis Using 26 Letters and Space
[2]Single Letter Frequency Analysis Using 26 Letters (No Space)

Figure 12-5. Percent of Plaintext Recovered as a Function of Ciphertext Length Using a Single-Letter Frequency Analysis and a Digram Frequency Analysis for Simple Substitution on English

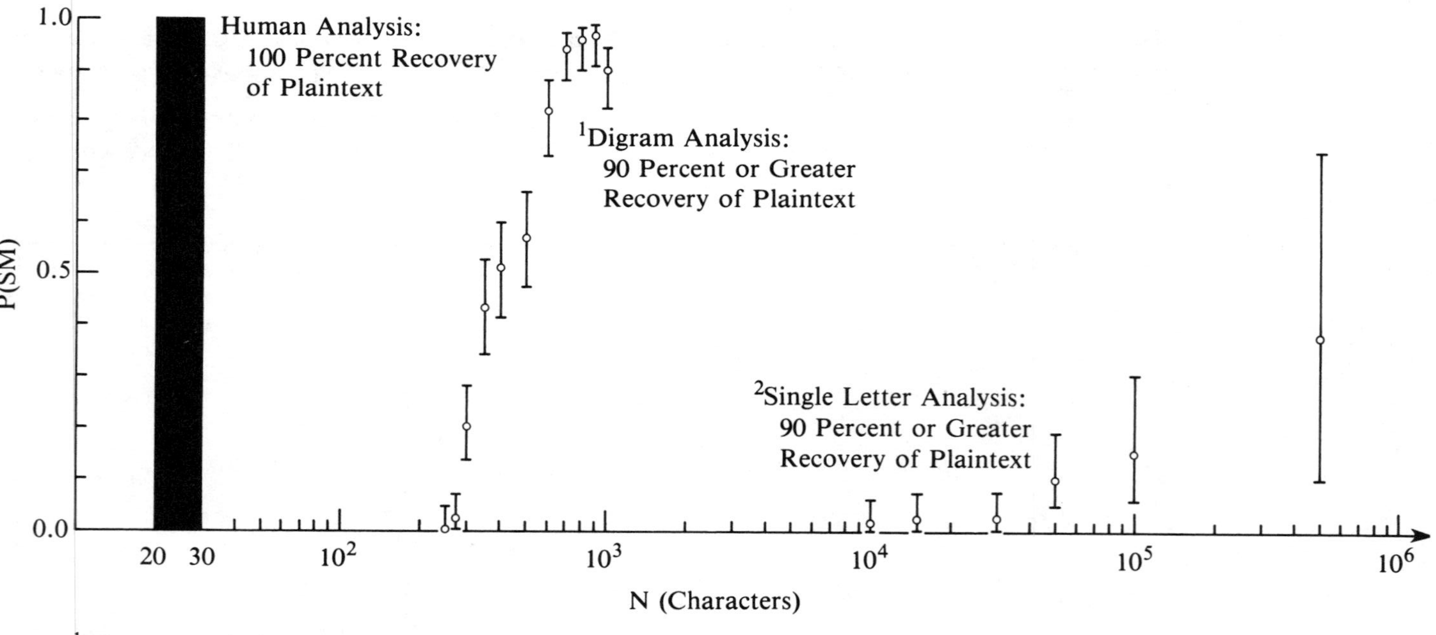

[1]Digram Analysis Using 26 Letters and Space
[2]Single Letter Frequency Analysis Using 26 Letters (No Space)

Figure 12-6. Comparison of p(SM) as a Function of Ciphertext Length Using a Single-Letter Frequency Analysis and a Digram Frequency Analysis for Simple Substitution on English

other hand, required about 30 CPU seconds on the same machine, and required 3000 bytes of storage. Both CPU time and storage can easily be converted to a monetary value. Hence it generally follows that the more powerful the attack (when higher order language statistics are used), the greater the associated cost. It follows also that the opponent may have some degree of freedom in selecting a method of analysis which will both be successful and keep his cost to a minimum. For example, with simple substitution on English, 1000 characters of ciphertext are not enough to allow a solution using only 1-grams. On the other hand, there may be no advantage in using trigrams in the analysis when digrams will do the job.

The analysis using digrams presented here shows that about 500 characters of ciphertext are needed for a successful attack. A more recent result obtained by Bahl [11] indicates that only about 300 characters are required.

REFERENCES

1. Diffie, W. and Hellman, M. E., "Privacy and Authentication: An Introduction to Cryptography," *Proceedings of the IEEE*, **67**, No. 3, 397–427 (1979).
2. Shannon, C. E., "Communication Theory of Secrecy Systems," *Bell System Technical Journal,* **28**, 656–715 (1949).
3. Francis, W., *A Standard Sample of Present-Day Edited American English for Use with Digital Computers,* Linguistics Department, Brown University, Providence, RI, 1964.
4. Shannon, C. E., "Predictions of entropy in printed English," *Bell System Technical Journal,* **30**, 50–64 (1951).
5. Parzen, E., *Modern Probability Theory and Its Applications,* Wiley, New York, 1960.
6. Hildebrand, F. B., *Advanced Calculus for Applications,* Prentice-Hall, Englewood Cliffs, NJ, 1962.
7. Friedman, W. F., "Cryptology," *Encyclopedia Britannica,* p. 848 (1973).
8. Raisbeck, G., *Information Theory, An Introduction for Scientists and Engineers,* M.I.T. Press, Cambridge, 1964.
9. Gallagher, R., *Information Theory and Reliable Communication,* Wiley, New York, 1968.
10. Browlee, K. A., *Statistical Theory and Methodology in Science and Engineering,* Wiley, New York, 1961.
11. Bahl, L. R., *An Algorithm For Solving Simple Substitution Cryptograms,* International Symposium on Information Theory, Ithaca, NY, October 10–14, 1977.

Other Publications of Interest

12. Peleg, S. and Rosenfeld, A., "Breaking Substitution Ciphers Using a Relaxation Algorithm," *Communications of the ACM,* **22**, No. 11, 598–605 (1979).
13. Hellman, M. E., "An Extension of the Shannon Theory Approach to Cryptography," *IEEE Transactions on Information Theory,* **IT-23**, No. 3, 289–294 (1977).
14. Blom, R. J., "Bounds on Key Equivocation for Simple Substitution Ciphers," *IEEE Transactions on Information Theory,* **IT-25**, No. 1, 8–18 (1979).
15. Lu, S. C., "The Existence of Good Cryptosystems for Key Rates Greater than the Message Redundancy," *IEEE Transactions on Information Theory,* **IT-25**, No. 4, 475–480 (1979).

16. Lu, S. C., "Random Ciphering Bounds on a Class of Secrecy Systems and Discrete Message Sources," *IEEE Transactions on Information Theory,* **IT-25**, No. 4, 405–414 (1979).
17. Kullback, S., *Statistical Methods in Cryptanalysis,* Aegean Park Press, Laguna Hills, CA, 1976.
18. Dunham, J. G., "On Message Equivocation for Simple Substitution Ciphers," *IEEE Transactions on Information Theory,* **IT-26**, No. 5, 522–527 (1980).

APPENDIX A

FIPS Publication 46

FIPS PUB 46

FEDERAL INFORMATION
PROCESSING STANDARDS PUBLICATION
1977 JANUARY 15

U.S. DEPARTMENT OF COMMERCE / National Bureau of Standards

DATA ENCRYPTION STANDARD

CATEGORY: ADP OPERATIONS
SUBCATEGORY: COMPUTER SECURITY

U.S. DEPARTMENT OF COMMERCE • Elliot L. Richardson, *Secretary*

Edward O. Vetter, *Under Secretary*

Dr. Betsy Ancker-Johnson, *Assistant Secretary for Science and Technology*

NATIONAL BUREAU OF STANDARDS • Ernest Ambler, *Acting Director*

Foreword

The Federal Information Processing Standards Publication Series of the National Bureau of Standards is the official publication relating to standards adopted and promulgated under the provisions of Public Law 89-306 (Brooks Bill) and under Part 6 of Title 15, Code of Federal Regulations. These legislative and executive mandates have given the Secretary of Commerce important responsibilities for improving the utilization and management of computers and automatic data processing systems in the Federal Government. To carry out the Secretary's responsibilities, the NBS, through its Institute for Computer Sciences and Technology, provides leadership, technical guidance, and coordination of government efforts in the development of technical guidelines and standards in these areas.

The series is used to announce Federal Information Processing Standards, and to provide standards information of general interest and an index of relevant standards publications and specifications. Publications that announce adoption of standards provide the necessary policy, administrative, and guidance information for effective standards implementation and use. The technical specifications of the standard are usually attached to the publication, otherwise a reference source is cited.

Comments covering Federal Information Processing Standards and Publications are welcomed, and should be addressed to the Associate Director for ADP Standards, Institute for Computer Sciences and Technology, National Bureau of Standards, Washington, D.C. 20234. Such comments will be either considered by NBS or forwarded to the responsible activity as appropriate.

ERNEST AMBLER, *Acting Director*

Abstract

The selective application of technological and related procedural safeguards is an important responsibility of every Federal organization in providing adequate security to its ADP systems. This publication provides a standard to be used by Federal organizations when these organizations specify that cryptographic protection is to be used for sensitive or valuable computer data. Protection of computer data during transmission between electronic components or while in storage may be necessary to maintain the confidentiality and integrity of the information represented by that data. The standard specifies an encryption algorithm which is to be implemented in an electronic device for use in Federal ADP systems and networks. The algorithm uniquely defines the mathematical steps required to transform computer data into a cryptographic cipher. It also specifies the steps required to transform the cipher back to its original form. A device performing this algorithm may be used in many applications areas where cryptographic data protection is needed. Within the context of a total security program comprising physical security procedures, good information management practices and computer system/network access controls, the Data Encryption Standard is being made available for use by Federal agencies.

Key Words: ADP security; computer security; encryption; Federal Information Processing Standard.

Nat. Bur. Stand. (U.S.), Fed. Info. Process. Stand. Publ. (FIPS PUB) **46, 17 pages (1977)**
CODEN: FIPPAT

For sale by the National Technical Information Service, U.S. Department of Commerce, Springfield, Virginia 22161

Federal Information Processing Standards Publication 46

1977 January 15

ANNOUNCING THE

DATA ENCRYPTION STANDARD

Federal Information Processing Standards are issued by the National Bureau of Standards pursuant to the Federal Property and Administrative Services Act of 1949, as amended, Public Law 89-306 (79 Stat 1127), Executive Order 11717 (38 FR 12315, dated May 11, 1973), and Part 6 of Title 15 Code of Federal Regulations (CFR).

Name of Standard: Data Encryption Standard (DES).

Category of Standard: Operations, Computer Security.

Explanation: The Data Encryption Standard (DES) specifies an algorithm to be implemented in electronic hardware devices and used for the cryptographic protection of computer data. This publication provides a complete description of a mathematical algorithm for encrypting (enciphering) and decrypting (deciphering) binary coded information. Encrypting data converts it to an unintelligible form called cipher. Decrypting cipher converts the data back to its original form. The algorithm described in this standard specifies both enciphering and deciphering operations which are based on a binary number called a key. The key consists of 64 binary digits ("0"s or "1"s) of which 56 bits are used directly by the algorithm and 8 bits are used for error detection.

Binary coded data may be cryptographically protected using the DES algorithm in conjunction with a key. The key is generated in such a way that each of the 56 bits used directly by the algorithm are random and the 8 error detecting bits are set to make the parity of each 8-bit byte of the key odd, i.e., there is an odd number of "1"s in each 8-bit byte. Each member of a group of authorized users of encrypted computer data must have the key that was used to encipher the data in order to use it. This key, held by each member in common, is used to decipher the data received in cipher form from other members of the group. The encryption algorithm specified in this standard is commonly known among those using the standard. The unique key chosen for use in a particular application makes the results of encrypting data using the algorithm unique. Selection of a different key causes the cipher that is produced for any given set of inputs to be different. The cryptographic security of the data depends on the security provided for the key used to encipher and decipher the data.

Data can be recovered from cipher only by using exactly the same key used to encipher it. Unauthorized recipients of the cipher who know the algorithm but do not have the correct key cannot derive the original data algorithmically. However, anyone who does have the key and the algorithm can easily decipher the cipher and obtain the original data. A standard algorithm based on a secure key thus provides a basis for exchanging encrypted computer data by issuing the key used to encipher it to those authorized to have the data. Additional FIPS guidelines for implementing and using the DES are being developed and will be published by NBS.

Approving Authority: Secretary of Commerce.

Maintenance Agency: Institute for Computer Sciences and Technology, National Bureau of Standards.

Applicability: This standard will be used by Federal departments and agencies for the cryptographic protection of computer data when the following conditions apply:

1. An authorized official or manager responsible for data security or the security of any computer system decides that cryptographic protection is required; and
2. The data is not classified according to the National Security Act of 1947, as amended, or the Atomic Energy Act of 1954, as amended.

However, Federal agencies or departments which use cryptographic devices for protecting data classified according to either of these acts can use those devices for protecting unclassified data in lieu of the standard.

In addition, this standard may be adopted and used by non-Federal Government organizations. Such use is encouraged when it provides the desired security for commercial and private organizations.

Data that is considered sensitive by the responsible authority, data that has a high value, or data that represents a high value should be cryptographically protected if it is vulnerable to unauthorized disclosure or undetected modification during transmission or while in storage. A risk analysis should be performed under the direction of a responsible authority to determine potential threats. FIPS PUB 31 (Guidelines for Automatic Data Processing Physical Security and Risk Management) and FIPS PUB 41 (Computer Security Guidelines for Implementing the Privacy Act of 1974) provide guidance for making such an analysis. The costs of providing cryptographic protection using this standard as well as alternative methods of providing this protection and their respective costs should be projected. A responsible authority then should make a decision, based on these analyses, whether or not to use cryptographic protection and this standard.

Applications: Data encryption (cryptography) may be utilized in various applications and in various environments. The specific utilization of encryption and the implementation of the DES will be based on many factors particular to the computer system and its associated components. In general, cryptography is used to protect data while it is being communicated between two points or while it is stored in a medium vulnerable to physical theft. Communication security provides protection to data by enciphering it at the transmitting point and deciphering it at the receiving point. File security provides protection to data by enciphering it when it is recorded on a storage medium and deciphering it when it is read back from the storage medium. In the first case, the key must be available at the transmitter and receiver simultaneously during communication. In the second case, the key must be maintained and accessible for the duration of the storage period.

Hardware Implementation: The algorithm specified in this standard is to be implemented in computer or related data communication devices using hardware (not software) technology. The specific implementation may depend on several factors such as the application, the environment, the technology used, etc. Implementations which comply with this standard include Large Scale Integration (LSI) "chips" in individual electronic packages, devices built from Medium Scale Integration (MSI) electronic components, or other electronic devices dedicated to performing the operations of the algorithm. Micro-processors using Read Only Memory (ROM) or micro-programmed devices using microcode for hardware level control instructions are examples of the latter. Hardware implementations of the algorithm which are tested and validated by NBS will be considered as complying with the standard. Procedures for testing and validating equipment for conformance with this standard are available from the Systems and Software Division, National Bureau of Standards, Washington, D.C. 20234. Software implementations in general purpose computers are not in compliance with this standard. Information regarding devices which have been tested and validated will be made available to all FIPS points of contact.

Export Control: Cryptographic devices and technical data regarding them are subject to Federal Government export controls as specified in Title 22, Code of Federal Regulations, Parts 121 through 128. Cryptographic devices implementing this standard and technical data regarding them must comply with these Federal regulations.

Patents: Crytographic devices implementing this standard may be covered by U.S. and foreign patents issued to the International Business Machines Corporation. However, IBM has granted nonexclusive, royalty-free licenses under the patents to make, use and sell apparatus which complies with the standard. The terms, conditions and scope of the licenses are set out in notices published in the May 13, 1975 and August 31, 1976 issues of the Official Gazette of the United States Patent and Trademark Office (934 O. G. 452 and 949 O. G. 1717).

Alternative Modes of Using the DES: The "Guidelines for Implementing and Using the Data Encryption Standard" describe two different modes for using the algorithm described in this standard. Blocks of data containing 64 bits may be directly entered into the device where 64-bit cipher blocks are generated under control of the key. This is called the electronic code book mode. Alternatively, the device may be used as a binary stream generator to produce statistically random binary bits which are then combined with the clear (unencrypted) data (1-64 bits) using an "exclusive-or" logic operation. In order to assure that the enciphering device and the deciphering device are synchronized, their inputs are always set to the previous 64 bits of cipher that were transmitted or received. This second mode of using the encryption algorithm is called the cipher feedback (CFB) mode. The electronic codebook mode generates blocks of 64 cipher bits. The cipher feedback mode generates cipher having the same number of bits as the plain text. Each block of cipher is independent of all others when the electronic codebook mode is used while each byte (group of bits) of cipher depends on the previous 64 cipher bits when the cipher feedback mode is used. The modes of operation briefly described here are further explained in the FIPS "Guidelines for Implementing and Using the Data Encryption Standard."

Implementation of this standard: This standard becomes effective six months after the publication date of this FIPS PUB. It applies to all Federal ADP systems and associated telecommunications networks under development as well as to installed systems when it is determined that cryptographic protection is required. Each Federal department or agency will issue internal directives for the use of this standard by their operating units based on their data security requirement determinations.

NBS will provide assistance to Federal organizations by developing and issuing additional technical guidelines on computer security and by providing technical assistance in using data encryption. A data encryption testbed has been established within NBS for use in providing this technical assistance. The National Security Agency assists Federal departments and agencies in communications security and in determining specific security requirements. Instructions and regulations for procuring data processing equipment utilizing this standard will be provided by the General Services Administration.

Specifications: Federal Information Processing Standard (FIPS 46) Data Encryption Standard (DES) (affixed).

Cross Index:

a. FIPS PUB 31, "Guidelines to ADP Physical Security and Risk Management"

b. FIPS PUB 39, "Glossary for Computer Systems Security"

c. FIPS PUB 41, "Computer Security Guidelines for Implementing the Privacy Act of 1974"

d. **FIPS PUB—, "Guidelines for Implementing and Using the Data Encryption Standard" (to be published)**

e. Other FIPS and Federal Standards are applicable to the implementation and use of this standard. In particular, the American Standard Code for Information Interchange (FIPS PUB 1) and other related data storage media or data communications standards should be used in conjunction with this standard. A list of currently approved FIPS may be obtained from the Office of ADP Standards Management, Institute for Computer Sciences and Technology, National Bureau of Standards, Washington, D.C. 20234.

Qualifications: The cryptographic algorithm specified in this standard transforms a 64-bit binary value into a unique 64-bit binary value based on a 56-bit variable. If the complete 64-bit input is used (i.e., none of the input bits should be predetermined from block to block) and if the 56-bit variable is randomly chosen, no technique other than trying all possible keys using known input and output for the DES will guarantee finding the chosen key. As there are over 70,000,000,000,000,000 (seventy quadrillion) possible keys of 56 bits, the feasibility of deriving a particular key in this way is extremely unlikely in typical threat environments. Moreover, if the key is changed frequently, the risk of this event is greatly diminished. However, users should be aware that it is theoretically possible to derive the key in fewer trials (with a correspondingly lower probability of success depending on the number of keys tried) and should be cautioned to change the key as often as practical. Users must change the key and provide it a high level of protection in order to minimize the potential risks of its unauthorized computation or acquisition. The feasibility of computing the correct key may change with advances in technology. A more complete description of the strength of this algorithm against various threats will be contained in the Guidelines for Implementing and Using the DES.

When correctly implemented and properly used, this standard will provide a high level of cryptographic protection to computer data. NBS, supported by the technical assistance of Government agencies responsible for communication security, has determined that the algorithm specified in this standard will provide a high level of protection for a time period beyond the normal life cycle of its associated ADP equipment. The protection provided by this algorithm against potential new threats will be reviewed within five years to assess its adequacy. In addition, both the standard and possible threats reducing the security provided through the use of this standard will undergo continual review by NBS and other cognizant Federal organizations. The new technology available at that time will be evaluated to determine its impact on the standard. In addition, the awareness of any breakthrough in technology or any mathematical weakness of the algorithm will cause NBS to reevaluate this standard and provide necessary revisions.

Comments: Comments and suggestions regarding this standard and its use are welcomed and should be addressed to the Associate Director for ADP Standards, Institute for Computer Sciences and Technology, National Bureau of Standards, Washington, D.C. 20234.

Waiver Procedure: The head of a Federal agency may waive the provisions of this FIPS PUB after the conditions and justifications for the waiver have been coordinated with the National Bureau of Standards. A waiver is necessary if cryptographic devices performing an algorithm other than that which is specified in this standard are to be used by a Federal agency for data subject to cryptographic protection under this standard. No waiver is necessary if classified communications security equipment is to be used. Software implementations of this algorithm for operational use in general purpose computer systems do not comply with this standard and each such implementation must also receive a waiver. Implementation of the algorithm in software for testing or evaluation does not require waiver approval. Implementation of other special purpose cryptographic algorithms in software for limited use within a computer system (e.g., encrypting password files) or implementations of cryptographic algorithms in software which were being utilized in computer systems before the effective date of this standard do not require a waiver. However, these limited uses should be converted to the use of this standard when the system or equipment involved is upgraded or redesigned to include general cryptographic protection of computer data. Letters describing the nature of and reasons for the waiver should be addressed to the Associate Director for ADP Standards as previously noted.

Sixty days should be allowed for review and response by NBS. The waiver shall not be approved until a response from NBS is received; however, the final decision for granting the waiver is the responsibility of the head of the particular agency involved.

Where to Obtain Copies of the Standard:

Copies of this publication are for sale by the National Technical Information Service, U. S. Department of Commerce, 5285 Port Royal Road, Springfield, Virginia 22161. Order by FIPS PUB number and title. Prices are published by NTIS in current catalogs and other issuances. Payment may be made by check, money order, deposit account or charged to a credit card accepted by NTIS.

Federal Information Processing Standards Publication 46

1977 January 15

SPECIFICATIONS FOR THE

DATA ENCRYPTION STANDARD

The Data Encryption Standard (DES) shall consist of the following Data Encryption Algorithm to be implemented in special purpose electronic devices. These devices shall be designed in such a way that they may be used in a computer system or network to provide cryptographic protection to binary coded data. The method of implementation will depend on the application and environment. The devices shall be implemented in such a way that they may be tested and validated as accurately performing the transformations specified in the following algorithm.

DATA ENCRYPTION ALGORITHM

Introduction

The algorithm is designed to encipher and decipher blocks of data consisting of 64 bits under control of a 64-bit key. Deciphering must be accomplished by using the same key as for enciphering, but with the schedule of addressing the key bits altered so that the deciphering process is the reverse of the enciphering process. A block to be enciphered is subjected to an initial permutation *IP*, then to a complex key-dependent computation and finally to a permutation which is the inverse of the initial permutation IP^{-1}. The key-dependent computation can be simply defined in terms of a function *f*, called the cipher function, and a function *KS*, called the key schedule. A description of the computation is given first, along with details as to how the algorithm is used for encipherment. Next, the use of the algorithm for decipherment is described. Finally, a definition of the cipher function *f* is given in terms of primitive functions which are called the selection functions S_i and the permutation function *P*. S_i, *P* and *KS* of the algorithm are contained in the Appendix.

The following notation is convenient: Given two blocks *L* and *R* of bits, *LR* denotes the block consisting of the bits of *L* followed by the bits of *R*. Since concatenation is associative $B_1B_2 \ldots B_8$, for example, denotes the block consisting of the bits of B_1 followed by the bits of $B_2 \ldots$ followed by the bits of B_8.

Enciphering

A sketch of the enciphering computation is given in figure 1.

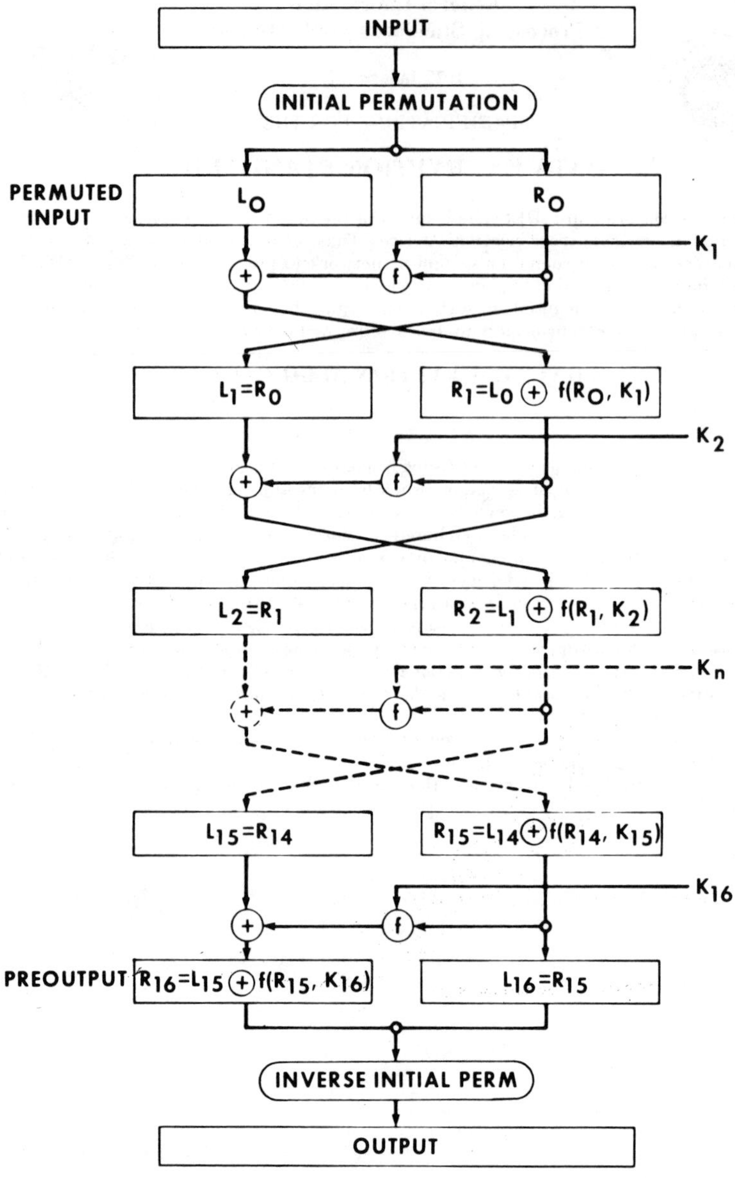

FIGURE 1. *Enciphering computation.*

The 64 bits of the input block to be enciphered are first subjected to the following permutation, called the initial permutation *IP*:

IP

58	50	42	34	26	18	10	2
60	52	44	36	28	20	12	4
62	54	46	38	30	22	14	6
64	56	48	40	32	24	16	8
57	49	41	33	25	17	9	1
59	51	43	35	27	19	11	3
61	53	45	37	29	21	13	5
63	55	47	39	31	23	15	7

That is the permuted input has bit 58 of the input as its first bit, bit 50 as its second bit, and so on with bit 7 as its last bit. The permuted input block is then the input to a complex key-dependent computation described below. The output of that computation, called the preoutput, is then subjected to the following permutation which is the inverse of the initial permutation:

IP^{-1}

40	8	48	16	56	24	64	32
39	7	47	15	55	23	63	31
38	6	46	14	54	22	62	30
37	5	45	13	53	21	61	29
36	4	44	12	52	20	60	28
35	3	43	11	51	19	59	27
34	2	42	10	50	18	58	26
33	1	41	9	49	17	57	25

That is, the output of the algorithm has bit 40 of the preoutput block as its first bit, bit 8 as its second bit, and so on, until bit 25 of the preoutput block is the last bit of the output.

The computation which uses the permuted input block as its input to produce the preoutput block consists, but for a final interchange of blocks, of 16 iterations of a calculation that is described below in terms of the cipher function f which operates on two blocks, one of 32 bits and one of 48 bits, and produces a block of 32 bits.

Let the 64 bits of the input block to an iteration consist of a 32 bit block L followed by a 32 bit block R. Using the notation defined in the introduction, the input block is then LR.

Let K be a block of 48 bits chosen from the 64-bit key. Then the output $L'R'$ of an iteration with input LR is defined by:

(1)
$$L' = R$$
$$R' = L \oplus f(R,K)$$

where $\oplus$ denotes bit-by-bit addition modulo 2.

As remarked before, the input of the first iteration of the calculation is the permuted input block. If $L'R'$ is the output of the 16th iteration then $R'L'$ is the preoutput block. At each iteration a different block K of key bits is chosen from the 64-bit key designated by KEY.

With more notation we can describe the iterations of the computation in more detail. Let *KS* be a function which takes an integer n in the range from 1 to 16 and a 64-bit block *KEY* as input and yields as output a 48-bit block K_n which is a permuted selection of bits from *KEY*. That is

(2) $$K_n = KS(n, KEY)$$

with K_n determined by the bits in 48 distinct bit positions of *KEY*. *KS* is called the key schedule because the block K used in the n'th iteration of (1) is the block K_n determined by (2).

As before, let the permuted input block be *LR*. Finally, let L_0 and R_0 be respectively L and R and let L_n and R_n be respectively L' and R' of (1) when L and R are respectively L_{n-1} and R_{n-1}, and K is K_n; that is, when n is in the range from 1 to 16,

(3) $$L_n = R_{n-1}$$
$$R_n = L_{n-1} \oplus f(R_{n-1}, K_n)$$

The preoutput block is then $R_{16}L_{16}$.

The key schedule *KS* of the algorithm is described in detail in the Appendix. The key schedule produces the 16 K_n which are required for the algorithm.

Deciphering

The permutation IP^{-1} applied to the preoutput block is the inverse of the initial permutation IP applied to the input. Further, from (1) it follows that:

(4) $$R = L'$$
$$L = R' \oplus f(L', K)$$

Consequently, to ***decipher*** it is only necessary to apply the ***very same algorithm to an enciphered message block,*** taking care that at each iteration of the computation ***the same block of key bits*** K ***is used*** during decipherment as was used during the encipherment of the block. Using the notation of the previous section, this can be expressed by the equations:

(5) $$R_{n-1} = L_n$$
$$L_{n-1} = R_n \oplus f(L_n, K_n)$$

where now $R_{16}L_{16}$ is the permuted input block for the deciphering calculation and L_0R_0 is the preoutput block. That is, for the decipherment calculation with $R_{16}L_{16}$ as the permuted input, K_{16} is used in the first iteration, K_{15} in the second, and so on, with K_1 used in the 16th iteration.

***The Cipher Function* f**

A sketch of the calculation of $f(R, K)$ is given in figure 2.

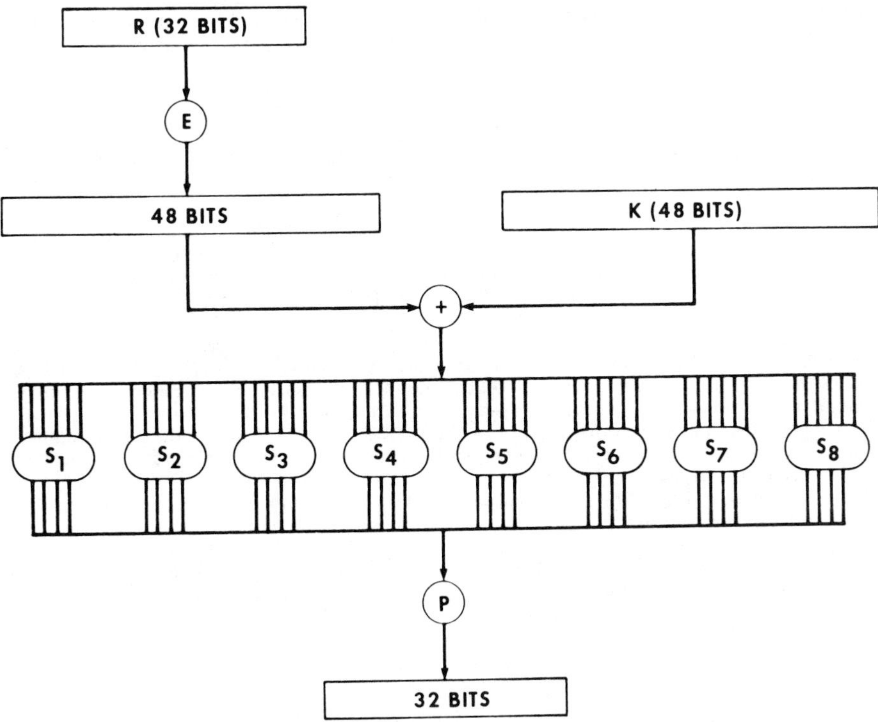

FIGURE 2. *Calculation of* f (R, K).

Let E denote a function which takes a block of 32 bits as input and yields a block of 48 bits as output. Let E be such that the 48 bits of its output, written as 8 blocks of 6 bits each, are obtained by selecting the bits in its inputs in order according to the following table:

E BIT-SELECTION TABLE

32	1	2	3	4	5
4	5	6	7	8	9
8	9	10	11	12	13
12	13	14	15	16	17
16	17	18	19	20	21
20	21	22	23	24	25
24	25	26	27	28	29
28	29	30	31	32	1

Thus the first three bits of $E(R)$ are the bits in positions 32, 1 and 2 of R while the last 2 bits of $E(R)$ are the bits in positions 32 and 1.

Each of the unique selection functions $S_1, S_2, \ldots, S_8$, takes a 6-bit block as input and yields a 4-bit block as output and is illustrated by using a table containing the recommended S_1:

$\underline{S_1}$

Column Number

Row No.	0	1	2	3	4	5	6	7	8	9	10	11	12	13	14	15
0	14	4	13	1	2	15	11	8	3	10	6	12	5	9	0	7
1	0	15	7	4	14	2	13	1	10	6	12	11	9	5	3	8
2	4	1	14	8	13	6	2	11	15	12	9	7	3	10	5	0
3	15	12	8	2	4	9	1	7	5	11	3	14	10	0	6	13

If S_1 is the function defined in this table and B is a block of 6 bits, then $S_1(B)$ is determined as follows: The first and last bits of B represent in base 2 a number in the range 0 to 3. Let that number be i. The middle 4 bits of B represent in base 2 a number in the range 0 to 15. Let that number be j. Look up in the table the number in the i'th row and j'th column. It is a number in the range 0 to 15 and is uniquely represented by a 4 bit block. That block is the output $S_1(B)$ of S_1 for the input B. For example, for input 011011 the row is 01, that is row 1, and the column is determined by 1101, that is column 13. In row 1 column 13 appears 5 so that the output is 0101. Selection functions $S_1, S_2, \ldots, S_8$ of the algorithm appear in the Appendix.

The permutation function P yields a 32-bit output from a 32-bit input by permuting the bits of the input block. Such a function is defined by the following table:

$\underline{P}$

16	7	20	21
29	12	28	17
1	15	23	26
5	18	31	10
2	8	24	14
32	27	3	9
19	13	30	6
22	11	4	25

The output $P(L)$ for the function P defined by this table is obtained from the input L by taking the 16th bit of L as the first bit of $P(L)$, the 7th bit as the second bit of $P(L)$, and so on until the 25th bit of L is taken as the 32nd bit of $P(L)$. The permutation function P of the algorithm is repeated in the Appendix.

Now let $S_1, \ldots, S_8$ be eight distinct selection functions, let P be the permutation function and let E be the function defined above.

To define $f(R, K)$ we first define $B_1, \ldots, B_8$ to be blocks of 6 bits each for which

(6) $$B_1 B_2 \ldots B_8 = K \oplus E(R)$$

The block $f(R, K)$ is then defined to be

(7) $$P(S_1(B_1)S_2(B_2) \ldots S_8(B_8))$$

Thus $K \oplus E(R)$ is first divided into the 8 blocks as indicated in (6). Then each B_i is taken as an input to S_i and the 8 blocks $S_1(B_1)$, $S_2(B_2)$, . . ., $S_8(B_8)$ of 4 bits each are consolidated into a single block of 32 bits which forms the input to P. The output (7) is then the output of the function f for the inputs R and K.

APPENDIX

PRIMITIVE FUNCTIONS FOR THE DATA ENCRYPTION ALGORITHM

The choice of the primitive functions *KS*, $S_1, \ldots, S_8$ and P is critical to the strength of an encipherment resulting from the algorithm. Specified below is the recommended set of functions, describing $S_1, \ldots, S_8$ and P in the same way they are described in the algorithm. For the interpretation of the tables describing these functions, see the discussion in the body of the algorithm.

The primitive functions $S_1, \ldots, S_8$ are:

S_1

14	4	13	1	2	15	11	8	3	10	6	12	5	9	0	7
0	15	7	4	14	2	13	1	10	6	12	11	9	5	3	8
4	1	14	8	13	6	2	11	15	12	9	7	3	10	5	0
15	12	8	2	4	9	1	7	5	11	3	14	10	0	6	13

S_2

15	1	8	14	6	11	3	4	9	7	2	13	12	0	5	10
3	13	4	7	15	2	8	14	12	0	1	10	6	9	11	5
0	14	7	11	10	4	13	1	5	8	12	6	9	3	2	15
13	8	10	1	3	15	4	2	11	6	7	12	0	5	14	9

S_3

10	0	9	14	6	3	15	5	1	13	12	7	11	4	2	8
13	7	0	9	3	4	6	10	2	8	5	14	12	11	15	1
13	6	4	9	8	15	3	0	11	1	2	12	5	10	14	7
1	10	13	0	6	9	8	7	4	15	14	3	11	5	2	12

S_4

7	13	14	3	0	6	9	10	1	2	8	5	11	12	4	15
13	8	11	5	6	15	0	3	4	7	2	12	1	10	14	9
10	6	9	0	12	11	7	13	15	1	3	14	5	2	8	4
3	15	0	6	10	1	13	8	9	4	5	11	12	7	2	14

S_5

2	12	4	1	7	10	11	6	8	5	3	15	13	0	14	9
14	11	2	12	4	7	13	1	5	0	15	10	3	9	8	6
4	2	1	11	10	13	7	8	15	9	12	5	6	3	0	14
11	8	12	7	1	14	2	13	6	15	0	9	10	4	5	3

S_6

12	1	10	15	9	2	6	8	0	13	3	4	14	7	5	11
10	15	4	2	7	12	9	5	6	1	13	14	0	11	3	8
9	14	15	5	2	8	12	3	7	0	4	10	1	13	11	6
4	3	2	12	9	5	15	10	11	14	1	7	6	0	8	13

S_7

4	11	2	14	15	0	8	13	3	12	9	7	5	10	6	1
13	0	11	7	4	9	1	10	14	3	5	12	2	15	8	6
1	4	11	13	12	3	7	14	10	15	6	8	0	5	9	2
6	11	13	8	1	4	10	7	9	5	0	15	14	2	3	12

S_8

13	2	8	4	6	15	11	1	10	9	3	14	5	0	12	7
1	15	13	8	10	3	7	4	12	5	6	11	0	14	9	2
7	11	4	1	9	12	14	2	0	6	10	13	15	3	5	8
2	1	14	7	4	10	8	13	15	12	9	0	3	5	6	11

The primitive function P is:

16	7	20	21
29	12	28	17
1	15	23	26
5	18	31	10
2	8	24	14
32	27	3	9
19	13	30	6
22	11	4	25

Recall that K_n, for $1 \leq n \leq 16$, is the block of 48 bits in (2) of the algorithm. Hence, to describe *KS*, it is sufficient to describe the calculation of K_n from *KEY* for $n = 1, 2, \ldots, 16$. That calculation is illustrated in figure 3. To complete the definition of *KS* it is therefore sufficient to describe the two permuted choices, as well as the schedule of left shifts. One bit in each 8-bit byte of the *KEY* may be utilized for error detection in key generation, distribution and storage. Bits 8, 16, . . ., 64 are for use in assuring that each byte is of odd parity.

Permuted choice 1 is determined by the following table:

$\underline{PC\text{-}1}$

57	49	41	33	25	17	9
1	58	50	42	34	26	18
10	2	59	51	43	35	27
19	11	3	60	52	44	36
63	55	47	39	31	23	15
7	62	54	46	38	30	22
14	6	61	53	45	37	29
21	13	5	28	20	12	4

The table has been divided into two parts, with the first part determining how the bits of C_0 are chosen, and the second part determining how the bits of D_0 are chosen. The bits of *KEY* are numbered 1 through 64. The bits of C_0 are respectively bits 57, 49, 41, . . ., 44 and 36 of *KEY*, with the bits of D_0 being bits 63, 55, 47, . . ., 12 and 4 of *KEY*.

With C_0 and D_0 defined, we now define how the blocks C_n and D_n are obtained from the blocks C_{n-1} and D_{n-1}, respectively, for $n = 1, 2, \ldots, 16$. That is accomplished by adhering to the following schedule of left shifts of the individual blocks:

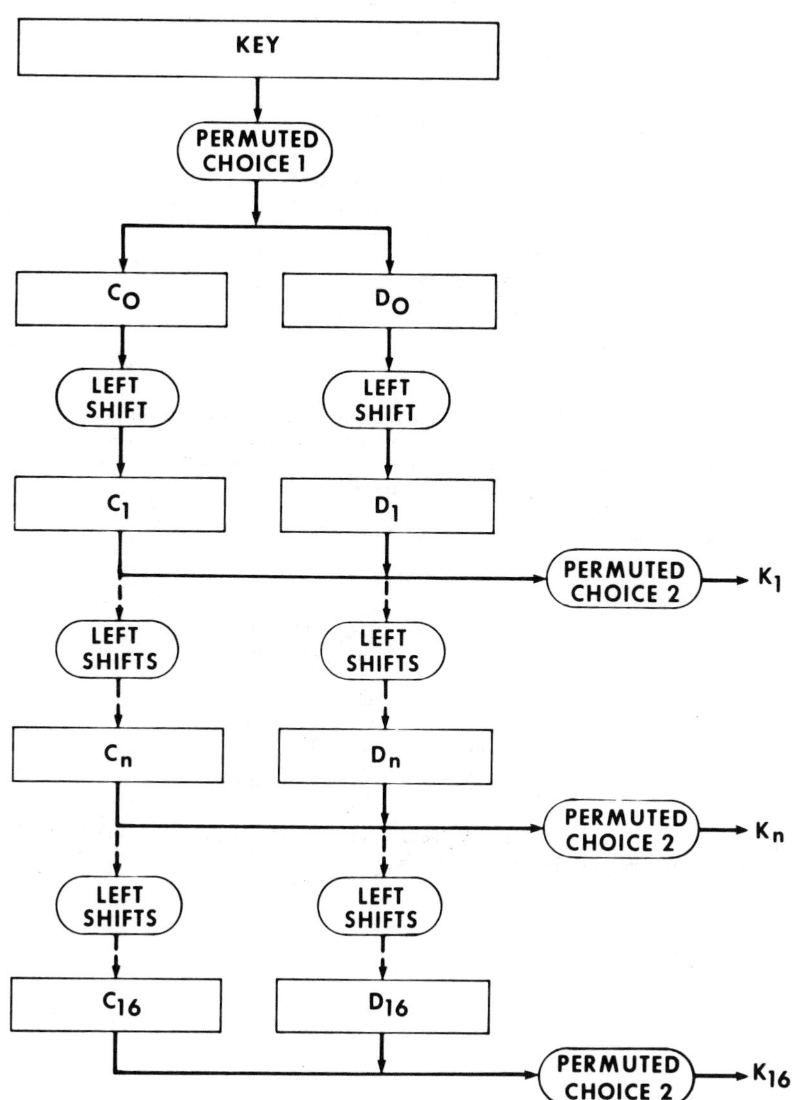

FIGURE 3. *Key schedule calculation.*

Iteration Number	Number of Left Shifts
1	1
2	1
3	2
4	2
5	2
6	2
7	2
8	2
9	1
10	2
11	2
12	2
13	2
14	2
15	2
16	1

For example, C_3 and D_3 are obtained from C_2 and D_2, respectively, by two left shifts, and C_{16} and D_{16} are obtained from C_{15} and D_{15}, respectively, by one left shift. In all cases, by a single left shift is meant a rotation of the bits one place to the left, so that after one left shift the bits in the 28 positions are the bits that were previously in positions 2, 3, . . ., 28, 1.

Permuted choice 2 is determined by the following table:

PC−2

14	17	11	24	1	5
3	28	15	6	21	10
23	19	12	4	26	8
16	7	27	20	13	2
41	52	31	37	47	55
30	40	51	45	33	48
44	49	39	56	34	53
46	42	50	36	29	32

Therefore, the first bit of K_n is the 14th bit of C_nD_n, the second bit the 17th, and so on with the 47th bit the 29th, and the 48th bit the 32nd.

APPENDIX B

Further Computations of Interest

TIME-MEMORY TRADE-OFF

In certain cases, the number of trials needed in a cryptographic attack can be significantly reduced by making use of a table of precomputed values. In effect, the attack is made more efficient by trading off computational time for memory. The technique is referred to as a *time-memory trade-off.* A method of searching key space using a time-memory trade-off is described by Hellman [1]. (Storage requirements may be quite large depending on the size of the precomputed table.)

Let R represent the total number of combinations associated with a particular cryptographic parameter under attack. For example, an attack against CE(M) is possible by precomputing the CE of $R = 2^m$ messages, where m is the number of bits in CE(M). If R different CEs are computed and the messages and CEs are stored in a table, an opponent can replace any intercepted message with another one by finding a message in the table with the same CE-value. Although only one table look-up is necessary, the attack requires R CE-values and messages to be stored.

The attack can be made more efficient by finding a better trade-off between table size and computation time. To illustrate this, let r1 be the number of precomputed values and r2 the number of intercepted values. Note that the attack succeeds if there is at least one match between the two sets; otherwise, the attack fails. Let p be the probability of success and $q = 1 - p$ the probability of failure. Assuming statistical independence, one obtains

$$q = (1 - r1/R)^{r2}$$

Taking the logarithm of each side of the equation and replacing $\ln(1 - r1/R)$ by its series expansion, one obtains

$$\begin{aligned} \ln q &= r2 \ln (1 - r1/R) \\ &= r2[-(r1/R) + (1/2)(r1/R)^2 - (1/3)(r1/R)^3 \dots] \end{aligned}$$

for $r1/R \neq 1$, where ln stands for the natural logarithm. Thus q becomes

$$q = e^{(-r2\,r1/R)[1 - (1/2)(r1/R)^2 \dots]}$$

The probability of success is thus

$$p = 1 - q = 1 - e^{(-r2rl/R)[1-(1/2)(rl/R)\dots]}$$

Since, in most cases, $rl/R \ll 1$, the probability of success is approximated by

$$p \simeq 1 - e^{(-r2rl/R)}$$

Moreover, since rl is a measure of storage (as well as of preattack computation time) and r2 is a measure of computation time, a trade-off can be made between rl and r2. For example, if $rl = r2 = R^{1/2}$, there is a probability of success of $p = 1 - (1/e) = 0.63$.

BIRTHDAY PARADOX

A closely related, but different example is the celebrated problem of repeated birthdays, or *birthday paradox* [2]. Suppose there are r people gathered together. What is the probability q that no two persons have the same birthday. To answer this question, assume that each person can have his birthday on any one of the 365 days in the year and that each day of the year is equally likely to be the person's birthday. Each group of r people can then be characterized by r numbers between 1 and 365, where each number refers to a specific birth date. There are thus 365^r such sets of numbers. To assure that no two birthdays (no two numbers in each set of r numbers) are equal, any one of the 365 days can be chosen for the first person, any one of the remaining 364 can be chosen for the second person, and so on. Thus, for the rth person, there are $365 - r + 1$ days that can be chosen. Altogether there are $(365)(364) \dots (365 - r + 1)$ different ways in which r birthdays can be selected. Thus, q is evaluated as follows:

$$q = (365)(364) \dots (365 - (r - 1))/365^r$$

The probability that two or more of the r people have the same birthday is given by $p = 1 - q$. Table B-1 gives the values for p and $1 - p$ for different values of r. From the list, one sees that p is about 0.5 for $r = 23$. Thus, if 23 people are gathered together, there is about a 50-50 chance that some two of them have the same birthday, which is a much smaller number than most people would guess.

In general, if one can choose among R (instead of 365) outcomes, the probability for q becomes

$$\begin{aligned} q &= R(R-1)(R-2)\dots(R-(r-1)/R^r \\ &= (1-1/R)(1-2/R)\dots(1-(r-1)/R) \end{aligned}$$

Using again the logarithmic transformation, one obtains

$$\ln q = \sum_{i=1}^{r-1} \ln(1 - i/R)$$

r	q	p
4	0.984	0.016
8	0.926	0.074
12	0.833	0.167
16	0.716	0.284
20	0.589	0.411
22	0.524	0.476
23	0.493	0.507
24	0.462	0.538
28	0.346	0.654
32	0.247	0.753
40	0.109	0.891
48	0.039	0.961
56	0.012	0.988
64	0.003	0.997

r denotes number of people and p denotes the probability that two or more of the r people have the same birthday.

Table B-1. Probabilities for the Birthday Problem

If $(r - 1)/R \ll 1$, then ln q can be approximated by using only the first term in the series expansion of ln, which results in

$$\ln q = -\sum_{i=1}^{r-1} i/R$$

$$= -(r - 1)(r/2R)$$

For $r \gg 1$, this reduces further to

$$q = e^{-r^2/2R}$$

Thus, p is given by

$$p = 1 - q = 1 - e^{-r^2/2R}$$

In that case, the probability of at least one match (p) is about 1/2 when $e^{r^2/2R} = 2$ or $r^2 = 2R(\ln 2)$. For the case where $R = 365$, one obtains $r = 22.5$, which is in good agreement with the actual result (Table B-1).

REFERENCES

1. Hellman, M. E., "A Cryptanalytic Time-Memory Trade-Off," *IEEE Transactions on*

Information Theory, **IT-26**, No. 4, 401–406 (1980).
2. Parzen, E., *Modern Probability Theory and Its Applications,* Wiley, New York, 1960.

APPENDIX C

Plastic Card Encoding Practices and Standards

GENERAL PHYSICAL CHARACTERISTICS

A strip of magnetic material applied to the back of a plastic card has the capacity to handle multiple bands of encoded data. Track 1 is encoded as the uppermost band followed by Track 2 and then Track 3. Original specifications for the magnetic material allowed for Tracks 1 and 2 only, which are read only tracks. The additional Track 3 provides a capability for read or write or both.

TRACK 1

The International Airlines Transportation Association promulgated the development of Track 1 as the official track for airline use and, in fact, even defined the data and encoding format(s) for the [American National Standards Institute (ANSI)] standard. Its reason for developing this standard was to allow for use of customer-operated ticket dispensing machines to alleviate the congestion at airport ticket counters [1].

Today, other parties besides the airlines are interested in Track 1 because it is the only encoded track that permits the encoding of the cardholder's name. With this alphanumeric capacity, the cardholder's name can be printed on an EFT terminal receipt inexpensively; otherwise, the name would have to be sent from the computer which, most likely, will be more time consuming and costly [1].

There are 26 formats for Track 1, which are designated by format codes A through Z. The Track 1 format corresponding to format code B is shown below (proposed revised format [2]).

Field Name	Length (characters)
Start sentinel	1
Format code = "B"	1 (alpha only)
Primary Account Number	Up to 19
Separator (SEP)	1

Field Name	Length (characters)
Country Code	3
Name	2 to 26
Surname	
Surname separator = "/"	
First name or initial	
Space (when required)	
Middle Name or Initial	
Period (when followed by title)	
Title (when used)	
SEP	1
Expiration Date or SEP	4 or 1
Discretionary Data	(the balance up to maximum record length)
End sentinel	1
Longitudinal Redundancy Check (LRC)	1
MAXIMUM TOTAL	79

Format code A is reserved for proprietary use by the card issuer. Format codes C through M are reserved for ANSI use in connection with other data formats of Track 1. Format codes N through Z are available for use by individual card issuers.

TRACK 2

The American Bankers Association (ABA) led the development of Track 2 on behalf of the two credit card companies (Interbank and Visa) and their members. The intent was to have a standardized plastic card which could be used at point-of-sale (POS) terminals to obtain authorization for credit card transactions [1].

Today, in the financial industry, Track 2 is the most widely used encoding method for plastic cards. It has a strong following because most EFT terminals are connected (on-line) directly to a computer that accesses the cardholder's account data files. Also, it is the preferred choice of the ABA and is the only track recognized and supported by Visa and MasterCard in their debit/credit programs [1].

The format of Track 2 is shown below (proposed revised format [2]).

Field Name	Length (characters)
Start sentinel	1
Primary Account Number	Up to 19
Separator (SEP)	1

Field Name	Length (characters)
Country Code	3
Expiration date or SEP	4 or 1
Discretionary Data	(the balance up to maximum record length)
End Sentinel	1
Longitudinal redundancy check (LRC)	1
MAXIMUM TOTAL	40

Although Track 2 is widely accepted, there is a serious potential concern about it because of its limited encoding capacity—only 40 positions. The argument supporting the current capacity stresses that all the necessary information to authorize a transaction is at the data center thereby eliminating the need to encode extraneous data. On the other hand, those suggesting that capacity be increased feel that greater capacity would allow certain transactions to be approved directly at the terminal, or, at least, minimize the data sent between terminal and computer for each transaction. Those who hold this view are investigating the alternatives of using Tracks 1 and 3 with their on-line terminals in order to take advantage of the increased capacity [1].

TRACK 3

Track 3 was developed for use in off-line EFT terminals but was designed to be compatible with the other current plastic card standards. Thus, Track 3 is compatible with the ANSI standard for embossing plastic cards (ANSI X4.13-1979) and the ANSI standard for physical characteristics of magnetic stripes (ANSI X4.16-1973). More recently, financial institutions have started to consider its use in on-line systems because of its greater data storage capacity [1].

The format of Track 3 follows [3]:

Field Name	Usage[1]	Status[2]	Length (Characters)
Start sentinel	M	S	1
Format code	M	S	2
Primary account number (PAN)	M	S	19
Separator (SEP)	M	S	1
Country code or SEP	M	S	3 or 1
Currency	M	S	3
Currency exponent	M	S	1
Amount authorized per cycle period	M	S	4
Amount remaining this cycle	M	D	4
Cycle begin	M	D	4

Field Name	Usage[1]	Status[2]	Length (Characters)
Cycle length	M	S	2
Retry count	M	D	1
PIN control parameters or SEP	M	S	6 or 1
Interchange control	M	S	1
Type of account and service restriction (PAN)	M	S	2
Type of account and service restriction (SAN-1)	M	S	2
Type of account and service restriction (SAN-2)	M	S	2
Expiration date or SEP	M	S	4 or 1
Card sequence number	M	S	1
Card security number or SEP	M	D	9 or 1
First subsidiary account number (SAN-1)	O	S	variable[3]
SEP	M	S	1
Second subsidiary account number (SAN-2)	O	S	variable
SEP	M	S	1
Relay marker	M	S	1
Crypto check digits or SEP	M	D	6 or 1
Discretionary data	O	D	variable
End sentinel	M	S	1
Longitudinal redundancy check (LRC)	M	D	1
MAXIMUM TOTAL			107

[1] "M" indicates that usage is mandatory; "O" that it is optional.

[2] Dynamic fields (denoted by "D") shall be updated as appropriate by interchange partners. Static fields (denoted by "S") shall be updated by the card issuer only.

[3] There is no maximum length for a variable length field, except that the total number of characters in track 3 must not exceed 107.

Details of the specific data elements encoded on Track 3 are contained in reference 3.

REFERENCES

1. Thomas, O. T. "Funds Transfer Research Department Working Paper #4," United States League of Savings Associations, Chicago, IL (June 1980).
2. Proposed American National Standard X4.16, *Magnetic Stripe Encoding for Financial Transaction Cards,* American National Standards Institute, X4, New York (Draft, October 1980).
3. American National Standard X9.1-1980, *Magnetic Stripe Data Content for Track 3,* American National Standards Institute, X9, New York, 1980.

APPENDIX D

Some Cryptographic Concepts and Methods of Attack

FURTHER DISCUSSION OF AUTHENTICATION PARAMETERS

One Way Functions

As stated in Chapter 11, a one-way function is defined as follows:

> *A function f is a* one-way function *if, for any argument x in the domain of f, it is easy to compute the corresponding value y = f(x); yet for almost all y in the range of f, it is computationally infeasible, given a value of y and knowledge of f, to calculate any x whatsoever with the property that f(x) = y. It is important to note that a function is defined which is not invertible from a computational point of view, but whose non-invertibility is entirely different from that normally encountered in mathematics. A function f is normally called "noninvertible" when the inverse of a point y is not unique, i.e., there exist distinct points x1 and x2 such that f(x1) = y = f(x2). This is not the sort of inversion difficulty that is required here. Rather, it must be overwhelmingly difficult, given a value y and knowledge of f, to calculate any x whatsoever with the property that f(x) = y [1].*

The intent of this section is to demonstrate that the design of one-way functions is not as straightforward as might be expected at the onset. It is particularly true if constraints are introduced. This is shown by discussing the case where a growth path is provided from a system using an authentication parameter which is not one-way (i.e., PIN ⊕ ID) to one which is one-way [i.e., PIN ⊕ ID ⊕ f(KP, PIN, ID)].

To discuss details, let it be assumed that personal verification is achieved with the aid of authentication parameters stored in a verification table together with the corresponding user ID (Table D-1). (The APs are generated at the entry point and compared with the appropriate AP of reference at the issuer as discussed in Chapter 11). Also, let AP be a one-way function f of KP, PIN, and ID, i.e.,

$$AP = f(KP, PIN, ID)$$

Since AP is one-way, a secure implementation must allow that AP be public. (An opponent could get AP information, for example, if he could read the verification table.)

ID1, AP1 of Reference
ID2, AP2 of Reference
⋮ ⋮ ⋮ ⋮
IDn, APn of Reference

Table D-1. Verification Table

The condition that KP and PIN must not be derivable from AP and ID is usually easily satisfied by treating KP and PIN as keys. For example, $AP = E_{KP \oplus PIN}(ID)$ satisfies such a condition. But a more stringent condition is that it must not be possible to derive a set of KPs and PINs such that the same AP is generated with the appropriate ID (assumed to be known). In other words, it must not be computationally feasible to find equivalent values KP* and PIN* (Figure D-1) such that

$$AP = f(KP^*, PIN^*, ID)$$

This condition is also satisfied with $AP = E_{KP \oplus PIN}(ID)$, since the evaluation of $KP^* \oplus PIN^* = KP \oplus PIN$ for a given ID, AP pair is equivalent to the effort of key exhaustion. (ID can be considered plaintext and AP the corresponding ciphertext for which the key must be found.)

An example of a weak one-way function is

$$AP = E_{KP \oplus PIN}(ID \oplus PIN)$$

because a KP* and PIN* can be found such that

$$E_{KP^* \oplus PIN^*}(ID \oplus PIN^*) = E_{KP \oplus PIN}(ID \oplus PIN)$$

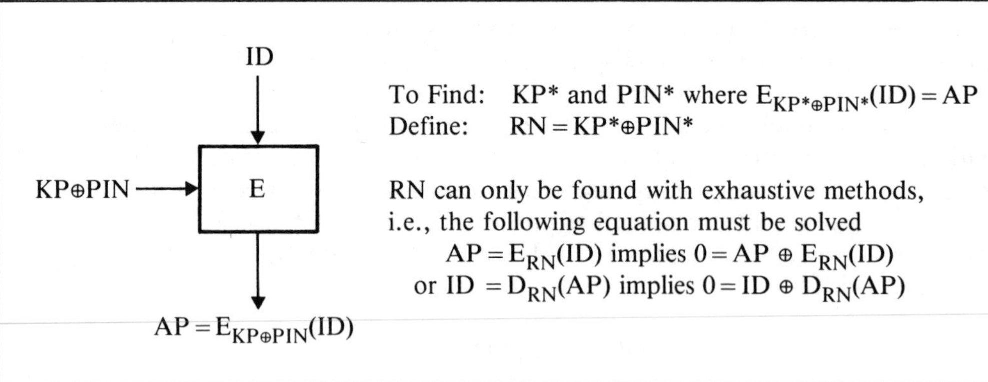

Figure D-1. Example of a Strong One-Way Function

To show this, let RN = KP* ⊕ PIN* be an arbitrarily selected quantity. The equation for AP can thus be rewritten as

$$AP = E_{RN}(ID \oplus PIN^*)$$

from which it follows that

$$PIN^* = ID \oplus D_{RN}(AP)$$

(It is assumed that the implementation allows up to 16-digit PINs even though 4-digit PINs may be used most frequently.) Furthermore, from the definition of RN, one concludes that

$$KP^* = RN \oplus PIN^* = ID \oplus RN \oplus D_{RN}(AP)$$

Thus, the equivalent values are only an easily computed function of the given ID, AP pair and an arbitrary quantity RN. The reason for the weakness is that changing the argument from ID in $AP = E_{KP \oplus PIN}(ID)$ to ID ⊕ PIN introduces an additional degree of freedom which allows the evaluation of equivalent KPs and PINs.

In Figure D-2 it is shown that $AP = E_{KP \oplus PIN}(ID \oplus KP)$ and $AP = KP \oplus E_{KP \oplus PIN}(ID)$ are not one-way functions either.

Attack Using Repeated Trials

The weak examples discussed so far have allowed the direct evaluation of equivalent parameters. But even if this is not the case, a candidate for a one-way function must be tested under the assumption that an opponent has a large set of (ID, AP) values, since he may, for example, obtain access to a verification table storing these values (Table D-2). Let the number of (ID, AP) pairs available to an opponent be equal to n and let the total number of possible AP values be N (i.e., 2^{64} if AP is represented by one block of the DES output).

If m trials are performed to obtain KP* and PIN*, the probability, q, of not generating a correct table entry is thus

$$q = \left(1 - \frac{n}{N}\right)^m$$

Taking the natural logarithm (ln) on both sides yields

$$\ln q = m \ln\left(1 - \frac{n}{N}\right)$$

Using the first two terms in a series expansion of $\ln\left(1 - \frac{n}{N}\right)$ results in

$$\ln q \simeq -m(n/N) + m(n^2/2N^2)$$

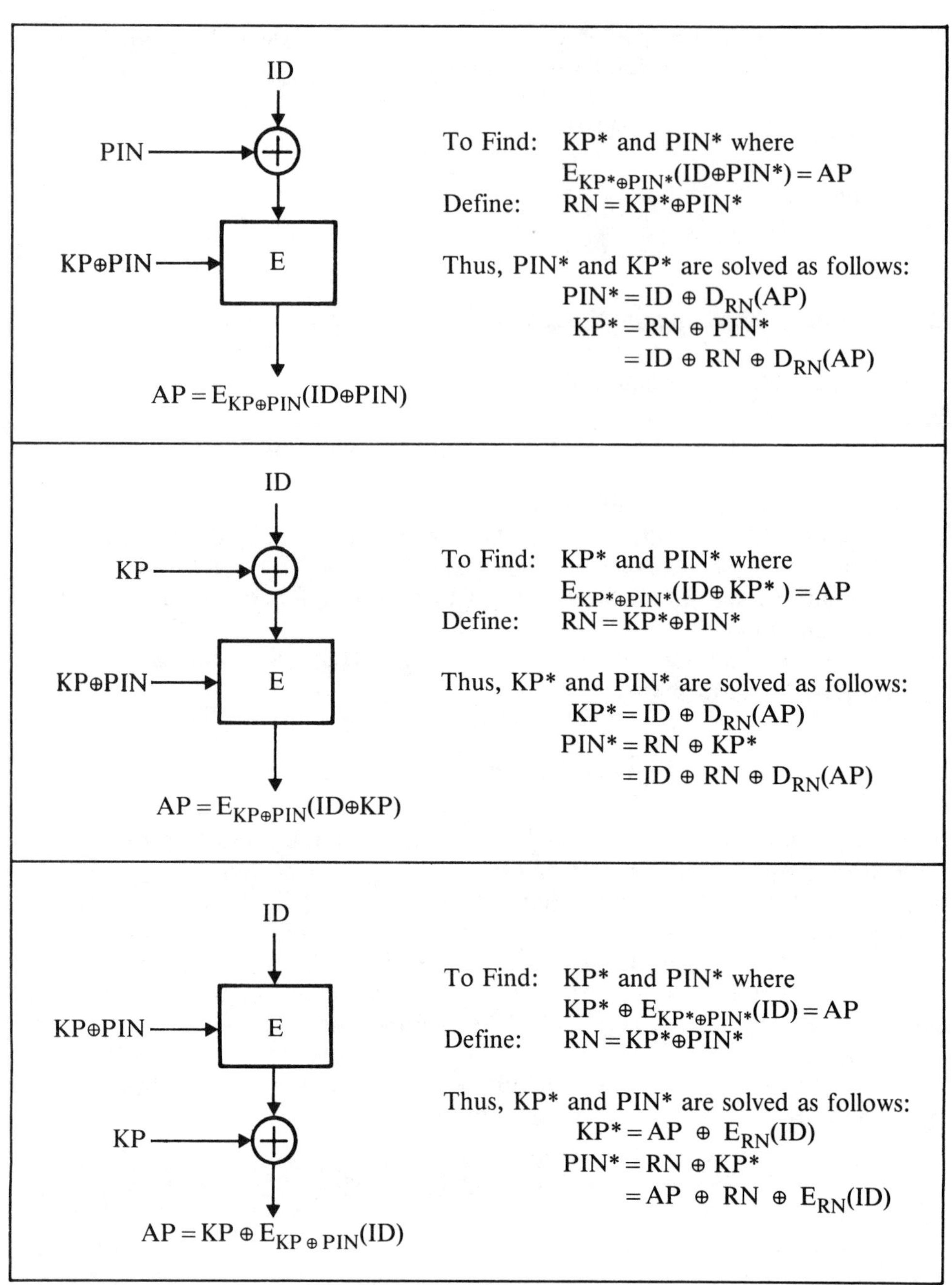

Figure D-2. Examples of Functions that are Not One-Way

If $n^2/2N^2 \ll n/N$ or $n/2N \ll 1$ (which is an easily satisfied condition), then the second term can be neglected and one obtains

$$\ln q = -m(n/N)$$

$$q = e^{-mn/N}$$

The probability, p, of finding at least one correct table value is thus $p = 1 - q$, or

$$p = 1 - e^{-mnN}; \qquad n/2N \ll 1$$

Values of p as a function of mn/N are given in Table D-2.

For $mn/2N \ll 1$, the probability p can be expressed as

$$p = mn/N; \qquad mn/2N \ll 1$$

If m and n are given, p is determined entirely by the number of bits ($\log_2(N)$) in the output (or range) of the one-way function. The minimum tolerable number of test combinations for AP is therefore determined by (1) how many trials (m) can be economically performed by an opponent and (2) how much information (n) the opponent has available. Since this information can be thought of as a dictionary, the attack falls into the category of dictionary attacks (discussed in Chapter 2) and will be labeled as such.

mn/N	$e^{-mn/N}$	$p = 1 - e^{-mn/N}$
16	0.000^+	1.000^-
8	0.000^+	1.000^-
4	0.018	0.982
3	0.050	0.950
2	0.135	0.865
1.5	0.223	0.777
1.0	0.368	0.632
0.5	0.607	0.393
0.25	0.779	0.221
0.20	0.819	0.181
0.10	0.905	0.095
0.05	0.951	0.049
0.01	0.990	0.010

Legend:

N = total number of possible AP values
n = number of AP, ID pairs available to an opponent
m = number of exhaustion trials to obtain equivalent values for KP and PIN

Table D-2. Values of p as a Function of mn/N

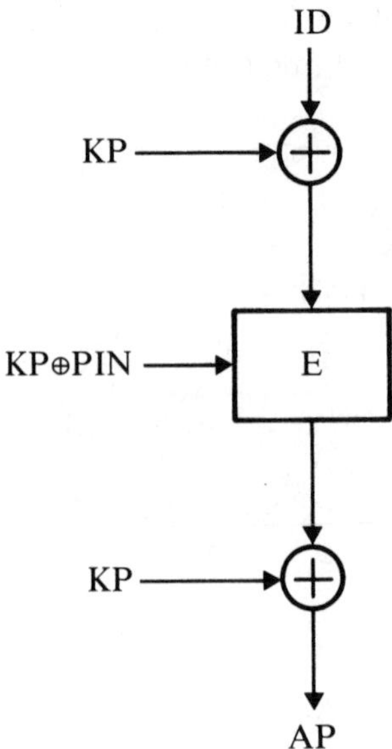

Figure D-3. Example of One-Way Function Which Yields to a Dictionary Attack

A weak one-way function which yields to the dictionary attack is $AP = KP \oplus E_{KP \oplus PIN}(ID \oplus KP)$. AP can be thought of as the ciphertext corresponding to a triply encrypted ID. Two encryption steps are defined by modulo 2 addition and the third by the DES (Figure D-3).

An equivalent way of looking at it is to consider $X = (ID \oplus KP)$ to be the plaintext and $Y = AP \oplus KP$ to be the corresponding ciphertext (Figure D-4). The weakness which can be exploited is that $X \oplus Y = AP \oplus ID$, since KP is canceled out in the operation. But knowledge of a set of valid (ID, AP) pairs also implies knowledge of a valid set of $(AP \oplus ID)$ pairs.

To solve for

$$AP = KP^* \oplus E_{KP^* \oplus PIN^*}(ID \oplus KP^*)$$

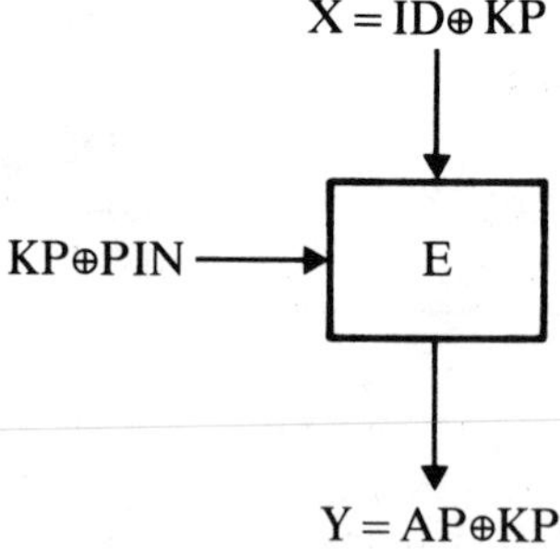

Note that $X \oplus Y = AP \oplus ID$.

Figure D-4. Equivalent Representation of the One Way Function in Figure D-3.

select two arbitrary quantities, RN1 and RN2, and define them to be

$$RN1 = ID \oplus KP^*$$

$$RN2 = KP^* \oplus PIN^*$$

According to Figure D-4, RN1 can be considered equivalent plaintext, X*, and $E_{RN2}(RN1)$ can be considered equivalent ciphertext, Y*. The attack of finding equivalent values for RNi and KP succeeds when $X^* \oplus Y^*$ is an element in the set of known $AP \oplus ID$ values.

Thus RN1 is encrypted with RN2 and the result is added modulo 2 to RN1. If this quantity is in the set of known ($AP \oplus ID$) values, the attack has succeeded, since in that case, it can be concluded that

$$RN1 \oplus E_{RN2}(RN1) = ID \oplus AP$$

i.e., plaintext added modulo 2 to ciphertext equals an element in the given table. But, by definition

$$RN1 = ID \oplus KP^*$$

Thus

$$KP^* = AP \oplus E_{RN2}(RN1)$$

and

$$PIN^* = RN2 \oplus KP^* = AP \oplus RN2 \oplus E_{RN2}(RN1)$$

If there is no match with a given table entry, a different RN1 and RN2 are selected and the process continues (RN2 could actually be fixed and RN1 could be variable, or vice versa). By making N sufficiently large the attack can be blocked (Table D-2).

To further illustrate the problems associated with designing one-way functions, consider a design in which a weak authentication parameter ($AP = ID \oplus PIN$) is to be made into a strong one (which is one-way) at some future time by simply Exclusive-ORing $ID \oplus PIN$ with an additional quantity. To solve the problem, let

$$AP = (ID \oplus PIN) \oplus f(KP, PIN, ID)$$

where AP and f(KP, PIN, ID) must be strong one-way functions of KP, PIN, and ID. Again, it must be assumed that KP and PIN cannot be deduced from ID and AP. Furthermore, it must not be possible to find equivalent values such that

$$AP = (ID \oplus PIN^*) \oplus f(KP^*, PIN^*, ID)$$

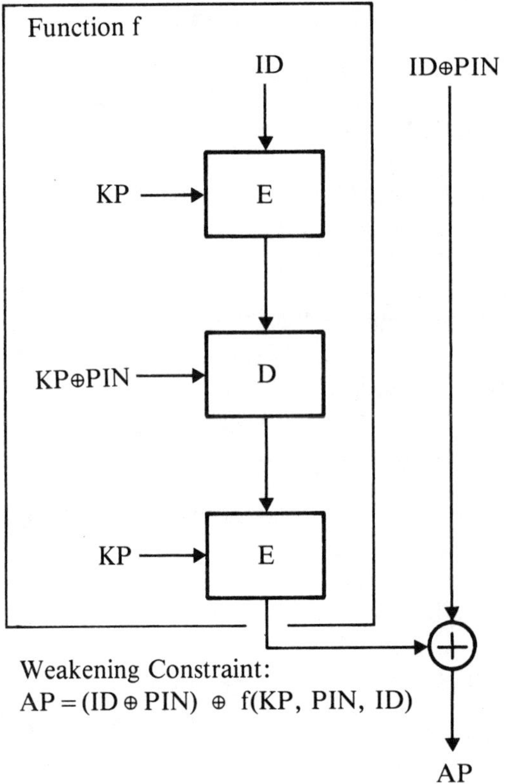

Figure D-5. Example of a One-Way Function Even with a Weakening Constraint

The problem at hand is more difficult than the one previously discussed, since the presence of (ID ⊕ PIN) makes it more difficult to design a strong one-way function. For example, let

$$f(KP, PIN, ID) = E_{KP \oplus PIN}(ID)$$

which was shown to be strong if used alone to define AP. In this case, AP is now defined as

$$AP = (ID \oplus PIN) \oplus E_{KP \oplus PIN}(ID)$$

Again, consider whether it is possible to solve for a KP* and PIN* such that

$$AP = (ID \oplus PIN^*) \oplus E_{KP^* \oplus PIN^*}(ID)$$

Defining, as before,

$$RN = KP^* \oplus PIN^*$$

one obtains

$$\text{PIN}^* = \text{AP} \oplus \text{ID} \oplus E_{RN}(\text{ID})$$

$$\text{KP}^* = \text{PIN}^* \oplus \text{RN} = \text{AP} \oplus \text{ID} \oplus \text{RN} \oplus E_{RN}(\text{ID})$$

Thus, choosing an appropriate ID, AP pair, together with an arbitrary quantity, allows the evaluation of PIN* and KP* in one trial. Therefore, the suggested AP is extremely weak. The lesson to be learned is as follows.

Coupling a strong one-way function with additional information may result in a weak one-way function.

To make sure that no exploitable degrees of freedom are introduced, a function f is defined that uses triple encryption (Figure D-5). The function defining AP is thought to be a strong one-way function of KP, PIN, and ID.

FURTHER DISCUSSION OF AUTHENTICATION PARAMETERS AND PERSONAL AUTHENTICATION CODES

Implementation Examples

To analyze the authentication parameter AP = ID ⊕ PIN, let two cases be assumed.

1. Personal verification is done with the aid of a verification table which stores the following quantities

   $$\begin{array}{l} \text{ID1 } E_{KA}(\text{ID1} \oplus \text{PIN1}) \text{ of reference} \\ \text{ID2 } E_{KA}(\text{ID2} \oplus \text{PIN2}) \text{ of reference} \\ \vdots \\ \text{IDn } E_{KA}(\text{IDn} \oplus \text{PINn}) \text{ of reference} \end{array}$$

   where ⊕ indicates modulo 2 addition and KA is a system key. In this approach, ID and ID ⊕ PIN are routed through the network securely, and ID ⊕ PIN is translated into E_{KA} (ID ⊕ PIN) at the issuer. If this quantity is identical to the stored reference, the user is accepted. Otherwise, he is rejected.
2. Instead of storing E_{KA} (ID ⊕ PIN) in a verification table, it is stored on the bank card as a Personal Authentication Code (PAC). The authentication key, KA, is stored at the node where authentication takes place (e.g., the issuer, the switch, or at any other designated node). In this approach, ID, PIN ⊕ ID, as well as PAC are routed throughout the network.

At the authenticating node, the received ID ⊕ PIN is encrypted, as before, with the stored authentication key, KA. The result is compared with the received PAC. If both quantities are identical, the user is accepted; otherwise, the user is rejected.

Attack Against a 16-Digit PIN

Consider the following attack against implementation method 2 above. An opponent opens an account at a bank. The assigned ID and PIN, and the calculated value of ID ⊕ PIN, are thus known quantities. The opponent also knows PAC = E_{KA} (ID ⊕ PIN) since it is stored on the bank card.

If he wants to attack account number ID*, he only has to use an equivalent PIN defined PIN*, which can be evaluated as follows.

$$\text{PIN}^* = (\text{ID} \oplus \text{PIN}) \oplus \text{ID}^* \tag{D-1}$$

The appropriate PAC* is

$$\text{PAC}^* = E_{KA}(\text{ID}^* \oplus \text{PIN}^*) = E_{KA}(\text{ID} \oplus \text{PIN}) = \text{PAC} \tag{D-2}$$

which is identical to his own PAC, since by definition (Equation D-1)

$$\text{PIN}^* \oplus \text{ID}^* = \text{ID} \oplus \text{PIN}$$

Even with method 1, the system is vulnerable since an opponent knows how to change the reference in the verification table (which could be done temporarily during the attack). He only has to change the PAC of the user under attack to his own PAC according to Equation D-2.

Attack Against a 12-Digit PIN

To show an attack against a shorter PIN (i.e., 12 digits), the PIN and ID blocks are defined using the proposed ANSI method (see PIN Block Construction and Account Block Construction, Appendix E). If the PIN block and the account number block are added together, modulo 2, the result is as follows.

$$\begin{aligned} \text{AP} = {} & \text{C, N, P1, P2, A1} \oplus \text{P3, (A2} \oplus \text{P4)} \oplus \text{F,} \\ & \ldots, (\text{A10} \oplus \text{P12}) \oplus \text{F, A11} \oplus \text{F, A12} \oplus \text{F} \end{aligned} \tag{D-3}$$

The nature of the attack is to make the input to the algorithm equal to a known value. In that case, the resulting output is also known. In other words, the personal authentication code arrived at by encrypting the authentication parameter is predictable.

From Equation D-3 it follows that for a 12-digit PIN all quantities except the last two (i.e., A11 ⊕ F and A12 ⊕ F) are constant or can be controlled by an opponent. The control field C, is fixed and determined by the character set. The PIN length field, N, is determined by the institution and hence is also fixed. (It is assumed that every user of the institution has a 12-digit PIN.) The next two fields (P1, P2) can be controlled by an opponent who knows what PIN information he has. The next ten quantities, A1 $\oplus$ P3 through (A10 $\oplus$ P12) $\oplus$ F, can be made equal to a predetermined value by requiring that

$$AN \oplus P = AN^* \oplus P^*$$

$$P^* = AN \oplus AN^* \oplus P; \qquad N = 1, 2, \ldots, 10$$

where AN and P are the parameters associated with the account the opponent opened. AN* is the nth digit of the account number to be attacked, and P* is the (n + 2)nd PIN digit the opponent must use to attack the system.

Thus the only two quantities not constant or under the control of the opponent are A11 $\oplus$ F and A12 $\oplus$ F. Any account number to be attacked must therefore have A11 and A12 as the least significant digits. Since they represent only a total of 100 combinations, 1% of all accounts can be attacked. However, the probability of success can be increased if the opponent opens several accounts. If he opens ten accounts, roughly 10% of all accounts can be attacked. If he opens a few hundred accounts, then all or nearly all the accounts can be attacked.

Proposals for Authentication Parameters and Personal Authentication Codes

A recommended solution to the general method of attack against PIN given above is to redefine the authentication parameter AP as

$$AP = E_{CI \oplus PIN}(ID) \qquad \text{(D-4)}$$

where CI represents information stored on a user's card. This would be implemented in addition to the authentication parameter recommended by the American Bankers Association (ABA):

$$AP = ID||PIN \qquad \text{(D-5)}$$

where ID||PIN represents the concatenation of ID and PIN. (Since this is a preliminary proposal, the information is subject to change.)

If CI is public, both authentication parameters (Equations D-4 and D-5) have equal cryptographic security. In either case, AP is routed through the network in enciphered form. If CI represents secret card information (e.g., a personal key), then the first method is stronger since AP is, in that case, a one-way function of CI and PIN. Since the system must be able to determine which authentication parameter is used, a bit is stored on the card to indicate this.

A preliminary ABA proposal for the computation of a PAC is shown in Figure D-6. To generate n PIN digits, the set of 16 hexadecimal digits in the triply encrypted PIN||ID are scanned for digits that fall in the range 0 to 9

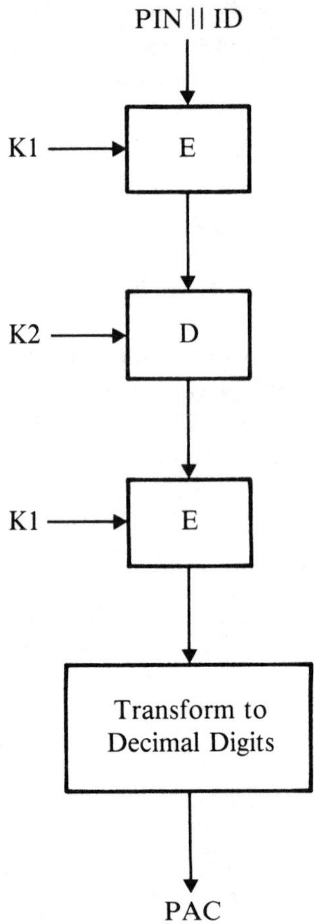

Note: || denotes concatenation.

Figure D-6. Preliminary ABA Proposal for Personal Authentication Code

(i.e. decimal digits). If the number of decimal digits found is equal to or larger than n, the first n digits are defined the PIN. If the number is less than n, say r, then n-r additional decimal digits are generated from the first n-r hexadecimal digits in the range A to F by subtracting 10 from their values. The scheme has two disadvantages.

1. The transformation is biased towards certain digits (0 through 5), which reduces the effective number of PIN combinations.
2. Only a limited number of PIN digits are used (e.g., up to four).

To eliminate the first disadvantage, a different transformation could be devised. For example, instead of generating 64 bits (16 hexadecimal digits) with one triple encryption step, 128 bits (32 hexadecimal digits) could be generated using two triple encryption steps. In that case, the probability of obtaining decimal digits directly is much higher (i.e., there are fewer instances in which it is necessary to transform hexadecimal digits A through F to decimal digits). The second disadvantage could be overcome by allocating

64 bits for both the ID and PIN and couple both by introducing another encryption under K1 as shown in Figure D-7. In a more secure approach, PIN is replaced by a one-way function of CI and ID as shown in Figure D-8. If the additional encryption of ID with CI is not acceptable, ID could be coupled to AP as shown in Figure D-9. The entry of ID at both points [labeled (a) and (b) in Figure D-9] is necessary. If only one entry were used, the approach would be weak for the case where K1 = K2.

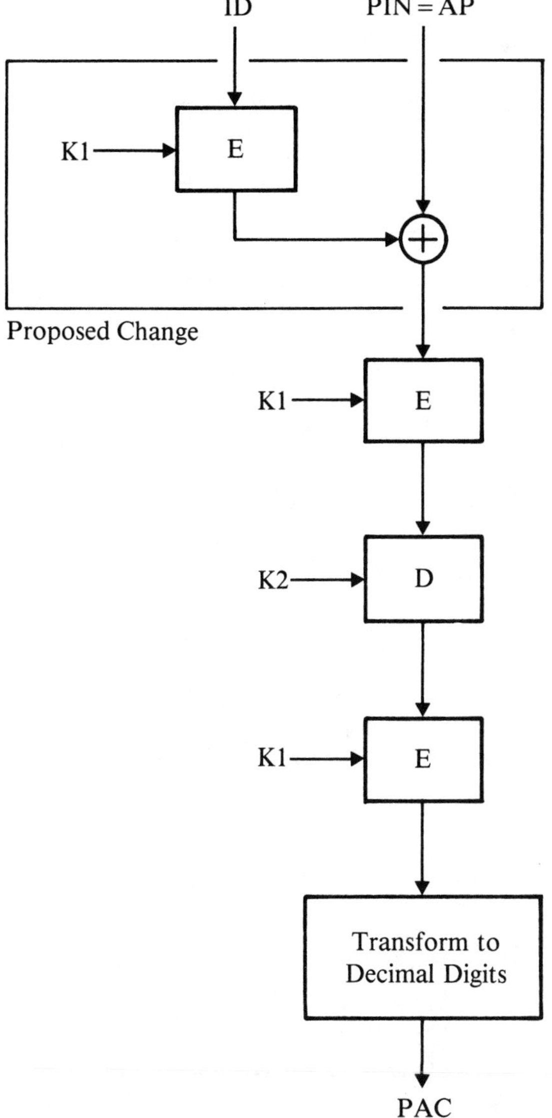

Note: The proposed change allows the use of up to 16 PIN digits and, at the same time, achieves coupling with ID.

Figure D-7. Modified Preliminary ABA Scheme

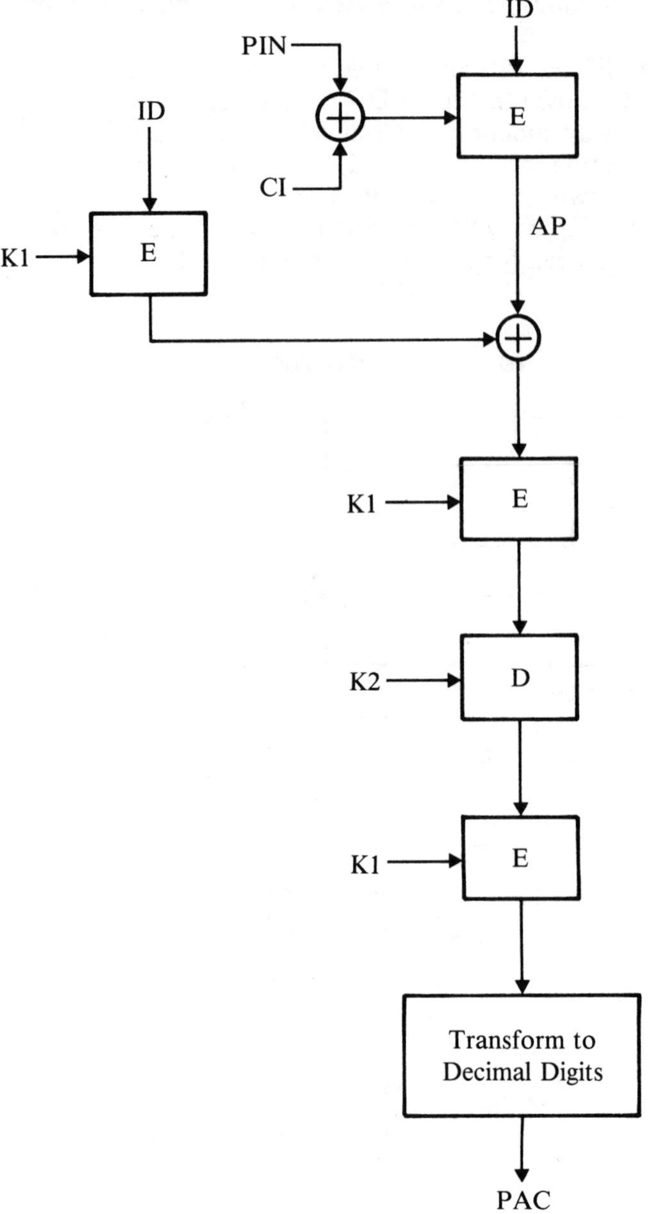

Legend: AP = Authentication Parameter
CI = Card Information
ID = Used Identifier
PIN = Personal Identification Number
PAC = Personal Authentication Code

Note: During initialization at the issuer, an AP is calculated for each given ID, PIN, and CI. ID and AP are also used to calculate PAC, which is stored on the bank card. During personal verification, AP is calculated at the entry point from the entered values of ID, PIN, and CI. The entered ID and AP, and the calculated PAC are then sent to the authenticator.

Figure D-8. Generation of Authentication Parameter and Personal Authentication Code—Method 1

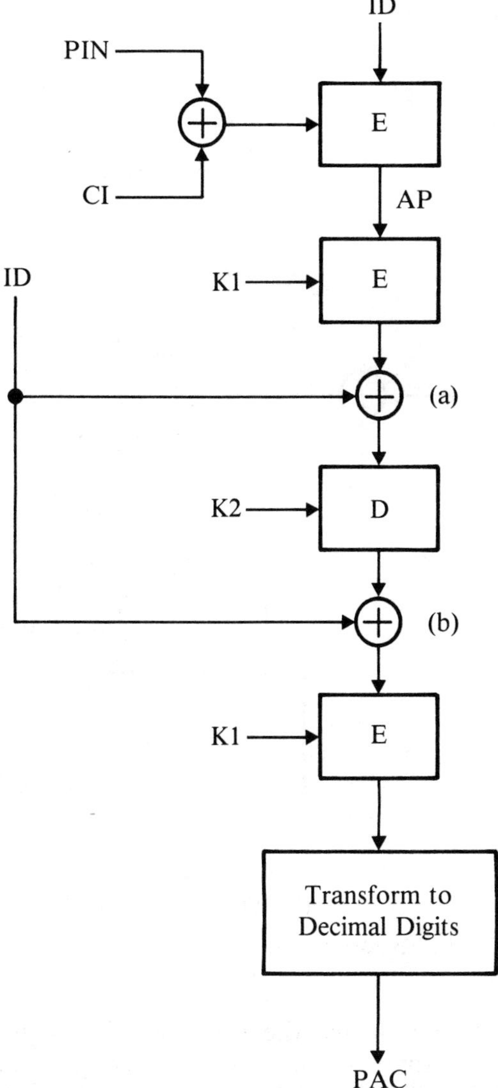

Note: During initialization at the issuer, an AP is calculated for each given ID, PIN, and CI. ID and AP are also used to calculate PAC, which is stored on the bank card. During personal verification, AP is calculated at the entry point from the entered values of ID, PIN, and CI. The entered ID and AP, and the calculated PAC are then sent to the authenticator.

Figure D-9. Generation of Authentication Parameter and Personal Authentication Code—Method 2

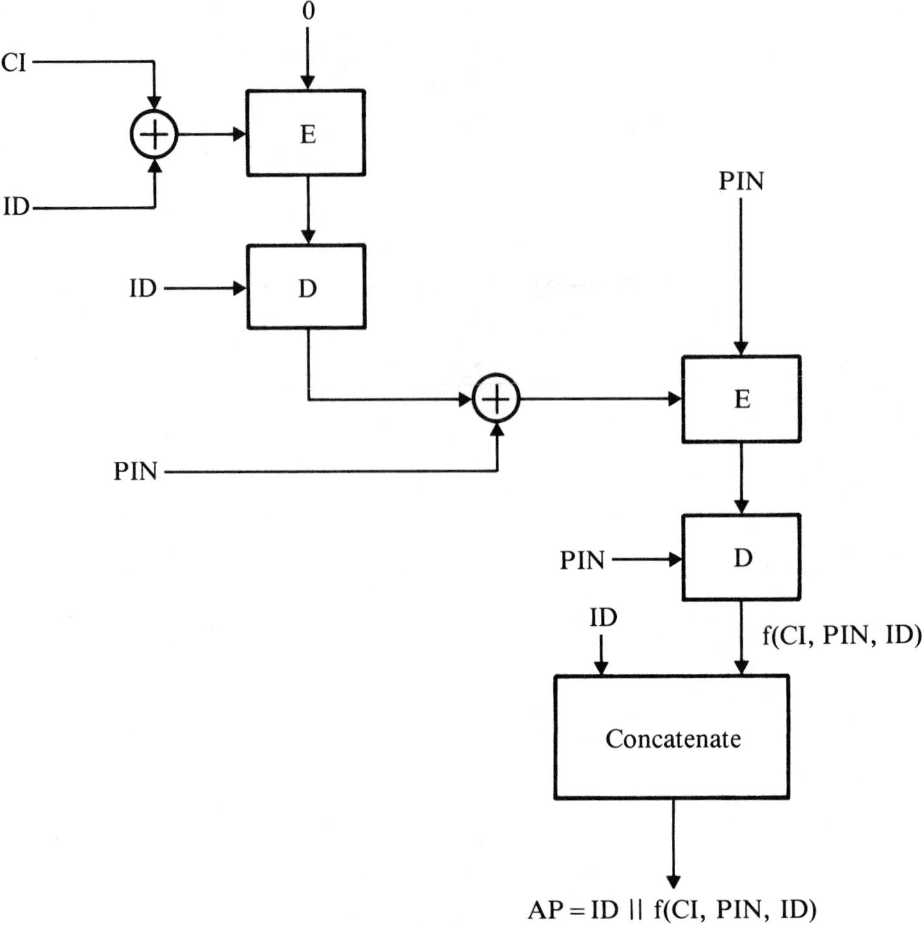

Figure D-10. Computation of AP with Migration Properties.

The AP value defined in Figure D-10 has the advantage that it provides a migration path to a very secure approach incorporating secret card information. Thus when CI ≠ 0, AP = ID||f(ID, PIN, CI), where f(ID, PIN, CI) is a one-way function and CI is secret card information. In the degenerate case (where CI = 0), AP = ID||PIN (i.e., the output of the function is equivalent to that defined by the ABA proposal, Figure D-6.

The Advantage of an AP that Depends on ID

The advantage of using ID as well as PIN in generating an authentication parameter is shown by the analysis of three different methods, where AP is a function of

1. PIN only, e.g., AP = PIN
2. PIN and ID, e.g., AP = E_{PIN}(ID)
3. PIN, KP, and ID, e.g., AP = $E_{KP \oplus PIN}$(ID)

Furthermore, let m be the number of different PIN combinations and n the number of different user IDs. To simplify the discussion, the assumption $n \leqslant m$ shall be made such that each user has a unique PIN. (Although, in general, this assumption will not hold, it is nevertheless useful to analyze this simple case to demonstrate the usefulness of coupling ID and PIN.) In that case, there are then m PIN choices for user 1, $m - 1$ PIN choices for user 2, and so on. In general, there are $m - (i - 1)$ PIN choices for the ith user.

Assume also that PAC = E_{KA}(AP) is stored in a verification table and that it is possible to obtain E_{KA}(AP*) for a trial value of AP*. (A good key management scheme would prevent this.) If $E_{KA}(E_{PIN*}(ID))$ can be related to each table entry $E_{KA}(E_{PIN}(ID))$, there are at most m (on the average about m/2) trials required to obtain the correct PIN for a given ID. On the other hand, to obtain all PIN/ID correspondences, the maximum number of trials needed would be:

$$S = m + (m - 1) + \cdots + [m - (n - 1)]$$
$$= mn - [1 + 2 + \cdots + (n - 1)] = mn - [n(n - 1)/2]$$
$$= n[m - (n - 1)/2]; \qquad n < m$$

whereas on the average only about half of that number (S/2) are required.

To simplify the computation, assume that there are as many users as there are PIN combinations ($m = n$). Then the number of trials an opponent needs to get all PIN/ID combinations is equal to the number of trials when $n = m - 1$ (because the last (nth) PIN is automatically determined if all the others are known). Using the above equation for S (with $n = m - 1$) yields

$$S = (m - 1)[m - (m - 2)/2]$$
$$= (m - 1)(m/2 + 1); \qquad n = m$$

It should be pointed out that the number of trials is drastically reduced if PAC is only a function of the PIN and not of the ID. For example, let PAC = E_{KA}(PIN). Then E_{KA}(PIN*) can be related uniquely to E_{KA}(PIN) and thus a proper ID can be evaluated with certainty for each trial of PIN (provided that the PIN is currently assigned to some user). Hence, the advantage of

Goal of Attack	Maximum Number of Trials Needed to Exhaust the Combinations of PIN, i.e., to Obtain the Correct PIN/ID Relationship		
	AP = PIN	AP = E_{PIN}(ID)	AP = $E_{KP \oplus PIN}$(ID)
Arbitrary (ID, PIN)	1	m	more than 10^{17}
Particular (ID, PIN)	m	m	more than 10^{17}
All (ID, PIN)s	m	$(m - 1)(m/2 + 1) \simeq (m^2/2) + (m/2) - 1$	more than 10^{17}

Table D-3. Maximum Number of Trials Needed to Exhaust the Combinations of PIN

coupling the ID together with the PIN is clearly demonstrated for the case where n = m. The results are summarized in Table D-3. The same advantage can be gained for the case where n > m, although the computations are omitted from the discussion.

INCREASING EXHAUSTIVE ATTACK WORK FACTOR BY IMPLEMENTATION METHODS

Multiple Encryption and Block Chaining

Usually the main emphasis is placed on the strength of the algorithm. An equally important factor on overall strength, however, is how the algorithm is implemented. For example, the work factor for exhaustive attacks can be significantly increased by using the DES with multiple encryption. A particularly attractive approach is one which allows compatibility between a basic single encryption scheme and a more secure multiple encryption scheme. This can be achieved by defining the cryptographic operations

$$Y = E_{K1} D_{K2} E_{K1}(X)$$

$$X = D_{K1} E_{K2} D_{K1}(Y)$$

where K1 and K2 are independently chosen (56-bit) keys [2] as shown in Figure D-11. This operation has the property that for the case where K1 = K2 = K, the relationships $Y = E_K(X)$ and $X = D_K(Y)$ hold.

Thus a high security multiple encryption implementation using K1 and K2 could communicate with a less secure single encryption scheme just by setting K1 equal to K2. Although, technically speaking, the method is not quite as strong as a method using three different keys, it is much stronger than double encryption with two different keys as analyzed below.

If arbitrary plaintext and corresponding ciphertext are known, (single encryption is assumed), the key can be determined by enciphering the plaintext with one key after the other until the correct ciphertext is produced. This requires, on the average, 2^{55} trials for the DES. Such an attack is, in theory, always possible regardless of the implementation. This is so because it must be assumed that some encrypted data will at some time become public.

A significant decrease in the exhaustive work factor is possible if plaintext (selected by an opponent) and corresponding ciphertext can be obtained (called a selected plaintext attack). One way to defend against the selected plaintext attack is to introduce "noise" into the encryption procedures such that the system itself does not encrypt the plaintext selected by the opponent. Block chaining achieves this via an initializing vector, as discussed in Chapter 2. *As a consequence, all attacks described below will fail when block chaining is used (a recommended mode of DES operation).* This represents an additional powerful argument in favor of chaining methods.

To determine the consequence of a weak implementation which allows a selected plaintext attack, some cryptanalytic techniques are discussed em-

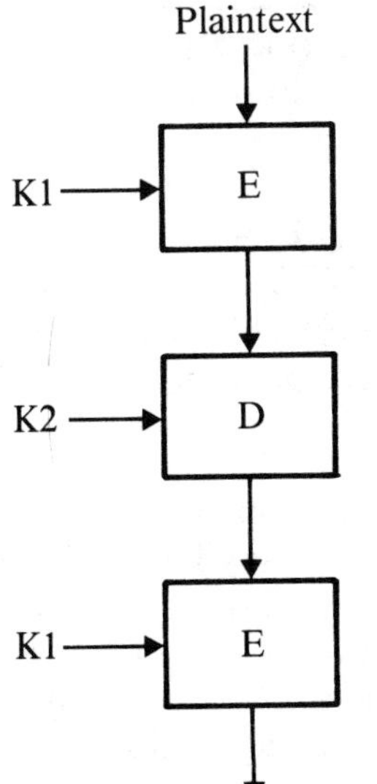

$E_{K1}(D_{K2}(E_{K1}(\text{Plaintext}))) = \text{Ciphertext}$

Note: $E_{K1}(D_{K2}(E_{K1}(\text{Plaintext}))) = E_{K1}(\text{Plaintext})$ when $K1 = K2$.

Figure D-11. Multiple Encryption Process with Migration Properties Using Two Independent Keys

phasizing the possible tradeoffs between them in terms of the storage requirements and time requirements needed to conduct the analysis. To show how such an attack, if it were possible, reduces the exhaustion work factor, let it be assumed that $E_K(P) = C$ (where C represents ciphertext) is available to an opponent who can select the plaintext, P.

The attacks discussed below are mostly of academic interest. As a practical matter, it appears that a viable business case cannot be made for development of a special purpose computer capable of key exhaustion, and storage of large tables, on the order of 2^{56} entries, is technically infeasible.

Reduction of Exhaustion Work Factor for Selected Plaintext Attack

Time-Memory Tradeoff: Approach 1

The time needed to attack a key after ciphertext C for selected plaintext P has been obtained (i.e., $C = E_K(P)$) can be minimized if a table of all plaintext and matching ciphertext is precomputed for each possible key (k1, k2, . . . , kn), where $n = 2^{56}$ as shown in Table D-4. All ciphertext values are then sorted and properly stored. Once this initial task is completed (which may require years or even hundreds of years depending upon the capability of the opponent), the attack against any key requires now a lengthy table lookup but no exhaustive encryption procedure since that was done beforehand. In this case the attack time against any key is drastically reduced at the expense of precomputing, sorting, and storing a table with 2^{56} entries.

k1	$E_{k1}(P) = C1$
k2	$E_{k2}(P) = C2$
⋮	⋮
kn	$E_{kn}(P) = Cn$

Table D-4. Precomputed Ciphertext Values for a Selected Plaintext, P, Using a Single Encryption Step

This attack is the most straightforward one and it trades maximum storage space for minimum time needed to attack any key once the appropriate cryptogram (i.e., $E_K(P)$) has been obtained. A variation of this procedure suggested by Professor Martin Hellman of Stanford University, at the 1977 National Computer Conference held in Anaheim, California, is possible by reducing storage requirements at the expense of computation time.

Time-Memory Tradeoff: Approach 2

Instead of storing $Ci = E_{Ki}(P)$ in a table together with Ki, a string of encryptions, say t, is performed for a selected starter key, ki, as shown in Figure D-12. Let there be T tables of m double word entries and let a key (randomly or systematically) selected out of the N possible keys ($N = 2^{56}$) be stored in the first word of each of the possible Tm table entries. (Note that t is related to computation time and m is related to memory size.)

Each key stored in the first word of each table entry is used to calculate a corresponding ciphertext (using t encryption processes as indicated in Figure D-12), which is stored in the second word of the table entry. Let the transformation shown in Figure D-12 be different for each of the T tables for reasons explained below. In that case, mt encryption steps are needed to create each table containing starter keys k1,1 through km,1 and corresponding ciphertext C1,t through Cm,t where each ciphertext is arrived at by encrypting a selected plaintext, P, a number of times, t, in the way shown in Figure D-12. After that the ciphertexts (C) are sorted for each of the T tables. This completes the process of precomputation.

The attack against an unknown key, K, proceeds as follows: If the obtained $Y1 = E_K(P)$ is equal to a table entry, $Cr,t = E_{kr,t}(P)$, then it can be concluded that K is equal to kr,t.[1] Since the seed key in that case is equal to kr,1 the unknown key, equal to kr,t, can be obtained by performing $t - 1$ encryption steps starting with kr,1 according to Figure D-12. (A different transform from 64 to 56 bits is used depending on which one of the T tables Cr,t is found in.) If $Y1 = E_K(P)$ is not found in any of the tables, Y1 (which is 64 bits long) is transformed with the T different transforms to create Y1trans1, Y1trans2, . . . , Y1transT (which are 56 bits long).

[1] To avoid unnecessary complexity, a third subscript to indicate a particular table is not introduced. It should be understood that the starter keys for each table are different (as well as the transformations).

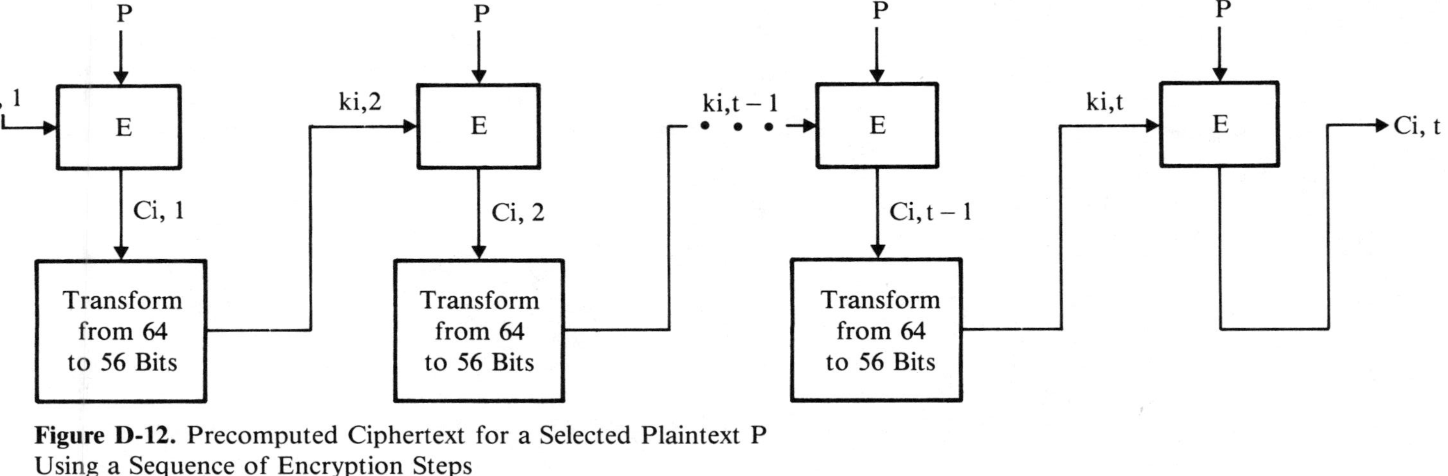

Figure D-12. Precomputed Ciphertext for a Selected Plaintext P Using a Sequence of Encryption Steps

P is next encrypted with Y1transl through Y1transT. If $E_{Y1trans1}(P)$ is equal to the value Cs,t in Table 1, then it can be concluded that ks,t − 1 is the correct key and that ks,1 is the corresponding seed key to generate ks,t − 1. To generate the correct key, ks,t − 1, requires, in this case, t − 2 encryption steps starting with ks,1 in addition to the T encryptions with Y1transl through Y1transT and the one to generate $E_K(P)$. If $E_{Y1trans1}(P)$ is not in table 1, a test is then made to determine if $E_{Y1trans2}(P)$ is in table 2; if $E_{Y1trans2}(P)$ is not in table 2, a test is then made to determine if $E_{Y1trans3}(P)$ is in table 3; and so on. If no match is found, then $E_{Y1trans1}(P)$ through $E_{Y1transT}(P)$ are transformed under their respective 64-bit to 56-bit transformations to produce Y2transl, Y2trans2, . . . , Y2transT and these values are used as keys to encrypt P to produce $E_{Y2trans1}(P)$, $E_{Y2trans2}(P)$, . . . , $E_{Y2transT}(P)$. Again, $E_{Y2trans1}(P)$ is checked against table 1, $E_{Y2trans2}(P)$ is checked against table 2, and so forth. If no match is found, the entire procedure is repeated until the t-1 encryptions are exhausted (i.e., the procedure ends with $E_{Yt\text{-}1trans1}(P)$, $E_{Yt\text{-}1trans2}(P)$, . . . , $E_{Yt\text{-}1transT}(P)$). In any case, if the correct key is kr,s, then there are s − 1 encryption steps performed starting with kr,1. In addition, there is the initial step to create $E_K(P)$ (which is performed on the system storing the secret key K) plus (t − s)T steps (maximum) to pinpoint the correct row (s in this case) in the precomputed T tables. Hence altogether there are (s − 1) + 1 + (t − s)T = s + (t − s)T encryption steps required.

The parameters mT (number of starter keys) and t (number of encryptions to arrive at C from the appropriate starter key) must be selected such that the key to be attacked can, for all practical purposes, be obtained with high probability. Since the total number of keys which come into play in the table generation process is equal to mtT, the attack will always succeed if all N possible keys (i.e., 2^{56} for DES) are present. To evaluate the probability, po(mt,N), that none of the N keys are missing in the mtT possible locations, the following approach can be taken.

From a probabilistic point of view the different mtT slots in the table generation process can be considered balls which are placed randomly into N cells. If a cell is not selected it means that the key corresponding to that cell cannot be obtained with this method. The probability, po(mtT,N), that all N cells are selected (i.e., that none of them is empty), is evaluated in reference 3 as follows.

$$\text{po}(\text{mtT},\text{N}) = \sum_{i=0}^{N} (-1)^i \binom{N}{i} [1 - (i/N)^{\text{mtT}}] \tag{D-6}$$

where

$$\binom{N}{i} = \frac{N!}{i!\,(N-i)!}$$

The direct numerical evaluation of the equation is practical only for the case of relatively small N and mtT. For larger values of interest, a good approximation can be found [3] if

$$\Delta = Ne^{-mtT/N} \quad \text{(D-7)}$$

remains bounded. Since this is the case here (as shown below) one can use

$$po(mtT,N) = e^{-\Delta} \quad \text{(D-8)}$$

Solving for mtT/N yields

$$mtT/N = \ln(N) - \ln\{\ln[1/po(mtT,N)]\} = \ln\{N/\ln[1/po(mtT,N)]\} \quad \text{(D-9)}$$

Choosing different values for N and po(mtT,N), the required ratio mtT/N can be evaluated. The results are shown in Table D-5. Note that $N = 2^{56}$, 2^{112}, and 2^{168} can be related to the situation where a time-memory tradeoff is used to attack single encryption, double encryption, and triple encryption, respectively. It is, however, shown below that double encryption can be attacked more efficiently with another exhaustive technique. For triple encryption, on the other hand, the work factor is so high that no viable exhaustion method is available.

It must be realized that Table D-5 covers the (unrealistic) case where it is possible to recover any key. In the practical situation, one is content with recovering a certain percentage of keys. Hence, in that case, it is not necessary to have all keys represented in the matrix of mtT entries. Let it therefore be assumed, that on the average, a certain fraction of the keys cannot be evaluated. In that case the ratio mtT/N can be smaller than the ones quoted in Table D-5. For example, the probability pr(mtT,N) that exactly r keys out of the total N keys are missing in the matrix of mtT entries can be evaluated as [3]

$$pr(mtT,N) = e^{-\Delta}\Delta^r/t!$$
$$\Delta = Ne^{-mtT/N}$$

This represents the Poisson distribution. The expected value of the number of keys that cannot be recovered is thus Δ with a variance also equal to Δ.

The expected (average) value of the fraction of keys which cannot be recovered is thus

$$E(r/N) = E(r)/N = \Delta/N = e^{-(mtT/N)} \quad \text{(D-10)}$$

and the variance is

$$\text{Var}\,(r/N) = \text{Var}\,(r)/N^2 = e^{-mtT/N}/N \quad \text{(D-11)}$$

As long as $E(r/N)/[\text{Var}(r/N)]^{0.5} \gg 1$ (i.e., $[Ne^{-mtT/N}]^{0.5} \gg 1$), the distribu-

	N		
po(mtT,N)	2^{56} ln(N) = 38.816	2^{112} ln(N) = 77.633	2^{168} ln(N) = 116.449
1/N	35.2	73.3	111.7
10^{-11}	35.5	74.3	113.1
10^{-10}	35.6	74.4	113.2
0.000001	36.2	74.9	113.7
0.00001	36.4	75.0	113.8
0.0001	36.6	75.4	114.2
0.001	36.9	75.7	114.5
0.01	37.3	76.1	114.9
0.1	38.0	76.8	115.6
0.25	38.5	77.3	116.1
0.5	39.2	78.0	116.8
0.75	40.1	78.9	117.7
0.9	41.1	79.9	118.7
0.99	43.4	82.2	121.0
0.999	45.7	84.5	123.3
0.9999	48.0	86.8	125.7
0.99999	50.3	89.1	128.0
0.999999	52.6	91.4	130.3
$1\text{-}10^{-10}$	61.8	93.7	132.6
$1\text{-}10^{-11}$	64.1	96.0	134.9
1--(1/N)	77.6	155.3	232.9

Legend:

mtT: Number of keys generated in the table generation procedure
N: Total number of possible key combinations
$mtT/N = \ln\{N/\ln[1/po(mtT,N)]\}$

Table D-5. Ratios mtT/N for Different Probabilities, po(mtT,N), of Having All Keys Present in the Precalculation Process

tion of r (Poisson) does not have to be considered. In that case the expected value alone (which is only a function of the ratio mtT/N) determines mtT/N.

Thus for a given expected value E(r/N) the quantity mtT/N can be evaluated as follows.

$$mtT/N = \ln[1/E(r/N)] \tag{D-12}$$

Some numerical results are given in Table D-6.

The difference between the results shown in Table D-5 and Table D-6 is as follows. In Table D-5 a value of mtT/N can be obtained as a function of the probability that all keys are represented in the precomputed matrix requiring mtT computations. In Table D-6 a value of mtT/N can be obtained as a function of the average fraction of nonrecoverable keys. Choosing, for

E(r/N) Fraction of Keys Which, on the Average, Cannot Be Obtained	mtT/N Total Number of Precalculations Divided by Total Number of Keys
10^{-11}	25.3
10^{-10}	23.0
0.000001	13.8
0.00001	11.5
0.0001	9.2
0.001	6.9
0.01	4.6
0.1	2.3
0.25	1.4
0.3679	1.0

Legend:

mtT: Number of keys generated in the table generation procedure

N: Total number of possible key combinations

mtT/N = ln[1/E(r/N)]

Table D-6. Ratio mtT/N for Different Average Fractions of Nonrecoverable Keys E(r/N)

example, mtT/N = 11.5, practically guarantees that 99.999% of the keys can be obtained (Table D-6).

The underlying assumption made so far is that all keys occur at random. To justify the assumption that keys are generated randomly requires that certain conditions for m and t are met to prevent (with high probability) the following situation from happening. Assume that a key is duplicated in two rows of one of the T tables (e.g., ki,r = kj,s). In that case this accidental equivalence of two row entries leads to an equivalence of the rest of the two rows.

To evaluate the probability of such an event, let pi represent the probability that all keys in row i are different from each other and are different also from the previously generated keys (i − 1)t. Thus

$$pi = \prod_{j=1}^{t} [N - (i-1)t - (j-1)]/N$$

Since the last term (j = t) represents the smallest factor, (N − it + 1)/N, which in turn is larger than [1 − (it/N)], a lower bound for pi can be found as follows.

$$pi > [1 - it/N)]^{t}$$

Taking the natural logarithm and approximating $\ln[1-(it/N)]$ with $(-it/N)$ results in

$$pi > e^{-(it^2/N)}; \qquad it/N \ll 1 \tag{D-13}$$

Since pi is close to one, the number of different keys in each of the T tables can be made close to mt by requiring that $mt^2 \ll N$. Furthermore, by choosing a different 64-bit to 56-bit transformation for each of the T tables it can also be assumed that the key generation processes in the different tables are statistically independent.

If the transformation selects 56 bits out of the 64 bits, there are actually $(64)(63)(62) \cdots (10)(9) = 64!/8!$ such transformations. With such a scheme accidental equivalence of two row entries in the different T matrices does not lead to an equivalence of the rest of the two rows. Thus choosing individual transformations for each table entry justifies the assumption of random generation of keys.

Now consider the problem from a different point of view. In principle, the relationship between mt and N is arbitrary. However, the ratio mt/N represents the average number of balls per cell (i.e., the average number of keys in the table generation process per possible key). If this ratio is excessively large, then there will probably be no empty cells (i.e., the attack will always work). In this case po(mt,N) is near unity. On the other hand, if mt/N tends to zero, then practically all cells must be empty (i.e., the attack will most likely not succeed). In this case po(mt,N) is near zero.

An approximation for this latter case can be derived as follows. Assuming that $mt \ll N$, one can also assume that all mt keys in the table generation process are different. The probability of finding the correct key is then mt/N. To increase the probability of success one could generate T tables. In that case the probability, q, of not finding the correct key is $q = [1-(mt/N)]^T$ provided that all keys in the T tables are different. (The justification for treating the key generation process in the different tables as independent is that each of them uses a different transformation.)

Taking the logarithm and using the fact that $mt^2 \ll N$ one arrives at

$$\ln(q) = T\ln(1-(mt/N)) = -mtT/N$$

$$q = e^{-mtT/N} \tag{D-14}$$

The probability of finding the correct key is $p = 1 - q$ and hence

$$p = 1 - e^{-mtT/N}; \qquad mt \ll N$$

This is the same result obtained in Equation D-12. Solving for mtT/N one obtains

$$mtT/N = \ln(1/q)$$

The Meet-in-the-Middle Attack Against Double Encryption

Method Using an Off-Line Attack

Let $Y = E_{K2} E_{K1}(X)$ represent the double encryption scheme to be analyzed where K1 and K2 are independently chosen as shown in Figure D-13. Assuming, as before, that selected plaintext, P, can be used, a table of ciphertext $E_{ki}(P)$ is constructed for all possible keys, after which the ciphertext is sorted (see also Table D-4). To evaluate the unknown keys, the given Y (i.e., P enciphered under the unknown keys K1 and K2) is decrypted with a trial key, $D_{K2trial}(Y)$, and the value is located in the aforementioned table. The corresponding key from the selected table entry is the trial key for K1 (i.e., K1trial). It is clear that $E_{K2trial}E_{K1trial}(P) = Y$ by design. To check if K1trial is indeed equal to K1 and K2trial is indeed equal to K2, some additional pairs of plaintext and corresponding ciphertext (in the order of ten) must be used. This can be done by encrypting additional plaintext (arbitrary in this case) with the unknown keys. If these additional pairs can also be generated with K1trial and K2trial the keys are accepted as correct. Otherwise, the procedure is repeated.

This attack requires precomputation and sorting of 2^{56} ciphertexts (as in Table D-4) as was the case in the attack against a single encryption scheme. In addition, about 2^{55} trial values, $D_{K2trial}(Y)$, must be generated which are used to determine a candidate for K1 (i.e., K1trial) before the correct keys are determined. To evaluate the actual work factor also requires taking into account the sorting procedure and table lookup time to find the match of

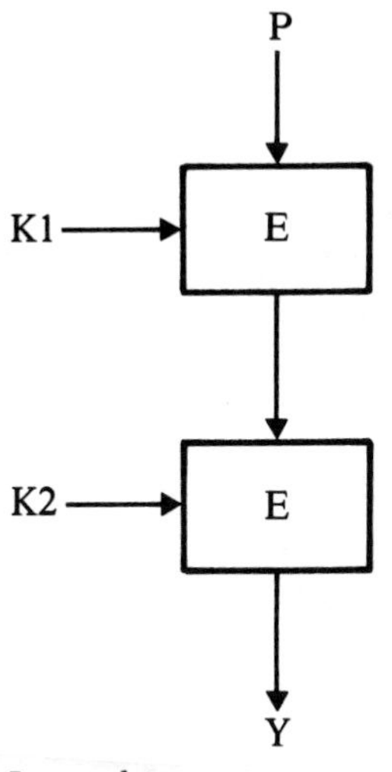

Legend:
P = Plaintext
$Y = E_{K2}(E_{K1}(P))$ = Ciphertext

Figure D-13. Double Encryption Process

$E_{K1trial}(P)$ with $D_{K2trial}(Y)$. But, importantly, it is possible to do all this on a system that is under the control of the opponent (off-line attack).

Method Using Combinations of Off-Line and On-Line Attacks

A reduction of the exhaustion time (after ciphertext for selected plaintext is obtained) to attack a key is possible at the expense of additional precomputations. These precomputations, however, must be done on the system that contains the key or keys to be attacked (on-line attack).

Assume that an input (PP for plaintext to be doubly encrypted) is used in a double encryption scheme to yield a known bit pattern P as an intermediate result as suggested by Figure D-14. Let YY be the ciphertext obtained using PP and a method of double encryption. Since PP and YY are corresponding pairs of plaintext and ciphertext for double encryption, there is only a certain set of keys (K1 and K2) which satisfy the condition that the intermediate result is equal to a selected value, P.

To evaluate the set of these keys, a relationship between K1 and PP and between K2 and YY must be established. To do this two tables are created as shown in Table D-7. Each of the quantities PPi [Table D-7 (a)] are doubly encrypted with the (unknown) keys K1 and K2, which are to be evaluated. But since unknown keys are involved, this set (in contrast to the ones in Table D-7) must be created on the system that contains K1 and K2. In other words, an on-line attack is necessary to generate the needed quantities enumerated in Table D-8.

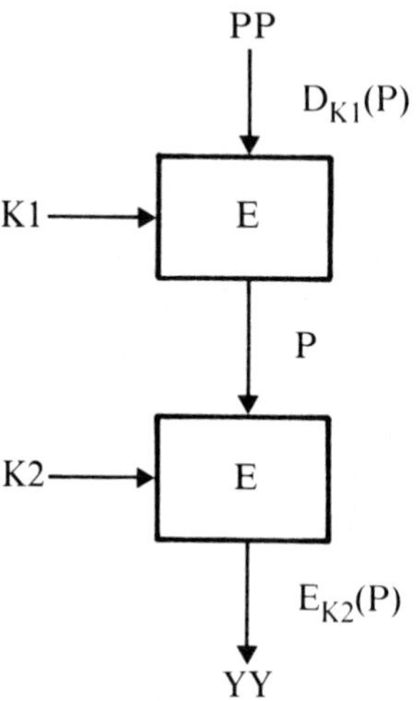

Legend:
PP = Chosen Plaintext
YY = $E_{K2}(E_{K1}(PP))$ = Corresponding Ciphertext

Figure D-14. Generation of Selected Plaintext Set (PP) for On-Line Attack on Double Encryption

(a)		(b)	
k1	$D_{k1}(P) = PP1$	k1	$E_{k1}(P) = C1$
k2	$D_{k2}(P) = PP2$	k2	$E_{k2}(P) = C2$
⋮	⋮ ⋮	⋮	⋮ ⋮
kN	$D_{kN}(P) = PPN$	kN	$E_{kN}(P) = CN$

Note: The entries in the table can be obtained on a system different from the one in which the keys to be attacked are installed.

Table D-7. Relationship Between Plaintext (PP), Ciphertext (C), and Keys (k1, . . . , kN) for a Given Selected Intermediate Result (P)

Table D-8 can now be used to find a trial key K1trial determined by PP [with the aid of Table D-7 (a)] and a trial key K2trial determined by YY = C [with the aid of Table D-7 (b)] for each PP/YY pair in Table D-8. In each case the relationship $E_{K1trial}(PP) = P$, $D_{K2trial}(YY) = P$, and $E_{K1trial}E_{K2trial}(PP) = YY$ holds. To check for the correct keys (i.e., if K1trial = K1 and K2trial = K2), additional plaintext and corresponding ciphertext values must be used as discussed above.

Since Table D-8 contains a large set of PP/YY pairs, these table entries could also be used to do the actual checking. To summarize, the attack takes place as follows.

1. All N (2^{56}) keys are exhausted to generate a table [Table D-7 (a)] whose entries are {ki, $D_{ki}(P) = PPi$; i = 1, 2, . . . , N}. Since in the on-line attack these PP values are used as selected plaintext against the double encryption method, the table does not have to be sorted. (Note that one PP value after the other can be used as originally generated.)
2. All N (2^{56}) keys are exhausted to generate a table [Table D-7 (b)] whose entries are {ki, $E_{ki}(P) = Ci$; i = 1, 2, . . . , N}. The C values must

PP1	$E_{K2}E_{K1}(PP1) = YY1$
PP2	$E_{K2}E_{K1}(PP2) = YY2$
⋮	⋮ ⋮ ⋮
PPN	$E_{K2}E_{K1}(PPN) = YYN$

Note: The entries in the table can only be obtained on the system which allows operations with the unknown keys (K1 and K2) to be performed.

Table D-8. Relationship Between Selected Plaintext Set (PP) and Corresponding Ciphertext Set (YY) for Double Encryption

be sorted to locate the proper entry satisfying the condition YY = C. in step 5 below.

3. All N (2^{56}) PP values created in step 1 are now used as selected plaintext in the double encryption scheme to be attacked. The resulting ciphertext values are recorded serially in a table where entries are {PPi, $E_{k2} E_{k1}$ (PPi) = YYi; i = 1, 2, . . . , N}. Since K1 and K2 are the actual keys, the entries in this table can only be created on the system which allows operations with K1 and K2 to be performed (on-line attack).
4. From Table D-7 (a) the key associated with PP1 is identified with K1trial.
5. From Table D-7 (b) the key associated with YY1 = Cj is identified with K2trial provided that such a match occurs.
6. A sufficient number of PP/YY pairs are selected from Table D-8. (e.g., ten) to check if K1trial = K1 and K2trial = K2. This is done by doubly encrypting each of the selected PP values with K1trial and K2trial and checking for equality with the corresponding YY values. Only if all tests are positive are the keys K1trial and K2trial accepted as being correct. Otherwise, Steps 4, 5, and 6 are repeated using PP2 and YY2 next, thence PP3 and YY3, and so on; in which case, at each iteration different keys for K1trial and K2trial are selected (steps 4 and 5) and tested (step 6).

The major disadvantage of this method is the requirement of an on-line attack to create Table D-8 (step 3). As a matter of fact, it can be stated that such an attack is not a viable one since it will take an enormous amount of time to create such a table. A special purpose computer cannot be used, since the attack must take place on the system wherein the keys to be attacked have been installed. Furthermore, this activity must continually be conducted in secrecy if it is to be of any value.

The reason for this discussion is to highlight a concept. If precomputation is performed on a system under the control of an opponent (which allows the use of special purpose computers), then there exists at least the possibility of a meaningful time-memory tradeoff. On the other hand, if precomputation must also involve the use of the system to be attacked to any significant degree, then such an attack is really only of academic value and thus not of much practical interest.

Thus the most viable attack against double encryption is the one discussed above using an off-line attack. This involves creating a table of 2^{56} sorted entries and about 2^{55} encryption steps using a selected plaintext/ciphertext pair.

Attack Against Triple Encryption With Three Independent Keys

To attack the triple encryption scheme of Figure D-15 using a combination of on-line and off-line attacks, the basic ideas discussed to attack a double encryption scheme (Figure D-14) also apply. The fundamental concept re-

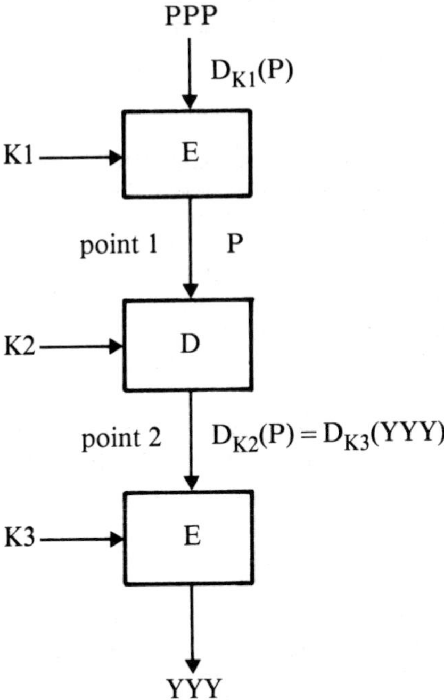

Figure D-15. Generation of Selected Plaintext Set (PPP) for On-Line Attack on Triple Encryption

quires that a preselected intermediate value P exist, as shown in Figure D-15. Going backwards, this allows the generation of a set of preselected plaintext (PPP) for any possible key (K1). This is accomplished by creating the entries in Table D-9 (see also Table D-7).

The same table can be used to determine the result at point 2 in Figure D-15 for any selected trial key K2trial. Thus only one table is needed here in contrast to the attack on double encryption (Table D-7). This is because the double encryption method of Figure D-14 employs the E-E operation whereas the triple encryption method of Figure D-15 uses the E-D-E operation. (This is the security price paid, although a small one, for the migration property.)

k1	$D_{k1}(P)$	= PPP1
k2	$D_{k2}(P)$	= PPP2
⋮	⋮	⋮
kN	$D_{kN}(P)$	= PPPN

Note: The entries in the table can be obtained on a system different from the one in which the keys to be obtained are installed.

Table D-9. Relationship Between Plaintext (PPP) and Keys (k1, k2, . . . , kN) for a Given Selected Intermediate Plaintext (P)

PPP1	$E_{K3}D_{K2}E_{K1}$(PPP1) = YYY1	
PPP2	$E_{K3}D_{K2}E_{K1}$(PPP2) = YYY2	
⋮	⋮	⋮
PPPN	$E_{K3}D_{K2}E_{K1}$(PPPN) = YYYN	

Note: The entries in the table can only be obtained on the system to be attacked (i.e., on the system where encryptions/decryptions under the unknown keys K1, K2, and K3 can be performed). This requirement puts the attack into the class of attacks that are of academic interest only (i.e., the attack is not viable).

Table D-10. Relationship Between Selected Plaintext Set (PPP) and Corresponding Ciphertext Set (YYY) for Triple Encryption

Each of the PPPi quantities in Table D-9 are next used as input data and triply encrypted with the (unknown) keys K1, K2, and K3. But since the unknown keys are involved, this set (in contrast to Table D-9) must be created on the system that contains K1, K2, K3. In other words, an on-line attack is necessary to generate the needed quantities enumerated in Table D-10.

This attack falls into the category described in Reference 4. Since the groundwork to understand this attack has already been de cribed in the previous section, only a summary of the attack is given here.

1. All N (2^{56}) keys are exhausted to generate a table (Table D-9) whose entries are {ki, D_{ki}(P) = PPPi; i = 1, 2, . . . , N}. Since in the on-line attack these PPP values are used as selected plaintext against the triple encryption method, the table does not have to be sorted. This establishes the set {PPPi; i = 1, 2, . . . , N} to be used in the selected plaintext on-line attack. Since the second operation is a decrypt operation in the multiple encryption scheme, the same table can be used to predict the output at point 2 (Figure D-15). This requires Table D-9 to be sorted.
2. All N (2^{56}) PPP values created in step 1 are now used as selected plaintext in the triple encryption scheme to be attacked. The resulting ciphertext values are recorded serially in a table whose entries are {PPPi, $E_{K3}D_{K2}E_{K1}$ (PPPi) = YYYi; i = 1, 2, . . . , N}. Since K1, K2, and K3 are the actual keys, the entries in this table can only be created on the system which allows operations with K1, K2, K3 to be performed (on-line attack).
3. A value for K3trial is selected and used to decrypt YYY1 to create $D_{K3trial}$(YYY1). Using this value with the table created in step 1 (Table D-9), a match is sought and if found identifies the corresponding key as K2trial. If no match is found, another K3trial is selected

and the procedure repeated. The possible values of K3trial are thus exhausted until a value is found such that $D_{K3trial}$(YYY1) matches some PPP value in Table D-9. If a match is found, the procedure continues with steps 4 and 5. If steps 4 and 5 fail to recover K1, K2, and K3, then step 3 is continued. That is, values of K3trial are again selected and tested until all N (2^{56}) trial values have been exhausted. At this point, the trial ciphertext YYY1 is discarded and step 3 is repeated using ciphertext YYY2 (i.e., the 2^{56} K3trial keys are again tested, if necessary, using YYY2 as the trial ciphertext). If YYY2 fails to recover the keys K1, K2, and K3, then YYY3 is used, and so on. Eventually a value of YYY, say YYYi, will be tested that allows K1, K2, and K3 to be recovered. This will occur, on the average, after 2^{55} YYY values have been tested. Note that up to this point 2^{56} K3trial keys are tested for each trial YYY value.

4. From Table D-9, the key associated with PPPi (PPP1 if YYY1 is the ciphertext selected at step 3, PPP2 if YYY2 is selected at step 3, and so on) is identified with K1trial.
5. A sufficient number of PPP/YYY pairs are selected from Table D-10 (e.g., ten) to check if K1trial = K1, K2trial = K2, and K3trial = K3. This is done by triply encrypting each of the selected PPP values with K1trial, K2trial, and K3trial. By checking for equality with the corresponding YYY values, a decision can be made to accept or reject the trial keys. Only if all tests are positive are the keys accepted as being correct. Otherwise, step 3 is continued until another match is found, whereupon steps 4 and 5 are again repeated.

Therefore the attack against three independent keys requires:

1. Generating and sorting a table of 2^{56} entries via an off-line attack (i.e., Table D-9).
2. Generation of 2^{56} related plaintext and corresponding ciphertext values via an on-line attack (i.e., Table D-10).
3. Generation of 2^{56} candidates for K3 for about 2^{55} PPP/YYY pairs, which must take place after the on-line attack is completed.
4. Test for correctness of trial keys via selected elements in Table D-10.

Thus the attack takes in the order of 2^{56} words of memory and 2^{112} operations. The described attack is presented only to illustrate exhaustion of E-D-E using three independent keys. Other more advantageous tradeoffs between memory space and computation time are very likely possible.

Attack Against Triple Encryption with Two Independent Keys

In this case K1 = K3, so that a selected PPP also determines K1 and K3. Thus trial keys for K3 do not have to be generated. Hence the 2^{56} trials to arrive at the correct K3 can be eliminated, and the attack reduces to:

1. Generate and sort a table of 2^{56} entries (i.e., Table D-9).
2. Generate 2^{56} selected plaintext and corresponding ciphertext values in an on-line attack (i.e., Table D-10).
3. Select PPP1/YYY1. The value of PPP1 is used with Table D-9 to determine k1, which is the value for K1trial. YYY1 is deciphered under K1trial and a check is made to see if $D_{K1trial}$(YYY1) matches some value of PPP (say PPPj) in Table D-9. If a match occurs, then the value of PPPj determines a key, kj, where kj becomes the trial key K2trial. K1trial and K2trial are then tested via selected elements in Table D-10 (e.g., 10) created in step 2 (i.e., the plaintext PPP is triply encrypted using K1trial and K2trial and the result is compared for equality with the corresponding ciphertext YYY). If there is ciphertext agreement, then K1trial and K2trial are accepted as K1 and K2. Otherwise, reject K1trial and K2trial and repeat step 3 using PPP2/YYY2. If PPP2/YYY2 fails to recover K1 and K2, then step 3 is repeated using PPP3/YYY3, and so on. Eventually (after about 2^{55} trials) a PPPi/YYYi will be found that recovers K1 and K2.

Thus the attack takes in the order of 2^{56} words of memory and 2^{55} operations.

REFERENCES

1. Diffie, W. and Hellman, M. E., "New Directions in Cryptography," *IEEE Transactions on Information Theory,* **IT-22**, No. 6, 644–654 (1976).
2. Matyas, S. M. and Meyer, C. H., *Cryptographic System Using Multiple Encipherment,* Filed US Patent Office (June 1980).
3. Feller, W., *An Introduction to Probability Theory and Its Applications,* Third Edition, Wiley, New York, 1968.
4. Hellman, M. E. and Merkle, R. C., "On the Security of Multiple Encryption," *Communications of the ACM,* **24**, No. 7, 465–467 (July 1981).

APPENDIX E

Cryptographic PIN Security—Proposed ANSI Method[1]

STORAGE OF PINS

When stored, the PIN must always be encrypted. Encryption for PIN storage may be reversible or irreversible.[2] The encryption must conform to the following requirements:

1. The Data Encryption Algorithm (DEA) is used with a 56-bit secret cryptographic key composed of 56 random bits.[3]
2. PIN encryption (reversible or irreversible) must incorporate the account number (or some other card or account related data), or a portion thereof, in such a way that the verification process would provide detection of substitution of one stored value for another stored value.

When derived PINs are calculated for use in verification, any temporary or transient computer storage area used in the calculation must be cleared immediately after use.

TRANSMISSION OF PINS

Whenver the PIN is electronically transmitted, it must be provided with a high level of protection. This protection may be provided through physical means whenever the transmission medium (wire, cable, fiber-optics, etc.) or network nodes can be physically protected. Whenever the communica-

[1] The material in this appendix is based on an ANSI (American National Standards Institute) Draft Standard for PIN Identification Number Management and Security [1], which is subject to change.

[2] *Reversible encryption* is defined as a cryptographic transformation of plaintext to ciphertext such that the ciphertext can be converted back to the original plaintext. *Irreversible encryption* is defined as a cryptographic transformation of plaintext to ciphertext such that the ciphertext cannot be converted back to the original plaintext by other than exhaustive procedures.

[3] The DEA is the ANSI equivalent of the DES.

tion medium and/or network nodes cannot be physically protected (e.g., common carrier facilities, circuit switched facilities, EDP facilities), the PIN is cryptographically protected using the DEA. Additional requirements to assure that the PIN has not been replaced or modified during transmission will be set forth in another ANSI document.

In an interchange environment, the minimum level of protection provided to the PIN anywhere in the path of transmission is to be equal to the highest level required by any financial institution whose liability for a financial transaction can be affected by the misuse of the PIN.

Reversible PIN Encryption

For the purpose of security of the PIN between financial institutions, DEA shall be used in a reversible encryption mode as specified by the technique described in this section. The technique specifies the number, position, and function of bits within a 64-bit block used as input to the DEA operating in the Electronic Code Book (ECB) mode (64 bits in, 64 bits out). The 64-bit output of the DEA is transmitted (or stored in the case of file protection) in its entirety.

Cleartext PIN Block Format

The PIN is assumed to consist of 4–12 decimal digits which the customer enters, with the first digit entered referred to as digit 1 and the last referred to as digit N. The cleartext PIN format specified must be used in interchange and may be used in the terminal to acquirer segment of the network. Bit positions are specified based on numbering the bits in the DEA input block, i.e., 1 to 64 from left to right.

The cleartext PIN and customer's account number are constructed as follows:

PIN Block Construction

Bit	1	5	9	13	17	21	25	29	33	37	41	45	49	53	57	61	64
	C	N	P	P	P	P/F	P/F	P/F	P/F	P/F	P/F	P/F	P/F	P/F	F	F	

C - Control field. Currently, the only defined value is 0000 (binary) which designates the block as containing 4 to 12 four-bit decimal PIN digits representing user-entered characters. Further use of different values of this field could accommodate different character sets.

N - PIN length entered field. Four-bit binary number with permissible values of 0100 (=4) to 1100 (=12).

P - PIN digit. Four-bit field having possible values from 0000 to 1001 (the binary representation of the decimal numbers 0 through 9).

F - Fill digit. A hexadecimal digit "F" (1111 binary) which must not depend upon PIN value.

P/F - PIN digit or fill digit, as determined by PIN length entered field (N).

Account Number Block Construction

Bit	1	5	9	13	17	21	25	29	33	37	41	45	49	53	57	61 64
	0	0	0	0	A1	A2	A3	A4	A5	A6	A7	A8	A9	A10	A11	A12

A - The first 12 digits of the account number where A12 is the least significant digit (right-most) and A1 is the most significant digit (left-most). Account number check digits are excluded.

0 - A decimal pad digit-zero. The first four-bit fields of the account number block are always padded with this value.

Next the PIN and account number blocks are Exclusive-ORed and the result is transferred to the DEA input register. Any network or interchange node having access to the cleartext PIN block (i.e., during a decryption/reencryption or during PIN verification) should reject transactions having any of the following:

1. Initially a PIN format field of value other than 0.
2. A PIN length field of value less than 4 or greater than 12.
3. Any PIN digit from P1 through PN of value greater than 9 (binary 1001).

This serves as a reasonableness check on PIN encryption/decryption processing but does not serve as any indication of validity of the customer-entered PIN.

Ciphertext PIN Format

The formatted cleartext PIN block, defined above, is then encrypted using the DEA in Electronic Codebook Mode (ECB). The 64-bit output cipher block is called the reversibly encrypted PIN (or encrypted PIN). The encrypted PIN is transmitted between financial institutions as a 64-bit entity in bit-oriented communications, as eight 8-bit bytes in 8-bit transparent character oriented communications, as sixteen characters representing hexadecimal digits (0, 1, . . . , 9, A, . . . , F), or by any other data representation agreed upon by sender and receiver.

The order of transmission is from left to right. For example, in 8-bit transparent communications the first byte transmitted will contain bits 1 through 8 of the DEA output block; the eighth byte will contain bits 57 through 64 of the DEA output block.

Received Ciphertext PIN

The receiver collects the 64-bit encrypted PIN as transmitted and enters it into the decrypting DEA device which must contain the same cryptographic key that was used to encrypt it. The decrypted PIN must then be physically protected while it is being verified or while it is being reencrypted using a different cryptographic key.

A PIN that does not verify must not be accepted. The entire transaction must be suspect until a PIN is received from the acquiring source that does verify in its entirety.

REFERENCES

1. *American National Standard for Personal Identification Number Mangement and Security, Draft Standard*, American National Standards Institute, Technical Committee X9.A3, Revision 5 (November 5, 1980).

APPENDIX F

Analysis of the Number of Meaningful Messages in a Redundant Language

A language is *redundant* whenever for some value N it can be shown that not all possible sequences of N characters occur with equal probability. That English is a redundant language is easily demonstrated by examining the probabilities of individual letters: p(A) = .080, p(B) = .015, . . . , p(Z) = .001 (based on a count of individual letters in a large sample of English text, see Table 12-1). Similar nonuniform distributions are observed for digrams, trigrams, and longer phrases. For example, the phrase "Hit th_ ball" (where _ denotes a missing letter) is clearly understood to mean "Hit the ball," which demonstrates that the various choices for the missing letter (and the resulting phrases upon substitution) are not equally likely.

If the 26-character English alphabet (no blanks) is reduced to a 2-character alphabet consisting of a vowel marker ("v") and a consonant marker ("c"), where vowels = {A, E, I, O, U}, the resulting language is also redundant. Table F-1 contains vowel and consonant N-grams for English ($N \leqslant 5$).

An approximation for the number of meaningful messages of N characters can be obtained by using a discrete Markov process to simulate the creation of text. A discrete Markov process consists of a finite number of states, q1, q2, . . . , qn, and a set of transition probabilities $\{p_i(j)\}$, where $p_i(j)$ represents the probability that the system will go to state qj given that it is in the state qi. If each state transition produces an output symbol, the Markov process can be treated as an information source that produces a stream of output characters.

For an nth order Markov process, the probability that a given character will be the next one depends on the previous n output characters, but not on characters preceeding those. Conforming to this model, a Jth order Markov approximation for message probability is given by

$$p(a_1 a_2 \ldots a_N) \simeq p(a_1 a_2 \ldots a_J) \prod_{i=J+1}^{N} p_{B_i}(a_i) \qquad \text{(F-1)}$$

where

$p(a_1 a_2 \ldots a_N)$ is the probability of message $a_1 a_2 \ldots a_N$,

5-gram		4-gram		3-gram		2-gram		1-gram	
VVVVV	7								
VVVVC	165	VVVV	172						
VVVCV	2476								
VVVCC	5417	VVVC	7893	VVV	8065				
VVCVV	8500								
VVCVC	65543	VVCV	74043						
VVCCV	74499								
VVCCC	57585	VVCC	132084	VVC	206127	VV	214192		
VCVVV	3634								
VCVVC	89792	VCVV	93426						
VCVCV	200227								
VCVCC	260828	VCVC	461055	VCV	554481				
VCCVV	65403								
VCCVC	387921	VCCV	453314						
VCCCV	220012								
VCCCC	82956	VCCC	302968	VCC	756292	VC	1310773	V	1524965
CVVVV	167								
CVVVC	7729	CVVV	7896						
CVVCV	71580								
CVVCC	126698	CVVC	198278	CVV	206174				
CVCVV	84927								
CVCVC	395481	CVCV	480408						
CVCCV	378868								
CVCCC	245362	CVCC	624230	CVC	1104638	CV	1310812		
CCVVV	4266								
CCVVC	108434	CCVV	112700						
CCVCV	280141								
CCVCC	363438	CCVC	643579	CCV	756279				
CCCVV	47306								
CCCVC	255599	CCCV	302905						
CCCCV	82943								
CCCCC	22096	CCCC	105039	CCC	407944	CC	1164223	C	2475035

Based on a sample of 8000 excerpts of 504 letters taken from the Brown University Corpus of Present-Day American English [1]. Vowels = { A, E, I, O, U }.

Table F-1. Vowel-Consonant N-gram Frequencies in 4 Million Characters of English Text (N⩽5)

$p_{B_i}(a_i)$ is the conditional probability that character a_i follows block B_i, and

$B_i = a_{i-J} a_{i-J+1} \ldots a_{i-1}$ is a block of J characters.

The symbol $\simeq$ denotes approximately equal to.

In a zero-order approximation, output characters are independent. Hence, for a zero-order approximation, message probability can be expressed by

$$p(a_1 a_2 \ldots a_N) \simeq \prod_{i=1}^{N} p(a_i) \tag{F-2}$$

where $p(a_i)$ is the probability that character a_i appears next. For example, with the values for p(a) given in Table 12-1, the probability for the word CIPHER is approximated by

$$\begin{aligned} p(\text{CIPHER}) &\simeq p(C)p(I)p(P)p(H)p(E)p(R) \\ &\simeq (.031)(.073)(.020)(.055)(.125)(.061) \\ &\simeq 1.90 \times 10^{-8} \end{aligned}$$

Suppose that the word CIPHER is reduced to its corresponding vowel-consonant pattern, cvccvc. A first-order approximation for the probability of cvccvc is given by

$$p(\text{cvccvc}) \simeq p(c)p_c(v)p_v(c)p_c(c)p_c(v)p_v(c)$$

Using the N-gram frequencies in Table F-1, it follows that

$$\begin{aligned} p(c) &\simeq 2{,}475{,}035/4{,}000{,}000 = .619 \\ p_c(v) &\simeq 1{,}310{,}812/2{,}475{,}035 = .530 \\ p_v(c) &\simeq 1{,}310{,}773/1{,}524{,}965 = .860 \\ p_c(c) &\simeq 1{,}164{,}223/2{,}475{,}035 = .470 \end{aligned}$$

and therefore p(cvccvc) is computed as

$$\begin{aligned} p(\text{cvccvc}) &\simeq p(c)p_c(v)p_v(c)p_c(c)p_c(v)p_v(c) \\ &\simeq (.619)(.530)(.860)(.470)(.530)(.860) = .060 \end{aligned}$$

An approximation for the number of meaningful messages in message space $\underline{X}$ can be obtained using the zero-order approximation of message probability given by Equation F-2. When message length (N) is very large, each message will contain about Np1 occurrences of the first character, Np2 occurrences of the second character, and so on. Hence for very large N, most messages will have roughly the same probability, p, i.e.,

$$p \simeq p1^{Np1}p2^{Np2} \ldots pn^{Npn} \tag{F-3}$$

where n is the number of different characters.

If s is the number of different sequences with probability p, then s is approximated by

$$\begin{aligned} s &\simeq 1/p \\ &\simeq p1^{-Np1}p2^{-Np2} \ldots pn^{-Npn} \\ &\simeq \prod_{i=1}^{n} 1/pi^{Npi} \end{aligned}$$

$$\simeq 2^{\left[\log_2 \prod_{i=1}^{n} pi^{-Npi}\right]}$$

$$\simeq 2^{\left[-N \sum_{i=1}^{n} pi \log_2 pi\right]}$$

$$\simeq 2^{NG_1}$$

where

$$G_1 = -\sum_{i=1}^{n} pi \log_2 pi \tag{F-4}$$

is called the *entropy per character* for the message source.

Using the values for p(a) in Table 12-1, the value for G_1 is computed as 4.17. Moreover, using this value for G_1 allows the zero-order approximation of s, given by Equation F-4, to be written as

$$s = 2^{N4.17}$$

When a higher-order approximation for message probability is used (see Equation F-1), it is possible to obtain a correspondingly higher-order approximation for s. Before this result can be derived, a few terms must be defined.

Let U be a discrete probability space in which the elementary events {u1}, {u2}, . . . , {un} have probabilities p(u1), p(u2), . . . , p(un). The *entropy* of U is defined as

$$H(U) = -\sum_{u} p(u)\log_2 p(u) \tag{F-5}$$

(The notation, $\sum_{u}$, means that the summation is over all elements u in the set U.)

H is an information theoretic measure of uncertainty which can vary between the limits 0 and $\log_2 n$, where n is the total number of elements in the probability space U. It can be shown that H(U) = 0 if and only if there is a single u in U such that p(u) = 1. Consequently, when there is a single u in U such that p(u) = 1, so that no uncertainty exists over which event in U will occur, the measure H(U) has the value zero. But H(U) = 0 is interpreted to mean that there is no uncertainty over which event in U will occur. Moreover, it can be shown that H(U) = $\log_2 n$ if and only if each of the n elements in U is equally probable. Consequently, when there is maximum uncertainty over which event in U will occur, the measure H(U) is maximized.

When the entropy measure H is applied to the message (plaintext), transformation (key), and cryptogram (ciphertext) spaces, the following interpretation is obtained. $H(\underline{X})$ and $H(\underline{K})$ represent the uncertainty over which message and key were used during encipherment; $H(\underline{Y})$ represents the uncertainty over which cryptogram was produced.

Let G_N represent the *entropy per character of blocks of N characters.* G_N is expressed as

$$G_N = -\frac{1}{N}\sum_{B} p(B)\log_2 p(B) \tag{F-6}$$

where

B is a block of N characters, and

p(B) is the probability that B is produced by the message source.

Let the union of U and V be a joint discrete probability space. The conditional entropy of U given v, an element of V, is defined as

$$H(U|v) = -\sum_{u} p(u|v)\log_2 p(u|v) \tag{F-7}$$

where $p(u|v)$ is the conditional probability of u given v. The *average conditional entropy of* U *given* V, or the *equivocation of* U *given* V is defined as

$$H(U|V) = \sum_{v} p(v)H(U|v) \tag{F-8}$$

Conditional entropy and equivocation have the following meanings when applied to enciphering systems. $H(\underline{X}|y)$ measures the uncertainty regarding which message in $\underline{X}$ was enciphered to produce cryptogram y. $H(\underline{X}|\underline{Y})$, on the other hand, measures this same uncertainty, except that it is averaged over all possible cryptograms. $H(\underline{X}|\underline{Y}) = 0$ may be interpreted to mean that regardless of the particular cryptogram y there is no uncertainty regarding which message produced it. Moreover, $H(\underline{X}|\underline{Y}) = 0$ implies that $H(\underline{X}|y) = 0$ for each cryptogram in $\underline{Y}$.

The conditional entropy of the message source is a measure of the uncertainty regarding the nature of the Nth character given that the previous $N - 1$ characters are known. As N increases, this measure accounts for more and more of the interdependencies between characters.

Let

$$F_N = -\sum_{B,a} p(B, a)\log_2 p_B(a) \tag{F-9}$$

where

B is a block of $N - 1$ characters,

a is a single character following B,

p(B, a) is the probability of N-gram (B, a), and

$p_B(a)$ is the conditional probability that character a follows block B and is equal to $p(B, a)/p(B)$.

From Equations F-6 and F-9, it follows that

$$F_N = NG_N - (N-1)G_{N-1} \tag{F-10}$$

G_N and F_N are two different measures which allow the entropy per character of a message source to be evaluated. It can be shown that both G_N and F_N are monotonically decreasing with N and bounded below by 0. Moreover, according to [2, Theorem 5], the limit of G_N, as N approaches infinity (∞), exists and is equal to R, called the *rate of the language,*

$$\lim_{N \to \infty} G_N = R \tag{F-11}$$

and, moreover, according to [2, Theorem 6]

$$F_N \leqslant G_N \tag{F-12a}$$

and

$$\lim_{N \to \infty} F_N = R \tag{F-12b}$$

From the asymptotic equipartition property [2, Appendix 3], it can be shown that when a Jth-order approximation to message probability is used and $N \gg J$, then most sequences produced by the message source will have the same probability of occurrence, p, and the number of different sequences, s, with probability p is approximated by

$$s = 1/p = 2^{NF_{J+1}} \tag{F-13}$$

(The notation $\gg$ means much greater than.) According to the asymptotic equipartition property, for all practical purposes, the possible messages of N characters can be divided into two groups: one group of high and fairly uniform probability, the second group of negligibly small total probability. The high probability group consists of those messages that are intelligible or meaningful. It contains approximately $2^{NF_{J+1}}$ sequences. The low probability group contains those messages that are meaningless.

Actually, the Equation F-13 demonstrates that s is a function of message length, N, and the order of the approximation of message probability, J. This relationship can be expressed notationally by defining $s_{N,J}$ as

$$s_{N,J} = 2^{NF_{J+1}} \tag{F-14}$$

The following interpretation of $s_{N,J}$ can now be made with respect to cryptanalysis. The situation in which F_{J+1} is used to compute s (i.e., when a Jth-order approximation of message probability is employed) is comparable to the situation where the analyst has no more than (J + 1)-grams, or (J + 1)-order statistics, available to attack the system. Consequently, if digrams are used to attack an enciphering system, then the number of meaningful messages that the analyst must cope with ought to be 2^{NF_2}. The cryptographer or designer of a cryptographic system, on the other hand, is interested in knowing what is the minimum number of meaningful messages that the analyst must always cope with. This number applies, of course, when the analyst is able to employ high-order statistics to attack the system. From Equations F-12b and F-14, it follows that

$$\lim_{J \to \infty} s_{N,J} = 2^{NR}; N \geqslant J \tag{F-15}$$

where

$$s_{N,0} \geqslant s_{N,1} \geqslant \cdots \geqslant s_{N,J} \geqslant s_{N,J+1} \geqslant \cdots \geqslant 2^{NR}$$

for all $N > 0$. It follows from this discussion, then, that meaningful messages are actually those which the decision procedure admits as being meaningful, whatever the sequences may be. The disparity between what a computer procedure admits as meaningful when, for example, digram statistics are used, and what the human recognizes as meaningful, may be substantial.

If $\underline{X}$ is the set of all N-letter messages, it follows from Equation F-5 that

$$H(\underline{X}) = -\sum_{x} p(x)\log_2 p(x)$$

where p(x) is the probability of message x (see Equation F-5). But, when the analyst uses (J + 1)-gram statistics to attack the system, p(x) must be computed via Equation F-1, and it follows that

$$p(x) = p(a_1 a_2 \ldots a_N)$$

$$\simeq p(a_1 a_2 \ldots a_J) \prod_{i=J+1}^{N} p_{B_i}(a_i)$$

(see Equation F-1).

Hence, when Equation F-1 is used together with Equation F-5, it follows that

$$H(\underline{X}) \simeq NF_{J+1}; N \gg J \tag{F-16}$$

and so, from Equation F-14, it follows that

$$s_{N,J} \simeq 2^{H(\underline{X})}; N \gg J \tag{F-17}$$

The important aspect of this result is that $H(\underline{X})$ depends on the order of the Markov approximation for message probability.

For small values of N ($N \leqslant 3$), G_N and F_N can be computed directly from Equations F-6 and F-9 using N-gram frequencies (see Table F-2 for com-

Alphabet Type	F_0	F_1	F_2	F_3
		(Bits per Character)		
26-letter[1]	4.70	4.17	3.62	3.22
26-letter[2]	4.70	4.14	3.56	3.30
27-letter[3]	4.76	4.03	3.32	3.10

[1]Computed from a sample of 1 million N-grams.
[2]Obtained from Reference 3.
[3]Space (blank) is included as an additional letter.
F_0 is defined as $\log_2$(Alphabet Size).

Table F-2. Computed Values of F_N for English ($N \leqslant 3$)

puted values of F_N). However, N-gram frequencies could not be used to evaluate R, as illustrated by the following example. Suppose that R is equal to 1 bit per character (R = 1.0 bpc). This means that, on the average, 100 bits would be required to represent a block of 100 characters, and there would be roughly 2^{100} meaningful English sequences of 100 characters (2^{100} is approximately equal to

1,000,000,000,000,000,000,000,000,000,000

or 10^{30}). Since most of these (10^{30}) sequences have never even been written down, it is impossible to measure their relative frequencies or estimate their respective probabilities.

In order to determine the value or R, one must be able to evaluate F_n for $N > 3$. One such way, described in reference 3, is based on the fact that anyone who can read and write a language possesses an enormous built-in knowledge of the statistics of that language. This can be demonstrated by measuring a person's ability to predict the Nth character in a message after seeing the preceeding $N - 1$ characters. Table F-2 gives upper and lower bounds on F_N that were obtained in this manner from an actual experiment involving a human subject [3,4]. In this experiment, a 27-letter English alphabet was employed (26 letters plus blank). Since the blank is almost completely redundant when sequences of one or more words are involved, the values of F_N in the 27-letter case will be 4.5/5.5 of F_N for the 26-letter alphabet when N is reasonably large [3]. Thus, F_N for a 26-letter alphabet can be obtained from F_N for a 27-letter alphabet via the relation

$$F_n(26 \text{ letters}) = (5.5/4.5)F_N(27 \text{ letters}) \qquad \text{(F-18)}$$

According to Shannon [3] (Table F-3), the value of R for a 27 letter English alphabet is approximately 1.0 bits per character. From Equation F-18, it can be seen that the value of R for a 26 letter English alphabet thus becomes about 1.22 bits per character.

N (Characters)[1]	F_N Upper Bound (Bits per Character)[2]	F_N Lower Bound (Bits per Character)[2]	F_N Upper Bound (Bits per Character)[3]	F_N Lower Bound (Bits per Character)[3]
1	4.03	3.19	4.72	3.95
2	3.42	2.50	3.81	3.19
3	3.0	2.1	3.34	2.44
4	2.6	1.7		
5	2.7	1.7	2.9	2.2
6	2.2	1.3		
7	2.8	1.8		
8	1.8	1.0		
9	1.9	1.0	2.5	1.9
10	2.1	1.0		
11	2.2	1.3		
12	2.3	1.3		
13	2.1	1.2		
14	1.7	0.9		
15	2.1	1.2		
17			2.4	1.3
33			1.9	1.1
65			2.0	1.2
100	1.3	0.6		
129			1.9	1.1

[1]Based on a 27 letter English alphabet (includes blank).
[2]Obtained from Reference 3.
[3]Obtained from Reference 4.

Table F-3. Bounds on F_N for a 27-Letter English Alphabet (Human Prediction Experiment in which the Preceding N-1 Characters were Known)

When the 26-letter English alphabet is reduced to a 2-character alphabet consisting of vowels and consonants, Equations F-6 and F-9 can be used to compute values of G_N and F_N for larger values of N than can be computed when a 26-letter alphabet is considered. Table F-4 contains computed values of G_N and F_N for $N \leqslant 10$ that were obtained from an N-gram analysis using 4 million characters of English text. It can be seen that F_N rapidly approaches a value of R = .80 bits per character.

A vowel-consonant alphabet also permits the accuracy of the approximation for $S_{N,J}$ (given by Equation F-14) to be evaluated in situations where N and J are small. Let J = 1 (use a first-order approximation of message probability) and let N take on values 2, 3, . . . , 15. For each value of N, compute

N (Characters)	G_N (Bits per Character)	F_N
0	1.000	1.000
1	.959	.959
2	.900	.840
3	.871	.812
4	.855	.807
5	.845	.806
6	.838	.805
7	.834	.805
8	.830	.805
9	.827	.804
10	.825	.804

G_N is computed from 4 million English N-grams using Equation F-6.
F_N is computed from the relation $F_N = N(G_N) - (N\text{-}1)(G_{N\text{-}1})$.

Table F-4. Computed Values of G_N and F_N for English Vowel-and-Consonant N-grams

N	2^N	$2^{N(F_2)}$	$p(2^{N(F_2)}$ most probable)
2	4	3.2	0.96
3	8	5.7	0.93
4	16	10.3	0.93
5	32	18.4	0.92
6	64	33.0	0.91
7	128	59.0	0.90
8	256	110	0.90
9	512	189	0.90
10	1024	339	0.89
11	2048	607	0.89
12	4096	1086	0.88
13	8192	1945	0.88
14	16384	3482	0.87
15	32768	6434	0.87

$p(2^{N(F_{J+1})}$ most probable) represents the sum of the probabilities of the $2^{N(F_{J+1})}$ most probable messages out of the 2^N total messages, the probability of which is approximated by Equation F-1 under the condition that $J = 1$.
Vowels = { A, E, I, O, U }.

Table F-5. Accuracy of Approximation ($s_{N,J} = 2^{N(F_{J+1})}$) Using a Vowel-Consonant English Alphabet.

the probability for each of the 2^N possible N character messages using Equation F-1. This list of 2^N messages is then sorted in descending sequence according to the computed value of message probability (most probable message to least probable message). Using this sorted list, obtain the sum of the probabilities for the first $2^{NF_J + 1}$ messages. This value is denoted by $p[2^{NF_J + 1}$ most probable]. The amount that $p[2^{NF_J + 1}$ most probable] differs from 1 is a measure of the accuracy of the approximation. Table F-5 contains the results of this analysis.

REFERENCES

1. Francis, W., *A Standard Sample of Present-Day Edited American English for Use with Digital Computers,* Linguistics Department, Brown University, Providence, RI, 1964.
2. Shannon, C. E., "A Mathematical Theory of Communication," *Bell System Technical Journal,* **27**, Part I 479–523, Part II 623–656 (1948).
3. Shannon, C. E., "Predictions of entropy in printed English," *Bell System Technical Journal,* **30**, 50–64 (1951).
4. Burton, N. G., and Licklider, J. C. R., "Long-Range Constraints in The Statistical Structure of Printed English," *American Journal of Psychology,* **68**, 650–653 (1955).

APPENDIX G

Unicity Distance Computations

In the following discussion of unicity distance computations, it is assumed that only ciphertext is available for analysis. It is further assumed that the reader is familiar with the information measures and unicity distance results given in An Expansion of Shannon's Approach Using Information Theory, Chapter 12.

TRANSPOSITION

Let $x = a_1 a_2 \ldots a_N$ be a message of N characters, which has been segmented into j blocks of T characters:

$$x = B_1 B_2 \ldots B_j$$

where

$$Bi = a_1(i), a_2(i), \ldots, a_T(i)$$

In a transposition cipher, encipherment is performed by rearranging the characters in each block of x according to a permutation function f:

$$\begin{aligned} f(x) &= f(B_1), f(B_2), \ldots, f(B_j) \\ &= C_1, C_2, \ldots, C_j = y \end{aligned}$$

Decipherment is performed using the corresponding inverse permutation function f^{-1}:

$$f^{-1}(y) = f^{-1}(C_1), f^{-1}(C_2), \ldots, f^{-1}(C_j) = x$$

For example, suppose

$$f = \begin{array}{|cccccccc|} 7 & 4 & 5 & 1 & 8 & 3 & 2 & 6 \\ 1 & 2 & 3 & 4 & 5 & 6 & 7 & 8 \end{array}$$

is a permutation of the integers 1, 2, . . . , 8, which is interpreted to mean that the character in position 7 is written in position 1, the character in position 4 is written in position 2, and so on. Then encipherment of the message x = "data encryption standard" with spaces removed and appropriate fill characters added, results in cryptogram

$$\begin{aligned} y &= f(x) \\ &= f(\text{dataencr}),\ f(\text{yptionst}),\ f(\text{andardxx}) \\ &= \text{caedrtan} \quad \text{sioyttpn} \quad \text{xaraxdnd} \end{aligned}$$

In this case, decipherment would be carried out with the inverse permutation

$$f^{-1} = \begin{array}{|cccccccc|} 4 & 7 & 6 & 2 & 3 & 8 & 1 & 5 \\ 1 & 2 & 3 & 4 & 5 & 6 & 7 & 8 \end{array}$$

Since there are T characters in each block, the number of possible permutation functions is (T)(T − 1) . . . (1) = T!.[1] Effectively, encipherment cancels or breaks down the usual 2-gram, 3-gram, and so on, language statistics between adjacent and neighboring characters, and spreads them over the entire block. Except for interblock dependencies, which can be ignored for moderate and large values of T, only the frequencies of individual characters remain undisturbed or unaltered.

The unicity distance for a transposition cipher is the value of N for which

$$H(\underline{K}) - H(\underline{Y}) + H(\underline{X}) = 0$$

where

$$\begin{aligned} H(\underline{K}) &= \log_2(T!) \\ H(\underline{Y}) &= NF'_{J+1} \\ H(\underline{X}) &= NF_{J+1} \end{aligned}$$

(see Equation 12-8). F'_{J+1} is a measure of the entropy per character of the cryptogram space, $\underline{Y}$ (see Equation F-9). Substituting and solving for N(ud), one obtains:

$$ud = \log_2(T!)|(F'_{J+1} - F_{J+1}) \tag{G-1}$$

Consider a transposition cipher on English in which 1-gram language

[1] Actually, if one omits the arrangement in which the block is unchanged, there are T! − 1 permutation functions. However, for moderate values of T, the difference between T! and T! − 1 is negligible.

statistics are used to attack the cipher. In that case, J = 0 and the entropy per character in the cryptogram space is

$$F_1' = -\sum_{i=1}^{26} p(b_i)\log_2 p(b_i)$$

where $b_1, b_2, \ldots, b_{26}$ denotes the cipher alphabet, $a_1, a_2, \ldots, a_{26}$ denotes the plain alphabet, and $b_1 = a_1$, $b_2 = a_2$, . . . $b_{26} = a_{26}$. Since there are about 8.0% As, 1.5% Bs, 3.1% Cs, and so on, in the messages being enciphered, there will also be about 8.0% As, 1.5% Bs, 3.1% Cs, and so on, in the produced cryptograms. In that case, $p(b_i) = p(a_i)$, $F_1' = F_1 = 4.17$, and ud equals infinity. This shows that 1-grams cannot be used to break a transposition cipher.

For large T, the usual 2-gram, 3-gram, and so on, language statistics in the message space are no longer present in the cryptogram space. This implies that F_2', F_3', and so on, are about equal to F_1' (4.17). Thus Equation G-1 can be written as

$$ud = \log_2(T!)/(4.17 - F_{J+1}); \qquad \text{for large T} \qquad \text{(G-2)}$$

In situations where J and T are of comparable magnitudes, values for F_2' and F_3' can be evaluated as follows. A large sample of English text is enciphered with each of the T! permutation functions. The resulting T! cryptograms are combined to form a single sample, which can then be used to determine the frequency of each (J + 1)-gram. The (J + 1)-grams are then used with Equation F-9 to compute F_{J+1}'.

Unicity distances for transposition on English (26 character alphabet) are given in Table G-1. These values were computed from Equation G-2 using T and J as variables.

J	F_{J+1}	T (Characters per Block)				
		10	20	50	100	1000
0	4.17	∞	∞	∞	∞	∞
1	3.62	40	111	390	954	15502
2	3.22		65	226	553	9473
6	2.81			150	386	6269
14	2.02				244	3966
99	1.22					2890

∞ denotes infinity. For each value of J, (J + 1)-grams are presumed to be used to attack the cipher. F_1, F_2, and F_3 were obtained from Table F-2. F_7, F_{15}, and F_{100} were computed from Equation F-18 using an average of the upper and lower bounds on F_N for a 27-character alphabet (see column 1, Table F-3). Unicity distance was computed using Equation G-2.

Table G-1. Unicity Distance in Characters for Transposition on English (26 Letter Alphabet)

SIMPLE SUBSTITUTION

In Chapter 12, the unicity distance for simple substitution on English was computed with a random cipher in which the approximation $\{H(\underline{Y}) \simeq \log_2 r = N4.70\}$ was made. A more accurate value of $H(\underline{Y})$, derived below, shows that for small N, the approximation $\{H(\underline{Y}) \simeq \log_2 r\}$ is fairly good.

A cipher is *pure* if the keys in $\underline{K}$ are equally likely and, for every k1, k2, and k3, in $\underline{K}$, there is a k4 such that

$$E_{k1}(D_{k2}(E_{k3}(x))) = E_{k4}(x) \qquad \text{for all x in } \underline{X}$$

(see reference 1). For example, simple substitution is a pure cipher if its keys are equally likely. In a pure cipher, the messages and cryptograms can be divided into sets of residue classes $C_1, C_2, \ldots, C_s$, and $C_1', C_2', \ldots, C_s'$, respectively, such that

1. Each message and cryptogram is an element of one and only one residue class.
2. Enciphering any message in C_i with any key produces a cryptogram in C_i'. Deciphering any cryptogram in C_i' with any key leads to a message in C_i.
3. The number of messages in C_i, say t_i, is equal to the number of cryptograms in C_i' and is a divisor of n the number of keys.
4. Each message in C_i can be enciphered into each cryptogram in C_i' by exactly n/t_i different keys. The same is true for decipherment.

In a simple substitution cipher, the residue class corresponding to a given cryptogram y is the set of all cryptograms that are obtained from y via the operation $E_{ki}(D_{kj}(y))$, where ki and kj vary over each key in $\underline{K}$. Thus all the cryptograms in a residue class have the same pattern of repeated letters. For example, if cryptogram abaabc is in residue class C_i', then so are the cryptograms babbax, abaabd, jqjjqt, mammae, and pippin. Therefore, each y in C_1' is equally likely and

$$p(y) = p(C_i)/t_i; \qquad \text{for each y in } C_i' \tag{G-3}$$

where $p(C_i)$ is the probability of residue class C_i and t_i is the number of different cryptograms in C_i'. Hence, $H(\underline{Y})$ is computed, as described in reference 1, by

$$\begin{aligned} H(\underline{Y}) &= -\sum_i t_i(p(C_i)/t_i)\log_2(p(C_i)/t_i) \\ &= -\sum_i p(C_i)\log_2(p(C_i)/t_i) \end{aligned} \tag{G-4}$$

Values of $H(\underline{Y})/N$ $(N = 1, 2, \ldots, 8)$ were computed for simple substitution on English using Equation G-4 (Table G-2). Values for $p(C_i)$ were obtained

Ciphertext Length N	Number of Residue Classes	H(Y)/N			
		N-gram Sample Size			
		50,000	100,000	500,000	1,000,000
1	1	—	—	—	4.700
2	2	—	—	—	4.700
3	5	—	—	—	4.699
4	15	4.695	4.696	4.696	—
5	52	4.690	4.692	4.692	—
6	203	4.684	4.686	4.686	—
7	877	4.677	4.679	4.680	—
8	4140	4.666	4.670	4.673	—

H(Y)/N = 4.70 for the Random Cipher.

Table G-2. Computed Values of H(Y)/N for Simple Substitution on English (26 letter alphabet)

from samples of English text by counting the number of N-grams in each residue class C_i and dividing the result by the sample size. For values of N greater than 8, the number of residue classes rapidly becomes large. In that case, it is not possible to obtain accurate estimates for $p(C_i)$ unless very large sample sizes are used.

The approximation $\{H(\underline{Y}) \simeq \log_2 r = N4.70\}$ is quite good for small values of N. This could account for the close agreement between computed unicity distance and the observed number of characters needed to break simple substitution on English when high-order language statistics are used in the cryptanalysis, since the observed value of N = 25 is still reasonably small. However, for large values of N, the approximation $\{H(\underline{Y}) \simeq \log_2 r = N4.70\}$ no longer holds. This could account for the disparity between computed unicity distance and the observed number of characters needed to break

J	F_{J+1}	Expected Number of Different Letters	Number of Keys	Unicity Distance (ud)	Approximate Value of N to Break the Cipher (Observed Values)
0	4.17	26	26!	167.0	Several Thousand (Fig. 12-5)
1	3.62	24	26!/2!	81.0	About 500 (Fig. 12-5)
2	3.22	23	26!/3!	58.0	About 100 (Ref. 2)
14	2.02	14	26!/12!	22.2	About 25 (Ref. 3)

Unicity distance is computed from Equation 11-8. It is assumed that $H(\underline{Y}) \simeq N4.70$.
For an explanation of J and F_{J+1}, see Table G-1.

Table G-3. Unicity Distance in Characters for Simple Substitution on English (16 Letter Alphabet)

simple substitution on English when low-order language statistics are used in the cryptanalysis, since the observed values of N are much larger (Table G-3).

When unicity distance is computed with Equation 12-8 using $F_{J+1} = 4.17$ ($J = 1$), a value of ud = 167 characters is obtained. However, observed results indicate that several thousand characters of ciphertext are needed to break a simple substitution cipher when only single letter probabilities are used (see Figure 12-5).

HOMOPHONIC SUBSTITUTION

In a *homophonic substitution* cipher (sometimes called substitution with variants, substitution with multiple substitutes, or multiple substitution), each character in the plain alphabet $a_1, a_2, \ldots, a_t$, has a corresponding set of unique cipher characters, or substitutes, $S_1, S_2, \ldots, S_t$, such that

1. The cipher characters in each set, S_i, are different from those in any other set, S_j.
2. L_i denotes the number of characters in S_i ($L_i = |S_i|$).
3. L denotes the total number of characters in the cipher alphabet ($L = L_1 + L_2 + \ldots + L_t$).

Simple substitution is therefore just a special case of homophonic substitution in which $L_1 = L_2 = \ldots = L_t = 1$. In all other cases, $\log_2 L$ (the bits needed to represent a character in the cipher alphabet) is greater than $\log_2 t$ (the bits needed to represent a character in the plain alphabet), thus indicating that homophonic substitution is an expansion cipher.

Encipherment is accomplished by replacing each character in the message with one of its allowed substitutes: plain character a_1 is replaced by an element in S_1, a_2 is replaced by an element in S_2, and so on. (It is assumed that substitutes are selected randomly, i.e., the probability of selecting any particular element in S_i is $1/L_i$.) Decipherment is the reverse of this process: cipher characters in S_1 are replaced by a_1, cipher characters in S_2 are replaced by a_2, and so on.

Consider an example in which the substitutes for each character in the plain alphabet are as follows:

e: c u 7	r: 1 9	m: 2	v: h
t: e r w	h: b	f: s	k: o
a: p 0	l: k	p: q	x: a
o: 3 5	d: d	g: x	j: i
i: f 8	c: g	w: t	q: z
n: j v	u: 6	y: m	z: 4
s: n #		b: y	

The message "data encryption standard," with spaces removed, can be enciphered in $1 \times 2 \times 3 \times \ldots \times 2 \times 1 = 331{,}776$ ways. One character can be substituted for d, two characters can be substituted for a, three characters for "t," and so on, as shown below:

plaintext:	d a t a e n c r y p t i o n s t a n d a r d
1st choice:	d p e p c j g l m q e f 3 j n e p j d p l d
2nd choice:	0 r 0 u v 9 r 8 5 v # r 0 v 0 9
3rd choice:	w 7 w w

In a homophonic substitution cipher, encipherment of message xj with key ki defines a set of candidate cryptograms, Yij:

$$E_{ki}(xj) = Yij$$

where, as part of the encipherment process, the communicant selects or generates (usually randomly and on a character-by-character basis) one of the cryptograms in Yij. However, only one message is recovered upon decipherment:

$$D_{ki}(yij) = xj; \quad \text{for each yij in Yij}$$

Since ki determines a set of cryptograms instead of one cryptogram, homophonic substitution does not satisfy our definition for a cipher (see Chapter 12, A Cipher with Message and Key Probabilities). The problem is easily avoided if one assumes that the enciphering algorithm E has a fixed rule for deciding which of the substitutes should be used to encipher each plaintext letter. For example, substitutes could be selected on a rotating basis, on the basis of the plaintext letter's position in the message, on the basis of the message's context (surrounding letters), and so forth. However, this has not been done here, since it would introduce an additional degree of complexity that can be avoided in the present discussion.

Since each ki defines a set of cryptograms, the assumptions leading to Equation 12-8 are not satisfied (i.e., Equation 12-8 cannot be used to calculate unicity distance). Hence, a new equation for computing unicity distance is derived.

From the general relation

$$H(U, V, W) = H(U|V, W) + H(V, W)$$

(see Equation 12-7i) it follows, with an appropriate change of variables, that

$$H(\underline{X}, \underline{K}, \underline{Y}) = H(\underline{X}|\underline{K}, \underline{Y}) + H(\underline{K}, \underline{Y})$$

and

$$H(\underline{Y}, \underline{K}, \underline{X}) = H(\underline{Y}|\underline{K}, \underline{X}) + H(\underline{K}, \underline{X})$$

Hence, it follows that

$$H(\underline{K}, \underline{Y}) - H(\underline{K}, \underline{X}) = H(\underline{Y}|\underline{K}, \underline{X}) - H(\underline{X}|\underline{K}, \underline{Y})$$

In a homophonic substitution cipher, since $x = D_k(y)$ (i.e., a knowledge of k and y permits x to be recovered), it follows that

$$H(\underline{X}|\underline{K}, \underline{Y}) = 0$$

and consequently that

$$H(\underline{K}, \underline{Y}) = H(\underline{Y}|\underline{K}, \underline{X}) + H(\underline{K}, \underline{X})$$

(Note that $H(\underline{Y}|\underline{K}, \underline{X}) > 0$, since $E_k(x)$ defines a set instead of only one element.) But, by Equation 12-7h, $H(\underline{K}, \underline{Y})$ can be rewritten as

$$H(\underline{K}, \underline{Y}) = H(\underline{K}|\underline{Y}) + H(\underline{Y})$$

Moreover, since messages and keys are selected independently, it follows from Equations 12-7h and 12-7j that

$$H(\underline{K}, \underline{X}) = H(\underline{K}) + H(\underline{X})$$

A general equation for $H(\underline{K}|\underline{Y})$ is thus obtained:

$$H(\underline{K}|\underline{Y}) = H(\underline{K}) - H(\underline{Y}) + H(\underline{Y}|\underline{K}, \underline{X}) + H(\underline{X})$$

The unicity distance of a homophonic substitution cipher in which only ciphertext is available for analysis is the value of N (N = cryptogram length in characters) for which

$$H(\underline{K}) - H(\underline{Y}) + H(\underline{Y}|\underline{K}, \underline{X}) + H(\underline{X}) = 0 \qquad \text{(G-5)}$$

provided that such an N exists. Except for the extra term, $H(\underline{Y}|\underline{K}, \underline{X})$, Equation G-5 is the same as Equation 12-8.

How many keys there are in a homophonic substitution cipher depends on whether the information is requested by the communicant who uses the cipher or the opponent who attacks it. The opponent's idea of how many keys there are in the cipher can be quite different from that of the communicant. For example, the number of substitutes per character in the plain alphabet ($L_1, L_2, \ldots, L_t$) and the number of characters in the cipher alphabet (L), are apt to be secret parameters of the cipher system. They would be known to the communicant but not to the opponent. An intercepted cryptogram would not always reveal the entire cipher alphabet. Thus, if L' denotes the number of different characters in the intercepted cryptogram, the analyst would not know whether $L' < L$ or $L' = L$. In that case, the opponent would have to approximate n, the number of keys, without knowing $L_1, L_2, \ldots, L_t$ or L.

Since any character in the cipher alphabet can be assigned to any character in the plain alphabet, an upper bound on n is obtained as follows:

$$n \leqslant t^T \tag{G-6}$$

In the worst case, where the analyst has no knowledge about the structure of the key space, t^T could be used for n. This would provide an upper bound on unicity distance.

However, if the analyst has a prior knowledge of $L_1, L_2, \ldots, L_t$, the number of keys can be obtained as follows:

$$\begin{aligned} n &= \binom{L}{L_1}\binom{L - L_1}{L_2}\cdots\binom{L - L_1 - L_2 \ldots - L_{t-1}}{L_t} \\ &= L!/[(L_1!)(L_2!)\ldots(L_t!)] \end{aligned} \tag{G-7}$$

In those cases where the analyst does not know $L_1, L_2, \ldots, L_t$, but has some knowledge of the key space, it may still be possible to approximate n using Equation G-7. For example, if the analyst knows or suspects that each plain character has an equal number of substitutes ($L_1 = L_2 = \ldots = L_t$), then this value can be approximated by L'/t, the observed number of characters in the cipher alphabet divided by the number of characters in the plain alphabet. If the analyst knows or suspects that the number of substitutes per character is proportional to the probability of that character appearing in the plain alphabet, $L_i = (pi)(L)$, then L_i' can be approximated by $(pi)(L')$ (rounding up or down to the nearest whole number, as appropriate).[2]

Theorem: In a homophonic substitution cipher

$$H(\underline{Y}|\underline{K}, \underline{X}) = N \sum_{i=1}^{t} p(a_i)\log_2 L_i; \qquad N \geqslant 1 \tag{G-8}$$

where $a_1, a_2, \ldots, a_t$ are the characters in the plain alphabet of $\underline{X}$.

Proof: The proof follows directly from Equation 12-7e if the relationship

$$p(b_{i1}b_{i2}\ldots b_{iN}) = p(a_{i1}a_{i2}\ldots a_{iN})(1/L_{i1})(1/L_{i2})\ldots(1/L_{iN})$$

is used, where $b_{i1}b_{i2}\ldots b_{iN}$ is an arbitrary cryptogram in $\underline{Y}$ (over the alphabet $b_1, b_2, \ldots, b_L$), $a_{i1}a_{i2}\ldots a_{iN}$ is the corresponding message in $\underline{X}$ (over the alphabet $a_1, a_2, \ldots, a_t$), and b_{i1} is one of the L_{i1} substitutes for a_{i1}, b_{i2} is one of the L_{i2} substitutes for a_{i2}, and so on.

[2] A better approximation of n could be obtained if L_i' were allowed to assume values in an interval about $(pi)(L')$ (e.g., the interval obtained using a method of confidence limits for some chosen level of confidence).

Corollary: From the above theorem, it follows that

1. If $L_1 = L_2 = \ldots = L_t$, then $H(\underline{Y}|\underline{K}, \underline{X}) = N(\log_2 L - \log_2 t)$
2. If $L_i \simeq p(a_i)(L)$ for $i = 1, 2, \ldots, t$, then $H(\underline{Y}|\underline{K}, \underline{X}) = N(\log_2 L - F_1)$

where F_1 is a measure of the entropy of $\underline{X}$.

If the approximation $N\log_2 L$ is used for $H(\underline{Y})$ and the values

$$H(\underline{K}) = \log_2 n$$

$$H(\underline{Y}) = N\log_2 L$$

$$H(\underline{Y}|\underline{K}, \underline{X}) = N \sum_{i=1}^{t} p(a_i)\log_2 L_i$$

$$H(\underline{X}) = NF_{J+1}$$

are substituted into Equation G-5, one obtains (solving for N):

$$N = \log_2 n/[\log_2 L - F_{J+1} - \sum_{i=1}^{t} p(a_i)\log_2 L_i] \qquad \text{(G-9)}$$

From the above corollary, when $L_1 = L_2 = \ldots = L_t$ Equation G-9 reduces to

$$N = \log_2 n/(\log_2 t - F_{J+1}) \qquad \text{(G-10)}$$

For English, $\log_2 t = \log_2 26 = 4.70$. Hence Equation G-10 shows that the analyst can attack the cipher using 1-grams ($J = 0$). This confirms one's intuition that $L_1 = L_2 = \ldots = L_t$ should not cause 1-gram, 2-gram, and so on, language statistics to be destroyed during encipherment. However, from the corollary, when $L_i \simeq p(a_i)(L)$, Equation G-9 reduces to

$$N = \log_2 n/(F_1 - F_{J+1}) \qquad \text{(G-11)}$$

For English, the value of F_1 is 4.17. Hence Equation G-11 shows that the analyst can no longer attack the cipher using 1-grams ($J = 0$). Again, this confirms one's intuition that 1-gram language statistics are destroyed during encipherment, since L_i is proportional to pi.

Two notable examples of homophonic substitution are the Beale Ciphers [4] and the Zodiac Murder Ciphers [5]. The Beale Ciphers consist of three numeric cryptograms, denoted B1, B2, B3, allegedly constructed by one Thomas Jefferson Beale in the year 1820. The purpose of these cryptograms was to describe the location, contents and respective heirs of a treasure in gold, silver, and jewels. B2, which describes the contents of the treasure, was broken several decades later, after Beale's key to B2 was discovered. This key

Cryptogram	N	L′	$Log_2 n$	Unicity Distance in Characters				
	(Length in Characters)	(Cryptogram Alphabet Size)	(n = Number of keys)	F_2 3.62	F_3 3.22	F_6 2.81	F_{15} 2.02	F_{100} 1.22
B1	520	279	1094.7	1990	1152	805	509	371
B2	763	179	685.5	1246	722	504	319	232
B3	618	263	1029.0	1871	1083	757	479	349
Z1	408	46	151.5	275	159	111	70	51
Z2	340	63	217.6	396	229	160	101	74

''B'' denotes Beale Ciphers; ''Z'' denotes Zodiac Murder Ciphers.
B2 and Z1 have been solved; B1, B3, and Z2 have not been solved.
Unicity distance is computed using Equation G-11.

Table G-4. Computed Unicity Distances for the Beale Ciphers and the Zodiac Murder Ciphers

was constructed by sequentially numbering each word in the Declaration of Independence ("When in the course of . . .") and assigning each number to the corresponding initial letter of each word (1 = w, 2 = i, 3 = t, 4 = c, 5 = o, etc.). The key to B2 did not, however, provide the solution to B1 or B3. Subsequently, amateur and professional cryptanalysts have expended untold amounts of time and money attempting to decipher the remaining cryptograms. No solution is known to exist.

The Zodiac Murder Ciphers, denoted Z1 and Z2, were constructed by the so-called Zodiac Killer who haunted the San Francisco Bay area in the late 1960s. Z1 was broken by an amateur cryptanalyst shortly after it was published by the news media. No solution to Z2 is known to exist.

Will cryptanalysts, or even amateur cryptogram buffs ever be successful in decoding these yet unbroken cryptograms? Some insight into this question can be gained if the unicity distances for these cryptograms are computed (Table G-4).

In each case, the number of keys (n) was calculated from L′ (the number of different characters in the cryptogram) using the following procedure: Let p1, p2, . . . , p26 represent the values of p(a) in Table 12-1, which have been sorted into descending sequence (i.e., p1 ⩾ p2 ⩾ . . . etc.). The values of $L'_1, L'_2, \ldots, L'_{26}$ were calculated as follows:

$$L'_i = q_i - q_{i-1}; \qquad i = 1, 2, \ldots, 26$$

where

$$q_0 = 0$$

$$q_i = L' \sum_{j=1}^{i} pj; \qquad i = 1, 2, \ldots, 26$$

and the values of q_i are rounded off to the nearest whole number.

For example, the values of $L'_1, L'_2, \ldots, L'_{26}$ for cryptogram B1 in Table G-4 were obtained from L′ = 279 as shown in Table G-5:

i	Character (i)	p(i)	$\sum_{j=1}^{i} p(j)$	$L' \sum_{j=1}^{i} p(j)$	L'_i
1	E	.1251	.1251	34.9	35
2	T	.0925	.2176	60.7	26
3	A	.0804	.2980	83.1	22
4	O	.0760	.3740	104.3	21
5	I	.0726	.4466	124.6	21

Remainder of Computation is not Shown

Table G-5. Computation of $L'_1, L'_2, \ldots, L'_{26}$ for L′ = 279

The procedure guarantees that $L'_1 + L'_2 + \ldots + L'_{26} = L'$.

There are two interesting results obtained as a consequence of these computations. Z1, which was broken by an amateur analyst, is well beyond the unicity distance, even when only digram statistics are used to attack the cipher. On the other hand, even when 7-gram language statistics are employed, B1 and B3 are still below the unicity distance. Moreover, B1 and B3 remain unsolved, even though they have been subjected to repeated cryptanalysis for more than 100 years. Thus, theoretical results (and the conclusions naturally inferred from these results) agree with observed results.

REFERENCES

1. Shannon, C. E., "Communication Theory of Secrecy Systems," *Bell System Technical Journal,* **28**, 656–715 (1949).
2. Matyas, S. M., *A Computer Oriented Cryptanalytic Solution for Multiple Substitution Enciphering Systems,* Doctoral Thesis, University of Iowa (1974).
3. Friedman, W. F., "Cryptology," *Encyclopedia Britannica,* p. 848 (1973).
4. Ward, J. B., *The Beale Papers,* Virginia Book and Job Print, Lynchburg, Virginia, 1885.
5. "Vallejo Mass Murder," *San Francisco Examiner and Chronicle,* August 3, 1969, Section A, p. 9; August 10, 1969, Section A, p. 26.

Other Publications of Interest

6. Deavours, C. A., "Unicity Points in Cryptanalysis," *Cryptologia,* **1**, No. 1, 46-68 (1977). (1977).
7. Lu, S. C. and Lee, L. N., "Message Redundancy Reduction by Multiple Substitution," *COMSAT Technical Review* **9**, No. 1, 37–47 (Spring 1979).
8. Tanaka, H. and Kaneku, S., "Data Compression Approach to Cryptography," *Proceedings 1979 Carnahan Conference on Crime Countermeasures,* University of Kentucky, Lexington (May 16–18, 1979).
9. Reeds, J. "Entropy Calculations and Particular Methods of Cryptanalysis," *Cryptologia,* **1**, No. 3, 235-254 (1977).

APPENDIX H

Derivation of p(u) and p(SM)

In this appendix, emphasis is placed on analysis of the random cipher with the objective of obtaining the correct message for an intercepted cryptogram, but not necessarily the correct key. Primarily, this analysis is carried out to provide the reader with additional insight into the problems of cryptanalysis.

In the definitions given below, y represents an intercepted cryptogram (i.e., y is an element of the set $\underline{Y}'$). Recall that

1. M is the random variable defined as the number of keys that will decipher an intercepted cryptogram into a meaningful message.
2. M′ is the random variable defined as the number of keys, except for the key originally used to produce the given cryptogram, that will decipher an intercepted cryptogram into a meaningful message.
3. U is the random variable defined as the number of different meaningful messages produced when an intercepted cryptogram is deciphered with all possible keys.

Now let the mutually exclusive events U1 and U2 be defined as follows:

1. Event U1 occurs if at least one incorrect key deciphers the intercepted cryptogram into the correct message when an intercepted cryptogram is deciphered with all possible keys.
2. Event U2 occurs if no incorrect key deciphers the intercepted cryptogram into the correct message when an intercepted cryptogram is deciphered with all possible keys.

(See Figures H-1 and H-2.)

It follows from the definition of U, U1, and U2 that

$$p(U = u) = p(U = u, U1) + p(U = u, U2)$$

(Note that event U1 or U2 can occur, but not both.) For the case where $u = 1$ occurs in conjunction with U1, it is implied that all m' ($m' \geqslant 1$) incorrect keys

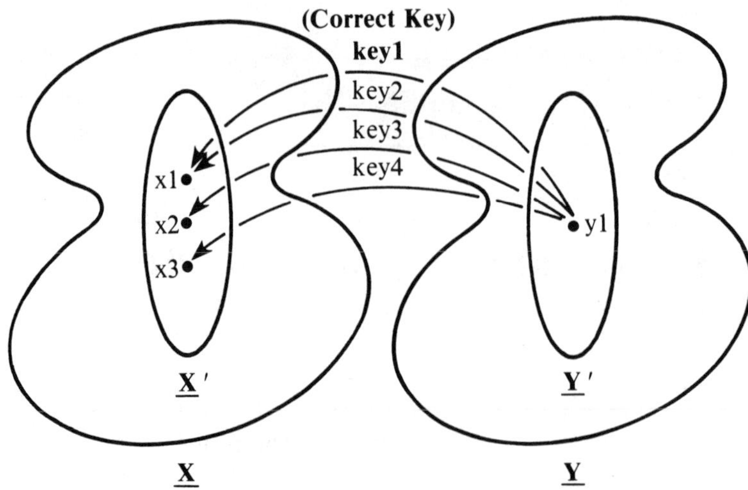

Figure H-1. Example in which U = 3 and Event U1 Occurs

must decipher the intercepted cryptogram into the correct message, and so

$$p(U = 1, U1) = \sum_{m'=1}^{n-1} \left(\frac{1}{s}\right)^{m'} p(m')$$

On the other hand, u = 1 in conjunction with U2 implies that there cannot be any incorrect keys that decipher the intercepted cryptogram into a meaningful message, and so

$$p(U = 1, U2) = p(m' = 0)$$

Consequently,

$$p(U = 1) = p(m' = 0) + \sum_{m'=1}^{n-1} \left(\frac{1}{s}\right)^{m'} p(m') \tag{H-1a}$$

and so, from Equation 12-3b, it follows that

$$\begin{aligned} p(U = 1) &= e^{-\lambda'} + \sum_{m'=1}^{n-1} e^{-\lambda'} \frac{(\lambda'/s)^{m'}}{(m')!} \\ &= e^{-\lambda'} e^{\lambda'/s} \qquad \text{for } s/r \ll 1 \end{aligned} \tag{H-1b}$$

For the case where u ⩾ 2, conditional probabilities can be used to obtain

$$p(U = u) = \sum_{m'=u}^{n-1} p(U = u, U1|m')p(m') + \sum_{m'=u-1}^{n-1} p(U = u, U2|m')p(m')$$

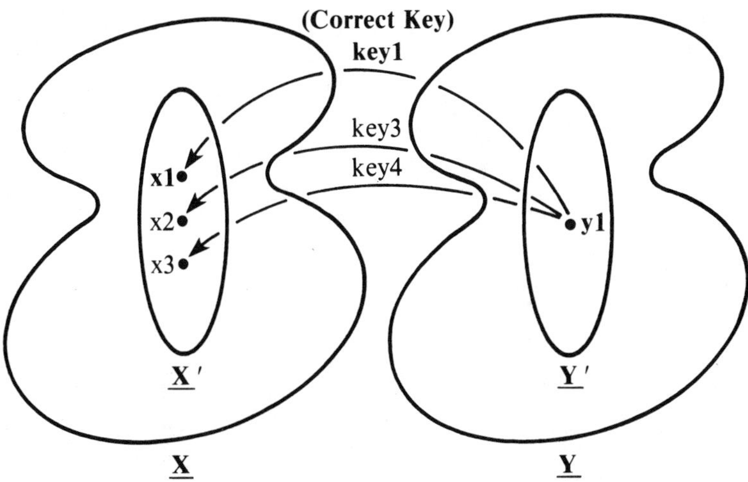

Figure H-2. Example in which U = 3 and Event U2 Occurs

Consider the situation where m′ balls are randomly placed into u cells. The probability that each cell will contain at least one ball is given by

$$\mathrm{po}(m', u) = \sum_{v=0}^{u} (-1)^v \binom{u}{v} \left(1 - \frac{v}{u}\right)^{m'}$$

(see reference 1). Because m′ decipherments produce only messages within the set of u specific messages, it follows for a random cipher that po(m′, u) represents the probability that these m′ decipherments will lead to each of the u specific messages at least once. A special case of interest is m′ = u, which results in

$$\mathrm{po}(u, u) = u!/u^u \tag{H-2}$$

Consider the situation in which m′ decipherments result in any of s possible messages. If u specific messages are designated out of s possible messages, then the probability that the m′ decipherments will lead only to the designated u messages, and that these m′ decipherments will lead to each of the u messages, at least once, is given by

$$(u/s)^{m'} \mathrm{po}(m', u)$$

Since for U1 to occur the correct message must always be included, there are $\binom{s-1}{u-1}$ different ways to select u messages out of s possibilities. Hence it follows that

$$p(U = u, U1 | m') = \binom{s-1}{u-1}\left(\frac{u}{s}\right)^{m'} \mathrm{po}(m', u)$$

Using similar reasoning, it follows that

$$p(U = u, U2|m') = \binom{s-1}{u-1}\left(\frac{u-1}{s}\right)^{m'} po(m', u-1)$$

and so,

$$p(U = u) = \binom{s-1}{u-1}\left[\sum_{m'=u}^{n-1}\left(\frac{u}{s}\right)^{m'} po(m', u)p(m') + \sum_{m'=u-1}^{n-1}\left(\frac{u-1}{s}\right)^{m'} po(m', u-1)p(m')\right]; \qquad s \geqslant u \geqslant 2 \tag{H-3}$$

In order for the process of cryptanalysis to be successful, the value of u should be much less than s. In that case, the following approximation for $\binom{s-1}{u-1}$ is obtained:

$$\binom{s-1}{u-1} = \frac{s^{u-1}}{(u-1)!}\prod_{i=1}^{u-1}\left(1-\frac{i}{s}\right) \simeq \frac{s^{u-1}}{(u-1)!} e^{-u(u-1)/2s}; \qquad u \ll s \tag{H-4}$$

Using Equations H-2 and H-4 together with the change of variable $m' = u + i$ allows Equation H-3 to be rewritten as

$$p(U = u) = p(m' = u-1)e^{-u(u-1)/2s} \times \left[1 + \sum_{i=0}^{n-1-u}\left(\frac{u}{s}\right)^{i+1}\frac{po(u+i, u)}{po(u, u)}\frac{p(m' = u+i)}{p(m' = u-1)} + \sum_{i=0}^{n-1-u}\left(\frac{u-1}{s}\right)^{i+1}\frac{po(u+1, u-1)}{po(u-1, u-1)}\frac{p(m' = u+i)}{p(m' = u-1)}\right] \tag{H-5}$$

for $u \geqslant 2$.

Equation 12-3a, which is the accurate expression for $p(m')$, can now be used in Equation H-5. In the present situation, where it may be assumed that $s/r \ll 1$, the Poisson approximation to the binomial given by Equation 12-3b is used for $p(m')$. Hence it follows that

$$p(m' = u+i)/p(m' = u-1) = (\lambda')^{i+1}(u-1)!/(u+i)!$$

which can be substituted into Equation H-5 to obtain

$$p(U = u) = p(m' = u - 1)e^{-u(u-1)/2s}$$
$$\times \left[1 + \sum_{i=0}^{n-1-u} \left(\frac{\lambda' u}{s}\right)^{i+1} \frac{(u-1)!}{(u+i)!} \frac{po(u+i, u)}{po(u, u)} \right. \tag{H-6}$$
$$\left. + \sum_{i=0}^{n-1-u} \left[\frac{\lambda'(u-1)}{s}\right]^{i+1} \frac{(u-1)!}{(u+i)!} \frac{po(u+i, u-1)}{po(u-1, u-1)} \right]$$

for $u \geqslant 2$.

Neglecting terms of order $(1/s)^2$ and higher, and using

$$\frac{po(u, u-1)}{po(u-1, u-1)} = \frac{u}{2}$$

whose derivation is left to the reader as an exercise, Equation H-6 can be written as

$$p(U = u) \simeq p(m' = u - 1)[1 + \lambda'/s + (u-1)(\lambda' - 1)/2s - (u-1)^2/2s] \tag{H-7}$$

Neglecting terms of order $(1/s)^2$ and higher in the accurate equation for $p(U = 1)$, Equation H-la, it follows that

$$p(U = 1) \simeq e^{\lambda'}(1 + \lambda'/s) = p(m' = 0)(1 + \lambda'/s)$$

Hence, it follows that Equation H-7 is valid for $u \geqslant 1$. Recognizing that the first three moments of the Poisson distribution are λ', $(\lambda')^2 + \lambda'$, and $(\lambda')^3 + 3(\lambda')^2 + \lambda'$, respectively, and using Equation 12-3b for $p(m')$, results in the expected value

$$\begin{aligned} E(U) &\simeq \sum_{u=1}^{s} u\, p(U = u) \\ &\simeq (\lambda' + 1)[1 - (\lambda'/2s)(\lambda' + (2/\lambda') + 1)] \\ &\simeq E(M)[1 - (\lambda'/2s)(\lambda' + (2/\lambda') + 1)] \end{aligned} \tag{H-8}$$

From Equation H-8, it can thus be seen that $E(U) \leqslant E(M)$, as expected.

Recall, from Equation 12-2, that p(SM) is the probability of solving for the correct message. Hence it follows from Equation H-7 that

$$\begin{aligned} p(SM) &\simeq \sum_{u=1}^{s} (1/u)p(U = u) \\ &\simeq (1/\lambda)(1 - e^{-\lambda})(1 + (\lambda'/2s)) \\ &\simeq p(SK)(1 + (\lambda'/2s)) \end{aligned} \tag{H-9}$$

From Equation H-9, it can be seen that $p(SM) \geqslant p(SK)$ as expected. However, the factor by which p(SM) is larger than p(SK) is $1 + \lambda'/2s$. At the unicity point for the random cipher, where $\lambda = 1$, it is observed that $1 + \lambda'/2s \simeq 1$. Consequently, when $\lambda \leqslant 1$, it is the case that $p(SM) \simeq p(SK)$. Therefore, Equation H-9 gives the reader additional insight into cryptanalysis, but does not provide an equation for the computation of p(SM) that would be used in practice.

REFERENCE

1. Feller, W., *An Introduction to Probability Theory and its Applications,* 3rd ed., Wiley, New York, 1968.

Index